Beneath the Mask:
An Introduction to Theories of Personality

Sixth Edition

Christopher F. Monte
Manhattanville College

Harcourt Brace College Publishers

Fort Worth   Philadelphia   San Diego   New York   Orlando   Austin   San Antonio
Toronto   Montreal   London   Sydney   Tokyo

Publisher	Earl McPeek
Acquisitions Editor	Carol Wada
Market Strategist	Kathleen Sharp
Developmental Editor	Janie Pierce-Bratcher
Project Editor	Laura Miley
Art Director	David A. Day
Production Manager	Andrea A. Johnson

Photo credits/Cover credit: © Ron Krisel/Tony Stone Images

ISBN: 0-15-505199-7
Library of Congress Catalog Card Number: 98-72354

Address for Orders
Harcourt Brace College Publishers, 6277 Sea Harbor Drive, Orlando, FL 32887-6777
1-800-782-4479

Address for Editorial Correspondence
Harcourt Brace College Publishers, 301 Commerce Street, Suite 3700, Fort Worth, TX 76102

Web Site Address
http://www.hbcollege.com

Printed in the United States of America

9 0 1 2 3 4 5 6 7   039   9 8 7 6 5 4 3 2

Harcourt Brace College Publishers

For my Mother and Father

A VOICE SAID, LOOK ME IN THE STARS
AND TELL ME TRULY, MEN OF EARTH,
IF ALL THE SOUL-AND-BODY SCARS
WERE NOT TOO MUCH TO PAY FOR BIRTH.

Robert Frost,
"A Question"

Preface

Theories of personality are psychological models of human nature that with surprising frequency reflect the nature of their creators. This sixth edition of *Beneath the Mask* presents classic theories of human nature much as each theorist might if the theorist were to teach his or her ideas to people coming into contact with them for the first time. Center stage is given to the theorist's progression of ideas, for often the *sequence of the theorist's thinking* and the changes embodied in the stream of ideas over time are more engaging and valuable than the final product. It is my intention to make it possible for the reader to go directly from an account of a theory in *Beneath the Mask* to the theorist's own works without the disorientation that comes from learning ideas in predigested textbook form.

A sympathetic approach to theories of personality is not new. What makes the six editions of *Beneath the Mask* unique is this continuing emphasis on presenting the ideas of personality theorists *developmentally*. A developmental account of a personality theory necessarily incorporates the *personal origins of ideas* to illuminate the links between the psychology of each theorist and that theorist's psychology of persons. This developmental emphasis has at least two consequences for teaching personality theories.

First, ideas about human psychology proceed from human beings, each with his or her own psychology that shapes the thoughts they think. To be complete and consistent, a developmental approach to theories of personality requires some exploration of how the personal histories, conflicts, and intentions of the theorist entered that thinker's portrait of people. *Beneath the Mask* has emphasized the importance of understanding these personal sources from its first edition. My experience in the classroom with this approach is that it not only leads to a fuller understanding of the theories, but that it makes them memorable by scaling them to human proportions. Put another way, *Beneath the Mask* explores the impact of the personalities of the theorists on their theories of personality.

The second consequence of a developmental approach for teaching is that the efficiency of reducing complex theories to concise summaries of a few basic principles is lost. Gained is the more time-consuming, but also more interesting and exciting, task of following the theorist's creative process, with all of its false starts puzzling personal questions and, one hopes, eventual solutions. There is an advantage in this approach that is as subtle as it is certain. Observing the thinking processes of idea-makers is an apprenticeship in cognition: Sometimes totally unaware that they are doing so, readers find themselves inductively reasoning to the solution of a problem as the theorist that they are reading about has done, or they deduce questions, see anomalies, or discover exceptions to a new theory in the way that a previously studied theorist might have done. Attention to thinking about psychological issues, along with its errors and sequential changes, teaches psychological thinking.

NEW IN THE SIXTH EDITION

Beneath the Mask, Sixth Edition includes two new chapters representing the addition of two object relations theorists (Melanie Klein and D.W. Winnicott) and one existential/humanist (Rollo May) who makes a return in this edition. One previously represented theorist (Lewin) has been removed to make room for the new. Numerous brief updates to the content of individual chapters, graphic revisions to tables and charts, and additions of historically relevant photographs enhance the reading experience. Overall, substantial revisions have been made throughout the remaining chapters of the sixth edition to update the work of theorists who continue to expand their thinking and writing, to incorporate the ever growing historical scholarship that continues to probe the classical theories, and to provide new conceptual tools that permit what I believe is a deeper understanding of these theories of human nature. At the same time, great care has been taken to preserve the continuity of substance and style from the earlier editions. Readers of earlier editions will find most of the familiar landmarks along with some new signposts.

Specific Changes

CHAPTER 1 (Varieties of Theory and Basic Issues) has been extensively rewritten and expanded to provide a more real and life-like introduction to the puzzles of personality theory, highlighting the clinical phenomena that are so often at issue. The discussion of normal and abnormal personalities ("The Short Course on Psychopathology") has been retained and updated and new graphic elements and tables replace the old ones for increased clarity. The clinical nosology introduced in Chapter 1 is *compatible* with the fourth edition of the *Diagnostic and Statistical Manual of Mental Disorders (DSM-IV)*, but it is, I believe, a far better teaching tool. More conceptual, developmental and, above all, clearer than the *DSM*, the clinical nosology permits a grasp of the developmental severity of psychopathologies by using cognitive and emotional severity markers to chart each disorder's impact. At the same time, the clinical nosology is a teaching tool that avoids overwhelming the learner with clinical jargon or unreliable and invalid taxonomic details. Personality and individuality are placed at the heart of a deep understanding of psychopathology that the "glossary of diseases" approach taken by the *DSM* altogether misses. Chapter 1 also now includes an expanded Chronology of Theorists that also can be used for alphabetical searches.

CHAPTERS 2 AND 3 (Freud) have been updated, some historically relevant photographs have been added, and the scientific evaluation section of Chapter 3 has been updated and expanded.

CHAPTER 4 (Anna Freud) retains most of the previous edition's material on ego psychology and expands to present coverage of *Freud's neurological model* ("The Project for a Scientific Psychology") as part of the historical analysis of "what Freud left undone." Heinz Kohut has been moved from this chapter into Chapter 5 to join the newly added object relations theorists in whose company, no doubt, Kohut would feel less like brown shoes in a world of tuxedos.

CHAPTER 5, a new chapter, presents two object relations theorists newly added for this edition: Melanie Klein and D.W. Winnicot. These two new arrivals are joined by

Heinz Kohut, who was formerly in the chapter with Anna Freud. The chapter also expands previous discussion of the historical development of object relations theory and its impact on classical psychoanalysis.

CHAPTER 10 (Rollo May) is a new chapter in this edition and replaces the previous edition's Kurt Lewin. Rollo May is a returning theorist whose work was presented in *Beneath the Mask, Fourth Edition.*

CHAPTER 16 (Watson, Skinner, Miller and Dollard, and Albert Bandura: Radical and Cognitive Behaviorism) has been updated with Bandura's *latest ideas on self-efficacy,* including his developmental analysis of the differing and progressive demands on self-efficacy at various phases of the life cycle.

CHAPTER 17 (Eysenck) expands in two ways. A new Personal Sources section has been added that explores the links between Eysenck's childhood experiences and his characteristic professional "tough-mindedness." A detailed account of *J.A. Gray's proposed modifications* of Eysenck's dimensions with considerations of his concepts of biologically based reward and punishment sensitivity has also been added to the chapter.

CHAPTER 18 (So, Which Theory Is Right?) has been updated, including a discussion of the parallels between the newly added *Object Relations Theorists' Personal sources* and their ideas to spotlight the themes of inferiority and unwantedness that appear repeatedly in the majority of theorists' lives.

Pedagogical Changes

- Further Reading sections have been updated.
- Many figures have been redrawn and expanded for clarity and precision.
- New art has been added to several chapters for enhanced historical detail.
- The *Instructor's Manual* has been completely revised for this edition.

Readers familiar with *Beneath the Mask* will find much that is changed or expanded, for the better I hope, along with many familiar themes and emphases. Readers' comments, as always, are welcomed.

My thanks to Carol Wada, Executive Psychology Editor; Janie Pierce-Bratcher, Developmental Editor; Laura Miley, Project Editor; David Day, Senior Art Director; and Andrea Johnson, Production Manager.

C.F.M.
E-mail:
cmonpsy@aol.com

Contents

SO, WHICH THEORY IS RIGHT?   932

VARIETIES OF
THEORY AND BASIC ISSUES

Masks are arrested expressions and admirable echoes of feeling, at once faithful, discreet, and superlative.

George Santayana, *Soliloquies in England*

In Confession the sinner tells what he knows; in analysis the neurotic has to tell more.

Sigmund Freud, *The Question of Lay Analysis*

PROBLEM OF THE MASK: AN ILLUSTRATIVE CASE

The director of the seminary called before 5 A.M. that morning to ask the psychologist's opinion on a troubling matter. Still half asleep, the psychologist did his best to elevate the level of his phone demeanor to daytime coherence, but through the lifting fog of sleep he could only croak "uh-huh." Pause. Silence. Auto pilot engaged. "Tell me more."

Dark Angel

The director's story was eye opening. Gabriel Grandé, a first-year Brooklyn seminary student and candidate for the Roman Catholic priesthood, had emerged from his room—bedraggled, pajama top torn at the shoulder, back and shoulders scratched and bloodied—with the announcement that he had fought with a "dark angel," in a struggle for his soul.[1] From Gabriel's viewpoint, the good news was that he had won the battle. From the seminary director's viewpoint, the bad news was that Gabriel was telling everyone about it.

As the details emerged, the psychologist began to grasp the outlines of the dilemma that was so troubling the seminary director before sunrise. In the middle of the night Gabriel awakened his seminary residence mates in the adjoining suites with several screams, sounds of a scuffle, and three loud thumps on the connecting wall. Within minutes, a half-dozen startled seminary students were dribbling sleepily out of their rooms to check on the commotion. Commotion was rare in the seminary, and middle of the night Satanic confrontations were unprecedented. Seemingly oblivious to tradition, Gabriel Grandé had launched a world-class precedent-setter.

The Diagnostic Dilemma

The seminary director voiced his dilemma directly. What, he wanted to know, was needed here: an exorcist or a psychologist? Was Gabriel Grandé's "unusual experience" a spiritual or psychological problem? To the psychologist, the answer seemed obvious. "I'm pretty sure even without evaluating the man," the psychologist told the worried seminary director, "that it's a psychological problem." The director was unconvinced. "How can you be so certain it's *not* a spiritual matter?" he wanted to know. The psychologist's willingness to entertain a supernatural explanation for the man's behavior might have been greater during normal business hours. "I doubt that the devil would make the trip to Brooklyn," he said. The remark was greeted with silence. More silence. Prolonged silence. "Oy. This will be no piece of strudel, Uncle Sigmund," the psychologist told himself.

A clash of cultures was operating here. In the seminary director's world, reports of "dark angels," and battles between personified good and evil were, if not routine, at least plausible events. In the psychologist's world, battles with dark angels instantly called into question a person's grasp on reality. Both of these experienced and astute

---

[1] The complete case of Gabriel Grandé with clinical assessment data and life history details can be had in Monte (1993).

evaluators of human behavior were wrong. But at that moment neither of them could envision the possibility that their long-established convictions would prove to be simply inapplicable.

The Psychological Evaluation

Gabriel Grandé was frustratingly contradictory. True to his name, Gabriel was flamboyant in the way he dressed and in the language he used, but he professed a deeply felt humility in accord with the vocation he had chosen. He appeared for his psychological evaluation in clerical collar and tunic worn with jeans and studded motorcycle boots. He exuded an air of complexity and mystery, but did so with such transparent pretentiousness that he impressed people as pompous, not charismatic. He made such a show of being guarded about his feelings and thoughts that he revealed instantly the depth of his low self-regard. This bundle of contradictions now claimed that his battle with the "dark angel" was only the most recent episode of an ongoing war he had fought with satanic influences since his teen years. He spoke of his repeated experiences with the "occult" in arcane jargon, and stated that he could not be too detailed so that he would "not violate confidences." Neither the psychologist's nor the seminary director's worldviews could tolerate such contradictions in a person without generating an extreme explanation for them. Where the psychologist assumed psychosis, the seminary director entertained the possibility of demonic intervention.

Gabriel Grandé's psychological evaluation upon entry into the seminary about a year before the dark angel episode revealed little that could be interpreted as anticipating the current crisis. The evaluating psychologist administered a battery of tests and assessments and noted tendencies for Gabriel to be enthusiastic but defensive about admitting his insecurities. Gabriel's interpersonal relationships were described as tending toward the "superficial," but the only really negative finding at the time of admission was that Gabriel's

> frustration tolerance tends to be low and when things don't go his way he can become evasive, argumentative, and angry. It seems that he is not sure of himself or others and experiences anxiety as well as a wary attitude towards the environment (quoted in Monte, 1993, p. 165).

In the present crisis, the consulting psychologist administered a similar battery of objective and projective personality tests supplemented by an extensive life history and clinical interview. To the psychologist's surprise, no indications of defective reality testing, incipient psychosis, or overtly delusional thinking were found. The seminary director's dilemma had suddenly become the psychologist's puzzle.

The personality data were as definitive as they ever get: There was no demonstrable defect in Gabriel's contact with reality. If Gabriel's reports of battles with dark angels were not the products of psychotic or delusional thinking, then the alternative explanation was left unchallenged. One had to conclude that Gabriel was accurately reporting authentic occult experiences. But explanations rooted in the occult had no place in the psychologist's worldview. Demonic intervention or defective reality testing? "If these are my only choices, Uncle Sigmund," the psychologist thought, "then either I'm in the wrong business or there is a third possibility that I am simply not seeing." It took substantial rethinking, but eventually the psychologist captured the unthinkable "third possibility" that had been eluding everyone.

Gabriel Grandé was neither psychotic nor possessed. He was a liar. *Dissimulating* is the clinically polite term for Gabriel's level of truth distortion. He was a skilled actor beneath a very theatrical mask. Enacting the leading role in a drama of his own creation, Gabriel was pretending, not heroically defending. Masks reveal what they conceal. By donning some masks, but not others, people disclose precisely what they would most shield. Indeed, a person does not hide behind a mask so much as struggle beneath the weight of it. But the realization that Gabriel was dissimulating raised a host of new questions: What sort of person must he be to mount such a skillful show of what he was not? Had the poseur become the pose, a player living his role? Had the actor become his mask? If so, is not that level of self-deception a personality pathology in itself?

In his final report to the seminary director, the psychologist pointed out that some vulnerable people who communicate their worlds of make-believe come to believe what they have made. Pretender and pretense become one. Where, the psychologist wondered, in all this effort to mask personal reality, is the person? Or is the apparent dilemma more illusion than substance? Perhaps role playing in the extreme version enacted by Gabriel Grandé ought to be understood as reflecting some authentic—if nevertheless eccentric—facet of Gabriel's personality.

THE QUESTIONS FOR PERSONALITY THEORY

A central issue for theories of personality, first framed with care by Gordon Allport (1968, p. 377), is the crucial and difficult decision to be made about what characteristics of a person evidence personality. Allport put the question this way: "How shall a psychological life history be written? What processes and what structures must a full-bodied account of a personality include? How can one detect unifying threads in a life, if they exist?"

If this small fragment ripped from the stream of episodes that comprise the life of Gabriel Grandé has any meaning whatsoever, how shall the personal narrative of confrontation with a dark angel be construed by the investigator of personality? Is not enacting a pretense as much a quality of personality—not to say "dysfunction"— as courage and cowardice, generosity and stinginess, or truth-telling? "If someone obstinately and for a long time wants to appear something," the philosopher Nietzsche wrote, "it is in the end hard for him to be anything else."

Is the *real* Gabriel somehow different from Gabriel the storyteller? Or is this incident so unusual as to have no connection to the "unifying threads" of Gabriel Grandé's ongoing life history? Are Gabriel's actions situationally determined? After all, this candidate for the priesthood created a dark angel fantasy not a secret agent or a war hero fantasy. *Personally determined? Biologically determined? Parentally determined? Actor or mask? Person or situation? Enduring characteristic or momentary aberration?* Even more fundamentally, it is possible to ask whether questions such as these are of any use to psychologists.

Almost every personality theory to be considered in this book explicitly employs the ancient metaphor of the actor and mask to distinguish between surface and deeper human qualities. Indeed, historically the most profound question of personality theory as a field of human psychology has been *Where is the person?* The theorists whose ideas are presented in this book have, with uneven success, looked for the person:

hidden within unobservable private thoughts,

displayed in observable behavior,

enacting roles across differing situations,

encoded by various parts of the central nervous system,

emerging from the spirals of the person's relationships with others,

embodied in the spirals-within-spirals of the person's view of those relationships,

imprisoned behind maladaptive signs and symptoms of psychopathology.

Even when one of these answers to the "where" question succeeds in satisfying someone's curiosity about the nature of personality, the classic "grand" theories of personality aspire to more. At the most fundamental level, psychological theories of personality are theories of human nature. It is from this more profound and older tradition of viewing human conduct that a deeper question emerges. *Who* is the person portrayed by a given theory? How authentically, believably, wholly does a theorist represent the people about whom he or she theorizes? And, for better or worse, is that theoretical representation scientifically *testable*? Can we know with some precision the validity or accuracy of a given theoretical portrait?

We shall see repeatedly that some theories meet this deeper and older question head-on, vigorously attempting to capture the "real," "private," "inner" agent who is only glimpsed in the façade presented for public scrutiny. Other theories take a different stance in the assumption that such questions are scientifically irrelevant because "what you see is what you get" and "what you see is all there is to get." And, of course, there are theories that aim to take possession of the best of both worlds by assuming that inferences can be made in scientifically testable ways about private thoughts from the person's public self-report of them.

SOME WAYS PERSONALITY IS UNDERSTOOD: THE THEORIES

In this book, 25 discrete, sometimes overlapping, theories of personality are presented. Almost always, a particular theorist's viewpoint is recounted with careful attention to the detail and emphasis that characterized the theorist's own development of those concepts. Each of the 25 theories, insofar as it is possible, is given full and sympathetic treatment. Along these lines, we have tried to imagine how a given theorist might present his or her theory to people learning it for the first time. This approach results frequently in what Robert White (1981) has called "studying personality the long way." In the present context, the long way means that each theory is permitted to expand to its fullest dimensions, narrate the history of its development, and demonstrate its progression through the many "changes of mind" that its creator experienced. The goal is to expose each theory in a light that reflects its contribution to the field of personality in its entirety and in a way that does not violate the theorist's own struggle to understand human nature.

The consequence of this sympathetic approach is that some residue of disappointment is inevitable. "But which theory is right?" students protest. "That is an inappropriate question because it is unanswerable," instructors reply. To some extent, the students' question is a good one, an inquiry deserving of reply on its own terms. It represents the timeless desire to know with some precision whether human existence is meaningful—whether, in fact, anyone has discovered a strategy for making sense of human nature.

Yet the instructors' traditional reply is a fair one, for it suggests that absolute truths, unbending certainties, are not to be found in psychology's study of personality. The Socratic dictum, "Know thyself," is always interpreted, never merely obeyed. The dilemma boils down to a single issue: How are we to decide among the *interpretations* of human personality? Psychologists are reluctant to answer this question because a unified strategy of determining the validity of competing theories is not yet within reach. And even if such validity tests were agreed upon, some theories are constructed in ways that defy tests of their accuracy.

Unfortunately, it is precisely such questions about the accuracy of personality theories that engender student frustration. A *scientific* theory of personality is likely to be far different in structure and content from any commonsense notion of what a useful theory of human nature should be. Restrictions imposed by scientific method make it a near certainty that satisfying generalizations about human conduct will yield to unsatisfying, sometimes trivial experimental abstractions (more about this restriction later). Rae Carlson (1971, p. 207) has listed the limitations of current research methods in personality:

> We cannot study the organization of personality because we know at most only one or two "facts" about any subject. We cannot study the stability of personality, nor its development over epochs of life, because we see our subjects for an hour. We cannot study the problems or capacities of the mature individual, because we study late adolescents [i.e., college students]. We cannot study psychosexuality, because we avoid looking at distinctive qualities of masculinity and femininity as a focal problem. We cannot study how persons strive for their important goals, because we elect to induce motivational sets. We cannot study constitutional, temperamental variables because . . . we do not consider biological bases of personality. We cannot study the development and power of friendship—nor the course of true love—because we choose to manipulate interpersonal attraction.

Personology: Studying Personality the "Long Way"

None of the theories we present here can convey the essence of Gabriel's personality as richly as a series of anecdotes can. Critical incidents in Gabriel's life are more satisfying, aesthetically more pleasing, than any scientific theory of personality could ever be. But no collection of anecdotes, no grouping of revealing crises, can effectively explain or predict *general* human behavior. If the question "Which theory is right?" remains unanswerable, it nevertheless requires some patience, some forbearance, to understand why. In the last chapter of this book, we return to this question.

A related issue concerns the reasons that some personality psychologists have preferred to be called *personologists*. This term is meant to indicate a distinctly different research tradition and conceptual strategy from that of psychologists who have traditionally been known as personality theorists. Henry A. Murray, an early pioneer of personology, defined the concept this way:

> The branch of psychology which principally concerns itself with the study of *human lives* and the factors that influence their course, which investigates *individual differences* and types of personality, may be termed "personology" instead of "the psychology of personality," a clumsy and tautological expression. Personology, then, is the science of men, taken as gross units. . . . (1938, p. 4; italics added)

As Robert White, one of Murray's students and himself an eminent personologist explained, Henry Murray came from a tradition of medical research where multiple sources of information, detailed diagnostic interviews, and complete histories were routine procedure. What was not routine was Murray's incorporation of these detailed, clinical methods into personality psychology. At Harvard, in the 1930s, Murray set up a Diagnostic Council of clinical psychologists and graduate students in clinical psychology. Members of the council included students and faculty who would later go on to shape the field of personality, among them Gordon Allport, Erik Erikson, Robert White, and Murray himself. The goal was to examine in detail individual life histories using every method they could devise or borrow: experimentation, observation, interviewing, personality testing, life history analysis, and direct contact of every member of the council with every subject in the research program. The work led eventually to Murray (1938) and his collaborator's classic book *Explorations in Personality*, a monumental achievement by anyone's standards. Here are some of Robert White's recollections of that fertile period in personality study:

> The use of a diagnostic council was no novelty to a veteran of medical staff conferences. It had not, however, been offered before in the study of personality, presumably because the information collected was so sparse and superficial as hardly to deserve a conference. But with mountains of data, and with variables that did not show themselves in just one way, it would have been perilous indeed not to rely on multiple judgments. The diagnostic council of *Explorations* [*in Personality*] consisted of seven people whose duty it was to become familiar with all the material on each subject. A taxing aspect of this duty was the rating of each subject on a six-point scale on each of the variables. This was done in conference with the goal of reaching consensus on each rating. You can easily imagine that these conferences were not brief, that argument and the calling up of evidence could develop a good deal of heat, and that the ultimate consensus might be surrounded by a halo of frayed tempers. Interpretations, conclusions, the development of the total picture, went through the same strenuous mill, and the life history that emerged as the final product was thus protected from the risk of purely personal bias by resting on a foundation of collective judgment. (White, 1981, p. 11)

Personology Versus "Studying Personality Without Looking at It"

The personologist is concerned with the *life history*, the coherent stream of feelings, events, traits, and situations that characterize individual personalities. Thus the question "How shall a psychological life history be written?" is a *personological* query. The question "Do subjects high in their need to achieve success cheat on exams more often than low need achievement subjects?" is not. The essential difference lies not so much in the content of the two inquiries as in the lack of breadth evidenced by the second one. Personologists are interested in whole persons, in their unique adjustment to the circumstances of their lives. The personologist would find the second question of interest only to the extent that research results obtained under its banner fit into an entire pattern of information about high need achievement subjects.

As White has pointed out, there has been a dearth of efforts in psychology to study personality in all of its complexity and richness (see also Sanford, 1985). We prefer sometimes to give two personality tests to a group of people and simply correlate the results as if that were somehow indicative of this intricate and elaborate system called personality.

> Of course there are many elaborations upon this design, introducing experimental situations, different treatments, and highly sophisticated statistical procedures. But none of these entail any real personal contact with the subjects or any attempt to think of them as more than momentarily living people. For some time I have described this type of research as *studying personality without looking at it*. Psychologists who are satisfied to work this way have either not read [Murray's] *Explorations* or have pushed it aside into some category which they do not feel obliged to take seriously. (White, 1981, p. 15; italics in original)

Most of the theories we examine have long historical development connected with them. And most of the theories reflect, sometimes to a surprising degree, the richness of the human personality in the tradition of personology. But something is lost for what is gained in detail and complexity. As we shall see, many of the theories are more literary and less scientific than we would like. Striking a balance between study of the individual and obtaining results that generalize to humanity is a very difficult art.

A USEFUL METAPHOR: THE MASK

Gordon Allport traced the etymological roots of the words *personality*. In classical Latin, the word *persona* was employed with a variety of meanings:

1. as one appears to others (but not as one really is)
2. the part someone (e.g., a philosopher) plays in life
3. an assemblage of personal qualities that fit a man for his work
4. distinction and dignity (as in a style of writing). (Allport, 1937, p. 26)

Allport further traced the meaning of the term persona to an antecedent phrase in Latin: *per sonare*, meaning "to sound through." The noun persona had originated as the designation for the masks worn by Greek actors and later adopted by their Roman counterparts. Thus the phrase *per sonare* referred to the mouthpiece of the theatrical mask through which the actor's voice was projected. The four meanings as cited by Allport demonstrate that the term persona slowly evolved to a more abstract designation indicating the dichotomy between appearance (the mask) and the actor.

The Greek equivalent, *prosôpon*, also designated the theatrical mask and the distinction between superficial and fundamental characteristics (Allport, 1937, p. 25).

The implication of Allport's survey of the linguistic roots of the word personality is that below the surface of *public* behavior there is a private, and perhaps different, person concealed from view. Nevertheless, it is possible to question the further implicit assumption that the inner person is more real or genuine than the surface phenomenon. Most contemporary psychologists, with the exception of the humanists (e.g., Rogers, Maslow) take a dim view of this distinction. To them it seems a great deal like magical thinking because they see no reason to look for inner persons when overt behavior is adequate for scientific study (cf. Bandura, 1986; Berlyne, 1968; Eysenck, 1963b; Kelly, 1955; Lundin, 1963; Mischel, 1985; Skinner, 1953, 1956, 1963, 1971, 1974; Wilkinson, 1973).

By contrast, other psychologists, such as Angyal (1941, 1965), Laing, Sullivan, and Allport feel that theories of personality which attend only to observable behavior with no inferences or assumptions about an inner core of experience lose contact with the very stuff they seek to understand. The legitimacy of the separation between the actor (inner person) and the observables (the mask) is assumed by these theorists to be a personality given—with the stipulation that eventually, as theoretical sophistication grows, personality psychology will be able to reconstruct the whole person and weld together the necessarily fragmented elements of actor and mask into a unified scheme.

Reducing Gabriel Grandé's personality to a description of his past reinforcement history or to a discussion of his degree of introversion/extroversion seems far removed from the "real" Gabriel. For our purposes, therefore, it is an acknowledged and convenient metaphor to conceptualize personality as the study of the actor and mask, as the person and persona. It is a metaphor, however, and not a precise description or evaluation of theoretical strategies. Convenient in its role of conceptualizing the degree to which a particular theory contacts the whole person, the actor-mask analogy increases the risk of creating pseudoproblems in personality psychology. It is risk, however, worth taking. The majority of theorists we discuss seem to agree, as evidenced by their use of the metaphor in their writings.

Throughout the following chapters, we indicate the many theorists who actually explicitly employ the actor-mask metaphor in their works (e.g., Freud, Chapters 2, 3; Jung, Chapter 7; Adler, Chapter 8; Laing, Chapter 10; Kelly, Chapter 12; Erikson, Chapter 6; Fromm, Chapter 13; Allport, Chapter 14; and Maslow and Rogers, Chapter 15). Theorists who prefer equivalent formulations to distinguish between central and peripheral personality phenomena (e.g., Anna Freud, Chapter 4; Horney, Chapter 13; Sullivan, Chapter 9; May, Chapter 11; and Miller and Dollard, Chapter 16) demonstrate the universality of this problem. Other theorists "solve" the problem by simple omission or by direct contradiction that such a problem exists (e.g., Eysenck, Chapter 17; Bandura, Chapter 16; and Skinner, Chapter 16). Yet, by their omission of inner and outer, central and peripheral distinctions, these theorists indicate the complexity of the task of conceptualizing real people.

The metaphor of the actor and the mask was used by Carl Jung to indicate the public self of the individual, the image presented to others, as contrasted with feelings, cognitions, and interpretations of reality anchored in the private self. Without adopting Jung's entire theoretical formulation, this usage of the term persona or mask will serve as our definition. Jung defined the persona in this way:

> Fundamentally the persona is nothing real: it is a compromise between individual and society as to what a man should appear to be. He takes a name, earns a title, exercises a function, he is this or that. In a certain sense all this is real, yet in relation to the essential individuality of the person concerned it is only a secondary reality, a compromise formation, in making which others often have a greater share than he. (1935, p. 158)

Jung seems to be identifying the persona with the concept of social role. The same use of the metaphor has also been made by Erving Goffman (1959; cf. 1961). Goffman has suggested, as had Jung, that the mask may become more real than the actor.

> [An] . . . illustration may be found in the raw recruit who initially follows army etiquette in order to avoid physical punishment and eventually comes to follow the rules so that his organization will not be shamed and his officers and fellow soldiers will respect him. (1959, p. 20)

Goffman employs a number of other distinctions drawn from theatrical vocabulary to illustrate the difference between the performance of a role and the actor's genuine belief that he or she *is* the role.

Sidney Jourard (1971a, 1971b) has investigated the conditions under which an individual will reveal various kinds of personal information to another person.

> The most powerful determiners of self-disclosure thus far discovered are the identity of the person to whom one might disclose himself and the nature and purpose of the relationship between the two people. More specifically, it has been found that disclosure of one's experience is most likely when the other person is perceived as a trustworthy person of good will and/or one who is willing to disclose his experience to the same depth and breadth. (1971a, p. 65)

Ironically, Viktor Frankl used the metaphor of the mask to describe the approach of the psychoanalytic therapist who tries to uncover hidden motives behind conscious reasons. Sometimes, according to Frankl, such "unmasking" approaches are carried away by their own momentum so that no motive is taken as genuine, accepted as real. All human tendencies are thus subject to continuous efforts to reduce them to more fundamental urges, with the result that "unmasking" becomes a goal in itself. Frankl (1959) comments, "What is needed, I would say, is an unmasking of the unmasker! Although in some cases unmasking may be right, the tendency to unmask must be able to stop in front of that which is genuine in man; else, it reveals the unmasking psychologist's own tendency to devaluate" (see also Erich Fromm's [1976] similar use of the metaphor in Chapter 13).

"NORMAL" AND "ABNORMAL" PERSONALITIES

On their face, theories of personality aim to describe "normal" interpersonal transactions and "normal" personality. From the very outset, however, theories of personality were constructed with close attention to the abnormal. Pathology was seen as an indispensable exaggeration, an extreme exemplar from which principles could be derived that would explain the typical by deciphering what had gone wrong in the atypical.

With precious few exceptions—only Abraham Maslow, George Kelly, and Gordon Allport come readily to mind—theorists of all intellectual stripes peered into the depths of their own and others' psychopathology to construct their vision of general personality functioning. Sigmund Freud began the trend as early as 1895 with his first, largely neurological, model of personality that he described as a "general psychology" with equal importance for normal and abnormal functioning (Freud, 1895, pp. 283–284). But, in truth, his neurology of 1895 was predominantly a brain model of personality derived from the treatment of hysterical conversion and other "neurotic" disorders.

Despite this history of the discipline, writers in personality, especially textbook authors, have sidestepped abnormal psychology in their accounts of personality and its theorists. Such sidestepping reflects the now outmoded belief that there is a clear demarcation between the normal and abnormal personality. Preserving what has thus come to be an increasingly unworkable convention, books on personality theory rarely explicitly treat the concept of the abnormal personality when discussing the classic theories. Abnormality sneaks in, of course, because it has to. Most of the classical and many of the contemporary theories of personality address issues of abnormality. Indeed, a majority of these theories originated in attempts to treat specific "abnormalities." But psychopathology in the context of personality theory has always been the country cousin—a poor relative that is tolerated only for the short term.

Fortunately, this narrowness of vision is broadening. Evolving work in the statistical analysis of traits that reliably cluster together on relatively few dimensions offers an opportunity to diminish the categorical thinking that has characterized the field of personality. Called the *Five Factor Model*, this increasingly accepted approach makes possible the rediscovery of the abnormal personality as an especially clear scientific window on some aspects of the normal personality, as well as enhancing the traditional value of looking through the window from the other side (McCrae, 1994; Widiger, Trull, Clarkin, Sanderson, & Costa, 1994). The "Big Five" model, as it is affectionately known by its supporters, also embodies a Galilean scientific outlook that permits normal and abnormal to be understood not as different in kind but as different in degree.

To understand these important changes in the psychology of personality we need the historical and conceptual context provided by the concepts of Aristotelian and Galilean thinking. Our aim is to understand how this evolving consensus in personality psychology about the nature of its subject is likely to widen as well as deepen our grasp of the normal and abnormal personality.

The Galilean Approach to Deep Understanding

It was Kurt Lewin (1935, 1936) who first clearly defined the differences between what he named *Aristotelian* (categorical) and *Galilean* (dimensional) scientific thinking. For the present discussion, the essential point is that Lewin explained how the Galilean thinker's more sophisticated strategy aims to understand nature by "homogenizing" *superficial* differences in seemingly unrelated phenomena. By making explicit the deeper commonalities natural phenomena embody, categorical distinctions and seemingly insurmountable incompatibilities evaporate. A more profound, frequently simpler, and more elegant understanding of nature and its causes is thereby achieved. An unintended but nevertheless fortuitous effect of the Big Five is the concept that personality *and its disorders* can be described in terms of a limited number of trait dimensions. If that hypothesis continues to receive support, the Big Five will thrust contemporary personality psychology squarely into the Galilean mode of thinking. Since the last edition of this text (Monte, 1995), where the importance of the Aristotelian-Galilean distinction for diagnostic taxonomies was introduced, the idea, apparently, has caught on (Carson, 1996).

To illustrate Galilean understanding, consider three seemingly diverse psychological phenomena. We might understand dreams, neurotic symptoms, and occasional slips of the tongue as behaviors marked by the enormity of their differences. Or, like Freud, we can look for a deeper property that homogenizes these behaviors by proposing a cause or common organizing principle that encompasses all. For Freud, this deeper property was the unconscious wish. The person who wishes is conflicted and wants simultaneously to gratify and to disavow a taboo urge. To achieve a compromise solution to the conflict, the person unconsciously creates a disguised or derivative version of the wish. Altered in this important way, the disguised wish is sufficiently different from the taboo wish that it is, at least superficially, renounced; but the disguised wish is also sufficiently similar to the taboo wish that it permits *some* gratification of the original urge.

This process of disguise, disavowal, and partial gratification is, appropriately enough, called *compromise formation* in classical psychoanalysis. Freud's explanation of these unconscious maneuvers, for good or bad, was an attempt to find a deep and common principle that would explain diverse behaviors. Thus the dreamer entertains in sleep a taboo wish that he or she could not gratify awake. A neurotic person's hysterically paralyzed arm prevents going to work, a guilty wish come true that is less guilt-provoking if one is sick. And the college professor who introduces an unwelcome guest speaker with the opening remark, "I would like to *prevent*, uhh, present—" is gratifying but simultaneously disowning a hostile wish. Diverse behaviors. Deep, Galilean explanation.

The validity of Freud's Galilean explanation for these behaviors is another matter. Psychoanalytic conceptual accuracy is discussed in Chapters 2 and 3. But the conceptual strategy is clear: Homogenization of diverse phenomena can enhance understanding of what nature has made. By searching for a limited number of underlying principles, rather than by categorizing each phenomenon as a unique entity, a deep understanding is achieved (cf. Wertheimer, 1959). For our present discussion of the Big Five personality factors and the changes they may bring to the study of normal and abnormal personality we need to familiarize ourselves with the range of abnormal behavior.

The Deep Understanding of Normal and Abnormal Personalities

One way that abnormal psychological functioning has been understood is to regard psychological dysfunctions as medical "disorders" that fit into discrete categories with little or no overlap between classes. It is important to recognize that once a descriptive category system is used, there is the risk that behaviors so categorized will be seen as "different in kind" from behaviors that lie outside the categories. Consequently, behavior categorized as "abnormal" can be seen as so different from behavior we agree to call "normal" that underlying links, commonalities, and causation shared with normality are lost. We may even assign such a profoundly influential category name—for example "disease"—to one class of behavior that the label foreclosing the possibility of any alternative explanations.

Since 1980, the prevailing diagnostic system in the United States has been the *Diagnostic and Statistical Manual of Mental Disorders-III* or *DSM-III*, and its more recent revised descendant, the *DSM-III-R* (APA, 1980, 1987). The current fourth edition, called the *DSM-IV* (American Psychiatric Association, 1994), adheres to the practices established in earlier versions and greatly amplifies the number of diagnostic categories and the level of their descriptive detail. The various *DSM*s serve as the official diagnostic system for abnormal psychological functioning, including personality disorders. Psychologists have not been always happy with the *DSM*, citing its perceived scientific, conceptual, and philosophical shortcomings. The debate over the *DSM* is a story so complicated that we cannot pursue it here. We can focus, however, on two central issues in the debate.

First, the *DSM* classifies mental disorders into discrete, nontheoretical categories that employ observable behaviors as *descriptive* criteria for diagnosis. Deliberate exclusion of overt conceptual or theoretical bases in favor of "pure" description has led some critics to argue that the *DSM* categories are adjectives in search of ideas. The second issue concerns the perceived poor reliability and validity (consistency and accuracy) of these categories. Certainly they are sufficiently far from ideal that clinicians sometimes fail to agree on the presence or absence of a syndrome in a specific patient, and sometimes cannot even identify in anyone syndromes that the *DSM* has established as diagnostic entities. Clinical psychologists want a system with descriptive power, but they prefer one that is founded solidly on developmental and psychological concepts.

An alternative to the *DSM*'s approach to abnormal psychological functioning is the rich historical tradition known as the *clinical nosology* (Monte, 1993, p. 7). A nosology is a classification system based on conceptual, sometimes developmental, principles. Informal and rarely taught directly, the clinical nosology is part of the "underground" wisdom of clinical psychologists and other mental health professionals (see the classic studies by Fey, 1958 and Fiedler, 1950a,b; 1951; and Howard & Orlinsky, 1970). Since the turn of the 20th century, clinicians have communicated with each other in the more or less precise and consistent language of the clinical nosology that describes abnormal behaviors as lying on a conceptual dimension of severity (Goldfried, 1980; Langs, 1973, pp. 235 ff.; Masterson, Tolpin, & Sifneos, 1991).

Position on the clinical severity dimension, and especially the psychological meaning of that position, can be tracked for each class of disorder by monitoring severity markers that clearly reflect the level of disorganization in the personality (for example, see Menninger, Mayman, & Pruyser's [1963] classic discussion of one such nosology, and Vaillant's [1993, 1994] similar approach to matching psychopathology, personality, and maturity of defensive functioning; the clinical nosology presented here shares much with their work). Our goal is to provide a concise conceptual road map to basic psychopathology because personality theory so often crosses paths with abnormal functioning, and because recent research developments associated with the Big Five promise a kind of universal descriptive system that will homogenize and reunify the study of normal and abnormal with disorders of personality at the center of the psychopathology universe. We turn, then, to the short course in psychopathology.

THE SHORT COURSE IN PSYCHOPATHOLOGY

Figure 1.1 displays the clinical nosology for the main psychological disorders. The disorder-free person at the zero level is, of course, a conceptual figment to serve as an anchor point in the scale, not as a paragon of mental stability. One might regard such a person in Freud's and Erikson's terms as one who can love and work and play, but who is not thereby necessarily free of conflict, anxiety, guilt, or stress (Erikson, 1950, p. 265).

From left to right along the continuum in Figure 1.1, the disorders are arranged in order of increasing severity. There are progressively more intense identifiable changes— "deteriorations" might be the better word—in the person's *reality testing* and *interpersonal relationships* as one proceeds toward the right end of the continuum.

Reality testing can be defined as the person's ability to distinguish the inner world of memory, fantasy, drive, and wish from the outer world of perceived events, time, people, and places. By the same token, reality testing includes the ability to process incoming perceptual and cognitive information *veridically*, that is, accurately. Hallucinations, for example, would be definitive evidence of a gross failure of reality testing whereas the *frequent* experience of déjà vu would represent only a lesser defect in reality testing.

Interpersonal relations—"object relations" as the psychoanalyst would prefer to call them—are an important indicator of the quality and stability of the person's transactions with the social world. Interpersonal relations can be mature, reciprocal, independent, and caring, or they can be destructive, manipulative, conflicted, and bizarre. In some cases, interpersonal relations can even be "fantastic," based on the person's gross failures to understand other people as independent entities with rights, needs, and wishes of their own. The range is quite broad, but in the clinical nosology the focus is on the degree of disruption to the person's interpersonal functioning as a sensitive indicator of severity.

These two cognitive-emotional functions—reality testing and interpersonal relations—are only an illustrative pair drawn from a dozen severity markers that might be tracked. For present purposes they will serve us well in the "short course" in psychopathology (see Bellak, Hurvich, & Gediman, 1973 for a complete profile of the severity markers that clinicians find useful). Although the clinical nosology is *DSM-IV* compatible, it is clearly far more conceptual and more deeply anchored in developmental and personality principles than any of the *DSM*s attempt to be. The clinical nosology is also compatible with all of the contemporary paradigms of psychopathology.

It is well to note that some common diagnoses, such as the sexual and eating disorders, are not listed in Figure 1.1. Disorders such as these may be found at virtually

FIGURE 1.1.   The Clinical Nosology

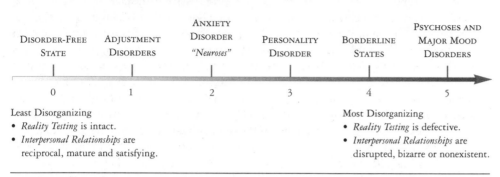

Note: The numbers in this scale are no more precise than rank orders indicating increasing severity and the width or range of each class. [Based on Monte, 1993]

any point in the continuum, a complication known as the problem of comorbidity. For the purposes of our short course in psychopathology, the sexual and eating disorders are therefore best understood only in the context of other disorders and other personality features of the person who embodies them. Thus a sexual or eating dysfunction in the context of an adjustment reaction is a quite different problem from either of these dysfunctions in the context of a borderline personality disorder or a major depressive episode, as we shall see.

Adjustment Disorders

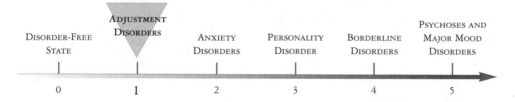

People who suffer with an *adjustment disorder* are displaying the psychological and physical effects of a recent stressful or even traumatic experience. Technically, such events are called *psychosocial stressors* and will date to the recent past of approximately three months and persist for not more than six months (American Psychiatric Association, 1994, p. 626). Unless other psychopathology is present, the person's reality testing remains intact, and only minor and temporary disruptions to their interpersonal relationships are likely. Of course, the precise meanings of qualifiers such as "minor" and "temporary" vary widely from person to person and also change with variations in the cause of the adjustment disorder. There are important differences of degree, for example, between the adjustment reaction of the person who experienced the disappointment of a failed bid on a new dream house and a person who witnessed the death of family and friends in an earthquake. Stressors can also be acute or chronic. There are vast differences in the phenomenology of experience between a person who undergoes a one-time acute trauma, such as a car wreck, and the person who experiences repeated and progressive physical or sexual abuse extending over many years at the hands of a family member (Coddington, 1989).

Severity of the symptoms associated with adjustment reactions vary widely with the individual. Generally, the symptoms are anxiety or depression, and sometimes both simultaneously (APA, 1994). Some few people in the throes of an adjustment reaction to a severe psychosocial stressor may exhibit the main features of a "disturbance of conduct" as the official diagnostic manual calls it. That is, they translate their anxious, angry, or sad feelings directly into behavior, thereby "acting out" the distress of the impulse they feel. Such changes in behavior, unusual for the person under normal circumstances, attract the attention of family and friends. Abrupt changes in eating and sleeping patterns, atypical angry outbursts, or highly unusual withdrawal into solitude are conduct disturbances that people familiar with the person undergoing the adjustment reaction will quickly detect.

In each case, however, as long as the psychopathology is an adjustment reaction *and nothing else,* the person's *reality testing* remains intact. *Interpersonal relationships* are only temporarily disrupted by the ongoing stress. The person may, for example, withdraw, be quick to anger or become sad, or perhaps, become unusually clingy and dependent. It is easy to envision, of course, that matters are rarely this uncomplicated. The problem of *comorbidity*—the simultaneous presence of more than one disorder and the nature of their associations—frequently complicates the clinical picture in adjustment reactions and in many other diagnostic categories.

The good news about adjustment reactions is that they are generally self-limiting disorders. If the stressor is removed or reduced, the person makes a substantial recovery (Coddington, 1989). In some extreme cases, professional intervention may be necessary, even when the stressor has been attenuated. The bad news from the afflicted person's point of view is that, during the course of the disorder, there is no good news. Knowing that adjustment reactions are self-limiting and the least severe of the psychopathologies is not comforting to the person experiencing one. A diagnosing professional may find some reassurance in the knowledge that the disorder is at a low level on the severity continuum, but the distressed person is not likely to feel thus blessed knowing that life has worse to offer.

Anxiety Disorders ("Neuroses")

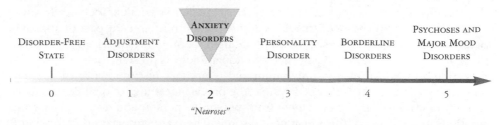

Marked primarily by symptoms that indicate high levels of anxiety and conflict, the aptly named *anxiety disorders* were known traditionally as the "neuroses." The person suffering from this class of disorder may not be able to identify the source of the anxiety—as is the case in *generalized anxiety disorder*—because several defense mechanisms are operating to protect the person from this self-awareness. Under such conditions, the anxiety is termed *free-floating* because the person does not experience it as anchored to a specific trigger idea or circumstance. From the afflicted person's point of view, the distressing feelings of fear, worry, and dread are a mystery. Reality testing is intact; indeed, some theorists would argue that the person is painfully attuned to reality (Adler, 1929b; Angyal, 1965; Horney, 1937, 1942).

By contrast, some anxiety disorders have focused symptoms in which the anxiety is anchored to specifics. These disorders include the classic *conversion hysterias* (currently called "Somatoform Disorders" in the *DSM*), made so well known by Freud in which a variety of sensory and motor dysfunctions mimic physical disease without real physical pathology, *phobias* that are unreasonable and unrealistic fears of places or things, and *obsessive-compulsive disorder* in which the person may carry out undoing rituals or other repetitive magical cancellations to cope with unwanted and persistent anxiety-provoking thoughts. There is also a class of neurotic-level disorders called *dissociative reactions* in the *DSM*, which involve psychologically triggered memory losses, typically for one's own identity. Another more controversial member of this subclass of "neuroses" is the dissociative disorder known as *multiple personality disorder*, which typically involves a person who reports several distinct, compartmentalized personalities.

There is even a kind of "neurotic" depression called *dysthymic disorder* also classed at this level of the clinical severity spectrum. The person suffering with dysthymic disorder is melancholy, lacks energy, and feels saddened and sometimes hopeless, helpless, and anxious all at once. Psychological stressors for dysthymic disorder, including personal losses and narcissistic injuries, are thought to be the necessary and sufficient triggers for this kind of mood disorder. But because reality testing remains intact and interpersonal relationships are, at worst, only conflicted, dysthymic disorder is not classed with the major mood disorders at level 5 of the nosology.

The neurotic person is a conflicted, anxious, and worried human being. Neurotic symptoms are said to be *ego dystonic*, meaning that they are unacceptable to and unwanted by the person who is not only aware of the distress he or she feels, but regards the symptoms as problematic and intrusive. Reality testing in the anxiety disorders is intact. Interpersonal relationships are conflicted; the very people the neurotic person wants most to love are simultaneously the targets of anger and hate. Nevertheless, interpersonal relationships provide at least modest satisfaction and have substantial durability, however rocky they may be at times.

A particularly severe form of anxiety disorder, *posttraumatic stress disorder*, may build on other psychopathology already present to exacerbate and prolong the intensity of the reaction to very severe stressors, such as war experiences, natural catastrophes, prolonged physical and sexual abuse, or hostage-taking. In instances such as these, the person may display a range of symptoms far in excess of the typical adjustment reaction or anxiety disorder to exhibit failures in reality testing, "flashbacks" and other recurring intrusive ideas, psychological numbing, depersonalization, and severely disrupted interpersonal relations. In some *very* extreme cases reality testing appears to fail, calling into question the placement of the disorder at this level or at least raising the question of comorbidity in the most severe cases (Horowitz, 1989). Careful research needs yet to be done to determine how best to understand and to classify this somewhat exceptional anxiety disorder (Coddington, 1989).

Personality Disorders

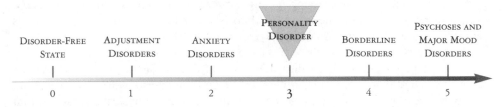

Marked primarily by the presence of troublesome and long-standing character traits, *personality disorders* put the person into conflict with the social environment. A long developmental history, sometimes dating from early childhood, is almost by definition a requirement for the emergence of these disorders. The key features of the person's history that shed light on his or her difficulties usually center on family interactions, crucial early learning experiences that were missed or went awry, overt "insults" to development, and a myriad of other cognitive and emotional abrasions throughout childhood (e.g., Bandura, 1986; Kernberg, 1992; Kirmayer, Robbins, & Paris, 1994; Millon, 1981; Smith-Benjamin, 1993).

Unlike the symptoms in anxiety disorder, personality disorders center on troublesome character *traits* that are *ego syntonic*, meaning that the person does not recognize the source of difficulties as stemming from the characteristics of self. The difficulties she or he experiences are attributed to other people or to circumstances beyond personal control, rather than to deficiencies of one's own character. Reality testing may be colored to some degree so that the person filters out negative information about self or perhaps employs other defenses to deny that there is anything wrong with self even in the face of substantial and repeated evidence to the contrary.

As you might expect, personality disorders embody substantial, pervasive, and persistent difficulties in interpersonal relationships. People with personality disorders may treat other people manipulatively, aggressively, selfishly, or indifferently (but see the historical review in Maher & Maher, 1994). In the more severe instances, such as *antisocial personality disorder*, the person may behave ruthlessly and without any awareness of, or concern for, the consequences to others of their destructive behavior. Reality testing nevertheless appears to be intact.

To take another example, for people with *histrionic personality disorder*, reality testing is intact, but interpersonal relationships are superficial and marked by strong, almost childish, needs for attention, and also are inappropriately intimate and easily disrupted. The histrionic person is dramatic, highly suggestible, and intensely emotional but with a superficial or shallow quality to the feelings that they seem to express so intensely. Such a person needs to be the center of attention and appears to view life as though it were a melodramatic soap opera replete with romantic villains and heroes (Shapiro, 1965; see also *DSM-IV* [APA, 1993]).

Similar elements of substantially disturbed interpersonal relationships with more or less intact reality testing are found in other disorders among the personality disorder group. Some examples:

Avoidant personality disorder is marked by chronic avoidance of intimate relationships, preoccupation with possible rejection and criticism, and enduring and profound feelings of inadequacy.

Dependent personality disorder centers around profound needs for constant reassurance and nurturance along with fears of abandonment and loss of approval so intense that the person cannot take responsibility for his or her own life, cannot make ordinary daily decisions or express routine disagreement with others for fear of losing their support.

Obsessive-compulsive personality disorder is reflected in preoccupations with rules, neatness, and organization to the point that such perfectionism blocks completing nearly any task. The person often misses the "big picture" in favor of trivial details, and this cognitive rigidity combines with moral inflexibility to produce a person who would be a very poor choice for a roommate.

Personality disorders are widely regarded as the most common diagnoses for people in distress. More important is the recently expressed view that personality disorders are fundamental, perhaps essential, to the development and course of other psychiatric illnesses (Millon, 1994; Walton, 1986; Watson, Clark & Harkness, 1994).

Borderline States

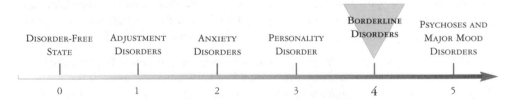

DISORDER-FREE STATE	ADJUSTMENT DISORDERS	ANXIETY DISORDERS	PERSONALITY DISORDER	BORDERLINE DISORDERS	PSYCHOSES AND MAJOR MOOD DISORDERS
0	1	2	3	4	5

The borderline states embody a different cluster of personality disorders that, as measured by our two severity markers, are more grave disturbances than those at level 3. Most recent of the diagnostic categories in the *DSM*, the concept of borderline conditions is one of the oldest ideas of the clinical nosology. *Borderline personality disorder (BPD)* was included for the first time in the official diagnostic system with the publication of *DSM-III* in 1980. Prior to the *DSM-III*, the term *borderline* was an unofficial label applied by puzzled clinicians in various ways to very different people who seemingly did not fit easily into the standard diagnoses. The history of the term borderline is a fascinating story in itself (Stone, 1980), but for our purposes we need to understand that the "border" in borderline states refers to the line between nonpsychotic and psychotic disorders; for example, any of the anxiety disorders versus schizophrenia.

The person with borderline personality disorder may display episodic losses of contact with reality, delusions (i.e., peculiar but moderately plausible beliefs that are rigidly held and resistant to change even in the face of contrary evidence), or hallucinations (sensory experiences without an external sensory stimulus, such as command voices). "Symptoms" such as these appear psychotic-like. But at other times, the borderline person's reality testing appears intact, much as it is in the lower levels of dysfunction, such as a personality disorder. However, almost always people with BPD have a lengthy history of primitive behavior in relationship to others, self-destructive acting out, possible antisocial aggressive behavior, substance abuse, extreme difficulties being alone, and extraordinarily poor judgment for the consequences of their own actions. A central feature of the disorder is what appears to be a major disturbance in personal identity resulting in profound consequences for the person's perception of self and others (Kernberg, 1986, 1992).

Similar features of episodically failing reality testing and primitive interpersonal relationships characterize other disorders that make up the borderline states group. Some examples:

Schizotypal personality disorder is marked by schizophrenic-like eccentric behavior and speech, magical thinking, and lack of intimate relationships. Some clinicians believe this personality disorder is a precursor of (premorbid for) schizophrenia.

Paranoid personality disorder describes a person who is hypersuspicious, has delusional, frequently grandiose beliefs, and may project angry, chaotic fantasies onto others, resulting in the belief that others will attack if one does not attack first.

Narcissistic personality disorder produces, in one of its variants, a grandiose self-centeredness with feelings of specialness and a firm belief that one is entitled to admiration and exceptional treatment from others.

We will see more of narcissistic personality disorder and how it became the basis for an object relations personality theory in Chapter 5 when we review the work of Heinz Kohut. People who have a narcissistic personality disorder have intense difficulties in interpersonal relations because they regard themselves as special and as entitled to admiration from other people. They generally have little regard for the needs or rights of others even though they ironically need others' esteem to bask in. Out of such need, the narcissistic person may momentarily overidealize a hero or rescuer, only to devalue that person completely within a short space of time. Sometimes grandiose, sometimes fragile, the narcissistic person can be preoccupied with fantasies of unlimited power and success. Such preoccupations frequently lead the narcissistic person to be opportunistic and exploitative. They can be skilled in manipulating others with no apparent appreciation of or empathy for their distress (*DSM-IV* [APA, 1993]; Kohut, 1971, 1977, 1984).

This panoply of symptoms and contradictory psychological experiences found in the borderline states indicates a severe level of dysfunction not captured by the description of the other "more routine" personality disorders at level 3 in the nosology. The problem of "comorbidity"—several disorders occurring together in the same person at the same time—may be especially acute in the case of borderline personality disorder. At minimum, borderline states seem to disrupt and distort the person's most basic personal identity (Kernberg, 1986), with resulting severe deteriorations in reality testing and interpersonal relationships.

The Psychoses and Major Mood Disorders

DISORDER-FREE STATE	ADJUSTMENT DISORDERS	ANXIETY DISORDERS	PERSONALITY DISORDER	BORDERLINE DISORDERS	PSYCHOSES AND MAJOR MOOD DISORDERS
0	1	2	3	4	5

Most severe of the psychiatric illnesses, the *psychoses* and the *major mood disorders* are devastating assaults on a person's ability to think clearly and experience feelings normally. Limiting our discussion to the schizophrenias as our example of psychosis, the schizophrenic person loses touch with reality, may experience hallucinations, and may have delusional beliefs and other problems in thinking. Reality testing is therefore grossly defective. The coherence of thinking and speech is disrupted to different degrees depending on the severity and type of schizophrenia. The schizophrenic person's thinking may exhibit *loosening of associations* so that the connections between thoughts grow increasingly remote and less and less understandable to an outside observer. Peculiarities of speech, including the use of *neologisms* or made up words, further impair communication with the social world. Interpersonal relationships are totally disrupted or completely devoid of intimacy in any meaningful sense of a *personal* relationship.

Arguments about the etiology of schizophrenia abound, but current thinking suggests a strategy that promotes the greatest understanding is likely to be a multicausal approach that incorporates concepts of genetic vulnerability, neurochemistry irregularities, perhaps structural defects in the brain, and psychosocial stressors that shape the course of the illness.

The major mood disorders, including *bipolar disorder*, once called "manic depressive psychosis," and *major depression* are included at this same level of dysfunction because of the extreme disruption to reality testing and interpersonal relationships evidenced by people with these disorders. The person's life can be totally devastated. Reality testing can completely fail, withdrawal from all social contact can occur, and suicidal thoughts and acts are frequently observed. Again causality is in some dispute, but most clinicians agree that neurotransmitter dysfunctions and other biological and genetic inputs play a major role in shaping this class of disorder. Antidepressant and other medications are very effective in treating these illnesses.

Transitional Summary

The clinical nosology is to be understood as a conceptual road map or clinical guide to the range of psychopathology that nature has created. Unlike the various editions of the *DSM*, it organizes the universe of psychopathology along a developmental dimension of severity that enriches our understanding of the relationships among disorders and the nature of the differences between them. The clinical nosology has traditionally also embodied these assumptions (Monte, 1993, p. 8):

- Psychopathologies lie on a continuum of severity that differentiates disorders by their developmental histories and by the amount of dysfunction found in basic cognitive and emotional skills.

- All psychopathologies are assumed to have multiple causes, so that biological, psychological, and social variables interact to shape the natural course of the disorder.

- Some multiple diagnoses can be assigned because the central features of the categories are mutually exclusive but several conditions may coexist simultaneously: Comorbidity is not only possible, it is probable.

TABLE 1.1 Illustrative Severity Markers in the Clinical Taxonomy

The clinical taxonomy is paired at each point in the spectrum with examples of the two severity markers of reality testing and interpersonal relationships. A full clinical profile consists of 12 such severity markers that track a range of cognitive and emotional dysfunctions (see Bellak, Hurvich & Gediman, 1973, and Bellak, 1989).

	Severity Markers		Main Diagnosis		
Least	DISORDER-FREE STATES	0	• Intact reality testing. • Stable, reciprocal, mature, long-term relationships.	0	Least
Severity	ADJUSTMENT DISORDERS	1	• Intact reality testing. • Temporary discord in relationships (e.g., withdrawal, irritibility).	1	Severity
	ANXIETY DISORDERS ("neuroses")	2	• Intact but vigilant reality testing. • Conflicted (love-hate) yet intimate and enduring relationships.	2	
	PERSONALITY DISORDERS	3	• Intact but self-protectively filtered reality testing. • Dependent, self-serving, or inappropriate relationships.	3	
	BORDERLINE DISORDERS	4	• Episodic failures of reality testing (e.g., magical thinking, delusions). • Explosive, manipulative, chaotic, exploitative relationships.	4	
Most	PSYCHOSES AND MAJOR MOOD DISORDERS	5	• Grossly defective reality testing (e.g., hallucinations, delusions). • Bizarre relationships, total lack of intimacy, isolation.	5	Most

- It is assumed that different people with the same diagnosis may differ considerably in the degree to which they evidence dysfunction so that a common diagnostic name does not always imply complete similarity.

- The clinical nosology uses person-centered rather than label-centered descriptions, focusing on the unique phenomenology of each person and not on the signs and symptoms associated with a diagnostic label.

Table 1.1 summarizes the main features of the clinical nosology with attention to the two severity markers of reality testing and interpersonal relationships we have tracked.

THE BIG FIVE: PERSONALITY DISORDERS THE GALILEAN WAY

Understanding the range of psychopathology puts us in a position to appreciate what appears to be an exciting development in the area of personality theory, especially with respect to the personality disorders. As many commentators have put the matter, there is a growing consensus among psychologists that a comprehensive, empirical, and coherent description of personality can be made in terms of five major traits. This phenotypic trait approach has been evolving since at least the mid-1880s with periods of enthusiasm and skepticism marking its progress in fits and starts. Commenting on one period in psychology's history when the study of personality traits fell into some disrepute during the late 1960s and early 1970s, Goldberg (1993) described the current enthusiasm for the Big Five approach in this way:

> Once upon a time, we had no personalities (Mischel, 1968). Fortunately times change, and the past decade has witnessed an electrifying burst of interest in the most fundamental problem of the field—the search for a scientifically compelling taxonomy of personality traits.

The history of this evolving consensus from Sir Francis Galton's pioneering attempt in the late 1880s to estimate the number of English language personality-related words to the work of early statisticians such as Thurstone in the 1950s is beyond our scope. Suffice it to say that an extraordinary range of research has repeatedly shown that large clusters of measurements of people's personalities can be organized reliably by a statistical procedure called factor analysis.

When large numbers of correlations are analyzed, it is generally true that five major personality traits or factors emerge. An individual person may be precisely described by measuring his or her location on each of the five trait dimensions. Called the "Big Five," these traits are conceptualized as lying on bipolar dimensions with persons at one end of the dimension exhibiting high degrees of the trait and persons at the other end exhibiting low degrees of the trait (or its opposite).

The Big Five are:

1. Neuroticism
2. Extroversion
3. Openness
4. Conscientiousness
5. Agreeableness

Of course, each of these main dimensions is composed of several secondary traits or "facets." Thus, for example, the *Neuroticism* (versus Emotional Stability) dimension has been shown to embody anxiety, depression, problems with intimacy, sensitivity to stimulation, impulsiveness, and narcissism, to name just a few (e.g., Schroeder, Wormworth, & Livesley, 1994; see also the application of the Big Five to the study of borderline personality disorder in the work of Clarkin, Hull, Cantor, & Sanderson, 1993; and Eysenck and M. Eysenck [e.g., 1985] whose work is presented in Chapter 17). In similar fashion, the *Extroversion* (versus *Introversion*) dimension embodies facets of sociability, warmth, assertiveness, and excitement-seeking, among others. Thus a "score" of high or low on a particular trait of the Big Five is actually a cluster of scores on the subfacets, providing for the uniqueness of individual combinations, a fact that would bring an I-told-you-so-smile to Gordon Allport's lips (see Chapter 14). It is this feature that surpasses the categorical approach to personality (see Chapter 17 for a fuller discussion of categorical versus dimensional description of personality in Eysenck's work).

The working clinician planning treatment for a patient might consider, for example, that the patient's high *Neuroticism* score includes anxiety, hopelessness, and unrealistic expectations. This same patient's low *Openness* score revealed a preoccupation with fantasy and daydreaming along with some eccentric thinking. And the patient's high *Agreeableness* score was associated with gullibility and indiscriminate trust of others (McCrae, 1994, p. 306). Given this kind of psychological description of personality functioning and malfunctioning using three of the Big Five dimensions as an illustration, the clinician may very well be guided not only to better understanding of the patient's personality and personality disorder but also to better avenues of providing educational and emotional "corrections."

The Real Significance of the Big Five

Although there is growing agreement about the utility of the five-factor model, skeptics and critics point out that factor analysis has certain limitations and weaknesses. For one thing, a surprising degree of creativity and subjectivity enters into organizing and naming clusters of correlations as factors (Eysenck, 1993; Shadel & Cervone, 1993 but see Watson, Clark, & Harkness, 1994).

A second surprise is that the number five may not be as inviolate as its supporters suggest. There is evidence for a simpler, three-factor "solution" to the data that results from factor analyses of many trait scores (Eysenck, 1993). On the other hand, the investigator can choose a more complex "solution" that includes many more than five dimensions (Cattell, 1993), or even choose a multilayered two-tier approach to the factors (Guastello, 1993).

There is also the nagging notion that what the Big Five offer in precision measurement they lack in explanation power. As Eysenck (1993) has pointed out on numerous occasions (see Chapter 17), the most productive research begins from and is guided deductively by a theory that makes predictions that can be tested. The Big Five evolved more or less the other way around, inductively collating and synthesizing sometimes unrelated measurements until they more or less coalesced into meaningful dimensions.

What, then, are we to make of the Big Five? Is it merely a chimera, as Eysenck (1993) suggests? Universal descriptive tool, as Goldberg (1993) suggests? Probably neither. What makes the Big Five model important in contemporary personality theory is the efforts of its supporters to devise a conceptual tool that permits psychologists to describe personality with precision, relevance, and, Galileo help us, simplicity (Widiger & Costa, 1994; O'Connor and Dyce, 1998). Whether the Big Five model lives up to its press clippings or to the hopes of its supporters remains to be seen. Millon (1994, p. 279) has correctly cautioned that current enthusiasm for the Big Five may wane with time and with continued research as have so many transient "enthusiasms" in psychology. But two beneficial outcomes are already in evidence.

1. REPSYCHOLOGICALIZATION OF DIAGNOSIS: The continuously expanding trend toward medicalization of psychological disorders—defining them as diseases—began with the publication of the *DSM-III* in 1980 and has continued unabated in *DSM-IV*. The Big Five model is currently generating new psychological research focused on the main diagnostic entities of the personality disorders to describe these dysfunctions in psychological and scientific terms. The dimensional approach advocated by Big Five enthusiasts is counter to the *DSM* categorical approach and may prove superior in its reliability, validity, and overall utility. The centrality of the personality disorders in the *DSM*, starting with the third edition and continuing into *DSM-IV*, is recognition that the characteristics of the person are the key to comprehending the person's distress. Explaining the *DSM* logic of assigning personality disorders a key diagnostic role, Millon (1994) describes the significance for personality psychology in this way:

> More relevant to this partitioning decision [assigning the personality disorders a special role in *DSM-III*] was the assertion that personality can serve usefully as a substrate of affective, cognitive, and behavioral dispositions from which clinicians can better grasp the "meaning" of their patients more transient or florid disorders. In the recent *DSM*s, then, personality disorders have not only attained a nosological status of prominence in their own right, but they have also been assigned a contextual role that makes them fundamental to the understanding of other psychopathologies. (pp. 279–280).

Costa and Widiger (1994, p. 320) capture the essence of the idea most succinctly: ". . . the best guide to personality pathology is an understanding of personality itself. . . . " Of course, Costa and Widiger believe that the best description of personality is provided by the Big Five approach, but if history is any predictor, it is likely that the need for a guiding theory or theories will make itself felt soon.

2. GALILEAN HOMOGENIZATION OF NORMAL AND ABNORMAL PERSONALITY PHENOMENA: If the best route to understanding personality disorder is to understand the complexities of personality, then the categorical separation of "normal" and "abnormal" personality begins to look artificial. The pathologist who wants to understand personality and other psychological dysfunctions can do so only by understanding personality functioning. Conversely, the personality psychologist who studies "normal" functioning may very well profit, as some of the pioneers tried to do, from understanding what goes wrong in personality functioning. In both instances, abnormal and normal

are not to be taken as separate categories, but as points on a dimension that can be occupied for shorter or longer periods of time by most people.

It may very well be that the time is rapidly approaching when psychology and psychiatry see the enduring interests, motives, conflicts, and wishes of people—their personalities—as the essential context for understanding why people do what they do both when they are in distress and when they are not.

PERSONALITY THEORIES AS PERSONAL THERAPIES: "CREATIVE ILLNESS"

At what point, we might well ask, does a personality theory cease to be a reflection of theorists' personal concerns and begin to be a form of personal therapy, subjective justification, for their own psychopathology? Ellenberger (1970) has advanced the notion that a wide range of influential psychological theories have their origins in the "creative illnesses" of their creators. A creative illness can take a variety of forms, ranging in intensity from mild anxiety through neurotic maladjustment to psychotic separations from reality.

> Whatever the symptoms, they are felt as painful, if not agonizing, by the subject, with alternating periods of alleviation and worsening. Throughout the illness the subject never loses the thread of his dominating preoccupation. It is often compatible with normal, professional activity and family life. (Ellenberger, 1970, p. 447)

The dominating preoccupation is absorption with some intellectual-creative problem, involving attempts to make social reality intelligible. The stricken, creatively ill persons become intensely preoccupied with a search for the truth; they become absorbed with self, suffering intense feelings of isolation until, suddenly, the suffering ends abruptly.

The termination period is often marked by feelings of exhilaration: "The subject emerges from his ordeal with a permanent transformation in his personality and the conviction that he has discovered a great truth or a new spiritual world" (Ellenberger, 1970, p. 48). Ellenberger regards such major figures as Sigmund Freud, Carl Jung, and Pierre Janet as illustrative cases of creative illness and its successful resolution through the creation of a generalized theory of human nature.

The concept of creative illness is a valuable one. It remains unclear, however, whether all far-ranging theories of human nature have their origins in such dramatic and acute personal disturbances. The clearest cases for creative illness can be made for Freud, Jung, Adler, Laing, Erikson, May, and perhaps for Horney and Sullivan, and with somewhat less certainty, for Carl Rogers and B. F. Skinner. In the chapters devoted to each of these theorists, we consider the personal sources of their creative illnesses. But it is acutely difficult to demonstrate the presence of creative illness in the case of some formulations, such as social learning theory.

It seems far more profitable to take the view that a large number of theories have their origins in personal motives and conflicts that fall short of Ellenberger's criteria for a creative illness. Thus the emotional upheaval that impelled Freud, Jung, Adler, and Laing to generalize their pain to all persons may not be a general tendency with all theorists. Sometimes a theory is just a theory.

EVALUATING PERSONALITY THEORIES

Recall the question we asked earlier in the chapter: "Which theory is right?" Recall, too, that the question was identified as inappropriate in the form in which it was asked. We need to ask a more complex question, and a question that does not demand right and wrong answers. To evaluate a theory of personality is not simple, and the job demands complex tools. There are so many dimensions on which to compare and to rate theories of personality that the task can be daunting. And for someone coming to the field for the first time, the wealth of qualities that can be assessed swamps out any opportunity to see common elements or important strengths and weaknesses.

Three Tools: Agency, Refutability, and Idiographic Focus

Our strategy is to employ three, and only three, fundamental dimensions to evaluate the theories in this book. At the end of each chapter, you will find an evaluation section in which we discuss the theory at hand in terms of three qualities that give substantial information about the empirical usefulness, validity, and view of human nature embodied in the theory. We turn next, then, to an examination of our evaluation tools. The first tool deals with the philosophical question of *agency*. How does a theory conceptualize a person's relationship to reality? Are people shaped by

- external "objective" reality,
- internal "subjective" reality,
- or do people shape both realities themselves?

Tool One: Active and Passive Human Agency

What promises to be a singularly useful tool in understanding how theories of human nature are formulated and how one theory reacts to another's vision of humanity has been formulated by Buss (1978). Borrowing from the philosopher Feuerbach, Buss argues that major psychological schools of thought can be understood by their efforts to do two things. First, each tradition or school reacts against the previous most influential historical conception rather than merely accumulating its own independent data. Second, each major psychological tradition attempts to solve this fundamental scientific puzzle: *Does the person construct reality, or does reality construct the person?* Put another way, each school, depending on the history to which it is reacting, asserts *either* that human beings are active, creative, relatively free constructors of their lives, or that people are passive, uninventive, determined receptacles of reality. In essence, each theory asserts that people are subjects or objects (Buss, 1978, p. 60; see also Fischer, 1977).

The problem, of course, is that neither view by itself is satisfactory. People are both subject and object, active creators and passive recipients of stimulation. As Buss persuasively argues, however, the history of psychology demonstrates that major theoretical traditions have adopted one or the other of these views exclusively. Because the two positions are mutually antagonistic, when one theoretical stance becomes a temporarily prevailing viewpoint, it is certain to provoke other thinkers to adopt the opposite viewpoint. However, there are only two extreme positions, and so psychology's history tends to be repetitiously reactionary (Buss, 1978, p. 62).

Buss applies his analysis to three main traditions in psychology: behaviorism, psychoanalysis, and humanistic theory. For most practical purposes, the theories we survey may be organized under one or another of the three traditions without doing major violence to the essence of the theories. Table 1.2 summarizes the three main types of theory.

It is possible to extend Buss's analysis in the direction of a psychobiographical question: *What are the personality traits in theorists that attract them to an active-subject or to a passive-object view of human nature?*

Put more directly and self-reflectively, what life events compel theorists to see themselves and others as shaped by inexorable external forces and inner urges? What life events compel them to interpret themselves and others as the independent steersmen of reality?

Psychoanalytic Theories: Reality Constructs the Person

Psychoanalytic or psychodynamic theories of human nature, in Buss's analysis, depict human psychology as the outcome of inexorable biological forces.

For Freud, irrational and unconscious psychological forces were what governed behavior. The latter, in turn, largely stemmed from the interaction of certain instinctive drives and past experiences. Thus Freud considered the individual to be a consequent of reality (biological drives plus environmental experiences), rather than an antecedent (Buss, 1978, p. 61).

TABLE 1.2   Types of Personality Theory

Theory	Active-Agent or Passive-Object Orientation	Definition of Personality
1. PSYCHOANALYTIC	Largely passive-object orientation: "Reality makes much of us."	Characteristic ways of resolving unconscious conflicts of sexual and aggressive drives with learned ethical values; or conflicts of impulses toward self-fulfillment with impulses toward self-fragmentation.
2. EXISTENTIAL-HUMANISTIC	Completely active-agent orientation: "We construct our reality."	Characteristic and habitual ways of actualizing the needs and values of the true self in the face of life's constant stresses, despite the realization that one must eventually face death.
3. RADICAL BEHAVIORISTIC	Largely a passive-object orientation: "The environment shapes our repertoire of behaviors."	Personality is a fiction. All behavior is learned and very much controlled by the situation.
3A. COGNITIVE BEHAVIORISTIC (Social Learning)	Interactional viewpoint, with person constructing reality by anticipating it, and reality constructing the person by meting out consequences.	Acquired observable response repertoire that may have "private" (cognitive) components, such as need to be masterful.

From his first model of the mind, literally a "psychology for neurologists" (1895), to his first dynamic conception of the mental terrain (1923a, 1923b), Freud never tired of depicting human psychology as fundamentally a struggle of the nervous system to cope with the physical demands of the body that houses it. For the body's drives to be met safely, the nervous system must find a way to adapt itself to the "exigencies" of the outside world and to the insistent demands of the inner world.

For Freud, reason and science were God. And science consisted of uncovering what Nature had fashioned for modern destiny. *Ananke*, the Greek personification of necessity and mother of the fates, was a frequent metaphor in Freud's writings (Freud, 1895; 1913b, p. 93; 1916, pp. 312, 355, 430).

> But we know the power which *forced* a development [of the ego and sexual instincts] upon humanity and maintains its *pressure* in the same direction today. It is, once again, *frustration by reality*, or, if we are to give it its true, grand name, the pressure of vital needs—*Necessity* . . . [*Ananke*]. *She has been a strict educator and has made much out of us.* (Freud, 1916, p. 355; italics added)

There was a streak of resignation in Freud, the resignation of a supreme rationalist who accepts what he believes he cannot change. And what cannot be changed is inner and outer reality. What can be changed—and the primary target of psychoanalysis—is human illusions about reality. "No, our science is no illusion. But an illusion it would be to suppose that what science cannot give us we can get elsewhere" (Freud, 1927, p. 56).

We can provisionally accept, therefore, Buss's analysis of the historical context of psychoanalysis as a theory that asserts "reality constructs the person." The central propositions of psychodynamic theory, including the dynamic unconscious, repression, and the Oedipus complex, can be understood not only as theoretical-intellectual constructs but as reflections of Freud's personal style, as mirrors of his need to accommodate himself to *Ananke*.

In Chapters 2 and 3, we consider some of the personal reasons underlying Freud's need to view human psychology as a process in which people submit passively to the demands of reality. To some degree, other psychoanalytically oriented theories follow in this same style, and where appropriate, the personal sources of their creators' outlook will also be discussed in subsequent chapters. Table 1.3 lists those theories contained here that fall under the heading of *psychodynamic* (psychoanalytically oriented) and that presumably fit Buss's analysis of this tradition as a "reality-constructs-the-person" viewpoint.

Behavioristic Theory: Reality Constructs the Person—Again

Much like Freud, John Broadus Watson (1878–1958), the founder of behaviorism, found salvation in a conception of scientific psychology as a purely objective study of what Nature had wrought. Unlike Freud, however, Watson sought the key to the human mystery not in what people *think* they are doing, nor in what they think *about* what they are doing, but only in what they observably do. For Watson, mental states, acts of introspection, or investigations of nonconscious impulses were simply not fit objects for scientific psychology. The famous opening passages of his 1913 paper dramatically announcing his position show clearly the vehemence of his rejection of things mental:

TABLE 1.3   Active-Agent, Passive-Object Classification of Major Theories

Theory	Central Human Motives
Psychodynamic	

Inner and Outer Reality Constructs the Person

1.	S. Freud	Sex, aggression, tension reduction.
2.	A. Freud	Sex, aggression, and warm interpersonal relations.
3.	Hartmann	Adaptation to one's life circumstances.
4.	R. White	Effectance motive (mastery).
5.	Jung	Reconciliation of life's opposites.
6.	Adler	Striving for personal perfection.
7.	Horney	Actualize true self.
8.	Sullivan	Freedom from anxiety.
9.	Erikson	Firm identity through acceptance of one's life history.
10.	Fromm	Creative freedom and courage to face own mortality.

Cognitive Behaviorism

(Social Learning Theory) Person Constructs Reality

1.	Miller and Dollard	Reduction of any strong stimulus.
2.	Bandura	Self-efficacy (mastery).

Radical Behaviorism

External Reality Constructs the Person

1.	Eysenck	Interaction of nervous system arousal and environmental stimulation.
2.	Skinner	Environmental consequences shape behavior.

Humanistic-Existential

Person Constructs Reality

1.	Laing	Need for congruence between feelings and behavior.
2.	Kelly	Anticipation of one's experiences.
3.	Allport	Ownership of feelings, and mature, realistic goal setting.
4.	Maslow	Self-actualization.
5.	Rogers	Self-actualization.

Psychology as the behaviorist views it is a purely objective branch of natural science. Its theoretical goal is the prediction and control of behavior. Introspection forms no essential part of its methods, nor is the scientific value of its data dependent upon the readiness with which they lend themselves to interpretation in terms of consciousness. The behaviorist, in his efforts to get a unitary scheme of animal response, recognizes no dividing line between man and brute. (Watson, 1913, p. 158)

As Paul Creelan (1974) has attempted to show, Watson seemed to be rejecting more than "unscientific" conceptions of human nature. For Watson, reality constructs the person, but reality is exclusively external. Inner reality is irrelevant.

Applying Buss's (1978) historical analysis to Watson's formulations, and to those theories that emerged in the behaviorist tradition, we can say that behaviorism construes human nature as passive, material, determined, and as very receptive to molding by reality. However, as Buss points out, within the tradition of behaviorism there has been a cognitive revolution: The inner states of the person have again become legitimate objects of scrutiny. Cognitive behaviorists such as Bandura still demand a scientific accounting of behavior and continue to require that a personality theory be couched in observable, measurable terms. However, cognitive behaviorists regard the individual as capable of internally processing information derived from the environment. For the cognitive behaviorist, persons are once again true active agents, constructing their own reality (Bandura, 1989). Table 1.3 lists two classical behaviorist positions: the work of H. J. Eysenck and B. F. Skinner. Table 1.3 also groups those theories that emerged from the behaviorist tradition but pursued a more mentalistic orientation.

Humanistic Theory: Person Constructs Reality

Humanistic theories emerged as a reaction to both behaviorism and Freudian theory (Maslow, 1970). Humanism is a broad term that encompasses a wide variety of viewpoints, ranging from pure phenomenological to existential. Generally, such theories emphasize the concept of the self as an active agent in charge of its own destiny. The person is regarded as essentially "good," free, and spontaneous (Buss, 1978, p. 60).

But the humanistic orientation includes a variety of other, more global emphases. Following Buhler (1971), the humanistic viewpoint can be further characterized as

1. emphasizing the person as a whole in the context of his or her unique life history;
2. embodying an active rather than passive conception of the person's relation to reality;
3. emphasizing self-enhancement, self-realization, or self-actualization as the fundamental human motive;
4. emphasizing persons' needs to integrate their strivings for pleasure, for security, and for belonging in a creative and personal way.

Thus humanistic theories, in Buss's terms, construe the person as an active constructor of reality. Table 1.3 lists those theories represented here that fall under such a heading. We must emphasize, however, that the classification of theories in Table 1.3 is somewhat ambiguous. Some psychoanalytic theories, for example, may very well be classed with the humanistic theories (e.g., Horney, Sullivan). To simplify matters, we have classed the theories in Table 1.3 into that category which seems appropriate in light of the theory's intellectual history and the tradition from which it emerged. For reasons of initial origin, Miller and Dollard's social learning theory, which emerged from Hullian behaviorism, is therefore classed with the cognitive behaviorists despite its psychodynamic content.

Transitional Summary: Human Agency

What can we extract from Buss's analysis that will serve as our first comparative tool? The meat of his analysis of theoretical changes is his concept of active versus passive human agency. As we have seen, theories impose a frame on their portraits of people. Sometimes the frame is flexible and sometimes it is not. The clearest contrast between humanistic theory and behaviorist theory is clear precisely because each position is so extreme. The radical behaviorist of John B. Watson's day quite literally understood people as infinitely malleable, infinitely plastic. Their interaction with reality shaped their conception of it, their learning experiences molded their actions, and their trial-and-error performances channeled their future deeds. At no point in Watson's scheme did the person's own view of reality, the person's expectations or the person's *thoughts* about the world, others, or self play any part. We would describe a radical behaviorism, such as Watson's (and perhaps Skinner's, but see Chapter 16) as embodying a *passive conception of human agency*. The reason? Radical behaviorism focuses on external reality and virtually ignores inner reality.

By contrast, the humanists and cognitive social learning theorists envision human beings as far more complex. For the humanist and cognitive social learning theorist, what people *think* about the world, what people have learned to *expect* from others and from self, and what a person *imagines* he or she can do shape their realities. People change the forces that act on them, create those forces, make decisions about them, and may even decide not to respond to pieces of reality. We would describe a humanistic or a cognitive social learning theory that incorporates this conception as embodying an *active conception of human agency*. The reason? Humanism, and many other forms of cognitive theory, focus on either the inner reality of the phenomenal world or on the interaction of inner with outer reality.

When we evaluate each theory we pay attention to the theory's underlying assumption about human agency. That assumption reveals much of its creator's worldview and exposes clearly the conception of human nature that the theory embodies.

Tool Two: Idiographic Versus Nomothetic Focus

Gordon Allport (1937) introduced into psychology a basic distinction and a fundamental dilemma with which philosophers had struggled for decades. He borrowed the terms *idiographic* and *nomothetic* from the philosopher W. Windelband (1894) to describe the apparent conflict between two basic interests of the psychologist. As a scientist, the psychologist is interested in obtaining data and results that apply generally to all people. A basic scientific finding derived from studying groups of people or even a handful of people should be applicable to a broader population of humans than those studied. Concerns such as these that focus on generalizability or even universality are called *nomothetic*.[2]

But consider the predicament of the personologist. He or she is interested in the individual human being, in the unique dynamics that resulted in *this particular person*. The personologist is concerned with the special combination of life history factors that contributed to the actions and thoughts of the person under investigation. The clinician who works in behalf of his or her client has the same concern: how best to gather the particular diagnostic information, the special or unique personality facts, and the unshared life events responsible for *this* client's distress. And the clinician wonders how best to use that knowledge therapeutically for this *sole* client who will make use of that set of insights in a unique way—seeing them differently from the way any one else might. Concerns for the *individual or for the unique case or for the atypical pattern* are called *idiographic*.

In many cases, the idiographic and the nomothetic can be complementary, so that information derived from the study of one person may very well have aspects that are shared by other, similar people. Conversely, nomothetic "laws" that purport to be universal may nevertheless apply to a particular individual in a particular way. Where's the rub?

The problem arises in the clash between the aims of the various subdisciplines of psychology. Where the personality psychologist is focused on individual differences, the experimental psychologist is likely to be more concerned with *grouping similarities*. Lee Cronbach (1957), in his presidential address to the American Psychological Association, called attention to this difference in aims, which he described as "the two disciplines" of psychology. Cronbach was distinguishing between the two research strategies of correlation and experimentation, but we need not concern ourselves with that distinction. The important point is that Cronbach urged that the two disciplines find a way to create a third, interactionist viewpoint that would capitalize on the concern for individual differences while simultaneously developing general "laws." Cronbach envisioned a third approach that would unite the aims of the idiographer and the nomotheticist. It will not surprise you that even in the 1990s, Cronbach's vision has yet to materialize completely fruitful results.

The tension between the idiographic and the nomothetic interests of psychologists continues. A variety of "solutions" have been proposed (e.g., Bandura's concept of reciprocal determinism [1986], see Chapter 16; Silverstein, 1988) so that most of contemporary personality psychology is focused on a kind of interactionism. But the classic and contemporary theories that we consider fall at various points between the two extremes. And, as they say in the real estate business, location is everything.

Transitional Summary: Idiographic Versus Nomothetic

What can we extract from Allport, Windelband, and Cronbach that will serve as our second comparative tool? We might expect that personality theories are idiographic

---

[2]Allport [1961, 1968] later changed the term "idiographic" to *morphogenic* to emphasize that uniqueness sometimes results from the *individual pattern* of general traits that an individual embodies rather than from strictly and absolutely unique qualities. But, on the whole, psychologists have stayed with *idiographic* as the preferred term.

in focus by definition. But that expectation has been violated many times in the history of personality psychology. There are theories, as we shall see, that take an extreme position on this issue and find themselves purely idiographic or purely nomothetic in principle. But in reality, as with nearly everything else in life, an extreme position in the abstract is a far distance from the compromises forced on a theory when we attempt to use it or test it in reality.

There are demonstrable consequences of taking a position on the idiographic versus nomothetic dimension that reflect on the theory's capacity to be tested scientifically. The idiographic focus, precisely because it is so centered on the "one time" event, does not lend itself to standard methods of scientific testing. And the nomothetic focus, precisely because it is centered on the generalizable-universal, begs for testing through standard methods of refutation. So, the question arises, how important is it to test a theory?

Tool Three: The Criterion of Refutability

All theories of personality must rely at some point on observed behavior. Each approach, however, begins with observable behavior to a different degree. Unconscious states, for example, are not directly observable in themselves. Yet even an orthodox Freudian analyst must focus attention on what people do, how they *behave* because of these underlying states. In the end, whether the theorist postulates an unconscious conflict, frustration of a biological drive, arousal of a brain mechanism, or the reinforcing effects of social approval, he or she must rely on observable behavior to construct and to test the theory.

In the sense described here, a scientific theory is very restricted in what may be included within its bounds (Popper, 1959, 1963). It is generally agreed that a scientific theory must be rooted in observational data if it is ever to be tested. Karl Popper proposed that such theories must, in principle, be refutable by observations that they themselves specify as incompatible. Thus the logic of refutability proceeds as follows:

1. Human beings behave in ways *A, B, C* because of motives *1, 2, 3.*
2. If this assertion (*A, B, C and 1, 2, 3*) is true, then observations *D, E, F* should be possible. Furthermore, if this assertion is true, then observations *G, H, I* should *not* be possible.
3. Observations *D, E, F* are made and confirm the theory. Observations *G, H, I* are attempted but cannot be accomplished. The theory is further confirmed. (Popper, 1963; cf. Campbell, 1969; Monte, 1975)

Thus, according to Popper, a theory must state not only what people are expected to do, but what, according to its own logic, they should be expected *not* to do. In effect, the scientific theory must state what observations it would take to disprove it. If such disconfirmatory observations can be made, the theory is refuted. This criterion of refutability guarantees that scientific theories will be stated in empirical, testable terms—in principle.

The problem is that the majority of personality theories are couched in terms that make it difficult to determine what phenomena, if any, could count against them.

Put in technical terms, the "good" theory specifies what it takes to falsify itself; the poor theory not only fails to specify falsification procedures, it is so vaguely stated that it can be compatible with any and all observations, depending on interpretation. Note, too, that there is a difference between a theory having the desirable property of *refutability* and the actual *refutation* of the theory. When a philosopher of science says that a theory is *refutable* there is no implication that the theory will, in fact, be refuted. The only necessary quality of a refutable theory is that it be *potentially refutable*, that is, testable.

You can probably surmise from the technical language used here that simple truth and falsity are not in the vocabulary of the philosopher of science. The criterion of refutability demands that a theory be testable, not that it be true. Theories that survive the challenge of careful tests increase our confidence in the theory to be a useful *summarizer* of myriad facts and a reliable *predictor* of new facts. The strongest test of a theory, in fact the strongest test of any kind of explanation, is its power to predict what will happen next. Nothing is so definitive as when someone gives an explanation of something and predicts on the basis of that explanation what will happen. We wait, and if it happens, we find the explanation compelling. For example, when my auto mechanic says that the chronic stalling I experience in my car is due to a clogged fuel filter, I watch as he pulls the filter (it's fairly dirty looking to the naked eye) and replaces it with a clean one. He says, "It won't stall anymore. Thirty-five dollars please." I fork over the money begrudgingly because the whole operation took five minutes and the part installed is worth only 75 cents. But I have to admit about a week later, the car does not stall. I paid for the mechanic's predictive knowledge, and that knowledge was tested.

But what happens when a theory seems to be stated in a way that allows for predictions to be made, yet any outcome could be interpreted as compatible with the theory? The mechanic says, for example, "It's just a minor carburetor adjustment," and then fiddles with a screw on my engine. The car keeps stalling, I keep returning to the mechanic, he keeps turning screws, assuring me that it could be nothing else. Eventually the car stops stalling. Is it because one of the many turns of the screw "fixed" the problem, or is there an alternative explanation, such as the clogged fuel filter passed through some of its dirt? I'll never know. I have no real basis on which to decide.

Consider another example of nonrefutability. The statement "heads I win, tails you lose" is unfalsifiable. This cliché con game has no outcomes that are not compatible with it. If the coin comes up heads, my prediction is confirmed. If the coin comes up tails, my prediction that I win is again confirmed. Barring the unlikely event that the coin stands on its edge (which would disqualify the coin toss and require a new toss), there are no possible outcomes that can disconfirm (or falsify) my prediction. Some personality theories are stated in terms like these. No conceivable observable outcome could count as evidence against the theory. A personality theory that postulates unobservable, unmeasurable processes easily falls into the trap of nonrefutability. Such a theory is so general and inclusive that the validity of its explanations must always be suspect. To be compatible with any and all outcomes is to be an explanation of none.

Transitional Summary: Refutability

What can we extract from Sir Karl Popper's principle of refutability to serve as our third comparative tool? The restriction of scientific theories to observable, refutable (testable) phenomena removes the flavor, the fullness of explanation that would be intuitively and aesthetically satisfying. No theory, in the present state of the art, and certainly none of the so-called grand theories from psychology's history, can both comprehensively and refutably account for the wholeness, for the uniqueness, for the universality of human propensities, foibles, drives, abilities, and desires.

The person represented in a scientifically testable way is not the real person demanded by common sense and by personologists. To the question "What is Gabriel Grandé really like?" we fully expect some answer that is readily understandable and that tells us something about the inner, private person that Gabriel *really* is. Are we naive? Yes and no. This expectation is irrelevant to scientific psychologists at the present state of their inquiries. They are more concerned with establishing general and valid propositions—nomothetic laws—than they are with idiographic (and frequently untestable) facts. The "real inner person," if such an entity exists, will have to be ignored for the present. But as human beings our interest in whole, real people is unabated by scientific argument. As personologists, our professional concerns remain focused on the idiographic. As psychologists, we struggle for ways to combine the two.

As we examine the many theories in this book, part of the evaluation section at the end of each chapter is devoted to a theory's refutability. For in the end, an untestable theory is less useful, less trustworthy, and less productive than a refutable one.

SUMMARY

The concept of personality is a hypothetical construct designed to bring order and consistency to the explanation of an individual's behavior. Theoretical orientations vary in how they construe the meaning of personality and in what questions they prompt the investigator to ask. But it is also true that all personality theories prompt some similar questions. Among these are the following:

1. *Developmental-historical question:* How did the person come to behave as he or she does now?
2. *Prediction-consistency question:* Will this person behave similarly in similar situations at a later time?
3. *Uniqueness-generality question:* To what extent are the effects of significant people and events on *this* individual similar to their effects on other individuals?

We consider 25 theories in the chapters that follow. Sometimes questions arise about a theorist's position in history, or about his or her location in the chronology of those who preceded or followed. A useful device for simplifying the conceptualization of the span of time involved in the construction of theories and of a particular theorist's position in the sequence are the lists in Table 1.4.

A convenient metaphor for concretizing the dilemma that personality theorists face when they try to understand human nature is that of the actor and the mask. Personologists, exemplified by Henry Murray or Gordon Allport, represent individuals in the context of their life histories. In more technical terms, a theorist may be concerned with peripheral variables that are easily observable (mask), or with central variables that touch upon the very core of some more "real" inner person (actor).

Normal and abnormal personality functioning have sometimes been treated simplistically as though they were very separate categories representing two very different kinds of human being. Kurt Lewin's concept of Galilean scientific thinking has shown historically that a deep understanding of nature results when seemingly unrelated phenomena are homogenized by penetrating to the underlying principles that they share. In similar fashion, the evolving consensus that personality can be accurately and comprehensively described by five major trait dimensions (Neuroticism, Extroversion, Openness, Conscientiousness, Agreeableness) offers the possibility of homogenizing the study of normal and abnormal personalities. The range of disordered psychological functioning can be understood using the clinical nosology, which organizes the main psychopathologies along a continuum of severity using changes in reality testing and interpersonal relationships as severity markers. The best understanding of personality disorders, indeed the best understanding of psychopathology across the continuum, is achieved by understanding personality.

Personality theories can also be understood as the very personal reflections of the psychology of their creators. One way to understand the personal origins of a theorist's conception of human character is to follow Buss's (1978) analysis of the major traditions of psychological enterprise into viewpoints that interpret persons as active agents and independent constructors of their reality, and those viewpoints that

TABLE 1.4   Chronology of Major Theorists of Personality

Chronological		Alphabetic	
Sigmund Freud	1856–1939	Adler, Alfred	1870–1937
Alfred Adler	1870–1937	Allport, Gordon	1897–1967
Carl G. Jung	1875–1961	Bandura, Albert	1925–
John B. Watson	1878–1958	Bowlby, John	1907–1990
Melanie Klein	1882–1960	Erikson, Erik	1902–1994
Karen Horney	1885–1952	Eysenck, Hans	1916–1997
Kurt Lewin	1890–1947	Frankl, Viktor	1905–1997
Harry Stack Sullivan	1892–1949	Freud, Anna	1895–1982
Heinz Hartmann	1894–1970	Freud, Sigmund	1856–1939
Anna Freud	1895–1982	Fromm, Erich	1900–1980
D. W. Winnicott	1896–1971	Hartmann, Heinz	1894–1970
Gordon Allport	1897–1967	Horney, Karen	1885–1952
Margaret Mahler	1897–1985	Jung, Carl G.	1875–1961
Erich Fromm	1900–1980	Kelly, George A.	1905–1969
Carl Rogers	1902–1987	Kernberg, Otto	1928–
Erik Erikson	1902–1994	Klein, Melanie	1882–1960
B. F. Skinner	1904–1990	Kohut, Heinz	1913–1981
George A. Kelly	1905–1969	Laing, R. D.	1927–1989
Viktor Frankl	1905–1997	Lewin, Kurt	1890–1947
John Bowlby	1907–1990	Mahler, Margaret	1897–1985
Abraham Maslow	1908–1970	Maslow, Abraham	1908–1970
Rollo, May	1909–1994	May, Rollo	1909–1994
Neal Miller	1909–	Miller, Neal	1909–
Heinz Kohut	1913–1981	Rogers, Carl	1902–1987
Hans Eysenck	1916–1997	Skinner, B. F.	1904–1990
Albert Bandura	1925–	Sullivan, Harry Stack	1892–1949
R. D. Laing	1927–1989	Watson, John B.	1878–1958
Otto Kernberg	1928–	Winicott, D. W.	1896–1971

regard individuals as passive objects who are constructed by reality. *Psychoanalytic* and classical *radical behavioristic* theories conceptualize reality as the constructor of the person. By contrast, *cognitive social learning* theories and *humanistic* theories regard the person as the constructor of reality.

Henri Ellenberger, an eminent historian of psychodynamic theories, has proposed that sometimes a theorist's life work is rooted in the successful resolution of a "creative illness." It is possible, therefore, that some personality theories (e.g., Freud's,

Adler's, Jung's, Laing's, Skinner's) may have resulted from the theorists attempts to justify and make his or her pain rational by seeing it as the common lot of all people.

We apply the following three fundamental tools to our study of theories so that we may evaluate them for their usefulness, accuracy, and view of human nature:

- *Human agency:* Does the theory picture people as passive receptacles of reality, or as active agents who shape their own inner and outer realities?

- *Idiographic versus nomothetic focus:* Does the theory emphasize the uniqueness or pattern of particular qualities that an individual embodies, or does the theory explore the general, universal aspects of human behavior? Or can a theory embody some interactive combination of idiographic and nomothetic focus?

- *Refutability:* Does a theory state what it would take to prove itself wrong? Scientific theories are refutable, and unscientific ones are not. In general, refutability assures some measurable degree of accuracy, usefulness, and predictive power, but it also curtails the human richness of any particular personality theory.

In all, it is probably not necessary to point out that the study of personality, the creation of personality theories, and the attempt to peer beneath the mask are all attempts to understand the understanders understanding themselves.

FOR FURTHER READING

To obtain an initial orientation to the historical scope of personality psychology, the easiest route is to browse through the annual editions of the personality research review contained in *Annual Review of Psychology* (Palo Alto, CA: Annual Reviews Inc.). These volumes may be found in any large college or university library and contain useful, succinct surveys of psychology's various subfields. Along these same lines, though now somewhat dated, E. Borgatta and W. Lambert's (Eds.) *Handbook of Personality Theory and Research* (Chicago: Rand McNally, 1968) contains informative reviews of several research traditions within personality psychology.

Problems of applying scientific method to the study of social and personality phenomena are cogently discussed by Howard Gadlin and Grant Ingle in their article "Through the One-Way Mirror; The Limits of Experimental Self-Reflection" (*American Psychologist, 1975,* **30**, 1003–1009).

We recommend specific readings for each of the theorists discussed in this book at the end of the appropriate chapters. However, some secondary sources on the various theoretical orientations may be helpful at the beginning of your study. The collection of chapters in Raymond Corsini's and Danny Wedding's (Eds.) *Current Psychotherapies* (Itasca, IL: Peacock, 1989) surveys the therapeutic applications of many of the theories covered here. Each of these chapters was written by a specialist in the particular theoretical orientation. Richard I. Evans has filmed and taped interviews with the "greats" of psychology for years and published transcripts of these dialogues as separate paperbacks. Included in the series are conversations with Ernest Jones, Carl Rogers, Neal Miller, Albert Bandura, R. D. Laing, Erik Erikson, Jean Piaget, B. F. Skinner, Gordon Allport, Erich Fromm, and C. G. Jung, to name only those who have immediate relevance to personality. Condensed versions of all these interviews were published in a single paperback, *The Making of Psychology*, edited by R. I. Evans (New York: Knopf, 1976), and each is well worth scrutiny.

Robert White's *The Enterprise of Living* (New York: Holt, 1976) is a particularly lucid and coherent account of the development of the healthy personality. Case studies of moderately healthy personalities may be found in R. W. White's *Lives in Progress* (New York: Holt, 1975).

A sound overview of general psychopathology can be had in Michael Hersen and Samuel M. Turner's *Adult Psychopathology and Diagnosis*, 2d ed. (New York: Wiley, 1991). A more detailed presentation of the clinical nosology and diagnostic issues can be found in Christopher F. Monte's *Still, Life: Clinical Portraits in Psychopathology* (Englewood Cliffs, N.J.: Prentice-Hall, 1993). The collection of theoretical and research papers in Paul T. Costa and Thomas A. Widiger's (Eds.) *Personality Disorders and the Five-Factor Model of Personality* (Washington, D.C.: American Psychological Association, 1994) will amply reward the reader interested in the Big Five and psychopathology.

An excellent and extraordinarily thorough historical and conceptual analysis of psychodynamic theory, including reference to the personal sources of a theorist's ideas, is provided by Henri Ellenberger in his *The Discovery of the Unconscious* (New York: Basic Books, 1970). Robert Stolorow and George Atwood's *Faces in a Cloud* (New York: Aronson, 1979) treats the subjective bases of a variety of personality theories lucidly. For more explicit information about radical behaviorism in its contemporary form there is no better spokesman than B. F. Skinner in his presentation in *About Behaviorism* (New York: Knopf, 1974). A dissenting viewpoint among the nonradical behaviorists but one that also argues against cognitive behaviorism can be found in Joseph Wolpe's article "Cognition and Causation in Human Behavior and Its Therapy" (*American Psychologist*, 1978, **33**, 437–446).

C H A P T E R 2

SIGMUND FREUD

Psychoanalysis:
The Clinical Evidence

They cannot scare me with their empty spaces
Between stars— on stars where no human race is.
I have it in me so much nearer home
To scare myself with my own desert places.

Robert Frost, "Desert Places"

About Freud's Clinical Psychoanalysis

Freud's theory is a history of one man's struggle to understand the conflict between human passion and reason. It was Freud's lifework to explore the convoluted ways that rationality clashes against irrationality.

In this chapter, the central concept to be distilled from the many changes Freud's ideas underwent is this: A person's wishes are not always what the person would consciously like them to be because:

1. *some basic wishes for pleasure violate conscious "rules" of conduct;*

2. *some wishes remain infantile and frozen in their intensity and primitive perversity;*

3. *some wishes can be partially satisfied and partially disavowed at the same time when a person's divided motives result in the creation of neurotic symptoms.*

Freud's classic theory remains a powerful influence on other thinkers' ideas, but much of what he wrote is likely never to be testable in the psychologist's laboratory. Passion and reason will occupy human thinking endlessly, and Freud's vision of the two will likely remain controversial for just as long.

THE HYSTERICAL NEUROSIS OF ANNA O.

Writhing in her bed with the pangs of labor, evidencing most of the usual signs of advanced pregnancy, 23-year-old Anna O. bore no child in her womb. The year, 1882, was to mark for Viennese physician Josef Breuer the termination of an intimate and lengthy doctor-patient relationship with this neurotic young girl. A two-year-long series of bizarre physical and mental symptoms was climaxing now with the most frightening and, for Breuer (who could intuitively read the symbolic meaning of the new symptom), the most painfully disconcerting outcome: pseudocyesis, or false pregnancy.

From Josef Breuer's work with Anna O. was to emerge a theory of hysterical nervous disorder, a method of psychological treatment nicknamed "chimney sweeping" by the patient herself, and the germ of a comprehensive theory of personality and psychotherapy yet to be formulated by Breuer's young colleague and friend Sigmund Freud.

Bertha Pappenheim, Anna O.'s real name (Jones, 1953, p. 223n.), was a charming, attractive, intelligent, and witty young woman who developed a series of disorders ranging from paralysis of limbs and disturbed vision to, at one point, a dual personality. The symptoms seemed to make their emergence subsequent to a protracted and fatal illness of her father. Though a variety of physicians was consulted, no physical basis could be found for her bewildering maladies. Breuer diagnosed Anna O.'s collection of symptoms as *hysterical neurosis*, a disorder that, though recognized from antiquity, had thus far defied satisfactory explanation.

FIGURE 2.1　Bertha Pappenheim (Anna O.)

The affliction received its name from the ancient Greeks' word *hystera*, meaning uterus. It was their opinion that hysteria was limited to women because the disease was the result of a wandering womb. By its travels to various parts of the body, the errant womb caused the symptoms of temporary paralysis of limbs or the dysfunction of sense organs whenever it came to rest in other than its customary place. Needless to say, Josef Breuer held no such mystical convictions about the nature of the disorder, although it can be said with equal certainty that he did not yet understand the full import of his observations on Anna O.

Breuer was originally consulted in the case because Anna had developed a severe and persistent cough while caring for her father during his terminal illness.

She was 21 years old at this time. Some months later, in 1881, Anna's father died and her own health showed signs of profound impairment. She refused food, became weak and anemic, and she then began to develop the even more bizarre symptoms of paralysis, muscle contractures, visual hallucinations, and loss of feelings in her hands and feet—the so-called functional anesthesias. Breuer described Anna's alternating states as follows:

> Two entirely distinct states of consciousness were present [in Anna O.] which alternated very frequently and without warning and which became more and more differentiated in the course of the illness. In one of these states she recognized her surroundings; she was melancholy and anxious, but relatively normal. In the other state she hallucinated and was "naughty"—that is to say, she was abusive, used to throw the cushions at people, so far as the contractures [in her limbs] at various times allowed, tore buttons off her bedclothes and linen with those of her fingers which she could move, and so on. . . . There were extremely rapid changes of mood leading to excessive but quite temporary high spirits, and at other times severe anxiety, stubborn opposition to every therapeutic effort and frightening hallucinations of black snakes, which was how she saw her hair ribbons and similar things. . . . (Breuer, in Breuer & Freud, 1893–1895, p. 24)[1]

In addition to the emergence of an incipient dual personality, young Anna O. began to exhibit other forms of disturbance in her relations with people. She occasionally omitted necessary words from her spoken language, and she gradually increased these omissions until her speech was rendered virtually nonsensical and totally devoid of logical and grammatical construction. The inevitable consequence of such behavior then occurred: complete mutism for a period of two weeks. Although she struggled mightily to speak, all of Anna O.'s efforts resulted in soundless frustration. When Breuer guessed that something had recently annoyed and offended her, causing her to resolve not to speak about it, his insistence that they discuss the problem robbed Anna's mutism of its efficacy (1893–1895, p. 25).

Anna, whose native tongue was German, now created a new symptom: She spoke only English. No amount of argument could convince Anna, who was seemingly unaware of her changed speech, that the people to whom she spoke English were as unable to understand her now as they had been during her weeks of silence.

"CLOUDS": SELF-INDUCED HYPNOSIS

Anna O.'s father died in April, nine months after these speech disturbances developed. "This was the most severe physical trauma that she could possibly have experienced. A violent outburst of excitement was succeeded by profound stupor which lasted about two days and from which she emerged in a greatly changed state" (Breuer, in Breuer & Freud, 1893–1895, p. 26).

---

[1] Reference citations throughout this chapter and the next that indicate the writings of Sigmund Freud (or, in this case of Josef Breuer) refer to the volumes of the *Standard Edition of the Complete Psychological Works of Sigmund Freud*, translated under the general editorship of James Strachey, with the collaboration of Anna Freud, and published by the Hogarth Press, London. Citations to the *Standard Edition* employ only the original publication date of the work, so that you may follow the chronology of Freud's thought.

Anna O.'s loss of feeling in her hands and feet and her paralysis returned, along with what would now be called tunnel vision; that is, her field of vision was greatly narrowed as when one looks through a narrow cardboard cylinder. For example, ". . . in a bunch of flowers which gave her much pleasure she could only see one flower at a time."

> She complained of not being able to recognize people. Normally, she said, she had been able to recognize faces without having to make any deliberate effort; now she was obliged to do laborious "recognizing work" [she used this phrase in English] and had to say to herself "this person's nose is such-and-such, his hair is such-and-such, so he must be so-and-so." (Breuer, in Breuer & Freud, 1893–1895, p. 26)

During the day, Anna was always upset, and she presented a picture of a harassed and tormented victim of her disease. She hallucinated, talked incoherently, and experienced grave anxiety. Toward afternoon, Anna became sleepy and quiet, sinking into a deep autohypnosis by sunset. For these self-induced evening hypnotic states she created the English term "clouds." When Breuer visited her in the evening, she was able to recount to him her day's hallucinations, and it was in this state of "clouds" that Breuer and Anna O. made a joint discovery.

Her family had noticed from Anna's mumblings that the content of these daytime hallucinations seemed to resemble a fantasy story. Anna's fantasies were surprisingly sad, yet they were also pretty and poetic because they had probably been modeled on a book of Hans Christian Andersen's fairy tales. After her father's death, these daytime hallucinations became even more tragic, and they usually involved, as at least one element of a complex structure, the character of an anxious young girl sitting near the bedside of a patient. Accidentally at first, a family member would repeat a few key words of Anna's mutterings, and this response would draw her out to narrate an entire story or hallucinatory fantasy. During her evening hypnotic clouds, Breuer took up the procedure of priming the conversation with several words or phrases from Anna's own fantasies. The significant point was that after Anna recounted the full content of her daytime hallucinations and stories to Breuer, she became quieter, more lucid and cheerful, and almost symptom-free for the rest of the night.

The Talking Cure: "Chimney Sweeping"

Little by little, through a combination of accident and intent, Anna and Breuer shaped a method to relieve Anna of her anxiety and symptoms, at least temporarily. By unburdening herself to Breuer in the evening, Anna was able to achieve some respite from her torment. She and Breuer had thus made an important discovery, a "talking cure" that involved a kind of verbal *catharsis* (literally, a cleansing or purifying).

Aristotle had used the term catharsis to describe the emotional release and purification engendered in the audience during their viewing of a tragic drama. As we mentioned earlier, Anna O., more to the point, perhaps, than Aristotle, called the emotional release produced by her semihypnotic conversations with Breuer "chimney sweeping."

The evening talking sessions were obviously beneficial for Anna O. and of medical interest to Breuer. Unfortunately for Breuer's scientific curiosity, however, no specific symptoms had yet been removed or explained by the cathartic talking cure method.

That such symptoms as paralysis, blindness, and mutism might be not just manifestations of the irrationality of the hysteric personality, meaningless expressions of "craziness" to be expected of the neurotic, had already occurred to Breuer. He became firmly convinced that neurotic symptoms had an explicable and rationally understandable cause to be found in the patient's life history, and that the *form* of the symptom was rooted in a deeply *personal meaning* attached by the patient to the past event.

Catharsis: Expressing Strangulated Feeling

As the talking cure progressed, Breuer found that some of the symptoms of Anna O.'s illness permanently disappeared. He was particularly surprised when a long-standing symptom disappeared during an unplanned conversation with Anna. Breuer provided an account of the removal of this specific symptom:

> It was in the summer during a period of extreme heat, and the patient was suffering very badly from thirst; for, *without being able to account for it in any way*, she suddenly found it impossible to drink. She would take up the glass of water she longed for, but as soon as it touched her lips she would push it away like someone suffering from hydrophobia. As she did this, she was obviously in an *absence* [self-induced hypnotic state] for a couple of seconds. . . . This [condition] had lasted for some six weeks, when one day during hypnosis she grumbled about her English lady-companion whom she did not care for, and went on to describe, *with every sign of disgust*, how she had once gone into that lady's room and how her [the lady-companion's] little dog—horrid creature!—had drunk out of a glass there. The patient [i.e., Anna O.] had said nothing, as she had wanted to be polite. After giving further *energetic expression to the anger she had held back*, she asked for something to drink, drank a large quantity of water without any difficulty and woke from her hypnosis with the glass at her lips; and thereupon the disturbance vanished, never to return. (Breuer, in Breuer & Freud, 1893–1895, pp. 34–35; italics added)

Here was the secret of the *origin* and the *form* of hysterical symptoms. An emotion had been experienced intensely, but it had been blocked from normal expression during the initiating event. The patient had been compelled to "strangle" the feeling, so to speak. However, even though the emotion had *then*—in the patient's past—been prohibited from expression, there was little cause, Breuer reasoned, to assume that the emotion had thereby ceased to exist. Indeed, the strangulated "affect," as Breuer and Freud would later call these unruly emotions, remained to haunt Anna O. She was able to solve partially the problem of the dammed-up disgust and anger by expressing these emotions behaviorally, symptomatically, as a feeling of disgust for water, and as a refusal to drink it. When the incident that had precipitated the *original* feelings had been recalled in hypnosis, those pent-up emotions were finally spent.

Following up his patient's success with that one symptom, Breuer systematically explored with Anna O. the possibility that other precipitating but no longer remembered incidents lay at the root of her remaining bizarre behaviors. Breuer adopted the procedure of asking Anna during hypnosis to tell him her thoughts on a particular symptom. The exploration was often difficult, and it required great concentration from both Breuer and his patient. On some occasions, the whole process ground to a halt because a particular symptom's initiating cause would not come to the surface of Anna's memory.

With time, however, concentrated effort relieved Anna of many of her difficulties. For instance, some of Anna O.'s visual disturbances, language problems, hallucinations, and the paralysis of her right arm were removed after she was able, under hypnosis, to recount the story of a particularly long and frightening night vigil she had spent at her sick father's bedside.

> She fell into a waking dream and saw a black snake coming towards the sick man from the wall to bite him. . . . Her right arm, over the back of the chair, had gone to sleep and had become anaesthetic and paretic; and when she looked at it the fingers turned into little snakes with death's heads (the nails). (It seems probable that she had tried to use her paralysed right arm to drive off the snake and its anaesthesia and paralysis had consequently become associated with the hallucination of the snake.) When the snake vanished, in her terror she tried to pray. But language failed her: *she could find no tongue in which to speak, till at last she thought of some children's verses in English, and then found herself able to think and pray in that language.* [Italics added]
>
> . . . on [another] occasion, when she was sitting by her father's bedside with tears in her eyes, he suddenly asked her what time it was. She could not see clearly; she made a great effort, and brought her watch near to her eyes. The face of the watch now seemed very big—thus accounting for her macropsia [tunnel vision] and convergent squint. Or again, she tried hard to suppress her tears so that the sick man should not see them. (Breuer, in Breuer & Freud, 1893–1895, pp. 38, 39, 40)

Breuer's account of the case history ends shortly after this incident is recounted, but that is not the end of the story. Anna O., Bertha Pappenheim, developed a new symptom that was to frighten Breuer so intensely and to engender such guilt in him that he could look to psychology in the future only with great trepidation.

Anna O.'s Treatment Ends

Symptom by symptom, feeling-event by feeling-event, the thread of Anna's hysteria was unraveled with the assistance of Breuer and the cathartic method. During the course of the treatment, a period lasting almost two years, an intimate and intense relationship developed between Breuer and Anna O. Breuer's wife became jealous of her husband's fascinating patient, and she provoked in Breuer a strong reaction of guilt. He decided to end his treatment of Anna, a decision strengthened by her improvement, and he announced this intention to her. Ernest Jones, Freud's official biographer, provides an account, based on a conversation with Freud years later, of what followed Breuer's announcement to his patient:

> . . . that evening . . . [Breuer] was fetched back to find . . . [Anna O.] in a greatly excited state, apparently as ill as ever. The patient, who according to him had appeared to be an asexual being and had never made any allusion to such a forbidden topic throughout the treatment, was now in the throes of an hysterical childbirth (pseudocyesis), the logical termination of a phantom pregnancy that had been invisibly developing in response to Breuer's ministrations. Though profoundly

shocked, he managed to calm her down by hypnotizing her, and then fled the house in a cold sweat. The next day he and his wife left for Venice to spend a second honeymoon. . . . (Jones, 1953, p. 224. Freud himself hinted at this story in his *Autobiographical Study*, 1925a, p. 26.)

There can be little doubt that Breuer had read the unconscious meaning of Anna O.'s symptom clearly and that he felt directly responsible. Despite the scientific importance of this further discovery, Breuer lost almost all professional interest in hysterical neurosis.

The Posttreatment Anna O.: Some Detective Work

The account of Anna O.'s illness and treatment by Breuer, and the historical additions provided by Jones (1953), seem to have been something less than complete. Ellenberger (1970, 1972) interviewed surviving relatives and acquaintances of Bertha Pappenheim and engaged in some clever detective work to find the sanitorium in which the patient sought refuge after the final episode with Breuer. In 1882 Bertha was far from "cured," and the severity of her illness suggests that she was not a hysteric neurotic but, perhaps, a borderline patient on the frontier of psychosis (review the Clinical Nosology in Chapter 1).

From an old photograph of Bertha Pappenheim that had been embossed with the still legible date 1882, Ellenberger uncovered an important clue. With the aid of the Montreal police laboratory, he was able to decipher the photographer's name and his address in the German town of Konstanz. Further legwork led Ellenberger to the Sanitorium Bellevue, in Switzerland, only a short distance over the border from Konstanz, where Anna had posed for her picture. Ellenberger obtained access to the patient's case file, which contained Breuer's original, unpublished case history and a follow-up report by the hospital's doctors.

Breuer's hitherto unknown case history, although substantially different from the published version in *Studies on Hysteria*, nevertheless matched the published case in lacking all reference to the hysterical childbirth. However, several new details about Bertha Pappenheim's life and illness are worth recounting here; the full document has not yet been published for reasons Ellenberger does not disclose.

In this version, Breuer more fully emphasized Bertha's "truly passionate love for her father," and revealed the strong antireligious sentiment Bertha harbored (Ellenberger, 1972, pp. 274–275). The death of her father, which had such a profound impact on Bertha, is now made more comprehensible.

> During the previous two months she had not been allowed to see [her father] and had continuously been told lies about his condition. . . . On April 5, at the moment when her father was dying, she called her mother and asked for the truth, but was appeased and the lie went on for some time. When Bertha learned that her father had died, she was indignant: she had been "robbed" of his last look and word. From that time on, a marked transformation appeared in her condition: anxiety replaced by a kind of dull insensitivity with distortions in her visual perceptions. Human beings appeared to her as wax figures. (Ellenberger, 1972, pp. 275–276)

At some time around the period of her father's death, Bertha made several suicide attempts (Ellenberger, 1972, p. 276). It might be possible, therefore, considering the severity of her reaction to the loss of her father, to equate her later loss of Breuer and its accompanying frightening symptom to the nearly psychotic mourning reactions she evidenced (Pollock, 1973).

Breuer's account mentions Bertha's quarrels with her brother and some difficulties with her "very serious" mother. Ellenberger quotes Breuer's assessment of the role of sexuality in Bertha's life as an "astonishingly undeveloped" element. Furthermore, "She had never been in love, 'insofar [as] her relationship to her father did not replace it, or rather was replaced by it' " (Ellenberger, 1972, p. 274).

The Bellevue Sanitorium doctors' follow-up report indicates that during her stay, Anna O. became habituated to large doses of chloral and morphine, administered to relieve severe facial neuralgia. Among other comments, the report cites the patient's "unpleasant irritation against her family," and her "disparaging judgments against the ineffectiveness of science in regard to her sufferings." In the evenings, she again lost ability to speak in German, substituting English phrases for sentences begun in her failing native tongue. Last, the report mentions that the patient would sit for hours under a picture of her father, and she would speak of visiting his tomb.

Eventually, Bertha Pappenheim was to transcend her illness to become an active feminist, writer, and leading figure in social work in Germany. In her later years she experienced a complete turnabout from her early antireligious attitudes to deeply religious, selfless but authoritarian traits (Ellenberger, 1970, p. 481). By the end of World War II, Bertha Pappenheim was revered as a legendary figure in social work, to the extent that in 1954 the West German government issued a postage stamp bearing her picture (Ellenberger, 1970, p. 481). The full continuing story of Bertha Pappenheim's—Anna O.'s—subsequent life is beyond the scope of our present purposes (see Freeman, 1972). She died in March, 1936, in time to escape the Nazi purge (Ellenberger, 1970).

PERSONAL SOURCES OF BREUER'S REACTION TO ANNA O.

Problem: How to account for Breuer's vulnerability to his patient's hysterical childbirth? Breuer was, after all, a physician, albeit a pioneering one in a field fraught with unconventional demands on his conventional medical skills, and astonishments that would swamp the most imperturbable doctor. But is astonishment and shock to one's sense of convention sufficient to account for Breuer's abrupt retreat?

Breuer's own belated explanation for his massive reluctance to pursue psychological investigations after his experience with Anna O. was given in a letter written some 25 years later, in 1907:

> The case which I described in the *Studies on Hysteria* as No. 1; Anna O., passed through my hands, and my merit lay essentially in my having recognized what an uncommonly instructive and scientifically important case chance had brought me for investigation. . . . Thus at that time I learned a very great deal: much that was of scientific value, but something of practical importance as well—namely, *that it was impossible for a "general practitioner" to treat a case of that kind without bringing his activities and mode of life completely to an end.* I vowed at the time that I would

not go through such an ordeal again. . . . The case of Anna O. . . . proves that a fairly severe case of hysteria can develop, flourish, and be resolved without having a sexual basis. I confess that the plunging into sexuality in theory and practice is not to my taste. But what have my taste and my feeling about what is seemly and what is unseemly to do with the question of what is true? (Cranefield, 1958, pp. 319–320; main italics added)

There are three important subjective elements in Breuer's retrospective account of his treatment of Anna O. The first element is his persistence in the belief (wish?) that his treatment "resolved" Anna's illness. Second, he remained convinced that his patient's illness was strictly a "fairly severe case of hysteria," a possible diagnostic error but one to which a pioneer is entitled. However, we now know that neither of these interpretations is completely accurate.

The third, and perhaps most important, subjective element in Breuer's explanation is his sardonic and self-effacing dismissal of his own offended sense of propriety in the matter of sexual motives. Breuer, apparently, maintained his original resistance to the idea that childhood sexual strivings were at the core of psychopathology. The idea was proposed by Freud during their collaboration on a book of case histories, as we see later in this chapter.

Thus, in Breuer's view, or at least in the version he was willing to express to his correspondent, treatment of Bertha Pappenheim had been terminated because her "hysteria" was "resolved" without the need to explore any sexual motives. All the more curious, then, is this protest against sexuality from the man who was the unwitting phantom father of his patient's imaginary child.

There is no reason to doubt the sincerity of Breuer's beliefs. He had done everything in his power for his patient, and she had improved immensely (Pollock, 1973, p. 331). But improvement is not cure, and, according to Jones's (1953) account, Breuer fled the hysterical childbirth scene in a "cold sweat," indicating, among other things, his partial awareness of how disturbed his patient remained.

It is more reasonable to assume that the discrepancy between Breuer's actual experiences and his interpretation of them has roots in very personal and painful meanings that his patient somehow resurrected in his memory.

Breuer's Identification With Bertha's Mournful Loss

"Benevolent" and "selfless" are words used repeatedly to describe Breuer (Ellenberger, 1970, p. 432; Pollock, 1976, p. 142). Ellenberger interviewed surviving relatives and friends of Breuer, and he was permitted to see correspondence from former patients, who wrote to thank Breuer for his generosity and humaneness in his treatment of them. One associate of Breuer, as later recalled by the associate's daughter, so admired him that he described Breuer's personality as "Christlike in character and charity, wise, restrained, lofty in spirit" (Becker, 1963, quoted in Pollock, 1976, p. 145n.). In every way, Breuer's identity was that of a man devoted to helping others, even at great personal sacrifice. In this respect, Breuer seems to have modeled himself after his father, Leopold Breuer, whom he deeply loved and admired (Ellenberger, 1970, p. 432; Pollock, 1976, pp. 142 ff.).

In a brief autobiography, prepared as a curriculum vitae, Breuer wrote of his father as "this man to whom I am indebted for everything" (Oberndorf, 1953). Breuer's mother died "in the blossom of her youth and beauty" during the birth of his younger brother. The boys' father, Leopold, together with the children's maternal grandmother, turned himself devotedly to the task of raising his motherless children. So complete was the elder Breuer's devotion, that Josef did not attend school but was successfully instructed at home by his father. Moreover, Leopold Breuer never remarried. This self-less devotion to the mother's memory probably intensified the closeness between himself and his children, while simultaneously heightening their sense of loss for one so idealized as to be irreplaceable.

Pollock (1976, p. 143) obtained evidence from members of the Breuer family that Josef's mother, *Bertha* Semler Breuer, died when Josef was between three and four years old; the child she died giving birth to contracted tuberculosis and died at the age of 20; Josef's father, Leopold, died when Josef was 30 years old. Pollock (1976) hypothesized, therefore, that the loss of his idealized mother at a critical period in emotional development, the subsequent death of the brother whom he may have unconsciously blamed and resented for the loss, and the repetition of profound grief at the passing of his father sensitized Breuer in a nonconscious and uncontrollable way to the whole painful issue of mourning for loved ones' deaths.[2]

Years later, struggling uncertainly on the frontier of new human knowledge, Breuer warily confronted the human unconscious in a patient named Bertha. Despite all their devious manifestations and symbolic linkages, Bertha Pappenheim's symp-toms centered on a theme frighteningly familiar to Breuer. In his patient's dispropor-tionate mourning for her father, Breuer found chilling resonances of his own losses. For her part, Bertha Pappenheim found herself in the hands of a caring, altruistic, humane, and fatherly physician, who was clearly interested in her suffering in ways that transcended the typical doctor-patient relationship.

Breuer could not have known, but his patient viewed him, as all future analytic patients were to view their therapists, as father, lover, confessor, friend, rival, villain, and hero, calling up emotions for these changing perceptions of the therapist from previous relationships to important people in her life. This process of projecting inap-propriate feelings and role images onto the therapist, known later in Freud's theory as *transference*, is a double-edged sword. For Bertha Pappenheim's transference of inappropriate love onto Breuer, there had to be Breuer's *countertransference* of sim-ilarly inappropriate emotions onto his patient. One other ingredient may have been present in the transference relationship between Breuer and Bertha. Contrary to Jones's (1953) chronology of events of this case, Breuer's wife gave birth to their daughter, Dora, a little less than a month *before* the death of Bertha Pappenheim's father (Pollock, 1976, p. 143; Ellenberger, 1972). It is reasonable to assume, conse-quently, that at the time of Breuer's announced intention to terminate treatment,

---

[2] Pollock's 1968, 1976 detailed marshaling of the evidence and his psychoanalytic interpretations of Breuer's unresolved Oedipus complex in relation to Bertha Pappenheim are not presented in the mater-ial that follows. Pollock's account is well reasoned and supported, but it requires knowledge of later psy-choanalytic theory that has not yet been presented in this chapter (see also Pollock, 1972).

Bertha was caught up in the conflicting feelings of desiring to posses her therapist as both lover and as father substitute, a contradictory emotional state further fueled by jealousy of Breuer's wife's pregnancy (see Pollock, 1972). With the threatened separation from Breuer rekindling her unresolved mourning for her real father, Bertha could magically but elegantly undo the unbearable recent loss, deny the impending separation from her imaginary lover, and obliterate all reason for jealousy with a single unconscious stratagem designed to bind Breuer permanently to herself: She "bore" his child.

Breuer now had to confront the full intensity of his own contradictory feelings. His attraction to this young and beautiful woman, his unconscious identification of Bertha Pappenheim with his mother, Bertha, and his dim recognition that his own mourning for lost ones was being played out hysterically by this agonized but kindred spirit combined to overwhelm Breuer's last reserves. It is small wonder that he fled the house in a cold sweat and refused to deal again with psychological matters.

Breuer's Contributions to Psychology

We should not overlook the immense contributions provided by Breuer's scientific astuteness prior to his embarrassing episode with Anna O. It was upon these contributions of Breuer that the young Sigmund Freud was to build the structure of psychoanalysis.

First, Breuer recognized that hysterical symptoms were *meaningful* and that they possessed a certain *emotional logic* beneath their bizarre appearance.

Second, Breuer regarded the *origin* of the hysterical symptom as some intense, *emotionally abrasive experience* in the life history of the patient. Though no longer remembered, the past experience *actively operated unconsciously*, pressing for release and goading the patient to find symbolic means of expressing the discomfort. It is not easy to determine how much Sigmund Freud contributed to this interpretation of hysterical symptoms. Freud was always generous in giving most of the credit to Breuer for the early theory of hysteria that they proposed in their joint publications, the "Preliminary Communication" of 1893 and their full monograph, *Studies on Hysteria* of 1895.

Third, the discovery that symptoms could be removed by promoting the expression of the strangulated emotion dating from the past traumatic experience gave further force to the theory that symptoms were the result of dammed-up emotional (affective) energy. The cathartic method, a joint discovery of Breuer and Anna O., was a uniquely *psychological* method for dealing with hysterical disorder. In the terminology of the *Studies on Hysteria*, the goal of the cathartic method was to enable the patient to "abreact" the painful feelings, literally to "react away" the trapped energy. As Breuer and Freud expressed the idea in their "Preliminary Communication," *"The hysteric suffers mostly from reminiscences"* (1893, p. 7).

It was also Breuer's conviction that the essential precondition for the occurrence of hysterical symptoms was the presence of a tendency to self-induced hypnotic states of consciousness. Thus, for Breuer, *any* intensely experienced emotion that occurred during one of these states of "absence" and that was prevented from immediate expression could serve as the origin of a hysterical symptom. It was with this idea that Freud was later to disagree and that he would modify by the time *Studies on Hysteria* had been published.

THE CATHARTIC METHOD IN FREUD'S HANDS: HYPNOTISM

The young Sigmund Freud, doctor in training at the University of Vienna, had been befriended by the older, more experienced Josef Breuer. In 1882, shortly after Breuer had terminated his treatment of Anna O., Freud heard the details of the strange case. He was greatly interested and requested Breuer to tell him the story again and again (Jones, 1953, p. 226). It was not until some years later, however, that Freud and Breuer began to treat cases together, employing for the most part the cathartic method. Apparently, Freud did not simply accept Breuer's technique on a wholesale basis. He was already experimenting with slight modifications on the application of the cathartic method to individual patients as the limitations of his hypnotic skill demanded.

Jean-Martin Charcot

Freud's early reliance on the technique of hypnotism—a necessary adjunct to catharsis—had other roots besides Breuer's successful treatment of Anna O. In 1885 Freud was awarded a traveling grant to attend the lecture-demonstrations of the famous neuropathologist Jean-Martin Charcot (1825–1893) in Paris, at the equally renowned Salpêtrière Hospital (Freud, 1925a, pp. 12–16).

Charcot was investigating the symptoms and causes of hysteria, and he had demonstrated that the bizarre behaviors associated with the disease could be removed and then restored under hypnosis at the suggestion of the physician. This famous French clinician had also demonstrated that hysterical symptoms parallel the hysteric's naive conception of physical disorder. Thus, for example, the patient who has recently been involved in a frightening horse-drawn carriage accident, but who emerges unscathed, may nevertheless exhibit all the symptoms of the paralysis he or she *expects* to have. Hence, in Charcot's view, *ideas*, rather than physical pathology, lie at the base of hysteria.

That a man of Charcot's professional standing could be scientifically interested in the clinical oddities of hysterical attacks was enough to impress Freud with the significance of the disease as a natural phenomenon worth investigation. Breuer's unusual experiences with Anna O. began to assume greater importance in Freud's estimation. He would, however, have a difficult time trying to convince the Viennese medical establishment to investigate what was then regarded as a malingerer's syndrome.

As if to underscore the incredulity with which the medical profession viewed hysterics' suffering, the Viennese society of physicians greeted the young Freud's report of Charcot's work with open hostility. Freud recounted in his *Autobiographical Study* the cool and unpleasant reception his presentation of Charcot's findings engendered (1925a, pp. 15 ff.).

Nevertheless, Freud had learned his lessons well with Charcot: Hysteria *was* a legitimate psychological disorder; there *were* cases of male hysteria; there were symptoms that could be removed, modified, or reinstated by hypnotism; there *were* ideas underlying the patient's symptoms. Freud was later able to demonstrate these truisms to the members of the *Gesellschaft der Aerzte* (Society of Physicians), but they expressed only grudging approval and little interest.

Liebeault and Bernheim

Meanwhile, in another part of France, two physicians, Ambroise-Auguste Liebeault (1823–1904) and Hippolyte Bernheim (1837–1919), founded a clinic at Nancy that rivaled the Charcot school of Paris in its employment of hypnotism in the treatment of hysteria (cf. Watson, 1963, pp. 303–304; and Zilboorg, 1941, pp. 361–378). The physicians associated with the Nancy School, as it came to be known, differed from Charcot's group by their emphasis on the purely pragmatic efficacy of hypnotism as a cure for their hysteric patients. Liebeault and Bernheim were more interested in *treating* the disease than in developing theories to explain its origin, or the action of hypnotism. In contrast to Liebeault and Bernheim's practical viewpoint, Charcot was *theoretically* interested in both hypnotism and in hysteria as manifestations of altered mental processes. He conceived of hypnosis as an essentially pathological or diseased state in itself, a state to which hysterics were peculiarly susceptible. Hypnotic trance, Charcot believed, was the precursor and necessary biological foundation on which the disease of hysteria was built. (It was, incidentally, from Charcot that Breuer adopted the idea that hysteria required a "hypnoid state" or condition of "absence" in order for the damming up of feelings to take place.)

Liebeault and Bernheim held the rather different view that hysteria and hypnotism were not necessarily related. The members of the Nancy School believed, furthermore, that Charcot's findings about the malleability of hysterical symptoms were an artifact of hypnotism imposed by the physician, and, therefore, hypnotic states in themselves could not be the biological *cause* of hysterical disorder (Murphy & Kovach, 1972, p. 156). History seems to have supported the views of Liebeault and Bernheim.

In 1889 Freud traveled back to France, this time to visit the Liebeault-Bernheim clinic at Nancy in an attempt to refine his hypnotic technique (1925a, p. 17). He came away from Nancy with " . . . the profoundest impression of the possibility that there could be powerful mental processes which nevertheless remained hidden from the consciousness of men."

Hypnotism Fails

Throughout the late 1880s, Freud continued to employ the cathartic method, but the difficulties and the dissatisfactions he experienced in its use continued to mount. For one thing, not all his patients could be hypnotized. Some individuals could not achieve the trancelike state of somnambulism so necessary to reliving and releasing the strangulated emotion of the forgotten traumatic event. Furthermore, Freud had begun to understand that even in cases where hypnotism was successful, the success depended deeply on the personal relationship between the physician and the patient.

The efficacy of the hypnotic act was thus a function of the emotional quality of the person-to-person contact between himself and his patient. If for some reason or other this personal relationship was disturbed, "even the most brilliant results [of hypnotism] were likely to be suddenly wiped away . . . " (Freud, 1925a, p. 27). Breuer's unwitting intimate involvement with Anna O. was proof enough of the partially erotic nature of the process.

Clearly, it was necessary for Freud to abandon hypnosis altogether if he was to pursue unimpeded his psychological investigations. Consequently, Freud was compelled gradually to reduce his reliance on hypnosis. His search for a new technique received its first important, if altogether unintentional, guidance from a new patient, Frau Emmy.

FRAU EMMY VON N.

"Keep still—Don't say anything!—Don't touch me!" These were the words which greeted Freud on an afternoon in May 1889 when he visited his new patient, Frau Emmy von N., for the first time.

Frau Emmy was lying on a couch when Freud entered, and as she greeted her new physician, interposed between perfectly coherent and logical, softly spoken amenities, came the bizarre utterance, "Keep still—Don't say anything!—Don't touch me!" She also evidenced several ticlike facial twitches, punctuated by grimaces of disgust and fear that contorted her pleasant face with each repetition of her magical formula: "Keep still!—Don't say anything!—Don't touch me!" Frau Emmy had a tendency to stutter, and her speech was often accompanied by a smacking sound that Freud, quite straight-facedly, tried to convey to the reader by describing it as comparable to the call of a forest bird (Freud, in Breuer & Freud, 1893–1895, p. 49n.). Freud's first suspicion was that these behaviors involved some form of protective ritual practiced by Frau Emmy to ward off a repetitive hallucination.

The Real Frau Emmy von N.: Fanny Moser

Frau Emmy von N. was actually the 41-year-old Fanny Sulzer-Wart Moser, born in 1848 of a large aristocratic Swiss family (Appignanesi & Forrester, 1992, pp. 91 ff.). Fanny was a middle child in the family with 13 brothers and sisters, the youngest born six years after her. In childhood, five of her siblings died, including a brother addicted to morphine who Fanny finally revealed to Freud as a central feature of her conflicts. At age 19, Fanny found her mother dead, probably of a stroke. At age 22 Fanny Sulzer-Wart married Heinrich Moser, a wealthy manufacturer who was 40 years her senior. Together they had two daughters, Fanny and Mentona, but Heinrich's two children by his first marriage treated Fanny as though she were the enemy.

When Heinrich died of a heart attack two days after the birth of their second daughter—Fanny was then 26 years old—her husband's children by the prior marriage accused Fanny of having poisoned him to take possession of his considerable estate and deprive them of their inheritance. The body was exhumed but no evidence of foul play was found, and Fanny Moser became one of the wealthiest women in Europe.

Unfortunately, in the more aristocratic social circles of European society, Fanny Moser was seen as a scandalous woman, and rumors about her participation in the death of her husband persisted for many years. Nevertheless, Fanny Moser became a salon hostess, entertaining celebrity artists and intellectuals, earned a reputation for eccentricity and extravagance, and lived out most of her life on a large estate in Switzerland.

By 1889, she was depressed, tortured by tics, hallucinations, insomnia, and pain (Appignanesi & Forrester, 1992, p. 91 ff.). Indeed, she had been ill since the death of her husband. She traveled to Vienna for medical treatment accompanied by her daughters, now aged 15 and 17 years. Josef Breuer casually recommended that she see Freud. Freud seems to have had a less than favorable opinion of the daughters and shaped his treatment of his new patient around this opinion. For the rest of the story, we return to Freud's case history of the woman he called Frau Emmy von N.

Tracing Symptoms to Their Origins

Freud suggested that Frau Emmy (i.e., Fanny Moser) place the girls with their governess and then enter a sanitarium, where he would visit her daily.

Fortunately, in this, one of the first cases that Freud treated by hypnosis and the cathartic method, Frau Emmy, unlike his later patients, proved to be an admirable subject. She was able to assume the sleeplike somnambulistic state readily, and she was cooperative in discussing her symptoms and their origins—to a point.

As the therapeutic relationship progressed, Freud attempted to trace each of Frau Emmy's symptoms to its root by asking her under hypnosis to explain its meaning. For example, Freud asked her to explain the meaning of her magical phrase, "Keep still!— Don't say anything—Don't touch me!"

> She explained that when she had frightening thoughts she was afraid of their being interrupted in their course, because then everything would get confused and things would be even worse. The "Keep still!" related to the fact that the animal shapes [hallucinations] which appeared to her when she was in a bad state started moving and began to attack her if anyone made a movement in her presence. The final injunction "Don't touch me!" was derived from the following experiences. She told me how, when her brother had been so ill from taking a lot of morphine—she was 19 at the time—he used often to seize hold of her; and how, another time, an acquaintance had suddenly gone mad in the house and had caught her by the arm; . . . and lastly, how, when she was 28 and her daughter was very ill, the child had caught hold of her so forcibly in its delirium that she was almost choked. Though these four instances were so widely separated in time, she told me them in a single sentence and in such rapid succession that they might have been a single episode in four acts. (Freud, in Breuer & Freud, 1893–1895, pp. 56–57).

Thus far, as Freud's account clearly indicates, he held to the conception of hysteria that Breuer had developed in working with Anna O. The patient's unconscious memory had to be searched through hypnotism for hidden emotional experiences that had not been fully expressed when they occurred. By allowing Frau Emmy to reexperience the strangulated affect of those events, catharsis was achieved. But it sometimes seemed as if Frau Emmy's list of traumatic experiences was endless.

For one thing, although Freud used hypnotic suggestion to remove these fears and the power of these memories to instill terror, Frau Emmy experienced relapses, and she sometimes succumbed to new fears and hallucinations. Freud realized that his hypnotic suggestions and emotional catharsis were only partially successful. Tracing the symptom to its origin and freeing the choked emotional energy could not of themselves explain why a particular event had been traumatic.

First Clue in the Discovery of Free Association: Freud Learns to Listen

It is perhaps surprising that Frau Emmy von N., the first patient with whom Freud employed the cathartic method, would also be the person who provided the first clue to the discovery of a new technique of conducting therapy. That clue assumed great significance in later years as Freud experienced difficulty with the hypnotic method.

Frau Emmy, despite Freud's hypnotic suggestions to the contrary, continued to recall frightening experiences with animals and terrifying hallucinations based on animal content. Freud, quite willing to accept the fact that each new instance of anxiety had to be removed separately, took to quizzing Frau Emmy closely on each occasion. She had reported intense stomachaches, and Freud noticed that reports of stomach pains coincided with each new animal terror. He questioned her under hypnosis on the possible origin of the stomachaches, but she seemed reluctant to continue examining each symptom with such exactness.

> Her answer, which she gave rather grudgingly, was that she did not know. I requested her to remember by tomorrow. She then said in a definitely grumbling tone that I was not to keep on asking her where this and that came from, but to let her tell me what she had to say. (Freud, in Breuer & Freud, 1893–1895, p. 63)

Frau Emmy's offhand and somewhat petulant remark was a momentous occasion in Freud's intellectual history. Jones, Freud's biographer, remarks with understatement worthy of Freud himself, that "he took the hint" and thus approached one step closer to a substitute for hypnosis (1953, p. 244).[3]

In more concrete and immediate terms, Freud's acceptance of Frau Emmy's "suggestion" meant that he would allow more free rein in the handling of his patient. He would permit her own feelings and strivings to direct the flow and the content of their therapeutic conversation.

False Connections: Deceptions of Memory

Freud had already begun to suspect that certain of the contents of mental processes revealed during hypnosis might be forms of self-deception designed to screen deeper

---

[3] It is interesting to note that Ernest Jones, in an uncharacteristic lapse, attributes Frau Emmy von N.'s irritable remark to Fräulein Elisabeth von R., a patient Freud treated some three years after Frau Emmy. The Fräulein Elisabeth case was also a landmark step in Freud's development of psychoanalysis and is considered at a later point.

and more threatening material. Thus he believed that one form of this self-protective deception involved an attempt by the unconscious mind to *falsely connect* one memory with another to obscure the real connections between thoughts. Such real connections, left undisturbed, might lead to the eventual recall of a threatening memory.

On one occasion, for example, Frau Emmy had a restless morning because she was worried that the hotel where her children and their governess were staying had a faulty elevator. She had recommended that the children use the elevator, and was now anxious over the thought that the elevator might fail. But a strange thing happened when Freud questioned Frau Emmy under hypnosis about the reason for her anxiety. Fully expecting to hear again the story of her concern for her children's safety, Freud was puzzled when Frau Emmy related instead a worry that her massage treatments would have to stop because her menstrual period might begin. The explanation for this hypnotic non sequitur, Freud reasoned, might be found in the self-protective tendency of the mind to distort and to obscure connections between anxiety-arousing ideas. Ideas can be rearranged into sequences that block conscious recognition of the correct sequence of ideas, the sequence that is connected to some anxiety-provoking thought.

Freud was able to decipher the meaning of Frau Emmy's jumbled thought train. Her real concern was for her oldest daughter, who was having some difficulty walking because of a severe attack of ovarian neuralgia. Frau Emmy had just that morning solicitously inquired of the children's governess if the girl, in her pain, had used the elevator to descend from the upper floor of the hotel instead of walking down. Then, blotting out the true source of her anxiety, her daughter's illness, Frau Emmy recalled only its oblique connection with the elevator. By displacing the anxiety to the least threatening component of the sequence, the elevator, the thought sequence became transformed:

Not afraid of consequences of daughter's illness, but afraid that elevator might fail.

The perceptive Freud noticed that the anxious impulse was not only displaced to another thought, but that the displacement had taken place along *meaningful* associative lines.

Daughter's menstrual problem → her own menstrual problem → elevator fear

Consequently, during hypnosis only the topmost displacement, *fear of the elevator*, had given way to the next item in the sequence, *her own menstrual problem*. Even though hypnotic exploration with her physician had enabled penetration one layer down through the sequence, the fundamental layer—*anxiety over the daughter's menstrual problem*—was left untouched.

Relapse: Intensification of Symptoms

Within seven weeks of the beginning of treatment, Frau Emmy's condition was sufficiently improved to warrant her dismissal from the sanitarium. It appeared that the cathartic method had once again worked its miracle. But this happy outcome was not long lived.

Seven months later, Breuer received word from Frau Emmy that her oldest daughter had suffered a recurrence of her ovarian difficulties, and this time the daughter had succumbed to a "severe nervous illness" as well. The girl had visited a gynecologist for her difficulty, and during the treatment she had manifested all the signs of a severe emotional disturbance. Frau Emmy had concluded that Freud was responsible for the daughter's condition because he had treated the subject so lightly during his therapy with her. Thus Frau Emmy relapsed into the state in which Freud had first encountered her. After much coaxing, Breuer persuaded Frau Emmy that Freud was not at fault, and one year elapsed before she again visited her old physician.

Overdetermination of Symptoms

Frau Emmy now began a period of self-inflicted semistarvation (anorexia). She refused to eat complete meals, and she drank very little. Freud ordered her to increase her intake of food and liquid, and there followed a somewhat uncharacteristic argument between patient and physician.

Two days passed and Frau Emmy mellowed a little. Freud put her into hypnosis and asked why she could not eat and drink normally.

"I'm thinking how, when I was a child [Frau Emmy began], it often happened that out of naughtiness I refused to eat my meat at dinner. My mother was very severe about this and under the threat of condign punishment I was obliged two hours later to eat the meat, which had been left standing on the same plate. The meat was quite cold by then and the fat was set so hard" (she showed her disgust) ". . . I can still see the fork in front of me . . . one of its prongs was a little bent. Whenever I sit down to a meal I see the plates before me with the cold meat and fat on them. And how, many years later, I lived with my brother who was an officer and who had that horrible disease [venereal disease]. I knew that it was contagious and was terribly afraid of making a mistake and picking up his knife and fork" (she shuddered) ". . . and in spite of that I ate my meals with him so that no one should know that he was ill. And how, soon after that, I nursed my other brother when he had consumption so badly. We ate by the side of his bed and the spittoon always stood on the table, open" (she shuddered again) ". . . and he had a habit of spitting across the plates into the spittoon. This always made me feel so sick, but I couldn't show it, for fear of hurting his feelings." (Freud, in Breuer & Freud, 1893–1895, p. 82)

We can discern in Frau Emmy's reminiscences a phenomenon that Freud called *overdetermination*. Each symptom, Freud discovered, had not one cause, not one root, but *multiple* determinants that had become associatively bonded together in the patient's thoughts. Consequently, one overt symptom represented many emotional threads woven to a single pattern. Conversely, a branching network of *emotionally related* ideas, impulses, and meanings supported each symptom. In Frau Emmy's case, the unitary symptom of refusing to eat capped a latent amalgam of previous experiences that centered on the arousal of disgust for the act of eating; *cold meat and fat*; *fear of contracting a "foul" disease through shared eating implements*; and *revulsion at the act of spitting into a spittoon over dinner*.

Freud again helped his patient to abreact these strangulated emotions. From that time on, Frau Emmy was able to eat relatively normally, and she began to recover her composure in most other respects as well.

THE THEORETICAL YIELD FROM FRAU EMMY'S THERAPY

The case of Frau Emmy von N. is important for a firm understanding of psychoanalytic theory because it provides a vivid illustration of the clinical data on which Freud exercised his powers of observation, imagination, and reason. There are at least five important features of the case that deserve consideration.

First, it would naturally be expected that a doctor using a new method of treatment for the first time would rigidly adhere to the inventor's technique to gain facility with its use. In so doing, he should be concerned with maintaining correct form and be temporarily blind to the method's shortcomings and limitations during the period of attempted mastery. None of these expectations is confirmed in Freud's use of Breuer and Anna O.'s cathartic method. Freud was sensitive not only to the limitations of hypnosis, but to the shortcoming of catharsis as well in achieving an understanding of the network of strangled emotions.

Second, we must not forget that it was Frau Emmy who provided for Freud a service similar to the one provided for Breuer by Anna O., namely, a timely hint about how to proceed. Frau Emmy's irritation with Freud's incessant probing, questioning, ordering, and badgering led to her modifying her physician's technique. She wished to be allowed to speak her mind without interruption. Instead of question-and-answer sessions, the flow of therapeutic communication should be at least partially under the patient's control. This hint was to stand Freud in good stead several years later as he searched about for a way to modify his procedure with patients not susceptible to hypnotic suggestion.

Third, Freud had been led to hypothesize that the workings of the mind could be directed toward *defending* the person's conscious self or ego from the recognition of unpleasant, frightening, or unacceptable thoughts. Frau Emmy's concern over her daughter's illness had been obscured by a conscious, but associatively related, concern for the safety of her children in the hotel elevator. The link in the chain between the *conscious* fear that the elevator might not be safe and the *unconscious* anxiety over her daughter's *ovarian* difficulties was revealed during hypnosis as the non sequitur of Frau Emmy's worry that she might have to forgo massage treatment if her own *menstrual* cycle interfered. This worry was the last of a chain of displacements. The conscious shield memories (elevator fear, menstrual-interference-with-massage) served to distract thought from the more threatening idea of her daughter's illness. Defense, not confusion, was responsible for the displacements.

Fourth, we can see evidence from this early case that Freud's attention was directed to the importance of childhood incidents, childhood emotions, and childhood conflicts in establishing the basis of an intricate associative chain of ideas that influences adult behavior. Frau Emmy's early dinnertime experiences with cold meat and fat and her terrifying experiences with death and disease had certainly not passed from memory with time.

Fifth, Freud understood the importance of following each symptom back to its cause. Partial abreaction led only to partial relief. He accepted only the permanent removal of that symptom as proof that a symptom had been fully explained. He did not accept the patient's verbal expression of relief as sufficient evidence that a symptom had been traced to its fundamental cause. Only his patient's subsequent behavior could satisfy that requirement. In consequence, Freud puzzled over the recurrence of Frau Emmy's symptoms after he had employed hypnotic suggestion to remove the memory traces of the strangled emotions. Such symptoms, he discovered, were overdetermined. Multiple causes, complex chains of experiences, contributed to the formation of a single symptom. Hence, to account for the persistence of some symptoms in the face of massive hypnotic suggestion to abandon them, Freud found it necessary to hypothesize that the fundamental cause of the symptom had not been reached (cf. Freud, 1896c). Deeper probing had to be undertaken; recall of a single traumatic experience was not sufficient.

Breuer's cathartic method became, in Freud's hands, not only a therapeutic tool of increased flexibility, but a method of investigation to be employed in understanding the psychology of the human animal.

THE EVOLUTION OF METHOD: FRÄULEIN ELISABETH VON R.

In 1892 Freud faced an intensification of his difficulties with the cathartic method: Fräulein Elisabeth von R., his latest patient, could not be hypnotized.

Hypnotism had been an invaluable adjunct in applying the cathartic method, widening the scope of the patient's consciousness and "putting within . . . [the patient's] reach knowledge which he did not possess in his waking life" (Freud, 1925a, p. 27). With some of his other patients Freud had experienced the same difficulty, and, in fact, some patients refused even to make any attempt to submit to hypnosis. Freud began to suspect that *unwillingness* to be hypnotized, whether verbally expressed or mutely evident in uncooperative behavior, formed the basis for all such failures (Freud, in Breuer & Freud, 1893–1895, p. 268).

Fräulein Elisabeth von R., therefore, posed a formidable problem because she was either unable or unwilling to achieve the customary somnambulistic state. Freud suspected that her hysterical symptoms of intense pain in her legs and her inability to stand or to walk for long periods were connected with some experience that she *could* recall if only she felt free enough. The greatest difficulty confronting Freud in the treatment of Fräulein Elisabeth was to devise a way to enable her to discuss her symptoms freely and without reservation in the absence of hypnosis.

The Real Elisabeth von R.: Ilona Weiss

Elisabeth von R. was actually Ilona Weiss, the youngest of three daughters of a well-to-do Hungarian family (Appignanesi & Forrester, 1992, pp. 108 ff.). She was an intelligent, ambitious, and independent young woman who wanted to pursue her education rather than the traditional role of wife and mother that prevailed as custom. Ilona had a close relationship with her father who by all accounts treated her as the son he had wanted. When he fell ill of what proved to be a fatal heart condition, Ilona nursed him until his death. Her leg pains began at that time, but the full paralysis did not occur until about two years after his death.

Freud learned from Elisabeth (i.e., Ilona Weiss) that she had nursed her father after his heart attack for a period of one and a half years. She was quite dutiful, sleeping in her father's room, attending to his needs morning and night, forcing herself to remain cheerful and encouraging. She had experienced an attack of severe pain in her legs during this period, an attack so intense that she had had to take to her bed and become a patient herself. Two years after her father's death, the pains returned, unbearably, and she discovered that she could not walk at all. Furthermore, because of the death of her father, the happiness of the family reached a new low ebb. In consequence, when Fräulein Elisabeth's sister married a talented and ambitious man, who unfortunately did not respect their mother, Elisabeth found herself expressing resentment both toward her new brother-in-law and toward her sister for deserting the family.

Elisabeth's younger sister also married in this period, but, fortunately, the couple remained close to the family. This sister then became pregnant and died in childbirth. The widowed brother-in-law was overcome with grief, and he withdrew from Elisabeth's family to seek solace with his own. Thus, in the space of a few years, Elisabeth had lost by death or by alienation those most important to her. She now began a period of almost total social isolation.

For Freud, the case history as thus far related by Fräulein Elisabeth was a great disappointment. True, it was a heartbreaking tale, but it contained no overt indication of the cause of her hysterical symptoms. Freud felt stymied. In the past, such obstacles had been overcome by the judicious use of hypnotism. His frustration was not helped much by Elisabeth's often biting remarks about the lack of effect his treatment exerted on her symptoms. With his usual candor, Freud conceded, "I was obliged to admit that she was in the right" (Freud, in Breuer & Freud, 1893–1895, p. 145).

SECOND CLUE TO THE FREE ASSOCIATION METHOD: THE CONCENTRATION TECHNIQUE

Freud's experiences with Bernheim and the Nancy Clinic came to his aid. He remembered an unusual demonstration during which Bernheim had suggested to one of his patients under hypnosis the negative hallucination that he, Bernheim, was no longer present in the room. Bernheim further encouraged her in the belief that no amount of effort would enable her to see him, despite any action he might take. Bernheim followed this hypnotic suggestion with a variety of threatening gestures directly in front of the subject's face, but she behaved in every way as if Bernheim truly no longer existed. Bernheim then added to his previous instructions the command to remember nothing of what had transpired, a typical posthypnotic amnesia command. Then, bringing the patient back to wakefulness, he proceeded to demonstrate just the opposite, that is, that the patient *could* recall what had transpired, despite the hypnotic amnesia, if only the hypnotist insisted strongly, urgently, and convincingly enough that the subject do so. To aid the process of recall, Bernheim would place his hand on the forehead of the awake subject and press firmly, while insisting that the memory of the previous events return. Much to Freud's surprise, the subject was able to recall the events of the hypnotic session. Thus Bernheim had shown Freud that the patient does remember but he does not know that he remembers until he is pressured to do so. Here was Freud's way out of his dilemma with the hypnotism-resistant Fräulein Elisabeth.

Willful concentration thus became the basis of Freud's new approach to therapy and the investigation of unconscious processes. Of course, the new concentration technique was no less dependent than hypnotism had been on the quality of the relationship between doctor and patient. The new method, in fact, was really another form of manipulating the patient's suggestibility. Freud described his new strategy as follows:

> I decided to start from the assumption that my patients knew everything that was of any pathogenic [disease-causing] significance and that it was only a question of obliging them to communicate it. Thus when I reached a point at which, after asking a patient some question such as "How long have you had this symptom?" or: "What was its origin?," I was met with the answer: "I really don't know," I proceeded as follows: I placed my hand on the patient's forehead or took her head between my hands and said: "You will think of it under the pressure of my hand. At the moment at which I relax my pressure you will see something in front of you or something will come into your head. Catch hold of it. It will be what we are looking for.—Well, what have you seen or what has occurred to you?" (Freud, in Breuer & Freud, 1893–1895, p. 110)

Using the new concentration technique with Fräulein Elisabeth brought immediate results. After a long silence, she admitted that the pressure of Freud's hand had brought forth the recollection of an evening in which a young man had romantically escorted her home from the social affair they had attended, the pleasure of their intimate conversation during the walk, and her feelings of distress on returning home to nurse her father. Bernheim had been right! Apparently, even the reluctant Fräulein Elisabeth could recall events that seemed meaningful in context without hypnotism. Freud's faith in a deterministic explanation of mental events would not allow that seemingly spontaneous thoughts were random thoughts. Thus whatever ideas were evoked by the pressure of the concentration technique *had* to be related to the problem at hand. The difficulty remained, however, to discover the relationship between these newly recalled incidents and the ongoing process of her neurotic symptoms.

Conflict, Symbol, Conversion

Freud observed that Fräulein Elisabeth's memories bore a very special emotional quality. *They conflicted.* She had known the young man for a short time, and because he could not yet support a wife, and because Elisabeth was dutifully bound to her ailing father, she had resolved to wait until she and her young man were both independent before marrying. But at the same time, she felt that her feelings for the young man were somehow incompatible with her equally worthy resolve to care for her father. She recalled that the night of the social affair, after which she had walked home with the man, marked the height of the conflict between her affection for the young man and her responsibility to her father.

When Elisabeth returned home late that night, she found her father's condition worsened, and she reproached herself for having sacrificed her father's care to her own pleasure. Elisabeth never again left her father for a whole evening. As a result, she saw her young man only rarely thereafter.

At the death of Elisabeth's father, the young man seemed to withdraw, but he probably did so only out of respect for her mourning. Eventually, his business affairs caused him to travel to distant regions, and contact with Elisabeth was completely severed.

Not only was the loss of her first love a painful experience for Elisabeth, but the relationship's premature end deprived her of ever resolving the conflict between her feelings for the young man and her self-imposed duty to her father. In effect, the solution to the conflict was made inaccessible, while the abrasively emotional quality of the incompatible feelings remained untouched.

On the basis of these revelations developed through the concentration technique, Freud reasoned that Elisabeth's symptoms were a technique of defense by which she had unconsciously converted the painful conflicting emotions into a bodily manifestation. Fräulein Elisabeth confirmed Freud interpretation by informing him that she now knew why her leg pains always began at the same point on her thigh: *This was the exact place upon which her father rested his leg every morning while she changed the bandages on his swollen leg.* Clearly, the pain in her own legs had arisen through association and symbolization with her father's painful leg. Furthermore, as Freud and Elisabeth discussed this interpretation, the pain in her legs intensified, or as Freud put it: "her painful legs began to 'join in the conversation' . . . " (Freud, in Breuer & Freud, 1893–1895, p. 148).

Freud followed up her several symptoms using the new concentration technique. When asked, for instance, why other areas of her legs were painful, Fräulein Elisabeth produced under the pressure of Freud hands a whole series of recollections of other emotionally painful events. Moreover, each of these events was connected by association or by symbolization with her legs or with the act of walking. For the pain she felt while *standing*, she produced a memory of *standing* at the door when her father was brought home after his heart attack. In her fright on that occasion, she had been frozen in place. When Freud asked her what else the notion of "standing" meant to her, she reproduced a memory of *standing* "as though spellbound" by her sister's deathbed.

Yet, despite the insights that had been attained, there seemed to be some hesitation, some difficulty in recalling certain feelings, desires, or events. It was almost as if Elisabeth, though desirous of cooperating with Freud in the removal of her symptoms, was nonetheless *resisting* the recollection of some important ideas. Freud wondered whether the new concentration technique was already proving to be a failure, or was there another psychological process at work here?

Resistance: Defensive Barrier to Psychological Pain

On those occasions when Freud applied the concentration technique and Elisabeth reported that nothing had occurred to her, Freud detected behind her tense and preoccupied facial expression a hint that ideas *had* come to her. For some reason, Freud suspected, Elisabeth did not want to communicate her thoughts to him:

I could think of two motives for this concealment. Either she was applying criticism to the idea, which she had no right to do, on the ground of its not being important enough or of its being an irrelevant reply to the question she had been asked: or she hesitated to produce it because—she found it too disagreeable to tell. (Freud, in Breuer & Freud, 1893–1895, p. 153)

Freud therefore decided to proceed as if he had the greatest confidence in his technique. He informed his patient that he knew full well that she had thought of something under the pressure of his hand, and that if she continued to conceal it, she would never be rid of her pains.

Freud had correctly surmised that the cause of her recalcitrance was emotional resistance. Elisabeth ultimately, but reluctantly, complied:

ELISABETH:	"I could have said it to you the first time."
FREUD:	"And why didn't you?"
ELISABETH:	"I thought I could avoid it, but it came back each time," or "I thought it wasn't what you wanted." (Freud, in Breuer & Freud, 1893–1895, p. 154)

It was at this point, with the concept of resistance in hand, that Freud was able to gather the several threads of evidence he had been collecting from his patients into one elegant skein. Resistance to recalling significant emotional events is another form of defensive maneuver that the conscious mind employs to protect the individual from threatening thoughts. But such thoughts, though consciously resisted, may nevertheless continue to exert unconscious pressure in their striving for expression, if not in their original form, then in disguised form. Thus Elisabeth's *symptoms* were not only the *result* of strangulated emotion, they were, indeed, the *unconsciously symbolic expression* of an unresolved conflict. The symptoms are substitute expressions of the conflicted emotions.

Such conflict has been pushed from conscious awareness because it has never been adequately resolved. It continues to be a source of painful and unacceptable self-perceptions. Fräulein Elisabeth's conflict over her duty to her father and her incompatible desire for the companionship of her young man certainly fit this mold. Yet, Freud discovered, there had to be more to it because the abreaction of these emotions had not completely removed Elisabeth's symptoms. There had to be a conflict still unresolved and continuing to operate behind some formidable resistance to its recall.

Symptoms as Self-Punishment

Covering old territory again from his new perspective, Freud began to requestion Elisabeth about the origins of her pains. Her thoughts turned back to the summer resort where she had stayed just before her sister died in childbirth, her worries over her mother's illness, and her feelings of despair and loneliness at having been unable to accomplish anything in life. Particularly strong at this period had been her desire for love, a desire that, contrary to her previous resolve to do without men after her unhappy love affair, had begun to soften her "frozen nature."

With these feelings uppermost in mind, the marriage of her sister to a man who cared lovingly and tenderly for her made a profound impression on Elisabeth. She knew that her sister regretted becoming pregnant again so soon after her first child's birth. But Elisabeth also knew, and marveled at, the way her sister bore the discomfort of the illness resulting from her pregnancy with absolute calm for the sake of her husband. At the summer resort, Elisabeth went on a walk with this brother-in-law. He had wanted to remain with his sick wife, but even she urged him to accompany Elisabeth, and he relented. Elisabeth enjoyed the afternoon she spent with her sister's husband tremendously because they talked freely and intimately, and, for the first time, she had the feeling that someone really understood her. In consequence, she became overwhelmed with the desire to possess a man like her brother-in-law. In fact, so strong was this desire that, a few days after their walk, Elisabeth returned to the place in the woods where they had been together and, in a reverie, dreamed of a man like him who might make her as happy as her sister. She arose from the reverie with her legs in pain.

The nature of her hidden conflict had become crystal clear to Freud: Elisabeth desired her brother-in-law, but she felt guilty over such feelings, particularly so because his wife—her own sister—was now ill and helpless. As clear as the conflict was to Freud, it was in the same measure obscure to Elisabeth. Because she had, apparently, never admitted the existence of these feelings, her guilty wish had remained utterly alien to her conscious personality. Ironically, several months after that fateful walk in the woods, Elisabeth's wish almost came true. She was called to her sister's sickbed but when she arrived, her sister was dead.

> At that moment of dreadful certainty that her beloved sister was dead without bidding them farewell and without having eased her last days with her care—at that very moment another thought had shot through Elisabeth's mind, and now forced itself irresistibly upon her once more, like a flash of lightning in the dark: "Now he is free again and I can be his wife." (Freud, in Breuer & Freud, 1893–1895, p. 156)

Here was the confirmation of Freud's burgeoning speculations about conflict and emotional resistance. Elisabeth had converted a series of painful ideas into bodily symptoms to exact a kind of self-punishment for the illicit wish for her brother-in-law and to atone for the reprehensible feeling of gladness at the thought that her sister's death had freed him to marry her. By the time she had come to treatment with Freud, the memory of her love and guilt had already been defensively isolated from her awareness.

Fräulein Elisabeth was devastated at the realization of her own feelings. Freud was kind to point out, however, that, strictly speaking, she was not responsible for her feelings and, more importantly, her symptoms and suffering were proof enough of her sound moral sense.

THE THEORETICAL YIELD FROM FRÄULEIN ELISABETH'S THERAPY

Freud had progressed sufficiently in his use of the cathartic method with Fräulein Elisabeth to consolidate his observations into important theoretical concepts.

Concentration Technique

Fräulein Elisabeth's lack of susceptibility to hypnotism had initially prodded Freud into the search for a new therapeutic technique. Thus, Fräulein Elisabeth von R. provided the occasion for Freud's incorporation of a second clue in the process of formulating his final psychoanalytic method of free association. Bernheim's demonstration at the Nancy Clinic that a posthypnotic patient could willfully remember her previous hypnotic experiences if she was authoritatively pressured to do so became the prototype for Freud's hand pressure concentration technique with the recalcitrant Elisabeth. (Freud's first clue, you may recall, was Frau Emmy's acid remark that he should allow her to speak her mind without interruption.)

Defense and Resistance

The discovery, through use of the concentration technique, that Elisabeth's thought processes were directed by *active resistance* to unacceptable ideas was a hard-won insight. Ironically, only through the loss of hypnotism as a therapeutic tool could the significance, cause, and direction of the process of resistance be uncovered. Because the patient in the hypnotic state is freed from active avoidance of unacceptable impulses and ideas, the *defensive* nature of this "forgetting" in the conscious state could not be discerned.

Freud's discovery clearly had brought about a drastic change not only in the way therapy was conducted, but also in the theoretical conception by which its effects were to be understood. Breuer's cathartic method focused on the problem of breaching the patient's conscious amnesia through hypnosis to reach dammed-up emotions. Once reached, these feelings could finally be spent in a therapeutic reenactment of the traumatic moment. Then, hypnotic suggestion was employed to help the patient forget the unpleasantness of his or her experiences and to conduct his or her life without the troublesome symptom. Freud, in contrast, had reshaped the rules of the game by zeroing in, not on the symptom and its backlog of unexpressed emotion, but on the patient's *unwillingness* to recall painful or unacceptable thoughts.

The goal of psychotherapy for Freud became the examination and interpretation of the patient's resistances in an attempt to enable the patient to deal with conflicts that had festered, defensively protected from real resolution. Thus, by working with, rather than by circumventing, emotional resistance, Freud discovered that hysterical symptoms were a form of psychological defense against threatening ideas and wishes. The symptoms of the neurosis were symbolic and associative replacements for the pain of unresolved, "forgotten" conflicts.

Repression and Conflict

If Fräulein Elisabeth could not willingly recall her desire for her sister's husband or her guilt feelings, and if she vigorously resisted the thought when pressured, then some psychological force that actively keeps the memory out of consciousness must have been operating. Furthermore, this same counterforce must have been responsible for originally removing the memory from awareness. Freud christened this hypothetical force *repression*.

Repression is a kind of motivated amnesia for certain impulses, ideas, or events. Resistance to recall is one evidence of motivated forgetting or repression. But the minute the word "motivated" is used, it becomes necessary to ask what that motive might be. The answer, it seemed clear to Freud, lies in the nature of the cognitive-emotional state known as *conflict*.

Not just any unpleasant thought, not just any painful memory succumbs to repression. Only memories, thoughts, ideas that are somehow connected to impulses or wishes *that are unacceptable to the individual's conscious ethical standards* are capable of the intense anxiety needed to trigger repression (Freud, 1910b, p. 24).

Removal from consciousness is one way of avoiding the emotional pain of the conflict when a solution to the discord is unavailable. Thus the thought that she was glad that her sister was dead because her sister's death freed the husband to marry again was a totally unacceptable idea to Elisabeth's ethical self. If the problem had been only a momentary desire for her sister's husband, Elisabeth would probably have only *suppressed* (not *repressed*) the thought. Suppression involves the conscious or deliberate avoidance of certain ideas with the individual's full awareness that he or she refuses to entertain them. Repression, on the other hand, is characterized by the *unconscious, automatic* nature of the "forgetting" that it accomplishes. When repression operates, the individual is *not* aware of avoiding certain thoughts or impulses. In fact, we could say along with R. D. Laing that when an individual represses an idea, he or she "forgets" it and then "forgets" that he or she forgot it (see Chapter 10 for Laing's treatment of this concept).

Sometimes suppression of a thought, though it begins as a deliberate act of mental avoidance, may grade imperceptibly into habitual "not-thinking" about the idea. When suppression has been practiced long enough, rigidly enough, and widely enough, it may become such an unthinking act that it is seemingly indistinguishable from an act of genuine repression. But the motive for such habitual "not-thinking" responses is vastly different from the motives that trigger repression, for repression is not brought about gradually but abruptly and automatically because its underlying conflict is unbearable.

In Elisabeth's case, this intensity of conflict was clearly present from the beginning. The fact that her illicit wish had become associatively connected with the even more reprehensible feeling of gladness that her sister was dead was too powerful a combination for Elisabeth to face consciously. The nascent conflict would become a two-pronged kernel of pain: the unacceptable wish for her brother-in-law and the wicked feeling of pleasure at her sister's death. Freud's most profound discovery about the nature of defensive repression was that it is not any *one* unacceptable thought that causes its removal from awareness; it is the *combination* of thoughts or feelings and their interrelationships that intensify psychological pain to the point where it cannot be consciously borne. Moreover, *each* element of the conflict clashes powerfully with the individual's ethical self-image.

A Dynamic Unconscious

Unfortunately, though removed from consciousness by repression, conflicts continue to operate unconsciously, producing symptoms that symbolically or through association with other ideas replace the conflict's psychological pain. Therefore, repression of wishes or impulses is not an adequate resolution of conflict at all. The symptom, Freud discovered, carries on the conflict in distorted form. In Fräulein Elisabeth's case, the symptoms of pain in her legs and the inability to walk or stand were shaped by a series of symbolic ("standing alone") and associative links (*standing* in shock by her dead sister's bed; *walking* with her brother-in-law; *walking* with her first love while she should have been caring for her father; father placing *leg* on her *thigh* to be bandaged).

Breuer had been right: The energy of the strangulated emotion had to be expressed somehow. But the cause of the neurotic's symptoms was not simply the damming up of emotional energy. First, Freud realized, there had to be a wish or an impulse that was *incompatible* with that individual's conscious self-perception. Such a wish would be at odds with his or her everyday ethical principles. Only this incompatibility could carry the conflict to an ego-threatening intensity. *Then* the conflict's associated emotions could be dammed up by repression. Conflict of a wish with a conscious ethical principle—this is the essence of defense by repression. It is an active, dynamic process giving painful, if mute, evidence of the power of unconscious forces.

It is interesting to note that some early attempts at experimental testing of the Freudian hypothesis of repression sorely missed the point. Some of these experimenters naively assumed, in their enthusiasm to design experiments, that *any* anxiety-provoking idea could trigger repression.[4] Often, this unsophisticated version of the theory led to the creation of mild forms of anxiety or unpleasantness as experimental analogs of Freud's ideas. In a great number of cases these attempts did not come close to the kind and the quality of anguish that Freud conceptualized as the basis of repression. The mechanism of repression remains a difficult phenomenon to study in the laboratory (see Monte, 1975, Chap. 3).

Postscript to Elisabeth's Treatment

Elisabeth (Ilona) recalled her treatment with Freud many years later in a conversation with her daughter. Her recollections are worth quoting:

> [Freud was] "just a young, bearded nerve specialist they sent me to" [who had tried] "to persuade me that I was in love with my brother-in-law, but that wasn't really so." (Quoted in Appignanesi & Forrester, 1992, p. 113)

Accurate recall of the events? Defensive and selective memory? The historical data do not permit a definitive answer.

---

[4] See Mackinnon and Dukes, 1962, for a review of the experimental literature on repression. Eriksen and Pierce, 1968, provide a broad overview of the methodological problems encountered in studying all defense mechanisms. See also Murray, 1938, Chapter 6, for some of the early studies on repression, and Rapaport, 1971, chapters 5, 7, 8, for a conceptual analysis of the early repression work. Interesting for the broad perspective it offers on experimental tests of Freudian hypotheses is the volume by Hans Eysenck and Glenn Wilson, 1973, which presents some of the original research reports and follows them with cogent, if pessimistic, criticism. A more optimistic view of the experimental tests of Freudian theory is given by Kline, 1972, and by Masling's (1983) collection of papers.

FREUD'S FINAL CLUE TO
THE METHOD OF FREE ASSOCIATION

For his final modification of his developing therapeutic procedures, Freud followed yet another clue, a recollection from his own youth. One of his favorite authors, Ludwig Borne, had offered the following advice to those who wish to write creatively:

> Take a few sheets of paper and for three days on end write down, without fabrication or hypocrisy, everything that comes into your head. Write down what you think of yourself, of your wife, of the Turkish War, of Goethe, of Fonk's trial, of the Last Judgement, of your superiors—and when three days have passed you will be quite out of your senses with astonishment at the new and unheard-of-thoughts you have had. (Quoted in Freud, 1920b, p. 265. See also Jones, 1953, p. 246)

The passage just quoted was part of a complete essay titled "The Art of Becoming an Original Writer in Three Days." At age 14, Freud was given a present of the collected works of Ludwig Borne. Ernest Jones reports that Borne had been such a favorite with the young Freud that only Borne's books survived Freud's adolescence to become part of his adult library (1953, p. 246). Freud himself acknowledged his debt to Borne for the latent seed of an important idea that was to revise his therapeutic method completely.

Borne's startling proposal apparently left a lasting impression on Freud, for he now began to follow Borne's advice, not for writing, but for allowing his patients free play for their thoughts during therapy. Freud developed a technique of therapeutic communication designed to permit patients to roam freely through their fleeting thoughts, verbalizing each idea as it occurred. He permitted his patients to omit *nothing*. Freud instructed each of his patients in the new technique of *free association* in the following way:

> You will notice that as you relate things various thoughts will occur to you which you would like to put aside on the ground of certain criticisms and objections. You will be tempted to say to yourself that this or that is irrelevant here, or is quite unimportant, or nonsensical, so that there is no need to say it. *You must never give in to these criticisms, but must say it in spite of them—indeed, you must say it precisely because you have an aversion to doing so. . . .* Finally, never forget that you have promised to be absolutely honest, and never leave anything out because, for some reason or other, it is unpleasant to tell it. (1913a, pp. 134–135; italics added)

Thus the "fundamental rule" of psychoanalysis, as Freud called it, was to say everything that comes to mind with no attempt to edit the stream of thought logically or emotionally. Sometimes patients had great difficulty following the fundamental rule. Freud had observed a similar difficulty earlier when using the concentration technique on those occasions when a patient world object: "As a matter of fact, I knew that the first time, but it was just what I didn't want to say" (Freud, in Breuer & Freud, 1893–1895, p. 111). In fact, patients would employ the most devious techniques of escaping the new fundamental rule. They would engage Freud in conversation about the decorations in his office, or in a discussion about the state of the weather, or they would pursue some abstract and irrelevant topic on which they considered themselves expert—anything rather than abandon logical and emotional censorship over their thoughts.

With careful prodding and urging, and with constant reminders and corrections, Freud eventually helped his patients to see the importance of abandoning the mind to its own directions. Actually, the notion that the associations dredged up in this way are "free" should not be taken to mean that they are random or accidental. Quite to the contrary, Freud discovered, the unconscious is bound by its own emotional logic that strictly determines the sequence, content, and speed of the flow of ideas.

COMPROMISE FORMATION: THE MEANING OF SYMPTOMS

Consider the following description of disordered behavior:

> An 11-year-old boy would not sleep each night until he had performed the following compulsive ceremony. He recounted to his mother every minute detail of the day; all scraps of paper, lint, or rubbish on the carpet in his bedroom had to be picked up; the bed had to be pushed up against the wall; three chairs, no more, no fewer, must stand by the bed; the pillows must be placed in a particular pattern on the bed. Finally, just before sleeping, the boy had to kick out with his legs a certain specified number of times and then lie on his side. Only then would sleep come. (Based on Freud, 1896b, p. 172)

The young boy's sleep ritual is evidence of a severe emotional disturbance known as *obsessional neurosis*. Obsessional neurotics practice a variety of ritualistic behaviors that bear the mark of anxiety. When the obsessive is prevented from carrying out the behavior in question, he or she succumbs to an intense anxiety attack. The obsessive patient suffers from ostensibly unwanted but continually intruding ideas that threaten to flood consciousness, despite attempts to control them. Performance of a ritual-like series of behaviors temporarily alleviates the discomfort produced by the constant succession of the obsessive ideas. The problem is to understand the connection between the obsessive ideas and the compulsive anxiety-reducing ritualistic behaviors. Utilizing his new conception of "defense," Freud sought to unlock the mystery of the obsessive's behavior by attempting to understand the *personal meaning* of symptoms.

> The nature of obsessional neurosis can be expressed in a simple formula. *Obsessional ideas* are invariably transformed *self-reproaches* which have reemerged from *repression* and which always relate to some *sexual* act that was performed with pleasure in childhood. (1896b, p. 169)

Unable to sleep until his ceremonial acts involving chairs, pillows, beds, and rug had been accomplished, along with a detailed explanation to his mother of the day's events, the 11-year-old boy was able to reveal in analysis the defensive nature of these compulsive behaviors. Some years earlier, a servant girl had abused him sexually at bedtime. She had lain on top of him in the bed, and this memory was forgotten until a recent similar experience revived it. The defensive meaning of the ceremony became clear:

The chairs were placed in front of the bed and the bed pushed against the wall in order that nobody else should be able to get at the bed; the pillows were arranged in a particular way so that they should be differently arranged from how they were on that evening; the movements with his legs were to kick away the person who was lying on him; sleeping on his side was because in the scene [with the servant girl] he had been lying on his back; his circumstantial confession to his mother was because, in obedience to a prohibition by his seductress, he had been silent to his mother about this and other sexual experiences; and, finally, the reason for his keeping his bedroom floor clean was that neglect to do so had been the chief reproach that he had so far had to hear from his mother. (Freud, 1896b, pp. 172n.–173n.)

Each of these compulsive behaviors served a double purpose. First, they served as a means of self-initiated, self-inflicted punishment for having engaged in behavior that was pleasurable but "bad." Second, performance of the ritual allowed the boy no time to think about the guilt-provoking memory or about possible future seductions. Thus preventive distraction, as well as self-imposed penance, formed the basis of his symptoms.

Paradoxically, the obsessive ideas and the compulsive acts were also the means to gratify the pleasurable (yet anxiety-triggering) impulse involved in the taboo sexual activity. Each night, through the symptomatic ritual, the original seduction was recalled or relived. The symptoms were, therefore, *compromise formations*: they balanced the anxiety and the guilt of the conscious personality against the pleasurable gratifications sought by the unconscious.

Only by assuming the defensively altered form of the somewhat magical ritual acts could the repressed memory of the seduction take a place in consciousness. In effect, the symptoms symbolically substituted for the sexual gratification that the boy would not allow himself in reality (Freud, 1916, p. 368). The patient reproached himself for "bad wishes" and guilt-provoking experiences, expiating the guilt by ritual, while his symptoms achieved partial gratification of the very same wish that he sought to repudiate. In performing his defensive ritual against seduction, the young boy reenacted, not any the less completely, the very experience he struggled to escape.

SEXUAL MOTIVES AS THE BASIS OF CONFLICT: ORIGINS OF THE HYPOTHESIS

The common denominator that Freud had discovered among his patients was the presence of erotic impulses from childhood that were frustrated or guilt-laden. Thus, to take but two examples, Fräulein Elisabeth suffered the pain of unacceptable desire for her brother-in-law because this desire clashed with her sense of moral responsibility; the 11-year-old boy's sleep ritual involved the stress produced by a pleasurable, yet anxiety-laden, seduction. Many of Freud's other patients revealed sexual themes in their free associations and, in each such case, Freud was able to trace the themes back to incidents and experiences of childhood. Additionally, Freud recalled some years later in writing the *History of the Psycho-Analytic Movement* (1914b) that offhand comments of Breuer, Charcot, and a gynecologist named Chrobak about the sexual nature of neurotic disorders in women had shown that the idea had fleetingly passed through the minds of other workers in the field. Chrobak and Breuer later denied any knowledge of such comments, and Freud concluded that Charcot, too, would have joined them in denial had he had the opportunity (Jones, 1953, p. 248). Could a 19th-century Viennese physician foist on the Victorian world the hypothesis that *erotic* conflict was the basis of neurotic disorder? Freud did not hesitate.

Seduction Hypothesis

Intrigued by the direction his clinical investigations were taking, Freud asked the logical question: Why should *sexual* experiences and *sexual* motives be the common denominator in the cases he had observed? The answer, he suspected, could be found only by examining the neurotic's fundamental defensive response: namely, repression.

Only emotional content intense enough to overwhelm the ego was ever subject to repression in the patients he had treated. One would, therefore, logically expect— if sexual motives were the common denominator—that any emotion connected with the sexual experience of patients would have been correspondingly intense. But there is a problem with this supposition. Most of Freud's patients were able through analysis to trace the critical sexual experiences to their childhood years when, presumably, their physical capacity for sexual stimulation had been undeveloped or nonexistent. Hence, the seduction by an adult in childhood could not have led to full understanding or to full sexual arousal with its normal accompaniment of emotional excitation. *How, then, could these relatively mild childhood feelings ever have been intense enough to trigger repression?*

The time sequence was wrong. Logically, the sequence should have been, first, some sexual experience like a forceful seduction by an adult; then, repression of the experience because of the intensity of the conflict between feelings of pleasurable arousal and feelings of guilt or anxiety; and, finally, the outbreak of neurotic symptoms in behalf of the repressed impulses. But if the traumatic seduction had taken place in childhood, as many of his patients reported, this sequence was impossible. There could not have been sufficient sexual arousal or pleasure in a child to establish an intense enough conflict to trigger repression *at that time*.

In order for repression to have occurred, a new, inverted sequence had to be postulated, placing repression at the end of the process: Sexual experience (seduction) occurs first; then amnesia for it until some stimulus or situation triggers by its similarity recall of the incident *at maturity*; then, finally, repression and symptom formation *after maturity has been reached*. In other words, neurosis was not a *product* of childhood, but a *process* begun in those early years and brought to fruition in maturity (Freud, 1896b, 1896c, and 1898, pp. 279–285).

Logic of the Seduction Hypothesis

Freud examined the new hypothesis carefully. Ordinarily, he knew, when thoughts are entertained that have sexual content, the *adult* thinker responds with simultaneous arousal of the sexual organs. This primary bodily arousal is always more intense than any later, secondary *memory* of the experience. But if his reasoning up to this point was correct, a sexual seduction experienced *before* physical maturity (that is, before eight to ten years) would be experienced only as a somewhat faded recollection years later in maturity. It becomes necessary, therefore, to assume that the memory is intensified from some other source of energy (cf. Freud, 1954, Letter No. 52, p. 174).

Suppose that source of energy was the bodily arousal associated with sexual excitation. Further suppose that physical sexual arousal could be rechanneled into psychological emotional arousal. In effect, the result would be a conversion of *physical*, biological energy into *mental*, psychological energy. If such a process was possible, then the *memory* of the earlier experience (that is, the seduction) would initiate the *deferred* bodily arousal some years after the experience, when the individual had developed the biological capacity for appropriate somatic response. In this delayed version it is the *memory* of the experience that leads to the kind of intense physical arousal that is stronger than the original passive-seduction experience itself.

Proportionate *adult* anxiety and guilt would accompany and augment the memory image—intensifying it—to bring about the conflicting psychological state of affairs that was not possible during the actual experience in childhood (cf. Freud, 1896b, pp. 172–175 and pp. 166n.–167n; see also 1916, Lecture XXIII, pp. 361–371). Thus, Freud reasoned, a memory could be more potent than the actual experience it represented *if* there was a biological process that lagged behind the psychological development of children. At maturity there would be sufficient incremental emotional arousal, freshly fueled by the slower developing biological events, for repression to operate.

Freud had managed to answer a key question as to why *sexual* content, above all else, was the basis of the neurotic disorders he had seen. Only the *sexual* experiences of individuals are subject to the delay in physical development that human biology imposes. So, of all the experiences and motives of childhood, only the *sexual* among them would succumb to repression because only the *sexual* experiences become intensified by the developments of puberty. *Neurotics, indeed, suffer from reminiscences.*

Abandonment of the Seduction Theory

The seduction hypothesis was an elegant one, for it accounted in one stroke for two observations: the reports of childhood seductions by Freud's patients, and the fact that his patients had been mentally healthy throughout childhood, succumbing to neurotic disorder only in adulthood. However, two new questions posed themselves: *What accounts for the period of childhood amnesia during which the seduction experience remains dormant?* and *What stimulates the recollection of these early seductions in adulthood?* In supplying answers to these questions Freud discovered that he had made a near-fatal error.

Reviewing the evidence on which the seduction hypothesis had been based, Freud discovered that he had been a victim of his own naiveté. In a letter written to his friend Wilhelm Fliess on September 21, 1897, Freud revealed how some critical rethinking had caused the collapse of his seduction theory (1954, pp. 215–217). He frankly enumerated the reasons: (1) the high improbability of universal sexual abuse of children by their fathers, though for a time it had seemed credible; (2) the failure of his patients' revelations of such seductions to accomplish any lasting therapeutic effect; (3) his hard-won insight that the unconscious cannot distinguish between reality and fantasy, an insight that had forced the conclusion that the reports of childhood seduction were not of real events but of *imagined* happenings; and (4) the discovery that, even in the severe psychoses, when the unconscious contents flood consciousness, no infantile sexual seductions are revealed.

Freud could only comment, years later:

> . . . If the reader feels inclined to shake his head at my credulity, I cannot altogether blame him. . . . When, however, I was at last obliged to recognize that these scenes were only phantasies which my patients had made up or which I myself forced on them, I was for a time completely at a loss. (1925a, p. 34)

Toward a Revised Theory: Childhood Sexuality

Freud did not long remain in this bewildered state. He began to revise his thinking in the light of the new evidence that seduction tales were fantasies, products of the imagination.

> If hysterical subjects trace back their symptoms to traumas that are fictitious, then the new fact which emerges is precisely *that they create such scenes in phantasy*, and this psychical reality requires to be taken into account alongside practical reality. This reflection was soon followed by the discovery that these phantasies were intended to cover up the autoerotic activity of the first years of childhood, to embellish it and raise it to a higher plane. And now, from behind the phantasies, the whole range of a child's sexual life came to light. (1914b, pp. 17-18; italics added)

Freud was gradually coming to the view that children are not *passive* participants in erotic activities imposed on them, as the seduction hypothesis had it, but they are, instead, *active initiators* of behaviors designed to bring sensual pleasure. Moreover, Freud had begun to understand the importance of fantasy in the mental economy of his patients. Imaginary events, he realized, occupied the same status as real events *in the unconscious*. It was only a short jump from this realization to the discovery that neurotics are not unique in this characteristic.

FREUD'S HONESTY QUESTIONED: AN ALTERNATIVE EXPLANATION

Freud's own account of the reasons for abandoning the seduction hypothesis have been challenged by Jeffrey Masson (1984a, 1984b). Masson charged that Freud needed for personal rather than clinical or theoretical reasons to abandon the seduction hypothesis to protect his professional standing and the professional image of his friend Wilhelm Fliess.

Masson (1984b) marshals a great wealth of detailed historical evidence gleaned from his access to an unedited version of the letters between Freud and Fliess. The bulk of this evidence cannot be reviewed here, but we can briefly summarize the main features of Masson's argument.

Freud's experiences in Paris with Charcot exposed him to an eminent pathologist, Paul Brouardel, who taught fellow physicians about the brutal effects of child

FIGURE 2.2   Sigmund Freud (left) and his colleague-friend, Wilhelm Fliess.

rape. Freud also had read several clinical texts on sexual abuse of children. Masson concludes that Freud was keenly aware of the reality of sexual seduction and assault, a fact that he chose to "forget" when he abandoned the seduction hypothesis.

One of Freud's earliest patients was Emma Eckstein, a 27-year-old woman who suffered a variety of hysteric symptoms and menstrual complaints. For reasons yet unknown, Freud referred Emma Eckstein to his friend Fliess for nasal surgery in an effort to control her menstrual difficulties. Fliess had developed a theory relating nasal difficulties with sexual functioning, and the surgery apparently made sense to both Freud and Fliess.

Fliess botched the surgery by leaving a piece of surgical gauze in Emma's nasal cavity, and during the weeks that followed, Emma hemorrhaged profusely to a point of near death. Freud eventually consulted another nasal surgeon and Emma's life was saved, but the woman remained badly disfigured for the remainder of her life. In fact, when this second surgeon began removing the gauze, Freud became sickened and dizzy and had to retreat to the next room. Freud reported that another member of the household gave him a small glass of brandy, which restored his composure. He wrote to Fliess that when he returned still somewhat shaky to the room where Emma and the surgeon were working, "She greeted me with the condescending remark, 'So this is the strong sex' " (Freud, 1985, p. 117).

It is unclear whether it was the hemorrhage he observed that sickened him or whether his feelings of guilt and responsibility overcame him. Freud's opinion was expressed to Fliess in a letter:

> I do not believe it was the blood that overwhelmed me—at that moment strong emotions were welling up in me. So we had done her an injustice; she was not at all abnormal, rather, a piece of iodoform gauze had gotten torn off as you were removing it and stayed in for 14 days, preventing healing; at the end it tore off and provoked the bleeding. That this mishap should have happened to you, how you will react to it when you hear about it; what others could make of it; how wrong I was to urge you to operate in a foreign city where you could not follow through on the case; how my intention to do my best for this poor girl was insidiously thwarted and resulted in endangering her life—all this came over me simultaneously. (Freud, 1985, p. 117)

It is fairly clear from the letter that Freud was overwhelmed by his feelings of uncertainty and, perhaps, guilt. He probably had serious doubts about Fliess's surgical treatment of someone he now realized was "not at all abnormal." Yet he avoids direct accusations or criticisms of Fliess.

Masson concludes that Freud needed to avoid blaming Fliess both for the strangeness of his treatment of Emma Eckstein's problems and for his lack of surgical skill. One way to defend Fliess and himself was to blame the victim. That is to say, Freud assumed initially that her continued nasal bleeding was another of her hysterical symptoms, not the result of Fliess's interventions. In this way, Freud abandoned the reality of sexual seduction as the cause of hysterical symptoms in favor of the patient's own fantasies and wishes. The stage was set to drop the seduction hypothesis in favor of seduction fantasies created by the patients themselves.

Masson adduces evidence from the Fliess-Freud correspondence that Wilhelm Fliess's son, Robert, later an eminent analyst, was abused-seduced by his father. The evidence for this conclusion is very speculative, as Masson readily admits, but sufficiently compelling for Masson to point to the irony of Freud's lengthy scientific discussion of the seduction theory concepts with the one man "least prepared to hear them." Masson writes, "Freud was like a dogged detective on the track of a great crime, communicating his hunches and approximations and at last his final discovery to his best friend, who may have been in fact the criminal" (1984b, p. 142).

Thus Masson argues that Freud abandoned the seduction hypothesis for these personally protective reasons:

1. his own knowledge of the reality and brutality of childhood rape was accompanied by his realization that the professional community would not look kindly on a psychiatrist who employed such data as the basis for his theories;

2. his complicity in the Emma Eckstein case, and the consequent guilt and shame;
3. probable indirect pressure from Fliess to abandon the theory because Fliess himself was a child abuser/seducer.

Given all these reasons, Freud had to abandon the seduction hypothesis in favor of a theory that emphasized fantasy rather than brutal reality. Masson stated the main consequence for psychoanalysis:

> . . . by shifting the emphasis from an actual world of sadness, misery, and cruelty to an internal stage on which actors performed invented dramas for an invisible audience of their own creation, Freud began a trend away from the real world that, it seems to me, is at the root of the present-day sterility of psychoanalysis. (1984b, p. 144)

Some troubling points cast doubt on his conclusions. For one thing, the Emma Eckstein case history (Freud, 1896c) shows no evidence of a real seduction or brutality in Emma's history, and the same lack of brutal seductions is to be found in most of Freud's published cases (1896c). It is interesting, too, in this context that Emma Eckstein and Freud apparently remained on very good terms for many years. She went on to become a psychoanalyst and apparently kept Freud informed of her work with her patients (Freud, 1985, p. 286; see also Gay, 1988, p. 87n.).

Freud's and his family's relationship with Emma Eckstein was a complex one. There is evidence that Emma had a "romantic" attachment to her therapist, which Freud interpreted as an erotic transference. There is also evidence that Emma played a substantial role in Freud's fantasy life and in his self-analysis, a story we cannot pursue here (see Appignanesi & Forrester, 1992, pp. 119 ff. for a fuller account). Some time after she had begun treating her own patients, Emma reapplied to Freud for treatment, but he declined. Emma nevertheless seems to have retained an affection for her therapist and for psychoanalysis through the subsequent years. What is clear from this case and several of the other early cases is that Freud and his early biographers, as well as his followers, daughter, and students, deliberately painted a rosier picture of the progress of psychoanalysis than was warranted by the facts. To accomplish this "psychoanalysis seen through rose-colored glasses," many of these people selectively reported the facts of some cases and sometimes blatantly omitted pertinent, not to say embarrassing, details. And no one was rosier in this undertaking than Sigmund Freud.

It would appear that Freud was being honest when he reported that one of the reasons he abandoned the seduction theory was that he could not find a *traumatic* history in every patient who was hysterical (Freud, 1896b, 1896c).

Even some of the evidence that Masson cites in favor of his own argument argues precisely the opposite viewpoint. For example, Masson (1984b, pp. 93–94) reproduces a previously unpublished letter from Freud to Fliess in which Freud recounts a case history of a young woman who learns that her brother kissed and licked his sister's feet at bedtime. Clearly this memory is sexual, but it is hardly a memory of a traumatically abusive or assaultive event (cf. Storr, 1984, p. 35).

In the end, for better or worse, Freud's psychoanalysis was constructed along certain lines, and it is unlikely that contemporary analysts will alter the main forms of the theory if that alteration requires abandonment of the importance of personal meaning, wishes, and fantasies. Reality counts, but if Freud had not focused on fantasy in 1895, latter-day analysts would certainly have had to invent the idea. Whether Freud assumed this focus to protect himself and Fliess is an issue that is not yet resolved by Masson's intriguing argument. The positive effect of Masson's thesis may be to alert the psychoanalytic community to the importance of the interaction between fantasy and reality.

PERSONAL SOURCES OF THE HYPOTHESIS: FREUD'S SELF-ANALYSIS

In the months before he announced to Fliess his not-quite-fatal error of the seduction hypothesis, Freud had begun to subject his own dreams and thoughts to careful scrutiny through the method of free association (Jones, 1953, pp. 319–323; Kris, 1954, p. 30). Beginning in the summer of 1897, Freud embarked on a process of self-exploration that was to occupy him for the rest of his life. Although we cannot trace the entire progress of his self-analysis here, several crucial discoveries deserve our consideration both for what they reveal about Freud and for the light they throw on the origins of some of his ideas. For, much to his own amazement, Freud uncovered a quasi-erotic love for his mother and an equally disturbing hostility toward his father, discoveries that were later to be incorporated into psychoanalytic theory as central tenets (Freud, 1900, pp. 318, 583).

The triggering incident for Freud's application of psychoanalytic method to himself seems to have been the emotional aftermath of his father's death in October 1896. Though Freud did not at this time begin his "official" self-analysis, the emotional upheaval of the loss and some resultant family discord over proper funeral rites occasioned a dream about his father that provoked in him some residue of unexpected guilt. The dream led Freud to suspect that he was not as sorry for the loss of his father as he should have been. Yet, as he wrote to Fliess, he experienced a feeling of "being torn up by the roots," and he continued to be troubled in this way for some months (1954, Letter No. 50, p. 170). Some years later, in *The Interpretation of Dreams* (1900, p. xxvi), Freud acknowledged that his father's death was "the most poignant loss of a man's life" and had played a significant part in both his self-analysis and in the writing of that book. We take up the matters of Freud's ambivalent relationship to his father and the effect of that relationship on his theory in the next chapter.

Another motive for Freud's undertaking the task of self-analysis was his discovery in himself of several mild neurotic symptoms (Schur, 1972, esp. Chapter 4). In addition to a very uncharacteristic overconcern with the prospect of an early death prompted by some cardiac symptoms, Freud also evidenced a phobia regarding travel. His concern for his health and the fear that he was developing severe heart disease may have had some element of neurotic anxiety at its core, though the physical symptoms were certainly genuine (Jones, 1953; Schur, 1972). Indeed, the only time in his life when he would abstain from his cherished cigars occurred during this period of somewhat superstitious worry over the possibility of an early, nicotine-aggravated death. To understand how out of character for Freud such concerns were, consider that, years later, stricken with cancer of the mouth and facing the certainty of an unpleasant death, he clung to his cigars all the more fervently.

A somewhat different neurotic symptom involved Freud's behavior when setting out on the journeys he professed to love so much. Throughout his life, he would frequently turn up at a railway station hours before his train was scheduled to depart, apparently in the compulsive attempt not to miss his train. But he would just as often enter the wrong rail station or board the wrong train. Freud recognized that these were symptomatic acts suggestive of anxiety and an unconscious unwillingness to embark on a journey.

Ever willing to face and accept the truth, Freud had a passion to be master of his fate, and it must have played no small role in his decision to turn on himself the same method of exploration he was so carefully shaping with his patients.

Self-Recognition of Oedipal Feelings: Freud's Two Mothers

Considering the concepts that Freud was to develop, it is no small irony that the man who discovered the Oedipus complex experienced the first years of life with strong attachments to two mothers: his natural mother, Amalie Freud, and a surrogate mother, his very religious and very devious Catholic nanny. To compound the irony, some biographers have speculated that later in childhood, the young Freud became aware that his father had married twice before his present union with Freud's mother. If these previous marriages were something of a family secret, could it have been that the future investigator of family myths was himself exposed to a protective family myth? Was his later self-discovered resentment toward his father somehow connected with these childish half-understandings? The facts suggest an affirmative answer to both questions.

Jakob Freud, Sigmund's father, was married three times. With his first wife, Sally Kanner, Jakob had two sons, Emanuel, born 1832, and Philipp, born 1836 (Schur, 1972, p. 20). After Sally Kanner's death, the date of which is not precisely known, Jakob married a woman named Rebekka, about whom almost nothing is known. In fact, until the actuarial research of J. Sajner (1968, cited by Schur, 1972), it was not known by any of Freud's biographers that Rebekka even existed. This blotting out of her existence, as Schur explains, probably indicates a certain amount of secrecy about this second marriage. Were it not for Sajner's uncovering a register of Jewish inhabitants for the year 1852 in the town where Sigmund was born, there would be no indication whatsoever in Freud's writings, in Jones's official biography, or in the record of Freud's self-analysis in the Fliess correspondence that Rebekka Freud ever lived. Schur comments on this startling fact:

> Obvious questions now arise: who *must* have known about the marriage and who *probably* knew about it? In addition to Jakob Freud, his two sons Philipp and Emanuel as well as Emanuel's wife must have known. It is possible, but unlikely that Freud's mother, Jakob's third wife, was completely unaware of the second marriage. There would have been no reason for her not to have been told about this previous marriage, unless there were some special reason for secrecy. We know, however, that it is very difficult to keep such information secret in a family in a small community. Even if such a secret is successfully kept, an "air" of secrecy is nearly always present. (1972, p. 21)

Schur suggests that Freud himself was not consciously aware of the "secret" second marriage of his father; but unconsciously the air of secrecy and the resulting family legend that would have grown from the necessary evasions probably created in Freud a special alertness for "disappearing persons" and for losses by death from his family circle. To the theme of disappearing persons we will shortly have to add several illustrations; but for the moment it is necessary merely to point out that Freud's dim awareness of the "secret" may have been one of the elements in his self-discovered hostility toward his father.

Marie Balmary (1979) has further enriched Schur's analysis with an even more detailed examination of Freud's personal history and writings. She has suggested that Rebekka Freud, the missing wife, may in fact have committed suicide, an event that would account for the family mystery surrounding this woman. Through a complicated series of turns and detours, Balmary has attempted to show that Freud's father Jakob married his mother Amalie after he had made her pregnant with the future founder of psychoanalysis. Thus it would appear that the family mystery surrounding Rebekka and Jakob Freud's own conduct was the result of accumulated shame, confusion, and deliberate concealment. The net effect, of course, was that Freud himself was later compelled to construct his theory of the Oedipus complex, as we shall see, in such a way that the *father's* role in the son's conflicts is minimized. In effect, Freud was unconsciously motivated to protect his own father from blame. See Balmary (1979) for the detailed account of this piece of historical detective work.[5]

More important in the present context was Freud's discovery during his self-analysis of several components of what he would later call the Oedipus complex within himself. As his self-analysis progressed, he was able to reconstruct and, with his mother's help, corroborate several memories from childhood. These reconstructions allowed him to piece together a fairly accurate account of his own emotional life in childhood. If his father had two wives before his present one, then Freud may be said to have surpassed his father's achievement with the discovery that he himself had two "fathers" and two "mothers."

One such memory fragment concerned the recollection of the elderly woman who had been the infant Freud's nanny along with the memory of a seemingly unconnected but especially important train ride with his mother:

> . . . the "prime originator" [of my troubles] was a woman, ugly, elderly, but clever, who told me a great deal about God Almighty and Hell and who gave me a high opinion of my own capacities; and that later (between the ages of two and two-and-a-half) my libido [sexual interest] was stirred up towards *matrem*, namely on the occasion of a journey with her from Leipzig to Vienna, during which we must have spent the night

---

[5] Silverstein (1984) has shown that Balmary gets some of her facts wrong and treats other historical data to sometimes inappropriate interpretation based not on evidence but on speculation. Silverstein argues cogently that Balmary's "analysis" of Freud's motives may reveal more about her own than about Freud's. Jakob Freud was probably less of a Don Juan than Balmary assumes, and Sigmund Freud may not have been as motivated to protect his father as she speculated. As with so much in the history of psychoanalysis, we must be cautious and conservative in drawing conclusions about the intentions of these historical figures. Details continue to emerge in what has become a virtual psychoanalytic historical industry, and the full narrative of this history will continue to grow more complex.

together and I must have had an opportunity of seeing her *nudam*. . . . (1897, Letter No. 70, p. 262)

This passage from Freud's correspondence with Fliess is remarkable for a number of reasons. First, it is a clear indication of the importance of an idea that Freud had been toying with for some time: namely, that the child experiences sexual impulses toward his mother. By "sexual" Freud meant to include all pleasurable and affectionate interactions, commonly called *love*, between mother and child (see, for example, Freud, 1925a, p. 38). (We pick up this idea again at a later point in the chapter.) Further on in this same letter, Freud hinted that his anxiety over traveling could be dated to the train ride with his mother and the residue of guilt that remained from his feelings toward her.

The second important aspect of this memory fragment is Freud's admission of such feelings in himself. Notice, however, that both the word for "mother" (*matrem*)

and the word for "naked" (*nudam*) are in Latin, as though writing them in his native German would have made them all the more unpalatable. Clearly, Freud experienced firsthand the kind of emotional resistance that his patients often exhibited.

Third, Freud evidenced another characteristic typical of a patient undergoing psychoanalysis, an erring sense of time. Freud could not have been only two or two-and-a-half years old, as he states. Ernest Jones, after careful research, places the date of the train ride somewhat later, at around the age of four (1953, p. 13). Max Schur, Freud's more recent biographer, concurs with Jones's estimate (1972, p. 120). Indeed, Schur suggests that it is probable that the infant Freud had many times observed some intimate scenes between his mother and father in the crowded conditions of their home.

Fourth, the "prime originator" mentioned in the letter was the nursemaid who had cared for Freud as an infant and for several years of his childhood. This enigmatic old woman had popped in and out of Freud's memories for years, haunting him like a ghost with a message to tell but no voice with which to announce it. During his self-analysis the memory finally yielded its secret. To substantiate his analysis, Freud asked his mother, now in her old age, to confirm the facts of his recollection.

She confirmed that he had indeed had a nurse who was elderly but clever, and that she had been arrested for stealing his silver coins and toys. At the time of the incident, Freud's mother had relinquished his care to the nursemaid because she was in the last stages of pregnancy with Freud's younger sister, Anna. Freud's self-analysis revealed that this nanny had a profound impact on his conception of himself, and that she had taught him a good deal about her religion, including a scary account of souls in hell. Moreover, this nanny was "my instructress in sexual matters, and chided me for being clumsy and not being able to do anything. . . . " (Freud, 1954, p. 220).

Thus this "elderly but clever woman" was in charge of the young Freud, associated with sexuality in his memory, and most important, equated with his mother (Grigg, 1973; see also Gedo, 1976, pp. 298 ff.). The identification in memory of the nanny and his mother had other determinants as well. Freud's older half brother, Philipp, had become a father substitute during the time of Freud's mother's pregnancy; and it was Philipp who had gone to fetch a policeman to arrest the nanny for her thefts. Freud's mother, helping her son to recollect these events, told Freud that Philipp's action had resulted in the nanny's *imprisonment* for 10 months. Thus, in the young Freud's mind, Philipp was responsible for the disappearance of one of his "mothers." Or, to put it another way, one of Freud's "fathers" enforced a separation between young Sigmund and one of his "mothers." With these facts in hand, Freud could focus his self-analysis on even more probing questions.

The Theme of Disappearing Persons

How had the equation between his nanny and his mother come about? Why was the nanny's disappearance so acutely felt? Freud's self-analysis provided the answers:

> I said to myself if the old woman disappeared so suddenly [on account of her imprisonment], it must be possible to point to the impression this made on me. Where is that impression, then? A scene then occurred to me which for the last 29 years has occasionally emerged in my conscious memory without my understanding

it. My mother was nowhere to be found: I was screaming my head off. My brother, Philipp, 20 years older than me, was holding open a cupboard for me, and when I found that my mother was not inside it either, I began crying still more, till, *looking slim and beautiful*, she came in by the door. What can this mean? Why was my brother opening the cupboard, though he knew that my mother was not in it, so that this could not pacify me? And then suddenly I understood. *I had asked him to do it. When I missed my mother, I had been afraid she had vanished from me just as the old woman had a short time before* [i.e., the maid's imprisonment]. Now I must have heard that the old woman had been locked up and consequently *I must have thought that my mother had been too*—or rather had been "boxed up"; for my brother Philipp, who is 63 now, is fond to this very day of talking in this punning fashion. *The fact that it was to him in particular that I turned proves that I knew quite well of his share in the nurse's disappearance.* (1897, Letter No. 7, pp. 264–265; italics added)

Freud's memory had condensed the account of the maid's disappearance with the memory of his mother's pregnancy. Analysis of the reconstructed memory revealed a peculiar pattern of motivation. There was the implied accusation against Philipp to the effect that he had made Freud's mother vanish. Philipp was represented as a rival who controlled the whereabouts of Freud's mother—a rival, that is, who possessed adult authority. From other details of Freud's life it was clear that Philipp also represented a specific father substitute. Note, too, that Freud's mother appeared in the memory as "slim and beautiful," emphasizing that her pregnancy was terminated.

Three elements, then, required interpretation: concern over his mother's pregnancy; the demand that his half brother open the *cupboard*; and an implied connection between Philipp's causing the maid's disappearance and the disappearance of his own mother. Freud's self-analysis allowed him to clarify the relations among these three elements, as he reported some years later in *The Psychopathology of Everyday Life*:

Anyone who is interested in the mental life of these years of childhood will find it easy to guess the deeper determinant of the demand made on the big brother [i.e., the request to open the cupboard]. The child of not yet three [i.e., Freud himself] had understood that the little sister [Anna] who had recently arrived had grown inside his mother. He was very far from approving of this addition to the family, and was full of mistrust and anxiety that his mother's inside might conceal still more children. *The wardrobe or cupboard was a symbol for him of his mother's inside.* So he insisted on looking into this cupboard and turned for this to his *big brother, who* [as is clear from other material] *had taken his father's place as the child's rival.* Besides the well founded suspicion that this brother had had the lost nurse "boxed up," there was a further suspicion against him—namely that *he had in some way introduced the recently born baby into his mother's inside.* (1901, p. 51n.; italics added)

The young Freud's disappointment when the cupboard was opened and his mother was not to be found inside was assuaged only by his relief when she reappeared *slim and beautiful*, that is, without any other unwanted children. Key emotions contained in these disturbing memories involved the desperate fear of losing his mother to an adult rival, the vague understanding that men somehow put babies inside women, and the defensive telescoping of the maid's having been "boxed up" at the hands of the same adult rival with the memory of his mother's disappearance. Freud had thus discovered within himself the essential elements of the emotional constellation to be known later as the Oedipus complex.

Freud was singularly and passionately attached to his mother. He idealized her, and she, in turn, idolized him (Bernstein, 1976; Fromm, 1959; Gedo, 1976; Grigg, 1973; Jones, 1953; Stolorow & Atwood, 1978). A good portion of his self-analysis had shown Freud that as a child he wished to share his mother with no one, and that he had viewed with enormous hostility every potential rival for her attentions. His enforced separation from his real mother by virtue of her pregnancy, and his experience of a similarly imposed separation from his surrogate mother by a surrogate father figure helped Freud to comprehend the strength of a child's attachment to his mother and the child's desire for her exclusive attentions (Stolorow & Atwood, 1979). Freud was even able to face the enormity of his own aggression against rivals for his mother's love in his reconstruction of his death wishes against one such competitor, his younger brother Julius.

Julius did in fact die when Sigmund was only 19 months old, and to the young, wishful Freud this death must have seemed like the magical fulfillment of desire. As he was to theorize years later in works such as *Totem and Taboo* (1913b), the neurotic personality behaves as though thoughts were omnipotent. He had wished for the death of Julius, and it must have seemed the thought itself was sufficient to bring reality into line with desire. During his self-analysis, Freud reported this discovery to Fliess:

> . . . I welcomed my one-year-younger brother (who died within a few months) with
> ill wishes and real infantile jealousy, and that his death left the germ of guilt in me.
> (Freud, 1954, p. 219)

It is no wonder that the theme of disappearing persons held such significance for Freud. In his lifetime he had been exposed to the possibility of a "disappearing" previous wife of his father, to a disappearing mother substitute, to a disappearing mother, and to a disappearing younger rival for his mother's attentions. Thus, in short succession, through what must have been a painful self-exploration, Freud discovered in his own mental economy hostile wishes toward his father and toward his siblings; erotic wishes toward his mother; and a tangled series of anxieties and guilt that had forced these experiences out of consciousness.

Perhaps it should again be mentioned that Freud never ceased his self-analysis, reserving the last half hour of his day throughout his life for such self-exploration (Jones, 1953, p. 327). Yet it was from the earliest self-analytic attempts that Freud derived his most fertile ideas, those which he sought to corroborate further with his patients. The implication of these early disturbing self-insights was clear: *Children are capable of diffuse sexual feelings, and the first objects of their erotic endeavors and resulting jealous aggression are their parents, the people with whom they have had the most intimate contact.*

It becomes necessary at this point to break off our essentially chronological treatment of psychoanalytic theory to gather together the several threads of Freud's continually evolving views of sexual development.

PSYCHOSEXUAL DEVELOPMENT: OEDIPUS AND ELECTRA

Human infants are born essentially helpless and vulnerable to all manner of painful and potentially lethal stimulation. It is only through the efforts of their caretakers that infants survive the first several years of life.

Erotogenic Bodily Zones

Consider the situation of the well-cared-for infant. When it experiences hunger, its cries bring its mother with nourishment in the form of breast or bottle. The sucking response with which it meets the nipple, though reflex at first, not only provides the needed nourishment to terminate the hunger pains, but soon itself becomes a pleasurable source of stimulation. Gentle stimulation of the lips and mouth, the infant quickly learns, is quite satisfying and sensually pleasing. Thus, even a thumb may become an object of sensual pleasure. In a sense, then, the infant is finding satisfaction through the stimulation of its own body; it is, in Freud's terms, behaving *auto*erotically (1905, pp. 181–182). The pleasurable activity of the mouth may be thought of as the prototype for various other potentially pleasurable zones of the body that yield satisfaction to rhythmic stimulation. Primary of such *erotogenic zones*, as they are called, are those areas of the body characterized by the presence of a mucous membrane, for example, the anus. But the infant's body pleasures are not restricted to mucous membrane areas. With time, these mucous membrane prototypes yield their dominance so that almost any part of the body may become an erotogenic zone. Thus the skin when tickled or stroked produces great delight; the anus during elimination provides a sense of satisfaction at the pleasure of discharging tension, and so on.

The important point is that children search their own bodies, seeking the sensations of pleasure that it will offer to the knowing touch. Consequently, Freud concluded, the infant's chief aim is the attainment of bodily or "organ pleasure" based on its experiences with the world, its body, and its caretakers. Food and the breast provided the first such experience and the mother was the medium through which that learning took place. Because the mother is directly connected with almost every other important—pleasurable and unpleasurable—activity of the infant's life, it follows that it will be the mother who becomes the object of the child's constantly developing modes of seeking new pleasures.

The Widened Meaning of "Sexual"

The biological force underlying the child's pleasure-seeking activity is the sexual drive or *libido* (cf. Freud, 1905, p. 135; and 1916, p. 313). (*Libido* is a concept we give much more detailed consideration in the context of Freud's theory of instincts in Chapter 3.) The term "sexual" cannot be confined to the adult sense in which it is customarily used to indicate *genital*, procreative activity. Genital primacy, one component of the generalized sexual instinct, or libido, is a relatively late, postpubertal development. Genital sexuality has origins far more diffuse and deeply rooted in infantile pleasure-seeking activity than is ordinarily realized. Adult, genital sexuality is only the final step in a long apprenticeship to pleasure.

The Oedipus Complex

The Oedipus complex occurs as a kind of emotionally climactic midpoint in the developmental sequence of the male child's ever-increasing interest in pleasurable sexual activity. In the first stages of psychosexual development, the child's dominant erotogenic zones are the oral and the anal areas. Eventually, however, through exploration of his own body, he discovers the pleasure to be derived from manipulation of a new zone, the genital area. It is at this point, when the mother first discovers the child's errant hand seeking out that "taboo" part of his body, that she is likely to take measures to prevent such "perversity." Her admonitions may take the form of direct or veiled threats to remove the tempting organ, or, more typically, she may delegate the responsibility to father (Freud, 1940, p. 189). Parental practices like these may have been widespread in the Victorian age, but it is doubtful that a contemporary mother or father would resort to such extreme threats. Freud nevertheless thought that children may invent such threats for themselves from even the most remote references to punishment.

If the threat is at first unbelievable, it easily becomes more real when it is reinforced by the sight, however accidental, of the female genitals. The young boy becomes convinced that castration is not only possible, but, in fact, has already been accomplished in some individuals. The distinction between the sexes is still obscure to the frightened and chastened boy.

In some diffuse and vaguely understood way, the pleasurable sensation produced by self-manipulation of the sexual organs is perceived by the child as connected with his relationship to his mother, displacing his earlier oral and anal interests.

> At this point in the developmental sequence, the child senses that his mother's attention and her warmly soothing ministrations are not exclusively his. Besides troublesome siblings, mother must be shared with father, and the child soon comes to resent and to be jealous of this interloper. Freud assumed that with increasing sophistication the child develops a belief that his father knows, or at least suspects, how much he would like to be rid of him. Anxiety-stricken and guilty, the young boy feels certain that his intense anger and avid pleasure-seeking are impossible to conceal. His submissive and overtly loving behavior, he feels, is but a transparent facade to an all-knowing, all-powerful father. What more appropriate retribution could father plan to exact than the removal of that organ that provides the most pleasure at this stage? Castration by the father becomes the overwhelming fear of the child's burgeoning ego, and this imagined outrage must be dealt with by the mechanisms of defense. Most notable of these is the mechanism of repression. (Monte, 1975, p. 100)

The period during which this emotional constellation of love, jealousy, and castration fear occurs is called the *phallic stage* of psychosexual development. Emotional ambivalence is the hallmark of the phallic stage, for the young boy not only must learn to give up his chosen love object, he must also reconcile his contradictory feelings of love for and anger at his father.

The Electra Complex

"Anatomy is destiny" was Freud's paraphrase of Napoleon and his own indication of the nature of the female version of the Oedipus complex (1924b, p. 178).

In the boy, it seemed clear that the Oedipus complex was dissolved by the real or fantasied threat of castration. However, since the girl, by virtue of her anatomical development, does not fear the *loss* of a penis, she must assume that its absence indicates that she has *already* been deprived. Consequently, for her the realization that she has been castrated *initiates* the Oedipus complex. Freud alternately rejected and then seemingly accepted the term "Electra complex" for the distinctly different feminine version of this emotional constellation (cf. Freud, 1931, p. 229 for his arguments against the use of the term; and 1940, p. 194, for his apparent acceptance). Regardless of the term employed, the Oedipus complex in the female involves several highly distinctive processes that differentiate her from the male.

ATTACHMENT TO MOTHER: "PENIS ENVY."   Just as the little boy takes his mother as the first love object, the little girl likewise attaches herself intimately to her mother. Thus, like the little boy, she will also eventually have to relinquish her first love object. More significantly, however, she will also have to relinquish her first erotogenic zone of pleasurable genital stimulation, the clitoris. When she first discovers that her clitoris is not a penis: ". . . she envies boys its possession; her whole development may be said to take place under the colors of envy for the penis" (Freud, 1940, p. 193).

With the discovery that she lacks what, in her view, is an essential anatomical item, the girl at first tries to convince herself that her perception is wrong. She has seized on the clitoris as the nearest approximately to the external male genitalia, but the choice has not been successful. Maturation forces her to abandon even more fully any notion of a comparable external genital to that of boys. Ultimately, the girl is forced to the realization that she is lacking not only the penis, but all the virtues of maleness that possession of such an organ implies.

A variety of outcomes is possible: The girl may develop a *masculinity complex*, in which she devoutly protests the injustice she perceives and comes to assume all the essential male personality characteristics in defiance of her alleged inferiority; or she may abandon sexual activity altogether in her attempt to avoid any reminder of her inferiority (Freud, 1931, p. 230).

DEVALUATION OF MOTHER.   In the light of her discovery that lack of a penis is a universal attribute of girls, devaluation of the mother and abandonment of her as a love object occurs (Freud, 1931, p. 233). Hostility accompanies this breaking off of the attachment for a variety of reasons. Some of these may include the real or fantasied idea that her mother deprived her of pleasures rightfully hers, or that her mother shortchanged her in affection, or, most important, that it was mother who deprived her of the envied organ. The hostility can reach a climax when a sibling is born:

> . . . what the child grudges the unwanted intruder and rival is not only the suckling but all the other signs of maternal care. It feels that it has been dethroned, despoiled,

prejudiced in its rights; it casts a jealous hatred upon the new baby and develops a grievance against the faithless mother. . . . (Freud, 1933, p. 123)

Consequently, it is to the father that the young girl now turns in her effort to obtain that which she "knows" her mother cannot provide.

SEARCH FOR A PENIS SUBSTITUTE.   Freud's earlier work with neurotic female patients had revealed the almost universal presence of a seduction-by-an-adult fantasy. In most of his published writings of the period he alluded to seduction, but Freud barely hinted that the seduction was accomplished by the patient's own father. He had, however, made the role of the father in the seduction tales of his patients known to his friend, Wilhelm Fliess, during the course of their correspondence (1897, p. 259; also in 1954, Letter No. 69, p. 215). In later published writings, Freud indicated that indeed it was the father who had been reported to have early seduced his own child (1925a, p. 34). It was not until 1931, however, almost 35 years after his ideas on the role of childhood sexuality had replaced the original seduction hypothesis, that Freud revealed, in a paper on female sexuality, that *mothers*, too, had been indicted in the seduction fantasies (1931, p. 238; see also 1933, pp. 120–121).

Of course, both types of seduction fantasy now made sense: They were products not of a perverse whimsy of hysterical patients, but of the female Oedipal stage of development. In the pre-Oedipal phase, the object of the seduction fantasy is the mother for both boys and girls. During the Oedipal period proper, the father becomes the focus of the girl's fantasy. She wishes for a penis from her father, since she cannot obtain one from her mother, who likewise lacks this vital equipment, or she desires a symbolic penis substitute, a baby. With the wish for a "penis-baby," the girl fully enters the Oedipal phase (Freud, 1925b, p. 256).

Resolution of the Oedipus Complex

Although a fully detailed description of the resolution of the Oedipus complex for the boy requires some knowledge of Freud's final model of the mind—and for that reason detailed discussion is deferred until Chapter 3—we can provide some general indications now. In a general way, Freud summarized the dissolution of the boy's Oedipus complex:

In boys . . . the complex is not simply repressed, it is literally *smashed to pieces by the shock of threatened castration*. Its libidinal cathexes are abandoned [i.e., the attachment to mother], desexualized and in part sublimated. . . . (1925b, p. 257; italics added)

In his final model of the mind, Freud extended this line of reasoning to show that the dissolution of the Oedipus complex results in the identification of the boy with his father and in the establishment of a "superego" or special agency of morality incorporated from the parents.

For the girl, however, the Oedipus complex (or Electra complex) has no such clear-cut, final issue. Because the threat of castration, the motive for its dissolution in the boy, has effected the *beginning* of the Electra complex, the same fear cannot be

TABLE 2.1   Successive Stages of the Oedipus and Electra Complexes Contrasted

Oedipus Complex (Boy)

Motive	Consequence	Outcome
1. Attachment to mother (feeding, bodily care)	Jealousy of rivals, particularly of father	Feelings of hostility toward father
2. Castration fear (sight of female genitals; possible threats)	Fear of punishment by father for his desires to possess mother	Intensification of rivalry with father; development of need to camouflage hostility
3. Need to appease father and prevent imagined attack	Creation of facade of meekness and love for father	Repression of hostility and fear; relinquishment of mother; identification with father

"A mother is only brought unlimited satisfaction by her relation to a son;
this is altogether the most perfect, the most free from ambivalence
of all human relationships" (Freud, 1933, p. 133).

Electra Complex (Girl)

Motive	Consequence	Outcome
1. Attachment to mother (feeding, bodily care)	Jealousy of rivals	General feelings of inferiority; discovery of genital differences from males
2. Penis envy (sight of male genitals)	Jealousy of male organ and of male privileges	Devaluation of mother and of female role; adoption of male behaviors
3. Attachment to father as more powerful than mother	Seeking from father a penis substitute—a baby	Identification with female behaviors to appeal to father; slow fading of penis envy and mother devaluation

" . . . girls hold their mother responsible for their lack of a penis
and do not forgive her for their being thus put
at a disadvantage" (Freud, 1933, p. 124).

the basis for its resolution. Instead, the female complex may undergo slow fading with time, or, in some cases, may meet its end through massive repression (Freud, 1925b, p. 257). The male and female Oedipus complexes are summarized in Table 2.1.

From the differences between boys' and girls' resolutions of the Oedipus complex, Freud drew several conclusions that today would be considered antifeminist. Among these was the notion that women do not develop as strong a conscience (superego) as men: Only the *full* resolution in the face of castration threat allows the Oedipal strivings to become the basis of strong conscience, a topic we treat in Chapter 3.

PSYCHOSEXUAL STAGES: LIBIDINAL ORGANIZATION

Along with the discovery that sexuality is wider in scope than adult genital activities imply, Freud was able to discern a sequence in the development of the expression of libido. Characteristic patterns of sexual instinct organization prevail at each stage; each pattern centers on an erotogenic zone that dominates the given age.

Actually a midpoint in psychosexual development, the Oedipus complex serves as a climactic demarcation between two earlier, *pregenital organizations* of libido and two subsequent *genital organizations* of the sexual instinct.

Pregenital Organizations: Oral and Anal Periods

Libido is organized, in the first year of life, around the pleasurable activities of the mouth. Thus the attachment to the breast is a prototype of pleasurable behavior for the infant, a behavior that is, incidentally, clearly pregenital in character (Freud, 1916, p. 328). In fact, as has already been mentioned, children are capable of finding pleasurable satisfaction in a variety of ways, from a variety of sources. If the same means of obtaining pleasure prevailed in adulthood, they would be labeled "perverse." For this reason, Freud characterized the infant as "polymorphously perverse" (literally, "many-formed perversity") (1905, p. 191).

Although the phrase is often misunderstood out of the context of the entire scheme of pregenital development, Freud meant to indicate by this description only the essentially malleable and plastic nature of the sexual instinct as it emerges in infancy. Adult sexuality must be thought of, consequently, as the long-range result of the unification of several component instincts that come to focus on genital sexuality only after an extended period of "polymorphously perverse" infantile expression.

The *oral* phrase is marked, first, by the pleasure obtained from feeding, then by the development of purely sensual sucking in which the infant obtains oral pleasure by sucking nonnutritive objects like the thumb. In this way, his or her own body provides sensual pleasure and this part of the oral period can be justly characterized as autoerotic (Freud, 1905, pp. 179–181). Further development tends toward the decreasing importance of autoerotic activity and a seeking for an *external* love object. Clearly, the dominant erotogenic zone during the oral phase is nongenital, but its flow of pleasure is analogous to sexual satisfaction of adult intensity:

> No one who has seen a baby sinking back satiated from the breast and falling asleep with flushed cheeks and a blissful smile can escape the reflection that this picture persists as a prototype of the expression of sexual satisfaction in later life. (Freud, 1905, p. 182)

With the development of the first teeth and with the possibility of chewing rather than simply swallowing food, children enter a phase of development characterized by a shift from a *passive* to an *active* orientation to their environment. From now on, the central concern for the infant is the attainment of self-mastery. From around the age of 18 months through the second year of life, children are subject to increased manipulation and discipline by the mother as she attempts to toilet train them. They discover that retention and expulsion of feces sets a rhythmic pattern of tension and relief that is associated not only with pleasure but with social approval and motherly love. When they retain their feces, or expel them in inappropriate places, they incur their mothers' wrath. When, on the other hand, they accomplish fecal elimination in a suitable place, at the appropriate time—a series of demands that must seem absurd to the child—each receives approval and other loving communications. Because the child is becoming biologically capable of controlling the sphincter muscle, each is also learning an important lesson about mastering the functions of his or her own body, with the anus as the prototype of such experiences. Again, the pleasures derived from elimination and self-mastery are clearly pregenital (1905, pp. 186–187).

Transient Genital Organization: The Phallic Period

Sometime at the end of the third year or in the beginning of the fourth year of the child's life and extending into the fifth year, a phase of libidinal organization is entered in which the genital organs play a brief and not yet adult role. Through their bodily self-explorations and through the attentions of their mothers to their physical care and cleanliness, children discover that manipulation of the genital region produces pleasurable sensations. There ensues a period of infantile masturbation, and because children do not yet know shame, they express an unabashed curiosity about the genitals of others, along with a guiltless exhibitionism of their own (Freud, 1905, p. 194). It is during this period of "sexual researches" that the Oedipus complex arises (Freud, 1908a). Freud called this period the *phallic stage* of psychosexual development because for both the boy and the girl, in their own ways, it is the male organ that dominates their thinking and inquiry.

The Latency Period

The sexual forces dating from infancy become the subject to mounting counterforces of suppression that require the sexual impulses to be rechanneled into nonsexual outlets. In the sixth year of life, the child's sexual activities, along with the Oedipus complex, are temporarily dethroned from their status as major elements of the child's developmental history, but the sexual drive does not cease to exist. Instead, libidinal impulses become latent, obscured by the overlay of learned shame, disgust, and morality. Freud, however, was of the opinion that the sexual impulses would become dormant at this stage even without cultural pressures because the phenomenon of latency is biologically determined (1905, pp. 177–178). In any event, the period of latency extends from the sixth to about the eighth year of life, or roughly from the resolution of the Oedipus complex to the onset of puberty. At puberty, truly adult, primarily genital, sexuality emerges.

The Genital Period

Biologically capable of procreating because his or her hormonal and anatomical development permit the production of viable sex cells, the pubescent child's sexuality is no longer dominated by its earlier infantile aim of the attainment of pleasure to the exclusion of all else. The adult sexual aim is the discharge of sexual products. It is probably an understatement to point out that this adult sexual aim also provides individual pleasure, despite its essentially altruistic, species-preserving goal (Freud, 1905, p. 207).

The important point is that the lengthy periods of development leading up to the adult's sexual status had as their ultimate goal the establishment of genital primacy. Stimulation of the genitals and the resulting production of sexual tension is the first step toward the species-preserving goal of procreation. Three sources of sexual stimulation are now possible for the adult: memories and impulses from the pregenital periods; direct manipulation and stimulation of the genitalia and other erotogenic zones; stimulation from the chemical, hormonal discharges from within the interior of the body (Freud, 1905, p. 208). Thus the genital period is the culmination of all those trends in development of the libido, begun in infancy, and played out through the biological development of the mature organism.

We summarize the psychosexual stages with their chief developmental issues and love objects in Table 2.2.

Fixation and Regression

Of course not all outcomes of the sequence of psychosexual development are satisfactory. *Fixation of libido* may occur at any of the stages, thereby stunting and distorting the sequence of development that follows.

Essentially, fixation involves a "lagging behind" in development of one of the components of the maturing sexual drive before genital activity becomes dominant. Thus

TABLE 2.2   The Psychosexual Stages

Psychosexual Stage	Libidinal Zone	Chief Developmental Issue	Libidinal Object
1. *Oral* [birth to 1 year]	Mouth, skin, thumb	Passive incorporation of all good through mouth; autoerotic sensuality.	Mother's breast; own body
2. *Anal* [2 to 3 years]	Anus, bowels	Active seeking for tension reduction; self-mastery; passive submission.	Own body
3. *Phallic* [3 to 5 years]	Genitals, skin	Oedipus and Electra conflicts; Possession of mother; Identification with same-sexed parent; Ambivalence of love relationships.	Mother for boy; Father for girl
4. *Latency* [6 to 8 years]	None	Repression of pregenital forms of libido; Learning culturally appropriate shame and disgust for inappropriate love objects.	Repressed previous objects
5. *Genital* [adolescence onward]	Genital primacy	Reproduction; sexual intimacy.	Heterosexual partner

(Based on Freud, 1905 and 1916.)

one of the child's pregenital modes of attaining pleasure may cease its progression toward adult expression. It then becomes a dominant, rigid means of attaining satisfaction. For example, the pleasure derived from periodic tension and tension release through retention and expulsion of feces during the anal phase may be so intense that the adultlike renunciation required by the mother's toilet training program is impossible for the child to accept. Though children eventually submit to the stress of the cleanliness routine, their final socialization may be fixated on the attainment of anal pleasures that were forcibly and prematurely relinquished. As an adult, compulsively defensive traits like stinginess ("not letting go") and compulsive concern about filth make their appearance.

An Illustrative Type: "Anal-Erotic Personality"

One kind of fixated personality is the anal-erotic character. In adulthood, this person is characterized by the presence of a triad of related traits: *orderliness*, *thriftiness*, and *obstinacy*. Freud pointed out that for those adults who exhibit all three traits in unusual potency, a common pattern of experiences occurred during the anal stage of their psychosexual development.

As children, they had more than the usual difficulty with toilet training, and they exasperated their parents by refusing to empty their bowels when, as Freud put it, "they were placed on the pot." Thus these children expressed their defiance and self-mastery in an anal way, forcing their parents' use of more and more extreme measures to accomplish this necessary act of socialization.

Knowing no shame or disgust at this early age, anal-erotic children find pleasure in examining or playing with feces and pleasure in retaining them until release of tension produces the greatest satisfaction. Eventually they succumb to parental pressures for rigid orderliness and cleanliness and to a learned disgust for unclean products of the body. By adulthood, therefore, anal-erotic children have had to develop defensive measures to guard against reemergence of the taboo pleasures. The result is a personality overladen with defensive reactions against its own impulses to obtain pleasure in anal, that is, "dirty," ways. The anal-erotic adult, consequently, becomes a model of cleanliness and orderliness, but a model who bears the hallmark of exaggeration in the pursuit of these desirable goals. Excessive, even compulsive, desire for order, neatness, and antiseptic spotlessness develops to ensure that the earlier and opposite traits remain submerged.

The trait of obstinacy is clearly related to children's attempts at self-mastery as indicated by their refusal to "go on demand." Instead, they prefer to "let go" only when *they* decide to experience the pleasure of tension reduction, and anal-erotic children prolong this release until an optimal amount of satisfaction can be obtained. Even today, as Freud pointed out in very modest language, we point to the buttocks and make suggestions to caress them as a gesture of defiance to someone who makes demands on us. Who has not thwarted a rival's aggressive utterances with a defiant shout of "Kiss my ass"?

Thriftiness is also related to early developments in the anal period, as can be seen from the similar tendency of the stingy adult who "never lets go" of anything. Tightness with money may unconsciously represent earlier attempts to control fecal elimination against the demands by others to "let go." In adulthood, money may come to be associated linguistically with filth—"filthy lucre" or "dirty greenbacks"—just as that other once desirable possession, feces, was labeled filth by adults in authority. Stingy persons may even express unwillingness to part with their money by saying, "Who would want the filthy stuff," or, "Money only brings ruin."

Tongue in cheek, Freud remarked in a letter to Fliess that, because he was immersed in working out the details of the anal period of libidinal development and because he had begun to see its wide significance for adult behavior, he considered himself to be the "new Midas," for everything he now touched turned to shit (1954, Letter No. 79, p. 240; Freud, 1985, p. 288; see also Freud, 1908b for a more detailed account of anal character types).

Regression

Another difficulty in psychosexual development may occur when there is cause for a return to an earlier stage's mode of response. Such a return is called *regression of libido*, and it usually implies a primitivization of behavior in the service of the personality's defense against stress. For example, the six-year-old who, for one reason or another, finds his or her school experiences anxiety provoking and intolerable may return to the infantile mode of attaining peace and tranquility in the face of stress by narrowing attention to pleasurable oral stimulation. He or she consequently regresses to thumb sucking, much to the dismay of parents and teacher.

Fixation and *regression* bear an important relationship to each other. The more intense the fixation of libido at early stages of development, the more susceptible that individual will be to regression (Freud, 1916, pp. 339–341).

EVALUATING CLINICAL PSYCHOANALYSIS

Much like the intimate relationships of the conflicted people he described so lucidly, Freud's theory has sustained a love-hate conflict with the rest of psychology. In 1934 the psychologist Saul Rosenzweig sent Freud reprints of some experimental studies that purported to support psychoanalysis. Freud responded in a brief postcard to Rosenzweig that psychoanalysis rested on so many reliable observations that it was independent of experimental verification. "Still," Freud added, "it can do no harm." This widely quoted anecdote has been taken as emblematic of Freud's ambivalent attitudes toward both the theory he created and the science he seemed to revere (e.g., Eysenck and Wilson, 1973, p. xi; Gay, 1988, p. 523n.; Postman, 1962, p. 702).

In fact, given the scope, breadth, and grand goals of psychoanalysis, it seems that Freud's attitude about the relevance of scientific verification to his theory was less a product of arrogance than it was a result of intellectual overload. By his own account, from the very beginning of his work, Freud wanted psychoanalysis to be a general psychology. Psychoanalysis was designed to encompass all of human action and thought. Normal and "abnormal" would yield to psychoanalytic principles. The net effect of this bigger-than-life ambition was a theory that "explained" virtually every human behavior or motive of which we can conceive.

We can admire Freud's ambition, but we have to temper our admiration with a dose of antigrandiosity. One of my college professors, John M. Egan, had a memorable way of describing this tension between the intellectual attractiveness of Freud's majestic ideas and the rude requirement that such ideas be accurate. Egan used to say that it would take a *hundred psychologists a hundred years just to devise experimental tests of one page of Freud's writing*. At the time I thought that was a very quaint apology for Freudian vagueness and a telling epitaph for a moribund psychoanalysis. With the passage of years, Egan's words have taken on deeper meaning. It was customary in psychology at the time to ask questions such as, "How *good* is Freud's theory?" or "How *valid* is psychoanalysis?" or, worse still, "Was Freud *right* about . . . ?" Like Mark Twain, who ironically pointed out that the older he became, the wiser his father grew, personality psychology is older now and Freud is smarter. The questions have changed: "What is Freud's theory good *for*?" and "*Which* concepts of psychoanalysis can be tested?" and "How useful is psychoanalysis for generating *new* ideas?"

I really can't answer these questions any more precisely than I could answer the more naive questions of college days. But now I understand Egan's "epitaph" differently. If we are to evaluate psychoanalysis fairly, we still need to ask global questions about its scientific testability, but we can't close the book there. We need also to ask questions that are more discriminating, more fine-tuned to the complexity of this enormous theory, and questions that are less self-answering.

For the purposes of this book, we introduced three main qualitative dimensions by which to compare theories of personality in Chapter 1: *refutability*, *human agency*, and *idiographic-nomothetic focus*. There are many, many other dimensions on which to evaluate theories and by which to compare them. But as we multiply the number of evaluative variables, what we gain in completeness is more than lost in confusion. Our all too human inability to track large numbers of multidimensional variables at once must be taken into account. Because Freud's theory is presented in two large parts, the early clinical observations discussed in this chapter, and the later, structural theoretical formulations in Chapter 3, we need to divide our evaluation into two corresponding parts. For now, we turn our attention to the refutability, human agency, and idiographic concerns of the "early Freud."

Refutability of Psychoanalysis

To be refutable, recall from Chapter 1 a theory has to state what evidence could count against one or more of its concepts. The theory is tested by attempting to construct or observe the situation under which that contrary evidence should be obtainable. In very crude terms, if the contrary evidence cannot be obtained, the theory is strengthened. Should disconfirming evidence be had, the theory is weakened. On paper, refutability is elegant and powerful. In reality, you just can't get there from here.

For one thing, Freud's basic propositions are stated in terms that are simply not testable. Egan's epitaph applies literally to this aspect of psychoanalysis. The variables and conditions that Freud wrote about are simply, by definition, not observable. For example, consider the proposition of repression and the Oedipus complex. By definition, a repressed wish or thought is absent from awareness. And by definition, all boys have experienced an erotic attachment to mother and ambivalent feelings of love and hate toward father. But, again by psychoanalytic definition, all conscious memory of the Oedipal events is repressed. *What evidence could count against the proposition that boys have Oedipus complexes if the very behaviors and memory that constitute this 'universal' emotional conflict are unavailable for examination by the person or by an outside observer?*

Imagine telling the mythical "man on the street" that sometime between ages three and six years, he lusted after his mother, hated his father, and was terrified that his father would remove his penis. If our man on the street protests that this is nonsense or berates us for being offensive, we must point out to him that he is incredulous or offended precisely because he is repressing these experiences! And, indeed, the more he protests, the more we are prone to assume that he is threatened by these ideas precisely because he, like all males, has *repressed* his Oedipal strivings. What possible evidence could the man produce that would *disconfirm* our theoretical assertion that he was Oedipal as a child? By our psychoanalytic definition, both the hypothetical phenomenon and its evidence are not directly observable.

The problem is not that the psychoanalytic constructs of repression or of the Oedipus complex are fantastic, bizarre, or untrue. The real problem is that they are not testable in the form in which Freud proposed them. Someone, perhaps soon, may find a creative and scientifically acceptable way to do so. But for each failure of a concept to provide the possibility of disconfirmation, the theory is weakened as an acceptable scientific account of human action and thought.

On the whole, with exceptions, the history of classical psychoanalytic theory is a story of profoundly interesting and engaging ideas that are colossal monuments to untestability. But that is not the whole story. For there are also ideas in Freudian theory that are testable and which have received both experimental and observational tests. In Chapter 3 when we examine the parts of Freudian theory that are more removed from clinical experience and description we discuss a few of these tests. For now, even allowing for those few Freudian concepts that lend themselves to test and for those potentially testable ideas that some creative psychologist will fashion from Freud's work, psychoanalysis has to be rated low in scientific testability.

Freud's Conception of Human Agency

As we saw in Chapter 1, theories of personality can be understood in terms of the way they picture a person's relationship to reality. At one extreme are those theories that picture a person as shaped by reality, as a passive receptacle to be filled by environmental influences. At the opposite extreme are those theories that portray people as active agents who shape the reality to which they respond (Buss, 1978).

Freud painted a portrait of his early patients as shaped by reality. His pioneering neurological model of the mid-1890s conceptualized the human nervous system as a tension-reduction machine whose evolutionary history designed it for quick discharge of tension in response to mounting needs. Left to its own devices, the human nervous system is a passive discharger of tension. It strives to quell irritations such as hunger, thirst, and sexual desire. Seen in this way, drives are irritants, and the nervous system responds only when an itch must be scratched. "Reality makes much of us," Freud wrote, but he failed to see how much we make of reality.

The person who emerges from Freud's early clinical work is one who "defends" *against* threatening wishes, one who tolerates conflict until tolerance fails and then is "forced" to *repress* it. People "involuntarily" *disavow* their own frightening wishes only to find disguised or "compromise" ways to satisfy them in neurotic "symptoms." Human psychosexual development proceeds, in Freud's earliest conception, as a halting process of advance and retreat, development and fixation. But only rarely in the Freudian universe are people pictured as actively striving toward goals of their own choosing, or as motivated by positive needs to master problems creatively rather than as driven by irritants they seek to quell. From Freud's point of view, the poet Emerson was right:

> Things are in the saddle,
> And ride mankind.

Freud's Focus on the Idiographic

There is an intimate and profound connection between the testability of a theoretical construct and its idiographic-nomothetic status. Idiographic concepts, if they are genuinely idiographic (unique to an individual) are difficult to test scientifically. By the same token, ideas that lack refutability tend to be idiographic with limited generalizability.

Freud's clear intention was to create a theory that was generalizable to all humans. His goal, from the initial neurological model of 1895 to the final structural model of 1937, was nomothetic theory design. The problem for Freud is that his way of creating theoretical concepts without clear empirical referents not only makes his ideas untestable but also makes them intensely idiographic. As we have seen, much, but not all, of Freud's major ideas do not lend themselves to direct observational or experimental tests because they are defined in terms of individual processes that have only indirect relationships to observable behavior. From Freud's point of view, such a strategy facilitates the *belief* that what the analyst infers from his own and his patient's behavior is universal. But the strategy blocks anyone from attempting to replicate the conditions under which the psychoanalytic idea is supposed to operate and automatically limits the concept to the particular case in which it was observed.

Furthermore, many of Freud's key early ideas derived from his self-analysis. This personal origin by no means invalidates the ideas, but it does create the suspicion that many of the emotional dynamics he wrote about were unique to Freud himself, to his time in history, and to his particular social conditions. The only way that such limitations could be confidently lifted is to demonstrate, by scientific test, that the dynamics he inferred from his own dreams and associations can be observed in other people under the same or nearly the same conditions. But that is precisely where we started, for only if the ideas lend themselves to scientific refutation can the scientist generalize them.

Pending the creative efforts of psychologists to test Freud's clinical theory scientifically, we have to conclude that Freud's theory, despite his aspirations to the contrary, is a highly idiographic (some would say *idiosyncratic*) theory of personality.

SUMMARY

Anna O.'s long array of hysterical symptoms were interpreted by her physician, Josef Breuer, not in their usual way as bizarre and meaningless ravings of a diseased mind, but as a coherent array of meaningful behaviors possessing a hidden emotional logic. Breuer soon discovered with Anna O.'s help that the coherence and logic had origins in strangulated emotions.

Sigmund Freud, Breuer's young colleague, was greatly interested in the case of Anna O., especially after his visit with Charcot in Paris, during which he observed the master remove and produce hysterical symptoms through hypnosis. Practicing Breuer and Anna O.'s method of catharsis, the "talking cure," Freud soon found that hypnosis could be achieved only with a rare few of his patients. His search for a new method led, eventually, to the technique of free association.

With the method of free association in hand, Freud soon discovered what had been hidden by hypnosis—emotional resistances. Examining and removing these resistances revealed to Freud one of the fundamental notions of his psychology, the mechanism of repression. Repressed ideas and impulses require a continual outlay of energy to prevent their return to consciousness, and the symptoms of neurotic disorder may be viewed as the return of the repudiated thought in compromise form. Symptoms allow the simultaneous satisfaction and rejection of the unacceptable impulse or idea in symbolic form.

Much to his own amazement, Freud found that sexual impulses were the common denominator for classifying unacceptable thoughts. For a time, Freud was convinced that the strongest evidence for the correctness of the sexual hypothesis was the almost universal occurrence among his neurotic patients of childhood seductions by their fathers. Soon, however, Freud saw how untenable the idea of universal childhood seduction was, and simultaneously he faced a momentous truth: children are not merely passive recipients of sexual attentions by adults, but, rather, they are active sexual creatures who seek pleasure in a variety of diffuse ways before the onset of purely genital sexuality at puberty.

For the infant, pleasure seeking is connected to developing erotogenic zones in a sequence of psychosexual maturation that shows the sexual instinct to be very much broader than adult notions of genital sexuality ordinarily admit. An emotional climax in sexual development is the Oedipal phase, in which the male child focuses his pleasure-seeking activities on the mother, and he views siblings and father as hostile rivals. The girl, on the other hand, who also initially takes her mother as the first love object, relinquishes mother for father when she realizes that girls, including mother, do not possess a penis.

The Electra and Oedipus complexes are only one part of Freud's scheme of psychosexual development, a scheme that involves five phases: (1) the *oral stage*, in which pleasurable activities center on the activities of the mouth; (2) the *anal stage*, in which the critical developments involve retention and expulsion of feces, as well as learning generalized self-mastery; (3) the *phallic stage*, the time period of the Oedipus and Electra complexes; (4) the *latency stage*, during which time the child's sexual interests and impulses lie dormant until puberty; and (5) the *genital stage* of adult sexuality and interest in the opposite sex.

Sometimes development does not proceed smoothly through the five stages because anxiety, threat, or frustration block further maturation. Such blocking is termed *fixation* in the Freudian scheme, and it is intimately related to another phenomenon of development called *regression*. Regression is a partial return to an earlier form of impulse gratification when current stresses frustrate the normal progression of the sex drive's development.

When we examine Freud's early formulations on the dimensions of refutability, human agency, and idiographic versus nomothetic focus, we find

- The theory is structured from a variety of assumptions that are simply not testable because they have no observable referents.

- Psychoanalysis credits reality with shaping humans, so that the person is pictured as a passive receptacle rather than as an active agent.

- Because so much of early psychoanalysis is focused on the unique characteristics and life events of individuals, its general flavor is idiographic rather than nomothetic.

In the next chapter we take up the matters of Freud's dream theory, his changing views of the instincts, and his final model of the mind.

FOR FURTHER READING

Freud's writings in psychology span over 43 years of theorizing and fill 23 volumes in the definitive translation of *The Standard Edition of the Complete Psychological Works of Sigmund Freud*, translated by James Strachey in collaboration with Anna Freud (London: Hogarth, 1953–1974). Perhaps the single best overview of Freud's early ideas is contained in his *Five Lectures on Psychoanalysis*, which has been published in paperback as *The Origin and Development of Psychoanalysis* (Chicago: Henry Regnery, 1965), and may also be found in Vol. 6 of *The Standard Edition*.

Freud's early neurological model of the mind deserves some scrutiny by the serious student of psychoanalysis and may be found under the title "A Project for a Scientific Psychology" in Vol. 1 of *The Standard Edition* and in a different translation as part of *The Origins of Psychoanalysis: Letters to Wilhelm Fliess*, edited by Marie Bonaparte, Anna Freud, and Ernst Kris (New York: Basic Books, 1954). A more recent and more complete translation of the Freud half of the correspondence to Fliess is provided by J. M. Masson (Ed.) in his *The Complete Letters of Sigmund Freud to Wilhelm Fliess: 1887–1904* (Cambridge, MA: Harvard University Press, 1985). Understanding the neurological model is a difficult task that can be made somewhat easier with the help of Peter Amacher's scholarly commentary, *Freud's Neurological Education and Its Influence on Psychoanalytic Theory,* Psychological Issues, Vol. 4, **16** (New York: International Universities Press, 1965). Along these same lines, Karl Pribram's "The Neuropsychology of Sigmund Freud" is an attempt to assess the contemporary significance of Freud's neurological model, and it may be found in *Experimental Foundations of Clinical Psychology*, edited by A. J. Bachrach (New York:

Basic Books, 1962). A particularly lucid account of the neurological model is provided by Raymond Fancher in *Psychoanalytic Psychology: The Development of Freud's Thought* (New York: Norton, 1973), Chapter 3.

Laurence Miller makes the argument in *Freud's Brain* (New York: Guilford Press, 1991) that psychoanalysis can survive into the next century only by a return to its roots in neurophysiology, and attempts to show how contemporary neurophysiology can be integrated with fundamental psychoanalytic concepts.

The clinical evidence on which Freud based his early concepts is to be found in Josef Breuer's and Sigmund Freud's *Studies on Hysteria* (1893–1895, Vol. II of *The Standard Edition*; also available in paperback from Beacon Press, Boston). Other case histories that have a bearing on Freud's developing theory of sexuality may be found in Vol. X of *The Standard Edition* under the titles "Analysis of a Phobia in a Five-Year-Old Boy" and "Notes Upon a Case of Obsessional Neurosis" (1909; also available in paperback editions edited by Philip Rieff: *The Sexual Enlightenment of Children* [New York: Collier, 1963]; and *Dora: An Analysis of a Case of Hysteria* [New York: Collier, 1963]).

Two important books summarize the recent wealth of new historical and personal materials from the history of psychoanalysis that have been made available. Lisa Appignanesi and John Forrester provide detailed accounts of Freud's early patients, colleagues, and family members in *Freud's Women* (New York: Basic Books, 1992). John Kerr's *A Most Dangerous Method* (New York: Knopf, 1993) details the complex relationship between Carl Jung, Sigmund Freud, and the nearly forgotten Sabina Spielrein, who was Jung's patient, lover, and nemesis.

An unusual opportunity is afforded the reader who would like to hear both sides of the story of a psychoanalytic patient's treatment by the publication of *The Wolf-Man by the Wolf-Man* (New York: Basic Books, 1971). This volume contains Freud's original case history of this young Russian nobleman whom he had treated for obsessional-compulsive neurosis and an account by the young man himself of his treatment with Freud.

Basic background reading into the details of Freud's personal life is best begun with Ernest Jones's three-volume masterwork *The Life and Work of Sigmund Freud* (New York: Basic Books, 1953, 1955, 1957). Peter Gay's *Freud: A Life for Our Time* (New York: Norton, 1988) is a comprehensive, recent biography that focuses on the personal sources of Freud's theoretical achievements. Max Schur, Freud's personal physician during the last years of his life, provides a glimpse into the personal incidents of Freud's life that shaped his attitude toward death in *Freud: Living and Dying* (New York: International Universities Press, 1972). Freud's correspondence with Carl Jung has been published as *The Freud/Jung Letters* (Princeton, NJ: Princeton University Press, 1974). These letters provide a rare glimpse into the personal lives of Freud and Jung, their attitudes toward their contemporaries (not always flattering), and the emotional abrasiveness of their theoretical and personal falling out.

There has been an explosion of psychoanalytic publications that make available previously unavailable personal documents and letters from Freud's early history. Especially noteworthy is the *The Letters of Sigmund Freud to Eduard Silberstein* (Cambridge, MA: Harvard University Press, 1990) because we get a clearer picture of Freud the adolescent, experiencing his first love, revealing his disappointment with his mother, and assuming a typically adolescent intellectual pretentiousness in the safety of his correspondence with his friend.

Freud's adoption of the Oedipus legend and the personal function it served for him in creating his theory is discussed by Arnold Bernstein in "Freud and Oedipus: A New Look at the Oedipus Complex in the Light of Freud's Life," (*The Psychoanalytic Review*, Fall 1976, **63**, 393-407). The possible connection between Freud's travel neurosis and his early experiences with his nanny, along with a discussion of Freud's ambivalence toward his father, is provided in Kenneth A. Grigg's " 'All Roads Lead to Rome': The Role of the Nursemaid in Freud's Dreams" (*American Journal of Psychoanalysis*, 1973, **21**, 108-126). Robert Stolorow and George Atwood's "A Defensive-Restitutive Function of Freud's Theory of Psychosexual Development" (*The Psychoanalytic Review*, 1978, **65**, 217-238) provides one intriguing explanation of the role of Freud's attachment to his mother in the development of his concepts of the Oedipus and Electra complexes.

For a sophisticated accounting of Josef Breuer's involvement with and abandonment of psychoanalysis, George Pollock's "The Possible Significance of Childhood Object Loss in the Josef Breuer–Bertha Pappenheim (Anna O.)–Sigmund Freud Relationship (*Journal of the American Psychoanalytic Association*, 1968, **16**, 711-739; also reprinted in Gedo and Pollock [Eds.], *Freud: The Fusion of Science and Humanism, Psychological Issues, Monographs* **34/35,** 1976 [New York: International Universities Press, 1976] provides an abundance of fact and theory. Fourteen different accounts and analyses of Bertha Pappenheim's neurosis are provided in *Anna O.,* edited by Max Rosenbaum and Melvin Muroff [New York: Free Press, 1984]).

For those with a taste for psychoanalytic trivia, albeit historical, Freud's last 10 years of daily desk diary and notebook entries have been published with a wealth of new photographs in *The Diary of Sigmund Freud 1929-1939* (New York: Scribner's, 1992). And Freud's extensive, but frequently unilluminating, correspondence with Ernest Jones, Freud's first biographer, is now available in *Sigmund Freud and Ernest Jones: 1908-1939* (Cambridge, MA: Harvard University Press, 1993). Of somewhat more historical significance is the recently published first volume of correspondence between Freud and Sandor Ferenczi (Eva Brabant, Ernst Falzeder, and Patrizia Deutsch-Giampieri [Eds.], *The Correspondence of Sigmund Freud and Sandor Ferenczi: Volume 1, 1908-1914* [Cambridge, MA: Harvard-Belknap, 1993]), in which the two friends gossip about their patients, discuss substantive theoretical issues, and reveal the important influence Ferenczi had on some of Freud's ideas.

Adolf Grünbaum's dense but important *Validation in the Clinical Theory of Psychoanalysis* (New York: International Universities Press, 1993) deserves the attention of the serious student of psychoanalysis. Grünbaum examines Freudian clinical concepts with reference to refutability and other logical tests of their validity and finds the entire enterprise wanting.

Additional recommended readings for Freud's theory are provided at the end of Chapter 3 and concern more directly his later theoretical efforts and final model of the mind.

CHAPTER 3

SIGMUND FREUD

Psychoanalysis:
The Dynamic Model of the Mind

Since I have started studying the unconscious I have become so interesting to myself.

Sigmund Freud, *The Origins of Psychoanalysis*

But these two discoveries—that the life of our sexual instincts cannot be wholly tamed, and that mental processes are in themselves unconscious and only reach the ego and come under its control through incomplete and untrustworthy perceptions— these two discoveries amount to a statement that the *ego is not master in its own house.*

Sigmund Freud, (1917a, p. 143)

About Freud's Dynamic Model

Central to Freud's early clinical work was the concept that observable behavior is a disguised derivative of unconscious wishes. The derivatives included neurotic symptoms, slips of the tongue, and many self-defeating behaviors. The story continues in this chapter with the study of dreams as disguised ways to satisfy taboo wishes.

Freud's struggle to understand the war between passion and reason reached a plateau in his creation of an abstract model of a divided mind. He moved away from direct reporting of his clinical experiences with patients and toward an increasingly complex intellectual representation of human self-division.

The key achievements of psychoanalysis by the time of Freud's death include

1. *a fairly complete picture of the "rules" by which the human unconscious operates to satisfy its urges;*
2. *a disturbing portrait of childhood sexual and aggressive wishes drawn largely from Freud's own analysis of his personal history;*
3. *a structural model of the mind that pictures the war between reason and passion as a conflict of mental agencies each obeying its own rules of operation.*

In the end, Freud was convinced that human passion was more potent, more real, and more enduring than human reason.

DREAMS AS WISH FULFILLMENTS

Consider the following dream of Freud's daughter Anna:

> My youngest daughter, then 19 months old, had had an attack of vomiting one morning and had consequently been kept without food all day. During the night after this day of starvation she was heard calling out excitedly in her sleep: "Anna Fweud, stwawbewwies, wild stwawbewwies, omblet, pudden!" At that time she was in the habit of using her own name to express the idea of taking possession of something. The menu included pretty well everything that must have seemed to her to make up a desirable meal. (Freud, 1900, p. 130)

Clearly, as can be discerned in Anna's menu, children's dreams are relatively transparent embodiments of wishes come true. There is no disguise here to obscure Anna's blatant craving for goodies that had necessarily been denied her during her illness. Anna's dream was an undisguised wish receiving undisguised fulfillment.

Freud had already come to the conclusion that dreams are mental states designed to bring about the fulfillment of wishes or desires. The dream, he reasoned in the "Project for a Scientific Psychology" (1895), is a hallucinatory state that serves to structure dream events, not as they are in the external world, but as we would like them to be. Sometimes, however, unconscious desire clashes with conscious restraint, so the dream processes pursue devious paths to wish fulfillment. Freud stated the fundamental implication of this insight in the dictum *"The interpretation of dreams is the royal road to a knowledge of the unconscious mind"* (1900, p. 608).

By examining a dreamer's nighttime productions, the skilled observer can detect those motives and wishes that are hidden from view during waking life, motives and wishes that the dreamer can entertain only in the disguised, compromise form that dream imagery represents. Compared with the dreams of children, adult productions rarely evidence the simplicity of Anna's stwawbewwies-and-pudden fancy.

Disguised Wish Fulfillment

Compare the following adult dream with Anna's innocently lucid construction:

> The patient, who was a young girl, began thus: "As you will remember, my sister has only one boy left now—Karl; she lost his elder brother, Otto, while I was still living with her. Otto was my favorite; I more or less brought him up. I'm fond of the little one too, but of course, not nearly so fond as I was of the one who died. Last night, then, I dreamt that *I saw Karl lying before me dead. He was lying in his little coffin with his hands folded and with candles all round—in fact just like little Otto, whose death was such a blow to me.* (Freud, 1900, p. 152; italics in original)

If it is true that dreams are the fulfillment of wishes, then surely this dream by one of Freud's patients must embody the wish that little Karl had died instead of little Otto.

Assured from *his knowledge of his patient* that she was not cruel, Freud considered the dream carefully. He asked her to tell him everything that came to mind when she thought of the separate elements of the dream. It is important to note that the interpretation of the dream is possible only when the past history of the dreamer, as well as the context provided by the dreamer's personality, is known to the analyst. Dreams are the dreamer's unique productions.

Thus Freud knew that after his patient had been orphaned, she had been raised in the house of an elder sister. A particular male visitor to the sister's home, nicknamed "the professor" by virtue of his occupation as professional lecturer, had made quite a romantic impression on Freud's patient. After marriage plans had been disrupted between the girl and the professor, he ceased to visit the sister's home. Freud's patient nonetheless secretly longed to see and to be with him. On the other hand, through hurt pride, she tried to convince herself to relinquish any romantic attachment to him. Her resolve was not an easy one to keep. Whenever she learned that he was to give a public lecture, she quietly became a part of the audience. Yet she would observe him only at a discreet distance, and she never allowed herself to confront him directly. In fact, she seized upon every opportunity, however trivial, to see her professor friend. *She had even experienced a moment of happiness at the funeral of little Otto when her professor had made an appearance to express his condolences.* It was this continual vacillation between approach and withdrawal that chiefly characterized Freud's patient.

Here, of course, was the key to her dream. If little Karl were to die, his funeral would provide another opportunity to see her professor without any direct attempt on her part to bring about the meeting. *Her wish, therefore, was not directly for Karl's death, but only for a meeting with her professor.* The dream had created from her past history of associations a perfectly logical pretext for furthering the satisfaction of her ambivalent desire. Thus the lucidity and directness of Anna's stwaw-bewwy dream is not to be found here.

There is clearly great similarity between adult processes and hysterical symptoms if we make the assumption, as Freud did, that both dreams and symptoms conceal ideas that are not acceptable to the conscious personality. Freud found evidence in several of his own dreams that particularly objectionable desires were frequently the kernels from which nighttime fantasies grew.

PERSONAL SOURCES: FREUD'S MOTHER AND FATHER DREAMS

We saw in Chapter 2 that Freud had begun a self-analysis in the summer of 1897, and that the precipitating incident for the task was his emotional disturbance over the death of his father. Throughout *The Interpretation of Dreams*, and in one or two of his other works, Freud employed his own dreams, elucidated by self-analysis, as examples of his concepts. Like his patient's Karl and Otto dream, Freud's own dreams revealed how important it was for the analyst to understand the personal symbols and meanings of the dreamer.

Immediately following his father's funeral, Freud had a dream about a sign hanging *in a barbershop that he visited every day.* In a letter to his friend Wilhelm Fliess, Freud reported that the dream occurred the night *after* his father's funeral; whereas in *The Interpretation of Dreams* he states that it occurred the night *before* the funeral (see 1954, Letter No. 50, p. 170). The analysis given in *The Interpretation of Dreams* provides the more detailed account:

> During the night before my father's funeral I had a dream of a printed notice, placard or poster [in a barbershop]—rather like the notices forbidding one to smoke in a railway waiting-room— on which appeared either
>
>
>
> "You are requested to close the eyes"
>
> OR
>
> "You are requested to close an eye.". . .
>
>
>
> Each of these two versions had a meaning of its own, and led in a different direction when the dream was interpreted. I had chosen the simplest possible ritual for the funeral, for I knew my father's own views on such ceremonies. But some other members of the family were not sympathetic to such puritanical simplicity and thought we should be disgraced in the eyes of those who attended the funeral. Hence one of the versions: "You are requested to close an eye," i.e., to "wink" or "overlook" [the simplicity of the services]. Here it is particularly easy to see the meaning of the vagueness expressed by the "either-or." (Freud, 1900, p. 318)

The dream was, upon analysis, clearly a form of self-reproach or self-chastisement for not providing the "proper" full-fledged funeral that members of the family expected and desired. Simultaneously, the dream represented the ultimate act of filial duty; namely, the closing of his father's eyes at death. It was as though the dream condensed the idea of "failing to do your duty" with the idea of "filial duty" in a clever word picture.

Freud suspected that the dream was in some way connected with ever deeper feelings of guilt. Might it be that he had not loved his father as much as he consciously protested? The family thought so, because on the day of the funeral Freud was actually late in arriving because he had been detained in a *barbershop*. The seemingly inexcusable lateness, coupled with his desire for relatively austere last rites for his father, must have seemed to members of Freud's family indications of supreme lack of respect. The important point is that to Freud, too, such behavior was an admission of an ambivalent attitude toward his father.

Personal Sources of Freud's Ambivalent Love for His Father

During his extensive self-analysis, Freud uncovered several roots of his hostility toward his father and its accompanying pangs of guilt. The barbershop dream just discussed had emphasized, in Freud's interpretations of it, the theme of *filial duty*, literally, a responsibility to provide his father with respect. Instead, Freud had shown neglect. Freud's father died in October 1896; by 1899 Freud had included in *The Interpretation of Dreams* several pieces of his self-therapeutic efforts to cope with the guilt and anger triggered by the loss. By 1904, on a vacation to Greece with his brother Alexander, Freud's guilt over his father's death reached a crisis. Eight years after the event, Freud was still painfully experiencing the reverberations of his own not quite completely analyzed Oedipus conflict.

The Acropolis Episode

In 1936, only three years from his own death, suffering terminal cancer of the jaw and mouth, Freud published an account of his crisis experience in Greece. Standing upon the Acropolis, surveying the majesty of the landscape and ruminating on the impressive history of the site, Freud was abruptly thrust outside of himself, as though he were suddenly two people. His own later description of the experience was that he endured a "splitting of consciousness." One part of himself was astonished to find that the fabled city of Athens existed! Freud thought, "So all this really *does* exist, just as we learnt at school!" (1936, p. 241). The other, more reality-oriented aspect of Freud's personality was astonished, too, as though unaware that Athens and its landscape had ever been the subject of doubt.

Freud interpreted his splitting of awareness as a form of "derealization," a kind of defensive disbelief in an effort to repudiate a segment of threatening reality. He was able to analyze the experience to uncover the chain of associations that underlay his defensive maneuver; the chain led straight back to his guilt and hostility associated with his father. Schur (1972) has provided additional details that Freud was apparently unwilling to publish as part of his analysis.

From Freud's own account, we learn that as a child he harbored doubts, not of the existence of Athens, but of the possibility that he would ever see it with his own eyes. To see Athens had the personal meaning of "going such a long way," that is, becoming successful enough to make the dream of distant travel possible. Because his youth was one of poverty, the wish to travel to distant places was a desire to escape the privations of his real existence. As Freud expressed the feeling,"When first one catches sight of the sea, crosses the ocean and experiences as realities cities and land which for so long had been distant, unattainable things of desire— one feels like a hero who has performed deeds of improbable greatness" (1936, p. 247). The symbolic meaning of travel to fabled cities, especially to the city of Rome, was, for Freud, intricately connected with a host of guilt-laden and aggressive feelings toward his father (for details of Freud's "Rome neurosis" see Grigg, 1973, and Schorske, 1975).

In the present instance, the visit to the Acropolis brought to Freud's mind the further association of Napoleon, during his coronation as emperor, turning to his *brother* to remark how pleasant it would be if their father could be present this day. But herein lay the crux of the defensive disbelief in Athens' reality. To "have come so far" was equivalent to success, the special success of having gone further than one's own father:

> The very theme of Athens and the Acropolis in itself contained evidence of the son's superiority. Our father had been in business, he had had no secondary education, and Athens could not have meant much to him. Thus what interfered with our enjoyment of the journey to Athens was a feeling of *filial piety*. (Freud, 1936, pp. 247-248)

Just as the barbershop dream after the funeral had contained an allusion to *filial duty*, the experience of derealization on the Acropolis embodied the feeling of *filial piety*: literally, loyalty to the father. It was as though the trip to Athens had been not merely a surpassing of father but a betrayal of him as well. Such intolerable guilt and its implied hostility had to be defended against. As Freud put it, he was overcome with the feeling that *"What I see here is not real."*

Suffering from terminal cancer, with thoughts of death nearly always in his mind, Freud concluded the Acropolis account with this sentence: "And now you will no longer wonder that the recollection of this incident on the Acropolis should have troubled me so often since I myself have grown old and stand in need of forbearance and can travel no more" (1936, p. 248). It is possible that at one level of his understanding, Freud was accepting his imminent end as fitting punishment for having surpassed his father; certainly, this last statement suggests his identification with the fate of his father, who similarly had grown old and stood in need of forbearance.

Freud's Death Fear
Schur (1972, pp. 225 ff.) has shown that there were other important determinants of the Acropolis episode that involved Freud's relationship with Wilhelm Fliess. A Berlin physician, Fliess played the role of father figure and confidant during Freud's self-analysis in an extensive interchange of letters and a series of personal meetings, or "congresses," as Freud termed them. Through a complex system of biological numerology and critical-period theory, Fliess had predicted the year of Freud's death—completely wrongly, as it turned out—and in so doing fed directly Freud's

already superstitious concern with the prospects of his own demise. Fliess's critical period calculations had set Freud's death near the age of 51; but Freud's superstitious turn of mind, after the death of his father, had its own chosen date. Freud was convinced that the year of his death would be between the ages of 61 and 62. He wrote jokingly but revealingly to Carl Jung of his trip to Athens with his brother Alexander

> . . . It was really uncanny how often the number 61 or 60 in connection with a 1 or 2 kept cropping up in all sorts of numbered objects, especially those connected with transportation. This I conscientiously noted. It depressed me, but I had hopes of breathing easy when we got to the hotel in Athens and were assigned rooms on the first floor. Here, I was sure, there could be no No. 61. I was right, but I was given 31 (which with fatalistic license could be regarded as half of 61 or 62), and this younger, more agile number proved to be an even more persistent persecutor than the first. From the time of our trip home until very recently, 31, often with a 2 in its vicinity, clung to me faithfully. (Freud, in Freud/Jung, 1974, p. 219)

Freud's own analysis of his superstition centered on the fact that his conviction that death would come at 61 or 62 appeared in 1899, the year *The Interpretation of Dreams* (postdated to 1900 by the publisher) was issued. In 1899, Freud was 43 years old and had just received a new phone number (14362) that contained a "43." In his compulsive frame of mind, with his nets spread very wide, almost any incident would have been scrutinized for some indication of the year of his death. Similarly, the fact of the publication of *The Interpretation of Dreams* that year was brought into the service of his *Todangst*, or death fear. Because he believed that this book was his masterpiece, he harbored the despairing conviction that there was nothing more to accomplish in his life. In essence, he might as well die.

When the new phone number contained not only the 43 of his present birthday but another pair of numbers—62—his superstitious inclination allowed him to convince himself that 62 would be the year of his death. He would thus outlive the present, forestalling his *Todangst*. As Schur points out, Freud's preoccupation with his own demise received several reinforcements in 1904, the year of the trip to Athens. For in that year, Freud's long and intimate relationship with Fliess ended bitterly, ostensibly over Fliess's belief that Freud had provided crucial information about his periodicity theory to a plagiarist.

Consequently, in 1904, Freud had in mind the death of his father and his guilt in having surpassed him, the death of a friendship with a father figure who was analogously accusing him of betrayal, and the prospects of his own death appearing magically and persistently as though in self-punishment for these filial misdeeds. Schur notes the irony in Freud's numerical death premonitions, for in his absurd calculations Freud was caricaturing Fliess's theory of critical number cycles. Freud was going Fliess one better, just as he had contemplated surpassing his father (Schur, 1972, p. 233). In his personal copy of another of his books, Freud wrote some remarks in the chapter on superstition that he apparently intended to add to some future revised edition. The essence of his note was that obsessive-neurotic superstitions have at their core murderous rage directed toward some loved one that is defended against by repression. The concluding line of the note states "My own superstition has its root in suppressed ambition (immortality) and in my case takes the place of that anxiety about death which springs from the normal uncertainty of life . . ." (1901, p. 260n.).

Thus the core of Freud's guilt was concerned with his personal ambition to surpass his father, to surpass his peers, to defeat death. Freud's fear of death was the fear of not being allowed to complete his work because the completion of his work personally meant to him the act of surpassing his father (cf. Wallace, 1978).

The Bedroom Episode

One last piece of evidence linking Freud's ambivalent feelings toward his father and his own need to achieve enduring success involves a recollection of a particularly painful incident from Freud's seventh or eighth year.

> One evening before going to sleep I disregarded the rules which modesty lays down and obeyed the calls of nature in my parents' bedroom while they were present. In the course of his reprimand, my father let fall the words: "The boy will come to nothing." This must have been a frightful blow to my ambition, for references to this scene are still constantly recurring in my dreams and are always linked with an enumeration of my achievements and successes, as though I wanted to say: "You see, I *have* come to something." (Freud, 1900, p. 216)

As Erich Fromm (1959, p. 56) has pointed out, this act can be interpreted as a form of rebellion against the father by symbolically taking possession of the parents' bedroom. More important, from the standpoint of Freud's relationship with his father, is the significance he himself attached to the memory, namely, the desire to be successful and to prove his father wrong. It was precisely this theme that the ascendance to the Acropolis embodied for Freud. He had, after all, proven his father wrong; but the accomplishment aroused such guilt that Athens ceased to be real.

What is abundantly clear is that Freud made greater use of the personal sources of his ideas as later theoretical constructs than is generally acknowledged. It should perhaps be mentioned that this personalizing of theory sometimes took the form of generalizing his personal pain to all humans. In *Totem and Taboo* (1913b) Freud raised the father conflict of the Oedipus complex to a universal, evolutionary trend by which our early human forebears, having murdered the primal father of the tribe to possess his power and his women, proceeded guiltily to spoil the fruits of their ambition by erecting incest taboos. As Wallace (1977, pp. 79–80) expressed it so lucidly, "By raising a personal dynamic to the level of a phylogenetic universal based on a deed done long ago, Freud is on the one hand distancing himself from his patricidal rage . . . but on the other he is metaphorically expressing its importance (by calling it a primal fact of world history) in his own psychic life" (cf. Wallace, 1976, and Schur, 1972, p. 474).

Freud's Relationship to His Mother: The Birds'-Beaked-People Dream

Another of Freud's dreams indicates the complexity of the verbal linkages that may be employed defensively to obscure threatening wishes. In his seventh or eighth year, Freud's self-analysis revealed, he had dreamt of his mother with a "peculiarly peaceful, sleeping expression on her features." In the dream, he saw her being carried into a room by two or three people with birds' beaks and laid upon a bed (Freud, 1900, p. 583). The bizarre creatures with birds' beaks brought to Freud's mind the association of the illustrations of bird-masked people in a particular edition of the Bible called the *Phillippson's* Bible.

Further analysis revealed an association to the name "Phillippson" in the form of a memory of an "ill-mannered boy" named Phillipp, who was the first person to reveal to the young Freud the vulgar word for sexual intercourse. In German, the word *vogeln* is slang for copulation, and it is derived from the proper form of the world *Vogel*, which means "bird." Hence, the associative chain from people with *birds'* beaks to the *Phillippson* Bible to the boy named *Phillipp* had revealed a sexual connotation to the dream images.

The expression of his mother's face in the dream reminds Freud of his dying grandfather, whom he had observed in a coma a few days before the grandfather's death. However, when the young Freud awoke from the dream, he had rushed into his parents' room to wake his mother and was quite relieved to discover that she was indeed alive.

Why, then, had the dream depicted her in a state similar to death—a state, that is, similar to his grandfather's coma? Surely the dream could not have been the representation of a wish that his mother die? On the contrary, Freud's anxiety at the thought of her death had forced him upon awakening to rush into her room to confirm that she was still alive. Perhaps the anxiety over her death was a form of disguise to prevent recognition of the sexual longing the dream had really depicted, a sexual longing for his mother.

Further analysis might be made along the path of the association of the grandfather's death. Could "grandfather" be a disguise for "father" so that the dream actually conveyed not only a sexual wish for mother but a death wish toward father? Unfortunately, Freud did not carry the analysis that far in his published writings.

However, it seems very likely that the ill-mannered Phillipp of this dream is the same Phillipp of the disappearing nanny dream, discussed in Chapter 2 (Grigg, 1973, p. 125). Recall that Freud perceived his half brother Philipp as a father substitute who put babies inside his mother and who controlled the whereabouts of both his nanny and his mother, a condensation based on the earlier imprisonment of the nanny. If indeed these two Philipps are the same, then significant strength is added to Freud's own interpretation that his anxiety in the present dream was over a sexual wish for his mother and hostile wishes toward his father (or toward the two father figures in the dream: Philipp and the comatose grandfather). The fact that the death imagery in the dream is both times associated with a father figure (*Phillipp*son's Bible Funeral Figures, and the dying grand*father*) and then condensed with the image of a sleeping mother suggests that death wishes toward the father are primary, and sexual wishes toward the mother are a secondary but related issue (see Bernstein, 1976).

Another interpretation of this dream is that the anxiety Freud experienced was due to a death wish directed toward his *mother*. This interpretation proceeds from the well-established fact that Freud's relationship to his mother was an especially close one. Freud consciously held a very idealized conception of the relationship between a mother and a son, suggesting at one point in his writings that it was altogether the most perfect and free from ambivalence of all human relationships (Freud,

1933, p. 133). Stolorow and Atwood (1978) suggest that Freud had an intense need to preserve an entirely positive image of his mother, an idealistic vision of her that had to be defended at all costs. When, as a child, he experienced resentment and rage toward her for having more children and for deserting him to do so, his only means of dealing with his hatred toward a figure he so dearly loved was repression, followed by "splitting" his image of her into a good mother and a hateful mother. Thus, in his interpretation of the birds'-beaked-people dream, Freud avoided the obvious meaning of hostility toward mother, and displaced the death wish interpretation onto father.

Stolorow and Atwood (1978) point out that Freud's theory of psychosexual development views the origin of personal conflicts as lying in the child's own internalized but universally biological urges. Actual parental influences on the child were minimized:

> In Freud's theoretical view of infantile development, the sources of evil were located not in the parents (mother), but rather in the child himself, in his own sexual and aggressive drives. . . . Specifically, through the relocation of the sources of badness into the child, Freud absolved his mother from blame for her betrayals of him and safeguarded her idealized image from invasions by his unconscious ambivalence. Freud's wish to banish (destroy) the treacherous mother ["treacherous" because she disappeared and gave birth to rivals] was thus replaced in his theory with the child's need to repress his own evil wishes. (Stolorow & Atwood, 1978, p. 232; see also Stolorow & Atwood, 1979, p. 67)

Stolorow and Atwood are probably correct in their assumption that Freud needed to locate the "sources of badness" in his own internalized biological states. They are probably also correct in assuming that in so doing, Freud exonerated his mother from the taint of his rageful impulses and defensive distortions. However, it seems clear that Freud also exonerated *himself* from guilt for these unacceptable impulses. By proposing that erotic attachment to mother and murderous rivalry with both father and siblings are biological and fixed universals (with a phylogenetic history, no less), Freud in effect absolved himself from personal compliance in very personal evils. As they say in some circles, that is the bottom line. Misery does love company.

It is also necessary to consider the fact that, even if Freud had rageful feelings toward his mother, the depth of his displaced rage toward his father matched or surpassed them. In principle, consequently, we would have to assume that, whether defensively displaced or genuinely, Freud harbored hostile wishes toward nearly every significant member of his family. In either case, the evidence supports the view that Freud distanced himself from his conflicting feelings by conceptualizing them as human inevitables. *Ananke.*

In fairness to Freud, it should be pointed out that his goal in the analysis of his dreams was not only self-therapy, but also the ambitious attempt to unmask the secret of all unconscious fabrications. Freud's own dreams point up the difficult nature of the task. For Freud sought no less an accomplishment than the explanation of how dreams are structured to conceal significant but unacceptable motives from consciousness—how dreams, that is, can satisfy in fantasy, desires conceived in reality. Without his efforts we would scarcely have the tools to probe so presumptively into the recesses of the toolmaker's workshop.

Manifest and Latent Dream Content: The Mask

In light of the disguised nature of wish fulfillment in adult dreams, even the most elementary description of dream processes must include a distinction between the readily accessible disguise and the less accessible ideas that lie behind the distortion. Freud referred to the dream's facade or mask consisting of all those recalled sights, images, ideas, sounds, and smells that compose the story of the dream. Behind the facade, beneath the mask of recallable elements, lie the "perverse," unacceptable impulses that, like "masked criminals," are far commoner in mental life than straightforward, undisguised urges (Freud, 1925c, p. 132).

Freud's use of the mask metaphor is an apt analogy for his more technical distinction between the *manifest* and *latent* content of the dream. The manifest content corresponds to the mask, whereas the impulses thus disguised like "masked criminals" are properly termed latent content. Manifest content is generally easily recalled by the dreamer. By contrast, the latent content can be arrived at only by careful interpretation of the manifest content.

The mental processes that convert strivings, wishes, and needs into the disguised images of the manifest content are called collectively *dream work*. In a sense, the analyst's interpretation of a dream is an attempt to undo the dream work, to unmask the manifest content and reveal the more fundamental latent content from which the dream was constructed.

The Dream Work

Once distortion or disguise is recognized as a general phenomenon of dream imagery, it becomes necessary to search for a cause of the distortion. Freud postulated that the wishes or needs that initiate the dream are unacceptable to a special agency of the conscious mind called the "censorship system." The censorship system is actually on the frontier of consciousness, a border guard, so to speak, between the unconscious and conscious systems of the mind.

The censorship system is very selective about the wishes and needs it allows the dreamer to entertain or remember consciously. Wishes that are morally unacceptable to the awake dreamer are also unacceptable to the sleeping dreamer's censorship system. In consequence, wishes or urges that arise from the unconscious during sleep are heavily censored by this ethical arm of the mental apparatus. Thus the distortion in those wishes as they appear in the manifest dream is a direct result of the efforts of the ever-watchful preconscious dream censor.

The two systems of the mind, the unconscious system from which the wishes emerge and the preconscious censorship system that prevents those wishes from freely entering consciousness, constitute the mechanism of dream formation (Freud, 1900, pp. 144–145). Unacceptable wishes can be prevented from gaining access to consciousness in only one way. The censorship system must selectively distort the wish, transforming it into an alternate form that does not clash with the conscious ethical standards of the personality. Conversely, the only way the unconscious can achieve satisfaction for its pressing urges is to evade the censor by masquerading the unacceptability of its wishes behind a facade of related but more neutral ideas. Hence the distortion in dreams is a joint product of two architects: the unconscious system and the censor. Freud was able to isolate four separate processes in the dream work of these two architects that account for the form of the manifest dream.

The Work of Condensation

One of the mundane facts about the interpretation of a dream, but a fact that contains a significant clue about dream distortion, is that a remembered dream (i.e., the manifest content) can be recounted in relatively few words. In contrast, the *interpretation* of the manifest dream, penetrating to the latent content, may produce as much as 12 times the amount of information (Freud, 1900, p. 279). Freud concluded, therefore, that the manifest content is an unsurpassed model of compression, or *condensation* as it was called in Freud's technical vocabulary.

It might be possible to conclude hastily that the work of condensation is merely a one-way editing process whereby only a select few elements of the mass of unconscious material are chosen for representation in the manifest content. In this simplistic view, condensation is accomplished by a process of omission. But free association to the few manifest elements of a dream usually reveals that each manifest element has multiple, two-way relationships with every other element, and each component is, therefore, at least partially redundant. Borrowing a concept from the study of hysterical symptoms, it can be said that the manifest dream content is *overdetermined*. Several unconscious ideas band together to contribute *as a group* some energy to direct the choice of *one* common manifest element. Simultaneously, each manifest element has connections to several other manifest elements, which, of course, have their own connections to other groups of unconscious, latent ideas that have similarly banded together. The picture that Freud paints of condensation is more like an associative web than it is like a chain.

Condensation, consequently, is not a process of simple omission. It is a technique of creative compression by telescoping elements together. Each segment of the manifest content is a nodal point upon which a great number of latent ideas converge (Freud, 1900, p. 283). The latent dream thoughts are thus condensed into the manifest dream content much as a composite photograph of a single person is constructed from the characteristics of several individuals: It may "look like *A* perhaps, but may be dressed like *B*, may do something that we remember *C* doing, and at the same time we may know that he is *D*" (Freud, 1916, p. 171).

The Work of Displacement

Displacement is a technique the censorship agency of the mind employs to replace a latent dream element in consciousness by a more remote idea, or to accomplish a shifting of the dream's recalled emphasis away from an important idea and toward an unimportant one. Thus displacement may proceed by two paths: replacement of one idea with a remote associate, or the shifting emotional accent from one thought to another. The dreamer is left with the impression of having dreamed a very strangely connected sequence of thoughts, or of having very absurdly made "much ado about nothing."

Freud employed an amusing anecdote in his *Introductory Lectures* to illustrate the concept of displacement:

> There was a blacksmith in the village, who had committed a capital offence. The Court decided that the crime must be punished; but as the blacksmith was the only one in the village and was indispensable, and as on the other hand there were three tailors living there, one of *them* was hanged instead. (1916, pp. 174–175)

Where condensation was responsible for compressing the latent thoughts into the abbreviated form of the manifest content, displacement is responsible for the "choice" of elements from which the manifest dream is constructed.

Beginning with the latent, unacceptable wish at the center, the dream work of displacement spins outward from this nucleus a web of increasingly remote associations. Each strand of this associative web is connected both to the central latent wish and to every other associated idea in the network. Hence, manifest elements are redundant in the sense that the unacceptable wish is dispersed simultaneously into many interconnected and mutually excitatory strands of the web. Because each of these strands shares a common origin, the nuclear wish, recollection of the ideas along any other strand excites recollection of nearby, connected strands of ideas.

One way to view the manifest dream, therefore, is to conceive of it as an associative "beating around the bush," whereby the unacceptable nucleus wish of the latent content is dispersed into any available channel of the web *except* one that leads directly back to the origin. The pattern of associatively connected, overlapping, and redundant ideas evoked by the dreamer during free association to a manifest element is evidence of this delicately tangled skein. Displacement robs the latent content of its normal sequence of ideas, substituting the sequence of the associative web, and it likewise rechannels the latent content's original focus of emotional intensity into the diffuse lattice of the web.

The Work of Visual Representation

Abstract ideas, wishes, and urges that form the latent thoughts of the dream are by themselves colorless and ephemeral. Within the scope of the dream, these abstract thoughts must be converted into concrete visual images with the kind of primitive pictorial quality that readily lends itself to the manipulations of condensation and displacement (Freud, 1900, p. 339). Although not all the elements of the latent content are converted into visual images, on the whole the translation of abstract thoughts into concrete pictures constitutes the essence of a dream (Freud, 1916, p. 175).

The translation of abstract thoughts into visual imagery typically follows the path of converting the symbolic labels representing the idea into a physical and concrete act. For example, the abstract idea of "possession" can be converted into the visually concrete act of "sitting on the object." Children often employ this strategy to protect a treasured possession from the grasp of an overwhelming playmate (Freud, 1916, p. 176n.).

To take another illustration, Freud reported the recollections of Herbert Silberer, who, in a sleepy, twilight state, often converted some abstract intellectual task into visual imagery. On one occasion, Silberer thought of having to revise an uneven or rough passage in an essay he was writing. He then pictured himself planing a piece of wood (Freud, 1900, p. 344). In another episode, Silberer had the experience of losing his train of thought so that he had to return to the beginning to pick up the thread of logic. Silberer subsequently had the visual image of a printer's typesetting form for a page with the last lines of type fallen away (Freud, 1900, p. 345).

It is easy to see that the translation of abstract thoughts into visual imagery represents a process of *personal, idiosyncratic symbolization.* The dreamer creates concrete pictures to represent abstract thoughts. The images employed are likely to be a function of his or her own creativity, unique experiences, and sophistication. But it is important to keep in mind that this kind of symbol formation proceeds from the abstract to the concrete, as opposed to the more usual literary case of transforming concrete acts into abstract symbols.

The Work of Secondary Revision

All the mechanisms of the dream work discussed thus far have as their common goal the appeasement of dream censorship. The dream work can condense, displace, and represent in visual form the latent dream thoughts in its attempt to disguise them. For the most part, these three mechanisms attend to distorting and to breaking apart the latent elements' form and organization. Thus, these mechanisms usually produce an absurd product. When the dreamer tries to recall and to make sense of the dream, however, the gaps, distortions, and substitutions strike a note of disharmony to the conscious mind. The dreamer's waking need is for logical coherence and consistency in mental activities. Consequently, to bring order to what otherwise would be experienced as chaos, that part of the mind which is between unconsciousness and consciousness exerts an organizing, sense-making influence on the confused and bizarre story. In those twilight moments just before waking from a dream, it is the preconscious system of the mind that struggles to mold the dreamer's creations into a form comprehensible to waking intelligence.

The preconscious thus attempts to patch together, into an understandable, coherent whole, the scattered and apparently nonsensical elements of the latent dream. In so doing, the preconscious is, in effect, subjecting the dream to an interpretation before the dreamer is fully awake. Whatever that interpretation is, the elements of the dream will be fitted to its outlines until what was scattered and diffuse becomes organized and reasonable.

It is this preinterpretation that introduces further distortion into the recalled manifest content. Freud called this process of constructing a coherent whole from the scattered dream elements *secondary revision.* In a sense, the preconscious treats the dream elements to a kind of further elaboration designed to mold what is patently unconnected and absurd into a logically consistent structure.

Sometimes the secondary revision occurs during the dream itself. For instance, a particular dream may be so laden with unpleasant emotional intensity that the various patterns of distortion introduced by the mechanisms of condensation and displacement are not sufficient to satisfy all the demands of the dream censorship. If the ever-watchful dream censor were to be aroused to action, the dreamer's sleep would surely be disturbed or disrupted in an effort to halt the dream. To lessen the impact of such a dream without recourse to interrupting the dreamer's sleep, there occurs instead a kind of judgmental interpretation on the part of the dreamer that, after all, *"it's only a dream"* (Freud, 1900, p. 489).

STUDY OF THE DREAM: THEORETICAL YIELD

Psychoanalytic dream interpretation is a careful labor of elucidating the apparent absurdities of the recalled dream by accepting such productions as evidence of the dreamer's nonconscious mental achievements. Accurate interpretation of the dream, therefore, lifts the disguise, makes intelligible the distortions, and replaces absurdity with understanding. The long hidden logic of the unconscious is made accessible. Freud considered the study of the dream one of his most fundamental and lasting achievements. A brief survey of the theoretical yield is in order.

Regressive and Archaic Nature of Dreams

The medium of dreams is visual imagery. It was Freud's opinion that visual imagery represents an earlier and more primitive mode of mental operation than verbal thought. Thus the dream is an *archaic production*—a return to a mode of thought characteristic of the early years of childhood before language achieves its prominence in our relations to the world. Each individual initially begins mental life, Freud asserted, with sensory impressions and memory images of such impressions. Words are attached to these images only later in development, so that, at the outset, the child does not code his mental activities into language labels (Freud, 1916, pp. 180–181; see also Freud, 1900, pp. 189 ff.).

Dreams are a return to this archaic mode of mental functioning, and often, when correctly translated, a dream's latent content may contain a wish that dates from childhood:" . . . to our surprise, *we find the child and child's impulses still living on in the dream"* (Freud, 1900, p. 191). Dream processes, then, are a *regression* to the earlier years of the dreamer's mental life.

Sexual and Aggressive Motives of Childhood

On the whole, adults retain very few memories of the first five or six years of life. With rare exception, most of us can recall but one or two incidents that we now presume, precisely because they are remembered, to have been overwhelmingly important at the time. But key memories and feelings are conspicuously absent from adult consciousness. Recollection of our Oedipal sexual and aggressive strivings remains inaccessible to consciousness because an *infantile amnesia* obscures the great wealth of experiences of the childhood epoch.

However, it was Freud's discovery that these memories are not simply "forgotten." Instead, they are only inaccessible or latent, and having become part of the unconscious, these childhood memories, strivings, and wishes may emerge during dreams when triggered by some current, thematically similar, incident.

The "Hellish" Unconscious

Consider the necessity of censorship in dreams. Dreamers entertain wishes and desires that would seem so perverse and unethical to them if awake that the dream work must disguise these thoughts beyond conscious recognition. What is the source of these monumentally "evil" inclinations? Obviously, since dreams are a product of the unconscious, the unconscious must be the source of the impulses that the conscious personality, the ego, finds objectionable. But during sleep, the censorship agency is less stringent, more easily pacified by partial disguise, and it allows the ego to be flooded with material that is customarily held in check.

> The ego, freed from all ethical bonds, also finds itself at one with all the demands of sexual desire, even those which have long been condemned by our aesthetic upbringing and those which contradict all the requirements of moral restraint. The desire of pleasure—the "libido," as we call it—chooses its objects without inhibition, and by preference, indeed, the forbidden ones: not only other men's wives, but above all incestuous objects, objects sanctified by the common agreement of mankind, a man's mother and sister, a woman's father and brother . . . Lusts which we think of as remote from human nature show themselves strong enough to provoke dreams. Hatred, too, rages without restraint. Wishes for revenge and death directed against those who are nearest and dearest in waking life, against the dreamer's parents, brothers, and sisters, husband or wife, and his own children are nothing unusual. *These censored wishes appear to rise up out of a positive Hell; after they have been interpreted when we are awake, no censorship of them seems to us too severe.* (Freud, 1916, pp. 142–143; italics added)

Are we to conclude, on the basis of the seemingly reprehensible content of adult dreams, that dreams simply expose the inherently evil character of humanity? On the contrary, Freud protested. It is not that dreams expose evil, hellish strivings of adults, but that adults *interpret* such feelings in themselves as evil when they become aware of them. Actually, the egoistic, unrestrained sexual and aggressive urges found in dreams date from childhood, when ethical and realistic standards of conduct, which we attribute to adult understanding, were yet undeveloped.

Against the standards of adult ethics, such wishes as sexual desire for a parent and murderous intent directed toward rivals are absolutely wrong, shocking, and condemnable. But for infants such reactions are the typical responses of organisms that are at once helpless, yet dominated by urgent needs for immediate gratification of their wishes. That gratification can come only from those persons who are in charge of their care, and who, therefore, are in intimate contact with them. For *infants* it is not morally outrageous to desire the exclusive possession of their mothers; it is not shocking that they expect this accustomed fulfiller of every pleasure also to be the object of their sexual explorations and curiosity; it is not a condemnable quality of *infants* that they harbor wishes for the annihilation of brothers, sisters, and father, along with anyone else who rivals their insistent and pressing commitment to mother, the satisfier. To the *infant*, unschooled in shame, disgust, or morality, such desires are the mere commonalities of day-to-day existence. To the *adult*, recollecting these feelings in dreams, guilt and horror seem the only appropriate responses.

It is with these memories, wishes, and strivings, then, that the ethical and realistic demands of later socialization will clash. The forces of repression will thrust them into the unconscious: "... *what is unconscious in mental life is also what is infantile*" (Freud, 1916, p. 210). Adult dreams regress to the archaic and amoral level of infancy, and they deceptively appear to shed light on the vileness of the adult unconscious.

The obvious question arises: "What triggers the reemergence of these latent, infantile strivings in adult dreams?" Freud suggested that something in the dreamer's current waking life, an incident, a frustrated desire, the emotionally abrasive happenings of the day, somehow connect by association to the stored memories of the unconscious and, together with them, initiate a dream. Archaic wishes in the unconscious link up with these "day's residues," as Freud called them, to produce the dream thoughts. Dream thoughts are thus dominated by events that have given us pause for reflection during the day and which bear some associative similarity to the archaic wishes in the unconscious. The explanation, of course, may apply the other way round: Events that give us pause during the day do so because they are connected with repressed wishes in the unconscious (Freud, 1900, pp. 169, 174).

Indeed, in either case, dreams *are* the royal road to an understanding of the unconscious mind.

Counterwishes: Anxiety Dreams

If dreams are indeed wish fulfillments, then why do we sometimes dream dreams that apparently run counter to our most cherished desires? Indeed, why do our dreams sometimes contain elements of our most dreaded fears? To answer these questions, and to account for the apparent contradiction, we must ask a further question: "*Whose* wish is fulfilled by a dream?"

> No doubt a wish-fulfillment must bring pleasure; but the question then arises "To whom?" To the person who has the wish of course. But as we know, a dreamer's relation to his wishes is a quite peculiar one. He repudiates them and censors them— he has no liking for them, in short. So that their fulfillment will give him no pleasure, but just the opposite; and experience shows that this opposite appears in the form of anxiety.... *Thus a dreamer in his relation to his dream-wishes can only be compared to an amalgamation of two separate people who are linked by some important common element.* (Freud, 1900, pp. 580–581; this passage was added as a footnote in 1919; the same paragraph is included in Freud, 1916, pp. 215–216; italics added)

The amalgamated personage referred to in this passage describes, of course, the conflicting relationship between the dreamer's *unconscious*, the source of the wish, and the *preconscious* censorship agency, the source of the repudiation. Thus although the wish fulfillment embodied in the dream brings pleasure to the unconscious, the anxiety element introduced by the distortion of the dream work is meant to satisfy the ever-watchful censor. Freud employed a clever analogy to describe how a wish could bring both pleasure and unpleasure simultaneously:

A good fairy promised a poor married couple to grant them the fulfillment of their first three wishes. They were delighted, and made up their minds to choose their three wishes carefully. But a smell of sausages being fried in the cottage next door tempted the woman to wish for a couple of them. They were there in a flash; and this was the first wish-fulfillment. But the man was furious, and in his rage wished that the sausages were hanging on his wife's nose. This happened too; and the sausages were not to be dislodged from their new position. This was the second wish-fulfillment; *but the wish was the man's, and its fulfillment was most disagreeable for his wife.* You know the rest of the story. Since after all they were in fact one—man and wife—the third wish was bound to be that the sausages should come away from the woman's nose . . . *if two people are not at one with each other the fulfillment of a wish of one of them may bring nothing but unpleasure to the other.* (Freud, 1900, p. 581; italics added)

If we conceive of the mind as divided between the two agencies—the unconscious pleasure-seeking system, and the preconscious censorship system—the compromise nature of anxiety dreams becomes apparent. On the one hand, the unconscious is allowed *some* expression and *some* satisfaction of its repressed urges in the dream. On the other hand, the ethical arm of personality is allowed *some* control over the unacceptability of the wishes (Freud, 1900, p. 581). *Dreams, just like neurotic symptoms, are compromise formations that allow both an outlet for the discharge of the wish's tension and a censorship mechanisms to repudiate the now gratified, but still unacceptable, wish.*

Repression and the Unpleasure Principle

Consider once again the state of human infants. Striving to obtain satisfaction for their needs and to avoid the unpleasure of mounting somatic tension, infants soon learn the distinction between a fantasied and a real satisfier. Frustration and unpleasure are the tutors in a curriculum that includes the lessons that fantasied food cannot be eaten, hallucinatory milk cannot be drunk, and an ephemeral mother cannot be cuddled. In order to survive, the infant must learn that the wish fulfillments embodied in dream states and fantasies have to be pursued in reality. When *real* satisfactions for its desires are not forthcoming, the infant experiences psychological and sometimes bodily pain that Freud termed *unpleasure*. Conversely, when the unconscious obtains gratification of its desires, the result is the physical and mental state of *pleasure*.

A further set of lessons, however, must be mastered to ensure a comfortable and safe existence. This "unpleasure principle" is a two-edged sword, not only motivating naive infants to avoid the discomfort of hallucinatory need satisfaction, but also pressing on their awareness the importance of *actively avoiding painful or noxious stimulation* as well. Hence, the newly developed *preconscious* reality-scanning system may operate to promote escape or flight from certain forms of excitation when, on the basis of past experience, it recognizes some stimuli as potentially threatening. This class of unpleasure-producing stimuli might include, for example, as the child matures, lighted matches, hot radiators, and angry-in-the-mood-for-a-spanking mother.

Furthermore, even in the internal, *mental representations* of such stimuli would trigger avoidance responses in the mental apparatus. But in the case of internal stimulation, the mental apparatus cannot engage in the physical act of flight. Instead, mental withdrawal occurs that takes the form of a removal of *cathexis*[1] (charges of mental energy, or the diversion of attention) from the *memory image* of the noxious stimulus. In brief, this "ostrich policy" is the prototype of the mechanism of repression.

THE REALITY PRINCIPLE

The infant's newest mental attainment under the tutelage of the unpleasure principle is the ability to delay the motor activity that is normally employed in obtaining gratification. The infant will now wait until there is a clear indication of reality from the preconscious perceptual system. It is this reality-testing orientation to the world that provides the infant with a reliable income of pleasure. We might, therefore, redefine a wish in these terms: *A wish is a quantity of unpleasurable excitation resulting from a need that can be completely satisfied only by a real object or by specific and instrumental activity in the external world.*

Thus infants' intercourse with the world is governed not only by the pleasure-unpleasure principle, but by the *reality principle* as well. With the adoption of this more sophisticated mental strategy, external reality increases in importance in the economy of the infants' mental lives, along with the rising significance they now attach to their sense organs. Infants will gradually increase the use of their senses to scan the environment for appropriate objects of satisfaction demanded by the reality principle (Freud, 1911, p. 220).

Primary and Secondary Process Thought

Our description of the unpleasure and reality principles is incomplete because their joint functioning is more complicated than this rigidly dualistic picture might suggest. The unconscious system, for example, apparently knows no bounds to its wishfulness, and it is well satisfied with only hallucinatory wish satisfaction. Behaving as if reality did not exist, the unconscious does not by itself discriminate between real and fantasied objects. Its only interest is in the distinction between pleasure and unpleasure. Moreover, as revealed in manifest dreams and in neurotic symptoms, the unconscious system's sum total of mental energy is highly mobile and capable of all sorts of shifts, condensations, and displacements. All of these mental acrobatics are, of course, directed to the attainment of satisfaction *at all cost.* Freud characterized this state of affairs in the unconscious as *primary process thinking.* The chief characteristics of

---

[1] The term *cathexis* is a translation of a German term Freud had first used in his "Project for a Scientific Psychology" (1895). The project was a detailed neurological model of the mind in which Freud postulated coordinated systems of neurons with the brain as the basis of various psychological processes, including repression and dreams. Certain of the neurons in this model become permeable to the flow of energy (electrochemical discharges) within the nervous system and they "fill up" with quantities of it. Freud used the German word *Besetzung*, which roughly means "to fill up," or "to occupy," in describing the flow of energy in and out of the neurons. His translators converted the German word to the more technical sounding *cathexis* from a Greek root meaning "to hold on to." Freud abandoned the neurological model, but not the analogous idea of psychic energy systems that could fill up and discharge their quantities of energy, that is, their cathexis of excitation. (See Chapter 4 for a discussion of Freud's neurological model.)

primary process thinking are the urgency with which tension reduction is sought, the plasticity or mobility of its energy, and its disregard for reality.

In contrast to the primary process functioning of the unconscious system, the preconscious system operates in accord with the reality principle by delaying gratification until appropriate moments. This kind of mental functioning, characterized by an *interest in the demands of reality* and an ability to *delay gratification*, Freud termed *secondary process thinking*. Because secondary process mental functioning develops later than primary process thinking, and because such reality-oriented mental activity is characteristic of truly adult thought, Freud considered secondary process thought to be a clear developmental advance over primary process functioning. Of course, during dreams, even the most mature adult regresses to primary process thought as the unconscious system gains control of the mental apparatus.

THE MEANINGS OF *UNCONSCIOUS* IN PSYCHOANALYSIS

The way in which Freud had used the term "unconscious" in his early writings led to some confusion about the reasons for which an idea might be removed from consciousness. Freud, therefore, distinguished three ways in which the term unconscious was used in psychoanalysis.

The first meaning, indicating the existence of ideas that are not *now*—at this precise moment—in consciousness, is a purely *descriptive* one. Thus, for example, although few of us keep our own phone number in the forefront of our minds at every minute of the day, we can nevertheless recall that item when necessary. Our phone number is only temporarily out of immediate awareness. There is no a priori reason why it cannot be brought into consciousness at will. Such items that can easily be made conscious are conceptualized as residing in the preconscious system (Freud, 1912, p. 262). Hence, this first meaning of "unconscious" is *descriptive* of those occasions when the limitations of consciousness and the human attention span necessitate the simple omission of some content.

In contrast with this purely descriptive sense, there are memories of early childhood incidents, impulses, and desires that are unacceptable to the conscious ego and cannot be recalled no matter how great the effort. Such memories are *repressed* from consciousness. Hysterical symptoms owe their existence to such unconscious ideas that, despite their intensity and their activity, remain apart from conscious awareness. *Repressed memories are never admitted to consciousness so long as repression operates successfully.* Because this meaning of unconscious indicates the forceful and energetic activity of ideas not in consciousness and implies the continual expenditure of energy required to keep them out of awareness, it is called the *dynamic* meaning (Freud, 1912, pp. 263–264). (Freud employed another explanatory term in connection with the concept of a dynamic unconscious. He would often refer to the fact that a dynamic conception of the energy which is required to keep a thought repressed raised questions of an *economic* nature, that is, of attempts to *quantify* various degrees of energy expenditure [1923a, p. 14].)

Last, Freud's investigations of dream processes had revealed that there are at least two types of mental functioning: the primary and secondary processes. The unconscious is characterized by the high mobility of its cathexes of energy as evidenced in its ability to condense, displace, and distort ideas. Furthermore, the unconscious responds to the demands of the pleasure principle by its continual press for immediate gratification of wishes, in contrast with the delayed, inhibitory, reality-testing orientation of the preconscious. In consequence, the unconscious must be conceptualized as a unique *system* operating in accordance with its own local rules of conduct side by side with the other systems of the mind that, likewise, operate in conformity with their intrinsic standards of conduct. This usage of the word "unconscious" conveys the *systematic* meaning of the term, indicating the independent status of the unconscious as a system among systems.

In summary, Freud distinguished among three meanings of the term "unconscious": the descriptive, the dynamic, and the systematic. Each of these usages might be thought of as corresponding to a question: *What* is unconscious? (*descriptive*); *Why* is it unconscious? (*dynamic*); and *Where* is the unconscious idea? (*systematic*).

The Concept of "Metapsychology"

The complexity of the term unconscious led Freud to the useful strategy of distinguishing among its separate but interrelated meanings. Using a similar approach, Freud now began to distinguish among the various facets of any psychological event. He resurrected a term from his earlier work to describe the process of conceptualizing mental processes from multiple viewpoints simultaneously. *Metapsychology* was the technical term to be used whenever a psychological process was understood from its descriptive, systematic, and dynamic aspects. Unfortunately, Freud introduced some confusion into the concept by changing his vocabulary each time he wrote about metapsychology (cf. Freud, 1915c, p. 181; 1933, pp. 70 ff.).

The *systematic* meaning was sometimes identified as the *topographic* viewpoint, indicating not only Freud's conception of different systems but also that he viewed the systems as spatially arrayed. At this point in his career, Freud pictured the unconscious, preconscious, and conscious systems as three adjacent compartments (see 1900, Chapter 7). Hence, the topographic viewpoint referred not only to the unique properties of a particular system of the mind but also to its particular location with respect to the other systems and the paths of its access to consciousness at any moment in time.

In a similar way, Freud enlarged the meaning of the term *dynamic* by suggesting that not only are there competing and conflicting forces behind psychological processes but also that the relative magnitudes or quantities of energy may be measurable. Hence, the term *economic* was coined to indicate the differing degrees of intensity with which dynamic interactions take place (1915c, p. 180).

To complicate matters further, other psychoanalysts point to another component of metapsychology inherent in Freud's way of understanding behavior. Any symptom, dream, or act has a psychological history within the chronology of a person's life. By reconstructing the many events (or memories of them) that coalesced into

TABLE 3.1   Components of Freud's Metapsychology

Metapsychological Viewpoint	Clinical Referent
1. Descriptive	Momentary absence from awareness of particular ideas or feelings that can easily be made conscious at will.
2. Systematic (or Topographic)	Special quality of a mental event due to the unique characteristics of the psychological system in which it originates, presently occupies, or to which it has access by virtue of its location.
3. Dynamic	Energetic mobility of the competing, conflicting forces that prevent an idea or feeling from becoming conscious, or allow it to enter awareness only in disguised form.
4. Economic	Relative intensities or quantities of the competing dynamic forces, and their changes in strength over time.
5. Genetic	Reconstruction of the multiple origins of any psychological event in the life history of the person.
6. Adaptive	Degree to which a psychological process or act functions in resolving unconscious conflicts and in the healthy management of life events.

one mental process, the ultimate origins of symptoms, ideas, beliefs, resistances, feelings, and so on are reached. This life history viewpoint is what Freud called the *genetic* approach, and it constitutes another facet of metapsychology (A. Freud, 1969a, p. 153).

Finally, analysts who followed Freud have also stressed the nonconflictive aspects of some psychological events. Thus Hartmann (1939, 1964) emphasized the *adaptive* quality of psychological processes that function not only to resolve individuals' personal conflicts but serve them in a healthy way to fit comfortably into the life they and their environment create. Hence, the adaptive viewpoint is added alongside the others as a component of metapsychology.

It is clear that the Freudian way of viewing any human event requires attention to the complex interplay of a host of determinants. Metapsychology requires that the human person be regarded as an intricate, but understandable, organism. The various facets of metapsychology are summarized in Table 3.1.

METAPSYCHOLOGY OF REPRESSION

Repression, you may recall, is the way in which the mental apparatus deals with wishful impulses from which physical flight is impossible. Instead, these unescapable and unacceptable impulses are denied direct access to awareness. Consider the paradox involved in proposing a mechanism like repression. Wishful impulses demand satisfaction because when it is forthcoming, the experience of pleasure is the usual result. But in the case of a repressed impulse, something has happened to a wishful idea that makes satisfaction so *unpleasurable* that denial of its existence is the only means of dealing with it. Yet, paradoxically, the impulse continues to press for release.

It thus seems that one of the preconditions for an impulse to be subject to repression is that satisfaction of the impulse be simultaneously pleasurable and unpleasurable. The only way to account for this disparity of aims is to assume that the reason a repressed impulse has been denied release into consciousness is because its satisfaction would create pleasure for one mental system at the expense of the even more grave unpleasure evoked in a competing system. Here, of course, we have the conflict between the unconscious wishful demands and conscious restraint.

A Balance of Pleasure and Unpleasure

Freud clearly conceived of repression as the expression of a *balance* between these two motives: *the seeking after pleasure* and the *avoidance of unpleasure*. In the case of a repressed impulse, however, the motive force of unpleasure is more intense than the pleasure to be obtained from satisfaction of the impulse. Repression occurs, consequently, when the balance between pleasure and unpleasure is tipped in the direction of unpleasure.

The process of repression requires that the preconscious system prevent the emergence of the unconscious impulse into awareness by withdrawing a sum of mental energy (cathexis) from the offending impulse. However, having lost the cathexis of the preconscious, the unacceptable impulse may still retain the cathexis of energy from the unconscious, where it originated. Consequently, the repressed impulse can continue to make assaults on the preconscious system indefinitely, drawing on its reserve of energy in the unconscious. The simple expedient of withdrawing preconscious energy from the impulse is not sufficient to prevent the impulse from unendingly repeating its attempts at entry into consciousness (Freud, 1915c, p. 180).

What is needed to accomplish the permanent subjugation of the impulse is another, opposing quantity of energy, strong enough to resist the unconsciously endowed impulse's cathexis of energy. Such an opposing supply of energy would, in effect, serve as a barrier against the reemergence of the rejected impulse. Freud called this barrier that is set up by the preconscious an *anticathexis*. Anticathexis is the primary mode of dealing with unacceptable unconscious content. Clearly, to enable repression to remain effective, an anticathexis requires a *continual* expenditure of energy by the preconscious.

Primal Repression and Repression Proper

With the development of the theoretical concept of anticathexis, Freud could account for the creation and presence of repressed derivatives in consciousness, like symptoms and seduction fantasies. He now conceived of repression as a two-stage process to effect this theoretical advance.

In the first stage, the ideational representative of the unacceptable impulse is denied access to consciousness by the preconscious setting up an anticathexis as a barrier. The first stage is called *primal repression. The immediate result of primal repression is that the repressed idea or impulse is fixated or frozen in development.* No further modification or maturation of the repressed content can occur (Freud, 1915b, p. 148). Significant acts of primal repression occur during the first six or eight years of life, and in their role of immobilized, unconscious memories they become important sensitizing or predisposing factors for later acts of adult repression.

The second stage of repression is called *repression proper*, and it is directed against any derivatives or associates of the originally repressed impulses that may enter consciousness. Repression proper is rather like an "after pressure," to use Freud's descriptive phrase, whereby ideas, trains of thought, or perceptions that are associatively linked to the primally repressed impulse are also denied access to consciousness. *Repression proper consists of the preconscious system's withdrawing its cathexis* (energy) *from the derivative.* Repression proper thus cooperates with primal repression to ensure that unacceptable impulses and associated ideas remain out of consciousness awareness.

Thus repression is not a unitary act. Or, more precisely, repressions of primal derivatives that occur after infancy depend on the mass of primally repressed impulses *already* present in the unconscious. An idea or an impulse cannot be removed from awareness by repression proper *unless there has already been an act of predisposing primal repression to exert a "pulling effect" on subsequent derivatives.* At the same time, the preconscious system actively strives from its vantage point on the threshold of awareness to eject these offending ideas by pushing them away from consciousness (cf. Freud, 1900, p. 547n.).

INSTINCTS OF THE UNCONSCIOUS

Terms like "excitation," "impulse," "wish," and "tension," dating almost from the very beginning of Freud's psychological writing, were replaced in his later work by the term *instinct*.

In his 1915 metapsychological paper, "Instincts and Their Vicissitudes," Freud carefully delineated the meaning of the term in psychoanalysis. First, Freud distinguished between a stimulus and an instinct by pointing out that physical stimuli impinge on the organism from the external environment, whereas instinctual urges develop from within the organism. Although the organism, through the use of reflexes, may escape or even terminate *external stimulation, internal instinctual* demand cannot be escaped by flight. An organism cannot flee the demands of its own body.

A second distinguishing feature of instinct Freud pointed out is that stimulation originating in the environment is only *temporary* in its impact on the organism. Instinctual, internal excitation is *constant*, terminating only when the tissue need that gives rise to the instinct is satisfied. Thus instincts may be thought of as needs seeking appropriate satisfactions (Freud, 1915a, p. 119).

Freud returned in his discussion of instinct to an earlier idea of his and Breuer's of the nervous system as an apparatus that functions to reduce stimulation and excitation to the lowest possible level. In Freud's view, the nervous system is assigned the task of "mastering stimuli" by discharging excitation almost as soon as it builds up (1915a, p. 120). Called the "principle of constancy" by Breuer and Freud, this idea of repeated returns to some optimal state of minimum arousal is similar to the modern biologist's concept of homeostasis. It follows, in consequence, that this essential task is complicated in the case of an instinct because the nervous system cannot master instinctual demands by the expedient of flight. Furthermore, because the nervous system is governed by the pleasure principle—the seeking after pleasure by the discharge of unpleasurable mounting tension—instincts must not be dealt with in a way that merely avoids their demand; the nervous system must find a way to reduce the biological deficit (or to satisfy the urge) that the demand represents.

For Freud, then, the concept of instinct was both a psychological and a biological one, a "frontier concept" on the border between bodily and mental phenomena. *An instinct is a mental representation of a physical or bodily need* (1915a, p. 122).

CHARACTERISTICS OF INSTINCTS

Freud distinguished four characteristics of an instinct.

Pressure

The amount of force or strength of the demand made by the instinct on the mind is described as *pressure*. Thus, for example, deprivation of food for 24 hours produces greater instinctual pressure (hunger) than deprivation for only four hours. A 24-hour-deprived individual is more strongly impelled to seek food, think about food, and to devour it, when food is available, than he or she would be after only four hours without a meal.

Aim

Instinctual impulses all strive toward one goal: satisfaction or tension reduction. Whereas satisfaction is clearly the universal *aim* of an instinct, a given instinct may operate to achieve its aim in differing ways, as circumstances dictate. Freud distinguishes, therefore, between *ultimate aim*, the immediate gratification of demand, and *intermediate aim*, the devious, roundabout, or substitute forms of satisfaction for which an instinct may strive when blocked from a directly suitable goal. The sexual instinct is particularly prone to this widening of its aims. For example, the aim of the sexual instincts is "organ pleasure," a pleasing sensation attached to a particular part of the body when stimulated. With maturation, the sexual instincts become focused on the aim of reproduction (Freud, 1915a, p. 126). The path from the goal of diffuse pleasurable sensation in infancy to the stage of genital primary at puberty is a long and tedious journey.

Object

To obtain its ultimate aim of satisfaction, the instinct must seek some concrete, usually external, *object* that has the power to reduce its tension. For example, an infant's hunger drive is directed toward the object of food; for the sexually aroused individual, an appealing member of the opposite sex is the appropriate and satisfying object.

However, the object of an instinct is its most variable characteristic. Appropriate objects may be changed many times during the course of the instinct's vicissitudes. Thus displacement from one satisfying object to another, a process so characteristic of the wish fulfillments in dreams, is possible. Prisoners, for example, confined with members of their own sex often resort to masturbation or to homosexual gratification as substitutes for heterosexual satisfaction, only to return to exclusive heterosexual gratification upon release.

Conversely, it is equally possible for a single object to satisfy several instincts simultaneously. Thus thumb sucking may partially alleviate the infant's hunger, soothe teething discomfort, and also provide pleasurable stimulation as a prelude to shutting out the world before sleep.

Source

The origin of all instincts, as we have seen, is to be sought in the physical-chemical processes of the body. These processes give rise to the tissue needs of the organism that make their demands felt in the mental operations that guide much of our behavior. The sexual instincts, for example, have their *source* in the genital zone of the body (and in some central nervous system activities); the hunger instinct originates in the viscera (and also in some parts of the central nervous system). It was Freud's opinion, however, that physical and chemical processes were beyond the scope of psychology.

DUALISTIC DIVISION OF THE INSTINCTS: HUNGER VERSUS LOVE

It is clear that Freud viewed the instincts, though biologically based, as essentially malleable and plastic in the course of an organism's life history. During their collision with life's circumstances, the instincts may undergo modifications or reversals of expression. These vicissitudes, to use Freud's translators' term, share the common motive of avoiding the psychological or biological discomfort that would result from free, undisguised expression of an instinctual urge. Repression, as we have seen, is one of the vicissitudes that an instinct may undergo.

Although instincts may be expressed and satisfied in diverse ways, Freud was hesitant to catalog a seemingly infinite list of biological demands and their mental representatives. Instead, he proposed a concise, bipolar division of all instincts into two great classes: instincts in the service of the preservation of the individual's life, and instincts directed toward the attainment of pleasure. *Life maintenance and pleasure*—these are poles around which the operations of the mental apparatus are organized.

According to this dualistic scheme, Freud asserted that the ego was the seat of the organism's instincts for self-preservation, whereas striving for pleasure was a function of the child's developing sexual equipment. Though Freud did not provide a name for the energy of the ego instincts, he employed the term *libido* to denote the energy of the sexual or pleasure instincts (e.g., 1916, p. 313). Libido, to reiterate an important concept, was to be broadly conceived as general pleasurable stimulation rather than as restricted to genital, sexual pleasure. Thus Freud's original dualistic classification of the instincts pitted the ego instincts against the sexual (pleasure) instincts: survival versus libido.

The ego instincts have as their main goal the preservation and continuance of the safety and bodily integrity of the *individual*. Sexual (pleasure) instincts, on the other hand, are directed to the preservation of the *species*. Consequently, in Freud's original dualism, the ego instincts are individual-centered and the sexual instincts are, ultimately, species-centered. This dichotomy, Freud pointed out, is roughly similar to the division between *hunger* (individual self-preservation) and *love* (other-centered pleasure).

Freud introduced this division of the instincts in a paper in 1910 (1910b, p. 214; see editor's footnote), and he maintained the dualism of which he was so fond for a number of years. The bulk of his writing in subsequent years, however, was focused on the sexual instincts with the effect of obscuring by neglect the role of the ego instincts. But the ego instincts were to come into their own in psychoanalysis as Freud's clinical practice revealed some disconcerting anomalies and violations of the dualistic hunger-love scheme.

Exceptions to the Hunger-Love Model: Narcissism

In the dualistic conception of the instincts, libido, the energy of the sexual or pleasure instincts, should be a separate quantity from that of the ego instincts. Freud noted a disconcerting exception to this separation hypothesis in the case of some psychotic patients.

One of the main characteristics of some forms of schizophrenia is the withdrawal of the patients' interest from the external world. They behave as if reality no longer existed and in every way as though only their own ideas, feelings, or urges mattered. Freud's instinct theory would characterize such withdrawal as the retraction of libido from external objects and persons. Simultaneously with this retraction of libido, however, there occurs what seems to be an *expansion* of ego instinctual energy, an increase in the ego's self-interest. In short, psychotics overvalue their own ideas, their own bodies, their own person. Why should this reciprocal increase in ego instinct occur at the same time as outwardly directed libido is diminished—unless the two forms of energy are *not* separate? Freud had to conclude that libido could be turned back on the ego and that libido could donate to the ego's disposal some of the energy normally expended outwardly:

> The libido that has been withdrawn from the external world has been directed to the ego and thus gives rise to an attitude which may be called narcissism. (1914a, p. 75)

Clearly the energies of the ego and sexual instincts are not separate. They commingle, one drawing on the reserves of the other at various times. Freud had thus introduced a new distinction into his theory of instincts. He postulated that in the earliest stages of life there is a supply of libidinal energy in the ego that produces a primary state of narcissism or self-love. It is from this pool of primary ego libido that the later, external object libido emerges. But the original pool of ego libido remains in the ego, and it is this supply that is expanded or contracted in the narcissism of psychosis. In consequence, ego instinctual energy and sexual instinctual energy are not completely independent, but initially emerge from a common pool. Thus in the beginning all instinctual energy was one, libido. Later developments cause the differentiation into ego libido and object libido.

Freud had thus revised his dualistic notion of the instincts, altering the nature of the conflict from that of a clash between ego instincts and sexual instincts to that of a clash between two forms of libido: *ego libido* conflicts with *object libido*. This seemingly unitary or monistic scheme of instinctual energy is more apparent than it is real. Freud was fond of dualistic, bipolar explanations of events and certainly ego and object libido fit the favored pattern. Yet even this partial dualism did not satisfy Freud, and he ultimately would again revise his conception of the instincts.

Return to a Dualism: Life Against Death

By considering the narcissistic pool of ego libido the primal source of all significant interactions with the world, Freud had virtually erected libido as the unitary scheme of explanation. He was not, as some of his critics accused, attempting to sexualize all human behavior. His distinction between the self-preservation nature of ego libido and the pleasure-seeking orientation of object libido had maintained and paralleled his original division between ego and sexual instincts. But the problem for Freud was that his clinical experience had uncovered the essentially conflict-ridden nature of human behavior and neurosis. A unitary scheme of instinctual dynamics based solely on libido deprived psychoanalytic theory of the ability to specify the elements of the conflict precisely. What was needed was a new dualistic scheme in which libido (both object and ego libido) could be contrasted against some other, independent pool of instinctual energy.

In 1920, Freud solved the problem. He published a startlingly speculative account of a profoundly revised instinct theory whereby libido was contrasted with a newly discerned instinctual energy, the *death instinct*. Thus Freud returned to a dualistic

FIGURE 3.1   Freud's changing views of the instincts.

1. ORIGINAL DUALISM: HUNGER-LOVE

EGO INSTINCTS   *versus*   SEX INSTINCTS (libido)

Individual self-preservation   Species-preservation
(hunger)   *(love, pleasure)*

2. QUASI-UNITARY SCHEME: EGO AND OBJECT LIBIDO

PRIMARY NARCISSISTIC LIBIDO

Ego libido (self-love)   Object libido (other love)
(self-preservation)   *(species-preservation)*

3. FINAL DUALISM: LIFE-DEATH

EROS: THE SEX INSTINCT   *versus*   THANATOS: THE DEATH INSTINCT
(libido)   *(aggression)*
Ego libido ⟷ Object libido   Self-directed   Other-directed

conception of mental energy. At the same time, he traveled beyond his earlier model of the mind by transcending even the seemingly secure dominance of the pleasure principle. For in revising his instinct theory, Freud replaced the pleasure principle as the fundamental mental rule with an even more basic "law," the *compulsion to repeat*. It is no wonder that Freud entitled the book in which he made these radical, and for some psychoanalysts disturbing, revelations *Beyond the Pleasure Principle*. Consequently, we turn now to a survey of the evidence on which Freud predicated his final, most radical revision. It may be of some help to refer to Figure 3.1 to obtain an overview of the sequence of changes in Freud's three revisions of his instinct theory.

A PHYLOGENETIC FANTASY: "PATHOLOGY RECAPITULATES PHYLOGENY"

Freud's metapsychology was to serve as the cherished core of his theorizing for the remainder of his career and as the ultimate critical target for skeptics and supporters alike. Of the group of "metapsychology" papers dating to the period from 1914 to 1915, only five were published by Freud over the space of about three years. He had intended to publish 12 such papers as chapters in a book, but until recently the fate of the missing papers had remained somewhat of a mystery, moderated only by the assumption that Freud had, for reasons of his own, destroyed the seven unpublished papers (see Silverstein, 1986, 1989a for an account of Freud's dissatisfaction with this series of papers and his possible motives in withholding them from publication). In 1983, Ilse Grubrich-Simitis (1987) was searching through a trunk of papers in preparation for an edition of Freud's correspondence with Sandor Ferenczi, his longtime friend and colleague, when she discovered a draft of the twelfth paper in Freud's own handwriting that he had apparently sent to Ferenczi as part of their correspondence.

Why Freud withheld this and the other papers of this series from publication is still unclear, but the content of this paper suggests that its editors appropriately chose Freud's own description of the work to entitle it a "Phylogenetic Fantasy." For in this singular essay, intended to be the last chapter of a 12-chapter book, Freud permits his imagination and creativity full expression, sketching themes that were to occupy him at length some years later in *Beyond the Pleasure Principle*, a work we will pursue shortly. Very little of the essay is grounded in empirical observation or anthropological evidence, and some of the ideas depend upon a Lamarckian view of evolution.

Transference and Narcissistic "Neuroses"

The central argument of the paper is a distinction that Freud had made for some time between the transference and narcissistic "neuroses." The term *neurosis* was used by Freud and others at this period as a rough synonym for psychopathology rather than in the contemporary sense that we discussed in Chapter 1. The *transference neuroses* correspond closely to what we now would describe as anxiety disorders or neuroses: anxiety hysteria (i.e., generalized anxiety disorder), conversion hysteria, and obsessive-compulsive disorder. People with a transference neurosis can form more or less intimate "object attachments," that is, engage in more or less conflicted interpersonal relationships because their libido is not totally narcissistically invested and may thus be directed outwardly to other people. By contrast, the *narcissistic neuroses* included the very severe pathologies of psychosis (dementia praecox or what is now termed schizophrenia, the paranoid disorders, and the major mood disorders of manic-depression or bipolar disorder; see Chapter 1). None of these disorders would now receive the label "neurotic," because their level of severity precludes intact reality testing and includes totally disrupted interpersonal relationships. Freud noted that the person with a narcissistic "neurosis" could not form object attachments, withdrawing protectively instead into a private, sometimes psychotic, inner realm. In such disorders, libido is turned inward, unable to "cathect" (attach to) external "objects" (people).

Freud proposes that the transference and narcissistic neuroses form a chronology that parallels and recapitulates in individual development the evolutionary development of the human race. Specifically, he proposed that if the transference and narcissistic neuroses are arranged according to the developmental period in which they typically occur, a pattern emerges that parallels evolutionary development:

> . . . anxiety hysteria, almost without precondition, is the earliest [neurosis], closely followed by conversion hysteria (from about the fourth year); somewhat later in prepuberty (9–10) obsessional neurosis appears in children. The narcissistic neuroses are absent in childhood. Of these, dementia praecox [schizophrenia] in classic form is [an] illness of the puberty years, paranoia approaches the mature years, and melancholia-mania the same time period, otherwise not specifiable. (Freud, 1915d, p. 12)

Of course, Freud was wrong about the absence of the narcissistic "neuroses" (especially schizophrenia) in childhood, but that was the prevailing view in his day. Nevertheless, he argued that each characteristic neurosis represents a "regression" to:

> phases that the whole human race had to go through at some time from the beginning to the end of the Ice Age, so that at that time all human beings were the way only some of them are today, by virtue of hereditary tendency and by means of new acquisition. (Freud, 1915d, p. 13)

Pathology Recapitulates Phylogeny

Freud proposed that our ancestors' social and biological evolution proceeded in six phases that are recapitulated in six chronologically arranged transference and narcissistic "neuroses":

1.   ANXIETY HYSTERIA = REALISTIC ANXIETY: Because of the privations of scarce food and the hardships of subsistence survival in a world they little understood at the approach of the Ice Age, humankind experienced realistic anxiety. The ego turned inward, abandoning interest in external objects in favor of investing energy in individual survival. New experiences were anticipated as threatening, just as in the developmentally earliest neurosis of Anxiety Hysteria seen in children.

2.   CONVERSION HYSTERIA = RESTRICTED PROCREATION: With the passage of time, early humans felt their existence increasingly threatened to the point at which the two instincts of self-preservation and species preservation through procreation came into conflict. Insufficient food supplies, Freud argued, forced primal humans to reduce

their numbers by abstaining from sex, by killing newborns, and by "perverse" (i.e., nonreproductive) satisfactions of the ungratified sexual instincts. Women were more affected than men, "who were less concerned about the consequences of sexual intercourse" (Freud, 1915d, p. 15). This state of affairs corresponds to Conversion Hysteria, which Freud and others regarded as at least partially caused by self-imposed sexual prohibitions and sexual guilt. Freud also thought for a time prior to his structural model that dammed-up libido could be transformed into anxiety.

3.   OBSESSIONAL NEUROSIS = MAGICAL OMNIPOTENCE OF THOUGHT: As evolution continued, pressures to adapt affected males to a greater degree than females (Freud, 1915d, p. 15). Intelligence increased and survival placed a premium on learning how to investigate causes and understand a hostile world to increase the chance of survival. Language developed and words and thoughts must have seemed magical. Thoughts were omnipotent as if ideas and words were as real as the things they represented. Inanimate objects and nature were invested animistically with spirits and feelings. These primitive techniques of understanding and controlling the world made the males feel, however unrealistically, all-powerful. "As a reward for his power to safeguard the lives of so many other helpless ones [early man] bestowed upon himself unrestrained dominance over them. . . . " (Freud, 1915d, p. 15). Early men came to believe, according to Freud, that they were invulnerable and that their "possession of women must not be challenged." By the end of this epoch, the human race splintered into hordes that were dominated by the "strong" and the "wise" brutal man acting as the authoritarian father figure to the whole horde. Obsessional neurosis thus recapitulates this phase of evolution in its overemphasis on thinking, the belief in the omnipotence of the obsessive thoughts to make things happen, and belief in the power of ritual.

4.   SCHIZOPHRENIA = LIBIDO EXTINGUISHED BY CASTRATION: After the development of the "primal hordes," a second generation of sons of the primal father emerged. This second generation was jealous of the domineering primal father who castrates them to prevent their competing with him for possession of the women. The castrated sons remain in the horde as "harmless laborers" whose libido is "extinguished." They no longer pose a sexual threat of competition to the primal father and, like the schizophrenic person (narcissistic neurotic), become withdrawn, isolated, and uninterested in others, especially females. Freud thought that this phase of evolution was especially recapitulated by hebephrenic schizophrenia because the hebephrenic schizophrenic person "gives up every love object" and returns to an exclusively autoerotic state of absolute narcissism. Hallucinations, thinking disorders, and speech peculiarities typical of this kind of schizophrenia, Freud argued, are "restitutive attempts" or desperate efforts on the part of the contemporary schizophrenic patient to restore the lost love object (1915d, p. 17).

5.   PARANOIA = HOMOSEXUAL ALLIANCE OF THE SONS: Eventually the generation of sons learned to avoid castration by fleeing the horde sometime before puberty, and formed their own alliance to survive. Living together in this all male society brought "social feelings" to the surface, which may have been founded by sublimating the only avenue of sexual expression left to them. "The social feelings that originated here, sublimated from homosexuality, became mankind's lasting possession, however, and the basis for every later society" (Freud, 1915d, p. 18). This phase of evolution is recapitulated by paranoid schizophrenia and other paranoid disorders, Freud suggested,

because in paranoia "secret alliances are not lacking, and the persecutor plays a tremendous role. Paranoia tries to ward off homosexuality, which was the basis for the organization of brothers, and in so doing must drive the victim out of society and destroy his social sublimations" (Freud, 1915d, p. 18).

6.   MANIC-DEPRESSION = KILLING THE PRIMAL FATHER: The members of the allied but exiled clan of sons eventually overpower and kill the primal father because fundamentally they share an identification with him, and their mixture of elation and sadness is thus a kind of narcissistic mourning for the loss of self while celebrating the restoration of their power and its rewards. This moment in phylogenetic history is recapitulated by the narcissistic pathology of adulthood known to Freud as manic-depressive psychosis: a succession of moods from expansive elation to profound melancholy.

Freud summarized his speculations:

> If the dispositions to the three transference neuroses [anxiety hysteria, conversion hysteria, obsessional neurosis] were acquired in the struggle with the exigencies of the Ice Age, then the fixations that underlie the narcissistic neuroses [dementia praecox or schizophrenia, paranoia and manic-depression] originate from the oppression by the father. . . . As the first struggle [castration of the sons] leads to the patriarchal stage of civilization, the second [alliance of the sons] (leads) to the social; but from both come the fixations which in their return after millennia become the disposition of the two groups of neuroses. Also in this sense neurosis is therefore a cultural acquisition. (1915d, p. 19)

Transitional Summary

What can we make of Freud's speculations? Certainly they are of a piece with his speculations along evolutionary lines in such works as *Totem and Taboo* and *Beyond the Pleasure Principle*. And, of course, they are fraught with biological, psychological, and anthropological errors and omissions. Nevertheless, they represent an imaginative attempt to bring order to a wealth of observations in a way that was consistent with Freud's central vision of metapsychology as the overarching theory of psychoanalysis as a science. In essence, Freud was here letting his imagination extend the biologist Haeckel's dictum ("Ontogeny recapitulates phylogeny"—development of the individual embryo parallels the stages of human evolution) with his own version: *pathology recapitulates phylogeny*. Freud apparently restrained his imagination and philosophical yearnings for a while after 1917. But by 1920, Freud was again ready to give his powers of speculation and creativity free rein, and the metapsychology took another leap forward with *Beyond the Pleasure Principle*.

BEHAVIORS BEYOND THE PLEASURE PRINCIPLE: THE CLINICAL EVIDENCE

Ernst's "Gone" Game

At one and a half years, Freud's eldest grandson, Ernst, played a strangely symbolic game. He would momentarily take hold of any available small object, throw it into a corner of the room or under the bed, and croon loudly the German word for "gone" (*fort*) with a peculiarly long, drawn-out "o-o-o-o" pronunciation. Immediately upon throwing his toys away from himself, Ernst would retrieve them only long enough, it seemed to Freud, to begin the dispersal again. Freud soon realized that the sole use Ernst made of his toys was to play this strangely compelling game of "gone."

Ernst was singularly attached to his mother and especially sensitive to periods of her absence. Not that Ernst ever cried or showed any other obvious form of protest to separation from his mother. In all respects, Ernst was a "good" child. In September 1915, while Freud was spending several weeks with his daughter Sophie at her home in Hamburg, he had the opportunity to observe Ernst's extraordinary game (Jones, 1957, p. 267). Freud found himself peculiarly moved by Ernst's pastime.

As if to confirm his growing feeling that the "game" was somehow strangely symbolic of Ernst's sense of loss at his mother's absence, Freud was able to make the following further observation: Ernst had as one of his toys a wooden reel (probably similar to a thread spool) with a piece of string firmly attached.

> It never occurred to [Ernst] to pull it along the floor behind him, for instance, and play at its being a carriage. What he did was to hold the reel by the string and very skillfully throw it over the edge of his curtained cot, so that it disappeared into it, at the same time uttering his expressive "o-o-o-o." He then pulled the reel out of the cot again by the string and hailed its reappearance with a joyful "*da*" ["there"]. *This, then, was the complete game—disappearance and return.* (1920a, p. 15; italics added)

On another occasion, when Ernst's mother had been away for several hours, her return was greeted by her son's exclamation, "Baby o-o-o-o!" In the light of Freud's earlier observations, such an utterance could only be meant to communicate: "Ernst (baby) was gone!"—an interpretation that was confirmed when it was discovered that Ernst had tried a variation of his "gone" game with a full-length mirror. Not quite reaching the floor, the mirror had provided the inventive Ernst with the opportunity to make himself "gone" each time he crouched below its bottom edge (Freud, 1920a, p. 15n.).

"Gone" was more than a game. It was a form of self-discipline by which Ernst had sought to master the unpleasurable prospect of his mother's periodic absences. He could not, however, symbolically act out the pleasurable *return* of a missing love object until he had first staged its unpleasurable *disappearance*. In his "game," Ernst was particularly successful because the disappearance and return of his toys were directly under *his* control, as contrasted with the absences of his mother, which he could experience only as a circumstance imposed from without.

Ernst had developed a technique of symbolically *repeating* an unpleasurable experience. In its original form, the experience had to be endured *passively*. By his recreations, Ernst could *actively* control the event, and he could express a kind of defiance: "All right, go away—I don't need you!"

Sadly, when Ernst was almost six years old, his mother died of pneumonia; in his terms, she was permanently "gone." Figure 3.2 shows Freud with his grandsons, Max and Ernst.

On the theoretical level, Freud offered Ernst's game as one example of a violation of the pleasure principle. It showed clearly that unpleasurable events could be

FIGURE 3.2   Freud and his grandsons Ernst and Max.

Ernst's (seated) "gone game" was immortalized by his grandfather's descriptions of the boy's ritualized but masterful effort to cope with his mother's (Sophie Freud) death.

Source:Freud, E., Freud, L., & Grubrich-Simitis, I. (1976), p. 228.

reworked, repeated, and relived, despite their painful quality, until they were mastered. Yet, Ernst's game was not a definite example. Freud pointed out that such cases could be interpreted as consistent with, rather than beyond, the pleasure principle because the *eventual* outcome was pleasurable. He searched about for another example of a behavior beyond the pleasure principle.

Recurring Posttraumatic Dreams

In the dreams of patients suffering from hysteria-like paralysis and apparent physical illness following upon some life-threatening accident like a railway collision or exposure to stress on the battlefield, Freud found another illustration of an urge to repeat unpleasant experiences. Traumatic neurosis resembles hysterical symptomatology in that the afflicted individual shows no organic basis or demonstrable physical cause for the symptoms. But, more important, in many such cases the individual experiences recurring dreams that each night re-create the traumatic situation of the accident or battlefield. By contrast, such patients in their waking state are usually more concerned with forgetting the trauma than with reliving it. The dream, however, instead of pleasurably fulfilling some wish, *returns* the patient to the situation and to the fright that was once helplessly endured.

Reliving Painful Memories

As a last example of an apparent violation of the dominance of the pleasure principle, Freud cited an observation from the realm of psychotherapy. Often, during a psychoanalysis, patients treat analysts as if they were particular authority figures from the patients' own past. They thrust onto their therapist attitudes and desires that would be appropriate only to the real figures of their past lives. In effect, the patients *relive* significant experiences and attitudes of their life histories with the therapist as their present target. ". . . [The patient] is obliged to *repeat* the repressed material as a contemporary experience instead of, as the physician would prefer to see, *remembering* it as something belonging to the past" (Freud, 1920a, p. 18).

Transference is the name that Freud gave to this tendency of patients to react to their therapists with emotions reproduced from childhood. Because the material that is thus repeated originates in the unconscious, and because the conscious ego is occupied with the repression of that material, Freud concluded that the compulsion to repeat must also originate in the unconscious. Therefore, in the conflict between the ego and the unconscious, reexperience of the repressed material must figure as a potent source of unpleasure for the beleaguered ego.

For every instance cited—Ernst's game, traumatic dreams, transference in therapy—the common denominator seems to be that these individuals are acting under the *compulsion endlessly to repeat unpleasurable experiences*.

REDUCTION OF THE PLEASURE PRINCIPLE TO A PLEASURE "TENDENCY"

Freud had in mind cases like Ernst's game, transference, and traumatic dreams when he modified his conception of the pleasure principle from a dominating influence to that of a trend in mental life:

> If such a dominance [of pleasure] existed, the immense majority of our mental processes would have to be accompanied by pleasure or to lead to pleasure, whereas universal experience completely contradicts any such conclusion. The most that can be said, therefore, is that there exists in the mind a strong *tendency* toward the pleasure principle, but the tendency is opposed by certain other forces or circumstances, so that the final outcome cannot always be in harmony with the tendency towards pleasure. (1920a, pp. 9-10)

The opposing forces were, of course, those underlying the *compulsion to repeat* unpleasurable experiences until, like Ernst's, they are mastered. Freud was now prepared to embark on a speculative reexamination of his previous accounts of the mental apparatus. His intention was to bring his discrepant findings about violations of the pleasure principle into harmony with the rest of psychoanalytic theory.

The Nirvana Principle

The overwhelming necessity governing the operation of the mental apparatus is the reduction of excitation, tension, or drive, and the need to maintain a relatively stable state of stimulation-free existence. Freud, following Breuer, had originally adopted the term "constancy principle" to describe the tension reduction efforts of the nervous system. Breuer had borrowed the term from the psychophysicist Gustav Fechner.

In *Beyond the Pleasure Principle*, Freud incorporated some new terminology from Barbara Low to replace the constancy principle. Freud now employed the "Nirvana principle" to indicate the homeostatic trend of nervous system functioning whereby it attempts to divest itself of disturbing tensions and excess stimulation. In fact, Freud had thought that the Nirvana principle and the pleasure principle were essentially intimately related so that the nervous system's adherence to the Nirvana principle was guaranteed by the operation of the pleasure principle. That is, reduction of tension and the maintenance of an almost stimulation-free state implied by the Nirvana principle are pleasurable. However, in a paper written in 1924, Freud changed his mind and distinguished between the two principles.

The distinction was necessary, Freud thought, because certain states of pleasure require *increases* in excitation rather than the reduction of excitation. One state, for example, that would violate the Nirvana principle, but accord with the pleasure principle, is sexual excitation, in which rising amounts of bodily tension in the genitals produce pleasurable sensation (Freud, 1924a, p. 160). Therefore, the Nirvana principle and the pleasure principle were distinguishable as separate, but complementary, trends in mental life.

Conservative Nature of Instincts

As Ernst played his evocative game of "gone," and as traumatic neurotic patients relive their frightful experiences in nightly dreams, so too the instincts, when viewed from the perspective of the nervous system's ultimate goal of tension reduction, seem to function to *repeat the past. Instincts operate to return to an earlier state—to the excitation-free state prior to stimulation.*

> *It seems, then, that an instinct is an urge inherent in organic life to restore an earlier state of things* which the living entity has been obliged to abandon under the pressure of external disturbing forces . . . or, to put it another way, instincts are the expression of the inertia inherent in organic life. (Freud, 1920a, p. 36)

Freud was postulating that mental life is essentially *conservative* in quality. The mental apparatus is periodically disturbed by outside stimulation and internal needs but, on the whole, strives to maintain itself in the state of quietude that characterizes its functioning prior to such disturbances. A "Nirvana-like" state of peaceful freedom from need is the principal goal of the mental apparatus, for it is this satiety that conforms faultlessly to the pleasure principle.

As primitive organisms evolved, however, their trend toward maintaining a constant state and inertial resistance to change would have been overcome by the continuous flux of external conditions, the constant change of environmental pressures, which make their demands on living things. Thus the instincts developed in unison with the increasing biological complexity of the evolving primitive organisms in order to maintain the capacity of the organism perpetually to restore an internal state of harmony in the face of a changing environment. The hunger instinct is a good example. When hunger tension mounts, we seek food and achieve satisfaction, but within a few hours, food again must be sought to return to the state of satisfaction, and so on.

Such striving is always *returning to* or *repeating* the earlier state of quietude before the world or internal needs made their demands. In its most fundamental form, the compulsion to repeat is the ultimate conservative trend: an urge to gain *complete* quietude, *total* freedom from stimulation and need, and *absolute* independence of the world. In short, the aim is death.

> It would be in contradiction to the conservative nature of the instincts if the goal of life were a state of things which had never been attained. On the contrary, it must be an *old* state of things, an initial state from which the living entity has at one time or other departed and to which it is striving to return by the circuitous paths along which its development leads. If we are to take it as a truth that knows no exception that everything living dies for internal reasons—becomes inorganic once again—then we shall be compelled to say *"the aim of all life is death"* and, looking backwards, that *"inanimate things existed before living ones."* (Freud, 1920a, p. 38)

Accidental death arising from *external causes* would cheat the organism of the completion of its *cycle* by merely terminating organic life. The organism would be deprived of achieving a *return* to the earlier state of inorganic existence that is an intrinsic part of its cellular structure. In consequence, accidental death, illness and injury merely short-circuit the process and circumvent the aim of life. The organism must gain death in its own way—the gradual burning out of the life energies. Any other means of death is evolutionary heresy.

REVISION OF INSTINCT THEORY: EROS AND DEATH

Freud's bold proposal of a death instinct brings the new theory into direct conflict with his original dualistic model of the instincts whereby one-half of the dichotomy was asserted to be constituted of self-preservation ego instincts. Of what use to the organism are self-preservation instincts if the ultimate aim of life is death? Freud ingeniously answered this question by placing the ego instincts in the service of the death instincts as their agent of successful discharge:

> [Self-preservative instincts] . . . are component instincts whose function it is to assure that the organism *shall follow its own path to death, and to ward off any possible ways of returning to inorganic existence other than those which are immanent in the organism itself.* . . . What we are left with is the fact that the organism *wishes to*

die only in its own fashion. Thus these guardians of life [i.e., self-preservative instincts] too, were originally the myrmidons of death. (Freud, 1920a, p. 39; italics added)

Although Freud himself never, except in conversation with colleagues, used the term *Thanatos* to refer to the death instinct, his followers have almost universally adopted the term as the official name (Jones, 1957, p. 273). (*Thanatos*, incidentally, is the name of the Greek god of death and was first used to refer to the death instinct by Freud's pupil Paul Federn.)

The other half of the original dualistic classification of the instincts, the sexual instincts, presented yet another problem to the hypothesis of a death instinct. How could instincts that serve the continuity of life, the longevity of a species, be brought into line with the penultimate conservatism of the death instinct in its striving toward the dissolution of life? The answer is that these two forces *conflict*.

Eros and Immortality

The instincts that guard the development of the germ cells, sperm and egg, that provide them with safety during their time of generativity, and that motivate the union of male and female are the sexual instincts, collectively termed *libido*. Clearly the sexual instincts are the true *life* instincts since they operate against the forces of death and dissolution by attempting to immortalize the organism through its progeny. Paradoxically, the other class of instincts, ego instincts, subserve death by striving to promote the self-preservation of the organism *until it dies in its own way*, of its own immanent causes. Thus, in *Beyond the Pleasure Principle*, the ego instincts presented Freud with a problem of classification. In which group, life or death, should the ego instincts be included? Freud eventually combined the ego instincts with the sexual instincts and considered them to be part of the libido's press for the continuity of life while they nevertheless serve the inexorable aims of death.

Freud had retained much of his desired dualistic classification by opposing the death instincts to be combined life instincts (ego and object libido) (1920a, p. 41). In honor of the changed scheme, Freud assigned to the unified sexual and ego instincts the term *Eros*, the name of the god of love and passion. Consequently, the dichotomy in Freud's theory was changed from the conflict between love and hunger to the opposition between life and death. All organisms die. If they bear the spark of immortality, it is evidenced only in their ability to confer equally transient life.

Eros and Bisexuality: Return to Unity

Freud had one further problem that had to be solved before his life-death dualism could be brought into the main body of psychoanalytic theory. How is Eros governed by the compulsion to repeat, a compulsion that is basic to all instincts? The death instinct operates to *return* the organism to the prior evolutionary state of inorganic existence. But what is Eros attempting to repeat; *to what does it seek return?*

The answer, Freud speculated, lies in the origin of the two sexes. He suggested, hesitantly at first, that Plato's myth of the origin of the human race may be a poetic representation of a fundamental truth. In the *Symposium*, Plato, speaking through the character of Aristophanes, recounts a myth in which the original human sexes existed in three varieties: male, female, and the union of the two. Those bisexual humans had double sets of hands, feet, and sexual organs, but, because they offended the gods, Zeus decided to cut them into two. After the division, each half human, desiring its missing component, sought out its mate. They threw their arms about each other, eager to merge again into unity. Freud commented,

> Shall we follow the hint given us by the poet-philosopher, and venture on the hypothesis that living substance at that time of its coming to life was torn apart into small particles, which have ever since endeavored to reunity through the sexual instincts? that these instincts, in which the chemical affinity of inanimate matter persisted, gradually succeeded, as they developed through the kingdom of protista, in overcoming the difficulties put in the way of that endeavor by an environment charged with dangerous stimuli—stimuli which compelled them to form a protective cortical layer? that these splintered fragments of living substance in this way attained a multicellular condition and finally transferred the instinct for reuniting, in the most highly concentrated form, to the germ cells? (1920a, p. 58)

Freud had returned to the concept of the inherently bisexual nature of the human constitution as the basis of the compulsion to repeat in Eros. Humans are striving in their sexual activity to attain the wholeness of sexuality that once was the hallmark of the earliest organisms. The compulsion to repeat is evidenced by Eros in the active striving of males and females to consummate sexual union—that is, in their striving to repeat evolutionary history.[2]

Death Derivatives: Aggression and Hate

Operating silently and invisibly, the death instinct is rarely observable in pure form. The existence of the death instinct can only be inferred from the operation of its more observable derivatives: namely, a tendency in humans to behave aggressively and their capacity to harbor destructive intent. These more observable derivatives of the death instinct emerge when the life instinct, Eros, succeeds in preventing the full self-destructive expression of Thanatos. Thus when Thanatos is deprived of expression within the individual, it emerges as other-directed, displaced aggression. Eros succeeds in preventing the death instinct from achieving the destruction of the *individual* by diverting the death instinct's energy to other individuals. The price of Eros's success is high.

Yet it was Freud's opinion that the death instinct and Eros are generally mingled throughout life. He believed that Eros generally succeeds in preventing Thanatos from attaining the organism's dissolution at the cost of creating outwardly directed human

---

[2] It is interesting that Freud later rejected this formula of the compulsion to repeat in Eros. In one of his last considerations of the subject, *An Outline of Psycho-Analysis* (1940), Freud came to the conclusion that the hypothesis that living substance was once a unity that, having been separated, now struggles toward reunion could not be supported by biological fact (1940, p. 149n.). He did not, however, offer an alterative basis for Eros's repetition compulsion, and by his omission, he left himself open to the criticism that Eros no longer fits his own definition of an instinct (cf. Fromm, 1973, Appendix).

hate and aggression. Where Eros succeeds in constructive unification of humans, the death instinct wins a victory for human misery (Freud, 1930, p. 119).[3]

Freud's changing views of how the instincts were organized, from the original hunger-love dualism to the final Eros-Thanatos dichotomy, are summarized in Figure 3.1.

THE FINAL, STRUCTURAL MODEL OF THE MIND

In 1923, in a book entitled *The Ego and the Id*, Freud again embarked on a major theoretical adventure. During the course of his career, he had constructed two major models of the mind. The first was a neurological model (1895), which he soon abandoned.[4] The second, proposed in Chapter 7 of the *Interpretation of Dreams* (1900), was a distinctly psychological theory based on a spatial or topographical analogy. It was from this topographical model that terms like *unconscious* and *preconscious* originated. Both of these previous models, however, had serious flaws and ambiguities, chief of which was their inability to depict unambiguously the interplay of combining and competing forces within the personality.

In *The Ego and the Id* (1923a), Freud created a final, *structural* model of the mind that no longer represented mental functioning as divided among sharply separated and rigidly frontiered subsystems. Freud's new structural strategy depicted the

---

[3] Although it is not our purpose to survey the body of criticism that exists for each personality theory, we should perhaps point out that the concept of a death instinct aroused enormous controversy and criticism from sources within and outside psychoanalysis.

Ernest Jones, Freud's biographer and himself a psychoanalyst, found very little support in biology or in medicine for the death instinct, and he suggested that Freud's proposal of the concept could be understood only in terms of Freud's personal reaction to the prospect of his own death. That eventually was periodically impressed on Freud's mind by the loss of members of his own family, some early recurring cardiac problems to which Freud reacted somewhat superstitiously, and by his ultimately fatal protracted illness of jaw cancer (Jones, 1957, p. 278; see also Wallace, 1976).

Max Schur, Freud's personal physician during the latter part of his life, criticizes the death instinct along much the same lines as Jones in his insistence that the theoretical concept served an important role in Freud's personal mental economy (1972, Chap. 12). Schur, however, goes a step further and concludes that the death instinct is based on an act of circular reasoning, an error very uncharacteristic of Freud. Thus, according to Schur, the conservative nature of the instincts is proposed on the basis of the Nirvana principle; the Nirvana principle is seen as the cause of the conservative trend of instincts to repeat compulsively (1972, p. 323).

Erich Fromm, a leading psychoanalytic thinker, accuses Freud of playing the game of theory construction by different rules at different times. Fromm points out that Freud confused the tendency to *repeat* with the motive to *destroy*. In so doing, Freud failed to bring the death instinct into line with his own semibiological definition of an instinct that emphasized the achievement of bodily satisfaction through tension reduction. The death instinct strives not for tension reduction within the organism, but for the actual dissolution of the organism's life integrity (Fromm, 1973, p. 366).

[4] In conversation with Anna Freud in July 1974, at her home in London, she suggested to me that her father had "dismissed" the neurological model he created in 1895 because he could advance no further with it. She was quite adamant that contemporary presentations of psychoanalysis, like this one, should exclude the neurological model from consideration because psychoanalysis is a *psychological* theory, not a modified neurology. She conceded that her father's early training in neurology had been influential in shaping his thinking and that his habit of framing his thoughts in biological terms was not easily overcome. When I suggested that, were her father alive today, he might adopt for his use some of the recent advances in biology and neurology, she again insisted that her father had created a psychology and not merely a neurology translated into psychological language. Apart from its historical significance, Freud's 1895 neurological model of the mind has little relevance to psychoanalytic theory or therapy as it is practiced today. She reemphasized that her father would not have returned to his neurological ideas under any circumstances. (See the discussion of Freud's neurological model in Chapter 4.)

mind as a complex of melding, combining forces whereby parts of the conscious personality could also harbor unconscious content. Three newly named agencies, the *id*, the *ego*, and the *superego*, subsumed all of the mental functions previously assigned to the unconscious and the preconscious.

Id, Ego, Superego Terminology

Because the unconscious could no longer be restricted to a distinct region of the mind, and because it could not be employed solely as a description of momentarily latent thoughts, the term *id* would from now on indicate that part of the human person's selfhood that is alien to or isolated from the conscious self, or ego. Freud adopted the Latinized term id (originally, the simple German pronoun *das es*, meaning "it") from Georg Groddeck (1922), a physician who had become interested in psychoanalysis. Freud's translators converted the terminology to Latin equivalents to preserve in English translation the technical flavor of the terms.

In a similar way, Freud's translators converted his other plain German pronouns to Latin equivalents, so that the simple German for "I" (*Ich*) became the Latin *ego*, and the German for "over-I" became *superego*.

THE ID

Developmentally, the id is the oldest portion of personality. The existence of the id dates from birth. "Originally, to be sure, everything was id . . ." (Freud, 1940, p. 163). Because the id is the most archaic portion of personality, already operative before the infant has had much in the way of transactions with the world, it must contain all of the unlearned, innate strivings that we have come to know "psychoanalytically" as the instincts. Thus Freud characterized the id as a "cauldron full of seething excitations," fueled by the energics of the organic processes of the instincts and striving toward one goal: *immediate satisfaction of its wishes*.

The id is to be regarded as the pool of mental representatives of the biological processes underlying bodily needs, a pool populated, therefore, by Eros and the death instinct: " . . . but it has no organization, produces no collective will, but only a striving to bring about the satisfaction of the instinctual needs subject to the observance of the pleasure principle" (Freud, 1933, p. 73).

Like its precursor, the unconscious, the id is an untrammeled, primeval chaos free of the laws governing logical thought. Contrary impulses exist side by side without canceling each other; the passage of time exerts no influence on the id; and wishful impulses, after the passage of decades, behave as if they had just occurred (Freud, 1933, p. 74). Freud summarized the characteristics of the id in much the same way as he had previously spoken of the unconscious:

> The id of course knows no judgments of value: no good and evil, no morality. The economic or, if you prefer, the quantitative factor, which is intimately linked to the pleasure principle, dominates all its processes. *Instinctual cathexes seeking discharge—that, in our view, is all there is in the id.* It even seems that the energy of these instinctual impulses is in a state different from that in the other regions of the mind, far more mobile and capable of discharge. . . . (1933, p. 74; italics added)

Because it is ruled by primary process thinking, condensations and displacements of its energy are not only possible for the id, they are an inevitable result of the id's striving for satisfaction without due regard for the goodness, evilness, realness, or appropriateness of its objects. In many ways, the id operates on the principle that whatever brings satisfaction to a want, desire, or wishful impulse is good; whatever hinders or frustrates such satisfaction is bad. "The id obeys the inexorable pleasure principle" (Freud, 1940, p. 198).

THE EGO

Left to itself, the id's unbridled striving would bring about the destruction of the organism. The id's lack of organization, its diffuseness and disregard for reality must be tamed in the service of survival. It is to the ego that the task of self-preservation falls.

The ego develops out of the id. In fact, the ego is a differentiated part of the id that has become specialized and organized in response to its constant exposure to external stimulation. Thus the ego is conceived as having an intimate relationship with the outermost layer of the organism, the perceptual and conscious systems that are localized in the cortical layer of the brain.

Clearly, Freud pictured the ego as developing from the id in response to the organism's need for a mediator between its internal needs and the demands of reality. The ego is thus the reality-oriented arm of the mental apparatus, though it is simultaneously responsive to internal conditions as well.

With reference to the *external environment*, the ego's functions are familiar ones: to become aware of stimuli and their location; to avoid excessively strong stimulation; and to learn to bring about changes in the external world that would be to its own advantage in pursuing survival. For this last activity, the ego must govern the muscular apparatus of the organism (Freud, 1933, p. 75).

Correspondingly, with reference to the *internal environment*, including the id, the ego functions to gain control over the expression of the instincts. The ego must decide whether the instincts are to be *immediately* satisfied as the id demands, or if their satisfaction is to be *postponed* to later times more favorable to wish fulfillment, or, finally, whether the instinctual demand should be totally denied expression, that is, whether the instinct should be *repressed*.

With the development of the ego as a specialized and efficiently organized portion of the id, the organism correspondingly increases in the degree of sophistication with which it approaches the tasks of life. For one thing, the pleasure principle is "dethroned" by the reality principle as the ego seeks to provide safe and realistically appropriate pleasures for the id. "To adopt a popular mode of speaking, we might say that the ego stands for reason and good sense while the id stands for the untamed passions" (Freud, 1933, p. 76).

Metaphorically, the ego is fighting a battle on two fronts: It must not only protect the organism from excessively strong demands from within, it must also seek to satisfy these demands in an external world fraught with danger. Such external dangers can be dealt with by flight, that is, by the removal of the organism from the dangerous situations. Internal threats to the integrity of the organism, that is, impulses whose satisfaction would bring the organism into contact with external dangers, are dealt with by the ego in an analogous way, namely, by *mental flight* or repression.

Thus there is a portion of the id-ego amalgam that becomes separated from the conscious functioning of the ego. That separated part, the repressed, then behaves in every way as if it were part of the unconscious. This zone of alien content is nevertheless part of the ego, though *functionally, dynamically separated* from it.

It is important in this context of defense by repression to note that it is the id that is the great reservoir of libido or sexual energy. In his previous writings, Freud had characterized the ego, in his then broad usage of the term as the reservoir of libido. But actually there is no contradiction, for the ego is a specialized aspect of the id, and while it is only the very tip of a deep iceberg, the ego is nonetheless an integral part of that mass (Freud, 1923a, pp. 30, 38).

In the original state of being at birth, the total energy of Eros, libido, is available to the undifferentiated id-ego amalgam. Eros's presence serves to neutralize the death instinct (Freud, 1940, p. 149). The ego is, therefore, primarily narcissistic at this stage, and it cathects *itself* with libido. Only when the ego becomes differentiated from the id will it direct its cathexes of libido to external objects. Once a quality of its libido is externalized as object libido, the ego's remaining store of libido comes into opposition with the death instinct. Ego libido, as contrasted with the externalized object libido, thus works in the service of the organism's own preservation, and ego libido operates to keep the organism from premature harm that might cheat the death instinct of its opportunity to bring the organism to its immanent destiny. Thus it is the particular developmental stage that determines whether it is the undifferentiated id-ego unity or the id alone that occupies the focus of attention as the reservoir of libido.

While the ego is fighting a two-front battle with the internal and external worlds, there is yet a third front that the ego is compelled to consider during its intercourse with life and death. This third front is the *superego*.

THE SUPEREGO

When the id is forced by circumstances beyond its control to give up its love objects, as for example, in the child's renunciation of the mother at the resolution of the Oedipus complex, it is compensated for the loss by the ego (Freud, 1916, p. 249; 1923a, p. 23 ff.). The ego undergoes an alteration by which it takes on the characteristics of the lost love object. This same process can be seen more clearly in adulthood when one marriage partner is widowed. After the immediate shock of the death, the powerful sense of loss is almost too painful for the remaining partner to bear. The surviving spouse may then unconsciously adopt the habits or the speech patterns of the deceased, or an item of the deceased's apparel, as if to compensate for the loss by reinstating at least a part of that person's identity in the survivor's own behavior.

> When the ego assumes the features of the [lost] object, it is forcing itself, so to speak, upon the id as a love-object and is trying to make good the id's loss by saying: "Look, you can love me too—I am so like the object." (Freud, 1923a, p. 30)

This process of modeling itself on the lost love object, as the ego attempts to pacify the id, is called *identification*. Identification is an important part of the processes by which the superego is formed.

Recall that the male child's first erotic love object is his mother. Since his first, and in some ways his most important, contact with the mother is through feeding, it is this most satisfying activity that serves as the prototype for the child's desire to possess this eminently pleasurable creature. When, however, during the phallic stage of libidinal development, the child continues to seek his mother as desirable love object in the new sexual sense, he comes to perceive that his father is his competitor. Without recapitulating the entire progress of the Oedipal situation (Chapter 2), you may recall that the child relinquishes his mother as love object, identifies with his father in order to be like him because father possesses desirable objects, and the child represses his libidinal cathexes toward mother.

There is an obvious inconsistency in this formulation of identification, as Roger Brown (1965, p. 379) has pointed out. According to Freud's account, since the boy must relinquish his *mother* as a love object, he should identify with *her*, not with his father. Likewise, the girl, having relinquished her father, should identify with him. Obviously this sequence won't do since, except in the most pathological cases, boys correctly assume their masculine sexual identity and girls similarly correctly identify with their mothers. Freud noted the discrepancy between his proposed mechanism of identification and the actual outcome (1923a, p. 32). As a result he returned to one of his long-standing ideas and concluded that the *inherent bisexuality* of human nature determines the outcome of the identification. Because boys are *more* male than female, they identify only partially with mother, but *mostly* with father. The converse is true for girls. As Brown put the matter, the assumption of inherent bisexuality makes the theory work, but "if that assumption is acceptable to Freud he does not need all the rest of his theoretical apparatus . . ." (1965, p. 379).

Undaunted by his own discovery of the inconsistency and relying on the concept of bisexuality, Freud proposed that the full Oedipus complex is comprised of both positive and negative aspects. It is *positive* in the sense that the boy *actively* strives to be like his father, to identify with him. But the Oedipus complex may also have negative properties because of the child's inherent feminine components. The boy may behave *passively* or "girlishly" toward the father because he has partially identified with mother when he was forced to renounce her as love object. In this way, the boy may also attempt to appease his father by an overtly submissive attitude. For girls, of course, the opposite set of behaviors dominates, for the girl has partially identified with father and so behaves in subtle *masculine* ways (Freud, 1923a, p. 33). The final outcome, however, is an expected one: Boys identify with their fathers, and girls model themselves on their mothers.

Sometime around the age of five, children internalize (identify with) the standards of rightness, morality, and goodness that were originally enforced by their parents. Where the parents had watched over them, guided them, and reprimanded them for "bad" behaviors, a new internal agency continues *from within* to exercise these judgmental functions autonomously. In terms of psychoanalytic theory, a *superego* has been formed. Through the process of identification with the mother and father, the superego becomes the "heir of the Oedipal complex." This formulation requires some explanation.

In becoming like the father, the child has internalized the standards of adult authority, but more important, he has also internalized a number of prohibitions that will form the basis of his superego. The child's ego not only must strive to be like the all-powerful father who possesses the all-desirable mother, it must also establish the boundaries that limit the degree to which he acts the role of father (Freud, 1923a, p. 34). Out of fear of his competitor, the child must not carry the identification as far as actual possession of the mother. Before they arouse the hostility of father, he himself must repress the id's Oedipal desires. Hence, the child *internalizes* the prohibitions that he imagines his father might enforce. Timely compliance thus averts what his hesitation would otherwise provoke. As a direct result, the superego is formed. The superego is a combination of the active striving to be like the father and the anxiety-motivated attempts to anticipate the father's proscriptions.

The next step in the sequence is for the child to repress his Oedipal strivings. Repression of desire for mother and hostility toward father is not an easy undertaking for the boy's ego. The force that such repression requires is a measure of the strength of the internalized superego. For it is the superego that embodies the anxiety and resultant identification with authority that remain after the Oedipal strivings are repressed. To say it another way, *the superego replaces the strength of the Oedipal wishes in the mental economy with the equal or stronger energy of the father identification.* Or, as Freud repeatedly stated it, "The superego is the heir of the Oedipal complex." Like the father, the superego can stand apart from the ego and master (Freud, 1923a, p. 48).

Superego as Conscience

An important quantitative relationship may be inferred from the fact that the superego becomes the repository of the quantity of energy that was required to master and to repress the Oedipal desires (Freud, 1923a, pp. 34–35; 1930, p. 123). *The greater the instinctual gratification that is renounced, the more severe the superego grows in its judgments of the ego* (Freud, 1923a, p. 54; 1930, p. 129).

In effect, the intensity of the impulse or desire that is mastered is assimilated by the superego, increasing its supply of energy for future moral judgments. In less technical language, the greater the temptation to which persons *fail to yield*, the greater will be the pangs of their consciences in future temptations. In short, the superego is fed by the energy of the renounced id impulse, and it grows more scrupulous with each moral triumph.

Since the superego is the internalized character of the father (through identification), the more fearsome and wrathful the child perceived that character to be, the stronger was the ego's fear of the id's unacceptable wishes. Consequently, a child in the Oedipal phase who harbors intensely aggressive feelings toward his father will be required for the sake of his ego to internalize an even more intense fear of the father's potential wrath in order to master his hatred. Thus it is the child who has renounced the strongest aggressive urges who will have the strongest sense of guilt about them and about similar desires in the future. The aggression not expressed toward the father becomes available to the superego for use against the child's own ego.

The paradox is clear: *The more aggression you virtuously renounce, the more your conscience reproaches you.* Common sense, contrary to psychoanalytic theory, suggests that the stronger a person's conscience, the more virtuous he or she will be. Freud reversed the temporal sequence in this apparent truism, and he suggested that

> . . . the more virtuous a man is, the more severe and distrustful is . . . [the behavior of his conscience], so that ultimately it is precisely those people who have carried saintliness furthest who reproach themselves with the worst sinfulness. (1930, pp. 125–126)

Clearly, Freud meant to emphasize that once the superego was established within the personality to be fed by the energy of renounced id impulses, it could be as harsh and unyielding in its demands as the id continually is in its relationship to the ego. "From the point of view of instinctual control, or morality, it may be said of the id that it is totally non-moral, of the ego that it strives to be moral, and of the superego that it can be super-moral and then become as cruel as only the id can be" (Freud, 1923a, p. 540).

ID, EGO, SUPEREGO INTERACTIONS

Because the superego was formed at a stage in developmental history when children idealized their parents and saw in them every perfection, it follows that the standards of the superego will likewise have the character of the parents' *idealized* image (Freud, 1933, p. 64). Conscience is thus a standard of perfection, an ideal, rather than a realistic appraisal of behavior. Consequently, in their rearing of children, parents exemplify not so much a standard of experience tempered by a realistic appraisal of life, but rather the idealistic standard of their own superegos (Freud, 1933, p. 67).

Freud employed a diagrammatic summary of his new structural model that, reproduced here as Figure 3.3, is helpful in recapitulating the essential points.

Figure 3.3 shows the location of the three mental structures: id, ego, and superego. It also indicates the important relationships that bind them.

The ego is situated near, and oriented toward, the perceptual-conscious end of the organism, and it is thus in direct contact with the external world. But the diagram also clearly demonstrates that the ego extends into the lower regions of the system, where it merges into the unconscious id. A segment of the ego, then, is in closer contact with the unconscious than it is with consciousness or perceptual activity. Furthermore, there is a segment of the ego that is equally rooted in the unconscious, but that is sharply separated from the rest of the ego's conscious activities. Even though this segment forms a structural part of the ego, it functions *dynamically* like the unconscious system.

In Figure 3.3 this ego-alien segment is illustrated in its separation from conscious ego activity by two diagonal lines that define the boundary of repressed content. The ego is thus both conscious in its orientation toward the perceptual end of the apparatus and dynamically unconscious by virtue of its repressions.

FIGURE 3.3   The dynamic model of the mind.

Note that the diagram depicts the three agencies of the mind with no sharp boundaries between them. In Freud's last model, the mind was represented as an amalgam of blending, combining, and competing forces. See text for explanation. Based on Freud (1933), p. 78.

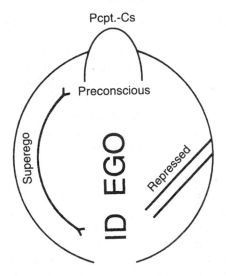

Although Freud did not include the superego in the diagram that he used in *The Ego and the Id* (1923a, p. 24), by the time he had written his *New Introductory Lectures*, almost 10 years later, he found a way to include the superego in such diagrammatic summaries. Lying along the left-hand margin of the drawing in Figure 3.3, the superego clearly merges into the unconscious id, for, as "the heir of the Oedipus complex it has intimate relations with the id; it is more remote than the ego from the perceptual system" (Freud, 1933, p. 79).

The superego, therefore, is structured of both conscious and unconscious components, and, as a moral or ethical agency, it functions both consciously and unconsciously. That is to say, the superego has relations with both the ego and the id.

In several respects, Freud pointed out, the diagrammatic summary of Figure 3.3 is misleading. For one thing, the space occupied by the unconscious id should be greater than that of the ego or preconscious. For another thing:

> In thinking of this division of the personality into an ego, superego, and an id, you will not, of course, have pictured sharp frontiers like the artificial ones drawn in political geography. We cannot do justice to the characteristics of the mind by linear outlines like those in a drawing or in a primitive painting, but rather by areas of color melting into one another as they are presented by modern artists. After making the separation we must allow what we have separated to merge together once more. (Freud, 1933, p. 79)

The ego's task is to balance the passions of the id against the censure of the superego while it simultaneously appraises reality and its exigencies. In Freud's words, for the ego "Life is not easy!" When the ego is overwhelmed and compelled to recognize its own weaknesses in carrying out successfully its Herculean tasks, anxiety results. Such anxiety may be the result of fear of the external world, fear of the id's passions, or fear of the superego's censure.

FREUD'S CHANGING CONCEPTIONS OF ANXIETY

In the earliest days of Freud's theorizing, he came to view anxiety as the result of unexpressed or dammed-up libido. The neurotic's badly distorted relations with the world and its people are often expressed in sexual difficulty. Normal, satisfying sexual relations are frequently foregone as a welter of neurotic symptoms and other defensive measures sap the individual's capacity for joyous living. Unexpressed libido, the dammed-up energy of the sexual impulses that have thus succumbed to repression, is then explosively released in a transformed state, the state of anxiety. In short, in Freud's early thinking, repression of sexual impulses is the cause of anxiety (cf. Freud, 1894; 1896a; 1896b; 1896c; and 1898).

According to this early view, anxiety was instinctual, arising from the repressed unconscious sexual urges. But if it were true that such feelings were restricted to unconscious origin, the conscious ego as depicted in the new structural model with its separation from the repressed would never experience the unpleasant affect of anxiety. Furthermore, if the ego did not experience the anxiety, it would never trigger repressive counterforces to cast the unacceptable, anxiety-producing impulses from consciousness in the first place (Freud, 1926a, pp. 140, 161). Freud's new structural model demanded that the ego be the seat of anxiety, and so Freud was required to rethink the problem.

Birth Trauma as the Prototype of Adult Anxiety

Through a slow return to and development of his neurological ideas, Freud renounced the view of anxiety as transformed libido. In his early neurological model of the "Project for a Scientific Psychology," Freud had experimented with the idea that anxiety originates in the feeling of overwhelming helplessness (1895). The ego experiences the perception of being overpowered or flooded with too much stimulation. In infancy, the first of such experiences is the act of birth. The neonate is thrust from its warm, dark, safe, parasitic existence in the mother's body into the confusing, demanding, changing, and irritating external environment (Freud, 1926a). In successive stages of life, other situations will evoke the same emotional response of helplessness, stimulus flooding, and the feeling of being overpowered. Separation from the mother (recall Ernst's "gone" game) provokes distress in most infants, and such separation is a good example of a later life situation that harbors the threat of helplessness.

The common denominator in all such cases of anxiety is the sense of abandonment, the feeling that life's demands will overwhelm the isolated ego because of its helplessness. When anxiety mounts to a level that individuals feel will threaten their survival, neurotic symptoms may be formed as attempts to stifle the tide of mental confusion and emotional pain. In a very real sense, adult neurotics develop symptoms to control their anxiety over threats that they perceive as truly life threatening, just as life threatening as early abandonment by mother. Overt symptoms thus unconsciously replace what they can no longer consciously bear (Freud, 1933, p. 85). The question of significance thus changed for Freud from how libido could be transformed into anxiety, to how anxiety was produced from the ego's perceptions.

As early as 1909, in a footnote to the *Interpretation of Dreams*, Freud pointed out that " . . . the act of birth is the first experience of anxiety, and thus the source and prototype of the affect of anxiety" (1900, pp. 400–401). In effect, Freud was postulating that the birth situation is every individual's first experience with the unpleasurable state of anxiety, and that it is the first experience which serves as the model against which the ego compares future situations in making its responses to reality and to the demands of the id and superego.

A colleague of Freud's, Otto Rank, broadened the concept of birth trauma beyond its status as the prototype for anxiety. Rank established the birth trauma as the central emotional constellation in psychological development (Rank, 1929; 1932). In emphasizing the significance of the birth trauma for neurotic symptomatology, Rank almost inadvertently dethroned the main psychoanalytic concepts of the Oedipus complex and sexual strivings from their etiological importance. For Rank, the trauma of birth was the nucleus from which all human development, neurotic and normal, proceeds. Freud thus felt compelled to repudiate Rank's ideas.

Freud's Chronology of Danger Situations

As the child's ego develops, Freud reasoned, anxiety becomes less and less an experience of flooding helplessness and more and more a signal to avoid such danger. The prototype for the danger situation of the ego disruption is birth. If an ego were present from birth, it would feel helpless. Only through the care of the mother does the infant survive, feel comforted, and become eventually tension-free. But at base, the danger situation of birth is the fear of nonsurvival.

Throughout infancy, the child learns that survival depends on this "love object," the mother, being present to minister to its needs. When she is absent—*loss of the object*—the burgeoning ego experiences a "signal" or danger, a feeling that mounting needs will go unsatisfied to the point of annihilation.

Later, after the first year of life during the anal period of two to three years, the toddler recognizes that absence of mother does not mean abandonment. Instead, what now counts for survival is getting the mother's love. For it is only by her loving anticipations of its needs that the child receives gratifications that assure safety and survival. An angry or aloof mother does not care. The danger situation for the ego is now transformed by learning into a *fear of the loss of the object's love*.

At the phallic phase, the time of the Oedipus complex around ages three to five, the male child learns that father can retaliate for his secret wishes to possess mother exclusively. Furthermore, beginning sexual interest has become vaguely attached to the person of the mother, and this interest becomes a source of additional fear should father detect these taboo wishes. The fear that assails the child's ego now is a *fear of castration*, for what more appropriate punishment could father exact than removal of the offending organ? In more general terms, the child experiences this new danger situation not only as an Oedipal fear but also as a broader fear of injury and physical insult to its body. What the analogous process for girls may be, Freud did not say. But the implication from his writing is that girls experience similar danger signals because their discovery that they do not have a penis is interpreted by them as meaning that they have already been injured.

Finally, in the post-Oedipal period persisting until adulthood, the ego responds to ever more sophisticated danger signals. Having internalized the moral standards of the parents in the form of the superego, the ego responds with anxiety to judgments of the superego that a particular id impulse is dangerous. Thus the final danger situation is *fear of one's own self-evaluations*.

It is clear that several common features are shared by all the danger situations. First, anxiety at its core is the experience of helplessness: feeling helpless to manage internal needs, helpless to cope with external threats and signals of disintegration, and feeling helpless to maintain survival. Second, each danger situation is a derivative or a representation of the experience of loss. In order, these losses are loss of complete dependence (birth), loss of the love object, loss of the object's love, loss of a body part, and loss of self-esteem or self-love.

We should mention that this final experience of loss contained in the fear of one's own self-judgments is strikingly similar to Freud's earliest theory of repression discussed in Chapter 2: Namely, wishes that clash with one's self-image are very threatening. Table 3.2 summarizes the chronology of the danger situations, and it should be apparent from the table that Freud's scheme implies that anxiety takes its meaning from the development processes active at a given moment in time.

TABLE 3.2   Freud's Chronology of Danger Situations

Development Period	Danger Situation	Ego Experience of Anxiety
Birth	Global feelings of flooding, distress, helplessness	No awareness of outside world, but survival is threatened.
First year (Oral Phase)	Fear of loss of the love object (mother)	Feelings of helplessness occur when mother is out of sight, understanding that she is needed for survival.
Two to three years (Anal Phase)	Fear of loss of the object's love	Learns that survival and need satisfaction depend on mother's loving and caring.
Four to six years (Phallic Phase)	Castration fear and anxiety over injury	Oedipal dynamics result in castration fear because of desire to possess love object exclusively; attack anticipated.
Post-Oedipal through adulthood	Fear of superego censure: fear of negative self-judgments	After internalization of parental standards, superego judges ego's efforts to satisfy id, and may condemn some wishes or ideas. Fear of self-evaluation.

Based on Freud, 1926a and 1933.

EVALUATING THEORETICAL PSYCHOANALYSIS

In Chapter 2, clinical psychoanalysis was evaluated in terms of its poor scientific testability, conception of human agency as essentially passive, and its focus on the idiographic aspects of human psychology. It is to be expected that much of what our evaluation of clinical psychoanalysis revealed applies to the more abstract elements created by Freud in later years. The later theory continues to picture people as passive entities shaped by reality, and its focus remains on the unique dynamics of the individual case. But a question poses itself: *Can testable propositions be derived from the later, more theoretical psychoanalytic psychology?* In this chapter, therefore, we do not retrace our steps in discussing human agency or the idiographic dimension. Instead, we focus on issues of deducing empirical propositions and subjecting them to scientific test.

Refutability of Psychoanalysis

As Freud built increasingly complex abstractions to represent his clinical observations, psychoanalysis grew more distant from clinical experience. Freud thought of his theoretical abstractions from about 1914 onward as a "metapsychology" in the sense that the theoretical concepts evolved out of but surpassed the observations on which they were based.

Were psychoanalysts willing to map their theory to observable brain structures and processes, and were they sufficiently patient to submit such ideas to laboratory tests, we would have to award high grades for refutability to psychoanalysis. There is no implication that all such tests would be confirmatory, but at least the theory could capitalize on established scientific method. Unfortunately, as always, things are not that simple.

Freud sometimes regarded his metapsychological creations as metaphors for unmapped brain processes and structures, not as "internal agents" in a literal sense. Rather, he seems to have hoped that his structural metaphors would someday be anchored to brain function and location when the sciences of neuroanatomy and neurophysiology had progressed. Yet there are lengthy theoretical discussions in some of Freud's major books where he intellectually manipulates metapsychological concepts as if they were real, as if they were to be understood as reality. In his popular lectures and essays, for example, he treats his model of the mind quite dramatically so that ego, id, and superego are described in terms of war metaphors, battle strategies, and advances and retreats, and as having motives and expectations of their own (Freud, 1910a, 1916, 1933, 1940). For his popular audience, he treated these "structures" as if they were individual people inside the person.

But in his more professional writings Freud clearly is aware that these "structures" are metaphors for something else (e.g., 1923a, 1926a). The puzzle for scholars and scientists is to discover the nature of the "something else," for it is from the interpretation of what the structural entities "really" represent that the empirical research flows (see the answers proposed by Parisi, 1987, 1988; B. Silverstein, 1985, 1988, 1989a, 1989b; Sulloway, 1979). The eminent contemporary psychoanalyst Roy Schafer (1976, 1983) has shown the many ways in which Freud's followers have taken his metaphors as literal and the difficulties such literalizing causes (see also Leites, 1971,

for a compelling analysis of the confusion between metaphor and reality in psychoanalytic theory).

Thus it is doubtful whether Freud really understood people as divided among
three agencies—id, ego, superego—that conduct warfare inside their heads. What is
not doubtful is that many of Freud's followers and adherents of classical analysis lost
sight of the metaphorical nature of Freudian metapsychology. Well-intentioned efforts
to test Freudian theory in the laboratory were doomed to failure because such tests
confused two very different levels of discourse. In principle, the researcher has to
decide at the outset whether the concepts to be tested are to be extracted from psychoanalysis *unchanged in definition* or to *translate the psychoanalytic metaphors
into a form that anchors them to observable, nonmetaphorical referents.*

If a researcher decides to test analytic theory unchanged, the main psychoanalytic concepts will prove to be stated in unrefutable terms, as we discussed in Chapter 2. Metaphors are neither confirmable nor falsifiable. On the other hand, if the
researcher decides to test psychoanalytic concepts by *translating them into some
empirical form,* such as referencing id operations to what is known about the brain's
limbic system or hypothalamus, then psychoanalysts will, rightfully, ask, "Is it really
Freud's psychoanalytic theory that is being tested?" By the same token, once an
empirical translation is made of a Freudian idea so that a testable idea is deduced from
the original untestable one, the rest of the scientific community is likely to ask, "So
what has this idea to do with psychoanalysis?" No one, it seems safe to say, will be satisfied. Whatever experiments are conducted to test this theory, they will always leave
room for more dispute, create more questions than those that are answered, and generate more confusion. As Mark Twain pointed out in *Puddn'head Wilson,* it is very
much a case of the oyster:

> We know all about the habits of the ant, know all about the habits of the bee, but we
> known nothing at all about the habits of the oyster. It seems almost certain that we
> have been choosing the wrong time for studying the oyster.

Some Illustrative Oyster Studies in Psychoanalysis

The story of actual attempts to verify or refute psychoanalytic theory is very much
like a psychology soap opera. For sheer number, discounting quality for a moment,
nothing ever devised by psychologists has so stimulated research as Freud's ideas. If
we evaluate the productivity of Freudian theory for motivating people to do research,
it rates very high. However, if we rate the quality, coherence, and reliability of the
research results associated with this theory, we enter a world of confusion. The story
of "refutable" research connected with psychoanalysis can be told simply by examining three standard anthologies of such work.

Eysenck and Wilson (1973), two psychologists well known for their anti-Freudian
sentiments, collected 19 empirical studies of psychoanalytic theory that ranged from
tests of oral sexuality to castration anxiety to dream wishes. In every instance, they
were able to identify serious methodological flaws that invalidated the results of
the study. Moreover, even in studies that evidenced only minor methodological
flaws, Eysenck and Wilson questioned whether the hypothesis tested really needed
Freudian theory as its basis.

By contrast to Eysenck and Wilson, Paul Kline (1972), a psychologist with a favorable estimation of Freudian theory, examined several hundred observational and experimental studies that tested psychoanalytic ideas. In many cases, Kline found the same methodological flaws as had Eysenck and Wilson, and for other studies, Kline concluded that the hypothesis tested was irrelevant to psychoanalytic theory. However, for a substantial number of studies, especially those concerned with repression and the Oedipus complex, Kline interpreted the outcomes as verifying some major psychoanalytic concepts. Here's a small excerpt from Kline's closing summary:

> Much of the metapsychology of psychoanalytic theory, it has been agreed, is unscientific in that it cannot be subjected to any kind of empirical test and so be refuted. Such concepts as the death instinct and the pleasure principle fall under this head. On the other hand we have shown much of psychoanalytic theory to consist of empirical propositions which can, logically at least, be tested. . . . Many of the Freudian concepts most important to psychoanalytic theory have been supported, for example, repression and the Oedipus complex. Finally, we have raised the fundamental question as to whether the verification of these Freudian concepts means that psychoanalytic theory should be retained. To this end, for those psychoanalytic propositions that were verified, we examined the predictions made from theories of learning. Here it was found that in most cases the Freudian phenomena could be fitted into a model derived from theories of learning but that these theories on their own could not have predicted the clinical phenomena. (Kline, 1972, p. 358).

Who is right here? Is the skepticism of Eysenck and Wilson too negative? Is the enthusiasm of Kline too positive? In some cases, both the Eysenck and Wilson book and the Kline book examine identical studies and draw opposite conclusions. How can opinion count so much, how can there be such disagreement if the evidence, experiments, and research designs being reviewed adhere to acceptable scientific criteria? The answer, we cringe at the realization, is that it depends on who is reviewing the evidence.

A third family of experimental studies comes from the long-term research program of Lloyd Silverman (e.g., 1976, 1983; Silverman, Lachmann, & Milich, 1982) using a subliminal presentation of verbal stimuli thought to enhance, gratify, or elicit unconscious wishes. Silverman and his students have published a large number of studies in which subjects are exposed to a visual presentation of a phrase such as *"mommy and I are one"* at exposure speeds that prevent *conscious* perception of the phrase. (A device called a tachistoscope that controls presentation speed in hundredths of a second, lighting intensity, and even placement in the visual field is used in such experiments.) In a typical study, schizophrenic patients or depressed patients compared with control subjects in other diagnostic categories and compared with nonpatient normals are exposed to the "mommy and I are one" stimulus. Control subjects, depending on the experimental design, are exposed either to a neutral verbal stimulus (e.g., *"People are walking"*) or to the same verbal stimulus as the experimental patient group.

The "mommy and I are one" stimulus is allegedly deduced from contemporary psychoanalytic theory and allegedly gratifies the symbiotic wishes that this version of psychoanalytic theory postulates as one of the psychological variables at work in disorders such as schizophrenia, obesity, and depression. Outcome measures include ratings of reductions in the patients' symptom severity, or ratings of before and after changes in nonverbal behavior or mood or sometimes direct performance measures on laboratory tasks. Silverman and his students have argued that their work tests psychoanalytic hypotheses empirically, and that their results overwhelmingly support one or another derivation from the theory.

The number of logical and methodological problems with Silverman's studies is substantial. Balay and Shevrin (1988) reviewed the bulk of the literature and made some important discoveries. Among those of relevance to the present discussion are the following points:

- In many studies, the measured favorable change in the people exposed subliminally to the message drawn from psychoanalytic theory was actually a statistical artifact. What appears to have happened is that comparisons of an individual's changes before and after subliminal exposure were made to the control group subjects who evidenced changes in a direction opposite to the subjects. Experimental subjects did not "improve." In fact, they changed very little from their exposure to "*mommy and I are one.*" It was the control subjects exposed to the neutral stimulus "*people are walking*" who changed, but the changes were typically those that would count as "negative" within the design of the study. For example, controls might become more depressed than their own preexposure ratings indicated whereas the experimental subjects tended to remain stable or change very little. Thus one could argue for a large number of Silverman's studies that the hypothesis drawn from psychoanalytic theory had little or no relevance in itself. Only when overall comparisons are made between experimental subjects and control subjects (who deteriorated) is there a significant difference between the groups, and that difference is not the one predicted. Seen in this light, some of Silverman's studies can be understood as demonstrating not the therapeutic power of "*mommy and I are one,*" but the toxic effect of "*people are walking*"!

- Carefully considered, there is no single example in the whole literature of a real replication of any one of Silverman's studies. Every time someone set out to test Silverman's method or to confirm one of his findings, they sufficiently changed the method or the outcome measures to disqualify the study as a replication. In fact, the Balay and Shevrin (1988) review suggests that whenever Silverman and his students found that there was the possibility that the outcome of a study might be dubious as a confirmation of Freudian hypotheses or the outcome was essentially disconfirmatory, the dependent measures were changed until one was found that lay in the predicted direction.

- Even if Silverman's method and measures were valid, there would still be difficulty interpreting the outcome of his studies as testing psychoanalytic ideas. The assumption that a subliminally presented verbal message such as "*mommy and I are one*" is somehow equivalent to an unconscious, developmental experience of "fusing with" a love object or with one's perceptions of the maternal figure is highly questionable. Does Silverman really mean that a verbal statement is *equivalent* to the developmental experience postulated by his interpretation of psychoanalysis? Or does he mean that the verbal statement presented subliminally activates some form of *memory* of an actual experience? Or does he mean that the verbal stimulus gratifies some kind of *universal longing* in people that enhances our psychological functioning (Balay & Shevrin, 1988, pp. 171 ff.)? The answer to all three questions is the same: It depends on when you study the oyster.

In any event, even this research that purports to derive from and to test psychoanalytic ideas does not satisfy most rigorous experimentalists and disappoints some psychoanalytic thinkers.

Refutability:"Couldn't Hurt—Much."

Fisher and Greenberg (1996) are among those commentators who, thankfully, are not deterred by the philosophical, methodological and historical critics who raise clouds of obfuscation. They updated their earlier reviews (1977, 1985) of the research studies testing Freudian hypotheses and arrived at what seems to be a balanced current assessment of the scientific status of Freud's ideas. Of course, Fisher and Greenberg are not immune to the Oyster phenomenon, and there are undoubtedly critics who will disagree with Fisher and Greenberg's evaluations. Nevertheless, these commentators have simply done their reviews more often and more thoroughly than anyone else and they deserve some consideration. Here are a few of Fisher and Greenberg's conclusions:

- Freud's notion that the experience of loss is the trigger for depression receives little support from the scientific literature. There is some evidence that accumulated early and late losses over a lifetime are linked to depression, but the evidence is weak. Freud's related idea that nonnurturing or disapproving parents make a child vulnerable to depression receives moderate support. The strongest support was for Freud's notion that depression is linked to a passive orientation marked by feelings of oral dependency and fixation to the oral stage of psychosexual development.
- Freud's concept of an orally dependent personality type prone to the use of repression and denial was supported by factor analytic research that demonstrated meaningful clustering of the personality traits described in Freud's theory.
- Freud's "anal retentive" and "anal erotic" personality types likewise received substantial support from factor-analytic studies that demonstrate a clustering of the relevant traits.
- The Oedipus theory advanced by Freud, including his hypotheses about the origins of homosexuality and the severity of individual moral self-judgment, had no support in the scientific literature. However, derivations of Oedipal theory based on the concept of "penis envy" in females, surprisingly, received some support in Fisher and Greenberg's view, possibly because they conducted some of the relevant studies.

- Freudian dream theory, especially his notion of dreams as disguised fulfillment of taboo wishes, was entirely contradicted by current dream research.

Greenberg and Fisher (1996, p. 267) point out that they did not review what seem to be supportive studies of Freud's concepts of repression and the unconscious. On the whole, they conclude that Freud's theory has far more scientific support than widespread stereotypes about its failings suggest, but much of the theory either defies scientific testing or has failed the tests made.

What, then, are we to make of the refutability of psychoanalysis? However pessimistic and cynical it may appear, history indicates that Freud probably made the best prediction of all in his laconic message to psychologist Saul Rosenzweig, who had sent some experimental studies for Freud to examine. Recall that Freud wrote to Rosenzweig that he felt such studies were more or less irrelevant, but that in the long run such research "could do no harm." Was Freud saying, "Won't do any good, but it couldn't hurt"? We suspect he was. Because the theory was stated originally in terms that actually defy any uniform interpretation or translation into empirically testable constructs, it is likely that no research will ever substantially affect what the adherents or the foes of psychoanalysis do or think about this theory.

SUMMARY

Anna Freud's "stwawbewwies" dream reveals with stark simplicity the essential nature of dream processes: the fantasied fulfillment of wishes. As Freud investigated dream processes, however, he soon learned that adult dreamers' productions were far from the lucid creations of children. Distortion and disguise are introduced into the story of the dream by the mechanisms of dream work, including displacement, condensation, visual representation, and secondary revision. Thus, Freud found, dreams have both a latent and a manifest content, as distinguishable from each other as the actor and the mask.

Freud embarked on a revision and a tightening of his psychological theory in a series of important "metapsychological" papers.

Freud now saw repression as a two-stage process: *primal repression against early unacceptable impulses* and *repression proper* against later adult derivatives.

Permitting his imagination free rein in constructing the metapsychology, Freud proposed that psychopathology recapitulates phylogeny. He outlined a six-phase evolutionary history of the human race that is recapitulated at different stages of some individuals' lives in the six transference and narcissistic "neuroses" of Anxiety Hysteria, Conversion Hysteria, Obsessional Neurosis, Paranoia, Schizophrenia, and Manic-Depression.

Because of the basic conflict underlying the neurotic behavior of the patients he observed, Freud sought to conceptualize the instincts in a dualism that contrasted the self-preservative instincts (e.g., hunger) with the instincts of pleasure (sex, libido). The dualistic classification of hunger versus love had eventually to be revised when Freud's speculations revealed the presence of an even more fundamental dichotomy in instinctual life: life versus death.

In *Beyond the Pleasure Principle* (1920a), Freud created a new picture of the workings of the mind. This altered view included Freud's argument that the nervous system had evolved in such a way as to minimize the excitatory level of the organism by directing the organism's efforts to satisfy needs immediately. The ultimate aim of an instinct is to return the organism to the unstimulable state of inorganic matter, namely, to the state of death. Since the death instinct cannot be directly observed, its derivatives of hate, anger, and aggression are the only overt evidence of its existence. When the life instincts, or Eros as Freud now called the combined ego and sexual instincts, oppose the death instinct, the energy of destruction is turned outward from the individual and displaced onto other individuals.

Freud proceeded from his revision of instinct theory to a total revision of his conception of the mind. He created a structural model that depicted the mind as a blending, merging amalgam of forces. The structural model had three divisions: id, ego, and superego. The id, formerly the unconscious, is the seat of the instincts, and is a cauldron of fury, striving to gain immediate satisfaction of its urges. To accommodate the id's desires and needs, a specialized portion, the ego, emerges from the id to steer a safe course through reality and to maintain satisfactory relations with the world. By the age of five or six, another agency, the superego, is internalized within the child. The superego is the "heir of the Oedipal complex," for it is based on identification with the parents, and assimilates the energy of the renounced Oedipal desires. The superego is the moral or ethical arm of personality, and it has final say in matters of ego-id relations.

Freud's conception of anxiety changed over the years from the view that anxiety is the result of dammed-up sexual impulses, to the concept that the ego responds to a variety of danger situations with signals of unpleasure. Freud experimented with the idea that the prototype of anxiety is the trauma of birth, but more generally, anxiety is an ego reaction to perceptions of being overwhelmed or flooded helplessly by intense stimulation.

As we saw in Chapter 2, Freud's theory does not lend itself to scientific testing easily. History suggests that even when hypotheses are derived from the theory that can be tested, such hypotheses will be perceived by Freudians as irrelevant to the theory, and by experimentalists as not actually testing the classic formulations. What research exists, and it is a vast literature, always dissatisfies everyone. The brief survey undertaken in this chapter suggests that between the methodological flaws and the logical inconsistencies, psychoanalysis will continue as a powerful theory in the hands of its adherents and as a straw man against which to rail in the hands of its critics.

Though the scope of our two chapters on Freud is extensive, it should not surprise you that the material presented merely scratches the surface of the mass of ideas and hypotheses that are to be found in Freud's collected works. For that reason, you are encouraged to pursue topics of interest in Freud's own writings.

FOR FURTHER READING

The best overviews in Freud's own writings of his later theory are to be found in two complementary sets of lectures. The first of these dates from his prestructural model of the mind and is entitled *Introductory Lectures on Psychoanalysis*, Vol. XV and XVI of *The Standard Edition* (or in paperback under the title *A General Introduction to Psychoanalysis* [New York: Washington Square Press, 1960, or Norton, 1935]). The second set of lectures dates from his development of the id-ego-superego model and can be found in Vol. XXII of *The Standard Edition* under the title *New Introductory Lectures on Psychoanalysis* (also available in paperback [New York: Norton, 1964]).

Possibly the simplest and clearest introduction to psychoanalysis ever written and one that can claim some measure of authority is Anna Freud's recently published *The Harvard Lectures* (New York: International Universities Press, 1992).

Freud's own historical accounts of the development of his system bear scrutiny. *An Autobiographical Study* (*The Standard Edition*, Vol. XX; paperback edition, Norton, 1935) was Freud's attempt to survey personal and intellectual factors that shaped his theorizing. A further historical effort by Freud, dating from somewhat earlier in his career (1914), can be found in *On the History of the Psychoanalytic Movement* (*The Standard Edition*, Vol. XIV; also in *The Basic Writings of Sigmund Freud*, translated and edited by A. A. Brill, New York: Random House, 1938).

Freud considered *The Interpretation of Dreams* to be his masterpiece (Vols. IV and V of *The Standard Edition*; also in *The Basic Writings of Sigmund Freud*, edited by A. A. Brill, New York: Random House, 1938), and Chapter 7 of this work contains the direct translation of his early neurological model into a topographical model of the mind. The serious student of psychoanalysis will also want to consult a series of papers collectively termed Freud's "Metapsychology," and published as "Instincts and Their Vicissitudes" (1915); "Repression" (1915); "The Unconscious" (1915); "Metapsychological Supplement of the Theory of Dreams" (1917); and "Mourning and Melancholia" (1917) (all contained in Vol. XIV of *The Standard Edition*). These papers form the heart of Freud's midcareer theorizing and his attempts to reconcile ambiguities and inconsistencies in his early formulations.

Freud's final model of the mind is to be found in his *The Ego and the Id* (1923) in Vol. XIX of *The Standard Edition* (also in paperback [New York: Norton, 1960]), and in more concise form in one of his last publications, *An Outline of Psycho-Analysis* in Vol. XXIII of *The Standard Edition* (and in paperback [New York: Norton, 1949]).

Freud's changing conception of defense and anxiety can be discerned by a comparative reading of one of his early papers, "The Neuro-Psychoses of Defence" (1894) and his later *Inhibitions, Symptoms and Anxiety* (1926); in Vol. XX of *The Standard Edition* (or in paperback under the title *The Problem of Anxiety* [New York: Norton, 1936]. Anna Freud elaborated her father's conception of neurotic defense mechanisms in a book that has now become a psychoanalytic classic and essential reading for all students of psychoanalysis, *The Ego and the Mechanisms of Defense*, revised edition (New York: International Universities Press, 1966). Robert Stolorow and George Atwood's *Faces in a Cloud* (New York: Aronson, 1979) considers the subjective sources of Freud's psychosexual theory.

Critical commentaries and summaries of Freud's thinking abound. A survey and analysis of the experimental study of Freudian concepts is provided by Paul Kline in *Fact and Fantasy in Freudian Theory* (New York: Harper & Row, 1972; originally published in Great Britain by Methuen). Where Kline is relatively optimistic about the empirical testability and validity of Freud's ideas, Hans Eysenck and Glen Wilson in their *Experimental Study of Freudian Theories* (New York: Harper & Row, 1973; originally published in Great Britain by Methuen) reproduce and sharply criticize several "classic" experiments purporting to demonstrate the validity of Freudian hypotheses. Richard Wolheim has edited a collection of philosophical essays and methodological criticisms of Freud's ideas that will repay the careful reader of his *Freud: A Collection of Critical Essays* (New York: Doubleday, 1974). A similarly critical viewpoint from a more psychological perspective is maintained throughout the essays contained in *Critical Essays on Psychoanalysis*, edited by Stanley Rachman (New York: Macmillan, 1963). Erich Fromm's *The Anatomy of Human Destructiveness* (New York: Holt, 1973) contains an incisive criticism of Freud's death instinct.

The areas of personality research in which Freud's theory have been applied are so numerous as to defy classification, but two clinically oriented studies deserve attention. Peter Blos modified and extended Freud's ideas for application to the stormy period of adolescence in two books: *On Adolescence* (New York: Free Press, 1962) and *The Young Adolescent: Clinical Studies* (New York: Free Press, 1970). The latter volume presents two detailed case histories of Susan and Ben, young people for whom psychoanalytic therapy proved invaluable. Kenneth Keniston's *The Uncommitted: Alienated Youth in American Society* (New York: Dell, 1960) brilliantly applies Freudian theory, especially the Oedipus complex, to the task of explaining why young, affluent, and well-educated males become disaffected with society and with their own lives.

ANNA FREUD

The Psychoanalytic Heritage:
Ego Psychology

. . . instinctual danger makes human beings intelligent.

Anna Freud (1936)

Healthy people too obey "musts."

Heinz Hartmann (1939)

Past theories of personality have not always made it clear that human beings have intrinsic urges which make them want to grow up.

Robert W. White (1975)

. . . the prerequisite for personality development . . . is contact with a human love object.

Margaret Mahler (1968)

About Ego Psychology and Object Relations Theory

By the time of Freud's death, psychoanalysis began to focus on the unique properties of the ego in guiding a person's capacity to master life's demands and not just react to them.

*   **Anna Freud** *began these subtle changes in her efforts to work psychoanalytically with children. Gradually she altered the theory of the ego from that of the helpless rider of the id horse described by Sigmund into a more intelligent rider concerned with the best routes to travel.*

*   **Heinz Hartmann**, *the "father of ego psychology," further strengthened the ego by theorizing that it originated not out of the id, but simultaneously with the id out of the same nervous system roots. This small change in conceptualizing the ego's birth effectively rewrote the psychoanalytic definition of humans as passion-driven creatures.*

*   **Robert W. White** *completely freed the ego from its dependence on the id by postulating that the ego has its own independent source of energy. Called "effectance motivation," this basic striving is the inherent urge to manipulate, to explore, and to master the environment from the earliest days of infancy.*

*   **Margaret Mahler** *explored the early roots of ego development in the interaction between infant and mother. Her work established a theoretical sequence of the formation of important ego skills, such as the capacity for empathy, restraint of action, and tolerance for being a separate person. With Mahler, early cognitive, emotional developments, and object relations were given importance equal to the importance given to post-Oedipal developments in classical theory. Mother-child love grew in stature in psychoanalysis, taking a place alongside the classical emphasis on mother-child-father conflicts.*

*   *This chapter can be understood, despite the diversity of thinkers represented, as an intellectual history of the changes wrought in classic psychoanalysis by thinkers who struggled to correct its contradictions rather than abandon it.*

WHAT HAD FREUD LEFT UNDONE?

From the distress of his patients, from the almost too painful revelations of his self-analysis, and from his formidable knowledge of neuroanatomy, Sigmund Freud composed his complex portrait of the hidden but inescapable war of human needs. In a near half century of psychological work, Freud structured his theory with observations of human beings in their times of self-defeating helplessness, during their crises of self-deceiving passion and despair. How shall we human creatures, then, construe ourselves differently because one such man as Freud lived, and loved, and worked? What weight shall we give to the new meanings that Freud distilled from his observations of self and others? What features had Freud neglected to include in his portrait? *What had Freud left undone?*

Consider the contribution to be made to psychoanalytic theory by widening its focus to include not merely the ego's vulnerabilities but the ego strengths that emerge and generalize to new situations as the person confronts life's adversities. An illustrative case is in order to concretize the contrast between classical and contemporary psychoanalytic theory.

Little Lulu and the Girls' Night Out

Because of her many hospital stays and separations from home during childhood treatment for her heart condition, Jean-Mary was especially sensitive to social privations. Any abrupt change in the continuity and sameness of her life was likely to be equated with the harrowing experiences of hospitalization. Thus Jean-Mary developed her own strategies to master the anxiety of a continually uncertain existence. Her goal, though of course she would not have verbalized it as such, was to bring as much of her life as possible under her own control.

One game of special importance to Jean-Mary around the age of nine or ten was playacting the cartoon character of Little Lulu. All children, quite normally, enact fantasy roles, but the typical fantasy involves a superhero or heroine capable of more than ordinary human feats. Jean-Mary was content to be Little Lulu.

In that role, she would roam easily around her neighborhood, pretending to look for her "friends" Tubby and Alvin. Looking back on the game from the perspective of adulthood, Jean-Mary recalls that its special attraction was the "homey" ordinariness of the characters, and the fact that Little Lulu was usually the boss who instigated the action.

Another pastime that occupied Jean-Mary around that same period involved more direct contact with children of the neighborhood. Called "girls' night out," this game required all of the eight- or nine-year-old young ladies of Jean-Mary's acquaintance to assemble under her direction near a large elm tree at the end of the block immediately after supper. Boys were explicitly excluded from the gathering, hence the significance of the name. More important, prior to a satisfactory "girls' night out," a whole afternoon had to be devoted to planning and scheduling the events, selecting the right dolls and their outfits, and organizing with great care the arrivals and departures of the participants. Almost invariably, however, the pregame planning was kept scrupulously the same. Needless to say, the chief organizer was Jean-Mary.

The Classical Psychoanalytic Account

In classical Freudian theory, Jean-Mary's games would be interpreted as compulsive ritualization designed to inhibit separation anxiety. By promoting the enforcement of sameness and repetition in her games, Jean-Mary's ego was able to assume an active rather than a reactive role. The enforced uncertainty of hospital admissions and releases was reflected in her attempts to create a limited area of life directly under her own control. Recall the similarly motivated game of Freud's grandson Ernst, discussed in Chapter 3, whereby the repetitive cycle of loss and gain was mastered symbolically as Ernst made his toys and himself "gone." The focus of the classical Freudian account of human behavior is on the vulnerability and weakness of the ego when confronted with powerful id demands or overwhelming external reality. If, for example, the id's pressure for secure and unbroken contact with gratifying love objects is violated, the ego may feel threatened and helpless. To restore mastery, the ego initiates a series of defensive adjustments, as in Jean-Mary's compulsively repetitive games.

Thus Freud's dynamic model represents neurotic maladjustment as a weakening of the ego's customary mastery of the three provinces of mental life: the pressing id drives, the demands of external reality, and the censure of the superego (Freud, 1940, pp. 172ff.). But the crucial subject of interest for Freud was the id. He envisioned this mental province as ceaselessly pursuing gratification for its sexual and aggressive urges. And what the id wants, the id gets.

Jean-Mary's attempts at life mastery through her games would have to be understood within Freud's scheme as partially derived from the id's anger at being deprived of satisfying love objects, and partially derived from the ego's double fear of the id's demands and of the real dangers of separation from home. The emphasis is not on the ego's strivings to master the world it experiences or to adapt to circumstances that cannot be changed; the emphasis is on the ego's defensive operations undertaken on the id's behalf.

Freud was adamant throughout his writings that the central contribution of psychoanalysis was its elucidation of unconscious instinctual dynamics. Psychology, for Freud, was the unmasking of human passion. What was psychologically most real, what was truly "mental" in classical psychoanalytic theory was the id. "The power of the id," Freud wrote, "expresses the true purpose of the individual organism's life" (1940, p. 148). Although the ego assumed increasing importance in Freud's theory from the 1920s onward, it nevertheless remained always only a participant in the id's power.

In comparison to the monolithic id, the ego was to be considered a "facade" or a "frontage" of the unconscious, owing its unique properties to and exercising its reality functions exclusively for the more extensive id from which it initially emerged (Freud, 1926b, pp. 195 and 200). In short, the ego owes its very reason for existence to the id. Freud bluntly summarized the character of his theoretical creation:

> If we accept the distinction which I have recently proposed of dividing the mental apparatus into an ego, turned towards the external world and equipped with consciousness, and an unconscious id, dominated by its instinctual needs, then *psychoanalysis is to be described as a psychology of the id (and of its effects upon the ego).* (1924c, p. 209; italics added)

The id and its biological processes persistently occupied center stage in Freud's thinking. One important reason for Freud's apparently one-sided approach was his commitment to an implicitly neurological conception of psychology, and we discuss Freud's "Psychology for Neurologists" at a later point in this chapter. However, at the moment we need to contrast this classical viewpoint with the wider contemporary psychoanalytic focus on ego strengths.

The Ego Psychological Account

Taken together, Jean-Mary's games have a common character: Each game aided her adaptation to a reality she did not create but in which she had to function productively.

More precisely stated, Jean-Mary recalls that each of these "games" had the very important personal meaning that life *could* be rational, *should* be reliable, *was* predictable. She understood in her childishly wise way that her separations from home and the unpredictable life of the hospital must not be allowed to overwhelm and sour her growing up. How shall we understand these needs for consistency, for predictability, and for mastery? How do we understand the ego's need for sensible meanings?

It makes little sense, logically or emotionally, to conceptualize these urges as exclusive derivatives of sexual pleasure or aggressive-destructive drives. Nevertheless, it is possible to do so, because the ultimate outcome of Jean-Mary's games is the production of pleasure and the reduction of tension, broadly conceived. Yet, the stretching of Freudian drive theory to human strivings that are beyond its realm is like explaining Picasso's achievements as a sublimation of his childhood struggle with the urge to smear feces. Such "explanations" can be made, but they sadly neglect the role of innate intelligence and unique personal interpretations of the meaning of one's life.

Freud himself took steps in this direction of broadening the ego's independence from the id's drives by proposing the concept of desexualized libido (1923a, pp. 43–45). In this form, libido provided the ego with a neutral and displaceable form of energy, severed from the id's passions. However, even with its neutral status, desexualized libido was conceptualized by Freud as emanating from the ego's original pool of narcissistic libido and as obeying the pleasure principle (1923a, p. 45). Freud went so far as to apply this concept of desexualized libido to the task of explaining thinking and the judgmental processes of the ego. But even in this limited sphere, Freud would not allow the ego full independence from the id's drives, for thinking was now to be interpreted as "the sublimation of erotic motive forces" (Freud, 1923a, p. 45).

Consider another difficulty in accounting psychoanalytically for Jean-Mary's games. Classical theory would have it that her actions were completely accounted for in the discovery of their defensive, anxiety-reducing nature. The fear of separation from love objects (mother-father) is derived from the infant's initial total dependence on adults for survival and for pleasure-producing tension reduction. Through development, this dependence is enlarged and elaborated into acceptance of the mother as an independently existing object who both provides and evokes love. But is the enigma of Jean-Mary's games completely dissolved by attributing their origin to defensive maneuvers designed to provide security substitutes for the lost love objects? How then shall we account for her unique choice of Little Lulu as the character of her "defensive" fantasies? It would appear that we require something more social, more reality-oriented, and more intellectually based to understand her choice of the particular strategies that suited her purposes so creatively.

A child's thoughts and fantasies are not always centered on new ways to obtain lost gratification. Maturation and growth present their own joys in the pleasures of exercising imagination and reason. Solving problems yields not only relief from frustration but positive intrinsic satisfactions:

> . . . the mastery of difficulties, the solving of problems, becomes a novel source of delight. And thinking itself yields gratification. Thought processes can operate on various levels; thought and fantasy interact. The child can imagine and pretend; he

can, in his fantasies, re-enact his relationship with his environment; he can play at being an adult—briefly, the child has created a world of his own. (Hartmann, Kris, & Lowenstein, 1946, p. 48)

Jean-Mary's games were not merely defensive maneuvers to restore lost security. Her games were also expressions of her innermost attitudes toward herself and toward her world. In devising her fantasy world and in organizing her girls' night out, Jean-Mary displayed a wide range of *adaptive* skills designed not only to resolve conflicts but to aid in healthy living. Her self-chosen image of Little Lulu reveals an ego struggling not only *against* anxiety but creatively *for* mastery of the present. Identification with Little Lulu was not a defensive strategy designed to provide disguised gratification for sexual and aggressive urges. What Jean-Mary found in Little Lulu was the means to lead an ordinary and healthy girlhood in the face of extraordinary circumstances. Little Lulu was the way to try out being a little girl, the way to test out her own sorely challenged ability to be competent in life.

It can be said fairly that Freud neglected none of these aspects of psychology. All of these ideas, and more, can be found scattered through his writings, as Hartmann (1939) has shown. But therein lies the problem; the ideas are scattered through Freud's work. Intentionally or by default, Freud left it to others to elaborate, extend, and apply these germs of insight (Blanck & Blanck, 1974, p. 24; see also Yankelovich & Barrett, 1970, especially chapters 4 and 5). Contemporary ego psychology must not be thought of as a sweeping revision or profound revolution in psychoanalytic thought, or in terms of any other simplifications meant to suggest an abrupt break with the past. Closer to the truth is a conception of ego psychology that depicts its various theoreticians as skillful extenders of Freudian concepts in pathways marked but not journeyed by its first explorer (Holt, 1975). Freud rightfully, but perhaps too one-sidedly, considered his discovery of unconscious forces and their diversity of expression to be fundamental achievements outweighing any other contribution psychoanalysis had made:

> *The* great discovery of psychoanalysis was the existence of these unconscious forces. It took quite a while to realize that this discovery does not compel us to embrace a solipsistic theory in which a chimney is primarily a phallic symbol and only secondarily the means for letting smoke out of the house. It was some time before we began to take account of the chimney as a smokestack, because these realistic meanings were not the focus of our early interests. (Rapaport, 1958, p. 14)

Building on Freud's achievements with increasing sophistication and heightened concern for whole persons rather than partitioned minds, the theorists who followed him stressed the autonomy and self-sufficiency of the ego. In contemporary ego psychology, humans are neither completely drive-bound nor fully emancipated from their biological heritage. By contrast, in classical Freudian theory, the drives predominate, and the ego is, to use Freud's own metaphor, like the rider of a spirited horse who leads it where the horse wants to go (Freud, 1923a, p. 25; 1933, p. 77).

What had Freud left undone? He left incomplete the picture of the ego's vital participation in maintaining the delicate balance that prevents individuals from tottering into slavery to their drives or into submission to their environment. And Freud omitted from consideration the fact that sometimes a rider prefers to walk.

FREUD'S TYRANT: THE FORTY-FOUR YEAR PERSISTENCE OF NEUROLOGY

There is another way to phrase the question "What had Freud left undone?" Why was Freud compelled to emphasize the id instincts in a mind portrayed as partitioned into competing systems? To represent the conflict he invariably found in his patients and in himself, Freud had constructed a theory of the mind that pictured the psyche as a house divided against itself. From Freud's pioneering viewpoint, how else could paradoxical self-deceptions be explained?

For example, in the case of a repressed impulse, the analyst observes the enigma of persons who *intend* what they do not know. Or, conversely, when a person says the exact opposite of what was meant, as in a slip of the tongue: "I would like to *prevent*, uh, present, the distinguished professor. . . ."—the slip seems to indicate that the person *knows* what he or she does not intend (Fingarette, 1974; Thalberg, 1974). Freud was acutely alert to such paradoxes, for their existence seemed to reveal that a person could be literally of two minds. In the case of the manifest dream content, to take one more example, the dreamer has fooled her- or himself by disguising the latent content of strong desires so successfully that when awake he or she seems not to know what was avidly wished for while asleep: ". . . I can assure you that it is quite possible, and highly probable indeed, that the dreamer *does* know what his dream means: *only he does not know that he knows it and for that reason thinks he does not know it*" (Freud, 1916, p. 101).

In order to explain such apparent self-division, Freud conceptualized seemingly whole personalities as a congregation of compartmented agencies. Each agency, in Freud's view, is capable of only imperfect knowledge of the others and quite able to disavow their existence. The psychological portrait that emerges is an abstraction of a person, what Schafer (1976, p. 86) calls an "assembly of minds." As a result, Freud was forced into a curious anthropomorphism, treating each of the agencies as though it were a human entity with feelings, wishes, motives, blind spots, and goals of its own. In short, the abstractions—designed initially only to represent observable conflict—became personified. To illustrate, consider some of Freud's more memorable statements:

> When the ego assumes the features of the [lost] object, it is forcing itself, so to speak, upon the id as a love-object and is trying to make good the id's loss by saying: "Look, you can love me too—I am so like the object." (1923a, p. 30)

> . . . [The ego] is not only a helper to the id; it is also a submissive slave who courts his master's love. Whenever possible, it tries to remain on good terms with id. . . . (1923a, p. 56)

> The poor ego has things even worse. . . . Its three tyrannical masters are the external world, the superego and the id. When we follow the ego's efforts to satisfy them simultaneously—or rather, to obey them simultaneously—we cannot feel any regret at having personified this ego and having set it up as a separate organism. (1933, p. 77)

It may well be argued that because Freud was a master writer, his analogies, metaphors, and similes are nothing more than elegant and deliberate devices for expression. It is necessary to point out, therefore, that contemporary psychoanalysts do not object to Freud's use of metaphor; they object to the concepts implicit in the metaphors. Specifically, the various personifications in Freud's writings were designed to communicate his underlying conception of forces, conflicts between brain systems, and expulsions and retentions of physiological energies. As Schafer lucidly stated the difficulty of confusing neuroanatomy with psychological description:

> In line with this strategy, reasons become forces, emphases become energies, activity becomes function, thoughts become representations, affects become discharges or signals, deeds become resultants, and particular ways of struggling with the inevitable diversity of intentions, feelings, and situations become structures, mechanisms, and adaptations. (1976, p. 103)

Ironically, the fundamental difficulty to which the ego psychologists address themselves is the impersonalization that results from theoretical personifications. Intended only to communicate in a facile way a natural science, mechanistic conception of psychology, the divided agencies became homunculi ("little people") inside the person. Presumably, each homonculus has a little person within, and so on in a never-ending succession. The metaphors and personifications accomplished their end, conveying Freud's meaning clearly: Persons are partitioned systems powered by biological energies.

To return to our rephrased question: Why was Freud compelled to emphasize biological instinct energies and to partition the mind into an assembly of minds? The answer lies in Freud's implicit conception of the mind as functionally and (initially, at least) anatomically related brain systems.

"I have found my tyrant, and in his service I know no limits," Freud wrote to Wilhelm Fliess in April of 1895. He was confiding to his friend the joyous and overriding ambition of his life:

> . . . a man like me cannot live without a hobby-horse, a consuming passion—in Schiller's words a tyrant. . . . My tyrant is psychology; it has always been my distant, beckoning goal and now, since I have hit on the neuroses, it has come so much the nearer. I am plagued with two ambitions: to see how the theory of mental functioning takes shape if quantitative considerations, a sort of economics of nerve-force, are introduced into it; and secondly, to extract from psychopathology what may be of benefit to normal psychology. Actually a satisfactory general theory of neuropsychotic disturbances is impossible if it cannot be brought into association with clear assumptions about normal mental processes. (Freud, 1954, pp. 119–120)

Freud's goal, almost from the beginning of his work with hysterical patients, was to mine those bizarre disturbances for what they would yield in universal scientific knowledge about all mental functioning. He seemed to feel embarrassed in reporting the dramatic case histories of the *Studies on Hysteria,* that his work with these troubled people had resulted in such interesting literary-sounding accounts of private worlds:

> . . . I have not always been a psychotherapist. . . . It still strikes me myself as strange that the case histories I write should read like short stories and that, as one might say, they lack the serious stamp of science. (Freud, in Breuer & Freud, 1893–1895, p. 160)

As a trained and exceptionally talented neurophysiologist, Freud wanted to emulate his teachers and colleagues in their scientific attack on the problems of brain anatomy and biological function (Amacher, 1965; Hartmann, Kris, & Lowenstein, 1953, p. 122). What was real, legitimate, and worth studying in the science of Freud's day were the physical concepts of energy powering living and nonliving systems alike.

"The Project for a Scientific Psychology"

By 1895, Freud's apprenticeship to Josef Breuer and his own tentative, searching efforts to understand his neurotic patients confronted him with the first of a host of intellectual dilemmas. On the one hand, Freud now understood that the hysteric's suffering and symptoms made *psychological* sense. Indeed, symptoms had their origins in the patient's personal emotional history. On the other hand, Freud was schooled in the deterministic and mechanistic faith of nineteenth-century science that all phenomena are reducible to their physical, material components (Jones, 1955; McCarley & Hobson, 1977; Schur, 1972). Psychological events, like other biological functions, have their seat of origin in material bodily processes and in measurable flows of energy. Freud thus conceived a way out of his dilemma by proposing a "Psychology for Neurologists." That is to say, he attempted to construct a neurophysiological model of psychological processes that would bear the "serious stamp of science" to legitimize his "strange case histories."

This first model of the mind was a complex and elegant scheme of neuron cell systems and their mutual interchange of metabolic energy. Within the 150 or so pages of his "Psychology for Neurologists" may be found the kernel of nearly every important idea that occupied Freud for the next 44 years of theorizing (Basch, 1975; Gill, 1977; Holt, 1963; Kris, 1954, p. 364; McCarley & Hobson, 1977; Solomon, 1974). Freud wrote to Fliess that the model he was constructing was his tyrant. Yet, upon completion, Freud's tyrant had become Freud's castoff. He now described it to Fliess as a momentary "aberration" to be abandoned as a failure (1954, p. 134).

What Freud had begun as an attempt to justify and gain scientific respectability for his clinical insights had shortly become the intellectual stepchild of Freud's family of scientific aspirations. Freud kept the model from publication during his lifetime, and it was not until 1954 (1950 in German) that the "Project for a Scientific Psychology" made its appearance. The crucial point, however, is that the neurological model, undertaken near the beginning of Freud's psychoanalytic work, demonstrates clearly his intention to create a *scientific* theory of neurosis that would at the same time be a general psychology of human behavior. Freud understood the sterility of restricting his conceptualizations to abnormal behavior.

A successful neurophysiological model should also be capable of explaining the broad range of normal human psychology. Thus in Freud's "Project," attempts are made to explain such processes as dreaming, thinking, perception, learning, and judgment. But Freud, apparently, was embarrassed by the futility of his efforts to bend neuroanatomical concepts to the task of psychological explanation. He turned away from *explicit* neurologizing of his clinical findings, but he never abandoned the implicit model of brain systems as his abiding hypothesis for rendering clinical observations scientifically sensible. The terminology in Freud's writing became psychological, but the concepts thus represented remained neurological.

To understand Freud's deep intellectual attachment to neurological explanations, it is necessary only to read his excited announcement to Fliess, during his period of enthusiasm for the project, that the model was seemingly successful:

> One strenuous night last week, when I was in the stage of painful discomfort in which my brain works best, the barriers suddenly lifted, the veils dropped, and it was possible to see from the details of neurosis all the way to the very conditioning of consciousness. Everything fell into place, the cogs meshed, the thing really seemed to be a machine which in a moment would run of itself. . . . I can naturally hardly contain myself with delight. (Freud [1895], 1954, p. 129; see also the alternate version of this quotation in Freud, 1985, p. 146)

Freud's tyrant was, for the moment, Freud's joy.

BASIC ASSUMPTIONS OF FREUD'S BRAIN MODEL

Freud (1895) began with a set of hypotheses about the central nervous system derived more or less from the concrete anatomical knowledge of the day and sufficiently anchored in representational reality to be recognizable as a *brain model* of psychological processes. Others in medicine and neurology had attempted similar feats of biological reductionism with varying degrees of success (Amacher, 1965). What made Freud's effort modestly original was his attempt to build a brain on paper that would explain psychopathologies such as hysteria using the clinical observations he had gathered with his fundamentally psychological method of free association.

"Q" and "Qn" as the Energies of the Mind: Cathexis

At this stage of his career, *mind is brain* for Freud. In Freud's brain, nerve cells empty and fill with physical and psychical energy in response to the external world of stimulation and to the internal world of need. Nevertheless, this early neurological model had the essential Freudian psychological elements: conflict between needs and reality, ebbs and surges of psychological energy, and specialized neuron systems that "test" reality and store memories, unconscious processes, and wishes. More important, the fundamental concepts that occupied Freud through the next 40-odd years of theorizing were crudely formulated here (Miller, 1991). Among these paradigmatic issues were the idea that the human nervous system evolved to achieve pleasure through the discharge of tension; tension-free states are pleasurable states; the concept of mental censorship by which one part of the mind remains ignorant of another part's activities reflected in the censorship of unconscious taboo wishes and urges; and the notion that psychological conflict can be represented theoretically as a clash in the aims (functions? goals?) of neuronal systems that competitively process a finite supply of psychic energy called simply Q.

FIGURE 4.1   Freud's 1895 neurological model.

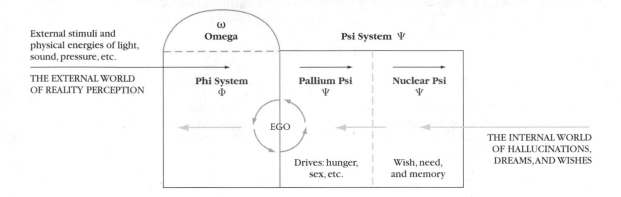

The Parts

Phi
Φ
A sensory receptor system with facilitative (nonresistant) contact barriers (synapses) that permits the energy (Q for "Quantity") of stimuli from the outside world to enter the internal world of the mind at the attenuated levels (Qn for "Neuronal-level Quantity") tolerable by living nerve cells.

Omega
ω
Sensitive to qualitative rather than quantitative differences between stimulation from the inner world of wish, need, and memory and to stimulation from the outer world of sights, sounds, and physical pressure, *Omega* is the neurological equivalent of reality testing. *Omega* sometimes gets confused. During sleep, for example, all incoming stimulation from the world is cut off and *Phi* neurons are "empty." What stimulation there is comes from the *Psi* memories, and fills the *Phi* neurons from the inside mental world. *Omega* believes the stimulation in *Phi* came from outside and mistakenly signals "this is real." The result is the hallucinatory realness of some dreams.

Psi
ψ
Two connected neuron systems that have resistant "contact barriers" or synapses and can store mental energy or what Freud called neuronal Quantity (*Qn*). *Pallium Psi* neurons have only partially resistant contact barriers and when they receive stimulation from the *Phi* system, they can pass it along to the deeper *Nuclear Psi* neurons, which have highly resistant contact barriers and store *Qn* as memory.

The Rules

Neurons communicate by exchanging Qn at their synapses, or "contact barriers." In Freud's neurological model, two rules govern cell interactions:

1. **Frequency.** The more frequently two or more neurons have exchanged Qn in prior interactions, the easier ("more facilitated") becomes such transmission between them. This principle states a fundamental rule of learning and memory.

2. **Magnitude.** The larger the volume of Qn stored by a neuron, the more that neuron can "attract" new Qn to itself through its contact barrier. In effect, Qn is a "magnet" for more energy, a principle that Freud used to great effect in explaining how the ego defends against pain and threat.

3. **The defense of repression.** The ego is a neuron system with strongly resistant contact barriers and an enormous reserve or "cathexis" of Qn. Acting like a flywheel or perhaps a magnet, the ego uses its stored Qn to attract Qn away from other neurons and direct the energy of threatening ideas away from their normal paths of association leading to consciousness. This "detouring" of ideas was Freud's first theory of repression.

In Freud's vocabulary of the time, neurons were "cathected"—a more or less Greek derivation meaning to "fill up" or "occupy"—with quantities of energy. By its very nature, this metaphor is linked to concepts of magnitude; hence, the Q for *Quantity*. Freud also recognized, however, that consciousness and other complex cognitive processes, such as distinguishing between inner and outer stimulation, could not be explained by raw changes in a cell's *quantity* of energy. So he introduced the idea that some neurons—*Omega* cells—are sensitive to the *quality* or patterning of the energy that passes through them. Freud retained the term *cathexis* to describe energy transactions within the mind long after Q and Qn became the more widely known *libido*. He had abandoned the neurological model and its neurons filled with energy, but the metaphor lingered.

Figure 4.1 visualizes Freud's neurological model based on his description of it and on his later incorporation of these ideas into the diagram he drew in his master-work *The Interpretation of Dreams*.

The *Phi* System: Perception of the External World

The energies of the world impinge on the organism's sensory receptors and are reduced to a magnitude that can be processed by the brain in the *Phi* system (Φ), which Freud labeled with this Greek letter as a kind of shorthand for "physical" or physiological. He conceptualized *Phi* as fundamentally a sensory-receptive system. The physical energy of the world's stimuli processed by *Phi* is called Q (for *Quantity*). Q passes through the sensory receptors of the *Phi* neurons where it is reduced to levels tolerable by living cells. At this point, the Q becomes the lesser magnitude Qn (for neuronal-level *Quantity*). Qn is further processed by the *Phi* neurons for immediate response by the organism, for storage as a short- or long-term memory image, or for more or less permanent burial deep inside the brain in what later would be called the unconscious.

Much of the time, physical stimulation from the outside world in the form of Q is simply the trigger for an immediate, frequently reflex, response. The Q loops no further than the *Phi* system in the lower brain centers. A mosquito buzzes in the ear, injects stinger into skin, hand shoots up, swat. End Q transaction. Neurons of the *Phi* system do not routinely retain traces of neuronal energy. Instead *Phi* neurons pass Q through their "facilitative" contact barriers (synapses) like water through a leaky sieve. In the case of the unlucky mosquito, Q went directly from sensory receptors (ears and skin) to the person's musculo-skeletal system for a quick, reflexive response. The probability that this particular mosquito, on this specific day, in this singular place will be remembered by the person is rather low.

The *Psi* System: Memory for Wishes and Urges

Sometimes, however, small traces of this energy are transferred to the next level of nervous processing, the neurons of the *Psi* (Ψ) system. Because *Psi* neurons have *resistant contact barriers*, they can dam the flow of Q and retain the energy as a kind of short-term memory. Put another way, *Psi* neurons storehouse experience: memories. *Psi* is divided into two subsystems. The topmost level are the *Psi Pallium* neurons, which can store small amounts of energy scaled to levels tolerable by neurons, called Qn for relatively short periods. Qn is Freud's shorthand for "neuronal magnitude Q." At another level of the brain are the *Psi Nuclear* neurons which are the cells most resistant to the passage of energy and represent the deepest and most durable storage areas of the mind, including the unconscious.

The *Omega* System: Reality Testing

Freud realized that he needed another neuronal system that would be able to differentiate stimulation originating in the outside world from excitation arising within the nervous system in the form of memories and urges. The *Omega* (ω) system distinguishes energy from the world that signals "reality" from energy stored in *Psi* that signals memory, fantasy, need, and wish. *Omega* (ω), is a kind of watchful mind's eye that interprets the origin of stimulation—the world or memory of the world—and thereby engages in reality testing. Defense against painful stored memories or perceptual stimuli that threaten to resurrect painful memories is left to a special collection of neurons called the *ego,* which stores significant amounts of neuronal energy to act like a magnet. Its large supply of stored *Qn* permits the ego to attract to itself energy from *Phi* and *Psi* neurons and redirect it down pathways that prevent painful memories, taboo wishes, or unruly urges from reaching awareness. Freud hypothesized that the neuronal ego differentiates between painful and pleasant memories because each kind of *Qn* is associated with the release of different brain chemicals.

Repression as Displaced *Qn*

In this model, the ego neuron system defends against threat, not by obliterating ideas and wishes (later called repression), but by detouring the energy (*Qn*) of painful ideas, wishes and fantasies into mental blind alleyways that do not lead to awareness. The ego neuronal system stores a permanent and large supply of *Qn* that it can use as a kind of psychological magnet. *Psi* neurons that store *Qn* behind their resistant contact barriers can generally attract more *Qn* to themselves, and the ego neuronal system is a powerhouse of such stored energy. Thus, when the neuronal ego detects a threatening or painful idea traveling along an associative pathway that leads to conscious recognition of the idea, it uses its stored *Qn* to detour the energy of the threatening idea into an alternate path that does not lead to consciousness. Repression by detour is the result. Sometimes the detours fail and a painful memory or taboo wish makes it down an unintended neuronal path all the way to consciousness. But at this stage of his work, Freud envisioned defense in the concrete terms of neuronal energy displacements and detours. Figure 4.2 illustrates this early conception of defense using Freud's own hand sketched neuron diagram as a template.

Enduring Limitations of Freud's Implicit Neurology

It is nearly impossible to turn to any of Freud's later work without catching a glimpse of hypotheses formulated originally in neurological terms. The most general premise that mental activity is an economics of energy transfer among neuronal systems was, of course, the basis for the concept of instinctual energy transfers among agencies of the mind. Implicit in this general postulate is the more fundamental premise that the nervous system is a passive receptacle of energy from the environment or from bodily processes that convert environmental energy into mental energy. Once received, the prime goal of the nervous system, in Freud's view, is to discharge this stimulation as quickly as possible. Because in Freud's erroneous neurological thinking neurons have no energy sources of their own, they inherently treat inputs of external energy as irritations to be discharged at all costs, with all possible speed. In effect, the nervous system strives to be completely passive, for total inertia is its natural state. Thus Freud convinced himself years later that the ultimate goal of all life is death (1920a, p. 38).

FIGURE 4.2   Freud's neurological model of ego defense.

Freud's first attempt to explain ego defense was the neuronal analog to displacement. The ego's main mechanism of defense against painful wishes, ideas or perceptions was to "inhibit" recognition of them. With its large permanent supply of QN, the ego is able to pull Qn from other neurons and reroute it away from logical associative paths (A → B) that might provoke a chemical pain reaction from "key neurons." Instead, the ego redirects the Qn toward alternate associative links (A → C) that do not lead to pain or to consciousness. Threatening or painful ideas are thus "repressed" or at least temporarily "not thought." See text.

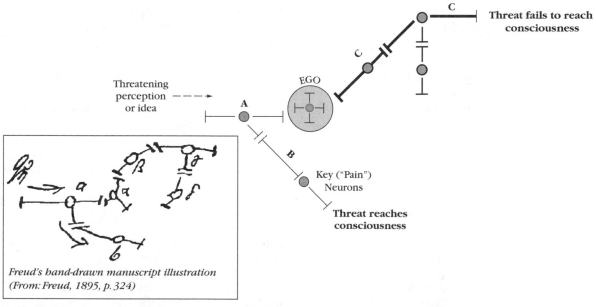

Freud's hand-drawn manuscript illustration (From: Freud, 1895, p. 324)

Modified from Freud (1895), pp. 324, 367–371.

McCarley and Hobson (1977) point out that modern neurophysiology conceptualizes nerve cells as active processors of energy that they themselves generate biochemically. Moreover, they stress that Freud's conception of the nervous system pictured no mechanisms of active inhibition of discharge whereby neurons could deliberately prevent responses. Freud had only the concept of the ego *diverting* energy from particular pathways and redirecting it to alternate pathways to prevent some neurons from discharging. In Freud's scheme, therefore, inhibition is a relatively passive process requiring specialized neurons to redirect, but not stop, energy flows. By contrast, it is now known that neurons can cancel excitation by altering their threshold sensitivity to stimulation, an active process of metabolic inhibition.

This conception of the nervous system as a passive processor of externally derived energies and as a protector of the organism's normally quiescent state was carried over into all of Freud's later theory. And it was this erroneous neurological formulation that became the central inconsistency that contemporary psychoanalytic ego theorists attempt to surmount:

The absence of self-generated activity and energy postulated by Freud's model for neuronal systems leads directly to the notion of lack of autonomy for psychological systems. The source of the postulate of ego dependence on drive energy originates in the physiology of the "Project," and one legacy of this inaccurate physiological model was the necessity of a long, difficult struggle by psychoanalytic ego psychologists to convince conservative analytic theorists that the ego should be regarded as autonomous. (McCarley & Hobson, 1977, p. 1217)

Thus, another answer to our persistent question—*What had Freud left undone?*—is that he neglected to revise his implicit neurological assumptions to take account of the active, independent nature of some psychological processes that function apart from instinctual economics. In Freud's theory, all psychological phenomena had to be derived from two and only two drives: At first, these drives were the ego and sex instincts in the hunger-love theory; later, two forms of sexual drive or libido were the fundamental instincts; and finally, libido and aggression drives, or Eros and death instincts assumed stature of Freud's final universal dualism (see Chapter 3). All such derivations of psychological events from pairs of competing instincts were conceptualized by Freud as acts of necessity, survival strategies of an organism exposed unmercifully to a continually intruding inner and outer world of energy. Against such intrusions, human nervous systems have no greater purpose, no more pressing commitment than to "tame" these "exigencies of life" in order to return to the pleasurable state of quietude. *Ananke,* destiny, was biological necessity. Robert Holt capsulized this element in Freud's intellectual heritage:

> The concept of a passive nervous system that strives to rid itself of externally imposed energies and the closely related ideas of the constancy principle, the pleasure principle, tension reduction, the need for a protective shield against stimuli, action, and affect as phenomena of energy discharge—all derive from the heritage of physicalistic physiology. Indeed, I believe that a good case can be made that most of the inherent difficulties of Freud's general theory derive from this heritage, which he could never get rid of, and not from his original ideas. (1963, p. 375)

It is difficult to resolve the issue of whether Freud was fundamentally biological or psychological in his thinking. Parisi (1987, 1988) has argued that Freud understood that psychological phenomena could not profitably be understood by a simple reductionism that interprets mental events as "nothing but" brain activity. Silverstein (1985, 1988, 1989a; see also Sulloway, 1979) has argued that Freud was a mind-body dualist with a rather sophisticated interactionist model of the relationship between biological and psychological variables. The historical record is ambiguous but suggestive. It would be hard to explain major portions of Freud's work (such as Chapter 7 in the *Interpretation of Dreams,* and several of his subsequent papers) as other than reflecting Freud's keen interest in and early admiration for neuroanatomy and physiology. By the same token, Freud ultimately created a *psychology* in which the biological and neurological substrate are hidden or only metaphorized. Freudian scholars and historians will probably debate for a very long time Freud's perceived commitment to a psychological, biological, monistic, dualistic, interactionist strategy for building psychoanalysis. We can almost hear Freud chuckling, "Couldn't hurt."

For Freud, the id horse was far more powerful than the ego rider. The ego was merely a necessity of the id's survival, a means to the end of tension discharge. A mind that always struggles to meet all-consuming inner and outer pressures is a mind that never acts to create its own environment. It is a mind whose ". . . cogs meshed . . ." [and] really seemed to be a machine which in a moment would run of itself. . . ." (Freud, 1954, p. 129).

What Freud Left Undone

Psychoanalytic ego psychology emerged as an attempt to extend and complete Freudian theory. Contemporary ego theory addresses itself to the inherent inconsistencies between the classical Freudian drive theory of competing energy systems and the clinical observations that people are able to transcend their passions. Humans struggle not only to satisfy id instincts but also to impose meaning on the events they experience. Satisfaction comes not only from passive tension reduction but also from the sense of active mastery in surmounting life's obstacles. Maladjustment is not exclusively the result of a clash among id, ego, and superego; neurosis may also be present in persons who have no life goals, who have been unable to establish a sense of harmony and order between themselves and their social world. What had Freud left undone? He left the following issues unresolved.

1. If the ego emerges from the id through the necessity of survival, how is it possible for some human behavior to become independent of its instinctual origins, to be capable of persisting after instinctual conflict is resolved or after instinctual urges are satisfied, to be enjoyed for its own sake?

2. If human psychology is understandable as a complex war of mental agencies, with their various attacks, retreats, defenses, and victories, where is the *person* who is their battleground? *Who* attacks, retreats, defends, and enjoys victories? Does the *person* feel pain, or does that person's ego? Does the *person* act inconsistently, self-deceptively, or does the id fool the ego, the superego chastise the ego, or the ego tame the id? As Merton Gill, from the viewpoint of the therapist, put it: "If we see the patient in natural-science terms as an object defined by an interaction of forces resulting from energies operating in structures, we are much less likely to see both him and ourselves as responsible agents involved as participants in a meaningful personal interaction" (1977, p. 594).

3. If Freud's implicit neurological conception of a passive nervous system that strives to discharge tension is characteristic of psychological functioning, how is it possible to explain a person's positive strivings for increased stimulation, for new excitations, for new challenges to confront?

4. If the mind is a compartmented pool of energies, how can we understand the relationship between body and mind? For example, *where* is a repressed impulse? *What* is a repressed impulse? Is it blocked energy? Compartmentalized idea? Self-deception? How does a bodily symptom "convert" mental conflict and its energy into physical energy and pain?

5. If neurosis develops when the id overwhelms the ego's capacities to find safe gratifications, how then was it possible for Jean-Mary to develop a healthy adaptation to her life? Her games did not resolve the separation anxiety, or shorten her hospital stays. They became sources of satisfaction in themselves, as well as ways of coping with an unpredictable life. But they did not provide

gratification for the id. These games may have emerged out of conflict, but they were soon freed from their origins.

ANNA FREUD

LEGITIMIZING EGO PSYCHOLOGY

Where Sigmund Freud reconstructed the patients' childhoods from their adult recollections, Anna Freud observed her child patients in the act of constructing their adult reminiscences. Sigmund Freud liberated his patients from ignorance of their own pasts. Anna Freud labored to nurture her patients' mastery of the past they had yet to live.

Beginning officially in 1922, with the publication of her first psychoanalytic paper, Anna Freud devoted nearly 60 years to the application of analytic technique to children and adolescents. Along the way, almost inadvertently it seems, she lent her prestige and her talents to legitimizing the direct study of the ego. Close inspection of her writings, however, reveals that Anna Freud's conception of ego psychology is a very orthodox Freudian enterprise. The ego, in her view, is a legitimate object of psychoanalytic study *if* the analyst remembers that fundamentally the ego is inescapably bound to the id and unavoidably regulated by the superego. For Anna Freud, the chief theoretical justification for study of the ego is that: "It is, so to speak, the medium through which we try to get a picture of the other two institutions" (A. Freud, 1936, p. 6).

For Anna Freud, widening the scope of psychoanalysis means applying the fundamental discoveries of her father to new realms of behavior, to children, to adolescents, to pediatrics, to family law, and to modified techniques in education and child care (A. Freud, 1972, 1978). A widened psychoanalytic theory of the ego does not include leaving behind her father's conception of the power of id instincts, his portrait of the ego as a survival-contingent outgrowth of the id, and his conviction that, after all, the ego rider leads the id horse where the id horse wants to go. But the story of Anna Freud's work is not the history of a student blindly devoted to her teacher's maxims. It is a narrative of innovation, revision, and creation accomplished almost reluctantly but with brilliance (Young-Bruehl, 1988, p. 208ff. and Chapter 11).

Reviewing her psychoanalytic career in 1964 as part of her acceptance speech for an honorary doctorate from Jefferson Medical School, Anna Freud pictured an essential difference between herself and many other contemporary psychoanalytic theorists:

> In contrast to many colleagues, I was never concerned one-sidedly with either id, ego, or superego, but always with the interactions between them. The dynamics of mental life which fascinated me, to my mind, found their clearest expression in the defense organization of the ego, with the attempts of the rational personality to deal with the irrational. (1967, pp. 514–515)

Within the body of Anna Freud's work we can detect the tension that inevitably must arise when an innovative student struggles to preserve the theoretical fundamentals of her teacher while hesitantly demanding fair consideration for new and independent ideas. For in the end, Anna Freud's position in contemporary psycho-analysis, indeed, in the overall history of the discipline, must be forever unique and exquisitely contradictory. In her primary role as Sigmund Freud's self-chosen, self-trained intellectual heir, she is the keeper of the keys, custodian of the faith, and con-servator of tradition. Balanced against these protective but understandable daugh-terly motives is her competing role as an independent theorist whose explorations into new territories must inexorably reduce the usefulness of old maps. Her family heritage not only ensures a protective attitude toward classical psychoanalysis, it also supports an adventuresome curiosity to make new discoveries. She is not, after all, a neo-Freudian; she is a Freud.

Personal Sources: From Being Unwanted to Becoming Indispensable

By the time Sigmund and Martha Freud realized that Martha was again pregnant, they had already agreed that their fifth child, Sophic, was to be their last. Indeed, the initial phase of Martha's pregnancy was misinterpreted and welcomed as an early onset of menopause (Roazen, 1969, p. 40; 1971, pp. 52 ff. and pp. 436 ff.; Young-Breuhl, 1988, p. 35 ff.). When it became clear that the pause in Martha's menstruation was not the end of fertility but the beginning of new life, Freud found himself hoping for another son. He wrote to his friend Wilhelm Fliess in October 1895, "You will not have any objection to my calling my next son Wilhelm! If *he* turns out to be a daughter, *she* will be called Anna" (Freud, 1954, p. 130). He *was* she, as Freud and Martha learned on the afternoon of December 3, 1895. Freud resignedly announced Anna's birth to Fliess in this most curious way:

> If it had been a son I should have sent you the news by telegram, as he would have been named after you. But as it is a little girl of the name of Anna, you get the news later. She arrived to-day at 3.15 during my consulting hours, and seems to be a nice, complete little woman. Thanks to Fleischmann's [Martha's obstetrician] care she did not do her mother any harm and both are doing well. (Freud, 1954, p. 136; see alternate form of this quotation in Freud, 1985, p. 153)

Despite the laconic birth announcement to Fliess, Freud seems to have been gen-uinely fond of all of his children. Anna, his youngest and last child, would mature to become the intellectual heir Freud was unable to find in Jung, Adler, Rank, or in any of his other male psychoanalytic colleagues.

On the basis of his extensive researches in the unpublished material of Jones's archives, his interviews with surviving relatives, colleagues, and former patients of Freud, Paul Roazen (1968, 1969, 1971) has pieced together the probable personal his-tory of Anna Freud's early years and her eventual entrance into her father's discipline. Roazen's research and conclusions have not gone unchallenged; however, the criti-cism has tended to come from quarters with more than a casual interest in the legend of the Freuds (See Eissler, 1974, 1978; Roazen's reply to Eissler, 1977, 1978; Anna Freud herself found Roazen's work objectionable, as reported by Young-Bruehl, 1988, p. 432ff.). We follow Roazen's account supplemented with some of Sigmund Freud's letters here.

FIGURE 4.3   **Anna Freud at about age sixteen.**

Source: Young-Bruehl, E. (1988). *Anna Freud: A Biography*. (New York: Summit Books).

Training Analysis With Freud

In addition to being an unwanted child at birth, Anna Freud grew into adolescence as a shy and withdrawn young woman, with few interests outside the family (Roazen, 1971, p. 438). Elisabeth Young-Bruehl, Anna Freud's most recent biographer, makes the case that Anna's adolescence was marked by a variety of normal sexual and romantic interests, but her strong attachment to her father and her masculine identification resulted in a more or less ascetic lifestyle for most of her years. There may be some substance to the obvious "Freudian" interpretation we could make that Anna was attached to her father so strongly that there was no room left for romantic interests in other men (Young-Bruehl, 1988, p. 288).

Sometime before 1918, when Anna was in her early twenties, she entered into analysis with her father. This unique relationship apparently continued for several years (Dyer, 1983, p. 26 feels that the duration was somewhat shorter; Roazen, 1971, p. 439; Young-Bruehl, 1988, gives the most complete and compelling account. See especially Young-Bruehl, 1988, p. 171). Thus, with no formal academic training or credentials in medicine or psychology, Anna Freud was nevertheless committed to psychoanalysis by the strongest of bonds: She was engaged in intellectual and emotional self-exploration with the founder of psychoanalysis, her own father, who had to function in the acutely contradictory roles of professional and paternal intimate. Roazen described the consequences for Anna Freud's development in this way:

> Freud's motives may have been the very best, but medically and humanly the situation was bizarre. As her analyst, he would inevitably mobilize her feelings of overvaluation, while at the same time invading the privacy of her soul; he added new transference emotions to their relationship, without the possibility of ever really dissolving them. A genius who was also naturally an immense figure in his daughter's fantasy life, as her analyst he tied her permanently to him. (1971, p. 440)

That Freud broke the rules he himself created for the proper conduct of a psychoanalyst by taking his own daughter into such a relationship testifies to the special importance he placed on having a trustworthy and competent intellectual heir after so many previous failures and betrayals. By teaching his daughter the techniques of his profession, Freud bequeathed to her his place as leader of the psychoanalytic movement.

Perhaps the best source for understanding the meaning of her analysis with her father is Anna Freud herself. In a letter advising her friend Eva Rosenfeld to enter treatment with her father Sigmund, whom Eva already knows in a social context and as the father of her friend, Anna made these poignant remarks:

> You know, there is no contradiction in your undergoing analysis in a place that you would prefer to come to for love's sake alone. I did the same thing, and perhaps because of it, the two things became inextricably bound together for me. In the end you will realize: it is the only way to go into analysis. Right now you are troubled by the feeling that where you love you would like to be especially good. You will see that being good and being in analysis finally amount to the same thing. (A. Freud, 1929/1992, letter 8, p.112)

Anna Freud began attending her father's lectures, and she was permitted to join the famous Wednesday seminars of the Vienna Psychoanalytic Society (Roazen, 1971, p. 438). She was even given her first exposure to classical psychiatry by being allowed to attend rounds in the psychiatric teaching hospital of Vienna, under Professor Wagner-Jauregg, a friend of Sigmund Freud's from his own medical school years (A. Freud, 1967, p. 512). Heinz Hartmann, known later as the father of ego psychology, served as a second assistant on these psychiatric rounds. In May of 1920, two years after her training analysis by one account, Sigmund bestowed one of his famous rings on his daughter. Freud gave such rings to members of his inner circle, and it was certainly his way of confirming Anna's special place as a full-fledged and accepted member of the Vienna Psychoanalytic Society (Dyer, 1983, p. 32).

Anna as an Early Analyst

By 1923, having already presented her first psychoanalytic paper to the society the previous year, Anna Freud was ready to enter psychoanalytic practice (A. Freud, 1922). Unfortunately, 1923 was also the beginning of the end for Sigmund Freud. His cancer of the upper palate was first detected and operated on that year, and the complications resulting from its removal were to mark the start of a 16-year struggle with pain.

Her first paper was an extension of one of her father's own essays on "beating fantasies" devised by children. The elder Freud (1919) had written a paper entitled "A Child Is Being Beaten" in which he described the fantasies of several of his female patients for what they reveal of the plasticity of sexual motives. Freud's analysis shows that the fantasylike daydream of his patients which pictured an older person beating or punishing a child is a disguised substitute for a taboo sexual wish that has been repressed.

Anna Freud's (1922) own first published contribution to psychoanalysis is an extension of the beating fantasy analysis with a major difference from her father's work. The female patient she describes in the paper is most certainly herself (Young-Bruehl, 1988, pp. 103ff.). Anna Freud describes the progressive fantasy stories of a girl from preschool age through adolescence in which the central theme is "a child is being beaten." We will not trace the details of her analysis here. The essential point, however, for our discussion of the personal sources of Anna Freud's ideas is that this 1922 paper reveals some of the personal experiences on which Anna Freud based her therapeutic method for working with children. The girl described in her paper eventually developed a set of "nice fantasies" that she thought had little or no connection with the "beating fantasies" she found so distressing. In fact, the nice fantasies were more deliberate on the surface, more under voluntary control. But, as Anna Freud reveals in the paper, through analysis, the "patient" learns that the "nice stories" are thinly disguised continuations of the beating fantasies. Like her father, she interprets the beating fantasy as an intermediate level of disguise for taboo, incestuous sexual wishes toward an adult figure, most likely the girl's father. Of course, what makes this paper so poignant is that Anna Freud is describing herself.

Anna Freud analyzes the progression from the beating fantasies to the "nice stories" as a study in repression and sublimation, two defense mechanisms she would later describe in much detail. She implies that the girl is developmentally more mature at the point when she can recognize the connection between the earlier unwanted beating fantasies and her even more defensive "nice stories." Anna Freud points out that the girl eventually turned her combination beating fantasies and "nice stories" into a creative and more rationally controlled enterprise by writing a compelling short story that she could share with others. In this early paper, the theme of creative mastery of conflict as a basic motive is already clearly in evidence, a theme that she later extended in the theoretical concept called "developmental lines." She concludes the paper with these words:

> By renouncing her private pleasure in favor of making an impression on others, the author has accomplished an important developmental step: the transformation of an autistic into a social activity. We could say: she has found the road that leads from her fantasy life back to reality. (A. Freud, 1922, p. 157)

Anna's Antigone Played to Freud's Aging Oedipus

Through those 16 years of the battle with cancer, Anna Freud became indispensable to the ailing but uncomplaining Sigmund. She was his emissary to psychoanalytic societies throughout the world, and she delivered his papers when his prosthesis, designed to replace excised oral tissue, made speaking difficult or impossible for her father. She typed his correspondence daily, and with Dr. Max Schur, Freud's personal physician and friend, administered to his personal and medical needs. That task required daily inspection of Freud's surgically brutalized mouth for any signs of new growth. Anna Freud accompanied her father on his journeys to Paris for radium treatments, on visits to his surgeon in Berlin, and on much-needed holidays in the woods to pick mushrooms and wild strawberries (Jones, 1957; Schur, 1972; Young-Bruehl, 1988, p. 118). In every possible way, Anna Freud devoted herself to her father's comfort and care.

Sigmund Freud himself understood how dependent he had become on Anna, and the discoverer of childhood sexuality chose an appropriate metaphor to describe the relationship between them. In his correspondence of the mid-1930s, Freud would refer to Anna as his "faithful Antigone," alluding to the dutiful and courageous daughter of the blind and ill Oedipus in Sophocles' plays. For example, to Arnold Zweig in 1934 Freud wrote,

> But it cannot have remained concealed from you that fate has granted me as compensation for much that has been denied me the possession of a daughter who, in tragic circumstances, would not have fallen short of Antigone. (Freud/Zweig, 1970, p. 66)

Thus, in Freud's mind, with Anna as his Antigone, he was the ailing and aged Oedipus. Freud has also written despairingly to Zweig that

> My mood is bad, little pleases me, my self-criticism has grown much more acute. I would diagnose it as senile depression in anyone else. I see a cloud of disaster passing over the world, even over my own little world. I must remind myself of the one bright spot, and that is that my daughter Anna is making such excellent analytic discoveries just now and—they all tell me—is delivering masterly lectures on them. An admonition therefore not to believe that the world will end with my death. (Freud/Zweig, 1970, pp. 110–102)

The world Freud referred to in this last letter to Zweig was, of course, the cosmos he himself had created, the inner world of psychoanalysis that had been constructed as much from the life histories of his patients as it had from Freud's self-analytic probing of his own desert places. Freud here implicitly acknowledged Anna as his successor. Like the blind Oedipus led by his faithful Antigone, Sigmund Freud's contacts with the outside world were made through Anna's skilled touch.

In a letter to Lou Andreas-Salomé, he also managed to express fatherly pride in a peculiarly objective—almost depersonalized—way that echoes the equally curious tone of his announcement of her birth to Fliess 40 years before:

> I of course rely more and more on Anna's care, just as Mephistopheles once remarked:
>
> > In the end we depend
> > On the creatures we made.
>
> In any case, it was very wise to have made her. (Freud [1935], 1960, p. 425)

From an unexpected and unwanted daughter, Anna Freud had matured into an indispensable Antigone, among whose virtues was the ability to clarify what other potential psychoanalytic "heirs" had managed only to cloud:

> She has grown into a capable, independent person who has been blessed with insight into matters that merely confuse others. To be sure, for her sake I would like—but she must learn to do without me, and the fear of losing vital parts of my still intact personality through old age is an accelerating factor in my wish. (Freud/Zweig, 1970, p. 140)

Freud's incompletely expressed wish not to die indicated some degree of concern that his daughter needed his continued presence. But the wish gave way to his more realistic appraisal that the ravages of his illness and age would ultimately render him unable to act as protecting father to Anna and as founding father of psychoanalysis. Anna's growing independence and mastery of psychoanalysis assured him that she would continue to prosper and so, in consequence, would his other "creation."

Anna's Relationship With Her Mother

Throughout the period of Freud's illness, Anna assumed increasing authority around the household in her role as private nurse, companion, and colleague to her father. Her widening sphere of dominance as a confidante of her father became a source of friction between Anna and Martha Freud. Roazen (1971, p. 452) quotes Martha as commenting that: " 'she *was* such a tender child,' but that the hardness in her had come out." Anna resented that her mother did not assume more responsibility for the care of her father, but seemed instead to become less and less capable of coping with the increasingly difficult situation. "The more incapable Martha became, the more Anna's feelings of being an unwanted child were reinforced, and thus the more her father meant to her" (Roazen, 1971, p. 452).

Years before family matters had come to this impasse, Freud had written to his then fiancée Martha on the theme of children and marriage, a theme that, in retrospect, yields some measure of irony:

> It is a happy time for our love now. I always think that once one is married one no longer—in most cases—lives for each other as one used to. One lives rather with each other for some third thing, and for the husband dangerous rivals soon appear: household and nursery. Then, despite all love and unity, the help each person had found in the other ceases. The husband looks again for friends, frequents an inn, finds general outside interests. But that need not be so. (Freud (c. 1884), quoted by Jones, 1953, p. 140)

Some of Freud's predictions had materialized, but not for the reasons he had prophesied. The "dangerous rivals" of nursery and household proved to be neither dangerous nor rivalrous; indeed, the nursery had yielded a creature on whom, in the end, he had to depend.

The Central Themes:
Devotion, Protection, and Reluctant Innovation

Three fundamental themes governing the course of Anna Freud's work emerge from our necessarily selective overview of her life history. First, Anna Freud's intellectual and emotional devotion to her father and to his work seems, in Freud's own terminology, to be overdetermined. Apart from the usual child-parent love, there were the extraordinary emotional bonds between Anna and her father created by Anna's position in the family as youngest, originally unplanned child, who seemed to have had less than the norm in the way of an affectionate relationship with her mother. As Anna grew closer to her father, she grew more distant from her mother. Both emotionally as his daughter and intellectually as his student, Anna found her whole life centered in one person. Freud's own need for an emotional and intellectual intimate intensified the momentum of their growing mutual dependence.

The second relevant theme of Anna Freud's life history is her understandably protective and conservative approach to psychoanalytic theory. As we have seen, Anna Freud regarded her father's basic discoveries as foundation stones that cannot be discarded or greatly modified without demolishing the entire edifice they support. This sense of protection for classical psychoanalytic doctrine is again overdetermined in origin. On the one hand, Anna Freud cogently argued that psychoanalysis historically achieved its uniqueness and value as the study of the whole personality in both its unconscious and conscious components (A. Freud, 1936, pp. 3–5; 1969a). Restricting investigation to one aspect of personality functioning or ignoring instinctual factors in favor of environmental-cultural ones severely distorts and violates psychoanalytic procedure and theory. On the other hand, her reluctance to move very far beyond classical boundaries is understandable when the extensive lifetime commitments and personal sacrifices that underlie her engagement with analysis are borne in mind.

In this context of personal sacrifices, it is difficult to read Anna Freud's own description of James Strachey's near lifetime of devotion to translating and editing her father's work without wondering how much self-reflection entered into its composition:

> It cannot be easy for any man to give up his own personal pursuits for the purpose of immersing himself wholly in the work of another. . . . The founder of psychoanalysis is considered fortunate to have found a translator of this stature. It may also be said that James Strachey was fortunate to find an author and a subject matter worthy of his efforts. (A. Freud, 1969b, pp. 277, 279)

Perhaps we may be permitted to extend Anna Freud's description of Strachey's devotion to her own, for we come to view our sacrifices and commitments on behalf of a beloved figure as justified in proportion to the worth of his or her cause; and to view his or her cause as worthy in proportion to the need to justify those commitments.

The third and last theme that is discernible in Anna Freud's life history follows directly from the conflicting nature of the first two themes. Caught between genuine loyalty to and belief in her father and his work, and the compelling evidence of her own innovative discoveries in child analysis and ego function, Anna Freud's contributions to contemporary psychoanalytic psychology are never presented by her as revisions or modifications of psychoanalytic theory. She envisions her own work as more in the nature of subtle refinements, sophisticated clarifications, or shifts in emphasis. Yet, despite her tendency to minimize the newness of her ideas as a solution to the conflict between her loyalty and creativity, genuinely new discoveries and fresh ideas are found in Anna Freud's writings. Some of these ideas have profoundly influenced other psychoanalytic workers to alter the course of contemporary psychoanalysis, moving the evolution of theory in directions never contemplated by Sigmund Freud in his lifetime.

There is no better way to illustrate and to summarize this enduring conflict between Anna Freud's loyal protectionist attitude and her own hard-won discoveries than to quote an instance of her own vacillating prose:

> . . . It is important to remember that some forty years ago, long before the time when cooperation with academic workers could have played a part, psychoanalytic child study itself had already *transgressed the strict confines* of the psychoanalytic technique and situation, and had created its own field of direct observation, in its own way. It is true that all the important data on which psychoanalysis has built its view of childhood . . . were derived from the analytic setting itself, reconstruction from the analyses of adults, and later from the analyses of children. But immediately after the discoveries were made, a host of observers set to work, outside of the analytic setting, unsystematically indeed, and following the opportunities offered by life situations as they arose, but providing in time a mass of useful data, which served to check and countercheck, add to or refute the analytic findings proper. (A. Freud, 1951a, pp. 139–140; italics added)

Anna Freud's muted claims for originality and independence of child analysis, her special branch of the discipline, are inseparably interwoven in this passage with her dutiful recognition of the primacy of classical psychoanalysis. Yet she ends the passage with the admonition to remember that the data of child analysis have the special status of serving as the "countercheck" by which classic theory is confirmed or refuted.

FIGURE 4.4   Anna Freud at age 85 with her puppy Jo-Fi.

WIDENING THE SCOPE OF ANALYSIS: LITTLE PATIENTS' PROBLEMS

By extending psychoanalytic technique from the reconstruction of childhood events in adults to direct exploration of children's life histories as they live it, Anna Freud quickly made two discoveries. Little patients are frequently exuberant free spirits but lackadaisical free associators. As might be expected, the use of disciplined verbal-analytic technique with verbal novices is an undertaking doomed to failure. Furthermore, unlike the adult patients who come to psychoanalysis voluntarily—indeed, desperately—seeking help with misery they can no longer tolerate, child patients typically do not perceive themselves as needing aid, do not comprehend the role of or need for a psychoanalyst's intrusion into their lives, and present themselves for treatment only at the urging or command of parents. Because successful psychoanalysis demands that the patients themselves be intellectually and emotionally engaged in their own treatment, child patients necessarily constitute a formidable challenge (A. Freud, 1927, p. 6; 1945, p. 8).

A further consideration arises from the fact of these patients' youth: How do we decide when a child requires psychoanalysis? One viewpoint, represented by other child analytic workers in the 1920s and 1930s, was that any emotional or intellectual disturbance in the child would benefit from psychoanalytic treatment. Anna Freud's own early view during this same period was that psychoanalysis was indicated only for children in whom a full-blown childhood neurosis was strangling further development (A. Freud, 1927).

After considerable experience, Anna Freud conceptualized the criteria for treatment of children in a different way. For adult patients, the severity of neurotic disturbance is indicated by the degree of damage to their capacities to lead a conflict-free love life and to work productively with satisfaction (A. Freud, 1945, p. 15). Clearly, these same criteria are inapplicable to children. Childhood, by its very nature, is a progression of increasingly sophisticated *changes,* transitions to new learnings, new physical attainments, and new emotional adjustments. Childhood is fluidity. Consequently, Anna Freud's criterion for the application of analytic method to children reflected these maturational necessities:

> In childhood there is only one factor of such central importance that its impairment through a neurosis calls for immediate action; namely, the child's ability to develop, not to remain fixated at some stage of development before the maturation process has been concluded. (A. Freud, 1945, p. 17)

In this subtle way, the first steps to a broadened and refocused psychoanalytic theory were taken. The broadening in theory to encompass the facts of childhood change was required by the unique demands of child patients whose unconscious processes were not accessible by strictly verbal procedures. The refocusing of theory was necessitated by the shift from treatments for outright pathology to therapy for developmental, transitional impairments (A. Freud, 1968). Thus the criterion by which a child's need for analytic treatment was to be assessed was no longer the presence of explicit neurotic symptoms. Threatened fixation to some single phase of development became a sufficient indicator to warrant analytic intervention.

MAKING THE CHILD ANALYZABLE: THE PREPARATORY PHASE

Coming from her experiences as a teacher of children (A. Freud, 1952), Anna Freud understood the importance of engaging children's interest at the outset in the task at hand and the necessity of capturing their respect for the superior skills of the adult participant. In the early years of formulating usable principles of child analysis, Anna Freud felt the necessity of a lengthy preparatory phase of give-and-take relationship building before analytic work was begun. This conception was modified later with Anna Freud and her coworkers' development of a "metapsychological assessment" procedure based on direct observation of a child's defensive strategies and indirect observations of his or her family interactions.

Engaging the Child's Self-Interest

Initially, Anna Freud undertook a preparatory period of "breaking the child in" for analysis by inducing him or her to see the need for the treatment, to view the analyst as helpmate and ally, and aiding him or her in forming a genuine resolve to endure the difficulties of self-exploration. Such goals have the sound of tightly reasoned abstractions, packaged with precision and enacted with reliable ease. In practice, however, the abstractions are transformed into creative strategies designed to confront the child gradually with tolerable doses of insight into difficulties, with ever-increasing demands for cooperation, and with the sincere interest and good wishes of the analyst for the child's eventual self-management.

To illustrate, consider Anna Freud's skillful approach to a 10-year-old boy presented for treatment by his parents for a variety of anxieties, nervous states, tendency toward lying and fabrication of stories, and for a series of thefts. With some children, the analyst may assume the role of helpful ally against a hostile adult world, or of potential helpmate in dealing with inner misery. For this child no such partnership could be proposed. His attitude from the outset was one of hostile rejection of his proposed analyst, and, on the surface at least, no obvious wish was present to alter himself or diminish his difficulties.

At first, therefore, Anna Freud spent their time together merely mirroring his moods. When he appeared cheerful, she was cheerful; when he was serious or depressed, she acted seriously. At one point, he preferred to spend the entire session under a table in the room, an activity that Anna Freud treated with no special attention. She merely lifted the tablecloth to speak with him as though it were the most ordinary conversation. Simultaneously, however, she also subtly demonstrated the superiority of her adult skills and wisdom:

> If he came with a string in his pocket, and began to show me remarkable knots and tricks, I would let him see that I could make more complicated knots and do more remarkable tricks. If he made faces, I pulled better ones; and if he challenged me to trials of strength, I showed myself incomparably stronger. (A. Freud, 1927, p. 12)

Throughout their conversations together, Anna Freud followed his every whim and choice of topic, with no subject too delicate or too adult for discussion. "My attitude was like that of a film or novel meant to attract the audience or reader by catering to their baser interests" (1927, p. 12). In this way, Anna Freud succeeded not only in making herself interesting to the boy, but also in obtaining a sample of his interests, attitudes, and typical actions.

Establishing the Analyst's Usefulness

A second stage in this preparatory phase was initiated when Anna Freud began to demonstrate to the boy that she could be useful to him in a variety of small ways, such as by writing letters for him on her typewriter, by recording his proudly created daydreams and stories in writing, and by creating small toys and odd playthings for him during their sessions. As Anna Freud remarked concerning another of her patients who similarly required a period of analytic preparation, ". . .I zealously crocheted and knitted during her appointments, and gradually clothed all her dolls and teddy bears" (1927, p. 13). If we take this last statement as typical, it suggests that such a preparatory phase is relatively long-lived, requiring a big store of patience to wait for some sign of commitment from the little patients. Of course, such seemingly trivial activities served a double role: The boy's analyst became interesting and useful to him; but more important, Anna Freud had gained access to his fantasy life.

Establishing the Analyst's Power and the Child's Vulnerability

The third stage of the preparatory period had its origins in yet another skillful maneuver designed to augment the boy's growing value for his analyst. "I made him realize that being analyzed had great practical advantages; that, for example, punishable deeds have an altogether different and much more fortunate result when they are first told to the analyst, and only through him to those in charge of the child" (A. Freud, 1927, p. 13).

Eventually the boy relied on Anna Freud to protect him from punishment for his rash acts, to confess to his parents for him, and to restore stolen money before he was caught. The chief result of this stage of preparation was that Anna Freud had now become not only interesting, helpful, and wise, but powerful as well, a person "without whose help he could no longer get along (1927, p. 13).

At this point came the crucial moment when Anna Freud could request his complete cooperation in unveiling his treasured and guarded secrets. She could demand of him the equivalent of the adult analytic rule: Surrender all, retain nothing in secret. Obviously, the child analyst cannot make this demand directly, but the fact that the child has learned to trust and to value the analyst's judgment and interventions on his or her behalf makes the demand for surrender understandable in an indirect way.

For example, another 10-year-old boy, who was presented for treatment because of noisy, violent attacks of rage and defiance without any discernible cause, was actually proud of his symptoms as a mark of distinction. In the language of analysis, his symptom was "ego-syntonic," that is, compatible with his ego's self-image. After winning his confidence, Anna Freud's task was to induce his ego to see the symptom as troublesome and frightening, that is, to convert the temper tantrums into "ego-alien" behaviors. Only when the boy himself found his behavior unacceptable and frightening would he be willing to surrender his secrets in the effort to rid himself of the newly recognized source of discomfort. Anna Freud employed this shrewd strategy:

> I inquired how far in such states he was in control of himself at all, and compared his fits of rage to those of a madman who would be beyond my aid. At that he was startled and rather frightened, for to be regarded as mad naturally did not accord with his ambitions. He began to try himself to master the outbreaks, to resist them instead

of encouraging them as he had done before. As he did so, he realized his complete inability to suppress them and this failure enhanced his feelings of suffering and discomfort. After a few vain attempts the symptom finally, as I had intended, turned from a treasured possession into a disturbing foreign body, in the battle against which he only too readily claimed my help. (A. Freud, 1927, p. 15)

The preparatory phase concludes when children have developed sufficient insight to recognize the necessity of external aid for their difficulties. Indeed, child patients must be made to understand that they have difficulties. The only clear signal of sincere willingness to attempt extended and painful self-exploration comes when the child has experienced his or her own vulnerability and needs to invest the analyst with complete and trusting dependence. In short, during the preparatory phase the analyst works very hard to establish a strong positive transference relationship.

In consequence, the analyst must become the child's ego ideal throughout the whole period of treatment. The analyst displaces the parents from this role and usurps their authority: "Before the child can give the highest place in his emotional life, that of ego ideal, to this new love object which ranks with the parents, he needs to feel that the analyst's authority is even greater than theirs" (A. Freud, 1927, p. 60). In some cases, where the parents themselves are either the source of the child's difficulties or are negatively disposed to the treatment, it becomes necessary for the child analyst to work actively against their influence.

THE CHILD ANALYSIS PROPER: TECHNIQUES

Once the affectionate and dependent attachment to the analyst is established, analytic treatment of the child, with its special focus on the unconscious, may begin. The success of the analysis depends heavily upon the firmness of this attachment, for "Children, in fact, believe only the people they love, and make efforts only for the love of such people" (A. Freud, 1927, p. 40). The question naturally arises of how to provide analytic interpretations to a child in the absence of free-associative verbal products. *What does the analyst interpret?*

Interpretation of Fantasy and Dreams

One avenue of approach that immediately suggests itself is the play activities of the child. The Berlin school of child analysis headed by Melanie Klein employed the technique of play interpretations. Anna Freud rejected this road to the child's unconscious because it implies that a child's manipulations of toys and construction of play fantasies are equivalent to adult verbal productions in the analytic situation, a proposition for which there seemed little justification (1927, p. 38). Compared to verbal expressions, the difficulty with play is understanding when a behavior is symbolic and when it is merely play.

Thus, at the beginning of her work with children, Anna Freud employed two tools adopted from adult psychoanalysis but in greatly modified form. The first of these modifications was the reliance of the child analyst on the child patients' verbal reports of their fantasies and dreams. As in adult analysis, these productions were treated as symbolic derivatives of unconscious processes, and they were therefore subject to interpretation. Anna Freud clearly drew here on her own experience ana-lyzing her own "beating fantasies" and "nice stories." With some children, direct encouragement of fantasy stories was employed, as in the case of a little girl patient who was asked to close her eyes and "see pictures" that she would then describe to Anna Freud. In a similar way, the analyst and child patient discuss the child's dreams, and with practice, the child becomes accustomed to seeking hidden meanings in his or her own productions.

Interpreting the Child-Analyst Relationship: Shared Transference

The second tool of child analysis in the initial period of Anna Freud's development of the technique was the interpretation of the relationship between herself and her patient. In adult analysis, the transference relationship and the development of a full-blown transference neurosis become the crucial focus of the therapy. However, with a child patient, as we have seen, the transference relationship involves elements of educational dependency and embodies an essentially positive, affectionate quality that is missing from the adult version. In fact, though negative feelings toward the analyst will eventually emerge, Anna Freud regards these as temporary interferences that should be dealt with as soon as possible to prevent rupture of the delicate bonds that hold the child to the therapist (1927, p. 41). The only really productive work with children, she feels, takes place in the atmosphere of positive emotional attachment.

The child's transference relationship to the analyst is different from the adult's in other important ways. Unlike adult counterparts, child patients are still in the throes of establishing their real love relationships to important persons in their lives. They do not recall and reexamine and relive these relationships in analysis; they live them in the present. Outside the analytic room, all of their pleasures and pains still depend on those figures who populate the daily course of their growing up. The analyst who attempts to interpose her- or himself in this scheme of things has to *share* the chil-dren's affection for their parents and merely *participate* in the children's hostilities, disappointments, and idealizations of their parents. By contrast, the analyst of adult patients becomes the full target of these same feelings *reconstructed* from the patient's past. The adult analyst becomes momentarily a blank screen onto which the patient can project unresolved and unrealistic feelings carried over from the patient's early parent-child interactions.

The situation is further complicated in cases where children have little or no real affection from their parents. Emotionally deprived children obtain from their analysts what they have never experienced in the reality of their lives. Such children do not project a fantasied reenactment of their emotional relationships onto the analyst; they satisfy a never-filled need (A. Freud, 1927, p. 45).

> For these reasons the child forms no transference neurosis. In spite of all his positive and negative impulses toward the analyst, he continues to display his abnormal reactions where they were displayed before—in the home. Because of this the child analyst must not only take into account what happens under his own eye, but also direct his attention to the area where the neurotic reactions are to be found—the child's family. (A. Freud, 1927, p. 46)

In this special way, then, the transference relationship in child analysis is a shared transference, an analysis of interpersonal bonds both in and outside of the analytic situation, both from the patients' own views and from the viewpoint of the adults with whom they have their most intimate contacts. Furthermore, child analysts must violate a basic premise of adult analysis in their reliance on and active seeking of information about the patient from outside sources.

Delicate Balance Between Permissiveness and Authority

If, as Anna Freud was discovering, children's neurotic disturbances were so dependent on their *present* relationship to the people and things in their own worlds, then it must follow with inevitable logic that (1) childhood neurosis is not limited to conflicts among the id, ego, and superego, but includes distorting and paralyzing influences exerted against developmental change by the environment; (2) because children are developing—becoming rather than being—their own persons, their egos and superegos are not only weak by virtue of unconscious conflict but also by lack of maturation.

Both of these consequences have a single profound effect on the technique of child analysis. If the analyst succeeds in liberating the conflicted instinctual forces of the child's id, will the environment provide a healthy context for continued growth? If the superego and ego are not fully mature and are not sufficiently experienced in modulating these liberated unconscious forces, will the environment, especially the parents, provide understanding acceptance of this unruly transition to emotional health?

In the case of the adult, the analyst need not be overly concerned with the fate of impulses freed from repression, because the adult liberated ego is able to take charge of them, manage them, and accept them for what they are. In the child's case, however, liberated impulses may easily find themselves translated into action.

To illustrate, a young girl Anna Freud was treating had gotten to a stage of her analysis in which she was producing a wealth of anal fantasies, marked by use of particularly vulgar imagery and language. Her analytic sessions were seen by the child as a period of freedom, a "rest hour" during which all of this repressed and suppressed anxiety-producing fantasy material could be openly expressed in the seclusion of the analytic room. However, with time she began to carry her fantasies, her "dirty" jokes, and her anal language into situations beyond the analytic "rest hour." Alarmed, the parents "consulted" Anna Freud, who took the matter lightly, suggesting that they neither reject nor condone such misbehavior but merely let it pass unnoticed. The effect was wondrous. Without external condemnation, the little girl reveled in her anal verbalizations, especially at the dinner table, where they produced the most dramatic effect:

> I had to acknowledge that I had made a mistake, in crediting the child's superego with an independent inhibitory strength which it did not possess. As soon as the important people in the external world had relaxed their demands, the child's superego, previously strict and strong enough to bring forth a whole series of obsessional symptoms, suddenly had turned compliant. . . . I had changed an inhibited, obsessional child into one whose "perverse" tendencies were liberated. (A. Freud, 1927, p. 63)

It is clear that the child analyst cannot depend on the strength of the patient's ego to keep both patient and therapist out of trouble. Experienced child analysts learn to steer skillfully between two dangerous extremes. On one side, they have to tease unconscious material into consciousness, educating children to employ healthy strategies for dealing with their frightening impulses. On the other side, the child analyst must somehow prevent the freed impulses from creating total anarchy in the child's life, a real threat in the light of the child's underdeveloped superego. "The analyst accordingly combines in his own person two difficult and diametrically opposed functions: he has to analyze and educate, that is to say, in the same breath he must allow and forbid, loosen and bind" (A. Freud, 1927, p. 65).

The Theoretical Yield: New Meanings for Familiar Analytic Concepts

It became increasingly clear to Anna Freud that child analysis was more complex than the mere application of orthodox psychoanalytic theory to children. Her earliest work with the technique laid the groundwork for the exploration of important new areas of human living that promised not only to establish child analysis as an independent, special branch of psychoanalysis, but also to open the door to fundamental modifications of classical theory.

The Therapeutic Alliance: Awe and Trust

The first theoretical yield derived from the fact that child analysis could not be undertaken with the usual tools of free association, dream interpretation, and transference analysis. Each of these procedures had to be either modified greatly or supplemented with more direct techniques that capitalize on the child's inherent striving to grow, to mature, to change, to master inner and outer reality. Thus Anna Freud learned the importance of a long preparatory phase designed to establish the analyst as an important, dependable, indeed, indispensable person in the child's current living. With a mixture of awe and trust, the child must come to accept the analyst as a very special kind of teacher, namely, as a specialist in self-knowledge and as an ally against an intruding and misunderstanding outer world. Although the adult analytic patient may fantasize this kind of relationship with the therapist, it is only the child patient who lives it.

Beyond Structural Conflict: Developmental Vulnerability

Second, the fact of a child's plasticity, the continual growth toward maturity, forces the child analyst to focus not on overt neurotic symptoms but on the distant goal of future healthy functioning. Anna Freud and her colleagues soon recognized that crystallized neurotic syndromes were only a small fraction of the problems of childhood. Developmental disturbances, threats to continued maturing, both physical and psychological, were more typically the objects of concern. Moreover, even when manifest neurotic symptoms were present in a child's behavior, these overt indicators of serious pathology often have a quite different meaning in the context of a child's evolving life history from their customary significance in an adult's more or less completed development.

What was sorely needed, and what Anna Freud and her coworkers eventually developed, as we shall see, was a formalized system of diagnosis that would emphasize the developmental sequence of personality formation and malformation, highlighting serious threats to the completion of personality growth while minimizing those less serious but unavoidable insults to a child's integrity (A. Freud, 1970b, pp. 163ff.). In effect, analytic therapy with children had forced Anna Freud to go beyond the classic conception of neurosis and maladjustment as an unconscious war of ego, id, and superego. Children manifest disturbances that stem from the vulnerabilities intrinsic to the enterprise of growing up.

Metapsychological Assessment

Third, Anna Freud had learned an important lesson from the length of the preparatory period required to make a child "analyzable." Not only do child patients require a relatively lengthy breaking-in to convince them of the value of analysis, but the therapist likewise requires a relatively lengthy period of assessment to understand each child's conflicts, deficits, and strengths. What was needed was a way to make such assessments at the outset. Observational and formal interviewing techniques modeled on the academic tradition of psychological testing were not especially attractive alternatives to psychoanalysts, but this relatively new field of child analysis seemed to require some compromise with formal academic psychology. With time, just such an assessment procedure was developed, and only recently has it been formalized into a metapsychological profile (A. Freud, 1965a, 1965b; W. E. Freud, 1972; Laufer, 1965).

The *metapsychological profile* is the psychoanalyst's way of organizing all of the information obtained about a patient during a diagnostic assessment. "Metapsychological" is applied as a descriptive term to this procedure because the diagnostician attempts to integrate the findings into a coherent picture of the person's dynamic, genetic, economic, structural, and adaptive functioning (see Chapter 3 for a discussion of metapsychological viewpoints).

Recall that the *dynamic* meaning of a psychological event refers to the *conflictful* nature of the competing drive energies as the ego attempts to provide satisfaction for the id; the *genetic* viewpoint refers to the multiple *developmental* experiences in the course of a person's life history that converge to produce a particular symptom, meaning, or defense; *economic* is meant to indicate the degree of drive *intensity* and changes in quantity of instinctual energy over time; the *structural* (or, earlier, topographical) viewpoint seeks to understand the *interactions* among the various structures or agencies of the mind as the ego, id, and superego perform their tasks; and the *adaptive* metapsychological perspective focuses attention on the ego's capacity to enable the person to resolve inner conflict and "fit in" with external reality's demands in a *healthy* way.

Metapsychological profiles have been developed for infants (W. E. Freud, 1972), for adolescents (Laufer, 1965), and for adults (A. Freud, 1965a; A. Freud, H. Nagera, & W. E. Freud, 1965). The version we present here was designed for children (A. Freud, 1965b). Table 4.1 outlines the major categories of the child's metapsychological profile. The categories in Table 4.1 range from biographical information, such as family

TABLE 4.1   Outline of Metapsychological Profile of the Child

I.   REASON FOR REFERRAL—arrests in development, behavior problems, symptoms.

II.   DESCRIPTION OF CHILD—personal appearance, moods, manner.

III.   FAMILY BACKGROUND AND PERSONAL HISTORY—life history, family constellation.

IV.   POSSIBLY SIGNIFICANT ENVIRONMENTAL INFLUENCES

V.   ASSESSMENTS OF DEVELOPMENT

  A. Drive Development

   Libido and aggression distribution toward self and others.

  B. Ego and Superego Development

   Ego functions, age appropriate behavior, defensive balance, emotional balance.

VI.   GENETIC ASSESSMENTS (Regression and Fixation)

  Behavior, fantasy, and symptoms from which can be inferred the level of psychosexual development that has been reached or whether regression or fixation to earlier stages is indicated.

VII.   DYNAMIC AND STRUCTURAL ASSESSMENTS

  Classify internal and external conflicts as to source in ego-id, ego-superego, or ego-reality clashes.

VIII.   ASSESSMENT OF GENERAL CHARACTERISTICS

  A. Frustration tolerance

   Ability to endure tension, drive blocking, and capacity to employ adaptive defenses.

  B. Sublimation Potential

   Ability to neutralize sexual and aggressive urges and channel them into healthy activities.

  C. Attitude to Anxiety

   Use of defenses against fears of external and internal stimuli; degree of capacity to master inner and outer fears and stress situations.

  D. Progressive versus Regressive Forces

   Estimate ability to continue to develop, to profit from learning, and treatment, to move forward to next developmental level.

IX.   DIAGNOSIS

  Integrate findings on degree of ego health, conflicts, frustrations, developmental level, superego severity, presence of organic disease, role of environment.

Based on A. Freud, 1965b, pp. 138–147.

background and current environmental situation, to descriptions of drive functioning to diagnosis based on an integration of all preceding metapsychological viewpoints.

The significance of the metapsychological profile is threefold. First, it provides a uniform and concrete set of *explicit instructions* to gather specific *behavioral and psychological* data. Little is left to the clinician's "intuition." Second, it requires the diagnostician to *integrate those observations* and supplementary life history data into a unified picture of the overall functioning and *developmental appropriateness* of the child's personality. Patterns of consistency, inconsistency, and outright deficits clearly emerge. Third, the profile requires sophisticated *use of psychoanalytic developmental theory, drive theory,* and *ego theory* to derive "metapsychological" meaning from the observations required. In effect, the profile demands that, for better or worse, psychoanalytic theory be used as a conceptual guide to diagnosis and as a predictive guide to specific therapy. In short, the metapsychological profile integrates theoretical propositions and observable clinical phenomena into a coherent psychological "map."

It should be mentioned, in passing, that the baby, adolescent, and adult profiles require somewhat different kinds of data from those required by the child profile. For example, the baby profile requires assessments of bodily functions such as sleeping, eating, and elimination. Adult profiles focus on the possible interferences of the patients' conflicts and regressions with their sexual functioning and with their ability to work productively.

The Inescapable Limits of Child Analysis: Unchangeable Lives

The fourth theoretical yield from Anna Freud's work with children was her discovery that there was a temptation to pursue therapeutic exploration too far. As other analysts entered the field of child therapy, there emerged the unwritten and unspoken goals of pursuing personality disturbances in children to their very roots—the first year of life. In trying to go beyond manifest disturbances to the earliest antecedents of personality, the child analyst runs the risk of prolonging the analysis interminably. Furthermore, such all-encompassing analyses, extending to the very beginning of the child's short life, may very well run headlong into unchangeable constitutional or environmental givens of personality that do not yield themselves to modifications through analysis:

> In my opinion, these earliest environmental influences on the child create states which are comparable to deficiency illnesses on the physical side. While the effects of such early deprivation can be mitigated by later favorable influences, they cannot be undone or reversed or solved in a new more age-adequate way, as conflicts can: this means that they are not in the true sense of the word a legitimate object of analytic effort. (A. Freud, 1970a, pp. 18–19)

In short, Anna Freud had to acknowledge that child analysis is not a universal preventative of human misery, no matter how early such interventions are begun. Certain environmental and constitutional givens cannot be undone. Specific elements of the human condition may mar a child's life, yet remain beyond the reach of even the most well-intentioned efforts. Failure to recognize these real limits leads to the unrealistic aspiration of extending a child's analysis through the full period of development into adulthood.

Significance of Contemporary Social Reality: Bulldogs Bank Children

The fifth theoretical yield from Anna Freud's work was her discovery that the analytic practitioner must recognize that, unlike adults, children are more greatly dependent on and more easily influenced by their current external realities. The child analyst must be prepared to accept the proposition that child patients' *current* dependencies on parents, their conflicts with siblings and peers, and their relationships to teachers and other authority figures are all reflected in their disturbances. Unlike adult analytic patients whose neurotic disturbances are almost entirely internalized and have their causes in past relationships or prior unresolved conflicts, children can be disturbed to an equal degree by their present relationships in present reality:

> In treatment, especially the very young reveal the extent to which they are dominated by the object world, i.e., how much of their behavior and pathology is determined by environmental influences such as the parents' protective or rejecting, loving or indifferent, critical or admiring attitudes, as well as by the sexual harmony or disharmony in their married life. . . . *The child analyst who interprets exclusively in terms of the inner world is in danger of missing out on his patients' reporting activity concerning his—at the time equally important—environmental circumstances.* (A. Freud, 1965b, pp. 50–51; italics added)

The child analyst must recognize that the little patient's disturbances do not exclusively reflect what has gone wrong, been distorted, or been blocked in the realm of the child's internal world. A child's disturbances may very well reflect his or her links to reality (A. Freud, 1958, p. 127).

The importance of children's external environments and their abilities to cope with grave threats was impressed on Anna Freud in her work with children separated from their parents during World War II in the London bombing raids. Children, with the consent of their parents, were evacuated from areas of extreme danger and relocated in safer foster homes outside the bombing zone. Suddenly, thousands of children who had never before been separated from home and family were under the guardianship of strangers (A. Freud, 1953, p. 511). Other less fortunate children suffered the permanent loss of their parents through the devastation wreaked on London by German air attacks. Such children had witnessed death and destruction firsthand and, therefore, had been even more traumatically separated from their parents.

In 1940 Anna Freud collected financial contributions from several sources to open and staff a children's center in Hampstead, London. Eventually a babies' rest center and a country house in Essex were also opened and all were filled with evacuated children. Collectively known as the Hampstead Nurseries, Anna Freud's residential homes were designed not as institutional settings but as substitute homes that would provide security, mothering, and love for the children (A. Freud & D. Burlingham, 1944).

The effects of separation took their greatest toll on the youngest children and infants. Children between five and 12 months responded with all manner of bodily disorders, ranging from eating difficulties, sleep disturbances, and feeding problems to respiratory troubles and loss of recently acquired abilities such as talking and walking. Other children evidenced uncontrollable grief reactions and refused all contact with their new environment. When reunited with their mothers or provided with a substitute mother, most of these grief-stricken infants returned to normal. In Anna Freud's view, the disaster of war and evacuation had demonstrated the validity of psychoanalytic hypotheses concerning the significance of the mother-child relationship (1958, p. 515).

Some years later, six young children, German-Jewish orphans whose parents were killed in gas chambers shortly after the children's births, were evacuated from one place and one family to another until they reached England in August 1945. For three years they had been in a concentration camp in conditions of nutritional and emotional deprivation. A former contributor to Anna Freud's Hampstead Nurseries donated a year's tenancy of a country house in Sussex named Bulldogs Bank. Together with Sophie Dann, one of the nurses in charge of Bulldogs Bank, Anna Freud published an account of their group life (A. Freud, 1951c).

> The Bulldogs Bank children functioned as a unit; no child wished to be separated from the others, nor would the group allow any of its members to be parted. Their insistence on being constantly together caused some difficulty in the staff's plans to treat them as individuals. For example, John, the oldest (3 years, 10 months), needed only to push away his plate at dinner for the other five children to cease eating. Unlike normal children, this group of orphans showed no envy, jealousy, or rivalry among themselves. They would spontaneously take turns at games, equally share every treasure, and were acutely sensitive to each other's needs and feelings. (A. Freud, 1951c, p. 174)

The Bulldogs Bank children rarely attacked or hurt one another during their first few months at the country house. Disputes were typically word battles, which ended in a massed attack against any outsider, such as an interfering adult. Their way of expressing aggression was less sophisticated than would be expected for children of their age. Biting and spitting were the usual modes of anger, although sometimes urinating on the floor or into their clothes were suitable alternates. All of these behaviors are more characteristic of younger children. But after a few weeks, they were able to add hitting and smacking adults to their growing repertoire.

Positive relations with adults were made on a group basis, as though generalizing from their tightly knit unit to the adults at large. For example, the children eventually began to insist that the adults take their turns or share, and began also to be concerned about the adults' feelings. In effect, the adults ceased to be outsiders and began to be equals. Individual personal attachments to the adults then began to appear and had the quality of child-parent relationships.

The children had been exposed to terror and deprivation during their stay in concentration camps. Though they had no clear memory of their past, they evidenced signs of their experiences. For example, all six children were terrified of dogs, probably because of the concentration camp guard dogs. "Once, when he met a strange large dog on a walk, John bit his lip in his terror and thought that the dog had bitten him when it bled" (A. Freud, 1951c, p. 216). In a similar way, the children were afraid of large trucks, presumably because they resembled concentration camp vans. That the children did not show an even greater range of fears and anxieties is probably attributable to their close cohesion and mutual defensiveness through which each member drew strength from the others. Anna Freud and Sophie Dann summarized their observations in this way:

> They were deprived of mother love, oral satisfactions, stability in their relationships and their surroundings. They were passed from one hand to another during their first year, lived in an age group instead of a family during their second and third year, and were uprooted again three times during their fourth year. . . . The children were hypersensitive, restless, aggressive, difficult to handle. They showed a heightened autoeroticism and some of them the beginning of neurotic symptoms. But they were

neither deficient, delinquent, nor psychotic. They had found an alternative placement for their libido [i.e., each other] and, on the strength of this, had mastered some of their anxieties and developed social attitudes. (1951c, pp. 228–229)

Thus, even in children who were severely deprived and traumatized, Anna Freud was compelled to recognize their strivings to adapt to, to cope with, and to master an environment that, in principle, should have devastated them.

Mastery of Life Tasks: Developmental Lines

The sixth and last theoretical yield from Anna Freud's child analytic work was her observation of how the ego masters problems posed by life. A *developmental line* is Anna Freud's term for a stage of id-ego interaction during which children outgrow in gradual steps their dependence on external controls and consequently gain in ego mastery of internal and external reality (A. Freud, 1965b, p. 63). In principle, however, the focus is not exclusively on the ego's growing mastery, for without the id drives, there would be little incentive for the ego's alertness to inner and outer demands.

Developmental lines, then, may be thought of as reliable sequences in the child's maturation from complete *dependency* to relatively complete *independence*, from being wholly *irrational* to being nearly completely *rational*, and from exclusively

TABLE 4.2   Six Developmental Lines

I. Dependency to Emotional Self-Reliance	II. Suckling to Rational Eating
1. Biological dependence on mother; no recognition of separation between self and other.	1. Being nursed by schedule or on demand.
2. Need-fulfilling relationship, with mother seen as partially externalized satisfier.	2. Weaning from breast or bottle initiated either by infant or by wishes of mother; new food difficulties.
3. Object-constancy phase, in which image of mother is retained even when she is not present.	3. Transition from being fed to self-feeding; "food" and "mother" still identified with each other.
4. Pre-oedipal, clinging stage, marked by fantasies of dominating the love object.	4. Self-feeding, disagreements with mother about quantity; meals as battlegrounds for other difficulties of mother-child relations.
5. Phallic-oedipal phase, marked by possessiveness of parent of opposite sex and rivalry with same-sexed parent.	5. Infantile sexual theories shape attitude toward food: fantasies of impregnation through mouth, pregnancy fear (fear of getting fat).
6. Latency phase with lessening of drive urgency, denigration of parental models, transfer of libido to peers, groups, authority figures.	6. Fading of sexualization of feeding, with pleasure in eating regained or increased; more self-determination of eating habits.
7. Preadolescent phase of return to early attitudes of need-fulfilling relationship with love object.	
8. Adolescent phase, marked by struggle to win independence and break ties with childhood love objects (parents), and need for establishing genital primacy.	

TABLE 4.2   (*continued*)

III. Wetting and Soiling to Bowel-Bladder Control	IV. Irresponsibility to Responsibility in Body Management
1. Complete freedom to wet and soil is controlled by mother, not self.	1. Aggression turned from self to external world. Self-injury from biting, scratching, picking limited by focus on external objects; child recognizes causes of self-induced pain.
2. Anal phase of child's direct opposition to control of elimination by others; feces treated as precious "gifts" to mother; battle of wills for toilet training.	2. Ego advances of understanding cause-effect principles, delay of dangerous wishes, recognition of external dangers such as fire, heights, water.
3. Identification with parental rules, self-control of bladder and bowel; cleanliness concerns based on learned disgust and shame. Orderliness and tidiness interests based on anal regularity.	3. Voluntary endorsement of rules of hygiene and medical necessity; avoidance of unwholesome foods, bodily cleanliness, compliance with doctor's orders only when fear or guilt enforces it. Belief that mother can restore endangered health.
4. Cleanliness concerns pursued for their own sake, regardless of parental pressures; autonomous ego and superego control of anal drives.	

V. Egocentricity to Companionship	VI. Body to Toy and Play to Work
1. Selfish, narcissistic outlook, in which other children do not matter or are seen as disturbers and rivals for parental love.	1. Infant play is body sensuality in fingers, skin, and mouth of own or mother's body with no clear distinction between the two.
2. Other children related to as lifeless objects or toys, to be manhandled and roughly treated with no response expected from them.	2. Sensual properties of own and mother's body transferred to some soft object; e.g., teddy bear, blanket.
3. Other children seen as helpmates in tasks; duration of partnership determined by task requirements.	3. Clinging to one specific "soft" object grows into general liking for such cuddly things; but all are inanimate objects and do not retaliate for toddler's ambivalent handling.
4. Other children seen as equals and partners in their own right; they can be admired, feared, or competed with, loved, hated, or identified with. True companionship desired.	4. Cuddly objects used now only at bedtime; other toys for day play.
	5. Pleasure in finishing play activities, and pleasure in achievement.
	6. Play grades into work via hobbies, daydreams, games, proficiency sports. Child can inhibit own impulses.

Based on A. Freud, 1965b, pp. 64–85.

passive to almost totally *active* relations with reality. These lines of development expose the ego's attempts to confront life situations successfully, without painful retreat and without overly defensive inhibition. Such life situations include separation from mother, birth of a brother or sister, illness, school, peer relations, play, emergence of sexual interest at puberty, and, of course, love (A. Freud, 1962, p. 34) (see Table 4.2).

1. From Dependency to Emotional Self-Reliance
2. From Suckling to Rational Eating
3. From Wetting and Soiling to Bladder and Bowel Control
4. From Irresponsibility to Responsibility in Body Management
5. From the Body to the Toy, and From Play to Work
6. From Egocentricity to Companionship

Anna Freud's introduction of the concept of developmental lines is a genuinely original contribution to psychoanalysis. Some of these areas have been pursued by other analytic thinkers, some of whose work we review briefly in a later section of this chapter. However, it is important to note in the present context that interest in these lines of development focuses attention on the ego's capacity to adapt to life's demands, and those demands can be situational, interpersonal, or personal. Thus Anna Freud has brought classic psychoanalytic theory one step closer to the people world and one step further away from the purely internal world of instincts.

THE EGO DEFENDS ITSELF:
PROFILES OF MASTERY AND VULNERABILITY

In the early phase of her development of an analytic method for application to children, Anna Freud searched about for a way to shorten the diagnostic stage of the preparatory period. The first step in that direction came with her investigation of the ego defenses as indicators of instinctual change, blocking, fixation, and sublimation. In effect, although the instinctual dynamics themselves are not directly observable, the ego's reaction to them is apparent from an examination of the individual's defenses.

In 1936 Anna Freud published her classic monograph, *The Ego and the Mechanisms of Defense,* and this book, more than any other publication, legitimized psychoanalytic interest in ego functioning. The main justification for interest in ego defenses as objects of scrutiny in their own right was simply stated:

> If we know how a particular patient seeks to defend himself against the emergence of his instinctual impulses, i.e., what is the nature of his habitual ego resistances, we can form an idea of his probable attitude toward his own unwelcome affects. (A. Freud, 1936, p. 32)

Anna Freud embarked on a systematization and expansion of Sigmund Freud's diverse pronouncements on ego defenses, ranging from his earliest conception of repression as the fundamental ego maneuver in the face of instinctual threat to his later elaboration of secondary defense strategies. Now, for the first time, the patients' maneuvers for adjusting to their social and biological needs, and their typical techniques of expressing emotional reactions to the inevitable course of their lives came under direct scrutiny. All of these ego functions, most of them involving observable behaviors, had been largely ignored or neglected by classical analysts in favor of the presumed more valuable knowledge to be gained by study of "deeper" unconscious drives. Defenses had been viewed merely as obstacles to a clear view of the unconscious.

Defenses as Diagnostic Indicators

Consider the paradox that confronts the psychoanalyst treating patients who navigate the obstacles of their lives with the aid of massive psychological defenses. Such patients have come to therapy because they feel that their lives are constricted, joyless, and devoid of spontaneity. Yet, so long as a patient's defenses hold, the analyst confronts an apparently intact personality, unneedful of the analyst's intrusion. It is ironic that only when the defenses fail and unconscious material reemerges into awareness that the analyst may discern trouble in the depths:

> So long as the defenses set up by a person's ego are intact, the analytic observer is faced by a blank; as soon as they break down, for example, when repression fails and unconscious material returns . . . a mass of information about inner processes becomes available. (A. Freud, 1969a, p. 125)

Defenses are successful protectors of the personality precisely because the ego remains unaware that it is defending itself.

In Anna Freud's terms, the ego's defenses are silent and invisible (1936, p. 8). Repression, for example, is only apparent by the *absence* of drive components that we expect to be present in a normal person. The child who is all sweetness and goodness, with no evidence of hostility, jealousy, or anger is a child from another solar system where these drives do not exist. More probable, such a child is one whose ego has been enfeebled by massive repression against anger and aggression. Thus the ego defenses are observable only by inference from the individual's behavior, when that behavior evidences signs of missing customary id derivatives. Looked at from the developmental point of view, people's defenses reveal their personal history of ego development, that is, life stories of mastering or succumbing to their passions, needs, wishes, and urges (1936, p. 21; Sandler & A. Freud, 1985).

Motives for Defense

Following her father's lead (S. Freud, 1926a), Anna Freud distinguished three sources of danger to which the ego responds defensively. First, in the case of the adult neurotic, there is the *danger of superego dissatisfaction* with the way the ego seeks to provide gratifications to id sexual and aggressive strivings. The irony of this form of anxiety is that the ego itself does not regard the sexual or aggressive impulses against which it so actively defends itself as dangerous or condemnable. "The instinct is regarded as dangerous because the superego prohibits its gratification and if [the instinct] achieves its aim, it will certainly stir up trouble between the ego and superego" (A. Freud, 1936, p. 55). Because the superego is capable of setting up an ideal standard of such intense rigidity, the neurotic's ego works to renounce *all* sexual and aggressive impulses to a degree that is incompatible with good mental health. In effect, the neurotic's ego becomes the superego's handmaiden, prosecuting its stringent moral wishes at the cost of internal conflict.

Second, in the case of the child neurotic who has not yet formed a severe superego, the ego may come to fear the *danger of the outside world.* Fearing the instincts because the parents have prohibited their expression, the child's ego is reacting to fear of *their* displeasure. This more "objective" anxiety is nevertheless sufficient to trigger the ego's defensive maneuvers against sexual and aggressive impulses (A. Freud, 1936, p. 57).

Third, there is the ego's direct fear of the *danger of the strength of unconscious impulses.* Sigmund Freud felt that this fear resulted from the ego's differentiation from the id in infancy and its gradual separation from id primary process function by the development of its own reality-oriented secondary process logical thought. Thus, when an instinct becomes too strong, the ego experiences the impulses as a threat to its independence, as a signal of disintegration through flooding with id primary process chaos (S. Freud, 1923a, p. 57). Rather than submit helplessly to invasion, the ego brings defenses into play. Freud summarized the three kinds of anxiety that trigger ego defenses:

> Thus the ego, driven by the id, confined by the superego, repulsed by reality, struggles to master its economic task of bringing about harmony among the forces and influences working in and upon it; and we can understand how it is that so often we cannot suppress a cry: "Life is not easy!" If the ego is obliged to admit its weakness, it breaks out in anxiety—realistic anxiety regarding the external world, moral anxiety regarding the superego, and neurotic anxiety regarding the strength of the passions in the id. (S. Freud, 1933, p. 78)

In Anna Freud's hands, analysis of ego defensive functioning became a diagnostic tool of extreme sensitivity. For the child analyst, severely limited in the use of free association, defense analysis became the indispensable means to an understanding of the child's personal history of instinctual development (A. Freud, 1936, pp. 37-39; Sandler & A. Freud, 1985). By permitting the deduction of the specific id passion, the period of life when it emerged, and the specific kind of blockage erected by the ego against it, defense analysis opened the way to the hidden depths of the child's life history.

Anna Freud listed 10 ego defenses hinted at or described by her father, and five elaborations of her own. Table 4.3 provides a definition and an illustration of each of these "classic" defenses. It should be pointed out that other psychoanalysts have added endlessly to this list, so that the total number of possible ego defenses is considerably larger than those represented in the table.

TABLE 4.3   Anna Freud's Ten Ego Defenses

Defense Mechanism	Definition and Characteristics	Illustration
1. REPRESSION [Motivated Forgetting]	Abrupt and involuntary removal from awareness of any threatening impulse, idea, or memory. Most dangerous and one of the most archaic defenses, repression or denial is the prerequisite for any of the other defense mechanisms listed below.	Adolescent girl feeling guilty over her sexual impulses, frequently "blocks" on her boyfriend's name when introducing him to family and friends.

TABLE 4.3 (*continued*)

Defense Mechanism	Definition and Characteristics	Illustration
1A. DENIAL [Motivated Negation]	Blocking of *external* events from entry into awareness, when perception of such stimuli is symbolically or associatively related to threatening impulses. Denial abolishes dangers "out there" by negating them.	A recent widow continues to set a place at the table for her deceased husband. She also fantasizes frequently about conversations she is having with him.
2. ASCETICISM [Renunciation of Needs]	Characteristic of puberty, asceticism is more of a character style than a defense. Preadolescents feel overwhelmed by their emerging sexual impulses and protect themselves by repudiating *all* desires, *all* pleasures. In extremes, adolescents may "mortify" themselves by limiting sleep and food intake, and retaining urine and feces as long as possible.	The adolescent who embarks on what seems to be a "fad" diet, or "fad" interest in rigorous physical exertion *may* be attempting to control his or her impulses.
3. PROJECTION [Displacement Outward]	Attribution to another person or object one's own unacceptable impulses, wishes, or thoughts. Then, these impulses become "ego-alien" as though not a part of self.	A husband who has barely resisted the temptation to be unfaithful to his wife, begins to be chronically suspicious about her fidelity to him.
3A. ALTRUISTIC SURRENDER [Sacrifice Self]	A form of projection in which the person fulfills his or her own needs vicariously by identifying with the satisfactions of another; in extreme form, person may even give up own ambitions to allow another to be fulfilled.	An employee who was too timid to ask for a raise for herself became a militant advocate on the rights of another worker, expressing extreme assertiveness.
3B. DISPLACEMENT [Redirection of Impulse]	Redirection of impulses, usually aggressive ones, onto a substitute target when the appropriate target is too threatening.	A young woman, who in childhood was very envious of her brother's relationship with their mother, could only express her feelings of rage toward other females, typically other female relatives.
4. TURNING-AGAINST-SELF [Self-as-Object or Target]	Redirection of impulses inwardly against oneself instead of outwardly toward the appropriate target. Usually results in masochistic feelings of inadequacy, guilt, depression.	Same woman as above (3B) also turned her hatred toward mother inward, becoming self-accusatory, passive, surrendering, and inferior feeling.
5. REACTION-FORMATION [Believing the Opposite]	Transformation of unacceptable impulses into their opposites and more acceptable forms; usually has the quality of "The Lady doth protest too much." Hate into love; love into hate.	A child who had been aggressive toward her mother became overly concerned for her safety, for her mother's welfare, and became excessively worried that some harm would befall her mother.

TABLE 4.3 *(continued)*

Defense Mechanism	Definition and Characteristics	Illustration
5A. REVERSAL [Active into Passive]	Similar to reaction-formation, reversal transforms an impulse from an active to a passive mode. Also similar to Turning-Against-Self.	Sadistic impulses may become masochistic, with the self as passive target of aggression and sexual impulses.
6. SUBLIMINATION [Acceptable Substitutes]	Transformation of an impulse into a socially productive and acceptable form.	A Vietnam veteran who, as a Green Beret, had enjoyed his soldiering, became a policeman who preferred assignments in the most dangerous neighborhoods.
7. INTROJECTION [Taking Within]	Incorporating into one's own behavior and beliefs the characteristics of some external object or admired person.	The adolescent who adopts the traits, mannerisms, and speech of an admired teacher. The widow who adopts items of apparel from her deceased husband, along with his tastes in food and entertainments.
7A. IDENTIFICATION-WITH-THE-AGGRESSOR [Adopting Feared Traits]	Adopting the traits or mannerisms of a feared person or object.	Hostages in skyjackings often feel protective of their captors. A little girl who was afraid to walk down the dark hallway of her house for fear of meeting a ghost solved the problem by "booing" her way down the hall: "You just have to pretend that you're the ghost who might meet you."
8. ISOLATION [Stripping of Emotion, Meaning]	Characteristic of obsessive-compulsive neurosis, unacceptable impulses are retained in consciousness but divested of emotion and separated from connecting ideas to achieve an emotional-intellectual quarantine.	Seventeen-year-old boy with acute masturbation guilt, divided all his thoughts into acceptable and unacceptable ones. Both categories of ideas could not be thought simultaneously without unacceptable ideas contaminating acceptable ones. (Fenichel, 1945)
9. UNDOING [Magical Cancellations]	Characteristic of obsessive-compulsive personality, who performs magical gestures, or rituals, to cancel unacceptable thoughts, or acts, once the thought or act has been completed.	Same boy as above (8), had to perform rituals whenever unacceptable and acceptable thoughts occurred together. For example, he had to recite the alphabet backward whenever he had a sexual thought, or turn around and spit whenever he met another boy he knew also masturbated.

TABLE 4.3 (*continued*)

Defense Mechanism	Definition and Characteristics	Illustration
10. REGRESSION [Developmental Retreat]	Probably not really a defense, so much as a primitivization of behavior in face of stress: return to earlier modes of response when confronted with anxiety.	At his first separation from mother upon hospitalization for a tonsillectomy, Timmy began thumb-sucking and soiling his pants, deeds he "outgrew" two years earlier.

Based on A. Freud, 1936; Undoing and Isolation examples from Fenichel, 1945; Sandler & A. Freud, 1985.

FIGURE 4.5   Anna Freud, age 79, in her home office, Maresfield Gardens, 1974.

The relatively poor quality of this photograph reflects the reluctance Anna Freud expressed in posing for it when I interviewed her at her home. I could not get her to move away from the bright side-light of the open window near her desk; but she did momentarily sit still for the picture. Her reluctance was not limited to picture taking. As late as 1974, almost 80 years after Sigmund Freud had created the brain model and 18 years since it was first made public, Anna Freud was still reluctant to attribute significance to it. She vigorously dismissed all my attempts to question her on the subject during the July interview at her home in Maresfield Gardens, Hampstead, London.

A FINAL WORD ON ANNA FREUD

Anna Freud's work represents one possible solution, or more precisely, a group of solutions, to the unfinished problems bequeathed by Sigmund Freud. The character of Anna Freud's "solutions" was threefold: First and foremost, she attempted to enlarge the boundaries of classical psychoanalysis with direct considerations of ego functioning in social reality without abandoning the bedrock of psychoanalytic instinct theory. For Anna Freud, the ego is still in partnership with the id, still bound primarily to fulfill its tasks at the id's behest. But it is also an ego capable of some independent functioning in the areas of life mastery.

Second, Anna Freud's theorizing has the character of systematizing what had been informal or scattered insights in her father's work. Thus her attention to ego defenses, her adaptation of analytic method for therapy with children, and her metapsychological classification scheme are all based on classic theoretical formulations; but at the same time each of these achievements transcends classical theory in subtle yet significant ways. The key modification was her emphasis on viewing personality development as more affected by the environment, as more easily shaped by interpersonal relations, and as more fluid than classical theory would have it.

Third, Anna Freud's work is far removed from the implicit neurological assumptions of Sigmund Freud's creation. For Anna Freud, the child, and presumably also the adult, are active, assertive, masterful creatures, who need not be the victims of their internal conflicts or of their overwhelming environments.

HEINZ HARTMANN

THE AUTONOMOUS, ADAPTIVE EGO

If Anna Freud may be said to have been the reluctant legitimizer of ego psychology, Heinz Hartmann may be justly described as its enthusiastic father. Hartmann set out to accomplish no less a task than to extend psychoanalytic theory beyond the neuroses into a general psychology of human conduct. It was Hartmann's belief that the time had come to push beyond conflict theory to explore the functions of the ego that are independent of id drives, that is, those functions which allow individuals to make a place for themselves among their fellows.

> We must recognize that though the ego certainly does grow on conflicts, these are not the only roots of ego development. . . . Not every adaptation to the environment, or every learning and maturation process, is a conflict. I refer to the development *outside of conflict* of perception, object comprehension, thinking, language, recall phenomena, productivity, to the well-known phases of motor development, grasping, crawling, walking, and to the maturation and learning processes implicit in all these and many others. (Hartmann, 1939, p. 8)

The Conflict-Free Sphere of Ego Function

Hartmann proposed that the term *conflict-free sphere* be adopted by psychoanalysts to designate that "ensemble" of ego activities occurring outside the region of mental conflict. Hartmann was not proposing a new region of the mind; rather he was suggesting that the ego's *style* of functioning could change in accordance with the goals *it* set out to accomplish (1939, p. 11).

In effect, Hartmann was pointing out that, although ego functions such as memory and learning may become enmeshed in conflict resolution attempts, they emerge in development *before* such attempts can be made. Memory, learning, association, and other ego functions are *prerequisites* of the ego's relationships to the id drives; they are not products of those interactions (1939, p. 15). The ego defenses even emerge first in essentially normal developments before their eventual induction into service by the ego in its war against the id. As Hartmann, Kris, and Lowenstein point out,

> . . . it is correct to say that the human personality is formed by psychic mechanisms which serve, also, the purpose of defense. Some of these mechanisms first operate in other areas; thus projection and introjection are used in order to establish the distinction between the self and the nonself; regression as a regular and temporary transformation of psychic functioning accompanies the daily cycle from awakeness to sleep; and denial of the unpleasant probably represents an initial phase in the elimination of all disturbing stimuli. (1946, pp. 45–46)

Thus for Hartmann the ego is more than a by-product of the id. Where Freud had emphasized that the id is psychologically and biologically "older" than the ego, and that the ego develops out of the id to serve the id's interests with reality, Hartmann interpreted the ego as a simultaneous psychological development, functioning independently of, but in synchrony with, the instincts (Hartmann, 1950b, p. 120).

In Hartmann's reformulation of psychoanalytic developmental psychology, both the id and the ego develop—differentiate—out of the same matrix of innate biological equipment. Parts of that biological equipment are the instincts or drives, from which the id emerges; but other, separate though equally biological, parts are the "inborn ego apparatuses." "Strictly speaking, there is no ego before the differentiation of ego and id, but there is no id either, since both are products of differentiation" (Hartmann, 1939, pp. 102–103). Hence, in Hartmann's view, the ego is not limited in its independence by virtue of its origins in the id, for the ego does not develop out of the id. It develops from its own biological roots, the innate processes that serve a person in adapting to the world.

The Primary and Secondary Autonomy of the Ego: Adaptation

Hartmann pointed out that in principle there are two kinds of ego autonomy. *Primary ego autonomy* refers to those biological, *maturational* roots of such conflict-free ego processes as perception, learning, memory, and motility. These functions "differentiate" out of basic biological properties innate to the organism and aid in its adaptation to the environment. But the ego is capable of a *secondary autonomy* when it is able to modify those of its functions that developed in conflict with the id into tools that also serve healthy adaptation to life (Hartmann, 1950b, p. 105). These secondary "ego autonomies" are the products of an interaction between physical maturation and learning.

As Hartmann later described secondary ego autonomy, some of the functions of the ego are "wrested" from the influence of the id and may even develop a degree of resistance to reinvolvement with conflict (Hartmann, 1959, p. 330). Slowly, even skills that had originally been developed to satisfy id drives may themselves become secondary independent sources of satisfaction. Provision of necessary gratifications to the id drives, for example, may generalize with development into a broader "self-interest," a healthy concern with social status, success, financial security, and comfort (Hartmann, 1947, p. 64).

As Hartmann himself pointed out, secondary ego autonomy bears a striking resemblance to Gordon Allport's notion of "functional autonomy" of motives (Hartmann, 1959, p. 330; see Chapter 14 for a discussion of Allport's concept). In effect, Hartmann was proposing that the ego could "neutralize" sexual and aggressive id drives for functions other than pleasure and destruction, for pursuits other than drive reduction.

Neutralization is ". . . the change of both libidinal and aggressive energy away from the instinctual and toward a noninstinctual mode" (Hartmann, 1955, p. 227). Freud had suggested, as we saw in the historical introduction to this chapter, that libido could be "desexualized" to provide the ego with relatively id-independent energy (Freud, 1923a). Hartmann and his colleagues, however, took the matter a step further and suggested that *both* sexual and aggressive drives could be severed from their instinctual roots (Hartmann, Kris, & Lowenstein, 1949, pp. 67ff.). There are, nevertheless, differences in the degrees of neutralization of the sexual and aggressive drives, so that one or the other may more easily at a given moment come under the ego's control (Hartmann, 1955, p. 228).

When an ego function becomes independent of the id and is practiced for its own sake, the process of neutralization has occurred. But so has the process of adaptation. Adaptation is thus the result of the ego's primary and secondary autonomies, that is, of the ego's attempts to maintain an equilibrium within the mental apparatus and between the person and the environment (Hartmann, 1939, pp. 23ff.).

> The observation underlying the concept of "adaptation" is that living organisms patently "fit" into their environment. Thus, adaptation is primarily a reciprocal relationship between the organism and its environment. (Hartmann, 1939, p. 24)

The process of adaptation is a continually evolving movement toward increased "fitting in" with the environment; it is not a static achievement. Hartmann employed Freud's terms of alloplastic and autoplastic change to conceptualize this gradual inner and outer mastery. *Alloplastic* refers to changes made by the person on the environment to make the environment more congenial. In effect, people change the world and then adapt to the changes they have created. *Autoplastic* refers to that part of this process which involves changes in the organism. For in order to adapt to self-created changes in the world, there must be some changes in the self as well. A third way in which adaptation may be accomplished is neither completely alloplastic nor completely autoplastic. It is simply the organism's choice of a new environment that is more advantageous for survival (Hartmann, 1939, p. 27).

Adaptation is a process involving constitution and environment, past and present, innovation and tradition:

> Man does not come to terms with his environment anew in every generation; his relation to the environment is guaranteed by—besides the factors of heredity—an

evolution peculiar to man, namely, the influence of tradition and the survival of the works of man. . . . The first social relations of the child are crucial for the maintenance of his biological equilibrium also. It is for this reason that man's first object relations [i.e., interpersonal relationships] became our main concern in psychoanalysis. *Thus the task of man to adapt to man is present from the very beginning of life.* . . . Man not only adapts to the community but also actively participates in creating the conditions to which he must adapt. Man's environment is molded increasingly by man himself. (Hartmann, 1939, pp. 30–31; italics added)

Hence, for Hartmann, humans' adaptive ability draws its central importance in human psychology from the fact that each of us collaborates in molding the human world that molds us, a kind of "social compliance." All healthy infant egos must develop within the context of an *average expectable environment* provided by the first and most crucial of their love objects: their mothers.

THE EGO FUNCTIONS AND THE REALITY PRINCIPLE

Clearly, Hartmann's conception of adaptation as a reciprocal process between an organism and its average expectable environment emphasizes the role of social processes. Because human beings are intelligent and inventive creatures, adaptation is never a unitary achievement, never restricted to one method of mastery. The concept of adaptation, for Hartmann, transcends a narrow conception of the human person as a rigid, pleasure-seeking creature, compulsively driven toward tension reduction. Because the ego is relatively independent of the id in both origin and development, it operates to aid the person's survival even when that survival necessitates endurance of pain or prolonged delay of gratification. The ego is governed by the reality principle in its broadest sense: namely, the need to anticipate future courses of action, which may secondarily bring pleasure to the id, but which primarily serve the continued "fitting in" of the person with his or her average expectable environment (Hartmann, 1939, pp. 44ff.). Because adaptation is reciprocal, the reality principle also demands that the human environment make efforts to "fit in" with the developing person.

To accomplish these goals, the ego must maintain four different kinds of inner and outer harmonies. First, the ego must maintain the delicate overall balance between complete individuals and their external physical and social realities. Second, because the id has several instinctual drives, all competing for satisfaction, the ego must establish harmony within the id's own domain. Third, the ego has to balance all three competing mental agencies: id, superego, and itself, the ego. Fourth, the ego must maintain harmony among its own disparate aims, that is, a balance between its role as helpmate to the id and its role as an independent agency with interests beyond drive gratification (Hartmann, 1939, p. 39).

To achieve these harmonies, the ego operates "synthetically." The synthetic function is the ego's ability to integrate and reconcile differing aims and conflicting information into a coordinated whole. Through its synthetic ability, the ego is able to achieve reconciliation of not only *intrasystemic* conflicts (i.e., clashes between systems, such as between ego and id, between ego and superego, and between ego and reality) but also *intrasystemic* conflicts (i.e., disharmonies within itself). Thus, for example, the ego can tolerate the conflict between its mission as a drive-satisfier and as a drive-opposer, or the conflict between its defensive functions and its goals of achieving a rational, uninhibited mastery of life (Hartmann, 1950b, p. 139).

Along this same line of reasoning, Hartmann felt compelled to list as many of the ego functions as he thought warranted by clinical observation. His list of ego functions, by no means an exhaustive one, is instructive for the breadth of human cognitive and social functioning it emphasizes beyond the classical conception of the ego's duties in drive taming:

1. Motility
2. Organization of perception of both inner and outer reality
3. Protective barrier against excessive internal and external stimulation
4. Reality testing
5. Thinking and intelligence
6. Translation of thinking into action
7. Inhibition or delay of tension reduction
8. Recognition of danger, providing the signal of anxiety, and defenses
9. Anticipation of future actions, goals, effects, consequences
10. Time perception
11. Character formation (personal style)
12. Synthetic ability (i.e., capacity to integrate all previous functions, to harmonize the three mental agencies, and to harmonize the organism's relations to reality). (Based on Hartmann, 1950b, pp. 114–115)

A FINAL WORD ON HARTMANN

Like Anna Freud, Hartmann attempted to reconcile some of Freud's conflicting statements and to provide new concepts to fill gaps in classical theory. In Hartmann's hands, the relatively weak ego of Freud became a relatively autonomous, relatively strong, and nearly central agency in the human person's attempts to live productively and joyously in a collaborative people world.

Hartmann's main achievements in supplying answers to problems posed but not solved by Freud may be condensed to three essentials:

1. Freeing of the ego from its passive role as handmaiden to the id's passions; but not a total freedom, for the id and ego are still mutual regulators of each others' aims.
2. Emphasis on adaptation to the social environment in the concept of the maternally provided "average expectable environment" for healthy development.
3. The theoretical explanation of *neutralization* of id drives for use by the ego in its secondarily autonomous transformation of sexual and aggressive energy into energy focused on mastery of the world.

Hartmann, however, did not take matters to their next logical step, for though Hartmann's conception of the ego allows it neutralization of id energies, it does not invest the ego with energy of its own. Moreover, though Hartmann tried, he did not escape the classical theory's emphasis on semipersonified internal "agencies" powered by surging and waning energies. His conception of an ego that regulates and is reciprocally regulated by its environment was, however, a giant step toward a more human and less mechanized psychoanalytic theory (see, for comparison, Bandura's conception of reciprocal determinism in Chapter 16).

Robert W. White

Complete Independence for the Ego: Effectance Motivation

From the vantage point of academic psychology, Robert W. White took the ego through its next logical development: complete motivational independence from the id's energies. Marshaling a variety of experimental and physiological evidence, White (1959) argued that the classical conception of drive theory as the sole basis of human and animal motivation failed to do justice to the inherent urge in living things to master the environment, to explore the world freely, and to flourish.

The classical drive reduction model, founded on the prototype of the hunger drive, conceptualized motivation as a biological need and pictured learning as behavior directly or indirectly acquired to satisfy such needs. In addition to hunger, the list of primary drives included thirst, sexual need, the need to avoid pain, and the need for sleep. Each of these primary drives has its primary reinforcer: for example, food and water for hunger. An organism will feel itself impelled to strive for this reinforcer and will acquire along the way new behaviors that are instrumental in obtaining it. (See the discussion of Miller's drive-reduction theory in Chapter 16.)

White pointed to evidence that suggested classical drive theory was too limited because it neglected other strivings characteristic of complex organisms that do not fit this hunger-consumption model. Monkeys, for example, will learn a new response for the "reinforcement" of being allowed to explore interesting places (Butler & Harlow, 1957; Miller & Myers, 1954; Zimbardo & Miller, 1958). Curiosity is clearly not a deficit drive in the strictly biological meaning of the term. Other research seemed to demonstrate that organisms have an inherent need for activity and for manipulation of their environments that can be intensified by depriving animals of their customary freedom of movement (Kagan & Berkun, 1954). When allowed to run in an exercise wheel, the animals persist at this activity seemingly for the sheer "pleasure" of running. There is no obvious consummatory response in running that might reduce any need conceptualized along classical lines (White, 1959, p. 302).

From the areas of physiological and neurological research, White drew evidence suggesting that the human nervous system embodies active, self-maintaining motivational brain centers that are relatively independent of environmental events (Olds & Milner, 1954; Olds & Olds, 1965). White was asserting, consequently, that complex organisms are motivated by "drives" that have exploration, activity, or manipulation as their goals rather than the reduction of some tissue need (1959, p. 305).

In White's view, an adequate model of motivation needs to take account of an organism's *competence* or fitness for dealing with its environment in the absence of intensely driving stimulation. "The competence of an organism means its fitness or ability to carry out those transactions with the environment which results in its maintaining itself, growing, and flourishing" (White, 1960, p. 275). The label "competence" is merely a description of the consequences of some behaviors that produce *intended* effects on the environment beyond drive reduction. The motive underlying competent actions is termed "effectance":

> Putting it picturesquely, we might say that the effectance urge represents what the neuromuscular system wants to do when it is otherwise unoccupied or is gently stimulated by the environment. Obviously there are no consummatory acts; satisfaction would appear to lie in the arousal and maintaining of activity rather than in its slow decline toward bored passivity. (White, 1959, p. 321)

Human infants are born almost totally helpless and completely dependent upon others for their survival. But as they develop, all of their seemingly insignificant play actions have the very significant effect of building competencies and establishing the range of their personal effectiveness:

> The infant's play is indeed serious business. If he did not wile away his time pulling strings, shaking rattles, examining wooden parrots, dropping pieces of bread and celluloid swans, when would he learn to discriminate visual patterns, to catch and throw, and to build up his concept of the object? . . . [Infancy is] a time of active and continuous learning, during which the basis is laid for all those processes, cognitive and motor, whereby the child becomes able to establish effective transactions with his environment and move toward a greater degree of autonomy. Helpless as he may seem until he begins to toddle, he has by that time already made substantial gains in the achievement of competence. (White, 1959, p. 326)

PERSONAL SOURCES OF WHITE'S IDEAS

"I think of myself as much more of a humanist, and my mind is working in that softer but sometimes more creative way. I was a humanist who wandered by mistake into the science of psychology," is the description that Robert White once gave of himself (Sollod & White, 1980, p. 18). His interests lay more in the direction of history, literature, church organ music, and, especially, life history than in science or experimental research. As with so many people attracted to personality psychology, White wanted to know why some people appear perfectly confident, or completely competent, whereas he felt so insecure. He hinted that his professional knowledge about competence had roots in personal doubts: ". . . if a person is very competent in all ways, they know practically nothing about competence" (Sollod & White, 1980, p. 20).

Effectance motivation and competence are together an elegant argument for conceptualizing people as active agents. White's introduction of the ideas into psychoanalysis not only alters the Freudian picture of the ego, but it also raises some questions about the personal issues that prompted White's ideas. Psychologist Robert Sollod, a student of White's at Harvard during the early 1960s, interviewed the inventor of effectance motivation at his home in Marlborough, New Hampshire, in July 1980. The discussion of personal sources relies on Dr. Sollod's transcript of the interview.

A Solitary but Independent Childhood

Compared with his older brother, White recalled, he was a shy and solitary child who could spend hours alone more comfortably than in the presence of others. His parents were relatively affluent and of English heritage dating back to the Pilgrims. They modeled and taught strong religious values, independence, and responsibility. White described his mother as "a bit of a snob" (1980, p. 13) whereas his father, a lawyer, was spontaneously more dedicated to community service from deeply felt religious conviction. White's older brother fit the family pattern well, and he was studying to become a lawyer like his father. But the family was concerned about young Robert's solitary habits and social isolation (1980, p. 22). White's mother, apparently, was more concerned than his father about her youngest son's lack of social skills. But White himself found his own path to competence in the development of intellectual skills and interests:

> Well, there should be some kind of fraction [i.e., balance] between social development and the internal development of what we call interests and occupying yourself without the necessity of social support. If you have a lot of that, and nobody pushes you too hard, which is very unlikely at present with all the emphasis on socialization, you may develop a lot along the line of private interests without feeling a great deal of need for social interaction, which may come as a sort of foreign intrusion on all that. And that will slow up socialization, whereas the people that haven't got much going on in their heads are sort of hungry to go with the crowd and have somebody stimulate them. (Sollod & White, 1980, pp. 22-23)

White recalled that he retained his shyness into adulthood (Sollod & White, 1980, p. 27). Years later as a professional psychologist studying individual lives, one of the themes that interested him was a person's degree of competence, security, and confidence (e.g., White, 1975). The Protestant (Episcopalian) ethic of independence and achievement that had been part of White's growing up had become important in his personal and professional interests but also the source of some self-doubts. White remembered that among the strongest of his family and religious values was the belief that everyone is responsible for self and for making something of one's life even if allowance is made for environmental influences. Fundamentally, however, will and deliberate decision making underlie a person's commitments and values: "People have the potential mastery of their destiny to a certain extent; they at least can strongly contribute to their destiny" (Sollod & White, 1980, p. 14).

Although Robert White was a shy child, he was also an independent one. There are indications that he resisted and resented parental pressure to be more sociable. In fact, as we shall see, White's style was to resist pressures to conform at each stage of his life. The issue of enforced social adjustment was an important theme for White the psychologist just as it had been for White the child. With both personal and professional irony no doubt intended, White (1961) titled one of his later professional papers "The Dangers of Social Adjustment." The main theme of this paper is parental overconcern with their child's socializing skills and relationship to peers:

> If we can get over the widespread compulsion to hurl children into each other's company, we shall be in a better position to recognize what is really involved in becoming a social participant. . . . What we really want is that children should become interested in each other. We want them to enjoy being with others, to take pleasure in companionship. We want them to find and to appreciate the happiness that comes from sharing activities with other members of a group. Social discipline, learning to give and take, pruning one's personal ambitions so that they do not injure others, come about readily when the child has real interest in other children, when he has a personal stake, so to speak, in improving an enjoyed social participation. (White, 1961, pp. 394–395)

It is clear that White is offering a corrective for parents and educators who unthinkingly encourage the acquisition of "social tricks" in children when they really intend to promote the child's social welfare (White, 1961, p. 395). In effect, White was suggesting that, barring unusual disruption of personality development, the typical child will spontaneously develop an interest in his or her agemates if he or she is freed from parental pressure and worries about it. We can speculate that White was here voicing his own experience and expressing a childhood wish.

An Adult Model of Competence

White's professional academic career began with the teaching of history at the University of Maine. He had obtained a master's degree in history from Harvard in 1926, but began to wonder about psychology as a professional path to pursue. This break with history was influenced partly by Arthur Schlesinger, one of White's history professors at Harvard. Schlesinger emphasized social and intellectual history, as well as the study of the individual, and White found himself more interested in individual life histories than in traditional historical studies (Sollod & White, 1980, p. 4).

But the break with history was also influenced in a more direct and more personal way by a clinical psychologist. In the fall of 1927, White met psychologist Donald Mackinnon, who joined the faculty at the University of Maine. White was impressed with Mackinnon and also puzzled by him. Mackinnon would become well known for his empirical studies in psychoanalysis, especially the study of repression. During the time White and Mackinnon were colleagues, their relationship was an informal one in which Mackinnon communicated his enthusiasm about clinical psychology and his studies with Henry Murray at Harvard (see Chapter 1 for more information about Murray and the tradition of personology).

Several faculty members gathered after class at the college inn, and during their dinnertime discussions White wondered how Mackinnon could be so confident, so competent, and so assertive.

> He was kind of a role model for me, although he was just about my age, of assertive and confident behavior. And I felt a great shortage of that in myself by comparison. . . . He did have definite values. That made me think erroneously that this [i.e., certainty about values] comes to you because you're a psychologist and I'm just sort of dribbling around in history, which is interesting but doesn't have very much intellectual structure. (Sollod & White, 1980, pp. 4–5)

In a way, White's admiration for Mackinnon's apparent certainty and competence represented a desire to break with his family's traditional Episcopalian religious views in the search for more certain values in "scientific" psychology. White felt that his family lacked a spirit of adventure and that they functioned largely to conform to tradition (Sollod & White, 1980, p. 7). He, on the other hand, would venture away from family tradition in the hope of becoming confident, assertive, and competent like Donald Mackinnon.

In 1928, White returned to Harvard and began preparation for doctoral studies in psychology. From 1930 to 1933, he taught at Rutgers University, and returned to doctoral studies in psychology at Harvard from 1933 to 1937, when he was awarded a Ph.D. in psychology. He was ready to be confident, competent, and assertive.

Formulation of the Theory of Effectance Motivation

At Harvard, White joined Henry Murray's group of personologists in the study of lives. He had contact with eminent thinkers in the field such as Gordon Allport, Erik Erikson, B. F. Skinner, and Morton Prince. White was influenced by these people and by the atmosphere created in the Harvard Clinic by Murray, but his long tradition of independence surfaced:

> . . . when I came into the [Harvard] clinic after being at Rutgers, which was the time when I was especially excited to be at the clinic, the whole atmosphere was full of psychoanalysis. Some of the graduate students were being analyzed. They had an analyst on the staff. Murray had his own analysis with Hans Sachs and had previously had one or part of one with Jung in Zurich. Everyone was struggling to get the money for their training analysis. They thought, "If I don't get that, my training will never be complete." And I was in the position that I could have paid for it, and I didn't want to. I thought I would do without analysis and see what happens. And it wasn't that I felt that I didn't have problems, I felt I had plenty of problems but I had the feeling, "Well, I'll work on them, I'll solve them myself in some way." (Sollod & White, 1980, p. 11)

Old values die hard. White found that his family tradition of independence, personal effort, and acceptance of personal responsibility were still with him. White recalled his feelings at the time:

> Becoming a full-fledged Freudian would have been going further away from my background than I did. And you could say, to put it very simply, that the concept of competence, when I finally got it formed, was an attempt to explain those things, that kind of thing in my background that I believed in before and that I still believed in up to a point and were [*sic*] not present in Freudian thinking. (Sollod & White, 1980, p. 12)

Conclusion: A Little Bit of Incompetence Is a Good Thing

White's candid account of his own development contains an interesting irony. The theory of competence and efficacy motivation evolved in White's thinking because he felt incompetent in social skills compared with others he admired. He entered psychology, as so many theorists have, searching for certainty, wisdom, and self-knowledge. Ironically, the strengths he sought were already available in those traditional values against which he gently rebelled as a young man. In fact, one way to understand White's theory of competence is to view it as an explanation of the dynamic motives that underlie mature self-responsibility.

It is also interesting that, as White pointed out, his feelings of insecurity or inferiority were confined to a particular sphere. He was not feeling generally incompetent, only socially insecure compared with people such as Donald Mackinnon:

> In my response to Mackinnon, for instance, I felt very incompetent to be like that, to be clear in my thoughts and communications and positive and downright sure of myself. I felt very incompetent in that sphere. And I wanted to get to be something the way I conceived that he was [*sic*]. On the other hand, in a great many ways, I was unusually competent. . . . I know the whole range of realms of things where you feel utterly incompetent to feeling totally competent. I think that's helped me make sense of the theory because I know the whole thing all the way around from personal experience. I doubt if I would have got as close to it if I hadn't had this sector of incompetence to know about. (Sollod & White, 1980, p. 20)

We can wonder along with White whether he would have gotten around to the theory of competence had he been less independent and more easily influenced by the prevailing Freudian atmosphere.

COMPETENCE THEMES IN THE PSYCHOSEXUAL STAGES

Freud's theory of the instincts puts the organism at the mercy of its drives. The history of individual development in Freud's theory is a narrative of emerging sexual and aggressive instincts, unavoidable frustrations, anxieties, and defenses centered on crucial pleasure-seeking, tension-reducing prototypes at different ages. In the oral stage, for example, the prototype is the infant at the breast; at the anal stage, the child on the toilet; during the phallic stage, the prototype is the child ruminating about sexual urges toward other family members; and by the genital stage, the sexual urge is focused on the prototype of heterosexual attraction and intimacy (White, 1960). But each of these phases also contains important elements of mastery learning entwined with instinctual satisfactions, piled on top of libidinal gratifications, stretching beyond id pleasures.

White's next step in developing his theory of effectance motivation was the reconceptualization of the Freudian psychosexual stages of development around the theme of mastery learning.

The Oral Stage

Central to the psychoanalytic description of the oral phase is the notion that sucking, feeding, and chewing are all satisfactions rooted in the organism's need to gratify its hunger drive, that is, that the hunger instinct underlies the pleasures of the first year of life. But is feeding the only theme of the first year? According to White, the feeding child not only gratifies its hunger, it also tests its capacity to cope with its environment. The child plays constantly with available objects, with its own body, even eating utensils that, in its mother's hands, would certainly provide food more efficiently and reliably.

When they begin to crawl, infants expose themselves independently to their environments, exploring, hiding, peekabooing, chasing, and being chased. They explore the people in their world, learn how to evoke responses from them, how to maximize loving gratifications and minimize loveless neglect (White, 1960, p. 284). Above all, infants learn a variety of ways to have fun and to make interesting things happen in their world. Not every activity can be derived from the libido-hunger gratification model of orthodox Freudian theory.

White concedes that the prototype of the feeding child is central to the oral period, but he rightly points out that there is no justification or compelling theoretical reason to limit understanding of the oral stage to this one prototype:

> . . .we lose rather than gain, in my opinion, if we consider the child's *undisputed* play, six hours a day, to be a continuous expression of libidinal energy, a continuous preoccupation with the family drama, as if there could be no intrinsic interest in the properties of the external world and the means of coming to terms with it. (White, 1960, pp. 284–285)

As White pointed out, the activities of the oral stage are expressions not only of libidinal derivatives but of inherent urges toward mastery. A child grows up not only for its mother's love, but for itself. "He does not have to do it wholly for mother; as an active living being he has his own stake in growing up" (1960, p. 285).

The Anal Stage

During the second and third years of life, the anus and bowels become dominant as the zones through which the child's pleasures now come. In the orthodox Freudian scheme, libidinal or erotic pleasure becomes increasingly associated with excretion as the child learns voluntarily to control the retention and passing of bowel movements. Interpersonal theorists emphasize the parent-child struggle over independence and self-mastery that is also embodied in anal learnings.

White, however, suggests that the decisive struggle of the anal phase is not restricted to the bathroom. Intrinsic to the second and third years of life is a more significant developmental crisis embodied in the two-year-old's *negativism*. Children of this age are unwilling to follow directions passively or to allow adults to perform routine tasks for them. They much prefer struggling by themselves with buttons that won't button, sleeves that defy entry, and water faucets not designed for small hands. They have learned or are learning to walk without toppling and without external supports, which means they can assert themselves both in loudly expressed verbal "No's" and in relatively expressive motility: They can walk away. More to the point, they can *intend* to walk away, *intend* to say no, *intend* to assert their rights.

Parents are sorely tested throughout this period, for their desire to prevail over the toddler at all costs can easily swamp the child's burgeoning sense of competence. At the other extreme, "apostles of permissiveness" may find themselves totally directionless and startled into disciplinary paralysis (White, 1960, p. 288).

> The bowel training model is wrong, I think, in two ways. First, it concerns a function that is governed by the autonomic nervous system, that never comes under direct voluntary control, and that does not carry the experience of initiative that goes with voluntary action. The child may be proud when he can meet parental expectations,

but it will be pride in meeting a somewhat mysterious process of habit formation, not the pride of mastering things directly by trial and by effort expended. . . . Second, it is a situation in which cultural requirements inevitably prevail. Every child is bowel trained. . . . The best outcome of the bowel training problem is that the child will come to will the inevitable. The best outcome of the struggle for social competence is that he will face the world with self-respect and a measure of confidence in his own strength. (White, 1960, p. 289)

White suggests that Freud's conception of the anal-erotic personality who defensively orders his or her life through the triad of anal traits—parsimony, stubbornness, orderliness—is better understood as one expression of a child's struggle for independence. (See Chapter 2 for a discussion of the anal-erotic personality.)

Although the first two traits of the triad, parsimony and stubbornness, make sense as oppositional strategies against strong parental pressure, orderliness presents a problem. Not a defensive opposition, orderliness seems to be an outright surrender to parental-cultural pressure. Viewed in this way, orderliness is the odd member of the triad.

But viewed from the perspective of White's effectance model, the discrepancy is reduced by interpreting all three traits in terms of their competence value—if they are not pushed to the extreme of obsessiveness. Orderliness, therefore, makes sense as a competent way of mastering life's complexities in an active rather than passive way. Parsimony and stubbornness are likewise attempts at active mastery in the face of passivizing parental pressure:

In these terms, then, stubbornness, parsimony, and orderliness are completely of a piece. They are ways of preventing oneself from being pushed around by the environment. . . . The fixation of the triad of traits happens when there is a relative feeling of incompetence in relation to the environment, especially the human one. . . . (White, 1960, p. 290)

In White's reconceptualization of the anal phase, the "anal personality" is one who has learned to mistrust its world; its triad of stubbornness, parsimony, and orderliness is evidence of the way in which it has adapted.

The Phallic Stage

In orthodox Freudian theory, the phallic period centers on maturation of the genital organs and the direction of sexual interest first to the mother, then to other family members. In the boy's case, fear and hostility toward father accompany this burgeoning of sexual interest in an emotional constellation known as the Oedipus complex. At the resolution of the Oedipus struggle, near the age of five, the superego takes on the parental character and the imagined prohibitions of the father, replacing it in the mental economy as the conscience and moral censor.

But at the same time that the oedipal strivings are emerging, children are developing at least three spheres of competence for dealing with the world. First, they are better able to move around independently. Second, their language facility is improving to the point where precise expression of feelings and urges is possible, and this more efficient attention to the meanings of others in their world expands their understandings of the human environment. Third, children's capacities for imaginative fantasy are expanding so that they can dramatize themselves in a variety of adultlike roles. Thus locomotion, language, and imagination do not replace the sexual themes but supplement them with the developmental strengths of interpersonal competence. White, therefore, does not want to abandon the Freudian oedipal themes; he merely wants to expand them with considerations of inescapable child world mastery transactions. White proposes that we imagine a child in the phallic era who does not experience the usual increased genital sensitivity:

> This child would still make locomotor, linguistic, and imaginative progress, would become interested in being like adults, would make comparisons to size, would be competitive and subject to defeats and humiliations, would be curious, ask endless questions and encounter rebuffs, would have bad dreams and guilt feelings over imagined assertive or aggressive actions, would learn about sex roles, would struggle to understand his relation to other family members, and might very well ask about marrying one of the parents. All of these things arise inescapably from progress in the growth of competence. (White, 1960, pp. 293–294)

The Latency Stage

In Freud's classical scheme, the latency period was somewhat theoretically undeveloped and characterized by the absence of eventful developments. At puberty, the end of the latency phase, the sexual motives arise from hibernation, but during latency proper, these most interesting urges decline in intensity. As White points out, Freud's assumption was wrong: "For once we can almost say that Freud underestimated the importance of sex" (White, 1960, p. 296).

The child of six to eight is moving in a more social direction, discovering peer competition, the challenges of schoolwork, and an identification with people who can *do* things, as Erikson, too, had suggested. Fantasy and imagination no longer suffice; the child needs some real income of mastery and competence. All children have to learn how to get along with others, how to compromise, how to compete, how to protect themselves from hurt, how to negotiate challenges so that a firm sense of competence is built rather than painful feelings of inadequacy (White, 1960, p. 298).

The first five years of life prior to this latency period can leave a residue of damaged feelings of esteem, unresolved oedipal strivings, and badly mangled self-confidence. The latency period may offer the opportunity to correct these developmental misadventures by providing successfully met challenges, warm chumships, and tentative but pleasing heterosexual contacts. For the child who successfully negotiates the realistic demands of the latency period, the rewards are many. Such healthy individuals have not lived crisis-free lives; they have simply had the opportunity to build ego strength in the form of a subjective sense of competence. They are not problem-free; they are simply capable of drawing on a wide range of social and personal skills to tackle problems with some measure of confidence.

The Genital Stage

The orthodox description of adolescence in Freud's theory emphasizes the reemergence of the sexual instinct directed toward the attainment of genital primacy over the previously diffuse, "polymorphously perverse" forms of drive satisfaction.

In White's view, emphasis needs to be laid upon the adolescent's strivings to be somebody, in the sense that Erikson employs the term "sense of identity" (see Chapter 6 for Erikson's psychosocial stage theory). Adolescents acquire a variety of sophisticated skills that prepare them for vocational enterprises that may very well turn into lifelong pursuits—into total-life investments. The central theme of making or failing to make these acquisitions of knowledge and skill is competence, not displaced sexual energy:

> My professional life is spent among late adolescents [i.e., college students] whose sexual problems and social relations have for the most part not overwhelmed them. We talk together about their plans for study, their abilities and limitations, their struggles with materials to be learned and skills to be attained, their occupational learnings, career plans, and concerns about modern society as the scene of their future endeavors. We talk, in other words, mostly about their competence, and I do not believe that understanding is fostered by interpreting these concerns too much as displacements of instinctual drives, defense mechanisms, or interpersonal relations. They are real. (White, 1960, p. 301)

White's reanalysis of Freud's psychosexual stages expands these phases of development with considerations of healthy adaptation and satisfying acquisitions in the realm of mastery and self-confidence. His competence model does not, nor did White intend it to, replace Freud's analysis of instinctual crises in each of the developmental epochs. The effectance motive never exists in isolation, and it is never the most significant or most salient trait of personality that is simultaneously enmeshed in a host of other strivings. But effectance motivation is, nevertheless, detectable as an independent drive apart from the basic id passions:

> We can detect it by horse sense; that, at least is what horses do when inexperienced riders are on their backs. A horse can apparently deduce from the first few physical contacts with the novice that the situation is right for a little fun along the bridle path or an unscheduled return to the stable. Similarly, though with less whimsical intent, a teacher making the acquaintance of a new class will notice how the children approach each activity. At the crafts table, for instance, she will see behavior ranging from picking things up quickly and using them firmly, through all grades of tentativeness and uncertainty, to hanging back or turning completely away. If the tools had horse sense, they could rate the confidence of the children who picked them up. (White, 1963, pp. 74–75)

A child's sense of competence is, therefore, the product of the cumulative consequences of past challenges met and mastered, or confronted and failed. In White's scheme, the child's developing sense of efficacy subsumes the whole range of learnings that shape all persons' expectancy of coping masterfully or meekly with their own world. Because our sense of competence is an enduring attribute that generalizes over time and across situations, it should be conceptualized as independent of the id's passions. White's next step was to propose effectance motivation as the ego's independent source of energy. To that development we turn next. Table 4.4 summarizes the differences between Freud's instinctual conflict model of development and White's expansions of the stages into the realm of competence learning.

TABLE 4.4 Instinct and Competence Models Contrasted

Stage	Freud's Emphases (Instinct Model)	White's Expansions (Competence Model)
1. ORAL	a. Hunger instinct striving for tension reduction.	a. Feeding as trial ground for self-mastery and for learning to master human environment.
	b. Passive dependence on love object for survival.	b. Learning to master others by maximizing love and minimizing neglect.
	c. Incorporation of food and love object as part of self.	c. Sensorimotor play as practice for later cognitive and motor skills.
2. ANAL	a. Libidinal pleasure from retention and expulsion of feces.	a. Intrinsic development of two-year-old's negativism.
	b. Learning submission to parental-cultural demands.	b. Locomotion and negativism employed in development of autonomy.
	c. Possible *defensive* reaction of anal-erotic personality with triad of parsimony, stubbornness, and orderliness traits.	c. Triad of traits seen as adaptive ways of preventing world from overwhelming child, when developed in *moderate* degree.
3. PHALLIC	a. Oedipus complex, with genital sensitivity.	a. Locomotion, language, and imagination develop in service of mastering world and building sense of competence.
	b. Development of superego through identification with father, and fear of father's wrath.	b. Self-dramatizing and imitating adult roles with emphasis on personal productivity.
	c. Sexual interests directed toward family members.	
4. LATENCY	a. Submergence of sexual motives.	a. Establishment of social competency in peer and school activities, and heterosexual relations.
	b. Period of relative quiescence.	b. Real work tasks in school, job, games.
		c. Learning personal compromise and how to protect self.
5. GENITAL	a. Heterosexual object-choices.	a. Sense of identity, feelings of past competence are now consolidated.
	b. Genital primacy of libido expression.	b. Vocational choices actively studied or prepared for.
		c. Dating as social and sexual satisfaction.

THE EGO AS THE LOCUS OF EFFICACY AND COMPETENCE

Robert White had taken Hartmann's adaptation theme several steps further along the path of ego independence. Leaving Freud's neurologically based instinctual model to its own domain, the scope of each psychosexual stage was expanded to describe phases in the ego's gradual accumulation of strength to master its world.

Hartmann and his colleagues had taken the ego just so far with their conception of the ego employing neutralized sexual and aggressive energies. It was further than Freud had gone, of course, for he had thought only of sexual energy as subject to neutralization for the ego's use. And, after all, neutralization of sexual or aggressive energy, or even of both simultaneously, is not the same as conceptualizing the ego as the autonomous source of its own energies. Neutralization is like a country importing foreign manufactured goods it cannot itself produce. Such goods always bear the import stamp of their origins. Independence is more like ownership of the factory.

In White's proposal (1963a), the ego was to be conceptualized as having its own natural endowments of energy reserves, the "energy" of effectance motivation. On the subjective side, the emotional and intellectual consequences of effectance motivation are experienced as *feelings of efficacy,* a sense of pleasure in being masterful: "Effectance thus refers to the active tendency to put forth effort to influence the environment, while feeling of efficacy refers to the satisfaction that comes with producing effects" (White, 1963a, p. 185). Effectance motivation *is* independent ego energy.

Although the effectance energies are conceptualized as equally fundamental, and equally intrinsic to human life as id energies, these independent ego motives are not directly related to specific bodily sources nor to particular consummatory acts that reduce tension. However, the biological significance of effectance motivation and the more subjective feelings of efficacy and a sense of competence lies in the improved survival chances a competent organism attains.

As he had done with the psychosexual stages, White now applied his broadening conception of the competence model to a selected few areas of psychoanalytic theory.

Reality Testing: Knowledge Through Action

In classical theory, the ego occupies the central position in the personality's relationship to reality and its "objective" demands. Infants turn more and more to reality to obtain satisfaction for their needs; but the only way such satisfaction can be obtained is through acting upon reality instrumentally, making alterations in the environment that bring forth satisfaction. At first, infants act reflexively but nevertheless instrumentally by simply crying. They passively receive gratification from their caretakers. Repeated frustration of id needs leads in turn to the formation of the ego as a reality mediator, that is, as an agency that is alert to the specific actions which must be carried out to obtain gratifications.

Hartmann (1956) pointed out that the classical Freudian explanation of the development of the reality principle as enforced necessity contained an important unexpressed assumption. The ego turns toward reality when the id cannot satisfy itself, but the ego must sometimes *postpone* immediate gratification until external circumstances are right or safe. Furthermore, to be able to postpone gratification, the ego must be able to *anticipate* subsequent reality developments (Hartmann, 1956, p. 242; see also White, 1963a, p. 45). These two ego functions—*postponement* and *anticipation*—cannot be accounted for strictly in terms of the id's frustration and its emerging need for a reality mediator:

Thus the question arises . . . how far does the development of ego functions enter as an independent variable into the processes described by Freud? It is true, we are wont to say that the "demands of reality" are responsible for them. But this is, of course, a metaphorical way of putting the case; it is correct only if we presuppose the existence of something in the individual that speaks out for reality—a tendency toward self-preservation which, in the mental life of man, we attribute mostly to the ego and to its precursors. *The question whether the ego plays a primary role in the institution of the reality principle will be answered differently, according to whether we view the ego as an agent active from the beginning, though only in a limited way (as Freud did in later writings), or as something traceable only to the impact of the interaction of reality and drives (as he did earlier).* (Hartmann, 1956, pp. 242–243, italics added)

Thus Hartmann was insisting on the ego's ability to anticipate and to postpone gratification as preformed functions, independent of the id's drives and their clash with reality.

White now proposed that the anticipation and delay functions implied by the ego's adherence to the reality principle be understood as direct consequences of the infant's own actions on the environment. The ego can delay and anticipate because infants *learn through their own efforts* that they are sufficiently competent to endure postponements whose duration they can foresee will be temporary. At first, infants only thrash, squirm, cry, and kick when they are hungry; but it is nevertheless *their* actions that bring mother running. If the cries are immediately and reliably met with soothing care and food, the infant *learns,* as Erikson (1950) puts it, to trust both his external environment and his own capacity to make things happen (White, 1963a, p. 46):

> According to action theory, reality testing is not undertaken solely because of instinctual frustration. Exploration occurs in its own right, and reality can be interesting and satisfying as well as frustrating. Even in Freud's model situation it seems clear that frustration leads to action and that the pleasure principle is transcended through the discovery of some action, like crying, which influences the environment and can be used to influence it again. *Tolerance of delay depends on a confidence, born of experience, that something efficacious can be done if need waxes painful.* (White, 1963a, p. 187, italics added)

SEPARATING SELF FROM NOT-SELF

A further consequence of adopting an action model founded on children's gradual learning of their own degrees of competence is the changed perspective it provides for understanding how self and not-self are discriminated by the infant. As Sullivan, Piaget, and other non-Freudian developmental psychologists have proposed, infants learn the differences between themselves and external objects by their own actions. Sucking a nipple on a bottle is a pleasurable experience, but infants do not distinguish themselves from the nipple. Both pleasure-giving object and self are fused. However, an infant sucking his own thumb again experiences the sucking pleasure, but this time also feels sucked. Gradually, from their own behaviors and their consequences, infants learn to distinguish that which is part of self from that which is not. The role of the mother in White's account of the self, not-self distinction is minimized:

> No one will challenge [the mother's] affective importance to the infant, but it is not a compulsory deduction from this that she will be the main arena of reality testing and the object most suitable for discriminating self and not-self. Indeed one might consider her, precisely because of her close and intimate interactions with the child, a rather unsuitable object for arriving at cool appraisals of reality. Both common experience and clinical observation suggest that in mother-fixated children the mother continues to be the one object not fully discriminated from the self even when this distinction has been achieved as regards all other objects. (White, 1963a, p. 52)

White was thus proposing that the child's relationship to reality is not passive, not born entirely out of the clash between urgent drives and satisfactions realistically delayed. Children's pictures of reality are their own constructions, mediated by their gradually learned sense of what is feasible for them to do, what is impossible to accomplish, and what is reliably forthcoming when they turn their heads to the world outside themselves, but that world cannot be interpreted solely on the basis of our own needs. If we were to relate to life's demands in this egocentric way, reality would wax and wane with our hungers.

Pathological Ego Development

In the original Freudian model, the psychoses were conceptualized as failures in normal ego development. Following Freud, other psychoanalytic workers extended the concept to mean that the ego fails to develop normal social responsiveness, with normal and stable defenses, and therefore becomes deficient in its reality testing capacities and vulnerable to id intrusions. Some of these early workers laid the blame for the child's ego deficiencies at the doorstep of the mother. Inadequate mothering, cool, mechanical handling, or guilt-motivated overprotection were deemed primary causes of ego failure and psychosis.

Using White's model of competence and effectance motivation, the focus of attention can be shifted from what goes wrong with the ego's capacity to deal with id energies to what goes wrong in the development of feelings of efficacy: *"What happens to obstruct the infant's tendencies to explore and interact with his environment?"* (White, 1963a, p. 76).

An infant's interest in his or her own efficacy is relatively independent of the id's passions. "Effectance is independent in the sense that it constitutes a push toward growth without any necessary collaboration by the instinctual drives, though it may be importantly influenced by them" (White, 1963a, p. 77). Effectance motivation can be thought of as an inherent urge to dispense gradually with the necessity of being mothered. In their growth toward independence, children behave in ways that slowly remove them from passive reliance on others' actions, although some mothers encourage such autonomy only halfheartedly. Yet it is widely believed that the mother retains her omnipotence in the causal links of pathology because it is *her* encouragement or discouragement of independence that produces a masterful or a defeated child (White, 1963a, p. 77).

But in truth, as White conceptualized it, the infant ego has its own urges toward independence and these urges are themselves independent of maternal encouragement and discouragement—to a degree.

. . . there exists in every child an independent urge to explore and interact with his surroundings, as a consequence of which he draws the lines of his own autonomy and establishes his competence in dealing with things and other people. . . . How the mother responds to it is always an important consideration, but not because she generates it, not because she can always stop it, not because it always needs her reinforcement. (White, 1963a, pp. 79–80)

Thus at least part of the fault in the ego's development of deficiencies lies on the child's side. Because society expects mothers to love, to care for, and to raise healthy children, the mother who confronts a child who will not behave, who is constitutionally hyperactive or uncontrollable, or who is temperamentally passive and unresponsive is confronting subjectively her own potential failure, in her acutely enforced sense of incompetence. The roots of ego pathology, then, lie in the various ways that the mother-child interaction may obstruct the development of feelings of efficacy or swamp out the budding energy of effectance motivation.

The first inhibition of effectance motivation is possible when maternal care is unreliable or physically impoverishing—that is, the child's instinctual needs of hunger and freedom from pain are aroused continually. In this tension-filled state, there is no opportunity for exploratory and manipulative interests to emerge. All of the infant's time is spent on survival strivings and pain endurance. The child has no spare time, so to speak, for actions that can lead to efficacy (White, 1963a, p. 85). "The ego does not gain its strength just through instinctual gratification; it must have enough time to itself, free from need tension, to explore its own way toward full development" (1963a, pp. 85–86).

The second possibility for the inhibition of self-efficacy developments can be found in the mother who is unresponsive to and unpraising of the infant's efforts. If the mother does not allow herself to be influenced by her child's actions, whims, and expressed desires, the child will necessarily be continually unsuccessful in manipulating his or her people world. In this case, the injury to the ego is less extensive than that done by instinct-swamping, and the resultant deficiency in development tends to be selectively focused on the sphere of social interactions (White, 1963a, p. 87). This child is learning a rather painful human lesson:

People can give you things and hurt your pride at the same time. They can be responsive at one moment, busy and preoccupied at another, inexplicably cross at another. This means that one must be careful, trying to assess cues before acting; for the hypothetical sensitive, distractible child such assessment may prevent action from being attempted at all. (White, 1965, p. 205)

The third way in which the ego's drive toward competence can be injured involves the direct deprivation or obstruction of play activities. In this instance, for a variety of reasons, the mother abandons the child in an unstimulating environment, devoid of all potential play materials and stimulation. For some mothers, such abandonment may be a reflection of their own repressed hostility toward the child, of their ignorance, or of their own psychopathology. But the result is the same. The independent energies of the ego are blocked from development through expression in action. Isolated, the child can only become increasingly reality-shy, increasingly incompetent. In effect, the anxiety of abandonment or outright fearfulness has developed, and these feelings, like unsatisfied drives, can easily swamp exploratory play.

THE OEDIPUS COMPLEX:
IDENTIFICATION WITH ADULT COMPETENCE

Freud had employed the concept of identification in a variety of ways, some of which resulted in contradictory explanations. At various times, Freud wrote of identification as an emotional tie to some person, typically marked by the unconscious desire to incorporate that person's attributes into our own behavior. The desire to incorporate may stem from loss of the love object, as in the case of the widow who adopts her dead husband's manner of talking, or some piece of his apparel and thus symbolically preserves his presence. The male child in the Oedipal phase who identifies with his father defensively incorporates into his conscience the prohibitions he fears his father might enact if the father knew of the child's sexual desires for mother. But Freud also used identification in the more typical sense of acting like someone whom one admires, without any connotation of loss, fear, or rivalry as the motive for the identification.

White (1963a) has suggested keeping both meanings in psychoanalytic theory, but applying them to different phases of development with different theoretical labels employed to distinguish the two different kinds of copying. For the emotional tie, based on an attempt to reconcile loss, fear, or rivalry with a model, the term *introjection* should be used. For the copying of an admired model, who is imitated because the model's apparent competence or strength is a desirable attribute, the term *identification* should be reserved.

Consequently, with this distinction between introjection and identification made, White argued that the Oedipus complex and its subsequent formation of the superego have to be understood as something more adaptive than conflict resolution by identification with the father's standards. Identification is one of the elements of superego formation, but the male child also has to act differently from his father. For, after all, the Oedipal resolution in Freudian theory requires that the boy renounce his mother as sexual object, a renunciation that his father does not model.

In White's view, the sociological evidence implies that children learn their sex roles from a variety of sources, beginning even earlier in this learning than Freud would have indicated. By the time of the Oedipal events, the child already has acquired rudimentary notions of "what boys do" and "what girls do" quite apart from any instinctual strivings. Thus, as we saw in Chapter 2, Freud's contradictory application of his concept that a person identifies with a lost love object added an element of confusion to the picture. For if the boy should, in principle, identify with the love object he must give up, why does he identify with his *father?*

Freud's answer leaned heavily on the innate biological masculinity and femininity components of human nature, implying that the boy does identify slightly with mother but mostly with father because they are both males. But as White argues, if we rely on the fact that children have knowledge of their sex roles from early learnings, we need not either propose constitutional mechanisms nor employ the concept of identification in its two different meanings to explain why the boy identifies with his father. "He is sticking to the choice dictated by his learned sex role" (1963a, p. 121).

The boy's renunciation of his mother as love object is not a complete renunciation of her as a person. A normal resolution of the Oedipus complex requires only that the boy learn a selective renunciation of his mother as a *sexual* object; she remains a source of affection and security in his life. The Oedipus resolution "requires the learning of a compromise, or, to put it another way, a discovery of the terms upon which the boy is permitted to love his mother—terms somewhat less inclusive than his urges tend to dictate" (White, 1963a, p. 122).

Thus in White's competence model the Oedipus complex and superego formation do not take place in one relatively brief period of development, through one unified process of conflict resolution. Rather, the male child gradually learns his sex role, his areas of special family competence, and his permitted avenues of affection and aggressive competition. The superego is established not through identification-introjection of the father's prohibitions, but through a slow and complex learning process "arising out of the necessity to work out a compromise among instinctual urges, parental frustrations, and need for parental support" (1963a, p. 123). Identification with the father docs take place, but the avenue through which it occurs lies at the intersection of desire to be competent like him and desire to have such an esteemed person express reciprocal love.

A FINAL WORD ON ROBERT W. WHITE

Robert White's competence model has its roots in academic general psychology and developmental psychoanalytic theory. His prime contribution to ego psychology was the complete freeing of the ego from its id moorings. Effectance motivation, an independent ego energy, is inseparably intertwined with other personality developments and rarely observed in isolation. Yet the theme of self-efficacy and adaptive mastery over one's life is a central organizing tenet that broadens and clarifies many psychoanalytic propositions. White's accomplishments can be summarized as three interlocking postulates:

1. The ego has its own fundamental energies that find expression in children's capacities to explore and manipulate their world when instinctual urgency and inhibiting anxiety do not swamp their free expression or sour the child's joy in being an active agent.
2. The psychosexual stages of development are broader phases of competency learning than Freud's instinctual prototypes of feeding, elimination, and genital pleasure imply. In each phase, children are gratifying not only libidinal and aggressive urges but expanding their sphere of interpersonal mastery and their competence in generating intentional effects on their world.
3. The sense of efficacy, fueled by the inherent effectance ego energy, can only develop in an interpersonal milieu, through interactions with people who reflect in their responses to the child's efforts their own competencies, and who model the rewards of personal mastery in their healthy and joyous living.

MARGARET S. MAHLER

PSYCHOTIC AND HEALTHY EGOS: SYMBIOSIS AND SEPARATION THEMES

The theme of the adaptive and masterful ego elaborated by Heinz Hartmann and Robert White brought psychoanalytic theory closer to Freud's original intent of creating a general psychology of the human person and his or her growth into healthy personhood. Erik Erikson elaborated the same basic themes into a rich portrait of the ego's progression from play to reason, from dependent trust to self-reliant integrity (see Chapter 6). Psychoanalytic theory had clearly changed from its initial emphasis on internal instinctual conflict to an emphasis on the whole person's relation to inner and outer reality, in conflict and in peace, in despair and in joyful living, in failure and in mastery, alone and with others.

Margaret S. Mahler's work began with her observation of severely damaged ego functioning in psychotic children whose cardinal difficulty seemed to be a total lack of comprehension of what human beings are (Mahler, 1968, p. 3). Such children, sometimes described as "autistic," seem to be encased inside a shell that is untouched by the outside human world and permits no entry from the world's people into the secrecy of the shell. Mahler was eventually able to differentiate the autistic child, as described by Kanner (1949), from the symbiotically psychotic child.

Truly *autistic* children seem from birth unable to utilize their mothers as auxiliary egos, that is, they show no interest in relating to mother, or to any person, as a needed partner in orienting themselves to inner and outer reality (Mahler, 1968, p. 67).

> [The autistic child's] . . . most conspicuous and characteristic behavior patterns are the classical features described by Kanner (1942, 1944): an obsessive desire for the preservation of sameness; a stereotyped preoccupation with a few inanimate objects or action patterns toward which he shows the only signs of emotional attachment. As a consequence, he shows utter intolerance of any change in his inanimate surroundings. . . . The primarily autistic child differs from the organic, as well as from the predominantly symbiotic psychotic child, by his seemingly self-sufficient contentedness—*if only he is left alone.* These autistic children behave like omnipotent magicians if they are permitted to live within, and thus to command, their static and greatly constricted segment of inanimate environment. (Mahler, 1968, p. 68)

Thus, in Mahler's view, the autistic child has regressed to the most primitive stage of life possible outside the womb. Such autistic children are shutting out the *living* world, which is, after all, the part of reality that demands emotional and social responses.

Symbiotic children, by contrast, are psychotic in a more sophisticated way. They are attached to their mothers; but the attachment is global fusing with her, so that they cannot tell where they begin and she ends.

> [Symbiotic psychotic] . . . children may be described by their mothers as "cry-babies" or as oversensitive infants. Their disturbance becomes apparent either gradually or fulminately at those crossroads of personality development at which maturation of

the ego would usually effect separation from the mother, and would enable the child to master an ever-increasing segment of reality, independently of her. As soon as ego differentiation and psychosexual development confront the child and thus challenge him with a measure of separation from and independence of the mother, the illusion of symbiotic omnipotence is threatened and severe panic reactions occur. (Mahler, 1968, p. 72)

Symbiotic psychotic children evidence their profound psychosis only around the third and fourth years, when their increased motor coordination and the demands of the beginning Oedipal period force them to face real independence from their mothers in the combined forms of physical and psychological distance.

Where autistic children cannot cope with unexpected stimulation from the external world, symbiotic psychotic children fuse themselves with one agent of that world. Autistic children fail to break out of their protective shells or primitive isolation, whereas symbiotic psychotic youngsters fail to create *any* distance between themselves and their mothers. For autistic children, the potential intrusion of outer human reality is unthinkable and intolerable; but symbiotic psychotic children regard one portion of outer human reality and themselves as narcissistically joined.

What has happened during the brief lives of each of these disturbed children to so fragment their egos? Why have each of these children, in their own way, failed to become *individuals*? To put these questions into more answerable form—can some reliable sequence of development be observed in the formation of a healthy child's ego that is somehow missing or injured in these disturbed children? Margaret Mahler set out to answer this question by gathering observational data on normal children and their relationships to their mothers from birth through the period when children establish themselves as separated and individuated persons.

PSYCHOLOGICAL BIRTH: SEPARATION AND INDIVIDUATION

Mahler had hypothesized (1968, pp. 32ff.) that the central issue in the fragmentation of these disturbed children's egos was their failure to develop a *normal* symbiotic relationship with their mothers, from which could emerge a strong, integrated, independent ego able and ready to treat self and others as persons: "The salient feature in childhood psychosis is that individuation, i.e., a sense of individual identity, is not achieved" (1968, p. 35).

From her study of severely disturbed children, Mahler turned to an investigation of normal children and their mothers at the Masters Children's Center in New York, beginning in 1959. Mahler and her colleagues set up an observation room containing an observation booth, a play area, and a separate sitting area for mothers. Groups of children and their mothers could be watched as they interacted with one another, played with toys, or experimented with their opportunities for separation from mother. Children from four months old through four years old were, at one time or another, participants with their mothers in the study.

With increasing experience in natural observation, Mahler and her colleagues devised a number of data-gathering techniques that revolved around several important questions. *How does a mother carry her child when she arrives?* Like a part of herself? Like another human being? *At what stage of growth does the child become aware of his mother?* Is there an invisible bond between mother and baby? How does she separate herself from her child? Gradually? Abruptly? *When separated from mother, how does the child bridge the gap between them?* Visually? Vocally? By physically approaching? *How does the mother respond to the child's needs?* Quickly? Consistently? Reluctantly? Neglectfully? And so on.

From the mass of data gathered over the years, Mahler began to construct a picture of the normal sequence of stages in the process of becoming a person, the process that had gone so sadly awry in her disturbed children patients. In essence, Mahler was studying the phenomenon of "psychological birth" (Mahler, Pine, & Bergman, 1975, p. 3). The separation-individuation process required for normal ego functioning begins optimally around the fourth month and climaxes at or near the end of the third year of life. Before separation-individuation begins, however, there are two "forerunner" phases, *normal autism* and *normal symbiosis,* in which the mother and child mutually lay the groundwork for the child's subsequent "hatching" in psychological birth as a potential person. Therefore, six interdependent phases are required altogether for normal ego development. The two forerunner phases and the four subsequent stages of the individuation-separation process are summarized with their approximate age ranges in Table 4.5 as a prelude to the detailed discussion that follows.

First Forerunner of Separation-Individuation: Normal Autism

During the first month of life, infants' physiological rhythms and needs outweigh all psychological processes. They spend most of the day in a half-sleeping, half-waking state, broken by full wakefulness only in moments of hunger or pain (Mahler et al., 1975, p. 41). In Freud's (1895; 1920a) language, the infant's *stimulus barrier* is strongly erected, enforcing a relative absence of cathexis of external objects.

Using another of Freud's concepts, Mahler and her colleagues characterize this *normal autistic phase* as a stage of *absolute primary narcissism:* Infants have no recognition of their mothers as external agents of satisfaction. As the first few weeks after birth proceed, the infantile *absolute* narcissism normally gives way to a dim recognition that needs are satisfied from somewhere outside the self (Mahler et al., 1975, p. 42). This secondary narcissism of the autistic phase might be termed "*conditional* hallucinatory omnipotence," for though infants recognize external need satisfiers, they nevertheless are convinced that their own *desires* alone are sufficient to assure their presence.

Although there is a relative disinterest in external reality, some stimuli may fleetingly penetrate the autistic shell of the stimulus barrier and evoke crude, global responses from the infant, but such responses show no precision of specificity, suggesting that the infant's various bodily reactions are all of a piece. Infants respond to every stimulus that can penetrate the barrier with the whole body, with their entire physical being (1975, p. 45). In effect, the stimulus barrier and its enforced autism protect the infant against extremes of stimulation fairly reliably, a situation similar to the fetal state, with the same goal of promoting unbroken biological growth.

TABLE 4.5 Forerunners and Subphases of Separation-Individuation

The Two Forerunners

1. Normal Autism (First month)
   a. strong stimulus barrier
   b. absolute primary narcissism
   c. conditional hallucinatory omnipotence
   d. *achievement:* homeostatic balance of physiological mechanisms

2. Normal Symbiosis (2 to 4 months)
   a. dim recognition of mother as object.
   b. good (pleasure) and bad (pain) distinguished
   c. no real separation of self from mother
   d. *achievement:* formation of inner core of self established through mother's handling of infant's needs

The Four Subphases

1. Differentiation and Development of Body Image (5 to 9 months)
   a. hatching process of tentative differentiation of self from mother
   b. checking back to mother pattern
   c. stranger anxiety
   d. *achievement:* movement toward active and separate functioning

2. Practicing (10 to 14 months)
   a. interest in early phase in inanimate objects supplied by mother
   b. expanded locomotor capacity
   c. low-keyed behavior when mother is absent; imaging mother
   d. *achievement:* building fear resistance to separation from mother and increased exploration of world

3. Rapprochement (14 to 24 months)
   a. increased awareness of separateness from mother
   b. shadowing of mother
   c. darting-away games
   d. rapproachement crisis, "losing" mother, and conflict between urge to separate and fear of loss
   e. splitting mechanism of defense
   f. *achievement:* ego eventually integrates good and bad images; beginning of gender identity

4. Consolidation of Individuality (2 to 3 years)
   a. verbal form of communication dominant
   b. time concepts
   c. emotional-object constancy
   d. *achievement:* formation of a stable self-concept, a notion of "me" separate from love object

Based on Mahler, 1968; and Mahler et al., 1975.

The main achievement of the autistic phase is the infant's gradual attainment of physiological stability in the new, demanding world outside the mother's body. Restricted only for the moment to bodily homeostatic mechanisms, the infant will nevertheless shortly cross the frontier into the realm of psychological functioning. The purely biological balancing mechanisms of the body will now be supplemented by a series of psychological harmonizing processes designed to adapt infants to their world, to themselves, and to the meanings they create themselves.

By the second month of life, the dim awareness of the external mother marks the transition to the next, symbiotic phase. For all practical purposes, the infant now behaves as though it and its mother were a dual unity within a common boundary (Mahler, 1968, p. 8).

Second Forerunner of Separation-Individuation: Normal Symbiosis

From the second month onward through the third month, the autistic shell begins to crack, and the child's ego begins gearing up for its sensory and perceptual tasks that require alertness to the outside world. But infants cannot differentiate between their own tension-reducing efforts and those of the mother in their behalf. Thus their own tension-relieving activities such as urinating, defecating, coughing, sneezing, spitting, regurgitating, and vomiting are indistinguishable at this point from their mothers' attentions to the wet diapers, to providing food and cuddling, and to supplying warmth and cleanliness (Mahler et al., 1975, p. 43). The combined result of the infant's own and the mother's actions is the gradually developing ability to distinguish between *good* (pleasure) and *bad* (pain) aspects of experience.

Thus the normal relationship during the second and third months of life between mother and infant is *symbiotic,* a term drawn metaphorically from biology to indicate the life-sustaining quality of two organisms living together.

> It is obvious that, whereas during the symbiotic phase the infant is *absolutely* dependent on the symbiotic partner, symbiosis has a quite different meaning for the adult partner of the dual unity. The infant's need for the mother is absolute, while the mother's need for the infant is relative. . . . The term "symbiosis" in this context is a metaphor. It does not describe, as the biological concept of symbiosis does, what actually happens between two separate individuals. . . . It was chosen to describe that state of undifferentiation, of fusion with mother, in which the "I" is not yet differentiated from the "not-I," and in which inside and outside are only gradually coming to be sensed as different. (Mahler, 1968, pp. 8–9)

The crude differentiation between good and bad, between pleasure and pain, allows the symbiotic child to deal with painful perceptions in only one way: projection of the bad outside the realm of the symbiotic partnership, in the same way that sneezing, coughing, urinating, vomiting, and defecating expel pain-producing material into the external world to provide tension-reducing pleasure. But the external world, for the symbiotic child, is everything outside of mother-self; it does not yet include mother alone.

> The essential feature of symbiosis is hallucinatory or delusional somatopsychic omnipotent fusion with the representation of the mother and, in particular, the delusion of a common boundary of the two actually and physically separate individuals. This is the mechanism to which the ego regresses in cases of the most severe disturbance of individuation and psychotic disorganization, which I have described as "symbiotic child psychosis." . . . (Mahler, 1968, p. 9)

Through their continued experience of pleasure and pain, infants begin to differentiate a sense of their own bodies and a sense of the distinction between "inner" and "outer," though these perceptions are still somewhat fused with perception of the mother's body. Inner sensations form the *core of the infant's self.* The primary narcissism of the autistic phase yields to the secondary narcissism of the pleasures to be derived from its own and its mother's body (Mahler, 1968, p. 10; Mahler et al., 1975, p. 47). Where, in the autistic phase, the mother's breast was experienced as part of self, it is now seen symbiotically as a "satisfying object" located outside the self but not independent of the self.

The mother's "holding behavior" during feeding shapes the infant's own style of reacting to the human environment. Thus a mother who feels proud and self-sufficient because she is able to breast-feed her child is likely to handle the infant differently and communicate different meanings from the handling and communications of a mother whose puritanical upbringing makes her feel uncomfortable nursing her infant with her own body (Mahler et al., 1975, p. 49).

A mother who genuinely enjoys her children, who smiles and talks to them during their intimacies, will encourage a smiling and talkative baby, who pleasurably anticipates human contacts of all kinds. For this reason, Mahler describes the holding behavior of mothers as "symbiotic organizers" of psychological birth.

We turn now to the first subphase of the separation-individuation process proper, beginning where symbiosis leaves off, at four months of age.

First Subphase: Differentiation and Development of the Body Image

At four to five months of age, when symbiosis is at its peak, infants have already begun to show signs of differentiating themselves out of the symbiotic orbit. Called the "hatching process," it marks the beginning of the child's emergence as a permanently alert, perceptually aware creature.

Hatching is psychological birth, for this first subphase marks the start of the child's tentative and healthy efforts to break away, in a strictly bodily sense, from the previously passive "lap-babyhood" during symbiotic unity with mother (Mahler et al., 1975, p. 55). The entire subphase of differentiation and development of the body image lasts from approximately five to nine months of age.

At the six-month mark, infants show tentative differentiation of self from mother through a variety of new behaviors: pulling mother's hair, ears, and nose; putting food into *her* mouth; straining back from her arms to better see her or other interesting things outside their orbit. The infant spends a good deal of time exploring the external environment when awake, and these investigations include examinations of the contours of mother's face, her eyeglasses or earrings, and any other object that can be grasped, mouthed, or yanked. Infants may even enjoy games of peekaboo, signaling in their delighted, throaty laughter vague comprehension that mother may disappear and reappear unexpectedly, that is, her presence and absence are independent of the *infant's* bodily control.

At seven or eight months, a "checking back to mother" behavior pattern emerges, in which a baby seems to compare his or her mother with other people, feature by feature: "He seems to familiarize himself more thoroughly, as it were, with what *is* mother, what feels, tastes, smells, looks like, and has the 'clang' of mother" (1975, p. 56). "Stranger anxiety" is also a development of this period, and the child is both apprehensive under a stranger's gaze and wondrously fascinated with the details of this "other-than-mommy" person.

From the period of this first subphase of separation-individuation onward, the child has embarked on a course that has two developmental tracks. The first track is the development of *separation from mother*, distancing with confidence, forming boundaries to the self, and a slow disengagement that results in subjective awareness of separateness as a positive, satisfying state. The second track is the development of *individuation* through the internal maturation of independent ego functions in the areas of perception, memory, cognition, and reality testing. Individuation is literally the psychological process of assimilating one's recognition of physical separateness from the mother into an intrapsychically harmonious acceptance of oneself as an *individual*. Separation is becoming a discrete entity; individuation is becoming a functioning person.

Second Subphase: Practicing

From approximately 10 to 14 months, children build on their accomplishments of the first subphase. They are now able to differentiate their bodies from those of their mothers, they recognize their own mothers as special, unique persons, easily detectable as different from all "non-mommies," and their egos have begun to develop autonomous perceptual, cognitive, and reality-testing capacities.

In the *early practicing* subphase, interest becomes partially focused on inanimate objects supplied by mother: a diaper, bottle, toy, or blanket, left with the child as they part for the night. But though children explore these objects visually, tactually, perhaps even tasting them, their primary interest remains centered on mother. Simultaneously, however, they are developing increased facility in locomotor coordination.

> Expanding locomotor capacity during the early practicing subphase widens the child's world; not only does he have a more active role in determining closeness and distance to mother, but the modalities that up to now were used to explore the relatively familiar environment suddenly expose him to a wider segment of reality; there is more to see, more to hear, more to touch. (Mahler et al., 1975, p. 66)

The way children will interpret their experiences in this new world will be subtly shaped by their still close relationship to mother. Her reactions to brief separations will amplify or minimize the apprehensions. In all such separations, however, the mother remains the "home base," an emotional refueling stop on the road to increasingly lengthy, increasingly distant separations.

The *practicing subphase proper* begins with the shift to upright walking near the age of 10 or 12 months. Now a child is truly physically independent, free to roam widely and proudly. Children become interested in the accomplishments of their own bodies and are more easily able to resist the knocks and bruises that this new sense of adventure will inevitably bring. Familiar adults other than mommy are easily accepted as substitutes, an accomplishment that they will relinquish in the next subphase.

However, some children become *low-keyed* when they become aware of mother's absence from the room. Motility and other performances slow, interest in surroundings decreases, and when a person other than mother offers comfort, toddlers may lose their emotional balance and burst into tears. It appears that the low-keyed state involves the child's inward concentration of attention on an image of the mother that helps build resistance to fear of love-object loss, until emotional individuation catches up with locomotion.

Third Subphase: Rapprochement

In the third subphase, *rapprochement,* lasting from about 14 months to two years, children become more aware of their separateness and are able to make greater use of cognitive faculties in the service of resisting frustration. Paradoxically, however, there is an increase in sensitivity to mother's absences, expressed in the child's nearly constant concern over mother's whereabouts (Mahler et al., 1975, p. 76). "As the toddler's *awareness* of separateness grows . . . he seems to have an increased need, a wish for mother to share with him every one of his new skills and experiences, as well as a great need for the [mother] object's love" (1975, pp. 76–77).

During this subphase, the toddlers begin to "*shadow*" their mothers, a kind of continuous vigilance and following of every move. They also begin games of "darting-away" so that they can be caught after a chase and swept into her arms. It is possible that darting-away games express both the child's wish for reunion with the love object and fear of reengulfment by her (1975, p. 77).

This rapprochement phase is a period of contradictions. As toddlers become aware of their separateness, they devise strategies for denying it, for preventing it, and for maintaining close contact. But they also "dart away." Verbal communication becomes easier and replaces gestural and bodily contact as the only ways to express meaning; yet, toddlers find it difficult to give up their sense of preverbal omnipotence and self-grandeur long enough to recognize that adults do not respond automatically to their magical wishes. Even though they can barely bring themselves to be parted from their mothers, they discover new love objects in their lives. They begin to see their fathers as unique persons, with special and interesting characteristics of their own.

Sometime near the 18-month mark, extending through the second year, a *rapprochement crisis* develops in which the toddler is nearly overwhelmed by a resurgence of separation fear. Rapid mood changes may be evident, temper tantrums may occur, or prolonged bouts of whining and clinging behavior suddenly make their appearance in a child who seemed just at the point of readiness to assert independence. It is as though toddlers struggle acutely with a conflict of pushing away a mother to whom they desperately want to cling. At the same time, there appears a resurgence of stranger fear, sometimes interpreted by adults as "shyness."

An odd reaction may also surface in the child at the crisis phase of the rapprochement stage. Toddlers may suddenly become intensely anxious because they believe their mothers have left the room, even though they are sitting next to each other. Mahler and her colleagues (1975, p. 96) suggest that this peculiar anxiety over "losing" mother is a form of projection on the child's part, stemming from a conflict between independence and separation fear: "The desire to function by one's own self may be particularly threatening to the child at the very point in development when one's own feelings and wishes and those of mother are still poorly differentiated. The wish to be autonomous and separate from mother, to leave her, might also mean emotionally that the mother would wish to leave him. . . ." (Mahler et al., 1975, p. 96).

Most often in the 20- to 21-month range, the child discovers the bodily differences between boys and girls. The boy's discovery of his own penis actually takes place earlier, but the new enlightenment is focused on the *differences* between boys and girls, and between parents and children. Generally, Mahler found, this discovery seemed to be more difficult for girls than boys to assimilate into their growing sense of identity (1975, p. 106). Consistent with Freudian theory, girls in the rapprochement crisis tended to blame their mothers for the sexual difference between themselves and boys, "to blame her, to demand from her, to be disappointed in her, and still be ambivalently tied to her" (1975, p. 106).

Boys, by contrast, seemed to be confronted with the classical conception of castration anxiety in relation to the father, but only later, after the rapprochement crisis had ended. As a result, boys were better able than girls to cope with their separation conflict and to find some restorative security in their growing gender identification with father.

From the viewpoint of ego development, the rapprochement phase may be crucial to the child's ability to internalize conflict and to reconcile clashes between an "all good" mother and an "all bad" one. The good mother is the person who has provided all pleasures, all securities, all warmth, and all companionship. In the symbiotic phase, this "good love object" was viewed as a part of self. But now the child's growing psychological sophistication confronts a serious conflict. Mothers unavoidably have their dark sides. Sometimes mother is a need-frustrator, or a pain-inflicter, or an indifferent and distracted caretaker, or, most painful of all her shortcomings, mother is sometimes absent altogether. For the child's newly developing ego, the "good mother" and the "bad mother" cannot be one and the same love object. She, who was once so long ago a part of me, cannot be bad; yet, undeniably, mother is not *always* good. If the good mother and the bad mother *are* one person, then, I too, must harbor some bad within me. That is not possible, for I am all good.

The rapprochement child may employ the defense mechanism termed *"splitting"* of the ego, to deal with such contradictory love objects by treating them in all-or-none fashion. Thus mother cannot be both good and bad simultaneously. There is a good mother, and there is a bad mother. The good mother is the love object that was internalized as part of the child's own narcissistic ego during symbiosis. The bad mother is externalized, projected to the outside world, outside me, where all pain-producing, threatening objects belong.

After all, one's mother cannot be both loving and unloving, cannot be loved and hated, approached and avoided at one time. "Hence the toddler may displace aggression onto the nonmother world while exaggerating love for (overidealizing) the absent, longed-for mother. When mother returns she disrupts the ideal image, and reunions with her are often painful, since the young ego's synthetic function cannot heal the split" (Mahler et al., 1975, pp. 292–293). In the case of the normally developing child, however, the ego gradually gains the ability to synthesize good and bad, to integrate divided feelings and perceptions into a unified, "synthetic" whole.

Fourth Subphase: Consolidation of Individuality— "On the Way to Object Constancy"

Toward the end of the second year, and extending through the third year of life, the image of the mother as a separate entity in the outside world is consolidated with the "good" and the "bad" images of her. As a result, the beginnings of the child's own individuality also emerge with a gradual recognition of separate personhood.

In psychoanalytic language, the child is said to have achieved a fair degree of *emotional object constancy*. Internally, mentally, such children are able to maintain an image of the mother even when she is not present. They cognitively grasp, however vaguely, that mother does not cease to exist just because she is out of sight, nor does her absence imply that she has stopped loving her child.

> But the constancy of the object implies more than the maintenance of the representation of the absent love object. . . . It also implies the unifying of the "good" and "bad" object into one whole representation. This fosters the fusion of the aggressive and libidinal drives and tempers the hatred for the object when aggression is intense. . . . In the state of object constancy, the love object will not be rejected or exchanged for another if it can no longer provide satisfactions; and in that state, the object is still longed for, and not rejected (hated) as unsatisfactory simply because it is absent. (Mahler et al., 1975, p. 110)

For the healthy child to achieve emotional object constancy, two prior essential steps are necessary. The first step is the establishment of basic trust in mother and self that comes from reliable, immediate, loving gratification of need. The second step is the cognitive development of mental imagery to allow the child to form internal representations that abstractly and symbolically embody external reality in relatively permanent memories.

Verbal ability, developed in rudimentary form during the third subphase, now assumes complete dominance as the means of communication. Play becomes more imaginative and purposeful, taking on aspects of role playing and dramatic fantasy. The concept of time (later, tomorrow, before) is meaningful to children in terms of their mothers' comings and goings, an attainment achieved in a similar way by Freud's grandson Ernst in his masterful "gone game" (see Chapter 3).

The main accomplishment of this last phase of separation-individuation is the attainment of a self-concept organized around a stable sense of "me." The process of forming a unique identity, the core of individuality, is not completed at the end of the third year, but continues throughout the later oedipal phase. In Mahler's view, the normal child has an intrinsic drive toward growth and personality integration:

> It bears special emphasis . . . that our study convinced us that the maturational pressure, *the drive for and toward individuation* in the normal human infant, *is an innate,* powerful *given,* which, although it may be muted by protracted interference, does manifest itself all along the separation-individuation process. (Mahler et al., 1975, p. 206, emphasis in original)

PERSONAL SOURCES OF MAHLER'S SEPARATION-INDIVIDUATION HYPOTHESIS

The central feature of Mahler's theory is the development of a helpless, symbiotically dependent, and unthinking biological creature into a quasi-independent, self-reflective psychological entity capable of other-recognition. Abstracted in this way, Mahler's description of the maturation of the pre-Oedipal ego is a narrative on becoming a person. We can ask, therefore, from what personal origins does Mahler's focus on autonomy stem?

Rejecting Mother, Confounding Father:
Self-Sufficiency Is Everything

Mahler's childhood memory of her mother was that she was a "deeply unhappy woman":

> I came far too early—nine months and six days after the wedding—and was very much unwanted by my mother, who was a mere girl of nineteen at the time. Very beautiful, very narcissistic, and greatly pampered, she blamed my father for my untimely arrival. . . . In her anger, she had as little to do with me as she could. During my first year of life, when I was quite sickly and had sleep disturbances, it was my father who, with my nurse, arose at night to attend me. My symbiotic stage of life was difficult: I must have been full of frustrated rage at the rejecting mother whom I greatly loved nonetheless. (Mahler, 1988, p. 4)

Born in the Hungarian village of Sopron in 1897, Margaret Mahler *née* Schön-berger grew up speaking two languages. Her Hungarian-speaking father, Gustav Schönberger, was a physician in general practice and chief public health officer of his district. Eugenia Wiener Schönberger, Margaret's mother, spoke primarily German at home. Much to the adult Margaret's amazement, during psychoanalysis she realized that she and her younger sister had spoken Hungarian with their father and switched automatically to German when their mother would enter the room (Mahler, 1988, p. 2). Mahler recalls that her father was socially prominent and active, especially in the political life of their town, whereas her mother devoted herself primarily to being an "excellent cook and homemaker."

Fueled by her own feelings of rejection, the four-year-old Margaret became a keen observer of her mother's elation at the birth of a second daughter. From Margaret's point of view, her new baby sister Suzanne was greeted with affection and delight—maternal responses Margaret now understood had been denied her. Indeed, the young Mahler began to assume that their mother wanted her dead (1988, p. 5).

In what appears to be utter candor, Mahler states in her *Memoirs* that it was this harsh contrast with the loving acceptance and attention her sister received that inspired her own interest in pediatrics, psychoanalysis with children, and especially the study of mother-child relationships (Mahler, 1988, pp. 4–5). Out of frustration, Mahler turned to her father. She recalls that at age four and one half, she observed her mother treating her sister lovingly, saying to her child, "I have brought you into this world, I love, I adore you . . ." and other endearments, to which the four-year-old Margaret is reported to have said, "And I, I was born by my father" (Mahler, 1988, p. 6).

Her mother did not like visitors or Margaret's friends or even her husband's patients to "intrude" into the house. On one occasion, Mahler recalled that her mother would permit her to have a birthday party only if she consented to give away her precious collection of chocolate animal figures as a prize for one of the party games. Reluctantly Margaret consented, but in the end her mother gave the entire collection to a child who was distantly related to her. Mahler recalls crying "inconsolably" at the end of the party (1988, p. 7).

Her Father's "Son": Gender Confusion as Self-Confidence

Out of such frustrations, rejections, and hurts, Margaret turned to the world of her father. Medicine, science, politics, and mathematics captured her interests and intelligence, and, supported by her father's enthusiasm, Mahler became the "son" her father wanted: ". . . it was my father's eager adoption of me as his 'son,' and my willing acceptance of this role, that confounded my childhood gender identity." Mahler reports that it never occurred to her that she might be a "pretty young girl," and her father's attention to her intellectual development did nothing for the development of her feminine self-esteem. To erode her tenuous grip on feminine identity further, her father would greet her schoolgirl avowals of admiration or love of a male teacher with the remark, "You are man enough for yourself" (1988, p. 8). Mahler's intellectual prowess provided for an intimidating reputation during the dating years of adolescence. When her sister attracted young suitors, Margaret was off reading Einstein's ideas on relativity. In what should have been a simple conversation, which she later regretted, she startled one young man who had taken her to a dance with the proposition that God existed in the fourth dimension! There was no second date.

> . . . I tended to deny my own femininity entirely. I refused to believe that any man worth having could love me; if one perchance expressed any feeling for me, he was instantly devalued. Never having learned how to compete with other women as a woman, I learned instead how to avoid defeat as a woman in a world of men. In short, I developed a strong drive for independence at an early age. . . . (Mahler, 1988, p. 9)

Years later, when the adult Margaret would return to Sopron and talk with her family about the young men who now courted her, her father voiced his unchanging refrain: "Why did I need to marry, he would ask, when I was so self-sufficient. I was really much 'better' than the average man" (1988, p. 77). When, at age 39, she introduced Paul Mahler to her father as the man she was going to marry, her father said to the startled young man: "You must know what you are doing; she is not average . . ." (1988, p. 10). From Mahler's psychoanalytic point of view in later years, she interpreted her father's comment to the erstwhile Paul Mahler as reflecting his deep resentment of her marriage:

> Psychoanalytically speaking, my father meant [to warn Paul]: "Watch out, for whatever her strengths and weaknesses, she is not castrated, and you had better watch out not to get castrated by her." (Mahler, 1988, p. 10)

Medical School: The Compromise Solution

It is not surprising that Mahler chose a career in medicine, in part to emulate the father who had so strongly, if inappropriately, nurtured her and in part to pursue her own intellectual strengths. During her early preparation she came into contact with psychoanalysis through friends and acquaintances, and her interest was sparked.

In 1917, she gained admission to the medical school of the University of Budapest. Throughout her schooling, her father was supportive, but he tried to persuade his daughter to avoid certain medical specialties that he felt were not suited to a pioneering woman pursuing a medical career. He especially tried to dissuade his daughter from a career in psychiatry, which he regarded as a more or less academic and custodial branch of medicine. But when he learned that his daughter was interested in Freud, he read Freud (Mahler, 1988, p. 22).

Anti-Semitism in the communist regime that ruled Budapest was intensifying, and if the chances that a Jewish medical student would be permitted to finish medical school were small, then the chances for a Jewish female medical student were practically nil. At about the same time, Mahler's younger sister, who was somewhat immature, wanted to move to Munich to study music. Mahler's parents would grant the younger sister permission only if the older Margaret would accompany her and serve as substitute parent.

So in 1919, Mahler entered the university in Munich. She became a star student and several young men became interested in her romantically. But she recalls that she was still under the influence of her father's disapproval of any interactions with the opposite sex and did not believe that she could really be attractive to men. As she recalls, "I had effectively embraced the meaning of my father's devaluation of my feminine strivings: that I was neuter" (1988, p. 25).

Consistent with her self-analyzed personal history, Mahler chose the medical specialty of pediatrics. "Pediatrics, I should perhaps explain, represented a compromise of sorts: it would enable me to be what my father was [i.e., a practicing physician], while simultaneously accommodating my desire—perhaps my outstanding 'feminine' trait—to work with children" (1988, p. 23).

Conditions in Munich deteriorated for Margaret and her sister. Anti-Semitism grew more blatant, and at one point, to encourage Jews to leave Munich, apparently random arrests were made of Jewish students. Mahler and her sister found themselves briefly in jail (1988, p. 28). By 1920, mounting indignities and aggressive prejudice, as well as a growing resentment that she was trapped in this situation by her sister's needs, led Mahler to the decision that it was time to transfer to the University of Jena in southern Germany near Weimar. Mahler's sister was forced to return to Vienna.

As assistant to an eminent pediatric researcher in Jena, Mahler got her first exposure to the serious illnesses and psychosomatic disorders of childhood. One case in particular left an enduring impression. A woodcutter brought his child for treatment with symptoms of failing to thrive and loss of weight, but with no other medical disorders apparent. The father and child had what Mahler would later recognize as a symbiotic relationship. Persuaded to leave his child overnight, the woodcutter returned home and dreamt that night in a symbolic dream that he had felled a tree and that the tree was his son. When the father returned to the clinic the next morning to reclaim his son, he was told that the child had died during the night. Mahler understood intuitively, and later psychoanalytically, that the father had been everything to the child, and when that symbiotic bond had been disrupted, the child could no longer survive (Mahler, 1988, p. 31). The significance of emotional and psychological variables was becoming salient to Mahler, a pediatrician training in a medical specialty that could be blind to the critical importance of psychology.

Despite the intellectual excitement and enjoyment Mahler was experiencing in Jena, the anti-Semitism continued unabated. At one point, despite academic excellence, Mahler was in danger of being expelled because she was an "East European Jewess" whom the general student body organization deemed unfit. Fortunately, influential friends intervened in Mahler's behalf and she was able to graduate *magna cum laude* from the university two years later, completing her final semester at the university in Heidelberg, a "fun" city where anti-Semitism was not yet rife.

Because she was not a citizen of Germany, Mahler's medical diploma did not entitle her to a German medical license. But she had acquired Austrian citizenship in preparation for this event, and she now returned to Vienna (close to her home village of Sopron) to obtain her license, to continue her training in psychoanalysis, and to begin the practice of pediatrics.

As part of her continued training, she became an assistant in a famous pediatric institute under the eminent Viennese pediatrician von Pirquet. Professor von Pirquet had created a well-known feeding system for very ill infants called the "nem system." An infant was placed in a sterile cubicle with one or more glass walls and fed precisely measured portions of milk called "nems." A nem is a unit of measurement that corresponds to the caloric value of one gram of breast milk. The entire feeding procedure involved no human contact with the infant!

In total contrast, Mahler spent her summer months in a rival pediatric institute that stressed the importance of the mother's nurturance of the sick child and the critical "communication" between the two in the care of its small patients. Well ahead of its day, the Leopold Moll Institute admitted sick children for treatment *with* their mothers, and operated strictly on the philosophy that "a baby not only 'belonged' to its mother but that the presence of the mother . . . was essential if a sick baby was to get well" (Mahler, 1988, p. 47). Babies were routinely assigned to special student nurses to provide "maternal" care so that both the nurse in training and the baby received nourishment from the experience. So dedicated and loving were these nurses that they would frequently don surgical masks and spend an entire night holding, cuddling, and talking to a dying child. To Mahler's amazement, many of these children recovered under this regimen. The contrast with the von Pirquet Institute and its nem-feeding was stark. Mahler's own childhood experiences had exquisitely sensitized and prepared her to absorb these crucial lessons about the power of the intimacy in the mother-child dualism.

Cinderella in Psychoanalysis Land

Mahler's interest in psychoanalysis continued. She met August Aichhorn, the child guidance movement leader and psychoanalyst. Aichhorn was an elusive and "mysterious man" who spoke frequently of his contacts with the criminal elements of Viennese society, especially among the adolescent gangs. He spoke the language of "delinquents" and seemed to earn their trust easily both in therapy and in institutional settings by communicating that he would always give them the benefit of a doubt. He was able, apparently, to attend meetings of gang members as they plotted their activities, and frequently "predicted" a particular crime well in advance of the actual event. Aichhorn's therapeutic approach to these children was a mixture of psychoanalysis and commonsense humanism. He understood them not as criminals but as abused and misunderstood children. In his counseling technique, Mahler recalled him as a master of drawing out the unconscious motivations in the child's recounting of circumstances and then showing the child how he had "chosen" a certain course of action. Making rounds and attending consultations with Aichhorn gave Mahler her first real exposure to child psychiatry and a firsthand experience with psychoanalytic method.

By 1926, Mahler entered a training analysis with the well-known analyst Helene Deutsch, but the match of patient and therapist was not made in heaven. Deutsch, acting somewhat authoritatively and regally, made it clear to the enthusiastic Mahler that she had agreed to accept her for analysis mostly because of a professional favor. At the time, Mahler was financially impoverished and had arranged a modified fee with this eminent analyst. What Mahler did not know at the time was that Helene Deutsch resented treating her for less than her usual fee. At the time, Mahler interpreted Deutsch's arrogant attitude as a personal rejection and was crushed. She spent the next 50 or 60 sessions trying to prove her worth to her analyst. Accustomed to being treated as special and intellectually gifted, Mahler chafed under the Deutsch regime of being treated like a "second-class citizen." After a series of missed appointments (canceled by the ambivalent Helene Deutsch), Deutsch terminated Mahler's training analysis, informing the patient that she was "unanalyzable."

What followed was a series of negative appraisals of Mahler by members of the analytic community in Vienna. Anna Freud wrote to Mahler informing her that her candidate status at the Vienna Psychoanalytic Institute was terminated until she undertook a therapeutic analysis to resolve her difficulties, at which point she might reapply to the Institute. By a circuitous route, Mahler sidestepped the officially recommended analysts and appealed to her friend August Aichhorn. He agreed to take her as a patient and evolved a characteristically "secret" plan whereby he would rescue and restore her to acceptable status in the professional psychoanalytic community. Seriously depressed and demoralized, Mahler was ready to be rescued by Prince Charming. In the end, she was in analysis with Aichhorn for almost three years, and during that time analyst and patient fell in love. With her usual candor, Mahler describes the familiar essence of the situation in which she found herself:

> Under Aichhorn's analytic care, I became a sort of Cinderella, the love object of a beautiful Prince (Aichhorn) who would win me the favor of a beautiful stepmother (Mrs. Deutsch). At the same time, my analytic treatment with him simply recapitulated my oedipal situation all over again—I was the daughter of both a rejecting mother (Mrs. Deutsch) and a father (Aichhorn) very partial to me. (Mahler, 1988, p. 68)

Realizing that the analytic "work" they accomplished together was far from "classical," Aichhorn and Mahler decided that she should continue her training analysis with another analyst. In the meantime, Aichhorn, as promised, secured Mahler's readmission to the Vienna psychoanalytic establishment.

Other difficulties ensued. As a member of Anna Freud's training seminar in child analysis, Mahler recalled that her relationship with Freud's daughter was "unpleasant" and distant. In general, Mahler's experience with the psychoanalytic establishment in Vienna was abrasive and disappointing for her. By the time the Nazis had risen to power, Margaret and her husband, as well as a host of other Jewish intellectuals, began to emigrate to safer places. Mahler and her husband Paul arrived in the United States in 1938, where she began the work that secured her place in psychoanalytic history. She died in 1985, at the age of 88.

Transitional Summary

Unlike nearly any other theorist for whom we have personal source information, Mahler has done our work for us. She candidly identified the three main themes of her early life that led to her interest in child psychiatry and eventually to the theory of separation-individuation:

1. Maternal indifference and rejection coupled with strong, frequently inappropriate, emotional support from her father.
2. Gender and personal identity confusion shaped by her father's attempts to treat her as the son he did not have.
3. Prematurely enforced self-sufficiency based on her father's need to have a son and her mother's need to distance her daughter.

Coupled with these self-identified themes, we might add the obvious underlying themes of insecurity and feelings of inferiority that Mahler strove so successfully to master. She had struggled firsthand with the experience of early rejection, with the pain of finding her own specialness unwelcome in the wider world, and with the belief that, as a woman, she could not ever be "good enough." Out of these experiences came her focus on pediatrics, on the emotional consequences of adequate "mothering," and her interest in what it takes to be a competent, self-sufficient person.

A FINAL WORD ON MARGARET S. MAHLER

Mahler's work shares much in the way of emphases and conception with Anna Freud, with Heinz Hartmann, and with Robert White. In all three cases, increasing degrees of stress have been placed on individuals' capacities for mastery of their own worlds in a healthy way. For Anna Freud, the roots of mastery are to be found in the ego's inherent capacities to *reconcile drive conflict and the "demands of reality."* For Robert White, the roots of mastery lie in the ego's *independent energies of effectance motivation* and the impact of the interpersonal environment that provides opportunities for self-testing one's degree of competence. Between these extremes, Heinz Hartmann interpreted the ego's strength as lying in its capacity to adapt to reality through its ability *to neutralize drive energy.*

Mahler's work draws from all three traditions, with emphasis on the need for adequate mothering as well as the virtues of inborn ego capacities. Thus we can condense Mahler's picture of the development of ego functioning and true individuality in this way:

1. Grave maladjustment of psychotic proportions has its ego origins in developmental failures to separate from mother as an autonomous agent, or in failures to use mother as a living aid in making sense of the living world. The *symbiotic psychotic* child exemplifies the former and the *autistic* child the latter form of ego pathology.
2. Psychological birth as a human person can be accomplished only by children whose inherent strivings toward individuality are undamaged and whose mothers encourage, however reluctantly, their burgeoning struggles toward separation, without overwhelming their capacities to endure aloneness.

3. The height of ego individuation embodies the ability to synthesize not only aggressive and libidinal strivings toward mother, but also the capacity to draw sustenance from an internalized representation of her. Thus Mahler's work has shown, contrary to Freud's classical scheme, that the roots of identity, conflict resolution, and ego strength lie much earlier in development than the Oedipus complex; and these ego functions are more influenced by the mother than Freud's paternalistic viewpoint would allow.

EVALUATING THE EGO PSYCHOLOGISTS

Much of our evaluation discussion of Freud's classical psychoanalysis is pertinent to the group of people whose work is represented in the present chapter. Like Freud's classical approach, ego psychology represents a collective attempt to understand both normal and abnormal human functioning. And like Freud's work, the ego psychologists aimed to clarify the connection and the conflict between reason and passion. But unlike Freud, the ego psychologists gradually shifted psychoanalysis away from its focus on passion and more toward a concern with human reason and mastery of life.

Refutability of Ego Psychology

It is necessary to understand that the ego psychologists are different in aim and method from those theorists identified as "neo-Freudians," some of whom we study in later chapters. The ego psychologists considered in this chapter explicitly attempted to preserve classical psychoanalysis insofar as that was possible. They certainly developed radical ideas that would qualify as "neo-Freudian" in the sense of being "new," but they invariably did not claim originality. Instead, Anna Freud, Heinz Hartmann, and Margaret Mahler paid ritual obeisance to Freud in their works, trying hard to show that their ideas were mere derivatives of seminal thoughts created by the master. By contrast, the neo-Freudian thinkers we examine later had no such concerns for the preservation of classical analysis. Thinkers such as Horney, Fromm, and Sullivan aimed to change (some historians would say demolish) classical analysis, and in their work they were able, in part, to escape the essentially nonrefutable style of the parent theory.

But the ego psychologists, for all their revolutionary changes, did little to provide a handhold for the empirical researcher. There is much in what we have seen that cries out for testing, but there are so few ways to translate ego psychology into testable hypotheses. To take one example, Daniel Stern (1985) has reviewed basic empirical findings from developmental psychology and has tried to correlate these data with Mahler's concepts of normal autism and normal symbiosis. The bottom line? Stern finds literally no evidence to support any of Mahler's concepts.

To take a different example, consider Robert White's concepts. Drawn initially from academic psychology, including the work of Piaget, we would expect that his reformulation of the Freudian ego as a cognitive agency would lend itself to empirical research. But it has not. As we shall see, however, the concept of mastery has empirical research supporting it, but the support has been generated within the behavioral, social leaning school of personality theory, with workers such as Albert Bandura (see Chapter 16).

What can we conclude? For the issue of refutability, concepts such as symbiosis, effectance motivation, ego synthesis, and Selfobject are not much improved over Freud's libido, id, or repression.

Ego Psychology's Conception of Human Agency

The greatest difference between classical psychoanalysis and the ego psychologists considered in this chapter concerns the issue of active versus passive human agency. Whereas in the classical theory the person is essentially a passive receptacle for reality, there can be discerned a steady progression away from this concept beginning with Anna Freud. Her conception of developmental lines emphasizes themes of mastery that partially free the ego from its passive stance in relation to the id and to reality. With Hartmann, the ego becomes more active, capable of independent action and decision. By the time we reach White, the ego is freed to be an active, independent, even creatively healthy "agency."

This progression from Anna Freud to Robert White is a reflection of one of the chief correctives that ego psychology offered for the aging classical conception of human action. With the ego psychologists, humans are seen, in part, as active agents who create the reality with which they interact and with which they sometimes do battle.

Having said that the ego psychologists lean more toward an active agent conception, we should also point out that their understanding of this active agency is still very far from what a humanistic thinker (see Carl Rogers, for example, or Abraham Maslow) would regard as a truly active agent.

Ego Psychology's Essentially Idiographic Focus

Again, like classical psychoanalysis, the focus in ego psychology is largely clinical, almost exclusively idiographic, and more or less completely aimed at understanding the dynamics of the individual. Despite Hartmann's claims to universality, and Mahler's aspirations to understand broad human developments, close examination of each of the theories in this chapter reveals no real difference from the classical analytic obsession with the unique dynamics of one person at a time. We may, in passing, point out that Robert White's reanalysis of the classical psychosexual stages in terms of mastery rather than sexual or aggressive themes turns his model slightly away from the idiographic. But without a refutable set of hypotheses, the outcome remains locked to the single case.

SUMMARY

Freud's classical picture of the personality in distress was built psychologically from his clinical experiences but conceptualized neurologically along the lines of 19th-century deterministic, materialistic physiology. Picturing the mind as a collection of competing agencies, Freud was forced into a number of dubious assumptions about the nature of human mental functioning.

Freud felt that his own greatest accomplishment had been the exploration of the irrational passions of the unconscious id. The ego was, for the most part, conceptualized as the helpless rider of the spirited id horse, directing the horse where the horse wants to go. If we ask the inevitable question, "What had Freud left undone?" we are compelled to provide at least three answers. First, he neglected the individual's direct relationships to interpersonal reality, especially to the reality of the mother in her role as the nurturing, shaping, esteem-building, trust-building partner in development. Freud's focus had been on conflict, with the powerful id passions seen as the foundation of all human endeavor.

Second, Freud failed to complete his picture of the ego as the *executive* of the personality, capable of more than safe and reliable id satisfactions. Although Freud implied that the ego could function relatively autonomously, his theory sorely lacked a coherent account of how persons adapt to the reality that they themselves helped to create. Without the id pulling the strings in the background, there is no way in classical Freudian theory to explain logically and convincingly the various ways that persons master obstacles beyond instinctual conflict or derive satisfactions from enterprises other than conflict resolution. Not every personal achievement, not every human satisfaction, not every human urge or pain can be derived from the war of sexual and aggressive impulses.

Third, the "assembly of minds" that *is* Freudian structural, dynamic theory runs the risk of losing sight of the person in whom they are assembled. Contemporary psychoanalysts are beginning to question the wisdom of compartmentalized explanations of mental events without proposing some overall synthesizing, integrating, coordinating function. In Freud's theory, the ego was to be the seat of such synthesis, but he failed to develop this idea beyond simple and scattered statements of its existence.

Anna Freud,   Freud's self-chosen psychoanalytic conservator, legitimized ego psychology by her publication of a book devoted to examining the ego defenses for what they could reveal of the history of instinctual conflict.

Through her work with child patients, with war orphans, and with children separated from their parents temporarily, Anna Freud was able to transcend classical drive theory without demolishing it. She developed a diagnostic classification system predicated on the plasticity of the child's healthy strivings toward increased maturity. Her most original contribution to psychoanalytic theory has been her elucidation of *developmental lines,* sequences of psychological and physical growth organized along the paths of dependency to independence, from irrational to rational, and from passive to active relations with reality. Developmental lines suggest an important *interactionist* vantage point from which to account for psychological functioning, a viewpoint neglected in classical Freudian theory.

Heinz Hartmann, the father of ego psychology, strengthened the ego by allowing it a *conflict-free sphere* of functioning in the areas of perception, memory, learning, and locomotion. Hartmann suggested that the ego had the capacity to neutralize sexual and aggressive energy, an improvement over Freud's own tentative proposal of the ego's capacity to desexualize some libido for nonconflictful uses.

In Hartmann's reorganization of psychoanalytic theory, both the id and the ego emerge simultaneously from an "undifferentiated" matrix of biological givens. The ego's essential tasks include not only the classically conceived reconciliation of inner and outer reality, but also the adaptation in a healthy way to the larger social, interpersonal reality of the "average expectable environment" provided by the child's caretakers. Thus, in Hartmann's view, the ego is the great synthesizer, promoting not only *intersystemic* harmony among the id, ego, and superego, but also *intrasystemic* equilibrium within the ego itself.

Robert W. White took Hartmann's reorganization of psychoanalysis a step further to the point of complete energic independence of the ego. In White's view, the ego has inborn motivational properties of its own, expressed in exploratory play, manipulation, and curiosity about the environment. Children not only adapt to the environment, in White's theory, they actively assert themselves within its context, learning their special areas of competence and weaknesses. Driven by "effectance motivation," the child proceeds through the psychosexual conflicts, not only experiencing instinctual pleasures and frustrations, but also acquiring important learnings about how to effect interesting and desirable changes in the world. In real measure, White's theory of effectance motivation restores to psychoanalytic theory a conception of active, striving, autonomous organisms, regulated by the environment that they, in turn, shape.

Margaret S. Mahler, in line with mastery themes, has chronicled the six stages through which a child's ego develops on the road to separation and individuation, that is, on the complex and winding pathway to becoming a self-reliant and unique person. Beginning in "forerunner" phases of *normal autism* and *normal symbiosis,* the infantile ego matures from its initial absolute narcissistic shell of isolation to dim recognition of an external, satisfying object world. Then, progressing in graduated steps, the child passes through symbiotic fusion with mother to a stage of primitive *differentiation of self,* then toward the *practicing* and *rapprochement* stages, marked by increasing awareness and acceptance of separateness from the love object. In the final subphase, children consolidate matured verbal, locomotive, and cognitive skills into a coherent unity, *self-reliantly* able to function apart from mother, and unfearfully capable of the recognition that each is a "me."

Our evaluation of the ego psychologists suggests three conclusions:

- Refutability is as difficult to achieve among the ego psychologists' concepts as it was for classical psychoanalysis—and largely for the same reasons.

- Human agency is conceptualized as a more active, more interactive quality of human beings among the ego psychologists and object relations theorists than the conception found in classical Freudian theory.

- Idiographic emphasis remains unchanged from classical analysis.

FOR FURTHER READING

General background exploration of ego psychology is best begun with two classic papers by David Rapaport: "The Autonomy of the Ego" (*Bulletin of the Menninger Clinic,* 1951, **15**, 113–123); and "The Theory of Ego Autonomy: A Generalization" (*Bulletin of the Menninger Clinic,* 1958, **22**, 13–35). Helpful for its historical breadth and comparative approach, Daniel Yankelovich and William Barrett's *Ego and Instinct: The Psychoanalytic View of Human Nature—Revised* (New York: Vintage Books, 1970) provides a clear theoretical account of classic theory's shortcomings, alternatives that have been proposed, and a lucid treatment of the philosophical underpinnings of classic and contemporary theory. With more emphasis on the therapeutic applications of contemporary ego psychology, Gertrude and Rubin Blanck's *Ego Psychology: Theory and Practice* (New York: Columbia University Press, 1974) provides relatively clear insights into the work of the major ego theorists and a close view of how ego pathologies are therapeutically treated. Thomas Parisi's "Why Freud Failed" (*American Psychologist,* 1987, **42**, 3, 235–245) is a well-reasoned account of why Freud abandoned biological, evolutionary, and neurological concepts in constructing his psychology.

Anna Freud's most important books and papers have been collected into the seven-volume *The Writings of Anna Freud* (New York: International Universities Press, 1965–1974). Essential readings in these volumes are *Introduction to Psychoanalysis and Lectures for Child Analysts and Teachers* (Vol. 1, 1974); *The Ego and the Mechanisms of Defense* (Vol. 2, 1966); *Normality and Pathology in Childhood: Assessment of Development* (Vol. 6, 1965); and the collection of papers in Part I of *Problems of Psychoanalytic Training, Diagnosis, and the Technique of Therapy* (Vol. 7, 1971).

Heinz Hartmann's classic monograph *Ego Psychology and the Problem of Adaptation* (New York: International Universities Press, 1958) deserves attention from the serious student of psychoanalysis. Hartmann's later papers are collected and edited in his *Essays on Ego Psychology* (New York: International Universities Press, 1964), and demonstrate Hartmann's refinements of his original position. In a similar vein, Hartmann's collaboration with Ernst Kris and R. M. Loewenstein, resulting in six important papers, may be sampled in their *Papers on Psychoanalytic Psychology (Psychological Issues,* Monograph **14**, New York: International Universities Press, 1964).

Robert W. White's initial papers on competence and effectance motivation are worth reading for historical background: "Motivation Reconsidered: The Concept of Competence" (in *Psychological Review,* 1959, **66**, 297-333) and "Competence and the Psychosexual Stages of Development" (In M. R. Jones [Ed.], *Nebraska Symposium on Motivation,* Lincoln: University of Nebraska Press, 1960, 97-140). White's most comprehensive presentation of his position is lucidly given in his monograph *Ego and Reality in Psychoanalytic Theory (Psychological Issues,* Monograph **11**, 1963, International Universities Press). White's comprehensive textbook on personality development, *The Enterprise of Living* (New York: Holt, 1976) contains chapters on the competence theme.

Margaret Mahler's classic monograph, *On Human Symbiosis and the Vicissitudes of Individuation* (New York: International Universities Press, 1968) is somewhat difficult reading, but still the best introduction to her concepts of symbiotic psychosis. Her collaborative effort with Fred Pine and Anni Bergmann, *The Psychological Birth of the Human Infant* (New York: Basic Books, 1975), contains a more readable introduction to both symbiotic psychosis and to the stages of the separation-individuation process.

Leopold Bellak, Marvin Hurvich, and Helen Gediman's *Ego Functions in Schizophrenics, Neurotics, and Normals* (New York: Wiley, 1973) presents a historical survey of the concept of the ego in Freud's and his followers' works, a system of classifying ego functions, and a procedure for rating the efficiency of ego function in the personalities named in the title. For comparative reading, Albert Bandura's "The Self-System in Reciprocal Determinism" (*American Psychologist,* 1978, **33**, 344–358) makes an interesting contrast to Robert White and to Heinz Kohut, discussed in Chapter 5. More relevant to White's sense of competence is Bandura's "Self-Efficacy: Toward a Unifying Theory of Behavioral Change" (*Psychological Review,* 1977, **84**, 191–215), also written from the social learning point of view. We treat Bandura's theory in Chapter 16.

MELANIE KLEIN

The Psychoanalytic Heritage: Object Relations Theory

. . . the infant's longing for an inexhaustible and ever-present breast stems by no means only from a craving for food . . .

> Melanie Klein, *Envy and Gratitude*

. . . you teach your child to say "thank you" out of politeness and not because this is what the child means. In other words, you start up teaching good manners and you hope that your child will be able to tell lies. . . .

> D.W. Winnicott, "The Concept of the False Self"

. . . the normal child's Oedipal experiences . . . contain, from the beginning and persisting throughout, an admixture of deep joy. . . .

> Heinz Kohut, *The Restoration of the Self*

About Object Relations Theory

Exploration of the psychoanalytic heritage continues. Like the ego psychologists, object relations theorists sought to revise Freud's classical psychoanalysis without demolishing the entire structure.

__Melanie Klein__ pictured the subjective world of the infant as a near-psychotic chaos of internalized images of people and parts of people. The child's imagination spurred by anxiety and anger transforms these images into terrifying phantasies of good and bad objects.

__D. W. Winnicott,__ pediatrician and child psychoanalyst, learned from Melanie Klein about the internal world of object relations in infancy. Winnicott advanced beyond the Kleinian scheme to study children, not as antagonists, but as persons capable of healthy spontaneity.

__Heinz Kohut__ made the constructive and destructive properties of human relationships, especially those in childhood, the keystone of his theory. Kohut constructed a picture of personality development linked to empathic parenting. Loving parents promote healthy self-structure in their children by providing a model of how to be human.

SO, WHO ARE THE OBJECT RELATIONS THEORISTS?

By the time of Freud's death in 1939, orthodox psychoanalysis was experiencing growing pains from sympathetic attempts to update it and unsympathetic efforts to dismantle it. Ego psychologists were working to modernize psychoanalysis without destroying the house that Freud built. NeoFreudians were vigorously relocating to a new neighborhood. Between these extremes were the object relations theorists who started modestly by remodeling Freud's basement. By the time the object-relations theorists were done, however, Freud's Victorian mansion had become a split-level sprawling ranch with central air conditioning and a two-car garage.

One irksome problem with so many architects working on the same project is that the label *object-relations theorist* is difficult to assign with precision. In contemporary psychoanalysis, the term *object-relations* is used sometimes as a synonym for interpersonal relations. However, to qualify as a psychoanalytic object relations theory, the theory must reach beyond social transactions to the private and unconscious meanings that precede, provoke, accompany, or follow them.

Precise labeling offers less clarity than it promises. Categories often overlap. Distinctions are clouded. For example, despite their name, several ego psychologists in the previous chapter theorized about interpersonal relations in terms that are indistinguishable from object relations concepts. Erik Erikson, considered in Chapter 6, can most certainly be counted as one of these hybrids. Some neo-Freudians to be discussed in later chapters (e.g., Adler, Fromm, Horney, and Sullivan) made interpersonal relations the prominent feature of their theories. Such efforts, however, did not make their ideas welcome within the emerging tradition of psychoanalytic object relations. Curiously, orthodox Freudians believed these early neo-Freudians were using cultural and interpersonal issues as rationalizations to distance themselves from controversial orthodox concepts such as libido, the Oedipus complex, and the motivational dominance of sex and aggression. Consequently, the interpersonal emphases of the neo-Freudians—often for reasons more political or personal than theoretical—had little initial impact on standard psychoanalysis and even less credibility as contributions to emerging object relations theory.

Matters get cloudier. In contemporary psychoanalysis, especially in Great Britain, anyone who is anyone claims the heritage of the object-relations tradition (see, for example, Schafer, 1997b; Summers, 1994, pp. 122 ff.). Indeed, it is now so fashionable to be an object relations theorist that some commentators are rewriting history to permit several of the ego psychologists and a few of the neo-Freudians to claim the title. We come full circle. Who, then, qualifies as a *true* object relations theorist?

The Two Meanings of *Object Relations*

History provides an answer. In the development of psychoanalysis, there have been two uses of the label *object relations.* One historical meaning was used informally and inclusively to refer to *gratification* of the basic drives. The other meaning with substantial historical precedent was used formally and more restrictively to refer to *interpersonal processes.*

The informal meaning derived from Freud's (e.g., 1917b; 1921; 1923a) use of the term *object* in his drive theory, as we discussed in Chapter 3. Freud referred to the specific *satisfier* of the sexual and aggressive drives: the "object" of the drive. Thus, libido "cathects" its love *object.* Destruction of anyone or anything perceived as frustrating the gratification of id needs is the *object* of aggression. Food is the *object* of the hunger drive.

The specifically interpersonal dimension of love objects momentarily caught Freud's eye as he constructed his final model of the mind. In *The Ego and the Id,* he hypothesized that lost or renounced love objects could be incorporated as trait-bearing images into the ego itself. The ego thus diminishes the id's frustration at the loss. Freud concluded that the very character of the ego—one might say its "personality"—is formed by incorporating lost love objects:

> When it happens that a person has to give up a sexual object, there quite often ensues an alteration of his ego which can only be described as a setting up of the object inside the ego, as it occurs in melancholia. . . . It may be that by this introjection, which is a kind of regression to the mechanism of the oral phase, the ego makes it easier for the object to be given up or renders that process possible. It may be that this identification is the sole condition under which the id can give up its objects. *At any rate, the process, especially in the early phases of development, is a very frequent one, and it makes it possible to suppose that the character of the ego is a precipitate of abandoned object-cathexes and that it contains the history of those object-choices. . . .*
>
> When the ego assumes the features of the object, it is forcing itself, so to speak, upon the id as a love-object and is trying to make good the id's loss by saying: "Look,

you can love me too—I am so like the object." [Freud, 1923a, pp. 29 and 30, italics added; see also Freud, 1917b)

It is important to grasp what Freud is *not* saying in this passage. He is not hypothesizing about the *origins* of the ego. More specifically, he is not suggesting that the ego owes its existence to identification with love objects. The ego's origins, recall from Chapter 3, are rooted in the id's experience of drive frustration. Infants gradually develop social intelligence—the ego—as the means of negotiating the demands of the outside world, a world about which the id is totally ignorant. Without the ego to take account of reality, the id would not have its needs gratified and could not survive. Drive frustration, not object incorporation, brings the ego into being. Object loss provokes the ego to identify with (imitate?) the attributes of a person for whom the id pines. But identification triggered in this primitive way is a mixed blessing. The id is provoking the ego to attempt the impossible: to have its cake by eating it.

> Identification, in fact, is ambivalent from the very first; it can turn into an expression of tenderness as easily as into a wish for someone's removal. It [i.e., the identification] behaves like a derivative of the first, *oral* phase of the organization of libido, in which the object that we long for and prize is assimilated by eating and is in that way annihilated as such. The cannibal, as we know, has remained at this standpoint; he has a devouring affection for his enemies and only devours people of whom he is fond. (Freud, 1921, p. 105)

Freud thus was specifying that the ego's *character*—its personal traits, if you will—is shaped in large part by its history of object choices. The ego learns how to be the executive member of the personality team by incorporating the qualities of the people it loves, hates, and sometimes loses. But through all of this Freud's focus was on the enduring *structures* of personality that are thereby altered. He appeared considerably less interested in the nature of the interpersonal processes that affected those structures. His hypotheses about internalized object images had the sense of a theoretical aside. It is, of course, at such points where Freud is perceived to have neglected significant issues that opportunity opens for an object relations theorist to make an original contribution. With a few deft theoretical gestures, Freud had introduced the very entanglement of object relations with personality structure that subsequent theorists could exploit in their bid for uniqueness. For Freud, however, the real pearls in the necklace were the id, ego, and superego as they engage in dynamic interchanges with or without the benefit of internalized interpersonal relationships.

The interpersonal sense of the term *object relations* evolved with time. Where Freud's main efforts had been spent explaining how the ego achieved the aims of the id *drives,* theorists such as Melanie Klein and D. W. Winnicott focused on the infant's interpersonal strivings for safety, love, empathy, admiration, and trust. Crucial significance was now assigned to the role such personal transactions play in building the infant's perceptions of self and other. Freud's pioneering drive model was being supplanted by a theory of human intimacy. Object relations was understood as interpersonally literal: *the person's relations with "objects" (mostly people) beyond the subjective world of the self, and the enduring changes that accrue to the developing person's private world.*

Unfortunately, there is yet another fly in the ointment: Some theories are about object relations in the *interpersonal sense,* but are simultaneously *structural drive theories* in the classical sense (e.g., Hartmann, 1939, 1950a; Kernberg, 1976, 1992; Klein, 1932, 1946; Mahler, 1975). Margaret Mahler is an especially relevant example. In the previous chapter, Mahler was classified as an ego psychologist, but with some justification, Mahler could claim a place in the present chapter. Her description of the development of the ego from birth to 36 months of life certainly focuses on interpersonal events, with the infant-mother relationship as its centerpiece. On the other hand, it was Mahler's intention to describe the psychological developments embodied in the process of ego development as a central *structure* in personality. Is Mahler an ego psychologist or an object relations theorist? Both? Neither? Hybrid?

Similar questions could be asked of Melanie Klein's work, one of the main theories of the present chapter. That it is not always clear from which tree theoretical fruit has dropped is one of life's mysteries, an enigma destined to irritate only those truly obsessive historians who cannot abide apples and oranges in the same basket. Widely acknowledged as experts on this issue, psychoanalysts Greenberg and Mitchell voice the frustration of many:

> Because of this ambiguity we reject narrow definitions of object relations. Dispute as to whose theory constitutes a "true" object relations approach is a barren enterprise that has caused endless confusion. . . . (Greenberg and Mitchell, 1983, p. 13; but see Summers, 1994, chapter 1)

For our purposes, a general rule of thumb may be helpful. The degree to which a psychodynamic theorist addresses the person's relationships with significant others and the person's conception of those relationships is a measure of whether the label "object relations" is appropriate for that theory. *Alternate version of this rule:* the further the psychoanalytic theorist is from describing personality as a result of *drives* emanating from personality *structures,* the closer that theorist comes to object relations.

WHAT WOULD FREUD SAY?

Most of the changes introduced by object relations theory would have alarmed Freud (e.g., Freud & Jones, 1993, pp. 579 ff., and especially pp. 627 ff.). The creator of psychoanalysis would necessarily worry that the designers of this new interpersonal landscape had forgotten to lay track for the unstoppable locomotive of the id. He might even view with considerable puzzlement how little attention his concepts of signal anxiety, repression, and compromise formation receive in object relations theory. But it is probable that the apex of Freud's irritation would be reached when he saw what became of the Oedipus complex, superego development, and the sexual and aggressive drives. The epic war between passion and reason, he might observe, had been retold as the history of a skirmish.

No doubt, Freud would console himself with thoughts of the debts owed to classical psychoanalysis by the object relations theorists. Carrying their first mortgage with the Bank of Orthodox Psychoanalysis, the object relations theorists necessarily invest their intellectual capital in the *unconscious* meanings of interpersonal relationships. They delegate the mere cultural details of interpersonal transactions to general social psychology and to anthropology. Freud might have expected more, but the ultimate consolation, he would realize, is that psychoanalysis is alive and well even if it is no longer precisely *his* psychoanalysis.

Transitional Summary: What's in a Name?

Ego psychology. Object relations. Neo-Freudian. What's in a name? Critics complained that in classical psychoanalysis Freud had the ego playing second banana. Ego psychologists answered the critics by giving the ego equal billing. They lengthened its developmental history and beefed up the ego's résumé with a host of accomplishments independent of the id. Then the critics of ego psychology complained that the ego was guilty of overacting. It was becoming a homunculus—an actor within an actor—thereby rendering extraneous the concepts of person and personality. Object relations theorists answered the critics by adding supporting characters from the audience. Each member of the child's family was now brought on stage as a potential model of identification whose ego qualities could enhance or inhibit the child's ego development. But it was the neo-Freudians who really stopped the show. They protested that the original playwright was obsessed with sex and judged *all* the actors to be unconvincing. So they left the theater.

By most criteria the three main theorists to be considered in this chapter, Melanie Klein, D. W. Winnicott, and Heinz Kohut, are psychoanalytic object-relations theorists. By some people's standards, they are also ego psychologists or even neo-Freudians. But then, according to some, Anna Freud, the mother of ego psychology, is also an object relations theorist, and so, we might add, was Sigmund Freud (the father of the mother of ego psychology). Clearly, object relations can be perplexing.

Melanie Klein

Psychoanalysis as Pedagogy: Educating Fritz

Melanie Klein took Freud at his word. The ego is the repository of the person's history of object choices. If drive satisfaction, character, and object relations are inextricably entwined in ego functioning, then it must follow that elucidating any one ego component necessarily sheds light on the others. Melanie Klein eventually chose object relations as her beacon, but her starting point was in classical psychoanalysis.

With no formal academic training in medicine or psychology, and only a personal analysis as clinical preparation, Klein was encouraged by her analyst, Sandor Ferenczi (1873–1933), to establish her credentials in the one psychoanalytic domain immediately accessible to her: informed observation of a child's "educational upbringing" based on psychoanalytic principles. Using her own son Erich as her first subject, Klein's earliest contributions were largely enthusiastic confirmations of prevailing psychoanalytic theory and naive ideas about the liberating effects of analysis on children. She therefore chose not to describe her first psychoanalytic efforts as treatment, per se. Her relationship to the child described in the paper is also concealed.

Instead, she advanced the near-transparent fiction in her first professional paper that she was narrating an "upbringing with analytic features" of a boy named "Fritz." She portrayed her role as one of a consultant in an educational process to which she was privy (Klein, 1921/1975a, p. 44).[1] In reality, Fritz was Klein's youngest son Erich, whose intellectual and emotional development beginning before the age of three is reported in Klein's first professional papers (Grosskurth, 1987, p. 75). These first papers are theoretically unremarkable and somewhat amateurish confirmations of the prevailing idea in the psychoanalytic community that children benefit greatly from an upbringing based on psychoanalytic principles (cf. Grosskurth, 1987, pp. 74 and 77 ff.). Klein expressed her passion for psychoanalysis with a beginner's enthusiasm masquerading as the prescriptions of an authority. "I am of the opinion that no upbringing should be without analytic help because analysis affords such valuable and, from the point of view of prophylaxis, as yet incalculable assistance" (Klein, 1921/1975a, p. 45).

In these early efforts, Klein took Freud at his word when he proposed that every adult neurosis has origins in a childhood neurosis that may have escaped attention. Freud had even argued for the special theoretical importance to psychoanalysis of childhood neurosis:

> . . . it may be maintained that analysis of children's neuroses can claim to possess a specially high theoretical interest. They afford us, roughly speaking, as much help towards a proper understanding of the neuroses of adults as do children's dreams in respect to the dreams of adults. (Freud, 1918, p. 9)

Klein certainly was eager to take Freud at his word, to demonstrate that she adopted Freud's rationale as her own and was merely logically extending it. In what would become a Kleinian hallmark, however, she often greatly amplified and altered Freud's intent:

> It would therefore be advisable, with most children, to pay attention to their dawning neurotic traits; if however we wish to get hold of and remove those traits, then the earliest possible interventions of analytic observation and occasionally of actual analysis becomes an absolute necessity. I think a kind of norm might be set up in this matter. If a child, at the time when his interest in himself and his environment is aroused and expressed, shows sexual curiosity and endeavours step by step to satisfy it; if he shows no inhibitions in this and fully assimilates the enlightenment received; if also in games and phantasies he lives through a part of his instinctive impulses, especially of the Oedipus complex, uninhibited; if for instance he listens with pleasure to Grimm's fairy-tales without subsequent anxiety-manifestations and shows himself in general mentally well balanced, even in these not-too-frequent cases it might be employed with benefit, as many inhibitions from which even the best-developed people suffer or have suffered would thereby be overcome. (Klein, 1975a/ 1921, p. 52)

From limited experience linked to seemingly boundless enthusiasm, Klein saw "upbringing with psychoanalytic features" as a means of ensuring and enhancing

---

[1] Citations to the works of Melanie Klein follow the convention introduced for Freud in chapters 2, 3 and 4. Whenever possible, the original publication date is cited first so that the chronology of her changing ideas can be easily monitored.

normal development. Perhaps more important is the notion implicit in her description of the benefits of such education. Klein believed that "neurosis"—or more generally, psychopathology—gets its first foothold in the personality as an anxious inhibition or a constriction of development (Klein, 1931/1975a). Psychoanalysis as education is not only liberalizing, it can be preventive, a kind of prophylaxis for the mind.

KLEIN'S BEGINNING ASSUMPTIONS

Among the achievements from her early observations of her own and friends' children, three stand out for their subsequent elaboration by Klein into fundamental concepts of her object relations theory. From the beginning, Klein emphasized the child's imaginative reconstruction of reality in phantasy, the necessity for plain talk, adult-like interpretations and explanations, and the power of interpretation to liberate and protect a child's development from the inhibiting influences of anxiety. She also sought to rectify Freud's emphasis on the psychodynamics of the male with her own maternal-centric view of infancy as a period dominated by the child's relationship to the breast.

Phantasy Versus Fantasy: The "Unreal Real"

She discovered that from the very earliest moments of life, children construct imaginative "phantasies"—as distinguished from photographically realistic images—of the people linked with their experiences. Klein used the word *phantasy* to mean the infant's unconscious world of the "unreal real" (Klein, 1930/1975a, p. 221). *Phantasy* with the "ph" spelling, as distinguished from "fantasy," thus describes for Klein unconscious thoughts and wishes that may be occasionally actively connected by imagination to reality but need not be (cf. Mitchell 1986, p. 22).

> In Klein's concept, phantasy emanates from within and imagines what is without, it offers an unconscious commentary on instinctual life and links feelings to objects and creates a new amalgam: the world of imagination. Through its ability to phantasize, the baby tests out, primitively "thinks" about, its experiences of inside and outside. External reality can gradually affect and modify the crude hypotheses phantasy sets up. Phantasy is both the activity and its products. (Mitchell, 1986, p. 23)

The phantasy image derived and elaborated from experience *is* the child's reality; hence, it is, in Klein's own words, the world of the unreal real. Use of the "ph" version of phantasy as a semantic convention has its counterpart in James Strachey's efforts to translate Freud's writings into consistent English for *The Standard Edition*. Strachey (1966, p. xxiv) explained that he had adopted the distinctions of the *Oxford English Dictionary* which restricts the word *fantasy* to meanings of "caprice, whim, and fanciful invention" whereas *phantasy* means "imagination, visionary notion." Strachey's intention was to use the "ph" version as a technical psychological term to indicate that a Freudian phantasy was weightier than a whim.

Klein, too, preferred the "ph" version for her technical meanings. Presumably, she reserved the alternate spelling of the word—fantasy—for *consciously* whimsical imaginative constructions. It is not clear, however, that she ever used the "f" word for anything. Nevertheless, the somewhat misleading equation *phantasy = unconscious* has become a widely adopted Kleinian convention. Her observations of Fritz/Erich and other children convinced Klein that the child's phantasy world, which rarely corresponds with adult reality, is nevertheless the child's reality: unreal but real enough.

Adult-Like Interpretative Technique: Phantasy *Is* Free Association

From the beginning, Klein's interpretations to her child "patients" were unflinchingly direct and adult-like. Her unpretentious, unvarnished style probably began as a product of inexperience. A beginning psychoanalyst whose only prior experience with interpretation was a personal analysis or reading about analytic method may very well directly voice her interpretations of the unconscious meanings of the patient's associations with little thought of gentle phrasing or customized doses. Neophytes tend to apply techniques literally as they work by trial and error to increase their level of mastery. With children, moreover, Klein was pioneering a frontier with few examples to imitate.

Klein believed that direct interpretation and sympathetic acknowledgment of the child's phantasies strengthened the child in dealing with inevitable clashes of conflicting feelings. Klein had in mind such normal developmental conflicts as learning to balance love and hate for the same person and discriminating between reality and illusion (cf. Segal, 1992, p. 59).

Although we take up this issue in more detail later, it is worth noting one prominent feature of Klein's interpretative style. Klein treats the child's verbal expressions and spontaneous narratives during play as direct equivalents of adult free associations. She encouraged verbalization by providing an assortment of toys, including human and animal figures, building blocks, vehicles of all kinds, and even capitalized on the child's interest in ordinary objects in the therapy room. But she did not limit her interpretations to what the child said. The child's play, actual *behavior* with the toys, was taken as representing, even symbolizing, unconscious ideas, wishes, and phantasies. Klein again took Freud at his word. The technique and aims of psychoanalysis—interpretations of verbal reports or behavior to make the unconscious conscious—are not changed when a child is the patient. Only the medium, play, is adjusted to accommodate the child. Play, Klein believed, employs the same archaic language as dreams to represent phantasies, wishes, and experiences, and is therefore an especially suitable vehicle for interpretation to the child (Klein, 1926/1975a, p. 134). Klein's willingness to interpret verbally reported phantasies and the child's play narratives as direct equivalents to free associations became a bone of contention in a bitter rivalry that later developed with Anna Freud. We will explore some aspects of this dispute at a later point in the chapter.

What probably began as a neophyte's excessively literal execution of technique while trying to learn it could also be seen as expert adaptation of established method by a gifted therapist. Comparison of Klein's early papers with her final and most detailed report of a child analysis (Klein, 1961) suggests that the bluntness of her interpretations probably did have their *origins* in her inexperience. However, tempered by increased sophistication and accumulated clinical experience, Klein's bluntness was transformed by the middle of her career into penetrating directness of interpretations skillfully phrased and paced. Accuracy of these interpretations is a separate issue to be dealt with in a subsequent section.

Interpretation Liberates, Strengthens, Protects

Lest the impression be conveyed that Klein's interpretations were somehow more blunt or rigidly adult only when working with children other than her own, consider Klein's efforts to provide Fritz/Erich with accurate sexual enlightenment. Klein's son had matured to the stage when natural curiosity about the origins of babies manifests itself. One morning, while sitting on the chamber pot, Fritz related a phantasy that equated "kakis" (feces) with children inside a mother's stomach. He evolved these phantasies from previously provided anatomical information that he had only partially understood. On a prior occasion, Klein had attempted to provide sexual enlightenment, but had dealt only with what she believed were the conscious issues. Fritz/Erich had been very resistant to the information. Klein decided it was time for the facts of life and their unconscious meanings:

> I ask him, "These [i.e., the kakis] are the children then that grow in the stomach?" As I notice this interests him I continue, "For the kakis are made from the food; real children are not made from food." He, "I know that, they are made of milk." "Oh no, they are made of something that papa makes and the egg that is inside mamma." (He is very attentive now and asks me to explain.) When I begin once more about the little egg, he interrupts me, "I know that." I continue, "Papa can make something with his wiwi that really looks rather like milk and is called seed; he makes it like doing wiwi only not so much. Mamma's wiwi is different to [sic] papa's (he interrupts) "I know *that!*" I say, "Mamma's wiwi is like a hole. If papa puts his wiwi into mamma's wiwi and makes the seed there, then the seed runs in deeper into her body and when it meets with one of the little eggs that are inside mamma, then that little egg begins to grow, and it becomes a child." Fritz listened with great interest and said, "I would so much like to see how a child is made inside like that." I explain that this is impossible until he is big because it can't be done till then but that then he will do it himself. "But then I would like to do it to mamma." "That can't be, mamma can't be your wife for she is the wife of your papa, and then papa would have no wife." "But we could both do it to her." I say, "No, that can't be. Every man has only one wife. When you are big your mamma will be old. Then you will marry a beautiful young girl and she will be your wife." (Klein, 1921/1975a, pp. 33–34)

Apparent in Klein's frank "Fritz-explanations" is a beginning psychoanalyst's innocence of faith that theoretical doctrine is literal. Repressed sexual curiosity is a primary cause of a child's difficulties with intimacy and one determinant of generalized inhibitions against learning (Klein, 1921/1975a, p. 30; 1926/1975a, pp. 136 ff.). Psychoanalytic doctrine has it that truth liberates and strengthens, and Klein believed that more was better than less. Bluntly delivered information may even be "prophylactic," protecting the child against future anxiety and inhibition. Her only written expression of surprise in all this was how little emotional protest Fritz/Erich offered to her explanations. The last two sentences in the passage quoted above also leave the reader puzzling over a poignant question: Which of the two participants in this educational process has the most regret for having confronted reality and the most difficulty coping with the result? Keeping in mind that "Fritz" is Klein's son Erich, the best one can do is wonder what the effect of Klein's "educational" efforts might have been on the mother-son relationship.

Klein did encounter and sometimes recognize resistances to her interpretations. It is clear in several of her early papers that such resistances often took the form of the child's stubborn refusals to continue a "session," or anxious pursuit of distractions designed to divert the conversation. From these experiences Klein gradually learned to adjust her interpretations, titrating them to tolerable intensity and condensing them to a manageable degree of detail to enable the work to proceed (e.g., Klein 1921/1975a, p. 40). Such resistances were also an early indication to her of the significance of children's anxieties in shaping their phantasies. Nevertheless, the hallmark of even Klein's mature style was her blunt, unsoftened, plain language interpretations that sometimes impress observers as excessive.

Maternal-Centrism

Klein took Freud at his word, but she made every effort to correct him at those points where she felt he had gone astray. She believed that Freud had taken a giant misstep in his theoretical neglect of the mother's role. Freud's version of psychosexual development tipped the explanatory balance toward male stuff. To name some: the significance of the penis for both genders in castration anxiety and penis envy, Oedipal strivings, superego formation, the boy's guilt in competing with and surpassing his father. By contrast, Klein assigned overwhelming significance to the loving, or rejecting, breast which was the origin and the enduring core of Klein's maternal-centric psychoanalytic point of view (cf. Hughes, 1989; pp. 174–175). It has become conventional wisdom to point out that Melanie Klein intended in this way to level the balance with a focus on female stuff (cf. Sayers, 1991, pp. 3–20 and pp. 261–268). However, conventional wisdom in this instance distorts the historical facts in the service of elevating Klein's uniqueness at Freud's expense. When it came to extolling the significance and lauding the virtues of the mother's breast, Freud was no slacker. Consider his well-known pronouncement on the subject:

> A child's first erotic object is the mother's breast that nourishes it; love has its origin in attachment to the satisfied need for nourishment. There is no doubt that, to begin with, the child does not distinguish between the breast and its own body; when the breast has to be separated from the body and shifted to the "*outside*" because the child so often finds it absent, it carries with it as an "*object*" a part of the original narcissistic libidinal cathexis. This first object is later completed into the person of the child's mother, who not only nourishes it but also looks after it and thus arouses in it a number of other physical sensations, pleasurable and unpleasurable. By her care of the child's body she becomes its first seducer. *In these two relations lies the root of a mother's importance, unique, without parallel, established unalterably for a whole lifetime as the first and strongest love-object and as the prototype of all later love-relations—for both sexes.* (Freud, 1940, p. 188; emphasis added)

Freud may have been necessarily constrained to the male viewpoint, but he knew a good thing when he saw it.

In growing legend, myth, and biography, Klein is portrayed as having corrected Freud's gender-induced tunnel vision. She nevertheless began with Freud's concepts—

taking him at his word, so to say—and then expanded the words to their limits. From her analyses of her own and her friends' children, Klein drew conclusions that created entirely new, often controversial, meanings for fundamental psychoanalytic concepts. We begin with the breast.

LOVE AND HATE—LOTS AND LOTS OF HATE—AT THE BREAST

The most important object in the world for the infant—indeed, initially it is the only object—is the breast. Concerned exclusively with the gratification of its needs, the infant is limited to processing its experiences within the structure of two categories: pleasure (gratification) and pain (frustration). Riveted in this way to a rudimentary hedonism, infants gradually perceive a world populated by *good objects* (satisfying = pleasurable) and *bad objects* (frustrating = painful). However, the "goodness" or "badness" of an object is never a simple product of the amount of pleasure or pain it provides. Good (gratifying) objects are idealized in phantasy, elevating them to absolute and superlative goodness. Under the influence of the death instinct, bad objects are phantasized into monoliths of distilled hate. Because mother is sometimes a satisfier, sometimes a frustrator of the infant's self-preservative needs, she is the first and most enduring influence on the way the child learns to manage love and hate beyond this first object relationship.

Mother as Part-Object

An infant's undeveloped cognitive abilities permit it to attach to a part of a person or even to parts of his or her own body. *Pars pro toto*—"the part *is* the whole"—is the infant's motto. Most of the infant's early relationships have this *phantastic,* sometimes fragmented, and always unrealistic character. The "mother" of early infancy thus need not be the whole, real person. Mother is little more initially than a nipple protruding from a breast (Klein, 1936/1975a, p. 290). That *part-object,* however, is the fount of all goodness or, sometimes, the agent of all that is frustrating:

> The baby's first object of love and hate—his mother—is both desired and hated with all the intensity and strength that is characteristic of the early urges of the baby. In the very beginning he loves his mother at the time that she is satisfying his needs for nourishment, alleviating his feelings of hunger, and giving him the sensual pleasure which he experiences when his mouth is stimulated by sucking at her breast. This gratification is an essential part of the child's sexuality, and is indeed its initial expression. But when the baby is hungry and his desires are not gratified, or when he is feeling bodily pain or discomfort, then the whole situation suddenly alters. Hatred and aggressive feelings are aroused and he becomes dominated by the impulses to destroy the very person who is the object of all his desires and who in his mind is linked up with everything he experiences—good and bad alike. (Klein, 1937/1975a, p. 306)

From the earliest days of life, Klein argued, children struggle no less than adults do with Thanatos, the death instinct. Thanatos feeds the destructive impulses that the infant constructs through the primitive mental activity of "phantasy building" or imaginative thinking:

> When a baby feels frustrated at the breast, in his phantasies he attacks this breast; but
> if he is being gratified by the breast, he loves it and has phantasies of a pleasant kind
> in relation to it. In his aggressive phantasies he wishes to bite up and to tear up his
> mother and her breasts, and to destroy her also in other ways. (Klein, 1937/1975a,
> p. 308)

The essence of phantasy building is that wish and reality are blurred. Unable to distinguish reliably between what phantasy squeezes from desire and what experience constructs from reality, the infant, for a time, is *magically omnipotent,* able to generate hallucinatory satisfaction from the mere presence of the urge. Got milk? "Oh yes, yes!" says the phantasying baby, "I got milk. And I got the thingy that gives milk. And I get them whenever I think about them. And I think about them a whole lot."

Devouring the Breast: Persecution and Guilt

Love and hate at the breast join the blur between phantasy and reality. The infant's relationship to the breast, and therefore to the world, is nearly completely oral, almost exclusively a passive-incorporative orientation with very little reality-based active initiative or differentiation between self and not-self. Consequently, the child's phantasy building takes aim at its "object of constant desire." The breast is possessed by incorporation:

> In phantasy, the child sucks the breast into himself, chews it up and swallows it; thus
> he feels that he has actually got it there, that he possesses the mother's breast within
> himself, in both its good and bad aspects. (Klein, 1936/1957a, p. 291)

The baby phantasizes that the breast-in-the-mouth is part of self because, after all, it is "inside." Breast *is* baby and baby *is* breast. Concealed by the influence of inborn aggressiveness in the form of the death instinct, the infant's angry or destructive wishes toward mother are equivalent to death wishes: the urge to annihilate a frustrator by making it "gone." The wish itself is all powerful, and the baby can believe that it has actually killed or destroyed the object; but the object, recall, is the relatively undifferentiated fusion of breast *and* baby. Thus, the "object" that is killed or destroyed is breast-baby, mother-baby, or both. Kleinian infancy is scary.

The object world of the very young infant thus consists of part-objects, some of which are gratifying, some frustrating, some welcoming and some hostile, some inside and some outside. Hostile objects are interpreted by the infant as "persecuting" and attacking (Klein, 1936/1975a, p. 293). To defend itself, the infant incorporates as much of the safe and gratifying good breast as possible, eventually extending its "greedy" impulses to the mother's entire body. Erotic and aggressive impulses are fused into *infantile sadism,* an actively aggressive stance toward love objects. "Greedy, erotic and destructive phantasies and feelings have for their object the inside of the mother's body. In his imagination the child attacks it, robbing it of everything it contains and eating it up" (Klein, 1936/1975a, p. 293). Kleinian infancy is very scary.

Parallel with the maturation taking place in the infant's emotional life is the child's growing sophistication in perceiving its love-objects. Some time after four or five months of life, mother is transformed from a pair of part-objects to a pair of contrasting whole objects. Good and bad *breasts* become good and bad *mothers.* Now the clash of love and hate—the fear of being attacked by a gratifying but frightening object—is targeted to the mother as a *person*. This developmental achievement not only permits the transformation of a fragmentary part-object image into a whole human being, it raises the stakes in the aggression game and heightens the risks.

The infant experiences an intensification of its conflict about good and bad objects. Things have gradually grown more complex: How can I cope consistently with a good-mother-who-is-also-sometimes-a-bad-mother? One strategy might be to protect the good object with a preemptive first strike against the bad. Annihilate bad mommy before she is really, really bad and attacks you. But such infantile logic clashes with infantile good sense. Good and bad are no longer separate part-objects. Mommy is a whole person. Therefore, it is possible, the infant now calculates, to destroy the loving good object even when one intends to destroy only the persecutory bad object. This dim awareness that the love object is in danger sharpens the infant's realization that it is he or she who, in fact, has created that danger (Klein, 1936/1975a, p. 295).

Guilt feelings are thus added to the pain of the conflict between love and hate. The infant now has a veritable laundry list of fears:

- persecution *by* the internalized bad object
- its own persecution *of* the hated bad object
- losing control of its own aggression toward the bad object and damaging or annihilating the good object
- death or loss of the mother, who is now perceived as a whole but endangered person.

Kleinian infancy is very, very scary.

SADISM AND THE OEDIPUS COMPLEX

To explain sustained human development—indeed just minimally to acknowledge that something resembling a civilized person rather than a mildly remorseful cannibal ordinarily emerges from childhood—Klein had to expand her scope beyond raw aggression.

The Littlest, Cruelest Superego

Klein's observations led her to believe that the Oedipus complex is triggered at the time of weaning from the breast, when sadistic oral and anal impulses are dominant. In her earliest papers, Klein (1921/1975a; 1923/1975a) had first reported observations that indicated the presence of a sadistic superego as early as age two. In contrast to Freud's view of genital dominance in the Oedipal phase, Klein believed that the dynamics of the classic Oedipus complex emerge only when they build on these earlier, more amorphous and more unruly impulses (Klein, 1929/1975a, p. 212; 1933/1975a, p. 251). Under the influence of the death instinct, an extremely sadistic, self-punishing version of the Oedipus complex was already being enacted, according to

Klein, as much as three years earlier than Freud had envisioned. Eventually, Klein (1933/1975) located the origins of the superego and a rudimentary Oedipus complex even earlier in development—in the first half of the first year of life.

"Epistemophilic Instinct" and the Femininity Phase

The infant's ego is undeveloped and poorly equipped to understand the nature of the oral and anal impulses that are mounting in intensity. Feeling overwhelmed in the face of these unruly urges, the infant's ego is nevertheless intensely curious about them. Because of the importance she attributed to the child's sexual curiosity, Klein christened it with the formal name *epistemophilic instinct.*

But about precisely *what* is the child sexually curious? Klein's interpretations of older children's phantasies led her to believe that infants and younger children, caught up in a confusing swirl of oral, anal and emerging genital impulses, are curious about those same processes in the love object. Therefore, the child's urge to know is directed at first to the mother's body which the child believes is the site of all sexual processes. The young child phantasizes that inside the mother's body are feces, sexual organs, and even father's penis. Still incorporative in its relation to the world and dominated by aggression, the child is not only curious about mother's body and its contents, but desires strongly to take possession of it. Klein called this phase of development the *femininity phase* because infants of both genders actively identify with and envy the mother they seek to possess (Klein 1928/1975a, p. 189). Both boys and girls are dominated early in infancy by their desire to possess the mother's "special sexual organs." Put another way, children of both genders experience "breast envy" and "womb envy."

The infant's intense sexual curiosity meets initially only with frustration because the primitive ego lacks language with which to ask questions about sexual urges, body parts and how they work. Even somewhat later, when the child can formulate rudimentary questions, frustration is rekindled because the child realizes that most of the interesting questions remain unanswered (Klein, 1928/1975, p. 188). Early and late frustrations turn to grievances, and the infant grows indignant.

Inhibition of the child's sexual curiosity can generalize over time to constrict all forms of the desire to know. Haunting feelings of being incompetent and impotent that are not limited to sexual matters may result. Angry grievances over "not knowing" may impede the child's development of generalized intellectual competency and skills needed to meet the demands that life makes.

The Oedipus Complex in Boys

Klein's version of the Oedipus complex trumps Freud's penis envy with "womb envy" as the universally prior and dominant oedipal motive. The sexual organs of interest to the boy include not only the womb, but the breasts and vagina as well. Nevertheless, unresolved sadistic and aggressive impulses are still operating toward this same love object, so that the male infant not only wants to learn about these organs and to possess them, but also to injure or destroy them. Yet, the infant also is fearful of retaliation for its hatred. Klein proceeds to a grand slam, completely reversing Freud's concepts, by suggesting that the mother, too, can be part of the male's castration fears:

> The boy fears punishment for his destruction of his mother's body, but, besides this, his fear is of a more general nature, and here we have an analogy to the anxiety associated with castration-wishes of the girl. He fears that his body will be mutilated and dismembered, and this dread also means castration. Here we have a direct contribution to the castration complex. In this early period of development the mother who takes away the child's faeces signifies also a mother who dismembers and castrates him. Not only by means of the anal frustrations which she inflicts does she pave the way for the castration complex: in terms of psychic reality she *is* also already the castrator. (Klein 1928/1975a, p. 190)

Klein further hypothesized that infants of both genders phantasize that the mother incorporates orally one or more of father's many penises. As a result, infants envy the mother, but also fear what might be inside her. For the boy, the mother-who-incorporates-father's-penis is a "woman with a penis," that is, an amalgam of father and mother. It does not go unnoticed by the boy that mother has "taken" a penis from a man. In short, mother can be a castrator (Klein, 1932/1975a, pp. 131, 245).

Thus the male child is caught in a painful clash of oral, anal and genital impulses. Overlapping toilet training, during which the mother must at least partially frustrate the child's anal impulses as she sometimes has frustrated its earlier oral urges, the femininity phase rekindles feelings of intense anger toward the frustrator. Klein (1928/1975, p. 189 ff.) believes that this new *anal frustration* is in fact a "second trauma" that prompts the child eventually to devalue the frustrating love object. Children of both genders may thus be prompted to turn away from the mother and move toward the father. But it is the boy who narcissistically learns to overvalue the penis. His insecurity over not being able to have a baby because he has no womb is concealed behind a façade of ever-escalating curiosity about wombs impelled by his epistemophilic drive. He can become an expert on where babies come from even if he can't have one. Hence, the boy directs his sexual urges and fears into curiosity and information gathering. In this way, intellectual challenges at which eventually he can feel superior displace the anatomical deficiencies that made him feel inferior (Klein, 1928/1975a, p. 191). Those who can't do, think.

Under the influence of his emerging genital impulses and natural sexual curiosity, the boy desires his mother as a love-object. But recall that he experiences her as a frustrator of his oral and anal needs, and his accumulated feelings of hatred are now amplified to encompass genital urges. To make matters more difficult, an early and incomplete version of castration anxiety in the form of jealousy and fear of the father makes itself felt, although full castration fear at the hands of the father will not materialize until later, around the ages of four and five years. Now, however, as early as age one or two years, the male child is caught on the horns of a three-pronged dilemma: desire to possess the mother, hatred of her as a frustrator-castrator, and an amorphous fear that father will take revenge.

The Oedipus Complex in Girls

After weaning, the girl turns away from her frustrating mother and is further encouraged to devalue her mother by the anal deprivations she feels mother imposes. Klein proposed that the girl infant unconsciously senses her vagina and other sexual equipment as soon as the stirrings of the oedipal impulses begin (Klein, 1928/1975a,

p. 192). Unlike her male counterpart, the female infant gains little gratification from masturbation for these newly emerging genital impulses. Envy and hatred of the mother arise because the girl believes that mother not only possesses the father but also the father's penis. As time progresses, the more classical form of oedipal dynamics (actually *Electra* dynamics) appear as the girl grows more attached to father, experiences his attentions erotically, and becomes increasingly resentful of mother.

> The little girl's epistemophilic impulse is first roused by the Oedipus complex; the result is that she discovers her lack of a penis. She feels this lack to be a fresh cause of hatred of the mother, but at the same time her sense of guilt makes her regard it as a punishment. This embitters her frustration in this direction, and, in its turn, exercises a profound influence on the whole castration complex. (Klein, 1928/1975a, p. 193)

Analogous to the boy's castration anxiety in the full Oedipus complex described by Freud, the girl, too, has a primal fear. She desires to empty her mother's body of all its goodness, including the father's penis she imagines within it, feces, and other children. But the girl phantasizes that the mother may turn the tables on her to retaliate by emptying the child's body of these good things. In short, the mother can attack the self and destroy, devour, or annihilate it. Klein regarded this terrible fear of being destroyed by mother to be the fundamental and universal danger situation among woman. At later stages of development, this fear of an attacking mother is transformed into a fear of losing the real mother (Klein, 1929/1975, p. 217).

Mother-as-love-object is thus closely associated with guilt and anxiety. Consequently, during infancy, Klein argued, the girl finds for a brief time that she can identify with the father more easily than with the mother. But the little girl, in Klein's portrayal of her, is a contrary creature. Guilt provokes another attempt to form a new love relationship with mother, but it bears the hallmarks of overcompensation and reaction formation. She overdoes it to the point of being saccharine and ungenuine. "Me thinks the little lady protests too much." Yet, even this new attempt at a loving relationship is doomed for the girl by a fresh round of hatred and rivalry with mother for father's attentions. The girl gives up her attempts to identify with father. Instead she comes to view father as a love object from whom she can obtain love and to whom she may give love without necessarily being like him. More or less by default, mother becomes the girl's object of identification (Klein, 1928/1975a, pp. 193–94).

In the end—and there is an end, thank you—the girl, unlike the boy, has to come to grips with unrelenting frustration. Despite the boy's fears to the contrary, he does actually possess a penis; but the girl must endure permanently unfulfilled desire for a penis and deferred desire for a baby.

HOW IT ALL TURNS OUT: KLEIN'S FIRST THEORY OF THE SUPEREGO

Ultimately, the girl models herself on her *phantasy* of the mother in both its cruel and nurturing aspects. "From the early identification with the mother in which the anal-sadistic level so largely preponderates, the little girl derives jealousy and hatred and forms a cruel super-ego after the maternal imago" (Klein, 1928/1975a, p. 195). Fortunately, as the little girl matures and as her genital impulses assume dominance over the oral and anal sadism of early infancy, she identifies more and more with mother's nurturing, kind, and generous qualities. She even phantasizes an idealized image of the "bountiful mother" who may be more a product of wish than reality.

The boy's development is along similar lines with a slightly different outcome for his superego. Initially, the boy also acquires a severe superego modeled on the cruel-sadistic image he has constructed of mother-breast in phantasy. And, like his female counterpart, maturity finds the boy incorporating in a more modest way the kinder, nurturing aspects of the maternal image. But boys ultimately have to identify more strongly with *father,* and it is the *idealized* father image that becomes the dominant quality in the boy's superego.

Klein (1927; see especially 1928, pp. 197 ff.) argued early in her career that her account of the Oedipus complex, including the infant's hatred and its origins in an early, cruel superego, did not contradict Freud's model. She felt that her ideas extended Freud's without substantially challenging his fundamental meanings. Nevertheless, Klein's ideas continued to evolve, and in her considerations of the extended process of personality development, she began gradually but discernibly to diminish the importance allotted to hatred. With little public fanfare, the psychoanalytic community began to notice, even if Klein apparently did not, that her "conceptual extensions" were appropriating Freud's ideas and inexorably transforming them into Klein's (e.g., A. Freud 1927, pp. 37–40; and A. Freud, 1952/1992, p. 63; Freud & Jones, 1993, pp. 621 ff., see especially Freud's letters to Jones, # 508, p. 624; and letter # 509. pp. 627 ff).

"RICHARD": EXTRACTS FROM AN ILLUSTRATIVE CASE

Near the end of her life, Klein decided to publish an extended case history of a ten-year-old boy she had analyzed for four months during World War II. At the height of the war in 1941, Klein moved to Pitlochry, Scotland, to treat two children and simultaneously evade the London bombings. Indeed, Klein was in the middle of two wars. Around her raged the world conflict of Axis and Allies, but on the home front she fought a different kind of war with Anna Freud. The dominant dispute within British psychoanalysis at the time was whether Anna Freud's verbal method or Melanie Klein's play technique was "really" psychoanalysis. More about the personal war shortly. For now, the case of "Richard" is a particularly effective illustration of the state of Klein's thinking through the 1940s.

Klein had used elements of this case history earlier to illustrate some of her papers on the Oedipus complex (e.g., Klein, 1945/1975a). However, in *Narrative of a Child Analysis,* Klein (1961) presented her detailed session notes along with some of the child's drawings from 96 daily meetings (not the 93 erroneously listed in the *Narrative*). Klein's biographer, Phyllis Grosskurth (1986, p. 267), who had access to Klein's calendar diary, was able to correct the session count. In the same way, Grosskurth was able to date exactly the period of therapy. The analysis began on April

FIGURE 5.1   Melanie Klein's ten-year-old patient "Richard."

28 and ended on August 23, 1941. One extended interruption of eight to ten days occurred when Klein traveled to London. A few additional sessions were skipped when Richard was sick or visiting family with his mother. Figure 5.1 shows "Richard" around the time of his analysis with Klein.

What is remarkable about the case is both its level of narrative detail and the especially clear window it opens on Klein's diagnostic and therapy techniques. The latter may have been considerably sharper than the former. The case also serves as an excellent account of how Klein translated her early theoretical concepts into interpretations to be made to a ten-year-old boy.

Richard's Presenting Problem and Family Background

Richard's mother referred the child to Melanie Klein because he had been unable to relate normally to other children in school, was aggressive and hard to control at home and in school, and eventually refused to go to school altogether. The mother, herself a rather anxious woman, seems to have had an ambivalent attitude toward her youngest son with some degree of resentment for his occasional clingyness. Richard's father appears to have been a detached and distracted man who was largely uninvolved with the child's daily care. An older brother by 11 years, then serving in the army, had been the preferred child.

Richard's older cousin, "Dick," had been in analysis with Melanie Klein, and the report of his treatment is widely regarded as the first published psychoanalysis of a psychotic or possibly autistic child (Klein, 1930/1975a; see Grosskurth, 1986, p. 266n). It was cousin "Richard," however, who became the subject of Klein's most extensive published case. Younger than Dick by six years, Richard exhibited severe interpersonal difficulties, confused thinking, and catastrophic levels of anxiety regarding the ongoing war around him. However, Richard's anxieties also had a paranoid quality that centered on fears of being poisoned and worries about being spied upon, and Klein soon found such anxieties to be linked to the images of his internal phantasy world. Indeed, Klein was critical of both mothers' relationships to their sons and appears to have concluded that neither child had been given the close, warm and empathic mothering she regarded as essential to normal development.

Dick's mother had convinced Klein to join her and her son in the Scottish mountain village of Pitlochry in order for Dick to resume his analysis with Klein. Around the same time, cousin Richard and his mother were evacuated to Scotland, and Richard also became Klein's patient. Shortly after leaving London, Richard's home was bombed, a sad and frightening reality of which Richard was aware and which made its impact on his imagination, intensifying his feelings of vulnerability.

From the outset, Klein knew that the period of treatment would be no more than four months, a relatively brief course of analysis for such serious presenting problems. Nevertheless, she undertook the task and saw Richard several times a week in a rented "hut" or cottage that was used by the Girl Guides (an organization similar to the American Girl Scouts) as their headquarters. The setting was a bit unusual because a variety of Girl Guide artifacts, such as wall maps, pots and pans and such, could not be removed from the room, but Klein's own living quarters were even more unsuitable for treating a child. To begin a session, Klein had to unlock the "hut," as it was called, gain entry, light a fire, and keep track of Richard.

Richard's First Session: Anxieties and Worries, Worries and Anxieties

Richard was able even in the first session to establish a workable rapport with Klein. He told her how frightened he was of going to school, how he often could not sleep because he was worried about his mother's health, and how interested but worried he was about the ongoing war. He described his experiences of the London bombings, and had once seen the results of a detonated bomb near his home. Not much damage, he reported, only some windows blown out and the green house in the garden had collapsed, but their poor cook had been alone in the house at the time and was badly frightened. He spoke about Hitler's cruel treatment of conquered countries, how Hitler was himself an Austrian but treated the Austrians very badly. And wasn't Mrs. Klein herself an Austrian?

Richard described how he worried that a "tramp" might break in during the night and kidnap his Mummy. He envisioned himself going to her rescue, and making the tramp unconscious by scalding him with boiling water. He would not mind being killed except for the fact that it would prevent him from saving Mummy. Klein interpreted to Richard that his fears were a parallel to his feelings about Hitler, the Austrians, and what happens at night in his parents' bedroom:

> At night he might have been afraid that when his parents went to bed something
> could happen between them with their genitals that would injure Mummy. . . . *Mrs.*
> *K.* Interpreted that he might have contradictory thoughts about Daddy. Although
> Richard knew that Daddy was a kind man, at night, when he was frightened, he might
> fear that Daddy was doing some harm to Mummy. When he thought of the tramp, he

did not remember that Daddy, who was in the bedroom with Mummy, would protect her; and that was, Mrs. K. suggested, because he felt that it was Daddy himself who might hurt Mummy. (Klein, 1961, p. 21)

One might suppose that the immediacy, adult level content, and directness of Klein's interpretations drove Richard screaming from the Girl Guides' hut. On the contrary, Klein reports that after she had clarified the meaning of "genitals" to him, Richard became thoughtful and appeared impressed with her interpretation.

And so it went for the next several months. Klein and Richard developed a close, almost tender relationship through which Richard learned the Kleinian vocabulary for inner distress. As he became more adept in the new idiom, Richard's verbal tolerance for anxiety seemingly strengthened, but his conversational stories and crayon drawings grew primordial. One explanation for this effect is that Klein's interpretations assisted Richard to detoxify and assimilate increasingly deeper unconscious phantasies. An alternative explanation is that Richard's growing attachment to Mrs. K. is reflected in an enhanced facility with her language and increased willingness to use it in playing this most interesting of games. Indeed, it may even be the case that some combination of the two processes operated throughout the treatment.

Overview of Richard's First and Last Sessions

As always, Klein had available some toys and drawing materials in the Girl Guides' hut, but after a time Richard chose to focus on constructing a series of drawings.

Figure 5.2 reproduces Richard's first and last drawings. The first drawing actually required two sessions, 12 and 14, to complete. The last drawing, of a total of 74 pictures reproduced in Klein's *Narrative of a Child Psychoanalysis,* was done in session 90. Beneath each picture is an extract of Klein's commentary on and interpretation of the drawing to Richard as recorded in her daily notes. The subject matter of Richard's first drawing makes clear the degree to which the reality of the war fueled the boy's anxieties, but Klein teaches Richard that his war stories are also a medium through which he expresses his internal phantasies. According to this scenario, which Richard accepted with interest, Klein interpreted to Richard that the British ships represented Richard's own family, whereas the "enemy" German U-boats are Richard and his brother John. Richard believes unconsciously that he and his brother are dangerous to the family, especially to mother. Klein explained to Richard that his drawing of U-boats and ships thus expresses his unconscious conflict: He desires both to protect and to attack his parents, and he imagines similar motives in them directed toward him.

After four months, near the end of his analysis, Richard produced the simply graceful and metaphorical DRAWING 74, shown as the *second* picture of Figure 5.2. He identified the picture as a "railway," and he ran his pencil through the curves repeatedly while drawing it. On its face, the drawing is certainly alive with far less anxiety than all of his earlier drawings, and even Richard's demeanor during the final sessions is far more reserved, almost melancholy, as he prepares to end his analysis with "Mrs. Klein." On the basis of Richard's associations, Klein interprets to him that the railway drawing is a representation of his mother's body, especially the breast, nipple, and stomach. The caption for Figure 5.2 elaborates the details of her interpretation.

FIGURE 5.2   First and Last Drawings of Melanie Klein's ten-year-old patient "Richard."

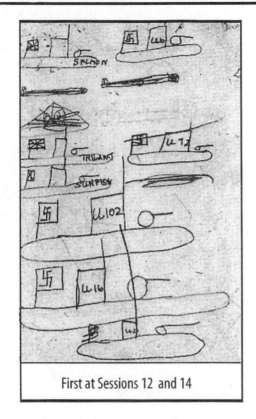

First at Sessions 12 and 14

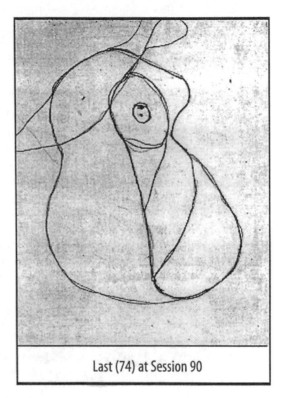

Last (74) at Session 90

"Richard said there was an attack going on, but he did not know who would attack first. . . . He pointed at U 102 and said that 10 was his own age; and to U16 he associated the age of John Wilson [another of Mrs. Klein's patients whom Richard knew]. He was . . . extremely interested to find that drawing could be a means of expressing unconscious thoughts. Mrs. K. pointed out that the number also indicated that he and John were represented by German U-boats, and were therefore hostile and dangerous to the British . . . , [and] that the British represented his own family and that he had already recognized that he not only loved and wished to protect, but also wished to attack them. . . ."

(Klein, 1961, p. 56)

"[Richard] . . . said it was a railway line and made his pencil go over it repeatedly; this stood for a train travelling. Mrs K. interpreted the exploration of Mummy's (now Mrs. K.'s) inside and pointed out that the drawing of the railway line was in the shape of a female body. After Mrs. K.'s interpretation he pointed to the circle near the top and said that this was the breast. The smaller circle was the nipple. He suddenly pounced on it with his pencil, making the dot in the centre, but at once restrained himself from making further dots— obviously preventing himself from destroying Mrs. K.'s breast and body."

(Klein, 1961, p. 451)

A crucial difference reflected in the first and last drawings of Figure 5.2 is the great change in the way Richard experiences and copes with anxiety. It is clear that some positive emotional change has occurred in this child that is probably not attributable solely to the passage of time, a mere four months. Richard's first and last artistic efforts reveal a developmental progression from a worried, vulnerable-feeling and chaotic child to a calmer, certainly more introspective ten year old who is more skillful in containing his fears. He has acquired the verbal and visual vocabulary of a Kleinian analysand, and the acquisition appears to have been beneficial.

Beginning Phase of Richard's Analysis: The Starfish Drawings

By session 15, Klein focuses Richard on the dynamics of his family life. His feelings toward his mother, father, and brother, and his conflicts about them are central opening issues of the analysis. His first "starfish" drawing, reproduced in Figure 5.3, shows Richard's anxious interest in the ongoing war, but the war has become a shaky metaphor for his own inner conflicts. Richard freely associates to the elements of his picture that the topmost fish is Mummy, who has swallowed a ragged-edge starfish who hurts her by breaking through her body with its sharp edges. The U-boat attacking the submarine in the drawing, Klein suggests to Richard, is Richard attacking Daddy to punish Hitler-Daddy for putting such a dangerous thing inside Mummy.

A similar drawing made in the next session began with Richard's exclamation that he was making a "wild picture." The starfishes surrounding the British ship *Emden* had grown "greedy." Klein pointed out to Richard that each starfish in the cluster was more jagged than previous ones. Perhaps, she proposed, these "greedy" destructive starfish represent teeth that want to attack Mummy's breasts (the ship's two funnels). Equally significant, Richard had drawn the *Emden* sunk below the surface of the water, a feature that Klein thought was worth interpreting. The caption to the second picture (DRAWING 8) in Figure 5.3 indicates the meaning that Klein attached to "sunk Mummy."

Early Middle Phase of Richard's Analysis: The Empire Drawings

By the 17th session, Richard's starfish had become larger and more colorful. Starfish became the central elements of his drawings. DRAWING 9, shown as the *first* picture in Figure 5.4, has a rather pointy, multicolored creature inside a circle. Klein reminded Richard of their work together in previous sessions which had "established" the starfish creature as Daddy's genital inside mommy. Now Klein suggested to Richard that the encircled paternal genital was making mommy bleed, as shown in the red circular border around the creature. Klein pointed out to Richard that the starfish actually has a double meaning, as related in the caption to the *first* picture in Figure 5.4.

By session 23, the compartmented starfish drawings are transformed in meaning by Richard to "empire drawings" which depict countries with all their various parts. "There was no fighting. 'They come in but the smaller countries don't mind being taken' " (Klein, 1961, p. 107). Most likely Richard's interest in the daily reports of the ongoing war and the maps on the walls of the therapy room stirred his imagination in the direction of a geography metaphor. Drawings 12 and 13, shown as the *second* picture in Figure 5.4, employ various colors to represent different countries but now

FIGURE 5.3   Starfish/War drawings of Melanie Klein's ten-year-old patient "Richard."

Drawing 7 at Session 15

Drawing 8 at Session 16

"[Richard said] . . . the starfishes were babies, the fish was Mummy who had put her head above the periscope so that the U-boat should not see the British ship. It would be deceived because it saw nothing but yellow. . . . The fat fish on top was also Mummy. She had eaten a starfish, which was now breaking through with its edges and hurting her. . . . Mrs. K. interpreted that the upper U-boat which was attacking the submarine represented Richard attacking Daddy. . . . Richard wanted to punish the Hitler-Daddy for having put such a dangerous starfish genital into Mummy—the fat fish on top—which injured her inside."

(Klein, 1961, p. 70)

"[Richard said] he was making a 'wild picture' . . . Richard explained that the starfishes were 'very greedy'; they were all round the sunk Emden and wanted to attack her. They hated her and wanted to help the British. . . . Mrs. K. interpreted that Richard's need to make a 'wild' picture was expressed by the starfishes having so many more jagged edges that in former drawings and, since Richard said that they were 'very greedy,' Mrs. K. suggested that these edges represented the teeth of the greedy babies. They came so close to the Emden because they attacked her breasts (the two funnels). The sunk Emden stood for Mummy who died because she was eaten and destroyed by the children. . . . "

(Klein, 1961, p. 73)

the countries are like the various members of Richard's family. The topmost "empire-starfish" (DRAWINGS 12, 13) was done in session 12, but the empire-starfish located at the bottom of the picture was added in the following session. Richard's color code for the various members of his family is given in the caption to the picture. Klein's interpretations to Richard throughout this period emphasize oedipal themes and persecution by internalized bad objects.

By the 24th session, Klein's interpretations appear to be having an effect. Richard shows some indications of resistance, including arriving late for his appointment, remaining silent much of the time, and generally looking unhappy (Klein, 1961, p. 110). Richard finally speaks about his current worry over a possible German invasion he has heard about from news broadcasts. He asks Klein whether she could continue to see him if there were an invasion. Worry or wish? As the conversation progressed, Richard completed DRAWING 14, shown as the *third* picture in Figure 5.4. The empire-starfish became expansive, and the sections assigned to mommy and to Richard himself had grown in size. At that point, Richard told Mrs. Klein that he was happy.

With a child's wisdom, Richard then asks, "Do I really think this of all of you? I don't know if I do. How can you really know what I think?" (Klein, 1961, p. 111). Richard's remark starkly points up the dilemma for the reader of an extended case such as this. From Klein's report, her interpretations elicit agreement from the child, promote further associations, and appear to have a positive effect on Richard's anxieties. But Richard's remark raises another possibility, that of a child eager to please his therapist-friend by colluding in an eccentric game, but helped more by the relationship with such an attentive person than by the actual content of the interpretations. That Richard voices his skepticism at all is rather remarkable evidence that at least to a small degree, this child is aware that he sometimes plays a role for the substantial benefit of sustaining the play.

Terminating Richard's Analysis: Portraits of Mrs. K.

Toward the end of the analysis, Richard's anger was coming to the fore. Family events and the therapy itself conspired to provoke angry outbreaks directed to Klein herself. At session 65, Richard drew a portrait of his therapist (DRAWING 55), shown as the *first* picture in Figure 5.5. The picture is hand-labeled and portrays Mrs. Klein with breasts but no arms. She has a small "v" above the right leg and a large "V" closed at the top placed between the breasts and extending the length of the trunk. Klein understood the victory letters to be not only expressions of Richard's oedipal rivalry with his father alluded to in her interpretation, but also a kind of triumph of Richard over his therapist (Klein, 1961, 424). The caption to DRAWING 55 in Figure 5.5 gives the details of Klein's interpretation of her portrait to Richard in her own words.

By session 83, Richard's anger is making itself known in furious scribblings and page tearings during the session. He completes the portrait shown as the *second* picture (PICTURE 68) in Figure 5.5, a rather primitive figure drawing showing Mrs. K. with breasts and a penis. The picture is labeled "sweet Mrs. Klein," and Richard has written "lovely eyes" on Mrs. K.'s forehead. Klein's interpretation is given in the caption to PICTURE 68 in Figure 5.5, and indicates that she was alert to Richard's desultory attempts to hide his anger toward her. As the session progressed, Richard's face became red, he

FIGURE 5.4   **"Empire" Drawings of Melanie Klein's ten-year-old patient "Richard."**

Drawing 9 at Session 17

Drawings 12 and 13 at Session 23

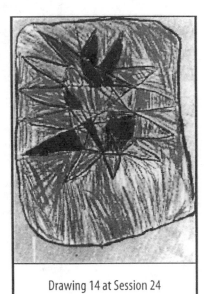

Drawing 14 at Session 24

"Mrs. K. reminded [Richard] that two days ago . . . a starfish had represented Daddy's devouring genital which the fish-Mummy had eaten, and he drew that at the time when Mummy had a sore throat. . . . In today's drawing the big starfish also seemed to represent Daddy's devoured genital which made her bleed because it ate her inside; this was shown by the red border round the starfish. The starfish also stood for the greedy and frustrated baby—himself—injuring and eating Mummy's inside when he wanted her and she did not come."

(Klein, 1961, p. 79)

"[Richard] . . . said this was an empire and the various colours represented different countries. . . . Mrs. K. suggested, referring back to the first drawing in this session, that this empire again represented the family. Richard at once agreed. He said that the nasty black was Paul, the light blue was Mummy, the puple was the maid (Bessie) and the cook. The very small area of heliotrope blue in the centre was himself, and the red was Daddy. Suddenly he said, 'And the whole is a greedy starfish full of big teeth.' "

(Klein, 1961, pp 107–108)

". . . as he was about to fill in the red sections [Richard] . . . announced, 'This is me, and you will see what a large part of the empire I get.' Then he coloured some sections light blue, and while doing so he looked up at Mrs. K. and said, 'I feel happy.' . . . A moment later . . . he said, 'Can you see how Mummy has spread herself. She has got much more of the empire.' . . . He left a few sections near the centre blank and now filled them in with black, saying that Daddy was squeezed in. . . . When he finished, he paused . . . and asked, 'Do I really think this of all of you? I don't know if I do. How can you really know what I think?' "

(Klein, 1961, p. 111)

FIGURE 5.5   Views of Melanie Klein by her ten-year-old patient "Richard".

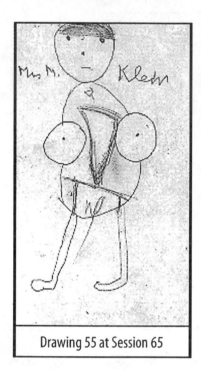

Drawing 55 at Session 65

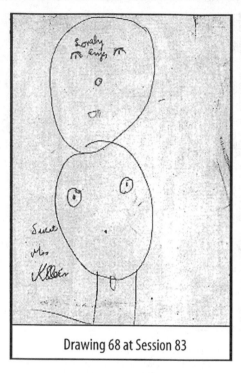

Drawing 68 at Session 83

"Mrs. K. asked what the uncompleted triangle had meant. Richard replied that it was V for victory. Mrs. K. interpreted that there was also a small V above the right leg, and asked who the bigger victory belonged to. Richard replied that it was his, and Daddy had the smaller victory."

(Klein, 1961, p. 323)

"[Richard] . . . leaned forward, looking into Mrs. K.'s eyes, and said that she had such lovely eyes. (This sounded entirely false and artificial.) After saying this, Richard added the penis on the drawing and asked Mrs. K. what the "tops of the breasts" (meaning the nipples) were called. Mrs. K. interpreted that her tummy was also a face—actually Hitler's—inside her, and that the penis he had added seemed to be Hitler's."

(Klein, 1961, p. 421)

scribbled furiously with far less control than usual, and he referred several times to the scribblings as showing Mrs. K. "in bits." Richard was angry with Klein both for symbolic and for real reasons. Symbolically, she has come to represent his parents toward whom he has conflicted feelings; but simultaneously, Richard had become attached to Mrs. Klein and was aware that their work together was drawing to a close. He discussed the train that she would take to leave Scotland, and he expressed his worries about what would happen to her in the bombings when she had gone back to London. On the whole, Richard was the embodiment of a miserable, angry, and anxious boy about to lose his therapist.

In the few remaining sessions, Richard is alternately sad and exuberant. Klein relentlessly continues to interpret the material Richard presents, but she does so at the same time that she cooperates with his play, joining him sometimes in doing tasks about the Girl Guides hut or in the garden and kitchen. It is clear that both therapist and patient are aware of the approaching termination. By session 93, on August 23, 1941, which Klein lists as the last session (although Grosskurth's [1986, p. 267] review of Klein's daily notes indicates there were 96 sessions), therapist and patient are determined to get the most out of their last meeting. Grosskurth published Klein's private notes written after the last session:

> 23rd Aug. 1941. Last day. Let's get the most out of it.—K. sad?—K. very sorry etc. R. Pleased—Is she going to cry? [His eyes watering]—R. pleased.—Should not kiss him, parting.—Some days ago when so clinging, asked to be kissed.—To-day's mood— serious, some depression, but determined & resolved. . . . (Quoted in Grosskurth, 1986, pp. 268–269)

Her final note also indicates that Richard spent part of the last session arranging two chairs under a table to represent himself and Mrs. K. staying together. Richard expressed his desire to return to London with Mrs. K. and Klein actually considered the possibility, but Richard's mother opposed the idea. Eventually, Klein and Richard decided on postcards to keep in touch.

For the next year or so, Richard's mother wrote to Klein, reporting continued difficulties in relating to other children, aggressive, even violent behavior toward other children and animals, and a tendency to be "deceitful" and disobedient (Grosskurth, 1986, p. 276). Despite these problems, Richard's mother wrote to Klein that she did not think the analysis had been completed without some positive effect because Richard did show some indications of gaining "insight into himself." Sometimes Richard's mother would "bombard" Klein with letters to which Klein occasionally responded by offering pragmatic parenting advice or an optimistic reframing of Richard's aggression as something positive. By January, 1942, the flow of letters subsided. Richard's mother began to see her son as a person with unique characteristics and had grown more accepting of him (Grosskurth, 1986, p. 277).

The Adult "Richard" Remembers Mrs. K.

Grosskurth (1986, pp. 272 ff.) reports that she "fortuitously" met the adult Richard and was able to obtain some of his recollections of his childhood analysis with Melanie Klein. He had not read Klein's *Narrative,* and until Grosskurth established that the man was indeed *the* Richard of the book, "Richard" had no idea that at least in psychoanalytic circles he was famous.

Grosskurth provided few identifying details, but she states that the man had no contact with psychoanalysis, and traveled widely, "usually to remote places covered most of the year in snow, under which lie extinct volcanoes" (1986, p. 272). He recalled Melanie Klein as a "sympathetic" woman who was somewhat ungainly, had bad feet, and a rather loose lower lip that hung down. When shown a picture of Klein on the cover of the *Narrative,* "Richard" kissed the photograph with the comment "Dear old Melanie." Clearly the man's memories of his therapist were warm ones.

He remembered that Mrs. K. talked a lot about "mummy's big genital" and "Daddy's big genital," and "good and bad Mommy-Daddy genitals." He recalled a discussion about the war in which the Allies were to seize Berlin and then the city of Brest. Melanie, he recalls, "seized" on Brest which, to no one's particular surprise, became "b-r-e-a-s-t." He remembers after Klein departed for London, he had been enrolled in a day school and had become "not unhappy" and a "sociable solitary." Grosskurth took the opportunity to ask the adult "Richard" the big question:

> "What kind of little boy do you think you were at the age of ten?"
>   "Well, dispassionately, looking back on it, I think I was a pretty appalling sort of kid. . . ."
>   "Why?"
>   "I always had quite a temper. I think I'm still somewhat like this. I flew into a panic several days ago at the office about something very trivial. Tiny things do rattle me. That's my nature. I've always been very impatient." (Grosskurth, 1986, p. 274)

Because "Richard" continued to suffer from depression, he once visited Melanie Klein as an adult, but she politely brushed him off. Richard thought that she had become old and tired and "didn't wish to become involved."

IMPLICATIONS OF THE "RICHARD" CASE

The main features of Klein's early theory are clearly discernible in her work with Richard. Direct interpretation of Richard's angry feelings toward family members are interwoven with educational explanations about sexuality, childbirth, and death.

Kleinian Oedipal Themes

Much of the work with Richard centers on his oedipal rivalry with his father and sometimes with his older brother. Klein's concept that the child internalizes phantasized object-images was directly interpreted to Richard using the medium of his "starfish-empire" drawings. Richard is told that he believes Mummy will be injured by the objects Richard imagines (projects) inside her, that he believes Daddy's penis has been incorporated into Mummy, and that he has even portrayed himself inside Mummy in the form of a hurtful "starfish." Furthermore, Richard is introduced to the idea that his feelings are conflicted and changeable. He both wants to injure and protect Mummy and Daddy just as the war raging outside injures some and protects others.

The Disagreement With Anna Freud

It is clear throughout the narrative that Klein was especially permissive and supportive of her child patients, joining them in their games and conducting spontaneous experiments with the materials at hand. She made a variety of toys available to Richard from the outset, but he preferred the medium of drawing, which Klein permitted and even encouraged at several points by joining in. Nevertheless, she used virtually every activity as a source of interpretation, and every interpretation embodied ideas drawn from Klein's vision of the unconscious. Klein clearly uses the child's play as a direct equivalent to the medium of adult free association. As such, all play activity is fair game for blunt, adult-like interpretation. On precisely these issues Anna Freud most disagreed with Melanie Klein.

As we saw in Chapter 4, Anna Freud did not regard child analysis as a simple equivalent of adult psychoanalysis. She insisted on specialized technique, a phase of preparation for analysis, and only then did she interpret the child's verbal associations elicited by play. Anna Freud avoided interpreting the play activity itself. In all respects, Anna Freud emphasized the unique developmental requirements that make working analytically with children different from working with adults. Given this fundamental divergence in orientation to the task, Melanie Klein's play technique seemed utterly wrong to Anna Freud on three counts, one of them linked to practical technique, and two of them linked to fundamental theory.

First, Anna Freud's own technique for child analysis (see Chapter 4) emphasized the child's *verbal,* productions during play or story telling. Interpretations to the child were limited to the immediately available evidence emerging from the child's associations after a period of preparation in which the child is made comfortable with and instructed in the procedure. Very young children were not suitable candidates for psychoanalysis precisely because they were not yet sufficiently verbal creatures. For Anna Freud, the transference relationship with a child is different from adult transference because the child's past relationships are necessarily also its *current* relationships (A. Freud, 1927, pp. 39 ff. and p. 45). From Melanie Klein's point of view, transference is transference. Object relationships begin almost from birth in Klein's view of infancy. Thus early object relations, real and phantastic, are sufficiently plentiful to form the basis of a child's transferential relationship to the therapist. Just as in adult analysis, the analyst must interpret the transference relationship to the child and link it with the child's inner world of phantasy objects.

Second, for Anna Freud the *goal* of the interpretations was shaped by Sigmund Freud's classical theory, and later by her own views on ego psychology, both of which did very little violence to the classical essentials. Thus, in the classical spirit, Anna Freud aimed to strengthen the child's ego in dealing with the id and superego at a point when the child reached sufficient maturity to have an ego. Melanie Klein (1927/1975a) aimed to weaken a primitively punitive superego at a point so early in development that it is difficult to envision the presence of real personality structures. To Anna Freud it made little sense to speak of primitive anxieties and a sadistic superego from the earliest days of life when, according to orthodox Freudian theory, there is yet no coherent ego (A. Freud, 1927, pp. 36, ff.; A. Freud, 1992, p. 63).

Third, the *content* of the interpretations for Anna Freud was also shaped by classical psychoanalytic theory. Klein's notion of play as a direct expression of unconscious phantasy seemed to Anna Freud to run the risk of molding the child's associations to the theory rather than the other way around (A. Freud, 1928). Klein's interpretations were often made to the child on the basis of symbolic meanings derived from her theory. She treated the child's games and play with toys as direct representatives of the phantasy objects her theory postulates in the child's unconscious. With Richard, for example, sharp-edged starfish were interpreted as symbols of a destructive baby inside mother; enemy U-boats symbolized father and brother; British ships were mummy and Richard himself. In working with other children, Klein capitalized on the child's use of toys and objects in the room as opportunities to interpret symbolic meanings. All sorts of toys, kitchen utensils and paints can cooperate in this enterprise as symbols of the child's interest in genitals, curiosity about the womb (a handbag), sadistic urges to tear up family members, or conflicted desires to poison loved ones. To Anna Freud it seemed possible that directly symbolic interpretations imposed meanings on the child's actions rather than elucidating their inherent meaning. Such technique amounted to "wild analysis" subtly teaching the child how to play in accord with the therapist's theoretical rules by steering the child's thoughts and actions into compliance with established code.

For her part, Melanie Klein considered Anna Freud's technique an extension of educational efforts, especially the long preparatory period upon which Anna Freud had insisted. Klein argued that Anna Freud's technique did not establish a "true" analytic situation for the child because Anna Freud seemed to believe that children were incapable of free association (Klein, 1927/1975a, pp. 142–143). At core, Klein suggested that Anna Freud saw children as very different beings from adults whereas she herself saw very little reason to treat a child patient differently from an adult patient. Using her own play technique with toys and drawings, Melanie Klein felt she had been able to access the most primitive layers of the child's unconscious, an achievement that lay outside the range of Anna Freud's more verbal technique. It seemed to Klein that Anna Freud's method minimized the analyst's role as the interpreter of the child's unconscious conflicts. Instead the analyst operating with Anna Freud's technique becomes an educational role model who encourages a positive, even submissive, transference relationship with the child. As a result of the analyst's failure to establish a "true analytic situation," the child becomes unable and unwilling to make its deepest feelings known (Klein, 1927/1975a, pp. 153–154, 167).

In the end, the dispute between Anna Freud and Melanie Klein resulted in permanent divisions in the profession of child analysis in London, with students and analysts becoming Kleinians, Anna-Freudians, or Middle-groupers. Some of the dispute no doubt was more a war of words and a clash of personalities in a power struggle than an expression of substantive differences about *technique*. In the consulting room with a child, *any* therapist learns quickly that play and games are the brushes and paints, patience and persistence are the canvas, and empathy is the language of successful communication.

Strengths and Weaknesses of Klein's Technique

On the positive side of the ledger, Klein demonstrates the skillful management of a child patient whose cooperation and motivation she enlists and maintains throughout the treatment. She is warm, empathic, permissive, tolerant, supportive, and caring, and knows well how to communicate these attitudes to her patient. Richard obviously makes a strong emotional connection to "Mrs. K.," one that he is reluctant to end when the agreed upon time arrives.

The behavioral evidence provided by Klein's reports of Richard's responses, supported by his drawings, suggests a certain progress in anxiety tolerance through the course of the treatment. Richard begins treatment with intensely disorganizing feelings of anxiety and anger, and he expresses these in highly detailed, highly compartmentalized, intensely colored, almost frantic war and "empire" drawings. By the end of treatment, his artistic productions are calmer, more organized, less frenetic, less intense, and more graceful. Compare the drawings in Figures 5.2 and 5.3 with the portraits of Mrs. K. in Figure 5.5. Or, for that matter, simply compare Richard's first and last drawings, as shown in Figure 5.2.

On the negative side of the ledger, the sophistication of the drawings, from beginning to end, remains at a more cognitively primitive level than expectable for a boy of ten years. There are indications of serious psychopathology in the portraits of Mrs. K. and the "empire" drawings. Aspects of these drawings reflect substantial disturbances of thinking, compulsive needs to compartmentalize anxieties and other feelings, and wishes felt so intensely as to be almost beyond Richard's ability to endure. Klein, however, apparently does not clinically conceptualize this child at such a severe level of dysfunction. She appears to believe that Richard is cognitively and emotionally more intact than either his behavior or his drawings indicate.

Summers (1994, pp. 118 ff.) has succinctly summarized criticisms of Klein, three of which we can apply to highlight the debatable aspects of Richard's analysis.

Over-Pathologizing

For Klein, the world of the infant's phantasies is akin to psychotic thinking. Recall the interpretations she made to Richard of his oedipal beliefs, expressed in a nightmarish vision of parts of people, mutilation, fear of attacking and being attacked, and fantastic delusions of poisoning, penetrating, and puncturing. Klein, of course, argued that the infant's phantasies were only *psychotic-like,* composed of the very stuff that the normal infant will eventually learn to moderate, assimilate, and control. Richard is told, for example, that he believes Mummy's insides can be devoured by the starfish, that the starfish is himself, that the starfish is also other "greedy babies" trying to devour Mummy, and that Daddy's penis is also inside Mummy's body because Mummy devoured it. To many observers, interpretations such as these seem extraordinary, eccentric, and excessively pathological. To Richard, apparently, they were reasonable, thought provoking and calming. Although Klein's account of the case can be challenged on this point, at the very minimum, her interpretations were tolerated by Richard. He adopted her vocabulary, almost always followed her lead, and appears to have found something of value in the relationship.

Aggression, Aggression and More Aggression

Klein's concept of the death instinct as the fountainhead of all aggression is theoretically fuzzy. For one thing, the death instinct is tied in classical theory to the concept of the repetition compulsion and the conservative aim of instincts (see Chapter 3). In Klein's theory, the death instinct is used virtually always as a simple synonym for aggression or hate. Used in this loose way, the death instinct is divested of its evolutionary and instinctual links and is therefore theoretically irrelevant. A related problem of fuzzy definition is that *any* behavior of the child can be interpreted as aggression or one of its derivatives. The distinctions between hate for another, envy of another, sadism for its own sake, and destructiveness for its own sake are not clear or precise in Klein's application of her theory to children. Thus Richard's presumed conflict over wanting to hurt his mother and father at the same time that he fears their retaliation is the common interpretative theme applied to nearly all of his "empire-starfish" drawings. Even Klein's transference interpretations to Richard more frequently target his anger and envy than his obvious affection for Mrs. K. One fact is certain. In Klein's psychological universe, there is no shortage of aggression.

"Wild" Analysis

It is easy to conclude that some of Klein's interpretations to Richard are wild speculations driven by a theory that is not always linked to the clinical observations at hand. Some of Richard's drawings, for example, lend themselves to other interpretations along the lines of distressed feelings rather than destructive phantasy. It could be argued that Richard's therapy consists of learning Klein's vocabulary which he then uses effectively to generate compatible ideas and drawings that are advantageous in preserving his attachment to her. One counterargument mounted by Kleinians points out that people find her conclusions alienating and fantastic precisely because they are unconsciously accurate. Labeling such unconscious content absurd or fantastic is merely a defense against recognizing that truth. Of course, the final word on validity, as with all theories, has to be refutability (see Chapter 1). We will consider this issue in the broader context of Klein's whole theory at the end of the chapter.

ANXIETY: FIRST MODIFICATIONS TO THE THEORY OF DEVELOPMENT

With growing experience and an increased number of observations from child analyses, Melanie Klein modified her basic formulations about the development of the superego and Oedipus complex. The changes take three forms. She added detail about the *content* of the child's phantasies, changed the developmental *timing* of them, and slightly *reduced the role of aggression* in all of them. The first change resulted in a significant population explosion of the infant's internalized objects whereas the second change pushed back the origins of personality structure to the earliest days of life. Klein postulated, for example, the existence *at birth* of a rudimentary ego, superego and innate oedipal-like motives. The third change was, and remained throughout her career, much more modest, infinitely more subtle. Klein moderated her concept of aggression as the primary motive of infancy and supplemented it with considerations of envy, guilt, anxiety, and love. But a moderated view of aggression is not the same thing as a completely revised one. Hate/sadism/envy/aggression remained first team players to the end.

Fear of Own Destructive Impulses: Projection

In amplifying her reasons for the severity of the infant's superego, Klein elaborated her theory of internalized objects. Her observations led her to believe that a regular part of a child's life centers around fears of phantastic frightening figures who threaten to dismember, devour or "tear the child to pieces." The child acquires some of this sadistic imagery from the usual fairy tales and ghost stories that are a regular part of growing up in virtually every culture. Klein believed, however, that the terrifying characters of fairy tales are transformed by phantasy into personalized constructions of real objects in the child's life:

> I have no doubt from my own analytic observations that the real objects behind those imaginary, terrifying figures are the child's own parents, and that those dreadful shapes in some way or other reflect the features of its father and mother, however distorted and phantastic the resemblance may be. (Klein, 1933/1975, p. 249)

If a child unconsciously equates the parents with wild beasts and fairy tale monsters, then the child clearly is not identifying with actual parents as they exist in reality. Instead, the child is identifying with transformed "imagos"—images— of the parents created by the child unconsciously. The cruelty and sadism of the child's superego thus derives secondarily from identifying with the cruelty of these transformed and *imaginary* objects. The primary transformation of the objects into malevolent persecutors, recall, was a product of the child's innate sadism. But how does a child's fear mount to a level that can transform loved ones into menacing object images? Surely most parents do little, other than reading fairy tales, to prompt such psychologically catastrophic transformations.

Klein's answer is that the child's immature ego is frightened of its own innate sadism. The danger of being destroyed by one's own death instinct is so terrifying that the immature ego mobilizes against the death instinct what libido or life instinct it has available (Klein, 1932/1975b, pp. 126 ff.) Then, using the relatively primitive defense of projection, the ego directs the uncontainable aggression outward onto external objects. In this way, the infant's fear of its own internal impulses becomes, in part, a fear of external objects (Klein, 1932/1975b, p. 128). Now the infant believes that it is the objects who want to destroy self rather than vice versa. Projections grow into persecutors. The infant's internalized and externalized objects have become ravaging terrorists within. In reality, the fear that the infant experiences is the dread of its own destructive urges toward love objects. Consequently, ". . . his fear of his objects will always be proportionate to the degree of his own sadistic impulses" (Klein, 1933/1975a, pp. 251).

The weapons of the child's sadism are ordinary infantile equipment and activities mutated by phantasy into agents of destruction. Thus wetting by urination becomes equivalent to drowning, cutting, stabbing, and burning; feces are equated with missiles and direct-contact combative weapons. With development, the more knowledgeable child can perceive feces as poisons and toxins of all sorts. The penis itself can be a target of injury or a weapon with which to inflict it. And of course there are the always available standbys of biting, chewing, and spitting which can become interchangeable equivalents of devouring, dismembering, and annihilation (Klein, 1930/1975a, pp. 219–220, 226).

With the focus thus firmly on sadism and fear as the motivating force, Klein moved the timing of the origins of the superego to the child's first oral introjections of objects, that is, to the first few months of life.

Oral, Urethral, and Anal Sadism: Cannibalizing Mother

In her reformulation, Klein continued to rely heavily on innate aggression as a primal motive. However, she tempered this reliance with a consideration of the child's *fears* of its own aggression and its displacement of that aggression onto phantastic internalized and external objects. Eventually, as we will see, she tempered sadism even further with considerations of love and guilt. For now, however, the *content* of the child's sadistic phantasies was given greater elaboration and increased developmental precision.

Taking Freud at his word once again, Klein distinguished between an early oral-sucking aggressive phase and a later oral-sadistic phase. In the first part of the first year of life during the *oral-sucking phase,* the child phantasizes taking the breast within itself; in the somewhat later *oral-sadistic phase,* the child imagines chewing it up, devouring the breast cannibalistically. In this later phase, presumably late in the first year, oral and aggressive needs are simultaneously gratified by the same phantasy. In the second and third years of life, the child enters the *anal-sadistic phase* in which the necessary focus on elimination becomes tied to aggressive urges once more. Klein believed that elimination of feces took on the meaning for the child of eliminating the love object—a "forcible ejection" of it—linked to destructive desires (1933/1975a, p. 253). Between the oral-sadistic phase and the anal-sadistic phase, Klein discerned a transitional *urethral-sadistic phase* and its associated phantasies:

> In its oral-sadistic phantasies the child attacks its mother's breast, and the means it employs are its teeth and jaws. In its urethral and anal phantasies it seeks to destroy the inside of the mother's body, and uses its urine and faeces for the purpose. In this second group of phantasies the excrements are regarded as burning and corroding substances, wild animals, weapons of all kinds, etc.; and the child enters a phase in which it directs every instrument of its sadism to the one purpose of destroying its mother's body and what is contained in it. As regards choice of object, the child's oral-sadistic impulses are still the underlying factor, so that it thinks of sucking out and eating up the inside of its mother's body as though it were a breast. (Klein, 1933/1975a, pp. 253–54)

When the child phantasizes attacking the insides of the mother, he or she thereby attacks a great many internalized objects. By extension of its infantile phantasy logic, Klein argued, the infant is attacking an entire world peopled by objects hostile to the self, including the father, mother, brothers, and sisters. "The world, transformed into the mother's body, is in hostile array against the child and persecutes him" (Klein, 1929/1975, p. 214). Destroy or be destroyed becomes the infant's strategy, but it is a strategy fraught with guilt and anxiety.

HATE VERSUS GUILT: REPAIRING THE RAVAGES OF SADISM

As the child matures toward the genital phase of development in the fourth and fifth years of life, innate sadism diminishes because life-affirming and creative motives take precedence. With these normal developments, in short, comes the emergence of the child's capacity for pity, sympathy, and empathy (Klein, 1929/1975, p. 214). In short, authentic object love becomes possible.

From Part Object Introjection to Whole Object Identification

Initially, as we have seen, the infantile ego is capable only of identifying with *part objects,* and often these partial persons are equated in phantasy with body processes and products such as feces, breasts, and penises. With development, the infantile ego becomes capable of perceiving and identifying with *whole objects* that more closely approximate reality. More important, given the choice, the ego more readily identifies with and incorporates good rather than bad objects because good objects can provide pleasure for the id and because bad objects installed into the self are likely to create pain. From the ego's point of view, preservation of the good internalized object is synonymous with survival of the ego (Klein, 1935/1975a, p. 264). Said differently, the ego is now capable of understanding that loss of or damage to the good object threatens its own existence.

> With this change in the relation to the object, new anxiety-contents make their appearance and a change takes place in the mechanisms of defence. The development of the libido also is decisively influenced. Paranoid anxiety lest the objects sadistically destroyed should themselves be a source of poison and danger inside the subject's body causes him, in spite of the vehemence of his oral-sadistic onslaughts, at the same time to be profoundly mistrustful of the objects while yet incorporating them. (Klein, 1935/1975a, p. 264)

Endlessly the child repeats the act of incorporating the good object. Each repetition is also a compulsive test of their goodness as the child tries to disprove its fears about them. In this way, the child fortifies itself against persecutory objects—which the child itself created by projecting its sadism—and can phantasize about protecting the good objects by safeguarding them within the self.

Protecting the Good Object: Paranoid Versus Depressive Anxiety

To the child's dismay repetition does not lead to success or finality. It soon discovers that it cannot protect internalized good objects from the sadism of internalized bad ones, even if it continually re-introjects them. Deep anxiety develops about the dangers that lie in wait for internalized good objects, including a phantasy that the "inside" of its own body can be a poisonous place in which good objects perish (Klein, 1935/1975a, p. 265). Every real and imagined act of destruction that objects have enacted against one another, including parental sexual relations which the child views as an act of violence, are seen as sources of continuing danger to the good object.

One irony, lost on the child, is that its new capacity to identify with whole objects occurs simultaneously with the development of its awareness that it cannot protect them from persecuting bad objects or from the id.

> It seems to me that only when the ego has introjected the object as a whole, and has established a better relationship to the external world and to real people, is it able fully to realize the disaster created through its sadism and especially through its cannibalism, and to feel distressed about it. . . . It requires a fuller identification with the loved object, and a fuller recognition of its value, for the ego to become aware of

the state of disintegration to which it has reduced and is continuing to reduce its loved object. The ego then finds itself confronted with the psychic reality that its loved objects are in a state of dissolution—in bits—and the despair, remorse and anxiety deriving from this recognition are at the bottom of numerous anxiety-situations. To quote only a few of them: there is anxiety how to put the bits together in the right way and at the right time; how to pick out the good bits and do away with the bad ones; how to bring the object to life when it has been put together; and there is the anxiety of being interfered with in this task by bad objects and by one's own hatred, etc. (Klein, 1935/1975a, p. 269)

Another irony is the close link between love and destruction:

For at this stage of his development, loving an object and devouring it are very closely connected. A little child which believes when its mother disappears, that it has eaten her up and destroyed her (whether from motives of love or of hate) is tormented by anxiety both for her and for the good mother which it has absorbed into itself.

It now becomes plain why, at this phase of development, the ego feels itself constantly menaced in its possession of internalized good objects. It is full of anxiety lest such objects should die. Both in children and adults suffering from depression, I have discovered the dread of harbouring dying or dead objects (especially the parents) inside one and an identification of the ego with objects in this condition. (Klein, 1935/1975a, p. 266; italics added)

Thus, for Klein, even the apparent love and empathic concern that develops with the maturation of the infant ego fundamentally has a selfish basis. The child fears that its good objects may die and is terrified that such dead objects will reside within the self. Every event that signals loss of the real good mother in the world of reality also indicates the potential loss of the internalized good mother in the world of phantasy. The feelings of sadness or remorse that result from imagining loss of the loved object is what Klein initially called *depressive anxiety.* At its core, depressive anxiety is a kind of sadness about the fate of the good object.

But there is also *paranoid anxiety* over what the objects might do to the self. Never secure in his or her possession of the good object, the child cannot reach certainty about the "goodness" and stability of the good object. Instead, "paranoid" fear and doubt become haunting. Even if good objects of the real world are not actually lost, it is nevertheless possible, the anxious and suspicious child believes, that bad objects of the phantasy world can still mount an assault on them. In Klein's account, the child's construction of the world is strictly a lose-lose proposition.

PARANOIAC AND DEPRESSIVE "POSITIONS": THE FIRST THEORY

A child's self-involved fears take one of two forms. When the central anxiety assumes the form of persecution of the ego itself—a fear that one's *own* ego is at risk of attack—then the anxiety is described, by Kleinian convention, as "paranoiac." If, however, the central fear is that the good object is at risk because it might be destroyed by internalized bad objects, the prevailing feeling is melancholy and therefore "depressive" (Klein, 1935/1975a, p. 269).

Persecution and Pining

The feelings of sorrow in the depressive position reflect a desire to regain or repair the lost or damaged love objects. Klein called this whole constellation of melancholy emotions "pining." The depressive position, therefore, constitutes anxiety that internalized bad objects will persecute and destroy internalized good objects, defenses against these fears, and subjectively experienced longing or pining (Klein, 1945/1975a, p. 349). It is characteristic of the *depressive position* to be anxious and remorseful about the plight of the damaged loved object, whereas the person in the *paranoiac position* is vigilant and fearfully alert to the possibility that a disintegrated object may reunify to emerge again as a persecutor (Klein, 1935/1975a, p. 272).

"Positions" of Normal Developmental
From Paranoid to Depressive

Fear of one's own annihilation, the paranoiac form of anxiety, is the developmentally earlier and more primitive form because its danger situation—annihilation—is innate. *Fear of losing the good object by destruction or mutilation,* the depressive form of early anxiety, is developmentally later and more complex because its danger situation requires a comprehension of whole objects, empathy for them, and a sense of guilt for one's own role in the process of loss. The depressive and paranoiac forms of early anxiety to perceived danger situations are actually a normal developmental personality progression, but one which is never completely surpassed with age or totally resolved in the sense that ordinary developmental stages are customarily outgrown. For that reason, Klein referred to these personality processes as the *depressive position* and the *paranoid position,* rather than to "stages" of melancholy and persecutory anxiety (Klein, 1935/1975a, p. 275n; see especially the last paragraph of the end notes in 1952/1975c, p. 93).

MANIC AND DEPRESSIVE POSITIONS IN
ADULT PSYCHOPATHOLOGY

The adult psychopathologies of manic excitation and depression can be understood, Klein argued, as derivatives of the paranoiac and depressive positions of childhood. In classical theory, Freud had argued that manic behavior was the ego's way of defending itself against feelings of depression at the loss of love object. Klein held the rather different view that the ego is seeking refuge not only from depressive feelings, but also trying to escape its tortured relationships with and paranoiac fears of internalized love objects. To do so, the ego attempts to take control of its love objects by dominating them. The ego supplements the familiar paranoid and depressive positions by adopting a *manic position* that serves the additional defensive aim of denial.

Omnipotence and Denial

The sense of omnipotence observable during some adult manic episodes is the central feature, Klein suggested, of this psychotic level psychopathology. (See the clinical taxonomy in Chapter 1 for the severity markers of psychosis and its cognitive-emotional position on the spectrum of severity relative to other disorders.) For Klein, the normal developmental version of the "manic position" also hinges on the child's belief in its own omnipotence. The person destined to be manic in adulthood attempted early in infancy to deny the presence of the internalized persecuting objects it had incorporated into the self. Even more painfully, the infantile ego of the person heading toward mania denied its dependence on good objects as well. This defense of denial has also to accomplish an additional aim. The child or adult in the manic position uses denial to obliterate all recognition of danger to good objects from the persecution of internalized bad objects. Freud had pictured personality dynamics as internalized warfare of the competing agencies of the id, ego and superego. Klein widened the war to the combat of real and internalized phantasy objects:

> What in my view is quite specific for mania is the *utilization of the sense of omnipotence* for the purpose of *controlling and mastering objects.* This is necessary for two reasons: (*a*) in order to deny the dread of them which is being experienced, and (*b*) so that the mechanism (acquired in the previous—the depressive—position) of making reparation to the object may be carried through. By mastering his objects the manic person imagines he will prevent them not only from injuring himself but from being a danger to one another. His mastery is to enable him particularly to prevent dangerous coitus between the parents he had internalized and their death within him. (Klein, 1935/1975a, pp. 277-78; italics in original)

By adulthood, infantile denial no longer works for the manic adult, even though the infantile techniques of magical omnipotence linger. Adult psychopathology results when the manic patient believes that he or she has destroyed the internalized love objects, but simultaneously omnipotently and magically believes he or she can reconstitute them at will.

Omnipotence and Devaluation: The Power of Life and Death

Omnipotence—essentially the belief in one's power over life and death—is coupled with the defense of *devaluation* whereby the adult resumes the "manic position" to belittle the worth and importance of its internalized objects. Contempt replaces love. "This *disparagement of the object's importance and the contempt for it* is, I think, a specific characteristic of mania and enables the ego to effect that partial detachment which we observe side by side with its hunger for objects" (Klein, 1935/1975a, p. 279; italics in original).

By detaching itself from its loved objects, the ego advances its development beyond the more dependent depressive position, but it does so at the price of increased anxiety and the need for perpetual vigilance. The new burden that has been presented to the ego is that it must gain mastery over its objects. Merely hungering for them and worrying about their safety are no longer sufficient. Sometimes, however, mastery over the persecuting and malevolent internalized objects includes killing them—with the intention, perhaps, of resurrecting them later.

Splitting and Triumph: The Troublesome Achievements of Defense

At a deeper level, the dynamics of the manic position reveal the fundamental ambivalence of children toward their internalized objects. Klein argued, as we have seen, that the infant eventually has to form a more realistic perception of the parents as real objects in the real world. To do so, it must maintain the separation between incorporated good and bad phantasy objects. But learning and development are making clear to the infantile ego that good and bad are often aspects of the same object, not separate objects as it once thought.

Splitting in Normal Development

As the child relates with increasing appropriateness to the real mother, there is the danger that the phantasy good and bad mother-breast will also unite into one contradictory and unmanageable object. To prevent this intolerable and confusing internal state, the ego *splits the imagos,* as Klein describes the process, into permanently separate and opposite object images. Notice that the splitting mechanism is aimed at the internal world of phantasy objects rather than the external world of actual people. Now the child can treat the internalized objects as simple instances of good *or* bad, loved *or* hated, while it puts increased trust in the more complicated real people who exhibit both qualities simultaneously (Klein, 1935/1975a, p. 287).

The child vacillates between depressive worry and manic omnipotence. Troubling thoughts that the good objects will be destroyed are warded off by manic efforts to exert life and death mastery over them. *Splitting* the phantasy objects into separate good and bad images helps confine this vacillation to the internal world of phantasy objects, and paves the way for the child to relate appropriately to its real objects. In Klein's view, when splitting is used as a strategy to protect the internalized good objects from the internalized bad ones, it is a normal component of personality development. Healthy adaptation to reality requires that the child perceive its real objects accurately and trust them more than its primitive phantasy objects as it matures to adolescence (Klein, 1945a, pp. 348 ff.).

Splitting as a "Flight to the Good"

The defensive advantage of splitting the internalized object images into loved and hated is that the paranoid anxieties of persecution and destruction can be directed to the hated *phantasy* images, leaving both the loved phantasy objects and the combined loved/hated *real* objects in relative safety. Further support for developing normal love relationships comes from a secondary defense Klein described as a "flight to the good" by which the child can vacillate between its external love objects and its internalized love objects, sidestepping the issues of fear and hatred for these same objects. If the flight is directed inwardly to the *good but internalized phantasy objects,* then the result is separation from reality and potential psychosis. On the other hand, if the person's flight is directed outwardly to the *good but external real objects,* there is the potential either for normal development or for slavish and neurotic dependence on others. In either case, the flight mechanism is the child's way of resolving its depressive and paranoiac anxieties. Thus splitting, for Klein, is both a mechanism of defense and a normal developmental process. But, of course, matters rarely remain definitively simple in the Kleinian world:

> It seems that at this stage of development the unification of external and internal, loved and hated, real and imaginary objects is carried out in such a way that each step in the unification leads again to a renewed splitting of the imagos. But, as the adaptation to the external world increases, this splitting is carried out on planes which gradually become increasingly nearer and nearer to reality. This goes on until love for the real and the internalized objects and trust in them are well established. Then ambivalence, which is partly a safeguard against one's own hate and against the hated and terrifying objects, will in normal development again diminish in varying degrees. (Klein, 1935/1975a, p. 288)

At this stage of her thinking, Klein used the term *splitting* in a narrow way to refer to the separation of good and bad *objects* in the child's phantasy. Subsequently, as we shall see, Klein (1946/1975c) elaborated her account of splitting to include *structural splits* in the child's id, ego, and self. In fact, she later makes clear that the infant cannot split its image of the love object without splitting its own ego into good and bad components as well. A particular split-off part of the id, Klein will later propose, becomes the prison of the psychoticlike and terrifying object images who seek to devour the child.

Triumph and Guilt in the Manic Position

If psychological development is normal, a balance is achieved between love and hate as the child's objects are unified into whole and more realistic images. With time, the child develops the desire to "out grow" its dependencies, to rival the achievements of its admired love objects, and to master fears of its own destructiveness. Eventually, mastery strivings become dominant. The child wants to reverse the parent-child relationship so that it can attain power over them, exceed their achievements, even subjugate them in phantasies of power and humiliation. Envisioning a time when the parents will have changed into helpless beings, like little children, as they become weak, old and frail adults, the child relishes its future triumph. But the ego also experiences these phantasies of triumph with feelings of guilt (Klein, 1945/1975a, pp. 351–52).

Triumph and guilt can impede the child's progression out of the depressive position because they compete with and block the ego's reparative work of restoring the damaged loved objects. Without the reparative work of normal mourning for lost or abandoned love objects, normal emotional development and healthy independence are put at risk. This destructive aspect of the manic position mobilizes the child's sadism and focuses it not only on healthy urges to be masterful, but on desires to humiliate and destroy the parental figures. But there is good news as well as bad. Triumph over one's objects can also promote emotional, intellectual, and physical growth. "The child's growing skills, gifts and arts increase his belief in the psychic reality of his constructive tendencies, in his capacity to master and control his hostile impulses as well as his 'bad' internal objects" (Klein, 1940/1975a, p. 353). Triumph thus leads to genuine mastery and ultimately to the capacity for authentic object love.

Of the three positions—paranoiac, depressive, and manic (psychotic)—Klein regarded the depressive position as the central feature of infantile development. The ways in which the child learns to resolve its depressive anxieties and establish real relationships with real objects is crucial to normal personality functioning (Klein, 1935/1975a, p. 289).

Love, Guilt, and Reparation

By the late 1930s, Klein was further moderating her emphasis on hate and sadism with an expanded analysis of love and guilt. Klein began to emphasize that infants have spontaneous feelings of love and empathy for others, a rather different focus from her previous pronouncements. In addition to all of the negative emotions infants experience, she pointed out, they can routinely feel love and gratitude toward the mother for the care she provides. Love, previously a rarely used term in Klein's lexicon, is now reintroduced. Following Freud's lead, love is seen as a derivative of the life instincts, ever present alongside the destructive urges of the death instinct and opposed to them:

> Side by side with the destructive impulses in the unconscious mind both of the child and of the adult, there exists a profound urge to make sacrifices, in order to help and put right loved people who in phantasy have been harmed or destroyed. In the depths of the mind, the urge to make people happy is linked up with a strong feeling of responsibility and concern for them, which manifests itself in genuine sympathy with other people and the ability to understand them, as they are and as they feel. (Klein, 1937/1975a, p. 211)

Restoring the Good Object: Restitution as Self-Serving Love

Guilt drives love in the Kleinian world. Because the child's ego is identified with the good object and can empathize with its plight, the ego is motivated to make restitution to the good object for all of its previous acts of sadism against it. As the superego develops, furthermore, the child's phantasies of attacking its objects are met with guilt. Feelings of regret surface in the child's awareness for the imagined damage it has inflicted. Desires to "make good"—restitution and reparation—emerge in the infant mental economy fueled equally by love and guilt (Klein, 1933/1975a, p. 254).

The infant's empathy for and identification with the love object also permits it to profit from its concern for the love object's welfare. Whatever sacrifices the child makes for the sake of the loved one, it is simultaneously making for itself because it identifies with the love object. As adults, we complete circle by assuming the role of caring parents where once we were cared-for children. In so doing, we reenact the love we received from our own mothers and now give to our children, but we also expiate our infantile guilt for the damage we imagine we, so long ago, inflicted on our mothers (Klein, 1937/1975a, p. 314).

An alternative scenario is presented by the mother who turns the tables and excessively identifies with her child. Caught up in a resurgence of her own infantile unconscious guilt for the harm she once wished on her love objects, the mother is attempting to revive a loving relationship to her own mother through her child. She becomes overly self-sacrificing because she sees far too much of herself in the child and far too much of her mother in the role she plays toward her child. Instead of repairing the damage to her own phantasy objects, however, the overly indulgent mother deprives her child of those experiences that will permit it to mature as a healthy, independent, and emphatic person. "It is well known that a child who has been brought up by a mother who showers love on him and expects nothing in return often becomes a selfish person" (Klein, 1937/1975a, p. 318).

For Klein, the infant's efforts to make reparations to its loved objects operate as a defense to keep guilt and despair at bay. When successful, the infant's reparative efforts open the child to the possibility of loving new objects without fear or guilt. "Thus making reparation—which is such an essential part of the ability to love— widens in scope, and the child's capacity to accept love and, by various means, to take into himself goodness from the outer world steadily increases" (Klein, 1937/1975a, p. 342).

PROJECTION + IDENTIFICATION = SPLITTING REVISITED

Klein revised her earlier views by now concluding that splitting was more of a universal process of defense against normally occurring psychotic-like anxiety states than she had earlier discerned. Klein wanted to make the implicit link between splitting and the paranoiac and depressive forms of anxiety more explicit.

Revision of the Paranoiac Position to the Paranoid-Schizoid Position

Recall that in Klein's earlier theory, the infant "splits" the love *object* into a good and bad object to isolate its own sadism to one aspect of a part-object rather than risk destroying the whole. The infant also "splits" its *relationships* with the object into love and hate—love for the good and hate for the bad object. Klein now elaborated this twofold concept of splitting and extended its reach from the early splitting of objects relationships to the splitting of personality structures, the self, and feelings.

To reflect the changes, she renamed the "paranoiac position," which henceforward was to be called the *paranoid-schizoid position.* Schizoid personality phenomena—dysfunctions of empathy, love, and hate in relating to objects and to the self— became for Klein a convenient synonym for all manner of personality pathologies; hence the inclusion of "schizoid" in the newly named paranoid-schizoid position.

How Shall I Split? Let Me Count the Ways.

From the very beginning of life, Klein now argued, the ego's experience of its own fear of annihilation is the foundation of all anxiety. Anxiety is always experienced in connection with objects, even from the earliest days of life. During the paranoid-schizoid position, the infant projects all of its fears onto part-objects, transforming them into hated persecutors. Other significant sources of anxiety included in Klein's new view are the trauma of birth and the frustration of bodily needs. Even these anxieties are experienced from the earliest moments as linked to objects or projected onto them defensively (Klein, 1946/1975c, pp. 4–5; Klein, 1958/1975c, pp. 23 ff.).

Splitting the Object: Defending Against Annihilation

In the early days and weeks of life, the normal state of the early ego is a lack of cohesiveness. Its natural tendency toward integration alternates with a tendency toward disintegration, a "falling into bits" when confronted with the immensity of its own destructiveness (Klein, 1946/1975c, p. 4). It is this vacillating pair of opposite "tendencies" that underlies the mechanism of splitting.

Some of the infant's annihilation fear is not projected outwardly onto objects. A residual component of the death instinct always remains unprojected and lurks within to magnify the primitive ego's feelings of helplessness. As helplessness mounts, the ego's natural tendency toward disintegration is accelerated. Thus threatened, the ego attempts to defend itself in one of three ways: by externalizing (projecting) the threat, by denying it altogether, or by splitting the object perceived to be the source of the threat into good and bad images. Consistent with her earliest formulations, Klein regarded this most elementary form of splitting as a defense directed to the control of annihilation anxiety under the impact of the death instinct. Splitting dichotomizes the internalized phantasied and the perceived external object into *good* and *bad.* Splitting also bifurcates the child's *relationships* to these images into love-and-hate/desire-and-fear. The destructive impulse and its associated anxiety is thus defensively dispersed, deflected, and isolated from the good objects and from self-identified-with-good-objects.

Splitting the Ego: The Idealized Breast and the Superego

In her revised formulation, Klein suggested that the ego cannot split the object without also splitting itself (1946/1975c, pp. 5–6; see also 1958/1975c). Because the infant incorporates its objects and identifies with them, what it does to the phantasy object it necessarily experiences as having been done to itself. When the infant took into itself the "good" and satisfying breast, this phantasy object was experienced as "whole" or integrated. In contrast, the split off "bad" and frustrating breast is experienced as fragmented, "broken into bits." Good feelings that derive from having a satisfying object "inside" can be disrupted by the anxiety of having a fragmented and poisonous bad object also inside. To the degree that the child's innate sadism prevails, the internalized object will be experienced as fragmented, and the more likely it is, therefore, that the child's own ego will sustain a split.

To enhance the effectiveness of splitting as a defense against the bad objects, the infantile ego *idealizes* the goodness of the good object images. "Idealization is bound up with the splitting of the object, for the good aspects of the breast are exaggerated as a safeguard against the fear of the persecuting breast" (Klein, 1946/1975c, p. 7). A secondary motive also governs idealization of the good object. Because the infant is also driven by its instinctual needs for food and love, it strives for unlimited gratification from an inexhaustible and always bountiful object, the idealized breast. Klein proposed that the process of idealization of split-off parts of the ego underlies the formation of the earliest superego. By the end of the first six months of life, splitting the breast into good and bad images, idealizing the good aspect, and identifying with it constitute the formation of the earliest and most primitive superego (Klein, 1958/1975c, p. 239). Said another way, one aspect of the splitting of the ego is the creation of the superego.

> In my view, the splitting of the ego, by which the super-ego is formed, comes about as a consequence of conflict in the ego, engendered by the polarity of the two instincts [i.e., life and death]. This conflict is increased by their projection as well as by the resulting introjection of good and bad objects. The ego, supported by the internalized good object and strengthened by the identification with it, projects a portion of the death instinct into that part of itself which it has split-off—a part which thus comes to be in opposition to the rest of the ego and forms the basis of the superego. (Klein, 1958/1975c, p. 240)

For Klein, the superego is a product of very early splitting of the ego and phantasied incorporation of the good (satisfying) and bad (frustrating) mother, rather than, as Freud's version would have it, the repository of the image of the father who punishes by castration.

To return to the general theory of splitting, the bad object is kept as distant as possible from the bountiful object. Toward this end, the infant's ego may even use denial to obliterate recognition of the very existence of the bad object, along with any frustrating situations linked in phantasy to the bad object. But this very selective obliteration of reality only works because the infant experiences itself for a time as omnipotent, capable of materializing gratification by mere experience of the desire:

> In hallucinatory [omnipotent] gratification, two interrelated processes take place: the omnipotent conjuring up of the ideal object and situation, and the equally omnipotent annihilation of the bad persecutory object and the painful situation. These processes are based on splitting both the object and the ego.
>   In passing I would mention that in this early phase splitting, denial and omnipotence play a role similar to that of repression at a later stage of development. (Klein, 1946/1975c, p. 7)

In the process of annihilating *recognition* of the bad object, an entire set of object relations is obliterated and along with them a part of the ego that supported those relations (Klein, 1946/1975c, pp. 7). In short, phantasy objects, reality objects, the relationship to both, and the part of the ego active in the process are all split off and denied.

Splitting the Id: Dividing Conscious From Unconscious
Another structural split is need to cope with the incorporated and terrifying bad object images that the child has split-off from the sadistic strivings of its ego. The id splits. In this way, the unmanageable terrifying persecutory objects—derived, you will recall, from the phantasy transformations of the mother and father—are "relegated to the deeper layers of the unconscious"—to the split-off section of the id. (Klein, 1958/1975c, p. 241). Two benefits result. First, the split-off aspect of the ego destined to become a superego is better tolerated once these horrific images are dissociated into the deeper unconscious. Second, the "extremely bad" images are not assimilated

or accepted into either the superego or the ego. They remain dissociated as "split-off" id content, or what Freud called "primal repressions."

Klein pointed out in passing that ego splitting is different from id splitting. The ego has to fuse together contradictory images and drives to create its split-off part of the superego. When the id splits, in contrast, images have to be "defused" so that the bad images are divorced from the good and then split-off or dissociated. In short, the first kind of splitting associated with the ego ultimately results in a synthesis whereas the second kind associated with the id results in a dissociation or a primal repression (Klein, 1958/1975c, pp. 243 ff.).

As a defense, splitting is developmentally prior to repression, and the nature of the splitting shapes the character of repression. In fact, for Klein, even the adult defense mechanism of repression is a kind of splitting whereby the fully integrated adult ego "divides itself off" from unconscious threat. Consequently, one might suppose that yet another sense in which Klein used the concept of splitting is the division of conscious from unconscious mental *content* as contrasted with defensive structural splitting.

Splitting the Self: Projective Identification

As development proceeds, the early oral incorporative and aggressive impulses are joined by anal and urethral aggressive impulses. The good object—idealized breast—and the mother's body as an extension of the breast become the targets of the infant's attacks.

> The phantasied onslaughts on the mother follow two main lines: one is the predominantly oral impulse to suck dry, bite up, scoop out and rob the mother's body of its good contents. . . . The other line of attack derives from the anal and urethral impulses and implies expelling dangerous substances (excrements) out of self and into the mother. Together with these harmful excrements, expelled in hatred, split-off parts of the ego are also projected on to the mother or, as I would rather call it, *into* the mother. These excrements and bad parts of the self are meant not only to injure but also to control and to take possession of the object. In so far as the mother comes to contain the bad parts of the self, she is not felt to be a separate individual but is felt to be *the* bad self. (Klein, 1946/1975c, p. 8; italics in original)

The infant thus splits off the bad parts of the self and projects them into the mother, but also necessarily expels some of the good parts of the self: excrements perceived as "gifts." For a time, the ego is weakened by these enforced excessive expulsions. The ego may even feel that it has no independent life or strength of its own. Ultimately, however, the infant can regain coherence and strength by identifying with an object who embodies the good and bad self-components the ego has projected into the object.

There is even a bonus to be had in all this projection and splitting: To the degree that the infant can idealize the good parts of self it has projected, it can reincorporate not only the original good aspects but the intensified and idealized ones it has created. It is truly a give and take world for the infant. Normal development, Klein suggested, is an exquisitely delicate balance of optimal degrees of introjection and projection (Klein, 1946/1975c, p. 11).

Because the infant can project self content into the object and then take it back by identification, Klein termed the process *projective identification.* In a way, the infant gets what it gives: predominantly hostile projections result in primarily hostile identifications. But another aspect of projective identification is that the intention of the infant is *forcibly to enter the object* to take control of it. This strategy can backfire during the identification part of the cycle. When identification is at its height, the infant ego may feel that others are controlling it, or can take retribution for the violent intrusion, or that its own body and mind can be controlled by others (Klein, 1946/1975c, p. 11).

Schizoid Object Relations: Guilt, Narcissism, and Projective Identification

Because the child projects the split-off hated part of the self into the object, it eventually realizes that it has placed the object in jeopardy. The child feels guilty at least to the small degree that it can experience responsibility for others who are representatives of the sadistic parts of the self. On the other hand, the projection and splitting enable the child to permit the "bad" object to carry some of the guilt.

There is also a narcissistic element in projective identification. The child, after all, is also projecting good aspects of the self, often idealized, into the object. Objects are

TABLE 5.1   The Meanings of Splitting in Klein's Theory

Splitting Type	Definition and Functions
Object	Good-satisfying breast split from the bad-persecuting breast. *Infant's earliest defense against "bad" objects.*
Object Relations	The infant can "hate" the bad and "love" the good object (breast). *Defense against guilt for sadistic urges to destroy the good object.*
Ego	Because the infant "incorporates" objects into itself, there is necessarily a split in the ego that parallels splits in the object and relations to the object. *Structure building: Split off parts are destined to become the superego but only if they can be reintegrated.*
Id	Terrifying and persecuting phantasy objects that the infant has projected onto the parents are "split off" from the rest of the unconscious and pushed to the "deepest" area of the id. *Defensive dissociation: These split-off images are never reintegrated and are like "primal repressions."*
Self	Split-off and hated "bad" parts of the ego and self are split off and projected into the mother to injure her and take possession/control of her. Some good parts of self are also split off and projected into mother: excrements intended as "gifts of self." *Structure building through projective identification and defensive protection against bad objects.*

loved and admired because they are so like the self. Correspondingly, the despised parts of the self can be "split off" and projected into others. Perceived as resembling the unacceptable self, objects embodying the unacceptable projections are transformed into targets of hatred. In either case, the schizoid position from which some children never emerge assures that their later object relations will be marked by themes of control. For narcissistic self-protection, the infant must dominate the people who carry its projected, split-off self-fragments.

If the child fails to resolve the paranoid-schizoid position on its way to the depressive position, there is also the possibility that later character development will be marked by a degree of artificiality and lack of spontaneity in relating to others. This characteristic "coldness" of the schizoid style reflects a severe disturbance of a self that has failed to reintegrate the split-off and projected aspects by identification with the available good objects. The various ways in which Klein applied the term *splitting* to the developmental process are summarized in Table 5.1.

REPARATION: THE LINK BETWEEN POSITIONS

Recall that the paranoid-schizoid (earlier called the "paranoic position") developmentally precedes the depressive position. The depressive position is the central feature of normal development, for the way in which the infant resolves its depressive longings sets the pattern for its later intimate interpersonal relationships. When the infant can introject a "complete" object near the end of the first six months of life, the split between good and bad (and those corresponding splits in the self and ego) are narrowed. The infant begins to construct a more realistic picture of reality and its people. Because loved and hated aspects of the breast and mother are now not so widely separated, the infant experiences a sense of loss or mourning when the whole object is not available. An increased sense of guilt for sadistic urges toward the object is the price to be paid for this achievement, a developmental advance that marks the infant's entry into the depressive position (Klein, 1946/1975c, p. 14).

The Drive to Reparation Promotes Ego Integration

The depressive position, Klein now proposed in more detail, has a beneficial early effect of integrating the fragmented ego that has been weakened by its earlier paranoid-schizoid phase of excessive projection and splitting. Depression, an infantile reaction to the phantasied damage inflicted on the love object, engenders strivings to repair or restore the object. This "drive to reparation" exhibited by the infantile ego during the second six months of life will remain in effect for the next several years of childhood. As the child's growing ability to process reality more realistically enhances its adaptation to the world, the depressive position is "worked through" as part of normal emotional development. However, if the earlier paranoid-schizoid position has not been successfully navigated, a successful resolution of the depressive position is also jeopardized. Under these circumstances, the impact of the depression and anxiety of the depressive position may thus mark not a developmental progression but the onset of a vicious circle:

> For if the persecutory fear, and correspondingly schizoid mechanisms, are too strong, the ego is not capable of working through the depressive position. This forces the ego to regress to the paranoid-schizoid position and reinforces the earlier persecutory fears and schizoid phenomena. Thus the basis is established for various forms of schizophrenia in later life; for when such a regression occurs, not only are the fixation-points in the schizoid position reinforced, but there is a danger of greater states of disintegration setting in. Another outcome may be the strengthening of depressive features. (Klein, 1946/1975c, p. 15)

Klein was adamant that during normal development no precise line could be drawn between feelings of persecution in the paranoid-schizoid position and guilty anxiety in the depressive position. One slowly grades into the other, and elements of both positions persist in later life.

ENVY AND GRATITUDE: THE FOREVER GENEROUS, TOLERANT, AND BOUNTIFUL BREAST

From the infant's point of view, the good breast is an inexhaustible and ever-present source of all that is satisfying. In the struggle against the innate death instinct, the good breast is the most powerful ally the infant can recruit to protect itself from its own destructive urges. So powerful, so generous, so satisfying is the good breast that the infant envies it and suspects that the good breast selfishly keeps for itself some of its unlimited milk, love, and power (Klein, 1957/1975c, p. 183).

Envy, Jealousy, and Greed Distinguished

Klein distinguished among the meanings of three related terms. *Envy* is an angry feeling that another person possesses and enjoys something desirable. The envious person wants to take away the object of desire, and failing that, to spoil the object of envy so that no one can enjoy it. *Jealousy,* by contrast, is found in the love relationship between two people. When one of the people feels that love is in danger of being taken away by a rival, he or she becomes *jealous* of the rival. The loved object itself is not the target of the emotion and is in no danger of being harmed. *Greed,* a related term, indicates an impetuous and insatiable craving that exceeds what the loved object can give and what the greedy person actually needs (Klein, 1957/1975c, p. 181). In short, the envious person cannot tolerate someone else's possession of the good, the jealous person is fearful of losing the good, and the greedy person is never satisfied by any amount of goodness.

Primary Envy of the Breast

Klein's previous descriptions of the infant's sadistic urges to scoop out the mother's body and breast and to defile or poison it with excrements were forerunners of her last major theoretical construct of envy for the breast. She now extended her earlier descriptions of the effects of frustration to include the child's feelings of envy for a mean and grudging breast that somehow deprives the child by keeping for itself what the child wants: milk, care, love. But the good breast can also be envied. "The very ease with which the milk comes—though the infant feels gratified by it—also gives rise to envy because this gift seems something so unattainable" (Klein, 1957/1975c, p. 183).

Envy Expressed as Grievances in Analysis

Klein pointed out that a primitive analog to this infantile envy exists within the transference relationship to the analyst in therapy. For example, when the analyst provides an interpretation that brings relief and changes the patient's mood from despair to hope, some patients respond with angry and destructive criticism of the analyst. The interpretation, initially experienced as enriching and nourishing, is quickly transformed into an experience of "not good enough." Focusing on what appear to be trivial details, the envious patient may say that the interpretation should have been given earlier, or that it was too long or short:

> The envious patient grudges the analyst the success of his work; and if he feels that the analyst and the help he is giving have become spoilt and devalued by his envious criticism, he cannot introject him sufficiently as a good object nor accept his interpretations with real conviction and assimilate them. (Klein, 1957/1975c, p. 184)

Feeling guilty for devaluing the help given him in analysis, the envious patient may also punish the self by feeling unworthy to benefit from the analysis.

A different but related devaluing maneuver is typical of the paranoid person. Particularly prone to concealing the split-off hostile and envious parts of self from the analyst, the paranoid patient exacts a kind of sneaky revenge against the helpful therapist who expects the patient to be grateful. The paranoid patient cannot permit the self to experience any gratitude to the therapist or incur any psychological debts to the therapist that might mean the therapist has superior insight, knowledge, or power. Instead such patients have abundant needs to devalue the therapist by defeating the analyst's efforts and "spoiling" whatever good might come of the process. A kind of perverse sadistic, but self-defeating, pleasure is experienced when the analyst's efforts can be disparaged. This "spoiling" strategy is fed by the split-off feelings of envy the patient experiences relative to the therapist. Pathological envy thus precludes any healing identification with the person of the analyst and swamps out all possibility that the analyst's interpretations can be meaningfully assimilated.

Another defense against recognizing unbearable envy is employed by patients who become "confused" and express their open doubts about the meaning of interpretations. Their confusion is designed to avoid open criticism of the analyst by substituting expressions of uncertainty and doubt. Klein hypothesized that such "confusion" stems from the earliest possible object relationship disturbances. Such patients in infancy were unable to keep apart the images of the good and bad, nurturing and persecuting, breast because the strength of their paranoid-schizoid and depressive fears were overwhelming. The result is that love and hate are not kept sufficiently separated and the infant is confused about what might be a good (safe) breast and what might be a bad (persecuting) breast. Infants who cannot adequately maintain the split between good and bad never know whether they will suck or be sucked dry, bite or be bitten. Put another way, it's a breast-eat-breast world out there.

For both kinds of patients, the infantile analogs of their contemporary envy include feelings that the breast was not available when wanted or that it provided milk too quickly or too slowly. Such infants may have turned away from the breast to suck their own fingers for a time. When they finally accepted the breast, they may not have drunk enough to satisfy hunger. Some infants overcome their grievances and eventually enjoy feeding, but others seem unable ever to be satisfied even by a satisfactory breast, just as some patients seem unable to accept what good the analyst can provide (Klein, 1957/1975c, p. 185). But at core, what the infant most wants from the bountiful breast, and entertains grievances for not having gotten, is safety and security from its own destructive and frightening urges.

Excessive Envy: Spoiling the Breast

Envy aims to spoil the primary envied object. Sadistic attacks on the breast are intensified by envy, sometimes to the point that the object loses its value utterly. The breast has become "bad" by being bitten and poisoned by urine and feces. Greed, envy and persecutory anxiety, all linked together, intensify one another and increase the level of the infant's destructive impulses toward the mother. The good object is never completely or reliably introjected. Doubts about the reliability, goodness, and generosity of the good object have repercussions for later object relationships. As adults, such infants may exhibit poor judgment about others, sliding into and out of inappropriately intimate relationships repetitively and too quickly. In the end, the infant's envious desires to spoil the good breast spoils it for everyone.

Gratitude and Love: Breast Bliss and Self-Trust

The infant who can overcome its own destructive impulses, incorporate a stable and nurturing object image of the good breast and good mother, can love. There is, Klein had to acknowledge, *some* enjoyment to be had at the breast for most infants. From these feelings of pleasure and joy the more subtle emotions of gratitude and love emerge. Gratitude precedes love and lays the foundations for it.

> A full gratification at the breast means that the infant feels he has received from his loved object a unique gift which he wants to keep. This is the basis of gratitude. (Klein, 1957/1975c, p. 188)

Gratitude is also the basis of trust. When the infant feels grateful for the sustenance and security provided by the breast, it begins an object relationship based on positive feelings for and trust in the object. Such feelings become the foundation for later feelings of unity with other people, pleasure in their happiness, and trust in their capacities to reciprocate. The infant who can incorporate the good object without envy and grievance disturbing the process excessively is the infant whose mother was trustworthy.

Recall Freud's (1905) earlier description of the infant's "bliss" in sucking at the breast as the prototype of all later sexual satisfactions. Klein took Freud at his word, again, and suggested that bliss at the breast is even more widely influential in permitting later intimate relationships, feelings of love for others, and feelings of being fully understood by others. Perhaps even more important, investing the good object with one's feelings of trust permits the infant to begin developing a sense of trust in self (Klein, 1957/1975c, p. 188).

Defending Against Envy:
The Most Deadly of Sins

Klein's ideas on envy and gratitude were proposed toward the end of her career, and she made them central components of her theory, displacing the earlier emphasis on sadism and hatred. One indicator of the importance she placed on these new concepts is her insight into the reasons why envy has traditionally been classed as one of the "seven deadly sins."[2]

> There are very pertinent psychology reasons why envy ranks among the seven "deadly sins." I would even suggest that it is unconsciously felt to be the greatest sin of all, because it spoils and harms the good object which is the source of life. This view is consistent with the view described by Chaucer in *The Parsons Tale:* "It is certain that envy is the worst sin that is; for all other sins are sins only against one virtue, whereas envy is against all virtue and against all goodness." The feeling of having injured and destroyed the primal object impairs the individual's trust in the sincerity of his later relations and makes him doubt his capacity for love and goodness. (Klein, 1957/1975c, p. 189)

When the infant's ego feels overwhelmed by envy, it may resort to an array of primitive defenses against envy. Some of these defenses specific to protecting the self from envy may evolve with time into adult personality features that disrupt interpersonal relationships. Klein enumerated eight defenses against envy:

1. IDEALIZATION. Klein originally described the infant's efforts to idealize the good breast as a protection against the persecution of the bad breast. Now she expanded her concept to include idealization as a means of protecting self from envy of the good object. Klein did not make definitively clear how this defense might work, but she indicated that for children in whom the normal splitting process of the object into good and bad has failed, "Strongly exalting the object and its gifts is an attempt to diminish envy" (Klein, 1957/1975c, p. 216). One can suppose that she means the infant attributes such godlike properties to the good object or breast that it realizes such attributes are unattainable by mere mortals.

2. CONFUSION. Recall the confusion and doubting of the resistant patient in therapy. For the infant who cannot achieve the normal splitting of the object, confusion between good and bad, love and hate are the result. "By becoming confused as to whether a substitute for the original figure is good or bad, persecution as well as the guilt about spoiling and attacking the primary object by envy is to some extent counteracted" (Klein, 1957/1975c, p. 216). In extreme form, such confusion may lay the groundwork for psychotic-level states of delusion and obsessive indecision later in adulthood.

3. FLIGHT FROM MOTHER TO OTHER. Both infants and adults may learn to avoid admired people because they are reminders of the primary envied object, mother. In

---

[2] From the Middle Ages, the seven "deadly sins" were pictured as the royal road to damnation. They are: *pride, greed, lust, anger, gluttony, envy,* and *sloth.*

this way, they protect the breast (and mother) from the destructiveness of their envy. Somewhat later in life, such behavior may lead to promiscuous relationships as the person flees from one love object to the next (Klein, 1957/1975c, p. 217).

4.   DEVALUATION OF THE OBJECT. Spoiling and devaluation are inherent in envy. A devastated or spoiled love object need not be envied. Even idealized objects are subject to such devaluation. Indeed they may be especially vulnerable to such devaluation. With devaluation comes a sense of ingratitude and the expression of grievances in the form of complaints about the object's failings.

5.   DEVALUATION OF THE SELF. Some adults are unable to use or exploit their own talents and abilities. By denying their own competencies, they avoid envy of and rivalry with admired figures who may provide occasions for unflattering competitive comparisons. As we have seen, even in analysis, the patient may admire and therefore envy the analyst. Only by further devaluing the self can some patients maintain any relationship with the analyst. One of the deepest roots of a person's defensive need to deny self success, Klein thought, was ". . . the guilt and unhappiness about not having been able to preserve the good object because of envy" (Klein, 1957/1975c, p. 218).

6.   GREED FOR THE GOOD. By greedily and rapaciously incorporating the good and admired object, the infant can believe that it possesses the object and controls it totally. Therefore, all the object's good attributes have become its own. All reason for envy is rendered unnecessary.

7.   AROUSE ENVY IN OTHERS. A frequent adult maneuver to conquer envy is to arouse it in others. In one stroke, the situations of envious subject and envied object are reversed. Klein suggested that this method is particularly ineffective because it backfires, creating worries of being persecuted. Envious people are prone to attack the object of their envy, which in fact was the initial reason for this defense. Another reason why this defense is so fragile, Klein suggested, is its link to the depressive position. "The desire to make other people, particularly loved ones, envious and to triumph over them gives rise to guilt and to the fear of harming them. The anxiety stirred up impairs the enjoyment of one's own possessions and again increases envy" (Klein, 1957/1975c, pp. 218–19).

8.   STIFLING LOVE AND INTENSIFYING HATRED. One way to prevent envy is to deny love for the admired object and express hatred for it instead. Freud referred to such transformations of impulses into their opposites as the defense of reaction formation. In this way, the most painful combination of love, hatred, guilt, and envy is avoided. On the surface, the hatred may not be evident, but a degree of studied indifference or coldness toward others is observable. An allied maneuver is simply to withdraw from all intimacy. The loner need not be envious or in competition with anyone.

For the infant who cannot work through the paranoid-schizoid persecutory position adequately, these defenses may signal later severe disturbances of personality. However, for the infant who achieves the depressive position and is able to work through his or her feelings of depression and guilt, the outcome is more favorable. Such an infant can learn not only to contain its own destructive impulses, but to care for, rather than envy, the admired object.

Some Personal Sources of Klein's Vision of the Infant's World

Because no one can read an infant's mind, Klein's conclusions about the infant's subjective world are necessarily inferential. But what guided her inferences? There are clues in what Klein envisioned. She construed the infant's subjective world as a frightening place of psychotic-like phantasy, need, and wish. Driven by fear, sadism, hate and more hate, triumph, and envy, the Kleinian infant seemingly experiences precious little happiness. Even triumphs lead, not to ultimate satisfaction, but to guilt. Guilt mobilizes the child to make reparations to its injured love objects, and the infantile equivalent of damage control ensues. For the Kleinian infant, life is hard: frighteningly difficult to endure or master, nearly impossible to comprehend, and stingy in its rewards. Small wonder that Klein thought infants were angry.

Childhood: No Breast for Melanie

The youngest of four children, Melanie Reizes had reason to believe that she had been an unexpected child and therefore an unwanted addition to the Reizes family (Grosskurth, 1986, pp. 10, 15, 57; Segal, 1992, p. 3). Her three older siblings were apparently "planned" pregnancies. Emilie, Emanuel, and Sidonie were born in the three consecutive years from 1876 to 1878. Melanie, born in 1882, was the exception to the pattern, following her nearest sibling Sidonie by four years. Indeed it was her own mother who told her that she had been "unexpected." Her father openly stated that he preferred his oldest daughter Emilie to Melanie, another hurtful revelation made more painful by Melanie's realization that her father could voice his preference with no awareness of its effect on her (Grosskurth, 1986, p. 11).

By the time she recounted these anecdotes for the autobiography she wrote in her mid-seventies, Melanie Klein claimed little significance for experiences that she would most certainly have interpreted for anyone else as unwelcome and decisive childhood revelations. Quite to the contrary in her own case, Melanie wrote in her autobiography, she had been untouched by her parents' disclosures: "I have no particular feeling that I resented this because there was a great deal of love towards me" (quoted in Grosskurth, 1986, p. 10).

Melanie was also aware that she had been the only child of the four Reizes siblings who had not been breast-fed. She had been handed over to a "wet nurse," who was, in her memory of it, a more than satisfactory substitute. The theoretical importance she later placed on the role of the breast as the first object and the significance she attached to breast-feeding as the first object relation lend weight to Grosskurth's (1986, pp. 10 ff.) surmise that Melanie harbored substantial resentment about her childhood despite her denials. That she mentions these aspects of personal history—being an "unexpected" child who was nursed by a woman other than her mother—indicates that she had *some* "particular feelings" about them. Clearly she attributed sufficient relevance and importance to these events to make them part of her autobiography.

Whether these autobiographical recollections are factual or not, their psychological significance is to be found in Melanie Klein's belief that she had been less than intimately and joyously cared for and was initially unwanted. Her facile denial of resentment suggests the operation of one of her own her theoretical concepts. Perhaps, like the anxious and angry infants she spent a lifetime describing, Melanie Klein experienced the same need to protect her primary love objects from the destructiveness of her own anger. Her autobiographical account portrays her mother and father as the sort of idealized parents that guilt-driven reparative urges are so skilled in creating for safe recall.

When Melanie was four years old, her nearest sibling in age, Sidonie (age 8) died from a particularly virulent form of glandular tuberculosis. The child was probably ill for a long time, and the fears and ignorance surrounding such diseases had an impact on Melanie. The two had enjoyed an especially close relationship. Melanie recalled that Sidonie had taught her to read and do arithmetic, although the accuracy of this memory is in some doubt because Melanie would have been only three or four years old at the time. Nevertheless, Sidonie treated her younger sister with memorable kindness by comparison with their older siblings who had less tolerance for their youngest sister and often made Melanie the target of their teasing.

Sidonie's death was the first of many that Melanie Klein would experience through her long life, and each of the losses she endured fed her earliest fears of illness and death (Grosskurth, 1986, p. 15). Substantial periods of unresolved mourning, feelings of anxious vulnerability over her own health, and episodes of overt depression recurred throughout her adult life and probably had their genesis in these early experiences of illness and death (cf. Sayers, 1991, p. 206). As we shall see, Melanie's feelings of physical vulnerability and susceptibility to illness were often preyed upon, if not actually manipulatively concocted, by her mother.

Intrusive Mother, Detached Father

Libussa Deutsch Reizes (1852–1914), Melanie's mother, was a smart, strong-willed, energetic but intrusive person. Figures 5.6 and 5.7 show Libussa and Melanie around the turn of the century. Twenty-four years younger than her physician husband, Libussa was in her mid-twenties when the couple settled in the Austrian town of Deutsch-Kreuz to raise their first three children. By 1882, the year Melanie was born, the family had relocated to Vienna. Moriz Reizes (1828–1900), Melanie's father, was a general medical practitioner in a small Austrian town whose very rigidly religious family was perceived by Melanie and her mother to be of lower social status than the maternal side of the family. Melanie regarded her mother's clan as "full of knowledge and education" whereas the paternal relatives were largely the objects of scorn (Grosskurth, 1986, p. 7).

Melanie wanted to feel close to her father and to find things about him she could admire, such as his knowledge of at least ten languages. But she had few memories of happy moments with him and no recollections of her father actually ever playing with her. She attributed this neglect largely to his age (an "old fifty") during her childhood. A favorite childhood anecdote about her father told of his brave conduct during a cholera epidemic in a Polish village. Her father volunteered to go to the village, and unlike the other doctors who stood at the windows of the villager's cottages and

FIGURE 5.6   **Libussa Reizes, Melanie Klein's mother in 1900.**

(From: Grosskurth, 1986, opp. p. 148)

FIGURE 5.7   **Melanie Klein in 1902 at the age of 20.**

(From: Grosskurth, 1986, opp. p. 148)

shouted directions to them, Moriz Reizes bravely entered their homes to treat the victims (Grosskurth, 1986, p. 6). The historical authenticity of the cholera story is unknown, but it gave Melanie something of the heroic father most children would want. Nevertheless, a Polish-Jewish doctor was not destined for great material success in the anti-Semitic climate of Vienna of that period. Moriz never achieved financial prosperity as a physician and eventually set himself up in practice as a dentist. Moriz's mediocre accomplishments in the medical and dental professions did not go unnoticed by the women in the family, notably Libussa, who communicated her disappointment in her husband to her children:

> In many little ways, Libussa conveyed to the rest of the family the contempt she felt for her husband. Scholarly, withdrawn, inept at business, he left the management of the household in the hands of his wife. The only way he could assert his superiority was by his intellectual prowess. . . . Libussa did not hide her pride in [her son] Emanuel and in [her daughter] Melanie, whose beauty was bound to catch a good husband. Emilie, on the other hand, is something of a cipher—not very pretty and not at all clever. Nevertheless, her father befriended her, preferring her to the assertive Melanie. It was made clear to father and daughter, in the subtle ways families express such things, that they were excluded from the humid, symbiotic entanglement of Libussa, Emanuel, and Melanie. (Grosskurth, 1986, p. 18)

Libussa Reizes was clearly the dominant member of the family. Melanie grew up observing firsthand a matriarchy that no doubt shaped much of Melanie's attitude toward her mother, motherhood in general, and herself in particular (Grosskurth, 1986, pp. 7, 18). Although no one said it aloud, Moriz was regarded as ineffectual, invisible, and irrelevant. To help the family cope financially, Libussa opened a shop where she sold reptiles and plants with substantial success even though she despised the reptiles. In Melanie's view, her mother's efforts were crucial to the family's survival (Sayers, 1991, p. 206).

As he aged, Melanie perceived her father growing increasingly ineffectual and detached. In her recollection, her father had grown not only old but "senile." As Grosskurth put it, ". . . Moriz Reizes gradually faded away until one day people realized that he was actually dead" (1986, p. 18). In reality, Moriz Reizes died of pneumonia on April 6, 1900, and his passing created even greater financial stresses for the family. Libussa seems to have spent the rest of her life worrying about money and Melanie's alleged poor health.

Melanie's Engagement: The Matriarchy Continues

Melanie was 17 years old when her 21-year-old second cousin, Arthur Klein proposed marriage (Gross, 1986, p. 19). Melanie was quite a beauty at age 17, and some of Emanuel's (her older brother) friends had indicated their interest. But, though she was to regret it later, Melanie and cousin Arthur had eyes only for each other. Even brother Emanuel was initially impressed with Arthur's intellectual gifts, although with time, Emanuel's almost incestuous jealousy soured his view of Arthur. Melanie had plans to go to medical school like her father, but she recalled later that her "passionate temperament" outweighed her intellectual aspirations when she met Arthur. She abandoned plans for medical school and stopped dating other young men.

Privately, however, Melanie was aware that passion was not love. She convinced herself that with time love would blossom. The two second cousins were not well matched. Arthur was rigid and could be inflexible about his strongly held opinions, a male assertiveness and oppositionalism to which Melanie was not accustomed. Arthur and Melanie decided to postpone their marriage for a few years, until economic circumstances stabilized and Arthur could earn a comfortable living. He was then a student preparing for his degree in chemical engineering, and his prospects seemed very good.

Meanwhile, the year of Moriz's death, Melanie's older sister Emilie married Leo Pick, a young doctor. Ostensibly to help the young couple get started on a happy life, Libussa suggested that Dr. Pick take over Moriz's dental practice. Libussa would renovate the Reizes's apartment to provide living quarters for the new couple, an office for Leo and, of course, living quarters for herself. Dr. Pick reluctantly agreed to the arrangement, and Libussa, whose talents for survival were proving exceptional, turned her attentions to Melanie in the hope of hastening this daughter's marriage. She encouraged Melanie to pay an extended visit to her fiancé's family while Arthur was completing advanced studies in America. Libussa's intention seems to have been to maintain the certainty of their eventual marriage during the couple's separation, but it was the first of many intrusions by Libussa into the relationship. Emilie and Leo, too, would soon find that their living arrangements with Libussa would provide her with endless opportunities to meddle in their marriage and manipulate their perceptions of each other.

Emanuel's Death, Melanie's Guilt

After the death of their father, Emanuel thought that Emilie and Melanie were being given preferential treatment by Libussa. Both sisters had the full attention of their mother and were the beneficiaries of what money she had. For her part, Libussa spent what she had to make the young women attractive to suitors. Emanuel, on the other hand, received little money and was given his dead father's madeover clothes. He had an "artistic temperament" and had been known to brood and become depressed, but after his father's death his behavior became even more eccentric. Emanuel also suffered from rheumatic heart disease, a vulnerability that combined with an eccentric and self-destructive lifestyle, ultimately did him in. Emanuel became involved with drugs and alcohol, preferred a nomadic existence and traveled initially to Italy where his romantic entanglements became very complicated and stressful.

Melanie and Emanuel corresponded frequently, but his letters created worries about his health and sanity. Emanuel grew discontented with a young woman with whom he was romantically involved, and they broke off the relationship. Emanuel descended further into depression, broken periodically by manic-like episodes. Melanie found herself trapped in a long engagement to a man she did not love. Her mother was more committed to the idea of Arthur as Melanie's husband than Melanie was, but that commitment reflected Libussa's needs not her daughter's. Melanie's plans for further education were stymied, and Libussa was very unhelpful in dealing with her daughter's worries about the deterioration Emanuel was displaying. Libussa, forever the strategist, did what she could to discourage Emanuel from returning home. She explained to him that his health would suffer more (!) if he returned to the hot summer weather of Vienna. Libussa also implied that Melanie might not love him as much in his present state (Grosskurth, 1986, pp. 24–25). Libussa's machinations were making Emanuel more depressed and angry, and he communicated those feelings through Melanie to his mother. Sensing defeat, Libussa designed a new strategy to keep Emanuel away from the newly renovated but crowded Reizes–Pick apartment-office. She attempted to persuade Emanuel to stay through the summer of 1901 with his sister Melanie at her prospective in-laws home in a Viennese suburb.

In the end, Emanuel did return to Vienna, where, for lack of space, he had to sleep in the same room as his mother. To some degree denying the seriousness of Emanuel's erratic behavior, Libussa nevertheless observed firsthand how Emanuel did not sleep at night, ate little, and fluctuated wildly in his moods. By 1902, Emanuel resumed the nomadic life that seemed to suit him. He moved to Switzerland, but kept in touch with the family, requesting increases in his allowance and advising Melanie on her upcoming wedding. Emanuel gambled with the money he received, and quickly squandered all of his resources. Libussa pressured Melanie to send him what money Melanie had.

Melanie wrote to Emanuel that her fiancé Arthur had obtained a job and that they were ready to marry. In an extraordinary letter to his sister, Emanuel revealed his true feelings about the wedding, about Arthur and, surprisingly, about Melanie. He clearly was jealous of his sister's romance and also of her place in the family. He informed Melanie that ". . . I rejoice in the awareness that Mother will be relieved now of the heaviest burden among her loving concerns, which she has always hidden with her pride and secrecy. I am almost as grateful to you for her sake as for mine!" (quoted in Grosskurth, 1986, p. 30). Melanie was again being told that she was an unwanted burden, and this time the impact of the message was heightened because it originated, despite its obvious anger, from a most trusted and admired source.

Emanuel also threatened his sister Melanie with predictions of dire consequences if she did not help him get money or ease his way with Libussa to return home. References to his own death appear frequently in his letters to Melanie, but he kept their mother more or less in the dark about the state of his mind. In this way, the burden for Emanuel's well-being had been subtly assumed from Libussa by Melanie. Some of Emanuel's letters also amplify an oedipal-incestuous theme that existed between them for some years. Emanuel expressed these uncomfortable thoughts in the guise of his concerns for Melanie's upcoming marriage and her unpreparedness for the sexuality that would accompany the union. Klein's biographer makes clear that Emanuel was jealous of any other man who would possess his sister (Grosskurth (1986, pp. 32 ff.). Emanuel's talent for troubling innuendoes about marriage and sex intensified Melanie's anxiety and guilt, especially because she was already worried about her fiancé's sexual fidelity. She suspected Arthur had been unfaithful to her repeatedly during his travels and could be something of a Lothario around other women. There can be little doubt that Melanie Klein earned her expertise in the area of guilt, envy, and triumph the hard way.

And so the Reizes family crises continued through 1902. Emanuel became even more involved with drugs, more reckless with money, and increasingly depressed and angry. He wandered from place to place throughout Europe, unable to go home to die (Grosskurth, 1986, p. 35). On December 2, 1902, one day after his arrival in Genoa,

Emanuel Reizes, age 25, died of "heart failure," alone in his hotel room. His failing rheumatic heart may have received a substantial push from the combined effects of the deteriorated state of his health, malnutrition, and the catastrophic combination of drugs and alcohol he was consuming. Some years later, Melanie wrote in her autobiography that Emanuel had been "the best friend I ever had." (quoted by Grosskurth, 1986, p. 39).

Melanie's Marriage: The Matriarchy Continues

Still in mourning for Emanuel, Melanie Reizes married her second cousin Arthur Klein on March 31, 1903. Melanie was 21 years old. In an autobiographical story written some 10 years later, Melanie described a fictional young woman who is shocked by her wedding night experience: "And does it therefore have to be like this, that motherhood begins with disgust?" (quoted in Grosskurth, 1986, pp. 40–41). The young heroine of the story, Anna, is consoled by her husband that decent women have a natural dislike for "these things," but Anna is haunted by unexpressed longings for unnamed fulfillment. Melanie was pregnant with her first child within two months of the wedding, and spent several weeks nauseated and miserable. Nausea, misery, and anxious apprehension were to be the dreaded hallmarks of Melanie's subsequent pregnancies. Emanuel's threatening innuendoes were proving to be eerily true. Figure 5.8 shows Arthur Klein during his student years.

Libussa was delighted to learn that she would be a grandmother again (Emilie and Leo had already bestowed grandmother status on Libussa), but she suggested to

FIGURE 5.8   Arthur Klein, Melanie's husband, as a student.

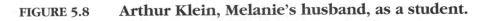

(From: Grosskurth, 1986, opp. p. 148)

Melanie that a boy would be preferable. To Melanie's delight, baby girl Melitta was born January 19, 1904, and took eagerly to being breast-fed. Years later, however, when Melitta had become a psychoanalyst, she would be her mother's most bitter professional antagonist and personal heartbreak. But during this period of Melitta's childhood things were looking up for the Klein family. Arthur's career was advancing steadily and financial security was within the couple's grasp. Never one to miss an opportunity, Libussa pressured Melanie and Arthur repeatedly with letters about the poor state of her own finances. Libussa's intrusion into Melanie's marriage was not restricted to money matters, nor was money the only topic about which she reshaped truth to fit her aims.

When Melanie confided to her mother that even though she was fundamentally unhappy with Arthur she wanted to be pregnant again, Libussa encouraged her to do so. But Libussa also expressed the wish that the next child be more like Emilie and "less nervous" than Melanie herself. Three years after Melitta's birth, on March 2, 1907, Melanie gave birth to her second child, Hans. During her pregnancy with Hans, Melanie was sick, depressed, nauseated, and felt increasingly confined in her marriage. Arthur moved the family to Krappitz, a small town in upper Silesia, now Poland, to take a new job as director of a paper mill, but Melanie experienced the move as one more burden enforced upon an already dismal existence. Krappitz (who names these things?) was crushing in its dreariness. Nevertheless, Arthur's new financial security permitted him to quiet Libussa's continual complaints by settling most of her debts. They invited Libussa to live with them, a move Melanie initially relished, but one which gave Libussa a better purchase from which to steer the unhappy marriage.

Arthur began traveling frequently, and Melanie suspected that he was frequently unfaithful to her. The more such worries fueled her unhappiness the wider the door opened to her mother's attempts to serve as chief arbitrator and intermediary between Arthur and Melanie. Libussa became the not-so-diplomatic link for letters between Melanie and her forever traveling husband. She even took command of the Klein household, as Melanie became more angry, withdrawn, and depressed. Libussa did everything she could to keep Arthur away from Melanie, even suggesting to both of them that it would be bad for Melanie's health for them to spend time together. She encouraged her daughter to travel to distant places "for her health," and told Arthur any story that was momentarily expedient to keep him away from home as he traveled on business.

> According to Libussa, Arthur blossomed when [Melanie] was away, the children were much better off without her, and her own mother needed the absence in order to achieve serenity. Melanie was a pampered object, not a loved daughter, but a lap dog who had been taught to sit up and beg and to lie down passively. (Grosskurth, 1986, p. 58)

Libussa tried to control each person's perception of the others. Melanie's eldest daughter Melitta, for example, was made to understand by grandmother Libussa that Melanie was so emotionally crippled and physically vulnerable that she had to abandon her daughter repeatedly just to survive (Grosskurth, 1986, p. 53). Libussa also made clear to Melitta that Hans was her preferred grandchild.

Arthur eventually negotiated a new job that required the family to move to Budapest, a compromise move that Melanie could tolerate better than Arthur's original proposal for a move to another small Silesian town bleaker than Krappitz. The move to Budapest had clear benefits for everyone. Arthur's career was advanced by the move, Melanie's depression was momentarily diminished by the cosmopolitan atmosphere, and Libussa could enjoy unbroken security in her living arrangements.

But Budapest also had its inevitable downside. World War I was raging and would quickly separate Melanie both from her husband and her analyst, as both were called into the military. On July 1, 1914, Melanie gave birth to her third child, Erich, with whom we are already familiar as "Fritz," the subject of Melanie's first published case history. Life in Budapest had even greater challenges in store for her. After a relatively brief illness that did not initially appear to be serious, Libussa Reizes died on November 6, 1914. In reality, Libussa had undiagnosed cancer and had been losing weight and vigor for some time. The inevitably lethal effects of the disease were hastened by a bronchial infection that ended Libussa Reizes's life within two weeks of its diagnosis.

In what must have seemed like the blink of an eye, Melanie was bombarded with devastating losses. She was deprived by the war of her husband and her analyst and had lost forever the mother on whom she had become dependent. Almost simultaneously, she had become a new mother for the third time with little emotional support or sustained help from Arthur in parenting their children. Arthur became director of several factories and family fortunes improved considerably, even if it meant that Arthur and Melanie spent even less time together. At some point in this period, around 1914, Melanie read Freud's (1901b) brief essay "On Dreams" and became convinced that she had found the answer to her own personal distress. In addition to the emotional relief that Freudian therapy seemed to promise, psychoanalysis as an intellectual pursuit might provide a substitute way to achieve her long blocked professional interests in a medical career (Grosskurth, 1986, p. 68).

Melanie sought psychoanalytic treatment for her ongoing depression, recently intensified by the death of Libussa, with the eminent Hungarian analyst Sandor Ferenczi (1873–1933). Ferenczi was not just another Budapest analyst. For a long period, Ferenczi was a confidante and close associate of Sigmund Freud, so close that Freud entertained hopes that Ferenczi would eventually marry his daughter Mathilde (Haynal, 1992, p. xx). Gradually, in the period between 1911 and 1912, the character of their friendship began to change around issues of Ferenczi's personal conduct with a patient with whom Ferenczi fell in love (Haynal, 1992, p. xxii). Both men committed indiscretions and conducted themselves in ethically questionable ways. Such behavior put them on the road to later personal and theoretical disputes. Nevertheless, Ferenczi underwent "experimental" personal analyses with Freud in 1914 and 1916, even though Freud warned that there was a danger that the analyses might result in "personal estrangement." And, in the end, that was indeed the outcome. Sometime around 1914, it was Sandor Ferenczi who first suggested to his patient Melanie Klein that child analysis would profit from her unique skills. Figure 5.9 shows Melanie around the period of her analysis with Ferenezi.

FIGURE 5.9   Melanie Klein in 1912.

(From: Grosskurth, 1986, opp. p. 148)

Divorce

By 1916, at the end of the war, an anti-Semitic revolution had turned the social climate in Budapest against Jews. Arthur Klein had been wounded and permanently injured, and he lost his job. Sometime in 1919 Arthur moved to Sweden where he was able to find work, leaving Melanie to care for their three children. Melanie understood that they would never again be together as a couple. For the remainder of his life, Arthur was not able to rise to the heights of success he had experienced prior to the war.

Melanie left Budapest with the children and returned briefly to Austria. By 1921, she moved again, this time to Berlin taking only her youngest son Erich with her. Apparently with the separation from Arthur, money was scarce. The two older children remained either in boarding school or with their paternal grandparents in Austria for the next two years until approximately 1923, when Melanie reunited all of her children in Berlin. The precise date of Melanie and Arthur's divorce is unclear. Melanie claimed 1922 or 1923 as the year in different autobiographical accounts, but Grosskurth (1986, p. 90) makes the case that the divorce could not have been final until 1926.

The divorce was both a much delayed ending and an energetic beginning for Melanie Klein. She focused her newfound energy and attention on making an impact in the psychoanalytic community to build a professional life that would sustain her and the children. Erich became the subject of her first published case of "Fritz's psychoanalytic upbringing," as we have seen, and in subsequent decades her reputation as a pioneering child analyst and her body of work grew enormously. Melanie Reizes

Klein had sustained many losses: her sisters Sidonie and Emilie, brother Emanuel, mother Libussa, husband Arthur. She would eventually lose two of her children: Melitta by embittered alienation and Hans in a hiking accident that led to his death in 1934, at the age of 27. She had weathered many conflicts and controversies: her marriage to Arthur, her clash with Anna Freud, and the attacks of her own eldest daughter Melitta in later years.

Melanie outlived Arthur by 20 years. Arthur Klein died in Switzerland in 1939. Melanie Reizes Klein died in London on September 22, 1960.

The Implications of Klein's Personal Sources

Melanie Klein described the development of human character with the earthy vocabulary of love and hate, envy and triumph, guilt and reparation. What links can we detect between Melanie Klein's theory and Melanie Klein's life?

Melanie's experiences with the dominating and intrusive Libussa Reizes surely fueled angry feelings in her. The utter detachment of the nearly invisible Moriz Reizes could only facilitate Libussa's fabrication of the Reizes matriarchy. Melanie's yearning for a competent father was thus thwarted equally by the very different behavior of both parents. Her mother and brother, each for their own selfish reasons, convinced Melanie that she had been an "unexpected" child and the "heaviest burden" to her mother. Like so many theorists we examine in this book, Klein felt unwanted. Rejection, too, breeds anger. Melanie Klein's understanding of the infant's mental life was thus captured—some would say "constrained"—by emotions derived from insecurity, frustration, threat, and conflict.[3] Klein's inferences about the nature of human nature bear the imprint of this unique vision. Kleinian infants are more angry than curious, more anxious than eager, and impelled more by hate than by love.

As an adult, Melanie's experiences with her own children led to the discovery that mothers can be seen as evil, devouring witches, or as trustworthy, comforting companions. As Pasteur pointed out, "chance favors the prepared mind." Melanie had been well primed. The concept of mother-as-evil-devouring-witch was not entirely unprecedented in her experience and not all that difficult to accept. She understood that the maternal phantasy image created by children was determined in large part by the character of the relationship between mother and child at that moment in development. And so it must be, she reasoned, for all children. There can be little doubt that Melanie applied this reasoning to her own conflicted feelings toward Libussa, and thereby insulated her mother from a great deal of anger. Used in this way, the concepts of phantasy and split objects are both theoretical constructs and personally protective rationalizations.

Klein's belief that she had been the unplanned and begrudgingly loved child among her more favored siblings instilled a motive beyond anger. We will see the same motivation again among other personality theorists who felt unwanted as children and in the search for self-knowledge and healing chose psychology or psychiatry as their life work. For Klein specifically, the path to psychoanalysis was paved with chronic depression and intolerable feelings of unworthiness. She was especially alert

---

[3] Chapter 18 presents a detailed comparison of the theme of unwantedness among the theorists.

to those feelings in others. If anger is the first reaction to feeling unwanted or inferior, the second is curiosity. Creative thinkers transcend the immediate grievance to question the meaning of what they experience. Such people, and Klein was certainly one of them, want to know if others share similar personal pain, and if so, *how* is it similar? Klein found herself focusing on this version of the puzzle: How can relationships with others be so contradictory? It was clear to her that even the earliest relationships generate pleasure with pain. They generate chaos and thereby instigate a need for order. Relationships trigger rage, but rage provokes guilt and anxiety. Love and admiration put the infant on the fast track to envy. These contradictory experiences were the ones Melanie Klein knew best and most intimately, and she chose to universalize them.

Klein's understanding of the infant's anger had eventually to be tempered by her more mature grasp of the child's complex world. The nuances and complexities of real children and the real distresses of her own relationships combined to moderate Klein's earliest, overly narrow obsession with infantile anger. Because parents are enviable for their superior power and knowledge, the child admires and envies them. In time, she recognized the child's need—and her own—not merely to destroy love objects, but to surpass them and bask in triumph until fleeting exultation yields to remorse.

She understood from experience the exquisite complexity of object relations. For example, the mother she loved and admired had nevertheless dominated and manipulated her. More painful still, Libussa contributed substantially but covertly to the failure of Melanie's marriage. Emanuel Klein, the much admired but fatally vulnerable brother, evoked taboo feelings in her. Their adult brother-sister relationship is described by Klein's chief biographer as all but overtly incestuous (Grosskurth, 1986, pp. 31 ff.). As a mother herself, she was often depressed and distracted, with the apparent result that her children created angry phantasies about her. As she had experienced her own mother, Melanie Klein must have been experienced as intrusive and manipulative by those of her children she employed as psychoanalytic patients. And their anger at having a mother who sometimes, frustratingly, was not a mother wrote profoundly influential passages in Klein's notebook of observations. It is small wonder that Klein proposed the fear of being attacked, devoured, or annihilated by mother as the fundamental and universal danger situation among women as compared with castration anxiety in men.

A FINAL WORD ON MELANIE KLEIN

Melanie Klein learned from her own relationships that the people to whom one is most attached are also the people who can provoke the most profound anger and the deepest envy. Hatred of one's nearest and dearest intimates inevitably leads to guilt. More painful still, when these people are gone through death or alienation, there is no recourse. Envy of love objects and triumph over them exacts a price. Only the residue of unresolved guilt grounded in the finality of loss remains constant. The need to protect them, one is compelled almost to say, "maternally," arises without logic, in spite of reason, guiltily from unmediated emotion. The raw power of feeling, not reason, is at the heart of the Kleinian worldview. In her emphasis on the irrational alone is a compelling explanation of Melanie Klein's insistence on chaotic infantile phantasy, aggression, love, and guilt-driven reparation.

D. W. WINNICOTT

"MAY I BE ALIVE WHEN I DIE."

Pediatrician turned child analyst, Donald Woods Winnicott (1896–1971) brought common sense and a wry spontaneity to the treatment of children. Compared to such luminaries as Melanie Klein and Anna Freud, D. W. Winnicott was restrained in his rhetoric, pragmatically playful in his clinical style, and fiercely protective of his intellectual independence. Above all other qualities, Winnicott was gifted in the art of communicating with children. He could be playful with youngsters, even ironic, without patronizing them. And he had the knack of "holding"—making them feel safe.

Compared with the Kleinian child, still fresh in memory, the Winnicottian child is a collaborator not an antagonist (Phillips, 1988, p. 52). Winnicott positioned himself as a sympathetic witness to a child's distress, acknowledging a child's need for "holding" in both realistic and metaphorical ways. In short, Winnicott was a good mother to his patients. A measure of the man can be had in three anecdotes. The first provides a glimpse into Winnicott's down-to-earth, use-what-you-got technique with children. The second displays the ineffable Winnicottian charm, a graceful mix of whimsy and wit that struck sparks from flint. The third provides a front row, center seat at a matinee performance of the flinty side of Winnicott's character, a personal style that, for all its playfulness, was provocative and contentious.

The Squiggle, the Spatula, and the Niffle

Winnicott drew a random-appearing line or an elaborate but ambiguous doodle on paper. He then invited a child to "make something" from this squiggle while encouraging the child to talk about the drawing and what it might mean. Then it was Winnicott's turn. The child was encouraged to create a squiggle which Winnicott, who had some talent for drawing, could turn into a meaningful picture. Of course, Winnicott's creations were often better than anything the child could accomplish with squiggles, and he was not reticent about pointing out this fact. Figure 5.10 illustrates Winnicott's use of squiggles with 12-year-old Patrick.

Winnicott sometimes enjoyed completing the child's squiggle with a wry or comic picture accompanied with humorous comments or even patently absurd, Dr. Seuss–like word play. On one occasion, for example, each time a child rose to place her latest squiggle drawing at the end of a row of pictures on the floor, Winnicott said "goodbye." She was greeted almost immediately with a Winnicottian "hello" as she returned to her seat beside him (Winnicott, 1964b, p. 308).[4] In another instance,

---

[4] Because his papers have appeared in so many overlapping collections at different periods in his career, the original publication date of Winnicott's work is cited wherever possible to permit the reader to follow the chronology of his thinking.

FIGURE 5.10   Squiggle Drawings of a 12-Year-Old Boy.

Patrick made the elephant in the left frame (1) from a squiggle drawn by Winnicott. The middle frame (3) shows Winnicott's transformation of Patrick's squiggle into what Patrick called "mother holding a baby." Sometime later, Patrick made the unusual picture on the right (11) from Winnicott's squiggle. He described it as person "who slipped into some dog food," and was probably mocking someone, perhaps Winnicott. The bottom corner inset of each frame shows the probable outlines of the starting squiggles, which are more apparent in the originals as variations of line density.

(From: Winnicott, 1965b, pp. 344, 346).

Winnicott interpreted a child's squiggle as defecation products, calling it a "busy" in the peculiar idiom of the girl's family.

> She looked at me as if it was interesting, but as if I was talking a language that was not hers, and she said it was a snake. So I put a plate round it and I suggested that we could have it for lunch. (1964b, p. 307)

Squiggle by squiggle, Winnicott permitted the child to tell the story of his or her world without hurry, often disjointedly, always interactively. After several "consultations" with Dr. Winnicott, inhibited children learned to work through play.

The Spatula

With infants, Winnicott invented a different but equally creative technique to enable them to communicate. The waiting room outside his office in the Paddington Green Hospital was often full to bursting with mothers and their infants. One by one, they entered Winnicott's consulting room to make a rather lengthy walk from the door to the desk and chair where the mother was invited to sit with her infant on her lap. The long walk provided Winnicott with an opportunity to observe the mother's handling of her child and the demeanor of both as they entered for the "consultation."

He then invited the mother and her infant to sit together next to a table on which he had placed a shiny, steel tongue depressor called a "spatula." Winnicott instructed the mother and any observers present in precisely how to behave, especially about the necessity to restrict their natural eagerness to prompt the infant.

. . . I ask the mother to sit opposite me with the angle of the table coming between me and her. She sits down with the baby on her knee. As a routine, I place a right-angled shining tongue-depressor at the edge of the table and invite the mother to place the child in such a way that, if the child should wish to handle the spatula, it is possible. Ordinarily, a mother will understand what I am about, and it is easy for me gradually to describe to her that there is to be a period of time in which she and I will contribute as little as possible to the situation, so that what happens can fairly be put down to the child's account. You can imagine that mothers show by their ability or relative inability to follow this suggestion something of what they are like at home; if they are anxious about infection, or have strong moral feelings against putting things to the mouth, if they are hasty or move impulsively, these characteristics show up. (1941/1992, pp. 52–53)

Over time, Winnicott's "set situation," as he called it, grew into a situational personality assessment of mother and child. Despite Winnicott's explicit instructions to remain silent and motionless, some mothers were unable or unwilling to accept the discipline of the situation. He observed, for example, mothers who "have a rooted objection to the child's mouthing and handling of objects. . . ." and communicated their disgust to their infants in subtle and not so subtle ways. Impulsive-anxious mothers, by comparison, could not restrain their eagerness to reassure and comfort their babies. Such over-eager reassurance often had the paradoxical effect of interfering with the child's spontaneous efforts to cope with the novelty of the situation. The set situation was seen as a test of intelligence by competitive mothers. Eyes on the prize, these mothers intrusively coached and prodded their infants toward "success" in grasping the spatula (1941/1992, p. 59).

In fact, the spatula game was a kind of test, but the primary subjects were the children. Winnicott used the set situation of mother, child, pediatrician, and spatula as a near-standardized but fundamentally projective assessment of infants' cognitive and emotional functioning. He described a three-stage sequence of "normal" behavior he had observed in the set situation with infants ranging in ages from four to 13 months. The beginning phase, called the *period of hesitation,* is one of initial stillness and expectancy with little overt action. In the second stage, the infant grasps the spatula and exhibits confidence and satisfaction in taking possession of and exerting control over the enticing object. Finally, the infant becomes playful, deliberately dropping the makeshift toy to hear it clang on the floor. Some infants in this third stage even engage the collaboration of an adult to "lose" and "find" the dropped spatula repeatedly. Table 5.2 provides a more detailed summary of a typical child's progress through the three stages.

Winnicott thought that the first stage in Table 5.2, or *period of hesitation,* was especially significant in revealing infants typical emotional reactions in unfamiliar situations. Most infants already have a characteristic way of handling curiosity in the face of anxiety, and that temperamental style is manifest in the set situation. For most normal infants, the period of hesitation can be more precisely described as a moment of expectation. The infant who spies the shiny spatula is at first very still, very alert. Most youngsters restrain the impulse to reach for it immediately. They wait warily. Normal infants, Winnicott observed in thousands of instances, rapidly overcome their initial hesitancy because desire and curiosity grow more intense than anxiety. To all appearances, normally curious infants are struggling with inner resolve: "I could just

TABLE 5.2   Behavior of Normal 4–13 Month Old Infants in Winnicott's "Set (Spatula) Situation"

Stage	Infant Behavior	Evidence of Anxiety
1. Period of Hesitation (*Expectation and Stillness*)	• Holds body still. Expectant but not rigid. • Touches spatula, hesitantly, warily. • Wide-eyed with expectation, watches adults. • Sometimes withdraws interest and hides face. • Momentary hesitation to summon courage and accept reality of own desire to touch the spatula.	Inhibited. Buries face in mother's lap. Ignores spatula completely or immediately seizes and throws spatula.
2. Confident and Collaborative Play (*Possession and Control*)	• Reaches for spatula decisively. • Excitement and interest mirrored in changes in baby's mouth: inside becomes flabby, saliva flows copiously, tongue looks thick and soft. • Explores spatula with mouth. • Free/flexible body movements linked to the spatula. • Exhibits confidence that he/she possesses the spatula and is in (magical?) control of it. • Plays with spatula, bangs it on table or on nearby metal bowl to make as much noise as possible. • Wants to play at being fed with adult as collaborator, but is upset if adult "spoils" game by really taking spatula into mouth. • Not obviously disappointed that spatula is inedible.	Persistent, prolonged hesitation. Brute force needed to bring spatula close to infant or put it in baby's mouth with resulting distress, crying, colic, or screaming.
3. Riddance and Restoration (*Loss and Return*)	• Drops spatula as if by mistake. • Pleased when it is retrieved. • Deliberately drops it after restoration. • Enjoys aggressively getting rid of spatula, especially if it makes sound when dropped.	Persistent (compulsive) repetition of riddance and restoration, with no evidence of boredom or waning interest.

(Based on the description in Winnicott, 1941/1992).

look at it. I should grab it. Maybe I shouldn't? But I *could.* I want it. I *will.*" As self-confidence grows, action replaces indecision. Delight displaces delay. Anxiety evaporates. The prize is seized. Drooling and cooing accompany the spatula as it enters baby's mouth for an examination unlike anything intended by the designer of the tongue depressor.

Winnicott also observed that acutely anxious infants were unable to master their hesitation and prolonged their delay indefinitely. In contrast, some anxiously impulsive infants circumvented the period of hesitation altogether and immediately seized the spatula to throw it to the floor. When Winnicott wrote his first paper describing this deceptively simple observational technique, he was still in the early phases of learning about child psychoanalysis. Melanie Klein's ideas loomed large in Winnicott's training, and he attempted to interpret the symbolic meaning of the spatula for the child. He hypothesized that the spatula signified to the infant a breast, a penis, and even a person or "bits" of a person (1941/1992, p. 61). Fortunately, Winnicott's empirical predilections and good sense eventually prevailed over his enthusiasm for

Kleinian speculations. He could see that the "set situation" was a window on the infant's interpersonal transactions and emotional maturity:

> In the set situation the infant who is under observation gives me important clues to the state of his emotional development. He may only see in the spatula a thing that he takes or leaves, and which he does not connect with a human being. This means that he has not developed the capacity, or he has lost it, for building up the whole person behind the part object. Or he may show that he sees me or mother behind the spatula, and behave as if this were part of me (or of mother). In this case, if he takes the spatula, it is as if he took his mother's breast. Or, finally, he may see mother and me and think of the spatula as something to do with the relation between mother and myself. In so far as this is the case, in taking or leaving the spatula he makes a difference to the relationship of two people, standing for father and mother. . . . The infant, if he has the capacity to do so, finds himself dealing with two persons at once, mother and myself. This requires a degree of emotional development higher than the recognition of one whole person, and it is true indeed that many neurotics never succeed in managing a relation to two people at once. (Winnicott, 1941/1992, pp. 64–65)

The Niffle

Tom, age five, was injured while on vacation with his family and evacuated to a distant city to be hospitalized. His mother accompanied him, but eventually left Tom alone in the hospital, where he found it hard to sleep without his "niffle." Tom's niffle, so named by his sister, was a square of woven material derived from a wool shawl. In fact, there had been three niffles, but only one of them was Tom's special niffle. He could distinguish his special niffle from the other two even in the dark (Winnicott, 1996a/1996, p. 105). Returned home, Tom's mother tried to ship the special niffle to her son's hospital, but the niffle failed to arrive and was never seen again.

Eventually Tom recovered and rejoined his family, but he seemed not to be the same child. He became oppositional toward his mother, and resisted being dressed and cleaned by her. Tom acted in a "generally annoying way" and spoke with a peculiar high-pitched voice that sounded girlish. Tom's mother was especially irritated by this voice. When questioned by Winnicott, Tom summed it all up: "But I wish I had this little niffle. It makes me feel . . ."—at which point Tom was at a loss for words. Fortunately Winnicott did not share Tom's loss, but understood the betrayal he was feeling and the angry mourning reaction he was experiencing.

We have all seen children attached to their teddy bears, comforted by soft blankets they drag around with them, and their delight in other cuddly things; but until Winnicott ventured into the field it is doubtful that anyone understood the child's active creation of attachment magic with these things. Winnicott intuitively grasped that the teddy bears, blankets, and niffles of this world are *transitional objects* that bridge the gap between the child's utter dependence on its mother and its profound need to progress to independence. Tom's missing niffle was experienced by him as a profound loss of love, security, and trust. Winnicott understood what Tom's mother did not, and he taught the rest of us that a niffle is not a trifle.

Winnicott clearly had the spontaneity, creativity, and playfulness to adapt ordinary activities and materials to the psychoanalytic task of interpreting the child's inner world. It is no small matter, as we shall see, that Winnicott's choice of the tongue depressor/spatula as one of his diagnostic instruments had the subtle consequence of emphasizing his professional and personal links to medicine. He nevertheless used this "doctor-tool" in the most "un-doctor" ways. Winnicott consolidated the observations that he made with this traditional instrument of pediatric physical examinations into the most untraditional of pediatric psychological assessments. It is important, therefore, not to underestimate how much Winnicott prized his originality and protected his independence. As a pediatrician/child psychiatrist, Winnicott worked hard to be seen as an innovator. It was no less important to Winnicott to be steadfastly, not to say defiantly, original as a psychoanalytic psychiatrist. It is a virtual certainty that Winnicott would be pleased to know that, among his other accomplishments, he is remembered as the theorist of the squiggle, the spatula, and the niffle.

The Pill for Folks Not Ill

Late in his career, Winnicott delivered an invited but informal talk to the members of the Progressive League entitled "The Pill." His opening remark was pure Mark Twain: "Actually, you know, I've never had the Pill" (p. 195). He then described how he tried to prepare for the talk, but instead of an organized outline, he managed to create only the following poem (Winnicott, 1969a/1986, pp. 196–97):

> O silly Pill for folks not ill!
> Why not wait till you know God's will?
> What's empty will in time refill
> And pregnant hill be razed to nil.
> Men! Have your will, put Jack in Jill;
> Girls! Drink your fill of his chlorophyll.
> Fear not the spill you know the drill,
> You know a still and silent kill . . . the Pill.
> So take my quill I sure will:
> Don't dally dill with silly Pill,
> Just wait until what happens will!
> Then pay the bill.

Winnicott's audience delighted in his humor, whereas a contemporary audience would probably polarize into armed camps.

"I died."

Toward the end of his life, Winnicott began preparing an autobiography, fragments of which have been published in the reminiscences of Clare Winnicott (1978; 1989). On the inside cover of a notebook, he copied several lines from T. S. Eliot[5] and followed

---

[5] The lines Winnicott quoted were from T. S. Eliot's *Four Quartets* ("Little Gidding") and reflect Winnicott's lifelong affinity for paradox and dialectical thinking:

> Costing not less than everything
> [and]
> What we call the beginning is often the end
> And to make an end is to make a beginning.
> The end is where we start from.

them with this prayer: "Oh God! May I be alive when I die." Immediately thereafter, Winnicott begins his autobiography: "I died." Not one to prolong the suspense, a few lines later Winnicott tells his readers that his prayer was answered, "I was alive when I died. That was all I had asked and I got it" (quoted in C. Winnicott, 1989, p. 4; see also C. Winnicott, 1978, p. 19).

UNCONVENTIONAL PSYCHOANALYSIS: THE PEDIATRIC CONSULTATION MODEL

Winnicott's primary professional training was in pediatrics. Throughout his career, even after years of preparation as a child analyst, Winnicott thought of himself as both a pediatrician and a psychoanalyst. Each professional identity, he believed, informed and enhanced the activities of the other (e.g., Winnicott, 1965a, pp. 140–141; Kahr, 1996; Phillips, 1986). In so doing, Winnicott found that he had become the proverbial man without a country, citizen of neither domain. As a pediatrician, Winnicott encountered the "unwillingness" of his medical colleagues to consider the psychology of physical illness. And a pediatrician of the late 1920s who took seriously the psychology of the unconscious was simply not a pediatrician (Winnicott, 1931/1958, p. 20). As a child analyst, Winnicott was expected to leave pediatric medicine and all its traditions behind. The analyst does not take detailed histories of the patient and patient's family, does not physically examine the patient, nor does the analyst directly observe the child-rearing environment provided by the parents. Above all else, the child analyst does not serve as a consultant who briefly sees a child in one or two sessions to provide child-rearing advice to the parents or make focused, often educational, interventions (Winnicott, 1963a/1965a; 1958/1965c). Such forays outside the analyst's traditional role were simply not done.

Winnicott did them. "I am a paediatrician who has swung to psychiatry," Winnicott wrote, "and a psychiatrist who has clung to paediatrics" (1948c/1992, p. 157). He sought nothing less than a personal synthesis of two antagonistic traditions. Compounding two disparate professions into one had the most welcome side effect of conferring an aura of originality on both. With originality came the added blessing of intellectual independence. Successful management of this novel, not to say subversive, blending of clinical roles elevated Winnicott to a unique position in medical and psychiatric circles. He became *the* pediatric child analyst (see Jacobs, 1995 for a similar view; and Phillips, 1988, pp. 48 ff.; Winnicott, 1971, "Introduction").

And the rich grow richer. Winnicott's singularity among child analysts caught the attention of Ernest Jones, the head of the British Psychoanalytic Society. In a 1936 letter to Freud, Jones described Winnicott as "our only man [child] analyst" (Freud and Jones, 1993, p. 755). Had he known, Winnicott would have been amused, then pleased. He abhorred following the crowd in anything.

Elements of a Winnicottian Consultation

Much of Winnicott's experience was gained in relatively brief consultations with parents and children, especially during the war years, and frequently in a hospital clinic setting. In these consultations, Winnicott provided a number of services, including diagnosis, advice on childcare, and recommendations for placement or specialized treatment. Khan (1975/1992, p. xvii) places the number of children and family members seen by Winnicott in consultation over a period of four decades at an amazing sixty thousand. Winnicott (1948c, p. 158) himself reported that he had personally taken histories from over twenty thousand mothers.

Although Winnicott (1972/1986; Little, 1990) conducted a fair share of the more traditional one-on-one "analyses," his pediatric training and personal preferences steered him in the direction of a consultative style characterized by precision focus, rapid tempo, and brief duration. Such encounters, sometimes episodically repeated, might consist of a single "diagnostic-history-taking-recommendation-session" or a series of comparatively leisurely meetings with a child, typically over the span of several weeks or months, but sometimes extending for years (Winnicott, 1957/1965c). Only the tiniest fraction of the children with whom Winnicott consulted were viewed as appropriate candidates for "standard" psychoanalysis. Straddling the two worlds of pediatric psychiatric consultation and child psychoanalysis demanded that Winnicott develop a singularly flexible perspective. The real world constraints of distressed children, and the living conditions provided for them by their parents, achieved special significance in Winnicott's thinking. A composite picture of the Winnicott consultative method highlights these techniques and assumptions.

Take a History, Make a Diagnosis

Winnicott was a bear about taking a detailed family history. His medical training persuaded him that children were people who could be understood only when a complete and chronologically ordered narrative of the child's life had been constructed. The clinician had to take the time to piece together the fragments of confusion that often blurs the meaning of the child's "symptoms." Simply disentangling the facts from the confusions was often therapeutic enough. Such history taking included the usual elements of presenting problem, chronology of developmental landmarks, parental descriptions of the child's problem, the child's description of the problem, and sometimes even direct observation of mother and child (or father and child) playing together. But the purpose of taking the history was not the mere gathering of data:

> It was as a practicing paediatrician that I found the therapeutic value of history taking, and discovered the fact that this provides the best opportunity for therapeutics, provided that the history-taking is not done for the purpose of gathering facts. Psycho-analysis for me is a vast extension of history-taking, with therapeutics as a by-product. (Winnicott, 1963a/1965a, pp. 198–99)

Diagnosing the patient's difficulty correctly was a central feature of Winnicott's work. His diagnosis began by taking the patient's history, but continued throughout their work together. Changes in the patient's behavior, alterations to the patient's circumstances, and "spontaneous" modifications in the nature or quality of the therapeutic relationship signaled Winnicott to alter his diagnosis and sometimes his therapeutic strategy. One size, Winnicott believed, does not fit all: ". . . by and large, analysis is for those who want it, need it, and can take it" (1962a/1965a, p. 169).

Take Charge, Take Notes, Take Your Time

From the vantage point of medical practice, Winnicott was a firm believer in taking charge of the consultation. As both a pediatrician and as a psychodynamic psychotherapist, Winnicott assumed that it was his responsibility to provide a setting in which both the child and parents felt safe enough to communicate the meaning they placed on the child's distressing symptoms. The responsibility of the clinician is to be reliable, truthful, calm, and authoritatively knowledgeable (Winnicott, 1961b/1990, p. 235).

Use What You Got, as Little as Needed, as Simply as Possible

For many consultations, Winnicott was creative in enlisting the aid of the child's parents, teachers, or caseworker to carry out "treatment" in the child's daily environment. As Winnicott pointed out, "In psychoanalysis we ask ourselves: how much can we do? At the other extreme, in my hospital clinic, our motto is: how little need we do?" (1961b/1990, p. 233; 1962a/1965a, p. 166). Winnicott was sensitive to the need for economy and efficiency in the treatment of childhood disorders, a sensitivity that he carried over into his psychoanalytic practice as well (Winnicott, 1955/1989). Even when working analytically, Winnicott strove to make his interpretations as brief as possible. He even limited himself to one interpretation per session, unless he was very tired (1962a/1965a). He did not hesitate to mix "standard" analytic method with other procedures that met the needs of specially primitive patients. In a very unanalytic way, he sometimes intervened directly into the patient's daily life. He aimed to provide more stability and security for those who functioned especially precariously or who exhibited the special needs of people with primitively organized personalities (e.g., Little, 1990).

Don't Be Eager to Be Clever. Shut up. Let the Patient Talk.

Winnicott learned a lesson unusual in medical education from a teacher of pediatrics—Dr. Thomas Horder—at St. Bartholomew's Hospital. The lesson was to listen to his patients. Horder told Winnicott "Don't you go in with your wonderful knowledge and apply it all. Just listen. They'll tell you quite a lot of things. You'll learn if you listen" (C. Winnicott, 1983/1991, pp. 188–89). Winnicott took the advice both for his pediatric consultations and, later, for his approach to psychoanalysis. He tried to restrict himself to one or at most two interpretations in a single session. When he was tired, he sometimes found himself talking too much in analytic sessions. At such times, he described himself as having drifted into a "teaching session" rather than "doing psychoanalysis." He even quipped that whenever he found himself using the word *moreover,* he knew he had drifted again (Winnicott, 1962a/1965a, p. 167). As Winnicott put it toward the end of his life,

> If only we can wait, the patient arrives at understanding creatively and with immense joy, and I now enjoy this joy more than I used to enjoy the sense of having been clever. *I think I interpret mainly to let the patient know the limits of my understanding.* (1968b/1989, p. 219; emphasis added)

Normal Life Is Normally Difficult. Symptoms Are Easier.

Winnicott recognized that a child's aberrant behavior often had multiple "uses" in the child's world. Symptoms can have various meanings that are not always "abnormal" even when extreme. Bed-wetting, for example, is

> . . . a common enough symptom which almost everyone has to deal with who has to deal with children. If by bed-wetting a child is making effective protest against strict management, sticking up for the rights of the individual, so to speak, then the symptom is not an illness; rather it is a sign that the child still hopes to keep the individuality which has been in some way threatened. In the vast majority of cases, bed-wetting is doing its job, and given time, and with ordinary good management, the child will become able to leave off the symptom and adopt other methods of asserting the self.
>
> Or take refusal of food—another common symptom. It is absolutely normal for a child to refuse food. I assume that the food you offer is good. The point really is that a child cannot always *feel* the food to be good. A child cannot *always* feel that good food is deserved. Given time and calm management the child will eventually find out what to call good, and what to call bad; in other words, will develop likes and dislikes, as we all do. (Winnicott, 1964a, p. 127; emphases in original; see also 1964c)

Normality is maturity; abnormality is immaturity (Winnicott, 1958/1965c, pp. 101–03; 1961a/1989). Sometimes, Winnicott argued, the most efficacious thing the child therapist can do is nothing. Waiting for the child's growth and maturity to attenuate the problem is often the pediatrician's/therapist's best strategy, and Winnicott often advised parents to do the same. Active intervention in what appears to be seriously pathological behavior is sometimes not necessary if the parents can provide an adequate and loving environment for the child to master its momentary distress.

> A normal child can employ any and all of the devices nature has provided in defence against anxiety and intolerable conflict. The devices employed (in health) are related to the kind of help that is available. Abnormality shows in a *limitation* and *rigidity* of the child's capacity to employ symptoms, and a relative lack of relationship between the symptoms and what can be expected in the way of help. (1964a, p. 126–27; emphases in original)

Winnicott's point, drawn from his pediatric medical experiences, was that "symptoms" are often indicators of the healthy child's ability to battle against disease and other adversities. Only when a child's "symptoms" are linked to failure of the child's natural defenses can we assume the presence of "abnormality."

> So, although bed-wetting, and refusal of food, and all sorts of other symptoms can be serious indications for treatment, they need not be so. In fact, children who can surely be called normal can be shown to have such symptoms, and to have them simply because life is difficult, inherently difficult for every human being, for every one from the very beginning. (Winnicott, 1964a, p. 127)

Why Normal Life Is Difficult: From Illusion to Disillusion

Under the best of circumstances, the developing infant confronts and must master a succession of disappointments. First, Winnicott pointed to the child's experience of the clash between its inner world of fantasy and the outer world of reality. With varying degrees of disappointment, babies learn that what is wanted is not always what is supplied. The illusion of wishfulness are inevitably disillusioned by the facts of reality (1964a, p. 128).

Second, babies learn that destructive urges and thoughts that are frightening sometimes accompany the feeling of excitement (1964a, p. 128). As the infant slowly recognizes and increasingly loves the person who supplies food, care, and affection, its spontaneous urges to devour and use up the good it receives from that person become increasingly troubling. "And, along with this, there comes a feeling that there will be nothing left if everything has been destroyed; and what happens then, should hunger return?" (Winnicott, 1964a, pp. 128–29). Consequently, the baby's eagerness for food disappears. The "symptom" of inhibition has replaced the infant's healthy greediness for food. Wise mothers intuitively know that simply "playing for time" is the necessary and sufficient intervention to make in these circumstances.

Third, the infant quickly discovers a new source of life's difficulties. "Only too soon, added to other troubles are those that belong to the child's recognition that there is also father to be reckoned with" (Winnicott, 1964a, p. 129). Perhaps, the discovery of siblings adds additional fuel to the fire. Jealousy rears its ugly head. The illusion of exclusive possession of mother dissolves into the disillusionment of a shared, sometimes unavailable, love object.

Fourth, the child's inner world of imaginary friends and foes, fantastic fairies and animals, and magical battles won and lost is an illusion that the child can omnipotently control. With time however, the stresses and strains of controlling this inner world are revealed in all manner of bodily aches, pains, and upsets (Winnicott, 1964a, p. 130). Transformed into an apparently possessed creature, the child indeed is possessed by the real and imaginary people from within making their way into the outside world. Aches, pains, and upsets are normal reflections of internal ups, downs, triumphs, and failures. The wise mother and father support the child's struggle to reconcile inner and outer worlds. They might, for example, acknowledge that they, too, could see the imaginary friend. Providing care for "both" children thereby demonstrates to one of them that life is doable, parents do understand, and imaginative play need not be shameful. Setting a place at the table for the friend, or at bedtime even tucking child and companion in for the night strikes some as pandering to the child's eccentricity, but the alternative is to invalidate the child's healthy childishness. Hence, parents who scoff at their child's imaginary world and its creatures are prematurely expecting maturity.

In Winnicott's description of it, life is hard. Early experiences are fraught with difficult things to learn, and often evoke disappointment because disillusionment is unavoidable. Such experiences, however, are normal, and momentary signs of psychological distress are not indications of abnormality. The degree to which a child remains sufficiently able to be playful through all of the adversities and disappointments of early life is the measure of that child's normality.

Commitment to Pediatrics

Clearly, Winnicott's early papers were blends of pediatric medical advice, Dr. Spockish admonitions to parents to trust their own abilities and those of their children, and psychological insights about development drawn from reading Freud (e.g., Winnicott,

1931a, 1931b, 1936, 1944). Winnicott had a wry, homey, avuncular style honed to perfection in his child care radio broadcasts during World War II. That same style, an entertaining and disarming mix of authority, wit, and soothing nurturance, continued to serve him well in print when his broadcasts were turned into papers and books (Winnicott, 1993, esp. Chapter 1). He was widely in demand as a speaker for medical, parent, and teachers' groups throughout his career, and he never failed to provide a humorous but psychological slant on seriously practical pediatric matters.

By the same token, however, Winnicott's commitment to his role as a pediatrician had important consequences for his theory of object relations. Pediatrics broadened his vision as a child psychiatrist and supported his intuitive and empathic grasp of child psychology. Pediatrics taught him patience with his patients. Most important, Winnicott was pragmatic, a psychoanalyst who recognized that life is difficult, and psychoanalysis cannot alter that fact.

> The best that can happen is that the person who is being analyzed gradually comes to feel less and less at the mercy of unknown forces both within and without, and more and more able to deal in his or her own peculiar way with the difficulties inherent in human nature, in personal growth, and in the gradual achievement of a mature and constructive relationship to society. (Winnicott, 1945b/1996, p. 12)

With these foundations, Winnicott's natural reluctance to "follow anybody's lead" intensified. The result was an object relations theory that, more often than not, fabricates playful paradoxes from orthodox concepts and stands traditional ideas on their heads.

EARLY THEORY: THE KLEINIAN INFLUENCE

As much as Winnicott wanted his independence, the reality of psychoanalytic training in the 1920s and 1930s demanded at least publicly professed allegiance to the ideas of the movement's leaders. Anna Freud and Melanie Klein dominated the specialized branch of child psychoanalysis to which Winnicott aspired. Perpetually wary of intellectual entanglements and demands for orthodoxy, Winnicott found himself in the awkward position of having to choose between the frying pan and the fire. He chose fire.

At the outset of his psychoanalytic career, Winnicott incorporated a multitude of Kleinian and Freudian concepts into his understanding of child psychology. He had assimilated the "classic" formulations of Freud both from his reading and from his personal analysis with James Strachey (1887–1967), the eminent British analyst and Freud's chief translator. However, during the analysis, Strachey recommended to Winnicott that he seek out Melanie Klein to learn more about the application of psychoanalysis to children (Winnicott, 1962b/1965a). Winnicott took Strachey's advice and made contact sometime in 1932, about two years before the end of his analysis with Strachey (Kahr, 1996, p. 58).

Winnicott's View of Melanie Klein

Winnicott initially found that Klein's work provided important insights about emotional functioning at the very earliest periods of infancy. As we have seen, Klein was almost daily pushing psychoanalysis to earlier and earlier periods of infancy. For a time, Winnicott found this Kleinian direction a congenial and enlightening path to follow. His own observations as a pediatrician had already paved the way for his ready acceptance of the idea that children could be "emotionally ill" with roots extending well before the oedipal period of ages five and six. Winnicott commented, "This was difficult for me, because overnight I had changed from being a pioneer into being a student with a pioneer teacher" (1962b/1965a, p. 173). Nevertheless, Winnicott recalled that Klein was an admirable teacher who could be surprisingly flexible and formidably attentive to the details of the cases he brought for supervision. Winnicott retained Melanie Klein as a clinical supervisor for the better part of six years, from 1935 to 1941 (Kahr, 1996, p. 59). More than 20 years later, Winnicott summarized the significance of his experiences with Melanie Klein in a capsule view of her importance to psychoanalysis:

> Klein was able to make it clear to me from the material my patients presented, how the capacity for concern and to feel guilty is an achievement, and it is this rather than depression that characterizes arrival at the depressive position in the case of the growing baby and child.
>
> Arrival at this stage is associated with ideas of restitution and reparation, and indeed the human individual cannot accept the destructive and aggressive ideas in his or her own nature without the experience of reparation, and for this reason the continued presence of the love object is necessary at this stage since only in this way is there opportunity for reparation.
>
> This is Klein's most important contribution, in my opinion, and I think it ranks with Freud's concept of the Oedipus complex. (1962b/1965a, p. 176)

Winnicott nevertheless insists on his independence, although he admits to some small degree of disappointment:

> Since those days a great deal has happened, and I do not claim to be able to hand out the Klein view in a way that she would herself approve of. I believe my views began to separate out from hers, and in any case I found she had not included me in as a Kleinian. This did not matter to me because I have never been able to follow anyone else, not even Freud. (1962b/1965a, p. 176)

It is no surprise, then, that Winnicott's first "official" psychoanalytic paper was primarily an elaboration of—with subtle modifications to— one of Melanie Klein's central concepts. On December 4, 1935, Winnicott presented his membership paper entitled "The Manic Defence" to the British Psychoanalytic Society. Such presentations carried the weight of a commencement ceremony intended to mark the culmination of a candidate's long preparation in becoming a qualified psychoanalyst by admitting that analyst to full membership in the society.

Of course, the ritual was as much a political and professional rite of passage as it was a theoretical contribution. Ostensibly, candidates for membership were required to present "original" theoretical or clinical ideas, but the wise aspirant understood that the presentation had to be managed with the skill and tact of a diplomat. Covert but mandatory etiquette governed the proceedings. Applicants first had to demonstrate that their "original" ideas derived from Sigmund Freud's concepts. The master said it, said it first, and said it mattered. Somewhere. Somehow. As convoluted a task as that sometimes proved to be, proper execution of the commencement ritual, the full Monty, so to say, demanded more. A candidate also had to acknowledge intellectual debts to the influential senior analysts in the candidate's area of specialization. Paradoxical as it seems, candidates mounted the podium eager to argue that their original ideas were derivative.

The Manic Defense: Inner and Outer Reality

Winnicott was master of this paradox. His "graduation paper" was a personalized reinterpretation of Kleinian concepts masquerading as debt acknowledgement (Winnicott, 1935/1992). Starting with the central Kleinian concepts of fantasy (i.e., phantasy) and the depressive position, Winnicott described how Klein helped him to distinguish among fantasy, inner reality and outer reality. Recall from our earlier discussion that a central aim of a person in the Kleinian "manic position" is to exert omnipotent control over external objects by magically manipulating their internalized or phantasized representations. The Kleinian infant believes that what is done to the phantasy object is done to the external object in reality. Because manic control is believed to be absolute, the infant can "devalue" powerful and persecutory bad objects into mere shadows of their former threatening selves, held in suspended animation between life and death.

Following Klein, Winnicott argued that fantasy—and he avoided the idiosyncratic Kleinian "ph"—is akin more to daydreaming and to ordinary imagination than to the processes of unconscious inner reality. With this subtle shift in perspective, Winnicott gives Klein's term new meaning:

> . . . it is part of one's own manic defence to be unable to give full significance to inner reality. There are fluctuations in one's ability to respect inner reality that are related to depressive anxiety in oneself. (1935/1992, p. 129)

Winnicott artfully redefines the manic position to moderate Klein's emphasis on the absolute power of the internal world. He argues that the developmentally "normal" manic defense against depressive feelings compels the defender to minimize, not maximize, as Klein would have it, the influence of internal object representations.

> Omnipotent fantasies are not so much the inner reality itself as a defence against acceptance of it. One finds in this defence a flight to omnipotent fantasy, and flight from some fantasies to other fantasies, and in this sequence a flight to external reality. This is why I think one cannot compare and contrast fantasy and reality. (Winnicott, 1935/1992, p. 130)

Sounds almost Kleinian. Might be Klein-friendly. Could be Klein-compatible. However, the core distinction between fantasies and inner psychic reality is not bona fide Klein. Winnicott was paving the way for a fundamental alteration to Klein's ideas. Recall his argument that normal life is normally difficult. He therefore simply asserted the importance of the role in development that ordinary reality plays. As a direct consequence, he normalized the pathological sounding—"manic" and "depressive"—developmental positions. Winnicott reasoned that manic defending is detectable in ordinary living inherent to the struggle all people make against the daily abrasions and sorrows of life:

For instance, one is at a music-hall and on the stage come the dancers, trained to liveliness. One can say that here is the primal scene, here is exhibitionism, here is anal control, here is masochistic submission to discipline, here is a defiance of the super-ego. Soon or later one adds: here is LIFE. Might it not be that the main point of the performance is a denial of deadness, a defence against depressive "death inside" ideas, the sexualization being secondary.

What about such things as the wireless [i.e., radio] that is left on interminably? What about living in a town like London with its noise that never ceases, and lights that are never extinguished? Each illustrates the reassurance through reality against death inside, and a use of manic defence that can be normal. (Winnicott, 1935/1992, p. 131)

For Winnicott, inner reality is an equal partner with outer reality, the world of ordinary life. "Life is hard," but that does not mean for Winnicott that strenuous coping with life's difficulties, including the struggle to feel alive in the face of death, is inevitably pathological. Winnicott thus depathologizes Klein's concept of manic defense by reframing it to encompass coping with life's unavoidable miseries. He elevates the external world to equal status with the inner world as a determinant of emotional development.

Depathologizing the Depressive Position: The Ruth and the Ruthless

In a later paper, he applied the same strategy to a fuller discussion of the Kleinian depressive position, more strongly emphasizing than did Klein herself the normal "achievement" of concern for the good object (Winnicott, 1954–55/1992). He proposed that the Kleinian term *depressive position* was a poorly conceived name for this essentially normal process, and suggested that *stage of concern* might better communicate the essence of the process. In subtle and not so subtle ways, Winnicott again normalized a Kleinian concept that implied greater abnormality than the typical infant exhibits. Winnicott agreed with Klein that the infant begins its relationship to the external object more or less "pre-ruth," that is, ruthless in attempting to satisfy its needs. With the whimsy of Lewis Carroll, Winnicott points out that the infant gradually passes from the pre-ruth stage to the stage of ruth. In more familiar, less whimsical English, the infant grows less ruthless and more able to feel concern and empathy for its love objects.

PRIMITIVE PERSONALITY DEVELOPMENT, WINNICOTT STYLE

Despite his obvious discomfort with the extremity of some of Klein's concepts, Winnicott nevertheless incorporated many of her ideas concerning psychological processes that hypothetically describe an infant's earliest days of life. Winnicott's own pediatric observations suggested that a series of important cognitive and emotional achievements had already unfolded in orderly progression prior to the stage of concern (i.e., Klein's "depressive position"). These capacities *must* develop in the first five or six months of life for the infant to be able to reach the stage of concern.

His observations of babies exploring the spatula had convinced him that infants of five months understood that the object for which they reach is localized in space "outside me." Furthermore, the baby who thrusts the spatula into its mouth is necessarily aware that there is an "inside me." Deliberately dropping the spatula demonstrates that "he knows he can get rid of something when he has got from it what he wants from it" (1945a/1992, p. 148). Parallel to these achievements, the infant of five or six months:

> . . . assumes that his mother also has an inside, one that may be rich or poor, good or bad, ordered or muddled. He is therefore starting to be concerned with the mother and her sanity and her moods. In the case of many infants there is a relationship as between whole persons at six months. Now, when a human being feels he is a person related to people, he has already travelled a long way in primitive development. (Winnicott, 1945a/1992, p. 148)

Thus, Winnicott argued that Klein's depressive position includes cognitive and emotional developments that have nothing to do with defensive maneuvers against depression. Winnicott now set himself the task of describing what happens before the stage of concern at five or six months. The big question, he pointed out, is whether anything matters before five or six months. Winnicott's answer was that at least three important achievements mattered to a great degree: personality integration, personalization, and realization.

Personality Integration: From Muddled to Cuddled

Winnicott hypothesized that at the very beginning of life, personality is in a primal state of "unintegration." With absolute literalness, Winnicott meant that in the earliest days of life there is no *person* to embody an integrated personality. There is only a bundle of biological needs and potentials. "What is there is an armful of anatomy and physiology, and added to this a potential for development into a human personality" (Winnicott, 1968a/1987, p. 89). Unintegrated infants do not comprehend themselves or others as whole people and are not yet aware that others do so all the time. Personality integration begins quickly and spontaneously after birth, and requires two sets of experiences to go forward smoothly.

The first is the baby's own internal world of need and drive which by their infinite repetition become the stabilizing routines of life around which a personality can form. Need and drive are, in their ways, reassuring experiences that signal one is alive. As long as mother and other caretakers satisfy the infant's needs reliably, survival is not threatened, and the natural process of integration proceeds unhindered. The inexorable repetition of appetite arousal and satisfaction gradually grows familiar and welcomed.

The second organizing experience is the quality of the care the infant experiences. The baby is handled, bathed, fed, rocked, named, and called by name, and cuddled, and each of these repetitive events helps to bring order to internal confusion. From these scattered fragments of need, maternal response, cuddling, and predictable care, a gradual synthesis of identity emerges. "Me" and "not-me" begin to have meaning for the infant. Mother's "holding" her infant in ways beyond physical cuddling promotes comfort and stability. As Winnicott used the term, *holding* elevates cuddling to a primary means of communication between infant and mother. Holding the infant securely in both the physical and psychological senses of the term enables the securely held infant to organize its muddled urges, wishes, and fears into predictable experiences. We return to a more complete examination of Winnicott's evolving concept of holding at a later point.

Personality integration continues to evolve with time, but the feeling of being "not quite whole" does not frighten the securely held infant. "There are long stretches of time in a normal infant's life in which a baby does not mind whether he is many bits or one whole being, or whether he lives in his mother's face or in his own body, provided that from time to time he comes together and feels something" (Winnicott, 1945, p. 150). Later in development, however, specific developmental failures that can provoke regression to an unintegrated state—the experience of *disintegration*—is very frightening and often associated with psychotic-level psychopathology. Primordial "unintegration," however, is the natural state of newborns and infants up to five months of age. In contrast to the astonishing cognitive resources of a Kleinian infant, Winnicottian babies come equipped with more homely logic. Psychological anachronisms are found only rarely in their repertoire. Winnicottian youngsters can fear the loss of personal integrity only after they have had it.

We should note Winnicott's creative, but nonetheless idiosyncratic, use of opposites. As he employs the term, the opposite of integration is not disintegration but "unintegration." Unintegration indicates a naturally occurring starting point on the road to the final destination of integration. Disintegration lies on an altogether different conceptual dimension—the dimension of psychopathology—rather than occupying the opposite end of the same dimension as unintegration. Disintegration is pathological because it "is an active production of chaos in defence against unintegration in the absence of maternal ego-support . . ." (1962c/1965a, p. 61). We have also seen in passing Winnicott's use of illusion and disillusion. As we shall see in the next section, Winnicott created another concept by converting the standard psychiatric term *depersonalization* into its Winnicottian opposite: *personalization*. Dialectical thinking—formulating concepts by contrasting pairs of opposites—was one of Winnicott's favorite theoretical strategies.

Personalization: From Cleaning to Weaning

Satisfactory personalization leads to the feeling that the infant is "in" his or her own body. As with integration, biological need and maternal care guide the process of personalization so that the evolving personality has a "place" to reside. Mother's attention to physical care and cleanliness quietly helps the infant reach the understanding that he or she has a body, "resides" in it, and is sometimes in control of it. In short, the infant achieves *personalization*. Put another way, the infant particularizes its inventory of recognizable physical equipment by personalizing each component. The particular "person" is either self or not-self. This waving digit is *my* finger because I can make it go in my mouth for a good suck, but this digit tickling my tummy is not mine because *I* can't stop it. This wiggling pink thing that lies just out of reach is *my* toe, but this bigger one that I can reach—and bite—is not mine because I don't feel bitten and because Daddy is doing the yelling. A very sore place I can feel but can't see is *my* tushy (bobo, heinie, butt, rear, tuchis) with *my* diaper rash.

Schizophrenic and near-psychotic people who abruptly feel uncomfortable with their own bodies or develop the delusion that they are not "in" their bodies sometimes experience the opposite phenomenon, called depersonalization. A less malignant variation of depersonalization is the belief that something is alarmingly and abruptly different, "not right," or "not real" about my body. However, the person frequently is unable to articulate the specific difficulty that he or she is experiencing. An even less malignant variation of depersonalization, in fact a common occurrence of childhood, is the creation of imaginary companions. Some children even use the imaginary companion as a magical defense to bypass the anxieties of childhood associated with eating, digestion, retention, and expulsion (Winnicott, 1945a/1992, p. 151).

Some primitive depersonalization phenomena, Winnicott hypothesized, have their roots in failures of the primary personalization experiences in infancy (1945a/1992, p. 151). Personalization, as Winnicott employed the term, is the achievement of a burgeoning personality attempting to complete the process of integration by taking possession of the body in which it finds itself and becoming increasingly comfortable with ownership.

Realization: From Dreaming to Scheming

The third early personality development is learning to take account of external reality. Rather than employ "reality testing," the standard psychoanalytic term, Winnicott chose to call this achievement *realization* (as a parallel to *personalization?*). He would later extend the list with a fourth process that emphasized "object relating," as we shall see. At this point, however, Winnicott focused on the more familiar psychoanalytic concepts of ego development.

Mother and baby each bring to the nursing situation their own capabilities and needs. The mother brings knowledge, tolerance, and adult judgment. The baby brings absolute dependence, need, and a readiness for hallucinatory gratification. Sights, sounds, smells, and touches experienced with each real feeding teach the baby what he can and cannot conjure up when the real object is not present but real need is exerting itself (1945a/1992, p. 153). Eventually, over substantial periods of time, the mother helps her infant accept and tolerate the limitations of reality, and to enjoy the real satisfactions that such acceptance makes possible:

> Real milk is satisfying as compared with imaginary milk, but this is not the point. The point is that fantasy things work by magic: there are no brakes on fantasy, and love and hate cause alarming effects. External reality has brakes on it, and can be studied and known, and, in fact, fantasy is only tolerable at full blast when objective reality is appreciated as well. The subjective has tremendous value but is so alarming and magical that it cannot be enjoyed except as a parallel to the objective. (1945a/1992, p. 153)

In the earliest phase of life, objects act according to magical laws. The object exists when desired, approaches when approached, hurts when hurt, and vanishes when not wanted. Vanishing is a terrifying experience for the infant because it represents annihilation. To not want—that is, to be gratified after a satisfactory feed—is to evoke annihilation of the object. From this dreamlike world of magic the infant progresses to the real world of planned actions. The change from dreaming to scheming is paralleled by the nature of the changes in the infant's relationship to the object. Initially, following Klein, Winnicott proposed a "ruthless" stage prior to the stage of concern in which the infant expects mother to tolerate its aggressiveness in play. Without this experience of a tolerant caretaker, the infant can show its ruthlessness only in dissociated states. In later life, the ruthlessness can be shown only in states of disintegration marked by abrupt regression to the primitive and magical world of infancy. In short, ruthless relations to objects reappear in psychotic-level psychopathologies.

"There's No Such Thing as a Baby"

"I once risked the remark, 'There is no such thing as a baby'—meaning that if you set out to describe a baby, you will find you are describing a *baby and someone.* A baby cannot exist alone, but is essentially part of a relationship" (Winnicott, 1964a, p. 88; 1969d, p. 253). This instance of Winnicottian hyperbole is a landmark in both object relations theory and in the public presentation of Winnicott's authentically original views. He had learned important lessons from Melanie Klein and from his own pediatric practice. Contrary to orthodox Freudian theory, Winnicott put the focus of child emotional development, not solely on the child, but on the "nursing couple": a child-in-an-adaptation-enhancing-relationship-with-a-mother who provides a "good enough" environment.

> *"There is no such thing as a baby."* I was alarmed to hear myself utter these words and tried to justify myself by pointing out that if you show me a baby you certainly show me also someone caring for the baby, or at least a pram with someone's eyes and ears glued to it. One sees a "nursing couple."
>
> In a quieter way today I would say that before object relationships the state of affairs is this: that the unit is not the individual, the unit is an environment-individual-set-up. By good-enough child care, technique, holding, and general management, the shell becomes gradually taken over and the kernel (which has looked all the time like a human baby to us) can begin to be an individual. (Winnicott, 1952/1992, p. 99)

Winnicott's insistence that babies make psychological sense only in relationship to their environments, specifically the "ordinary devoted mother," was an important corrective to Melanie Klein's often one-sided emphasis on the infant's instincts.

Holding: Primary Maternal Preoccupation of the Ordinary Devoted Mother

Winnicott hypothesized the existence of a special psychological state called "primary maternal preoccupation." Among its characteristics are:

It gradually develops and becomes a state of heightened sensitivity during and especially towards the end of, pregnancy.

It lasts for a few weeks after the birth of the child.

It is not easily remembered by mothers once they have recovered from it.

I would go further and say that the memory mothers have of this state tends to become repressed. (Winnicott, 1956/1992, p. 302)

Winnicott suggested that this special state is comparable to a psychiatric illness except for the fact of pregnancy. Indeed, the specific comparisons that suggested themselves to Winnicott were dissociation with fugue (i.e., amnesia for personal identity with flight to a new location) and schizoid states (for details, see the clinical taxonomy in Chapter 1). Winnicott argued that only by understanding this illness-like state of the mother and her recovery from it could the earliest relationship between infant and mother be understood. Nevertheless, in typical Winnicottian contrarian fashion, he referred repeatedly to the "ordinary devoted mother" or the "good enough mother" to describe the mother who undergoes this "illness" (Winnicott, 1966c/1987; 1971, p. 12).

The mother's special state provides a specific adaptive context for the unique infantile properties of her newborn to flourish and mature. The mother is "sensitized" to the newborn's state and she can empathically put herself in the infant's place. She "knows" her infant's needs and capabilities as she knows her own. In short, the primary maternal preoccupation results in a close identification of mother with her infant (Winnicott, 1960c/1965a, p. 147).

For their part, infants bring their biological constitution, innate developmental tendencies (conflict-free ego functioning), motility, and drives to the mutuality equation. Mother's heightened empathy permits the kind of silent communications that enable the infant's "innate equipment" to unfold, helps the infant experience free movement for the first time, and encourages the child to take ownership of its body and sensations (personalization). In short, the mother provides a "good enough" adaptation to infantile absolute dependency of need.

> . . . from these silent communications we can go over to the ways in which the mother makes real just what the baby is ready to look for, so that she gives the baby the idea of what it is that the baby is just ready for. The baby says (wordlessly of course): "I just feel like . . ." and just then the mother comes along and turns the baby over, or she comes with the feeding apparatus and the baby becomes able to finish the sentence: ". . . a turn-over, a breast, nipple, milk, etc., etc." We have to say that the baby created the breast, but could not have done so had not the mother come along with the breast just at that moment. The communication to the baby is: "Come at the world creatively, create the world; it is only what you create that has meaning for you. Next comes: "the world is in your control." From this initial *experience of omnipotence* the baby is able to begin to experience frustration and even to arrive one day at the other extreme from omnipotence, that is to say, having a sense of being a mere speck in the universe, in a universe that was there before the baby was conceived of and conceived by two parents who were enjoying each other. (Winnicott, 1968a/1987, pp. 100–01)

Winnicott grouped these various "good enough" maternal caretaking practices under the general, and metaphorical, label of *holding.* In its literal sense, the mother "holds" her infant securely in her arms while feeding, cleaning, and playing with it. This tight and intimate physical closeness provides the initial and most primitive level of maturational "holding." At a more sophisticated, metaphorical, level, holding embodies a number of interconnected more emotional communications from mother to child.

> In describing communication between baby and mother, then, there is this essential dichotomy—the mother can shrink to infantile modes of experience, but the baby cannot blow up to adult sophistication. In this way, the mother may or may not talk to her baby; it doesn't matter, the language is not important. (Winnicott, 1968a/1987, p. 95)

Holding communicates to the infant that it is alive—"I am seen and I exist"—as the child feels mirrored in the mother facial expressions and reactions (Winnicott, 1962c/1965a, p. 61). Inherent in these mirroring experiences are the infant's gradual realization that there *is* another, someone who is *not* me, who reacts to me. A "membrane"—another Winnicottian metaphor—develops between the infant "me" and the infant's experience of the other, "not-me." Personality integration, as we have seen, gets its impetus from these "holding" communications.

Holding and the Unthinkable Anxieties

Perhaps more important, holding provides a safety net for the infant to survive the earliest and most terrifying first fears. Influenced again by Klein, Winnicott described a series of infantile *unthinkable anxieties* or primordial fears that date to the earliest days of life. Unlike Klein, Winnicott saw these "anxieties" as normal developmental phases, not as derivatives of the death instinct. More important, unthinkable anxieties are not necessarily precursors of personality pathology but can become the core of serious psychopathology when mother's holding functions fail. Typically, however, the combination of maternal "holding" and an infant who is constantly on the verge of unthinkable anxiety is the recipe for normal personality integration, personalization, and realization. The unthinkable anxieties are:

- Going to pieces
- Falling forever
- Having no relationship to the body
- Having no orientation
- Complete isolation because of there being no means for communication.

Winnicott added the last item in the list some years after his initial formulation (1962c/1965a, p. 58; and 1968a/1987, p. 99). Maternal holding is the totality of the mother's loving physical and emotional care that, to extend Winnicott's metaphor, prevents the infant from toppling over the abyss of unthinkable anxiety.

Winnicott pointed out the parallel to the analyst's "holding" interpretations in therapy. The words sometimes are less significant than the nonverbal and spontaneous message that the analyst and the patient are both alive and continue to be real. For example, Winnicott related the incident of the patient who dug her nails into the back of his hand during an intense moment in therapy.

My interpretation was: "Ow!" This scarcely involved my intellectual equipment at all, and it was quite useful because it came *immediately* (not after a pause for reflection) and because it meant to the patient that my hand was alive, that it was part of me, and that I was there to be used. Or, shall I say, I can be used if I survive. (Winnicott, 1968a/1987, p. 95)

The medium of "holding" communications, as might be expected from Winnicott's metaphors, tends to be physical care. Rocking, cleaning, mother's breathing and heart beat, the sounds she makes, and the smells she has are all significant messages to the infant. Playing, not games, but the interplay between mother and baby constructs a "virtual space" or common ground between them. It is not physical play space, as in a specific area of the floor or table top, but an interactive "secret space" built from gesture and nod, affection and enjoyment. It is a "no-man's-land that is each man's land, the place where the secret is. . . ." (Winnicott, 1968a/1987, p. 100)

REAL AND FALSE SELVES

Good enough adaptation means, in Winnicott's vocabulary, encouragement and support for the infant's "going on being" (Winnicott, 1956/1992, p. 303). The mother protects the infant from "impingements." Impingements are any experiences that jeopardize "going on being." They can stem either from the external environment or originate in occasional maternal "failures" to provide "good enough" care. Unreliable need satisfaction, prolonged separation from each other, intolerance of infantile neediness and aggression, or an inability to make the infant feel safe are all forms of impingement because they threaten spontaneous and normal developmental progress (Winnicott, 1968a/1987, p. 95). Winnicott's focus here, as always, is on the spontaneous and healthy developments of infancy and those special maternal actions that enhance healthy personality formation. The infant must learn to be real to survive. To do so, the infant must feel safe enough to be spontaneous, secure enough to embrace a self that can sacrifice spontaneity, even die (Winnicott, 1956/1992, p. 304). The good enough mother makes "normally difficult life" tolerable, manageable, masterable:

> . . . without the initial good-enough environmental provision, this self that can afford to die never develops. The feeling of real is absent and if there is not too much chaos the ultimate feeling of futility. The inherent difficulties of life cannot be reached, let alone the satisfactions. If there is not chaos, there appears a false self that hides the true self, that complies with demands, that reacts to stimuli, that rids itself of instinctual experiences by having them, but that is only playing for time. (Winnicott, 1956/1992, pp. 304–05)

Winnicott's concept of the False Self seems to have originated from two sources. First, Winnicott had a keen interest in working therapeutically with severely regressed adult patients who were psychotic or near psychotic. Winnicott saw the dependency needs of the infant re-emerge in an exaggerated form that provided a window on a peculiar sort of personality splitting in his adult schizophrenic and borderline patients. In particular, one patient described to Winnicott how she had felt all her life that she had not been "real," and felt as though she had been looking for her "True" self (1960c/1965a, p. 142). From the patient's point of view, the first two years of her analysis had been conducted between what she called her "caretaker self" and Winnicott. This caretaker self had sought out treatment, protected the patient during the early phases, gradually handed over its role to Winnicott, and "hovered" nearby to resume caretaking whenever Winnicott "failed" to "hold" the patient safely.

The second origin for Winnicott's concept of the False Self was his experience with apparently cheery children who visited his hospital clinic displaying exuberance and delight in being alive. Nevertheless, these children, by definition, are at the same time *presented for psychological treatment* by their parents, often with maternally described problems of depression, listlessness, anger, and apathy. This marked discrepancy between direct observation and maternal report caught Winnicott's attention:

> It took me years to realise that these children were entertaining me as they felt they must also entertain their mothers, to deal with the mother's depressed mood. They dealt with or prevented my depression or what might be boredom in the clinic; while waiting for me they drew lovely coloured pictures or even wrote poems to add to my collection. I have no doubt that I was taken in by many such cases before I eventually realised that the children were ill and were showing me a false self organisation and that at home the mother had to deal with the other side of this, namely the child's inability to keep up counteracting the mother's mood all of the twenty-four hours.
>
> Indeed the mother had to endure the hatred belonging to the child's sense of having been exploited and of having lost identity. (Winnicott, 1969c/1989, pp. 247–48)

Winnicott discovered that some of these "entertaining" children had developed their False Selves not only to "cheer up" their depressed mothers, but also to fend off her hatred of them (1969c/1989, p. 249; 1948d/1996, pp. 91–92). We return to the concept of the mother's unconscious hatred of her child shortly. It is of some benefit at present, however, simply to note that Winnicott links the three concepts of maternal depression, hatred, and the False Self.

Origins of the False Self: The "Not Good Enough" Mother

From clinical observations such as these, Winnicott hypothesized that the primary purpose of the False Self is defense of the True Self. It is a mask that others perceive as real, and, when successfully executed, totally conceals the True Self. The question arises: Against what is the False Self protecting the True Self? Winnicott's answer is "exploitation" and "impingement."

The origins of the False Self are in failures of the mother-infant relationship during the phase prior to the integration of the infant's personality (1960/1965a, p. 145). The "not good enough" mother fails to hold her infant securely and reliably. She may permit external reality to "impinge" on the infant's world before the infant is ready. Or she herself may intrusively impinge on that world in a way that the infant cannot tolerate. Such "errors" of maternal care fail the infant in two ways. First, the "not good enough mother" does not validate or help make real her infant's spontaneous gestures. She does not mirror in her responses her empathic understanding of the infant's needs or wonderment at her infant's successes. In Winnicott's terms,

> The mother who is not good enough is not able to implement the infant's omnipotence, and so she repeatedly fails to meet the infant gesture; instead she substitutes her own gesture which is to be given sense by the compliance of the infant. This compliance on the part of the infant is the earliest stage of the False Self, and belongs to the mother's inability to sense her infant's needs. (1960c/1965a, p. 145)

The second failure of the not good enough mother is that she does not help her infant link its spontaneous gestures with observable effects in reality, including her own reactions. Thus the infant is unable to reach the stage of "giving up" omnipotence and hallucination in favor of manipulating the real. Consequently, the infant may not *feel* real. Instead, *illusionary* creating and manipulating are never critically questioned, and therefore never transcended.

In the extreme case, where the maternal failures occur from the very beginning of existence, the infant's survival may be in question. More often, however, the not good enough mother is not "bad enough" to disrupt infant survival totally. Instead, the infant complies with the maternal environment by creating the mask of the false self:

> Through this False Self the infant builds up a false set of relationships, and by means of introjections even attains a show of being real, so that the child may grow to be just like mother, nurse, aunt, brother, or whoever at the time dominates the scene. The False Self has one positive and very important function: to hide the True Self, which it does by compliance with environmental demands. (Winnicott, (1960c/1965a, p. 146–47)

Ultimately, the chief defensive efforts of the False Self are directed to protecting the True Self from exploitation, manipulation, and unjust demands. The most "unthinkable" anxiety of all is thus fended off: Annihilation of the True Self.

Levels of Organization of the False Self

Winnicott distinguished five different "levels" of False Self personality organization. They are organized along a spectrum of severity extending from gross maladaptation to ordinary healthy adaptation.

Extremely Maladaptive: Mask

The False Self is organized as "real" and observers see and relate only to the "real" False Self as it takes over relationships in work, love, play, and friendships. The True Self is completely masked. With time, however, the False Self shows signs of failure because life continues to present situations in which a whole person is required.

Moderately Maladaptive: Caretaker

The False Self defends the True Self and even serves as its "protector" or "caretaker." The True Self is dimly acknowledged as a "potential" self and is permitted to have a "secret life." Winnicott's constant search of the healthy silver lining exhibits itself most clearly when he wrote of the moderately pathological False Self that it is: ". . . the clearest example of clinical illness as an organization with a positive aim, the preservation of the individual in spite of abnormal environmental conditions" (1960c/1965a, p. 143).

Minimally Adaptive: Defender

The False Self can serve as a defender against exploitation of the True Self, biding its time until proper conditions for the emergence of the True Self can be found. If safe conditions are not encountered, the False Self may defend the True Self literally to death: suicide. When there is no hope left that the True Self can emerge safely, then the False Self can mobilize the psychological equivalent of a scorched earth policy. The False Self carries out suicide with the paradoxical intention of preventing the annihilation of the True Self by accomplishing the absolute destruction of the entire self. *Good news:* Having successfully executed, as it were, its defensive task, the False Self is needed no longer. *Bad news:* Suicide is the False Self's way of saying, "oops."

Moderately Adaptive: Imitator

A False Self is organized within the personality, but is modeled on caring, productive, and protective people. Although the person feels as though he or she is sometimes "not really real," or continually searching for him- or herself, the False Self comprised of benign identifications can negotiate a very successful life.

Adaptive: Facilitator

The False Self is organized "normally" as ordinary elements of socialization, including polite behavior, personal restraint, false-but-charming modesty, and deliberate control over personal wishes and urges. Without this benign False Self, a kind of socially sophisticated alter ego, the unvarnished True Self would not achieve a place in society as successful or as satisfying.

Table 5.3 summarizes the levels of False Self organization.

The True Self: Aliveness

The True Self is real, spontaneous, and creative. It originates in the "aliveness" of the body tissues and functions, especially the beating of the heart and the regularity of

TABLE 5.3 Winnicott's Levels of False Self Organization

False Self	True Self	Consequence
Extremely Maladaptive: *Mask*	Completely hidden beneath an utterly compliant False Self.	False Self fails when life demands a whole spontaneous person.
Moderately Maladaptive: *Caretaker*	Permitted secret life, regarded as potential self.	Preservation of individual in abnormal environments. Minimal spontaneity, aliveness.
Minimally Adaptive: *Defender*	Waits for safe/desirable conditions to reveal True Self.	Possible suicide if hope for safe conditions is lost; little aliveness.
Moderately Adaptive: *Imitator*	Identifies with caring or productive objects as models.	Successful life, but without realness, aliveness.
Adaptive: *Facilitator*	Normal socialization for politeness and self-restraint.	Humility, modesty, social success.

breathing (Winnicott, 1960c/1965a, p. 148). At the beginning, the True Self is linked to the primary process thinking of the unconscious and is therefore not responsive to external reality (see the discussion of primary process thinking in Chapter 3). Forever fond of opposites, Winnicott points out that the True Self acquires its greatest meaning when compared to the False Self. At core, True Self is a synonym for the "experience of aliveness." It is thus initially little more than sensory motor aliveness.

Gradually the True Self grows more complex and develops its own links to reality. At first, reality is understood as a projection of the inner world. Somewhat later, reality is actually "real" in the sense of having an objective, outside the self, existence. Finally, the strengthened True Self can tolerate two kinds of momentary breaks in personal continuity. First, physical trauma such as brief separations from mother or physical illness do not have the devastating effect after the emergence of the True Self that they would have had prior to it. Second, "normal" False Self experiences, such as being taught to say "thank you" when the child hardly feels thankful, are taken in stride as part of ordinary socialization without deforming or threatening the integrity of the True Self. In this sense, everyone develops a normal social mask or False Self which functions to provide superficial compliance in social contexts where conformity is routinely required (Winnicott, 1964d/1986, p. 67). Functioning in this way, the False Self is a social compromise.

An intermediate level of functioning of the False Self that lies between healthy compromise and pathological defense lies between dreaming and reality, the cultural life of the actor. People who develop a compliant self capable of manipulating symbols and language can use their skills to play roles deliberately, entertainingly, and convincingly in the world of drama. The False Self becomes a sublimation of the True Self rather than a defender. However, when the split between the True and False Selves is large, the person is impoverished in the use of symbols, language, and cultural skills.

> Instead of cultural pursuits one observes in such persons extreme restlessness, an inability to concentrate, and a need to collect impingements from external reality so that the living-time of the individual can be filled by reactions to these impingements. (Winnicott, 1960c/1965a, p. 150)

The greatest danger of the successful False Self is that it will be too successful. By hiding the True Self, the False Self may bury its potentialities so deep that they are no longer accessible, no longer constitute the core of the person's "going on being." That level of "success" means, ironically, that the defense actualizes the very fear—virtual obliteration of the True Self—that it was intended to prevent.

TRANSITIONAL OBJECTS AND TRANSITIONAL PHENOMENA

A *transitional object* in Winnicott's sense is, as its name implies, anything—even a part of the child's own body, such as a fist or thumb—to which the child "relates" with the behavioral/cognitive capabilities it has at that moment (Winnicott, 1959/1989, p. 53). It is, in Winnicott's phrase, the child's "first not-me possession." Early on, the infant's own tightly balled fist in the mouth is "explored" with tongue and lips in pretty much the same way as the breast or bottle are explored and comprehended. Later in development, external objects—rattles, stuffed toys, and the like—will become transitional objects with which the infant, guided by the sensitive assistance of the attuned mother, establishes a "relationship." Between the two extremes of completely subjective reality of one's self and one's own desires and the completely external reality of the world and its people, there are transitional phenomena, the world of the partly subjective, partly objective transitional object (Winnicott, 1971, p. 2).

At first, when the infant's needs are aroused, it provides its own objects on demand (the fist or thumb in the mouth). Sometimes the infant's crying and other signs of distress or excitement prompt the mother to provide the nipple or bottle. From the child's point of view, each time *desire created satisfaction.* Subjectivity is all there is. Objective reality, things that are "not me," and people who are "not me," simply does not exist. To the infant it appears that the subjective wish is sufficient to construct the gratification, a feeling that can be described in adult language as omnipotence. On some occasions, the infant will "conjure" up an image of what it wants, and because the sensitive mother is attuned and can read her child's signals of curiosity or distress, she "magically" seems to provide the exact object desired: a teddy bear, rattle, blanket, or the like. Again the infant has conjured an object, and it seemingly has materialized—a kind of "hallucinatory omnipotence." Winnicott calls this the "moment of illusion."

> The mother, at the beginning, by an almost 100-per-cent adaptation affords the infant the opportunity for the *illusion* that her breast is part of the infant. It is, as it were, under the baby's magical control. The same can be said in terms of infant care in general, in the quiet times between excitements. Omnipotence is nearly a fact of experience. The mother's eventual task is gradually to disillusion the infant, but she has no hope of success unless at first she has been able to give sufficient opportunity for the illusion.
>
> In another language, the breast is created by the infant over and over again out of the infant's capacity to love or (one can say) out of need. A subjective phenomenon develops in the baby, which we call the mother's breast. The mother places the actual breast just where the infant is ready to create, and at the right moment. (Winnicott, 1971, pp. 12–13)

Besides the breast, other "objects," such as a teddy bear or a favorite blanket, are dimly recognized by the infant as not belonging to the infant's body ("not me"). However, they are not necessarily fully comprehended as belonging to the outside world or to another person either. Such objects are *transitional* in the senses of:

- PLACE: bridging inner and outer
- AGENCY: bridging hallucinatory omnipotence and dependency on a real external agent
- SEPARATENESS: bridging not-me and me.

(Derived from: Winnicott, 1971, p. 2)

What is important for Winnicott is not the object itself, but the process of transition between subjective hallucination and objective reality-testing. These objects are not completely magical nor are they completely real. They are transitional.

> I have introduced the terms "transitional object" and "transitional phenomena" for designation of the intermediate area of experience, between the thumb and the teddy bear, between the oral erotism [sic] and true object relationship, between primary creative activity and projection of what has already been introjected, between primary unawareness of indebtedness and the acknowledgement of indebtedness (Say: ta! [i.e., "thanks"]). (Winnicott, 1951/1992, p. 230)

Thus, for Winnicott, transitional objects and phenomena are fundamentally intermediate between reality and illusion, landmarks on the road to full acceptance of the real. However, there are "rules" of ownership over the transitional object that the infant exercises with care:

- The infant assumes rights over the object, and we agree to this assumption. Nevertheless, some abrogation of omnipotence is a feature from the start.
- The object is affectionately cuddled as well as excitedly loved and mutilated.
- It must never change, unless changed by the infant.
- It must survive instinctual loving, and also hating, and, if it be a feature, pure aggression.
- Yet it must seem to the infant to give warmth, or to move, or to have texture, or to do something that seems to show it has vitality or reality of its own.
- It comes from without from our point of view, but not so from the point of view of the baby. Neither does it come from within; it is not an hallucination.
- Its fate is to be gradually allowed to be decathected, so that in the course of years it becomes not so much forgotten as relegated to limbo. By this I mean that in health the transitional object does not "go inside" nor does the feeling about it necessarily undergo repression. It is not forgotten and it is not mourned. It loses meaning. . . .

(Winnicott, 1951/1992, p. 233)

Winnicott assumed that at least for some infants in some circumstances, the transitional object served as a symbol for a part object. Thus a piece of cherished blanket symbolizes the nurturing breast for some infants; for others it may symbolize feces (1951/1992, p. 236). Yet the fundamental purpose remains the same: Transitional objects are the infant's first "tools" in negotiating the gap between the illusion of magical creation of desired objects and the disillusion that such objects have their own, willful, existence.

With time, of course, the infant learns to distinguish between "me" and "not-me," between "inner" and "outer," and between illusion and reality because at least some of the time its needs will not be instantly gratified no matter how intense the wish. Reality in the form of external frustration and obstacles makes itself known. And, of course, the mother herself will become a real "object" with whom the infant establishes a mutual relationship. Out of this relationship will come important psychological understandings about trust in self, trust in others, and how to "relate" to people.

Transitional phenomena are not restricted to infancy. Even as adults the task of relating inner to outer reality continues to make its demands felt. Is there anyone, for example, who does not have photographs of loved ones in his or her wallet? How many of us treasure some "keepsake" possession given us by a distant loved one? Lock of hair? Special letter or poem? At the other extreme, consider the sports fans who will pay huge sums of money to own a sweaty jersey worn by Refrigerator Perry or a golf club once used by John F. Kennedy. Are these transitional objects or fetishes? Winnicott left the issue open.

SEVERE PSYCHOPATHOLOGY AND FAILURES OF ADAPTATION

In what may prove to be an unfortunate extension of his ideas to very severe psychiatric disorders, Winnicott (1966b/1996; 1967/1996), late in is career, extended his model of maternal holding and infantile adaptation to childhood autism and schizophrenia. Winnicott hypothesized that these catastrophic disorders of childhood were failures in the adaptive context provided by "not good enough" mothering. Following the general outlines of a theory advanced by Bruno Bettelheim (1967) in his well-known book, *The Empty Fortress,* Winnicott insisted that the psychotic emotional and intellectual manifestations of autism and schizophrenia were not evidence of a *disease* in the medical sense (Winnicott, 1969b/1989, p. 246n). Bettelheim's psychological formulation and claims of treatment efficacy were themselves controversial in their time and have grown increasingly suspect (Sutton, 1995, pp. 10, 304, and especially 424–27). In his own description of these disorders, Winnicott did nothing to make a purely psychological model less controversial:

> The illness is a disturbance of emotional development and a disturbance that reaches back so far that in some respects at least the child is defective intellectually. In some respects the child may show evidence of brilliance.
>
> I am hoping that what follows may strengthen the argument that the problem in autism is fundamentally one of emotional development and that autism is not a disease. It might be asked, what did I call these cases before the word autism turned up? The answer is that I thought of these cases, and I still think of them, under the heading "infant or childhood schizophrenia." (Winnicott, 1966b/1996, p. 200)

Winnicott here condenses the two syndromes of schizophrenia and autism into one family of adaptive failures. By itself, this one theoretical maneuver puts Winnicott at odds with contemporary thinking about these disorders (e.g., American Psychiatric Association, 1994, pp. 75, 77, 273–85). Beyond the classification issues, however, Winnicott's hypothesized etiology for these disorders emphasizes failures in emotional attachment at the cost of dismissing biological causes. Most contemporary thinkers regard childhood-onset schizophrenia and childhood autism as neurological, probably neurochemical, disorders of the brain linked to a modest degree of genetic predisposition (e.g., Andreasen, 1984; Andreasen and Munich, 1995; Heinrichs, 1993; Torrey, Bowler, Taylor, and Gottesman, 1994).

By contrast, Winnicott argued that the essential feature of these disorders:

> Is the *mother's* (or substitute mother's) *capacity to adapt to the infant's needs through her healthy ability to identify with the baby* (without, of course, losing her own identity). With such a capacity she can, for instance, hold her baby, and without it she cannot hold her baby except in a way that disturbs the baby's personal living processes.
>
> It seems necessary to add to this the concept of the mother's *unconscious* (repressed) hate of the child. Parents naturally love and hate their babies, in varying degrees. This does not do damage. At all ages, and in earliest infancy especially, the effect of the repressed death wish towards the baby is harmful, and it is beyond the baby's capacity to deal with this. (Winnicott, 1967/1996, p. 222; emphases in original)

What is significant in Winnicott's formulation is his reference to the mother's repressed aggression toward her baby in the context of the mother's depression. This unusual link between maternal depression–aggression and the infant's attempts to survive reappears in Winnicott's final theoretical formulations. As we shall see in a subsequent "Personal Sources" section, coping with maternal depression was one of Winnicott's own early challenges.

"WASTELAND OF DESTROYED REALITY"

Near the end of his life, Winnicott turned his attention, once again, toward the paradoxical aspects of living and dying. The concepts of survival, creation, and annihilation had renewed fascination for the aging pediatrician. Always the master of puns and paradoxes, Winnicott now grew increasingly philosophical. His thinking became more abstract and drawn toward the ontological implications of psychoanalytic concepts. In this frame of mind, Winnicott introduced a distinction between *using* and *relating* to an object. The distinction embodied his last concerns in a formulation that elevated psychological paradox into metaphysical existentialism. The theme of survival was placed squarely at the center of the circle of creation, destruction, and recreation—the universal cycle of birth, death, and renewal.

Winnicott's Jungian Dream

While working on a review of Carl Jung's (1961) autobiography, *Memories, Dreams, Reflections,* Winnicott had a dream about a deep layer of destructiveness in human nature that he could master only in the most paradoxical way:

The dream can be given in its three parts:

- There was absolute destruction, and I was part of the world and of all people, and therefore I was being destroyed. . . .
- Then there was absolute destruction, and I was the destructive agent. Here then was a problem for the ego, how to integrate these two aspects of destruction?
- Part three now appeared and *in the dream* I awakened. As I awakened I knew I had dreamt both (1) and (2). I had therefore solved the problem, by using the

difference between the waking and sleeping states. Here was I awake, in the dream, and I knew I had dreamt of being destroyed and of being the destroying agent. (Winnicott, 1963b/1989, pp. 228–29; emphases in original)

During awakening, Winnicott was aware of a "splitting" headache. He even envisioned himself with his head divided showing a "black gap" between the two halves. While trying to reach full wakefulness, Winnicott lay pondering the dream and its meaning. His interpretation was that, in the dream, he had been split into three essential selves, corresponding to the three parts of the dream: a sadistic *destroyer,* a masochistic *victim* of destruction, and a *survivor* of destruction. But self number three was aware of being the agent of destruction as well as the object of destruction—and thus had survived. Without "I(3)," as Winnicott called his third self, he realized that he would be doomed to remain split, "solving the problem alternately in sadism and masochism, using object-relating, that is, relating to objectively perceived objects" (Winnicott, 1963b/1989, p. 229).

Having worked on the review of Jung's autobiography, Winnicott realized that he was "dreaming a dream for Jung and for some of my patients, as well as for myself" (1963b/1989, p. 229). Jung's autobiography, it should be mentioned in passing, contains numerous accounts of Jung's mystical, sometimes apparently psychotic, always magical experiences and dreams from which he drew many of the concepts of his theory (see Chapter 7 for a full account of the autobiography). One of Winnicott's further associations to his own dream was that he had the impression from reading about Jung's childhood that Jung was unaware of his own destructive impulses. Winnicott hypothesized that Jung's blind spot was related to having been cared for by a depressed mother. Thus, again, the theme of destructive but paradoxically creative aggression is linked by Winnicott to a child's attempt to cope with its mother's depression and unconscious aggressiveness.

In a letter to a friend, Winnicott provided the simplest statement of the profound insight he achieved in the dream: ". . . the individual child finds total destruction does not mean total destruction" (1963b/1989, p. 230).

The Cycle of Aliveness: Using an Object

Winnicott's formulation of transitional objects and phenomena already had laid the foundations for the recognition of the significance of paradox in object relations:

> I should like to put in a reminder here that the essential feature in the concept of transitional objects and phenomena . . . is *the paradox, and the acceptance of the paradox:* the baby creates the object, but the object was there waiting to be created and to become a cathected object. I tried to draw attention to this aspect of transitional phenomena by claiming that in the rules of the game we all know that we will never challenge the baby to elicit an answer to the question: did you create that or did you find it? (Winnicott, 1968b/1989, p. 221)

What Winnicott had accomplished in formulating the concept of transitional phenomena was to diffuse the usual psychoanalytic focus. Instead of the traditional understanding of the external world as interesting only to the degree that it is a projection of the internal world, Winnicott studied the external world on its own terms.

Transitional phenomena are the bridge between worlds. To exist at all, they require an interaction between subjective and objective reality. Transitional objects are paradoxically both projections and discoveries. Part illusion, part perception, transitional phenomena belong to the middle ground between unreal and real. They are projections sent into the objective world by an infant who creates them in the subjective world; but projections are, by definition, *projected onto something*. That suitable *something* is always also an *accessible* something. It is a *something* that happens to be available at exactly the moment the baby is ready to create. In this very metaphysical sense, then, the baby repeatedly creates and recreates its image and experience of the breast as love object (Winnicott, 1951/1992, p. 238).

In line with his insight of his "three-self" dream, Winnicott now argued that a baby progresses from *relating* to *using* the love object. The transition between relating and using presupposes destroying the object in fantasy. The specific sequence follows this logic: In the first phase, *relating to the object* requires that the infant advance from magical understanding of the object's existence as a projection under omnipotent control to realistic comprehension of the object as a real, independent, objectively existing entity. Mother becomes a person. At that point, following Melanie Klein's hypotheses, the baby's innate destructiveness meets an obstacle it had never before encountered. Real objects *survive* fantasies of destruction.

Indeed, the most significant developmental advance in distinguishing between fantasy and reality comes from this very stubborn refusal of real objects to be obliterated by wishing. "Aha!" says the infant, "total destruction is not total destruction" for objects that *really* exist continue to exist. The attempt at destruction—and most important, the *failure* of the attempt—is the trigger for the infant to place the object outside subjective reality and squarely into the world (Winnicott, 1968b/1989, p. 223). Winnicott summarized the paradoxical logic of his hypothesis in this way:

> This is a position that can be arrived at by the individual in early stages of emotional growth only through the actual survival of cathected objects that are at the same time in process of becoming destroyed because real, becoming real because destroyed. . . . (1968b/1989, p. 223)
>
> [And]
>
> *There is no anger* in the destruction of the object to which I am referring, though there could be said to be joy at the object's survival. From this moment, or arising out of this phase, the object *is in fantasy always* being destroyed. This quality of "always being destroyed" makes the reality of the surviving object felt as such, strengthens the feeling tone, and contributes to object-constancy. The object can now be used. (1968b/1989, p. 226; emphasis in original)

A main effect of Winnicott's hypothesis was to shift the emphasis in psychoanalysis away from the theory that the infant's understanding of external reality is based primarily on its own projections. In accord with his long-standing emphasis on the facilitating environment, Winnicott's "use of an object" concept split the focus equally between internal and external reality.

But what, precisely, does it mean to say that the infant progresses from relating to *using* the object? Winnicott argued that the infant's realization that the object survives its attacks—*without retaliating*—enables the baby not only to believe in its external existence, but also to trust the object. An object that survives the most intense destruction the infant can muster and that does not strike back is a "good enough" mother whose reliability and trustworthiness are usable—helpful—in learning how to cope with normally difficult life.

Reactions to the Hypotheses

When Winnicott first presented these ideas—the culminating but paradoxical achievements of a long career—to a meeting of the New York Psychoanalytic Society, they were not welcomed with enthusiasm. For one thing, Winnicott was understood to be equating object *relating* to subjective reality and object *using* to external reality. In Winnicott's scheme, the ability to use the object in the external world was the more sophisticated phase of emotional development. Thus some psychoanalysts perceived Winnicott's concepts as diminishing the importance of the internal world.

Even more resistance to Winnicott's ideas were couched in clinical terms. Winnicott's hypothesis implied that only through the patient's discovery that aggression toward the analyst does not destroy the analyst—and indeed is tolerated by the analyst without retaliation—can the patient "use" the therapist therapeutically. If the patient does not achieve this level of emotional development, the treatment is stalled at a subjective level of "self-analysis." The patient does not construct or use the analyst as a real person. Put another way, the analyst would be a projection of the self (Winnicott, 1968b/1989, p. 224). Thus Winnicott implied that psychoanalytic treatment was not exclusively a matter of interpretation. "Holding" and "good enough" therapeutic parenting that enable the patient to "use" the analyst as a collaborator in the search for maturity were at least equally important. Implications such as these were given a hostile reception by the New York analytic community in 1968, and Winnicott, who was already in declining health, suffered a heart attack the day after his presentation that prevented his return to London for more than a month.

PERSONAL SOURCES FROM WINNICOTT'S CHILDHOOD

If ever a man were born to be a mother, it was Donald Woods Winnicott. His near magical talent for communicating with children became legendary (cf. C. Winnicott, 1983/1991, p. 184). A particularly revealing and charming story is told, for example, of Winnicott's return visit to a Danish family after a period of some years. The children were eager to see him again because they remembered happily how he had played with them. They were delighted to talk with this Englishman who spoke Danish so well. But the children's father tried to forestall disappointment by telling them that Dr. Winnicott did not speak Danish. He failed to persuade them even though he was correct (anecdote reported in Goldman, 1993, p. 57). Language was no barrier in the children's memory of the man.

The majority of Winnicott's biographers agree that he had a strong identification with his mother and an empathic bond with all mothers (especially C. Winnicott, 1978, 1989; see also Goldman, 1993; pp. 47ff.; Jacobs, 1995; Kahr, 1996; Phillips, 1988). It is heartening, too, that Winnicott's childhood has been described by his second wife Clare as "too good to be true" in the particular sense that Donald was loved, knew he was loved, and thought of himself as lovable (1989, p. 9). He grew up fundamentally happy and secure. To judge from the substance of the theory he left behind, his vision of humanity was certainly individualized by his experiences—even, necessarily, idiosyncratic ones—but it does not appear to have been driven by psychopathology.

Taking Charge: Doctors, Darwin, and Death

If anything at all can be said to have driven Donald Winnicott's personality development it was his profound need to be actively and exclusively in charge of his life. For example, when he broke his collar bone at sports, he came to the realization that he would have to "depend" on doctors for the rest of his life everytime he "damaged" himself or became ill (C. Winnicott, 1989, p. 10). Enforced dependence on anyone meant vulnerability to Winnicott. Illness and "damage" were loathsome, if unavoidable, paths on life's road that Winnicott had already decided to travel only on his own terms. He would, quite directly, pursue an independent route. By becoming a physician, he would take active control over, and responsibility for, the vulnerabilities of his life. It is not difficult to see that the young Winnicott, as he observed in so many children throughout his career, was making first contact with the discomforting meanings of his own mortality. Characteristically, his response was to take charge.

In a similar vein, his encounter during his school years with the writing of Charles Darwin set the pattern of Winnicott's intellectual and philosophical life. Painting on a cosmically vast canvas, Darwin made life itself seem humanly comprehensible. To Winnicott, Darwin's ideas meant living things could be understood "scientifically." Gradually he envisioned the need for a psychological Darwin whose work would advance a unified understanding of human behavior in the same "scientific" way. Winnicott ultimately found his psychological Darwin in Sigmund Freud (Winnicott, 1945b/1996, p. 7). Such extraordinary yearnings for the independence of spirit to master life's vulnerabilities had the effect of elevating doctors, Darwin, and death to the ranks of the high rollers at Winnicott's table.

Donald Winnicott was also a playful man and remained so until his death. His wife Clare Winnicott (1983/1991) recalled that she and her husband rarely sat in chairs at home, preferring to spread out their books and papers on the floor for a good read or simply to watch television. And together they often played the squiggle game. Clare remembered fondly how Donald loved to ride his bicycle with his feet up on the handle bars, tearing exuberantly down Haverstock Hill. He rode like that until very late in life, when a policeman stopped him to say, "Fancy an old man like you setting an example to everybody" (1983/1991, p. 192). Driving his car was an opportunity for similar playfulness. He drove standing up, a walking stick propping the accelerator forward, while he stuck his head up through the open roof. "He was the most spontaneous thing that ever lived" (C. Winnicott, 1983/1991, p. 193).

Multiple Mothers

Donald was born on April 9, 1896, in Plymouth, England, the youngest and only male of three children born to John Frederick Winnicott and Elizabeth Martha Woods. His sisters were already five and six years of age when Donald joined the Winnicott family, self-described as "Wesleyan Methodists" (Phillips, 1988, p. 23). Clare Winnicott (1983/1991, p. 184) pointed out that the Methodist tradition is one of strong independence, self-reliance and nonconformity, characteristics that certainly describe Winnicott himself.

Donald recalled as an adult that:". . . in a sense I was an only child with multiple mothers and with a father extremely preoccupied in my younger years with town as well as business matters" (quoted in C. Winnicott, 1989, p. 8). Clare Winnicott recalled that Donald had thought he did not have enough contact with his own father:"So he says, 'I was left too much to all my mothers. Thank goodness I was sent away at thirteen!' " (1983/1991, p. 185). In fact, the members of the Winnicottian household in which Donald grew up were almost exclusively female. Two older sisters, his mother, a nanny, sometimes a governess for his sisters Violet and Kathleen, his Aunt Delia and another aunt, a cook and several parlor maids populated the Winnicott household, and all "doted" on Donald (Kahr, 1996, p. 5). As a child, Donald especially loved to spend time in the kitchen with the cook. His wife Clare later reported that this remained an interest though his adult life. The one place you were certain to find Dr. Winnicott was the kitchen (C. Winnicott, 1983/1991). All the Winnicott females loved children and all of them, well into their elderly years, maintained the knack of playing and talking with youngsters (C. Winnicott, 1983/1991).

> This unique constellation of a little boy fully enveloped by mothers and virtually deprived of a father seems to have left an indelible impression on Winnicott's psychological development, resulting in a powerful female identification. First of all, because young Donald received so much affection from so many women with whom he interacted in a reliable manner, he felt protected, safe, and secure, and this emotional stability provided him with a solid foundation for a sturdy, productive, and creative adult life. Secondly, the preponderance of women in Winnicott's childhood stimulated an extreme fascination with the inner world of the female. . . . (Kahr, 1996, p. 6)

As Winnicott's biographer concludes, life contrived to have him confront the nature of femaleness at nearly every turn down the path of childhood (Kahr, 1996, p. 6). One less positive legacy of a childhood spent with so many women and so little paternal attention was a high pitched and squeaky voice that Donald himself detested. Years later when he did his radio broadcasts for the British Broadcasting Corporation, he received a considerable number of letters addressed to "Mrs." Winnicott (Kahr, 1996, p. 7).

Donald's Mother: Elizabeth Woods

For all his focus on mothers, Donald's mother is a biographically indistinct figure about whom few details are known. There is some evidence that Elizabeth Woods struggled with episodes of depression throughout her life and that Donald's very absent father unconsciously assigned his son to care for and cheer up his mother (Kahr, 1996, p. 10). Clare Winnicott quoted her husband's observation that ". . . it is probably true that in the early years [my father] left me too much to all my mothers. Things never quite righted themselves" (C. Winnicott, 1989, p. 8; see also C. Winnicott, 1978, p. 24). At the age of 67, Winnicott wrote a poem about his mother entitled "The

Tree," which he sent to his brother-in-law with a note acknowledging the hurt he felt in composing it:

> Mother below is weeping
> weeping
> weeping
> Thus I knew her
> Once, stretched out in her lap
> As now on dead tree
> I learned to make her smile
> to stem her tears
> to undo her guilt
> to cure her inward death
> To enliven her was my living.

(quoted in Phillips, 1988, p. 29)

The tree referred to in the title was the special place to which the young Donald retreated to do his homework. Phillips (1988) points out that there is religious symbolism in Winnicott's choice of metaphor:

> In the poem Winnicott clearly identifies himself with Christ, and the Tree of the title is the Cross. . . . The chilling image of himself 'stretched out on her lap/As now on dead tree,' by omitting the definite article suggests that once it is dead it is no tree in particular, as anonymous as dead wood. (Phillips, 1988, pp. 29–30)

Is it worth mentioning that Donald *Woods* Winnicott's middle name is his mother's maiden name? It is probably more worthwhile to point out that his poetry alludes to the role that the young Winnicott played in combating his mother's "deadness." The poem poignantly also expresses themes that occupied Winnicott professionally for his entire career:

- feeling fully alive versus feeling dead numbness,
- maternal depression experienced by the child as aggression,
- the needs of the child for maternal holding,
- the protective role of a superficially compliantly cheerful False Self, and
- the False Self as caretaker.

Winnicott understood that at the beginning and at the end of his life that he had made, ". . . a living out of keeping his mother alive" (Phillips, 1988, p. 30).

Donald's Father: Sir John Frederick Winnicott

John Frederick Winnicott was a successful merchant, specializing in women's corsetery. He was a religious man with a simple but strong faith who attended church regularly and apparently viewed himself as the patriarch of the household. As the only male child, young Donald had the privilege of walking home from church as his father's solitary companion. John Winnicott was twice elected mayor of the town of Plymouth and was knighted in 1924 (Phillips, 1988, p. 23). "Sir Frederick," as he became known, was active in town politics and the business community, and even became Manager of the Plymouth Hospital and Chairman of the Plymouth Chamber of Commerce. Despite these accomplishments, Frederick Winnicott felt insecure throughout his adult life about his lack of a "proper" education (Phillips, 1988, p. 23). His aspirations to become a member of Parliament foundered on lifelong "learning difficulties," which John Frederick believed had robbed him of the confidence to enter the world of politics outside his local community (Kahr, 1996, p. 4).

For all of his success in local business and politics, John Frederick was a distant parental figure and inept father to his son. His relationship with Donald was formal rather than intimate, and sometimes surprisingly authoritarian. Indeed, Frederick Winnicott could be so insensitive to his son's needs that Donald risked the humiliation of his father's teasing for even minor infractions of Winnicottian decorum. On one occasion, 12-year-old Donald used the word *drat* as an expletive during the noonday meal:

> . . . my father looked pained as only he could look, blamed my mother for not seeing to it that I had decent friends, and from that moment he prepared himself to send me away to boarding school, which he did when I was thirteen. (quoted in C. Winnicott, 1989, p. 8)

Perhaps it was characteristic for Winnicott to "detoxify" the recollection into a more benign memory than the reality on which it was based, but Winnicott recalled in his autobiography that in fact his father fundamentally had been correct. The boy who was his closest friend in school was "no good," and left to their own devices, Winnicott envisioned that they would have gotten into trouble. The deeper meaning of the incident—abandonment by his father, or at the very least, banishment and punishment—did not altogether escape Winnicott's Klein-tutored attention. "So my father was there to kill and be killed, but it is probably true that in the early years he left me too much to all my mothers" (quoted in C. Winnicott, 1989, p. 8).

There is some indication that the nature of John Frederick's teasing was linked to issues of Donald's masculinity or sexuality. When Donald was only three, he ascended the grassy slope in the garden armed with his child-sized croquet mallet prepared to exact revenge and make a piece of personal family history. In the tall grass, he bashed flat the nose of a wax doll called "Rosie" that belonged to his sisters. Rosie was a particular source of irritation to young Donald because his father often teased him with the doll by parodying a popular song of the day in a voice intended to taunt:

> Rosie said to Donald
> I love you
> Donald said to Rosie
> I don't believe you do.

(quoted in C. Winnicott, 1989, p. 7)

Winnicott (1989, p. 7) says that he "knew the doll had to be altered for the worse, and much of my life has been founded on the undoubted fact that I actually *did* this deed, not merely wish it and planned it." Ironically, his father relieved some of his son's guilt by heating the wax of the doll's head with a series of matches and remolding it into a more or less recognizable face.

> This early demonstration of the restitutive and reparative act certainly made an impression on me, and perhaps made me able to accept the fact that I myself, dear innocent child, had actually become violent directly with a doll, but indirectly with my good-tempered father who was just then entering my conscious life. (Winnicott, quoted in C. Winnicott, 1989, p. 8)

It is a subtle autobiographical conceit, but Winnicott clearly and defensively presents the memory of his father as an admirable, even tempered, helpful man for whom he felt only admiration and love. Yet it was the father who provoked humiliation by repeated teasing of his son.

Implications of Winnicott's Childhood

At least three inferences can be drawn from the sample of episodes we have reviewed from the early life of D. W. Winnicott. First, compared to most of the theorists we examine in this book, Winnicott had a happy, secure, healthy childhood in a warm and loving family. For this reason, Winnicott's vision of personality development emphasizes spontaneous collaboration between children and their parents rather than the conflicts that are also inevitably enacted between them. The most frequently occurring personal theme among the theorists in this book (see Chapter 18) is the individual theorist's memory of having been an unwanted child. Winnicott is the only theorist for whom it appears virtually certain that this theme was irrelevant—both in his recollection of childhood and in the reality of his family life. There is a strong temptation to observe that one of the healthiest theories has sprung from the healthiest personal sources.

Second, Winnicott's freedom from childhood insecurity was not immunity from other forms of maternal rejection. Although the definitive biography has yet to be written, the existing body of life history data make it clear that Winnicott's sensitivity to failures in maternal "holding" stemmed from his own experiences trying to vitalize an emotionally numbed and depressed mother. His wish to "be alive" when he died, as we saw in the opening of this chapter, can also be understood as the desire of the man who described the caretaking False Self to not be depressed, to not be merely socially compliant, to not be inauthentic.

Third, Winnicott's theory mentions the contributions of fathers to the development of their children—but just barely. Fathers are not in the Winnicottian spotlight just as Sir Frederick was not in his son's daily life. Winnicott's affinity for and empathy with mothers, his tight focus on mothering, rather than parenting, and his own impressive talents "mothering" and "holding" his patients clearly had their origins in his family traditions of interest in children and in his personal experiences with "multiple mothers." With all due respect, Winnicott must share with Anna Freud, each for unique personal and historical reasons, the title of *mother of object relations theory*. He would be pleased.

A Final Word on Winnicott

Imagine a deserted island after civilization has been destroyed by nuclear holocaust. The island is populated by children who will reestablish human society. Half of the children are prototypical Kleinian and half of them are Winnicottian. Which group, do you suppose, could have inspired William Golding's novel *Lord of the Flies?*

HEINZ KOHUT

BEYOND THE EGO: PSYCHOANALYTIC SELF-THEORY

In many ways, Heinz Kohut's work with patients whose central disturbance involved feelings of emptiness and depression is a therapeutic extension of Margaret Mahler's observations of the roots of individuality. Kohut found the need to extend psychoanalytic theory beyond the ego concept to understand a patient's narcissistic vulnerability in terms of the patient's inadequately formed or damaged sense of self. Such "narcissistically disturbed" individuals seemed not to be suffering from castration anxiety or from conflicted id strivings in the classical sense; they seemed to be fixated at a stage in development where fear *of the loss of the love object prevails* (Kohut, 1971, p. 20).

In the psychoanalytic relationship, such patients form a unique kind of transference to the analyst. An *idealizing transference* develops in some patients who behave toward their therapists as though they were the all-good, all-powerful parent who is still part of the self. Such patients are projecting onto their therapist their idealized images of the "good love object," as though they were still searching and yearning for fusion with it. The obvious conclusion is that such patients suffered severe trauma in that stage of early development when the love object had not yet been entirely distinguished from self:

> Persons who have suffered such traumas are (as adolescents and adults) forever attempting to achieve a union with the idealized object, since, in view of their specific structural defect (the insufficient idealization of their superego), their narcissistic equilibrium is safeguarded only through the interest, the responses, and the approval of present-day (i.e., currently active) replicas of the traumatically lost self-object. (Kohut, 1971, p. 55)

Idealizing transferences may occur in a variety of forms, ranging from most archaic and primitive to most mature, depending on the point in development at which narcissistic injury took place. The key point is that such a narcissistically injured person was unable to form internalized capacities for self-control, for self-judgment, and for the maintenance of self-esteem as an independent entity.

A second kind of narcissistically disturbed patient forms a different kind of *mirroring transference* relationship with the analyst. In this form, the patient is regressing to an even earlier stage of development during which, in Mahler's terms, *absolute narcissism* prevails.

The mirror transference . . . constitute[s] the therapeutic revival of that aspect of a developmental phase (roughly corresponding to the condition which Freud referred to as the "purified pleasure ego") in which the child attempts to save the originally all-embracing narcissism by concentrating perfection and power upon the self—here called the grandiose self—and by turning away disdainfully from an outside to which all imperfections have been assigned. (Kohut, 1971, p. 106)

In the mirror transference, the roots of pathology go further back in development to the period before any recognition of the external love object (mother) was formed. The grandiose self is formed by internalizing "all good" and externalizing "all bad" experiences. Good (pleasure) is part of me; bad (pain) belongs out there. This process of assimilating "good" and expelling "bad" is thus a form of splitting in its most fundamental and autistic form.

In the *idealizing transference,* the experience of the mother's aid in satisfying tension needs revolved around the mechanism: "You are perfect, but I am part of you" (Kohurt, 1971, p. 27). By contrast, the more archaic *mirror transference* involves the mechanism: "I am perfect" in order to avoid any experience of "the bad" as part of self. In the idealizing transference, the therapist becomes the perfected mother-self image; in the mirroring transference, the therapist functions as a reflector of the archaic self-perfection of the patient. From the patient's viewpoint in a mirroring transference, the therapist is a looking glass in which can be seen displayed the patient's own grandiose, exhibitionistic self.

Origins of the Self

The idealizing and mirroring transference relationships that emerged in psychoanalysis with narcissistically wounded patients served as an important clue to the processes of development. Kohut began to understand that such patients used the therapist as a *Selfobject* rather than seeing the therapist as an independent human being.

Selfobjects are objects [people] which we experience as part of our self; the expected control over them is therefore closer to the concept of the control which a grown-up expects to have over his own body and mind than to the concept of control which he expects to have over others. (Kohut & Wolff, 1978, p. 414)

Like the mirroring and idealizing transferences observed in the treatment of patients with wounded selves, Kohut envisioned normal development as a process of interaction between the growing infant and his or her mirroring and idealizing Selfobjects. The mother serves as a *mirroring Selfobject* when she is able to confirm and admire the child's sense of strength, health, greatness, and specialness. The key ingredient, of course, is the mother's capacity to be attuned empathically to her child's needs for such personal confirmation and admiration.

Mother also serves as an *idealizing Selfobject* somewhat later in development when she encourages and permits the child to merge with her own strength and calmness as a powerful and caring adult. From the child's point of view, the idealizing Selfobject is a model of perfection, power, and soothingness who can be experienced in part as a component of self.

Unlike the classical psychoanalytic model, Kohut's theory of development pictures the mother's relationship with her child not in terms of drive satisfactions but in terms of emphatic, warm, loving responsiveness to the whole child. As a consequence, the child will experience self as a joyful, competent and valuable person, or as a rejected, depleted, empty self. When the Selfobject-child relationship is seriously deficient, as with a latently psychotic mother, the child is as unable to survive psychologically in a loveless relationship as he or she would be unable physically to survive in an oxygenless environment. Human warmth, responsiveness, and empathy are the oxygen, the crucial survival elements in the development of a self that is neither grandiosely isolated from reality nor delusionally idealizing of magical love objects (Kohut, 1977, pp. 75-76).

> The essence of the healthy . . . [parental relationship] for the growing self of the child is a mature, cohesive parental self that is in tune with the changing needs of the child. It can, with a glow of shared joy, mirror the child's grandiose display one minute, yet, perhaps a minute later, should the child become anxious and overstimulated by its exhibitionism, it will curb the display by adopting a realistic attitude *vis-à-vis* the child's limitations. Such optimal frustrations of the child's need to be mirrored and to merge into an idealized selfobject, hand in hand with optimal gratifications, generate the appropriate growth-facilitating matrix for the self. (Kohut & Wolff, 1978, p. 417)

Structure of the Bipolar Nuclear Self

Kohut hypothesizes that an adequate relationship with a healthy Selfobject results in the formation of a bipolar self that has three components:

1. *Nuclear Ambitions,* which are the child's learned strivings for power and success *mirrored* admiringly by the Selfobject;
2. *Nuclear Ideals,* which are the idealized goals and images derived from the child's recognition of the satisfying and soothing power *modeled* by the Selfobject; and
3. *Basic Talents and Skills,* which lie metaphorically between the two poles of ambitions and ideals and which form a kind of metaphorical "tension arc" of psychological activity as the person is "driven" by ambitions and "led" by ideals in the pursuit of life goals using what talent and skills he or she possesses. (Kohut, 1977, p. 188)

The nuclear ambitions are formed early in life, at or around the second or third year, whereas the nuclear ideals are incorporated into the self as a second pole around the ages of four or five years (Kohut, 1977, p. 179).

Kohut thus envisions the nuclear self as a bipolar entity, with the ambitions and ideals anchoring opposite poles. The central process in the formation of these two poles, as we have seen, is the relationship with empathic Selfobjects. The nuclear self, however, is not simply a direct copy of the Selfobjects. It is an assimilation of some aspects of their personality characteristics, but the main features of the Selfobject are depersonalized and generalized in a process Kohut calls "transmuting internalization."

Transmuting internalization is a kind of psychological digestion by which the usable and good features of the Selfobject are incorporated into the child's self in a pattern that is unique to that child. Mild frustrations and failures in empathy by the Selfobjects encourage the child to see them as "only human." Such occasional failures in empathy on the part of the Selfobjects permit the child to build his or her own self-structures without the need to incorporate the total personality of others.

Unlike Freud's emphasis on drive conflict, Kohut's emphasis is clearly on person-to-person interactions. Kohut suggests that one way to conceptualize the difference between classical psychoanalysis and his own self-psychology is to contrast the traditions of "Guilty Man" and "Tragic Man."

Guilty Man is the concept of persons as struggling always toward the satisfaction of their drives. They are pictured in classical psychoanalysis as living under the domination of the pleasure principle, striving endlessly to reconcile inner conflict. They are frequently blocked from their goal of tension reduction by their own inadequacies or those of the people who raised them.

Tragic Man, by contrast, is Kohut's picture of people struggling to fulfill the aims of their nuclear selves. That is to say, Tragic Man is attempting to express the pattern of his or her very being, the pattern of the ambitions and ideals that comprise the self-expressive goals of a human life (1977, p. 133). Where Guilty Man is driven, Tragic Man yearns.

An Illustration: Reinterpretation of the Oedipus Complex

As an example of the differences between Kohut's self-psychology and classical psychoanalysis, consider Kohut's interpretation of the child's experiences during the phallic phase of development.

In classical theory, this central development-instinctual conflict is the source of a variety of weaknesses and unresolved guilts in the area of identity. Kohut, on the other hand, prefers to view the Oedipus conflict as the source of potential strengths.

Without a firm sense of self, a cohesive and continuous realization of "who I am," an Oedipus conflict cannot take place (1977, p. 227). "Unless the child sees himself as a delimited, abiding, independent center of initiative, he is unable to experience the object-instinctual desires that lead to the conflicts and secondary adaptations of the Oedipal period" (1977, p. 227).

With the focus on the positive aspects of the oedipal period, Kohut suggests that the typical oedipal desires are experienced by the child as assertive-possessive, affectionate-sexual urges to possess the opposite-sexed parent, combined with assertive, self-confident, competitive feelings toward the same-sexed parent. Parents will typically react to both sets of feelings with different, contradictory feelings of their own. On the one hand, they will become counteraggressive toward the child's aggression, and on the other will "react with pride and joy to the child's developmental achievement, to his vigor and assertiveness" (1977, p. 230).

When parents are able to respond in *both* ways to the child's Oedipal feelings—neither overdoing the aggression nor exaggerating the joy and pride in assertiveness—they promote the child's mental health and capacity for self-confidence. "If the little boy, for example, feels that his father looks upon him proudly as a chip off the old block and allows him to merge with him and with his adult greatness, then his Oedipal phase will be a decisive step in self-consolidation and self-pattern-firming. . . ." (Kohut, 1977, p. 234).

> What, in other words, is the Oedipus complex of the child who has entered the Oedipal phase with a firmly cohesive self and who is surrounded by parents who themselves have healthy cohesive and continuous selves? It is my impression . . . that the normal child's Oedipal experiences . . . contain, from the beginning and persisting throughout, an admixture of deep joy that, while unrelated to the content of the Oedipus complex in the traditional sense, is of the utmost developmental significance within the framework of the psychology of the self. (Kohut, 1977, pp. 235–236)

Parents who themselves are cohesive personalities will pass along their joy in living to their child. Kohut, in essence, asks whether the Oedipus complex is not more joyful, less conflicted, less violent, and less wounding to self-esteem than classical theory would have it (Kohut, 1977, p. 246). Could it be, he asks, that the classical version of the Oedipus complex exists only in the case of the child whose parents are themselves narcissistically wounded?

When Selfobjects Fail: The Injured Self

Psychological disorder from the perspective of Kohut's theory is no longer viewed in terms of the ego's failures to balance reality, id wishes, and superego judgments. Abnormal psychological functioning is pictured in Kohut's theory as the result of defects in the formation of a cohesive self. Such defects represent developmental insults to normal narcissism. When the insult or injury is sufficiently intense, characteristic pathological distortions are introduced into the infant's developing self. Kohut has described four such distortions that correspond to four different kinds of Selfobject failure (Kohut & Wolff, 1978):

1. *The understimulated self* that develops in the child whose Selfobjects are seriously unattuned to his or her self-needs for mirroring and idealizing. The self loses vitality, and in later life, the mirrorless and ideal-less self experiences itself as deadened, empty, and numbed. Such people may turn to momentary and risky ways of experiencing "aliveness" in the abuse of drugs and alcohol, sexual adventurism, or compulsive gambling. But all such artificial "self-stimulants" can provide only fleeting experiences of an alive self, and even those flashes of aliveness may be experienced as alien intrusions from the outside world. The person's self even has a quality of alien, depersonalized existence.

2. *The fragmenting self* is formed in the child whose Selfobjects have inflicted some definite narcissistic injury on the child at a particularly vulnerable moment. The child's self-esteem is overtaxed in the face of humiliation that proves permanently damaging. As a result, the person experiences self as fragmented, uncoordinated, and lacking balance and cohesion. Hypochondriacal complaints of vague pains and chronic but undefinable illness may characterize the person's daily life. At base, the person experiences self as sickened, weakened, and at the mercy of life.

3. *Overstimulated self* develops in the child who is exposed to Selfobjects who inappropriately stimulate either the child's ambitions or ideals. If the

grandiose ambitions-pole of the self is stimulated intensely, the result is a self that attempts to avoid situations where the person may become the center of attention. Archaic "greatness fantasies" stimulated by the Selfobjects arouse much anxiety in adulthood and push the person to hide the self from scrutiny.

If, on the other hand, the ideals-pole of the self was inappropriately responded to by the Selfobjects, the result is a persistent need to merge with idealized people and share in their greatness. But such a need to merge with them can also be experienced as threatening because one loses one's self in a fusion with another. Thus the person is trapped: He or she is "ideal hungry" but afraid to be devoured by his or her own hunger.

4. *Overburdened self* is embodied in the child whose Selfobjects did not provide opportunities for the child to merge with their strength and calmness. The overburdened self that develops lacks an ability to soothe itself, and the person experiences the world as a threatening, dangerous, inimical place. Any stimulation is overwhelming and fearful, and there is no place to turn for comfort.

It should be clear from Kohut's various conceptualizations that he has attempted to move away from a drive model of psychological functioning toward a more interpersonal and phenomenological viewpoint. In fact, Kohut argues in his last and posthumously published book that the curative ingredient in psychoanalytic treatment is the analyst's ability to teach the patient how to look for and use healthy Selfobjects:

> According to self-psychology, then, the essence of the psychoanalytic cure resides in a patient's newly acquired ability to identify and seek out appropriate Selfobjects—both mirroring and idealizable—as they present themselves in his realistic surrounding and to be sustained by them. (Kohut, 1984, p. 77)

A FINAL WORD ON HEINZ KOHUT

Heinz Kohut's self-theory is the attempt to view personality development and the various ways in which it can go wrong in the light of the person's own evaluation of his or her success or failure in mastering the obstacles of life. The narcissistically injured patient, with whom Kohut primarily deals, evidences the kind of deficits and misinterpretations of reality that only make sense if a narcissistically damaged nuclear-self is postulated beyond the three agencies of the ego, id, and superego. Kohut perhaps summarizes his own contribution best when he explains the goal of psychoanalytic therapy with the narcissistically wounded personality:

> The successful end of the analysis of narcissistic personality disorders has been reached, when, after a proper termination phase has established itself and has been worked through, the analysand's formerly enfeebled or fragmented nuclear-self—his nuclear ambitions and ideals in cooperation with certain groups of talents and skills—has become sufficiently strengthened and consolidated to be able to function as a more or less self-propelling, self-directed, self-sustaining unit which provides a

central purpose to his personality and gives a sense of meaning to his life. (Kohut, 1977, pp. 138–139)

There is no doubt that Kohut wishes to preserve the essence of psychoanalysis; but there is as little doubt that he has moved psychoanalysis toward the humanistic position of such theorists as Carl Rogers and Karen Horney in which integration and personal purposiveness are the criteria of personality health.

EVALUATING OBJECT RELATIONS THEORY

Indebted as they were to classical psychoanalysis, Klein, Winnicott, and Kohut each in their own way, advanced psychoanalysis from a drive theory to an interpersonal, transactional, and highly developmental model of personality. But intellectual debts are still debts. Like the parent theory from which these object-relations models emerged, each of them shares the strengths and weaknesses of psychodynamic formulations.

Refutability of Object Relations Theory

It is ironic that the great strength of object relations theory—a concern with the developmental consequences of intimate relationships—is also its greatest scientific weakness. Because the major interest of each theorist in this chapter was the unconscious dynamics, rather than the observable interpersonal transactions, of relationships, most of Klein's, Winnicott's and Kohut's hypotheses are untestable. What transpires in the "mind" of the baby as it interacts with mother can only ever be an inference.

Some inferences impress us as more reasonable than others, but reasonableness is not equivalent to refutability. Klein's formulations appear on close examination to be wanting both in the consistency of their logic and in the vast distance between her inferences and the observations on which they are putatively based. Winnicott's proposals, influenced by Klein, lie closer to pragmatic common sense. Unfortunately, however, with the single exception of the transitional object, Winnicott's hypotheses are still inferences about unconscious dynamics that lie too distant from the possibility of empirical test. Kohut's formulations, more philosophical than his colleagues, are nevertheless similarly speculative.

What can we conclude? In some respects, object relations theory represents no improvement in refutability relative to classical psychoanalysis. Indeed in some ways— including reliance on the death instinct, emphasis on innate aggression, reliance on paradoxical formulations—object relations theory represents a regression.

Human Agency in Object Relations Theory

Each theorist in this chapter shares more with the ego psychologists than with classical psychoanalytic theory on the dimension of active-versus-passive agency. If we ranked the three theorists from the least-active to the most-active conception of agency, the order would be: Klein, Kohut, Winnicott. Klein's formulation preserves substantial elements of the classical drive theory and its reliance on a reactive model of the nervous system. Kleinian babies are tense infants who reactively discharge their drives on to available objects. Kohut's model clearly pictures humans as active constructors of their social reality, but his aim, necessarily, was a clinical one that emphasized the aberrant functioning of wounded people reacting to significant others who inflict their wounds. Winnicott, by far, is the theorist who most completely comprehends people from the earliest days of their lives as collaborative constructors of social reality. Winnicott's concepts of the infant's progress from omnipotent magical thinking to object relating and on toward *using the object by constructing it, destroying it, and happily rediscovering it surviving in reality* are active agent concepts. They are even interactive concepts of human agency. Unfortunately, they are also fuzzily metaphysical. No one is perfect.

The Idiographic Emphasis of Object Relations Theory

Shared with orthodox psychoanalysis is an almost religious fervor for understanding the individual. Personality development, and the ways in which it can go wrong, are strictly "one person at a time" phenomena for object relations theorists. It could hardly be otherwise for any theory with psychodynamic aspirations. The intention, however, is to generate clinical data that will by sheer accretion eventually cohere into nomothetic "laws" or rules of predictable behavior. But in object relations theory, as in Freud's pioneering attempts, that intention is stillborn. If there is a nomothetic principle *somewhere* in these formulations, then it is to be found in Winnicott's observations in the "set situation" or perhaps in the apparently universal human need for transitional objects.

Some Summary, Some Conclusions

Object relations theory advanced Freud's orthodox model in two ways. First, a more ambitiously developmental perspective based on direct clinical work with children was introduced into psychoanalysis. Second, Freud's passing references to the ego's propensity to retain the character of its lost objects was expanded substantially. Intimate relations, rather than drive gratification, became both the medium and the message of psychoanalysis. Unlike the neo-Freudians, whom we consider in later chapters, the object relations theorists wanted to preserve as much of orthodox psychoanalysis as they could.

Melanie Klein

Beginning with the observations of her own children, Melanie Reizes Klein's (1882–1960) earliest formulations were more or less overly enthusiastic educational applications of classical theory. She initially presented her formulations as "psychoanalytic educational upbringing" designed to be a kind of prophylaxis of the child's mind. In a number of other ways, Klein took Freud at his word, and then extended the words beyond anything Freud intended. She soon pushed psychoanalytic understanding backwards in time to the earliest days of life, where eventually she found a fully functioning ego, superego, and a remarkably active aggressive drive. She credited even the youngest child with an active unconsciously imaginative capacity, called "phantasy," to construct images of the important people in their lives. Phantasy images are real to the infant, as real as the people from whom they are derived and on whom they will eventually be projected. Klein's work is sometimes seen as a feminist corrective to Freud's male-dominated theory. In contrast to Freud's emphasis on the importance of the penis for both genders, Klein placed the female breast, the child's first love and most enduring love object, at the center of her psychological world.

Klein's conception of the infant pictures an inherently aggressive, sadistic, and opportunistic creature who becomes frightened by its own aggression. To protect itself from the retaliation it imagines its love objects might enact, the infant splits objects into good and bad. The worried infant anticipates persecution from its bad objects and idealizes its good ones for protection.

With time, Klein moderated the role of aggression in her theory, supplementing it with formulations of anxiety, guilt, envy, and reparation. The infant was now understood as envying the good object (breast) because of its bountiful goodness. Phantasies of destroying the good object not only evoke anxiety but provoke guilt feelings. The need to repair the love-object emerges and the infant omnipotently believes that it can accomplish this magical feat.

These various landmarks in the infant's progress toward conceptualizing the mother as a real person were called "positions" by Klein to emphasize that they are ongoing, lifelong processes. The first developmental position was called the *paranoid position* because the central anxiety is the infant's fear of its own annihilation. By a convoluted twist of logic, Klein argued that the infant fears that the destroyed object may reconstitute itself inside the infant and reinitiate its persecution. At a later moment in development, anxiety or concern for the welfare of the object becomes dominant. When the infant comprehends that the mother-as-a-person is in jeopardy from its own rage, the *depressive position* is entered. Now the baby's central concern is to protect the good object from its own attacks and those mounted against the mother by internalized bad objects. To supplement the reparative defensive strategy, the ego may temporarily adopt what Klein called the *manic position*. This developmental phase is marked by the need to take omnipotent control over the object, dominating it by exerting the power of life and death over it, and protecting it from its own sadistic impulses.

Although Klein originally proposed *splitting* as an elementary and primitive infantile defense against the recognition that good and bad object are one, she elaborated the concept into a series of complex developmental maneuvers. *Splitting* eventually referred to object division (good and bad), ego defensive splitting or repressive dissociation, object relations splitting (love and hate), and even splitting of enduring personality structures such as the id and superego. A supplementary and related defense is *projective identification,* whereby the infant identifies with the split-off good object and distances itself from the split-off bad object. But the target of the projection, mother, may find that the infant behaves in ways that subtly coerce her behavior into conformity with the infant's projection. Projective identification can thus be a kind of self-fulfilling prophecy by which the projector manipulates the projectee to comply with the wish embodied in the projection.

Klein's model of infant development relies on major inferences about the infant's mind. It strikes many observers that Klein's specific deductions tell us less about the infant's mind than they do about what was on Klein's mind.

D.W. Winnicott

Trained as a pediatrician, Donald Woods Winnicott (1896–1971) brought to psychoanalysis a pragmatic sensibility rooted in common sense. He had a gift for communicating with children and often could employ the simplest of games as diagnostic assessments. The squiggle game and his observations of babies mouthing a shiny tongue depressor (the "spatula") were part of Winnicott's consultative approach to child psychiatry.

He transferred that same flexible, spontaneous attitude to his psychoanalytic clinical work and to his theoretical formulations. Influenced by Melanie Klein, Winnicott was nevertheless adamant trying to maintain his intellectual and creative independence. He understood infants as collaborators rather than as sadistic aggressors. While he found value in Klein's developmental "positions," he made every effort to depathologize them by focusing on the achievements of the infant in coping with its interpersonal world. Life is normally difficult, Winnicott argued, and most babies momentarily display some forms of behavior that appears pathological. But on closer examination, coupled with a willingness to tolerate momentarily eccentric or disruptive behavior, adults soon discover that most children can cope with life's real difficulties if their mothers can provide sufficiently secure and comforting *holding*.

The basic developmental tasks for the infant whose mother provides the physical and metaphorical holding that facilitates development are threefold: integration, personalization, and realization. *Integration* refers to the organization of personality facilitated by the mother's attention to satisfying her infant's needs reliably. *Unintegration,* the Winnicottian opposite of integration, is a primordially natural phase of development that the infant does not find distressing. *Personalization* is Winnicott's term for the infant's achievement of linking inner and outer reality by recognizing the boundaries of its own physical body. He meant that the baby "personalizes"—takes possession of—its body with help from mother's ministrations so that "this is *my* finger" begins to have real meaning. Finally, *realization* was Winnicott's term for the baby's acceptance of external reality as real, as objective and as enduring contrasted with the inner world of fantasy. Here the mother helps her child achieve "disillusionment": the understanding that illusion, however satisfying, is simply not shared reality.

Winnicott suggested that the "ordinary devoted mother" provides "good enough mothering" to permit her child to master its own aggression, come to grips with life's real difficulties, and develop a spontaneous, authentic self that he termed the *True Self.* By contrast, "not good enough" mothering, exhibited, for example, by the depressed mother, the psychiatrically ill or the neglectful mother, promotes the development of a protective mask-like self, called the *False Self.* Children can develop differing levels of False Self protection that vary in degree of maladaptiveness. At the extremely maladaptive end of the continuum is the False Self that functions to conceal completely the spontaneous True Self in an effort to protect it from manipulation in social contact. At the opposite end of the spectrum, most children develop a kind of socially cooperative False Self that serves to facilitate social success rather than to wall off the True Self. Between these extremes, children find healthy and not so healthy ways of protecting their inner lives from "impingement" and potential betrayal. But it was Winnicott's belief that the more protectively powerful the False Self grew, the less "alive," spontaneous, and playful could the True Self feel.

As part of her skilled and empathic "holding," the good enough mother provides just those things that the baby needs at just those moments when the baby is ready for them. In Winnicott's famous phrase, "There's no such thing as a baby." Babies are best understood as an integral part of the "nursing couple." Winnicott envisioned the mother-child relationship as a collaboration of two very unequal partners. The mother's task is to "shrink down" to baby-size to understand her infant's needs because the baby cannot expand to adult size to tell her what they might be. The good enough mother provides sufficient holding for the baby to master its most primitive fears, the unthinkable anxieties:

- Going to pieces,
- Falling forever,
- Having no relationship to the body,
- Having no orientation, and
- Complete isolation because of there being no means for communication.

Along the way, the infant learns the difference between those parts of self and mother which belong to "me" and those that are "not-me." Once this division between inner and outer reality is achieved, the infant can tolerate increased separation from its love-objects. To bridge the separation, a *transitional object,* the infant's first "not-me" possession will be "created" in collaboration with the mother. A bit of soft blanket, a stuffed toy, even a handkerchief or piece of clothing ("the niffle"), can serve the role of transitional object. It is baby's choice in cooperation with a mother who facilitates and supports the choice.

Toward the end of his life, when personal survival was at issue, Winnicott created one final developmental distinction between *relating* to and *using* an object. On the basis of a dream evoked by reading Jung's autobiography, Winnicott came to the insight that the infant has to fantasize destroying its love object to discover that the object in reality nevertheless survives. This infantile discovery permits the infant not only to relate to the object in a dependent way, but to trust sufficiently in the reliability and durability of the object to *use* the object to facilitate its own growth toward independence. As Winnicott pointed out, the progression from relating to using involves creation by destruction.

Heinz Kohut

Heinz Kohut (1913–1981) proposed a psychoanalytic self-theory in which the classical tripartite division of the mind is not adequate to the task of accounting for the development of a person's ambitions and ideals. Beginning his work with narcissistically wounded patients, Kohut argued that classical drive theory excludes from its account of normal development some important interpersonal interactions responsible for the emergence of emphathic understanding, self-esteem, and healthy adaptation to life.

The nuclear-self, in Kohut's formulation, is structured around the bipolar anchor points of ambition and ideals. Between these poles lies a tensions arc of psychological activities representing the forces that drive the individual to attain his or her goals. Classical psychoanalytic theory regards humans as struggling under the domination of the pleasure principle to reduce the tension of their instincts. A picture of a person as *Guilty Man* emerges from such a viewpoint, whereas Kohut's self-formulation portrays a *Tragic Man* conception of personality, whereby persons are interpreted as struggling to fulfill the aims of the ambitions and ideals contained in the bipolar nuclear-self.

In all, ego psychology has greatly expanded the confines of classical theory. No longer is a human being an "assembly of minds" or a battlefield on whose terrain the battalions of the mind erect obstacles, conduct assaults, and sustain defeats. No longer is psychoanalytic psychology restricted to study of unhealthy personality disasters. The whole span of life, from birth through adulthood, and the whole range of possible adaptations, from inhibited and fearful withdrawals to psychotic and fragmented separations from reality to masterful and efficacious coping, are accepted as suitable areas for a general psychoanalytic psychology to explore.

Taken as a loosely related group of ideas, object relations theories share the strengths and weaknesses of their parent model, classical psychoanalysis. They rely on untestable, irrefutable inferences about the infantile mind. The three theorists in this chapter represent advances over orthodox psychoanalysis in conceptualizing humans as active agents, but ranked on their conceptualizations from least active to most active, the list puts Klein at the bottom, Kohut in the middle, and Winnicott at the top rank. Idiographically focused on the individual case, objects relations theorists intend to generate universal or nomothetic, law-like principles, but they have not done so thus far.

FOR FURTHER READING

Scope and History of Object Relations Theories

A thorough and readable overview of the history and variety of object relations theories is given by Frank Summers in his *Object Relations Theories and Psychopathology* (1994, New York: Academic Press). Judith M. Hughes provides a comparison of the lives and work of Klein, Winnicott, and Fairbairn in her *Reshaping the Psychoanalytic Domain* (1989, Berkeley, CA: University of California Press). Jay R. Greenberg and Stephen A. Mitchell survey the details, philosophy, and metapsychology of a wide range of object relations theories in their *Object Relations in Psychoanalytic Theory* (1983, Cambridge, MA: Harvard University Press). Roy Schafer's edited volume, *The Contemporary Kleinians of London.* (1997, New York: International Universities Press) fulfills the aims of its title.

Melanie Klein

The most detailed and compelling biography of Klein is Phyllis Grosskurth's psychologically insightful and monumental *Melanie Klein: Her World and Her Work.* (Cambridge, MA: Harvard University Press, 1989). Klein never wrote a simple overview of her fully developed theory, but two of her books taken together provide a good introduction. The first is Klein's *Envy and Gratitude* (*The Writings of Melanie Klein,* Vol III, 176–235; New York: The Free Press, 1975). The second is Klein's *The Psycho-Analysis of Children* (*The Writings of Melanie Klein,* Vol II, New York: The Free Press, 1975). Julia Segal's, *Melanie Klein.* (London: Sage Publications, 1992) gives a sympathetic overview of Klein's life and work.

D. W. Winnicott

The best introduction to Winnicott's own writings are the papers collected into D. W. Winnicott's *The Maturational Processes and the Facilitating Environment* (Madison, CT: International Universities Press, 1965). Winnicott's *Playing and Reality* (Harmondsworth, Great Britain: Penguin, 1971; a variety of paperback editions available) is easy reading and a worthwhile supplement to Winnicott's professional papers.

Heinz Kohut

Heinz Kohut's chief publications include *The Analysis of the Self* (New York: International Universities Press, 1971), which presents the concept of the narcissistic personality; and his *The Restoration of the Self* (New York: International Universities Press, 1977), which more comprehensively elaborates his theory of the self, treatment for the narcissistic disorders, and his speculations on the flaws in classical psychoanalytic theory. Kohut's final statement in which he answers his critics has been posthumously published as *How Does Analysis Cure?* (Chicago: University of Chicago Press, 1984) and contains some important clarifications of his position.

C H A P T E R 6

ERIK ERIKSON
Psychoanalytic Ego Psychology

As an old Jew put it . . ."Doctor, my bowels are sluggish, my feet hurt, my heart jumps—and you know, Doctor, I myself don't feel so well either."

Erik H. Erikson, *Insight and Responsibility*

. . . healthy children will not fear life if their elders have integrity enough not to fear death.

Erik H. Erikson, *Childhood and Society*

About Erikson's Ego Psychology

Erik Erikson's work is both a psychoanalytic ego psychology and a unique creation that he calls a psychosocial life span theory. The focus for Erikson, as for the other ego psychologists, is on the person's interaction with the significant people in his or her life. He might, therefore, also be considered an object relations theorist. Instincts or drives are important, but the chief concern for Erikson is how the person interprets those needs. Erikson also broadens the theoretical focus to include a concern for cultural rituals and values imparted to the developing child in the family.

Central to Erikson's formulation are his concepts of

1. *Ego identity formation, by which he means that the ego (person) stands outside itself judging the continuity, the reliability, and the consistency of life as it is lived;*

2. *Developmental progression of the human life cycle through eight stages from infancy to old age. A human life is a psychological success for Erikson if the earliest achievement is the acquisition of basic trust in self and others and the last achievement is a sense that one's life was good exactly as it was lived;*

3. *Ego strengths that mark each of the eight stages and that are actually classical virtues such as hope, will, purpose, and wisdom.*

Erikson's work made it possible for psychoanalysts to ask a question that would have been alien to classical analysts: "What is the person's conception of him or herself?"

INNER AND OUTER REALITY: CHILD'S PLAY

Ten-, 11-, and 12-year-old California boys and girls were invited by Erik Erikson to construct on a tabletop with the available toy figures and blocks an "imaginary moving picture" (Erikson, 1950, p. 98). Over the course of a year and a half, 150 young people constructed nearly 450 such scenes, although most of them failed to follow Erikson's instructions completely.

Much to Erikson's surprise, "after a moment of thoughtfulness, the children arranged their scenes as if guided by an inner design . . ." (1950, p. 98). For this and other reasons, Erikson regarded the play constructions as significant personality revelations. In fact, Erikson detected quite early in his sequence of observations certain *common elements* of design and topography that distinguished boys' use of blocks and figures from the girls' fabrications with these same materials. Figures 6.1 and 6.2 illustrate two representative constructions. With Freud's conception of psychosexual development in mind (see Chapter 2), even the most skeptical student of personality will not find it difficult to predict which of these drawings represents a boy's imaginary construction and which of them depicts the girl's.

FIGURE 6.1

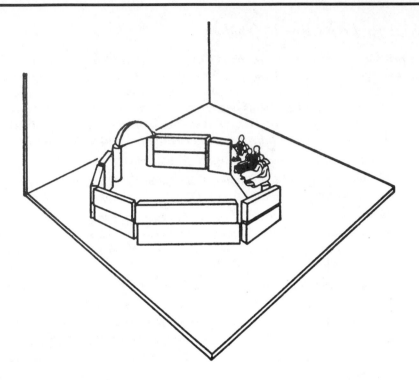

Inspection of Figures 6.1 and 6.2 reveals that the materials Erikson used were quite ordinary: dolls representing family figures, some uniformed figures representing policemen, an Indian, a monk, an aviator, wild and domestic animals, furniture, automobiles, and a large assortment of wooden blocks. Yet the constructions of Figures 6.1 and 6.2 are vastly different. Figure 6.1 depicts a circular *enclosure* with an arched entranceway within which are seated several family figures. The design of the construction in Figure 6.1 is relatively *static,* exhibiting little movement and no real action. In fact, the dominant feeling of Figure 6.1 is "peacefulness."

By contrast, Figure 6.2 is characterized by tall *projections* and *dynamic* or stressful activity. The whole feeling of Figure 6.2 is one of controlled energy and potential danger. A figure balances precariously atop one of the elevated buildings. There are automobiles and trucks present in the "streets" of the scene, suggesting bustling city activities. The central and tallest construction, resembling a rocket, is built from a teetering and shaky selection of blocks. The dominant tone of Figure 6.2 is "excitement."

If, in true psychoanalytic spirit, you have made predictions about the sex of the persons who constructed the figures, you will, no doubt, not be surprised that the peaceful enclosure of Figure 6.1 was fabricated by a girl, whereas the tense array of skyward projections in Figure 6.2 was created by a boy. Erikson summarized his overall findings with 300 boys and girls:

FIGURE 6.2

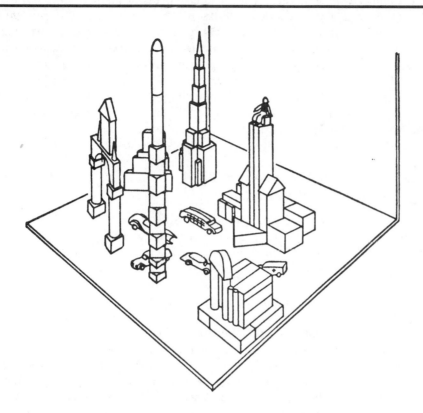

. . . the girl's scene is [typically] a house *interior,* represented either as a configuration of furniture without any surrounding walls or by a simple *enclosure* built with blocks. In the girl's scene, people and animals are mostly *within* such an interior or enclosure, and they are primarily people or animals in a *static* (sitting or standing) position. Girl's enclosures consist of low walls, i.e., only one block high, except for an occasional *elaborate doorway.* These interiors of houses with or without walls were, for the most part, expressly *peaceful.* Often, a little girl was playing the piano. In a number of cases, however, the interior was *intruded* by animals or dangerous men.

Boys' scenes are either houses with elaborate walls or facades with *protrusions* such as cones or cylinders representing ornaments or cannons. There are *high towers,* and there are entirely *exterior* scenes. In boys' constructions more people and animals are *outside* enclosures or buildings, and there are more *automotive* objects and animals *moving* along streets and intersections. . . . While *high structures* are prevalent in the configurations of the boys, there is also much play with the danger of *collapse* or downfall; *ruins* were exclusively boys' constructions. (1968, pp. 270–271, italics in original)

Erikson concluded from his study that a child's organization of play space parallels the morphology (structure) of his or her genital equipment. As Erikson put it in a statement that has drawn a great deal of criticism: ". . . in the male, an *external* organ, *erectable* and *intrusive* in character, serving the channelization of *mobile* sperm cells; in the female, *internal* organs, with vestibular *access,* leading to *statically expectant ova*" (1968, p. 271, italics added; cf. Erikson, 1950, p. 106; and 1951, pp. 690 ff.). Erikson acknowledged that the differences in spatial organization of the play materials might also be indicative of the social expectations enforced by parents in rearing boys differently from girls. Thus the boy's outward and upward projections may be his means of expressing his *learned* desire to achieve "high standing" and to be aggressive, mobile, and independent. Likewise, the girl's preoccupation with house interiors and enclosed, static space might be evidence of the social expectations modeled by parents to the effect that little girls eventually take care of a home, bear children, and rear them within its peaceful confines (Erikson, 1950, p. 106).

Biological, Cultural, and Psychological Components of Development

In a famous essay, "Womanhood and the Inner Space" (in Erikson, 1968), Erikson attempted to blend biological, cultural, and psychological interpretations of his findings. The purely *biological* interpretation asserts that preadolescents are overly concerned with their bodies and with their developing sexual equipment. Therefore, it is a natural consequence that play activities reflect in their structure the structure of the sexual equipment that is the object of the child's concern. The *social* interpretation restricts its explanation to the impact of learned attitudes and preferences. Thus boys learn to enjoy the outdoors, girls the indoors; boys learn to seek adventure and excitement, girls learn to seek the tranquility of family love and homemaking skills. The *psychological* (psychoanalytic) view emphasizes the unconsciously *symbolic* implications of the child's construction of play space. Hence, the psychological interpretation hinges on the boy's castration fear and on the girl's penis envy, an interpretation that requires some elaboration.

Following Freud's conception of psychosexual development, Erikson suggested that the girl experiences a genital trauma when she discovers that she does not have a penis. Again, following orthodox psychoanalytic doctrine, this early trauma causes the girl to turn from her mother to the father. She realizes that mother shares this lack and assumes that, indeed, it was mother who cheated her of the envied possession in the first place. Unlike Freud, however, Erikson shifted his focus of attention from this early "trauma" to the girl's growing sense of competence in being uniquely different from men. It is more important, Erikson argued, to understand the girl's transition from "a 'passive' renunciation of male activity to the purposeful and competent pursuit of activities consonant with the possession of ovaries, a uterus, and a vagina. . . ." (1968, p. 275).

In essence, Erikson shifted psychoanalysis's traditional concern with abnormal defensively motivated behaviors to a concern with the normal functioning of the healthy ego once the Oedipus and Electra complexes are resolved. Thus, rather than concentrate exclusively on the girl's defensive substitution of potential motherhood for the lost penis, Erikson preferred to focus attention on the girl's acceptance of the uniquely productive "inner spaces" of her own body. The issue, consequently, was changed from the girl's presumed resentment over not being a boy to her positive identification with womanhood, to her sense of solidarity with the femininely creative models at her disposal.

The differences, then, in spatial constructions evidenced by the boys and girls in the California study were to be interpreted as the result of *pervasive* and *combined* effects of one's sense of one's own body, one's social role, and one's psychosexual adjustments (Erikson, 1950, p. 108). In Erikson's view, significant differences in the way space is organized by boys and girls exist because "a profound difference exists between the sexes in the experience of the ground plan of the human body" (1968, p. 273).

Boys organize their play constructions in a way that parallels the anatomical construction and function of their genital equipment: *protrusive, extensive, intrusive,* and *mobile.* By contrast, because the biological ground plan of the girl's genital equipment revolves around internal, enclosing organs, girls organize their spatial constructions in a way that parallels the structure and function of their bodies: *enclosing, accessible, "expectant."*

Thus each child's play construction evidenced the *predisposing* effects of the individual's sense of his or her own body. But each play construction also evidenced the influence of social and psychological factors as they merged in the child's characteristic and personal way of dealing with a world that he or she creates. To some extent, Erikson was asserting that "anatomy is destiny," just as Freud had once paraphrased Napoleon's famous dictum that "history is destiny."

> Am I saying, then, that "anatomy is destiny"? Yes, it is destiny, insofar as it determines not only the range and configuration of physiological functioning and its limitations but also, to an extent, personality configurations. The basic modalities of woman's commitment and involvement naturally also reflect the ground plan of her body. . . . We may mention in passing woman's capacity on many levels of existence to actively *include,* to accept, *"to have and to hold"*—but also to *hold on,* and *hold in.* She may be protective with high selectivity and overprotective without discrimination. . . . So far I have only reiterated the physiological rock-bottom which must neither be denied nor given exclusive emphasis. For a human being, in addition to having a body, is *somebody,* which means an indivisible personality and a defined member of a group. . . . In other words, anatomy, history, and personality are our combined destiny. (Erikson, 1968, p. 285)

From his psychoanalytic perspective, Erikson identified the ego as the locus of the merging elements of biological, social, and psychosexual trends. The ego mediates between bodily and personal experiences, and between social and bodily experience:

> To do so, [the ego] uses psychological mechanisms common to both sexes—a fact which makes intelligent communication, mutual understanding, and social organization possible. . . . Here, then, the fact that a woman, whatever else she may also be, never is not-a-woman creates unique relations between her individuality, her somatic existence, and her social potentials and demands that the feminine identity be studied and defined in its own right. (Erikson, 1968, pp. 289–290)

Erikson thus emphasized that, although there are certainly commonalities for men and women in the way their egos function, substantial and real differences exist between the sexes that deserve special study and open acknowledgment.

Critique of Erikson's Study

The most telling criticism of Erikson's conceptualization of inner space came from Caplan (1979), who attempted a partial replication of the study and achieved largely negative results. Working with a sample of children younger than Erikson's sample, Caplan found no significant sex differences in the construction of towers and enclosures built by children ranging in age between two years, ten months and four years, eight months. In some cases, Caplan found complete reversals of Erikson's results. For example, there was a tendency for girls to use more blocks than boys, and when a variety of toys and blocks was available, girls tended to use more ornamental blocks than boys.

Caplan criticized Erikson on other grounds as well as the possibility of faulty methodology. But her criticism of Erikson's belief in a one-to-one correspondence between sexual physiology and a person's sense of space is worth quoting without further comment:

> The most important physiological factor to take into account is that there is no inner space. The walls of the uterus touch each other, as do the walls of the vagina. They are open only when separated by and filled with substances, as in intercourse or pregnancy. If girls' play constructions were to represent their uteri, they should look more like folded flapjacks than enclosures. (Caplan, 1979, p. 101)

THE EGO FUNCTIONS OF PLAY

It is important, within the scope of this discussion on sex differences in play constructions, not to lose sight of Erikson's basic premise: namely, that the children's manipulation of toys *spatially* reflects the organization of their egos *psychologically.* Play permits children to externalize, in a manageable fashion, what would ordinarily remain internalized and beyond the reach of their attempts at mastery. Recall that Erikson's instructions to the children emphasized that they were to construct an imaginary scene. Indeed, the actual wording of the instructions was designed to encourage projection of personal concerns:

> I am interested in moving pictures. I would like to know what kind of moving pictures children would make if they had a chance to make pictures. Of course, I could not provide you with a real studio and real actors and actresses; you will have to use these toys instead. Choose any of the things you see here and construct on this table an exciting scene out of an *imaginary* moving picture. Take as much time as you want and tell me afterwards what the scene is about. (Erikson, 1951, pp. 668–669)

As Erikson discovered, the pretense of make-believe motion pictures easily gave way to more personal dramas that seemed to reflect the child's interior designs.

For example, Erikson worked with a girl of 12 who had developed a severe neurosis after her parents dismissed her nurse for withholding the secret of her first sex play with a little boy. This child's second attempt at a play construction is pictured in Figure 6.3.

Erikson noticed some rather contradictory features of the girl's construction. The "house" she built consisted of two rectangular compartments. One half of this

FIGURE 6.3   Little girl's "house-body."

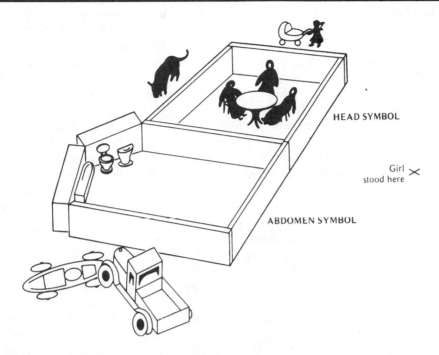

HEAD SYMBOL

Girl ✕
stood here

ABDOMEN SYMBOL

Redrawn from Homburger (1937), p. 145.

structure was a dining room with a family seated around the table, and the other compartment, occupying fully one half of her house, was a bathroom, complete with toilet. Outside the house, at the lower end of her construction, she staged a traffic accident between a race car and a truck. At the top of the house, she placed a little girl walking with her baby carriage toward a cow. One last detail of Figure 6.3 should be noted: The side wall of the bathroom, constructed of two pieces, bulged outward.

Erikson, writing under his adoptive name, Homburger (1937), hypothesized that the "house" as a spatial entity represented this girl's psychological experience of her body and the precipitating events of her neurosis. The girl's case history revealed several pieces of evidence in support of Erikson's interpretation. "Spoiling" the child when her parents were not around, the nurse allowed her to suck her thumb and eat goodies between meals. When the mother was absent, the little girl and her nurse created "their own world" in which to live and play. This private universe included the shared secret of the little girl's sex play with a little boy, a secret whose revelation was responsible for the firing of the nurse. At about the time of the sex play, the nurse became pregnant, and from the little girl's point of view, this startling development was a puzzle that the dismissal of the nurse prevented her from solving. To make matters worse, the girl's mother set out to break her daughter's "bad habits," acquired from the nurse, as soon as possible. The next result was the precipitation of a severe "neurotic" reaction in the girl.

The little girl began to hear "voices" inside herself commanding her: "Don't say anything, don't say anything." Other voices, speaking in a foreign language, objected to the command. To stop the voices, the girl ran to the kitchen and stayed with the cook, who was the one person in the house most similar in role to her former nurse. When Erikson saw her for the first time, he noticed the girl's peculiar posture, which included thrusting out her abdomen: ". . . my first impression was, 'She walks like a pregnant woman.' "

Clearly, the little girl was defensively identifying with the lost nurse and incorporating the nurse's pregnancy into her own stance. Furthermore, the girl expressed this identification in the structure of her house. The protruding bathroom walls were a symbolic equivalent of her protruding abdomen, itself a bodily metaphor for the missing pregnant nurse. But why bulge the walls of a *bathroom?* Because, Erikson concluded, the bathroom is a place of secrets for a child, a place where the door is closed for concealment of private doings. In this little girl's experience, the bathroom was a place where forbidden nakedness and masturbation occurred, where dirty things were to be disposed of, where she had seen bloody menstrual sanitary napkins. In her own unconsciously metaphorical way, the little girl equated these "bathroom secrets" with the "secret" of the nurse's pregnancy and the "secret" of her own sex play.

The dining room compartment symbolized the little girl's continuing conflicts with her parents about her eating habits—habits that had been "spoiled" by the nurse's permitting her to eat between meals. Moreover, the parents frequently spoke about the child during dinner in their native tongue, a foreign language the little girl had not been taught.

The little girl walking with a baby carriage toward a cow, placed around the periphery of the house, externalized the child's feeling that *outside the house* was freedom, where a little girl could seek the comfort of her milk-giving nurse. Danger also lay outside, however, as indicated by the crash of the racing car and truck. According to Erikson, the placement of the *accident* is at the lower end of the "abdomen" part of the house, a place where "it seems a girl can lose something, since boys have something there and girls do not" (Homburger, 1937, p. 146). No doubt, boy-girl differences in anatomy had recently come to the girl's attention in her sex play episode. But, Erikson continues, the lower abdomen, and hence the lower part of her house construction, is "Where people say girls will bleed. Where men do something to women. Where babies come out, hurt women and sometimes kill them. . . ." (Homburger, 1937, p. 146, see also 1938). A short time after the birth of her child, the nurse died.

Thus, for this confused little girl, the interior of her house-body was a place where conflicts, secrets, fears, and foreign voices speaking secretively about her reside. The exterior of her house is a conflicting blend of wished-for freedom and terrifying threat. Excitement and the danger of bodily harm are experienced as "outside"; dark secrets lurk inside. Constructed as a playful fantasy, this child's "imaginary moving picture scene" exposed the ego's painful labors to reconcile discordant inner and outer reality and to heal wounds inflicted in the name of growing up. Child's play.

The Types of Play

Developmentally, the earliest form of play is the infant's exploration of its own body, fingers, toes, voice, as well as any external objects near to a curious hand. Erikson termed this essentially self-centered form of play *autocosmic play* (Homburger, 1937, p. 170; Erikson, 1950, p. 220). From self-manipulations and explorations of nearby persons and objects, the infant constructs its first personal geography, its primitive maps for the ego's first orientation to the world.

At the next stage of development, the child "weaves fantasies" around the world of toys—a miniature world constructed by the child where the child is in control. Erikson gave the name *microcosmic play* to these attempts of the child to externalize the intuitively sensed laws of its own growing body onto the self-reflecting miniature world of its toys (Homburger, 1937, p. 170; Erikson, 1950, p. 221). Yet this external world has its own laws; it may resist the child's attempts to synthesize and to build, and fall to pieces. In this "thing-world" of the microsphere, the child "makes blocks 'grow' by placing them on top of one another; and, with pleasurable excitement in repetition he knocks them down, thus externalizing the trauma of his own falls" (Homburger, 1937, p. 170). Success at microcosmic play builds the child's sense of mastery and allows the child to "overhaul its ego," when such healing is demanded by the inevitable disasters of growing up.

By nursery school age, children extend their play into shared activities that depend on and take account of other players. Life-sized objects—chairs, tables, precious adult possessions—are utilized as the landscape of fantasy. Forcing a reluctant chair to be a horsie, the child imposes its omnipotence onto grown-up things by appropriating them for its own fanciful uses. Erikson called this form of play *macrocosmic* because the child slowly learns by trial and scream-producing error what parts of the larger world it is permitted to make its own and what parts arouse parental censure or rebuff (Homburger, 1937, p. 171; Erikson, 1950, p. 221).

Childhood play is work, not recreation, in Erikson's view. "The playing adult steps sideward into another reality; the playing child advances forward to new stages of mastery" (1950, p. 222).

Psychoanalytic Ego Psychology: Erikson's Psychosocial Perspective

Although Erikson was trained as a psychoanalyst, indeed his training analyst was Anna Freud, it is clear that in his own theorizing he has emphasized rather different personality dimensions from those of classical psychoanalytic doctrine. Grounding his analysis of sex differences in Freud's psychosexual concepts, Erikson has worked to broaden Freud's emphasis on instinctual dynamics with a consideration of *psychosocial* dynamics.

For Erikson, the fundamental personality problem is to determine how individuals adjust to the unique set of social and historical circumstances into which each is born. Consequently, Erikson's focus of attention is about equally divided among the id, ego, and superego. The process of adjustment to instinctual, cultural, and historical circumstance, and the development of one's *sense of self* in response to these determinants, are largely the tasks of the conscious ego.

Perhaps more than any other "ego theorist," Erikson has achieved wide recognition beyond psychoanalysis for his specification of the stages through which an individual ego develops. In response to the crises initiated by the biological and social givens of life, the child's ego matures in an *epigenetic* sequence of combined psycho*sexual* and psycho*social* stages.

The term epigenetic is drawn from biology and means that the structure of an organism and its sequence of development are precisely laid down in that organism's genetic code. For the organism to reach full development of its potential structure, the environment must provide specific stimulation. The structure that thus develops was rigidly predetermined by the organism's genetic endowment, but its unfolding was governed by environmental variables. For Erikson, social demands influence the ways in which the biologically determined psychosexual characteristics of the infant develop. To Freud's oral, anal, phallic, and genital stages, Erikson couples eight interpersonal crises that guide the flowering of these biologically determined developments. In short, for Erikson, Freud's psychosexual stages are biological, inescapable givens of development. The child's interpersonal milieu, however, is the psychosocial half of the equation, an aspect that pre-ego psychologists neglected (see Chapter 4 for a historical discussion of psychoanalytic ego psychology).

In somewhat simplified fashion, it is now possible to capsulize the difference between classical psychoanalytic doctrine and psychoanalytic ego psychology: Where Freud interpreted human behavior as the result of a clash between the biological drives of the unconscious id and the conscious ego-superego, *the ego psychologist, like Erikson, interprets human behavior as the product of an interaction between the ego-id-superego apparatus and the external, social world*. The difference may, at first, appear not to be significant. An example may underscore its importance.

For Freud, the nursing relationship between mother and infant was of supreme and lasting importance in the development of personality. In supplying the infant with breast or bottle, the mother not only relieves its accumulated hunger tension, she also establishes a reliable sequence of pleasurable stimulation. The pleasurable activities of feeding, cuddling, touching, and sucking are all motivated, in Freud's scheme, by the same generalized sexual or pleasure drive: libido. As a result, hunger reduction becomes the prototype for all later libidinal (pleasurable-sexual) satisfactions. The importance of feeding, for Freud, was the light it shed on the interaction between the biological drives of the id (e.g., hunger) and the efforts of the ego to secure satisfaction and pleasure from the external world (e.g., from mother). But Freud's focus of attention was narrowly restricted to the effects *on the id* of the ego's interaction with reality.

Like Freud, Erikson regards the nursing relationship as crucial for personality development. But unlike Freud, Erikson does not restrict his theoretical considerations to id-ego interactions or to the result of id satisfactions by the ego. Instead, the feeding situation is for Erikson a model of *social* interaction between the infant and its interpersonal world. Hunger is certainly a biological (id) manifestation, but the consequences of its satisfaction by the mother transcend the immediate pleasurable id gains. Reliable and timely satisfactions of the infant's hunger establish for it a sense of *basic trust,* a sense that external reality is trustworthy. Infants learn from their feeding experiences to anticipate interaction with significant others in one of two ways: They either view person-to-person contacts with pleasurable eagerness and relish because in the past such interchanges have been safe and comforting, or they anticipate with anxious concern all such personal contact because, in the past, people have proven to be frustrating and pain-provoking entities. Whereas Freud emphasized the consequences of biological drive reduction for the development of id-ego relations, Erikson emphasizes the personal, conscious impact of such interaction for the ego's adjustment to social reality. Once established, basic trust endures as an independent ego characteristic, free of the id drives from which it originated. Likewise, such ego functions as perception, problem solving, and the formation of an ego identity operate independently of the drives that gave them birth. Figure 6.4 illustrates the basic differences between orthodox, classical psychoanalysis, and psychoanalytic ego psychology.

It thus becomes possible to discern within Erikson's work several trends that are uniquely characteristic of psychoanalytic ego psychology.

FIGURE 6.4   Classical psychoanalysis versus ego psychology.

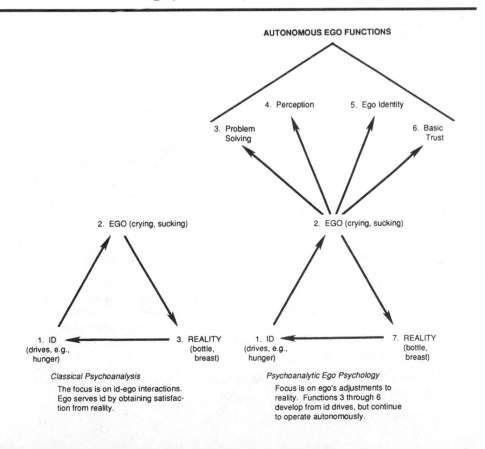

1. Erikson emphasizes the individual's conscious adjustments to social influences. Healthy maturation, rather than neurotic and conflicted maladjustment, is of central concern.
2. Erikson attempts to build upon the instinctual theoretical framework developed by Freud by adding his own epigenetic conception of personality development. Upon the psychosexual biological givens elucidated by Freud, psychosocial influences erect the structure of personality.
3. Erikson explicitly recognizes that motives may originate in unconscious or repressed id impulses, yet these motives may become freed of their id origins as the individual lives out his or her particular social and historical role.
4. Erikson has conceptualized the ego as the source of the person's self-awareness. During adjustment to reality, the ego develops a sense of its own continuity with the past and with the future. In brief, the ego comes to the realization that it is an "I."

EGO IDENTITY: SOURCES OF THE HYPOTHESIS

For life to be worthwhile, the individual must feel that he or she has willingly nurtured the power to shape existence, the intention to be an autonomous self-provider, and the desire to be competently equal to life's tasks. The healthy personality sees that the person of the past, the person of the present, and the person of the future are smooth continuations of the person he or she *must* be in the face of the realities that are his or hers (Erikson, 1950, pp. 250, 269). As the executor of personality, the ego must master at the various stages of development certain important biological and social tasks to facilitate the healthy adaptation of the individual to his or her life circumstances.

Erikson proposed that the individual's ego progresses through a reliable sequence of stages in the development of personality from infancy to adulthood. Each successive stage in the epigenetic sequence sees the ego adding new modes of competency for dealing with characteristic "crises" attending that phase of life. By adolescence, the central hurdle for the ego to mount is the crystallization of identity, of a sense, that is, of self-continuity. Knowing *who I am, who I am to become* is a crucial aspect of the ego's integrative task. Persons in whom the sense of self is tenuous and easily shaken are prone to a variety of pathological adaptations to life. The concept of ego identity is complex and continually under refinement in Erikson's thinking. Thus Erikson has wisely avoided providing any single restrictive definition of ego identity:

> I can attempt to make the subject matter of identity more explicit only by approaching it from a variety of angles. . . . At one time, then, it will appear to refer to a conscious *sense of individual identity;* at another, to an unconscious striving for a *continuity of personal character;* at a third, as a criterion for the silent doings of *ego synthesis;* and, finally, as a maintenance of an inner *solidarity* with a group's ideals and identity. (1959, p. 102)

A brief survey of Erikson's personal and clinical experiences that shaped his formulation of the concept of ego identity is in order.

Personal Sources of the Identity Hypothesis

In 1970, Erikson published an autobiographical essay in which he traced some aspects of his own identity formation. In true psychoanalytic spirit, Erikson employed the facts of his own early life to illustrate the concept of *identity crisis* and the ultimate resolution of the crisis in the formation of an acceptable personal identity. Yet Erikson's account is somewhat less than completely candid. As one reviewer of *Life History and the Historical Moment* (1975), the book in which the autobiographical essay was reprinted, commented, "The immediately troubling thing about . . . [the autobiographical essay] is that the crises are wholly left out. . . . Our first impulse may be to feel envious, until we realize that no human being this serene can ever have lived" (Berman, 1975, p. 22). Despite the facade of serenity, Erikson provided glimpses into the motives that underlay his own intense interest in the concepts of identity and identity crisis.

As a child, Erikson was raised by his mother, Karla *née* Abrahamsen and her second husband, Theodor Homburger. Homburger, a physician, had married Erikson's mother after her first husband had abandoned her before their son's (Erikson's) birth. Erikson's mother had been a resident of Denmark, and his father was apparently a native Dane. Throughout childhood, Erikson's mother and stepfather "kept secret from me the fact that my mother had been married previously. . . . They apparently thought that such secretiveness was not only workable (because children then were not held to know what they had not been told) but also advisable, so that I would feel thoroughly at home in their home" (1975, p. 27).

Nonetheless, Erikson developed a sense of "being different" from other children, and he entertained fantasies of being the son of "much better parents" who had abandoned him. Erikson's stepfather, however, did not fit the traditional image of stepfathers. Because Dr. Homburger was kindly and understanding, offering his name to the otherwise fatherless boy, Erikson adopted Homburger as his adult middle name. But it is clear that Erikson's own choice of name—Erik Erikson—reflects his longstanding need to make his own identity.

Sometime after the age of three, Erikson developed the beginnings of his later identity crisis. Because his mother and stepfather, Dr. Homburger, were Jewish, Erikson's Scandinavian heritage of blue eyes, blond hair, and "flagrant tallness" enforced and intensified his feeling of somehow not belonging to his family. Further intensification of his identity crisis was produced when, as a schoolboy, he was referred to as a "goy" in his stepfather's temple, whereas his schoolmates identified him as a Jew (1975, p. 27). Thus a conflicting family heritage, discordant social expectations and prejudices, and his own sense of not belonging to the family in which he grew up combined to create for Erikson an acute sense of identity confusion.

At puberty, having violated his stepfather's expectation that he, too, would become a doctor, Erikson consciously chose to be different. After graduation from a humanistic *Gymnasium,* roughly equivalent to high school, Erikson entered art school. Establishing for himself the identity of "artist," Erikson wandered through Europe, not completely aimless, but freely independent of socially enforced obligations to make something of himself: "I was a 'Bohemian' then" (1975, p. 28). At around this time, Erikson's identity crisis reached an apex of intensity, bordering on an "adolescent psychosis":

> . . . the choice of the occupational identity of "artist" meant, for many, a way of life rather than a specific occupation . . . and, as today, it could mean primarily an anti-establishment way of life. Yet, the European establishment had created a well-institutionalized social niche for such idiosyncratic needs. A certain adolescent and neurotic shiftlessness could be contained in the custom of *Wanderschaft* [journey or excursion]. . . . To be an artist, then, meant to have at least a passing identity, and I had enough talent to consider it for a while an occupational one. The trouble was, I often had a kind of work disturbance and needed time. *Wanderschaft* under those conditions meant neurotic drivenness as well as a deliberate search, even as today dropping out can be a time either of tuning in or of aimless negativism. . . . No doubt, my best friends will insist that I needed to name this crisis and to see it in everybody else in order to really come to terms with it in myself. (1975, pp. 25–26)

With the help of a youthful friend, Peter Blos, who later became a psychoanalytic expert on adolescence (e.g., 1962, 1970), Erikson overcame his crisis and learned to discipline himself to work regular hours. Joining the faculty of a school in Vienna founded by Dorothy Burlingham, Erikson met the circle around Anna Freud and, of course, her father, Sigmund Freud.

> It must be obvious now what Freud came to mean to me, although, of course, I would not have had words for it at the time. Here was a mythical figure and, above all, a great doctor who had rebelled against the medical profession. Here also was a circle which admitted me to the kind of training that came as close to the role of a children's doctor as one could possibly come without going to medical school. What, in me, responded to this situation was, I think, some strong identification with my stepfather, the pediatrician, mixed with a search for my own mythical father. (Erikson, 1975, p. 29)

Much to his own surprise, Erikson was accepted by the psychoanalytic group surrounding Freud. Yet, he reports, he struggled to avoid being totally assimilated to the identity of "psychoanalyst," preferring to keep in touch with his previously formed identity of "artist." The fact that psychoanalysis then "collected at least a few men and women who did not quite belong elsewhere" admirably suited Erikson's unconsciously formed identity of "stepson" or "outsider." His professional training, therefore, was the outcome of a set of unique personal and historical circumstances. Psychoanalysis was at that period in its history when it was considered "outside" the medical establishment. Not quite belonging elsewhere, Erikson found in this group of outcasts a congenial compromise solution to the conflict between his "Bohemian" identity and his growing need for commitment to a productive cause. If medicine treated psychoanalysis as an unwanted stepson, psychoanalysis accepted Erikson as a long-lost son.

Except for his formal training under Anna Freud in psychoanalysis with children, and the possession of a Montessori diploma, Erikson neither sought nor obtained any other professional credentials. His eventual complete identification with the profession of "psychoanalyst" satisfied two important requirements: As a psychoanalyst, Erikson followed his stepfather's wish that he, too, enter medicine; yet, as a psychoanalyst, Erikson was able to remain aloof from medicine in accord with his own need to be an outsider while still practicing a clinical specialty. Erikson's need to identify himself as an outsider led not only to a successful resolution of his identity crisis, but also to nearly 50 years of productive clinical and theoretical work.

Clinical Sources of the Identity Hypothesis: War Veterans

When Erikson left Nazi-dominated Europe to seek citizenship in the United States, he worked for a time at the Mt. Zion Veterans' Rehabilitation Clinic in San Francisco. In treating military casualties, Erikson first coined his now famous phrase "identity crisis" to describe the chaotic, profoundly confused mental state of soldiers hospitalized for "battle neuroses." As Erikson described these soldiers, it was as if their egos had lost their shock-absorbing capacity (1968, p. 66).

> Anxiety and anger were provoked by anything too sudden or too intense, a sudden sensory impression from outside, an impulse, or a memory. A constantly "startled" sensory system was attacked by external stimuli as well as by somatic sensations: heat flashes, palpitation, cutting headaches. Insomnia hindered the nightly restoration of sensory screening by sleep and that of emotional rebinding by dreaming. . . . Above all, the men felt that they "did not know any more who they were": there was a distinct loss of ego identity. The sense of sameness and continuity and the belief in one's social role were gone. (1968, p. 67)

Erikson reported an illustrative case of a marine who had suffered loss of ego identity sometime after discharge from the service. The soldier told Erikson of a particular incident during an assault on a beachhead in the Pacific under enemy fire. Lying in the darkness, the soldier had experienced intense anger, rage, disgust, and fear at the failure of the "brass" to provide supportive air cover and naval reinforcements. It was as though he and his group of marines had to take the enemy's fire "lying down." As a medical officer, Erikson's patient was unarmed on that beachhead, and the mounting rage and panic he had experienced, and the similar feelings expressed by the men around him, seemed to have little to do with his medical duties. His memories of the remainder of the night on the beach were fogged and incomplete. The soldier claimed that medical corpsmen were ordered to unload ammunition instead of attending to medical duties. Sometime during the night, he recalled, somebody handed him a submachine gun—the remainder of what transpired was a blank. The following morning he found himself in an improvised field hospital, suffering from a severe intestinal fever.

That night, the enemy attacked from the air, and though all able-bodied men found shelter, he was unable to move or to help others. For the first time, he experienced real fear, a fear that, unlike the emotions he had felt on the beach, he knew to be his. After evacuation from the beach, he succumbed to raging headaches, chronic anxiety, and "jumpiness" to all sudden sounds and sensory impressions. In therapy with Erikson, the young ex-marine was able to trace his difficulties back to the night of the attack when somebody had forced him to take the submachine gun. He had observed his superior officer swearing and violently angry, and perhaps a little afraid. He told Erikson that the officer's behavior had disillusioned him because such an outpouring of rage and anger by an officer was shocking conduct. Erikson immediately saw the contradiction: Why was this soldier so outraged by anger in others;

why was it necessary for him to see himself as a paragon of strength, insusceptible to anger or fear?

The soldier's free associations led back to his childhood and to an incident when his mother in a drunken rage had pointed a gun at him. Taking the gun from her, he broke it in half and threw it out the window. He left home for good, and, seeking the protection of a fatherly man (his school principal), he promised never to drink, swear, indulge sexually, or touch a gun (Erikson, 1950, p. 41). When his fatherly superior officer had exploded with violent oaths that night on the beachhead, and when someone had thrust a gun into his hands, his carefully formed sense of personal identity as a "good," moral, and benevolent person crumbled.

Thus three factors conspired to provoke the battle neurosis to which this young man succumbed. First, his sense of shared identity with his group was threatened by the growing panic and anger of the men on the beachhead. Second, the constant assault on the soldier's bodily integrity by the real dangers of the battle, exploding bombs and the like, combined with his intestinal fever, led to a breakdown of his ego's capacity to ward off and control external stimuli. Third, the loss of his inner sense of personal continuity, or ego identity, in the face of his officer's anger and fear and his own possession of a gun served to undercut the remaining supports binding together his personality functioning. His lifelong rigidity and adherence to idealized moral values had served as a defensive bulwark against disturbing life circumstances. Now, in battle, these defenses were crumbling as he began to feel fear, rage, and panic (Erikson, 1950, p. 43). Erikson summarized his findings in this way:

> What impressed me most was the loss in these men [i.e., war veterans] of a sense of identity. They knew who they were; they had a personal identity. But it was as if, subjectively, their lives no longer hung together—and never would again. There was a central disturbance of what I then started to call ego identity. At this point it is enough to say that this sense of identity provides the ability to experience one's self as something that has continuity and sameness, and to act accordingly. In many cases there was at the decisive time in the history of the breakdown a seemingly innocent item such as the gun in our medical soldier's unwilling hands: a symbol of evil, which endangered the principles by which the individual had attempted to safeguard personal integrity and social status in his life at home. (1950, p. 42)

Thus the concept of ego identity proved to be an indispensable tool in understanding the combined impact on personality of changes in the biological organism, changes in the ego, and changes in the social milieu (Erikson, 1950, p. 44).

Anthropological Sources of the Identity Hypothesis: Oglala Sioux

Erikson accepted an appointment with the Yale Institute of Human Relations within the medical school. Under the leadership of John Dollard, Erikson was able to secure financial support for a field trip to South Dakota to study childrearing practices among the Oglala subtribe of the Sioux at the Pine Ridge Indian Reservation.

The expressed purpose of the field trip was to "try to find out whence came the tragic apathy with which Sioux Indian children quietly accepted and then quietly discarded many of the values taught them in the immensely thoughtful and costly experiment of federal Indian education" (Erikson, 1950, p. 114). Teachers in the government-sponsored education program complained of a variety of character defects in the Indian children they taught.

> Truancy was the most outstanding complaint: when in doubt Indian children simply ran home. The second complaint was stealing, or at any rate gross disregard of property rights as we understand them. This was followed by apathy, which included everything from lack of ambition and interest to a kind of bland passive resistance in the face of a question or of a request. Finally, there was too much sexual activity, a term used for a variety of suggestive situations ranging from excursions into the dark after dances to the mere huddling together of homesick girls in boarding-school beds. . . . The discussion was pervaded by the mystified complaint that no matter what you do to these children, they do not talk back. They are stoical and noncommittal. (Erikson, 1950, p. 125)

Erikson detected in his discussion with these teachers a deep and unconscious "fury" that even the most well-disciplined educators had allowed to affect their professional judgments. So disappointed, so discouraged, and so disillusioned were many of the teachers at their lack of success with these children that they had come to regard their failures as the fault of some inherent Indian personality flaw. Erikson, operating from his psychosocial perspective, felt that the difficulty lay elsewhere.

To understand the behaviors to which the teachers objected so strenuously, Erikson undertook a historical investigation of the Indians' tribal identity. The members of the Oglala tribe lived on land allotted to them by the federal government in a final act of political and economic subjugation. In times past, when the Sioux ranged over their land as masters of territory and of themselves, the buffalo was central to their lives. As a source of food, clothing, and fuel, the buffalo was the very nucleus around which the Sioux shaped their nomadic hunting existence. The early white settlers disturbed the hunting grounds with their homesteads and domesticated cattle, and they "playfully, stupidly, slaughtered buffalo by the hundred thousands" (Erikson, 1950, p. 116). When gold fever struck these early settlers, they invaded the Sioux's holy mountains, game preserves, and winter refuge. An appeal by the Sioux to the U.S. Army generals, warrior to warrior, was of little help in setting matters right.

The outcome of the resulting chronic warfare between settlers and Sioux could be capsulized in the tragedy of two massacres. General Custer's decisive defeat by Sioux was avenged years later at Wounded Knee by the Seventh Army cavalry's massacre of a small band of Indians they outnumbered by four to one. Erikson summarized this climax to the gradual erosion of the Indians' tribal identity.

> The young and seething American democracy lost the peace with the Indian when it failed to arrive at a clear design of either conquering or colonizing, converting or liberating, and instead left the making of history to an arbitrary succession of representatives who had one or another of these objectives in mind—thus demonstrating an inconsistency which the Indians interpreted as insecurity and bad conscience. (1950, p. 117)

Thus the government policy of establishing reservations for the Indian, "guiding" the education of Indian children, and attempting to assimilate the Indian culture by foisting the larger society's values on this subculture resulted in the dissolution of the Indian's identity. Instead of fostering independence, enforced dependence of the

Indian on the government was accomplished. In place of mutual trust, chronic suspicion and disappointment were engendered by the government's inconsistencies of policy. Where the Indian had a right to a sense of history as a "man wronged," the over-complex government machinery regulating "Indian affairs" had substituted a sense of self as "one to whom something is owed" (Erikson, 1950, p. 119).

The crux of the problem, in Erikson's estimation, was the shock of contact between the two cultures. White, middle-class, competitive values modeled by the educators and government advisers were singularly inappropriate to the needs and traditions of the Indian. Teachers tried to alter age-old child-rearing practices, and the Indian family was forced to reconsider the meaning and the value of its existence. Erikson recounted many examples of the discordant effects of teachers' efforts and stoic Indian compliance, but one brief illustration serves here:

> During school time the child is taught cleanliness, personal hygiene, and the standardized vanity of cosmetics. While having by no means fully assimilated other aspects of white female freedom of motion and of ambition which are presented to her with historically disastrous abruptness, the adolescent [Indian] girl returns home prettily dressed and clean. But the day soon comes when she is called a "dirty girl" by mothers and grandmothers. For a clean girl in the Indian sense is one who has learned to practice certain avoidances during menstruation; for example, she is not supposed to handle certain foods, which are said to spoil under her touch. Most girls are unable to accept again the status of a leper while menstruating. (1950, p. 131)

Thus, as in his clinical work, Erikson demonstrated that the concepts of identity and of identity crisis were essential for an understanding of "disturbed" behavior.

THE LIFE CYCLE: EIGHT STAGES OF HUMAN DEVELOPMENT

The very heart of Erikson's concept of personality is a sequence of eight stages of ego development. Each of the first five stages in Erikson's scheme builds on Freud's psychosexual stages, treating them as prerequisite and fundamental determinants of personality. Erikson states that his own contribution in delineating the concept of ego identity has been to broaden rather than to revise or replace Freudian theory (Erikson, 1950, 1959, 1968). Thus Erikson's clinical and personal experiences demonstrated to him the necessity for a concept of identity. But his psychoanalytic training convinced Erikson that one's sense of self always develops in union with one's progress through the biological stages of Freud's psychosexual sequence.

Erikson's conception of the life cycle focuses on a series of sequential ego crises that begin in infancy and extend through life to old age. Successful resolution of each phase-specific crisis is the necessary preliminary to advancement through the entire sequence. Erikson describes the life cycle in terms of eight discrete crisis periods. However, his epigenetic scheme may be usefully previewed by grouping the ego crises into four broad life periods.

The four divisions of Table 6.1 represent a condensation of Erikson's scheme in which he distinguishes between early and later childhood, and between young

TABLE 6.1   Life Cycle Ego Crises

Infancy	Childhood	Adolescence	Adulthood
1. Trust versus Mistrust (Oral)	3. Initiative versus Guilt (Phallic)	5. Identity versus Role Confusion (Early Genital)	6. Intimacy versus Isolation (Genital)
			7. Generativity versus Stagnation
2. Autonomy versus Shame, Doubt (Anal)	4. Industry versus Inferiority (Latency)		8. Ego Integrity versus Despair

Note: Corresponding Freudian psychosexual stages appear in parentheses.

adulthood and adulthood proper (cf. Erikson, 1959, p. 120). Each of the eight psychosocial crises is to be viewed as having both positive and negative elements. Early misunderstanding of Erikson's proposals led many readers to assume that the negative and positive outcomes were mutually exclusive. Hence, in this mistaken view, a child who develops a sense of basic trust will not develop a sense of mistrust, and vice versa.

However, Erikson has carefully pointed out that, for healthy development to proceed, it is necessary for the person to experience and to incorporate into his or her identity both negative and positive aspects of each crisis. Without a sense of mistrust, the child would be vulnerable to all manner of manipulation and to gross invasions of its personal integrity at the hands of its personal contacts. Each crisis is favorably resolved when the *ratio* of positive to negative elements incorporated into the person's identity leans toward the positive (Erikson, 1968, p. 105). A little bit of mistrust, of shame, of guilt, and so on, are good things in negotiating the demands of life and its people.

Ritualization Versus Ritualism: The Way We Do Things

Erikson's later work involved a return to the theory of play. For each of the eight psychosocial ego crises, Erikson hypothesized a parallel pair of *ritualizations* and *ritualisms* that reflect the ego's growing sophistication in using playfulness and custom to master biological and social reality. A *ritualization,* the positive member of each pair, is an orienting or socializing mechanism formally prescribed by the culture in which the child matures. Subjectively, ritualizations are experienced as "the only proper way to do things," that is, as creative formalizations of custom.

Stemming initially from the ego's capacity for playfulness, ritualizations are translated into behavior as daily customs that make, through their endless repetition, the pattern of life within a culture familiar and consistent. Ritualizations confirm one's sense of identity, one's sense of belonging to a particular culture and fitting in with that particular version of human existence. "In this last sense, ritualization is a mixture of formality and improvisation, a rhyming in time" (Erikson, 1977, p. 79).

The term *ritualization* was borrowed by Erikson from Julian Huxley's description of evolutionary "ceremonial" acts of certain animals, such as the greeting ceremonies of some bird species (Erikson, 1982, p. 43). But Erikson uses the term for humans with less emphasis on evolutionary history and more emphasis on the "informal and yet prescribed interplay between persons who repeat it at meaningful intervals and in recurring contexts. While such interplay may not mean much more . . . than 'this is the way *we* do things,' it has, we claim, adaptive value for all participants and for their group living" (Erikson, 1982, p. 43).

On the negative side, each of the eight ritualizations is balanced by a *ritualism*, which is a form of estrangement from self and from one's community. Ritualisms result from the ambivalent character of all human relationships. The loving mother, for example, must also have a dark side that threatens abandonment and separation. Like trust and mistrust, love and the fear of separation can form either a healthy or a perverted ratio. The ideal balance for each ritualization is achieved when the ritualistic negative aspect is present but outweighed by the playful and formalized positive aspects. In short, a ritualism is a ritualization that has become stereotyped and mechanical, an empty ceremony devoid of meaning and lacking the power to bond individuals.

The Psychosocial Ego Functions of Ritualization

For Erikson, ritualizations serve at least seven important psychosocial functions:

1. *Social Function:* Ritualization elevates need satisfaction to a communal context by joining personal desire and right to the human group's shared sense of the importance and justice of its desires and rights.
2. *Destiny Function:* In teaching a sanctioned way of doing simple and daily things, ritualization transforms the infantile sense of omnipotence into a joint sense of manifest destiny.
3. *Worthiness Function:* Ritualization deflects feelings of unworthiness onto outsiders, both in and out of one's culture, who are excluded or exclude themselves from knowing the right way.
4. *Interpreting Function:* Ritualization puts emerging cognitive patterns in the service of a general vision shared by the community; it also uses and cultivates the growing cognitive capacity to discern what distinguishes the right class of things and people from the wrong one.
5. *Sanctification Function:* Each successive stage of ritualization helps develop essential aspects of all ritual sense.
6. *Moral Function:* Ritualization develops the experience of social differentiation between good behavior and shameful or guilty acts, which may, in adulthood, lead to legal sanction.
7. *Identity Function:* Ritualization provides the psychosocial foundation for the gradual development of an independent identity to be sealed in by adolescence with various rituals of "confirmation," which will integrate all childhood identifications in a worldview and belief system while marking as ideologically foreign all those wishes and images that have become undesirable and evil and are remindful of other, "lower" species of humans. (Modified slightly from Erikson, 1977, pp. 82–83)

ACQUIRING A SENSE OF TRUST VERSUS A SENSE OF MISTRUST: HOPE

The earliest sense of identity that the infant may be said to harbor arises from its contact with mother in the feeding situation (Erikson, 1968, p. 105). Throughout the first year of life, the infant's most crucial contacts with reality are those mediated by the mother as she attends quickly, reliably, and calmly to the infant's needs. From the repetitive handling, feeding, and love-motivated attentions of the mother, the infant acquires a fundamental attitude toward itself and toward its world. When mother's attentions have been given willingly, lovingly, and reliably, and in quick response to the infant's cries, the infant develops the attitude of *basic trust* (Erikson, 1950, pp. 247 ff.; 1959, p. 56).

A sense of basic trust is first evidenced by infants who show a willingness to let mother out of sight without showing signs of intense anxiety or rage. Because the trusting infant's experiences have been marked by consistency, continuity, and sameness in the mother's responses, the infant develops a dim recognition that what it has learned to anticipate nearly always materializes.

> Such consistency, continuity, and sameness of experience provide a rudimentary sense of ego identity which depends, I think, on the recognition that there is an inner population of remembered and anticipated sensations and images which are firmly correlated with the outer population of familiar and predictable things and people. (Erikson, 1950, p. 247)

When the child begins to develop its first teeth, the parents' patience is likely to be tried to the limits. Seeking to bite and to grasp desirable objects and persons, infants explore the boundaries of their capacities to trust and be trusted. Consequently, Erikson stressed that the sense of basic trust is not restricted to a perception of the outer world as trustworthy, "but also that one may trust oneself and the capacity of one's own organs to cope with urges; and that one is able to consider oneself trustworthy enough so that the providers will not need to be on guard lest they be nipped" (Erikson, 1950, p. 248).

It is important, too, in this context to understand that the infant's sense of trust is not damaged when the parents enforce restrictions or prohibitions. As long as the parental commands and prohibitions, "do's" and "don'ts," communicate to the infant a sense that the parents "know what they're doing," minor frustrations and repeated "No's" engender no lasting adverse effects on identity. Because parents have to model the prevailing cultural standards of socialized behavior, only discipline that is administered without confidence and without consistency can result in damaged trust (Erikson, 1950, p. 249).

On the opposite side of the coin, the infant who has failed to experience reliability, continuity, and sameness, and who has therefore failed to develop a sense of basic trust, succumbs to an overwhelming sense of *basic mistrust*. In the extreme case, the schizophrenic child exemplifies the degree to which identity is damaged in the child who fails to trust her- or himself and others. Withdrawal, bizarre behavior, and an inability to differentiate self from the environment, all characteristics of psychotic adjustment, may be traced to the missing sense of inner and outer "sameness."

Thus the central crisis of the first year of life is the development of a larger proportion of basic trust than of basic mistrust. For the healthy trusting infant, continued life becomes not one hurdle after another, but one beckoning challenge after another arising from each past masterful effort. In this sense of healthy, reality-oriented personality strength, Erikson has proposed a developmental schedule of psychological virtues (1964, pp. 111 ff.). Successful resolution of each crisis throughout development leads to the attainment of a different virtue. Thus the infant who has acquired a sense of basic trust that outweighs its sense of basic mistrust has also acquired one form of ego strength: namely, the capacity to *hope.*

The Latin root of the word "virtue" is *virilitas,* meaning "virility" or "strength." Coupled with this root is another Latin noun of the feminine gender, *virtus,* meaning "goodness." It is in the sense of these Latin roots that Erikson employs the term *virtue* and the specific virtues of *hope, will, purpose, competence, fidelity, love, care, wisdom.* At each of the eight developmental stages one of these virtues is added to the ego's changing and growing sense of continuity. Therefore, Erikson uses the term virtue to indicate the capacity of the ego for *strength, restraint,* and *courage* (Erikson, 1964, p. 113). In Erikson's own words, "I will call 'virtue,' then, certain human qualities of strength, and I will relate them to that process by which ego strength may be developed from stage to stage and imparted from generation to generation" (1964, p. 113).

For the infant who finds itself and its world trustworthy, *"Hope is the enduring belief in the attainability of fervent wishes, in spite of the dark urges and rages which mark the beginning of existence"* (Erikson, 1964, p. 118; italics in original). Because at each stage of development the trusting infant's desires and wishes have been reliably "verified" by the trustworthy environment, the infant now dares to "hope" for an ever-expanding array of achievements, masteries, possessions, and accomplishments. In short, the trusting infant has learned to dare, to risk, to gamble on disappointment of his or her desires. The infant trusts that failures, frustrations, losses will not be overwhelming; he or she hopes.

The ritualization characteristic of the trust-mistrust stage centers on the significance of the *mutual recognition and affirmation of mother and child.* Every day the infant is exposed to the repeated ritual of its mother's approach, her smiles, her calling the infant's name, relieving its discomfort, and amusing him or her. The infant experiences in its mother the ritualization of the *numinous* (*awe*-some, hallowed) quality of her presence, evidenced by her facial expression, voice quality, and the feel of her touch. The whole series of infant care events is highly stylized and superimposed on the periodicity of the infant's physical needs. The numinous quality of the mother is therefore related, on the one hand, to biological survival; but on the other, the ritualized aspects of her care, the repetitiveness and reliability of it, are related to the infant's emotional survival.

By her care and reliable concern—her custom—the mother confirms the infant's "I-ness"—the burgeoning sense of independent identity—while, paradoxically, she helps the infant to transcend fears of aloneness and separateness (Erikson, 1977, pp. 85 ff.).

The ritualism possible at this stage is *idolism,* a distortion of the numinous reverence into adulation. An illusory image of perfection is created between mother and child that binds the idolizing infant to the mother; conversely, compulsive adoration of mother leads eventually to narcissistic idealization of self. Instead of the mutuality of affirmation and recognition, idolism results in reciprocal dependence and rigid, unthinking adulation of impossibly unreal human perfection.

Acquiring a Sense of Autonomy Versus a Sense of Shame and Doubt: Will

Near the age of 18 months, the infant gains more precise control over its muscles. Of prime importance to the eager parents is that with increased voluntary muscular control comes the capacity for increased self-control. The child begins to experiment with two modes of muscular action: holding on and letting go (Erikson, 1950, pp. 251 ff.). Anyone who has stooped repeatedly to retrieve for the high-chaired child those treasured objects he or she endlessly delights in dropping to the floor knows what holding on to and letting go mean to the willful child.

In psychoanalytic terms, this period of muscular exertion and experimentation corresponds to the anal stage. Besides holding on to and letting go of tossable objects, the child also begins to learn how to hold on to feces and urine until the appropriate time and place is reached to let go of them with parental approval. Toilet training, consequently, is a battle of wills. Depending on the way the parents handle this important learning experience, the child either learns that holding on and letting go are powerful weapons to be employed against overly demanding parents, or that elimination is "a relaxed 'to let pass' and 'to let be' " (Erikson, 1950, p. 251). Parental guidance at this stage must be firm, but protective of that sense of trust achieved during the previous oral stage:

> Firmness must protect him against the potential anarchy of his as yet untrained sense of discrimination, his inability to hold on and to let go with discretion. As his environment encourages him to "stand on his own feet," it must protect him against meaningless and arbitrary experiences of shame and of early doubt. (Erikson, 1950, p. 252)

The crisis of this stage of ego development, then, revolves around the necessity for the child to achieve a sense of independence or willful autonomy in the guidance of its body. Experiences with self-control will set the pattern for later capacity to make free choices. If the child learns to overcontrol its impulses, it is likely that it has been needlessly and mercilessly shamed.

"Shame supposes that one is completely exposed and conscious of being looked at: in one word, self-conscious. One is visible and not yet ready to be visible . . ." (Erikson, 1950, p. 252). Thus the child who has learned control over self by having been made to feel small or shameful for unavoidable lapses wins only a "hollow victory." Shamed beyond the limits of its trust, such a child learns to distrust the shamers. Instead of learning to regard the products of its body as dirty or evil, it learns to regard its tutors as evil.

Harsh parental demands for self-control have a further negative consequence: Doubt. The child is made to feel that it is compelled by the will of others rather than by its own burgeoning sense of independence.

> Where shame is dependent on the consciousness of being upright and exposed, doubt . . . has much to do with a consciousness of having a front and a back—especially a "behind." For this reverse area of the body, with its aggressive and libidinal focus in the sphincters and in the buttocks, cannot be seen by the child, and yet it can be dominated by the will of others. The "behind" is the small being's dark continent, an area of the body which can be magically dominated and effectively invaded by those who would attack one's power of autonomy. (Erikson, 1950, p. 253)

Harry Stack Sullivan's concept of the Not-Me as the part of personality that lies outside of conscious reach, outside of self-acceptance, is similar in emotional flavor to what Erikson has here termed the "dark continent" of the child's being. The sense of ego identity—that feeling of sameness, continuity, and "me-ness"—depends on the freedom accorded to the child by the parents to be the self that has been trusted.

The quality of ego strength that emerges during the establishment of a sense of autonomy corresponds to the virtue of *will:* "Will . . . *is the unbroken determination to exercise free choice as well as self-restraint, in spite of the unavoidable experience of shame and doubt in infancy*" (Erikson, 1964, p. 119; italics in original). Thus the child who attains a favorable ratio of autonomy to shame and doubt evidences a capacity for "free will," for "good will," and for willful self-control. Reasonable tolerance and realistic firmness shown to the child by the parents result in reasonable self-tolerance and realistic self-firmness (Erikson, 1959, p. 70).

In this stage of autonomy versus shame, the ritualization that develops centers on the ego's capacity to discriminate good from bad. Erikson terms this capacity the *judicious* ritualization, whereby the child learns what is culturally sanctioned and what is out of bounds (Erikson, 1977, p. 92). The autonomy gained in this stage of development asserts itself through willful acts that test the limits—playfully— of peer and adult tolerance. Before this stage, the child's deeds and misdeeds were the responsibility of the parents; now the infant, rapidly entering childhood, is trained to "watch itself." "Giving himself away by blushing, he can feel furiously isolated, not knowing whether to doubt himself or all those who judge" (Erikson, 1977, p. 94). Sometimes, parents compare the child to negative images of what it might become if it does not learn the limits of good behavior, tolerated behavior; and herein lie the roots of a later negative identity to be formulated in adolescence precisely to shock and to punish the parents. The child may very well become just what it has been forewarned not to become.

> Behind the dreaded traits, of course, are often images of what the parents themselves had been tempted to become and therefore doubly fear the child might turn out to be—*potential* traits, then, which the child yet must learn to imagine in order to be able to avoid them. (Erikson, 1977, p. 95)

The ritualism that balances the judicious sense is *legalism:* "the victory of the letter over the spirit of the word and the law" (Erikson, 1977, p. 97). Legalism is marked by self-centered displays of righteousness and a moralistic insistence on right over justice. The reverse, of course, may also result, so that the legalistic individual learns to exploit the letter of the law to justify self-excess. This individual is motivated not by a compulsive sense of "rightness" but by a shrewdly manipulative lack of impulse control.

Acquiring a Sense of Initiative Versus a Sense of Guilt: Purpose

Resolving the crisis of autonomy, the child of age four or five enters the next phase of ego development with the firm sense that he or she *is* a person (Erikson, 1959, p. 74). The child must now discover what kind of person he or she is. In its most basic form, the crucial question for the child is to decide which of the parents will be the object of identification. Freud characterized this stage of development as phallic, and the chief crisis as the solution of the Oedipus complex.

In addition to the oedipal strivings, three important developments attend this stage and serve to bring the child closer to the point of crisis: (1) The range of movement is widened by the capacity to walk rather than crawl; (2) the use of language is more precise "to the point where he understands and can ask about many things just enough to misunderstand them thoroughly"; (3) language and locomotion combine to permit the child to expand the imagination, to create the impossible, to be frightened by his or her own thoughts (Erikson, 1959, p.75).

The key characteristic of this stage, therefore, is the child's growing capacity *to initiate* actions, thoughts, and fantasies. To the established hallmarks of trust and autonomy, the ego adds the capacity *to plan*. The child's increased capacity to anticipate or to reflect on the consequences of self-initiated activities can lead to jealous rage against siblings or against anyone who trespasses in what the child perceives to be its special area of privilege. For the male child, exclusive domination of mother's attention comes to a climax when he realizes that father is the stronger, more powerful competitor. To resolve these oedipal strivings, the child internalizes those prohibitions that he imagines his father might enforce. These internalized standards become the basis of the superego or conscience (see the discussion of the superego in Chapter 3). With the formation of the superego, the child also solidifies its identification with the same-sexed parent, taking on the sex-appropriate behaviors of that model.

During this stage, too, the child learns to cooperate with other children in planning mutual undertakings. The child emulates desirable models like teachers and pursues idealistic goals and causes. Hence, the crisis for the ego in this stage is to establish a favorable balance between initiative and the residue of oedipal guilt that was retained in the formation of the superego. In short, the child discovers what it *can* do and what it *may* do (Erikson, 1959, p. 75). Nowhere is this balance between ability and expectancy more apparent than in imaginative play:

> Play is to the child what thinking, planning, and blueprinting are to the adult, a trial universe in which conditions are simplified and methods exploratory, so that past failures can be thought through, expectations tested. (Erikson, 1964, p. 120)

The crucial increment to the ego's strength that results from a successful resolution of the crisis attending this stage is the virtue of purpose: *"Purpose . . . is the courage to envisage and pursue valued goals uninhibited by the defeat of infantile fantasies, by guilt and by the foiling fear of punishment"* (Erikson, 1964, p. 122; italics in original). With the internalization of conscience, that is, with the adoption of external standards as its own moral and ethical guidelines, the child may be said to have its own purpose. The child's ego may now make judgments and plans that in the past had to be made for it.

The initiative versus guilt stage of development has for its ritualization the sense of *authenticity*. Entering the play stage of childhood, boys and girls learn to manipulate the microsphere of toy-reality, to create dramatic elaborations of their inner and outer conflicts. This dramatic element combines with the established ritualizations of the numinous and the judicious to allow the child to relive, correct, recreate, and rework past experiences, and to anticipate future ones. The child can experiment—dramatically—with a variety of roles, arranging them into a hierarchy of sanctioned ideal and evil performances. A genuine sense of inner guilt—the capacity for self-condemnation—is developed as the child toys with fantastic events and roles it could not possibly enact in "real life." From play, there emerges a sense of congenial roles, comfortable situations, satisfactory coping strategies that combine, eventually, into authenticity, that is, into a feeling of what I really *want* to be and *can* realistically be.

Impersonation is the ritualism of the dramatic element, a form of ungenuine role playing untempered by realistic shame and guilt. "To be denied a true chance of authenticity . . . can force children (and youths) to compulsively assume the role of shameless evildoers—as preferable to being either nameless or overly typed" (Erikson, 1977, p. 103). The impersonating child is able to shift dangerously among a variety of roles because it lacks a genuine commitment to one role. It can appear as anyone because it is no one.

ACQUIRING A SENSE OF INDUSTRY VERSUS A SENSE OF INFERIORITY: COMPETENCE

In the first stage of basic *trust*, personality focused around the conviction, *"I am what I am given."* During the crisis of the second stage involving *autonomy*, personality was centered on the belief that, *"I am what I will."* At the third stage, when the sense of *initiative* reached critical proportions, the nucleus of personality was, *"I am what I can imagine I will be."* With the emergence of the fourth psychosocial crisis of industry versus inferiority, the central theme for personality development becomes *"I am what I learn"* (Erikson, 1959, p. 82). This fourth stage, consequently, coincides with the child's first school experiences.

With entrance into school and the enforced attention to the impersonal abstractions of the "three R's" that school brings, the child must forget past hopes and desires, taming its exuberant imagination in the service of productive learning (Erikson, 1950, p. 258). Corresponding to the Freudian latency period, this psychosocial stage finds the child leaving behind its efforts to win a place of privilege and mastery within the safety of the family. The child discovers, instead, that recognition outside the family is important. And that recognition is most easily obtained by producing—that is, by preparing for useful work.

The most important lesson that children derive from their school experiences is the pleasure to be gained from completing a task by steady attention and persevering diligence (Erikson, 1950, p. 259). They learn to handle the implements of their culture, to acquire the rudiments of technology, or, in nontechnological cultures, the rudiments of survival. The key danger is that children may despair of success; they may develop a sense of inadequacy and inferiority. When school life fails to maintain the accomplishments of the three previous ego crises, children may fail to identify with the productive adult models that surround them.

A successful resolution of the crisis between industry and inferiority leads to the ego's development of a new strength, the virtue of competence: *"Competence . . . is the free exercise of dexterity and intelligence in the completion of tasks, unimpaired by infantile inferiority"* (Erikson, 1964, p. 124). Children learn "by virtue of" their trust, autonomy, initiative, and industry that confident, independent, and active productivity is satisfying because it allows them to join and to effect changes in the adult human community.

The industry versus inferiority stage is marked by the ritualization of *formality*. Becoming accustomed to school tasks and their necessity for successful "making" and "producing," the youngster learns the value of methodical performance (Erikson, 1977, p. 103).

> [In school] . . . with varying abruptness, play is transformed into work, game into competition and cooperation, and the freedom of imagination into the duty to perform with full attention to the techniques which make imagination communicable, accountable, and applicable to defined tasks. (Erikson, 1977, p. 104)

School, in industrial societies, introduces children to the proper *forms* of "making" and "doing," competing, and cooperating. When children master the formal aspects of work, they are made to feel worthwhile, deserving of praise, success, gain, and acceptance. They learn that hard work, initiative, and "stick-to-itiveness" are the elements that allow their eventual accession in reality to the roles they have chosen in fantasy.

The ritualism side of formality is *formalism,* the forgetting of the purpose of methodical performance in favor of mere proficiency. As Karl Marx suggested, a "craft-idiot" is one who denies the human significance of his or her skills and becomes enslaved to the trappings of efficient method (Erikson, 1977, p. 106). Formalism is adherence to technique and blindness to purpose and meaning.

ACQUIRING A SENSE OF IDENTITY VERSUS A SENSE OF ROLE CONFUSION: FIDELITY

When the child's ego has assimilated an adultlike sense of industry, childhood ends. In reaching this point in development, the adolescent has constructed a sense of his or her own sameness, a sense that, although he or she is changing, the "he or she" who changes is also fundamentally the same. This sense of continuity is the foundation of ego identity.

In adolescence, however, the four earlier crises are resurrected and the sense of sameness is requestioned.

> In their search for a new sense of continuity and sameness, adolescents have to refight many of the battles of earlier years, even though to do so they must artificially

appoint perfectly well-meaning people to play the roles of adversaries; and they are ever ready to install lasting idols and ideals as guardians of a final identity. . . . The sense of ego identity, then, is the accrued confidence that the inner sameness and continuity prepared in the past are matched by the sameness and continuity of one's meaning for others, as evidenced in the tangible promise of a "career." (Erikson, 1950, pp. 261–262)

The adolescent period is thus a socially sanctioned interval of role experimentation, of delay in making final choices. A full and healthy ego identity can emerge only when all previous identifications are integrated. The varying senses of one's identity in infancy, childhood, and in the school years must merge to become a comfortable and workable whole. The early stages of trust and autonomy were dominated by a sense of *bodily identity:* hunger and elimination. The later stages of initiative and industry were concerned chiefly with *social roles* modeled by important adult others. In adolescence the bodily and social identifications must coalesce to bridge the division between childhood and adulthood. "A lasting ego identity cannot begin to exist without the trust of the first oral stage; it cannot be completed with a promise of fulfillment which from the dominant image of adulthood reaches down into the baby's beginnings and which creates at every step an accruing sense of ego strength" (Erikson, 1959, p. 91).

The danger of this period has become a rather faddish label affixed indiscriminately to all sorts of behavior. "Identity crisis," the term coined by Erikson in the context of his theory, rightly applies to the potential of the adolescent to become role-confused. Because a wide variety of adult roles are modeled in our complex culture, the adolescent may turn the socially sanctioned period of temporary delay in choosing a role into a combined or semipermanent moratorium (Erikson, 1950, p. 262; 1963, p. 13).

In proper perspective, the *psychosocial moratorium* of adolescence permits the youth to explore a range of opportunities without the necessity of immediate commitment. For the adolescent who has failed to integrate all previous crisis solutions, the moratorium on final role choice permitted by society to its young is extended to a paralyzing and interminable era of confusion. Like Erikson with his own youthful identity crisis as an "outsider," confused adolescents cannot become what their lives have prepared them to be:

The prime danger of this age, therefore, is identity confusion, which can express itself in excessively prolonged moratoria . . .; in repeated impulsive attempts to end the moratorium with sudden choices, that is, to play with historical possibilities, and then to deny that some irreversible commitment has already taken place. . . . The dominant issue of this, as of any other stage, therefore, is that of the active, the selective, ego being in charge and being enabled to be in charge by a social structure which grants a given age group the place it needs—and in which it is needed. (Erikson, 1963, p. 13)

Thus the sense of identity means "being at one with oneself," and harboring an affinity for one's community, both for its history and for its future (Erikson, 1974, p. 27). But with this positive sense of identity there is necessarily a negative aspect to one's sense of self. Each adolescent, consequently, harbors a *negative identity.* Healthy resolution of the identity crisis ensures for the adolescent the means of discarding the dark identifications and troublesome conflicts that compose the negative identity. However, for the adolescent who succumbs to the crisis of establishing a positive ego identity, "The loss of a sense of identity often is expressed in a scornful and snobbish hostility toward the roles offered as proper and desirable in one's family or immediate community. Any part or aspect of the required role, or all parts, be it masculinity or femininity, nationality or class membership, can become the main focus of the young person's acid disdain" (Erikson, 1959, p. 129).

Negative identity choices are most easily discerned among troubled or "disturbed" adolescents. Such young people willfully choose to become everything that parents and teachers had expressly indicated as undesirable. A negative identity is thus "an identity perversely based on all those identifications and roles which, at critical stages of development, had been presented to the individual as most undesirable or dangerous, and yet also as most real" (Erikson, 1959, p. 131). For example:

> A mother who is filled with unconscious ambivalence toward a brother who disintegrated into alcoholism may again and again respond selectively only to those traits in her son which seem to point to a repetition of her brother's fate, in which case this "negative" identity may take on more reality for the son than all his natural attempts at being good: he may work hard on becoming a drunkard and, lacking the necessary ingredients, may end up in a state of stubborn paralysis of choice. (Erikson, 1959, p. 131)

"Vindictive choices" of negative roles around which to integrate one's sense of self represent a desperate attempt to regain some control over one's fate. Many adolescents faced with chronic identity diffusion would "rather be nobody or somebody bad, or indeed, dead—and this totally, and by free choice—than be not-quite somebody" (Erikson, 1959, p. 132).

Despite the dangers of adolescent identity diffusion, the majority of ego-integrated youth evidence attainment of another form of ego strength, the virtue of fidelity: *"Fidelity is the ability to sustain loyalties freely pledged in spite of the inevitable contradictions of value systems"* (Erikson, 1964, p. 125; italics in original). Healthy youths, from their springboards of firm self-identities and strong egos, develop a high sense of duty to the tasks of rendering reality faithfully to themselves and to their culture. For youths who have attained the strength of fidelity, life becomes the living out of their established core identities. The roles they play are the roles they are.

Like other theorists, Erikson employed the theatrical imagery of the actor and his mask of roles. The danger in the roles to which adolescents turn in their experimentation with the multiple identities their life offers is that the role may become more real than the actor's core:

> But what if role-playing becomes an aim in itself, is rewarded with success and status, and seduces the person to repress what core-identity is potential in him? Even an actor is convincing in many roles only if and when there is in him an actor's core identity—and craftsmanship. (Erikson, 1974, p. 107)

Fidelity thus guarantees that adolescents with a firm sense of self will match their inner necessities with outer demands. For healthy "faithful" adolescents, the actor's mask is adjusted precisely to the actor's face.

The ritualization of the adolescent identity-formation period is the commitment to an *ideology*. Adolescence is the time to integrate all the conflicting self-images that have developed since infancy in some formal "confirmation" procedure. A formal *rite de passage* is needed to mark clearly the adolescent's transition from childhood to adulthood. Adolescents must be made to experience what Erikson calls "solidarity of conviction," that is, a sense that they belong to the generation of youth as distinguished from their elders (Erikson, 1977, p. 107). Adolescents often develop their own formal rituals of belonging, marked outwardly by the distinction of their clothes, preferences for music and literature, and, sometimes, open hostility to "adults." Inwardly, adolescents have to prepare to adopt the work roles chosen in the previous phase of development, committing themselves to be "fully grown" and to take a place in the technological system of their society. By their adoption of the work ethic prevalent in their culture, adolescents also implicitly adopt its ideological style and they are ready to exclude, by disdain, by moral repudiation, fanatic rebellion, or warfare, all alien ideologies (Erikson, 1977, p. 107).

The ritualism of this phase is *totalism,* "a fanatic and exclusive preoccupation with what seems unquestionably ideal within a tight system of ideas" (1977, p. 110). Ritualism is a partial regression to the idolism of infancy. Adolescents now find themselves a cause, an idea, a group to which they can totally commit themselves unthinkingly and in which they run the risk of losing themselves.

ACQUIRING A SENSE OF INTIMACY VERSUS A SENSE OF ISOLATION: LOVE

With entrance into young adulthood, the person becomes willing to risk his or her newly established identity by fusing it with the identities of others. "He is ready for intimacy, that is, the capacity to commit himself to concrete affiliations and partnerships and to develop ethical strength to abide by such commitments, even though they may call for significant sacrifices and compromises" (Erikson, 1950, p. 263).

A firm sense of personal integrity based on the fusion of past bodily and social identifications allows the young adult to face the fear of ego loss in situations and in unions that call for self-sacrifice. Thus the young adult faces intimate social commitments ranging from intense friendships or physical combat to hesitant sexual experimentation.

The danger of this period is that young adults may not be ready for the demands of intimacy. They may be unwilling to lend themselves to intimate sharing with another, and thus retreat into personal isolation. Freud was once asked what he thought the healthy person should be able to do well. His curt answer was *"Lieben und arbeiten"* (to love and to work) (Erikson, 1950, p. 265). In the shift among combative, cooperative, and intimate interpersonal relationships, new adults must learn not only to adopt personal formulas for intimate cooperation, but also their own unique modes of productivity.

True, healthy genital sexuality that marks this stage is characterized by

1. mutuality of orgasm
2. with a loved partner

3. of the other sex
4. with whom one is able and willing to share a mutual trust
5. and with whom one is able and willing to regulate the cycles of
   a. work
   b. procreation
   c. recreation
6. so as to secure to the offspring, too, all the stages of a satisfactory development. (Erikson, 1950, p. 266)

Clearly, Freud's formula, "to love and to work," is more complicated than is at first apparent. Freud and Erikson mean to indicate that the healthy adult personality is able to absorb him- or herself in intimate sexual fulfillment while *simultaneously* maintaining the independence of spirit necessary for productive and fulfilling work.

The key virtue attending the successful resolution of the conflict between intimacy and isolation in this stage is, of course, love: *"Love . . . is mutuality of devotion forever subduing the antagonisms inherent in divided function"* (Erikson, 1964, p. 129; italics in original). Love is thus the strength of ego to share identity for "mutual verification" of chosen identity while taking from this supportive relationship the strength to be "self-ish."

Growing from the core of intimacy achieved in this stage is the ritualization that Erikson calls the *affiliative* (Erikson, 1977, p. 110). Affiliation indicates that the identity achieved thus far is complementary to the identities of those people with whom life is shared. The young adult finds a partner with whom to share enthusiastic opinions and scathing judgments, and with whom to establish an enduring affiliation promising a productive and procreative life (1977, p. 110).

The ritualism counterbalancing the affiliative element is *elitism,* a sense of shared narcissism with one or several people that leads to exclusion and to "exclusive" group memberships. Elitism is an isolating trend rooted in the ego inflations of infantile idolism.

ACQUIRING A SENSE OF GENERATIVITY VERSUS A SENSE OF STAGNATION: CARE

"Mature man needs to be needed, and maturity needs guidance as well as encouragement from what has been produced and must be taken care of" (Erikson, 1950, p. 267). The loving and working mature adults thus need to feel some concern for the next generation as exemplified in their own offspring. Because children are the products of the intimate fusion of bodily and personal identities of the parents, mother and father have a "libidinal investment" in their offspring.

Merely wanting children does not ensure the attainment of a sense of generativity. The fundamental requirement is the ability to extend oneself, literally to give oneself to the future. Erikson chose the term *generativity* rather than synonyms like productivity or creativity because the key characteristic of the ego at this stage is its ability to transcend the immediate self-related interests of the person in favor of a view of generations to come (Erikson, 1968, p. 138).

The danger of this stage lies in the inability of some otherwise mature adults to find value in guiding and aiding the next generation. A pervasive sense of stagnation or boredom characterizes their approach to a variety of life tasks. There is present the feeling of living an adequate but unsatisfying life. A feeling exists that all accomplishments and all interpersonal intimacies are fundamentally impoverished because they lack relevance to one's diffuse sense of "Who I am."

The ego's strength in meeting the necessities of life is increased in the generative adult by the development of the virtue of care: *"Care is the widening concern for what has been generated by love, necessity, or accident; it overcomes the ambivalence adhering to irreversible obligation"* (Erikson, 1964, p. 131; italics in original). By postulating the stage of generativity and the attainment of the virtue of care, Erikson has extended the Freudian psychosexual stages beyond genital sexuality. Care assures for the mature ego the right to be needed and the privilege to need the young. Thus care includes not only work for those persons whom one has created, but for all of humanity's created works as well.

The hallmark of the adult generative period is the ritualization that Erikson calls the *generational* (1977, p. 111). This ritualization is a composite of a variety of adult ritualizations, including the parental, the teaching, and the curative. Generational means that the adult must be prepared to exercise authority with a conviction that "I know what I am doing" and receive reassurance from the various cultural images of authority, such as God, kings, and one's own parents, that "I am doing it right."

The corresponding ritualism of the adult period is *authoritism,* a self-convinced but spurious seizing of authority. Instead of functioning as a just transmitter of ideal values and as a sanctioned judge of evil, the adult who yields to authoritism becomes an oppressive model of insensitivity.

ACQUIRING EGO INTEGRITY VERSUS DESPAIR: WISDOM

The climax of the life cycle is reached when the foundations of infantile trust have made possible their adult counterpart: *integrity.* Adults who have been cared for, who have cared for others, can now care for themselves. The fruit of the previous seven stages ripens in adults whose egos can accept their life cycles "as something that had to be and that, by necessity, permitted of no substitutions: it thus means a new, a different love of one's parents" (Erikson, 1950, p. 268).

Adults in whom ego integrity has fully blossomed realize that their individual lives are but one life cycle in the flow of history. They are convinced that what had to be, was—and was satisfying. The danger is that the ego may have failed to integrate the crisis resolutions of the previous seven stages. The fear of death that emerges means that the individual is unable to accept his or her life cycle as the ultimate and one and only meaning that living embodies. *Despair* of what has been implies that what has been, has been in vain. Despair is the protest of a person who is not yet satisfied with a life that has never been satisfying. Despair indicates an unwillingness, paradoxical as it may be, to end a life that has failed to achieve fulfillment and that now culminates as the sum of a thousand little miseries.

The most important gift parents can provide their children is the strength, shown in their own example, to face ultimate concerns like death without the disintegrating effects of fear: "Healthy children will not fear life if their elders have integrity enough not to fear death" (Erikson, 1950, p. 269). Thus the virtue that serves as the hallmark of the climactic stage of the life cycle is wisdom: *"Wisdom . . . is detached concern with life itself, in the face of death itself"* (Erikson, 1964, p. 133; italics in original). Adults who embody the kind of integrity that Erikson describes are wise in the sense that they view their limited lives as a totality that transcends petty disgust at the feeling of "being finished." They are able to transcend the despair "of facing the period of relative helplessness which marks the end as it marked the beginning" (Erikson, 1964, p. 134).

This last stage of the life cycle brings us to the ritualization called the *integral,* literally an ability to integrate the previous phases into a confirmation of the life thus led. To have achieved the ego strength of wisdom means that the important achievements of the previous seven stages are synthesized and consolidated into the awareness that new ideas, new meanings, new persons have been personally created. In a real way, these creations are immortality—for the individual and for the human group. The ego that has achieved the ritualization of the integral affirms life, and the person of old age realizes a new affinity for what was childish. This paradox is expressed beautifully in the lines of William Blake that Erikson used as his book epigraph and title:

> The Child's Toys and the Old Man's Reasons
> Are the Fruits of the Two Seasons.

TABLE 6.2 Crises, Ego Strengths, and Ritualizations of the Life Cycle

	Ego crisis	Ego Strength	Ritualization Range
Infancy	1. Trust versus Mistrust	Hope	Mother-Child mutual recognition: Numinous to Idolism
Early Childhood	2. Autonomy versus Shame, and Doubt	Will	Good-Bad discrimination: Judicious to Legalism
Childhood (play age)	3. Initiative versus Guilt	Purpose	Dramatic elaboration: Authenticity to Impersonation
Childhood (school age)	4. Industry versus Inferiority	Competence	Methodical performance: Formality to Formalism
Adolescence	5. Identity versus Role Confusion	Fidelity	Solidarity of conviction: Ideology to Totalism
Young Adulthood	6. Intimacy versus Isolation	Love	Complementarity of Identities: Affiliative to Elitism
Mature Adulthood	7. Generativity versus Stagnation	Care	Transmission of values: Generational to Authoritism
Old Age	8. Ego Integrity versus Despair	Wisdom	Affirmation of life: Integral to Sapientism

Based on Erikson, 1950, 1977, 1978

The ritualism of this stage is a distortion of wisdom that Erikson names *sapientism,* "the unwise pretense of being wise" (Erikson, 1977, p. 112).

Table 6.2 summarizes the eight stages of the life cycle and their various crises, strengths, and ritualizations.

SOME CONCLUDING REMARKS ON ERIKSON

Erikson's psychosocial scheme of the life cycle has provided the conceptual tools for the analysis of the lives of significant historical figures. Erikson has thus examined the process of identity development in the lives of Martin Luther (1962) and of Mahatma Gandhi (1969). In both cases, Erikson sought to identify the historical, social, and psychological forces that uniquely combined with accidental circumstance to produce a human personality that changed the course of history.

Psychohistory, as this form of clinical investigation has come to be called, is gaining a wide foothold in a broad array of academic disciplines. It is not within the scope of this chapter to review this literature. But it is important to recognize the far-reaching acceptance Erikson's ideas have had. The concepts of identity, identity crisis, life cycle, ego strength, and psychosocial development, all pioneered by Erikson, have found their way into quarters where orthodox psychoanalytic doctrine would be most unwelcome. Perhaps the reasons for the respectability of Erikson's concepts in the eyes of critics who would otherwise be hostile to psychoanalytic notions lie in some unique combination of Erikson's personal, social, and historical presence.

EVALUATING ERIK ERIKSON

Erikson's theory is probably the most widely read, taught, and written about theory in contemporary psychology. We would be hard put to find a general psychology text or an adolescent or child psychology text in America that does not give substantial space to his ideas. Erikson's ego psychology has been welcomed in places where Freud's theory would be most unwelcome. People from different disciplines, with vastly different expectations about psychological theories of human nature, find in Erikson what they are looking for, even if each of them seeks something different. Developmentalists find a stage-phase theory of psychological growth; psychoanalysts find a Freudian account of identity formation; humanists find a holistic conception of the life span; theologians find cogent observations on aging and death; and social learning theorists find a cognitive translation of Freudian developmental tasks. The list could be expanded. But the point is that Erikson is a man of great erudition, with the humanist's eye for the uniqueness of personality, the psychoanalyst's ear for the unconscious personal meaning, and the artist's flair for bold but elegant statement.

Refutability of Erikson's Concepts

Erikson's concepts are easily translated into cognitive and emotional constructs, independent of the psychoanalytic assumptions from which he started. His own studies of play, reviewed in this chapter, are one example, and those studies were soundly refuted, as we saw. But that is the point: Some of Erikson's ideas are refutable, a relative novelty in psychoanalytic circles.

The most research productive of Erikson's concepts has been his notion of identity and identity formation. Some years ago, Marcia (1966) devised a set of criteria and a way to measure various degrees of crystalized identity formation in young people. Since then, there have been a variety of empirical, sometimes predictive, studies based on the Marcia-Erikson measures of identity status (e.g., Marcia, 1993; Marcia & Friedman, 1970; Rowe & Marcia, 1980).

In principle, there are other fundamental Eriksonian concepts that should be refutable because they are measurable. For example, Hamachek (1988) has developed cognitive-behavioral translations of some of Erikson's ego strengths and other features of the developmental stages. Such a translation should pave the way for empirical testing.

So we have to give Erikson a qualified high grade in refutability. Qualified, because so much else in the theory is philosophical (the "Virtues," ritualisms, and ritualizations) that large portions are simply not testable. Yet, we should not take lightly the substantial refutability that is present.

Erikson's Concept of Human Agency

Erikson has a balanced conception of human agency. On the one hand, as a Freudian theorist, Erikson regards unconscious processes and social reality as determining variables that shape the person. But, as we have seen, Erikson also portrays development as a matter of some personal choices, which implies an active agent view. How shall we characterize Eriksonian theory, then? It is a matter of judgment, based largely on whether one emphasizes the Freudian component to the theory or the cognitive component. Because Erikson has stressed repeatedly his allegiance to the basic psychoanalytic formulations, especially for the first four developmental stages, we can speculate that Erikson's view of people is more of a passive agent view—people are shaped by reality—than an active agent view. But it is a close call.

The Idiographic-Nomothetic Balance in Erikson's Theory

Erikson's theory deals with universals. His conception of the stages/phases asserts a universal human developmental scheme. As we have seen, Erikson even reiterated Freud's "anatomy is destiny" dictum and thereby earned a great deal of criticism. His conception of identity formation clearly has nomothetic components, some of which have received testing, as we discussed.

By the same token, Erikson has argued convincingly that each of us "solves" the crisis of a given developmental stage *uniquely,* in terms of our given social, historical, and familial context. His early clinical work with soldiers, Native American children, and his own psychoanalytic patients, along with his interest in psychohistory (Martin Luther, Gandhi, and Adolf Hitler, for example) are testimony to the idiographic, single-case concerns of his work.

In Erikson, as in few other theories, we find the idiographic perspective well balanced with the potential for nomothetic "laws" that can be tested.

SUMMARY

Erik H. Erikson's work falls within the realm of psychoanalytic ego psychology by virtue of the theory's stress on the ego's integrating and stabilizing influences in the person's life history, but he might just as well be considered an object relations theorist. Identifying himself closely with orthodox psychoanalysis, Erikson nevertheless has transcended classical Freudian instinct theory. He portrays the ego from a psychosocial perspective as the hub of individual identity. As the ego matures through life crises, it gains strength to master in increasingly sophisticated ways the puzzles posed by inner and outer reality. Perhaps Erikson's continued self-identification with psychoanalytic theory and his desire to preserve its essential elements were fostered by his own gratefulness for his early acceptance into the Freudian mainstream. His adolescent role confusion, the culmination of his development as an "outsider," was greatly reduced by his commitment to the role of psychoanalytic therapist. Neither completely Jewish nor completely Scandinavian, the young Erikson had long wondered who his real father was, why he was "Jew" to his school chums and "goy" to his stepfather's relatives, and how he would ever be somebody.

Erikson's interest in the development of the individual's reality functioning was spurred on by his early researches with California boys' and girls' fantasy productions. He found that basic biological and anatomical differences in bodily equipment were paralleled in a child's play constructions: Boys built high, tottering, exterior, protrusive scenes from the play materials. Girls constructed enclosing, static, interior scenes.

Erikson conceptualizes the healthy personality as one who, in Freud's words, is able to work and to love. That is, the healthy functioning personality has the capacity to share intimacy with another and to work fruitfully, with personal satisfaction. A healthy social milieu, initially provided by the parents, aids the individual to accept the inexorability of his or her own development. Erikson calls such acceptance—that what one has lived *had* to be—a "sense of ego integrity."

Erikson has proposed that such integrity or ego strength is achieved in an unalterable sequence of psychosocial stages. Beginning in infancy, the child's ego must first learn to trust itself and others to become autonomous and self-sufficient. With trust and autonomy come the virtues of *hope* and *will,* forms of ego strength that foster sufficient security for the child to risk the potential disappointment that hope entails, and sufficient independence of spirit for children to dare to initiate willingly their personal adaptation to their inescapable realities. Once these fundamental ego strengths are acquired, the child is able to acquire, in sequence, a sense of initiative (*purpose*), a sense of industry (*competence*), a sense of identity (*fidelity*), a sense of intimacy (*love*), a sense of generativity (*care*), and, finally, a sense of integrity (*wisdom*).

During the various phases in the acquisition of these ego strengths or virtues, the maturing person will also be exposed to age-appropriate *ritualizations* and *ritualisms* through which comes a special kind of learning, the mastery of "the only proper way to experience and to do things" in that person's culture. In the trust-mistrust stage, there is the ritualization of *mother-child recognition;* in the autonomy-doubt stage, the child learns *good-bad discriminations,* followed by acquisition of the ability to *elaborate dramatically* conflicts and concerns in the initiative-guilt phase of middle childhood. By school age, the ritualization of *methodical performance* is acquired, allowing the child to progress into adolescence with a more or less perfectly formed "worker" image that will be further shaped by the ritualization of *shared convictions* with other adolescent children. Young adulthood brings exposure to the *complementary identity* of one's intimate partner, with whom, by mature adulthood, the person seeks to perform the ritualization of *transmitting values* to the next generation. Old age, finally, sees a return, in Erikson's view, to the playfulness of childhood in the wise old person's *affirmation of the life he or she has led.*

An evaluation of Erikson reveals a theory that has the potential for refutable constructs and an established capacity for generating productive research. Erikson also achieves a balanced view of human agency in which social, biological, and cultural variables are seen as determinants, but the individual is capable of choice within these limits. Erikson's theory embodies a well-balanced concern for nomothetic or universal psychological "laws" with some traditional psychoanalytic concern for the uniqueness of the individual, especially in the areas of clinical application and psychohistory.

FOR FURTHER READING

Erikson's most comprehensive treatment of both his early and later theorizing is contained in *Childhood and Society* (New York: Norton, 1963), rev. ed. His *Life History and the Historical Moment* (New York: Norton, 1975) contains several essays concerning his views on women's liberation, the abuse of the term *identity crisis,* and the significance of his own adolescent identity crisis. In *Insight and Responsibility* (New York: Norton, 1964) Erikson considers the various "virtues" that may arise through healthy resolution of the eight psychosocial developmental crises.

Robert Coles has provided a detailed account of the personal and historical influences that shaped Erikson's ideas in *Erik Erikson: The Growth of His Work* (Boston: Little, Brown, 1970). Richard I. Evans, in Vol. 8 of his famous "Dialogs" series, interviews Erikson and provides commentary on his work. This interview may be read in the full-length version of *Dialog With Erik Erikson* (New York: Harper & Row, 1967) or in moderately condensed form in R. I. Evans's *The Making of Psychology* (New York: Knopf, 1976).

Erikson's most recent conceptual additions to this life cycle theory, the stages in the ritualization of experience, may be read in his *Toys and Reasons* (New York: Norton, 1977). Erikson's most recent restatement of the rationale underlying his famous "eight stages" is to be found in *The Life Cycle Completed* (New York: Norton, 1982) and is worth consulting for the new emphases that have emerged as Erikson himself writes from the perspective of old age. A more artful and literary approach to Erikson's conception of the eight stages may be witnessed in the collection of papers, including his own analysis of an Ingmar Bergman movie, edited by Erikson under the title *Adulthood* (New York: Norton, 1978). Erikson's wife, Joan Erikson, has written of a milieu, work-activity therapy program at the Austin-Riggs Center during the time she and her husband served as consultants in *Activity, Recovery, Growth* (New York: Norton, 1976).

J. Marcia has provided some confirmatory empirical evidence for Erikson's concept of ego identity in "Development and Validation of Ego-Identity Status," *Journal of Personality and Social Psychology* (1966, **3,** 551–558), and N. L. Toder and J. Marcia provided further support in "Ego Identity Status and Response to Conformity Pressure in College Women," *Journal of Personality and Social Psychology* (1973, **26,** 287–294). Two recent volumes give some indication of the scope of research and thinking on the concept of identity and some of its philosophical underpinnings. The collection of papers edited by Jane Kroger in *Discussions on Ego Identity* (Hillsdale, NJ: Lawrence Erlbaum, 1993) presents a wide range of interpretations of identity. The compendium edited by Marcia and his colleagues, *Ego Identity: A Handbook for Psychosocial Research* (New York: Springer-Verlag, 1993) provides a thorough survey of recent research, Marcia's most recent thinking, and several samples of ongoing projects.

C H A P T E R 7

CARL G. JUNG
Analytical Psychology

It would be so much simpler if I knew nothing; but I know too much, through my ancestors and my own education.

C. G. Jung, *Analytical Psychology: Its Theory and Practice*

The truly "mysterious" object is beyond our apprehension and comprehension, not only because our knowledge has certain irremovable limits, but because in it we come upon something inherently "wholly other," whose kind and character are incommensurable with our own, and before which we therefore recoil in a wonder that strikes us chill and numb.

Rudolf Otto, *The Idea of the Holy*

About Jung's Analytical Psychology

Carl Jung was for a short time Freud's hand-chosen successor. But personal and intellectual differences between the two men led eventually to Jung following a very different path through philosophy, psychology, and studies of the occult. Much of Jung's picture of the human personality derived from his affiliation with Freud, so that the familiar landmarks of unconscious motivation, neurotic defenses, and human conflict will be found here. But Jung's importance lies very much in the ideas he created that differed drastically from Freud's. In particular, Jung's most basic concepts are these:

1. *the personal unconscious described by Freud is supplemented in everyone with a transpersonal or "collective unconscious" that consists of universal images which transcend particular persons, times, and places;*

2. *the spiritual needs of humans are at least equally, if not more, potent than the basic biological needs, and these yearnings will be expressed differently in introverted and extroverted people;*

3. *the subjective, reflective, inwardly oriented introvert finds purpose in life by integrating the inner conflicts into a whole self; the action-oriented, outwardly directed extrovert finds purpose in life by harmonizing the self with social reality.*

Much of Jung's thinking emerged from his personal battle with near psychotic episodes of personal disorganization, which he felt he had transcended and used productively in his theory.

EXPERIMENTAL STUDY OF ASSOCIATIONS

In April 1907, after only a few exchanges of letters and one brief visit to Freud's home, Carl Gustav Jung became Freud's handpicked successor. On April 7, Freud wrote to Jung "that you have inspired me with confidence for the future, that I now realize that I am as replaceable as everyone else and that I could hope for no one better than yourself, as I have come to know you, to continue and complete my work" (Freud & Jung, 1974, p. 27). Part of Freud's enthusiasm for his younger colleague rested on Jung's published acknowledgment that Freud's ideas had been useful in his own clinical work; part rested on some clinical experiments that Jung had conducted with his cousin, Franz Riklin, that purported to demonstrate unconscious mental processes.

Subjects in Jung and Riklin's experimental studies of word associations typically found themselves confronted by the following circumstances. Professor Jung or Professor Riklin would sit or stand opposite the subject, a one-fifth-second stopwatch in hand, and instruct him or her to "answer as quickly as possible with the first word that occurs to you" at each of 100 stimulus words. Jung's entire list of stimulus words appears in Table 7.1 so you may get a firsthand feel for the procedure.

A variety of grammatical forms was included among the various stimulus words. The list was arranged in a specific sequence that Jung's experience had shown was suitable for eliciting maximum emotional reaction. In later experiments, Jung and his

TABLE 7.1 Jung's List of Stimulus Words

1. head	26. blue	51. frog	76. to wash
2. green	27. lamp	52. to part	77. cow
3. water	28. to sin	53. hunger	78. friend
4. to sing	29. bread	54. white	79. happiness
5. death	30. rich	55. child	80. lie
6. long	31. tree	56. to pay attention	81. department
7. ship	32. to prick	57. pencil	82. narrow
8. to pay	33. pity	58. sad	83. brother
9. window	34. yellow	59. plum	84. to fear
10. friendly	35. mountain	60. to marry	85. stork
11. table	36. to die	61. house	86. false
12. to ask	37. salt	62. darling	87. anxiety
13. cold	38. new	63. glass	88. to kiss
14. stem	39. custom	64. to quarrel	89. bride
15. to dance	40. to pray	65. fur	90. pure
16. village	41. money	66. big	91. door
17. lake	42. stupid	67. carrot	92. to choose
18. sick	43. exercise book	68. to paint	93. hay
19. pride	44. to despise	69. part	94. contented
20. to cook	45. finger	70. old	95. ridicule
21. ink	46. dear	71. flower	96. to sleep
22. angry	47. bird	72. to beat	97. month
23. needle	48. to fall	73. box	98. nice
24. to swim	49. book	74. wild	99. woman
25. journey	50. unjust	75. family	100. to abuse

From Jung, 1909a, p. 440

colleagues used additional procedures besides the simple stopwatch timing of the subject's reactions. Sometimes, the subject's respiration rate was measured, along with a recording of galvanic skin response (GSR). The GSR measures the skin's decrease in resistance to electrical current during sensory and emotional changes, a variable akin to one of the measures used in the modern "lie detector" or polygraph.

The word-association experiment was not unique to Jung's laboratory (cf. Woodworth & Schlosberg, 1954, Chap. 3 for a brief history of the method; and Jung, 1909a). Jung's contribution lay in his use of the method to study the subject's nonconscious emotional reactions. He found, for example, that "normal" men and women do not respond similarly to the stimulus words. Individual differences in reaction time, respiration rate, GSR, and ideational content were the rule. More important, in word-association experiments with neurotic and psychotic patients, Jung found that the method could aid in uncovering latent emotional difficulties by exposing content areas that produced hesitation, perseveration, or total inhibition of response.

EMOTIONAL COMPLEX INDICATORS

Usually, the stimulus word that triggered the subject's hesitation or inability to respond was connected *symbolically* with a deeply personal and emotionally abrasive set of ideas or experiences. Because such latent difficulties were often collections of various thoughts held together by common emotional themes, Jung and Riklin termed them *complexes*. A complex is thus a personally disturbing constellation of ideas connected together by common feeling-tone (Jung, 1913, p. 599). For example, the individual caught up in a conflict over relations with his or her father would be said to have a "father complex"; the individual experiencing anxiety and frustration in sexual matters would be characterized as having a "sex complex."

Complexes are revealed in word-association experiments through a number of diagnostic signs:

1. Longer than average reaction time
2. Repetition of the stimulus word by the subject as if he or she had not heard it
3. Mishearing of the stimulus word as some other word
4. Expressive bodily movements like laughing, twitching
5. Reaction composed of more than one word
6. Very superficial reaction to stimulus word, as in rhyming to the sound: e.g., to sin—subject responds with "to win"
7. Meaningless reaction: made-up words
8. Failure to respond at all
9. Perseveration of response: continuing to respond to previous word even after new stimulus word is presented
10. Defective reproduction: subject drastically altering responses when list is administered for second time
11. Slips of the tongue: stammering

In addition to these 11 unique patterns of response, there were, Jung discovered, also characteristic and stable differences between men and women, and between educated and uneducated subjects' responses. Consider Table 7.2.

In Jung's laboratory, women characteristically took longer to respond to the stimulus words than their male counterparts at both educational levels. Generally, Jung found that educated people responded faster than uneducated.

TABLE 7.2   Educational Level and Reaction Time (in seconds)

	Educated Subjects	Uneducated Subjects
Men	1.3	1.6
Women	1.7	2.2
Average	1.5	1.9

From Jung, 1905, vol. 2, p. 227

An Illustrative Case of Word-Association Diagnosis

One of Jung's clinic patients, a 30-year-old woman, had been diagnosed as a depressed schizophrenic, and most of the hospital staff agreed that the prognosis for her recovery was poor. Jung felt otherwise. He therefore administered a modified form of the association test. Some of the woman's responses were very suggestive. Consider the graph of her responses in Figure 7.1.

Each of the words graphed in Figure 7.1 has a reaction time that exceeds the average reaction time for an educated woman. The height of the bars indicates the relative differences in length of reaction time above the mean for educated women. Most outstanding of the woman's responses was her inability to offer any reply to the word "obstinate." Jung confronted the woman with the results of her word-association test. He asked her to comment on the various stimulus words that had produced such lengthy reaction times.

To "angel," the woman replied, "Of course, that is my child whom I have lost." There followed a great upheaval. To "obstinate," she responded, "It means nothing to me." To "evil," she again refused to comment. But to the word "blue" (not illustrated in the graph) she replied, "Those are the eyes of the child I have lost." Jung asked her why the child's eyes had so impressed her: "They were so wonderfully blue when the child was born." Jung noticed that this last reply was accompanied by much emotion. He again asked her why she was upset: "Well, she did not have the eyes of my husband." With further questioning, the entire story was told.

The child's eyes had so upset her mother because they resembled the eyes of a former lover. In the town where she was born, the woman had fallen in love with a wealthy young man of the aristocracy. Being herself of a well-to-do but nonaristocratic family, the girl and her parents had concluded that a romance with the young man was not feasible. At the insistence of her family, she married another young man and remained happy until the fifth year of the marriage. A friend from her hometown came

FIGURE 7.1   **Relative reaction time for critical stimulus words.**

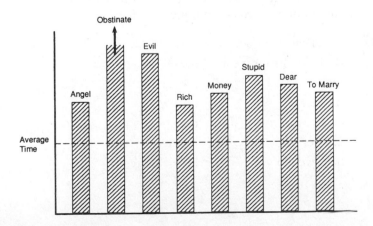

to visit in that fifth year and informed her that her present marriage had hurt and displeased the wealthy aristocrat she had once loved. For the first time she was made to realize that he had loved her in return. She immediately repressed her feelings.

Two weeks later, as she was bathing her two children, a small boy and the wonderfully blue-eyed girl, she noticed the girl sucking on the bath sponge. The woman knew she should stop the child because there was good reason to believe that the town's water supply was infested with typhus, and the bath water had not been boiled. She hesitated and finally purposefully did not interfere. Shortly thereafter, the girl got typhoid fever and died, but the little boy survived.

The act was symbolic, a denial of her marriage through murder of the first child. Jung felt obligated to confront her with the fact of her crime, the significance of which she seemingly failed to understand. Within three weeks she was sufficiently recovered from her depression to be released from the hospital:

> I traced her for fifteen years, and there was no relapse. That depression fitted her case psychologically; she was a murderess and under other circumstances would have deserved capital punishment. Instead of going to jail she was sent to the lunatic asylum. I practically saved her from the punishment of insanity by putting an enormous burden on her conscience. For if one can accept one's sin one can live with it. (Jung, 1968, p. 61)

Practical Uses of Word Associations

Jung became quite adept in the use of the word-association test for diagnosis of unconscious complexes. He even adapted the method for use in cases involving criminal proceedings. The guilt or innocence of the accused could be established by careful interrogation with the help of modified word lists containing critical words relating to key aspects of the crime (Jung, 1905, pp. 318 ff.).

Jung and his associates also employed the word-association tests for comparisons of unconscious complexes among members of a family. Thus, for example, Jung (1909b, pp. 466 ff.) investigated the associations of the members of 24 families, collecting in the process some 22,000 responses. The resulting data were analyzed in a variety of ways, but the outstanding overall result was the similarity of content among members of a single family. For example, the associations of a mother and daughter in different sessions to the same stimulus words were quite revealing:

STIMULUS WORD	MOTHER	DAUGHTER
law	God's commandment	Moses
potato	tuber	tuber
strange	traveler	travelers
brother	dear to me	dear
to kiss	mother	mother
merry	happy child	little children

(from Jung, 1909b, p. 469)

Not only do the content of the mother's and daughter's associations match, but the choice of response word is virtually identical in several cases. Clearly, the fleeting thoughts of members of a family are not random and richly varied, as we might expect. Rather, there is a striking mutuality of expression and feeling (cf. Laing's study of the family in Chapter 10).

JUNG'S CONCEPT OF LIBIDO

At the beginning of his career, Jung saw the possibility that his word-association studies could offer objective support for Freud's psychoanalytic concepts. It is easy to understand why. Subjects' inhibitions and long reaction times to the stimulus words, along with their heightened physiological responsivity, could serve as *quantitative* evidence that these individuals had latent feeling-toned ideas that they would or could not directly express but that produced demonstrable verbal and physiological reactions.

He had, Jung realized, developed a method of exploring the unconscious comparable to Freud's investigations of that domain with free association. In the early days, Jung and Freud agreed on what they found there: namely, repressed, unacceptable infantile sexual and aggressive strivings.

As Jung continued his explorations of the unconscious, he found it more and more difficult to accept Freud's insistence that sexual motives were the basis of neurosis (Jung, 1961, Chapter 5). The central Freudian concept of libido as a generalized and universal pleasure drive rooted firmly in an individual's developing sexuality caused Jung no small amount of difficulty. Early in their relationship Jung wrote to Freud and inquired,

> Is it not conceivable, in view of the limited conception of sexuality that prevails nowadays, that the sexual terminology should be reserved only for the most extreme forms of your "libido," and that a less offensive collective term should be established for *all* the libidinal manifestations? (Freud & Jung, 1974, p. 25)

Freud's reply to Jung's suggestion bears reporting:

> I appreciate your motives in trying to sweeten the sour apple, but I do not think you will be successful. Even if we call the unconscious "psychoid," it will still be the unconscious, and even if we do not call the driving force in the broadened conception of sexuality "libido," it will still be libido. . . . We cannot avoid resistances, why not face up to them from the start? (Freud & Jung, 1974, p. 28)

Jung's objections to Freud's sexual hypothesis abated for a while. But increasingly, as his own powers of perception and professional judgment grew, Jung discovered forces and content within the unconscious quite unlike anything in the Freudian scheme.

For Jung, then, the fundamental psychic energy was still to be termed *libido,* but his conception of this primal force drastically differed from the classical psychoanalytic view. In fact, in his English publications, Jung began to use the word *horme* for libido because he felt that the substitution avoided confusion with the established Freudian usage. *Horme* is a Greek word that means "force," "attack," "press," "urgency"

(Jung, 1914, p. 190n.). Thus *horme* more adequately conveyed Jung's conception of libido as a general psychic energy.

THE PRINCIPLES OF EQUIVALENCE AND ENTROPY

For Jung, libido was a more neutral form of general psychic energy, corresponding to an *intentionality* in living things (1912, p. 137). Libido, as a form of energy, may be shaped, channeled, suppressed, repressed, blocked, or expressed. In all cases, however, it is to be understood as a *creative* life force, the same creative force that underlies myths, religious dogma, and neurosis.

If libido is dammed up, repressed, an equivalent or substitute expression must take its place in consciousness. Hence, for Jung, as for Freud, repressed libido obeys what Jung called the *principle of equivalence:* When conscious psychic energy is repressed, an unconscious substitute, or symbolic alternative idea, assimilates the energy of the banished idea and takes a place in consciousness (Jung, 1948, p. 19; 1912, pp. 143–144). Following the laws of thermodynamics, Jung agreed with Freud that psychic energy never ceases to exist, despite transformations in form. Repressed ideas embodying psychic energy simply find expression in *equivalent* symbolic forms. Unlike Freud, Jung did not regard these transformations as necessarily neurotic. Rather, Jung defined such modifications as potentially healthy "canalizations of libido," that is, as creative, almost poetic, transfers of psychic energy to mythic or allegorical symbols.

Transformations or canalizations of libido are more than mere examples of psychic energy equivalence. Canalizations of libido from one form of expression to another are guided in humans by an inherent tendency toward symbol making. A symbol is, therefore, a "libido analog." Throughout history humans have created symbols and woven them into themes called myths. They have practiced rituals, both religious and magical, that center around unconsciously created symbols. In work with neurotic and psychotic patients, Jung found evidence that this process of converting libido into symbolic expressions has a certain continuity with the symbol making of our primordial ancestors. Though Freud had pointed to the symbolization of dreams as personally necessary disguises of unacceptable motives, Jung now focused attention on the transmission of symbol-making processes from human forebear to human descendant.

The principle of equivalence has a necessary and complementary coprinciple in Jung's theory. Based on the second law of thermodynamics, as the principle of equivalence had been based on the first law, Jung formulated a psychological counterpart to physical *entropy.* According to Jung's *principle of entropy,* transformations of psychic energy are possible only because there is a gradient of intensity among ideas. Some mental representatives are more intense, hold more energy, than others. The principle of entropy says, in effect, that psychic energy flows from the most intensely energized ideas to the least intensely energized ideas. Ultimately, the mental system strives to an equalization of differences (Jung, 1948, p. 26). Thus, for example, an individual torn between two opposite attitudes or feelings will eventually resolve the conflict by pursuing a less intense third course of action or thinking comprising the energy of the two more intense extremes (1948, p. 26).

Transcending the Unconscious: Sources of the Hypothesis

The Sun's Phallus

Staring out the window of the hospital corridor, a young schizophrenic patient beckoned Jung to his side. If you half shut your eyes, he told Jung, and stared at the sun, you could see the sun's phallus. If you then moved your head side to side, the sun's phallus would also move. The young man concluded his strange remarks to Jung with the matter-of-fact assertion that *the movement of the sun's phallus was the origin of the wind* (Jung, 1931, pp. 151–152; 1912, pp. 100, 157; and 1936, pp. 50–51).

Jung had this enigmatic encounter with a psychotic 30-year-old clerk in 1906. Under normal circumstances, Jung would have dismissed the episode as one more strange hallucination or fantasy characteristic of schizophrenia. Four years later, however, in 1910, while researching in the field of mythology, Jung came across a book that reproduced the rituals of the ancient Mithraic Greek religious cult. Professor Albrecht Dieterich, the author of the book, quoted one of the cult's visions:

> And likewise the so-called tube, the origin of the ministering wind. For you will see hanging down from the disc of the sun something that looks like a tube. And towards the regions westward it is as though there were an infinite east wind. But if the other wind should prevail towards the regions of the east, you will in like manner see the vision veering in that direction. (Quoted in Jung, 1931, pp. 150–151; italics added)

Jung was startled by the correspondence between this ancient pre-Christian myth and the young schizophrenic clerk's hallucinatory vision. There was no doubt that the clerk could not have read Dieterich's book, having been institutionalized before its publication. Nor could Jung explain the correspondence as a product of the young man's educational and cultural training because he had only the equivalent of a secondary school education and his occupation and habits precluded any possibility of travel. Further mythological study convinced Jung that the notion of a sun phallus, or its equivalent, a divine phallus, was a common theme in many cultures of the past. The problem remained to account for the presence of the myth in the unconscious and conscious mind of a contemporary schizophrenic.

The Snake Dream

Another of Jung's patients, a young military officer, succumbed to a hysterical neurosis characterized by three symptoms. First, he suffered severe attacks of pain in the chest. Second, he experienced several episodes of choking "as if there were a lump in his throat." Finally, he was unable to walk normally because of stabbing pains in his left heel (Jung, 1931, p. 146).

In psychotherapy with Jung, the source of the first two symptoms was uncovered and followed the usual patterns of hysterical neurosis. The young man had been hurt and humiliated by a love affair that terminated when the girl became engaged to another man. He had denied his hurt and shattered self-esteem, but unconsciously he felt that "his heart was broken," and the idea that she had terminated the affair was "hard to swallow." Thus, as Freud had suggested, a painful psychological experience had been converted into a painful and symbolic cluster of bodily symptoms. Though the pain in the throat and the choking attacks, along with the chest pains, were eliminated when these feelings were made conscious, the young soldier's third symptom, a stabbing pain in his left heel, remained intractable.

Jung turned to an analysis of the man's dreams. The officer reported a dream in which *he was bitten in the heel by a snake and instantly paralyzed.* Analysis of the dream revealed the expected associations of the girl as a "snake" who had betrayed him; of a mother who had overprotected and thus "crippled" him; of a certain tendency to "girlishness" in himself for which he overcompensated by joining the military. But Jung felt that he detected something more fundamental, more primitive and universal in the man's dream. It was as though the Genesis saying: "And I will put enmity between thee and the woman, and between thy seed and her seed; it shall bruise thy head, and thou shalt bruise his heel . . ." had been transformed by the man's unconscious mind into a personal mythic symbol of his recent romantic upset.

For some reason, this singularly unreligious soldier had felt the *need for mythic expression* of his psychic pain. Jung concluded that the man's knowledge of the Bible, scanty though it was, had lain dormant until his unconscious seized upon it (1931, p. 147). For the Bible story had provided just the right medium for conversion of a personal conflict into an opportunity to express a deeper sentiment in allegorical fashion (Jung, 1968, p. 116). Certainly, the soldier's unconscious could have chosen a more secular form of symbolism to express his pain. But, in fact, he chose a universal myth.

Consequently, Jung was convinced that a part of the unconscious mind transcends the personal experiences of the individual, as exemplified by the sun's phallus fantasy. This unconscious subsystem embodies some of the past experiences of the human race. Moreover, that same transpersonal unconscious domain may employ personal experience as a vehicle for mythological, allegorical expression of age-old themes, as exemplified by the soldier's snake dream, "for the dream of the snake reveals a fragment of psychic activity that has nothing whatever to do with the dreamer as a modern individual . . ." (Jung, 1931, p. 148). Such a dream could not be a product solely of the soldier's personal experiences. Fantasies like the sun's phallus and the snake dream could have originated only in the individual's recognition of the cumulative experiences of the human race. To the part of the mind responsible for universal myth transmission Jung gave the name *collective unconscious.*

PERSONAL SOURCES OF JUNG'S INTEREST IN MYSTICAL AND TRANSPERSONAL CONCEPTS

Jung's writings are studded with a seemingly endless array of mythological examples and their similarities to the dreams, paintings, and fantasies of normal and abnormal personalities. But there was an even more fundamental source of Jung's conviction that a suprapersonal unconscious exists. In his autobiography, *Memories, Dreams, Reflections,* written just before his death in 1961 with the collaboration of his personal secretary and confidante, Aniela Jaffé, Jung provided his readers with a series of rare and penetrating glimpses into his inner life, indeed, into the intimate workings of his own unconscious. The entire book is laden with gods, spirits, and fantasy figures that populated Jung's inner mental life. One event in particular is relevant in the present context of our discussion of the collective unconscious, because out of it grew Jung's conviction that "... there are things in the psyche which I do not produce, but which produce themselves and have their own life" (1961, p. 183).

Jung reported that between 1913 and 1917 he was seized by a series of visions, fantasies, or mystical experiences. Several personages made contact with Jung during these experiences; that is, they emerged from his collective unconscious. Several of these figures subsequently had long conversations together with Jung about topics of which Jung could have consciously known very little. One particular figure, whom Jung named Philemon, arose from the metamorphosis of an earlier fantasy figure, Elijah:

> Philemon was a pagan and brought with him an Egypto-Hellenistic atmosphere with a Gnostic coloration. His figure appeared to me in the following dream. There was a blue sky, like the sea, covered not by clouds but by flat brown clods of earth. It looked as if the clods were breaking apart and the blue water of the sea [was] becoming visible between them. But the water was the blue sky. Suddenly there appeared from the right a winged being sailing across the sky. I saw that it was an old man with the horns of a bull. He held a bunch of four keys, one of which he clutched as if he were about to open a lock. He had the wings of a kingfisher with its characteristic colors. (1961, pp. 182–183)

At first Jung did not understand the dream. He tried to impress it upon his memory by painting it. During the time he was painting that picture, he discovered in his garden a dead kingfisher bird. "I was thunderstruck, for kingfishers are quite rare in the vicinity of Zürich and I have never since found a dead one" (1961, p. 183).

For Jung, the significance of the Philemon figure lay in the insight that such apparitions represented a force beyond himself, and beyond his personal experiences and personal unconscious mind. Philemon said things during the fantasies that Jung felt he himself had not consciously thought. "He confronted me in an objective manner, and I understood that there is something in me which can say things that I do not know and do not intend, things which may even be directed against me" (1961, p. 183).

The Philemon "fantasy" occurred sometime between the middle of December and early January 1913, approximately one year after Jung's acrimonious break with Freud. Jung had been extending his theoretical talents in directions that Freud found quite unacceptable, both because Jung's ideas clashed with his own and because he felt sure Jung was heading in a mystical direction. For Jung's part, he saw himself poised on the edge of a precipice. Visions and fantasies had been bombarding his consciousness and threatening to take complete control. Jung knew, as of course a trained psychiatrist would, that he might be on the verge of engulfment by a full-blown psychosis. In his view, therefore, he was faced with a momentous decision: Should he attempt to fight off these assaults of the unconscious to remain, as it were, in the land of the living, or should he willfully make the descent and attempt to make rational sense of his experiences?

> My enduring these storms was a question of brute strength. Others have been shattered by them—Nietzsche, and Hölderlin, and many others. But there was a

demonic strength in me, and from the beginning there was no doubt in my mind that I must find the meaning of what I was experiencing in these fantasies. When I endured these assaults of the unconscious I had an unswerving conviction that I was obeying a higher will, and that feeling continued to uphold me until I had mastered the task. (Jung, 1961, p. 177)

Thus, between 1913 and 1917 Jung thought himself engaged on a voluntary exploration of his own personal and collective unconscious. There is considerable division of opinion over whether Jung's descent into his fantasies and dreams was as voluntary as he suggested in his memoirs. On at least one occasion, for example, after Jung had allowed himself to be engulfed by a vision in which he and a "brown-skinned savage" murdered a mythological Germanic hero, he was so overcome with disgust that he came close to suicide. He heard a voice that demanded he immediately interpret the vision or shoot himself with the loaded revolver he kept in his night table drawer (1961, p. 180). Experiences like this one, so characteristic of psychotic disorganization, have caused scholarly commentators on Jung to be divided into two camps.

The first of these schools of opinion is represented by writers like Aniela Jaffé (1971) and Laurens Van der Post (1975) who have accepted Jung's own view that his 1913 to 1917 "stormy period" was a careful and deliberate voyage of exploration. According to this view, Jung was a visionary, who skillfully charted unknown psychological realms with courage and determination. Jung phrased it this way:

It is of course ironical that I, a psychiatrist, should at almost every step of my experiment have run into the same psychic material which is the stuff of psychosis and is found in the insane. This is the fund of unconscious images which fatally confuse the mental patient. But it is also the matrix of a mythopoeic imagination which has vanished from our rational age. . . . Unpopular, ambiguous, and dangerous, [such an imagination] is a voyage of discovery to the other pole of the world. (1961, pp. 188–189)

In the contrasting school of opinion, represented by writers like Paul J. Stern (1976) and Henri Ellenberger (1970), there exists the equally certain conviction that Jung's voyage was not visionary but psychotic, not voluntary but uncontrollable. It must immediately be pointed out, however, that the question cannot be definitively answered on the basis of the published evidence. Each of us will form our own opinion, but it is important that such opinion be informed. For even if we decide that Jung had indeed undergone a psychotic episode, we cannot deny that he emerged from his descent with ideas and concepts that stand as creative, if yet untested, contributions to psychology.

The 1913 to 1917 period of engulfment was not an isolated episode of visionary experience for Jung. From childhood, Jung engaged in confrontations with his own, seemingly independent, inner life. Many of the concepts of his later theoretical writings can be traced to Jung's gift for universalizing and externalizing his inner turmoil (cf. Atwood & Stolorow, 1977b; Jaffé, 1979).

Themes of Jung's Boyhood

To judge from the evidence of his memoirs and from information provided by his biographers, Jung appears to have been beset with a series of (perhaps) serious emotional difficulties in childhood. Two personal themes in particular seem to have arisen by the age of 12 from Jung's attempts to deal with his difficulties. The first theme was embodied in his conviction that he was actually two persons: the child he objectively seemed to be and an authoritative wise old man who had lived in the 18th century, some hundred years before Jung's birth. So powerful was his belief that at least part of him belonged to the previous century, that, occasionally in doing school-work, he would write "1786" instead of the correct date, 1886. The second theme, closely allied to the first, was contained in Jung's secretly held belief that certain thoughts, dreams, visions, and fantasies he periodically experienced were truly important, externally derived revelations, "secret" wisdom that only rare few people were privileged to acquire.

Both of these themes, as we shall later see, became cornerstones of Jung's theoretical style. But it is important at the outset of our brief survey of the personal sources of his concepts to acknowledge with Paul Stern (1976, p. 10) that an examination of the origins of Jung's ideas in no way prejudges their validity.

The Stone

Between the ages of seven and nine, Jung had several experiences that helped form his belief that he was two personalities. The first experience involved a game that Jung played with a large chunk of stone that jutted from a garden wall. Frequently, when alone, Jung would mount the stone and pass the time in reverie:

> "I am sitting on top of this stone and it is underneath." But the stone also could say "I" and think: "I am lying here on this slope and he is sitting on top of me." The question then arose: "Am I the one who is sitting on the stone, or am I the stone on which *he* is sitting?" This question always perplexed me, and I would stand up, wondering who was what now. The answer remained totally unclear, and my uncertainty was accompanied by a feeling of curious and fascinating darkness. (Jung, 1961, p. 20)

Jung's ability to shift mental perspective to that of the stone was interpreted by him as his first discovery of the "mysterious" in life. When the very religious adults around him (his father was a minister and his mother a minister's daughter) tried to "pump" religious teachings into him, Jung would think to himself: "Yes, but there is something else, something very secret that people don't know about" (1961, p. 22).

The Mannequin

When Jung was 10 years old, he carved from a wooden ruler a small male figure, a "mannequin" approximately two inches long. With ink and small bits of wool, Jung created for the mannequin a frock coat, shiny black boots, and a top hat; from a wooden pencil case, he devised a little bed for the figure. Inside the pencil case, Jung deposited, along with the mannequin and makeshift bed, an oblong blackish stone that he had painted with watercolors: "This was *his* [the mannequin's] stone. All this was a great secret. Secretly I took the case to . . . the attic at the top of the house . . . and hid it with great satisfaction on one of the beams under the roof—for no one must ever see it! . . . I felt safe, and the tormenting sense of being at odds with myself was gone" (Jung, 1961, p. 21).

Thereafter, whenever Jung felt under stress, he would conjure up in his mind the image of his hidden mannequin and feel secure. Sometimes he would create for the mannequin small scrolls of paper on which, in a secret language of his own invention, he would write a particularly pleasing saying. Each addition of a scroll was treated as a solemn ceremonial act to be guarded as an inviolable secret, "for the safety of my life depended on it" (1961, p. 22).

It is possible to interpret both the philosophical stone dialogue and the creation of the wooden mannequin as attempts by Jung to concretize and therefore control his frightening belief that he was two persons. The stone and the mannequin may be thought of as externalizations of the second personality that Jung felt he harbored. Jung's own interpretation was that he had early come into contact with one of the great secrets of human nature: the existence of the collective unconscious from which these urges and actions had emerged. However, in the light of Jung's family circumstances, it seems possible that there were more mundane causes for his actions.

Jung's father, the Reverend Dr. Paul Jung, had many of his own boyhood dreams crushed. Failing to become a university professor of Oriental languages, he settled for the vocation of country parson, a wife who was stronger willed and an opposite personality, and a lifelong history of worry over his health. Jung reports that his father's depressed spirits and morose personality were due to a religious crisis in which his father was consumed by doubts (1961, p. 73). Toward the end of his life, his father became extremely hypochondriacal and believed that he suffered from a variety of diseases.

Jung's mother, Emilie, was, on the surface, an exact opposite personality to his father. Relations between Jung's parents were strained, and at least part of his own childhood sorrow stemmed from the parental disputes he observed. To make matters worse, Jung was convinced that his mother was possessed of two personalities: one, the observable character of the pleasant, plump housewife; the other, a witch, prophetess, and seeress who communicated with spirits. Jung described his mother in this way:

> By day she was a loving mother, but at night she seemed uncanny. Then she was like one of those seers who is at the same time a strange animal, like a priestess in a bear's cave. Archaic and ruthless; ruthless as truth and nature. (1961, p. 50)

The "uncanny" personality in his mother seems to have emerged only at special moments. "She would then speak as if talking to herself, but what she said was aimed at me and usually struck to the core of my being, so that I was stunned into silence" (1961, p. 49). Jung early decided to keep his own inner life hidden from her because he was unsure just how much control the uncanny personality exerted over the housewife personality (cf. Atwood & Stolorow, 1977b, p. 199).

Jung's propensity for endowing people with two personalities may have had its origins in his need to cope with feelings of inferiority. Thus his mother's uncanny personality emerged frequently when she was scolding young Carl or trying to instill in him good manners so that he would not embarrass the family with friends. It may have been easier for him to believe that a second personality within his mother administered these lessons. Likewise, his conviction that he himself was two persons seems to have emerged completely during a scolding he received from a friend's father for some misbehavior related to the man's boat.

. . . I was seized with rage that this fat, ignorant boor [i.e., the friend's father] should dare to insult ME. This ME was not only grown up, but important, an authority, a person with office and dignity, an old man, an object of respect and awe. Yet the contrast with reality was so grotesque that in the midst of my fury I suddenly stopped myself, for the question rose to my lips:"Who in the world are you, anyway?" . . . Then, to my intense confusion, it occurred to me that I was actually two different persons. One of them was the schoolboy who could not grasp algebra and was far from sure of himself; the other was important, a high authority, a man not to be trifled with, as powerful and influential as this [friend's angry father]. This "other" was an old man who lived in the 18th century, wore buckled shoes and a white wig, and went driving in a fly with high, concave rear wheels. . . . (Jung, 1961, p. 34)

The exact imagery of Jung's other personality had been adopted from a piece of terra cotta sculpture that depicted a well-known medical doctor of the day and his patient. The motive for adoption of this second personality is transparently clear in Jung's own account. It is similar to the motives that lay behind his earlier confusion regarding who was the stone and who was the stone-sitter:

. . . it was strangely reassuring and calming to sit on my stone. Somehow it would free me of all my doubts. Whenever I thought that I was the stone, the conflict ceased. "The stone has no uncertainties, no urge to communicate, and is eternally the same for thousands of years," I would think, "while I am only a passing phenomenon which bursts into all kinds of emotions, like a flame that flares up quickly and then goes out." I was but the sum of my emotions, and the Other in me was the timeless, imperishable stone. (Jung, 1961, p. 42)

Jung's uncertainties and doubts drove him near the edge of madness, for two dreams revealed to him secrets so blasphemous that he was terrified even to think them.

The Phallus-God

The first of Jung's terrifying secret dreams occurred between the ages of three and four. Descending a stone stairway, he came upon a rounded archway closed off by a green curtain. In the dream, he pushed aside the curtain to expose a large rectangular chamber constructed of stone. In the center of the chamber stood a magnificent golden king's throne:

Something was standing on [the throne] which I thought at first was a tree trunk 12 to 15 feet high and about one and a half to two feet thick. It was a huge thing, reaching almost to the ceiling. But it was of curious composition: it was made of skin and naked flesh, and on top there was something like a rounded head with no face and no hair. On the very top of the head was a single eye, gazing motionlessly upward. (Jung, 1961, p. 12)

Jung was paralyzed with terror at the sight of this huge column of flesh and was consumed with the fear that at any moment it would crawl off the throne. "At that moment I heard from outside and above me my mother's voice. She called out, 'Yes, just look at him. That is the man-eater!' " (1961, p. 12). The dream haunted Jung for years, causing him nightmares when he could sleep, and enormous fear on those nights when sleep would not come.

Jung later interpreted the dream as a condensation of his childhood fears of "Jesuits," about whom he had heard some frightening things. The column of flesh was, of course, a phallus, a phallus-god, in fact. For Jung, the Lord Jesus was the "above-ground" counterpart of this subterranean monster. "Lord Jesus never became quite real for me, never quite acceptable, never quite lovable, for again and again I would think of his underground counterpart, a frightful revelation that had been accorded me without my seeking it" (1961, p. 13).

It is possible that the Christian doctrine Jung had been taught by his mother and father, and which had engendered such skepticism, Jung later thought to have been somehow connected with this dream. In any event, on its surface, the dream suggests a small child's confusion about the Christian doctrine of eating the body and blood of Christ condensed with the notion of "man-eater" in the form of a wormlike column of flesh. It is also possible that in his later recollection of the dream, Jung added to it some of the anger he felt when being "pumped" full of religious teachings.

The Throne

Jung experienced one other dreamlike vision that has relevance to our discussion. One afternoon upon leaving school, his thoughts were occupied with the beauty of the day, the beauty of the nearby cathedral roof glinting in the sunlight, and the magnificence that God displayed in such creations. The image of God sitting on his golden throne in the beautiful clear blue sky came into Jung's mind. Suddenly he froze. No other thoughts would come, but deep within he knew that something momentous, something monstrous and blasphemous, was about to occur to him. For days he went about in a fog, attempting to ward off the dreaded thought and fearing that were he to entertain the idea, he would be plunged immediately into hell.

Three nights later, awaking from a restless sleep, Jung was struck with the thought: "Now, it is coming, now it's serious! *I must think.* It must be thought out beforehand. . . . Who wants to force me to think something I don't know and don't want to know?" (1961, p. 37). Jung finally convinced himself that it was God who intended that he think the unthinkable as a critical test of faith. Gathering his courage, Jung allowed the image he had been choking back for three days and nights to flood into awareness:

> I saw before me the cathedral, the blue sky. God sits on His golden throne, high above the world—and from under the throne an enormous turd falls upon the sparkling new roof, shatters it, and breaks the walls of the cathedral asunder. (1961, p. 39)

Jung immediately experienced relief from his turmoil. He explained to himself that his image of God befouling his own cathedral was God's way of revealing to him that "God could be something terrible." This dream became Jung's boyhood sorrowful secret, a secret that motivated him to explore his father's theological books in search of further clarification and reassurance. But the only result was his conviction that all these wise authors could shed very little light on genuine religious experiences.

The Welcomed Attack

Jung did not get on very well with his schoolmates. One day in his 12th year, during morning recess from class, another boy shoved young Carl from behind so hard that

Carl struck his head on a curbstone and nearly lost consciousness. "At the moment I felt the blow the thought flashed through my mind: 'Now you won't have to go to school anymore' " (Jung, 1961, p. 30).

For the next six months, Carl did not attend school because he was overcome with fainting fits that mimicked epileptic seizures. His worried parents consulted a variety of doctors, one of whom actually diagnosed his condition as epilepsy: "I knew what epileptic fits were like and I inwardly laughed at such nonsense" (1961, p. 31). The young Carl was rather enjoying himself with his free time away from school, but the enjoyment was soon to end shamefully.

Hiding behind a shrub in his father's garden, young Carl eavesdropped on a conversation between a friend of the family and his own worried father. To the friend's polite query about his son, Carl's father replied,

> "Ah, that's a sad business. . . . The doctors no longer know what is wrong with him. They think it may be epilepsy. It would be dreadful if he were incurable. I have lost what little I had, and what will become of the boy if he cannot earn his own living?" (Jung, 1961, p. 31)

Jung recalls that his father's remark galvanized him to action. He resolved to change his malingering ways and rushed to his father's library to begin studying his Latin grammar book. Within 10 minutes he had the "finest of fainting fits." He recovered and deliberately resumed studying through a succession of three more fainting attacks. His days of freedom from school were over:

> Gradually the recollection of how it had all come about returned to me, and I saw clearly that I myself had arranged this whole disgraceful situation. That was why I had never been seriously angry with the schoolmate who pushed me over. I knew that he had been put up to it, so to speak, and that the whole affair was a diabolical plot on my part. . . . The neurosis [i.e., the fainting fits] became another of my secrets, but it was a shameful secret. (Jung, 1961, p. 32)

The net effect of Jung's dreams, visions, and secrets was the creation of a lonely and withdrawn boy:

> My one great achievement during those years was that I resisted the temptation to talk about it with anyone. Thus the pattern of my relationship to the world was already prefigured: today as then I am a solitary, because I know things and must hint at things which other people do not know, and usually do not even want to know. (1961, pp. 41–42)

We have thus come full circle, returning to the two major themes of Jung's life with which we started. The first theme was the conviction that he was actually two persons. It is now easy to see the motives that shaped this belief. Jung's family dissatisfaction, his sense of inferiority, his religious skepticism in a home where religion was paramount, and his desire for inner peace necessitated the creation of the second personality as a haven, an immutable and stress-immune sanctuary. The second theme, namely that his inner experiences originated from some external source of revelation, later became the basis for Jung's ideas on the *collective unconscious,* the *archetypes* or inherited images that reside there, and *synchronicity* between internal psychic events and external equivalents. We take up each of these concepts in subsequent sections of this chapter.

Jung seems to have experienced an intense need to endow an external source, or at least an entity apart from himself, as the genesis of the feeling, dreams, and visions he experienced. In some acutely anguished way, Jung found it necessary to find a more believable substitute for the God that he suspected his own father doubted. He thus regarded his two personalities as real, that is, as genuine psychological achievements and as manifestations of higher, perhaps religious, wisdom. He viewed his visions and dreams as gifts of the same kind of wisdom, bestowed from the same unimpeachably holy source. He was thus adamant that his personalities were not evidence of a personality "split" or schizophrenic dissociation (1961, p. 45), and equally sure that his descent into the unconscious was a foray after psychological truth, not a folly of psychotic delusion. Whatever your opinion on these matters, the indisputable fact remains that Jung's theorizing was shaped by Jung's personalities.

STRUCTURE OF THE PSYCHE: EGO, PERSONAL, AND COLLECTIVE UNCONSCIOUS

In light of his clinical observations with schizophrenic patients such as the young visionary clerk, along with his own self-analysis from 1913 to 1917, Jung's approach to personality theory was necessarily different from Freud's. In Jung's view, the chief problem was to explain the individual's construction of fantasies and dreams that embody symbols and themes unlikely to be part of the individual's strictly personal experiences. He hypothesized, therefore, that the mind or total personality was divided into three major zones: the *conscious ego,* the *personal unconscious,* and the *collective unconscious.*

The Conscious Ego

The conscious ego, for Jung, corresponds roughly to what Freud meant by the same term. Functioning as the conscious part of personality, the ego includes all sense impressions and self-awareness. Consciousness, therefore, consists of all those internal and external events that are within our awareness at a given moment. By the same token, the ego can experience all that is conscious by simply directing attention to one or another sensory experience or to memories of such experiences.

The Personal Unconscious

Jung conceived of the second division of the mind, the personal unconscious, in a somewhat different way than Freud. Mental content that through disuse or inattention does not at the moment occupy our awareness, but which can become conscious at will, is classed as unconscious. (Freud would have called such momentarily latent content *preconscious.*) Even out of awareness, however, all the activities that normally take place consciously can also occur unconsciously (Jung, 1931, p. 144).

Therefore, the personal unconscious consists of all those contents that became unconscious simply because they lost their intensity and were forgotten or not attended to. Jung agreed with Freud, however, that the personal unconscious also contains ideas and impulses that have been actively withdrawn from consciousness by repression. Such content is unconscious because in the personal experience of the individual it involved motives unacceptable to his or her ego (1931, p. 151).

Despite the apparent agreement with Freud, Jung viewed the personal unconscious as more complex than simply the repository of *past* experience. For Jung, the unconscious is both *retrospective* and *prospective.* It is oriented not only by the individual's past but also by anticipations of his or her future. Jung's patients often had dreams that could aptly be described as "forward looking" in the sense that, though the individual was not yet aware of his or her decision or feelings, the dream revealed that the unconscious had already solved some problem or had already made some decision (1916, p. 255).

The unconscious also has a *compensatory* function. When an individual's conscious attitude leans too one-sidedly in a single direction, the unconscious may compensate for the imbalance by producing dreams or fantasies that emphasize the opposite tendency (Jung, 1916, pp. 252–253). Compensation may also be seen in dreams that make available to consciousness all that was subliminal or not attended to during the day.

Prospection and *compensation* may combine to aid in the individual's adaptation to life, as for example when the individual is confronted with a difficult problem. In the morning, the solution may pop suddenly into mind as if the problem had been continuously worked on while the individual was sleeping.

The Collective Unconscious

At a deeper level than the personal unconscious lies the *impersonal* or *transpersonal* unconscious. This transpersonal domain is "detached from anything personal and is common to all men, since its contents can be found everywhere" (Jung, 1917, p. 66). Consequently, as we previously pointed out, Jung termed the transpersonal layer of the unconscious the collective unconscious.

Stored within the recesses of the collective unconscious are the primordial images and ideas that have been common to all members of the race from the beginning of life. These images are not preformed; they have no concrete content. They are simply *possibilities* of action; *predispositions* to respond to external events in specific ways; *potentialities* of shaping experience in certain directions. They are, in short, flexible templates or models for current experience to follow (Jung, 1936, pp. 66 ff.).

These primordial images of the collective unconscious were termed by Jung the *archetypes,* in the sense of *prototypes* or molds of emotional reaction. As a kind of template or model, the archetypes serve to organize and shape the course of an individual's interactions with the external world and with the inner world of the personal unconscious. In this sense, Jung seems to have conceived of the *personal* unconscious as only the most superficial veneer of the entire unconscious domain.

ORIGIN OF THE ARCHETYPES

The collective unconscious is not a development of any *individual's* experience. It is inherited. Jung's arguments in this regard bear careful scrutiny because his various writings on the subject are often vague, contradictory, and abstract to a degree that makes unequivocal interpretation impossible.

Within the course of the history of the human race, certain fundamental day-to-day events *had* to be experienced by all members of the human family. For example, the rising and setting of the sun surely did not escape the notice of even the most primitive humans.

> One of the commonest and at the same time most impressive experiences is the apparent movement of the sun every day. We certainly cannot discover anything of the kind in the unconscious, so far as the known physical process is concerned. What we do find, on the other hand, is the myth of the sun-hero in all its countless variations. It is this myth, and not the actual physical process, that forms the sun archetype. The same can be said of the phases of the moon. *The archetype is a kind of readiness to produce over and over again the same or similar mythical ideas. Hence it seems as though what is impressed upon the unconscious were exclusively the subjective fantasy-ideas aroused by the physical process.* We may therefore assume that the archetypes are recurrent impressions made by subjective reactions. (Jung, 1917, p. 69; italics added)

Archetypes, therefore, are the cumulative effect of perpetually repeated experiences on the human nervous system's development. To say it another way, perhaps more precisely, it is *not* the memory of the actual *physical experience* itself that is inherited. The repetitive *subjective emotional reaction* to the event is impressed on human unconscious mental processes, and it is this *internal state,* this predisposition to react in a similar way to repetitions of the physical event, that is transmitted to future generations. Thus the collective unconscious's archetypes are a residue of ancestral emotional life (Jung, 1917, p. 77).

Symbol-Making Processes

Jung himself asked the most significant question of his theory: ". . . why does the psyche not register the actual process, instead of mere fantasies about the physical process?" Jung's answer centered around some well-known hypotheses about the mind of primitive humans, namely, James George Frazer's notion of *sympathetic magic* and Lévy-Bruhl's treatment of the *"participation mystique."*

Frazer postulated that early humans interpreted their world magically by assuming that events, though separated in time or space, could nevertheless affect one another. Frazer called this assumption "sympathetic magic." Such mental functioning is based on the conviction that through some *mysterious* or *unknowable* means, events and objects may exert a mutual reaction, a kind of sympathetic effect without physical causality. For example, some early people believed that the fingernail clippings and hanks of hair they stole from an enemy could be used to gain control over that individual. What was done to the nail fragments and hair, would, mysteriously, be done to their owner (Frazer, 1963).

Lévy-Bruhl went a step further and suggested that for the primitive mind the distinction between self and object, between what is "me, mine" and what is external to me, was vague and confused. For the primitive, what happens outside *is* happening inside (Jung, 1931, p. 154).

For early humans, then, what was of supreme importance was not the external physical event, or an objective conception of cause and effect. In fact, they probably did not make these distinctions. For these people, the ultimate reality was the self, its emotions, and its desires. Crucial for early humans was the net effect of reality on *them,* for "his emotions are more important to him than physics; therefore what he registers is his emotional fantasies. . . . It is not thunder and lightning, not rain and cloud that remain as images in the psyche, but the fantasies caused by the affects they arouse" (1931, pp. 154–155).

Hence, the descendants of early humans do not store within their brains the exact photographic copies of their ancestors' experiences. Each successive culture, each individual, creates afresh the myth of the sun god, or the hero, or the god of thunder when external events demand reaction. The *mythological tendency,* the predisposition to respond to these external events in specific ways, and the disposition to be emotionally affected by such events are the real legacy of past generations. "The primitive mentality does not *invent* myths, it *experiences* them" (Jung, 1940, p. 154).

Jung subsequently devoted a significant part of his life to discovering and elucidating specific archetypal images as they appeared in mythological stories, dreams, fantasies, and in paintings. Presumably, there is no a priori limit to the number of archetypes that are possible. Among the most frequently appearing, however, were the following.

Child-God Archetype

The Christ Child and personifications of children as elves or dwarfs are depicted throughout legend and religious lore as having divine or mystical powers. Among his patients Jung discovered cases of women who believed that they had an imaginary child. Symbolically, in a purely psychological sense, a *child* represents what Jung called "futurity." That is to say, children are *potentially* the adults they are in the process of becoming. A child may symbolize anticipation of future events and is likely to make its appearance as an archetype when an individual is in the process of important life decisions (Jung, 1940, p. 164).

Mother Archetype

The Mother archetype may be elicited from an individual's collective unconscious in response to a real mother, mother-in-law, grandmother, or stepmother. Even figurative mothers may provoke the emergence of the Mother archetype as symbolized by a wife, Divine Mother (Virgin Mary), an institution: Alma Mater, the Church, or any event, place, or person associated with fertility and fruitfulness.

The Mother archetype can be either positive or negative, light or dark, good or evil. For example, the goddess of fate (Moira) can be kind and generous, or remorseless and heartless. Evil-Mother archetype symbols abound: the witch, the dragon (or any devouring and entwining animal) (Jung, 1938, p. 82). Thus the Mother archetype includes both the loving and the terrible mother.

Trickster or Magician Archetype

Jung explored the figure of the Trickster or Magician through a variety of myths, most notably in Native American mythology. Characteristic of this mythical figure is his fondness for sly jokes, malicious pranks, and his dual nature: half animal, half human. The demonic figures of the Old Testament, even the characterization of Yahweh himself as Trickster undergoing transformation into a divine savior, embody this age-old myth (Jung, 1954, p. 256).

Hero Archetype

According to Jung, the finest expression of the symbol-making capacity of the collective unconscious is the figure of the Hero, or its opposite, the demon (e.g., Anti-Christ, Satan). Hero myths are common to many cultures and tend to share the same characteristics. The Hero defeats evil, slays the dragon or monster, usually near water, suffers punishment for another, or rescues the vanquished and downtrodden (Jung, 1917, p. 99).

Shadow as Archetype

Within our personal unconscious there are repressed, unacceptable motives, tendencies, and desires. There is thus within us an inferior, undesirable aspect to our personality. Jung calls this side of our inner life the Shadow, the "dark half" of personality. It is the side of ourselves that we would prefer not to recognize.

Mythologically, Shadow symbols include demons, devils, and evil ones. This archetype may be evoked in our relations with another when we feel terribly uncomfortable with a person but are unable to specify exactly what provokes the distress. We sense an immediate dislike for some people without being able to verbalize the cause. In such cases we may be projecting our shadow side onto them because we recognize in these persons something that we do not like in ourselves (Jung, 1917, p. 95).

There is danger in the Shadow archetype. If we fail to recognize the "inferior" dark side of ourselves, there is the possibility of dissociation of the Shadow from the ego. In this case, the personality would be incomplete, truncated. One or the other aspect could gain dominance. Thus the Shadow is common to all people. It is both a personal and a collective unconscious phenomenon (Jung, 1968, pp. 21–22). It may be used as a synonym for the personal unconscious, or as the name of an archetype.

Animus and Anima Archetypes

During the period when Jung was experimenting with the descent into his unconscious, he asked himself the question "What am I really doing?" Abruptly, a "voice" within said: "It is art." Jung was astonished and somewhat annoyed—astonished because the voice was a woman's, and annoyed because he did not agree with her assessment.

Then I thought, "Perhaps my unconscious is forming a personality that is not me, but which is insisting on coming through to expression." I knew for a certainty that the voice had come from a woman. I recognized it as the voice of a patient, a talented psychopath who had a strong transference to me [i.e., an emotionally inappropriate but strong attachment to her therapist]. She had become a living figure within my mind. (Jung, 1961, p. 185)

Jung struck up a conversation with this new feminine personality, which rapidly turned into an argument over whether Jung's exploration of his unconscious was science, art, or something else. The conflict was resolved when Jung insisted to his inner feminine personality that what he was doing was neither science nor art; it was nature. He now encouraged her to speak through himself and felt both awed and perturbed:

I was greatly intrigued by the fact that a woman should interfere with me from within. My conclusion was that she must be the "soul," in the primitive sense, and I began to speculate on the reasons why the name "anima" was given to the soul. Later I came to see that this inner feminine figure plays a typical, or archetypal, role in the unconscious of a man, and I called her the "anima." The corresponding figure in the unconscious of woman I called the "animus." (Jung, 1961, p. 186)

Once again, Jung had found his own interior world divided and populated by autonomous personalities. It was only a short step from this experience of personal division to the proposition of universal sexual opposites. No man is entirely masculine, exclusively male. Feminine elements, attitudes, intuitions are sealed into every man's character. Traditionally, men strive to repress their "weak, soft, feminine" traits. Such repression causes a buildup of libido tension within the unconscious. In striving to win a woman as a mate, a man unconsciously projects these feminine traits and the feminine image of himself that he has so actively repressed (Jung, 1917, p. 189). This internalized feminine image is based on his real experiences with women (his mother, sister, etc.) and on the collective experiences of men throughout history (Jung, 1917, p. 190). The projected image of femininity from a man's collective unconscious is his *anima*. The anima determines a man's relationship to women throughout his life and shapes his understanding of those relationships. In a sense, a man's anima helps to compensate for the otherwise one-sided masculine nature of his interactions with and perceptions of others.

Likewise, the woman has her inherited masculine image, her *animus:* "If I were to attempt to put in a nutshell the difference between man and woman in this respect, i.e., what it is that characterizes the animus as opposed to the anima, I could say only this: as the anima produces moods [in the male], so the animus produces [in the female] *opinions* . . ." (Jung, 1917, p. 207). Jung suggested that the opinions of a woman's animus have the character of solid convictions with unassailable validity. The moods of the man's anima are often expressed in sudden changes in temperament, or character, so that a man may say, "I was not myself today."

The woman's animus, unlike the man's anima, usually does not consist of a single personification, but rather of a plurality of masculine figures. "The animus is rather like an assembly of fathers or dignitaries of some kind who lay down incontestable 'rational' *ex cathedra* judgments" (Jung, 1917, p. 207). The animus is thus the embodiment of all of a woman's ancestral experiences of man.

The danger of the anima and the animus lies in the possibility that the entire psyche may come under the exclusive sway of these images so that a man loses his masculinity and a woman her femininity (Jung, 1917, p. 209). Yet, without recognition of their inherent opposites, man and woman run the risk of incompleteness.

Persona Archetype

Persona is the Latin word for the mask that actors in Roman and Greek drama wore to depict their roles (see Chapter 1). Thus the persona in Jung's scheme is the front we present to others because social living makes demands for certain kinds of behavior. Society establishes certain expectations and certain roles around which we must shape our public selves, and behind which we hide our "private" selves (Jung, 1917, p. 192).

There is danger in the persona, for "people really do exist who believe they are what they pretend to be" (Jung, 1917, p. 193). When the mask and the ego become identical, the personal unconscious must find an alternate means of expression and representation for its demands in consciousness. Thus "Whoever builds up too good a persona for himself naturally has to pay for it with irritability" (Jung, 1917, p. 193).

As described thus far, the persona is an individual creation, rather than an archetypal form. But there is also an *impersonal* or *transpersonal* aspect to the persona. It comes into existence to smooth the individual's *collective* existence as an individual among individuals. "It is, as its name implies, only a mask of the collective psyche, a mask that *feigns individuality,* making others and oneself believe that one is individual, whereas one is simply acting a role through which the collective psyche speaks" (Jung, 1917, p. 157).

Fundamentally, therefore, the content and form of the individual's persona is a projection of the collective unconscious. There are individual differences in the choice of collective unconscious themes that the individual will role-play, but the themes themselves are born of universal and impersonal archetypal images. The persona is an ideal image, a desirable actor's part, a compromise between the individual and humanity as a whole, past and present, as to what a person should appear to be (Jung, 1917, p. 158).

ARCHETYPES AND SYNCHRONICITY

Archetypes invariably involve great emotion. Jung pointed out that sometimes an archetype may even take control of the personality so that individual behavior from that point onward is modified and directed by the collective unconscious. In fact, Jung felt that groups of people, whole civilizations, may project a given archetype at a single moment in history. The course of that civilization may thus be directed by the universal theme that emerges. For example, a satanic or demonic archetype may have made its appearance during the years of the rise to power of the Nazis under Adolf

Hitler. The reverse may, of course, also occur. A return to religious commitment or faith may be preceded by the emergence of the God archetype or the Wise Old Man.

On an individual basis, archetypes may make their appearance in times of tension, whether or not the individual consciously experiences the stress. Jung even suggested that the archetypes could transcend causality as we know it. He proposed a principle called *synchronicity* to account for events that are related through meaning rather than by the usual cause-and-effect sequence. For example, one might dream of a relative with whom little contact has been had in recent years. A day after the dream, a telegram announces that relative's death. The two events, dream and relative's death, are not related *causally.* The dream did not cause the relative's death any more than the future demise could have caused an anticipatory dream. Nonetheless, the two events are related through *meaningful simultaneity,* which Jung termed *synchronicity* (1952).

Jung's explanation of synchronistic events involved the emergence of an archetype from the collective unconscious. During moments of great stress, the individual's collective unconscious knows more than the individual does. In the case cited, the dream and death, the archetypal figure of death had begun to penetrate into the dreamer's consciousness. For the collective unconscious, time is relative; future, present, and past are one. For the dreamer, the dream and subsequent death are uncannily coincidental, but to the collective unconscious the death of the relative was a certainty. In a sense, the collective unconscious experienced the dream imagery and the actual future death as one and the same, as happening simultaneously.

Jung's concept of the collective unconscious and its archetypes was severely criticized, unfairly he thought, as akin to the discredited Lamarckian notion of evolution. In Lamarck's view, parental *experiences* could be transmitted to offspring. Modern biologists no longer accept the view that characteristics acquired in the organism's lifetime can be transmitted to offspring. Only those traits coded into the organism's genes are capable of transmission. Jung's critics interpreted his concept of the collective unconscious as a special case of inheriting acquired characteristics. Jung's repeated explanations did not help much in dispelling the suspicion, for Jung often treated the subject abstractly and with vague, imprecise language that could be interpreted as supporting a Lamarckian view. Yet, on the other hand, biologists readily confess that we have only begun to understand patterns of inheritance and their mechanisms. The optimist and Jung supporter will interpret such statements as indications that potential hard evidence for the collective unconscious concept is just around the corner.

JUNG'S VIEW OF FREUD AND ADLER: INTERPRETING A CASE OF NEUROSIS

Here is a brief description by Jung of a case of neurotic misery:

> A young woman begins to have attacks of anxiety. At night she wakes up from a nightmare with a blood-curdling cry, is scarcely able to calm herself, clings to her

husband and implores him not to leave her, demanding assurance that he really loves her, etc. Gradually a nervous asthma develops, the attacks also coming during the day. (Jung, 1917, p. 35)

A strictly Freudian approach to this woman's difficulty, according to Jung, would begin by eliciting from the patient her associations to the nightmare, exploring her past anxiety dreams, and by investigating the circumstances of her childhood and familial relations. With such a thorough evaluation of the patient the following facts would be discovered: (1) Her prior dreams involved ferocious bulls, lions, tigers, and evil men attacking her. (2) She had lost her father when she was 14; before his death, when she was on an outing in Paris with him at the *Folies Bergères,* a dancer had looked at her father in a brazen way, and he had returned her gaze with an "animal look." From then on, the girl's relationship with her father changed. The patient reported that the dancer's gaze and her father's return stare had reminded her of the look in the wild animals' eyes in her dreams, and of the look of a former lover of her own who had treated her badly. (3) The first appearance of her neurosis came when she had her second child and discovered that her husband evidenced a "tender interest" in another woman. (4) One additional fact is pertinent: After her father's sudden death, she succumbed to fits of uncontrolled weeping followed by equally uncontrollable episodes of hysterical laughter.

Jung pointed out that the Freudian interpretation of this data would center on the woman's inability to break with her father as a young girl, her Electra complex, and on the sexual imagery of the animals in her dreams in relation to her father's animal stare at the dancer. Furthermore, the connection between her own husband's "tender feelings" for another woman after she herself had become a *mother* for the second time bore a powerful unconscious similarity to the relationship of her own mother and father. Her hysterical laughing and weeping fits betrayed the ambivalence she felt toward her husband, and more fundamentally, toward her father.

What would happen, Jung wanted to know, if the same case history were subjected to a different theoretical analysis? Alfred Adler, one of Freud's early colleagues, developed a different way of approaching such cases. For Adler, the key human motivation was a struggle to compensate for any perceived sense of inferiority. Compensation for inferiority feelings takes the form of a struggle for its opposite, superiority, and emerges as a fight for power in human relationships (Adler, 1959; we discuss Adler's theory in Chapter 8). Thus, according to Jung's application of Adlerian theory, Adler would see in this same case a struggle to dominate the father's attention, jealousy provoked by the dancer episode, and a repetition of these same motives in the woman's relationship with her husband. Her "sickness," asthma, her terrible plea for her husband not to leave her, and her demands for assurances of love are all techniques of interpersonal domination and striving for power (Jung, 1917, p. 39).

Whether Adler and Freud would have agreed with Jung's application of their viewpoints is an unanswerable question. What is important, however, is that Jung was troubled by the drastic difference in interpretation that resulted from different psychological theorists viewing the same case. Each would approach the personality of his patients from the perspective of his own theory—and from the constraints imposed by his own personality.

Jungian Attitude Types: Freud the Extrovert and Adler the Introvert

For Jung, the Freudian and Adlerian explanations both had merit, and neither could be totally dismissed (1917, p. 41). Jung felt that the key problem was to account for the difference in approach between two skilled men treating the same case. The essence of the difference, Jung hypothesized, lay in the two men's personalities. Not only were Freud and Adler different in intellectual skills and theoretical viewpoint, but, more important, each was a distinctly different *type* of personality.

The Freudian interpretation of the case just discussed centers on the woman's problem with unresolved sexual and affectional dependence on the father. That pattern of dependence on a significant *external love object* is repeated, in the Freudian view, throughout the woman's life (e.g., with her husband). For Freud, according to Jung, the key element is the individual's conscious and unconscious relationship to people and things in the external world (1917, p. 41).

For Adler, on the other hand, the focus is more *subjective* with the accent on the individual's striving for *inner* security and compensation for perceived *personal* inferiority, as interpreted by Jung.

Out of his ruminations on the differences in approach of Adler and Freud, Jung formulated a problem:

> The spectacle of this dilemma made me ponder the question: are there at least two different human types, one of them more interested in the [external] object, the other more interested in himself? (1917, p. 43)

Adler, it seemed to Jung, was an *introvert* whereas Freud appeared to be more of an *extrovert.*

> The first attitude [introversion] is normally characterized by a hesitant, reflective, retiring nature that keeps itself to itself, shrinks from objects, is always slightly on the defensive and prefers to hide behind mistrustful scrutiny. The second [extroversion] is normally characterized by an outgoing, candid, and accommodating nature that adapts easily to a given situation, quickly forms attachments, and, setting aside any possible misgivings, will often venture forth with careless confidence into unknown situations. (Jung, 1917, p. 44)

Thus personality type constrains an individual's perception of events. Both Freud and Adler were bound by their own personality type, to see only one viable interpretation of the psychology of others.

It is possible to speculate that Jung's explanation of how Adler's and Freud's personal differences gave rise to his own notion of two fundamental personality types is incomplete. It seems reasonable to conclude from Jung's personal history of several times experiencing within himself and those close to him contradictory personalities, competing selves, that the division of personality types in all people was more an inner reflection than a theoretical accomplishment.[1] It will not be difficult for the astute reader to predict the outcome of Jung's theory: namely, as we shall see

---

[1] I am grateful to my former student, Cynthia Albright Dowd, for this interpretation.

somewhat later, the proposal of a unifying component in the human person that can weld together all the contradictory fragments. Jung proposed such a construct and termed it the *self* (Atwood & Stolorow, 1977b, pp. 200ff.).

Jung also proposed that the differences between introverts and extroverts in relation to subjective and objective experience were not absolute. In some cases, introverts will be more interested in the objective, external world, *when that world affects their inner lives.* Conversely, extroverts are more interested in the subjective world *when the objective world has caused them disappointment.* Then, the extrovert will withdraw into moodiness and subjective, egocentric behavior.

At all events, it is clear that Jung was not satisfied with the simple division of personality into two gross, rigid types (1921, p. 6). He postulated, in addition to the attitude types of introversion/extroversion, four *functional types:* (1) sensation; (2) intuition; (3) thinking; (4) feeling. Thus, the introvert and extrovert personalities have gradations and variety. In all, disregarding the infinite variety that *degree* of expression may provide, there are eight combined attitude-function types of introvert and extrovert. A brief consideration of the four functions is in order before we undertake a survey of these eight types.

THE FUNCTIONS OF THE PSYCHE

Jung postulated that the mind has a number of specific functions, directed on the one hand to mediating intercourse with the external world, and on the other, focused on relations with one's own inner world, the world of the personal and collective unconscious. To those functions of consciousness directed outwardly to the world, Jung gave the name *ectopsychic.* To the functions of the unconscious in its relations with the ego, Jung gave the name *endopsychic* (1968, p. 11). The endopsychic functions were not emphasized in Jung's theory and we omit them in the present discussion.

Ectopsychic Functions

The ectopsychic functions were those that Jung emphasized in constructing his introversion/extroversion typology. The first ectopsychic function is *sensation,* "which is the sum total of external facts given to me through the functions of my senses" (Jung, 1968, p. 11). Thus sensation is concerned with orientation to reality: "Sensation tells me that something *is;* it does not tell me *what* it is" (Jung, 1968, p. 11; 1921, p. 461, definition 47).

The second ectopsychic function is *thinking* and is complementary to sensation, for thinking "in its simplest form tells you *what* a thing is. It gives a name to the thing" (Jung, 1968, p. 11; 1921, p. 481, definition 53). For Jung, the term *thinking* was to be restricted to "the linking up of ideas by means of a concept, in other words, to an act of judgment, no matter whether this act is intentional or not" (1921, p. 481).

The third ectopsychic function is *feeling.* For Jung, the concept of feeling had a somewhat restricted meaning. "Feeling informs you through its feeling-tones of the values of things. Feeling tells you for instance whether a thing is acceptable or agreeable or not. It tells you what a thing is *worth* to you" (1968, p. 12).

Feeling may give rise in isolated circumstances to *mood,* an emotional state of acceptance or rejection. Thus feeling is a subjective process that is independent of external stimuli (Jung, 1921, p. 434, definition 21).

The fourth and last ectopsychic function is *intuition.* Sensation tells us that a thing is; thinking tells us what that thing is; and feeling tells us what that thing is worth to us. The only conscious function left is an awareness of time, the past and the future of a thing, where it has come from and where it is going. Intuition is composed of hunches about the origins and the prospects of a thing (Jung, 1968, p. 13). Jung found it very difficult to define intuition, but he pointed to the conditions, familiar to almost everyone, under which we use intuition: "Whenever you have to deal with strange conditions where you have no established values or established concepts, you will depend upon that faculty of intuition" (1968, p. 14). Thus intuition is the psychological function that mediates perceptions in an unconscious way so that our experience of intuitive problem solutions is that they spring on us suddenly, without conscious intent (Jung, 1921, p. 453, definition 35).

Rational Versus Irrational Functions

The four ectopsychic functions can be further classified as *rational* or *irrational,* depending on the degree of judgment or reasoning involved. Hence, *sensation* and *intuition* are classified as *irrational* because conscious reasoning is, by Jung's definitions, virtually absent. By contrast, *feeling* and *thinking* are classed as *rational* functions because both involve the judgmental process and the "supremacy of reason" (Jung, 1921, pp. 359ff.; 1968, p. 12).

During the course of his famous Tavistock Lectures, Jung employed the diagram shown in Figure 7.2 to summarize the four ectopsychic functions and their

FIGURE 7.2 The functions of the psyche.

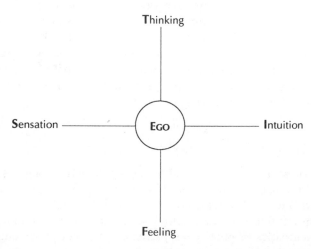

FIGURE 7.3   **The Jungian combined attitude and function typology.**

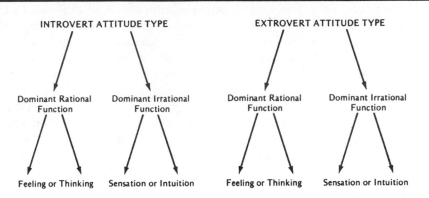

relationships in the psyche. In the central circle of Figure 7.2 is the ego, the center of conscious self-awareness and possessor of the psychic energy. At the top of the compasslike diagram is thinking (T) and its direct opposite on the lowest spoke, feeling (F). Thus the diagram represents the type of person whose *superior function* (topmost in the diagram) is reason or thought, and whose *inferior function* (lowermost spoke) is feeling, "for when you think you must exclude feeling, just as when you feel you must exclude thinking" (Jung, 1968, p. 16).

To represent the opposite type of personality, the individual for whom feeling is the superior function and thinking the inferior, the T and F spokes would be reversed. The two other possible types of personality may be represented, depending on the dominance of either sensation or intuition, by rotating the spokes of the compass accordingly.

Each of these four functional types may dominate the basic introvert or extrovert attitude orientation. The eight resulting personality types are summarized in Figure 7.3.

Jung's typology of introversion/extroversion bears scrutiny because it has been a source of fruitful empirical research for a variety of investigators. Foremost among these has been Hans Eysenck. His experimental and factor analytic work in exploring the biological bases of introversion/extroversion and neuroticism/normality dimensions has progressed for many years (Eysenck, 1967).

THE EXTROVERT TYPES

From our discussion thus far, it is clear that Jung's typology is not a gross classification of individuals into mutually exclusive categories. Rather, Jung pictured his typology as having the breadth and flexibility to allow for an infinite number of possible permutations of function, attitude, and degree. However, because they exemplify in clear-cut fashion the characteristics of pure types, extreme cases were the dominant illustrations Jung employed in delineating his scheme.

Recall that the extrovert is dominated by the external object to the detriment of subjective experience. Powerfully influenced by their social surroundings, extroverts are consequently shaped by the moral and ethical climate of their culture, and therefore by the opinions and values of those close to them. Greatest of the dangers for the extreme extrovert is that he or she gets "sucked into objects and completely loses himself in them" (Jung, 1921, p. 336). Thus, in Jung's view, the most typical neurosis of the extrovert is hysteria, for hysterical reactions are essentially attention-getting primitive, dependent attitudes toward people and things in the environment. Eysenck (e.g., 1953a, 1953b, 1967) has marshaled a good bit of empirical evidence that supports this view.

Extrovert Thinking Type (Rational)

Thinking extroverts are "captured" by external ideas and objects; they are unable to escape their influence in solving problems. They may give the impression of a certain shortsightedness or lack of freedom in the drawing of logical conclusions, because they refuse to go beyond the objective facts at hand.

Emotionally, thinking extroverts subjugate everything to the intellect, refusing to see any other principle for themselves or others to follow than the power of their own decision making. Their moral code is correspondingly rigid and intolerant of exception. Their struggle is for objective and valid universal truths (Jung, 1921, p. 347). "Oughts" and "musts" dominate the thinking extroverts' approach to values, and their thinking tends to be dogmatic.

Since thinking is their superior function, the feeling side of their lives is suppressed. They may, therefore, give the impression of being cold or indifferent. Key concise trait descriptions are *objective, rigid,* and *cold.*

Extrovert Feeling Type (Rational)

Dominance by the feeling function is most characteristic of women, according to Jung (1921, p. 356). Like thinking extroverts, *feeling extroverts* seek harmony with the external world. Their thinking function is kept suppressed behind a facade of loud gushing talk and intense displays of extravagant emotional responsiveness. There is, of course, a tendency to make friends easily and to be influenced by the feeling-tone of social situations. Key trait descriptions are *intense, effervescent,* and *sociable.*

Extrovert Sensation Type (Irrational)

The *sensation extrovert's* lifestyle is a search for new sensory experiences and the accumulation of actual experiences of concrete objects (1921, p. 363). They may refine their sensory powers to a high pitch so that they are not merely gross sensual types, but rather connoisseurs of fine wines, discriminating judges of art. Sensation extroverts are usually good company, for they suppress any tendency to introspection and self-concern, favoring instead minute attention to objective, external detail.

They tend to be well adjusted to reality and concerned for the welfare of others. Key trait descriptions are *realistic, sensual, jolly.*

Extrovert Intuitive Type (Irrational)

The *intuitive extrovert* has difficulty maintaining an interest in any one thing for very long. Usually, this type flits from one novel idea to another and stays with each only until the novelty wears off. Because thinking and feeling, the rational functions, are at a minimum, this individual tends to make decisions without conscious, reflective thought. Yet such persons' decisions are likely to be good ones, though based on hunches, because intuitive extroverts are closely in touch with the wisdom of their own unconscious. Consideration for the welfare of others is weakly developed in the intuitive extrovert. However, the intuitive extroverts are valuable to society because they have the capacity to inspire confidence and enthusiasm for new causes and adventuresome undertakings. Thus key trait words describing the intuitive extrovert are *visionary, changeable,* and *creative.*

THE INTROVERT TYPES

The introvert attitude, you may recall, implies that such individuals are aware of external conditions, but that they emphasize their subjective reactions to them as decisive. The introverts' orientation to life may be characterized as a struggle to keep their egos independent of external influences and tugs. Typically, if the extreme introvert succumbs to neurosis, it will be to what was called psychasthenia in Jung's day. This neurosis is, as might be expected, characterized by intense anxiety reactions, chronic fatigue, and exhaustion. The diagnosis of "psychasthenia" is no longer used. Instead, as we discussed in Chapter 1, some combination of the diagnoses of *anxiety disorder* and *dysthymic disorder* (neurotic depression) would probably be assigned to Jung's "neurotic" introvert. Eysenck has marshaled evidence that this neurotic disposition was more than a haphazard guess on Jung's part (see Chapter 17).

Introvert Thinking Type (Rational)

When the introvert's consciousness is dominated by the thinking function, each presents a picture of the stereotypical intellectual, the "egghead." Concerned with abstractions and with the creation of theories for their own sake, the *thinking introvert* has a tendency to ignore the practicalities of everyday living. "His judgment appears cold, inflexible, arbitrary, and ruthless, because it relates far less to the [external] object than to the subject [himself]" (Jung, 1921, p. 384).

The *thinking introvert* develops an intense desire for privacy and is horrified when anyone threatens to invade his or her solitary domain. Hence, the key trait descriptions of the thinking introvert are *theoretical, intellectual, impractical.*

Introvert Feeling Type (Rational)

More common among women, dominance of consciousness by feeling in the introvert produces a picture of cold indifference to others. Sometimes this impression is fostered by a suggestion that "still waters run deep." The *feeling introvert* seemingly has no concern for the feelings or opinions of others. There is even a faint air of superiority and critical neutrality in the feeling introvert's relations with others. Emotional expression is kept to a minimum, for inwardly the feeling introvert's emotions are intense and troublesome. Sometimes, this individual's emotions are so intense that they are expressed in the writing of poetry that is scrupulously kept from the prying eyes of others. Key trait descriptions are *silent, childish,* and *indifferent.*

Introvert Sensation Type (Irrational)

The *sensation introvert* is dominated by the changing flux of external events. Their subjective influence is of paramount importance, for the only thing that matters to the sensation type of introvert is personal reaction to objective sensory events. Such individuals' thinking and feeling functions are primitively expressed, and they are oriented mythologically or poetically to interpret their world. That is, they evaluate their sense impressions in terms of clear-cut categories of good and evil—strictly, of course, with reference to what is good and evil *for them.* They sometimes misinterpret reality and become separated from the external world, but they remain calmly undisturbed when others point this out to them. Key trait descriptions are *passive, calm,* and *artistic.*

Introvert Intuitive Type (Irrational)

When intuition gains the ascendancy in introverts, they tend to be aloof and unconcerned about concrete reality or external events. They present the stereotypical picture of the "peculiar artist" or the slightly "mad genius" whose productive efforts result in strange but beautiful creations. Perception is the main problem for *intuitive introverts.* They are enmeshed in shaping meaning from their perceptions that will satisfy the inner self. Thus they may become estranged from those around them and be viewed as a "wise person gone wrong" or as a "crank and oddball." Key descriptive traits are *mystic, dreamer,* and *unique.*

Summary

Jung emphasized that the extremes depicted in the previous list of eight combined attitude-function types rarely exist in pure form. Furthermore, he suggested that individuals of a given type may undergo change as conditions of their personal and collective unconscious change (1921, p. 405). Precisely which of the functions will be superior or differentiated fully within an individual's total personality depends on each one's need for auxiliary or compensatory functions to achieve adaptation to the life circumstances.

THE PROCESS OF INDIVIDUATION: "ENANTIODROMIA"

With Jung's emphasis on the collective unconscious, inherited archetypal images, and on the classification of personality types, it might seem that he was uninterested in *individual* personality development. Nothing could be further from the facts. Jung spent a good deal of the latter part of his life exploring the processes by which a person becomes a complete individual; that is, he investigated the psychological process of *differentiation* by which individuals develop their unique patterns of traits and their idiosyncratic relationship to each one's personal and collective unconscious. Jung called this development of a clearly personal pattern of traits *individuation*. Individuation, in short, is the process by which a person harmonizes the unconscious with the ego (1939, p. 287).

Jung believed that every human has an innate tendency to pursue this inner harmony, which he called the *transcendent function*. The transcendent function is the motive force behind the individual's desire to come to terms with all aspects of the self and guides the need to accept the content of the unconscious as "mine" (Jung, 1916, p. 73). Individuation and the transcendent function are thus opposite sides of the same coin. Individuation refers to the attainment of full development of all sides of oneself into a unique configuration. The transcendent function is the guiding force in the achievement of this idiosyncratic "wholeness."

Jung's method of helping his patients to attain individuation involved the process of *active imagination*. Jung instructed his patients in the art of consciously focusing on dream images or on fantasy figures in an effort to elaborate them willfully and to embellish such unconscious creations purposefully. Active imagination might best be compared to a form of meditation that enables the individual to capitalize knowingly on self-knowledge that would otherwise remain untapped. By active imagination, Jung's patients could truly examine every aspect of their personalities.

Within every personality Jung discerned a multiplicity of conflicting themes, discordant opposites, and antagonistic forces. Thus, for the anima, there is the animus; for introversion, there is extroversion; for thinking, sensation; for sensation, feeling; for the personal unconscious, there is the collective unconscious; the ego is opposed by the shadow; the God archetype has its counterpart in the demon; causal explanations should be complemented with acausal, synchronistic ones; and dreams can be analyzed not only in terms of the dreamer's past, but also in terms of his or her future.

Jung employed a term from Heraclitus, the 5th-century B.C. Greek philosopher, to label the conflicting, sometimes complementary, but usually opposed themes of the human condition. Jung referred to these opposites as examples of *enantiodromia*, literally as a "running counter to" (1921, p. 425, definition 18). Initially, Jung restricted the term to the emergence of an unconscious function or idea that was opposite to an individual's conscious dominant function. Eventually, however, Jung began to see the development of personality as a goal-directed enterprise, marked by a striving toward the *equal* development of *all* parts of the psyche. Thus opposites must coalesce in the individual person. Each of us not only must develop our rationality, but also must accept our irrationality with equal fervor; not only must we strive to adapt our egos to life, but we must also recognize the shadow's influence; not only must we venerate what is God-like in ourselves, but we must also respect what is most base. Failure to recognize the opposite tendency within ourselves can lead only to the feeling of being torn apart (Jung, 1917, p. 73; 1957, pp. 302 ff.). Success at individuation means the acceptance of inherent enantiodromia.

Individuation, however, is a product of the mature years. Throughout life, the individual's development is oriented toward the attainment of one goal: the reconciliation of opposites. Within the fully differentiated, individuated personality, then, a final psychological organization develops that embodies all the discordant elements, slighting none, emphasizing all equally. To this reconciler of opposites, Jung gave the name *self* (1950b, p. 267). "In the end we have to acknowledge that the self is a *complexio oppositorum* precisely because there can be no reality without polarity" (Jung, 1950b, p. 267). The self is the ultimate individuation.

DEVELOPMENT OF THE SELF: A TELEOLOGICAL VIEW OF LIFE

Jung had treated a variety of middle-aged patients who, although not mentally ill by any definition, were nonetheless discontented. They were ill at ease with themselves and alienated from any possible satisfaction in life. These patients had, in Jung's view, developed much too one-sidedly. One particular psychic function had become differentiated at the cost of others. These alienated middle-aged patients could be helped by psychotherapy only if Jung could aid them in developing the stunted functions of their psyches. In short, the process of individuation, the creation of the self as reconciler of opposites, had not occurred for them.

These individuals had arrived at middle age with their sense of purpose completely undeveloped. For Jung, life does not proceed randomly. It is purposive or *teleological,* and shaped by beckoning goals. The purpose of an individual's life is attained when that person is fully integrated, completely in harmony with the self. Some individuals find their purpose in religion, some discover their life's goal in helping their fellow humans, and yet others find purpose in simply living each day with care. But in every case, the purposive individual has accepted the basic enantiodromia of life.

The Self as Archetype

The most perfect mythological symbol of the self is Christ. "He [Christ] is our culture hero, who regardless of his historical existence, embodies the myth of the divine Primordial Man, the mystic Adam. . . . *Christ exemplifies the archetype of the self.* He represents a totality of a divine or heavenly kind, a glorified man, a son of God *sine macula peccati,* unspotted by sin" (Jung, 1950b, pp. 36–37).

Even the divine archetypal figure of the self is a composite of opposites: Christ and Anti-Christ, God and Satan, the Prince of Light and the Prince of Darkness (1950b, p. 44).

Thus the self, that totality of opposites, that unique combination of perfection and baseness, was prefigured in humanity's mythology and religion by symbols of the God-man. The early Christian concept of Christ implied an "all embracing totality that even includes the animal side of man" (1950b, p. 41). It is clear, therefore, that Jung regards humans' need for religion, for God, as an inherent drive directed toward self-fulfillment. Without God to aspire to, people are forever condemned to the incompleteness of their own existence. For Jung's theory the question of God's existence is nearly irrelevant because it can never be answered with certainty. What is important is humanity's *belief* in God's existence, for without that belief, the inherent need for wholeness is denied.

Expressions of the Self's Harmonies: Mandala Paintings

Jung found in his explorations of mythology and alchemy that the self was often arche-typically symbolized by a *mandala*. Mandala is a Sanskrit word meaning "circle." In various mythologies, religious rituals, and in the dreams and fantasies of his patients, a variety of mandalalike figures could be observed. Sometimes the mandala is divided into four segments, around which is drawn the characteristic circular enclosure. Figure 7.4 illustrates a mandala drawing by one of Jung's patients. The coiled snake within the circle is seemingly trying to wend its way out of the enclosure. Jung himself was seized on occasion with the compulsion to create mandala figures in paint:

> My mandalas were cryptograms concerning the state of the self which were presented to me anew each day. In them I saw the self—that is, my whole being—actively at work. . . . I had the distinct feeling that they were something central, and in time I acquired through them a living conception of the self. The self, I thought, was like the monad which I am, and which is my world. The mandala represents this monad [i.e., unity], and corresponds to the microcosmic nature of the psyche. (Jung, 1961, p. 196)

Three of Jung's own mandala paintings are reproduced in Figure 7.5. *Picture a* in Figure 7.5, a group of interlocking circles, with human figures in the four most

FIGURE 7.4   A mandala drawing by one of Jung's patients.

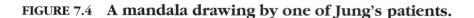

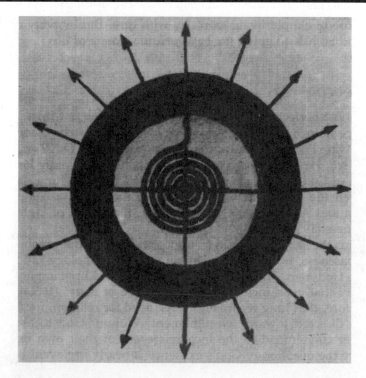

Source: Jung (1950b) "Concerning Mandala Symbolism."

FIGURE 7.5A   Four archetypes of the self, painted by Jung.

Source: Jung (1950a).

peripheral circles, was intended by Jung to illustrate four complementary aspects of the self. To the right and left of center are two female figures, with the left woman representing the "dark" side of the anima and the right one symbolizing the nurturing aspect. The top and bottom peripheral circles contain the Wise Old Man archetype and the Trickster archetype, respectively. The sixteen "globes" surrounding the center star are symbolic "eyes," and stand for "observing and discriminating consciousness" (Jung, 1950a, p. 374).

Picture b in Figure 7.5, a star-shaped motif within which lie concentric circles and mazelike compartments, was designed by Jung to represent a medieval city with walls, moats, streets, and churches, arranged in units of four. The buildings all open inward, facing center, which in turn is a castle with a golden roof. The castle center is surrounded by black-and-white tiles, representing united opposites, that is, the self.

Picture c in Figure 7.5 is the most interesting of Jung's mandala paintings because it was the last mandala he painted, and because he reported fully the circumstances surrounding its creation.[2] Entitled "Window on Eternity," *picture c* was produced

---

[2] Jaffé (1979, pp. 91–93) has published Jung's own paintings with his marginal notations, and it is clear that "Window on Eternity" was not his last. Jung's (1961, pp. 197–198) contradictory statements about this picture's finality in the sequence may have been a reflection only of his sense of emotional finality as expressed in the dream which provoked the painting of "Window on Eternity." The picture was painted in 1927, and "The Medieval City" was finished in 1928.

FIGURE 7.5B Medieval city, painted by Jung.

Source: Jung (1950a).

following a dream Jung had in which he found himself in the city of Liverpool, traveling with three younger companions. He had the impression in the dream of a dirty, sooty city; it was dark and raining. His companions were Swiss, and together they climbed a plateau to a broad square illuminated dimly by streetlights, and into which many city streets converged. All of the parts of the city were arranged radially around the square in which Jung and his companions stood. In the center of the square was a round pool with an island in its middle, strangely blazing with sunlight. On the island stood a single tree, with a shower of reddish magnolia blossoms; but the tree itself seemed to be the source of the sunlight. Jung's traveling companions commented on the abominable weather and apparently did not see the sunlit tree. They spoke of another Swiss who lived in the city of Liverpool, and they were surprised

FIGURE 7.5C   Window on eternity, painted by Jung.

Source: Jung (1950a).

that he had settled there. Jung's dream ended with the feeling, "I know very well why he has settled here" (Jung, 1961, p. 198; see also 1950a, p. 364).

> This dream represented my situation at the time. I can still see the grayish yellow raincoats, glistening with the wetness of the rain. Everything was extremely unpleasant, black and opaque—just as I felt then. But I had a vision of unearthly beauty, and that was why I was able to live at all. Liverpool is the "pool of life." The "liver," according to an old view, is the seat of life—that which "makes man live."
>
> This dream brought with it a sense of finality. I saw that here the goal had been revealed. One could not go beyond the center. The center is the goal, and everything is directed toward that center. Through this dream I understood that the self is the principle and archetype of orientation and meaning. Therein lies its healing function. (Jung, 1961, pp. 198–199)

Jung's own mandala paintings show his efforts at healing the painful self-division he harbored. His paintings demonstrate his strivings to mold unity and order from the chaos he felt within, and Figure 7.5c represents the culmination of the self-therapy. The "Window on Eternity" painting is at once the final and the most harmonious of Jung's mandalas.

In the delicately balanced harmonies of the mandala, Jung discerned a mythic expression of the self as the reconciler of opposites. The precise juxtaposition of colors and shadings and the fourfold spatial division of the circle symbolize the harmony of the self. This fourfold division of many mandalas is the instinctive expression of human desire to create organization from chaos, to plot on a schema of four coordinates the confusing flux of the inner and outer life. Each individual's approach to the attainment of self-harmony is unique and occurs only once in time, as the Christ figure symbolizes. But even the Christ figure has to be expressed in antagonistic terms, a complementarity of opposites.

Figure 7.6 expresses an analogy of the self through the historical and mythical figure of Christ. "As an historical personage Christ is unitemporal [once in time] and unique; as God, universal and eternal. Likewise the self: as the essence of individuality it is unitemporal and unique; as an archetypal symbol it is a God-image and therefore universal and eternal" (Jung, 1950b, p. 63).

Christ also embodied another fourfold division of opposites: *good* (Christ) versus *evil* (Anti-Christ) and *spiritual* (divine) versus *material* (human). Thus Jung illustrated this composite of opposites with another set of coordinates, shown here in Figure 7.7.

Because the self is a totality, it must embody both light and dark, good and evil. Fully individuated persons can freely accept both aspects of their psyches and can willingly strive to unite the two into wholeness.

In consequence, for Jung, the goal of psychotherapy, indeed, the goal of the well-lived life, is the attainment of wholeness, individuals' recognition of the opposites within themselves, and the achievement of harmony through the articulation of the separate parts.

FIGURE 7.6   Christ as an archetype of the self—the first set of opposites.

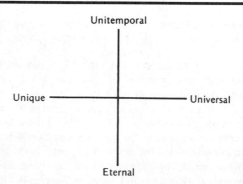

After Jung (1950b), p. 63.

FIGURE 7.7   **Christ as an archetype of the self—the
second set of opposites.**

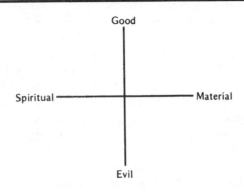

After Jung (1950b), p. 63.

Jung was able to face ambiguity and uncertainty. In fact, it would be fair to say that Jung was fascinated by antimonies and by paradoxes. Toward the end of his life, Jung was able to accept the rational and the irrational as copartners in the events of the psyche. He was, furthermore, capable of welcoming the mysterious with a relish no less than his acceptance of the merely logical. Perhaps the period of his own turmoil in childhood, and his self-analysis of the 1913 to 1917 "stormy period" prepared the way for his resignation to the conflicting pulls of a complex existence.

EVALUATING CARL JUNG

Of all the theories we present, Jung's is the one that best fits Ellenberger's (1970) idea that some theories emerge from a thinker's "creative illness." The historical and biographical evidence, as well as the content of the theory itself, link most of Jung's more controversial ideas to his attempts to resolve his own substantial conflicts. But unlike other theorists, for whom the same relationship exists between their ideas and their lives, Jung's personal difficulties included periods of hallucination, suicidal depression, and regression, as documented in his autobiography *Memories, Dreams, Reflections.* As a consequence, Jung's critics tend to dismiss his ideas without considering them and to criticize his work for all the wrong reasons.

As we discussed in Chapter 1, the fairest, most powerful, and most comprehensive test of a theory is provided in the criterion of refutability. A theory cannot be dismissed because it has demonstrable links to the personal distress or interests of its creator. The theory must be tested against reality, not against opinion. In fact, we could easily argue that a psychological theory originating in the personal distress of its creator is likely to be a more accurate description of *some* aspects of human personality than had it originated in the laboratory. At all events, the strangeness of some of Jung's ideas (e.g., synchronicity, the collective unconscious) encourages liberties among empirically minded psychologists when criticizing Jung's work that we do not find directed to even the most primitive "theories" that merit high skepticism.

Refutability of Jung's Ideas

It should not be surprising that, like Freud's theory, Jung's is a composite of empirical and nonempirical ideas. Jung's early work with the word-association test was certainly empirical, and though the standards of evidence have grown more stringent than they were in Jung's day, his basic research technique would qualify as a refutable way to test his hypothesis of "emotional complexes."

Jung's conception of personality types, especially the fundamental dimension of introversion-extroversion, is, in principle, eminently testable. Eysenck's work (e.g., 1967; Eysenck & Eysenck, 1985), which we review later, has certainly established the basic dimension and its correlates in the laboratory. However, beyond only the most elementary trait descriptions, Eysenck's concepts of introversion-extroversion are much, much different from Jung's. Nevertheless, taking Jung's ideas about this dimension, there is at least one paper-and-pencil personality test devoted to measuring the Jungian personality types and their attitudinal correlates (Myers, 1972). And, we should point out, the descriptions that Jung gave of the types, subtypes, and attitudinal variations lend themselves to a variety of empirical tests using already available psychological instruments. By the same token, however, not much actual research has been stimulated.

What of Jung's most original and central ideas? The collective unconscious, archetypes, synchronicity, to name a few, are simply not stated in testable form. By definition, synchronicity is a nonempirical, noncausal concept, and we really cannot get much further from refutability than that. The scientific problem with each of these ideas is not their strangeness nor their possible origins in Jung's personal conflict resolution. The problem is that none of these main ideas has a measurable referent that can be manipulated, predicted, or even observed directly. For the phenomena that Jung indicates as belonging to any one of these main concepts, it is possible to generate alternative and simpler explanations. The burden of proof, then, lies with Jung and his followers to show that their explanation, and only their explanation, covers the facts.

On the whole then, Jung receives low grades for the refutability of his most unique concepts.

Jung's Conception of Human Agency

Jung's work anticipated much of the later ideas of the American existentialist and humanist writers, such as Rollo May, Carl Rogers, and R. D. Laing, in their emphasis on the person's active creation of meaning from mere reality. Although Jung, more than any of these thinkers, was a dyed-in-the-wool psychoanalyst, at least to begin with, the ideas of his later years focus on the self, on actualizing the self, and on a holistic conception of personality that is quite contemporary in flavor and conception. Jung believed, apparently, in determinism, the determinism of our primordial ancestry and our personal history. But he emphasized that the person's responsibility lies in an active synthesis of the discrete parts of his or her life into a harmonious whole.

Jung's emphasis on the spiritual side of life, his concern with teleology or goal-oriented behavior, and his willingness to see the determinants of behavior in a person's remote past, personal past, and future strivings certainly argue for a complex, largely active conception of human agency.

Jung's Combined Idiographic-Nomothetic Emphases

Jung envisioned his theory as providing a nomothetic basis for understanding behavior by transcending the individual, by going beyond the immediate past, and by allowing for the influence of the future. In a way, his concepts of the collective unconscious and synchronicity are the clearest examples of a nomothetic or universal focus in personality theory. The problem, as we have seen, is that such concepts may be acceptable philosophical or metaphorical expressions of some truths in human experience, but they have no observable, empirical referents that permit the making of precise predictions about human behavior. Each of these concepts—collective unconscious, synchronicity, archetypes—is said to be universal and timeless, but in fact they serve as explanations of a phenomenon only after the fact. They are "post-dictions" not predictions, and therefore lie outside the realm of acceptable scientific theory.

On the other side of the coin, Jung clearly proposed idiographic concepts that have fared better. His word-association procedure is an idiographic one by definition. His psychoanalytic-like analysis of dreams and symptoms is, like its psychoanalytic cousin, strictly idiographic. And Jung's conception of the self as the psychological structure that harmonizes the conflicting pulls of an individual life proceeding toward self-actualization is wholly idiographic.

Thus our evaluation of Jung reveals a pattern of strengths and weaknesses that are not much different from those to be found in theories considered less mystical and less strange. But, for now, it also is disappointing that we do not find much here that lends itself to stimulating new ideas or new research.

SUMMARY

Beginning his career in the tradition of classical clinical psychiatry, Carl Gustav Jung soon developed a tool of investigation that brought his thinking close to that of Sigmund Freud. The word-association test, in Jung's innovative hands, revealed that normal and neurotic subjects harbored latent and inexpressible ideas and feelings. These emotional complexes, as Jung called them, could be objectively demonstrated in the pauses, hesitations, and inhibitions of the subjects as each reacted to a list of stimulus words.

Eventually, however, Jung pursued a path different from Freud's when he found himself unable to accept the exclusively sexual nature of Freud's "libido." With his own patients, Jung discovered residues of racial history in their fantasies. His own childhood experiences with visions and alternative personalities had prepared him to accept the possibility that some psychic content might arise from sources external to the individual. His self-analysis (from 1913 to 1917) of the dreams, visions, and nightmares that flooded his consciousness convinced him more strongly that a "higher" power was responsible for at least some of the content of mental life. He therefore postulated a personal unconscious similar to Freud's concept, and a collective unconscious that transcends the personal experiences of the individual.

Within the collective unconscious there are stored inherited predispositions to respond with great emotion to specific events. These predispositions, which Jung called *archetypes,* include the animus and anima, the hero, God, the shadow, and the persona. Jung felt that the archetypes were solid evidence of the innate symbol-making tendency humans had inherited from their ancestors.

In trying to resolve the differences between himself and Freud, and between Freud and Adler, Jung postulated two personality types: the introvert and the extrovert. Introverts are characterized by their withdrawal from social stimulation, their intensely subjective interest in things intellectual, and their reliance on the power of their own feelings. The extrovert, much the opposite, is dominated by objective, external reality and is socially oriented. In addition to these attitude types, Jung proposed four functions: thinking and feeling (rational), and intuition and sensation (irrational). Introverts and extroverts each can be dominated by one or more of these functions, leading to an eightfold combined typology.

In his later years, Jung came to emphasize the spiritual side of humanity's existence. Jung postulated that to achieve full individuality, or *individuation* as he called it, the person must form a psychological organization that can reconcile all of the opposing and contradictory trends within the psyche. To this reconciler of opposites, Jung gave the name *self.*

An evaluation of Jung's theory indicates that some parts are, in principle, testable, especially his early work on word association and his conception of the basic introversion-extroversion personality dimension. Jungian theory is essentially an "active agent" theory that anticipated much of the concerns of the American existentialists who focused on the person's capacity to create meaning actively from reality. It is a complex blend of nomothetic universals (e.g., collective unconscious, archetypes) and idiographic particulars (e.g., introversion, the self).

FOR FURTHER READING

Jung wrote, for various purposes, three relatively concise introductions to his work that serve as useful first contacts with his writing. In order of value to the serious student, these introductions are *Analytical Psychology: Its Theory and Practice* (New York: Pantheon, 1968), which is the published version of Jung's Tavistock Lectures, and the most readable of his writings; *Two Essays on Analytical Psychology* (Vol. 7 of *The Collected Works of C. G. Jung* [Princeton, NJ: Princeton University Press, 1953]), a work that is somewhat more difficult but also more characteristic of Jung's style; and *Man and His Symbols* (New York: Doubleday, 1964; available in paperback), which is a lavishly, though at times superficially, illustrated compendium of Jungian thought by both Jung himself and several of his collaborators as an attempt to more widely disseminate Jung's thinking to contemporary readers.

To gain some of the flavor of Jung's religious and spiritual researches, his *The Archetypes of the Collective Unconscious* (Vol. 9 of *The Collected Work* [Princeton, NJ: Princeton University Press, 1968]), though difficult in style, will introduce you to his characteristic form of presenting hypotheses drawn from clinical, mythological, and historical sources.

Three recent biographies of Jung present drastically different pictures of the same man and should be read together to achieve balance. Laurens Van der Post's *Jung and the Story of Our Time* (New York: Pantheon, 1975) is a spiritual rather than intellectual account of Jung's life and influence based on Van der Post's personal relationship with Jung. Very sympathetic and mystical, approaching almost hero worship, van der Post emphasizes Jung's image as a "wise old man." A somewhat more realistic view that sometimes borders on hostility is provided by Paul J. Stern in *C. G. Jung: The Haunted Prophet* (New York: Braziller, 1976). Stern attempts to make the case for Jung's personal psychotic episodes as the basis of his later theoretical ideas and succeeds in providing a more objective view of Jung's personality than Van der Post. Finally, Vincent Brome's *Jung: Man and Myth* (New York: Atheneum Books, 1981) offers, perhaps, the most balanced account of Jung's life and work. None of these biographies should be consulted without Jung's own account of his life and work given in his *Memories, Dreams, Reflections,* edited by Aniela Jaffé (New York: Pantheon, 1961). Further personal insights may be gleaned from *The Freud/Jung Letters,* edited by William McGuire (Princeton, NJ: Princeton University Press, 1974), in which the development, course, and final breakup of Freud and Jung's relationship may be witnessed.

Richard I. Evans's interview with Jung is contained in *Conversations With Carl Jung and Reactions From Ernest Jones* (New York: Van Nostrand, 1964), or in condensed form in Evans's *The Making of Psychology* (New York: Knopf, 1976). Gerhard Adler's *Studies in Analytical Psychology* (New York: Putnam, 1969) shows Jungian therapy at its best through studies of dreams and detailed case histories. A view of how the contemporary Jungian analyst operates may be obtained from E. C. Whitmont and Y. Kaufmann's "Analytical Psychotherapy," in Raymond Corsini (Ed.), *Current Psychotherapies* (Itasca, IL: Peacock, 1973), Chapter 3.

Aniela Jaffé, Jung's longtime student and colleague during the later part of his life, attempts to explicate some controversial aspects of Jung's thinking and career in her

From the Life and Work of C. G. Jung (New York: Harper & Row, 1971; available in paperback). Jaffé's essays are particularly worthwhile in the areas of explaining Jung's alleged anti-Semitism and his equally dubious sympathy for the Nazi philosophy. In contrast, Gustav Jahoda provides some criticism of Jung's ideas, especially his concept of synchronicity; in *The Psychology of Superstition* (Baltimore: Penguin, 1969), Chapter 7.

Three paperback books attempt to provide a comprehensive treatment of Jung's ideas. The classic one and the easiest to read is Frieda Fordham's *An Introduction to Jung's Psychology* (Baltimore: Penguin, 1953). Anthony Storr's *Jung* (New York: Viking, 1973) is more detailed than Fordham's book and somewhat less authoritative. Calvin Hall and Vernon Nordby's *A Primer of Jungian Psychology* (New York: New American Library, 1973) is the most sympathetic and uncritical account of the three. For fans of psychoanalytic soap opera, John Kerr's *A Most Dangerous Method: The Story of Jung, Freud, and Sabina Spielrein* (New York: Knopf, 1993) recounts in detail the nature of the relationship between Freud and Jung, and the story of one of Jung's lovers who had also been his patient. What gives this book its value is that it restores Sabina Spielrein's name to psychoanalytic history and focuses some attention on her real contributions.

Aniela Jaffé's *C. G. Jung: Word and Image* (Princeton, NJ: Princeton University Press, 1979) provides a rare glimpse into many of Jung's private concerns and artistic productions. For comparison purposes you may want to explore Hans Eysenck's biological introversion-extroversion theory in Chapter 17. Eysenck began with but soon abandoned Jung's formation.

CHAPTER 8

ALFRED ADLER
Individual Psychology

The most important question of the healthy and the diseased mental life is not whence? but, whither?

Alfred Adler, *The Individual Psychology of Alfred Adler*

About Adler's Individual Psychology

As did so many others, Alfred Adler began as a tentative adherent of Freud's theory, but his tolerance for Freud's orthodoxy ended after a brief period, and the two men parted bitterly. Crucial to understanding Adler's accomplishments are these ideas:

1. *Each person strives for superiority or personal competence, struggling not just to survive but to master life.*

2. *Each person develops a life plan or "style of life" that is partly deliberate and partly unconscious but one that steers the person toward self-fulfilling goals and gives a person's life consistency in action and thought.*

3. *The most important component of the healthy personality is an acquired capacity for "fellow feeling" or what Adler called* Gemeinschaftsgefühl. *That is, Adler felt that a person had to transcend the self, escaping the egocentrism implicit in Freud's picture of people as drive satisfiers.*

Adler's theory can be interpreted as a form of ego psychology or even as an object relations theory, but perhaps because the central feature of the theory is enhancement and growth of the self, Adler's work is best thought of as a psychoanalytic theory of mastery.

THE CEMETERY THAT WASN'T THERE

The men and women who create personality theories have sovereign personalities of their own. Consequently, some part of each theorist's comprehension of human character is always a reflection of his or her self-comprehension. For the young Alfred Adler, the reigning themes of childhood existence were fear and anger: fear in the face of death, and anger at the frailty thus imposed. Adler was able to recall a particularly revealing episode of his boyhood attempts to master what his five-year-old mentality perceived as cowardice:

> I remember that the path to the school led over a cemetery. I was frightened every time and was exceedingly put out at *beholding the other children pass the cemetery without paying the least attention to it, while every step I took was accompanied by a feeling of fear and horror.* Apart from the extreme discomfort occasioned by this fear I was also annoyed at the idea *of being less courageous than the others.* One day I made up my mind to put an end to this fear of death. Again, I decided upon a treatment of hardening. I stayed at some distance behind the others, placed my schoolbag on the ground near the wall of the cemetery and ran across it a dozen times, until I felt that I had mastered the fear. (Adler, 1959, pp. 179–180; italics added)

Of significance to Adler-the-theorist was the fact that this recollection showed Adler-the-child attempting bravely to confront his fear and to master the sense of helplessness and inferiority it evoked.

At the age of 35, in conversation with a childhood school chum, Adler learned that there had never been a cemetery on the way to their school (Adler, 1959, p. 180; Orgler, 1963, p. 37). This poignant "memory" had been a "poetic" expression of Adler's striving to overcome the fear of death. Death had been Adler's ready companion throughout childhood, and the struggle to overcome the fear of it, Adler later recognized from his theoretical perspective, was the central goal of his life.

Fear of Death and Anger at Being Helpless

Adler's unconscious had woven what Freud called a "screen-memory" around an illusory cemetery and feelings of fear and anger. This screen-memory was the culmination of a childhood series of brushes with death. As a young boy, Adler had twice been run over in the streets, and he could recall regaining consciousness on the living room sofa (Orgler, 1963, p. 2). When he was only three years old, Adler's younger brother died in a bed beside his. At the age of five, the period to which the cemetery recollection dates, Adler became so profoundly ill with pneumonia that the family physician gave him up for lost. Fortunately, another physician prescribed some treatment and within a few days the "lost" boy was well on his way to recovery. Adler recounted the lasting emotional significance of this brush with death:

> In the joy over my recovery, there was talk for a long time about the mortal danger in which I was supposed to have been. From that time on I recall always thinking of myself in the future as a physician. *This means that I had set a goal from which I could expect an end to my childlike distress, my fear of death.* Clearly, I expected more from the occupation of my choice than it could accomplish: The overcoming of death and the fear of death is something I should not have expected from human, but only from divine accomplishments. Reality, however, demands action, and so I was forced to modify my goal by changing the conscious form of the guiding fiction [life-goal] until it appeared to satisfy reality. So I came to choose the occupation of physician in order to overcome death and the fear of death. (Adler, in Ansbacher & Ansbacher, 1956, p. 199; italics added)

But even as a physician Adler could not tolerate death. Hertha Orgler (1963), Adler's biographer and friend, reports that Adler gave up his general medical practice after the death of several of his diabetic patients. Powerless to forestall these patients' deaths in the days before the discovery of insulin, Adler was overwhelmed by his old enemy.

In addition to his intimate contacts with death throughout his youth, Adler was a chronically sick and weak child. He suffered from rickets, a deficiency disease that results in softening of the bones. He was thus unable to compete well with his older brother or with peers in the physically active pastimes of childhood (Bottome, 1957; Orgler, 1963). Another of Adler's childhood recollections drawn from the age of two again indicates his special sensitivity to feelings of inferiority:

> I remember sitting on a bench bandaged up on account of rickets, with *my healthy elder brother* sitting opposite me. *He could run, jump, and move about quite effortlessly,* while for me, movement of any sort was a strain and an effort. *Everyone went to great pains to help me* and my mother and father did all that was in their power to do. (Quoted in Bottome, 1957, pp. 30–31; italics added)

The importance of this memory lies in Adler's comparison of himself with his older brother, who apparently made Adler feel all the more acutely his physical limitations. Moreover, as Mosak and Kopp (1973, p. 158) point out in their analysis of Adler's early recollections, the young Adler had discovered that there was much to be gained from one's organ defects in the way of sympathy and concern from the powerful people in one's life.

In addition to his acute sense of inferiority, Adler succumbed to a deep resentment over the birth of his younger brother, for this child "dethroned" him from his place of distinction in his mother's heart. It was, however, the mother, not his younger brother, who became the target of Adler's resentment. Therefore, Adler came to prefer his father, who encouraged his son to master life's difficulties on his own terms.

By the age of three, Adler had come to the extraordinary insight that another of his physical problems, contractures and spasms of his vocal cords, was caused by his own feelings of anger and resentment toward his mother and older brother. As with his fear of the cemetery, or more precisely the fear of death, he resolved to confront these unruly feelings and to bring his anger and resentment under control (Orgler, 1963, p. 215). He became a model young man, sociable, affable, outgoing, and altruistic. The hallmark of his style of life was concern for the welfare of others, a theme of existence for which Adler coined a new German word, *Gemeinschaftsgefühl* (most meaningfully translated as *social interest,* in his later theory of personality).

Three essential elements, then, marked Adler's early personality development and, consequently, the structure of his theory of personality. First among these personal elements were his repeated brushes with death, his own and those of loved ones. Second, his physical disability and clumsiness in comparison with his older brother and peers forced Adler into a position of inferiority he struggled consciously to overcome. Finally, he harbored resentment toward his mother for transferring her affections to his younger brother; what degree of guilt emerged from this childish anger when the younger brother died Adler's biographers do not tell us. The key element in Adler's early life history remains his boyhood exposure to and attempts to master the fear of death. Perhaps with his own life history in mind, Adler was later to theorize,

> In all probability none but human beings are conscious of the fact that death is in the destiny of life, and this consciousness alone is enough to give mankind a sense of being terribly overpowered by Nature. If a child experiences a brusque contact with death at an early age, the whole style of life may be largely moulded by that single impression. In such a case the importance of death to life is invariably over-valued, and we can often perceive how the child's actions and reactions are so directed as to find relief from this oppressive idea, or compensate for it. (Adler, 1929b, p. 145)

Adler further suggested that the confrontation with death could have far-reaching consequences for the direction the remainder of the child's life might take. To circumvent personal death, individuals may seek to *prolong their lives through their children* and thereby to gain a small measure of immortality through a contribution to the continuity of the species. Other individuals may seek to defy death through *the attainment of personal greatness in art or science,* thus assuring their survival in the works and ideas they leave for posterity. Finally, the fear of death may be allayed by commitment to *the belief in the immortality of one's soul,* a religious faith that, after all, death is not the final victor of life's struggle. Clearly Adler chose for himself the second of these directions, for in the act of selecting the vocation of physician, he chose to struggle actively against death.

Adler's, Freud's, and Jung's Early Recollections

Interestingly, there is some evidence to suggest that among personality theorists, Adler was not alone in according death a special place among the influences of his life. Mosak and Kopp (1973) compared Adler's early recollections with several of Freud's and Jung's early memories, drawn from their own and their biographers' writings. Freud's early memories seem to indicate that he was a doubter and a skeptic, but once he was convinced of death's inevitability, his doubt was supplanted by awe:

> When I was six years old and was given my first lessons by my mother, I was expected to believe that we were all made of earth and must therefore return to earth. This did not suit me and I expressed doubts of the doctrine. My mother thereupon rubbed the palms of her hands together—just as she did in making dumplings, except that there was no dough between them—and showed me the blackish scales of *epidermis* produced by the friction as a proof that we were made of earth. My astonishment at this ocular demonstration knew no bounds and I acquiesced in the belief which I was later to hear expressed in the words: "*Du bist der Natur einen Tod schuldig*" ["Thou owest Nature a death"]. (Freud, 1900, Vol. IV, p. 205)

In light of Freud's later theory of the death instinct as an inexorable force inherent in living matter, it is not difficult to agree with Mosak and Kopp that Freud was awed by death. (See Chapter 3 for a discussion of Freud's death instinct.)

Jung, on the other hand, was fascinated by death, attracted by the mystery and uncertainty of it. Two incidents he recorded from approximately his fourth year of life are suggestive of his attitude:

> And once there was a great flood. The river Wiese, which flowed through the village, had broken its dam, and in its upper reaches a bridge had collapsed. Fourteen people were drowned and were carried down by the yellow flood water to the Rhine. When the water retreated, some of the corpses got stuck in the sand. When I was told about it, there was no holding me. I actually found the body of a middle-aged man, in a black frock coat; apparently he had just come from church. He lay half covered by sand, his arm over his eyes. Similarly, I was fascinated to watch a pig being slaughtered. To the horror of my mother, I watched the whole procedure. She thought it terrible, but the slaughtering and the dead man were simply matters of interest to me. (Jung, 1961, p. 15)

It is possible to interpret each theorist's early recollection of an experience with death as one indicator of that person's style of life. Mosak and Kopp contrasted the significance of each theorist's early recollections for understanding the life goals of Adler's, Jung's, and Freud's adult personalities:

> Although all three show an interest in death, they differ in their approach to it. Jung is intrigued by death, Freud is awed by death's inevitability, while Adler resolves to work to overcome death. . . . Finally, the dominant life goals of each man emerge from their recollections. Adler's goal is to overcome inadequacy through effort and resolve. Freud

> strives to comprehend through analysis and interpretation, while Jung moves toward communion with nature through sensual awareness. (1973, pp. 164–165)

For Freud, death was a biological process he struggled to comprehend *intellectually, theoretically,* perhaps in an effort to master his own uneasiness. For Jung, death was but another aspect of an already paradoxical existence, inviting one to explore its spiritual and psychological reality. For Adler, death was the ultimate enemy, the supreme obstacle to self-fulfillment, the paramount state of helplessness against which one must struggle at all costs.

FREUD AND ADLER: DISSENT OVER THE FUNDAMENTAL HUMAN MOTIVE

It is small wonder, given Adler's early life history, that he disagreed drastically with Freud over the issue of the central motive force in human personality. Adler felt that human motivation could not be subsumed under the exclusive category of pleasure or sexuality, however broad these concepts had become. A new model of personality was needed, a model that accorded weight to other fundamental human strivings. As Robert White (1960) succinctly put the matter, with the neo-Freudians like Horney, Fromm, and Adler, the libido instinct model was replaced by the interpersonal model. People's search for success, for superiority, for freedom from their own helplessness, for escape from their own fears, and for perfection and personal completeness became Adler's fundamental coordinates upon which to plot human lives in process. While Freud labored to demonstrate the sexual and pleasure-seeking strivings that underlie a broad range of human behaviors, Adler was already inwardly attuned to a human desire he considered more fundamental: *the striving to compensate for one's own perceived inferiorities, for one's enforced states of helplessness.* As Adler had learned, nothing can make one feel more inferior, more powerless than death.

Although there is some confusion over the exact sequence of events, Adler's and Freud's biographers seem to agree that in 1902 Freud sent Adler and several others an invitation to meet with him for informal seminars (cf. Ansbacher & Ansbacher, 1973, p. 336n.; Furtmüller, 1973; Jones, 1955). Sometime shortly before this invitation, Adler had written a defense of Freud's *Interpretation of Dreams* in one of Vienna's foremost newspapers; thus Freud was apparently motivated to contact what he believed to be a kindred spirit. However, Adler's published defense of Freud has never been located. In any event, it seems clear that even though Adler joined the select group of intellectuals surrounding Freud, he was never as completely committed to the Freudian viewpoint as most of the others.

By 1911, at the culmination of continually widening personal and theoretical differences, Adler resigned from the Freud group to pursue his own psychological formulations. Some of Freud's recently published correspondence with Jung reveals the depth of personal and intellectual animosity that arose between himself and Adler. In March 1911, shortly before Adler's resignation, Freud wrote to Jung, expressing his disappointment at the direction Adler's theorizing was taking:

I see now that Adler's seeming decisiveness concealed a good deal of confusion. I would never have expected a psychoanalyst to be so taken in by the ego. In reality the ego is like the clown in the circus, who is always putting in his oar to make the audience think that whatever happens is his doing. (Freud, in Freud/Jung, 1974, p. 400)

Freud's own opinion about the significance of the ego would change drastically by the 1920s, but at this juncture in history Freud was convinced that Adler's psychology was too superficial, too concerned with conscious functioning, and too neglectful of the unconscious determinants of behavior. Freud was particularly alarmed that Adler seemed to ignore the most fundamental tenet of psychoanalytic motivation theory:

The crux of the matter—and that is what really alarms me—is that [Adler] minimizes the sexual drive and our opponents will soon be able to speak of an experienced psychoanalyst whose conclusions are radically different from ours. Naturally in my attitude toward him I am torn between my conviction that all this is lopsided and harmful and my fear of being regarded as an intolerant old man who holds the young men down, and this makes me feel most uncomfortable. (Freud, in Freud/Jung, 1974, p. 376)

The members of the informal seminar group, who now called themselves the Vienna Psychoanalytic Society, decided to clear the air by having a formal debate on the differences between Freud and Adler. Adler was therefore invited to give a systematic presentation of his ideas, beginning on January 4, 1911, and extending over the course of the next several sessions. On February 22, after the members of the group had discussed Adler's ideas and Freud had commented on the significance of the difference between Adler and himself, Adler resigned from the presidency of the Vienna Psychoanalytic Society. By May 24, Adler terminated all contact with the group and, at Freud's suggestion, withdrew as coeditor of the *Zentralblatt,* an important psychoanalytic journal. Freud wrote to Jung in early June:

I have finally got rid of Adler. After I had pressed Bergmann [the journal's publisher] to dismiss him from the *Zentralblatt,* he twisted and turned and finally came up with a strangely worded statement which can only be taken as his resignation. At least, this interpretation is supported by his announcement that he is leaving the Psychoanalytic Society. And then he came out with what he had been holding back: "Despite its unprecedented resolution at one time to that effect, the Society has not had sufficient moral influence on you to make you desist from your old personal fight (!!) against me. Since I have no desire to carry on such a personal fight with my former teacher, I hereby announce my resignation." The damage is not very great. Paranoid intelligences are not rare and are more dangerous than useful. As a paranoic of course he is right about many things, though wrong about everything. (Freud, in Freud/Jung, 1974, p. 428)

For Adler's part, the society's meetings devoted to the differences between himself and Freud had allowed him to crystallize the essential tenets of his own developing viewpoint. Before undertaking a study of Adler's theory, we briefly explore Adler's own presentation of his divergence from orthodox psychoanalysis.

Adler's View of His Differences With Freud

Years after his original dispute with Freud, Adler published an essay summarizing his differences from orthodox psychoanalysis (Adler, 1931). The views he expressed in this essay are a useful means of understanding the directions his theorizing took upon his official break with the Freudian circle.

The Ego

Adler viewed the ego not as the servant of the id's desires but as a creative intelligence independently operating to effect a healthy adaptation to life's circumstances. For him, the ego was the seat of the individual's sense of wholeness, of the person's identity as a complete and willful organism (1931, in 1973, p. 206). Freud, of course, initially viewed the ego as only one part of a complex series of interactions between the individual's drives and reality. The emphasis, for Freud, was on the ego's *relationship to the unconscious,* not on the ego's interactions with reality. Adler focused his attention on the ego as a mediator of social and physical reality, upon, that is, the individual's conscious striving to be someone.

The Oedipus Complex

In Adler's view, the Oedipus complex was not to be interpreted as a purely sexual phenomenon in which the male child vainly attempts to possess the mother. Rather, he felt that equal if not greater weight should be attached to the child's striving to compete with the father, to secure for himself equal strength and power, not merely equal pleasure. The personality theorist must recognize not only the sexual attraction between child and mother but also the fact "that the boy wants to grow beyond himself, wants to attain a superiority over his father" (Adler, 1931, in 1973, p. 207).

Narcissism

When Freud developed the concept of narcissistic ego libido, he had in mind a protective channeling of energy into the self, a healthy self-interest or self-love. Adler, however, felt that the Freudian notion of narcissism indicated a personality turned in on itself, a style of life that by definition excluded healthy *social* interest. The narcissistic attitude, contrary to Freudian theory, is not innate or instinctual, but learned or acquired by those personalities that doubt their own strength. The narcissistic individual fears that he or she is essentially too weak, too powerless to survive, and can control this fear only by excluding any obligation to others (1931, in 1973, p. 208).

Fragmentation of Personality

Adler felt that Freudian theory had fragmented the person into a set of competing parts that defied any attempt to understand the person as a *whole entity,* as a complete functioning unity. For Adler, as we shall later see, personality can be understood to have one fundamental, innate, evolutionary tendency: to grow, to become whole, to seek happiness by becoming fully what one is, rather than by satisfying one's discrete drives. For Adler, human motivation cannot be understood in terms of attempts to reduce the discomfort of mounting biological tensions like sex, hunger, and fatigue; humans struggle *toward* goals they set for themselves, not away from states of deprivation. Adler put the matter this way:

The main problem of psychology is not to comprehend the causal factors as in physiology, but the direction-giving, pulling forces, and goals which guide all other psychological movements. (1931, in 1973, p. 216)

The Meaning of Dreams

Adler disagreed strongly with Freud's conception of the function of dreams. According to Freud, a dream is a disguised fulfillment of a wish that would be quite unacceptable or unattainable in the waking state (cf. Chapter 3). Thus the dream stories that can be recalled by dreamers are bizarre, confused, and incomprehensible to the dreamers to protect them from recognition of their own unacceptable id impulses. The distortion and disguise of the manifest content is merely a protective mask defensively obscuring illicit latent urges.

For Adler, dreams were not to be interpreted as the fulfillment of unacceptable wishes; rather, they represent dreamers' attempts to resolve problems they are unwilling or unable to master with their conscious powers of reason (Adler, 1973, p. 214). Like Freud, Adler felt that the dream was disguised, but in marked contrast to Freud, Adler was convinced that the *purpose* of the dream was to be *not understandable:*

> It is the intention of the dreamer not to understand his dreams. He *wants* to withdraw the dream from understanding. This must mean that something happens in the dream which he cannot justify with reason. *The intention of the dream is to deceive the dreamer.* The person attempts in a certain situation to deceive himself. I have also understood why one does not understand the dream. Its purpose is only to create a *mood.* This emotion must not be clarified; it must exist and act as an emotion, created from the individuality of the dreamer. This apparently corresponds to the desire to solve a problem by an emotional episode and in accordance with his lifestyle, since he is not confident of solving his problem in accordance with the common sense. (Adler, 1973, p. 214)

Thus, for Adler, the dream is an attempt by the dreamers' unconscious to create a mood or emotional state upon waking that will force them to take action that they were reluctant to attempt. In effect, the dream provides them with the excuse and the strength to actualize their true feelings.

In Freud's view, the dream itself is satisfying, whereas in Adler's view, the dream is merely the means to an end, an act of emotional fortification enabling one to live what one thinks. When dreamers cannot provide a conscious and logical justification for their actions, they create a dream that will leave behind a residue of emotion to stimulate action, to provoke the behavior they had been hesitant to accept.

There are many other differences between Freud's and Adler's approaches to personality, and some of these will become apparent in subsequent sections. The five areas we have surveyed—the ego as mediator of social reality, the Oedipus complex as a striving for superiority, narcissism as unhealthy self-centeredness, fragmentation of personality into parts versus the goal striving of the unified person, and dreams as problem-solving self-deceptions—signify substantial differences of opinion between Freud and Adler in their basic view of human nature.

Freud and Adler never reconciled their differences, and, as Freud's system continued to evolve, Adler's disenchantment with his former teacher grew. Freud's increasing pessimism and fatalism about the nature of humans was in direct contrast to Adler's view of humans as essentially good creatures capable of altruistic social concern. In 1930 Freud gave vent to his pessimism in a remarkable passage in *Civilization and Its Discontents,* where he commented on the age-old precept: "Thou shalt love thy neighbor as thyself":

> What is the point of a precept enunciated with so much solemnity if its fulfillment cannot be recommended as reasonable? . . . Not merely is this stranger in general unworthy of my love; I must honestly confess that he has more claim to my hostility and even my hatred. He seems not to have the least trace of love for me and shows me not the slightest consideration. If it will do him any good he has no hesitation in injuring me, nor does he ask himself whether the amount of advantage he gains bears any proportion to the extent of the harm he does to me. Indeed, he need not even obtain an advantage; if he can satisfy any sort of desire by it, he thinks nothing of jeering at me, insulting me, slandering me and showing his superior power; and the more secure he feels and the more helpless I am, the more certainly I can expect him to behave like this to me . . . Indeed, if this grandiose commandment had run "Love thy neighbour as thy neighbour loves thee," I should not take exception to it. . . .
>
> The element of truth behind all this, which people are so ready to disavow, is that men are not gentle creatures who want to be loved, and who at the most can defend themselves if they are attacked; they are, on the contrary, creatures among whose instinctual endowments is to be reckoned a powerful share of aggressiveness. As a result, their neighbour is for them not only a potential helper or sexual object, but also someone who tempts them to satisfy their aggressiveness on him, to exploit his capacity for work without compensation, to use him sexually without his consent, to seize his possessions, to humiliate him, to cause him pain, to torture and to kill him. *Homo homini lupus* [Man is a wolf to man]. (Freud, 1930, pp. 110–111)

Adler was genuinely shocked by Freud's statement (Orgler, 1963). It seemed to him contrary to all reasonable views of human nature to assume that humans were inherently evil:

> And, indeed, if we look closely we shall find that the Freudian theory is the consistent psychology of the pampered child, who feels that his instincts must never be denied, who looks on it as unfair that other people should exist, who asks always, "Why should I love my neighbour? Does my neighbour love me?" (Adler, 1931, p. 97)

Transitional Summary

Stepansky (1983) has reviewed the available evidence on the dissolution of the relationship between Freud and Adler, and he has summarized those features of Adler's developing theory that most alarmed Freud.

First, Freud initially regarded Adler's focus on concepts such as organ inferiority as "too biological" to qualify as a psychological contribution (Stepansky, 1983, pp. 99 and 131).

Second, Adler focused on "surface" issues rather than on the unconscious (Stepansky, 1983, p. 132). In effect, Freud was calling Adler an ego psychologist, a pejorative term at that moment in history.

Third, Freud was concerned about Adler's move away from libido and sexuality in general as the key motivating forces in human behavior (Stepansky, 1983, p. 132

ff.). Adler, it seemed to Freud, was more concerned with the person's personal "safe-guarding" strategies than he was with libido threatening to overwhelm the ego, as orthodox psychoanalytic theory of the time emphasized.

Of the three objections he had to Adler's ideas, Freud apparently considered the second one, the surface focus of Adler's psychology, to be the most important (Stepansky, 1983, p. 127). It is not difficult to understand why: At the time, and probably for many years to come, Freud thought his most unique contribution in creating psychoanalysis was his investigation of the unconscious and its power. Here was Adler, to all intents and purposes, saying that complex psychopathology and behavior could be understood without that contribution.

INFERIORITY-SUPERIORITY: FROM MINUS TO PLUS SELF-ESTIMATES

In light of Adler's childhood infirmities and his experiences with death, it is not surprising that he gave to psychology the concept of the *inferiority complex* (1927, 1929a, 1931, 1964). An individual's sense of helplessness, of powerlessness in the face of death, is not the only way that such persons may arrive at the conclusion that they are inferior. Children may, as had Adler himself, experience the physical inferiorities of damaged or diseased organs that prevent successful competition with peers. Or they may perceive that their elders are powerful controllers of their fate, of their satisfactions, of the very direction their lives are to take. In comparison with these potent manipulators, children feel weak, impotent, and inferior, and like Adler himself, they embark on a lifelong struggle to compensate for their perceived inferiority, to erect a facade of compensatory superiority to conceal their sense of worthlessness.

For Adler, the striving to master inferiority feelings, whatever their origin, is an inherent characteristic of living things, a product of organic evolution: "Set in motion at one time or other the material of life has been constantly bent on reaching a plus from a minus situation. . . . This movement is in no way to be regarded as leading to death; on the contrary, it is directed towards achieving the mastery of the external world and does not by any means seek a compromise with it or a state of rest" (Adler, 1964, p. 97). For Adler, in contrast to Freud, the basic striving of life is not to achieve pleasure, nor final rest; the fundamental urge of life is to achieve "superiority," to achieve, that is, a sense of competence and fulfillment.

It may be helpful at the outset to indicate the sequence of changes through which Adler's thinking progressed on the subject of the organism's striving from minus to plus self-estimates. The concepts of superiority and inferiority underwent several transformations as Adler sought to refine his theory. At first, Adler began with a very concrete, physiological conception of inferiority as rooted in physical *organ defects*. Slowly, this medical conception was modified in the direction of a psychological theory to account for the person's own perception of physical inferiorities. Adler's interest subsequently shifted from this emphasis on the *perceived sense of inferiority* to the strivings of individuals to compensate for their inadequacies.

TABLE 8.1   An Overview of Adler's Changing Views of the Fundamental Human Motive

Organ Inferiority

Least or most poorly developed organ succumbs fastest to environmental demands. Disease strikes only such predisposed organs.

Aggression Drive

Hostile attitude toward perceived helplessness in obtaining satisfactions. May be reversed into an opposite drive of humility or submission.

Masculine Protest

Every child desires to be competent, to be superior, and in control of his own life. Overcompensation to be "manly" and admired results.

Superiority Striving

Inherent biological urge toward self-expansion, growth, and competence.

Perfection Striving

Seeking after a chosen goal, or dream, fulfillment. Based on subjective or fictional estimates of life's values.

Cultural and social factors were thus brought into the theory. *Aggressive* impulses, the *masculine protest, superiority* strivings, and *perfection* strivings rapidly took their respective places as successive transitions in Adler's developing theory of personality. A schematic overview of these transitions is provided in Table 8.1 as a prelude to more detailed discussion in the sections that follow.

Organ Inferiority: Compensatory Strivings

Adler had fought his own childhood battles with organ inferiority in struggling to compete with his older brother and peers in physical activities despite the weakness induced by rickets. When he later chose the vocation of physician in his continuing efforts to combat his own sense of helplessness, he characteristically located his first medical office in a lower-class Viennese neighborhood, where his patients would be drawn from society's least economically favored working men and women.

Situated near the famous Prater amusement park, Adler's practice brought him into contact not only with the "common folk" of Viennese society but also with the entertainers, acrobats, and artists of the Prater. Adler's interest in organ inferiority may have therefore received some impetus from the unusual nature of the patients who sought his help. Furtmüller (1973) has suggested in his biographical essay on

Adler that the entertainers of the Prater directed Adler's attention to the importance of physical strength and weakness in making a successful adaptation to life:

> All these people [i.e., Prater entertainers], who earned their living by exhibiting their extraordinary bodily strength and skills, showed to Adler their physical weaknesses and ailments. It was partly the observation of such patients as these that led to his conception of overcompensation [for perceived inferiority]. (p. 334)

In 1907 Adler published a novel theory of disease that would now be classed as a contribution to psychosomatic medicine. Entitled "Study of Organ Inferiority and Its Psychical Compensation," the essay asserted that all persons succumb to disease in that organ which has been less well developed, less successfully functioning, and generally "inferior" from birth. Thus, for example, some people are born with weak eyes, weak stomachs, badly functioning hearts, or damaged limbs. Whatever the inherent bodily weakness, environmental demands and stresses have their greatest impact on the inferior organ, and the way individuals adapt to life is likely to be shaped by their reactions, both physical and psychological, to their organ inferiorities.

The notion of organ inferiority did not mean, in Adler's development of the concept, that the individual suffers disease only through inherited organ defects. Rather, organs that are biologically inferior to the demands made upon them by the environment are the ones most likely to become sites of origin for physical disease. Adler later emphasized individuals' subjective reactions to their physical infirmities as of crucial importance for the direction their lives would take. The entertainers of the Prater—jugglers, acrobats, and strongmen—would be a case in point. Organ inferiority, one's attempts to compensate for it, and one's sense of self-worth are inextricably interwoven with the individuals' biological-medical statuses and their unique reactions to their social environment:

> We wish to replace the obscure concept of "pathological disposition" by the following proposition: Disease is the resultant of organ inferiority and external demands. The latter are limited in duration and to a particular cultural environment. Changes in the external demands represent cultural progress, changes of the mode of living, or social improvements. (Adler, 1907, p. 25)

Adler postulated that because the entire organism is governed by a principle of equilibrium or balance, the inferior organ under the guidance of the central nervous system would *compensate* for the defect of underdevelopment or damage. Physiologist Walter B. Cannon would some years later propose a similar principle called *homeostasis.* Undergoing increased growth and functioning power, the initially inferior organ, or allied organs, may "overcompensate" for the previous deficit as individuals consciously center their attention on that area of functioning. For example, the individual with an early speech defect may become so involved in mastering stuttering that he or she turns the inferiority into a career. Becoming a speech therapist, or an orator, or an actor, the individual overcompensates for what had been a perceived inferiority (1907, p. 29).

In this early stage of his theorizing, Adler did not yet include his characteristic later emphasis on the individual's subjective perception of inferiority. Compensation and overcompensation were still thought of as biological-environmental processes in the service of equilibrium or homeostasis.

The Aggression Drive

Adler's next step, taken in 1908, was the assertion of an inherent drive of aggression in humans. Ironically, Freud himself was not ready to admit the possibility of aggressive strivings in humans on an equal footing with the drive of sexuality. Yet, from his attempts to work within the frame of psychoanalytic thought, Adler developed this very concept. He was still within the circle of Freud's followers and sought to account for behavior with Freud's basic pleasure principle.

Thus Adler proposed that two basic drives govern the course of the individual's life: the drives of sexuality and of aggression. Along with these two primary biological urges, a number of diverse secondary drives associated with sensory processes like seeing, smelling, and hearing had to be included in any account of motivated behavior. But Adler's key contribution to this scheme was that no drive stands alone. Drives always enter into a *confluence,* an amalgam of interaction whereby each separate component drive is subordinated to the whole (Adler, 1908, p. 30). Furthermore, drives could be transformed and displaced from their original form and goals into new channels of expression:

A. *Transformation of drive into its opposite:* the unconscious drive to eat, for example, becomes the conscious refusal to eat;

B. *Displacement of drive to another goal:* unconscious love for father becomes a conscious love for a teacher or other authority figure;

C. *Direction of drive to one's own person:* the unconscious repressed drive to see, becomes the conscious drive to be looked at; in other words, exhibitionism;

D. *Displacement of the accent on a second strong drive:* the repression of one drive may enhance the expression of another. Thus, blocking of the sex drive's direct expression may increase the drive to "look" at sexual objects. (Adler, 1908, pp. 32–33)

In his paper "Instincts and Their Vicissitudes" (1915a), Freud elaborated the first two of these transformations, for which he gave Adler some credit. Adler, however, developed the concept of "confluence of drives" in a different direction from Freud. The drive of aggression became the dominant and governing force shaping the confluence of drives:

> From early childhood, we can say from the first day (first cry) we find a stand of the child toward the environment which cannot be called anything but hostile. If one looks for the cause of this position, one finds it determined by the difficulty of affording satisfaction for the organ [i.e., the sites of drive; e.g., hunger]. This circumstance as well as the further relationships of the hostile, belligerent position of the individual toward the environment indicate a drive toward fighting for satisfaction which I shall call "aggression drive." (Adler, 1908, p. 34)

Pure expressions of this superordinate striving toward aggression take form as fighting, beating, biting, and outright cruelty. But aggression, following the principle of transformation or plasticity of drives, may also be expressed in less direct form.

Athletic competition; religious conflict; social, national, and race struggles; politics; and even art embody this fundamental human motive. When the aggression drive is turned inward, the individual displays the resultant opposite traits of humility, submission, or in the extreme case, masochism (Adler, 1908, p. 35).

This ability of aggression to be reversed into its opposite at the demands of cultural and parental censure lends the complexity of a "hidden-figure puzzle" to human motivation:

> Charity, sympathy, altruism, and sensitive interest in misery represent new satisfactions on which the drive, which originally tended toward cruelty, feeds. If this seems strange, it is nevertheless easy to recognize that a real understanding for suffering and pain can only come from an original interest in the world of torment. The greater the aggression drive, the stronger will become this cultural transformation. Thus the pessimist becomes the preventor of dangers. Cassandra becomes a warner and prophet. (Adler, 1908, p. 36)

In contrast to his emphasis on the aggression drive as the basic striving governing the confluence of lesser drives, Adler also pointed out the importance of love and affection in the development of the child's personality. Parts of the drives to look, to touch, and to listen join in a unique confluence called the *need for affection:*

> Children want to be fondled [i.e., to be touched], loved, and praised [i.e., to be looked at]. They have a tendency to cuddle up, always to remain close to loved persons, and to want to be taken into the bed with them. (Adler, 1908, p. 40)

Where Freud had seen sexual strivings, Adler found striving for affection. Manipulation of children's drives for affection is the parents' tool of education, for by partially satisfying children's love needs, their behavior can be shaped in the direction of social interest, concern for their fellow beings. By partially denying them, they can be taught healthy independence.

MASCULINE PROTEST: A GENERAL STRIVING FOR SUPERIORITY

Adler's theorizing to this point emphasized the biological nature of the organism and its defects: organ inferiority and the confluence of drives. In 1910, however, Adler shifted his focus to purely psychological phenomena. These psychological formulations were, of course, derived from his early physiological concepts of inferiority and aggression, but now the center of interest was the individual's *interpretation,* his or her phenomenal experience, of organ inferiorities.

Adler first coordinated the biological fact of organ inferiority with its psychological counterpart, the *feeling* of inferiority. Thus children with marked defects like stuttering, clumsiness, deafness, visual deficits, or extreme ugliness or disfigurement develop a subjective feeling of inferiority in relation to the stronger, more competent persons in their sphere. "Such children are thus often placed in a role which appears to them as unmanly. All neurotics have a childhood behind them in which they were moved by doubt regarding the achievement of full masculinity" (Adler, 1910, p. 47).

In an unfortunately chosen metaphor, Adler had identified "superiority" feelings with masculinity and "inferiority" feelings with femininity. Masculinity and femininity were to be understood in their *cultural meanings* as well as biological genders:

> . . . any form of uninhibited aggression, activity, potency, power, and the traits of being brave, free, rich, aggressive or sadistic can be considered masculine. All inhibitions and deficiencies, as well as cowardliness, obedience, poverty, and similar traits, can be considered as feminine. (Adler, 1910, p. 47)

In Adler's view, then, children begin life with one conviction pressed on their awareness in relation to the powerful adults around them: *They are powerless, weak, and dependent* (Adler, 1927, p. 66). When the adults in the child's world insensitively treat their children as passive "toys" to be guarded as valuable property, or dismiss them as worthless "freight," the child learns that only two things are in *his* power: "the pleasure or displeasure of his elders" (Adler, 1927, p. 66).

In consequence, the "feminine tendency" toward passivity provokes in the child a need to combat this enforced inferiority. A *"masculine protest,"* or overcompensatory striving to demolish dependency, to assert autonomy, and to achieve *superiority* similar to that which children witness in those around them emerges. It should perhaps be pointed out that girls, too, engage in the "masculine protest." The identification of inferiority with femininity and masculinity with superiority may have been a poorly chosen set of terms, but until recently they were culturally accurate metaphors. Neither boys nor girls, according to Adler, wish to be locked into the "minus" role assigned to the traditional concept of the female. All persons, therefore, engage in *protest to be superior;* Adler happened to succumb to the historical moment in choosing to call this phenomenon "masculine."

RELATION BETWEEN INFERIORITY AND SUPERIORITY

The core of the feeling of inferiority is organized around a network of character traits that have as their common denominator the feeling of "smallness" and "powerlessness." On this emotional pattern of fundamental inferiority, the masculine protest overlays a defensive network of *compensatory traits:* for timidity there is courage; for submissiveness there is rebelliousness; for feelings of smallness, feelings of grandeur substitute, and so on, as illustrated in Table 8.2.

Striving for superiority, or in contemporary terminology, the need for an income of self-esteem, is a two-phase process. In the first phase, children's sense of inferiority in relation to the adults around them and perhaps founded on biological handicaps fosters a timid, passive, and insecure feeling of smallness.

In the second phase, a superordinate striving for superiority, for autonomy, and for assertive expression of "masculinity" compensates for the inferiority feelings. In the special sense that the terms have been used in this book (cf. Chapter 1), the compensatory traits of the masculine protest can be seen as the mask covering the actor's fundamental character flaws.

TABLE 8.2 Traits of Superiority Striving

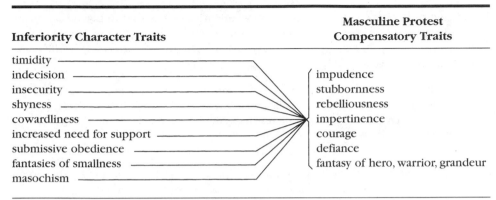

Inferiority Character Traits	Masculine Protest Compensatory Traits
timidity	impudence
indecision	stubbornness
insecurity	rebelliousness
shyness	impertinence
cowardliness	courage
increased need for support	defiance
submissive obedience	fantasy of hero, warrior, grandeur
fantasies of smallness	
masochism	

Based on Adler (1910), p. 53.

At a later point in his theorizing, Adler understood that these compensatory "superior" traits were more than attempts at mere cover-up of one's inferiority. They were, instead, indicators of persons' interpretations of their inferiority, for the traits they choose to adopt outwardly are shaped by their perception of those they inwardly despise. Therefore, such compensatory traits are *signs of what individuals have planned to do about their inferiority.* Table 8.2 pictures the relationship between the underlying network of perceived inferiorities and the individual's compensatory mask of superior "masculine-protest" traits.

The Mask Must Fit the Drama

The remainder of an individual's life takes shape and direction in accordance with an unconscious plan to overcome sensed inferior traits. People create, to use Adler's later terminology, *fictional goals,* that is, subjective guiding ideals that represent *to them* mastery of their character flaws. This fictional ideal of mastery, furthermore, becomes the achievement toward which, throughout life, every fantasy, thought, and action are directed. The mask of compensatory "superior" traits must be consonant with this abiding life goal and must, in an unconscious fashion, foreshadow this most desirable of all possible life outcomes. Adler himself employed the metaphor of the actor and mask to describe this fundamental continuity of personality:

> The fictional, abstract ideal is the point of origin for the formation and differentiation of the given psychological resources [of the individual] into preparatory attitudes, readinesses, and character traits. The individual then wears the character traits demanded by his fictional goal, just as the character mask (*persona*) of the ancient actor had to fit the finale of the tragedy. . . . The self-ideal [i.e., fictional goal] . . . carries within itself all abilities and gifts of which the so-disposed child considers himself deprived. (Adler, in 1956, pp. 94 – 95)

We return to Adler's notion of the fictional final goal or self ideal at a later point. First, we must turn to an illustrative case history to translate into more concrete human terms the abstraction of striving for superiority.

AN ILLUSTRATIVE CASE: LYING FOR SUPERIORITY

Philip, age nine, tells lies that portray him as a fearless hero, able to master all obstacles, willing to enter on new and bold adventures. "For example, he says, 'I was in England. From where I was standing *I looked around the corner of a wall,* and I saw a tiger' " (Adler, 1930a, p. 97; italics added). Adler commented:

> In itself, this is a big lie. But what interests me particularly is that he does not just look, he looks "around the corner of a wall." This is virtuosity. Not everyone can do it. And it tells us even more: The boy's interest is particularly marked, and he is eager to conquer difficulties—difficulties which would be insurmountable for anyone else. (1930a, p. 97)

Philip has a visual problem; he is cross-eyed (strabismus). For this acutely felt organ inferiority, Philip has learned to compensate with adventuresome tales that involve acrobatic feats in the visual mode: "I looked around the corner of a wall." He has turned a handicap into a marvelous feat.

Philip is described by his mother as a "problem child" because he is terribly restless and unable to learn. In school, Philip feels unsure and "unequal to the demands of the situation." But in everyday life, in his play on the street, he misses nothing. He is paradoxically incompetent at tasks favored by his parents and teachers, and quite competent at those of his own choosing. His mother describes him further as cowardly: "He is afraid of everything and runs away from any kind of danger."

Philip's mother understands that he would like to be brave and smart in school, and to be a person that everyone admires. She tries to help him, but Adler reveals that her "help" is more like pampering. She makes his decisions for him; she decides what dangers force her to protect him; she cares for his every need. Her husband confirms Adler's conclusion, for he too feels that she "spoils" Philip. Adler was very specific in his definition of the pampered child:

> A pampered child is one who has been relieved of his independent functioning. Someone else speaks for him, recognizes the dangerous situations, and protects him from them. In short, the child is taken in tow by someone else. *He has another person at his disposal, and he builds his life in symbiosis with her. Such a child has a parasitic trait: he tries to get everything he wants through the aid of his mother.* (Adler, 1930a, p. 97; italics added)

Despite his mother's attention, Philip is unlikely to give up his lies, for lying is the only source of independent superiority. In fact, the sole route open to Philip is to construct ever more subtle lies in an effort to avoid losing what remains of his own sense of selfhood: ". . . he cannot give up his lying and run the risk of appearing to be a 'zero' . . ." (Adler, 1931, p. 99).

Philip's lies continued to grow. For a school theme he wrote about a trip he and his father had made to a cemetery. The entire account was fictional, but Philip went so far as to indicate that he had even surpassed his father in courage: His father had cried, but "I didn't cry. A man doesn't cry."

Unable to win any sense of personal worth without lying for superiority, Philip's response was flight, the flight into a *fantasy* of superiority.

FICTIONALISM: THE PHILOSOPHY OF "AS IF"

To a considerable extent, the young Philip lived by a fiction. Philip's fiction was not identical with the lies he told but rather with the *motive* underlying his specific tales: namely, his desire to be brave, assertive, aggressive, and independent. The resulting lies and exaggerations were merely the tissue covering a skeleton of *subjectively real* interpretations by which Philip managed to navigate the obstacles of his life.

Philip's "lies" were transparent fictions, easily detectable by virtue of their exaggeration. With somewhat less transparency, most people live by similar objectively false ideals. Despite their contradiction of reality, such idealistic "fictions" as "all men are created equal" serve us well as rules-of-thumb or as working hypotheses in daily living (Ansbacher & Ansbacher, 1956, p. 77). Hans Vaihinger (1911) published a book devoted to explaining the ways in which people create and live by such "as if" thinking. Entitled *The Philosophy of "As If,"* Vaihinger's book so impressed Adler that he modified and adopted several of its concepts for his theory.

For Vaihinger, fictions are *subjectively useful interpretations of reality* that, despite their falsity, are valuable to the user in making sense of his life. Thus, although Vaihinger was personally skeptical, he acknowledged that behaving "as if" there were a God lent meaning to people's lives. Similarly, the legal profession must operate "as if" corporations were persons. Physicists sometimes proceed "as if" electricity were a fluid or "as if" light were discrete packets of energy. Some behavioristic psychologists conduct human experimentation "as if" the mind does not exist.

Vaihinger specified five types of fiction whose precise definitions need not occupy us here. The important point is that all such fictions are cognitive devices for representing reality in understandable, livable terms. The fiction may not coincide with the "truth" or objective fact it seeks to represent, but it does capture the essence of a form that is useful to the thinker. For Vaihinger, "truth is merely the most expedient degree of error, and error the last expedient degree of ideation"; but all ideation (thinking) is nevertheless fictional. What counts to the pragmatic Vaihinger is the degree of usefulness of any idea, the degree to which the idea is productive in negotiating the demands of life.

What seemingly attracted Adler's interest in Vaihinger's philosophical position was Vaihinger's emphasis on the *subjective perceptions* of the thinker. As Adler saw it, what matters to a given personality is not what is, but what he or she thinks is. Moreover, Adler was impressed by Vaihinger's stress upon the *individual, idiosyncratic* nature of the process of creating fictions. All individuals create fictions that are unique to them, that are singular creations of their personal inventiveness. Vaihinger even made clear that at least part of the time the creation of fictions was "carried on in the darkness of the unconscious," a proposition for which Adler's psychoanalytic experience had prepared his ready acceptance (cf. Ansbacher & Ansbacher, 1956, p. 88).

Like the "liar" Philip, each personality can be understood fully only when we expose to scrutiny the fictions by which goals and dreams, passions and promises are created.

PERSONALITY AS UNIFIED GOAL STRIVING: FICTIONAL FINALISM

Vaihinger's concept of fictions became for Adler the means to understanding the goal directedness of personality. He adopted the notion of a "fictional" *final goal* in the sense of an *ultimate* ambition that stands at the center of a person's existence. Although Adler eventually dropped the term *fictional* from his designation of this ultimate goal, the three meanings of the concept derived from Vaihinger remained in his usage: *the goal is subjective and personally meaningful; the goal is created by the individual to navigate the obstacles of existence; and the goal is unconscious* (Ansbacher & Ansbacher, 1956, p. 90).

The immediate motive underlying the creation of the fictional goal is the need to gain superiority, attain a state of "plus existence" from a position of minus:

> . . . the movement of the psyche is analogous to the movement of organic life. In each mind there is the conception of a goal or ideal to get beyond the present state, and to overcome the present deficiencies and difficulties by postulating a concrete aim for the future. *By means of this concrete aim or goal the individual can think and feel himself superior to the difficulties of the present because he has in mind his success of the future.* (Adler, 1929a, p. 2; italics added)

Adler pictured the creation of this superordinate goal, or process of *fictional finalism,* as beginning in early childhood. Like the "liar" Philip, the child formulates a "prototype" of his later mature personality in interaction with his environment from the base of his feelings of inferiority:

> A child, being weak, feels inferior and finds itself in a situation which it cannot bear. Hence it strives to develop, and *it strives to develop along a line of direction fixed by the goal which it chooses for itself.* . . . Children look for the strongest person in their environment and make him their model or their goal. It may be the father, or perhaps the mother, for we find that even a boy may be influenced to imitate his mother if she seems the strongest person. . . . Later on, the ideal may become the doctor or the teacher. For the teacher can punish the child and thus he arouses his respect as a strong person. (Adler, 1929a, pp. 3–4)

Thus Adler strongly emphasized the *teleological* or goal-directed character of the human personality, the "mysterious creative power of life." In Adler's own words, the creativity of the personality is "that power which expresses itself in the desire to develop, to strive, and to achieve—and even to compensate for defeats in one direction by striving for success in another" (1929a, p. 1).

In 1912 Adler introduced new terminology for this final fictional goal. He referred to a "guiding self-ideal" as the unifying principle of personality, as in the idea of the role models referred to in the previously quoted passage. Consequently, Adler's view of personality began to emphasize more strongly the "wholeness" or unity of personality as it is entwined and goal seeking, ultimate "becoming."

STRIVING FOR PERFECTION: FOCUS ON THE NORMAL PERSONALITY

In his earliest treatments of the subject, the striving for superiority that emerges from feelings of inferiority is conceptualized by Adler as concerned with power, aggression, and a need to be "masculine." However, Adler began to modify his views of superiority as he moved his focus from the neurotic personality's defensiveness to the normal's goal centeredness.

Adler had described the core of the neurotic personality as a balance between inferiority and the striving for compensatory superiority as expressed in gaining power over others:

> We can consequently always recognize, as the unconscious premises of the neurotic goal-striving, the following two facts:
>
> 1. *Human relations in all circumstances represent a struggle.*
> 2. *The feminine sex is inferior and by its reactions serves as the measure of masculine strength.* (1913a, p. 35)

Note that Adler *was not* asserting that the feminine sex *is* inferior, but that the neurotic personality, man or woman, believes in that inferiority as part of the struggle, masculine protest, to achieve superiority. Neurotic personalities struggle with an overexerted sense of their importance, their "godlikeness," in their efforts to win security:

> All neurotic symptoms have as their object the task of safeguarding the patient's self-esteem and thereby also the life-line [later, lifestyle] into which he has grown. *To prove his ability to cope with life the patient needs arrangements and neurotic symptoms as an expedient.* He needs them as an oversized safeguarding component against the dangers which, in his feeling of inferiority, he expects and incessantly seeks to avoid in working out his plans for the future. (Adler, 1913b, p. 263; italics added)

Thus in Adler's view, the essential characteristics of neurotics are their self-centeredness, their inflated perception of self and their overcompensation for their feelings of inferiority. For the neurotic the dominant goal is *self*-security through personal *superiority.* A healthy interest in the being of others, in their welfare, in their commonality with the self, is excluded from the neurotic's personality development and life plan.

STRIVING FOR PERFECTION: "SAFEGUARDING" THE NEUROTIC PERSONALITY

All persons have feelings of inferiority, in Adler's view, but only the neurotic has blown them up into the central fact of existence. Whereas normal individuals are always ready to abandon their fictional goals, their self ideals, as they mature beyond them, neurotics are fixated, defensively rigid, unable to budge:

More firmly than the normal individual does the neurotic fixate his God, his idol, his personality ideal, and cling to his guiding line, and with deeper purpose he loses sight of reality. *The normal person, on the other hand, is always ready to dispense with this aid, this crutch.* In this instance, the neurotic resembles a person who looks up to God, commends himself to the Lord, and then waits credulously for His guidance; the neurotic is nailed to the cross of his fiction. The normal individual, too, can and will create his deity, will feel drawn upward. But he will never lose sight of reality, and always takes it into account as soon as action and work are demanded. *The neurotic is under the spell of a fictional life plan.* (Adler, 1912, pp. 246–247; italics added)

Adler clearly had evolved a new scheme for interpreting the striving for superiority. He now saw this motive as a ceaseless *yearning for perfection,* a yearning that is inherent to organic life:

The origin of humanity and the ever-repeated beginning of infant life impresses with every psychological act: "Achieve! Arise! Conquer!" This feeling, this longing for the abrogations of every imperfection, is never absent. . . . The unreluctant search for truth, the ever-unsatisfied seeking for solution of the problems of life, belongs to this longing for perfection of some sort. (Adler, 1956, pp. 103–104)

The striving for perfection in one's life is inherent to the processes of life itself, "something without which one could not even conceive of life" (Adler, 1973, p. 31).

Neurotic Self-Absorption

Adler portrayed the neurotic person as self-involved and self-absorbed.[1] Feelings of inferiority are intensified in the neurotic person because real or imagined threats to self-esteem abound in every interaction with another, in every task attempted, and in every memory recalled. The neurotic becomes focused on protecting self:

When scrutinized, the neurotic will be found to be an individual placed in a test situation who is attempting to solve his problems in the interest of his own personal ambition rather than in the interest of the common welfare. This holds true of all neuroses. All neuroses grow out of the psychic tensions of an individual who is not socially well prepared when he is confronted with a task which demands for its solution more social interest than he is capable of. (Adler, 1932, p. 91; italics in original)

Safeguarding self-esteem and personal security become paramount to the neurotic person, and neurotic symptoms may be thought of as tools for safeguarding:

All neurotic symptoms are safeguards of persons who do not feel adequately equipped or prepared for the problems of life, who carry within themselves only a passive appreciation of social feelings and interest. (Adler, 1932, p. 95)

---

[1] It must be remembered that the term *neurosis* was used by Adler, and by most clinicians of the period, as a generalized term for a broad range of psychological dysfunction. Today the term would be employed in a narrower sense to refer to conditions that involve mostly high levels of anxiety with focused symptoms. The *Diagnostic and Statistical Manual of Disorders, Revised* (APA, 1987) would classify neuroses, if the term were still used, as *anxiety disorders.* Thus *neurotic* in Adler's vocabulary is only a general label for psychologically dysfunctional people with no attempt to be more specific about differences in dysfunction. From this perspective, neuroses and personality disorders are more or less blended into a single category; see the discussion of the clinical nosology in Chapter 1.

Neurotic Safeguarding Strategies

Because the neurotic person's self-esteem is so vulnerable, a "far-flung net of safe-guards" becomes part of the person's coping style (Adler, 1913c, p. 264). *Safeguards* are defense mechanisms. Unlike the Freudian version of defense mechanisms, which are focused most on protecting the ego from instinctual (internal) dangers, Adler's safeguards are aimed more at protecting self-esteem from external, usually interpersonal, threats. Adler enumerated three classes of safeguarding tendencies, each with its own subtypes:

1. Excuses or Rationalizing Strategies
2. Aggressive Strategies
3. Distancing Strategies

Excuses and Rationalizations

The neurotic develops symptoms that inhibit or impede some kinds of functioning in the social world. But behind this "barricade of symptoms," he or she feels secure because a certain freedom to do less, achieve less, and demand less of self develops. It is as if the neurotic were excusing self from the usual demands of life by saying, "See, I have this illness or this symptom, so I can't be expected to perform at my best." In Freudian theory, neurotic symptoms not only solve the neurotic conflict, but also provide secondary gain, that is, sympathy from people and a lessening of demands. Adler's concept of "excuses" is akin to the Freudian concept of secondary gain. Table 8.3 summarizes Adler's safeguards and provides a listing of comparable Freudian mechanisms. The similarities between safeguards and defense mechanisms range from substantial to superficial, and it might be helpful to consult Chapter 4 for a more complete account of Anna Freud's classic ten defense mechanisms.

Aggressive Strategies

To safeguard self-esteem, the neurotic person can also express open or disguised hostility to others and to self. Adler distinguishes three kinds of aggressive safeguarding.

   1. Depreciation is a strategy that the neurotic employs to devalue other people so that in comparison to self they are not superior and are not threats. A similar maneuver involves overvaluing self in relationship to others. Instead of expressing hostility directly toward competitors, the neurotic can accomplish the same end by inflating his or her own importance relative to others. Other people are perceived as inferior, just as when they are depreciated directly, but the neurotic can console self that he or she is not disparaging other people, only comparing them to his or her magnificent self (1913c, p. 268).

   In a similar way, the neurotic can depreciate others subtly by comparing real people to impossible ideal standards. The neurotic says to self, "I must be careful not to yield to submission; what I want is a wife (or husband) who is strong (or smart, or powerful, etc.)." But, of course, no real person ever lives up to the ideal, somewhat magical standard, and the result is depreciation of most candidates for an intimate relationship.

   Finally, Adler describes another, more subtle, even "backhanded" form of depreciation. Neurotic people can be overly solicitous for the welfare of others. They behave

TABLE 8.3   Adler's Safeguards and Freud's Defense Mechanisms

Adlerian "Safeguard"	Description	Comparable Freudian Defense Mechanism
Excuses	Neurotic symptoms used as reasons to escape life's demands or not perform at one's best.	• *Rationalization* • *Secondary Gain*
Aggression	1. *Depreciation:* strategies for feeling superior by making others feel inferior, or *overvaluing self* relative to others or being *overly solicitous* of others' welfare as a way to control them.	• *Reaction formation* • *Altruistic surrender* • *Reversal*
	2. *Accusation:* unconscious feelings of deprivation lead to blaming others for one's own feelings of inferiority and frustration. Sometimes person blames fate.	• *Displacement* • *Rationalization* • *Projection*
	3. *Self-accusation (guilt):* blaming self, "cursing" self, and suicidal thoughts and acts sometimes to gain attention, sometimes as a displaced intention to really hurt someone else. Or sometimes self-blame is a way of punishing others by making them feel guilty.	• *Turning against self* • *Reversal* • *Asceticism*
Distancing	Reflects the basic neurotic conflict between feelings of inferiority and strivings for superiority.	
	1. *Moving backward* by using symptoms to avoid social obligations, being helpless, "can't do anything."	• *Fixation* • *Regression*
	2. *Standing still* by refusing to do anything or participate in life, especially when demands are made.	• *Inhibition* • *Regression*
	3. *Hesitation* and procrastination around a self-created difficulty and attempts to master it. Obsessions and compulsions.	• *Rationalization* • *Undoing*
	4. *Constructing obstacles* by focusing on a symptom and blaming failure on it. Usually the least severe form of safeguarding because there is some success.	• *Rationalization* • *Inhibition*

as if they are altruistically concerned that the people in their lives are exposed to dangers, confusions, and demands that only they can help them master. The neurotic seems to believe that without his or her help, other people are incapable of caring for themselves:

> They always give advice, want to do everything themselves, find new dangers and never rest until the other person, confused and discouraged, confides himself to their care. Neurotic parents thus create much damage. . . . The neurotic aspires to make the laws for the others. (1913c, p. 269)

This kind of loving concern hurts. With friends like the neurotic people Adler is describing, we do not need enemies.

2.   *Accusation* involves a more direct expression of anger. The neurotic feels unconsciously deprived and frustrated by others. He or she embarks on subtle blaming of others, sending the covert message that others are at fault for his or her own failures. The person blames parents, siblings, or fate for his or her own difficulties. Adler

referred to this strategy as the "Cinderella" fantasy because the essence is to look for something or someone to take responsibility. In Freud's terms, this kind of substitutive behavior is called displacement and may be combined with rationalization.

3. Self-accusation is putting the blame for one's misfortunes on self, but doing it in such a way that it attracts attention, sympathy, concern, or help from others. Unconsciously, the neurotic person who accuses self also provokes guilt as a kind of atonement for being inferior. Self-accusation, making oneself a pitiable target of criticism can also be a way of inducing guilt in others—making them feel blameworthy for one's misery. It is even possible, in the guise of accusing oneself, to accuse another person by implication. Adler (1913c) provides the example of a depressed woman who suddenly told her husband how she had deceived him by having an affair with another man 25 years earlier. In fact, self-accusation was her way of hurting him for what she believed was his current "disobedience." The comparable Freudian mechanisms are turning-against-the-self, reversal, and asceticism.

Distancing Strategies

The person can also safeguard self-esteem by restricting his or her participation in life. By not exposing oneself to challenge, or by not entering into situations where there is some risk of failure, the person protects his or her self-image. Adler described four overlapping forms of distancing strategy. There is not much difference among them, despite the fact that Adler gave them four different names.

1. Moving backward is a strong indicator of the basic conflict of the neurotic person because he or she is caught between wanting success and wanting to avoid failure. As a result, the person becomes motivationally frozen. The person "moving backward" can either do nothing or develop symptoms that are equivalent to doing nothing, such as mutism (can't talk), hysterical paralyses (can't move), abulia (can't decide), agoraphobia (can't go out into the world), anorexia (can't eat), or amnesia (can't remember). According to Adler the person can also display severe anxiety attacks or even criminal behavior. The point, however, is that the neurotic symptoms put a great deal of distance between the person and the demands of life. Comparable, but not identical Freudian defenses are fixation and regression.

2. Standing still is not much different from "moving backward"; the person shows the same motivationally frozen attitude, but the symptoms are less dramatic. The person again uses the neurotic symptom as a way of not putting self in jeopardy of evaluation. Examples are complaints of weak memory, insomnia that produces fatigue and prevents work, or premature ejaculation that prevents a sustained intimate relationship. The trigger for such behaviors is some life demand, such as an examination, a job task, or a relationship demand that all serve to prompt the person to find a way of "standing still" and not participating. When the external demand or test is removed, the safeguarding strategy disappears. Analogous Freudian defenses are inhibition and regression.

3. Hesitation is a "back and forth" strategy of safeguarding by procrastinating so that whatever effort the person makes, it is "too late." The person may unconsciously create his or her own difficulties, and then, just as unconsciously, create a way of mastering it that becomes a neurotic symptom. Washing compulsions, touching compulsions, leaving things unfinished, destroying nearly completed work because it has to be done over to be right are all ways of wasting time and never committing oneself to be evaluated. Analogous Freudian mechanisms are undoing and rationalization.

4. Construction of obstacles is similar to hesitation and to the strategy of excuses because the person looks for problems that will prevent him or her from expending effort. However, this version is usually the least restrictive form of the safeguarding strategies, because the person has some successes, some achievements that required some effort. But the person rationalizes by saying, "If only I wasn't handicapped by such and such, I could have achieved so much more." The person does not use the obstacle to break off his or her efforts. Rather the obstacle is a challenge that can be overcome even with partial success (and therefore partial effort) so that he or she can say, "Oh, what I could have done had I not been ill."

Adler pointed out that there is a complex relationship between anxiety and the safeguarding tendencies. The safeguards are attempts to avoid the anxiety of perceived low self-esteem. But anxiety can also be a person's first response to any new challenge, such as looking for a job, leaving home, looking for a companion. All the person can think about is the anxiety, not the task, and in this way is already distanced from life. The safeguards that the person will develop will be maintained by this anxiety at the same time that the anxiety serves as a distancing mechanism.

The Completed Transition

Adler construed the striving for perfection as one more evolutionary trend evidenced in the Darwinian principle of adaptation to the environment. The striving for perfection is a never-ending struggle to better adapt to the world; it is, however, a "*victorious* adaptation to the external world."

With the concept of perfection striving as a basic evolutionary process of adaptation to life's circumstances, Adler had maintained continuity with his earliest notions of organ inferiority and the striving to compensate and win a sense of superiority. By the assumption of an inherent biological trend toward better adaption (i.e.,

TABLE 8.4   Transitions in Adler's Conception of Human Motivation

Motive or Personality Goal	Antecedent or Cause
1. Organ Inferiority	Physiological-environmental interaction
2. Aggression Drive	Frustrated biological needs and perceived helplessness
3. Masculine Protest	Cultural attitudes toward "maleness," and feelings of passivity or inferiority
4. Superiority Striving	Evolutionary trend toward successful adaptation; personal feelings of inferiority
5. Perfection Striving	Subjective interpretation of life's meaning, life's values, the fictional final goal

toward perfection), Adler also maintained the goal-seeking or teleological aspect of his personality theory. The steps involved in Adler's achievement of this final conception of perfection-striving as the superordinate goal of life are summarized in Table 8.4.

It may be of some help to compare the contents of Table 8.4 with the items outlined previously in Table 8.1.

SOCIAL INTEREST: THE TASKS OF LIFE

Though the striving for perfection is common to normal and neurotic personality alike, the neurotic's motives are isolated from any interest in the rest of humanity. Indeed, they are isolated from any interest even in those closest to them. Adler indicated the essentially normal sympathy of feeling for one's fellow humans by a German coinage "*Gemeinschaftsgefühl*," a term that defies precise translation. Eventually, the English equivalent of "social interest," which Adler himself favored, was decided on as the uniform translation of Adler's unique German neologism (Ansbacher & Ansbacher, 1956, p. 134).

Social interest is the key difference between the neurotic's striving for superiority and the normal's:

> It is always the want of social feeling, whatever be the name one gives it—living in fellowship, co-operation, humanity, or even the ideal-ego—which causes an insufficient preparation for all the problems of life. (Adler, 1964, p. 110)

The problems of life, which can be successfully solved only by a person with strong social interest, are grouped under three major headings. Each of these tasks was conceptualized by Adler as a universal life problem that all humans must master because they are embedded in a social fabric:

- *Occupational Tasks.* In the selection and pursuit of a vocation as a productive mode of existence, a person "arrives at a feeling of his worth to society, the only possible means of mitigating the universally human feeling of inferiority. The person who performs useful work lives in the midst of the developing human society and helps to advance it."

- *Societal Tasks.* Because individuals live within the context of humankind, they must adapt to others and interest themselves in them. Friendship, social interest, is the normal human means of adapting to societal life: "it was only because man learned to cooperate that the great discovery of the division of labor was made, a discovery which is the chief security for the welfare of mankind."

- *Love Tasks.* The relationship between the sexes is the last significant task of life to be mastered. "On his approach to the other sex and on the fulfillment of his sexual role depends his part in the continuance of mankind." (Adler, 1933, p. 132)

Adler emphasized the relatedness of the three tasks:

The three problems are never found apart, for they all throw cross lights on one another. A solution of one helps toward the solution of the others, and indeed we can say that they are all aspects of the same situation and the same problem—*the necessity for a human being to preserve life and to further life in the environment in which he finds himself.* (Adler, 1933, pp. 132–133; italics added)

The individual who embodies a healthy social interest is expressing an evaluative attitude toward life: "*To see with the eyes of another, to hear with the ears of another, to feel with the heart of another*" (Adler, 1956, p. 135).

STYLE OF LIFE: INDIVIDUAL PSYCHOLOGY

Adler chose the phrase *individual psychology* to identify his system for what by now must be obvious reasons. He emphasized the essential subjective nature of the individual's goal striving, the innate creativity of human psychological adaptation, and the wholeness of the individual's unified personality. Each of us, in an analogy to evolution, fits into our own niche in our own way. And then, individuals subordinate all drives, needs, and strivings to the context of their entire style of life, the very pattern of their existence as social beings *as they create it.*

> The goal of superiority, with each individual, is personal and unique. It depends upon the meaning he gives to life; and this meaning is not a matter of words. It is built up in his style of life and runs through it like a strange melody of his own creation. . . . Understanding a style of life is similar to understanding the work of a poet. A poet must use words; but his meaning is more than the mere words he uses. The greatest part of his meaning must be guessed at; we must read between the lines. . . . The psychologist must learn to read between the lines; he must learn the art of appreciating life-meanings. (Adler, 1931, pp. 57–58)

To the degree that individuals have developed healthy social interests, their strivings for superiority will be shaped into a style of life that is warmly receptive of others and focused on friendship and interpersonal ties. They will be characteristically expectant that other people are similarly warmly receptive of them and are therefore sources of satisfaction and pleasure.

Style of life, then, is based on individual's unique interpretations of their inferiority. Adler illustrated his meaning for "style of life" with the following analogy:

> Perhaps I can illustrate this by an anecdote of three children who were taken to the zoo for the first time. As they stood before the lion's cage, one of them shrank behind his mother's skirts and said, "I want to go home." The second child stood where he was, very pale and trembling, and said, "I'm not a bit frightened." The third glared at the lion fiercely and asked his mother, "Shall I spit at it?" The three children really felt inferior, but each expressed his feelings in his own way, consonant with his style of life. (1931, p. 50)

One's style of life is the product of a *creative* personality trend to overcome one's unique sense of inferiority. The goal that beckons one becomes the guiding force of one's life because it is one's goal. One decides to shape one's life in the direction of that goal because *one's own* feelings of inferiority form a unique constellation with one's own striving for superiority.

Every individual represents both a unity of personality and the individual fashioning of that unity. The individual is thus both the picture and the artist. He is the artist of his own personality, but as an artist he is neither an infallible worker nor a person with a complete understanding of mind and body; he is rather a weak, extremely fallible, and imperfect human being. (Adler, 1956, p. 177; see also 1930c, p. 24)

In Adler's view, therefore, the individual is a *creative artist* of personality, an *active constructor* of his or her life events (cf. Kelly (1958a), Chapter 12, for a similar proposition).

AN ILLUSTRATIVE CASE: JEAN-MARY'S LIFESTYLE

That the style of life of a child may be shaped by personal reaction to a perceived inferiority or to a physical limitation is illustrated by the direction Jean-Mary's life followed. Recall that Jean-Mary suffered from a congenital heart defect that required constant medical supervision and hospitalization during her childhood.

> When Jean-Mary was six years old, the congenital heart defect from which she suffered imposed a low ceiling on the physical activities that she could pursue. Unable to run, skate, or skip rope as well as the other children, Jean-Mary never assumed for a moment that there was anything wrong with *her.* It was simply a matter of ability. Her strengths lay elsewhere.
>
> For example, when the girls on the block skipped rope, Jean-Mary was always a "steady-ender," the girl who turned the rope as the others jumped. But when it came to school activities, Jean-Mary was at the top of her classes.
>
> Slowly her whole style of life was shaped in the direction of intellectual pursuit, helped on the one hand by her lack of physical prowess, and on the other by her positive intellectual superiority. Most of her spare time was spent devouring books. So great was her appetite for reading that daily trips to the library for new books were not unusual. In fact, a book was usually begun on the walk home, a journey that consequently took a meandering snail's pace. Once, while deeply absorbed in a particular juicy romance, Jean-Mary walked headlong into a sidewalk tree, excused herself without looking up, and continued homeward oblivious to the fact that her politeness had been inappropriately bestowed. Her later choice of career was therefore not surprising. As a manuscript editor for a university publisher, Jean-Mary was more concerned with Elizabethan prose than with the demands of daily life, as her friends would often tell her.

Jean-Mary's style of life was shaped by two important factors: Her physical restrictions fostered the development of interest in things intellectual, and her native superior intelligence made her interest fruitful. Thus Jean-Mary's style of life was a product of inferiority and superiority merging into a unique and unified personality.

PERSONALITY TYPES: DEGREES OF SOCIAL INTEREST

Adler developed a scheme of personality types based on the degree of social interest and activity level embodied in different personalities. His personality typology was not strongly emphasized in his whole personality system, but is of some interest in relation to other theorists' typologies.

Early on, Adler had written about the four classic types of temperament described in the writings of Hippocrates and Galen in ancient Greece. According to temperament theory, individual personality types can be classified into four categories on the basis of individual dominance of one of four body fluids or humors: blood, black bile, yellow bile, and phlegm. The *sanguine personality,* for whom blood is the decisive determinant of temperament, is accepting of life and greets it on its own terms with a certain joyousness. The sanguine individual does not take things too seriously, and optimistically attempts to see the good side of things. In terms of individual psychology, "The Sanguine individual seems to be that one who has been least exposed to the feeling of inferiority in his childhood, who has shown fewest important bodily infirmities, and has been subjected to no strong irritations, with the result that he has developed quietly with a certain love for life . . ." (Adler, 1927, p. 148). Thus Adler conceptualized the sanguine type as the healthiest of the four.

The *choleric type,* for whom yellow bile is the dominant humor, is irascible and easily irritated. Explosions of anger and perpetual pessimism are characteristic of the choleric type. In Adler's terms, "the choleric individual is one whose striving for power is so tense that he makes more emphatic and violent movements, feeling that he is forced at all times to produce evidence of his power. He is interested only in overcoming all obstacles in a straight-line aggressive approach" (Adler, 1927, p. 147).

The *melancholic type,* in whom the influence of black bile is strongest, is introspective and brooding, sad and "melancholy." "Individual Psychology sees in him the outspokenly hesitating neurotic who has no confidence in ever overcoming his difficulties or of getting ahead, who prefers not to risk a new adventure, who would rather remain standing still than proceed to a goal . . ." (Adler, 1927, p. 148).

Finally, the *phlegmatic type,* for whom, of course, phlegm is the dominant humor, is the slow, lethargic, uninterested-in-life individual. This type makes few friends and "of all types he perhaps stands at the greatest distance from the business of living" (Adler, 1927, p. 148). In individual psychology, the phlegmatic temperament is interpreted as "a defense mechanism, a meaningful response to the challenge of existence . . ." (Adler, 1927, p. 150).

In 1935 Adler expanded his views on personality types and created new terminology to describe them. Though the four new personality types correspond to the four classical Hippocratic types, Adler stressed two new variables in their classification. The *degree of activity,* or what would probably now be called arousal level (cf. Eysenck, 1967), and the *degree of social interest* were used to define and categorize the newly named *ruling, getting, avoiding,* and *socially useful* types.

Some individuals can be described in terms of activity level from childhood as wild or unbridled; others are characteristically shy, withdrawn, and calm. Individuals' styles of life will be molded in some degree by the basic attitude they have acquired in interaction with their environments through their activity levels. We would expect the wild, unbridled type of personality to have a more active, aggressive attitude toward life than the quieter, more withdrawn type. The four specific types are as follows:

A. *The Ruling-Dominant Type.* These personalities are assertive, aggressive, and active. They manipulate and master the life situation and the people in it. Their activity levels are high but are combined with minimal social interests. The danger is that the activities will be directed into antisocial behaviors.

B. *The Getting-Leaning Type.* These types of individuals expect others to satisfy their needs and to provide for their interests; they are "leaners." The getting-leaning types are combinations of low social interests and low activity levels.

C. *The Avoiding Type.* These individuals are inclined to achieve success by circumventing a problem, by withdrawing from it. In effect, they achieve mastery by avoiding defeat. Their social interests are about as low as those of the getting-leaning types, but their activity levels are even lower.

D. *The Socially Useful Type.* This personality type is the healthiest of them all in Adler's view. The socially useful person attacks problems head on with a realistic appraisal of their difficulty. This type is socially oriented and prepared to cooperate with others to master the tasks of life. Thus the socially useful person has a combination of high activity level and high social interest (based on Adler, 1935, pp. 167–168).

In all cases, the important consideration for Adler was the degree of social interest embodied in a particular type, for the feeling of human empathy is the determinant of a goal-directed life that avoids the excesses of self-centered neurotic striving. The four social interest types correspond to the classical humoral types and Adler's early description of them. These correspondences are summarized in Table 8.5.

EARLY RECOLLECTIONS AS INDICATORS OF STYLE OF LIFE

Adler used a number of diagnostic indicators in dealing with his patients. Among these he employed dream analysis, interpretation of early recollections, and the birth-order sequence within a family. Adler felt that one of the most significant roads to

TABLE 8.5   Correspondence Between Hippocratic and Adlerian Types

Classical Greek Types		Adler's Social Interest Types	
Humors	*Types*	*Types*	*Social Interest*
Yellow bile	Choleric →	Ruling-dominant	Low
Phlegm	Phlegmatic →	Getting-leaning	Low
Black bile	Melancholic →	Avoiding	Lowest
Blood	Sanguine →	Socially useful	High

Note that the sanguine and socially useful types were considered by Adler to be the healthiest personalities because of their degree of social interest and willingness to tackle the problems of life, namely, vocational, social, and love tasks.

investigating individual personalities could be traveled by analyses of their earliest recollections. We have already seen an application of this technique to aspects of Adler's own life. The incidents, feelings, and people that the individual recalls from early in life are significant exactly because these and no others are available to the individual's conscious recollection. With them the meaning he or she has placed on life is expressed:

> There are no "chance memories": out of the incalculable number of impressions which meet an individual, he chooses to remember only those which he feels, however darkly, to have a bearing on his situation. Thus his memories represent his "Story of My Life"; a story he repeats to himself to warn him or comfort him, to keep him concentrated on his goal, and to prepare him by means of past experiences, so that he will meet the future with an already tested style of action. (Adler, 1931, p. 73)

Thus, if one lives one's life "as if" others are always trying to humiliate one, the memories one is likely to recall are those of humiliation or those that can be interpreted as humiliating experiences (Adler, 1956, p. 351).

The most significant of the individual's early recollections is the one that he or she chooses to verbalize first. This incident will reveal the basic life attitude, "his first satisfactory crystallization of his attitude." Adler in no way accepted the individual's recollections as statements of fact. He seems, rather, to have treated them more as a form of projective test whereby the *individual's construction* of meaning, not the objective truth of the memory, is the key indicator. "What is altered or imagined is also expressive of a patient's goal . . ." (Adler, 1956, p. 352). Adler thus adhered to the same conviction that Freud had established as a major principle of psychology: Psychical events are determined. Or, as Adler stated it, "There are no chance memories." However, where Freud viewed the determinism of mental life as located in the patient's past, Adler interpreted early recollections as shaped by the patient's goal, that is, by his or her view of the future.

EARLY RECOLLECTIONS OF A PAMPERED CHILD

Adler treated a 32-year-old man, suffering for two years with hysterical aphasia. He could not speak above a whisper. He had been involved in an accident on the street in which he fell suddenly against the window of a taxi. For two days, he vomited and suffered intense headaches; he probably sustained a concussion. At this time he lost his voice, although his throat showed no organic changes and no signs of injury from the accident. Eventually, the man decided to sue the taxi company for damages resulting from his injuries. As Adler diplomatically stated it, "We can understand that he is in a much better situation with his lawsuit if he can show some disability. We need not say that he is dishonest; but he has no great stimulus to speak loudly" (1931, p. 86). Adler asked the man for his earliest memory:

> I was hanging in the cradle, lying on my back. I remember seeing the hook pull out. The cradle fell and I was badly hurt. (1931, p. 87)

Adler suggested that the man's recollection revealed an important aspect of his style of life: Because his mother had been horrified when she discovered his mishap, and because she showered him with atypical attentiveness, he learned a technique to gain her attention. It was his opinion that he deserved the increased concern and attention because before the accident "she did not take good enough care of me." Indeed, the accident occurred largely because, in the man's opinion, his mother had failed to prevent it. Of course the taxi incident followed the same pattern, for the company and the cab driver "did not take good enough care of him" (Adler, 1931, p. 87).

The character of these recollections suggested to Adler that the man had been a "pampered child," a favorite descriptive phrase for Adler. By that description Adler meant to indicate a child whose daily life involved the delegation of responsibility for living to others. Allowed to make none of his own choices, protected from every danger, the child soon fails to develop genuine autonomy, and he resents people who do not shower him with favor. The previous case history of Philip "the liar" is a similar example of a pampered child.

The man's next recollection followed in this path: "At the age of five I fell twenty feet with a heavy board on top of me. For five or more minutes I was unable to speak" (1931, p. 87). Again, his mother was horrified and excited, and, of course, very attentive. Adler's interpretation needs no elaboration:

> He was a child who wanted to be pampered, to be the center of attention. We can understand how he wants to be paid for his misfortunes [i.e., the taxi accident]. Other pampered children might do the same if the same accidents happened. Probably, however, they would not hit on the device of having a speech defect. This is the trademark of our patient; it is part of the style of life he has built up out of his experiences. (1931, pp. 87–88)

Early recollections, as employed by Adler, are an adjunct to psychotherapy that aims to reorient patients' lives to enable them to reinterpret their past misinterpretations of their experiences (cf. Dreikurs, 1963, p. 254). The technique can be used, of course, to interpret patients' early recollections from a variety of theoretical viewpoints (Mosak, 1958).

ORDINAL POSITION WITHIN THE FAMILY AS INDICATOR OF STYLE OF LIFE

Another diagnostic indicator Adler pioneered by systematizing his clinical insights was interpretation of the birth-order relationships of children within a family. Adler pointed to the myriad differences that exist between the first born and the last born, to the differences between an only child and a child with many siblings, and so on. *First born, second born, youngest child,* and *only child* are considered significant roles by Adler.

First Born (Oldest)

Because it is first born, the oldest child lives a favored existence for a time as an "only child." It is given central place until another child is born to remove its favored status. Adler comments,

> Now he must share the attention of his mother and father with a rival. The change always makes a great impression and we can often find in problem children, neurotics, criminals, drunkards, and perverts that their difficulties began in such circumstances. They were oldest children who felt deeply the arrival of another child; and their sense of deprivation had moulded their whole style of life. (1931, p. 144)

Though skillful at gaining attention, the oldest child eventually learns that mother is too busy, too harassed, or too unconcerned to tolerate its demands. It turns to father. By directing attention-getting behaviors to father, the deprived oldest child seeks to "reproach his mother" (1931, p. 146). The outcome of this family struggle is that the oldest child "trains himself for isolation." It masters the technique of surviving alone and independently of the need for anyone's affection or attention. Because the happiest time of life was *before* the birth of the new child, oldest children often show an unusual interest in the past. "They are admirers of the past and pessimistic over the future" (1931, p. 147).

A healthy outcome is also possible. An oldest child may imitate father and mother in their attentions to the other children. As such imitation progresses, the oldest becomes a helper to the younger children or a mother or father figure to playmates.

Second Born

From birth, a second-born child is raised in a world in which mother divides her attention and ministrations between her two children. This second child's existence is the more favored of the two since it has, so to speak, a "pacemaker" in the form of an older brother or sister. It is thus stimulated, or perhaps provoked, to match the older child's exploits.

> He behaves as if he were in a race, as if someone were a step or two in front and he had to hurry to get ahead of him. He is under full steam all the time. (Adler, 1931, p. 148)

When, however, the oldest child, the pacemaker, beats the younger sibling, the younger child is likely to feel incompetent. The most difficult combination occurs when the oldest is a boy and the second child is a girl. If the girl beats the older boy at his own game, he fares worse than if the younger child had been another boy. On the other hand, if the older child sets a pace to which the girl cannot match her stride, her personal and culturally reinforced feelings of inferiority will be intensified. Generally, however, the second child is the conqueror, using direct and devious means to surpass the pacemaker (Adler, 1929b, p. 106).

The Youngest Child

Although in a large family each succeeding child "dethrones" the previously born one, the last or youngest can never be removed from its pampered position. This child has many pacemakers, but because it retains the position of "most pampered," the baby of the family group, it often outstrips its brothers and sisters in achievements.

Adler felt, however, that the second largest proportion of problem children come from the group of youngest:

The reason for this generally lies in the way in which all the family spoils them. A spoiled child can never be independent. He loses courage to succeed by his own effort. Youngest children are always ambitious; but the most ambitious children of all are the lazy children. Laziness is a sign of ambition joined with discouragement; ambition so high that the individual sees no hope of realizing it. (1931, p. 151)

Because of the multiplicity of its pacemaker models, the youngest child is driven to desire success in everything. Because universal accomplishment is unlikely, he or she may be driven to discouragement.

The Only Child

The only child's rival is the father. Pampered by the mother because she is afraid of losing her child, the only child becomes "tied to the mother's apron strings." In later life, when no longer the center of attention, this enforced timidity and passivity will operate to the child's detriment.

Only children are often very sweet and affectionate, and later in life they may develop charming manners in order to appeal to others, as they train themselves in this way, both in early life and later. . . . We do not regard the only child's situation as dangerous, but we find that, in the absence of the best educational methods, very bad results occur which would have been avoided if there had been brothers and sisters. (Adler, 1929b, pp. 111–112)

Adler's homely positional psychology is another outstanding example of his differences from Freud. Whereas Freud focused on the instinctual interactions between children and parents, Adler preferred the commonsense approach of direct observation of children's behavior. His formulations contain many insights recognized from antiquity as "truisms," but as with all homespun theory, the exceptions to the rule outnumber the agreements.

Transitional Summary

Adler's chief contribution was to provide the framework for a unified, holistic account of personality. His emphasis on human creativity is matched by later theorists (e.g., George Kelly, R. D. Laing, Carl Rogers, Abraham Maslow).

But Adler's influence on contemporary psychology has been slight, with improving prospects in recent years largely through the systematic efforts of the Ansbachers (1956, 1973). As contemporary theorists seek to formulate theories more adequate to the task of dealing with people's humanity, Adler's stature will rise. But only when Adler's clinical and insightful hypotheses are translated into empirically testable constructs, if that is possible, will his system achieve a place in the broader field of a unified behavioral science.

EVALUATING ALFRED ADLER

A large portion of what Adler wrote and thought that was criticized by the orthodox Freudians has become mainstream ego psychology or accepted into humanistic psychology. It was Adler, striving to promote his own unique theory, who focused on some of the blind spots in the psychoanalytic conception of human beings well before the "orthodox revisionists" within psychoanalysis did the same thing to expand the theory into the arena of ego psychology. Freud did not like it when Adler did it as a competitor, and it is probable that he would not have liked much of what the ego psychologists did in his behalf. (Some of these issues are dealt with fully in Chapter 4.) But Adler nevertheless anticipated many later developments in psychoanalytic theory, humanistic theory, and even social learning theory for which he was given little credit at the time. The difficulty, as we might expect from our review of Freud and the ego psychologists (chapters 2 to 4), is that Adler shares much with Freudian theory, including the problems.

Refutability of Adler's Concepts

It is of some historical importance that Karl Popper's criterion of refutability was created in part in relationship to Adler's and Freud's ideas. Popper conceived of the idea of refutability when he realized that Freud's, Adler's, and Karl Marx's theories could explain any kind of human behavior, and that psychosocial theories such as these are different from physical theories, such as Albert Einstein's theory of relativity. Popper's account of how he first came to the concept of refutability is instructive both for its historical value and for its relevance to Adler's work. Popper (1965, p. 35) said that he was, in fact, "much impressed" by his experience of working with Alfred Adler in 1919 when he discussed a case with Adler and found that Adler could account for a child's behavior easily with his theory of inferiority feelings. Popper asked Adler how he could be so sure of his interpretation, and Adler replied, "Because of my thousandfold experience." Popper responded wryly, "And with this new case, I suppose, your experience has become thousand-and-one-fold" (1965, p. 35). Popper was not simply being sarcastic. The interchange with Adler set him thinking:

> What I had in mind was that his previous observations may not have been much sounder than this new one; that each in its turn had been interpreted in the light of "previous experience," and at the same time counted as additional confirmation. What, I asked myself, did it confirm? No more than that a case could be interpreted in the light of the theory. But this meant very little, I reflected, since every conceivable case could be interpreted in the light of Adler's theory, or equally of Freud's. I may illustrate this by two very different examples of human behaviour: that of a man who pushes a child into the water with the intention of drowning it; and that of a man who sacrifices his life in an attempt to save the child. Each of these two cases can be explained with equal ease in Freudian and in Adlerian terms. According to Freud the first man suffered from repression (say, of some component of his Oedipus complex), while the second man had achieved sublimation. According to Adler the first man suffered from feelings of inferiority (producing perhaps the need to prove to himself that he dared to commit some crime), and so did the second man (whose need was to prove to himself that he dared to rescue the child). I could not think of any human behaviour which could not be interpreted in terms of either theory. It was precisely this fact—that they always fitted, that they were always confirmed—which in the eyes of their admirers constituted the strongest argument in favour of these theories. (Popper, 1965, p. 35)

What Popper realized, of course, is that precisely this "strength" of the theories—that they apply to and are confirmed by so much—is their greatest weakness. To be compatible with any outcome is to predict no one outcome (see also Stepansky, 1983, pp. 37ff. for a similar view of Adler's difficulties with refutability).

Adler's theory, like Freud's and like the theories of the other psychoanalytically oriented thinkers, is largely unrefutable. The basic concepts, such as superiority striving, or the inferiority complex, or even the "safeguarding" strategies, are empirically empty. None of these concepts specifies measurable, observable consequences that ought to exist if they are inaccurate. In Popper's language, such concepts are not falsifiable.

There are sections of Adler's thinking that, in principle, are empirical. For example, his ideas on the effects of birth order should lead to some measurable consequences in the real world. And, in fact, a great deal of research has been done on the personality effects of birth position. But one review of a major portion of such studies (Ernst & Angst, 1983) concludes that the studies are methodologically flawed, based on post hoc explanations and correlations of data, and so ambiguous as to be able to explain virtually any personality effect by appeal to the child's position in the family.

As we saw with Freud, the theory clearly has value in clinical terms, but its propositions are not yet formulated in a way that permits adequate scientific testing.

Adler's Conception of Human Agency

Almost from the beginning, Adler argued that a person was not trapped by personal history, biology, or social circumstances. It was within the person's power to alter or adapt creatively to these conditions. When we read Adler's essays, our impression is that people who passively accept their limitations or who create their own obstacles to "safeguard" self-esteem angered him.

Adler's adoption of Vaihinger's concept of the "as if," and his insistence on the subjective meaning that people impose on reality as more important than reality itself, argue strongly for an active agency conception of people. It might be argued, however, that Adler allowed for an interaction between unchangeable determinants and complete freedom of choice, as for example in his concept of organ inferiority. But by the final phases of his theory construction, it is quite clear that Adler placed the greatest emphasis on a person's power to choose, capacity to interpret, and willingness to try to change the conditions of his or her life in the direction of social interest.

The Idiographic Nature of Individual Psychology

As its very name suggests, the focus of Adler's theory is idiographic. For the same reasons discussed under his conception of human agency, Adler stressed the individual's unique and creative interpretation of reality as the most important element of his understanding of psychology. And, like the other thinkers who share psychoanalytic propositions, Adler's own efforts were largely clinical and educational, working with individual cases and using such work as support for his ideas.

SUMMARY

As a child, Alfred Adler had been singularly sensitized to cues indicating his own frailty and powerlessness. Poor health prevented him from competing successfully with his older brother and peers in the athletic pursuits of boyhood. Repeated brushes with death impressed Adler with the fragility of human nature and with the necessity for struggling against imposed helplessness. A powerful resentment toward his mother and younger brother was also influential in shaping Adler's conception of human nature, for he became convinced that such undesirable impulses had to be controlled and replaced by a healthy concern for others. In his later theory of personality, Adler referred to this essential quality of the healthy personality as *Gemein-schaftsgefühl* (social interest).

Having joined Freud's intellectual circle in Vienna in 1902, Adler, never completely committed to psychoanalysis, slowly drew further apart from orthodox Freudian theory. By 1911 the split between Freud and Adler reached a climax, and Adler set off to develop his own school of individual psychology. His differences from Freud were many, but key theoretical discrepancies can be discerned in the following six areas: (1) The ego was not merely the handmaiden of the id, but an independent, creative entity mediating intercourse with social reality. (2) The Oedipus complex was not exclusively a sexual phenomenon but an indication of the boy's attempts to gain superiority and power as possessed by the father. (3) Narcissism was not a retraction of energy into the ego as a protective self-interest, but an unhealthy, antisocial, and egocentric withdrawal of interest in others. (4) Personality could not be studied piecemeal or in fragments of discrete id, ego, or superego functioning; the *human person is a whole entity,* striving toward self-determined goals. (5) Dreams are attempts to create a mood that will induce awake dreamers to take action they were previously reluctant to pursue; dreams are not satisfactions, as Freud held, but attempts to solve problems from waking life. (6) Freud's pessimism concerning the inherent evil of human nature offended Adler's philosophical convictions to the contrary.

For Adler the central core of personality is a state of perceived inferiority for which the individual feels compelled to compensate by striving for superiority. The notion of inferiority compensation underwent several changes in Adler's thinking:

Organ Inferiority

↓

Aggression Drive

↓

Masculine Protest

↓

Superiority Striving

↓

Perfection Striving

Adopting Vaihinger's concept of "fiction," Adler postulated that all persons have a *fictional final goal* in the sense of a *subjective* (fictional), unconscious, and creative striving to master the obstacles of their lives. Individuals' life-meanings can be understood only by comprehending the goals toward which they strive.

Adler developed a typology of personality organized on the principles of activity level and degree of social interest. Four personality types were described: ruling-dominant (choleric); getting-leaning (phlegmatic); avoiding (melancholic); and the socially useful (sanguine) type. Adler felt that only the socially useful type, embodying a high degree of social interest and a high degree of activity, was healthy enough to master successfully the three life tasks.

Adler's diagnostic indicators employed in psychotherapy included the analysis of early recollections and the interpretation of the child's ordinal position within the family. Early recollections are important indicators because they reveal the central concerns and unconscious goals (fictions) of the personality through its conscious choice of key memories. Positional or ordinal psychology is concerned with the child's relationship to parents and siblings. The first born is independent and initially favored; the second born is also favored because it has the "pacemaker" older sibling to model itself after, though there is the danger that it may feel incompetent by comparison, as had Adler with his older brother; the youngest child has many pacemakers to follow and is customarily the "most pampered"; and, finally, the only child, who, like the first born, learns to be independent, is initially pampered, but may ultimately become timid and passive because it lacks pacemakers and siblings with whom to compete.

Our evaluation of Adler's theory indicates that most, but not all, of its concepts are nonrefutable. In fact, Karl Popper created the criterion of refutability largely out of consideration for the capacity of Freud's and Adler's theories to be compatible with nearly any human behavior. Adler is a strong proponent of an active agency conception of human motivation and behavior, as evidenced in his adoption of Vaihinger's "as if" subjectivity. And for the same reasons, it is clear that *individual psychology* is exactly that: idiographic.

FOR FURTHER READING

Adler's definitive work is *The Practice and Theory of Individual Psychology* (Totowa, NJ: Littlefield Adams, 1959). Two biographical accounts are worth pursuing for what they reveal of the sources of Adler's ideas on inferiority and superiority. The most comprehensive biography is Phyllis Bottome's *Alfred Adler: A Portrait From Life* (New York: Vanguard, 1957). More concerned with explicating Adler's concepts than his life is Hertha Orgler's *Alfred Adler: The Man and His Work* (New York: Putnam, 1963).

Harold Mosak, an eminent Adlerian therapist, has edited a collection of papers that place Adler's work in historical perspective and evaluate his contemporary influence: *Alfred Adler: His Influence on Psychology Today* (Park Ridge, NJ: Noyes Press, 1973). Some of the papers in this collection seek to extend Adlerian theory to family and child therapy. In a similar vein, Rudolf Dreikurs and Loren Grey develop an approach to child rearing and teaching from the Adlerian perspective in *A New Approach to Discipline: Logical Consequences* (New York: Hawthorne, 1968).

Heinz and Rowena Ansbacher have collected some of Adler's writings and edited them into a coherent account of his theory in *The Individual Psychology of Alfred Adler* (New York: Harper & Row, 1956); this volume serves as an excellent sourcebook for students of Adlerian psychology. The Ansbachers have performed the same service with a collection of Adler's later writings in *Superiority and Social Interest: A Collection of Later Writings* (New York: Viking, 1973), and this volume contains Furtmüller's previously unpublished biography of Adler. An interesting collection of case histories with Adler's comments is provided in *The Problem Child* (New York: Putnam, 1963) and in *Problems of Neurosis,* edited by Philip Mairet (New York: Harper, 1929).

For contrasting points of view on why Adler and Freud ended their relationship, consult Vol. 2 of Ernest Jones's *The Life and Work of Sigmund Freud* (New York: Basic Books, 1955) for the Freudian camp's opinion. The Adlerian consensus on the breakup may be gleaned from H. Mosak and R. Dreikurs's "Adlerian Psychotherapy," in R. Corsini (ed.), *Current Psychotherapies* (Itasca, IL: Peacock, 1973), Chapter 2.

9

HARRY STACK SULLIVAN

Interpersonal Theory

A multiple personality is in a certain sense normal. . . .What we have here is a situation in which there can be different selves, and it is dependent upon the set of social relations that is involved as to which self we are going to be.

George Herbert Mead, *Mind, Self and Society*

Properly speaking, a man has as many social selves as there are individuals who recognize him *and carry an image of him in their mind. To wound any of these images is to wound him.*

William James, *Principles of Psychology*

About Sullivan's Interpersonal Theory

For Sullivan, personality exists only in the emotional exchange between and among people. A person does not "possess" personality so much as reflect one in responding to the perceptions of significant others. Sullivan was among the most eclectic of the neo-Freudians, and one of the first psychodynamic theorists to see the importance of thinkers such as Jean Piaget. Among the most important organizing elements in Sullivan's thought are these concepts:

1. *At the core of personality is the self-system, a protective organization of a person's experiences with other people who have judged, punished, and loved the person.*

2. *Anxiety is the great "motor" of personality, but it is not a drive in the Freudian sense. Anxiety for Sullivan is a social enterprise, an interpersonal event first experienced when mother responds out of her anxiety to her infant's behavior and body. In this sense, the unpleasant sensation of anxiety is psychologically contagious.*

3. *The development of personality is a composite of cognitive and emotional experiences centering around increasing use of cause-and-effect logic to structure reality. Such structuring is self-protective, in that reality is not perceived objectively but subjectively in a way that is consistent with one's own "good-me."*

AN INFANT'S VIEW OF THE UNIVERSE

During approximately the first four months of life, an infant's world is identical with the infant itself. When it closes its eyes, or when an object is moved out of sight, the world and the object cease to exist. Consider, for example, an observation made by Jean Piaget of his infant son, Laurent, reacting to the disappearance of his bottle:

> If the bottle disappears from his perceptual field this is enough to make it cease to exist from the child's point of view. At 0;6 (19) [six months, 19 days], for instance, Laurent immediately begins to cry from hunger and impatience on seeing his bottle (he was already whimpering, as he does quite regularly at mealtime). *But at the very moment when I make the bottle disappear behind my hand or under the table—* he follows me with his eyes—*he stops crying.* As soon as the object reappears, a new outburst of desire; then flat calm after it disappears. I repeat the experiment four more times; the result is constant until poor Laurent, beginning to think the joke bad, becomes violently angry. (1954, p. 32; italics added)

From observations such as this one, Piaget attempted to construct a picture of the infant's universe. Laurent's behavior at the disappearance of his bottle may be taken as evidence that objects in the infant's world do not have independent and permanent existence once they are outside its perceptual field.

If we pause for a moment before taking up Sullivan's ideas, Piaget's elegant observations can give us a frame of reference to make Sullivan's ideas clearer. In fact, Sullivan himself may have derived some of these ideas directly from Piaget, but Sullivan's way of expressing his concepts of how we perceive reality is quite abstract. So we need a little help from Piaget's children.

With a Little Help From Piaget

For another example of the infant's view of the universe, consider what happens if a child of five to seven months is shown a dangling pocket watch. The child will reach up to grab for it, more or less smoothly coordinating its perception with its motor responses. But if the pocket watch is suddenly removed from the line of sight, dropped behind the edge of the crib, for instance, its sudden disappearance elicits no systematic search behavior by the child. At this stage of its life, the infant does not seek out the watch, for once out of sight it ceases to exist. It is *not,* however, a case of the old maxim "out of sight, out of mind," because that saying implies simple forgetting as the cause of the child's lack of continued interest. Rather, in the infant state, out of sight means *out of existence,* for there is no mental image of the sensory object to be forgotten.

Piaget concluded that in the early months of infancy, the child's universe has no real stability or permanency. Objects exist only to the extent that they are immediately present as sensory experiences. Stop the flow of sensation, and the continuity of experience is erased. In Piaget's terms, the infant lacks a sense of *object permanence.*

To return for a moment to Laurent's behavior at the disappearance of his bottle, Piaget drew from this observation a further inference about the nature of Laurent's universe. Just because he ceases to cry when the bottle disappears, Piaget reasoned, does not mean that

> . . . the vanished bottle has been fundamentally forgotten; the child's ultimate rage reveals clearly enough that he believes he can count on the object. But this is precisely because *he considers it as being at the disposal of his desires* . . . and not as having a substantial existence under my hand or under the table. Otherwise he would have behaved quite differently at the moment of its disappearance; he would manifest, at that exact moment, a still more intense desire than during normal perception [i.e., while the bottle is in view]. (1954, p. 32; italics added)

In short, not only does the infant lack object permanence, but its conception of the object when present is an *egocentric,* magical view that its own desires and wishes are responsible for its timely appearance. Piaget referred to this worldview as *magicophenomenalistic* causality (Piaget & Inhelder, 1969, p. 18). "Magical" refers to the fact that the infant has no conception of physical causality governing the sequence of events it experiences; "phenomenalistic" is meant to indicate the subject immediacy of the infant's interpretations of reality: Its own wishes and desires are what count, for the infant's power controls its own universe.

Jean Piaget, the Swiss psychologist-biologist, studied the development of children's awareness and interpretations of reality for more than half a century. What is remarkable is that Piaget's descriptions of the child's progressively abstract constructions of reality are similar to the developmental sequence proposed by Harry Stack Sullivan to account for the same cognitive-emotional phenomena. In fact, Sullivan himself, in the first book he wrote, though delayed from publication for more than 40 years, called attention to Piaget's observational techniques and findings (1972, pp. 40n.–41n.).

Those phenomena that Piaget's scheme terms "magico-phenomenalistic" were termed by Sullivan the "parataxic" mode of experience. For both Sullivan and Piaget, parataxic and magico-phenomenalistic organization of reality are middle stages in a sequence of development that begins with even more primitive interpretations of events and ends with logical, predictive thought.

MODES OF EXPERIENCE: PROTOTAXIC, PARATAXIC, SYNTAXIC

Piaget's description of the child's development of the concept of causality and of its eventual recognition of a permanently existing universe of which it is only one part is organized into a progressive sequence of six stages. For present purposes, the stages can be grouped into pairs, each pair roughly corresponding to one of Sullivan's three stages of experience: prototaxic, parataxic, and syntaxic. By considering Piaget and Sullivan together, we can lend some descriptive precision to Sullivan's terms. Piaget's observations also provide approximate age ranges and coordinated behavioral referents lacking in Sullivan's account. Indeed, it is probable that Sullivan had Piaget's early observations in mind when he conceived of the three modes of existence (cf. Sullivan, 1972, p. 41n.).

Prototaxic: Serial Sensation

The simplest, crudest, and most exclusive mode of experiencing reality at the beginning of life is what Sullivan called the *prototaxic mode* (1953b, p. 29). For the first few months of life the infant's world is composed of a stream of sensory experience upon which it is unable to impose order or consistency. The infant's contact with and representation of the universe is limited to the continually changing flow of information provided by its sense organs. Generally, each sensory experience in the prototaxic mode is isolated from and uncoordinated with all other sensory experiences. As a result, the world is perceived, or "prehended" as Sullivan would say, as a flux of *unconnected* and *discrete* moments of sensation (1953b, p. 108). Even though some sensory events may be repetitive, the infant is unable to generalize from one event to another. Experiences occur in succession, but the infant does not apprehend that one event "goes with," "goes before," or "comes after" another.

In Piaget's terms, prototaxic experience corresponds to the first two stages of the development of causality: Stage one is called *global causality*, and stage two is termed *feelings of efficacy* (1954, pp. 250 ff.). In the first stage, extending roughly from the first few weeks of life to approximately four months, the infant makes no distinction between self and not-self. All its experience is fused into one global mass in which all that is "self" and all that is "not-self" are the same, a proposition with which Sullivan agreed. Some of Piaget's observations of his son's behavior in the early days of life had shown, for example, that the infant is unable even to keep track of the parts of its own body.

> Laurent at 0;0 (21) [21 days] is lying on his right side, his arms tight against his body, his hands clasped, and he sucks his right thumb at length while remaining completely immobile. . . . I take his right hand away and he at once begins to search for it, turning his head from left to right. As his hands remained immobile due to his position, Laurent found his thumb after three attempts: prolonged sucking begins each time. But once he has been placed on his back, he does not know how to coordinate the movement of the arms with that of the mouth and his hands draw back even when his lips are seeking them. (1952, p. 27)

Objects do not exist permanently or independently of the child's experience of them. A simple change of bodily position is sufficient to cause Laurent to "lose" his thumb.

Around the fifth month of life, extending to approximately seven months, the child's experience of the world becomes slightly more organized. It begins to recognize that some events do go together; that, for example, a given smell accompanies food, or a particular face is present when the bottle is available. But, as Sullivan suggested, the child is unable to anticipate one stimulus (food) from the presence of the other (face). They occur together, and they are responded to similarly, but the presence of only one does not evoke an "image" of the other. Piaget calls this period of development the *stage of feelings of efficacy* in the sense that the infant believes that its *desires* are responsible for the presence of both stimuli. When it is hungry, mother-with-bottle appears. Sullivan would call this personification of mother the "mouth mother." The infant does not, of course, understand that its crying is a *causal* signal to mother that feeding time is at hand. If the infant were left unfed, its crying would reach rageful proportions, and it would be confused as to why this time its feelings of hunger went unsatisfied. But it would not necessarily comprehend that it was mother's failure to bring the bottle that was responsible for its frustration.

Consequently, from the child's point of view, it understands that something is happening, but it does not know *why*. It senses its own existence, but only in egocentric fashion. Its own existence is everything that exists, for without its own immediate perception of objects, there simply are none. By the end of the stage of feelings of efficacy, the child's reflexes like sucking and crying have become organized into sequences of reliable habits. At this point, when events have *temporal connection*, Sullivan speaks of the parataxic mode of experience. Thus Piaget's second stage overlaps and grades into Sullivan's second mode.

Parataxic: Sequential Sensation

The cycle of mounting hunger tension and its reduction when food is available leads eventually to the child's *foresight* or *anticipation* of satisfaction when it experiences hunger (Sullivan, 1953b, p. 38). Before this achievement, the infant's experience of tension, or "disturbed euphoria," as Sullivan conceptualized it, and its eventual satisfaction after eating are simply two successive and unrelated events. With the establishment of the ability to predict or anticipate one event from another's presence, the dimension of time is imposed on the infant's universe. Temporal contiguity, the occurrence of one event immediately after or immediately before another event, comes to the center of the infant's attention. This dominance of temporal sequence as the only conception of causality is what Sullivan calls the *parataxic mode* of experience.

Sullivan made no precise statements on the duration of the period of parataxic experience in the infant's developmental history. If we take Piaget's observational sequence as a guide, the period extending from about the eighth month through the eleventh month probably encompasses the same phenomena Sullivan termed parataxic. The period is divided into two stages in Piaget's scheme: eight to nine months is the stage of *magico-phenomenalistic causality,* with which we are already familiar; from the end of the ninth through the eleventh month the child is in the stage of *elementary externalization of causality.*

Parataxic thinking is magical thinking, for in the parataxic mode events that occur close together in time are construed as causally related. For example, consider the following observation made by Piaget of his daughter Jacqueline:

> At 0;8 (9) [eight months, nine days] Jacqueline is lying down looking at a saucer which I swing 50 centimeters in front of her eyes. She reveals a lively interest and expresses her pleasure by the well-known behavior of arching herself upward, with her weight on her feet and shoulder blades, and then letting herself fall in a heap. I pass the saucer before her again. She watches it smiling, then stares at it seriously and attentively and arches upward a second time. When Jacqueline has fallen back again I pass the object before her once more; the same play three more times. After this I hold the object motionless before her; she arches herself again two or three times, then proceeds to something else. I resume twice; as soon as the saucer is motionless Jacqueline arches upward again. I then definitely pause in my game; Jacqueline nevertheless draws herself up five or six times more, while looking at the object, then tires of it. Every time the child's gesture has been followed by the saucer's movement, Jacqueline has manifested great satisfaction; otherwise, an expression of disappointment and expectation. (1954, p. 269)

Jacqueline believes that her arching response is the *cause* of the saucer's movement. Because in her past experience, the two events—arching and movement of saucer— have occurred in close *temporal* sequence, she assumes that her arching is the cause of the movement. Parataxic thinking is like Jacqueline's magico-phenomenalistic response. The infant understands that she may *intend* to bring about some effect. But what she fails to comprehend is the physical and spatial contact necessary to success. If she wants the saucer to move, either she or someone else must move it. Simple desire and unrelated body movements (arching) have no power to cause the observed effect. Most superstitions are based on parataxic reasoning. If a gambler on a losing streak at the roulette table suddenly strikes it lucky, he or she is likely to assume that the person who just sat down nearby was the cause of the good fortune.

When the infant enters the parataxic mode of experience, it has progressed to the point at which it can generalize experiences and identify similarities and differences among events. The infant is thus now able to respond differentially to different stimuli on the basis of past experience (Sullivan, 1953b, pp. 82–83). For example, the infant is able to see that it is the same person who ministers to different needs: The mother who produces a nipple when it cries with hunger is the same mother who produces a blanket when it cries with cold. Prior to this achievement, in the proto-taxic mode, each of these personages was identified only by the bodily zone through which satisfaction was obtained: thus there was a "mouth mother," a "skin mother," an "anus mother," and so on.

Piaget's fourth stage, *elementary externalization and objectification of causality,* extending from nine to eleven months, also overlaps with Sullivan's concept of parataxic thinking. In this stage, according to Piaget, the child is able to distinguish crudely between that which is "self" and that which is not. Sullivan, in a concept that we examine more fully later, proposed that parataxic thinking is accompanied by the ability to differentiate the body from the rest of the world (1953b, p. 163). Out of this differentiation emerges a personification of self called the "not-me."

Though the child's egocentrism is diminished during the stage of elementary externalization, it still tends to judge events only by their effects on itself. For example, though it realizes there are other people in the world, and that it, like them, is a member of an even larger universe, the only importance others have is in terms of what they do for and to the child.

Syntaxic: Causal Sensation

The syntaxic mode of experience corresponds to adult, logical, analytic thought. Syntaxic experience of reality thus presupposes the ability to understand physical and spatial causality, and the ability to predict causes from knowledge of their effects. As an example, consider another of Piaget's observations:

> At 1;4 (4) [one year, four months, four days] Laurent is seated in his carriage and I am on a chair beside him. While reading and without seeming to pay any attention to him, I put my foot under the carriage and move it slowly. Without hesitation, Laurent leans over the edge and looks for the cause in the direction of the wheels. As soon as he perceives the position of my foot he is satisfied and smiles. (1954, p. 335)

Laurent was able to infer from the movement of his carriage that something was the cause of it; that something, he surmised, had to do with the wheels on which the carriage must roll. From experience of the effect (movement), he was able to hypothesize a cause and test his hypothesis (looked at the wheels).

This kind of logical synthesis of present, past, and future experience is what Sullivan calls the syntaxic mode. It is characteristic of adult functioning. Piaget locates the origins of this kind of logical thought in two separate stages: *real objectification and spatialization of causes* (12 to 15 months) and *representative causality* (18 months to 2 years). From the 12th to the 15th month, the child is able to perceive that causes of the events it experiences are located *outside itself.* No longer magically phenomenalistic, nor totally egocentric, the child can perceive itself as an object in a world of independently existing and relatively permanent objects. The child realizes that it is only one cause among many causal agents.

In the last Piagetian stage, *representative causality,* the child of approximately 18 months to two years has learned to use a new tool to structure reality: language. As Sullivan had pointed out, in a vein similar to that of Piaget:

> . . . the first instances of experience in the syntaxic mode appear between, let us say, the 12th and the 18th month of extrauterine life, when verbal signs—words, symbols— are organized which are actually communicative. (Sullivan, 1953b, p. 184)

and

> . . . I should stress that syntaxic symbols are best illustrated by words that have been *consensually validated*. A consensus has been reached when the infant or child has learned the precisely right word for a situation, a word which means not only what it is thought to mean by the mothering one, but also means that to the infant. (Sullivan, 1953b, pp. 183–184; italics added)

Sullivan, like Piaget, also emphasized the predictive function of syntaxic thought (1953b, p. 233). Language allows children to store information from past experiences for use in understanding future novel events. Not only can they generalize from past experience, syntaxic thinkers can choose to focus on only certain events that make sense in terms of their past accomplishments:

> At 1;8 (11) [one year, eight months, eleven days] Jacqueline, observing from her window the mists on the side of the mountains, says, "Mist smoke papa." The next day, confronted by the same sight, she says, "Mist papa." The following day, on seeing me smoke my pipe she says, "Smoke papa." It would seem to me difficult not to interpret the first of these circumstances by a causal relation which can be formulated as follows: "It is papa who has made those mists with his pipe," or more cautiously, "There is in those mists something connected with the smoke papa makes with his pipe." (Piaget, 1954, p. 335)

Jacqueline's explanation of mist as pipe smoke may be wrong, but she has sought to apply her knowledge of similar events in a causal way. It is not the particular error that is important. From the child's point of view she has made an estimate of the high probability that because pipe smoke and mountain mist are similar, they have a common cause: Papa Piaget.

The three modes of experiencing, and their correspondences to Piaget's stages of causal thinking, are summarized in Table 9.1.

SCHIZOPHRENIA AS PARATAXIC EXPERIENCING: DISSOCIATION

Sullivan began his psychiatric career with an intense interest in schizophrenia. Influenced strongly by the then innovative ideas of Carl Jung and Sigmund Freud, Sullivan tried to account for the bizarre, seemingly unconnected cognitive and verbal processes of his psychotic patients. He adopted from Jung the concept that the disorganized thoughts of schizophrenics were the products of ideas and feelings that had been split off from waking consciousness and thereby freed from control by the ego (Sullivan, 1962, p. 19).

Set adrift from the rest of the personality, these "disassociated complexes," as Jung called them, ceased to obey the usual laws of logic and reason. They appeared, instead, to be isolated fragments of experience absurdly and madly strung together by the patient and spewn forth in jumbled speech patterns called "word salad."

TABLE 9.1   A Comparison of Sullivan's Modes of Experience and Piaget's Stages of Causal Thought

Sullivan's Modes	Piaget's Stages	Characteristics of Experience
Prototaxic (Literally, "placing one before the other in series")	1. Global causality (birth to 4 months) 2. Feelings of efficacy (5 to 7 months)	Lack of object permanence; egocentric interpretation of world as indistinguishable from self; constant flux of sensory events, unconnected and discrete; causality is vague conception of power when events accidentally coincide with desires.
Parataxic (Literally, "placing side by side without causal connection")	3. Magico-Phenomenalistic (8 to 9 months) 4. Elementary externalization and objectification of causality (9 to 11 months)	Discovery that one may intend an action; egocentrism persists; temporal connection between events perceived as causal; magical or superstitious thinking based on view that intentions are causes; causes are partially externalized in others, but only to extent they affect self; self/not-self distinction; crude memory.
Syntaxic (Literally, "placing together in logical connected order")	5. Real objectification and spatialization of causes (12 to 15 months) 6. Representative causality (18 months to 2 years)	Egocentrism absent; perception of difference between physical and temporal connections; language used to predict causes from their effects; consensual validation; mutually agreed-upon meanings; past, present, and future can be synthesized; interpersonal contacts grow in importance.

Jung had also proposed another idea adopted by Sullivan. Employing his word-association test with psychotic patients, Jung had detected a similarity between the "meaningless" verbal productions of the schizophrenic and the fantastic distortions of thought that occur during normal dreaming. Freud had elucidated the mechanisms of dream work—displacement and condensation, among others—that produce the disguised manifest content of the dream story. Furthermore, he had shown that the construction of dreams in normal personalities obeyed the same laws of impulse disguise that govern neurotic symptom formation (see Chapter 2). Jung sought to apply these principles to an explanation of schizophrenic thought processes. Sullivan picked up the threads of this psychoanalytic tradition, and from them and others he eventually created the fundamental tenets of his theory of personality.

Implications for Sullivan: The One-Genus Postulate

Jung's innovative approach to schizophrenia, particularly his early adoption of unpopular Freudian concepts, does not seem particularly startling or unique from the perspective of the present (cf. R. D. Laing in Chapter 10). No contemporary psychological investigator regards schizophrenic processes and verbal productions as meaningless or totally chaotic. Yet, at Jung's period in history, and even later in Sullivan's day, such insights were novel and controversial. Particularly controversial were the psychoanalytic tenets that Jung introduced into the clinical treatment of psychotics. Some of the implications of Jung's work bear summarizing, for these concepts, among others, were the building blocks from which Sullivan constructed many of his important conceptions of personality dynamics.

First, Jung's approach emphasized the possibility that certain feelings and thoughts could be split off from the bulk of conscious functioning, yet remain in consciousness in an isolated, encapsulated form. In a sense, the disassociation of these ideas and feelings was a case of repression in reverse. Instead of submergence to the unconscious, these unacceptable feelings were separated from the ego but kept within awareness as isolated fragments deprived of apparent meaningful connection with each other and with the self or ego. Sullivan construed schizophrenic functioning in much the same way. But Sullivan extended the idea of disassociation (or dissociation) to include normal personality developments. Each of us, Sullivan postulated, develops an aspect of self that is dissociated from the bulk of our self-conceptions. Called the Not-Me, this personification of self embodies all the unacceptable behaviors that are accompanied by "uncanny" feelings of anxiety. These emotions prevent our recognizing some behaviors as "ours." We consider Not-Me in more detail shortly.

Second, Jung saw no reason to assume that the processes of schizophrenic thought were different in kind from normal thought. As Freud saw neurotic and normal mental processes lying on the same continuum, Jung felt that "when we penetrate into the human secrets of our patients, the madness discloses the system upon which it is based, and *we recognize insanity to be simply an unusual reaction to emotional problems which are in no wise foreign to ourselves*" (1908, p. 165; italics added). Compare to Jung's formulation Sullivan's later statement of his position:

> In approaching the subject of mental disorder, I must emphasize that, in my view, persons showing mental disorder do not manifest anything specifically different in kind from what is manifested by practically all human beings. . . . From my viewpoint, we shall have to accept as a necessary premise that what one encounters in various stages of schizophrenia—the odd, awe-inspiring, terror-provoking feelings of vastness and littleness and the strange strewing-about of relevance—are part of the ordinary experience of these very early stages of personality development in all of us [namely, parataxic thinking and the Not-Me]. Most of us, however, experience these processes in later life only as strange fragments carried over from sleep or in our fleeting glimpses of what I call anxiety. (Sullivan, 1956, p. 3)

Sullivan was quite explicit that schizophrenia was to be regarded as lying within the range of processes found in normality:

> Schizophrenic thinking shows in its symbols and processes nothing exterior to the gamut of ordinary thinking, including therein that of revery and of dreams. . . . It is, as a whole, a peculiarly inadequate adaption of the cognitive processes to the necessities of adult life. . . . (Sullivan, 1962, p. 92)

Sullivan's reference to the normal personality's experience of the mental state of the schizophrenic only in dreams is reminiscent of Jung's conceptualization. Sullivan, of course, took matters a step further by establishing a developmental chronology of events leading to schizophrenia. Furthermore, Sullivan's emphasis on the continuity of mental processes from normality through psychosis led him to a rather important philosophical statement of human similarities. "Everyone and anyone is much more simply human than otherwise, more like everyone else than different" (1962, Frontispiece). This concise statement was originally called the species identity theorem by Sullivan in his early unpublished notebooks, and later expanded to the *one-genus postulate:*

> . . . the differences between any two instances of human personality—from the lowest-grade imbecile to the highest-grade genius—are much less striking than the differences between the least-gifted human being and a member of the nearest other biological genus. *Man*—however undistinguished biologically—*as long as he is entitled to the term, human personality, will be very much more like every other instance of human personality than he is like anything else in the world.* (1953b, pp. 32–33; italics added)

Because "everyone and anyone is much more simply human than otherwise," Sullivan felt it necessary to rescue psychiatry from the "ivory tower myth" of objective, uninvolved commitment to "scientific" truth finding (1964, p. 15). For Sullivan, the psychiatrist is certainly a scientific observer of behavior, but he is also a *participant observer* who is no less human, no less involved, no less of a participant, and no less changed than the patients he treats. As Sullivan pithily summarized his concept, "The crying need is for observers who are growing observant of their observing" (1964, p. 27).

The third implication of Jung's work for Sullivan's theory was Jung's emphasis that the wish-fulfilling tendencies observed in the schizophrenic's bizarre speech and thoughts *are derived from important concerns of his life before his illness began.* Jung had summarized his view in this way:

> . . . we can assert that the pathological ideas dominate the interests of the patient so completely *because they are derived from the most important questions that occupied him when he was normal.* In other words, what in insanity is now an incomprehensible jumble of symptoms was once a vital field of interest to the normal personality. (Jung, 1908, p. 173; italics added)

Sullivan's later conceptualization of schizophrenic personality development is nearly identical to Jung's:

> The disorder [i.e., schizophrenia] is one in which the total experience of the individual is reorganized. . . . It is a disorder which is determined by the previous experience of the individual—regardless of whether it is excited by emotional experience (psychic traumata), by the toxaemia of acute disease, by cranial trauma, or by alcoholic intoxication. (Sullivan, 1962, p. 12)

and

> Schizophrenia is considered tentatively as an evolution of the life process in which some certain few motivations assume extraordinary importance to the grave detriment of adjustive effort on the part of the individual concerned. This disturbance of adjustive effort is shown as an interference in the realm of social experience. (Sullivan, 1962, p. 160)

The comparison between Jung's approach to schizophrenia stemming from his adaptation of psychoanalytic theory and Sullivan's early conceptualizations of the disease could be extended into several other areas. That Sullivan read widely in the psychiatric literature, and adopted for his own purposes the conceptions that most suited his interpersonal theory, is an example of one of the common processes of science. To name just a few of Sullivan's intellectual antecedents and influences, we can list Piaget, Freud, Jung, Adler, William Alanson White, George Herbert Mead, and Kurt Lewin. But Sullivan's development and interweaving of their concepts resulted in a unique product.

ANXIETY: THE STATES OF EUPHORIA AND TENSION

From his work with schizophrenics, Sullivan had observed the effects of dissociated systems of experience in extreme form. The cause, it seemed clear, was the patient's struggle to master unacceptable and anxiety-provoking interpersonal situations. Because he intended to provide a developmental scheme of personality description, Sullivan's chief questions became *"How does the experience of anxiety originate?* and *How does the experience of anxiety cause dissociation of certain feelings and ideas?"*

> It is demonstrable that the human young in the first months of life . . . exhibits disturbed performance when the mothering one has an "emotional disturbance." . . . Whatever the infant was doing at the time will be interrupted or handicapped—that is, it will either stop, or it will not progress as efficiently as before anxiety appeared. . . . I have reason to suppose, then, *that a fearlike state can be induced in an infant under two circumstances:* one is by the rather *violent disturbance of his zones of contact with circumambient reality;* and the other is *by certain types of emotional disturbance within the mothering one.* (Sullivan, 1953b, pp. 8 – 9; italics added)

Sullivan had embarked on a theoretical assumption that anxiety was communicable from mother to child, and from child to mother. Sullivan conceptualized anxiety, however, in a very specific way. He distinguished between two hypothetical states of the organism: *absolute euphoria* and *absolute tension.* Absolute euphoria is roughly similar to total peace, complete freedom from desire and need, a state of utter well-being experienced, for example, by the infant in the state of deep sleep (Sullivan, 1953b, p. 35). Absolute tension is defined as the "maximum possible deviation from absolute euphoria" as, for example, the state of terror or panic. These bipolar opposites are hypothetical extremes that are only rarely experienced by any individual. Most of the organism's lifetime is spent in states of experience lying near the middle of the extremes.

Sullivan's next major assumption about personality development concerned the reciprocal relationship between mother's and child's tensions: *"The observed activity of the infant arising from the tension of needs* [e.g., hunger, thirst] *induces tension in the mothering one, which tension is experienced as tenderness and as an impulse to activities toward the relief of the infant's needs"* (1953b, p. 39). In simpler language, Sullivan conjectured that bodily tensions of hunger cause the infant to cry, and this pattern of behavior induces a state of tension in the mother that can be satisfied only by attending to the infant's needs. Thus, from the earliest moments of life, anxiety and tension involve interpersonal relationships.

THE COMMUNICATION OF ANXIETY

Because tension arising in the infant can induce tension in the mother, then it follows that tensions arising in the mother are likewise communicable to the infant: *"The tension of anxiety, when present in the mothering one, induces anxiety in the infant"* (Sullivan, 1953b, p. 41). Since the infant experiences reality in the prototaxic mode, its experience of anxiety is fragmented, isolated from other experiences, and diffuse. From the infant's perspective, anxiety is another increase in tension similar to tensions produced by needs like hunger and thirst. In fact, because the infant does not yet differentiate itself from its environment, but experiences itself and its world as one global, fused mass, the mothering one's anxiety *is* the infant's anxiety. They are linked by *empathy,* the capacity of the child to feel the mother's feelings, and vice versa.

Since it cannot differentiate the experience of anxiety from other unpleasurable tensions, the infant possesses as yet no specific means of reducing the anxiety. To reexperience the comforting state of euphoria, the infant must rely on the mothering one to reduce its anxiety as it relies on her to satisfy bodily needs. But because *she* is the origin of its anxiety, she cannot of herself reduce the infant's tension until she eliminates hers:

> . . . the infant's capacity for manipulating another person is confined, at the very start, to the sole capacity to call out tenderness by manifesting needs; and the person who would respond to manifest need in the situation in which the infant is anxious is relatively incapable of that response because it is the parental anxiety which induces the infant's anxiety. . . . Therefore, there is, *from the very earliest evidence of the empathic linkage, this peculiar distinction that anxiety is not manageable.* (Sullivan, 1953b, p. 43; italics added)

Once experienced, the affect of anxiety cannot be removed, nor destroyed, nor escaped for the remainder of the organism's life (Sullivan, 1953b, p. 53). Having been inoculated with the first dose of this unmanageable emotion, the human organism is made a human person, sensitive, vulnerable, insecure. Thus anxiety is the most potent, the earliest, and the most pervasive interpersonal force that can affect the human infant.

NURSING AS THE PROTOTYPE FOR INTERPERSONAL SITUATIONS

Because the infant experiences reality in the prototaxic mode, the sum of its perceptions is no more than momentary and fleeting states of sensory awareness. One of the most important of its sensory experiences is nursing, or more specifically, the experience of "nipple-in-the-lips." He "prehends" the nipple-in-the-lips event as a series of discrete bodily sensations including tactile, thermal, and olfactory stimuli.

From the repetitive nature of the experience, the infant slowly begins to develop a rudimentary conception of the nipple-person, the mothering one. His conception of her in no way corresponds to the completeness of reality. Instead, the infant's prototaxic, and later parataxic, experience of these discrete sensations constitutes a *personification* of the mother. She becomes identified with her primary transactions with the infant, namely, the nipple-in-the-lips image. In this sense, the nipple *is* the mothering one.

Depending on the degree of satisfaction supplied by her feeding behavior, the infant develops several different personifications of the nipple-in-the-lips mothering one:

1. *Good-and-Satisfactory Nipple* personification is the nipple in the lips that supplies milk when the infant is hungry [Good Mother].
2. *The Good-but-Unsatisfactory-Nipple* personification is the nipple that supplies milk when the infant is not hungry [Good Mother].
3. *Wrong-Nipple-in-the-Lips* is an unsatisfactory nipple because it does not supply milk when he is hungry; infant rejects this nipple and searches for a better nipple [Bad Mother].
4. *Evil-Nipple* is the nipple of an anxious mother who communicates a profound degree of anxiety and tension; this tension is a signal for avoidance; "not that nipple in my lips" [Bad-Anxious Mother]. (Based on Sullivan, 1953b, p. 80)

Thus the nursing situation is an important prototype for the development of the infant's relationships with future "significant others":

> . . . the infant is bound to have two personifications of any mothering person [Good and Bad Mother], barring the most incredible good fortune, and . . . the infant in the earliest stages of life need have only two personifications for any number of people who have something to do with looking after him. (Sullivan, 1953b, p. 122)

DIFFERENTIATION OF SELF FROM THE UNIVERSE

Toilet training and bodily care for urine and fecal elimination are clearly interpersonal situations that bear enormous potential for the learning of new personifications about oneself, and about one's own body. The way in which the mothering one responds to the infant's body—with disgust, with delight, or with simple acceptance—will be the key determinant in the infant's personification of itself. Coupled with these interpersonal effects are the infant's first clues that it is an independent object in the universe. As Piaget, too, has suggested, the infant learns it is a self through the activity of its hands, feet, and mouth.

For example, the infant lies in the crib and studies the movement of its own hands. The infant may grasp an object, bring it unsteadily to its mouth, and then insert it into its lips. The infant soon discovers that it is not a nipple; but it also discovers that *its own* hand—has brought about the event. When, moreover, it brings an *empty* hand to its mouth, and sucks the thumb, the infant learns an even more important lesson:

> . . . That the thumb is uniquely different from any nipple by reason of its being *in itself* a source of zonal sentience. *The thumb feels sucked.* (Sullivan, 1953b, p. 136)

Sucking the thumb is also different from the nursing situation in an important way: Unlike its attempt to bring mother-with-satisfactory-nipple *on demand,* its attempts to bring its thumb to its mouth are always successful, and invaryingly satisfying.

> The thumb-in-the-lips is dependable, and is independent of evoking the good mother; the infant can bring it into being, as it were, without cooperation—in isolation from any of his personifications, whether of the good mother or the bad mother. (Sullivan, 1953b, p. 139)

By its experiences with self-evoked satisfactions, the infant learns to foresee and to control some of its own behaviors. More important, the infant learns that *it is;* that it has a certain independence from the sequence of activities that engulf it. When, however, the infant naturally seeks further exploration of itself, in the genital or anal zones, it unwittingly brings the personification of the bad mother, the anxious mother, into play:

> The hand manipulating the anus, as any mother knows, will shortly be the hand that is in the mouth; thanks to the great development of the doctrine of germs and to the doubts about physical and sexual purity and cleanliness . . . many mothers feel that a finger conveying anything from the perineal region to the mouth would be disastrous. . . . *And even if these things are not so regarded by the mothering one, she will know that they are so regarded by a large number of other people.* (Sullivan, 1953b, pp. 143–144; italics added)

Thus the infant quickly discovers that although it is an independent being, it is not independent of the mothering one's "forbidding gestures" directing it not to experience certain parts of itself.

PERSONAL SOURCES OF SULLIVAN'S EMPHASIS ON HUMAN RELATIONSHIPS

Harry Stack Sullivan's early life may very well have sensitized him to the theme of boyhood loneliness and to the pain of the sensitive child who is ridiculed or ignored by his fellows because he is somehow ineffably "different." For Harry Stack Sullivan was different from other boys in his rural village. He was an Irish Catholic in an all-Protestant community; he was an only child, emotionally isolated from unaffectionate parents; and he was homosexual. Although he later wrote that "everyone and anyone is much more simply human than otherwise, more like everyone else than different," Sullivan was stating as theory what he poignantly missed in life.

A. H. Chapman was the first to pull together the known facts and speculations about Sullivan's early life, and Helen Swick-Perry (1982) has published the first complete biography of Sullivan. We follow both of their accounts here.

The young Sullivan was never accepted by the other children at school or in his rural village. Sullivan's social isolation seems to have been a mixture of shyness that triggered withdrawal and compensatory disdain for his school peers (Swick-Perry, 1982; cf. Thompson, 1962). Harry was thus shy, socially awkward, and eccentric. Perry reports a poignant image of the lonely boy standing in a pressed serge suit in the church courtyard after attending Sunday Mass:

He seemed miserable. . . . This standing alone on the edge of a group is a picture of Sullivan that persists. While close friends remember him as merry and witty in a social setting, people who saw him in situations of less intimacy think of him as testy and caustic—and often obviously miserable. Junior colleagues, who saw him usually in seminars, are apt to discount the idea that he could be kind and merry. (Swick-Perry, 1982, p. 89)

Boyhood on an isolated New York farm was lonely, and the one enduring value Harry seems to have taken from it was a fascination with horses. He used the symbol of two horses' heads, one facing up and the other facing down, intertwined within a circle as his personal emblem throughout his life. The covers of his books always bear this design (Chapman, 1976, p. 21). Swick-Perry (1982, pp. 342–343) has suggested that the horse symbol may have embodied a number of personal meanings for Sullivan by serving as a visual metaphor for evil versus good, male versus female, and homosexual intimacy.

Sullivan's Relationship With His Parents

Harry's mother was the dominant figure in his early life. He had been her third child, but the two previous children died in infancy. Mrs. Sullivan was a semi-invalid who appears to have been profoundly depressed and sufficiently disturbed to require periods of hospitalization (Swick-Perry, 1982). Among her chief concerns was her belief that she had married below her social station, and she communicated this belief to Harry in a variety of ways.

For reasons that remain a mystery, Harry's mother disappeared for a time when he was about two-and-a-half years old. Swick-Perry (1982) has been unable to determine the exact cause of the disappearance, but it is clear that Harry's mother was in some way too ill to care for her son. Her own mother took over Harry's care, but the demands of farm life resulted in a somewhat distant and detached form of child care. Harry's own mother may have suffered a "mental breakdown," or possibly attempted suicide (Swick-Perry, 1982, p. 39). Eventually, however, mother and son were reunited.

Harry's relationship with his father was also distant, and Harry described the man as "remarkably taciturn." Harry was nearly 30 years old before he was able to establish a closer relationship with his father. At this late date, Sullivan had come to understand that it was his mother who had prevented him from really knowing his father, largely out of her own disappointment in the marriage. Figure 9.1 shows Harry with his mother and father.

Sullivan's First Intimate Relationship

At the age of eight and a half, Harry found friendship with an older boy of 13. Chapman (1976) suggests that the relationship, "chumship" as Sullivan was to term such peer relations, was probably homosexual. However, Swick-Perry (1982, p. 89) has argued on the basis of more thorough research that the relationship was not homosexual. At the time, however, the relationship between Sullivan and Clarence Bellinger was widely regarded as homosexual by the people of Sullivan's hometown. This public "knowledge" no doubt added to the boys' sense of ostracism and increased their sense of unity in the face of outsiders.

**FIGURE 9.1   Harry Stack Sullivan with his mother (Ella)
and father (Timothy) about 1925.**

Source: Perry, H. S. (1982). *Psychiatrist of America: The Life of Harry Stack Sullivan.* (Cambridge, Mass.: Belknap Press of Harvard University.)

For Harry, the relationship with Clarence was one of trust and tenderness. Clarence, on the other hand, seems to have been somewhat of a bully, and it is possible that he manipulated the younger Harry's loneliness. Years later, Harry recalled that early relationship with more pleasure than pain, whereas Clarence appears to have come to hate his earlier chum.

It is ironic that both Clarence and Harry became psychiatrists, as if their own experiences of psychological pain and stress steered them into professional careers in search of answers to personal puzzles. When Sullivan had become somewhat famous in the profession, Bellinger, himself a hospital psychiatrist, let the staff know he had grown up with Harry, but dismissed Sullivan as "a homosexual son of a bitch" (quoted by Swick-Perry, 1982, p. 313).

In his first book, withheld from publication for a variety of reasons until 23 years after his death, Sullivan wrote of the sexual adjustment of the "isolated" pre-adolescent:

> Three special cases of isolation call for comment. The first and most unfortunate is that of boys who, because of serious deviation of personality growth, are excluded from gangs and chumships. Those whose progress was fair into the juvenile era are one class. One of these boys is usually clearly conscious of his "difference" from the other boys, of being an "outsider," of his being distrusted, if not despised, by the

"regular fellows." Often he has earned a nickname cruelly indicative of the most conspicuous social manifestation of his limitation. . . . His self-respect is gravely impaired. His authority-attitudes are upset. His schoolwork suffers. If he can he becomes loosely associated with some other "failures," often under quasi-leadership of an older, badly beaten boy. It may be that the boy is so unhappy that he submits to manipulation for criminal purposes. It may be that, while he is incapable of submitting himself thus far, he is glad to participate in activities clearly damaging to those who "belong." (Sullivan, 1972, pp. 177–178)

The autobiographical nature of this theoretical discussion is further strengthened by a later passage in which he describes the case of boys isolated merely by virtue of their geographical location. This kind of loneliness is enforced by the typical rural community, Sullivan states, and the boy usually suffers a prolongation of adolescence:

Fantasy processes and the *personification of subhuman objects* are called on. Loyalty is developed to abstract ideals, more or less concretely embodied in fanciful figures, rather than to concrete groups. The capacity for sympathy becomes peculiarly differentiated because of the elaboration of its underlying tendencies in loneliness, among fanciful objects. (Sullivan, 1972, p. 180; italics added)

In this passage may lie the explanation for Sullivan's adoption of the horse emblem as his personal symbol. His own loneliness as a child may have resulted in loyalty to "personified subhuman objects" who could neither reject nor ridicule their chum.

In an earlier passage in the same book, Sullivan was even more overtly autobiographical in speaking of a "rural community—a fair-sized village of the Middle East," where he had observed firsthand the matter of gang sexuality:

. . . a large number of the early adolescents participated in overt homosexual activities during the gang age. Most of them progressed thereafter without let or hindrance to the customary heteroerotic interest in later adolescence. Some of the few boys in this community who were excluded from the gangs as a result of their powerful inhibitions, who missed participation in community homosexual play, did not progress to satisfactory heterosexual development. (Sullivan, 1972, p. 171)

It is not unreasonable to assume that Sullivan was here writing about his own exclusion from "gang" friendships, and his own later failure to "progress to satisfactory heterosexual development."

Sullivan's College Years

Having won a state scholarship to Cornell University in the fall of 1908, Sullivan entered college at the age of 16. By the end of his second term at Cornell, he was suspended for failure in all his subjects. Moreover, Harry seems to have been involved in some illegal activities that included tampering with mail sent to other students at Cornell (Swick-Perry, 1982). Another version of the "trouble at Cornell" depicts Harry as selling something illegal through the mail. The exact facts are not known, but Swick-Perry (1982, p. 146) suggests that Harry may have been a "cat's paw" in the schemes of older students at Cornell who attempted to obtain chemicals illegally by ordering them on stolen drugstore stationery.

In any event, Harry left Cornell and seems to have "disappeared" for two years. Swick-Perry (1982) reports that Sullivan suffered a "schizophrenic break" during this time and was probably hospitalized at Bellevue in New York for an indeterminate period. Throughout his writings, Sullivan (see especially 1972) makes oblique reference to the fact that he had personal experience with "schizophrenic states," and his first contributions to his profession involved the treatment of male schizophrenic patients.

Sometime in 1911, having never returned to college, Sullivan gained entrance to a "diploma mill" medical school in Chicago. He was 19 years old and so impoverished that he was barely able to afford tuition. Education at this medical school was rudimentary and included little psychiatric study, the subject in which Harry received some of his lowest grades. Although he graduated within four years, he failed to receive his diploma because he could not pay his final tuition bill. Two years later, having earned money by working as a physician for insurance and steel companies in Illinois and Indiana, Sullivan redeemed his diploma.

Eventually, he became affiliated with a branch of the federal government serving war veterans, and in 1921 accepted a position as liaison officer at St. Elizabeth's Hospital in Washington, D.C. At St. Elizabeth's, Sullivan received wide exposure to psychiatric cases and seems to have acquired his knowledge of psychiatric procedure by on-the-job training. By 1923, Sullivan had moved to Baltimore to work at Sheppard and Enoch Pratt Hospital, under the direction of Ross McClure Chapman. He developed a reputation for remarkable empathic contact with male schizophrenics, establishing a famous special ward from which females were barred. Sullivan found that women made his patients uncomfortable, and he devised a number of then novel procedures for working with schizophrenic patients that soon established his reputation in American psychiatry.

He carefully selected six male aides and intensively instructed them in the art of relating to patients. Sullivan's goal was to employ healthy human relations between the staff and patients as a therapeutic procedure, reasoning that schizophrenia had its origins in initially unhealthy interpersonal relations (Chapman, 1976, p. 45). He also assumed that many male schizophrenic patients had prior homosexual conflicts, and even indicated that he himself had firsthand experience with that kind of stress (Swick-Perry, 1962, p. xii).

Sullivan encouraged the staff members to share their own experiences of "normal" preadolescent homosexual activity and to indicate that such activities are not depraved but simply part of the human condition. On the basis of his personal experience, Sullivan firmly believed that a period of homosexual interaction in puberty was part of healthy male development. Thus his special ward at Sheppard-Pratt was, in a sense, a corrective preadolescent society, a milieu from which women were "logically" to be excluded (Swick-Perry, 1962, p. xxi; see also Sullivan, 1962, pp. 104 and 251).

Sullivan's procedures brought remarkable success. Although his patients were selectively chosen, a possible factor in the success rate, approximately 80 percent were substantially improved and able to resume more normal interpersonal functioning.

As a therapist, Sullivan held daily interviews with his patients and demonstrated a "fine disregard" for the rules and procedures of classical psychiatry (White, 1977, p. 317). Excerpts of verbatim transcripts of Sullivan's sessions with three patients at Sheppard-Pratt during the period 1923 to 1930 have been published (Schulz, 1978). Sullivan frequently had a stenographer present to record the interviews, and at one point had a microphone concealed on his desk so that his secretary could record the sessions from another part of the building (Swick-Perry, 1962, p. xxi).

As Schulz (1978) points out, Sullivan's style was not focused on "helping" the patient or on trying to make him feel more comfortable. Rather, the patient was treated as a person, as one who knew his problems better than the psychiatrist. Sullivan would often confront a patient directly with the illogicalities of his statements or with his deliberate untruths. He would attempt to show the patient the nature of his evasions, and Sullivan could sometimes be deliberately sarcastic to make a point.

Sullivan's Last Years

In 1927, Sullivan adopted unofficially a 15-year-old boy who lived with him until Sullivan's death on a trip to Paris in 1949. There is some confusion surrounding the circumstances of the "adoption," but Swick-Perry (1982, p. 209) reports that the boy had been brought to Sullivan for treatment after he had been found in a kind of catatonic pose on the street.

For more than 20 years, this young man, now called James Inscoe Sullivan, served as confidant, household staff, cook, and office staff combined. Sullivan regarded Jimmie as his "beloved foster son," and there is no doubt that the relationship was genuinely intimate for both men (Swick-Perry, 1982, p. 211).

Sullivan moved to New York in 1930 to open a Park Avenue private practice. During this period, he received what was probably his first psychoanalysis with Clara Thompson. Chapman (1976) has shown that Sullivan's statements that he had about 75 hours of psychoanalysis much earlier were probably not true but merely an attempt to win needed prestige among colleagues.

The last 10 years of his life were spent in relative loneliness, living on a small tract of land in Maryland. On January 14, 1949, while attending a meeting of the World Federation of Mental Health, Sullivan suffered a brain hemorrhage. He died in his hotel room, as isolated in death as he had been in youth.

Even in death, however, there is mystery surrounding Harry Stack Sullivan. Swick-Perry reports that Harry had been in treatment for a heart condition for some years, and that at the time of his death he was depressed, lonely, far from home, and contemplating the anniversary of his mother's death. Under these circumstances, Harry may have felt a heart attack beginning, and deliberately failed to take his medication (Swick-Perry, 1982, p. 419). He had even predicted his own death in 1931 from almost the exact cause of his actual demise years later. In such a state of mind, Sullivan may simply have wished to die.

The Lessons of Sullivan's Life

The three central tenets of Sullivan's personality theory are that (1) interpersonal relations are the heart of human existence; (2) one's sense of self is, for good or bad, the product of others' appraisals; and (3) the single most powerful human motive is the need to avoid anxiety, that is, to achieve interpersonal security. Sullivan's life had been an attempt to reconcile all of these themes, to abstract them for his professional work, and to undo the core of loneliness in others that had been the source of anguish in himself.

PERSONIFICATIONS OF SELF: GOOD-ME, BAD-ME, NOT-ME

For Sullivan, it is clear, the most important kinds of learning in infancy, indeed throughout life, occur in the discovery that some behaviors eliminate or reduce the intensity of interpersonal anxiety (1953b, p. 152). The great steersman of development is the *gradient of anxiety* attached to different behavioral situations. By trial and anxious-error, the infant gauges the desirability of particular behaviors in its repertoire:

> The infant plays, one might say, the old game of getting hotter or colder, in charting a selection of behavioral units which are not attended by an increase in anxiety. (Sullivan, 1953b, p. 159)

The gradient of anxiety ranges from relatively mild tension-evoking behaviors to behaviors that elicit such intense feelings of emotion that they are best described as "uncanny," "*awe*-full," or "*dread*-full." Out of its games of hot or cold, the infant shapes its conceptions of "me."

Good-Me Personification

All those infant behaviors to which the mothering one has responded with tenderness, praise, emotional warmth, or physical reward become amalgamated into a self-perception of *Good-Me*. The Good-Me personification is thus a product of satisfying or pleasing interpersonal relations with this significant other, the mothering one (1953b, p. 162). The Good-Me personification is largely conscious and usually indicated in verbal behavior by everything to which a person can freely apply the pronoun "I," as in "I am . . ." or "I would like to be . . ." or "I have . . ."

Bad-Me Personification

Increasing degrees of anxiety and tension on the part of the mothering one are directed to certain behaviors of her infant: touching objectionable parts of its body, unruly crying, refusal to eat certain foods, struggling over bodily care like bathing. All those behaviors that cause increasing tension in the mother also evoke anxiety in the infant. Over time, these undesirable, anxiety-provoking behaviors become amalgamated into the personification of the *Bad-Me*. The Bad-Me personification is also conscious to a large degree, but it may grade imperceptibly into behaviors that are unconscious because they evoke stronger degrees of anxiety.

Not-Me Personification

The *Not-Me* personification is almost outside the realm of description. It is the part of personality that is rarely experienced consciously by the normal person, except perhaps during dreaming. For the schizophrenic, on the other hand, experience of the Not-Me personification is continual. The Not-Me is the dissociated cluster of feelings and images that exists side by side with the more neutral content of consciousness, but which seemingly does not belong to consciousness. Thus the Not-Me lies outside the realm of description by language. It is a product of intense, "uncanny" emotion in the parataxic mode:

> This [Not-Me] is a very gradually evolving personification of an always relatively primitive character—that is, organized in unusually simple signs in the parataxic mode of experience, and made up of poorly grasped aspects of living which will presently be regarded as "dreadful," and which still later will be differentiated into incidents which are attended by awe, horror, loathing, and dread. (Sullivan, 1953b, p. 163)

The feelings of dread and terror, disgust and loathing that attend the Not-Me personification are difficult to place in words because they were attached to certain behaviors and perceptions through forbidding gesture and empathic expression of anxiety from the mothering one. To a greater or lesser extent, all personalities have a Not-Me personification, a part of oneself that seems alien and hideous. For a good example of Not-Me experience common to everyone, turn to Chapter 14 and consult Allport's concept of the proprium.

Another rather potent example from the case history of one of Sullivan's schizophrenic patients may serve to indicate the "uncanny," "*awe*-full" nature of dissociated feelings of the Not-Me. This patient evidenced, among other dissociated systems operating in his psychosis, strong homosexual and incestuous impulses so loathsome and frightening that they had been split off from the rest of consciousness. In the development of the normal personality, if we are to take Freud at face value, incestuous and erotic impulses of childhood are repressed along with autoerotic wishes at the time of the resolution of the Oedipus complex. In addition, the child's normally uninhibited desire to play with and to smear his own feces is abandoned after "education" in the shame and disgust lessons of parental example and horror. In Sullivan's patient, most of these impulses lingered on in consciousness, but only in the dissociated form that intruded into his conscious fantasies and delusional thinking. Particularly problematic was his habitual masturbation accompanied by fantasies that could be described in the normal personality only as Not-Me:

> He masturbated frequently, to the accompaniment of homosexual anal phantasies. *On an occasion when about 17,* he, having inserted a candle into the rectum "to increase satisfaction," as the orgasm approached, withdrew the candle and thrust it into his mouth. The orgasm, he remembers vividly, was very powerful. This recollection was strongly resisted. He had never repeated the procedure. (Sullivan, 1962, p. 36; emphasis in original)

The revulsion we experience upon reading of this schizophrenic person's behavior is some evidence of the uncanny Not-Me nature of the oral-anal impulses that we have learned to disconnect from one another early in infancy. Because of the reaction of the mothering one, all normally socialized adults have acquired a sense of loathing and disgust for anything connected with anal or fecal content.

Ordinarily, the close association between the mouth and the anus for the infant is not connected with disgust or revulsion until shame, learned through anxiety, is established. From that point, the early willingness to manipulate feces, to smear them, or to raise them to the mouth evokes intense horror. Any connection between oral and anal impulses and genital sexual activity is likewise deeply submerged. In effect, these impulses have become Not-Me:

> The not-me is literally the organization of experience with significant people that has been subjected to such intense anxiety, and anxiety so suddenly precipitated, that it was impossible for the then relatively rudimentary person to make any sense of, to develop any true grasp on, the particular circumstances which dictated the experience of this intense anxiety. (Sullivan, 1953b, p. 314)

THE SELF-SYSTEM: SECURITY OPERATIONS

From its experiences with reward and anxiety, with forbidding and tender gestures, the infant learns another important lesson: Anxiety can be reduced by certain specific behaviors that are approved by the mothering one; and anxiety is sometimes increased to an unbearable degree by behaving in ways that she disapproves. In effect, it is desirable to be the Good-Me; undesirable to be the Bad-Me; and unthinkable to be the Not-Me.

To maintain the division between "good" and "bad" forms of living, the infant learns to interact only in certain ways with the significant others of its world. The habitual pattern of behaviors that the infant develops to gain the greatest satisfaction and to keep anxiety at a minimum in dealing with significant others is the *self-system,* or *self-dynamism.* The self-system is thus a cluster of "security operations."

In Sullivan's attempt to establish a scientific conception of interpersonal relations, he chose the term *dynamism* to indicate habitual patterns of behavior like the self-system because it offered the possibility of objectivity. Like the physicist, the psychiatrist should be able to specify what *energy transactions* characterize the human life he or she is studying because

> . . . the present view of the universe, as held by a great majority of mathematicians, physicists, and other scientists, makes the discoverable world a dynamism. This is implied in the fundamental postulate that the ultimate reality in the universe is energy, that all material objects are manifestations of energy, and that all activity represents the dynamic or kinetic aspect of energy. (Sullivan, 1953b, p. 102)

For Sullivan, the study of the personality is really the investigation of the organism's energy transactions with the world of things and people. Sullivan therefore defined dynamism in psychological and biological terms:

> . . . the ultimate entity, the smallest useful abstraction, which can be employed in the study of the functional activity of the living organism is the dynamism itself, *the relatively enduring pattern of energy transformations which recurrently characterize the organism in its duration as a living organism.* (1953b, p. 103)

The concept of dynamism may be thought of in psychological terms as a *habitual reaction pattern.* As always, Sullivan emphasized his fundamental belief that we are all "much more simply human than otherwise" by suggesting that minor variations in habitual reaction patterns were relatively unimportant. It was his opinion that such variations were merely "the envelope of insignificant particular differences." Thus his earliest definition of personality was constructed along these same lines:

> Personality is the relatively enduring configuration of life-processes characterizing all of the person's total activity pertaining to such other persons, real or fantastic, as become from time to time relevant factors in his total situations. (1972, p. 47)

In Sullivan's final, definitive lectures on his conceptualizations, he changed the definition of personality somewhat to emphasize the concept of person-to-person contact as the fundamental unit of study:

> Personality is the relatively enduring pattern of recurrent interpersonal situations which characterize a human life. (1953b, pp. 110–111)

Personality is thus composed of a series of interpersonal dynamisms; of, therefore, *habitual patterns of relating to others.* Originally founded on the need to reduce anxiety and obtain satisfaction for needs, the self-system is the dynamism of "educative experience called into being by the necessity to avoid or to minimize incidents of anxiety" (1953b, p. 165). The self-system's sole function is to aid the infant in reducing anxiety, first with the mothering one, and later as an adult, with all significant others.

Unfortunately, the self-system also embodies some troublesome characteristics. Since it is the product of parental censure and praise, it embodies the prevailing cultural standards by which the parents themselves have been molded. The self-system, therefore, functions to screen the child's repertoire of possible behaviors and to focus them into a smaller number of socially acceptable ones. Thus the self-system narrows attention to those aspects of living that generate praise and blame, and it attempts to perpetuate only those experiences that are least likely to generate anxiety. In this sense, the self-system is a stumbling block to growth:

> [The self-system] permits a minute focus on those performances of the child which are the cause of approbation and disapprobation, but, very much like a microscope, it interferes with noticing the rest of the world. *When you are staring through your microscope, you don't see much except what comes through that channel.* So with the self-dynamism. It has a tendency to focus attention on performances with the significant other person which get approbation or disfavor. (Sullivan, 1953a, p. 21; italics added)

The self-system refuses awareness to all experiences, all impulses, that are not relevant to parental approval and disapproval. Experiences that generated parental approval become part of the Good-Me; experiences that generated disapproval become part of the Bad-Me; but experiences that generated superdisapproval, intense disfavor, are dissociated from the personality and relegated to the Not-Me. In effect, the self-system is a selective filter, restricting attention, and consequently personality growth, to the reflected appraisals of others (Sullivan, 1953a, p. 29). Sullivan called this process of filtering "selective inattention."

SELECTIVE INATTENTION

Selective inattention may occur in emergency situations, for example, when it is necessary to focus awareness only on the problem at hand. In this case, selective inattention is a very adaptive and useful response. But when selective inattention to important aspects of living is habitual in the service of allaying anxiety, it is a mechanism of defensive perception, a "security operation."

To illustrate, Sullivan reported an experience with a patient who provided an elegant and extreme example of selective inattention. Sullivan had been seeing this patient every week for a number of years and soon became accustomed to the man's ritualistic way of beginning the therapeutic hour. Each week the patient would recount an experience he had while on the train en route to Sullivan's office. Each week it was the same experience. And each week the man reported the experience with the same fresh amazement, as if none of the other reported experiences had happened. Sullivan commented,

> I had heard it perhaps two hundred times when one day, for some reason or other, all the factors added up in my mind and I interrupted before he finished. After he had recounted his fantasy of kissing some man and then biting a piece out of his ear I said, "And you were amazed!" He said, "Yes, what do you mean? . . . I *was* amazed. But why did you say so? What do you know about it?" [Sullivan responded:] "Why, only that you have told me the same story two or three hundred times. . . ." (1956, pp. 44–45)

To a large extent, selective inattention resembles Freud's mechanisms of denial and repression. But Sullivan saw selective inattention as an integral part of the self-system's functioning. On this basis, Sullivan proposed a *Theorem of Escape:*

> The self-system unlike any of the other dynamisms . . . is extraordinarily resistant to change by experience. This can be expressed in the theorem that *the self-system from its nature . . . tends to escape influence by experience which is incongruous with its current organization and functional activity.* (1953b, p. 190)

As maturity is attained, whole segments of activity related to anxiety are relegated to the self-system. As with the train-riding man, parts of the self are isolated from the rest of personality. Though we behave in particular ways, we may be reluctant to recognize our actions as our own, or to incorporate new experiences into the self.

ME-YOU PERSONIFICATIONS

Even in maturity, the individual's self-system and its processes of selective inattention operate to shape in important ways his or her conception of the self and of significant others. For example, consider the possibilities inherent in the multiple relationships of Mr. A to Mrs. A in the course of their married life. Because both partners' self-systems are differentially attuned to reality, and to maintaining self-images founded on others' reflected appraisals, they respond to *personifications* of the other, not to the reality of the other's presence. As the conditions of the interpersonal situation change, Mr. A's image of his wife will shift. He may personify her one moment as the illusory image "loving and tender wife-mother," and in the next situation she will become for him the illusory image "feminine viper and tauntress." Likewise, Mrs. A responds not to the objective Mr. A, but to a series of multiple "you's" she has created in relationship to her personification of herself, her "me" image.

In a sense, at least eight personages are involved (based on Sullivan, 1964, pp. 46 ff.):

> *Mr. A and Mrs. A as they really are*
>
> *Mr. A[1] as his wife personifies him* [loving husband]
>
> *Mr. A[2] as his wife personifies him in another situation* [selfish and despicable husband]
>
> *Mrs. A[1] as her husband personifies her* [loving wife]
>
> *Mrs. A[2] as her husband personifies her in another context* [viper and tauntress]
>
> *Mr. A[3] as he sees himself* [peacemaker; long suffering]
>
> *Mrs. A[3] as she sees herself* [victim; belittled wife]

Additionally, the list of personifications might be supplemented with the subsequent changes in self-perception as the other's "you" image changes the situation and is reflected in changed self-images: Mr. A[4,5,6,7] $\cdots$ and Mrs. A[4,5,6,7] $\cdots$ and so on.

If we could observe a quarrel between Mr. and Mrs. A, we could record the shift in me-you patterns that takes place. In the quarrel, Mrs. A has assumed the role of victimized wife; she resents frequently being left alone on her husband's nights out. Mr. A, on the other hand, remarks to his wife that her choice of friends is so utterly boring and ridiculous that he can barely tolerate being present. That is why he seeks out his own friends. Mrs. A now unleashes some pent-up fury to inform the man she now views as an *utterly selfish belittler of women* not to "judge my friends by the fools you spend your evenings with" (Sullivan, 1964, p. 45). In response, Mr. A assumes the role of *wounded husband, long-suffering peacemaker* who has finally suffered enough at the hands of this malicious person. In his view, Mrs. A has become "the epitome of malicious persecutions, a human viper whom the law protects while she taunts him with her ability to destroy his every chance of happiness" (Sullivan, 1964, p. 45).

The interaction between Mr. A and Mrs. A has shifted among mutual *illusory* "me-you" patterns. The fact that the partners can respond to each other, to each other's image of self, and to their own illusory personifications of the other led Sullivan to propose that

> The incongruity in the coincident me-you patterns may grow to such a point that [Mr.] A comes to think "something is wrong" with Mrs. A, and consults a psychiatrist about her. He reports that "she seems to have undergone a complete change. She misunderstands everything I do, thinks I deceive her about everything. . . ." (1964, p. 47)

Thus the label "mental illness" may be applied to one partner on the basis of discrepant mutual and illusory me-you personifications. For Sullivan, the goal of psychiatry is "the study of the phenomena that occur in interpersonal situations, in configurations made up of two or more people, all but one of whom [the psychiatrist-observer] may be more or less completely illusory" (1964, p. 33).

R. D. Laing has extended Sullivan's concepts of me-you personifications into an elaborate and sophisticated set of postulates. In addition, with his colleagues, Laing has constructed a paper-and-pencil instrument to assess the impact of incongruent mutual perceptions. Laing et al. (1966, p. 3) rather poetically summarized these ideas:

> The human race is a myriad of refractive surfaces staining the white radiance of eternity. Each surface refracts the refraction of refractions of refractions. Each self refracts the refractions of others' refractions of self's refractions of others' refractions. . . . Here is glory and wonder and mystery, yet too often we simply wish to ignore or destroy those points of view that refract the light differently from our own.

In the next chapter, we consider Laing's work in some detail.

DEVELOPMENTAL EPOCHS: FROM INFANCY TO LATE ADOLESCENCE

Sullivan divided the course of personality development into six epochs. Each of these is marked by a distinctly different quality of interpersonal relations and by functioning in one of the three modes of experience. The six epochs are infancy, childhood, juvenile epoch, preadolescence, early adolescence, and late adolescence.

Infancy

Extending roughly from birth to the development of language, the period of infancy is primarily prototaxic in nature. The infant experiences reality as a discrete flux of momentary states. It does not differentiate self from the world; its experience of reality is global, diffuse.

Most significant of the developments of infancy are the personifications of self and significant other. Good-Me, Bad-Me, and Not-Me have already been surveyed, as well as the personifications of the Good and Bad Mother (nipple). Out of its experiences with the significant others of its world, the infant develops a particular orientation to the world. These dynamisms can include *apathy* and *somnolent detachment* when the infant's experiences with the mothering one have been anxiety provoking and frustrating.

Apathy refers to the capacity of the infant to deal with emergency situations of unsatisfied needs by developing a withdrawing "I don't care" orientation to its own experiences of hunger, thirst, and pain (Sullivan, 1953b, p. 55). (See Horney's description of the detached personality in Chapter 13.)

Somnolent detachment literally means the separation from reality that occurs by being sleepy. In effect, the infant's withdrawal response of apathy may be extended to cope with anxiety situations that are persistent and prolonged. Somnolent detachment is not distinguishable observationally from apathy in the infant. However, from the infant's point of view, somnolent detachment involves not only a "don't care" attitude about objects of need satisfaction, but also a forthright *indifference to significant persons* responsible for the neglected satisfactions. Apathy is called out by aggravated and unsatisfied needs; somnolent detachment is evoked by prolonged anxiety in interpersonal contacts (Sullivan, 1953b, p. 57).

An example of what prolonged anxiety and unsatisfied emotional needs can do to a child is provided by the work of René Spitz, a psychoanalytically oriented developmental psychiatrist. Spitz conducted studies of severely emotionally deprived children in hospitals and nursing homes. These children were provided with every material necessity but were totally lacking in experiences of emotional warmth and security, tender mothering, or even simple intellectual stimulation. For one reason or another, usually illness, they were separated from their mothers for an unbroken period of two to three months. A characteristic pattern of behavior emerged in these children which Spitz named *anaclitic depression* on the basis of psychoanalytic theory. The term "anaclitic" literally means "leaning on," "dependent," or "attached" (cf. Freud, 1914a, vol. XIV, p. 87). It is an approximate translation of a German word that Freud used to describe one form of narcissistic object choice. Spitz observed a reliable sequence in the establishment of anaclitic depression through the first three months of separation:

> *First month:* The children become weepy, demanding and tend to cling to the observer when he succeeds in making contact with them.
> *Second month:* The weeping often changes into wails. Weight loss sets in. There is an arrest of the developmental quotient.
> *Third month:* The children refuse contact. They lie prone in their cots most of the time. . . . Insomnia sets in; loss of weight continues. There is a tendency to contract intercurrent diseases; motor retardation becomes generalized. Inception of facial rigidity. (Spitz, 1965, pp. 270–271)

If satisfactory reunion with the mother is not accomplished within five months, permanent and irreversible physical and psychological effects result. In Sullivan's terms, these children are extreme cases of somnolent detachment.

Childhood

The childhood epoch extends roughly from the acquisition of language to the appearance of a need for playmates or "compeers" (1953b, p. 33; 1953a, p. 37). The basic mode of experience in childhood is parataxic. Though language is present, it is used in some very magical, parataxic ways:

> . . . in so far as a verbal statement by a child is taken by the acculturating adults to have a superior quality of reality to other of his behavioral acts, the child is being trained to be incapable of dealing with life. . . . In a good many homes, the following kind of statement is a conspicuous ingredient in the alleged education of the young: "Willie, I told you not to do that. Now say you are sorry.". . . If Willie dutifully says he is sorry, that is supposed to markedly mitigate the situation, although it is something that Willie is almost absolutely incapable of understanding. (Sullivan, 1953b, pp. 200–201)

To extend Sullivan's example, we can return to Jean-Mary. Her magical use of language illustrates the same phenomenon. She, too, had learned to say "sorry" or "pardon me" or "no offense" as a propitiatory gesture. She assumed that therefore it was all right to say or do anything to a playmate as long as one followed it with a "sorry" or a "no offense." Thus she would say to a playmate that her dolly was ugly or funny-looking, following this crass insult with a "no offense!" Having offered the magical cancellation, Jean-Mary was always amazed when her playmate was hurt or argumentative.

Another important development of the childhood epoch is the possibility for the child to undergo what Sullivan called a *malevolent transformation* (1953b, p. 213):

> For a variety of reasons, many children have the experience that when they need tenderness, when they do that which once brought tender cooperation, they are not only denied tenderness, but they are treated in a fashion to provoke anxiety or even, in some cases, pain. A child may discover that manifesting the need for tenderness toward the potent figures around him leads frequently to his being disadvantaged, being made anxious, being made fun of. . . . Under those circumstances, the developmental course changes to the point that the perceived need for tenderness brings a foresight of anxiety and pain. The child learns, you see, that it is highly disadvantageous to show any need for tender cooperation from the authoritative figures around him, in which case he shows something else; and that something else is the basic malevolent attitude, *the attitude that one really lives among enemies.* . . . (Sullivan, 1953b, p. 114; italics added)

Later, in adolescence, children who have learned that this is a hostile and unfriendly world may deliberately behave in ways that make it impossible for anyone to love them or to show them affection and kindness. In effect, they have learned to forgo any demonstration of a need for tenderness, and they treat others with a similar malevolence.

On the positive side, the epoch of childhood is marked by a number of *"as if" performances* or role-playing the significant behaviors modeled by parents. "As if" performances may eventually be practiced as defensive maneuvers by the child who has been exposed to manipulative and anxiety-provoking rearing.

Instead of a healthy identification with parents, children may play roles to conceal their real feelings in the *dramatization* of behaviors demonstrated by mother and father (1953b, p. 209). In a dramatization the "as if" performance shifts from "acting like" the parents to acting as if they *were* the parents. For the most part, however, dramatizations are an essential and normal part of the childhood epoch, and they facilitate adoption by the child of each one's appropriate male or female role.

The second kind of "as if" performance is the technique of seeming preoccupied with something in order to be left alone. Children learn to behave "as if" some activity were highly important to them, riveting their attention and demanding all their energy. In actuality, the seeming preoccupation is really a technique of avoiding disturbing and painful interactions with anxiety-provoking significant others, or it is a means of escaping their demands (1953b, p. 210).

Juvenile Epoch

The transition from childhood to the juvenile epoch is marked most clearly in Sullivan's thinking by the changing role of playmates in the child's estimation. In childhood, the need for a playmate was essentially egocentric, even selfish. Children play side by side, but they do not necessarily interact. Though the child is aware of the playmate, more important to it are the child's own pursuits, own ideas, and own speeches. The child may even invent an imaginary playmate to satisfy its own wishes.

But in the juvenile epoch, a true need, a need for genuine cooperative play, for mutuality of experience emerges (Sullivan, 1953b, p. 226).

The juvenile epoch thus extends from the grammar school years through that phase when the child experiences a need for an intimate relationship with a same-sexed "chum." Most of the juvenile's experiences are in the syntaxic mode, and language has become the chief tool for coping with the demands of authority.

Education and the authority figures of the school play a significant role in the juvenile's life. The chief contributions to personality development occur through two avenues of social activity. *Social subordination* occurs when the child learns to respect and to obey a succession of parental authority substitutes: the teacher, the crossing guard, the gym coach, and so on. *Social accommodation* involves "a simply astounding broadening of the grasp of how many slight differences in living there are; how many of these differences seem to be all right, even if pretty new; and how many of them don't seem to be right, but nonetheless how unwise one is to attempt to correct them" (Sullivan, 1953b, p. 229). In short, through exposure to a variety of new and significant others, the child learns to tolerate familial and social diversity.

Preadolescence

The key characteristic of preadolescence is the strong emergence of a trend that was already present in the juvenile epoch; namely, the need for intimacy with a "chum" or best friend of the same sex. The preadolescent epoch thus extends from the establishment of an intimate friendship with a same-sexed peer to the emergence of an interest and a need for a partner of the opposite sex.

The significance of the need for a chum is in the character of the relationship. For the first time, the chum is a person who has equal importance to self; his or her interests, needs, and fantasies are on the same level of importance as the preadolescent's own. The preadolescent has developed a real sensitivity to the needs of the other person.

> And this is not in the sense of "what should I do to get what I want," but instead "what should I do to contribute to the happiness or to support the prestige and feeling of worth-whileness of my chum." (Sullivan, 1953b, p. 245)

The relationship that develops between chums is termed *collaboration* because each of the chums validates the personal worth of the other. They collaborate mutually to validate desires, conceptions of the world, and interpretations of the self:

> Because one draws so close to another, because one is newly capable of seeing oneself through the other's eyes, the preadolescent phase of personality development is especially significant in correcting autistic, fantastic ideas about oneself or others. (Sullivan, 1953b, p. 248)

Early Adolescence

Extending from the emergence of genital sexuality, that is, from puberty, to a focused interest in the opposite sex, early adolescence is characterized by feelings of "lust" (1953b, p. 263). The adolescent has experienced orgasm, and the feelings of sexual arousal are a new and continual component of his or her self-image.

A variety of collisions between the feelings of lust and the needs for security and intimacy occur. It is typical of adolescence that the burgeoning sexual needs cause a reevaluation of the self-image in the light of growing doubts about sexual competence and proficiency.

> Ridicule from parents and other elders is among the worst tools that are used on early adolescents. Sometimes a modification of ridicule is used by parents . . . and this modification takes the form of interfering with, objecting to, criticizing and otherwise getting in the way of any detectable movement of their child toward a member of the other sex. (Sullivan, 1953b, p. 268)

There are also collisions between the need for intimacy and lustful feelings. Not uncommonly, the adolescent feels awkward and clumsy in his or her first advances to a member of the other sex, particularly so when that person has already been idealized and idolized. Male adolescents may create among their groups distinctions between "good" girls and the more permissive ones. Genital activities are thought to apply only to the latter group, with the "good" girls reserved as more or less potential marriage partners.

It is now clear from the newly available biographical material on Sullivan's childhood that his description of the whole adolescent epoch was colored by his own painful struggle in the area of male sexuality.

Late Adolescence: The Mask

Late adolescence extends from the focused expression of genital sexual activity through the establishment of a full repertoire of adult interpersonal relations (1953b, p. 297). The predominant mode of experience is, of course, syntaxic. The most important behavioral characteristics of late adolescence are the establishment of vocational identity or the decision to pursue an educational course leading to some professional role.

For the first time, adolescents may experience real "restrictions in living." Inhibitions or hindrances based on past developmental failures or other handicaps stemming from their past emotional interactions may curtail their range of adult choices for a job, for education, or for a mate. Respect for self must be based on learned respect for others; without this mutuality of concern and performance, the adolescent is likely to develop a variety of techniques for isolating and preventing further development to full maturity.

To cope with the puzzling inner and outer changes that they experience, adolescents on the threshold of adulthood may experiment with aspects of all the "selves" they have been up to now. Sullivan described this compartmentalization of character with the metaphor of the mask in the first book he wrote:

> The adolescent may begin the "life behind a mask" that tends to characterize numbers of our urban denizens. The mask, however, requires so much energy for its successful maintenance that personality growth is apt to end with its successful construction. As the necessities for masking certain motivations vary from one to another interpersonal situation, it may be easier *to avoid further integration of the self,* and to develop, from this point onward, specialized accommodations and interests for various groups. (Sullivan, 1972, p. 201)

TABLE 9.2   Sullivan's Developmental Epochs

Developmental Epoch	Chronology	Outstanding Achievements/Failures
1. Infancy	Birth to Language (0 to 18 months)	Prototaxic experience of reality: differentiation of Good, Bad, and Not-Me; personifications of Good/Bad Mother; defensive reactions of apathy and somnolent detachment.
2. Childhood	Language use to Need for playmates (18 months to approx. 5 years)	Parataxic experience of reality; egocentric relationship with peers; magical use of language; malevolent transformation possible; "as if" performances: dramatizations and preoccupations.
3. Juvenile Epoch	Grammar school to Need for a chum (6 to 8 or 9 years)	Parataxic and syntaxic experiences of reality; mutuality and cooperation in play; social subordination and social accommodation in school experiences.
4. Preadolescence	Intimate friendship to Puberty (9 to 12 years)	Mostly syntaxic experience of reality; need for a same-sexed chum; strong collaboration with chum; consensual validation of experiences; establishment of a capacity for selfless love.
5. Early Adolescence	Puberty to Interest in other sex (13 through 17 or 18 years)	Syntaxic experience of reality; need for expression of lust; need for partner of opposite sex; collisions between lust and security-intimacy needs.
6. Late Adolescence	Heterosexual activity to Adult interpersonal relationships (19 or 20 years to maturity)	Syntaxic experience of reality; vocational identity established; restrictions in living experienced on basis of past developments; establishment of adult friendships; need for a life partner of other sex.

Based on Sullivan, 1953b

In effect, the adolescent who has failed to integrate the many self-conceptions and reflected appraisals that constitute the personality into a functioning unity will remain a disjointed group of "selves" whose nucleus is the juvenile or childhood self that has never been outgrown.

The developmental epochs are summarized in Table 9.2.

EVALUATING HARRY STACK SULLIVAN

Sullivan is frequently considered a neo-Freudian, but he does not fit that label easily. Unlike the other neo-Freudians, Sullivan did not rebel against Freud's ideas so much as he merely ignored those he found uncongenial. And Sullivan was a borrower, although the more polite word is eclectic. He had a broad range of interests in the social sciences, linguistics, and anthropology, and each of these is, in some way, integrated into his theory. But Sullivan was first and foremost a psychiatrist whose primary duty was the treatment of patients, and much of his focus was clinical rather than theoretical. Out of this clinical, social, and scientific mixture arose interpersonal theory.

Refutability of Sullivan's Concepts

Because the main thread that runs through Sullivan ideas is a psychodynamic one, he shares the basic lack of refutability such theories embody. Many of his main concepts, however, are in principle testable, but not in the form he stated them. For example, his conception of the self-system as a group of self-protective processes with selective inattention as the "motor" of self-protection could certainly be reconceptualized in cognitive and perceptual terms. But his more abstracted and psychodynamic constructs, such as the "Not-Me" and the "Bad-Me," are couched in terms of nonobservable referents and are beyond testing in empirical terms.

As we shall see in Chapter 10, R. D. Laing and his colleagues at the Tavistock Institute were able to translate at least part of Sullivan's conception of personifications into an empirical assessment instrument (Laing et al., 1966). But on the whole, Sullivan's theory is not a generator of empirical research. It is widely respected, however, in clinical circles as a fountain of treatment wisdom.

Sullivan's Conception of Human Agency

The issue of agency is not a Sullivan concept. In fact, the active-passive, subject-object dichotomy would strike Sullivan as odd. Nevertheless, we can map his concepts to this dimension to see how the theory fares.

Sullivan has an essentially interactive viewpoint with respect to personality functioning. He emphasized that personality develops in social interaction, so that without the multiple perspectives of others' views of self, the self is empty. But Sullivan also acknowledged that the person constructs his or her own interpretations of others, the "personifications" supported by selective inattention, and he believed that the person acts on that set of beliefs. The balance therefore appears to be toward an active (interactive?) agency viewpoint, although Sullivan was certainly also a determinist who believed in the power of unconscious forces. Interpersonal relationships shape us, but we have the power to shape our relationships.

The Nomothetic Aims of Sullivan's Theory

More than other psychodynamic theorists, Sullivan emphasized the relationships between and among people, and the influence of cultural variables. His focus was technically nomothetic. But, as a clinician, his focus on psychopathology and its treatment raised idiographic issues, including such concepts as the development of the self-system through the "contagion" of anxiety from the "mothering one."

It is clear that Sullivan's *aspiration* was to produce a nomothetic theory with broad societal implications. But it is just as clear that the theory has substantial idiographic elements. On balance, Sullivan's theory would be classed as nomothetic, but, unfortunately, as a "sterile" nomothetic theory that has yet to generate empirical support for its generalizations. His scheme of development through the various "epochs" from infancy to adolescence would certainly lend itself to nomothetic research—very time-consuming nomothetic research—but to date, it has not done so.

SUMMARY

Sullivan viewed personality as the set of characteristic and habitual interpersonal relations that mark a human life, the most significant of which is with the mothering one in infancy. Because the mothering one can communicate anxiety to the infant, and because the infant's needs arouse in her a corresponding need to show her infant tenderness, Sullivan characterized the relationship as an "empathic linkage."

The ways in which the mothering one responds to the infant's behaviors shapes the three personifications of the self: Good-Me, Bad-Me, and the uncanny Not-Me. With the focus on interpersonal relations, Sullivan also emphasized the unity of human endeavor in his species identity theorem: We are all much more simply human than otherwise. Thus even psychiatrists' professional activities are to be conceptualized as *participant* observation, for they, too, bring to the therapeutic relationship strictly human experiences and qualities.

As infants progress through the various stages of growth and psychological development, they experience reality in vastly more abstract ways than were possible in the first months of existence. As Piaget had also shown, the infant's first perceptions of itself and its universe are fused, vague, and in continuous flux. Called the prototaxic mode, this early form of experience is primarily sensory, not cognitive, and predominantly egocentric. As the infant progresses to the parataxic mode, temporal contiguity is interpreted as causality. Finally, the child enters the syntaxic mode in which reality is interpreted on its own terms, and the most important tool that the child brings to bear is language.

Sullivan's conception of me-you patterns of personification was yet another indication of his growing sense of the importance of social interaction as the basic datum of psychiatry. In a close dyadic relationship, for example a marriage, the partners respond not to the reality of each other's person, but to illusory images of the other created in the situational context. R. D. Laing later extended some of Sullivan's ideas on interaction into a sophisticated interpersonal theory of perception-personality processes.

Sullivan divided personality development into six epochs: infancy, childhood, juvenile epoch, preadolescence, early adolescence, and late adolescence. The significant advances represented by the successive stages center, of course, on the child's acquisition of more sophisticated modes of experiencing reality and on its growing need for intimate relationships with significant others.

Our evaluation of Sullivan's theory suggests that it is a largely unrefutable one, with one or two exceptions, such as his concept of selective inattention, his developmental scheme, and his notion of "personifications." But each of these concepts would require very creative psychologists to derive an empirically testable version from Sullivan's loose theoretical prose. His theory leans toward an interactive conception of human agency, so that the person is shaped by relationships which he or she may shape in turn. It was suggested that Sullivan aimed to be nomothetic, but that large segments of the theory are fundamentally idiographic. In either case, the model has led to precious little empirical research.

The most important aspect of Sullivan's view of personality may be summarized by pointing out that this is a people world, and feelings—painful and joyful—are wisely or unwisely tied up with our relations to significant others.

FOR FURTHER READING

During his lifetime, Sullivan published rarely. His major work, *The Interpersonal Theory of Psychiatry* (New York: Norton, 1953), is actually a series of lectures skillfully edited into a coherent work. To gain some historical perspective on the development of Sullivan's ideas, you will find *Personal Psychopathology* (New York: Norton, 1972) quite illuminating. Sullivan had postponed the publication of this volume several times during his career, until it was finally published posthumously.

Some of Sullivan's early papers on schizophrenia and psychotic disorganization have been organized into a single volume under the title *Schizophrenia as a Human Process* (New York: Norton, 1962); a careful reading of these papers will reveal Sullivan's debts to Jung and to Freud. Another collection of Sullivan's papers, *The Fusion of Psychiatry and Social Science* (New York: Norton, 1964), more clearly exposes his methodological assumptions, including his one genus (species identity) theorem. Sullivan's other published works are cited throughout the chapter, and a careful reading of any of them will repay the effort involved.

For comparative purposes, you may want to explore some of R. D. Laing's works in which he expands and modifies some of Sullivan's conceptions on interpersonal perception. Particularly useful in this regard are Laing's *Divided Self* (Baltimore: Penguin, 1959), and his *Self and Other* (New York: Pantheon, 1969). (Laing's work is treated in Chapter 10 of this book.) A reading of George Herbert Mead's *Mind, Self and Society From the Standpoint of a Social Behaviorist* (Chicago: University of Chicago Press, 1934; available in paperback) will reveal another source of Sullivan's ideas on the nature of selfhood.

Indirectly influenced by Sullivan, Jurgen Ruesch has written two books that emphasize the power of language in shaping a person's worldview. The two volumes are *Disturbed Communication* and *Therapeutic Communication* (New York: Norton, 1957 and 1961, respectively).

The papers published in Patrick Mullahy's *The Contributions of Harry Stack Sullivan: A Symposium on Interpersonal Theory in Psychiatry and Social Science* (New York: Hermitage Press, 1952) attempt to place Sullivan's work in historical perspective.

The style of Sullivan's psychotherapy is treated by Mary Julian White in her "Sullivan and Treatment" (*Contemporary Psychoanalysis,* 1977, **13,** 317-347), and by C. G. Schulz in his publication of some verbatim transcripts of Sullivan's patient interviews at Sheppard-Pratt in "Sullivan's Clinical Contribution During the Sheppard-Pratt Era—1923-1930" (*Psychiatry,* 1978, **41,** 117-128).

10 CHAPTER

R. D. LAING

Existential Analysis and Phenomenology

In a lie the spirit practices treason against itself.

Martin Buber, *Good and Evil*

I have thought about the problem of how not to think a thought one is not supposed to think. I cannot think of any way to do so except, in some peculiar way, to "think" what one must not think in order to ensure that one does not think it.

R. D. Laing, *The Politics of the Family*

About R. D. Laing's Existential Analysis

R. D. Laing celebrates human experience on its own terms. His work is a mixture of humanism, existentialism, and psychoanalysis. But the mixture is a volatile one, full of surprises, pessimism, and challenges to traditional ideas. For Laing, the following ideas are human truisms:

1. *A person's experiences and interpretations of them are as valid and as real as the "reality" from which they are derived.*

2. *People make demands on each other that can be psychologically destructive in forcing people to be not what they are but what satisfies the demands.*

3. *Severe psychological disorders such as schizophrenia result in behavior that appears bizarre, but which is explainable as the person's desperate attempt to comply with an identity forced on him or her by members of the family.*

Laing's work reveals a rich humanism with detours into a philosophy of the absurd. People can be so divided within themselves that life seems without real meaning. Laing's point, of course, is that by being true to self one creates the meaning.

FLY ON THE WALL OF AN INSANE PLACE

You are to be accorded a rare privilege. Largely unnoticed and unhindered, you will spend some weeks in a mental hospital. As one of eight pseudopatients, you are a faker, a "normal" individual, perhaps even a professional mental health worker, who, by deception and guile, has gained voluntary entry to the hospital. As a disguised observer, you will be the proverbial fly on the wall, from whose view nothing is concealed, from whose hearing nothing is withheld.

Some duties, however, attend this privilege. For one thing, you will have to forgo your personal freedom, your real identity and name, and your normal daily activities. Most of your time will be spent taking notes, recording personal interactions between staff and patients, and making observations of your own reactions to the environment of the hospital. You will be, in effect, consumed by days and nights devoted to covert social-psychological observation.

Despite your initial misgivings, it was relatively easy to commit yourself to the institution. Presenting yourself at the admitting office, you reported a straightforward complaint: "I hear voices that say 'empty,' 'hollow,' and 'thud.' " Though you displayed no bizarre behavior nor acted in any way other than normally, the diagnosis of "schizophrenia" was affixed to you and to six of your seven comrades enacting the same drama in hospitals of five other states.

The chances of being detected as "sane" were unbelievably slim once the diagnostic label had been applied. None of the pseudopatients was, in fact, released from the hospital in less than a week. The longest period of time in which a pseudo-patient went undetected was 52 days, and 19 days was the average length of time for the group as a whole. In all cases, when release finally came, it was not because you were discovered to be a sane faker. Your discharge diagnosis read "Schizophrenia in remission."

Thus the absence of symptoms was interpreted as "spontaneous" recovery. Even more surprising, no hospital administrator, nurse, attendant, or physician ever discovered the true state of any pseudopatient's mental health. Only the real patients ever caught on to the deception: "You're not crazy. You're a journalist or something. You're checking up on the hospital."

The Illness of Mental Myths

David Rosenhan (1973), the man responsible for the design and execution of the pseudopatient study of mental hospitals, attacked several myths implicit in psychology and psychiatry. One myth states that the *"normal are detectably sane."* Rosenhan, who served as the first pseudopatient, and the seven other men and women enacting that role, went undetected as sane by people who presumably should be able to do so—but not by the real patients.

Another myth debunked by the Rosenhan study is the age-old tradition in the mental health professions that a trained diagnostician can correctly identify the specific "mental illness" syndrome from which a patient suffers. A corollary of this myth states that having diagnosed the patient's illness, the differential diagnostic label affixed to him or her is a humane and reliable guide for therapeutic procedure. Both of these myths evaporated under Rosenhan's critical scrutiny.

To illustrate, in a substudy related to the one described, Rosenhan informed the staff and professional workers of a teaching mental hospital that during the next three months one or more pseudopatients would attempt to gain admission to their facility. The staff were particularly skeptical about Rosenhan's previous results so they were even more on guard than the implied challenge to their professional competence would indicate. During the three-month period, judgments about 193 patients admitted to the hospital were obtained from the staff who had primary contact with them. "Forty-one patients were alleged, with high confidence, to be pseudopatients by at least one member of the staff. Twenty-three were considered suspected by one psychiatrist *and* one other staff member. Actually, no genuine pseudopatient . . . presented himself during this period" (Rosenhan, 1973, p. 252).

Rosenhan's findings imply that diagnostic labels and professional acumen are weak in two ways. First, it is clearly possible to affix a diagnostic label indicative of "mental illness" to someone who suffers no disease. On the other hand, it is possible to err on the side of overcaution and skepticism. *If one's suspicions are aroused,* it is possible to label as *sane* people who come for treatment out of a sincere belief in their own illness, as was the case with the alerted hospital staff. Evidently, therefore, in the normal order of things, when the physician does not expect patients to give false reports, all the people who present themselves for admission to a mental hospital are uncritically accepted as ill. They receive a diagnostic label that brands them members of a special class of people who suffer from *disease* that is "mental." The label is likely to follow them for the rest of their lives, influencing everyone with whom they come into contact, from relatives and friends to employers and government agencies.

Thomas Szasz (1960, 1961, and 1970) has been arguing for a long time that the concept of *mental illness* is a myth. It is his thesis that the so-called mentally ill are not *ill* in the medical sense. Disordered behavior does not fit the pattern of disease states. Neurotic and most psychotic reactions, according to Szasz, are more accurately conceived of as failures to adjust, mistakes in socialization, and as problems in assuming the tasks of living. In his view, so-called mental illness falls more sensibly within the scope of social, ethical, legal, and political specialists.

Szasz has traced the history of the medical model of mental illness as a transition from the witchcraft explanation of disturbed behavior. Initially, the medical model was heralded as a more rational and more humane conception than its predecessor model of demonic possession. But, Szasz argues, adoption of the medical model's view of disturbed persons as sufferers of disease unfortunately did not include the abandonment of depersonalizing and dehumanizing techniques in dealing with them (1970, Chapter 8). Just as accused witches were persecuted by the members of the medieval Inquisition clinging to their belief in demons and spirits, modern psychiatry clings to its myth that disturbed persons suffer disease. Torture wrung from many a "witch" her confession of complicity with the devil, and her inquisitors felt secure in having thus obtained salvation for her soul. Similarly, as compulsory salvation was practiced for witches, modern psychiatry treats its patients as people who have to be saved—even against their own will (Szasz, 1970, p. 112).

It is possible to interpret Rosenhan's pseudopatient study as supporting Szasz's contention that however personally disruptive and painful psychological disorder may be, it cannot be classed as a clear-cut, diagnosable, medically treatable illness. Yet there is the equally strong possibility that *some* difference between "normal" and "mad" individuals exists, for *real* patients were able to detect the sane.

R. D. Laing, like Szasz, has argued that schizophrenia is not a "disease." Schizophrenic patients' behavior is explicable, not as a medical disorder, but as a desperate attempt to survive conflicting and irrational demands made upon them by a world that, more than the patients, deserves the label "mad." *From the viewpoint of the patients themselves,* it is the situations into which they are thrust, not their minds, that are disordered. Laing's argument is an extreme position that, like the medical model it seeks to redress, is not by itself adequate to the task of describing and explaining disordered personalities. But, as we shall see, arguments like Szasz's and Laing's have served as much needed correctives to rigidly narrowed conceptions of disordered human lives (see also Goffman, 1959, 1961; and Redlich & Kellert, 1978).

Pseudopatients' Experiences

Life within a mental hospital is unbelievably boring, consisting of tedium and regimentation, broken very rarely by normal social enjoyments. This fact rarely intrudes itself into the professional staff's awareness because they themselves have little experience with enforced monotony.

> One psychiatrist pointed to a group of patients who were sitting outside the cafeteria entrance half an hour before lunchtime. To a group of young residents he indicated

that such behavior was characteristic of the oral-acquisitive nature of the [schizophrenia] syndrome. It seemed not to occur to him that there were very few things to anticipate in a psychiatric hospital besides eating. (Rosenhan, 1973, p. 253)

The psychiatrist's medical orientation, betrayed in his interpretation of the patients' cafeteria "waiting behavior," forces him to mold every observation, every patient trait into a uniform picture consistent with "disease." Given that he believes institutionalized patients suffer from mental illness, then surely it must follow that their every action is a result of the disease. For a mental patient, boredom is not possible. To illustrate, when Rosenhan's pseudopatients first entered the hospital, they kept their note taking secret. However, when no staff member paid attention to them, they began openly recording their observations. " 'Patient engages in writing behavior' was the daily nursing comment [in the patient's chart] on one of the pseudopatients who was never questioned about this writing" (Rosenhan, 1973, p. 253). Thus even this activity was made consistent with the role as patient, for "writing *behavior*" is surely different from the normal person's "writing."

To obtain a clear conception of the atmosphere of the psychiatric hospital and the flavor of the patient-staff interactions, consider the encounters recorded by the pseudopatients, as shown in Table 10.1.

The percentages recorded are based on the observations of Rosenhan's pseudopatients with 13 psychiatrists and 47 nurses. To flesh out the figures a bit, consider the quality of a typical encounter between a professional staff member and a pseudopatient. When the pseudopatient approached to ask, "Pardon me, Dr. X, could you tell me when I am eligible for grounds privileges?" the psychiatrist's reply was: "Good morning, Dave. How are you today?" (Moves off without waiting for a response.) Rosenhan points out that the psychiatrist's reply can be classed only as bizarre, and his behavior as strangely aloof (1973, p. 255). As Table 10.1 indicates, the majority of patient-staff contacts are aloof (71 to 88 percent), and only rarely is the depersonalizing environment transcended by simple human amenity (2 to 4 percent).

Rosenhan concludes his report by emphasizing that the hospital environment, and all it implies by way of atmosphere, expectations, and efficiency, is essentially countertherapeutic. Rosenhan cautions, however, against attributing the pseudopatients' experiences to malice or stupidity of the hospital staff. Quite to the contrary, Rosenhan's impression of the hospital staff was that they were concerned, dedicated, and uncommonly intelligent. "Where they failed, as they sometimes did painfully, it would be more accurate to attribute those failures to the environment in which they, too, found themselves than to personal callousness" (1973, p. 257). To emphasize the

TABLE 10.1   Staff-Patient Encounters (in percentages)

Type of Contact	Psychiatrists	Nurses and Attendants
Moves on, head averted	71	88
Pauses and chats	2	2
Stops and talks	4	0.5

Adapted from Rosenhan, 1973, p. 255.

role that environmental setting plays in shaping staff and patient roles, Rosenhan entitled his published study:"On Being Sane in Insane Places."

Implications of the Rosenhan Study

The one implication that emerges clearly from Rosenhan's study is the immensity of the task confronting mental health workers. Should they conceptualize mental illness and disordered personality as a disease state? Or, perhaps, the professional specialist should follow Szasz's recommendations that such patients be treated as people with problems in living. The question is reducible to the form:"How shall disordered personality be construed?"

R. D. Laing provides an answer to this question that favors the social, problems-in-living approach. Laing, however, would ask, "How does the *patient* view his or her 'disordered' behavior?"

Going a step further than Szasz's position that mental illness is a myth, Laing has suggested that the schizophrenic experience has its own validity as a mode of being, as a strategy of coping with an insane world (Laing & Esterson, 1964; and Laing, 1967, p. 115). Laing feels that *some* individuals are labeled mentally ill or schizophrenic when their mode of adapting to an insane situation conflicts with commonly held convictions about appropriate or "healthy" forms of behavior (1959, p. 36). Rosenhan's pseudopatient study concretizes and lends some support to Laing's thesis. But Rosenhan's findings should not be taken as a definitive rebuttal of the medical model of mental disorder, nor as the ultimate verification of Laing's position. Rosenhan's results should be interpreted as one indication of the degree to which mental health workers have continued to need to refine and reshape their conceptions of the disordered personality.

LAING'S VIEW OF "MENTAL ILLNESS"

To describe patients waiting outside the cafeteria as people evidencing the "oral-acquisitive nature of the syndrome" is an act of utter obscenity to Laing. For him, such facile application of terminology confuses labeling with explanation. Labels drawn from classical clinical psychiatric models obscure the fundamental humanity of patients who strive to make sense of the existence *they perceive as theirs.* Laing gave an extraordinary example of the discrepancy in viewpoints between the physician and the patient in his reanalysis of a classic lecture "demonstration" of schizophrenia by Emil Kraeplin, a pioneer in psychiatry. The following passage is part of Kraeplin's account (1905) to a lecture room of his students of a patient diagnosed as catatonic (quoted by Laing, 1959, p. 29):

> "The patient I will show you today has almost to be carried into the rooms, as he walks in a straddling fashion on the outside of his feet. On coming in, he throws off his slippers, sings a hymn loudly, and then cries twice (in English), 'My father, my real father!' He is 18 years old. . . . The patient sits with his eyes shut, and pays no attention to his surroundings. He does not look up even when he is spoken to, but he answers beginning in a low voice, and gradually screaming louder and louder. When asked where he is, he says, 'You want to know that too? I'll tell you who is being

measured and is measured and shall be measured. I know all that, and could tell you, but I do not want to.' When asked his name, he screams, 'What is your name? What does he shut? He shuts his eyes. What does he hear? He does not understand; he understands not. . . .' "

Kraeplin, committed to the medical model, which he had had a hand in creating, interpreted the patient's lack of responsiveness and seeming excitable incoherence as symptoms of the *disease* called catatonia. He concluded that the patient had not provided a single piece of useful information to the series of questions because his disease fostered catatonic disorganization.

Laing suggested that there is another way to interpret the same behaviors. If the psychiatrist had been successful in entering the patient's phenomenal world *to see things as the patient saw them,* Kraeplin would have understood that the patient was mocking him:

> Surely [the patient] is carrying on a dialogue between his own parodied version of Kraeplin, and his own defiant rebelling self. "You want to know that too? I tell you who is being measured and is measured and shall be measured. . . ." Presumably he deeply resents this form of interrogation which is being carried out before a lecture-room full of students. He probably does not see what it has to do with the things that must be deeply distressing him. But these things would not be "useful information" to Kraeplin except as further "signs" of a "disease." (Laing, 1959, p. 30)

The patient expressed not only his resentment at being "demonstrated" before an audience, he also adopted a survival strategy. He failed to cooperate with the "demonstrator," "his real father," and he resisted this authority figure's probing questions by parrying all inquiry with queries of his own. Of course, for Kraeplin, such resistive behavior was additional evidence of the effects of disease. For Laing, such behavior is rational and explicable once the psychiatrist is able to escape the case history approach to patients.

EXISTENTIAL PHENOMENOLOGY

Laing's viewpoint might be characterized as existential phenomenology informed by psychoanalysis. In his early writings, Laing shares much with the European existential psychiatric tradition expressed in the work of Ludwig Binswanger (May, 1958a) and Medard Boss. Though we cannot survey the major tenets of existential psychology within the scope of this chapter, some comment on the existential tradition is necessary.

Owing much to the philosophy of Heidegger and Jaspers, Binswanger and Boss adopted an existential phenomenological approach to the treatment of their patients. They had found classical psychoanalysis to be wanting when it came to understanding their patients as pained human beings. In the United States, a foremost exponent of the existential approach has been Rollo May, and he, perhaps more than anyone, has lucidly defined the existential viewpoint:

> [The existential approach] is the endeavor to understand the nature of this man who *does* the experiencing and to *whom* the experiences happen. (1961, p. 12)

and

> Existentialism means centering upon the *existing* person; it is the emphasis on the human being as he is *emerging, becoming.* The word "existence" comes from the root *ex-sistere,* meaning literally "to stand out, emerge." (1961, p. 16)

Thus the existential psychologist is concerned with a *process* conception of human nature. Existentialism emphasizes the *living immediacy* of experience as the *individual lives it.* There is, consequently, an emphasis on the *here* and the *now,* in contrast to psychoanalysis's emphasis on the patient's past.

In some ways, though the existentialists find much of value in Freud's work, existential psychology can be understood as a reaction to classical psychoanalysis. Where Freud had adopted a deterministic conception of behavior as a product of *past* causes, the existentialists prefer to view the human person as a complex of conscious *processes,* ongoing, changing, and continually striving toward a *future* state of self-fulfillment. Humans are unique among creatures of the living world, the existentialists point out, for they alone have the capacity to become aware of their own strivings, of their own *being.* Binswanger and other existentialists use the German word *Dasein* for this aspect of human existence. *Dasein* may be translated literally as "being" (*sein*) and "there" (*da*).

> *Dasein* indicates that man is the being who is *there* and implies also that he *has* a "there" in the sense that he can know he is there and can take a stand with reference to that fact. The "there" is moreover not just any place, but the particular "there" that is mine, the particular point *in time* as well as space of my existence at this given moment. Man is the being who can be conscious of, and therefore responsible for, his existence. (May, 1958a, p. 41)

As May indicates, the term *Dasein* is not exhausted by the English translation "being." It is extraordinarily difficult, most commentators agree, to speak and write about *being* with the full meaningfulness of the term as used by the existentialists. In English, the word *being* has a connotation of a thing, of a static state, or of a unit that contains being as in "a human being." For the existentialists, *Dasein* indicates a dynamic state, *becoming,* a continual *process*—the activity of *being something* not yet realized. In consequence, May (1958a, p. 41) has suggested that the term "becoming" probably conveys the import of *Dasein* more meaningfully to English-speaking readers.

Freud named his approach to the study of human nature psychoanalysis because he conceived of his task as the elucidation of the connection between mental states and their underlying physical processes. The existentialists, on the other hand, reject any assumption of a split between mind and body. For them, what is of importance in man is *being*—in both mind and body—as an inseparable amalgam of physical and spiritual. Thus the existentialists term their approach *Daseinanalyse.*

Where Freud conceived of anxiety as the threat of deprived instincts, the existentialist conceptualizes anxiety as a threat of nonbeing. Anxiety as the existentialist describes it is a sense of *dread,* of being *choked out of life,* a sense of exquisite *anguish* that the being one is and has must change with life's circumstances, causing one to forfeit present security in one's striving to become future potentiality (May, 1958a, pp. 51, 55; Binswanger, in May, 1958a, p. 315).

Modes of Being

Human beings are not isolated within themselves—they are *beings-in-the-world.* For the existentialists, humans are interrelated with the *world.* They frown on the word "environment" because it bespeaks a conceptualization of the human person that is fragmented. Existentially, *humans imply their world,* and *their world implies them:* ". . . there is neither without the other, and each is understandable only in terms of the other" (May, 1958a, p. 59).

> *World is the structure of meaningful relationships in which a person exists and in the design of which he participates.* Thus world includes the past events which condition my existence and all the vast variety of deterministic influences which operate upon me. But it is these *as I relate to them,* am aware of them, carry them with me, molding, inevitably forming, building them in every minute of relating. For to be aware of one's world means at the same time to be designing it. (May, 1958a, pp. 59–60)

Hence the existential conception of *world* is not restricted to what is ordinarily meant by environment. It is more forward looking and centered more on *possibility* than on biological givens. The existentialists have refined their concept of world by distinguishing three *modes of world,* which each person embodies as being-in-the-world.

1. *Umwelt,* translated literally as "world around," includes the biological drives, needs, and instincts of the individual. *Umwelt,* considered alone, corresponds roughly to what we mean by environment, the impersonal world of natural law and biological cycle. Even if we were totally without self-awareness, the *Umwelt* would continue to exist (May, 1958a, p. 61). In some respects, Freud's conception of human nature focused almost exclusively on the *Umwelt,* a narrowness of vision with which the existentialists profoundly disagree.

2. *Mitwelt* is literally the "with-world," the world of being-with-others, one's fellow humans. *Mitwelt* is not to be confused with the concept of group behavior, for *Mitwelt* includes the *meaning* I make out of my relationship with others, and the *meaning* that these others design into the relationships. The essence of *Mitwelt* interrelationship is that *"in the encounter both persons are changed"* (May, 1958a, p. 63). Laing, although he does not use the term, has focused much of his theorizing on the *Mitwelt,* and he probably would not have much difficulty in accepting this terminology.

3. *Eigenwelt,* or "own world," is the mode of relationship to one's self. "It is a grasping of what something in the world—this bouquet of flowers . . . means to *me*" (May, 1958a, p. 63). Thus the concept of *Eigenwelt* is not restricted to the inner, subjective world, but includes our subjective reactions to the world at large. Again, since Laing has emphasized what he calls the individual's *metaperspective,* as we shall see, he would have no difficulty in accepting the terminology of *Eigenwelt.*

The three modes of world, *Umwelt, Mitwelt,* and *Eigenwelt,* are lived in simultaneously. Our reality of being-in-the-world is lost or damaged if one of the modes is emphasized to the detriment of the other two. To understand an individual's being-in-the-world is a task of enormous complexity, requiring literally that the observer crawl inside the observed's three modes of world and that he or she live them as the observed lives them. In brief, this is the meaning of the phenomenological method that the existentialists have adopted.

Phenomenology as practiced by the existentialists is almost atheoretical. To see the world as another sees it, we must abandon most of our theoretical preconceptions to let experience speak for itself (see Macleod, 1964). Thus the assumption of phenomenology is that *the more categories of analysis the psychologist employs,* like drives, instincts, libido, *"the more you are talking about abstractions and not the existing, living human being"* (May, 1961, p. 18). The phenomenological strategy means that the psychologist accepts the individual's experiences on that individual's terms, unaltered by strategies of analyses, unshaped by theoretical predictions, and unhampered by technical verbalizations. The raw data of existence, the unprocessed, unvarnished *experiences,* are the existential phenomenologist's field of study.

R. D. Laing follows closely in this tradition, as evidenced in his criticism of Kraeplin. For what Laing proposes to do is nothing less than to accept the phenomenological world of the patient as real, as valid, and as essential to an understanding of what that patient is striving to do in those of his or her behaviors that outsiders construe as diseased. However, Laing does not follow the existentialists' preference for leaving the machinery of theory behind. He prefers a form of abstraction that closely follows the contours of experience, but a form of abstraction that is nonetheless theoretical.

ONTOLOGICAL INSECURITY: THE LOSS OF SELF

For Laing, the central problem in the development of human personality is what the existentialists call *ontological insecurity,* or the feeling that one is threatened by nonbeing. In his first major work, *The Divided Self* (1959), Laing remained very much within the mainstream of existential phenomenology, and he described three modes of ontological insecurity.

Engulfment: Loss of Identity

Some persons' sense of self is so tenuous that any relationship (*Mitwelt*) with another threatens to overwhelm them (i.e., to cancel the *Eigenwelt*). Any such interaction fosters the feeling that even minimal contact with another is a struggle to preserve their own existence, to maintain their own identity (Laing, 1959, p. 44).

The most typical strategy used by persons fearing engulfment is to isolate themselves totally, to provide themselves with a cloak of total "aloneness." Laing has dramatically illustrated the phenomenological sense of engulfment in one of the intricate poems of *Knots* (1970, pp. 14–16), a collection of patterns of "human bondage" written in the metalanguage of experience. What follows is an abbreviated excerpt of one of these knots, the knot of engulfment:

> Once upon a time, when Jack was little,
> he wanted to be with his mummy all the time
> and was frightened she would go away

later, when he was a little bigger
he wanted to be away from his mummy
and was frightened that
she wanted him to be with her all the time

when he grew up he fell in love with Jill
and wanted to be with her all the time
and was frightened she would go away

when he was a little older,
he did not want to be with Jill all the time
he was frightened
that she wanted to be with him all the time . . .

Jack feels Jill is devouring him.
He is devoured
by his devouring fear of
being devoured by
her devouring desire
for *him* to devour her, . . .

It can easily be seen that Laing has managed to capture the flavor of subjectively experienced emotional and cognitive states from the perspective of the perceiver's confusion. Laing is here suggesting that early experience of emotional knotting in relation to the other is a pattern of bondage that will haunt us throughout life.

Implosion: Vacuum of an Empty Self

When the individual senses that at any moment the external world will rush in and "obliterate all identity as a gas will rush in and obliterate a vacuum," he or she experiences what Laing (1959, p. 45) calls *implosion*. In effect, ontologically insecure individuals experiencing this dread assume that like the vacuum, they are empty. They may long for the emptiness to be filled, but they dread that eventuality, for their emptiness, they suspect, is all that they can be.

Phenomenologically, the experience of implosion has this flavor (Laing, 1970, p. 83):

One is inside
then outside what one has been inside
One feels empty
because there is nothing inside oneself
that inside of the outside
that one was once inside
once one tries to get oneself inside what
one is outside:
to eat and to be eaten
to have the outside inside and to be
inside the outside. . . .

Petrification: Doubt of Being Alive

Petrification is a form of terror that we will be turned into stone, made into a robot or machine without feelings, without subjectivity, without awareness. The feeling of petrification can be described by an outside observer as depersonalization. Petrification is accomplished in the act of treating another as not human, as an object, not as a being (1959, pp. 46–48). From the petrified person's viewpoint, this fear that others may manipulate the self through indifference is described this way (Laing, 1970, p. 24):

> . . .You are frightened of being boring, you
> try to be interesting by not being interested,
> but are interested only in not being boring.
>
> You are not interested in me.
> You are only interested that I be interested in you.
>
> You pretend to be bored
> because I am not interested
> that you are frightened
> that I am not frightened
> that you are not interested in me.

Depersonalization of the subject, however, may also be a product of his or her attempts to dehumanize another, for the act of greeting the other as an object reduces the actor to object (1959, p. 57).

Laing has published an additional volume of his "poetry" of human foibles and despairs. Entitled *Do You Love Me?* (1976c), the book is essentially a continuation of the previously quoted *Knots*, but contains more whimsical verses with a somewhat lighter touch of gallows humor (see also Laing, 1977).

ON DRIVING ONE MAD: EMBODIED AND UNEMBODIED SELVES

Use your imagination to construct images of the following acts:

1. Swallow the saliva in your mouth.
2. Take a glass of water; sip and swallow it.
3. Spit in the glass; swallow the saliva-water mixture.
4. Sip some water; spit it back into a glass; sip and swallow what you have spat back. (after Laing, 1969a, p. 92)

Although the demonstration just described is not Laing's creation, he used it effectively to illustrate the distinction most people phenomenologically make between "inside" and "outside." Most individuals are unable to perform all four acts and are disgusted particularly by numbers 3 and 4. "One is aware that there is a difference between saliva inside one's mouth, and that same saliva, one inch in space outside one's mouth. . . . *We* feel ourselves to be inside a bag of skin: what is outside this bag is not-us. Me—inside. Not-Me outside" (Laing, 1969a, p. 92).

Gordon Allport, a personologist, used roughly the same example in describing the self as a compartmentalized entity:"What I perceive as belonging intimately to my body is warm and welcome; what I perceive as separate from my body becomes, in the twinkling of an eye, cold and foreign" (1955, p. 43).

If you remain unconvinced that what is intimately a part of you may nonetheless become revolting and alien, try Allport's suggestion to imagine having pricked your finger with a needle. Few of us would hesitate to raise that finger to our lips to gently suck the wounded tip. But now imagine a bandage over that finger soaked in your blood. Further imagine sucking the blood from the bandage, the same blood that came from your pin-pricked finger: *your own blood.* This "bandage-blood" is no longer mine; it is something hideously alien.

The shortest route to madness is traveled by those persons who lose their abiding conviction that they are one within their bodies. An uncanny feeling of disembodiment, of being external and alien to self, a material object apart from a subjective mind, floods the waking consciousness of many schizophrenics. For the "mad," the distinction between "inner" and "outer" is heightened to the point that individuals feel themselves to be two selves: a *true,* authentic *self* that is the core of their very beings, and a *false self* that is the empty shell of the detached material body (Laing, 1959, p. 69).

The divorce of true self from body-shell produces a peculiar split in consciousness by which schizophrenics experience themselves both as perceiver and as perceived, both as observer and as observed, as *me* and as *other.* Sometimes, such states of dissociation occur in "normal" people under great stress. For example, prisoners in concentration camps tried to disembody their feelings and perceptions as a technique of survival. The goal was to produce the protective feeling expressed in such phrases as "this is a dream," "this is not happening to me," "this seems unreal" (Laing, 1959, p. 79).

The strategy of the individual who compartmentalizes many aspects of self is to escape or to transcend the real external world by relegating all interaction with it to one compartment—to the false self. In this way, safety is sought, but emptiness is achieved. The inner compartment, true self, becomes like a vacuum, empty and devoid of experience, activity, and need. "The detachment of self means that the self is never revealed directly in the individual's expressions and actions, nor does it experience anything spontaneously or immediately. The self's relationship to the other is always at one remove" (Laing, 1959, p. 80).

CHARACTERISTICS OF THE FALSE SELF: THE MASK

Because the individual relegates all intercourse between self and others, or between self and the world, to a system "within his being which is not 'him,' then the world is experienced as unreal, all that belongs to this system is felt to be false, futile and meaningless" (Laing, 1959, p. 80). Thus, much as Jung (cf. Chapter 7) had spoken of individuals who too closely identified with their persona, Laing interprets disordered behavior as a product of the individual's striving to produce a false front. The false self is a facade through which others cannot penetrate to his or her security.

The most important immediate result of the establishment of a false self is that the "individual's acts are no longer self-expressions" (1959, p. 94). Laing is another of many theorists who employ the imagery of the actor and the mask. He is at pains to point out that the false self, or mask, is fairly typical in situations other than madness. " 'A man without a mask' is very rare" (1959, p. 95; see also 1969b, p. 31). To some extent, all of us wear masks, but there is a key difference. In the normal individual, the mask or false front presented to others is not the medium of that individual's gratification of true-self desires. For the normal individual, the mask is a convenient social necessity. For the schizophrenic, the mask is the very vehicle of survival—a necessity without convenience.

Indeed, the false-self system is at once the most dangerous and the most treasured component of the schizophrenic's life. It is cherished and nurtured as a buffer between others and the real self; but the false-self mask is nevertheless fearsome in its power to assimilate the whole of being.

In a very real sense, the false self is a product of the individual's struggle to comply with *his or her* world, with the significant people who mold his or her life, with the members of the immediate family on whom life security is dependent. When interaction with these significant others is not bearable, or the demands of intimate living become intolerable, the false self is formed to comply with and to pacify these others. All the while, the mask protects the true inner self from likewise having to comply with unpleasant reality.

Thus the inner self stagnates. It pursues a course of development divorced from what transpires in the world. In its role of mediator with the external world, the false self may so effectively mimic normality that the distortions of experience transpiring in the protectively isolated genuine self go undetected for some time. Impersonating the characteristics of those others from whom withdrawal is attempted, the false self caricatures the personalities and traits of the very individuals most hated and feared by the true self.

The false self presents to the world what the world's troublesome people expect. To the extent that the false self adopts the behaviors modeled by significant others for the purpose of pacifying them and preventing these people from penetrating to the true self, it is playing a role. More precisely, *the false self is role-playing normality.* Laing called this kind of role playing *impersonation* (1959, p. 100). Impersonation is a minimizing technique. By superficial adoption of the other's behaviors, the false self prevents total loss of identity that would come with global commitment to the trappings of normality.

Split Between Behavior and Experience

All of Laing's early theorizing can be brought into focus around two central propositions, much as the spokes of a wheel are arranged around its hub. The first proposition is that *for individuals who succumb to ontological insecurity, there is a massive discrepancy between their behavior and their experience.* For such individuals, who incidentally are likely to get themselves diagnosed "schizophrenic," an unbridgeable gulf exists between what they phenomenologically experience, and what they publicly do. Yet their behavior is intelligible once *their* experience is understood.

Because only the "mask" behaviors receive validation from others, the gap between the actor and mask eventuates in the actor's annihilation.

Second, *the discrepancy between inner self and outer public behavior is a product of social interaction that is duplicitous and unintentionally designed by others to drive one "mad."* The focus of Laing's investigations of such pathogenic social interaction began with the study of two-person combinations called "dyads." He then expanded his view to the study of families, for it is within the family that the first and most important forms of public and private, "inner" and "outer," communications are experienced.

ON BEING UNWANTED: THE PERSONAL SOURCES OF LAING'S IDEAS

Laing's model of personality and personality disturbance stresses interpersonal communications, expectations, and frustrations as the crucial factors shaping human existence. Personality theorists of widely different theoretical perspectives have argued that children's view of self and of significant others is sculpted, wittingly or unwittingly, to the design modeled by their families. When the family pattern, by intention or accident, is disturbed, children struggle to cope with the mismatch between what they have learned of life and its people within the irrational family cloister and what they glimpse of life's meaning beyond it.

Laing's sensitivity to the irrationality of some family interactions seems to have grown from his experiences with his own. Born on October 7, 1927, Laing spent his boyhood in Glasgow, Scotland, amid a particularly raucous set of relatives. In a semi-autobiographical essay (1976a), he described some of the events of his boyhood in the same matter-of-fact (yet poetic) style he has used in describing the phenomenal world of others. In deliberately ambiguous and disjointed prose, he has implied that the central theme of his childhood in Glasgow was his discovery that he was unwanted by his parents:

> My parents and I lived in a three-room flat.
> My mother and I slept in one room in separate beds,
> and my father slept in another room.
> According to both of them, all sexual activity had ceased
> between them irrevocably before I was conceived.
> My mother and father still swear they do not know how
> I was conceived.
> But there is a birthmark on his right knee and one
> on mine.
> A fact against immaculate conception. (1976a, p. 8)

Laing further reports that his father could not "admit" his son's birth for several days after the event. His mother immediately entered a "decline," and a nurse was engaged to care for the newborn Laing. Unfortunately, this woman "turned out to be a drunken slut." A second nurse likewise proved to be a drunken slut, so Laing's mother resumed caring for the infant.

Laing's father's reluctance to reveal to others the birth of his child seems to have originated in a long-term family "rule" or taboo concerning sexual intercourse. As Laing remembers, "My father was the only one in his family to marry and, with one possible exception, the only one ever to commit sexual intercourse" (1976a, p. 3). So fraught with negative emotion was the topic of sexual relations that Laing had only the vaguest idea of "the facts of life" well into his mid-teens.

When Laing was 10 months old, his maternal grandmother and a maternal aunt arrived to live with Laing's family for eight months. In a nearby house, the paternal side of the family set up their housekeeping arrangements. The maternal and paternal branches of the family thus brought into such close proximity did not get along well together. Laing became rapidly aware of the impossibility of coping with so many conflicting adult viewpoints:

> From as far back as I can remember, I tried to figure out what was going on between these people. If I believed one, I couldn't believe anyone else. Especially at the time when my mother, my mother's mother, and my mother's younger sister were all part of the same household—from 10 months to 18 months—I could not believe all of them, one of them, or none of them. (1976a, p. 4)

As we shall later see, in establishing the phenomenological portion of his theory, Laing was to make much of the effects on family members of their own conflicting viewpoints.

Irrational Rules for the Laing Family

Growing up in Scotland, the young Ronald Laing frequently had to cope rationally with the irrationality of his mother's conception of discipline and loving concern. For example, Laing (1985, pp. 48 ff.) remembers in his somewhat selective autobiography that when he was five years old, he had "running eczema," a skin condition marked by water blisters that became easily infected. His mother was hypervigilant about the condition and was convinced that Ronald's eating habits were responsible. He was especially forbidden by her to eat sweets, such as jam, candy, soda, and so on. On his first day at school, another boy offered him a bite of a jelly sandwich, which he remembers enjoying very much. But when he returned home, his mother made him look her in the eye and "tell the truth." He lied. She detected the lie. He was given a sound "thrashing" by his father when he came home.

That same evening, Laing's mother made him promise that he would never lie to her or his father again. He kept his promises not to lie and not to eat sweets, but soon the eczema returned in full force. After about three months from the time of the eczema outbreak, Laing's forearms, wrists, and hands were almost always swathed in bandages. Another two months passed, and the eczema vanished. Everyone was puzzled. Young Ronald had not cheated on his promise, and he rather doubted that his condition came from the few sweets he'd had. He reasoned as follows on the occasion of a friend offering him a "jelly baby" candy:

> . . . I got this eczema without eating sweets, or other forbidden things. Then, after a while, it went away and I've been clear of a rash for months. Since I've got it *anyway,* why not accept that jelly baby, put it between my teeth, then pick it out of my mouth, deftly and throw it away when no one is looking? This way it could not be said to have

entered my mouth, I would not have bitten it, my lips would not have touched it, none of it would have come into contact with more than two fingers, two teeth, and the tip of my tongue. (Laing, 1985, p. 50)

He put his plan into effect. When he returned home, his mother asked the usual questions about whether he was keeping his promises, and he assured her that he had. What he did not know was that a neighbor had told his mother of the jelly baby incident, and his mother was testing him. Laing proceeded to deny that he had actually *eaten* the jelly baby. At that moment, the boy who had given him the candy appeared at the door wanting Ronald to come out to play. Laing says that never before had that boy come to his home. The boy was interrogated briefly by Laing's mother, and admitted to giving Ronald the candy, despite Laing's protestations. He was caught. He admitted taking the candy and tried to explain what he had actually done with it. Mrs. Laing asked which two teeth he had held it between, apparently tauntingly. That evening he was "soundly thrashed" again by his father.

Sometime later, Laing recalls letting his guard down at a dinner one evening and commenting that the cabbage he was eating "tasted like a lead pencil." His mother, ever alert, asked how he knew what a pencil tasted like. He was down on the floor in the blink of an eye, receiving yet another "thrashing." In the Laing family, one simply did not put anything disapproved of by Mrs. Laing into one's mouth.

Laing recounts a rather long list of other incidents in the family that centered on creating great guardedness in him. His sensitivity to the irrationality of parental demands and beliefs probably originated in these experiences. But we also have to ask what the emotional effects on the growing child might have been. What was Laing learning about himself from experiences such as these?

When Laing was 15, he recalls a particularly telling incident. It had been customary from childhood for him to have a hot bath each night and a cold one each morning. His mother's custom was to scrub his back, though as the years went on, the amount of scrubbing was considerably reduced. By the time he was 15, Laing became concerned about his mother coming into his bath, especially because the first signs of sexual development were beginning. He tried negotiating a compromise with her. She would not permit him to lock the bathroom door, but she would come in only when he called to her that he was ready. Her stated reason for her insistence that she scrub his back was that a "spot" might develop there where he could not reach, and his eczema might start again.

One night, Laing locked the door. His mother stood outside, beating on the frosted glass:

> She quickly escalated from yelling (Open this door at once. Come on now. This is your mother. Open this door.) to even higher pitched yells and screams through which she threatened to break the door down.
>
> At this point, my father dragged her away from the door. The yelling and screaming were unabated and her intention persisted. He remonstrated with her to no effect, then he yelled at her yell for yell, "if you don't stop it, I'll go out on the stairhead and shout my bloody head off!" The neighbours! That did it. She quieted down. I was already out of the bathroom.
>
> I was deeply grateful to my father that when it came to the crunch he took my side. It would have been awful if he too had ordered me to open the door. (Laing, 1985, p. 75)

It is likely that among the lessons Laing learned from these early experiences were these:

1. Don't believe what people tell you just because they tell it to you (Laing, 1985, p. 55).
2. Family rules have to be obeyed, however irrational they may be.
3. Maternal love is not always pure, but may contain elements of hostility, teasing, distrust, and intrusiveness.
4. Things that are not your fault are your fault, so appear to cooperate but privately resist.

Irrational Family Disputes: "Old Pa" and "Young Pa"

The pervading sense of adult irrationality to which Laing was exposed and to which he refused to submit completely is revealed in several of Laing's family anecdotes. For example, his father was convinced that his own father had "systematically murdered" Laing's grandmother over the years. On one occasion, when "Old Pa," as Laing's paternal grandfather was called, visited the Laing household, a fight erupted between Old Pa and Laing's father. Old Pa had told Laing's mother to shut off the radio, whereupon Laing's father told her not to touch the radio. The verbal dispute escalated to a physical struggle in which Old Pa and Laing's Pa fought a battle throughout the house. The outcome of this bizarre struggle was a clear but bloody victory for Laing's father. Dragging Old Pa into the bath, Laing's father submerged him in cold water and then "heaved him out [of the bath] drenched with blood and water, dragged him to the door, kicked him out, and threw his cap after him. Then he stood at the window and waited to see how [Old Pa] would manage to stagger or crawl away.'He held himself up very well,' Dad said.'You've got to hand it to him' " (Laing, 1976a, pp. 4–5).

Physical battles around the Laing household were not confined to those between Laing's father and grandfather. Old Pa's younger brother, "Uncle Jack," reputed to have gone "daft" with heat stroke in China during World War I, allied himself with Old Pa. For some years after the critical battle between Old Pa and Laing's Pa, Uncle Jack would occasionally come to the Laing household seeking to avenge his brother's defeat. Each of these reenactments was carefully orchestrated, and each time the outcome would be the same. First, Laing's mother would push all the furniture aside, then diplomatically leave the room. Hiding behind the curtains, the young Laing would watch his father and uncle go at each other, until Jack was down and called it quits. Before leaving, Uncle Jack would pause for a cup of tea provided by Laing's mother (because she felt sorry for him), and he would press a coin or two into Laing's hand. The entire sequence was enacted with chilling deliberateness, or so it must have seemed to young Laing. (See also Laing, 1985, pp. 103ff.)

Laing's perception of the irrational and unspoken rules that governed his family life was sharpened in adolescence. When Laing was 16, his father deemed it time to instruct his son in that most taboo of all topics, the facts of life. Hitherto the mere mention of sex was cause for grave anxiety. To escape the parental lecture, Laing lied: "Dad, it's all right. I've learned about them at school. . . . (This was the first lie I had told for, as far as I can remember, over eight years. I was terrified he would try to tell me. I didn't know what they [the facts of life] were, but I did not want to hear them from him. And by now I was so sorry for him I wanted to spare him the ordeal)" (1976a, p. 10).

Laing eventually established for himself what the facts of life were by covertly consulting, among other sources, the *Encyclopaedia Britannica* in the library and the local bookstore's selection of volumes on venereal disease. But more important, Laing had learned the potential power of others to shape one's experience and one's self-experience:

> For as early as I remember I never took my self to *be* what people called me. That at least has remained crystal clear to me. Whatever, whoever I may be is not to be confused with the names people give *to* me, or how they *describe* me, or what they *call* me. I am not my name.
>
> Who or what I am, as far as they are concerned, is not necessarily, or thereby, *me,* as far as I am concerned.
>
> I am presumably *what* they are describing, but not their description. I am the territory, what they say I am is their map of me. And what I call myself to myself is, presumably, my map of me. What, or where, is the territory? (Laing, 1976a, p. 24)

The Medical School Years

It is not difficult to detect a note of rebelliousness in Laing's self-description, an unwillingness to be contained by the perceptions and expectations of others. It is small wonder, then, that this characteristic unwillingness to be another's object extended to his years at medical school in Glasgow. Laing found medical practice to be lacking in human warmth, in human concern for those to be treated. During his internship, Laing attended a childbirth that had extended through 16 hours:

> Finally it started to come—grey, slimy, cold—out it came—a large human frog—an encephalic monster, no neck, no head, with eyes, nose, froggy mouth, long arms. . . . Maybe it was slightly alive. We didn't want to know. We wrapped it in newspaper— and with this bundle under my arm to take back to the pathology lab, that seemed to cry out for all the answerable answers that I ever asked, I walked along O'Connell Street two hours later.
>
> I needed a drink. I went into a pub, put the bundle on the bar. Suddenly, the desire to unwrap it, hold it up for all to see, a ghastly Gorgon's head, to turn the world to stone. (Laing, 1967, pp. 178–179)

In the cool professionalism that pervaded his medical training Laing had found no precedent for what he felt at this childbirth. We can surmise that the physicians and nurses attending this birth had shown no shock, horror, or sadness. And we can further speculate that Laing somehow wanted to express his own shock and sadness by shocking others.

When Laing began to specialize in psychiatry, as we shall see in more detail later, he observed what he felt were something less than humane methods of dealing with the troubled. In his fourth year in medical training, he witnessed an interview between a psychiatric consultant and a 17-year-old boy whose chief observable difficulty was an extensive case of acne. At one point in the interview, the patient stated that he was afraid that people were looking at him in the street. To this item of information, the psychiatrist replied to the effect that he, the boy, was really afraid that other people knew he masturbated. From there, the psychiatrist proceeded to interrogate the boy as to the details of his masturbation. Laing recalled the effect of that demonstration on his developing view of psychiatry:

> I had never heard the word "masturbate" used "in public" before. I cringed in terror at the prospect of the [psychiatric] consultant asking us the questions he asked this patient, but he did not. (1976a, p. 90)

Although Laing later trained in psychoanalytic technique and theory, he never forgot the lessons of his boyhood and years as a medical student. If one is to treat disordered persons, one must not forget in the welter of psychological theory and speculation that it is a *person* to whom the label "disordered" is attached. The ideas and tools of Freudian psychoanalytic theory were profoundly useful to Laing, but they were also constraining and insufficient to the task of accounting for the facts of life as each person lives them.

INTRAUTERINE LIFE AS A REFLECTION OF THINGS TO COME

Laing (1976b; 1982) has carried the theme of the effects of being unwanted by one's parents a giant step backward, to the time when the fetus is carried in the mother's womb. Could it be, he asks, that prebirth existence in the womb and the processes of birth set up causes whose effects will be felt only later, only in analogous ways, only in ways that are somehow "resonances" of life before birth?

> . . . it seems plausible to me that the intrauterine experience, from conception to birth and afterbirth experiences are mapped into our system in some way or another, and stored to express themselves later, especially surfacing after physical growth ends, and postpubertal life begins. One discovers as one gets older that the present situation, whatever it happens to be, doesn't entirely seem to account for one's present behavior. (Laing, 1976b, p. 5)

To take one, perhaps trivial, example of a "resonance," Laing reports that at 5:15 P.M. each day for several years he was taken with the desire for a drink. The time of his birth was 5:15 P.M. Often, he says, he knows when it is 5:15 P.M. by the feelings that well up within him, a desire for the calming effects of alcohol being only one of these subjective indicators.

Thus the act of birth itself may be an unnecessarily brutal experience that sets up lifelong resonances to be experienced and reexperienced in diverse ways. Following this line of logic, Laing suggests that it might be possible for the feeling of being unwanted to also be communicated to the fetus—perhaps even from conception. Carried to its most extreme form, Laing argues, it may be that some schizophrenic patients need literally and metaphorically to be reconceived, to be reborn—this time to confront volitionally the prospect of a hostile, rejecting world, prepared anew to master the cues that signal unwantedness (1976a, p. 72). Laing did, in fact, adopt the procedure of "birthing" some of his patients, modeling his technique on that of the late Elizabeth Fehr, a New York therapist he admired.

Extending this line of reasoning in another direction, Laing asks whether it is possible that the physical environment surrounding the unborn fetus might become the prototype or analog for later interpretations of life. To take one example, the placenta is the most critical tissue connection between fetus and mother, for it permits the exchange of nourishment and oxygen from mother to child, and the elimination of wastes from child's to mother's bloodstream:

> Could the placenta
> be the original
> life giver
> life sucker
> persecutor
> our first friend or our first
> tormentor?

(Laing, 1976a, p. 61)

Laing credits Francis J. Mott, a relatively neglected writer on this subject, with having proposed this analogy. Laing extends the analogy in specific psychological ways. Thus physically, chemically, the placenta is the membrane that serves as the two-way (in and out) physiological door through which the fetus receives nourishment and expends its wastes:

$$\text{(in) fetus} \longleftrightarrow \begin{array}{c}\text{feces}\\\text{placenta (out)}\\\text{food}\end{array}$$

Psychological analogs of these primary "in-out" functions may be indicated by the following metaphors:

$$\begin{array}{ccc} & \text{life} \rightarrow \text{death} & \\ & \text{death} \leftarrow \text{life} & \\ & \text{loss} \rightarrow & \\ & \leftarrow \text{renewal} & \\ & \text{giving} \rightarrow & \\ \text{(IN)} & \leftarrow \text{receiving} & \text{(OUT)} \\ & \text{going} \rightarrow & \\ & \leftarrow \text{coming} & \\ & \text{exports} \rightarrow & \\ & \leftarrow \text{imports} & \\ & \text{money} \rightarrow & \\ & \leftarrow \text{energy} & \end{array}$$

(modified from Laing, 1976a, p. 63)

Laing is here hypothesizing that our earliest interactions on the purely physiological level are impressed psychologically upon "our organism" (awareness?) before we are born. After-birth life may thus be a complex set of resonances of these, our first patterns of transaction with another.

Whatever may be Laing's intention regarding the possibility of incorporating such resonances into his procedures for treating disturbed personalities, it is clear that Laing is only at the beginning of his efforts to explicate the interactions between persons, and between persons and the lasting effects of their environments.

Inner and Outer Reality: Embryology, Experience, and Myth

Laing (1982) is asserting that prenatal experience can be "mapped" onto postnatal experience and vice versa. Laing has elaborated these ideas into a multilevel set of perspectives that permit mapping between embryological biology, psychological experience, and mythological representation of both. He is suggesting that certain patterns occur over and over in human experience and represent conceptual-mythological bridges between the facts of human biology and our experience of those facts. Patterns in embryology are called *embryologems;* corresponding patterns in psychological experience are *psychologems;* and universal, artistic rendering of those patterns in mythology are called *mythologems* (Laing, 1982, p. 109).

Laing's account of these correspondences among prenatal experience, postnatal experience, and mythological expression of the two is poetic, ambiguous, and paradoxical. Nevertheless, here are two examples of his thinking, in lieu of concrete definitions:

Prenatal Pattern One: Catatonic Schizophrenia
Prenatal patterns recur in postnatal life in many variations, and they come into view from different perspectives.

In the 1950s I would see someone in a padded cell, curled up on the floor, naked, cowering from the stimuli, indifferent to food, fed through a tube, incontinent. The comparison with a foetus in the uterus, complete with umbilical cord (tube) and placenta (funnel), is so irresistible that intrauterine regression is used as virtually a descriptive term to characterize this pattern. But what does it mean? A question not yet answered by anyone, at least to anyone else's complete satisfaction. (Laing, 1982, p. 113)

Prenatal Pattern Two: Dreams
A woman notes in her dream book a dream she made no sense of at the time, and which she did not remember. A year later, now a mother of a three-month-old baby, turning over the pages in her dream book, she came across the following dream: "A piece of gum is going along an escalator into a garage."

This dream, she reckoned, had occurred three or four days after she had conceived. She had no conscious knowledge of the anatomy of the internal genitals, nor of the physiology of impregnation, though, who knows, she may have looked at illustrations and repressed her impressions. A piece of gum, an escalator, a garage, are remote in themselves. They are brought together by what they bring together, that is to say, symbolize. . . . The piece of gum is the blastocyst, the escalator is the oviduct, and the garage, the uterus. (Laing, 1982, p. 103)

Laing is clearly willing to explore the personal meanings that people create to account for their experiences, and he is here attempting to abstract them into some kind of universal principles. The alert reader will detect some of Jung's influence in Laing's attempts.

A SCIENCE OF PERSONS:
SOCIAL PHENOMENOLOGY

"I cannot experience your experience. You cannot experience my experience. We are both invisible men. All men are invisible to one another. Experience is man's invisibility to man" (Laing, 1967, p. 54).

With these words, Laing sought to erect a science of persons' experience that would bridge the gulf between the superficial study of the mask and the phenomenological penetration to the actor's perspective.

For the individual constructing a false self to appease the world of others, there is an irredeemable split between inner experience and outer behavior. Experience is a very private matter, invisible to all, even to the experiencing agent. But it is *experience* that Laing sees as the central datum for his science of persons:

> We can see other people's behavior, but not their experience. . . . The other person's behavior is an experience of mine. My behavior is an experience of the other. The task of social phenomenology is *to relate my experience of the other's behavior to the other's experience of my behavior.* Its study is the relation between experience and experience: its true field is *interexperience.* (1967, p. 17; first italics added)

It is now clear why Laing would find the psychiatrist's comment about the "oral-acquisitive" nature of schizophrenia obscene. The comment is not merely an error; it betrays a monumental presumption that the observed person's experience of the act, interpretation of what he or she does, is irrelevant.

For Laing, as for the existentialists, the normal condition of modern persons is estrangement from themselves, from their experience of self and from others' experience of their selves:

> As a whole, we are a generation of men so estranged from the inner world [of experience] that many are arguing that it does not exist; and that even if it does exist, it does not matter. (1967, p. 54)

To some degree, we are all self-divided: "Man cut off from his own mind, cut off equally from his own body—a half-crazed creature in a mad world" (1967, p. 55). But, "The 'normally' alienated person, by reason of the fact that he acts more or less like everyone else, is taken to be sane" (1967, p. 27). Therefore:

> Long before a thermonuclear war can come about, we have had to lay waste our own sanity. We begin with the children. It is imperative to catch them in time. Without the most thorough and rapid brainwashing their dirty minds would see through our dirty tricks. . . . By the time the new human being is 15 or so, we are left with a being like ourselves, a half-crazed creature more or less adjusted to a mad world. This is normality in our present age. (Laing, 1967, p. 58)

Laing's proposal for a science of persons, a discipline to study the interaction and interexperience of humans adjusting to a mad world, might be regarded as pessimistic, indeed as cynical, if Laing's assumptions are valid. Specifically, Laing finds it offensive that from birth we are taught *what* to experience, instructed to *act* on what we experience at the behest of others, and indoctrinated in what *not* to experience in compliance with their demands. Eventually, we act, reflect upon our actions, act on our reflections, or even "act out" our reflections because we have been molded by the most violent force available to humans: love by and for significant others (Laing, 1967, p. 59). For it is with love that parents socialize their children into the culture by which they themselves are shaped. It is in the name of love that schools socialize students into the intellectual and practical skills that normalize their lives in the culture. It is for spiritual love that religions coerce the faithful into forfeiting experience for transcendent ethics. And it is for love that one marries and produces novices to initiate into this tradition of split experience. Sadly, these recruits are programmed to perpetuate the cycle of violence.

In Laing's (1982, p. 15) view, then, a science of persons is the study of *political* violence in the original meaning of the word "politic" as relating to a citizen of a particular culture:

1. wise, prudent, sagacious in devising and pursuing measures; shrewd, expedient; . . .
2. prudently or artfully contrived; . . .
3. crafty, unscrupulous, cunning . . .

(*Webster's Unabridged Dictionary,* 2d ed.)

Laing wrote two books in which the titles juxtaposed the word "politics" with more traditional psychological subject matter: *The Politics of Experience* (1967) and *The Politics of the Family* (1969a). The central theme of both books is that "madness" is a prudent, sagacious, and cunning measure artfully contrived to make an insane situation livable.

Laing is especially critical of psychologists and other social scientists who attempt to encompass experience with traditional scientific method:

> The scientific objective world is not the world of real life. It is a highly sophisticated artifact, created by multiple operations which effectively and efficiently exclude immediate experience in all its apparent capriciousness from its order of discourse. (1982, p. 15)

because

> A fact makes no difference to me personally unless I realize it. The *realization* of the difference is decisive in making any difference make a difference to me. It is very much easier to realize something one experiences personally than something one does not, perhaps cannot, experience at all. We even often fail to realize what we do not wish to recognize. (1982, p. 13)

STUDY OF DYADS: TWO-PERSON PERSPECTIVES ON EXPERIENCE

The split between inner experience and outer behavior is a problem for schizophrenics only because they have failed to master the division and are torn apart. This self-division is the core of Laing's view of disordered personality. The task at hand is to understand how the split originates.

When two individuals interact, communicate, interpersonally behave, they each bring to the situation a set of expectations, cognitions, and desires. Sometimes their two perspectives uniformly mesh; sometimes they clash. It is the clash that is most instructive.

To illustrate: Peter is upset about something. Paul hopes to help him by himself remaining calm. Peter, however, feels that Paul is not genuinely friendly because a true friend would share his upset. Paul is unaware of Peter's expectation, and he does not communicate the friendly solicitude that underlies his exterior calm. And he remains unaware of his failure to communicate his concern. Consider the following resulting *spiral of reciprocal perspectives,* ignoring for the moment the bracketed notations:

Peter	Paul
1. I am upset. [Pt → Pt]	1. Peter is upset. [Pl → Pt]
2. Paul is acting very calm and dispassionate. [Pt → Pl]	2. I'll try to help him by remaining calm and just listening. [Pl → (Pl Pt)]
3. If Paul cared about me and wanted to help, he would get involved and show some emotion also. [Pt → Pl → (Pl Pt)]	3. He is getting even more upset. [Pl → Pt] I must be even more calm. [Pl → (Pl Pl)]
4. Paul knows that this upsets me. [Pt → (Pl Pt)]	4. He is accusing me of hurting him. [Pl → Pt → (Pl Pt)]
5. If Paul knows that his behavior upsets me, he must be intending to hurt me. [Pt → Pl → (Pl Pt)]	5. I'm really trying to help. [Pl → (Pl Pt)]
6. He must be cruel, sadistic. Maybe he gets pleasure out of it. [Pt → (Pl Pt)]	6. He must be projecting. [Pl → Pt → Pl → Pt]

Modified from Laing, Phillipson, & Lee, 1966, pp. 21–22

A basic sense of mistrust is responsible for Peter's and Paul's mismatched experiences of their relationship. Laing, Phillipson, and Lee (1966, p. 23) call the result a spiral of reciprocal perspectives. Each of the involved individuals is capable of assuming at least three different levels of interpretation or *metaperspectives* of their mutual experiences.

First of these perspectives are the various *direct views* by each person of her- or himself and of the other. *Direct perspectives* come in four varieties.

The Direct Perspectives

The following four direct perspectives and the notations used by Laing and his coworkers are simply a list of the logical possibilities inherent in the dyadic situation:

1. Peter → Peter: "Peter's view of himself."
2. Peter → Paul: "Peter's view of Paul."
3. Paul → Peter: "Paul's view of Peter."
4. Paul → Paul: "Paul's view of Paul."

The notation system thus far is relatively uncomplicated; the arrows simply denote the subject's view of the other or of himself. Laing and his colleagues, however, emphasize that each participant in the dyad may have a direct perception not only of himself and the other, but of his own perception of the other's perception of himself, and of the other's perception of his perception of the other, and so on. In essence, the important perspectives of the dyad are the individual's views of these *relationships* between one's self with one's self, between one's self and the other, and between the other's self and one's self, and so on.

At first these multiple perspectives seem mind-boggling and arouse the suspicion that Laing, Phillipson, and Lee are parodying schizophrenic discourse. The algebraic notation system created by Laing and his team, which further abstracts these person-perspectives into a more-or-less workable form, does not do much to dispel the suspicion of a possible "put-on." If there is some element of whimsy in Laing's system, it is present with a purpose, for in using the notation system one is rapidly put into the position of struggling desperately to comprehend the meaning of communications from multiple viewpoints. This struggle perhaps is the point.

To express the direct perspective of each individual's relationship to her- or himself and to the other, Laing, Phillipson, and Lee (1966, p. 53) adopt the following shorthand:

1. Peter's relationship with himself (PtPt)
2. Peter's relationship with Paul (PtPl)
3. Paul's relationship with himself (PlPl)
4. Paul's relationship with Peter (PlPt)

By "relationship," Laing and his team mean to symbolize the phenomenologically experienced feelings, as in "Peter *likes* or *dislikes* himself" (PtPt), or "Peter *likes* or *dislikes* Paul" (PtPl), and so on. The relationship may take any form; the notation simply records the existence of the relationship. There is a further complication, however, in the fact that each of these individuals' unique *perception of the relationship* must also be specified:

PETER →
1. Pt → (PtPt): "Peter's perspective of Peter's relationship with Self"
2. Pt → (PtPl): "Peter's perspective of Peter's relationship with Paul"
3. Pt → (PlPl): "Paul's perspective of Peter's relationship with himself"
4. Pt → (PlPt): "Paul's perspective of Peter's relationship with Peter"

Likewise, Paul may experience his own direct perspective of the four relationships. Paul's direct perspectives can simply be added to the notation for Peter's. They are read backward, from right to left:

PETER → ← PAUL
1. Pt → (PtPt) ← Pl: (Paul's perspective of Peter's relationship with Peter)
2. Pt → (PtPl) ← Pl: (Paul's perspective of Paul's relationship with Peter)
3. Pt → (PlPl) ← Pl: (Paul's perspective of Paul's relationship with himself)
4. Pt → (PlPt) ← Pl: (Paul's perspective of Peter's relationship with Paul)

Metaperspectives

To completely capture the process of spiraling perspectives in dyadic relationships, it is necessary to describe the possible *metaperspectives* that may accrue to the direct perspectives of Peter and Paul. In phenomenological language we have not only: "My view of myself," but also "my view of the other's view of me," and, "how I think you see *me*" (Laing et al., 1966, p. 5). This form of internalizing the other's view of self, a kind of second-level perspective, is called a metaperspective.

Whereas "How I see me" defines my ego identity, "How I think *you* see me" defines my *metaidentity.* Self-identity (my view of myself) and metaidentity (my view of your view of me) may interact so that my views of others' views of myself begin to define a new self-identity (Laing et al., 1966, p. 6). Laing's conception of identity and metaidentity is very similar to what Harry Stack Sullivan meant by the Self being a product of "reflected appraisals" (e.g., 1953a, p. 22).

It is consequently theoretically possible to have not only a first-order metaperspective of a person-to-person relationship, but second and third orders of metaperspective as well: *meta-meta,* and *meta-metametaperspectives.* In fact, the layering of perspectives upon perspectives can continue indefinitely—in theory. However, mere practicality limits the number of layers that can be piled to one which is within the reasonable grasp of the observer. Perspectives numbering much beyond the meta-metaperspective level would be so removed from the phenomenological description of the event that they would be useless. Laing, Phillipson, and Lee do not exceed the meta-metaperspective in their presentation.

In the relationship that we have been considering, Peter's perception of Paul is the result of the objective-Paul who exists *and* of the *Paul-for-Peter* that Peter constructs from his expectations, fantasy, and imagination. To extend the Peter-Paul example, assume that the issue of immediate significance is Peter's upset over Paul's seeming indifference. The following layered metaperspectives are possible:

1. Peter's view of Peter's upset [direct]
2. Peter's view of Paul's view of Peter's upset [meta]
3. Peter's view of Paul's view of Peter's view of his upset [meta-meta]

The complementary perspectives from Paul's point of view are, of course, possible. To gain facility with the notation system, you should try to compile Paul's three perspectives.

If we convert Peter's layered perspectives to Laing's notation system it looks, with some modifications for clarity, like this:

1. Pt → (upset)[direct]
2. Pt → Pl → (upset)[meta]
3. Pt → Pl → Pt → (upset)[meta-meta]

To grasp what these notations mean, number three can be translated into words: "Peter's view of Paul's view of Peter's view of his upset." It is important to recognize that the "upset" in parentheses is always *Peter's* in all three notations. Of course, as always, Paul's complementary views are equally possible. Both Peter's and Paul's differing metaperspectives may be combined and expressed in abbreviated form. If we let X stand for the issue of "Peter's upset," then:

PETER → ← PAUL
1. Pt → (X) ← Pl [Direct]
2. Pt → Pl → (X) ← Pt ← Pl [Meta]
3. Pt → Pl → Pt → (X) ← Pl ← Pt ← Pl [Meta-meta]

To grasp the meaning, consider how number three is translated into words from *left to right* for Peter: "Peter's view of Paul's view of Peter's view of Peter's upset." And, from *right to left,* the translation for Paul is: "Paul's view of Peter's view of Paul's view of Peter's upset."

At this point, armed with a knowledge of the workings of the notation system, return to the original Peter-Paul reciprocal spiral and translate the bracketed notations into words. A clear conception of the system in context should emerge.

ASSESSING PATTERNS OF PERSON PERCEPTION: THE IPM

Laing, Phillipson, and Lee developed a self-report inventory called the *Interpersonal Perception Method* (IPM) (1966). The IPM is used by two individuals in a dyadic relationship to ascertain their direct, meta, and meta-metaperspectives on 60 important issues. These 60 issues are grouped into six categories:

A. Interdependence and autonomy
B. Warm concern and support
C. Disparagement and disappointment
D. Contentions: fight/flight
E. Contradiction and confusion
F. Extreme denial and autonomy

(Laing et al., 1966)

Husbands and wives, for example, may answer the items of the IPM, a process that takes about 70 minutes, to compare their direct, meta, and meta-metaperspectives on such issues as "He/she loves me." Within each of the six classes of issue, complementary questions are provided in separate booklets for each partner. Each set of questions on a particular issue is given in three levels with four choices in each question. The respondent's own direct perspective on one of the 60 issues is called an *A-level* question; *B-level* questions on the same issue provide an assessment of the respondent's metaperspective on the issue: "How he/she thinks the *other* has answered the equivalent question"; and *C-level* questions measure the respondent's meta-metaperspective on that issue: "How he/she feels the other feels he/she has answered the question."

After careful sorting and classification of the responses, their mutual three-level perspectives may be evaluated in terms of their similarities and differences, or *conjunctions* and *disjunctions* of perspective, as Laing and his coworkers call them. To illustrate, here are three questions on one issue from the IPM at each of the three levels. Note the change in phrasing of the stem of the question from level A through level C. The questions are answered by indicating with appropriate plus and minus signs for each of the four choices whether it is *very true* (+ +); *slightly true* (+); *very untrue* (– –); or *slightly untrue* (–).

A-LEVEL: How true do YOU think the following are? [direct perspective]
1. She belittles me. [H → (WH)]
2. I belittle her. [H → (HW)]
3. She belittles herself. [H → (WW)]
4. I belittle myself. [H → (HH)]

In brackets beside each of the A-level choices is the notation for the particular issue under scrutiny. In the real test booklet, of course, the notations are not included. Here is the B-level item on the same issue, measuring the husband's metaperspective, that is, how he thinks his wife has answered the questions in her booklet:

B-LEVEL: How would SHE answer the following? [metaperspective]
1. I belittle him. [H → W → (WH)]
2. He belittles me. [H → W → (HW)]
3. I belittle myself. [H → W → (WW)]
4. He belittles himself. [H → W → (HH)]

and

C-LEVEL: How would SHE think you have answered the following?
1. She belittles me. [H → W → H → (WH)]
2. I belittle her. [H → W → H → (HW)]
3. She belittles herself. [H → W → H → (WW)]
4. I belittle myself. [H → W → H → (HH)]

The C-level item has the phenomenological meaning: "How do you think she thinks you think." Thus, taken together, the total complex of items on the IPM provides an overall assessment of:

$$H \rightarrow W \rightarrow H\ (X_{60}) \leftarrow W \leftarrow H \leftarrow W$$

where X indicates one of the 60 issues. The important result of the IPM is not the mere matching of responses and detection of discrepancies or disjunctions. "What matters instead is whether or not the husband's *view* of how his wife treats him is concordant or discordant with how *she sees herself* to be in treating him, and how *she sees him* viewing her treatment of him" (Laing et al., 1966, p. 60; italics added).

IPM PROFILES OF RECIPROCAL PERSPECTIVES

Laing and his coworkers also developed a technique to profile the relationship between the two points of view assessed by the IPM. In purely operational terms, several important patterns of reciprocity emerge. Laing's team emphasized the following particular comparisons.

Agreement/Disagreement

A comparison between the two persons' direct perspectives on the 60 issues provides a measure of their agreements or disagreements. In notation form, the comparison is:

$$H \rightarrow (X_{60}) \text{ compared to } (X_{60}) \leftarrow W$$

In more concrete terms, disagreement/agreement comparisons involve tabulations of the A-level responses for husband and wife. To take one item as an illustration, if the husband answered the A-level item: *She belittles me* with the response of "very true," and the wife answered her A-level item: *I belittle him* with the response of "very true," it is clear that they agree that she belittles him. The truth or falsity of the assertion is another matter. The point is that they agree.

Understanding/Misunderstanding

A comparison of the metaperspective of one dyad member with the direct perspective of the other provides an estimate of the pair's understanding of each other's viewpoint. In notation, the comparison is given by:

$$H \rightarrow H \rightarrow (X_{60}) \text{ compared to } (X_{60}) \leftarrow W$$

The complementary comparison of the wife's metaperspective with the husband's direct perspective is also made. If the comparison shows that the other person is *aware* of the first person's view by being able to predict that person's A-level answer, then understanding may be said to exist. For example, to the B-level question: "How would SHE answer the following: *I belittle him*"—the husband replies, "very true." But to the A-level, direct-perspective complementary question in the *wife's* booklet: *I belittle him,* she answers, "very untrue." It is then clear that the *husband* misunderstands the wife's viewpoint because he cannot predict her answer to her question. It may be true that she does *not* belittle him, but the point is that the husband fails to understand her interpretation of the issue. Of course, once again, the reverse comparison of the wife's understanding of the husband's point of view is also made:

$$W \rightarrow H \rightarrow (X_{60}):(X_{60}) \leftarrow H$$

Realization of Being Understood/Misunderstood

Comparison of one person's metaperspective to the other's meta-metaperspective provides an estimate of whether the first person realizes that he or she is understood by the other. Simply being understood by the other is of no benefit unless the understood *knows* he or she is understood. In notational form, the comparison involves:

$$H \rightarrow W \rightarrow (X_{60}) \text{ compared to } (X_{60}) \leftarrow W \leftarrow H \leftarrow W$$

To illustrate in more concrete terms, suppose that the husband's response to a B-level question: "How would SHE answer the following: *He belittles himself*" is "very true." The wife agrees in her answer to the complementary C-level item: "How would HE think you have answered the following: *He belittles himself?*" She responds "very true." In this case, the wife's reply indicates that she knows her husband understands her, for he can predict her reply, and *she realizes that he can.*

If the wife had responded "very untrue" to the C-level item, her reply would indicate that she fails to realize that her husband understands her point of view, for she is *unable* to assume *his point of view* of her viewpoint. In neither case do the replies indicate the truth or falsity of the response. Wives may belittle husbands and vice versa, but the significant issue is whether they realize that the other realizes how they feel. If this last fails to make sense to you, it is time to put the book down and take a rest. I know how you feel. And we both understand that I know that you realize I know you are confused.

Despite the complexity of their method, Laing and his colleagues have focused attention on the intricacy of human relationships. It is doubtful that once having wended your way through the maze of the notation system, you can ever again view a dyadic interaction as a straightforward relationship of one person to another. With Laing's abstractions in mind, any such relationship will seem crowded with at least four personages.

In some cases, the convoluted thinking required to score and interpret the results of the IPM questionnaire seems to be more burdensome than the relationship being observed. But certainly Laing and his coworkers' strategy has the desired effect of making explicit what Sullivan calls "reflected appraisals" of the self. Laing has forced psychologists to conceptualize the knotted, often discrepant, viewpoints, perceptions, and perceptions of perceptions that are involved in human encounters.

DISTURBED COMMUNICATION: THE DOUBLE-BIND HYPOTHESIS

Ponder the following communication to her son from a mother who is feeling hostile and simultaneously guilty over her hostility (Bateson et al., 1956, p. 214):

"Go to bed, you're very tired and I want you to get your sleep."

Overtly, this statement is an expression of parental concern and love; covertly, the statement is a knot of conflicting messages. It asserts, first, that the outside observer, mother, can detect an internal feeling state in the observed, her son, before he himself is aware of it.

Second, *her* interpretation of that alleged state is the only one that is valid: "You're very tired." Her son's genuine state of feeling may directly contradict her assertive appraisal of his condition, but the *tone* of her statement, "Go to bed," precludes any possibility of protest or correction by the son. His feelings are automatically classified as irrelevant because his mother asserts her point of view: "*I* want . . ." Only at the cost of the implied punishment of withdrawal of love can the boy correct her assertion.

Third, the statement is simultaneously a command and a denial that it is a command by the expedient of coupling to the order an implied loving concern: "I want you to get *your* sleep."

Finally, the initial purpose of the communication is concealment. She must hide her hostility and guilt from the target of her message *and* from herself. But the mother's tone of voice, bodily gestures, and verbal timing will nonetheless convey all of these conflicting feelings to the son.

If the mother said, "Listen, I'm absolutely fed up with you. Go to bed and get out of my sight!"—the child could deal with the message without being torn in two directions at once. In this case, although the message is hardly pleasant, at least both parties to the communication agree on its content, the reason for its content, fair or unfair, and the emotional tone of the situation. The child can go to bed, recognizing that mother is angry, and that he in turn is angry, or he can thumb his nose at mother, and suffer the consequences. But at least the reason for *his* feelings, *her* feelings, and *her* command are clear to both parties. The command may not be just or pleasant, but it is after all openly acknowledged to be a command. It is, therefore, understandable. In the case of the first communication, however, "the result is that the mother is withdrawing from him and defining this withdrawal as the way a *loving* relationship should be" (Bateson et al., 1956, p. 214).

Laing has acknowledged the influence of Bateson's group on his own conceptualization of the importance of disturbed communications within families of schizophrenics (Laing, 1969b, Chapter 9). Gregory Bateson and his colleagues named the general class of knotted communications like the one we have been considering *metacommunications,* using the Greek prefix in its meaning of "along with," or "after." Jurgen Ruesch (1961, p. 423) has provided a concise definition of metacommunication as all ". . . the events that go along with language—specifically, a device which the speaker uses to instruct the receiver and which the latter uses to interpret a statement." Following Ruesch, metalanguage may be conceptualized as "communications about communication," in the sense that gestures, verbal tone, phrasing, and timing may change the meaning of verbal content. Bateson's team has focused on one particular variety of metalanguage, which they call the *double-bind* communication.

A double-bind communication is a message that conveys at least two meanings, and sometimes three, all of which conflict with the ostensible purpose of the message. The first meaning is a primary negative injunction: "Do not do so and so, or I will punish you." The punishment typically takes the form of withdrawal of love or a thinly disguised expression of hate and anger. The second meaning is another injunction, enforced by the same threats. This time, however, the receiver is enjoined to "not see this command as punishment; do not see me as punisher; do not question my love, or do not think of what you must not do" (Bateson et al., 1956, p. 207). The third meaning is yet another injunction, a tertiary injunction that implicitly prohibits the victim of the double bind from escaping the situation. This prohibition is enforced by the statement's implication that endurance of the conflict (primary and secondary injunctions) will evoke love or acceptance.

An overweight child at a birthday party is invited by the guest of honor to have some ice cream. The child's own mother stares coolly at her son, not wishing him to eat more goodies than necessary because his overweight reflects poorly on her, and she says, *"You don't want any more ice cream, do you?"* Again, this message is laden with auxiliary meanings and enforced interpretations. It sets up a full-fledged double-bind "can't win" situation. If the child says, "I *do* want more ice cream," he violates the primary and secondary injunctions and provokes the threatened withdrawal of love. If the child says, "O.K., I don't really want more ice cream," he thereby accepts his mother's definition of *his* feelings. *He* thus deprives himself in the presence of other conspicuously consuming children whose obvious enjoyment serves as an additional cue that his self-imposed denial is without reasonable foundation. In short, he's damned if he does, and damned if he doesn't.

Bateson's group proposed that single instances of double-bind communications could not by themselves cause distorted personality development. Only a constant environment of double binds is sufficient to evoke disorder. However, when individuals have been repeatedly exposed to double-bind communications, their mode of perception becomes permanently altered to accept "can't win" situations as normal. The complete ingredient package is no longer necessary; they have internalized this mode of "madness" to the extent that double-bind communications are autonomously present in their responses to others' messages even when such messages are simply ambiguous.

In the simplest case of disordered communication, taking the mother as the only double-bind inflicter, Bateson has suggested that the crux of the problem is her constant sending of messages that simultaneously convey hostility and simulated love. When the child responds to the latent hostility by withdrawing, she ambiguously verbalizes its apparent lack of love and provokes its guilt. Schizophrenia, in Bateson's view, is very much a case of disturbed communication between the "victim" and significant others.

In Laing's terms, the split between a person's behavior and his or her inner experience is fostered by such disturbed communications. The resultant spiral of reciprocal perspectives is the very heart of double-bind communication. To map the ice cream situation into Laing's notation system of such spirals is relatively easy. The mother wishes to replace the son's perspective of his liking or desire for ice cream with her own perspective of how he should view ice cream:

From: Son's $\rightarrow$ (S ice cream)

To: M $\rightarrow$ S $\rightarrow$ (S ice cream)

She further hopes that the substitution of perspectives will not be discovered, or will be discovered only at great cost.

FAMILY RULES AND METARULES

For Laing, disturbed communication patterns are not only the cause of disordered behavior, but also the result of prior communication disturbances. Thus schizophrenia is evoked in children by disturbed communication or metacommunication from the members of their families, and in turn, they respond to the disturbances with tangled metacommunications of their own designs. Their deranged utterances are more than mere response: they are strategies of survival. They must master not only the meta-language and meta-metalanguages of the network of persons, they must also learn to obey the covert rules on which the communications are based. For these hidden rules dominate the family's existence.

Every family, disturbed or otherwise, develops a set of rules that govern the behavior and the expectations of its members. The disturbed family, however, also develops *metarules* that are injunctions "not to see the rules." There can likewise be meta-metarules that are comprised of injunctions not to see the prohibitions against seeing the rules, and so on.

To illustrate the flavor of family rules, consider the dichotomy "good" and "bad." Within the family, certain events and persons are overtly labeled "good" and some are labeled "bad." There are "good" relatives and there are "bad" relatives. In a family dominated by one parent, all the "bad" relatives are, of course, on the side of the other spouse. Each member of the family is "good" or "bad" to the degree "onc has good thoughts about what one is supposed to think good about, and bad thoughts about what one is supposed to think bad about" (Laing, 1969a, p. 104). Or, one may be "bad" if one thinks bad about things one is supposed to think good. Double-bind communication establishes the boundaries for such evaluative thinking. Mother to six-year-old son: "What do you mean you don't want to go to Grandma's house? You know you like to visit Grandma!" Mapping this statement into Laing's notation system, we can see that the mother tries to replace the son's expressed viewpoint of his relationship with Grandma $[S \rightarrow (SG)]$ with her own: $[M \rightarrow S \rightarrow (SG)]$.

There may be further sets of family rules about what is to be put into words and "what words one may use to put something into" (Laing, 1969a, p. 111). One *must* say that a visit to the bathroom is to "wash my hands," when in fact one has to urinate. One may *not* say, "I have to urinate in the bathroom." But one may say, "I have to take a leak" if one is imitating Uncle Harry's use of this phrase, because Uncle Harry is a "good" relative who is always humorous.

As if rules and metarules were not complex enough, some rules may be contradictory, paradoxical, or incompatible. "A paradoxical order is one which, if correctly executed, is disobeyed: if disobeyed, it is obeyed. Don't do what I tell you. Don't believe me. Be spontaneous" (Laing, 1969a, p. 110). For example, the Great Subway Token Hustle practiced by scores of parents is an order not to do something in order to comply with what I have ordered you to do. Specifically, a mother gives her two girls, 11 and 12 years old, respectively, tokens for the subway, but she instructs them to try to pass under the turnstile for free while she engages the token seller in conversation. If he notices the hustle, she angrily demands of them, "Are you trying to pull that stunt again? You're not six years old anymore. Didn't I give you the tokens?" All the while, of course, the unspoken premise is "I'm only yelling at you to save me from embarrassment at the hands of this outsider." But sometimes the game goes too far. When caught in the act, the mother may genuinely scold her offspring, forgetting the game, because they have put her into a position of intolerable jeopardy. "Don't do what I tell you. Don't believe me *before,* believe me now."

The problem with rules and metarules of the family is that sometimes the members develop a conception of the family not as a collection of individual persons, but as a set of relations among rule makers and rule followers. This internalized conception of one's family Laing indicates by surrounding the word with quotation marks: "family." An individual may become more aware of his or her experience of the "family" than of the family (Laing, 1969a, p. 6).

It is easy to see why the "family" is important to survival. The "family" is the *internalized set of person relations* that makes living sensible, makes survival possible, and serves as a "bulwark against total collapse, disintegration, emptiness, despair, guilt, and other terrors" (Laing, 1969a, p. 14). Because it is a fully shared image, the world can be dichotomized into "Us" and "Them."

"Schizophrenics" in the "Family"

The complex influence of mutually exerted perspectives within the family became the focus of concern for Laing's research. It was clearly a logical outgrowth of his concern with dyadic perspectives, for the family can in some ways be conceptualized as multiple dyads and triads. As had many personality theorists before him, Laing turned to the clinical "laboratory" of disordered personality to find support in the data of raw experience for his ideas about interpersonal processes. With a colleague, Aaron Esterson, Laing (1964) published an important social-phenomenological study of the families of 11 women diagnosed by at least two independent psychiatrists as schizophrenic.

The premise on which Laing and Esterson's original research attempt was based included a genuine reluctance to accept the existence of schizophrenia as a disease entity. For Laing and Esterson, and later for another of their colleagues, David Cooper (1967, 1970; cf. Speck & Attneave, 1973), "schizophrenia" is another word to be used only in quotation marks to indicate the tenuous nature of the concept's reality. The only significance of the concept of "schizophrenia" is the social one evidenced in the number of psychiatrists willing to label the behavior of some individuals "schizophrenic." The problem, as we have seen from the outset, is that, having diagnosed "schizophrenia" as the source of the person's "problem," the psychiatric profession deceives itself into believing it has thus explained the person. The person's family is equally but deceptively secure now that the "problem" has been named, recognized, and located in one blamable, avoidable, treatable member of the "family" (cf. 1969a, p. 44).

Laing and Esterson framed a deceptively simple question about the families of "schizophrenics" (1964, p. 12): *". . . are the experience and behavior that psychiatrists take as symptoms and signs of schizophrenia more socially intelligible than has come to be supposed?"* (Italics added.)

The question clearly contains its own implicit affirmative answer. Laing and Esterson were able to demonstrate in their 11 case histories, and in later publications (Esterson, 1970), that the behavior and experience of the family member consensually designated the "schizophrenic" was explicable in terms of the relations among family members. The "schizophrenic" patient's "psychotic" behaviors made rational sense when viewed from the *patient's* perspective of her own family. The pattern of communication, the system of rules and metarules that the "schizophrenic" had internalized as the "family," could make her and her relatives' behavior intelligible.

Laing and Esterson borrowed some terminology from Jean-Paul Sartre to describe the variables that operate within the family. Their primary interest was the family *nexus,* "that multiplicity of persons drawn from the kinship group, and from others who, though not linked by kinship ties, are regarded as members of the family (Laing & Esterson, 1964, p. 21; cf. Laing & Cooper, 1971, for an indication of the importance that Laing attaches to Sartre's philosophy. However, this book is so dense as to be nearly unreadable). The important attribute of the family nexus for making intelligible the "schizophrenic's" behavior is the face-to-face influence that members of the network exert on each other's behavior and experience.

An entire pattern of relationships must thus be studied to make sense of family or individual events and to discern the *process* of *what* is going on within the network (cf. Speck & Attneave, 1973). The "what" in the last sentence refers, of course, to the flavor of communications within the network and their effect on the members of the network. But it is also important to know *who* within the nexus is doing the *what* with, for, or against the group. When an observer is able to specify the *who* of the process, he or she is concerned with *praxis. Praxis* and *process,* the *who* and the *what* distinctions, are terms borrowed from Sartre. The important point remains that the "schizophrenic" behavior attributed to the "ill one" could rationally be described as a more or less successful coping strategy in her struggle to survive the world *she* has experienced within the nexus (Laing, 1967, p. 115). Her behavior "made sense" once the praxis and the process were made explicit.

COPING STRATEGIES AGAINST DISTURBED AND DISTURBING COMMUNICATIONS

Family experience is not only tolerated but actively sought and maintained as a form of personal protection. Protection against what? Against real or invented dangers. When real danger cannot be found, the family nexus must invent it to ensure the maintenance of a reason for its existence as a "family" (Laing, 1967, p. 87). The result is a family fantasy of the external world as extraordinarily dangerous to the "family":

> The family's function is to repress Eros; to induce a false consciousness of security; to deny death by avoiding life; to cut off transcendence; to believe in God, not to experience the Void; to create, in short, one-dimensional man; to promote respect, conformity, obedience; to con children out of play; to induce a fear of failure; to promote a respect for work; to promote a respect for "respectability." (Laing, 1967, p. 65)

It should not be surprising that families, in Laing's view, foster the adoption among the members of coping strategies against *disturbing* communication with the threats of the world, against *disturbed* communications of other family members who have succumbed to such threats, and against the possibility of *being disturbed* further by recognition of *disturbance* within the family. Laing calls such coping strategies "operations," and some of them may be conceptualized as similar to the classic psychoanalytic defense mechanisms like repression, projection, and reversal. These coping techniques, Laing points out, are properly characterized by the psychoanalysts as "mechanisms" because the persons adopting them feel them imposed on their beings like impersonal machinery (Laing, 1967, p. 35; 1969a, p. 13). They are *intrapersonal* techniques of acting on oneself and treating the self as object.

But defenses are not only intrapersonal, they can also be *transpersonal* in the sense that they operate on another's experience. The development of direct, meta, and meta-metaperspectives in dealing with others can be forms of transpersonal defense in the same way that a double-bind inflicter tries to control self and other. However, there are also several specific transpersonal defenses whereby *"self attempts to regulate the inner life of the other in order to preserve his own"* (Laing, 1969a, p. 13). Within the triads and dyads of the family, transpersonal coping mechanisms are shared, traded, clashed, and supported to maintain the integrity of the nexus. Some of the main forms of these transpersonal strategies are *complementary identity, confirmation and disconfirmation,* and *collusion.*

Complementary Identity

Sometimes one's identity can be realized only in terms of the other. In fact, for some persons, identity does not exist in the absence of a complementary personality. A mother, for example, cannot be a mother without a child (Laing, 1969b, p. 66). But sometimes complementarity may be carried to extreme forms. The mother who comes to *need* her child to maintain her self-integrity is a good example of complementarity carried to the realm of transpersonal defense. For the mother must maintain her identity by manipulating the identity of her child in ways that are not consistent with the child's need for autonomy. Without the child, she is a different person to herself.

To illustrate, Laing cites the case of John, son of an emotionally rigid naval officer and a prostitute. Entrusted to his father's care at the age of six, John experienced a changed world living with this new and exacting "stranger." As John grew up, he disappointed his father in many ways: He failed to become a naval officer; he failed the university entrance exam; he even disgraced himself by failure as a common seaman. John's father was thus prompted to remark repeatedly that he was *unsure such a boy could be his son.* Eventually, John's father, severing all ties and kicking the boy out of his house, made good the symbolic threat and completely disowned his "fatherhood." "What his father taught him was: 'You are my son if I say you are, and you are not my son if I say you are not' " (Laing, 1969b, p. 79).

John eventually succumbed to an acute manic psychosis by which he adopted a basic premise for living: *He could be anyone he wanted, merely by snapping his fingers.* His father had destroyed his identity by withdrawing his own identity as father. The son was able to recover only when he realized that he was not who his father said he was (i.e., "nobody"), any more than he was what his father said he was not (i.e., his father's son). John's "psychosis" had been another form of identity deception by which he deluded himself into negating his father's negation.

Confirmation and Disconfirmation

A sign of recognition from another confirms one's presence in the world. All forms of interaction between persons require some minimum of confirmation from the other to maintain the interaction. Total disconfirmation, absolute indifference to the other's existence, is a fine strategy for driving one mad. Irrelevant recognition, that is, paying attention only to the marginal details of another's existence, is as powerfully damaging as the total disconfirmation of absolute indifference.

To illustrate, Laing cites the case of a five-year-old who, holding up a big fat worm, runs to his mother. He says, "Mummy, look what a big fat worm I have got." She says, "You are filthy—go away and clean yourself immediately" (Laing, 1969b, p. 85).

The mother's response to the boy is irrelevant, or what Ruesch has called a tangential response. The mother expresses no horror, delight, disgust, approval, or disapproval of the *worm*. She instead responds by calling attention to an aspect of the boy that he himself has not considered. "She may be saying either, 'I am not interested in looking at your worm unless you are clean,' or 'Whether or not you have a worm is of no importance to me—all that matters to me is whether you are clean or dirty, and I only like you when you are clean'" (Laing, 1969b, p. 86). The mother has failed to confirm the boy's being.

Collusion

Collusion is a "game" played by two or more people whereby they agree to deceive themselves. Their agreement to deceive and be deceived may not be conscious, but then part of the "game" is the rule not to see the game (Laing, 1969b, p. 90). The dynamics of collusion involve one or more persons' projecting a false self that is somehow more desirable than the real self. Then, the projector must find others who will confirm the existence of the false self-image by behaving in ways that are consonant with the projection.

> Collusion is always clinched when self finds in other that other who will 'confirm' self in the false self that self is trying to make real, and vice versa. (Laing, 1969b, p. 93)

To illustrate, some families must maintain the myth of being a "happy family." If one member is unhappy, he or she must conceal the unhappiness from the family and from her- or himself to maintain the myth of "happy family," for if he or she did not deny the unhappiness to her- or himself, his or her membership in the family would demolish its happiness. He or she thus projects an image of happiness. Conversely, the other members of the family must deny they detect unhappiness in any of their members and collude with the individual's projection. But colluding to keep unhappiness a secret causes unhappiness over having to keep it a secret. However, if the secret is well guarded by mutual denial and collusion, then unhappiness cannot arise in such a happy family (Laing, 1969a, pp. 99–100).

EVALUATING R. D. LAING

Laing has blended existentialism, psychoanalysis, and phenomenology into a unique synthesis that ranges from the philosophical to the empirical to the controversial. He has taken strong positions on issues and those positions earned him a reputation as an "antipsychiatrist." The reality is far more complex. Out of his own early experiences with irrational family members, Laing developed a strong need to test experience for himself. His suspiciousness of traditional diagnostic and treatment forms in psychology and psychiatry was an extension of his childhood suspiciousness of family rules and myths that seemed to operate to obscure his own view of reality. His criticisms of orthodox psychiatry and psychology have sometimes been taken less seriously than they deserve, because Laing has expressed those criticisms in writing that is at once poetic, ambiguous, and infuriatingly paradoxical.

Refutability of Laing's Existential Analysis

With the exception of the deliberately empirical IPM method, most of Laing's work is not stated in terms that permit testable hypotheses to be derived. In some places where his opinion has clashed with the facts, we might argue that Laing's ideas have received a disconfirmation. For example, from the late 1950s through the late 1960s, Laing appeared to be arguing that schizophrenia was not a mental disease in the biological sense of that term. It was, rather, he seemed to feel, a "voyage of discovery" that stemmed from purely psychological chaos to which the schizophrenic person had been exposed. But the last 20 years of neuropsychological, genetic, and neurochemical research into schizophrenia clearly demonstrate that there is a biological basis, probably causative, for schizophrenia. Such agreement as there is in the scientific community clearly undermines Laing's positions on the nature of this disease.

What can we say of Laing's even more controversial ideas, such as his hypothesized "resonances" between prenatal and postnatal experiences? Clearly, the ideas are intriguing, and clearly they are not, in principle, automatically untrue, despite the unusualness of their content. But just as clearly, such ideas are more the subject matter of mythology, theology, and philosophy than they are empirically psychological.

Over all, then, Laing receives mixed reviews on the issue of refutability for his theory. His IPM method has received too little scientific attention to date. But his poetic pronouncements have received too much.

Laing's Conception of Human Agency

Because so many of Laing's ideas are derived from existentialism and phenomenology, he portrays human beings as active agents in the extreme. Laing has criticized, as have the existentialists, the traditional subject-object dichotomy in our thinking about ourselves. For him, the treatment of a human being as a passive object, in life or in theory, is a grave error. Even in his controversial treatment of schizophrenic patients in the short-lived Kingsley Hall "experiment," Laing encouraged his patients to take active charge of their own lives and "illnesses."

On the other side of the coin, however, Laing has written extensively about the shaping power of others' views of ourselves. He acknowledges that people, out of fear, can relinquish their responsibility and their personal control and become passively shaped "false selves" that accommodate the outside world. But Laing's belief is that such "divided self" behavior is pathological and does not represent the natural state of the human being.

The Idiographic Character of Laing's "Science of Experience"

Like so many other theories derived from clinical work, Laing's theory is focused on the idiographic. He shares much with theorists such as Carl Rogers, Rollo May, and the

European existentialists in their insistence in taking the person on the person's own terms. Phenomenology, by definition, seeks not to abstract a person into theoretical constructs that apply to all people; rather, each person is understood empathically in terms of how that person sees self and the world. Laing's "science of experience" is fundamentally a phenomenal, humanistic, and existential attempt to study people through their own unique modes of communication. It is a highly idiographic enterprise, and to date, it has generated little in the way of nomothetic research data.

SUMMARY

Like Thomas Szasz, R. D. Laing has taken the position that the label "schizophrenia" does not necessarily indicate a disease entity. The "schizophrenic's" behaviors are more intelligible if viewed as a strategy for coping with an intolerable life. In this respect, David Rosenhan's pseudopatient study of psychiatric hospital environments lends some credence to Laing and Szasz's position by demonstrating that diagnostic labels are more a function of the situation and the psychiatric staff's expectations than of the behavior of the person so labeled.

Laing's theorizing may be classed as a modified form of existential phenomenology informed by psychoanalysis. The existentialists, notably Binswanger, Boss, and May, interpret humans as being-in-the-world. Humans' unique gift is for self-awareness, a consciousness that one *is*. One's being, the *Dasein,* is conceived of by the existentialists as a process of continual development, of growth toward fulfillment. Unlike the psychoanalytic conception of people as products of their pasts, the existentialists view humans as potentiality, guided more by their choices for the future than by their clashes with their own history. Each person occupies three modes of world, *Umwelt, Mitwelt,* and *Eigenwelt.* The *Umwelt* is the natural world of biological cycle and drive; the *Mitwelt* is the world of others, of relationships with one's fellow humans; and the *Eigenwelt* is one's subjective experience of inner and outer reality. Laing's emphasis has been on the last two modes, and he has developed a unique phenomenological style of representing *Mitwelt* and *Eigenwelt.*

In his semiautobiographical essay, he has recounted the early irrationalities of family living to which he was exposed. In addition to a strictly enforced taboo on matters concerning sexuality, Laing's relatives fought some quite literal battles in the family living room. His medical school experiences left Laing with the impression that medicine as a profession, in particular the specialty of psychiatry, is sometimes coldly inhuman—as inhuman as it seemingly construes the "diseases" it attempts to treat.

Laing has extended the theme of unwantedness from his own childhood into the beginnings of a theory to account for parental rejection of children from conception to birth, the period of intrauterine life. Laing suggested that certain physical and chemical patterns rhythmically established for the fetus during its mother's pregnancy may produce afterbirth "resonances," that is, psychological analogs of the physiological patterns of life before birth. Laing proposes that a science of experience might be able to map "resonances" across three domains of experience: prenatal biology (embrylogems), psychology (psychologems), and mythology (mythologems). His goal is to show the parallels in given prenatal embrylogems with their counterparts in experience, the psychologems, and in mythological representations of these experiences, the mythologems. In some extreme cases, schizophrenic and other psychotic patients may need to be metaphorically "reborn" to reestablish a satisfactory relationship with the circumstances and people of their lives.

Laing and his colleagues have developed a notational system to represent individual's perspectives of themselves, of the other, and of their own perceptions of the other's perception. More important, Laing has also developed means to concretize the very complex ways that the members of a dyad perceive the relationships between each other, and between the subject and one's self.

Out of his concern with understanding experience as the individual experiences it, Laing and his team developed the Interpersonal Perception Method (IPM) to assess the direct, meta, and meta-meta perspectives of intimately related twosomes. Both parties' direct, meta, and meta-metaperspectives may be compared to assess their understanding, their agreement, and their realization of understanding.

Bateson's work with double-bind communications served as an important influence on Laing's conceptualization of disturbed communication in families. A double-bind communication involves tangled statements of commands and denials of the statement's commanding aspects, coupled with implied punishments for noncompliance with the denied command. Laing suggests that the families of "schizophrenics" practice such disturbed communication to the extent that some family members can cope with the "can't win" situation thus constructed only by erecting a false self to pacify them.

Laing has pointed out that a variety of transpersonal coping mechanisms are possible, in addition to the traditional defense mechanisms elucidated by Freud and his followers. Thus, whereas classic psychoanalytic defense mechanisms like repression, denial, and projection are intrapersonal because they operate on the self, Laing has described coping techniques designed to operate on the experiences of others: Complementary identity involves defining one's own identity in terms of another's being; disconfirmation is the failure to respond to another as a human person, dismissing him or her as object; and collusion is the active striving of two or more persons to deceive and be deceived in accepting false projected self-images.

Our evaluation shows that Laing's theory is a mixture of refutable and nonrefutable ideas. His conception of people pictures them as active agents, with a strong idiographic focus.

FOR FURTHER READING

The development of Laing's thought from Freudian psychoanalytic premises through his existential-phenomenological modifications can be surveyed by successive reading of three books: *The Divided Self* (Baltimore: Penguin, 1959), the first statement of his position; *The Politics of the Family* (New York: Vintage, 1969), which contains some of his propositions on the importance of interpersonal relationships in guiding the individual's interpretation of reality; and *Self and Others* (New York: Pantheon, 1969), which sets forth his concept of how individuals feel themselves forced to distort reality by the demands of significant others.

An interview with Laing, along with one of his previously unpublished papers on the genetic basis of schizophrenia (and the futility of this concept), are contained in R. I. Evans's *R. D. Laing: The Man and His Ideas* (New York: Dutton, 1976; the interview may also be found in condensed form in Evans's *The Making of Psychology* [New York: Knopf, 1976]). A semiautobiographical account of some of the sources of his ideas is provided by Laing in his ironically titled *The Facts of Life* (New York: Pantheon, 1976). This same book contains his speculations on the importance of uterine life in shaping one's later feelings of acceptance or rejection within the family. Laing kept a record of his own family interactions (his son's, daughter's, and wife's) over a period of six years and published it as *Conversations With Adam and Natasha* (New York: Pantheon, 1977). A more complete, but nevertheless selective, autobiography is Laing's *Wisdom, Madness and Folly: The Making of a Psychiatrist* (New York: McGraw-Hill, 1985) in which Laing elaborates more details of his childhood family experiences as well as his training as a psychiatrist.

Two recent biographies of Laing deserve careful consideration for the light they throw on Laing's last and most controversial years as he slid self-destructively into angry alcoholism. Daniel Burston's *The Wing of Madness* (Cambridge, MA: Harvard University Press, 1996) is a combined biography and discussion of Laing's main ideas. Laing's son, Adrian Laing's *R. D. Laing: A Biography* (Chester Springs, PA, and London: Thunder's Mouth Press, 1994) is a compelling, unvarnished portrait of Laing's contradictions as a man, father, and psychiatrist. Zbigniew Kotowicz's *R. D. Laing and the Paths of Anti-Psychiatry* (New York and London: Routledge, 1997), is a relatively brief but cogent overview of Laing's life and work.

Laing's blunt, sometimes painfully honest self-revelations are recorded in Bob Mullan's (Ed.), *Mad to Be Normal: Conversations With R. D. Laing* (London, Free Association Books, 1995). In a more formal context, with the focus on theory rather than person, Richard Evans *Dialogue With R. D. Laing* (New York: Praeger, 1981) provides a glimpse of Laing's own estimate of the intellectual value of his ideas.

David Cooper, a colleague of Laing's, has carried forward some of Laing's propositions on the pathological potential of family life in *The Death of the Family* (New York: Vintage, 1970). Cooper has also set forth his own unique criticisms of classical psychiatry with a major debt to Laing in *Psychiatry and Anti-Psychiatry* (London: Paladin, 1967). Along these same lines, the collection of papers in Robert Boyers and Robert Orrill's *R. D. Laing and Anti-Psychiatry* (New York: Harper & Row, 1971) provides a useful overview of Laing's growing impact on the mental health professions. Ross Speck and Carolyn Attneave describe an approach to family therapy heavily influenced by Laing's concepts in *Family Networks* (New York: Vintage, 1973).

An account of Laing's unique approach to treatment of psychotic patients in his short-lived Kingsley Hall community is given from both the therapist's and the patient's viewpoints in Mary Barnes and Joe Berke's *Two Accounts of a Journey Through Madness* (New York: Ballantine, 1971). A similar but briefer version of the Kingsley Hall experiment is provided by Morton Schatzman in his "Kingsley Hall: The Politics of Madness" (*Contemporary Psychoanalysis,* 1971, **8,** 107–121).

Thomas Szasz's criticisms of the medical model of mental illness, which share much with Laing's philosophical assumptions, can most easily be had in *The Myth of Mental Illness: Foundations of a Theory of Personal Conduct* (New York: Harper & Row, 1961; available in paperback) and in *The Manufacture of Madness* (New York: Dell, 1970). Bruno Bettelheim's review of Laing's *The Facts of Life* contains some interesting comparisons of Szasz's work with Laing's and may be read in the *New York Times Book Review,* May 30, 1976, p. 5.

CHAPTER 11

ROLLO MAY

Existential Analysis

Life is not superficial. The real problem is how you exist in a world that is antagonistic, that hates you. How are you able to live in a world where we are all alone, where we all die?

Rollo May (1989)

The unconscious seems to take delight (if I may so express it) in breaking through—and breaking up—exactly what we cling to most rigidly in our conscious thinking.

Rollo May *The Courage to Create*

About Rollo May's Existentialism . . .

Some theories in personality psychology are "small potatoes" theories that focus on narrow but manageable issues that can eventually be synthesized into a bigger picture. May's work is a "big potatoes" theory, or perhaps a better metaphor might be a "bread and butter" theory. He has focused on the broad, historically enduring, and deeply philosophical issues close to the heart of human experience. Even the range of the chapter subheadings that track major transitions in May's ideas are impressive: Being, Death, Love, Evil, and Destiny. Clearly, May is not a "small potatoes" theorist.

Rollo May can be credited with bringing classical existential thinking to the attention of psychology. Through the anthologies of existential writings that he edited and through his own contributions to existential psychoanalysis, May's work shaped the thinking of a whole generation of clinical and counseling psychologists.

Central to May's conception of humanity are these issues:

1. *Human beings are aware in a way no other living creature can be of the possibility of death, and this awareness can shape a whole lifetime of living.*

2. *Anxiety can be a vague fear but it can also be a reflection of a person's feelings of separation from self or of not being in control of one's life, and at a deep level, anxiety always involves a confrontation with the possibility of nonbeing.*

3. *A human being is a process, not a thing. We are change, not accomplishment. And people create the change that they experience as they experience it.*

4. *Human nature is good and evil, partaking of the ancient Greek conception of the daimonic as both a creative force that affirms self and promotes creativity and as a destructive force that can overpower the individual.*

EXISTENTIAL PSYCHOANALYSIS

There is a subtle irony and a blatant contradiction inherent in an existential psychoanalysis. The existentialist tries to understand a person's *experience in the way that the person experiences it.* Classical psychoanalysis, for better or worse, became in Freud's hands a model of *experience-distant* theorizing. Direct descriptions of people, what they do, and what they feel are replaced in later psychoanalysis by an elaborate language sometimes known as Freud's "metapsychology." Freud's final model of the mind is thus a complex set of abstractions (such as id, ego, and superego) that represent in symbolic terms the clinical observations on which they were based.

Existentialism, by contrast, attempts to comprehend people as they are with a minimum of theoretical abstraction. For the existentialist, the central problem of human psychology is *being* and the person's awareness that someday he or she will *not be.* In metaphysics, a branch of philosophy, the study of being and reality is termed *ontology.* Many of Rollo May's (1958a, 1983) concepts and those of other existential thinkers are "ontological" in character. That is to say, although the vocabulary sounds like familiar psychology—for example, anxiety, guilt, repression—the terms are interpreted by the existentialist as reflecting the core processes of *being* and *non-being,* categories that do not come spontaneously to the average psychoanalyst's thinking. For the classical psychoanalyst, by contrast, the central problems of human psychology are *need* and *wish,* and the person's attempt to achieve satisfaction safely and ethically.

How, then, do we reconcile these divergent intellectual traditions? Rollo May achieves his unique integration by synthesizing those parts of psychoanalysis that are experience-near with the existentialist's interest in the person's own view of reality. By avoiding the abstract psychoanalytic metapsychology of Freud's later years, May creates a more or less uniform analytic existentialism. Or is it an existential psychoanalysis? May received his psychoanalytic training at the William Alanson White Institute and became a senior training analyst there. The White Institute was cofounded by Harry Stack Sullivan.

As a concise review of the principles of Existentialism, Table 11.1 summarizes the discussion of modes of being from Chapter 10 (R. D. Laing) as understood by the European existentialists and introduced into American psychology by Rollo May. It may be of some help to return to Chapter 10 to read the full discussion presented there.

ONTOLOGICAL PRINCIPLES: "MRS. HUTCHENS"

May began with a basic assumption that Freud's contribution to our understanding of the unconscious was fundamental (May, 1950, 1960). But May wanted to broaden the psychoanalytic horizon and emphasize active human agency and the contributions of ontology:

> The "unconscious," then, is not to be thought of as a reservoir of impulses, thoughts, wishes which are culturally unacceptable; I define it rather as *those potentialities for knowing and experiencing which the individual cannot or will not actualize;* that it cannot be adequately comprehended in *"ego"* and *"not-ego"* terms, or even "self" and "not-self"; and that it inescapably raises the question of the human being's margin of freedom with respect to his potentialities, a margin in which resides his responsibility for himself which even the therapist cannot take away. (May, 1960, p. 178; see also May, 1983, pp. 17–18)

It is clear that for May there is much of value in psychoanalytic ideas, but that the concepts have to be transformed into first-person actions from their status as theoretical, third-person "things." The unconscious, in this example, is not a place, not a reservoir, not an internal structure. It is, rather, the process of the whole person in the acts of *wishing, fearing, knowing, and choosing not to know.* By these standards, a person does not "have" defenses; he or she *defends* against threats. Similarly, a "neurotic" person is not a person "with" a psychological disorder, nor can he or she be said to "have" symptoms. Rather, the person, along with all of his or her other human qualities, behaves anxiously or conflictedly because of the way he or she *decides to*

TABLE 11.1   Modes of Being in European Existentialism

Being (Dasein) Defined

Binswanger and other existentialists employ the German word *Dasein* for this aspect of human existence. *Dasein* may be translated literally as "being" (*sein*) and "there" (*da*) (Binswanger, in May, 1958, p. 315).

   Dasein indicates that man is the being who is *there* and implies also that he *has* a "there" in the sense that he can know he is there and can take a stand with reference to that fact. The "there" is moreover not just any place, but the particular "there" that is mine, the particular point *in time* as well as space of my existence at this given moment. Man is the being who can be conscious of, and therefore responsible for, his existence. [May, 1958b, p. 41]

   As May indicates, the term *Dasein* is not exhausted by the English translation "being." In English, the word *being* has a connotation of a thing, of a static state, or of a unit that contains being as in "a human being." For the existentialists, *Dasein* indicates a dynamic state, *becoming,* a continual *process*—the activity of *being something* not yet realized. In consequence, May (1958b, p. 41) has suggested that the term "becoming" probably conveys the import of *Dasein* more meaningfully to English-speaking readers.

Modes of Being: Some Terminology

World is the structure of meaningful relationships in which a person exists and in the design of which he participates. Thus world includes the past events which condition my existence and all the vast variety of deterministic influences which operate upon me. But it is these as *I relate to them,* am aware of them, carry them with me, molding, inevitably forming, building them in every minute of relating. For to be aware of one's world means at the same time to be designing it [May, 1958b, pp. 56–59]. The existentialists have refined their concept of world by distinguishing three modes of world which each person embodies as being-in-the-world.

1. ***Umwelt:*** translated literally as "world around," includes the biological drives, needs, and instincts of the individual. *Umwelt,* considered alone, corresponds roughly to what we mean by environment, the impersonal world of natural law and biological cycle. Even if one were totally without self-awareness, the *Umwelt* would continue to exist (May, 1958b, p. 61). In some respects, Freud's conception of human nature focused almost exclusively on the *Umwelt,* a narrowness of vision with which the existentialists profoundly disagree.

2. ***Mitwelt*** is literally the "with-world," the world of being-with-others, one's fellow humans. *Mitwelt* is not to be confused with the concept of group behavior, for *Mitwelt* includes the *meaning* I make out of my relationship with others, and the *meaning* that these others design into the relationships. The essence of *Mitwelt* interrelationship is that "*in the encounter both persons are changed*" (May, 1958b, p. 63).

3. ***Eigenwelt,*** or "own world," is the mode of relationship to one's self. "It is a grasping of what something in the world—this bouquet of flowers . . . means to *me*" (May, 1958b, p. 63). Thus the concept of *Eigenwelt* is not restricted to the inner, subjective world, but includes one's subjective reactions to the world at large.

(In the interests of scholarly accuracy, May's generic use of the male pronoun is preserved throughout this table.)

interpret his or her life. A neurosis is not an alien entity imposed on the person. It is one facet, albeit a distressing one, of the whole human being. Neurosis may even be one way that a person strives to preserve his or her own way of being, a way of adjusting to perceived threat.

   We can obtain an initial orientation to the six ontological principles that governed May's early views by following his account of the difficulties of "Mrs. Hutchens," one of the first patients May wrote about.

Principle One: Phenomenal Centeredness

May argues, as the European existentialists do, that genuine understanding of a person comes not from seeing people as composites of drives and deterministic forces nor by conceptualizing people as individual statistical units in the group we call humanity. If people are defined in this way for psychological understanding, "you have defined for study everything except the one to whom these experiences happen, everything except the existing person himself" (May, 1960, p. 179).

May offers the extended example of one of his patients. "Mrs. Hutchens" is a woman in her thirties who presents herself as sophisticated, in control, and poised. But in her eyes, May detected "something of the terror of a frightened animal or lost child." She was referred for psychotherapy by her neurologist because of an hysterical tenseness of the larynx so severe that she can speak only in a hoarse whisper. May administered a Rorschach projective inkblot examination:

> I have been given the hypothesis from her Rorschach that she has felt all her life, "If I say what I really feel, I'll be rejected; under these conditions it is better not to talk at all." (May, 1960, p. 178)

As Freud discovered at the turn of the century, hysterical symptoms rest on personal meanings, some of which are unconscious. The symptom is not random but develops coherently out of the person's life experiences and the person's interpretation of those experiences. Thus Mrs. Hutchens's life history reveals an intimidating relationship with her authoritarian mother and grandmother, along with experiences that resulted in becoming guarded: choosing not to reveal any "secrets" at all. This information is *historical* and it is helpful in understanding some of the reasons why Mrs. Hutchens behaves as she does. But May argues that mere historical understanding is an incomplete understanding of the whole person. Tracing the events in the development of Mrs. Hutchen's hysterical hoarseness does not provide an understanding of Mrs. Hutchens. She is not her history. Mrs. Hutchens must be grasped as an *existing person* with the "terror of a lost child" in her eyes along with her unique *continuing* reasons for *choosing to be* hoarse, controlled, guarded, and distressed. Ontological principle number one describes this profoundly significant human core of subjectivity:

Centeredness:
Every person is centered in self and therefore lives, loves, hates, is creative or destructive, flexible or rigid, blind or perceptive by reason of that center.

Mrs. Hutchens can be understood only by grasping the world as *she sees it and lives it.* For Mrs. Hutchens, like every other existing person, organizes her understanding of reality and self through her experience of it. If we do not understand her experience, we do not understand her. Only by empathy and by avoiding theoretical abstractions can the observer get a glimpse of Mrs. Hutchens's world.

Principle Two: Courage for Self-Affirmation

May defines self-affirmation as the "courage to be," relying on the concepts of Paul Tillich, a theologian who influenced him greatly (May, 1973; Tillich, 1952). Without courage, according to Tillich, a person "loses being." It is courage that permits choice.

Courage to be does not remove anxiety, according to Tillich. Nor can courage, by itself, lead to personality health. Rather, courage permits the healthy person to confront anxiety and avoid despair, as given in ontological principle number two:

Self-affirmation and courage:
Every existing person has the character of self-affirmation, which is the need to preserve his or her centeredness, and can mobilize courage to do so.

In Mrs. Hutchens's case, the possibility exists that she was confronted with three choices as she grew up. She could succumb to the authoritarian and frightening relationships and become what her elders wanted her to be. Or, second, she could rebel against their wishes and pressure, acting out her anger in some destructive way. Or, third, she could yield to despair, giving up hope and retreating from reality and life into nonbeing. What, in fact, has happened appears to be a compromise outcome partaking of all three possibilities. Freud suggested in his concept of symptoms as "compromise formations" that sometimes symptoms permit gratification of unacceptable wishes at the same time the neurotic person disowns the unacceptable wish. Mrs. Hutchens has somehow found a way to avoid destructive rebellion, complete despair, and complete capitulation. Her hysterical neurosis is, from this point of view, to be understood as an act of courage, an act of dignity, as well as a process of psychological dysfunction. Tillich, from whom May borrows much, made these points well:

> Anxiety turns us toward courage, because the other alternative is despair. Courage resists despair by taking anxiety into itself. . . . He who does not succeed in taking his anxiety courageously upon himself can succeed in avoiding the extreme situation of despair by escaping into neurosis. He still affirms himself but on a limited scale. *Neurosis is the way of avoiding nonbeing by avoiding being.* In the neurotic state self-affirmation is not lacking; it can indeed be very strong and emphasized. But the self which is affirmed is a reduced one. (Tillich, 1952, p. 66)[1]

Mrs. Hutchens's previous therapist had, in fact, informed his patient that she was "too controlled" and "too proper." She became very upset and broke off treatment. The therapist, in a way, was correct, but he missed the essence of this controlled and proper person. Although these qualities may appear to be part of the "neurotic" process, the existential point is that they *are* Mrs. Hutchens. "Controlled" and "proper" and even the hysterical hoarseness are the adjustments to her life as she interprets it out of the center of her being. To interpret her personality qualities and behaviors as her "problem" is to attack precisely those ways of being in which she is centered and those ways of being that she has chosen to protect herself as a person. No doubt Mrs. Hutchens felt misunderstood by that therapist. She probably experienced his

---

[1] As in other chapters we make no attempt to edit the pronoun usage in the original writings of the thinkers who are quoted. In the interest of scholarly accuracy, despite the irony inherent in an *existential* thinker's use of the male pronoun exclusively, Tillich's and May's original words are presented as they wrote them. In May's later writings, he adopts the more flexible and inclusive use of both gender pronouns we now regard as customary.

interpretations and advice to change as an assault. From the therapist's viewpoint, he was addressing "neurotic symptoms" or dysfunctional character traits. From Mrs. Hutchens's point of view, it was *her very center of self* that was the target of attack. She *is* everything she *is* at this moment, including the "neurosis."

There is to be found in Mrs. Hutchens's actions a further act of self-affirmation. Mrs. Hutchens gathers the courage to seek out another therapist who may also demand that she change this center of being. How does she muster willingness to risk her identity again? Whence this fresh act of courage?

Principle Three: Participation in Other Beings

In seeking out her new therapist, Mrs. Hutchens confronts a new risk of losing her identity. "If the neurotic [person] is so afraid of his own conflicted center that he refuses to go out but holds back in rigidity and lives in narrowed reactions and shrunken world space, his growth and development are blocked" (May, 1960, p. 181). Mrs. Hutchens sits with her new therapist:

> Now as Mrs. Hutchens talks hoarsely, she looks at me with an expression of mingled fear and hope. Obviously a relation exists between us not only here but already in anticipation in the waiting room and ever since she thought of coming. She is struggling with the possibility of participating with me. (May, 1960, pp. 180–181 and 1983, p. 27)

Ontological principle number three formalizes this conclusion:

Participation in others:
All existing persons have the need and possibility of going out from their centeredness to participate in other beings.

May points out that it is also possible for the "neurotic" person to cope with the experience of threat to self by "overparticipating" in others. The neurotic may "lose self" by diffusing it in overidentification with others. In Mrs. Hutchens case, she has enacted neither of these losses of self. She has acted from courage and pain to confront her neurosis. Understanding her diagnostic category would obscure these more important issues (May, 1967b, p. 8).

Principle Four: Awareness

As May uses the term, *awareness* means vigilance. The person is wary of external threats and dangers. In the first few therapy sessions with May, for example, Mrs. Hutchens regards him as a threat who may put herself in jeopardy. She is "wary." It is her lifelong vigilance that is responsible for Mrs. Hutchens's guardedness. Ontological principle number four is thus:

Awareness:
The subjective side of centeredness is awareness.

May distinguishes such awareness from "consciousness." Awareness is a proto-type of anxiety at a primitive cognitive level, which May believes has numerous coun-terparts in the vigilance systems of animals lower in the evolutionary scale than humans. Such vigilance is self-protective, but not uniquely human (May, 1953, p. 75 ff.). It is probably best understood as an "early warning system" common to animals and humans who feel themselves in danger. But there is a more sophisticated cogni-tive development that takes place exclusively in humans which enhances this funda-mental alarm system, and it is called *self-consciousness.*

Principle Five: Self-Consciousness

Consciousness is the ability to know oneself as the being who is threatened. Only a human person can experience self as the subjective agent who has a world. Only a human can be *self*-conscious. Self-consciousness permits the person to transcend the immediate, concrete situation, to live in terms of the possible, and to use abstractions (May, 1960, p. 182). But there are two sides to self-consciousness, for not only can the person be conscious of self as an active subject, the person can also be conscious of self as a passive object (May, 1967b, pp. 8 ff.).

As an example, May cites his experience of writing a book under the time pres-sure of a deadline. His first state of self-consciousness is bound by attention to exter-nals. He looks at the clock, decides how much longer he will spend writing that morn-ing, wonders how best to get the most done before his afternoon consultation hours begin, and he continues working. He realizes something he has written will be criti-cized by a colleague and wonders whether to change the wording. He criticizes him-self for worrying about what his colleague will think. He is aware that this thought is intruding on his writing. He refocuses on the writing, asking himself what is the best way to write this, what is the most efficient way to get it done, meet the schedule, make the ideas palatable to others?

As he continues to write, May becomes excited by a new idea. He enters a sec-ond state of self-consciousness. "Ah, here is something that has been playing around the fringes of my consciousness for years—what an alluring prospect to work it out now, form it, see where it leads!" (May, 1967b, p. 7). For a while he is engaged in reorganizing the writing around the new idea. He wonders briefly whether his colleague will approve, then suddenly does not care because the idea is a good one. He looks at the clock and discovers that it is half an hour later than he had planned to stop.

In this brief episode, May has shown both kinds of self-consciousness. During the first part of the writing, musing about how to meet the deadline, setting time limits for himself, and wondering how best to phrase something so as not to offend a col-league, May is aware of himself as an object. He is a man bound by clock and calen-dar. But in the second phase of his writing, when the exciting idea has emerged, he becomes engaged in the idea and the process of working the idea through its many implications. His thinking reflects the change because he no longer experiences self as a "slave of time," bound by schedules. In the first state, the emphasis was on *extrin-sic* parts of the process, whereas in the second state, the focus shifted to *intrinsic* choices and interests. In the first state, May's self-consciousness is of himself as an *object.* But in the second state, the moments of the interesting idea, he treats himself as an active *subject* who wishes, is curious, and has feelings about what he does. Hence we arrive at ontological principle number five:

Self-consciousness:
The uniquely human form of awareness is self-consciousness.

In a parallel way, May points out, the therapist can be aware of his or her patient as an object or as a subject. If May were to be aware of Mrs. Hutchens as an object, he would focus on her life history, on the diagnostic category that best described her difficulties, and on the information reported by her neurologist. And as a consequence, Mrs. Hutchens would be an object of his thought, but little empathic understanding of Mrs. Hutchens as an existing person would result. May offers another clinical example:

> When consulting with a borderline patient . . . I must consider whether he needs hospitalization and in such case what is the best method, and so on; but at the moment I am standing outside him and not doing therapy. If I am to do therapy with him I must not be preoccupied with how bizarre and meaningless are his utterances, but what is the hidden meaning in his symbols? If he asserts two times two is five, I must ask not what kind of psychosis does this indicate, but can I discover what meaning it has for him to assert this? (May, 1967b, p. 8)

Human consciousness vacillates between the experience of self as object and the experience of self as subject. For the existential therapist, the same kind of vacillation is possible in relating to another. The therapist may experience the other as object or as subject. The key difference in the therapeutic setting is the degree of active empathy that the therapist can muster.

Principle Six: Anxiety and Nonbeing

From the existential point of view, human beings are unique in their capacity not only to be aware of self-being-aware, but they are also unique in their realization that ultimately self will end. Consciousness of death, of the possibility of the state of nonbeing, even the possibility of consciousness killing itself, is a powerful influence on the person's experience of self (cf. Feifel, 1962). Nothing so heightens living as the possibility of dying.

> Death is . . . the one fact of my life which is not relative but absolute, and my awareness of this gives my existence and what I do each hour an absolute quality. (May, 1958b, pp. 48–49; see also May, 1961)

We come therefore to ontological principle number 6:

Anxiety and nonbeing:
Anxiety is the state of the person in the struggle against what would destroy his or her being.

To illustrate, consider a dream reported by Mrs. Hutchens after approximately 25 hours of therapy with May:

> She was searching room by room for a baby in an unfinished house at an airport. She thought the baby belonged to someone else, but the other person might let her take it. Now it seemed that she had put the baby in a pocket of her robe (or her mother's robe) and she was seized with anxiety that it would be smothered. Much to her joy, she found that the baby was still alive. Then she had a strange thought, "Shall I kill it?" (May, 1960, p. 183)

During therapy May and his patient discovered that the house was at an airport where Mrs. Hutchens had learned to fly solo at the age of 20. That achievement had been a landmark in her developing independence from her parents. The baby in the dream was associated with her youngest son, with whom she identified. Some years before Mrs. Hutchens had entered therapy, she had changed her church affiliation, leaving behind the authoritarian relationship to her parents' church and customs. She never told her parents about her change of religious affiliation, and their visits were often marked with tension and anxiety that one of her children would reveal the secret. After 35 sessions of therapy, while Mrs. Hutchens discussed writing to her parents to tell them of her changed religious beliefs, she experienced several spells of "partially fainting" during therapy sessions. "She would become suddenly weak, her face would go white, she would feel empty and 'like water inside,' and would have to lie down for a few moments on the couch. In retrospect, she called these spells 'grasping for oblivion' " (May, 1960, pp. 183–184).

For a while, Mrs. Hutchens was very worried that her fainting spells might mean that she was going crazy, entering a psychotic state. May reassured her that the probable meaning lay elsewhere. From May's point of view, the dream of the baby at the airport and the fainting spells were personal metaphors for Mrs. Hutchens's confrontation with her own conflicts and the possibility of nonbeing. The baby represents Mrs. Hutchens's own consciousness and a desire to kill her own consciousness in the struggle for a healthy way of being. Likewise her fainting spells are not early signs of psychosis, but Mrs. Hutchens's symbolic way of saying, "If only I did not have to be conscious, I would escape this terrible problem of telling my parents [about her religious independence]" (May, 1960, p. 184).

The terrible anxiety that Mrs. Hutchens feels stems from her confrontation with the possibility of her own death. May interprets her anxiety as a sign that she realizes nonbeing is reflected in her relationship to her parents because that relationship causes her to forfeit her independence and identity. Forfeiting one's identity is a kind of death.

In therapy, Mrs. Hutchens learns to identify these issues, accepting the hatred of her past, her parents, the aggression of her family toward her, and, ultimately, her own motives of destructive anger.

Transitional Summary

The six ontological principles we have discussed and illustrated in the context of Mrs. Hutchens's therapy are a road map of the concerns that occupied Rollo May from the late 1950s through to the 1990s. In a way, May's forty-year career has been spent returning to each of these basic principles and elaborating on them with care and enhanced detail. But the main themes of May's work are all represented in these six basics:

1. Every person is centered in self and lives life through the meaning he or she places on that center.
2. Every person is responsible for mobilizing the courage to protect the self, to affirm it and enhance its continued existence.
3. People need other people with whom they can empathize and from whom they can learn.
4. People are vigilant about potential dangers to their identities.
5. People can be aware of themselves thinking and feeling at one moment and may be aware of themselves as the person who thinks and feels in the next moment.
6. Anxiety orginates, in part, out of a person's awareness that one's being can end.

THE PROBLEM OF NOTHINGNESS

"To grasp what it means to exist, one needs to grasp the fact that he might not exist . . ." wrote May, voicing one of the central concerns of the existential movement (1983, p. 105). As we have seen, such awareness is a dialectical process, for the awareness of death enhances one's sense of living. Life becomes real, vivid, flavorful only when one confronts the possibility of nothingness. From this understanding of the significance of death comes May's definition of anxiety:

> Anxiety is *the experience of the threat of imminent nonbeing.*

> and

> Anxiety is the subjective state of the individual's becoming aware that his existence can become destroyed, that he can lose himself and his world, that he can become nothing. (May, 1983, pp. 109–110)

This ontological meaning of the term *anxiety* derives in part from the philosopher Kierkegaard, who, along with Freud and other European thinkers, used the German word *Angst* to describe this feeling of "losing being" (May, 1950, p. 36), and in part the definition derives from theologian Paul Tillich's ideas (1952). Angst is not adequately translated into English by the word *anxiety,* for Angst carries the connotations of "anguish" and "dread." As Tillich conceptualized the problem, "The basic anxiety, the anxiety of a finite being about the threat of nonbeing, cannot be eliminated. It belongs to existence itself" (1952, p. 39).

Ontological Anxiety: Normal and Neurotic

May distinguishes between anxiety and fear. When a dentist aims to drill a sensitive tooth, we feel fear. The feeling a person experiences when someone he or she respects passes by without acknowledgment is probably less intense than the fear of the dentist. But the "gnawing threat" of this personal slight will reverberate for a long time, invading dreams and daydreams, whereas the fear of the dentist evaporates when the person leaves the chair (May, 1983). The feeling deriving from the slight is anxiety.

> The difference is that the anxiety strikes at the central core of his self-esteem and his sense of value as a self, which is the most important aspect of his experience of himself as a being. Fear, in contrast, is a threat to the periphery of his existence; it can be objectivated and the person can stand outside and look at it. (May, 1983, p. 110)

Anxiety has more profound effects, according to May, for the experience of this emotion can overwhelm the person's "discovery of being," demolish the person's sense of time, dull the memory of the past, and anxiety even "erases the future" (May, 1983, p. 110).

May distinguishes between two kinds of anxiety (1967b, p. 80; see also May, 1950, 1975):

- *Normal anxiety* is proportionate to the threat, does not involve repression, can be consciously faced and discussed, and is diminished or eliminated if the anxiety provoking situation is changed. Normal anxiety is found at nearly every stage of normal development as the child learns to walk, talk, and relate to others outside the family. Healthy personality growth stems from confronting these normal anxieties, mustering the courage to change one's values or give up actual security for potential security.

- *Neurotic anxiety is* ". . . a reaction which is disproportionate to the threat, involves repression and other forms of intrapsychic conflict, and is managed by various kinds of blocking-off [of] activity and awareness" (May, 1967b, p. 80). Neurotic anxiety can develop when a person fails to face normal anxiety. In a way, neurotic anxiety can block growth because the person fails to expand and to affirm self in new situations because his or her judgment and courage are overwhelmed by the anxiety.

It is clear that both normal and neurotic anxiety occur when a possibility for a new way of being opens for a person. But that very possibility is anxiety laden because it carries with it the seeds of destruction for the person's old way of being (May, 1950, p. 36; 1983, p. 111). To give up the old is to give up security and induce angst. But by the same token, to close oneself off from the possibility of change is to risk losing freedom.

As Freud, too, wrote, anxiety reflects inner conflict. However, May conceptualizes the poles of the conflict as derivatives of the being–nonbeing dialectic. His conception of ontological anxiety and the potential for blocking freedom and creating guilt is best illustrated by his earliest research. As part of his inquiry into the nature of anxiety for his doctorate, May tested a hypothesis about anxiety drawn loosely from psychoanalysis. He reasoned that vulnerability to anxiety can be heightened by an early experience of maternal rejection (May, 1950; 1975, p. 56). He studied a sample of unmarried mothers in their late teens and early twenties in a shelter home in New York City. May assumed that the situation of being unwed and pregnant would trigger more anxiety in those women whose personal histories included rejection by their own mothers. However, using largely clinical methods such as the Rorschach and clinical interviewing, he found that only about half of his subjects confirmed his hypothesis. The other half, with equivalent histories of maternal rejection, did not. Despite their histories of maternal rejection, their anxiety levels on the measures May employed were not heightened as predicted.

> . . . it suddenly struck me "out of the blue," as the not-unfitting expression goes, that those young women who didn't fit my hypothesis *were all from the proletarian class.* And as quickly as that idea struck me, other ideas poured. . . . I saw at that instant that it is not rejection by the mother that is the original trauma which is the source of anxiety; it is rather *rejection that is lied about.*
>
> The proletarian mothers rejected their children, but they never made any bones about it. The children knew they were rejected; they went out on the streets and found other companions. . . . But the middle-class young women were always lied to in their families. They were rejected by mothers who pretended they loved them. This was really the source of their anxiety, not the sheer rejection. I saw, in that instantaneous way that characterizes insights from these deeper sources, that anxiety comes from *not being able to know the world you're in, not being able to orient yourself in your own existence.* (May, 1975, p. 58)

Considering anxiety from an ontological point of view reveals its intimate connection to personal disorientation combined with a devastating assault on one's self-esteem, trust, and capacity to anticipate the actions of others. If life is made unpredictable, a person is forced into a position of helplessness and the potential for despair is established. As we see later in the chapter, the theme of helplessness is an important one in May's work.

Ontological Guilt

From May's point of view, the two kinds of anxiety share a common theme. Anxiety is always intimately related to inner conflict. The nature of the conflict is clear: To pursue new possibilities of living is anxiety provoking as we give up the familiar and with it our security. But to deny those possibilities, to deliberately fail to fulfill them to preserve security provokes guilt (May, 1983, pp. 112 ff.).

It is ironic that it is precisely because humans have the freedom of choosing among possibilities that they are subject to the anguish of anxiety or the pain of guilt. May is careful to point out that his conceptions of guilt and anxiety are both *onto-logical* conceptions. That is, these experiences stem from the processes of being and its confrontation with nonbeing or "nothingness" and not from particular relationships, failures, or rule violations (May, 1983, p. 115).

May distinguishes among three ontological levels of guilt that correspond to the three modes of being discussed earlier in this chapter. Recall the *Umwelt* or the "world around" of natural drives and needs, the *Mitwelt* or the "with world" of being with others, and the *Eigenwelt* or the "own world" of subjective meaning.

- The first form of ontological guilt, then, corresponds to the *Umwelt* and is referred to as "separation guilt" in the sense of alienation or separation from the natural world. Our own technology continually distances us from nature, but the process is subtle and insidious so that we remain unaware of this kind of ontological guilt (May, 1958b, p. 54; 1983, p. 115).

- The second form of ontological guilt corresponds to the *Mitwelt* (with world) and arises from ". . . the fact that since each of us is an individual, he necessarily perceives his fellow man through his own limited and biased eyes. This means that he always to some extent does violence to the true picture of his fellow man and always to some extent fails to understand fully and meet the other's needs" (May, 1958b, p. 54). May asserts that this kind of guilt is inescapable because we each have no choice but to see the world through our own eyes.

- The third form of ontological guilt is equivalent to the *Eigenwelt* and returns us to our starting point of the person who forfeits potentialities in order to preserve security. It is that forfeiture that produces ontological guilt at the most personal level.

Ontological guilt has four characteristics (May, 1958b, p. 55; 1983, pp. 115 ff.):

1. Everyone participates in ontological guilt because each of us distorts the reality of others and each of us fails to fulfill some of our possibilities.
2. Ontological guilt does not rely on cultural prohibitions. "Ontological guilt does not consist of I-am-guilty-because-I-violate-parental-prohibitions, but arises from the fact that I can see myself as the one who can choose or fail to choose" (May, 1958b, p. 55).
3. Ontological guilt is not neurotic or morbid. If a person can become aware of his or her ontological guilt, the person may be able to accept it rather than repress it.
4. Ontological guilt does not lead to symptom formation, but may in fact be constructive in personality development. One possibility is that awareness of ontological guilt, an alertness to the vulnerability and universality of the human condition, leads to humility (May, 1958b, p. 55).

PERSONAL SOURCES OF MAY'S EXISTENTIALISM

If we take a step back from the ideas of Rollo May presented so far, three broad themes emerge. First, May emphasizes the fragility of human life as well as its beauty. Like so many other personality theorists, much of May's professional concerns grew from his clinical work. There is, then, a thread of concern for the vulnerability of people to anxiety and despair and the struggle against helplessness. As we have seen, May began his career in clinical psychology with the study of anxiety. The opening quote for this chapter gives some indication of these elements in May's thinking:

> Life is not superficial. The real problem is how you exist in a world that is antagonistic, that hates you. How are you able to live in a world where we are all alone, where we all die? (May, in Rabinowitz, Good, & Cozad, 1989, p. 439)

The second theme that emerges from the theory thus far presented is May's profound concern with ultimate existence and death. His close association with theologian Paul Tillich is ample testimony to the importance of this theme in his work (May, 1973).

The third theme we can trace is May's concern with loneliness and alienation in human existence. His ideas on the nature of ontological guilt that we have explored thus far can be understood as a concern with alienation from others and self, but a kind of alienation that is universal, inescapable, and experienced as profound loneliness. Read again the quotation from May after the first paragraph of this section.

The three themes are not separate. They are all of a piece with links to each other that suggest a remarkable personal, if not theoretical, coherence. Put into words, May's view of self, of others, and of the world emphasizes the needs for intimacy and acceptance, the human struggle against uncertainty and helplessness, and the confrontation with death (nonbeing).

May's Needs for Intimacy and Acceptance

Rollo May's childhood and family life were discordant and lonely. He was born April 21, 1909, in Ohio; the family moved to Michigan early in May's life. His father was a secretary for the YMCA and moved his family frequently. Rollo's immediate family consisted of five brothers and a sister who later became psychotic. The marital relationship was "discordant" with a rather unhappy family life as the result (Rabinowitz et al., 1989, p. 436). His experience of this family discord sparked May's interest in psychology and counseling and provoked escapes to the shores of the St. Clair River to watch the ships go by. May suggested that he learned more from the river than from his school years because the river was a "clean, deep, demonic, and beautiful friend" (quoted by Rabinowitz et al., 1989, p. 436). As a boy, Rollo found peace at the river, away from the sooty, noisy industrial Detroit area in which he lived.

In recollecting his early life, May attributed his two failed marriages to the effects of the models provided by his parents' marriage and his conflicted relationship with his mother:

> My marriages were not successful. I think this is very much related dynamically to the fact that my mother was a "bitch-kitty on wheels." My sister, who was older than I, was psychotic and spent some time in a mental hospital. I've always had good friends and lovers, but I'm scared to death of marriage. I will probably be married again in a couple of months, if I can get over being so scared. I've been going steadily with a woman I love very much. But the first two marriages didn't work and this was terribly difficult. I knew I had to get out of my first marriage, which lasted 20-some odd years, and I knew it rather quickly, but I didn't want to leave until the children were through college, so I did not. (May in Rabinowitz et al., 1989, pp. 438–439)

May's early personal history is not unlike the histories of other personality theorists we have examined. It is clear that his childhood was a time of conflict and emotional pain from which he sought relief in the peacefulness of solitude at the river, his sole source of harmony. But it is also evident that these experiences sensitized May to the pain of loneliness and the anxiety associated with an unpredictable family life.

That these themes are central to existentialism and that May was drawn to the existential school of thought should not be surprising.

May's Struggle against Uncertainty and Helplessness

May describes himself as a somewhat angry adolescent and "rebellious" in school. During his college years at Michigan State College, May "irked" the school authorities with a student literature magazine he started, and transferred to Oberlin College in Ohio at the suggestion of a friend. His experience at Oberlin was positive and fed his interests in the humanities, especially Greek art and literature. He was hired by a Greek gymnasium (a kind of high school and junior college) to teach English to boys between the ages of 12 and 18, and he stayed in Greece for about three years teaching and studying art and painting.

> The boys were effusive, lovable, emotionally changeable. It was a case of an immediate love affair between the students and myself, but I was later to learn how unstable such adoration could be. . . . All this seemed to make my first year happy enough. But as the year went on *I found that my habits and principles, coming from a typical small-town, midwestern childhood, such as hard work, fidelity, honesty and so on, stood by me less and less as the year progressed.* (May, 1985, p. 6; italics added)

May grew lonely. There were only a few Americans at the Greek college, and they soon ran out of things to talk about. Two new American teachers came on staff and ". . . the boys in the school found these new teachers to lavish their inconstant affection and charm upon" (May, 1985, p. 8). We can assume that feelings of rejection were now added to the loneliness May felt, especially in light of his early family history. May tried to work harder, but found that the more effort he expended, the less effectively he taught. The loneliness was overwhelming:

> Finally in the spring of that second year I had what is called euphemistically a nervous breakdown. *Which meant simply that the rules, principles, values by which I used to work and live simply did not suffice anymore.* I got so completely fatigued that I had to go to bed for two weeks to get enough energy to continue my teaching. I had learned enough psychology at college to know that these symptoms meant that something was wrong with my whole way of life. I had to find some new goals and purposes for my living and to relinquish my moralistic, somewhat rigid way of existence. (May, 1985, p. 8)

Had he been in America, May says that he would have sought psychotherapy. Instead, a sympathetic couple who were teachers at the same college invited May to spend time at their home. May spent some time alone, and when he wanted to talk, the couple made themselves available. One late night in March, after a long talk with these new friends, May left the house and walked toward Mt. Hortiati about ten miles away. His friends did not interfere. It began raining, but May continued up the mountain, his clothes freezing to his body.

Some six hours later he reached a plateau in the darkness, and heard the barking of wolves. The pack circled around May a few times, but he reports that he was absorbed in his own inner turmoil and paid little attention. Fortunately for him, the wolves eventually left. By dawn, May made his way to the small village of Hortiati, woke up the café owner, and arranged to rent his upstairs room. After some sleep, May went down to the café, where some of the village men gathered around a stove to eat roasted fish, drink, and talk. May sat as near to them as he could "to keep warm" (1985, p. 10). He spent hours writing on the back of laundry slips he had carried from the school in his coat. Soon the village men became curious and asked about what May was writing:

> I knew they would not understand if I talked about philosophy, and furthermore it wasn't quite true that I was writing that anyway.
> So I answered in my halting Greek, "I write, *what is life?*"
> They all leaned back with guffaws of laughter. One of them spoke out, "That's easy! If you have bread you eat, if you do not have bread you die." (May, 1985, p. 10)

May had come far from his Detroit childhood. Caught in his own distress, lonely, feeling rejected and unable to make sense of the world in which he found himself, his companions' earthy philosophy must have felt even more alienating for all of its simplicity and directness. He was struggling for survival, the survival of his own identity and searching for familiar landmarks by which to navigate this alien existence that threatened his understanding of the world and self.

After two days, May started down the mountain again to return to the home of his friends. He spent his remaining time at their home walking around the surrounding hills and meadows. On one day, he climbed a hill and found himself knee-deep in a field of poppies that were so beautiful, their "perfect movements seemed like children in a ballet" (1985, p. 11). He sketched those poppies that morning in 1932, and he made an important discovery that was to stay with him for many years:

> I realized that I had not listened to my inner voice, which had tried to talk to me about beauty. I had been too hard-working, too "principled" to spend time merely looking at flowers! It seems it had taken a collapse of my whole former way of life for this voice to make itself heard. (May, 1985, p. 13)

The drawing of the poppies, reproduced here in Figure 11-1 from May's book *My Quest for Beauty* (1985, p. 13), is a black-and-white pencil sketch of about a dozen flowers and foliage. Despite his description of his emotional state on that May morning, the drawing is suggestive of a melancholy mood in the drooping stems of the flowers and the somewhat isolated quality of each of the individual flowers. Contrasted with other May drawings and paintings in the same book from other times in his life, the poppy drawing shows clear signs of the profundity of his distress and the depth of his depression at that time.

Ironically, the chapter of the book following the one that describes this emotional crisis is "Beauty Has Kept Me Alive," which May hastily informs the reader is only a metaphorical statement, not a literal one. Yet the close association of the description of that depressed episode in his life and his later concern with nonbeing leads us to speculate about how closely May examined the issue of continued living during his crisis.

Some years later, May recalled the thoughts that were on his mind after that summer of crisis in Greece. When he returned to America, his interest in psychology centered on substantive issues he could not find in most graduate psychology programs of the time.

FIGURE 11.1   **Rollo May's drawing of a field of poppies in Greece, 1932, during his time of emotional crisis.**

R. M.

Poppies, drawn at "White House," May 22, '32

Source: May (1985), used by permission.

American psychology, to which I came back, seemed naive and simplistic, omitting exactly what made life most rich and exciting. I longed for some community in which one could ask questions about the meaning of despair, suicide, and normal anxiety. . . . (May, 1973, p. 2)

Beauty is harmony, as May explains later in the book, and harmony within himself, oneness with his own identity, and with his fellows and with nature (*Eigenwelt, Mitwelt,* and *Umwelt*) were to be theoretical concepts that would occupy most of May's later professional life.

May survived his "breakdown" by returning to the lessons he first learned in childhood: Seek peace, harmony, beauty. Like his experience with the St. Clair River, which permitted escape from the chaos of his childhood, May's discovery of the beauty and peace that lay around him was salvation. May found his identity by turning inward. The fragments, the rigidity and "moralistic" concerns of which he speaks, and the personal uncertainty he experienced had brought him to the edge of personal dissolution. There is every reason to believe that such an experience sensitizes us to the issues of existence, identity, and death, themes which were to occupy May some years later as an existential psychologist.

May's Confrontation with Helplessness and Death

That June, following the emotional crisis, on summer vacation from his job at Anatolia College in Saloniki, Greece, May traveled to Vienna to study with Alfred Adler. His recollection of that experience was that Adler was "absolutely psychic in his therapy with children" (May in Rabinowitz, 1989 et al., p. 67). His interest in psychodynamic psychology was strengthened. May was imbued with the spirit of the European thinkers such as Adler, Freud, and Jung. He returned to America in 1933, with the intention of becoming a psychologist by taking a graduate degree at Columbia University. But the program at Columbia was behavioral, not psychodynamic. Issues such as war, death, love, hate—these were the questions that Rollo May wanted to investigate, and the standard psychometrics and behavioral psychology of the day were not satisfactory substitutes (Rabinowitz et al., 1989, p. 436; May, 1973, p. 2).

May enrolled at Union Theological Seminary, where the questions in which he had become interested were being discussed by professors who had fled Europe with the rise of the Nazi regime to power. At Union Theological, May began his friendship with theologian Paul Tillich, a European émigré who had left his homeland to escape the persecution of the Nazis. May earned a bachelor's degree in divinity, but initially had no intention of a career in the ministry. He was called home after graduation to "hold the family together" after his father left his mother (Rabinowitz et al., 1989, p. 437). Once home, he accepted a combined teaching and church position at Michigan State College in 1936. His interest in psychology and counseling combined along with his brief studies with Alfred Adler led to lecturing on counseling procedures and to the writing of a book on counseling (May, 1939/1967a). May decided to return to graduate school to study the process in more detail and enrolled in the clinical psychology program at Teacher's College of Columbia University. Working hard in graduate school, researching his dissertation, and trying to earn a meager living by teaching at the City College of New York, May came down with tuberculosis.

At that time, tuberculosis was a killer disease for which the only treatment was complete rest. May spent most of the next two years in upstate New York at Lake Saranac in a sanatorium, the occasion for a profound change in viewpoint. May had to confront the possibility of his own death in the face of a disease about which he could do little, or so he was told on the basis of prevailing medical wisdom. He achieved the insight that his helpless and passive attitude was enhancing the disease process and made the inner decision to combat it. He reports that only when he took this more active stance to take control over his life, as he had earlier in Greece, did he recover:

> For a year and a half I did not know whether I would live or die. As best I could, I tried to do what my doctors instructed me to do. This meant, as I then interpreted it, accepting the program of rest and giving my healing over to others. I could only lie in

bed, tracing with my eye patterns of light on the ceiling of my room, waiting for the monthly X-ray which would tell whether the cavity in my lung had enlarged or decreased.

But I found, to my moral and intellectual dismay, that the bacilli were taking advantage of my very innocence. This innocence had transformed my helplessness into passivity, which constituted an open invitation to the bacilli to do violence to my body. I saw, too, that the reason I had contracted tuberculosis in the first place was my hopelessness and sense of defeatism. . . . I could see in the apparently innocent patients around me in the sanatorium that passively accepting their powerlessness in the face of the disease meant dying. Not until I developed some "fight," some sense of personal responsibility for the fact that it was *I* who had the tuberculosis, an assertion of my own will to live, did I make lasting progress. (May, 1972, pp. 13–14; see also May, 1969, p. 239)

It was during this illness that May was working on his book about anxiety (1950), and he read the existential philosopher Soren Kierkegaard on anxiety as a struggle against despair and Freud's psychoanalytic ideas on anxiety. He found Kierkegaard to be the more cogent thinker on the subject and was deeply influenced by him and by the work of Paul Tillich (1952), who also presents an existential account of anxiety as a struggle against nonbeing.

Some years later, in the context of psychology's relevance to disease and health, and particularly its relevance to the disease of tuberculosis, May briefly discussed an old theory that attempted to explain why so many creative people seemed to have had tuberculosis. One physician apparently advanced the theory that the bacilli responsible for the disease release some substance into the blood that stimulates genius. May scoffed at this explanation and offered a psychological hypothesis instead:

This explanation seems to me absurd. It makes much more sense to hold that the way of life of the genius—intensive work, unquenchable enthusiasm, the fire in the brain—puts too much of a strain on the balance, and hence the individual becomes ill as a necessary way of withdrawing into himself for a time. (May, 1981, p. 215)

The pattern of withdrawal from chaos and stress into serenity and rest was certainly one that characterized May's early childhood and adulthood. It may be that May's comment was also a self-statement describing the lessons that had been true for him. He described the three types of patient he had observed in the sanatorium. Some patients become conditioned by the facts of their disease, the restrictions on movement, the limitations of sanatorium life. They become passive and helpless and "invite their own deaths" by essentially giving up the struggle for life (May, 1953, pp. 140 ff.). Other patients in the same sanatorium adhere to the prescribed regimen, but spend most of their time resenting their misfortune. Such people don't die, May observed, but they do not recover either. "Like rebels in any area of life, they remain on a plateau perpetually marking time" (1953, p. 141). Finally, there are those tuberculosis patients, one presumes like May himself, who confront the fact of their illness, spend time reflecting on the meaning of their lives, trying to understand what was wrong with their living before their illness. These patients use the opportunity as a means to new self-knowledge and self-discipline. "They are the ones who not only achieve physical health, but who also are ultimately enlarged, enriched, and strengthened by the experience of having had the disease" (May, 1953, p. 141).

In effect, May was saying that we become healthy by taking the responsibility to choose health. He quotes the letter of a "tuberculosis patient" to a friend. This patient had apparently achieved these insights, but more important, the letter writer is probably May himself:

> The disease occurred not simply because I overworked, or ran athwart some T.B. bugs, but because I was trying to be something I wasn't. I was living as the "great extrovert," running here and there, doing three jobs at once, and leaving undeveloped and unused the side of me which would contemplate, would read and think and "invite my soul" rather than rushing and working at full speed. The disease comes as a demand and an opportunity to rediscover the lost functions of myself. It is as though the disease were nature's way of saying, "You must become your whole self. To the extent that you do not, you will be ill; and you will become well only to the extent that you do become yourself." (May, 1953, p. 95)

May's confrontation with death led back to a reliance on his own resources, his own strengths. We have to admire May for his insistence on personal responsibility. And we have to admire him for his willingness to use what others have found to be a formidable limitation in the service of expanded knowledge. His confrontation with nonbeing led, not to nothingness, but to a productive struggle to survive.

LOVE AND WILL

The problems of existence to which May had turned his thinking encompass a broad range of human pain and struggle. Throughout the history of civilization, people have sought either love or "will power" as the solution to many of these problems of existence. But, as May (1969) pointed out, the solutions have become problems. Two great miscalculations govern the way contemporary people try to solve the dilemmas of life. On the one hand, there is the belief that love heals all and that if one does not have it, one is a failure. On the other, the heritage of our Victorian ancestors is the belief that the solution to life's problems lies in rationally choosing the right thing to do. One must *will* the good, *intend* the rational and, inevitably, life's problems will yield (May, 1969).

The rising divorce rates, plummeting self-esteem and violence in "loving families," and the trivialization of sex in the pursuit of intimacy suggest that love may be an illusory solution but a real problem. In a similar way, people seek out therapy to learn how to "release emotion" or how to "let the unconscious speak" in an effort to decide wisely at the choice points of their lives. But May characterized the illusion of this "solution" well: "Now it is no longer a matter of deciding what to do, but of *deciding how to decide. The very basis of will itself is thrown into question*" (May, 1969, p. 15).

Apathy, Alienation, and the Schizoid World

We have convinced ourselves that love and will are illusions. Contemporary life, according to May, has produced a schizoid withdrawal. He is not using the term *schizoid* in its technical psychopathological meaning. Rather he is referring to a kind of empty numbness that people can use as a way of avoiding or defending against the dilemmas of existence (May, 1969, pp. 27 ff.). If a person feels powerless or helpless to change his or her life, the concepts of will and love have little meaning. What is immediately lost is concern for other people and concern for self. What is lost somewhat later is any concern for the dangers of this kind of empty feeling, and violence can erupt out of apathy. The person does not merely stagnate; he or she grows destructive, emotionally calloused, and increasingly apathetic:

> When I use the term "apathy," . . . it is because its literal meaning is the closest to what I am describing: "want of feeling; lack of passion, emotion or excitement, indifference." Apathy and the schizoid world go hand in hand as cause and effect of each other. (May, 1969, p. 29)

Apathy undermines love and will: "a condition in which men and women find themselves experiencing a distance between themselves and the objects which used to excite their affection and their will" (May, 1969, p. 29). A kind of numb indifference sets in as a protection against the depersonalizing, schizoid world. But the numbness breeds violence because

> When inward life dries up, when feeling decreases and apathy increases, when one cannot affect or even genuinely touch another person, violence flares up as a daimonic necessity for contact, a mad drive forcing touch in the most direct way possible. (May, 1969, pp. 30–31)

Contemporary civilization has fostered apathy as a protective mechanism against stimulus overload, information flooding, and the depersonalizing, dehumanizing effects of our cities. But the protection that apathy affords us from these assaults has a heavy price. Love and will are the first casualties. In fact, from May's point of view (1969, p. 29), the opposite of love is not hate. It is apathy. And the opposite of apathy is *care.*

In principle, May distinguishes among four different forms of loving:

1. *Agapé* or *Caritas* or *Care:* the love devoted to the welfare of others, the prototype for which is the love of God for man. It is the foundation for all of the other forms.
2. *Sex* or lust or what Freud called libido.
3. *Eros,* the drive to procreate.
4. *Philia,* or brotherly love and friendship.

Care or Agapé

For the person who *cares,* things matter, people matter. There is a sense of relatedness between the person who cares and the object of care. The ancient Romans' Latin word is the root of our own: *Caritas.* Sometimes in theology the word *Agapé* is applied, as in the biblical account of God's *caring or love for humankind.* At the more human level, one cannot be indifferent if one cares. Care is essential from birth, for the infant whose mother does not care for it will not survive. And caring can be directed toward self as well. If we do not care for ourselves, we neglect our health and well-being, producing injury and disease.

Care is associated with compassion and with empathy. It is likely that as infants we learn to care for others by the care we are shown. Care is also the foundation for wishing and willing, for we would not wish or will anything unless we care for it. But we must not assume that care is a feeling. It is, according to May (1969, p. 292), an ontological state, a state of being. It may lead to feeling and passion and even to motivated action, but the phenomenon of *caring* is part of being and the source of love and will. It is, metaphorically speaking, throwing the weight of one's being in a particular direction—*tending* toward another, as in psychotherapy when the therapist's wish is for the patient to be well. Thus caring is a form of intentionality in which the carer "throws his or her weight on the side" of the patient. Caring is the prerequisite for love as it manifests itself in the remaining three forms: Sex, Eros, and Philia.

Sex: The Flight From Eros

May argues that it is only in relatively recent times that sex has become so important that it occupies us in all facets of our lives. The ancients, he believes, took sex for granted. Biology gives sex its evolutionary importance, as Freud had pointed out. But when we turn to an examination of the relationship between sex and love, a myriad of contradictions emerges.

Up to Victorian times, the topic of sex was difficult to talk or write about. In Freud's day, sexuality was the chief target of both personal and social repression. But, May argues, in the 1920s a minor revolution occurred. A belief developed in liberal circles that the opposite of sexual repression would have healthy effects. "In an amazingly short period following World War I, we shifted from acting as though sex did not exist at all to being obsessed with it" (May, 1969, p. 39). But despite our obsession with sex, we have trivialized it, turned it into a commodity by exchanging passion-for-proper-technique for passion.

There are ironies in our newfound freedom with sex. Guilt and performance anxiety have been increased by the new emphasis on good technique and the implication that health requires a vigorous sex life. If you don't perform well, so this distortion goes, you are not healthy. There is also what May calls the new "puritanism" (spelled with a lowercase "p" to distinguish it from the historical Puritans).

> I define this puritanism as consisting of three elements. First, *a state of alienation from the body.* Second, the separation of emotion from reason. And third, *the use of the body as a machine.* (May, 1969, p. 45)

The "new" puritanism is really a form of depersonalizing sexuality. We substitute machine-like terms and passive verbs (we "have" sex or get "laid" rather than "make love" or, more simply, "love") for sexual intercourse, and some counseling manuals even recommend the use of the "f word" when doing psychotherapy with married couples to promote a liberalized attitude and less defensiveness (May, 1969, p. 47). The picture May paints of contemporary sexual attitudes and behavior is one of depersonalized, mechanized, obsessive human interaction devoid of caring, relatedness, and joy.

May asks the difficult question that arises from these observations: What are the motives that underlie such depersonalized, confused, and uncaring sexual preoccupations? He offers several answers. First, there is the motive of *trying to prove one's identity* based on a misguided egalitarianism of the sexes. "Egalitarianism is clung to at the price of denying not only biological differences—which are basic, to say the least—between men and women, but emotional differences from which come much of the delight of the sexual act" (May, 1969, p. 54). The motive that is troublesome here is the need for lovers to prove they are identical, a misguided effort that results in loss of personal identity and uniqueness.

Second, there is the need behind some sexual behavior to overcome isolation, loneliness, and feelings of emptiness: ". . . partners pant and quiver hoping to find an answering quiver in someone else's body just to prove that their own is not dead; they seek a responding, a longing in the other to prove their own feelings are alive" (May, 1969, p. 54).

Third, there is the need to prove oneself competent. Men, for example, may feel inferior or insecure if their "technique" is unpracticed or not in line with the "latest" advice of media experts. Sex therapists have developed all sorts of "cures" and remedies for sexual performance difficulties, some of which are truly more demeaning than the problem itself. Obsessive concern with performance ironically lessens sexual enjoyment. One man whom May cites as an example was concerned with "premature ejaculation" even though he frequently experienced periods of penetration of ten minutes or more before ejaculation. His physician prescribed an anesthetic ointment that would reduce penile sensitivity and prolong performance. May notes the absurdity here: Feel less, and perform better (1969, p. 55). The man was willing to give up personal pleasure in his striving to prove himself a competent male.

What is missing in all of these confused sexual motives, May argues, is true passion—a desire to "make love" to one's partner because there is healthy lust, mature caring, and satisfying communication between the two people. In May's terms, sex has been separated from *Eros*.

Eros and Death

We have learned to anesthetize feelings for better sexual performance, to use sex as a test of our competence, and to give up identity in the search for intimacy. May's thesis is stated rather boldly: "We fly to *the sensation of sex in order to avoid the passion of eros*" (1969, p. 65; italics in original). May argues that contemporary people have faith in the power of technological advances to free them from the anxiety of unwanted pregnancy and from venereal disease. But there are signs that this belief is false. The number of illegal abortions each year, the increasing rate of premarital pregnancies, and the decreasing age of the women with unwanted pregnancies seems to argue that the more birth control we develop, the more problematic pregnancies there are (May, 1969, p. 67).

May is persuaded that we must examine the unconscious motives that underlie the apparent contradictions between our actions and our beliefs:

We observe in many of these illegitimate pregnancies—or their equivalent—a defiance of the very socially ordered system which takes away affect, where technology is felt to be a substitute for feeling, a society which calls persons forth to an arid and meaningless existence and gives them, particularly the younger generation, an experience of depersonalization which is more painful than illegal abortion. (May, 1969, p. 71)

How then to understand? May points attention to the fact that in Greek mythology, Eros is not synonymous with eroticism. Eros was one of the four original gods: Chaos, Mother Earth (Gaea), and Tartarus (the pit of Hell). Eros is a progenitor, a creator, the source of life. According to the myths, Eros created life on earth. Sex, clearly, is not Eros, although Eros may incorporate sexuality. Eros is life, yearning, desire to transcend ourselves. Sex, for some people, is equivalent to orgasm, but Eros is union. Sex is satisfaction, whereas Eros is delight in the beloved.

But there is a dark side to love as well. To love another, one must open self to the possibilities of grief, sorrow, disappointment, and loss. To "fall" in love, one is swept away, one's reason is suspended in the service of Eros's passion. From the ontological perspective, May pits the positive delight of love against the possibility of nonbeing or death.

For death is always in the shadow of the delight of love. In faint adumbration, there is present the dread, haunting question, Will this new relationship destroy us? When we love, we give up the center of ourselves. We are thrown from our previous state of existence into a void; and though we hope to attain a new world, a new existence, we can never be sure. . . . This experience of annihilation is an inward one and, as the myth [of Eros] rightly puts it, is essentially what *eros* does to us. To love completely carries with it the threat of annihilation of everything. This intensity of consciousness has something in common with the ecstasy of the mystic in his union with God: just as he can never be *sure* God is there, so love carries us to that intensity of consciousness in which we no longer have any guarantee of security. (May, 1969, p. 101)

The relationship between death and love can take at least three forms, according to May. First, recognition of our own mortality heightens our appreciation of those things that give us pleasure. In a way, the being–nonbeing dialectic prevails here too, for love partakes in part of the mortal and immortal (May, 1969, p. 102).

Second, mythology and popular figures of speech ("I love you so much, I could die!") and patients' dreams and associations in psychotherapy provide a metaphorical connection between love and death. The experience of orgasm, May suggests, is possible only when one can "let go" completely or surrender one's being completely, as in death.

Third, there is a defensively disguised connection between love and death. It is possible, for example, to pursue obsessive concern with sex as a way of avoiding the fear of death. In a way, the person reenacts this potentially life-producing behavior to defy death. Or, along a different defensive pathway, the person may invest self so completely in sexual love that he or she can simply repress the fear of death because contemporary people have fewer defenses against the idea of death than they do against sexuality. We rarely speak about death openly, but we encourage free expression of sexuality. Sex is a way of "making ourselves infinite" in the face of our own mortality, the eventuality we fear most and speak of least (May, 1969, p. 106). In short, sex is a readily available way to silence fears of death at the same time that its procreative potential symbolically triumphs over death.

Philia: Brotherly Love and Friendship

Eros cannot long endure without *Philia*. The continued tension and passion of Eros cannot be tolerated forever. At some moment must come relaxation in the presence of the loved one. Philia is a kind of acceptance, in which the lover accepts, and enjoys, simply being with the beloved. May asserts that Philia is friendship or "brotherly love" in its most direct form. In a way, Philia provides Eros with time to grow stronger, sink deeper roots (May, 1969, p. 317). Recall the similar concept in the work of Harry Stack Sullivan of the "chum" relationships of adolescence. The chum is the developing person's first opportunity to care for someone as much as he or she cares for self. Sullivan believed that prior to the "chum period" (approximately ages 8 to 12), the child is not capable of "loving" in any genuine sense. Without the chum experience, Sullivan felt that heterosexual love relationships would be difficult to form (Sullivan, 1953b, pp. 223 ff.). In a way, Sullivan, and May, are pointing to the necessity for learning mutuality and cooperative interaction with peers as a sound basis for relationships later between the sexes. Out of the experience of "brotherly love" grows the possibilities of truly loving another.

In turn, as Philia supports Eros, Agapé supports Philia. Agapé, recall, is a kind of esteem for the other in which there is no intention of getting something from the other. It is a genuinely disinterested love for another, modeled on the biblical accounts of God's love for man (May, 1969, p. 319). The New Testament renders the concept of Agapé as *charity*, which may be a poor translation but portrays the *selfless* quality of Agapé. Philia, then, needs agapé to flourish, for the mutuality and acceptance embodied in Philia can flourish only when it is truly selfless. And, as we might expect, all three kinds of loving—Sex, Eros, and Philia—rest on a foundation of caring or Agapé.

GOOD AND EVIL

It is fairly clear that the range of May's ideas encompasses some of the most enduring and profound human motives considered by thinking people since the beginning of written history. Fear, anxiety, love, sex, death, being, and nothingness constitute just a partial list. It should also be apparent that May's existentialism is far from picturing humans as saints, and just as far from picturing them as sinners. May has consistently taken the position that humans are both good and evil, gentle and destructive, restrained and assertive. People participate in this dialectical seesaw between good and evil, being and nonbeing because of the *daimonic* element in human nature.

The Daimonic

Eros is a daimon. The word *daimon* is to be distinguished from the more typical word *demon,* and May has been at pains to make a clear distinction between the two (May, 1986b).

> The word can be spelled "demonic" (the popularized form), or "daemonic" (the medieval form often now used by the poets—Yeats, for example), or "daimonic" (the derivative from the ancient Greek word "daimon"). Since this last is the origin of the concept, and since the term is unambiguous in its including the positive as well

as the negative, the divine as well as the diabolical, I use the Greek term. (May, 1969, p. 123n.)

The daimonic in May's usage is "*any natural function which has the power to take over the whole person*" (1969, p. 123). It can be a creative "taking over," as in love-making, or it can be destructive, as in sexual compulsion. May is not using the term with any implication of some substantive thing or entity, such as a demon or devil. Rather, he uses it as a metaphor, a descriptive archetype of universal human experience, much as Jung used the archetypal terms *anima* and *animus*.

What is daimonic in people can be the best that they are capable of, such as poetry, art, dance, literature, and ethical and religious convictions. The daimonic can be contagious, as when a charismatic figure exhorts others to his or her cause. The daimonic in us can even lead to "ecstasy," as in the feeling of lovers for each other or the religious mystic's feeling of being swept away in the presence of the divine. But the daimonic can also be an expression of the worst in humans, the void of nothingness or nonbeing. The daimonic can assert itself in psychosis, or in a destructive cause led by a charismatic leader such as Adolf Hitler.

When the daimonic is repressed in us, it tends to erupt in some derivative form. May gives as examples episodes of assassination, torture, brutality, crime, and war. Violence is the daimonic unleashed without the balancing forces of reason and love. May rightly credits Freud with detailing the power of the daimonic gone mad in his description of the dark urges and fantasies of which we are all capable. As Freud, too, understood, the daimonic can be productive assertiveness, reaching out to create, to protect, and to expand. But when the daimonic takes over, the unity of the self is broken, a fact revealed frequently in psychotherapy when the patient says, "I felt like I had no control. I couldn't help myself" (May, 1969, p. 146 ff.).

WILL

If it is true that human nature is both good and evil, light and dark, positive and negative, then are we creatures of bipolar fate? Is it accurate to conclude that the daimonic is responsible for our actions, for our decisions? Are we the creatures of fate? Or do we intend our actions and therefore assume responsibility for the daimonic in ourselves? These are the questions that May raises, questions of the will.

Who Is Responsible?

May believes that Freud's greatest contribution was to peel away the illusion of Victorian "will power" to show that unconscious urges, drives, and wishes prompt much of our behavior. "Under his penetrating analysis, Victorian 'will' did, indeed, turn out to be a web of rationalizations and self-deceit" (May, 1969, p. 183).

But Freud's picture of humans as driven, rather than as drivers, undermined a more rational conception of human agency. Freud, and other intellectuals, fostered a tendency for people to view themselves as passive, pushed by forces for which they have little responsibility. The dilemma that arises from this self-picture is that will and responsibility are undermined. On the one hand, people sometimes believe that even if they make decisions, exert effort, their actions will inevitably be futile in the face of deterministic forces that they cannot control. On the other hand, our pride in our technology deludes us into believing that our machines can do anything for us—from massive nuclear destruction to extending the life span. The problem with this second belief is that it requires a passive acceptance of the technology. For example, as advances in medical technology proceed, the process of medical treatment becomes more impersonal, less in the hands of the patient, more removed from personal decisions.

Intentionality: The Subject-Object Bridge

May's proposed alternative to the deterministic conception of human action rests on his analysis of a way of knowing termed *intentionality.* Intentionality is not to be confused with "intention" because intentionality is the prerequisite for intending. Intentionality is a bridge between subject and object, between knower and known. Intentionality, therefore, is the person's application of meaning to objects and people in his or her world. It is a relationship to the things perceived which permits us to make decisions about them and to act on those decisions willfully:

> [Intentionality] . . . is the structure of meaning which makes it possible for us, subjects that we are, to see and understand the outside world, objective as it is. In intentionality, the dichotomy between subject and object is practically overcome. (May, 1969, p. 225)

May is arguing that we impose subjective meaning on the people and things we observe at the same time that those people and things elicit from us a perception of their objective meaning. He (May, 1969, p. 224) gives the example of examining a house to rent. If the house hunter approaches the search for a suitable house in which to spend the summer months, issues such as how much sun the house gets, how soundly it is built, and whether there are guest rooms for friends will be paramount in shaping the meaning of "house" as "shelter." But if the house hunter examines houses from the viewpoint of a real estate speculator, then issues such as can a rundown "house" be fixed cheaply and resold for more than its purchase price, and can the "house" be made attractive to a particular group of buyers transform the meaning of "house" into "profit." Or, finally, if our house hunter is an artist looking for an aesthetically pleasing arrangement of house, hillside, and trees, the meaning of "house" becomes "beauty." If it is the same house in each instance, and we can imagine that it is the same person each time with a different motive, we can readily see that both the "objective" house and the "subjective" house must interact in the person's decision.

Intentionality is a way of saying that we really cannot know a thing, nor make a decision about it, unless we in some way already participated in it. "I take this to mean that in the process of knowing, we are *in-formed* by the thing understood, and in the same act, our intellect simultaneously *gives form* to the thing we understand" (May, 1969, p. 225). Intentionality, from this viewpoint, is *epistemology,* a way of knowing. The act of knowing bridges the perceiver and the perceived, the knower and the known.

May argues that in psychotherapy, the therapist works to help the patient expand the sphere of his or her knowing. Working through resistances and defenses, the wishes of the unconscious can be consciously known. Or, put another way, the therapist aids the patient to *attend* to parts of self that formerly were not conscious. It is a matter of *attending to hidden intention,* for only when we know something can we reach decisions about it, act in relationship to it, and *will* freely our behavior toward or away from the thing known.

The psychoanalyst encourages the patient to go beyond conscious intention— which may be a desire to "forget" particular feelings and wishes—and attend to unconscious intention (wishing). Then, when the patient consciously *knows* what until then he or she only unconsciously *intended,* the patient can take responsibility for his or her actions rather than feeling passively driven by inner forces. Seen in this light, Freud's method of free association is a technique of penetrating conscious *intention* and giving over one's self to the realm of *intentionality* (May, 1969, p. 235). Intentionality is the basis, therefore, of both conscious and unconscious intention, but it is an ontological concept rooted in the person's very being, not merely in the person's momentary motivations.

Will and Intentionality: Envisioning the Future

Will and intentionality are linked. The connection between them is the fact that an intention and its resulting act are one and the same. It is only an artificial separation to assume that one first intends something and then does it. Rather, the act is in the intention, and the intention is in the act. The only difference is time. We are capable of projecting the future, as when we say, "I *will* go to England next week." One verb in that last sentence, *will,* is both the customary future tense first-person verb, and it is the same word for intentionality: *will.* The fact that the traveler projects an act for the future means that the act already exists in his or her projection of it. And, conversely, when the act is carried through—that is, the intention accomplished next week—it will embody the intention that preceded it a week before.[2]

May argues that in acts of intentionality and will a person experiences his or her identity as an existing person. Descartes' famous dictum, "I think, therefore I am," is wrong. Existence is posited on the capacity to imagine the future. According to May, "I conceive—I can—I will—I am" (May, 1969, p. 243). The depression of some patients in therapy can be usefully understood as an incapacity to imagine their own futures: The patient says "I can't," and the therapist's job is to help the patient see the possibility for "I can." For it is in the "I will" and the "I can" that we are most authentically ourselves, most fully aware of our own existence, and most completely conscious of our identities.

Love and Will United

Loving and willing are not opposites, according to May. They are related experiences because they both involve reaching out to someone or something and attempting to produce an effect. Love and will aim at influencing others.

---

[2] If you are confused at this point, do not be alarmed. Existentialism can sometimes give you an ontological headache. Take a pause, and return when your being and nonbeing are more in harmony. That is to say, continue reading whenever you intend. If you are reading this chapter immediately after reading the previous chapter on R. D. Laing, you will, no doubt, intend a longer rest.

> Both love and will are ways of molding, forming, relating to the world and trying to elicit a response from it through the persons whose interest or love we covet. Love and will are interpersonal experiences which bring to bear power to influence others significantly and to be influenced by them. (May, 1969, p. 276)

At birth, love and will are not united by biological growth. Our task as adults is to unite love and will consciously. For the well-loved infant, all is harmony. The infant's drives are satisfied by mother, its body cared for by mother, its every need met reliably. At first, the infant is one with the mother, but as development proceeds, the infant will eventually separate from mother. Mother will be seen as an object, internal need and wish will be sometimes frustrated, and the environment may make demands on the child that permit the child the first experiences of will. The child is no longer at one with its world. As any parent knows, children exert their will in opposition to love. They say "no" loudly and clearly in their actions and in their speech to a variety of parental demands. We think of these developments as the emergence of individuality and independence, but they are also reflections of the beginning of a clash between love and will.

If the developing child had no restraints on individuality, no "reality tutoring" in the satisfaction of its wishes, the child would grow into a self-centered, narcissistic, and selfish creature incapable of relating to others. Instead, the child learns by watching and by parental discipline to say "no" to self in a variety of tempting situations. Slowly, the developing person learns to reach out to others, giving as well as getting.

As adults, we need to learn, again, to reunite love and will. May sees the unity of love and will as an important developmental task, and when it is accomplished, the result is mature integration and harmony.

FREEDOM

If intentionality is the meaning by which we understand reality and bridge the subject-object dichotomy, then freedom is the capacity to make choices. The problem, of course, is the degree to which our choices are determined by factors other than our will. It is the essence of freedom to *change* or at least to have the *possibility of change*. To take one example, May asks what value we would place on a person's love if we knew that the person were forced to love us (1981, p. 6). Unless we are convinced that love is given freely, it loses much of its value as love. May distinguishes between two kinds of freedom: freedom of doing and freedom of being.

Freedom of Doing

Freedom of doing is defined by May as ". . . the capacity to pause in the face of stimuli, from many directions at once, and, in this pause, to throw one's weight toward this response rather than that one" [May, 1981, p. 54]. It is the kind of freedom we experience in everyday activities when we make the myriad choices and decisions that constitute a day's activities. When we select one product rather than another from the supermarket's shelves, or when we watch one TV program rather than another, we are experiencing freedom of doing. One of the most interesting examples of freedom of doing is our ability to ask questions. The fact that questions occur to us implies that the question has more than one answer, or there would be no point in asking the question.

Freedom of Being

May distinguishes *freedom of being* as a second category of freedom that may also be called "essential freedom." Freedom of being is the origin of freedom of doing and goes to a deeper level of human existence. Instead of focusing on the act, or on the process of decision, freedom of being is concerned with the context of acts and the ability to choose one's attitude toward events whether one acts or not (May, 1981, p. 55).

May offers as an example the accounts of psychoanalyst Bruno Bettelheim, who was imprisoned in a Nazi concentration camp during World War II. Bettelheim had no freedom of action whatsoever, but he could choose his attitude toward his captors. Bettelheim could reflect, ponder, and ask spoken or unspoken questions about the situation and the people who controlled his daily life. Thus freedom of being is an inner, spiritual freedom that may or may not be reflected by external behavior.

DESTINY

Cooperating With Destiny

May resolves the conflict between determinism and freedom by conceptualizing these apparent opposites as dialectical:

> *Freedom and determinism give birth to each other. Every advance in freedom gives birth to a new determinism, and every advance in determinism gives birth to a new freedom.* Freedom is a circle within a larger circle of determinism, which is, in turn, surrounded by a larger circle of freedom. And so on *ad infinitum.* (May, 1981, p. 84; italics in original)

May is saying that freedom and determinism need each other, for one cannot be free from determinism unless determinism is possible; and one cannot be determined unless it is possible to remove a person's freedom (1981, p. 95). May, therefore, acknowledges the possibility of determinism, but he prefers to use the more humanly relevant term "destiny" to describe the limits of freedom. Billiard balls struck by other billiard balls are "determined" in the flight across the table. But humans are limited by their "destinies."

May defines *destiny* as the "pattern of limits and talents that constitutes the 'givens' in life" (1981, p. 89). May believes that it is our confrontation with these limits, with these "givens," from which our creativity and freedom emerge.

Forms Destiny Takes

Destiny has many levels, and each of the levels differs in the degree to which it yields to human intervention. May distinguishes four levels:

1. *Cosmic Destiny,* which is termed, sometimes, "an act of God." Included here are birth, death, earthquakes, volcanoes, and other relatively unpredictable natural events that affect our lives but about which we can do nothing. The concept of "fate" belongs in the category of cosmic destiny, as well as the notion of determinism.

2. *Genetic Destiny,* which governs the physical traits with which we are born, including the color of our eyes or skin and the gender of a person. Genetics may also play a role, in part, in the special "talents" we have for art, music, mathematics, and so on. We can enhance or cooperate with our genetic givens to a degree, but there is little we can do to change what we inherit.

3. *Cultural Destiny,* which includes the family and society into which we are born. We do not get to choose these "givens," although we may influence their effects greatly.

4. *Circumstantial Destiny,* which includes human-made events over which we individually have no control, such as the rise and fall of the stock market, or the attack upon Pearl Harbor. Once these events occur, there is no way to "undo" them, nor ignore them, nor avoid them.

Figure 11.2 summarizes the spectrum of limitations that May envisions as forms of destiny. As you move across the spectrum in Figure 11.2 from left to right, the degree of human control or choice increases.

May points out that there are at least five ways that a person can relate to his or her destiny.

1. *Cooperate with destiny* and accept that one's life is shaped by it.
2. *Acknowledge destiny* in our limitations, such as size, weight, and death.
3. *Engage destiny* by actively seeking out the challenge of our limitations and trying to transcend them.
4. *Confront and challenge destiny* by attempting to see the most productive path that destiny provides and trying to overcome the destructive directions destiny tries to enforce.
5. *Rebel against destiny* by refusing to accept it or cooperate with it. We can, for example, rage against death, as in Dylan Thomas's famous poem. ("Do not go

FIGURE 11.2   Degrees of human intervention in destiny.

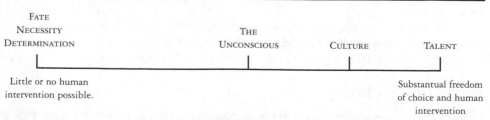

The Dimension of Destiny

Drawn from a description in May (1981), p. 91.

gentle into that *good* night.") It is not clear, however, what such "rebelling" can do to affect destiny.

May points out that if there were no limitations on our existence, no death, no illness, we would never develop freedom (1981, p. 95).

EVALUATING ROLLO MAY

The breadth of May's "theory" is astounding, for it encompasses most of the major philosophical questions and ideas of the last two thousand years of human thought. May's existentialism borrows heavily from psychoanalysis, ego psychology, philosophy, and theology, but the result is not a *theory* of personality in any commonly accepted meaning of the term "theory." May wastes no time on "small potatoes." His concepts are grand, philosophical, sometimes ambiguous, sometimes paradoxical, and always intriguing.

Refutability of May's Analytic Existentialism

Almost by definition, the existentialist would find the concept of scientific refutability inappropriate, if not irrelevant, to the task of existential thinking. However, because May has attempted to synthesize psychoanalytic ideas into his existential account, there are some questions about refutability that pose themselves.

In May's earliest work on anxiety, the definitions he provides of normal and neurotic anxiety, and the hypotheses drawn loosely from psychoanalytic theory, surely lend themselves to empirical test. In fact, May's own doctoral dissertation, a part of which found its way into May's 1950 book on anxiety, was just such an attempt. But then there is the rest of May's work. What scientific psychological sense can we make of concepts such as "ontological principles," "nonbeing," and "will?" Because these terms and their associated ideas deal with unobservables, and with processes that do not have measurable empirical referents in action or thought, they remain outside the scope of refutability altogether. We are not even certain that the concept of refutability is the right question to ask about concepts such as these.

But even in this thicket of metaphysics there lurk some ideas that have a possibility of translation into refutable statements. *Destiny,* as conceived by May, may not of itself be a refutable concept, but what about the person's conception of destiny? Using May's hypothetical dimension of destiny, as illustrated in Figure 11.2, could we not devise a measure of people's reactions to the limitations that life hands them? Could we not develop a way of measuring the subjective reaction to destinies, such as the chance events of earthquakes, and the social constraints of other people's reactions to our handicaps and infirmities? In a way, the social learning theorists have begun to consider the power of destiny in shaping our perceptions of our lives, but Bandura (1986, 1989) avoids the term destiny in favor of the term "chance" or "fortuitous events."

On the whole, May's analytic existentialism is a composite of largely nontestable ideas, with small pockets of potentially empirical constructs that would probably not engage most scientifically minded researchers.

May's Conception of Human Agency

It is clear from May's ideas on will, intentionality, destiny, and helplessness that he regards the person as capable of both active and passive agency. In fact, a main theme running through European existentialism is the significance of the split in human consciousness between active and passive experiencing of self.

However, May's philosophical argument puts the body of his work on the side of an active agency conception of the person. May argues forcibly, recall, for intentionality as a bridge between subject and object from which active willing emerges. It seems to be May's view that psychopathology (alienation, apathy, despair, and violence) are the result of blocking the person's freedom. Mature personality integration is possible, therefore, in May's estimation, only when the person is free to exercise will in decision and in action.

The Idiographic Nature of Existentialism

Like so many things about existentialism, May's focus is a composite of particular and general, of specific and universal. Existentialism, at its most abstract, deals with universals: existence, being, nonbeing, destiny, freedom, and so on. But the existentialist places the highest value on understanding the *individual's* unique embodiment of these universals. In fact, May's particular version of the existential position emphasizes individual meanings, individual perceptions, and centeredness in the individual self.

May also borrows much from psychoanalysis, itself a highly idiographic account of people. Because such a large portion of May's work has centered on the clinical issues of treatment for psychological disorder, we would expect his focus to be idiographic rather than nomothetic. And because so much of the theory is couched in untestable terms, the usual relationship between degree of idiography and testability prevails: The more idiographic a theory is, the less likely will it generate empirical referents to permit its concepts to be tested in the laboratory.

SUMMARY

Rollo May attempts to blend the more clinical and experience-near ideas of psycho-analysis with the philosophical issues raised by the European existentialists. His earliest efforts involved introducing existential theory into American psychology.

The existential position focus on ontological issues, that is, issues involving the conceptions of *being* and *being in the world*. Every person is conceptualized as an *existing person* to emphasize the ongoing, continuously becoming aspects of human personality. The classical existentialists distinguish among three modes of being:

- *Umwelt,* or the "world around," meaning the natural world of biological urge and drive;
- *Mitwelt,* or the "with world," meaning the social, interactive, interpersonal aspects of existence;
- *Eigenwelt,* or the "own world," meaning the subjective, phenomenal world of the self.

May adapts some of the ideas of existentialism to propose six ontological principles, discussed in the context of the case of Mrs. Hutchens:

1. Every person is centered in self and lives life through the meaning he or she places on that center.
2. Every person is responsible for mobilizing the courage to protect the self, to affirm it, and to enhance its continued existence.
3. People need other people with whom they can empathize and from whom they can learn.
4. People are vigilant about potential dangers to their identities.
5. People can be aware of themselves thinking and feeling at one moment and may be aware of themselves as the person who thinks and feels in the next moment.
6. Anxiety originates, in part, out of a person's awareness that one's being can end.

May defined anxiety as the active confrontation with nonbeing. Only the human person, he points out, is capable of envisioning a time when he or she will not be. And the realization of one's own mortality is a powerful determinant of our behavior. Within this conception of anxiety as a confrontation with one's own death, May distinguishes between normal and neurotic anxiety. Normal anxiety is proportionate to the cause, does not involve repressed elements, and can be removed by removing the threat. By contrast, neurotic anxiety is disproportionate to the threat, involves various unconscious defense mechanisms, and is responsible for blocking personality growth. Both kinds of anxiety reflect a basic conflict: being versus nonbeing.

When a person yields to anxiety and refuses to make choices or retreats from living, the result is feelings of helplessness, despair, and ontological guilt. Ontological guilt parallels the three kinds of being in the world, so that we can feel ontological guilt in a separation from the natural world (*Umwelt*), or experience guilt as alienation from self (*Eigenwelt*), or be aware of ontological guilt as alienation from others (*Mitwelt*).

We traced the personal sources of May's interest in existentialism in terms of his early discordant family life and subsequent sensitivity to loneliness, his personal confrontation with death as a tuberculosis patient, and his personal desire to struggle against feelings of helplessness and despair at all costs.

May dealt with the theme of apathy in his discussion of love and will. He distinguishes among four kinds of loving:

1. *Agapé or Caritas or Care:* the love devoted to the welfare of others, the prototype for which is the love of God for man. It is the foundation for all of the other forms.
2. *Sex* or lust or what Freud called libido.
3. *Eros,* the drive to procreate.
4. *Philia,* or brotherly love and friendship.

He argues that modern society has trivialized sexuality, separated it from passion, undermined the human motivation for procreation contained in Eros, and forced people into uncaring and indifferent attitudes toward each other.

The issues of good and evil have occupied May at some length. He has argued that human nature is a composite of both good and evil, and he writes metaphorically about this composite in his conception of the *daimonic,* which is defined as any natural human function which can reach such intensity that the person is overcome by it. On the positive side, the daimonic is the force underlying creativity and self-affirmation. On the negative side, the daimonic can be destructive addiction to power or fascination with death.

May has addressed the issues of freedom, responsibility, and determinism with his conception of destiny. In his view, destiny is a kind of dimension ranging from cosmic acts that affect us but over which we have no control to the inheritance of talents and handicaps, about which we may exert some choice. He argues that ultimately people are free in being, if not in action, because they can choose the meaning they will place on what reality provides. Intentionality, to be distinguished from intention, is a kind of subjective bridge between the passive and the active, between the subject and object in existence. Reality may provide its own input into our lives, but we make much of the reality that we interpret.

Our evaluation of May indicates that his blend of existentialism and psychoanalysis avoids "small potatoes" issues and focuses on broad, philosophical questions. As such, May's theory is largely, but not completely, untestable, strongly pushed toward the idiographic end of the idiographic-nomothetic spectrum, and it conceptualizes people as largely active agents with the freedom to choose how they will permit fate or destiny to affect them.

FOR FURTHER READING

The clearest overview of existentialism in psychology that May provides is to be found in an anthology he co-edited entitled *Existence: A New Dimension in Psychiatry and*

Psychology (R. May, E. Angel, & H. F. Ellenberger [Eds.], New York: Basic Books, 1958). A more recent presentation of much of the same theoretical material may be found in May's *The Discovery of Being: Writings in Existential Psychology* (New York: Norton, 1983). To round out the historical and philosophical picture, William Barrett's classic *Irrational Man: A Study in Existential Philosophy* (New York: Doubleday Anchor, 1962) remains a scholarly and readable approach. Existential psychiatrist Medard Boss's *Existential Foundations of Medicine and Psychology* (New York: Jason Aronson, 1994) is another comprehensive existential theory informed by psychoanalysis. Boss's discussion of the psychological issues surrounding perception of one's own mortality is especially clear and engaging.

May's earliest theoretical writing on anxiety gives some indication of the development of his thinking—see *The Meaning of Anxiety* (New York: Washington Square, 1950, updated 1972). For comparison purposes, you might want to consult May's later writings, which expand upon many of the fundamental issues with which he began. A good starting place is May's *Love and Will* (New York: Norton, 1969).

Glimpses into May's personal history can be most efficiently accomplished, until a definitive biography is written, by examining May's *My Quest for Beauty* (Dallas: Saybrook, 1985). This book also includes a sample of May's paintings and drawings, which are well worth more than a casual glance.

For comparative purposes you may also want to consult our Chapter 10, R. D. Laing, for comparative reading in the work of a different existential-analytic theorist. Along these same lines, Viktor E. Frankl's *The Unheard Cry for Meaning: Psychotherapy and Humanism* (New York: Simon & Schuster, 1978) gives a concise overview of yet another way to interpret existential philosophy in personality psychology. Finally, our Chapter 14, Gordon Allport, provides yet another view of a humanistic personality theory that shares much with existentialism.

CHAPTER 12

GEORGE A. KELLY
Personal Construct Theory

Each time one man reveals himself in privacy to another, a secret society springs into being.

Sidney M. Jourard, *The Transparent Self*

On Wednesday, when the sky is blue,
And I have nothing else to do,
I sometimes wonder if it's true
That who is what and what is who.

A. A. Milne, "Winnie-the-Pooh"

About Kelly's Personal Construct Theory

For Kelly, humans are thinking creatures who try to anticipate their own and others' actions on the basis of experience. Kelly has worked out in a very organized fashion the "rules" by which people create their own personalities and by which they judge the personalities of the people in their lives. These main concepts are central to Kelly's work:

1. *People need to predict accurately how other people will behave and how life will generally proceed.*

2. *Such personal predictions are made continuously and revised continuously as experience fulfills expectation or disconfirms it.*

3. *Traditional personality concepts such as anxiety, guilt, and defense have to be newly understood as consequences of prediction failures.*

WHEN WHAT IS WHO

When George A. Kelly turned his hand to theorizing about human nature, he abandoned time-honored concepts like motivation, drive, the unconscious, emotion, and reinforcement. Instead, Kelly saw each individual to be like himself, a unique theorist of human nature. All persons are personality scientists who devise and test predictions about the behavior of significant people in their lives. In Kelly's view, each of us constructs anticipations of others' behavior on a what-for-who basis: What makes some whos similar, and what makes them different? Consequently, individuals who came to Kelly for counseling would be asked to make explicit their private personality theories. They would complete one or more versions of Kelly's *Role Construct Repertory Test (REP)* to provide some indication of how they construed important people in their lives. You are invited to participate.

REP TEST PART A: ROLE TITLE LIST

Instructions

Write the name of the persons indicated in the blanks provided. Do not repeat names. If any role appears to call for a duplicate name, substitute the name of another person whom the second role title suggests to you (based on Kelly, 1955).

1. Your mother or the person who has
   played the part of mother in your life.

1._____

2. Your father or the person who has played the part of a father in your life.

    2._____

3. Your brother nearest your age. If you have no brother, the person who is most like one.

    3._____

4. Your sister nearest your age. If you have no sister, the person who is most like one.

    4._____

5. A teacher you liked or the teacher of a subject you liked.

    5._____

6. A teacher you disliked or the teacher of a subject you disliked.

    6._____

7. Your closest girl (boy) friend immediately before you started going with your wife (husband) or present closest girl (boy) friend [Ex-Flame].

    7._____

8. Your wife (husband) or closest present girl (boy) friend.

    8._____

9. An employer, supervisor, or officer under whom you served during a period of great stress [Boss].

    9._____

10. A person with whom you have been closely associated who, for some unexplainable reason, appears to dislike you [Rejecting Person].

    10._____

11. The person whom you have met within the past six months whom you would most like to know better [Sought Person].

    11._____

12. The person whom you would most like to be of help to, or the one whom you feel most sorry for [Pitied Person].

    12._____

13. The most intelligent person whom you know personally.

    13._____

14. The most successful person whom you know personally.

    14._____

15. The most interesting person whom you know personally.

    15._____

REP TEST PART B: CONSTRUCT SORTS

Instructions

The sets of three numbers in the following sorts refer to the numbers 1 to 15, inclusive, in Part A.

In each of the following sorts three numbers are listed. Look at your Part A sheet and consider the three people whom you have listed for these three numbers.

In what important way are two of these three people alike and at the same time, essentially different from the third?

After you have decided what the important way is, write it in the blank opposite the sort marked CONSTRUCT.

Next encircle the numbers corresponding to the two people who are alike.

Write down what you believe to be the opposite of the construct in the blank marked CONTRAST.

NUMBERS		CONSTRUCT	CONTRAST
Sort	Part A	(EMERGENT)	(IMPLICIT)
1.	9,11,14	_____	_____
2.	10,12,13	_____	_____
3.	2,5,12	_____	_____
4.	1,4,8	_____	_____
5.	7,8,12	_____	_____
6.	3,13,6	_____	_____
7.	1,2,9	_____	_____
8.	3,4,10	_____	_____
9.	6,7,10	_____	_____
10.	5,11,14	_____	_____
11.	1,7,8	_____	_____
12.	2,7,8	_____	_____
13.	3,6,9	_____	_____
14.	4,5,10	_____	_____
15.	11,13,14	_____	_____

When all of the construct and contrast blanks are filled, the Role Construct Repertory Test is completed. The form of the test that appears here is a slightly modified and shortened version of an early form of the Group REP Test. Number combinations making up the 15 sorts are, for practical purposes, virtually unlimited. In fact, subjects could be asked to repeat their constructs and contrast evaluations with a new set of sorts, depending on the judgment of the administering psychologist.

The ways in which psychologists can choose to analyze the subject's sorts are also virtually unlimited. Generally, however, they either embark on an informal *impressionistic* analysis, guided by the give-and-take of the clinical situation in which the subjects have provided comments and answered questions about their constructs and contrasts, or they analyze the themes revealed in the construct and contrast columns more *objectively* by tabulating the frequency with which key phrases are repeated, and the relations among the descriptions assigned to various crucial figure-combinations like Mother–Father, Teacher–Boss, Husband–Ex-Flame.

TABLE 12.1   Mildred Beal's Constructs

Sort Number	Similar Figures	Similarity Construct	Dissimilar Figures	Contrasting Construct
2	Rejecting Person (10) Pitied Person (12)	Very unhappy persons	Intelligent Person (13)	Contented
3	Father (2) Liked Teacher (5)	Very quiet and easygoing	Pitied Person (12)	Nervous, hypertensive
4	Mother (1) Sister (4)	Look alike Both hypercritical of people in general	Boyfriend (8)	Friendliness
11	Mother (1) Ex-Flame (7)	Socially maladjusted	Boyfriend (8)	Easygoing, self-confident
13	Disliked Teacher (6) Boss (9)	Emotionally unpredictable	Brother (3)	Even temperament

A sample REP protocol of a subject identified by Kelly as "Mildred Beal" appears in Table 12.1. Only five of her sorts need be reproduced for the sake of illustration (after Kelly, 1955, pp. 242 ff.).

A number of interesting personal meanings stand out from Mildred Beal's partial protocol. For example, in sorts numbers 3 and 11, the description "easygoing" is applied by Mildred to Father, Liked Teacher, and Boyfriend. In sorts numbers 4 and 11, Mother is described as "hypercritical of other people" and as "socially maladjusted." It is clear that Mildred construes her sister as different from her father and boyfriend in the same way that her mother is. Impressionistic analyses like these yield important insights about the way Mildred construes the people in her world, and the relationships of the various figures in Mildred's estimation.

GRID FORM OF THE REP: THE PERSON'S OWN PERSONALITY THEORY

Mildred's responses to the role constructs of the REP test may also be analyzed with the tools of mathematics. Factor analysis and its more lowly cousin, the correlation coefficient, can be applied to a grid form of the test. In this version, the subject is asked to make the sorts several times, applying each of his or her constructs developed in response to particular pairs of figures successively to all 15 roles. (Actually, the full form of the REP test may include 22 figures, of which the *Self* is one; it has been shortened in this presentation for the sake of simplicity.)

The first time around, the subject is presented with the standard sort-combinations in the form of a 15″ × 15″ grid, as illustrated in Figure 12.1. He or she is

FIGURE 12.1   A grid analysis of Mildred Beal's role construct repertory test.

SORT NUMBER	ROLE FIGURES	EMERGENT POLE (Two as Similar)	IMPLICIT POLE (One as Different)
1	9, 11, 14	Are related to me	Unrelated
2	10, 12, 13	Very unhappy persons	Contented
3	2, 5, 12	Quiet and easygoing	Nervous, hypersensitive
4	1, 4, 8	Look alike, hypercritical	Friendliness
5	7, 8, 12	Feel inferior	Self-confident
6	3, 13, 6	Socially better than adequate	Unpleasant
7	1, 2, 9	Hypersensitive	Easygoing
8	3, 4, 10	Hypercritical	Understanding
9	6, 7, 10	Feelings of inferiority	Assured of innate worth
10	5, 11, 14	Pleasing personalities	High-powered, nervous
11	1, 7, 8	Socially maladjusted	Easygoing, self-confident
12	2, 7, 8	Relaxing	Uncomfortable to be with
13	3, 6, 9	Emotionally unpredictable	Even temperament
14	4, 5, 10	Look somewhat alike	Look unlike
15	11, 13, 14	Dynamic personalities	Weak personality

Role figures (grid columns): 1 Mother, 2 Father, 3 Brother, 4 Sister, 5 Liked Teacher, 6 Disliked Teacher, 7 Ex-Flame, 8 Boyfriend (Wife/Husband), 9 Employer, 10 Rejecting Person, 11 Sought Person, 12 Pitied Person, 13 Intelligent Person, 14 Successful Person, 15 Interesting Person.

Constructed after Kelly (1955), pp. 242 ff.

instructed to indicate which two of the figures in the first sort (9, 11, 14) are similar by placing an "X" in the appropriate circles of the grid. The circles are placed in each line only in the boxes corresponding to the three figures the subject is asked to compare. Thus, for example, in Figure 12.1, Mildred has placed an "X" in the circles of numbers 9 and 14, Employer and Successful Person, indicating that she construes these two as similar (Emergent Pole). She has left number 11 unfilled, indicating that Sought Person is, in her view, different from the other two. On the first line of the emergent pole column, she then writes in her own words the way in which 9 and 14 are similar. Likewise, in the implicit pole column, she writes her ideas of what makes figure 11, Sought Person, different. Reading from Figure 12.1, Mildred regards Employer and Successful Person as similar because they are "related to me." Sought Person is different by being "unrelated."

The second time, after Mildred has completed all 15 sorts and listed her constructs, she is asked to make systematic comparisons of her 15 similar and different constructs to all of the remaining figures on each line. Mildred is thus instructed to start again with the constructs she listed for sort number one, namely, "related to me" versus "unrelated," and systematically consider this dichotomous construct in relation to the 12 remaining figures on line one. For each figure to which the construct of Sort 1 applies, Mildred is asked to place a check mark in that figure's box on the Sort 1 line.

Mildred proceeds down the remaining 14 constructs, repeating her search for applicable figures for each of the constructs on that line. For the sake of simplicity, Sort 11 has been abstracted from the total grid and enlarged in Figure 12.2. The first time that Mildred sorted the figures of line 11, she chose Mother and Ex-Flame as similar by placing an "X" in the circles for those roles. Now Mildred is asked to take the remaining 12 roles and to indicate whether her construct "Socially maladjusted" versus "Easygoing, self-confident" applies to any of them. For the sake of illustration, figures 4, 6, 9, 10, and 11 have been checked to indicate that Mildred feels the similarity construct "Socially maladjusted" applies to them. Those she has left blank indicate that the similarity (emergent pole) construct cannot be used to describe them.

The resulting grid pattern of checks and "Xs" may be converted to a series of numbered coordinates without reference to Mildred's verbal labels. All that matters is the *pattern* of expressed similarity and difference indicated by the check marks, not the verbal labels that led Mildred to assign these marks. The procedures employed in mathematically analyzing the data are very complex and need not concern us here.

The grid or matrix of Mildred's REP test represents her own unique personality theory, the system of personal constructs or interpretations by which she conducts her life. Reading *across* Mildred's grid we can answer questions about the *figures* she construes as similar on a particular dimension of her theory. Reading *down* the columns, we can ask questions about *how* Mildred construes each person on a whole series of *dimensions*. To illustrate, consider what is learned about the way Mildred construes the world when columns 1 (Mother) and 12 (Pitied Person) are read *downward* together, as shown in Table 12.2.

In a way, Kelly's approach is similar to Laing's (cf. Chapter 10), in that both of these theorists are interested in the ways that subjects interpret their own world and the significant people in it. Where Laing employs the terms "direct, meta-, and meta-metaperspectives," Kelly prefers the term *construct*. There are some important

FIGURE 12.2   **A single construct from Mildred Beal's grid REP analysis.**

Mother	1	⊗
Father	2	
Brother	3	
Sister	4	✓
Liked Teacher	5	
Disliked Teacher	6	✓
Ex-Flame	7	⊗
Boyfriend (Wife/Husband)	8	○
Employer	9	✓
Rejecting Person	10	✓
Sought Person	11	
Pitied Person	12	✓
Intelligent Person	13	
Successful Person	14	
Interesting Person	15	

SORT NUMBER	ROLE FIGURES	EMERGENT POLE (Two as Similar)	IMPLICIT POLE (One as Different)
11	1, 7, 8	Socially maladjusted	Easygoing, self-confident

TABLE 12.2   Constructs Compared

(1) Mother	(12) Pitied Person
(1) Are related to me	(1)
(2) Very unhappy person	(2) Very unhappy person
(5) Feels inferior	(5) Feels inferior
(7) Hypersensitive	(7) Hypersensitive
(8) Hypercritical	(8)
(9) Feelings of inferiority	(9) Feelings of inferiority
(11) Socially maladjusted	(11) Socially maladjusted
(13) Emotionally unpredictable	(13)
(14) Looks like sister and rejecting person	(14) Looks like sister and rejecting person

differences between Kelly and Laing, but one clear similarity emerges: Both Kelly and Laing are primarily interested in the way individuals *experience* their world through the meanings that *they* attach to others' behavior. In fact, both Laing and Kelly focus their attention on the way individuals *anticipate* the feelings and behavior of significant others. Where Laing assesses individuals' metaperspective (how each thinks the other thinks), Kelly evaluates individuals' anticipations of important people's roles.

"THE HUMAN SCIENTIST": THE FUNDAMENTAL POSTULATE

Tongue-in-cheek, Kelly caricatured the traditional attitude of most psychologists: " 'I, being a *psychologist,* and therefore a *scientist,* am performing this experiment in order to improve the prediction and control of certain human phenomena; but my subject, being merely a human organism, is obviously propelled by inexorable drives welling up within him, or else he is in gluttonous pursuit of sustenance and shelter' " (1955, p. 5).[1]

Psychologists' *professional* pursuit of the sometimes elusive goals of prediction and control tend to dominate their habitual mode of being with others. But of course, in their view, those others never themselves create or test hypotheses about psychologists or about the behavior of other people with whom they have contact. In consequence, psychologists easily succumb to the fallacy of believing that *their* theoretical constructs are real *things* with objective existence in the people they observe. These mere mortals are likely to surprise them when their behavior suggests that they too seek understanding—about themselves, about their psychologists, about people in general (Kelly, 1955, p. 5; 1958a, p. 87).

---

[1] Kelly wrote his theory at a time when our current conventions of language and our attention to gender differences did not prevail. In the interests of scholarly accuracy, Kelly's own words have been left unedited with respect to the use of the male pronoun and nouns such as "man."

Out of preconceptions like these, countless theoretical constructs have been created to predict and to control human behavior, only to be discarded when the human scientist got a real look at human beings. Kelly suggested that psychologists would do better to take the long-range view of human beings by adopting a perspective of centuries to chart the influences that shape the direction of the species' progress. Such a broadened perspective, Kelly predicted, would reveal that questions of appetite, tissue needs, and sex impulses were largely secondary to a more fundamental human characteristic: *The human need to know and to control one's own universe.*

> Might not the individual man, each in his own personal way, assume more of the stature of a scientist, ever seeking to predict and control the course of events with which he is involved? Would he not have his theories, test his hypotheses, and weigh his experimental evidence? (Kelly, 1955, p. 5)

A return look at Mildred Beal's REP protocol easily demonstrates the truth of Kelly's hypothesis that all of us behave *as if* we were scientists. Mildred has created explanatory hypotheses about her mother and father and the rest of the significant figures in her life. She presumably can predict their behavior on the basis of her past experiences with them; she can even discern similarities and differences among subgroups of these important people. In short, she has made sense of her world by attempting to *anticipate* the behavior of the people in it.

Kelly divorced himself from the view of humans as *reactive beings,* perpetually provoked by their environment to mere survival behaviors. For Kelly, humans are *creative* creatures with the capacity to abstract meaning from their environment and to impose their own representations on it (1958b). Because they can create their own interpretations of what they experience, humans are not restricted to inexorable reactions—unless they *choose* to interpret their lives that way. Furthermore, their being is not restricted to one-time interpretations; they are endlessly free to change their minds, to place *alternative constructions* on their experience when it is different from expectation. Thus all persons share with the scientist an enduring need to practice their skills as predictors and hypothesis testers.

Kelly described his position on humans' freedom to create alternative explanations of their world as *constructive alternativism* (1955, p. 15):

> We take the stand that there are always some alternative constructions available to choose among in dealing with the world. No one needs to paint himself into a corner; no one needs to be completely hemmed in by circumstances; no one needs to be the victim of his biography.

The central notions, then, in Kelly's approach to understanding human nature involve a belief in people's *active striving to understand,* their *creativity* in construing events of importance, and their *freedom* limitlessly to revise their "theories" about their world: *"A person lives his life by reaching out for what comes next and the only channels he has for reaching are the personal constructions he is able to place upon what may actually be happening"* (1955, p. 228).

It is not surprising, therefore, that the fundamental postulate by which Kelly described his theoretical position on human nature is couched in the language of the scientist's attempts to predict and control:

FUNDAMENTAL POSTULATE: *A person's processes are psychologically channel-ized by the ways in which he anticipates events* (1955, p. 46).

Kelly did not seem to be completely comfortable with the label "phenomenological" for his theory (1955, p. 517). Nevertheless, his emphasis clearly demonstrates a concern with immediate experience and the individual's interpretation of it. The key word in the fundamental postulate is "anticipates," because it is the person's need for reliable knowledge that Kelly sees as the distinguishing feature of human existence. Were it not for this urge to "anticipate," Kelly's theory would be virtually devoid of motivational concepts (cf. Sechrest, 1963, p. 212).

SOURCES OF KELLY'S CONCEPTION OF HUMAN NATURE

Toward the end of his life, Kelly traced, as well as the deceits of memory permitted, the possible origin of his ideas about the human scientist. Kelly recounted his first exposure to psychology as a graduate student in a lecture class and the mounting disappointment that he experienced with classical psychology. One day the professor wrote on the blackboard an "S" with an arrow pointing to an "R." Anticipating that after several weeks of dull course work, the crux of psychology's explanation of humans was about to be discussed, Kelly listened attentively: ". . . [T]he most I could make of it was that the 'S' was what you have to have in order to account for the 'R' and the 'R' was put there so the 'S' would have something to account for. I never did find out what the arrow stood for—not to this day—and I have pretty well given up trying to figure it out" (Kelly, 1963, pp. 46–47).

So much for stimulus-response psychology. Kelly graduated from the University of Iowa in 1931 with a doctor of philosophy degree, and he ran headlong into the Great Depression. He spent 12 years at a small college in western Kansas, the "dust bowl" region, and soon discovered that his professional training in academic physiological psychology and speech pathology was useless in helping the young people who did not know what to do with their lives during the hard times. At first, he returned to Freudian theory, having once dismissed it as preposterous in his student days, and now found that Freud had skillfully described the same pain and despair that he was discovering in his informal attempts to counsel students. "Through my Freudian interpretations, judiciously offered at those moments when clients seemed ready for them, a good many unfortunate persons seemed to be profoundly helped" (Kelly, 1963, p. 51).

Although Kelly experienced no out-and-out failures with his new Freudian orientation, something gnawed at him, the kind of unscratchable itch that sometimes precedes discovery of the obvious. Consequently, despite his apparent success with Freud's "language of distress," he continued to grow uneasy: "It was that I was beginning to take them [Freudian concepts] for granted" (1963, p. 52). In short, Kelly found his Freudian "insights" too certain, too pat, too prescriptive, and too boring.

In the depression climate of the 1930s, Kelly's informal Freudian psychological counseling was regarded by the local Kansans as "pretty far out." His Freudianisms may have seemed strange, but they worked most of the time because Kelly's clients' unsophisticated acceptance of them, their anticipation that to be effective such interpretations had to be bizarre, guaranteed success. Thus there was precious little in his patients' ready acceptance of his seemingly authoritative interpretations to pose challenge, scant few problems to provoke questions. In consequence, Kelly tried an informal experiment:

> . . . I began fabricating "insights." I deliberately offered "preposterous interpretations" to my clients. Some of them were about as un-Freudian as I could make them—first proposed somewhat cautiously, of course, and then, as I began to see what was happening, more boldly. My only criteria were that the explanation *account for the crucial facts as the client saw them,* and that it *carry implications for approaching the future in a different way.* (1963, p. 52; italics added)

Kelly might tell a client, for example, that his or her nervous stomach was "rebelling against nourishment of all kinds—parental, educational, and nutritional." Surprisingly, his clients felt that the interpretations were worth a try, and they often successfully changed the direction of their lives by adopting the new outlook implied in Kelly's "preposterous" suggestions. In Kelly's terms, they had developed alternative constructions about themselves.

Additional evidence began to mount for Kelly's slowly developing view that patients could change their own lives if somehow they would make the deliberate attempt to see things differently. When, for instance, more clients than he could handle applied to him for treatment, he started the practice of spending just a little time with these people to give them a few hints about what to do in the period while waiting their turn. Months later, when their turn came, Kelly often found that without formal therapy they had solved or were well on the way to resolving the difficulty for which they had initially come to see him. His few "hints" about how to proceed while waiting were sufficient to muster the patients' own creative resources in restructuring their perspective of the problems. These patients had not been "cured" in the interval, but now they viewed the problem as more manageable.

Kelly therefore began to formulate a new clinical perspective of his own. ". . . I began to pursue the notion that one's current acts and undertakings might have as much to do with the development of his personality as did the imprint of events with which he came in contact or the insights he was able to conjure up with the help of his therapist" (1963, p. 56).

With the help of some graduate students, he established a statewide traveling clinic to visit schools and other agencies in an effort to reach those many people experiencing difficulty in living through the circumstances of a nation in crisis. Often, during a visit to one or another school, teachers would complain about a student's behavior. To Kelly it seemed clear that such teacher complaints represented the child's disruptive influence on the *teacher's* life, and were not a description of that child in its life situation. A teacher's complaint of "laziness," for example, was hardly useful to the psychologist as a motivational construct, because the label described the teacher's construction of events, not the child's character. The child was lazy when it came to doing things the teacher thought it should do.

To obtain a picture of how persons construe their own lives, Kelly and his students began using an early personality test called the Maller Inventory. This test consisted of cards containing self-descriptive statements the subject was asked to sort in various ways; for example, those most like self, next most like, and so on. It was an early version of the Q-sort technique used by Stephenson and Rogers and a forerunner of Kelly's own REP test. From the person's response, Kelly and his students would write a characterization of the person that differed in significant ways from the way she or he viewed her- or himself. An attempt was made to make the description embody a new outlook on life and to offer specific examples of how this outlook would influence behavior. The "person" described was sometimes given a new name to emphasize the difference between the client's previous constructions and this new viewpoint. The client was then invited to pretend he or she was this "new person" and to enact the role for two weeks or so.

This role-playing procedure later became the basis of what Kelly called *fixed-role therapy* (1955, Chapter 8). Role playing helped clients to construe afresh the events of their lives. Fixed-role therapy is thus an invitation to the client to experiment with alternative modes of living. In principle, Kelly conceived of his procedure as a means of freeing the curious and inventive scientist that lies hidden in each of us. Although not a panacea, fixed-role therapy helped a great many clients to see things differently, to anticipate life with more relish, and to construe themselves and the significant people in their lives in wholly new and productively fresh ways. In the words of the fundamental postulate: *"A person's processes are psychologically channelized by the ways in which he anticipates events."*

Kelly created 11 corollaries to the fundamental postulate, which provide the overall skeleton of personal construct theory. It may be of some help to preview this basic outline and the grouping of the 11 postulates that follows here. For the better part of the remainder of this chapter we are concerned with examining these 11 corollaries:

FUNDAMENTAL POSTULATE

1. Construction Corollary
2. Individuality Corollary
3. Organization Corollary
4. Dichotomy Corollary
5. Choice Corollary
6. Range Corollary
7. Experience Corollary
8. Modulation Corollary
9. Fragmentation Corollary
10. Commonality Corollary
11. Sociality Corollary

CONSTRUCTION AND INDIVIDUALITY COROLLARIES: THE PERSON AS PROCESS

As Laing had been concerned with the power of labels to shape an observer's perception of the person so labeled, Kelly too had expressed concern lest psychologists be trapped by the traditions of Western civilization's language habits. Consider, for example, what happens when a person labels her- or himself:

> . . . on occasion I may say of myself . . . "I am an introvert." "I," the subject, "am an introvert," the predicate. The language form of the statement clearly places the onus of being an introvert on the subject—me. What I actually am, the words say, is an introvert.
>
> . . . the proper interpretation of my statement is that *I construe* myself to be an introvert, or, if I am merely being coy or devious, I am inveigling *my listener into construing me* in terms of introversion. The point that gets lost in the shuffle of words is the psychological fact that I have identified myself in terms of a personal construct—"introversion." (Kelly, 1958a, p. 70)

The form of the statement easily deceives the listener into believing that it is *objectively* true, that when a predicate is applied to a subject, the subject must undoubtedly *be* what the predicate asserts.

> . . . when I say that Professor Lindzey's left shoe is an "introvert," everyone looks at his shoe as if this were something his shoe was responsible for. Or if I say that Professor Cattell's head is "discursive," everyone looks over at him, as if the proposition popped out of his head instead of out of mine. Don't look at his head! Don't look at that shoe! Look at me; I'm the one who is responsible for the statement. After you figure out what I mean you can look over there to see if you make any sense of shoes and heads by construing them the way I do. (Kelly, 1958a, p. 72)

Thus the focus of Kelly's theory is on individuals and on their interpretations of events, not on the events themselves. Kelly believed that persons erect structures of meaning to be imposed on the events they experience, and these structures embody both similarity and contrast. The person notes the similarities among various events, and groups them together under one construct; but that same construct derives some of its meaning from those events that were excluded by contrast. Hence, the construct "introvert" not only indicates all traits the person associates with introversion but also defines what introversion is not for that person.

Time exerts an important influence on the manner in which a person construes his or her world. With the passage of time, the individual is able to detect recurrent themes, repetitive events, and their onset and termination. "Once events have been given their beginnings and endings, and their similarities and contrasts construed, it becomes feasible to try to predict them, just as one predicts that tomorrow will follow today" (Kelly, 1955, p. 53).

Kelly therefore formulated a first corollary to the fundamental postulate:

CONSTRUCTUION COROLLARY: *A person anticipates events by construing their replications* (1955, p. 50).

This construction corollary says that human beings can deal with their lives because they are able to detect and interpret through time similarities, regularities, and recurrences of events. They are, in short, able to make sense out of the chaos of the future only by predicting its occurrence on the basis of past experience. But most important, it is *each person's* past experience and *each person's* construction of that experience that dominates his or her life, not the events as they actually exist.

It follows from Kelly's emphasis on *personal* interpretation that individual differences in construction of events may exist. Kelly called this commonsense proposition the

INDIVIDUALITY COROLLARY: *Persons differ from each other in their constructions of events* (1955, p. 55).

HIERARCHY OF EXPERIENCE: ORGANIZATION AND DICHOTOMY COROLLARIES

A person's system of constructs is not static. The interpretations each imposes on the universe constantly change and are perpetually modified by new experience. Often, contradictions and conflicts between constructs emerge. The individual must then develop a way to resolve or to transcend the inconsistency—*if he or she perceives it.*

One way to resolve the conflicts that are perceived is to organize one's constructions of events into a hierarchy in which particular constructs may subsume many other constructs in the system. When one construct subsumes another, it is called *superordinal;* conversely, the construct so subsumed is termed *subordinal.* It is possible sometimes for super- and subordinal constructs to change places in the hierarchy depending on the demands of immediate events. For example, the construct *good* versus *bad* may include the two poles of the *intelligent* versus *stupid* dimension of experience. *Good* subsumes *intelligent,* and *bad* subsumes *stupid. Good* and *bad* may, of course, assimilate other constructs as well. Furthermore, *good* and *bad* may change ordinal position with *intelligent* and *stupid:*

Another way in which constructs may be ordinally ranked is for one to create categories that subsume complete dimensions under *one* pole of a superordinal construct. For example, the *good-bad* construct might itself be subsumed under one pole of a broader superordinal construct: *evaluative* versus *descriptive.* Thus the pair *good-bad* would be globally subsumed under *evaluative,* whereas other constructs like *light* versus *dark* would be subsumed under *descriptive:*

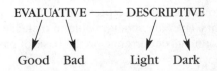

To make sense out of the world, people systematize their constructs into hierarchies for convenience in anticipating occurrences of events.

Kelly formulated an organization corollary to embrace his hypotheses about the

ORGANIZATION COROLLARY: *Each person characteristically evolves, for his convenience in anticipating events, a construction system embracing ordinal relationships between constructs* (1955, p. 56).

Kelly postulated that ordinal groupings were not the only way in which personal constructs are "filed." Each construct has meaning for the individual only because it is applicable to some events and is clearly inapplicable to others. A personal construct has a *range of convenience,* a collection of events that the individual construes as similar. For these events, the construct is "convenient." But the construct's range of convenience would make little sense if it were not precise enough to *exclude* some events as opposite or different. Kelly therefore proposed that every personal construct is dichotomous, bipolar in structure. In order to derive meaning from a construct, it must indicate at least two elements as similar, and a third as contrasting. Recall the structure of the REP test in which the subject is asked to find similarity between two figures and to determine how they differ from a third.

To illustrate further, suppose that there are two men, A and B. There is also a woman, C. An individual may abstract these people on the basis of a construct concerned with sex. A and B are construed as similar because they are men; C is outside the range of convenience of this construct that denotes "masculine sex." But note that the concept of masculinity would be meaningless were it not for the implied contrasting construct of " femininity."

Suppose further that the individual had the following elements in mind: A and B (men), C (woman), and D (a dog). If the individual's personal construct is "masculinity," would he now group C and D, woman and dog, together as equally different from A and B? Of course not, because the woman and dog are different from the concept "masculinity" in different ways. The woman is much "more relevantly unmasculine" than the dog (Kelly, 1955, p. 60). It is *her* femininity that is opposite to masculinity. The dog is only relevant to the construct's range of convenience if the person chooses to abstract the dog as "feminine dog" or as "masculine dog." Even then, however, the construct "dog" would still fail to be as relevant to the construct "masculinity" as the woman is in establishing *human* masculinity.

Kelly's assertion that persons think in terms of dichotomies does not accord with classical logic. He felt, however, that it would accurately represent the way people actually think. In classical logic, a thing is either "A" or "not-A": masculine or not-masculine; feminine or not-feminine. But in Kelly's system, *three* elements are required to establish the identity of a thing: two similar and one contrasting. In the formal language of a theoretical postulate, the fourth thus far, Kelly formulated these implications into a corollary:

DICHOTOMY COROLLARY: *A person's construction system is composed of a finite number of dichotomous constructs* (1955, p. 59).

The word "finite" suggests that Kelly viewed the breadth of a person's construction system as limited. Indeed, several variables serve to set limits to the individual's anticipations.

CHOICE, RANGE, AND EXPERIENCE OF COROLLARIES: LIMITATIONS OF ANTICIPATION

Individuals are perpetually confronted with choices between the dichotomous poles of their anticipations of events. People must adopt as their guiding constructs one or the other pole of a contrasting pair. It is at this point that people experience uncertainty, the conflict of decision. Two choices confront them: They may decide to widen their perspectives, including more, and therefore possibly uncertain, elements into their decision making; or they may decide to restrict their perspectives, to "stand pat" with what they already know as a means of ensuring their continued predictive power with familiar people and events. In either case, whatever their conduct, they will be changed by it, for, as Kelly describes it, the individual "places relative values upon the ends of his dichotomies" (Kelly, 1955, p. 65). As individuals choose one of each of their dichotomous constructs to live by, they simultaneously choose among and thereby rank their values.

People are guided in their choices of personal constructs by a basic urge to enhance and maintain their abilities to anticipate events reliably. Thus their eventual choices will be those that in their view provide greater or more reliable predictive power. Their choices are designed to achieve what in other psychologists' language would be called self-security, defense of the self, or anxiety reduction. Kelly formulated his fifth corollary around these ideas about individuals' choices:

> CHOICE COROLLARY: *A person chooses for himself that alternative in a dichotomized construct through which he anticipates the greater possibility for extension and definition of his system* (1955, p. 64).

A sixth corollary stated the limits of the individuals' choices:

> RANGE COROLLARY: *A construct is convenient for the anticipation of a finite range of events only* (1955, p. 68).

Thus individuals' personal construction systems are limited in their range of application by their interpretation of what is relevant to them and to the reliability of their predictions. For example, if we wish to ascertain what an individual means by the construct "respect versus contempt," we need to know not only those acts or behaviors that he or she regards as evidencing "respect," but also those considered on the basis of experience as evidencing "contempt." So far we are on familiar ground. For to understand an individual's construction of "respect," we must know both what is *excluded* from one pole of the construct and what is considered by him or her as relevant to the other. This concept was previously implied by the dichotomy corollary. But there is a further implication contained in the range corollary.

The range corollary implies, according to Kelly's elaboration of its stark language, that any construct is *limited* to a finite range of events that fall within the *experience of the individual* and that he or she considers *relevant. Relevancy* is the limiting factor. What is outside the range of a given construct is not considered as contrasting or opposite; it is viewed as *irrelevant.*

People do change their interpretations of relevancy, to include more or fewer events in their worldview, as experience demands. Kelly was prompted to take the fact of change into account by proposing a seventh proposition:

> EXPERIENCE COROLLARY: *A person's construction system varies as he successively construes the replications of events* (1955, p. 72).

When individuals' anticipations of events are violated and fail to conform to expectations, they are compelled to modify their construct systems. They change their predictions. If people did not change with changing events, they would grow more and more distant from reality. But individuals are never merely passive reflections of life's stream of events:

> A person can be a witness to a tremendous parade of episodes and yet, if he fails to keep making something out of them, or if he waits until they have all occurred before he attempts to reconstrue them, he gains little in the way of experience from having been around when they happened. *It is not what happens around him that makes a man experienced; it is the successive construing and reconstruing of what happens, as it happens, that enriches the experience of his life.* (Kelly, 1955, p. 73; italics added)

Clearly, Kelly meant to emphasize that it is only individuals who actively participate in their world who are changed by it. For in striving to make sense of the continuous flux of life's events, individuals simultaneously change themselves with each imposition of a new sense-making construction. The need to know what to expect is therefore the great driving force of human nature.

Taken together, the Choice, Range, and Experience corollaries were designed to make obsolete such classical psychological terminology as drive, motivation, anxiety, and learning. It is not that Kelly abandoned these concepts. Rather, he viewed them as inherent in the more fundamental process of individuals' attempts to predict, control, and modify their predictions in the light of experience. For Kelly, humans are intellectual animals.

Motivation in Kelly's system may therefore be subsumed under the concept of the human need to predict; anxiety is construed as the product of the violation of anticipations; and learning is inherent in the process of continual modification and definition of the construction system as individuals attempt to preserve the order and regularity each has imposed on life.

MODULATION AND FRAGMENTATION CORROLLARIES: VARIATION VERSUS STABILITY

When people make changes in their construction systems, those alterations are themselves events capable of being construed. People construe themselves as changing. In fact, the very changes they are likely to make emerge only from the framework of their entire system of constructs. Any change in construction must therefore be placed in context, must be interpreted in the light of its effect on the entire system. Just as scientists may use their theories as guides to making new observations, individuals employ their construction systems to make new constructions. And just as the scientist's theory may become a set of intellectual blinders, the individual's construction system permits him or her to see as possible only certain changes.

Certain of the individual's constructs are uniquely susceptible to change. Such constructs are said to be *permeable.* "A construct is permeable if it will admit to its range of convenience new elements which are not yet construed within its framework" (Kelly, 1955, p. 79). Conversely, constructs that will admit of no new elements are said to be *impermeable.* The implications of permeable and impermeable constructs were formulated by Kelly into an eighth proposition:

MODULATION COROLLARY: *The variation in a person's construction system is limited by the permeability of the constructs within whose range of convenience the variants lie* (1955, p. 77).

For example, early in life we may divide the people in our world into the two classes of the construct "fear versus domination." There are, consequently, in one's view those whom one fears, and those whom one may dominate. With the passing of years, this dichotomy may be interpreted as somewhat childish. The notion of "childishness," being itself a construct, has, of course, its opposite pole: "maturity." If this new construct, "childishness versus maturity," is *permeable,* we may be able to subsume our previous construct, "fear versus domination," under "childishness" as a rejected value. Under the pole of "maturity" we incorporate a totally new construct: "respect versus contempt." We are now, consequently, in a position to redivide our acquaintances in what we perceive to be a more mature fashion: those whom we respect versus those whom we hold in contempt (1955, p. 82).

The permeability of the superordinal construct, "childishness versus maturity," allows for this *modulation* or "fine-tuning" of the construct system whereby the respect-contempt variant is assimilated under the permeable "maturity" construct.

Sometimes, however, an individual may use subsystems of permeable superordinal constructs in such a way that one subsystem is not logically derivable from another. Yet, on the whole, from the point of view of the entire construct system, the new construct is compatible with the individual's broad view of life. Kelly termed this theoretical assumption, his ninth, the

FRAGMENTATION COROLLARY: *A person may successively employ a variety of construction subsystems which are inferentially incompatible with each other* (1955, p. 83).

Kelly emphasized the significance of the fragmentation corollary:

> It should make even clearer the assumed necessity for seeking out the regnant construct system [that is, the larger whole system and its dominant themes] in order to explain the behavior of men, rather than seeking merely to explain each bit of behavior as a derivative of its immediately antecedent behavior. (1955, p. 83)

It is thus possible for us to act in a way that is contradictory to our previous views, but which we *feel* is consistent with a momentarily dominant interpretation of events. Despite the piecemeal inconsistencies, the entire pattern of our life, our global anticipations of our world are always consistent with our *immediate* behavior. It is in this larger sense that our behavior is "logically" derivable from our "master life plan."

> . . . while a person's bets on the turn of minor events may not appear to add up, his wagers on the outcome of life do tend to add up. He may not win each time, but his wagers, in the larger contexts, do not altogether cancel themselves out. (Kelly, 1955, p. 88)

Kelly's modulation and fragmentation corollaries strike an intuitively satisfying balance between the inconsistency that we observe in people's daily activities and the general trend for individuals to behave in ways that are recognizably typical of them.

COMMONALITY AND SOCIALITY COROLLARIES: SHARED EXPERIENCE

Two people may be exposed to the same objective events but construe them differently. If their constructions, that is, the meanings that they impose on events, are different, then their experience of the events is different. This argument is the essential burden of the individuality corollary we previously discussed. But, if individuals can construe things differently, it follows that at least sometimes individuals may construe events similarly. Hence, in addition to an individuality corollary, there is a need for a commonality corollary.

> COMMONALITY COROLLARY: *To the extent that one person employs a construction of experience which is similar to that employed by another, his psychological processes are similar to those of the other person* (Kelly, 1955, p. 90).

Kelly added some important distinctions to clarify the commonality corollary:

> It is important to make clear that we have not said that if one person has experienced the same events as another he will duplicate the other's psychological processes. . . . One of the advantages of this position is that it does not require us to assume that it would take identical events in the lives of two people to make them act alike. Two people can act alike even if they have each been exposed to quite different phenomenal stimuli. It is the similarity in the construction of events that we find the basis for similar action, not in the identity of the events themselves. (1955, pp. 90–91)

It is probably worth pointing out that nowhere does R. D. Laing come as close to Kelly's position as in his similarity to Kelly's discussion of shared anticipations. Laing, as we have seen, used stunningly similar terminology. Where Laing labeled the process of mutual expectations *a spiral of reciprocal perspectives,* Kelly had used the term *spiralform model* to describe the way personal construct theory could be applied to interpersonal experiences:

> James anticipates what John will do. James also anticipates what John thinks he, James, will do. James further anticipates what John thinks he [James] expects John will do. In addition, James anticipates what John thinks James expects John to predict that James will do. And so on! (Kelly, 1955, p. 94)

The similarity of concept and language between Kelly and Laing is striking, but not surprising, for both theorists are deeply concerned with phenomenal processes.

If two interacting people share similar constructions of the events in which they are involved, it follows that they may socially influence each other. Kelly's statement of this potential mutual influence is again so similar to Laing's later elaboration of the concept as to give those familiar with Laing's position a feeling of *déjà vu:*

> In order to play a constructive role in relation to another person one must not only, in some measure, see eye to eye with him but must, in some measure, have an acceptance of him and his way of seeing things. We say it in another way: the person who is to play a constructive role in a social process with another person *need not so much construe things as the other person does as he must effectively construe the other person's outlook.* (1955, p. 95; italics added)

As Laing systematized his similar formulation of direct perspectives and meta-perspectives, Kelly formulated his thinking into his eleventh and last proposition:

> SOCIALITY COROLLARY: *To the extent that one person construes the construction processes of another, he may play a role in a social process involving the other person* (1955, p. 95).

Kelly clearly meant to emphasize that the basis of social interaction was interpersonal *understanding,* not simply shared experience. If one can anticipate (predict) another's behavior, one can modify one's own behavior in response.

An important part of the sociality corollary is its use of the concept of social role. Kelly defined roles as "psychological processes based upon the role player's construction of aspects of the construction systems of those with whom he attempts to join in a social enterprise" (1955, p. 97). To put it another way, the behavior of a person evoked by his or her interpretation of the other's interpretation of the task on which they are engaged is his or her role. In Laing's terms, a role is how you act because you think the other thinks such and such about this task. Kelly's definition of role is consistent with the cognitive orientation of his theory. The definition emphasizes the subjective interpretation of the role player and his or her audience.

With Kelly's personal construct theory, the imagery of the actor and the mask is again offered as an appropriate analogy of the personality that runs the risk of yielding to confusion of the role player with the role:

It may be helpful at this point to ask ourselves a question about children at Halloween. Is the little youngster who comes to your door on the night of October 31st, all dressed up in his costume and behind a mask, piping "trick or treat, trick or treat"— is that youngster *disguising* himself or is he *revealing* himself? Is he failing to be spontaneous? Is he *not* being himself? Which is the *real* child—the child behind the mask or the barefaced child who must stand up in front of adults and say "please" and "thank you"? I suspect costumes and masks worn at Halloween time, as well as uniforms worn by officers on duty, doctoral degrees, and the other devices we employ to avoid being seen as we are, are all ways we have of extricating ourselves from predicaments. . . . *But masks have a way of sticking to our faces when worn too long.* (Kelly, 1964, p. 158; last italics added)

Kelly used the mask analogy to illustrate how individuals may be trapped by "objective" language labels into believing they are the label that they portray. A social role may be played without the awareness of one or both parties to the performance, or played even when both parties do not share the same understanding of the task on which they are engaged.

KELLY'S CONSTRUCTION OF "PERSONALITY"

As Sechrest (1963, p. 229) has pointed out, Kelly's two-volume *Psychology of Personal Constructs* does not contain an explicit definition of personality. No doubt Kelly would point to the fundamental postulate and the 11 corollaries and say that they are his definition. In a later paper, Kelly came close to saying exactly that with a summary statement: "[Personality is] our abstraction of the activity of a person and our subsequent generalization of this abstraction to all matters of his relationship to other persons, known and unknown, as well as to anything else that may seem particularly valuable" (quoted by Sechrest, 1963, p. 229).

Kelly's basic system emphasizes the intellective nature of humans. He does not dismiss unconscious determinants or dynamics, but rather construes them with the same "as if" decision-making formulation that characterizes his approach to fundamental human character. Persons may not actually be scientists, but for Kelly it is theoretically useful to construe them as if they were. Humans are anticipatory animals, not reactive ones.

Envisioning a New Self: Fixed-Role Therapy Revisited

Kelly's conception of personality implies that persons are what they psychologically represent themselves to be (Kelly, 1955, p. 362). In essence, you are what you believe you are. If individuals find themselves trapped by the person they have been, they are free to envision a new self, a new way of being—to themselves and to others. Fixed-role therapy, mentioned in passing earlier in the chapter, was Kelly's attempt to aid his clients to construe themselves deliberately differently.

Recall that fixed-role therapy involves the clinician's writing a narrative sketch for the client that contains a précis of a new personality, new ways to behave, and even carries a fictional name to emphasize the character differences between the person in the sketch and the client. The therapist says, in effect, to the client: "Here is another way of construing yourself. *Pretend* for two weeks or so that you are this person. See what happens."

For Kelly, fixed-role therapy was a creative process mutually shaped by client and therapist. It was not to be understood as a "repair" technique for wounded personalities (Kelly, 1955, p. 380). Unique self-experimentation, rather than healing, describes Kelly's hope for the technique most accurately and reveals most lucidly his conviction that no one need be trapped by their life history just because some theories construe people as bundles of conflicted drives.

Kelly developed some simple rules for the writing of fixed-role sketches by clinicians (1955, pp. 368 ff.):

1. It should ideally be constructed by a panel of clinicians familiar with the client.
2. The sketch should develop a major theme rather than attempt to correct minor personality faults.
3. The sketch should sharply contrast with the client's real character, for it will be easier to pretend to be a person he or she believes is totally opposite from the one he or she presently is.
4. The sketch should attempt to engage the client's own personality growth processes and mobilize his or her own resources for change.
5. Testable hypotheses that the client can immediately check in his or her own life should be part of the sketch so that it is plausible and real to the client.
6. The client should be given the full protection of "make-believe," so that he or she can experiment with the role without making a permanent commitment. Kelly called this protective screening a "protective mask" (1955, p. 373).

Writing the Fixed-Role Sketch

The basis for constructing new fictional personalities is the clients' writing "self-characterization" sketches, in which they spell out, more or less clearly, the way they now construe themselves. From these personal essays, the clinician draws inferences about the clients' self-picture from the way they have organized the sketch, emphasized certain phrases, highlighted certain themes or omitted them altogether, and how they have embodied in the essay their personal constructs revealed by the REP test.

The actual construction of a fixed-role sketch then demands not only clinical acumen but a healthy measure of artistry. Table 12.3 contains, side-by-side, excerpts from the self-characterization sketch of "Ronald Barrett," a patient of Kelly's, and the fixed-role sketch written for him as the fictional Kenneth Norton.

Close inspection of both the client's self-characterization and Kelly's fixed-role sketch reveals that the central theme Ronald was invited to rehearse was *the seeking of answers in the subtle feelings of other people rather than in literalistic dispute with them* (Kelly, 1955, p. 375). After a period of time, Ronald Barrett was able to change his way of construing himself; he was able to be more open and friendly with others and he generally began selectively to adopt aspects of "Kenneth Norton" that he now found congenial.

TABLE 12.3   Excerpts from Ronald Barrett's Self-Characterization and Fixed-Role Sketches

Ronald Barrett's Self-Characterization
[original misspellings]

An overall appearance of Ronald Barrett would give one the impression that he has a rather quite and calm personality. Furthermore, he dislikes doing or saying anything that will draw unfavorable attention in public. . . . However, he has been known to flare up (not in public, though) very easily and often gets quite worked up or frustrated over something done or spoken by (usually not his friends or anyone with him) someone that he feels should know better. . . . He very rarely shows signs of anger toward his friends. On the other hand, he is apt to be inconsistent in that it sometimes takes a lot to get him worked up over some subject at hand, while at other times he will very easily get very worked up. . . . A feeling of guilt often comes over him if he thinks he has not been kindhearted enough. . . . His tendency to criticize and correct people, esp. in his family, on major as well as minor issues, shows some decrease outside his family, but not too much within. Proving his point, or arguing his point, and arguing against other people's points, seems to be one of his major "hobbies." . . . He has some ideas concerning girls that seem odd or just plain crazy to most people. He completely refrains from calling a girl "beautiful." She may be cute, pretty, attractive . . . but he uses the word "beautiful" only [to] describe material things that have no "feeling" as humans have. Although he listens attentively to stories or general discussion about sex, he rarely enters into the conversation. One may say that he puts too much meaning and thought into kissing a girl. . . . He is usually lost for conversation when meeting someone new, or seeing a girl he knows, but if he once "breaks the ice," he can usually talk freely. (From Kelly, 1955, pp. 326–328)

"Kenneth Norton": Fixed-Role Sketch

Kenneth Norton is the kind of man who, after a few minutes of conversation, somehow makes you feel that he must have known you intimately for a long time. This comes about, not by any particular questions that he asks, but by the understanding way in which he listens. It is as if he had a knack of seeing the world through your eyes. The things which you have come to see as being important he, too, soon seems to sense as similarly important. Thus, he catches not only your words but the punctuations of feeling with which they are formed and the little accents of meaning with which they are chosen.

Kenneth Norton's complete absorption in the thoughts of the people with whom he holds conversations appears to leave no place for any feelings of self-consciousness regarding himself. If indeed he has such feelings at all, they obviously run a poor second to his eagerness to see the world through other people's eyes. . . .

Girls he finds attractive for many reasons, not the least of which is the exciting opportunity they provide for his understanding the feminine point of view. Unlike some men, he does not "throw the ladies a line" but, so skillful a listener is he, soon he has them throwing him one—and he is thoroughly enjoying it.

With his own parents . . . he is somewhat more expressive of his own ideas and feelings. Thus his parents are given an opportunity to share and supplement his new enthusiasms and accomplishments. (From Kelly, 1955, pp. 374–375)

The CPC Cycle

Consider the predicament in which Jean-Mary found herself when some key personal constructs were threatened with obsolescence and note the phases through which her thinking progressed as she wrestled with various solutions:

> In the fall of her 13th year, when Jean-Mary was in the eighth grade, a teacher precipitated a crisis in the relationship between Jean-Mary and her younger sister, Robin.

Called from her own to the sixth-grade classroom by a note from Robin's teacher, Jean-Mary was startled to find her sister tear-stained, hotly flushed, and trembling beside the blackboard in front of the class. Unable to complete an arithmetic problem in long division to the satisfaction of the teacher, Robin had to endure a tirade from the teacher, the gist of which was an unfavorable comparison to her former student, Jean-Mary.

Jean-Mary appraised the situation, caught in the conflict between obedience to a respected authority figure and compassion for and loyalty to her own sister. Unable to decide between defiance and submission, Jean-Mary froze. She was finally made to solve the long division problem for Robin in view of the whole class. But in her own perceptive way she understood the damage that had been done to her sister and to their relationship.

In that moment of humiliating comparison a wall had been built separating the two sisters in a way that neither of them could verbalize, though the emotional import was intense.

For her past, Jean-Mary was faced with an awful realization. Up to this time, teachers had always been objects of respect and admiration. They were people to be obeyed without question. But clearly, as her experience had so painfully shown, teachers could be cruel and stupid. The problem was a triple conflict: She felt guilt for having participated against her own sister in a situation that required the wit to change one's views quickly and decisively; she experienced anger at her own gullibility in having uncritically accepted teachers as paragons of virtue; she struggled against an emerging distaste for all teachers and for schoolwork in general.

Surmounting her personal difficulties, Jean-Mary was able to reason that *some* teachers are less than perfect, and that *sometimes* being a teacher was no safeguard against cruelty and stupidity. Jean-Mary was even able to redefine her own self-image to admit that she had acted with less courage than her personal values had demanded. She resolved never again to be an unwitting pawn of her own preconceptions.

Jean-Mary's predicament illustrates a cyclic sequence of thought involving the reconstruction of important anticipations. Up to the time of her experience with the long division episode, her construction of "teachers" could be characterized as rigidly stereotyped: "Anyone who is a teacher also has to be good, kind, intelligent, just." Kelly calls such stereotypes *constellatory constructs* (1955, p. 155). The elements of the constellatory construct are dogmatically applied to anything and to anyone labeled "teacher." A whole "constellation" of persons who are expected to be no different from those with whom she has had experience is the result.

Fortunately, Jean-Mary's constellatory construct of "teacher" also has the characteristic of permeability. Recall that a permeable construct is one that is susceptible to change through the addition of new elements to its range of convenience. Constellatory constructs, however, take a bit more prodding than some less rigid forms of thought before they can be modified. When confronted with a violation of her expectancy in the form of a teacher who was mean, unjust, and stupid, Jean-Mary experienced some confusion and anxiety: "*This* teacher is not at all like 'teachers' whose behavior I think I can anticipate."

The conflict induced by the discrepancy between her anticipation and her new experience can be resolved only by a restructuring of the construct "teacher" into a more relativistic prediction that admits of variation to the stereotype of "good, just, and intelligent." From start to finish, the change in Jean-Mary's construct system involves three phases, collectively termed by Kelly the *CPC cycle* (circumspection, preemption, and control).

Phase One: Circumspection

When confronted with a situation that required her to act in a way that violated several personal constructs, Jean-Mary was forced to view the elements that composed her "teacher" construct with *circumspection.* Circumspection, in Kelly's theory, is the opposite of the rigid, dogmatic thinking characteristic of constellatory constructs. Circumspection involves the use of *propositional constructs* that allow one to reason relativistically. "A teacher is good, just, kind, and intelligent, but may *sometimes* also be cruel, stupid and unjust—and a lot of other incompatible things."

A propositional construct is a mode of thinking that avoids black/white pigeon-holing and "nothing but" thinking. Propositional thinking is hypothetical, tentative, and relativistic. Fortunately, Jean-Mary's construct was becoming permeable and flexible. She was thus able to enter the first phase of the CPC cycle, circumspection, and survey the situation and the persons involved for possible alternative constructions.

Phase Two: Preemption

The circumspection phase must come to an end if we are to be able to act on the propositions evolved. If Jean-Mary stayed in the circumspection phase, her thinking would have been largely devoted to creating more and more alternative ways of construing those painful events and the people involved. Circumspection had the fortunate consequences of freeing her from the rigidity of her constellatory construct of "teacher" and providing her with a more propositional version. But unless she can leave the circumspection phase, she will be permanently caught up in "rehashing" the incident and attempting to decide among the various interpretations made possible by her propositional position.

Jean-Mary must consequently narrow her range of focus and begin thinking more preemptively, more decisively. She must choose the *relevant* elements from among her propositional alternatives, pick those issues she regards as crucial, and ignore the rest. Temporarily, she must *preempt one* issue as most important to her.

She did. The issue was loyalty to her sister, and prevention of needlessly inflicted hurt, despite the admonitions of her teacher to the contrary. Unfortunately, Jean-Mary took a bit longer than circumstances required in the circumspection phase to prevent that particular incident. Kelly described the preemptive phase in this way:

> The preemption of issues characterizes the "man of action." He is likely to see things in what may appear to his associates to be an oversimplified manner. He consolidates all the possible perspectives in terms of one dichotomous issue and then makes his choice between the only two alternatives he allows himself to perceive. (1955, p. 516)

Jean-Mary finally preempted the issues to one dichotomous theme: "*defiance of a heretofore respected authority figure versus allegiance to my sister.*"

Phase Three: Control

Having reduced the field to one dichotomous issue, the individual still has to make the choice between the opposing poles. In Jean-Mary's case, the choice was for loyalty and the prevention of gratuitous hurt. Unfortunately for her sister, the choice stage of her thinking was a little behind schedule. Yet, in the future, when confronted with similar situations, Jean-Mary would not hesitate to act on her new constructions of events. The futurity of her new constructions is an important aspect of this final phase of the CPC cycle, for Jean-Mary was now in *control* (the final "C") of possible future conflicts.

Had the cycle come to an abrupt halt at the preemption phase with Jean-Mary unable to make the choice, she would be thrown back to the beginning of the cycle to view the situation again with circumspection and redefine the issues. She would, in a sense, be destined to speculate forever.

SOME TRADITIONAL PERSONALITY VARIABLES AS KELLY CONSTRUES THEM

Kelly's willingness to engage in propositional constructions about personality led him to propose some unique formulations of traditional personality variables. Time-honored concepts like the unconscious, anxiety, hostility, and guilt were given systematic redefinitions. In effect, Kelly reconstrued them in terms of personal construct theory.

The Unconscious

For many years following the long division classroom episode, neither Jean-Mary nor Robin was able to verbalize the change that took place in their relationship. If asked how they behaved differently, Jean-Mary could only reply that there *was* a perceptible difference, but one to which she could give no precise label. The important things were the way the relationship "felt" after the incident; the subtle nonverbal changes in communication; and the unvoiced hesitancy of both sisters in assuming that they could treat each other as they always had.

In Kelly's terms, both sisters had developed a preverbal or nonverbal construct. Jean-Mary and Robin construed events in ways that influenced their behavior, but to which they were unable to attach a verbal label or word symbol (Kelly, 1955, p. 459). The only cognitive representatives of their constructions of their changed relationships were behavioral, gestural, subtle impressionistic cues that defy word description.

The concept "unconscious" is partly subsumed under Kelly's notion of pre- and nonverbal constructs. His idea is similar to that of Freud himself. Freud had proposed that repression proper consisted of the preconscious system's removal of language "cathexes" from threatening ideas that have a relationship with content already primally repressed into the unconscious (cf. Chapter 3). Kelly, however, suggests that lack of a word label alone is not sufficient to prevent a construct from entering awareness. For a personal construct to be truly removed from consciousness, it must be *submerged* along one of its two poles.

Recall that each construct has a "similarity" pole by which two or more elements are construed as alike, and a "contrast" pole by which at least one other element is seen as different. One or the other pole of the construct may be submerged so that, for example, the similarity elements are kept out of awareness. Thus, in Jean-Mary's case, the construct "I acted *similarly* to an unjust teacher" may be submerged, while the opposite end of the construct "I am *not* like that mean, stupid teacher," is all that remains to be verbalized.

The important question is, How does one pole of a construct become submerged? In effect, we are asking, How does repression occur according to Kelly's theory? The motivated forgetting of her perceived similarity to the disliked teacher occurs through a shifting of many constructs from the total system into a new arrangement of fewer units. The threatening end of the construct is "mislaid" in the shuffle because the construct in which it formerly resided as one pole has been "refiled" or subsumed under another superordinal construct that has no room for that pole. In short, "repression" involves a redefinition of the construct system to exclude some constructs.

Submergence of one pole of a construct implies the *suspension* of whole categories of constructs from the total system. In contrast with some notions of repression, suspension implies that the idea or element is forgotten simply because the person cannot tolerate any structure within which the idea would have meaning. Once he or she can entertain such a structure, the idea may again become available within it (Kelly, 1955, p. 473).

Thus, for Kelly, the unconscious is translated into the concepts of nonverbal constructs, submergence, and suspension.

Anxiety

The feelings of threat that Jean-Mary experienced when confronted with a violent discrepancy between her "teacher" construct and her experience of a particular teacher could be characterized as anxiety. What made the threat so damaging was the close connection it had with her self-concept. Forced complicity in the humiliation of her sister threatened to violate Jean-Mary's *core constructs*. Constructs that compose the central anticipations by which people set their life goals and construe *themselves* in relation to these outcomes are called core constructs (Kelly, 1955, p. 482). In every way, Jean-Mary's core constructs were in danger of imminent change.

The feeling of anxiety that results from such threats is defined by Kelly as *"the recognition that the events with which one is confronted lie outside the range of convenience of one's construct system"* (1955, p. 495). In simpler language, Jean-Mary experienced anxiety because she felt that she had totally lost her ability to understand significant people in terms of her past expectations, and what was worse, she no longer understood herself.

An individual can tolerate some incompatibility between expectancy and experience, but the degree of conflict may not be very great before changed behavior results. In Jean-Mary's case, the discrepancy between her habitual mode of thinking teachers to be kind and just, and her experience with this stupid, unjust, and cruel one was too large. Furthermore, the enforced compliance with this outrageous person threatened to provoke an entire reconstruction of her construction of her self.

Similar ideas to those of Kelly have been emerging in recent years within cognitive dissonance theory (Festinger, 1957). The notion that perceptions which violate the self-concept are motivators for attitude change has received extensive empirical investigation (cf. Aronson, 1969). Rokeach (1973, especially Chapters 8 and 12) has even extended the analysis to the study of values in relation to self-consistent perceptions.

Guilt

Jean-Mary felt guilty long after the classroom episode because she had acted in a way that was inconsistent with her self-image. In Kelly's terms, guilt is defined as a *"Perception of one's apparent dislodgment from his core role structure"* (1955, p. 502). What differentiates guilt from anxiety in Kelly's theory is the concept of *core role structure.*

Core role structure is roughly similar to what the existentialists call being-for-the-other and to what Laing has termed metaidentity (cf. Chapter 10). The child's core role structure is his or her construction of who he or she is *in relation to significant people,* like parents. Thus, as Sechrest has concisely stated the experience of guilt from Kelly's perspective, "Guilt arises when the individual becomes aware that he is alienated from the roles by which he maintains his most important relationships to other persons" (1963, p. 228). Hence it was alienation from her role of "loving sister" that evoked Jean-Mary's guilt.

Aggressiveness

Kelly defined aggressiveness in a way that is clearly different from the usual usage of the term. *"Aggressiveness is the active elaboration of one's perceptual field"* (1955, p. 508).

For Kelly, the individual who actively seeks to construct a greater number of alternative choices is acting "aggressively": "They are always precipitating themselves and others into situations which require decision and action" (1955, p. 508). Kelly's manner of construing aggressiveness, therefore, includes situations that normally would not be labeled aggressive, as well as those that anyone would agree display aggression.

For example, an individual actively pursuing the hobby of autograph collecting may continually place him or herself in situations in which he or she can confront celebrities to demand their autographs. In restaurants, on the street, at theaters, despite security guards, press agents, and milling mobs, the dedicated autograph hunter braves all manner of obstacles, insults all kinds of people, and pursues the prey aggressively. The aggressive person in Kelly's view may be a "social pusher" (1955, p. 509).

EVALUATING KELLY'S PERSONAL CONSTRUCT THEORY

Had George Kelly formulated his theory in the 1970s and 1980s, instead of in the 1950s and 1960s, it would have been hailed as a "cognitive" theory rather than as an eclectic one. The psychology of personal constructs has been construed by other psychologists in a variety of ways. It has been interpreted as everything from existential and phenomenological to Adlerian and Jungian. Kelly did not mind any of these labels. He resented such constructions only when they were applied preemptively as if personal construct theory were "nothing but" Adlerian psychology, or "nothing but" phenomenology.

In many ways, Kelly's insistence on the accurate measurement and description of experience anticipated some of the phenomenological theories current in psychology. And his hypothesis of the human scientist, his conception that all persons create and test their own hypotheses about others, has only recently come to fruition in experimental psychology where shortly before it would have been blasphemy. The work of Martin Orne on demand characteristics (1962, 1969, 1973), Rosenthal and Jacobson's study of "Pygmalion Effects" (1968a, 1968b), and even the implications of signal-detection theory as a decision model of behavior (cf. Monte, 1975, Chapter 4) seem to be delayed recognition that Kelly was correct. The whole area of artifact in behavioral research and the contaminating influences of subjects' hypotheses about the experimenter would profit from a consideration of Kelly's position (cf. Rosenthal & Rosnow, 1969).

Kelly's ideas are also compatible with contemporary cognitive psychology in a way that is surprising for a theory whose origins preceded psychology's current willingness to focus on what people think. There was a time in our history as a science, especially during the 1960s, when the prevailing radical behaviorism made "thinking" a dirty word in psychology. Kelly was well ahead of his time in discussing thinking, decision making, and the cognitive activity of "anticipating" consequences.

Refutability of Kelly's Ideas

In principle, much of personal construct theory is refutable, or perhaps less technically put, it is testable. Certainly the REP test grid approach to the assessment of a person's private meanings lends itself to empirical manipulation (Bannister & Fransella, 1971, especially Chapters 3 and 6). It is also possible to list at least three other central concepts from Kelly's theory that, on the face of it, appear to be eminently testable:

- Repression as a kind of "refiling," "mislabeling," or "redefining" threatening ideas could certainly be tested in the laboratory with a verbal learning design or with a recognition memory design drawn from signal detection theory.
- Kelly's fixed-role therapeutic technique is, at the very least, empirically comparable to other therapeutic techniques so that its efficacy and range of application might be ascertained.
- The power of expectation or anticipation has, in its way, already been tested in a variety of research paradigms in psychology that range from social psychology studies to current social learning theory research (e.g., Bandura, 1986, reviews many of these studies on expectancy effects and observational learning).

The problem is that, although many of Kelly's ideas are suitable for research, most of them have been ignored. Except for a number of passing references, especially in the British psychological literature relevant to organizational psychology, Kelly's ideas are not especially influential in American psychology. So, the real question for Kelly's theory is not whether it is refutable, but why those portions of it that are have not been more seriously tested. Jankowicz (1987) titled a tentative answer to these questions with an ironic question that says it all: "Whatever Became of George Kelly?" Jankowicz's (1987) answer has three parts:

1. Kelly was an influential administrator and psychology activist, but a relatively shy man who did not establish a "school" of personal construct psychology. Kelly preferred simply to let his ideas speak for themselves and with the passage of time, fewer and fewer psychologists received exposure to them. Result: little research that originates from or even acknowledges Kelly's work.
2. In England, a small group of enthusiasts led by some of Kelly's former students has applied Kelly's ideas to problems of management, where his work has proved congenial and successful. But the group is small, the applications are few, and the focus is not on research.
3. Jankowicz (1987, p. 485) feels that Kelly's theory is essentially idiographic, with its focus squarely on the individual's idiosyncratic meanings and expectations. An idiographic theory does not lend itself well to broad research issues, a problem we have seen with several other theories.

Human Agency in Personal Construct Theory

Without hesitation, Kelly constructed a theory that emphasizes active human agency. Remember, it is the person who constructs meaning from reality. It is the person who tests personal hypotheses and confirms or disconfirms anticipations, much as a scientist does. Kelly's concepts of "man the scientist" and the fundamental postulate of anticipation are just now coming to partial fruition in the work of Albert Bandura and the social learning theorists, although Bandura does not acknowledge Kelly (Bandura, 1989, p. 1181). A great deal of "reinventing the wheel" occurs in psychology when psychologists are ignorant of their own history (cf. Jankowicz, 1987).

Personal Constructs Are Idiographic

It should be fairly obvious from the theory itself and from our previous discussion of refutability that Kelly's theory is idiographically focused. It is worth repeating, however, that the concepts of refutability and the idiographic-nomothetic dimension are linked in practice. Idiographic theories tend to be *ipsative,* a term drawn from psychometrics and psychological testing. *Ipsative* tests (and theories, and constructs) compare the individual with his or her own past and future performances, but they do not permit comparison across individuals. Although an ipsative (or strongly idiographic) approach to personality theory does not preclude refutability, it clearly does not make scientific testing of the theory any easier.

SUMMARY

George A. Kelly's theory of personal constructs is built upon his firm conviction that all persons behave "as if" they were scientists. Each of us, out of the fundamental human need to understand the world, creates and tests hypotheses about the behavior of significant others. Kelly formulated a fundamental postulate to embody this concept: *"A person's processes are psychologically channelized by the ways in which he anticipates events"* (1955, p. 46).

Eleven corollaries expand this basic theme:

1. *Construction Corollary:* A person anticipates events by construing their replications.
2. *Individuality Corollary:* Persons differ from each other in their construction of events.
3. *Organization Corollary:* Each person characteristically evolves, for his or her convenience in anticipating events, a construction system embracing ordinal relationships between constructs.
4. *Dichotomy Corollary:* A person's construction system is composed of a finite number of dichotomous constructs.
5. *Choice Corollary:* A person chooses that alternative in a dichotomized construct through which he or she anticipates the greater possibility for extension and definition of his or her system.
6. *Range Corollary:* A construct is convenient for the anticipation of a finite range of events only.
7. *Experience Corollary:* A person's construction system varies as he or she successively construes the replications of events.
8. *Modulation Corollary:* The variation in a person's construction system is limited by the permeability of the constructs within whose ranges of convenience the variants lie.
9. *Fragmentation Corollary:* A person may successively employ a variety of construction subsystems that are inferentially incompatible with each other.
10. *Commonality Corollary:* To the extent that one person employs a construction of experience which is similar to that employed by another, his or her psychological processes are similar to those of the other person.
11. *Sociality Corollary:* To the extent that one person construes the construction processes of another, he or she may play a role in a social process involving the other person.

On the basis of his theory Kelly created an instrument of appraisal, the Role Construct Repertory Test (REP), and a therapeutic auxiliary technique called fixed-role therapy. The REP test requires the individual to compare systematically his or her personal interpretations of the roles of significant people. Such comparisons can then be analyzed impressionistically or objectively with the tools of correlation and factor analysis. Fixed-role therapy involves the psychologist's writing a personality sketch that differs in significant ways from those by which the client construes his or her life. The client is then invited to enact the role for two or more weeks. In many cases the alternative construction of events embodied in the fixed-role sketch is sufficient to aid the client in construing differently the events of his or her life and him- or herself.

Personal constructs may be conceived as a person's means of making sense of life. Sometimes complex interactions among a person's constructions are necessitated by the demands of reality. Thus, for example, the circumspection-preemption-control cycle (CPC) involves the person in a restructuring of his or her construct system in three phases: (1) the circumspection phase, which involves propositional construction of events so that violations of old constructs or new evidence can be appraised and assimilated; (2) the preemption phase, during which the individual must narrow constructions to one significant dichotomous construct that he or she interprets as most relevant; and (3) the control or choice phase, in which the individual commits him- or herself to action on the basis of his or her decision to accept one or the other pole of the dichotomous construct seized upon in phase two.

Kelly's system has led to often novel formulations of basic personality constructs like the unconscious, anxiety, aggression, and guilt. Generally, each of these variables is defined in terms of the individual's capacity to modify and rearrange his or her system of constructs, and the emotional by-products of those constructs that fail to predict events reliably.

Kelly's theory has been less widely influential than, on the face of it, one would expect. Our evaluation of personal construct theory shows that it

- is refutable in principle, but rarely actually tested;

- emphasizes an active agent conception of human beings, especially in Kelly's fundamental postulate of the "person as scientist";

- is focused on the idiographic and therefore limited in the ways it can be tested or applied.

FOR FURTHER READING

Kelly's influence as a personality theorist has waxed and waned with changing fashion in psychology. In consequence, the number of research studies or original theoretical works connected to personal construct theory is limited. Kelly's own comprehensive masterwork is the two-volume *Psychology of Personal Constructs* (New York: Norton, 1955). The first three chapters of Vol. 1 of this work have been published as a self-contained paperback introduction to Kelly's theory under the title *A Theory of Personality: The Psychology of Personal Constructs* (New York: Norton, 1963).

Some of Kelly's theoretical papers have been organized by Brendan Maher into a single volume, *Clinical Psychology and Personality: Selected Papers of George Kelly* (New York: Wiley, 1969). Of particular significance among the papers in this volume is the one entitled "The Language of Hypothesis: Man's Psychological Instrument." Lee Sechrest, a student of Kelly's, provides an overview of Kelly's theory in his chapter "The Psychology of Personal Constructs," in Wepman and Heine (Eds.), *Concepts of Personality* (Chicago: Aldine, 1963), pp. 206–223.

The collection of research papers contained in D. Bannister and J. M. Mair's (Eds.) *The Evaluation of Personal Constructs* (New York: Academic Press, 1968; especially Chapters 3, 4, and 10) will provide some indication of the investigations stimulated by Kelly's ideas. In a similar way, J. C. Bonarius's review, "Research in the Personal Construct Theory of George A. Kelly: Role Construct Repertory Test and Basic Theory," in Vol. 2 of B. A. Maher (Ed.), *Progress in Experimental Personality Research* (New York: Academic Press, 1965), indicates the kinds of questions that have been asked with Kelly's concepts.

More recent research efforts can be surveyed in D. Bannister's (Ed.) collection of papers entitled *Perspectives in Personal Construct Theory* (New York: Academic Press, 1970). Bannister and F. Fransella have put together a paperback book summarizing Kelly's theory and surveying their own and others' research efforts on its behalf: *Inquiring Man: The Theory of Personal Constructs* (Baltimore: Penguin, 1971).

KAREN HORNEY & ERICH FROMM

Psychoanalytic Social Psychology

For the very reason that love in our civilization is so rarely a genuine affection, maltreatment and betrayal abound.

Karen Horney, *Our Inner Conflicts*

In the nineteenth century the problem was that *God is dead;* in the twentieth century the problem is that *man is dead.*

Erich Fromm, "The Present Human Condition"

About Horney's and Fromm's Social Psychoanalysis

Karen Horney and Erich Fromm began as psychoanalytic theorists. But each of them found classic Freudian ideas too restrictive by their emphasis on sexual and aggressive motives to the exclusion of social motives.

Karen Horney widened classical psychoanalysis with her concepts of

1. *childhood as a period of anxious helplessness and hidden anger toward all-powerful but indifferent adults;*
2. *strategies to cope with the anxiety and anger that alienate the person from the true self, so that the neurotic personality is one who cannot simply be, but must avoid, attack, or completely comply with others;*
3. *a desexualized Oedipus complex in which the key issues are power and love instead of sexuality and fear.*

Erich Fromm also widened classical psychoanalysis with concepts initially from Karl Marx and later from the existential philosophers. Fromm wrote about the human need for meaning in life, and he believed that people can find that meaning only if they can accept the responsibility for their choices. Fromm's central tenets are these:

1. *Freedom to make choices, to regulate one's life, and to assume responsibility for the consequences of decisions is a frightening experience for people. Used productively, such freedom leads to genuine intimacy and caring between people; used unproductively, such freedom becomes license to exploit and manipulate others.*
2. *Some personality types become malignant in their handling of aggression. The necrophilous type of personality is a lover of death, decay, and destruction.*
3. *The fundamental dichotomy between healthy and unhealthy personality types is in the distinction between the having and being modes of existence. The having mode is consumptive, based on the malignant belief that one is what one has. The being mode of existence is an embracing of life, a belief that one is as one lives.*

Both Horney and Fromm transcended Freudian classical theory in their search to understand how people create order in their lives rather than merely gratifying their drives.

KAREN HORNEY

THE WAY THE WORLD LOOKS: COPING

Individuals differ in the way they view the world and in their perception of the best way to conduct their lives in relation to the people in it. Some individuals are human doormats, inviting an endless succession of significant (that is, emotionally important) others to tread all over them. These compliant personalities behave as if the most crucial aspect of existence were to please and pacify other people.

At the opposite extreme, there are persons who operate with a typically hostile strategy for dealing with others. These aggressive personalities seem to be behaving in a world that they view as dangerous. Only by constant vigilance, they seem to believe, can the continually hostile efforts of others be thwarted.

Yet a third form of interpersonal strategy is exemplified by individuals who remain coldly aloof and withdrawn from any genuine interaction with significant others. These detached personalities seem to construe the world and its people as essentially troublesome and unjustly demanding. The only reasonable solution, they feel, is avoidance.

Karen Horney brilliantly described these three views of the world and the corresponding coping strategies. Although nearly everyone adopts from time to time each of these stances toward others, neurotics are unable to shift posture. Because they have become entangled in the web of their own efforts to ward off anxiety, neurotic personalities adopt *one* mode of interaction as a rigidly unshakable coping technique. The first task, therefore, in exploring Horney's account of personality is to understand the neurotic's striving for safety and control over his or her world.

THE NEUROTIC TRENDS

On the basis of theoretical assumptions derived partly from psychoanalytic theory and partly from her own clinical observations, Karen Horney postulated that the neurotic personality is governed by one or more of 10 needs or trends. Each of these trends is directed toward *interpersonal control and coping,* that is, toward making life and its necessarily people-oriented contacts bearable. Horney separated herself from the rest of the psychoanalytic school in an important way:

> Freud believed that the [neurotic] disturbances generate from a conflict between environmental factors and repressed instinctual impulses. Adler, more rationalistic and superficial than Freud, believes that they are created by the ways and means that people use to assert their superiority over others. Jung, more mystical than Freud, believes in collective unconscious fantasies which, though replete with creative possibilities, may work havoc because the unconscious strivings fed by them are the exact opposite of those in the conscious mind. *My own answer is that in the center of psychic disturbances are unconscious strivings developed in order to cope with life despite fears, helplessness, and isolation. I have called them "neurotic trends."* (1942, p. 40; italics added)

Each of the neurotic trends is characterized chiefly by its *compulsive rigidity.* Although a neurotic trend for affection, to take one example, may resemble the normal need for love, neurotics are unaware of the *indiscriminate* nature of their need. Their need for affection is out of all proportion to reality: "If it is affection that a person must have, he must receive it from friend and enemy, from employer and bootblack" (Horney, 1942, p. 41). Thus the 10 neurotic trends superficially resemble healthy values but are different in four important respects: They are *disproportion-*

ate in intensity; indiscriminate in application to all other persons; evidence an extreme *disregard for reality;* and show a tendency to provoke *intense anxiety* when they remain unsatisfied. These 10 neurotic "needs" are (Horney, 1942, pp. 54 – 60) as follows:

1. *The neurotic need for affection and approval:* an indiscriminate desire to please others and to be liked and approved of by others. The person's "center of gravity" is in others, not in self.

2. *The neurotic need for a "partner" who will take over one's life:* a partner who will fulfill all expectations the neurotic has in life; who will take responsibility for good and evil, success and failure. The neurotic so inclined has a tendency to overvalue "love" because love can solve everything.

3. *The neurotic need to restrict one's life within narrow borders:* a necessity to be undemanding and contented with little; a need to remain inconspicuous, belittling one's potential.

4. *The neurotic need for power, for control over others, and for a façade of omnipotence:* domination over others craved for its own sake; essential disrespect for others; indiscriminate adoration of strength and contempt for weakness; belief in the power of reason and intelligence; extreme value placed on foresight and prediction; tendency to relinquish wishes and to withdraw because of dread of failure.

5. *The neurotic need to exploit others and get the better of them:* others evaluated primarily according to whether they can be exploited or made use of; dread of being exploited or made to look "stupid."

6. *The neurotic need for social recognition or prestige:* self-evaluation dependent entirely on public acceptance; all things and people evaluated only in terms of prestige value.

7. *The neurotic need for personal admiration:* inflated image of self; need to be admired not for what one possesses or presents in the public eye, but for the imagined self.

8. *The neurotic ambition for personal achievement:* self-evaluation dependent on being the very best—lover, athlete, writer, worker—particularly in one's own mind, recognition by others being vital too, however, and its absence resented.

9. *The neurotic need for self-sufficiency and independence:* necessity never to need anybody, or to yield to any influence, or to be tied down to anything; necessity to avoid any closeness that involves the danger of enslavement.

10. *The neurotic need for perfection and unassailability:* ruminations or recriminations regarding possible flaws; relentless driving for perfection; feelings of superiority over others because of being perfect.

There are obviously overlaps and similarities among the 10 needs or trends. Horney devoted a great deal of her later theoretical efforts to grouping and categorizing these 10 discrete trends into clusters descriptive of particular personalities. The important fact to be kept in mind is that none of these trends is by itself abnormal; only when the trend is disproportionate, indiscriminate, relentless, and anxiety-provoking when frustrated can it be classed as neurotic.

Basic Anxiety and Basic Hostility

Very much like Adler, Horney assumed that one of children's most potent early perceptions of themselves was the discovery of their helplessness. In the face of powerful and authoritative, manipulative and decisive "giants" such as parents, they perceive themselves to be weak and small. Children thus soon learn that their needs, their safety, and their comfort are wholly dependent on these powerful people. Their very survival depends on evoking in them a favorable and responsive attitude toward themselves.

Parental Indifference: The "Basic Evil"

Horney felt that the "basic evil" that lies at the source of later neurosis is a coldly indifferent, perhaps hostile, rejecting attitude of the parents toward the child:

> The basic evil is invariably a lack of genuine warmth and affection. A child can stand a great deal of what is often regarded as traumatic—such as sudden weaning, occasional beating, sex experiences—as long as inwardly he feels wanted and loved. . . . *The main reason why a child does not receive enough warmth and affection lies in the parents' incapacity to give it on account of their own neuroses.* . . . We find various actions or attitudes on the part of the parents which cannot but arouse hostility, such as preference for other children, unjust reproaches, unpredictable changes between overindulgence and scornful rejection, unfulfilled promises, and not least important, *an attitude toward the child's needs which goes through all gradations from temporary inconsideration to a consistent interfering with the most legitimate wishes of the child,* such as disturbing friendships, ridiculing independent thinking, spoiling its interest in its own pursuits . . . *altogether an attitude of the parents which if not in intention nevertheless in effect means breaking the child's will.* (1937, pp. 80–81; italics added)

The main result of such parental indifference, inconsistency, and interference is the creation within the child of an attitude of *basic hostility.*

Basic Hostility: Repression for Survival and Security

Like mature persons, children sense the injustice of their treatment at the hands of emotionally manipulative elders, and they rightfully resent both the manipulation and the manipulators. Unfortunately, unlike mature adults, children are in no position to alter the circumstances by a direct expression of hostility and anger; they must repress their angry feelings—drive them right out of awareness—in the service of continued survival. Repression of the hostility is triggered by a combination of feelings on the child's part: feelings of helplessness, fear, love, or guilt (Horney, 1937, p. 85). But whatever the motive for repression, the result is the creation of feelings of increased unworthiness and anxiety. Because children are caught between dependence on their parents and the growing feeling of hostility toward them, they may actually intensify the conflict by turning those feelings against the only available "safe" target, their own selves. Their feelings of helplessness are thus magnified and the need to maintain the repression of hostility is reinforced. In mottolike form, the child's behavior says *"I have to repress my hostility because I need you"* (Horney, 1937, p. 86).

In some cases, parents actively strive to dominate their children by teaching them fear of the world and its people. They impress their children with the "great dangers of life": germs, cars, strangers, other children, and on and on. In consequence, such children become apprehensive lest they be unable to survive in such a dangerous world without their parents' help. Furthermore, they learn to fear the parents themselves because they have the awesome power to evoke images of the dangers. For such children, repression of hostility is a product of their fear: They do not *dare* to express it. *"I have to repress my hostility,"* their motto goes, *"because I am afraid of you"* (Horney, 1937, p. 86).

In other families, where genuine affection and warmth are lacking, there occurs a kind of verbal substitute expression of love in the form of continual protestations by the parents of how much they are sacrificing for the child. In this case, the child may cling desperately to this mock emotion and feel *"I have to repress my hostility for fear of losing love"* (Horney, 1937, p. 86).

All three cases are essentially similar in that the child's fundamental motive is to sustain satisfying contact with the powerful people of his or her world. Survival need, fear, and love are in most ways closely related by the thread of helplessness that runs through the child's entire pattern of existence.

Basic Anxiety: Lonely and Helpless in a Hostile World

The danger of children's repression of basic hostility toward their parents is that they will generalize that "grudging and anxious" attitude to people in general. The more they cover their hostility and their "grudge against their own family," the more likely they are to project their anxiety to the outside world and its people. They will soon convince themselves that the whole world is, as their parents' behavior may have suggested, a dangerous place:

> The condition that is fostered or brought about by the factors I have mentioned . . . is an insidiously increasing, *all-pervading feeling of being lonely and helpless in a hostile world.* . . . This attitude as such does not constitute a neurosis but it is the nutritive soil out of which a definite neurosis may develop at any time. Because of the fundamental role this attitude plays in neuroses I have given it a special designation: *the basic anxiety;* it is inseparably interwoven with a *basic hostility.* (Horney, 1937, p. 89; italics added)

Horney's concept of *basic anxiety* sounds similar to Adler's notion of the inferiority feelings of childhood. Her explicit definition of basic anxiety strengthens the similarity:

> It [basic anxiety] may be roughly described as a feeling of being small, insignificant, helpless, deserted, endangered, in a world that is out to abuse, cheat, attack, humiliate, betray, envy. (Horney, 1937, p. 92)

The most immediate consequence of the combination of basic hostility and the resultant basic anxiety is the creation of a characteristic mode of reacting to the world and to significant others. Originally, Horney proposed four such character types (1937, p. 96); later, however, in keeping with her tendency to formulate concepts in threes, she reduced the number (1945).

If children come to feel that they can survive only by *complying with others* and by placating them—*"If you love me, you will not hurt me"*—they may solve their survival problems by offering the world a passive, nonassertive, appeasing personality (Horney, 1937, p. 97).

Other children may develop the attitude that life is a struggle which must be fought by maintaining an aggressive stance toward others: *"If I have power, I shall not be hurt"* (Horney, 1937, p. 97). These children's characteristic interaction with others solves their survival problems by keeping others at arm's length or by exerting dominance over them.

Last, children may solve the conflict between unexpressed basic hostility and anxiety by withdrawal from others: *"If I withdraw, nothing can hurt me"* (Horney, 1937, p. 99). The habitual mode of dealing with others is to create a protective shell of isolation, thereby removing themselves from *any* significant emotional interactions.

Transitional Summary

We will give each of these character attitudes fuller treatment. For now, however, it is important to retrace the sequence of Horney's ideas about the nature of personality development to emphasize the importance of basic hostility and basic anxiety.

Out of the fundamental feelings of hostility and anxiety develops a set of values for living. As we have seen, Horney initially proposed 10 such values or neurotic trends, and later she regrouped them in terms of the three character attitudes of *compliance, aggression,* and *withdrawal.*

The child has been made aware that his or her feelings of hostility and anger cannot be openly displayed; he or she represses them and the repression is reinforced by parental indifference, inconsistency, or withdrawal of love. His or her feeling of helplessness is thus also intensified. The world and its people become a source of anticipated pain and anxiety. Out of these anticipations the child develops a series of needs that are rigid, compulsive, and indiscriminate strivings to predict, control, and survive the manipulations and the indifference of a hostile world.

Horney's lucid portrait of a child's basic hostility and basic anxiety—feelings, that is, of resentment to parental indifference and of impotence in the face of a hostile world—may have had important personal sources. We turn next to a recent biographical study of Karen Horney to trace out the roots of her special sensitivity to children's feelings of rejection and their strategies for coping with them.

PERSONAL SOURCES OF THE BASIC-ANXIETY AND BASIC-HOSTILITY HYPOTHESES

Like so many other personality theorists, Karen Horney felt she had been an unwanted child. This theme is so prevalent in the life histories of people who later made important contributions to psychology that it surely must lead historians to wonder whether feelings of unwantedness are a prerequisite in the career of a personality theorist. Sigmund Freud, Anna Freud, Harry Stack Sullivan, Alfred Adler, Carl Jung, Gordon Allport, R. D. Laing, and Erik Erikson evidence similar childhood themes. To this list of "unwanted" children who became eminent theorists of human personality the name of Karen Horney must be added. Rubins (1978) and Quinn (1987) have written the first full-length biographies of Horney, and they provide much insight into the personal sources of her theoretical concepts. In what follows we rely on Rubins and Quinn and on Horney's (1980) own diaries and letters.

Karen Horney was born on September 16, 1885, to a ship's captain, Berndt Wackels Danielson, and his second wife, Clotilde. Captain Danielson already had four children by his previous marriage, and his search for a second wife may have been motivated by the desire to have a mother for them (Quinn, 1987, p. 20; Rubins, 1978, p. 8). However, Captain Danielson's children never accepted his new wife, and they resented the two new children born into the marriage, Berndt and his younger sister, Karen. Moreover, the marriage between the gruff and masterful sea captain and his 18-year-younger bride, despite all appearances, was not made in heaven. In August 1904, Clotilde Danielson could stand her husband's tyrannical personality no longer, and with her two children, separated from Captain Danielson completely.

Karen's Relationship With Her Mother and Father

When Karen's brother Berndt was born, he fulfilled the family tradition by carrying on the family name. He was a boy, he was wanted, and he became his parents' darling (Rubins, 1978, p. 10). Karen's birth, four years later, came at a time when the relationship between her parents had grown abrasive. "Karen questioned whether she had really been wanted" (Rubins, 1978, p. 11).

Captain Danielson was an authoritarian personality, drawing his rigidity and tyrannical style from his avid fundamentalist religious beliefs. It was biblical truth that he sought to impose on his wife and children. On occasion, after a long period of silent Bible reading, he would erupt into one of his frequent explosions of anger and throw his Bible at his wife. The children later referred to their father as *der Bibel-schmeisser* (Bible-thrower), when he was not present (Rubins, 1978, p. 11). For the God-fearing Captain Danielson, women had been created second to men, in talent, in morality, and in privilege. The Bible itself had shown that a woman had yielded to temptation in the Garden and was therefore the source of evil. "What was permitted the male could not be tolerated in the female. His son Berndt would be allowed freedom, privilege, education; these were not necessary for his wife or youngest daughter" (Rubins, 1978, p. 11).

Danielson's wife, nicknamed "Sonni," was beautiful and a more sophisticated person than her husband. Karen's relationship with her mother was close, loving, and devoted. Rubins (1978, p. 13) speculates that Sonni so often came to the girl's rescue in disputes with the father because she identified with her daughter's talents and wishes, vicariously fulfilling her own blocked ambitions. As the children grew older, the three of them formed a "protective alliance" against the father (Rubins, 1978, p. 13).

On the other hand, Karen had rather contradictory feelings toward her father. She admired and respected him and was caught up in the romantic vision of his far-ranging sea travels. For his part, Captain Danielson took his daughter on at least three lengthy voyages aboard his ship, and he occasionally brought her gifts from exotic places. At one point, when she was in her thirties, she took to wearing a captain's style cap, indicating at least some positive and sympathetic feelings for the memory of her father (Rubins, 1978, p. 12). Karen may even have lied late in her life about traveling to South America on one of the ships her father commanded. She told several people, including her daughter, that it was the first time she had tasted bananas (Quinn, 1987, p. 36). Clearly the "lie" was more of a wishful fantasy that betrays at least some urge to be close with her father. On the whole, however, she felt rejected by her father, and less loved by him than her brother Berndt.

In childhood, Karen felt deprived of affection, and her coping style up to the age of eight was to behave "like a little lamb" (Rubins, 1978, p. 13). She even once placed some of her toys on the street for some poorer child to find, telling no one about her altruistic deed because self-sacrifice was her way of being the good child she hoped her parents would love. (See Horney's semiautobiographical case history and comments in Horney, 1950, p. 20, and 1942, pp. 190 ff.) By the age of nine, Karen shifted strategies, becoming rebellious and openly ambitious in the company of her schoolmates. Partly to escape the intolerability of her home life, and partly because of her native intelligence and curiosity, Karen attacked her schoolwork with a passion. Her sense of basic inadequacy was further intensified by concern over her physical appearance. "As she said years later to her daughter, 'If I couldn't be beautiful, I decided I would be smart' " (Rubins, 1978, p. 14). In reality, Karen was a strikingly good-looking young girl. Yet, schoolwork and achievement were seized upon as a way of compensating for her self-perceived defects.

At puberty, Karen's open and excessive affection toward her brother, stemming initially from her attempts to cope with her more genuine feelings of resentment toward him, was rebuffed by Berndt, who found his sister's loving protestations embarrassing. This rejection proved overwhelming for Karen: "It was a blow to her pride; . . . she felt ashamed and humiliated" (Rubins, 1978, p. 14). She became depressed, and believing a family doctor, who said that the strain of schoolwork had been responsible, her parents placed her in a lower grade. The result of these machinations was that Karen vowed to be first in her class always!

By the age of 12, she had decided on a career in medicine, a choice that her stern father regarded with amazement and opposition, and one that her mother encouraged. Through both her mother's and her brother's intercession with her father, Karen finally convinced him to provide the tuition to enter a school that would prepare her for later admission to medical school. Karen even gave him a statement written in verse, wherein she promised to ask nothing more of him if he would help her through this new undertaking (Rubins, 1978, p. 21).

The Religious Crisis

It is not surprising that, in the light of her ambivalent relationship with her father and his less than exemplary biblical interpretations, Karen developed a painful hostility to religion in adolescence. A growing theological skepticism emerged in her expressed as a doubting of authority figures and fundamental religious belief. She immersed herself in religious studies, and in typically adolescent fashion, her zealousness for truth turned into metaphysical questioning of the divinity of Jesus. Her brother Berndt guided her to one way of understanding the contradiction contained in the belief that Jesus was both man and God; and his explanation was as vague as it was loving. Karen confided to her diary: " 'Something like a stone fell from my heart. . . . He [Jesus] became dearer to me' " (Rubins, 1978, p. 18).

Her religious skepticism (really her form of rebellion) continued to mount, so that at the time of her confirmation, religious authority and her father's authoritarianism were roughly identical to her, and, in consequence, equally worthy targets of her despair and anger. Karen wrote in her diary:

> It must be grand to have a father one can love and esteem. The Fourth Commandment stands before me like a specter, with its "Thou shalt." I cannot respect a person who makes us all unhappy with his hypocrisy, egocentricity, crudeness and illbreeding. . . . [These are] indescribable days for Mother and us under the fearful domination of the master of the house and our pastor. Pen and paper would rebel against writing down anything so coarse and mean. Confirmation was no blessing for me. On the contrary, it was a great piece of hypocrisy, for I professed belief in the teachings of Christ, the doctrine of love, while carrying hatred in my heart (and for my nearest at that). I feel too weak to follow Christ. Yet I long for the faith, firm as a rock, that makes oneself and others happy. (Quoted by Rubins, 1978, p. 19; see also Horney, 1980, p. 37)

As Rubins notes, such hostile feelings could not be expressed openly, for Karen was rebelling against her father, his edicts, and her own deepest childhood beliefs (1978, p. 19). As she confided years later to her friend Franz Alexander, such grave doubts meant " 'standing up to the frightening gaze of my father's blue eyes' " (Rubins, 1978, p. 19).

Horney's Relationship With Her Husband and Children

In 1906, Karen entered one of the few medical schools that permitted women to study for the degree in Freiburg, Germany. Strongly competing with her brother's accomplishments at law school and finding herself in a virtually all-male atmosphere, Karen nevertheless relished her newfound sense of freedom and independence. During this exciting time, she met Oskar Horney, an economics student on vacation from his own studies at the University of Brunswick, and they struck up a close friendship. Karen was apparently attracted to the strong but stern Oskar, who radiated emotional and physical strength, intelligence, and independence, because she valued these qualities in her own character. She wrote letters to him for the next year in which she expressed her most private feelings, including her changing attitudes toward her mother. Sonni had become, in her daughter's less idealized view of her, a basically good person but one who was nevertheless coldhearted and lacking in self-control (Rubins, 1978, p. 31).

In 1909 Karen and Oskar were married. He had earned a law degree and was employed by an investment firm that was eventually to fail disastrously, taking his fortunes with it. By 1910, Karen was pregnant with her first of three daughters, Brigitte. Shortly before Brigitte's birth, Sonni suffered a stroke; she died one week later in February 1911. Thus in a relatively short space of time, Karen had experienced profound changes—her marriage, a death, and the giving of new life. At this time she was also undergoing her own personal psychoanalysis with Karl Abraham in preparation for her career in psychiatry. The net effect of all these experiences, along with the reexamination of childhood conflicts necessitated by the analysis, has been well summarized by Rubins (1978, p. 38):

> Karen's ambivalent feelings toward her father, her dependency upon her mother and her struggle to free herself from this dependency, her longstanding resentment at playing a secondary role to her brother, the conflict within herself between the roles of assertive professional woman and the compliant childbearing homemaker—all these had to be confronted.

The outcome of her analysis was not satisfying to Karen, and she remained depressed, asking in a letter to her analyst," 'Does not the real work begin after the analysis? The analysis shows one her enemies but one must battle them afterwards, day by day' " (Quinn, 1987, pp. 157 ff. and pp. 193 ff; Rubins, 1978, p. 39).

The Horneys eventually had three children, all daughters. In matters of discipline, Oskar was as severe and demanding as Karen's own father had been with her, but Karen never intervened. One Christmas, Marianne, the middle daughter, leaned back too far in her chair at the dinner table; she grasped the tablecloth and took with her to the floor an entire new dinner service and the Christmas meal. Oskar spanked Marianne with a dog whip, while Brigitte, the eldest, cried in sympathy, but Karen showed no outward reaction to her daughter's plight (Rubins, 1978, p. 51).

All three of the girls recalled that Karen had a "laissez-faire" and detached attitude toward their own concerns. Both parents believed in encouraging independence and in avoiding coddling, an amazing attitude on the part of a mother who herself had been so desperate for parental warmth and affection, and who would later construct an entire theory around parental indifference as a "basic evil."

> She would not interfere with their growing up, with their comings and goings. But the children felt that this noninterference might have bordered at times on neglect: Their clothes were often too long or too short, their stockings did not fit. A governess was no longer needed now that they were all in school, and the maids did not look after them personally. (Rubins, 1978, p. 83)

Due partly to her own hectic schedule, and partly to genuine personality differences with her husband, Karen's marriage began to disintegrate. In 1923 Oskar's investments collapsed and his salary with his bankrupt firm was worth little in the rising inflation of the day. He borrowed heavily, contracted encephalomeningitis during a business trip to Paris, and eventually returned home a broken, defeated, spiritless man. He became morose, withdrawn, and argumentative, losing friends and possessions with equal speed. As their finances deteriorated, so did the marriage—by 1926 the couple was emotionally, if not physically, separated by a wide gulf. Karen and her daughters actualized the separation later that year by moving into a small apartment with their few possessions. Some 10 years later, Karen filed for divorce, which became official in 1939.

The Depressions

Throughout her life, beginning with her brother's rejection of her effusive protestations of love for him in adolescence, Karen Horney suffered periodic bouts of dejection bordering on depression. In 1923, at the height of her husband's financial difficulties, her brother Berndt died of a pulmonary infection. He was 40 years old, and she was devastated at the senselessness of his death. Profound depression was the consequence. Writing to Georg Groddeck some months after Berndt's death, Karen expressed a curiously ambivalent kind of acceptance.

> . . . in the beginning I considered [the death of my brother] as something totally senseless—he belonged to those people who seem to burst with the joy of living. In the face of this, after many weeks I arrived at the conclusion: something in him had wanted to die. That insight I tend to accept in general and I have only one suspicion about it, and that is that it is too much of what we want to believe. (Quoted in Rubins, 1978, p. 72)

Her ambivalence, and her self-skepticism of her explanation, are understandable in the light of Karen's early belief in Berndt's favored position with her father. But the loss of this idealized yet resented person was too potent for even Karen's psychoanalyzed adjustment to life.

Shortly after Berndt's death, while on vacation at the beach with her family and friends, Karen went alone for a swim. When she failed to return after more than an hour, Oskar found her clutching a piling in deep water, ruminating on whether to end her life or swim back to the beach (Rubins, 1978, p. 87). Much pleading was required by Oskar and his friends to convince Karen her life was worth living.

Overall, the central conflicts of Karen Horney's life were profound feelings of inadequacy and guilt-provoking resentment toward her parents and her brother for making her feel that way. The death of her brother evoked such profound depression in Karen possibly because Berndt's demise fulfilled her darkest, rageful childhood wishes and simultaneously triggered the most intense adult guilt: self-punishment in suicidal longings. It is small wonder, then, that Karen Horney's theory stressed interpersonal relations as the core of neurotic conflicts. Tracing over her life history, three themes emerge. First, her sense of her own unwantedness and unattractiveness initially had produced a compliant, meek, over-eager-to-please child. From this stance of selflessness emerged a rebellious, skeptical, and defiant young woman, who sought by her intellectual achievements to compensate for her presumed weaknesses and to exact revenge with the evidence of her hard-won competence.

Second, Karen found herself almost unwittingly married to a man who bore more than superficial resemblance to the authoritarian father she so resented. Almost as though attempting to master in her marriage what she felt she had failed to master as a child, she professionally and parentally surpassed her husband.

Third, achieving in a frowned-upon profession for women in the early 1900s, Karen adopted psychoanalytic theory, drew what intellectual and emotional sustenance she could from it, and then abandoned some of its central tenets in favor of her own insights. She rebelled against paternalistic psychoanalysis in much the same way as she had rebelled against religion and her father's conception of it, and through that revolt, against the father himself. As Rubins (1978, p. 113) tactfully phrased it: "It was the same old conflict within her that she had experienced so often before, how to be aggressive yet friendly and loving at the same time."

Relationship With Erich Fromm

Karen had gotten to know Erich Fromm and his wife, Frieda Fromm-Reichmann, from her days in Berlin, where all three had studied psychoanalysis together (Quinn,

1987, p. 269). Although Fromm was 15 years younger than Horney, a close friendship and intellectual relationship developed. Once in America, in Chicago, they renewed their relationship, initially on an intellectual-professional level. At some point during the next several years, the relationship deepened into a romantic one, and the closeness intensified (Quinn, 1987, p. 270). As Quinn points out, it becomes impossible to separate the degree of influence they each had on the other in their writings, but the clear similarities of theme and content are testimony to the closeness they shared.

During this time, Horney's revisionist views on the psychology of women were creating some degree of divisiveness in the psychoanalytic society to which she belonged. Quinn's (e.g., 1987, p. 274) portrait of Horney indicates a strong, somewhat authoritative demeanor, fueled by no little amount of competitiveness with her male colleagues. It was not a personality recipe destined to soothe troubled waters in the intensely opinionated atmosphere of psychoanalytic circles. In 1934 Horney decided to leave Chicago for New York. Her reasons for leaving were part political, part frustration with the intellectual climate, and part a rumor that she had seduced a younger candidate at the psychoanalytic institute. Quinn (1987, p. 262) has sorted the evidence and presents the hypothesis that *if* Horney had seduced a candidate, and the truth of that assertion is likely never to be known because the analyst involved is now dead, it probably grew from her depression and despair with which she fought a lifelong battle. After the move to New York, Erich Fromm joined her there within the year. Friends remembered them as inseparable weekend companions.

The relationship with Fromm had a bitter ending. Eventually, a kind of competitiveness developed between the two. When students at the psychoanalytic institute wanted to study with Fromm, Horney suggested that a nonphysician (Fromm was a Ph.D., not an M.D. like Horney) should not teach courses to analytic candidates (Quinn, 1987, p. 363). When the matter came to a vote, Horney's view prevailed, and Fromm resigned from the institute along with Harry Stack Sullivan, Clara Thompson, and Janet Rioch. Together they made plans to establish an alternative institute, but the bitterness between Fromm and Horney was now crystallized.

Quinn (1987, pp. 366 ff.) points out that the romantic relationship between the couple had ended by the early 1940s, and these political-competitive disputes merely reflected that personal bitterness. Quinn believes that the relationship probably ended because Horney perceived Erich Fromm as not being able to provide the degree of intimacy she wanted. Perhaps marriage, too, had been an issue. A further complication involved Karen Horney's daughter, Marianne, who had gone to Fromm for psychoanalysis during the time of the relationship at her mother's suggestion. The analysis was a success, and Marianne reported that she lived a fuller life because of it (Quinn, 1987, p. 368). But it is possible that Horney resented the outcome or perhaps interpreted Marianne's increased independence from her as Fromm's fault. At all events, the relationship was complex, fraught with conflicts from the start, and ended sourly.

We turn next to the case history of Clare, which, there is good reason to believe, contains thinly disguised autobiographical elements of Karen Horney's own family history. In the case of Clare, we can catch a glimpse of Karen Horney's view of her own struggle (cf. Rubins, 1978, p. 17).

AN ILLUSTRATIVE CASE: CLARE, AN UNWANTED CHILD

Despite several of her mother's abortion attempts, Clare was born into the unhappy marriage. Her parents' first child, a boy, had been born at a time when the marriage was a happy one, and in some ways he remained the only object of genuine parental approval and affection. Not that Clare was in any material way mistreated or abused. She always received the same quantity and quality of gifts, trips, lessons, and educational opportunities as her brother.

> But in less tangible matters she received less than the brother, less tenderness, less interest in school marks and in the thousand little daily experiences of a child, less concern when she was ill, less solicitude to have her around, less willingness to treat her as a confidante, less admiration for looks and accomplishments. (Horney, 1942, p. 49)

Always away from home, Clare's father, a doctor, became the object of the mother's ridicule and loathing. As the "dominating spirit" of the family, mother's evaluation of father soon was converted into a family law of contempt. So great was the bitterness against the father that open death wishes were often expressed by Clare's mother and these "contributed much to Clare's feeling that it was much safer to be on the powerful side" (Horney, 1942, p. 49).

The most immediate result of the family atmosphere on Clare's development was her lost opportunity to develop a sense of confidence and self-trust. As Clare matured, her feelings of unworthiness and her sense of total unlikableness grew:

> This shift from essentially true and warranted accusations of *others* to essentially untrue and unwarranted *self*-accusations had far-reaching consequences. . . .*And the shift meant more than an acceptance of the majority estimate of herself. It meant also that she repressed all grievances against the mother. If everything was her own fault, the grounds for bearing a grudge against mother were pulled away from under her.* (Horney, 1942, p. 50; italics added)

Clare thus relinquished any possibility of genuine rebellion against the injustice of her own treatment at the hands of her family. Instead, she became a "joiner," a compliant member in the circle of admirers surrounding the powerful mother. "By admiring what in reality she resented, she became alienated from her own feelings. She no longer knew what she herself liked or wished or feared or resented" (Horney, 1942, p. 51). In short, she began to act on the unconscious premise "that it is safer to admire others than to be critical." In a word, Clare had become *compliant*.

The essentially self-effacing quality characteristic of compliance was expressed in a variety of ways in Clare's behavior. One way was her compulsive modesty, a tendency to "put herself into second place," and to judge herself more critically than anyone else ever could. In effect, Clare had lost the capacity to take control of her own life; she lived life only to appease and placate others. Beneath the façade of compliance, passivity, and modesty, however, there developed an unconscious need to surpass others, to beat them at their own game, a striving aimed at restoring some much needed self-esteem. But of course that need had to remain submerged.

At the age of 30, Clare felt the need of analytic treatment. As an editor for a magazine, she had submerged her ambition to do creative fiction writing. Her life and interests had become so constricted in the service of compliance that she was able to perform only routine work on the writing of others, but was totally incapacitated when it came to original or creative writing of her own.

Fortunately an incident occurred that allowed Clare to see the anxiety that underlay her compulsive humility and modesty. She had developed a plan for improving the magazine, a plan she knew to be sound but which would occasion much protest and argument from other members of the staff. During the staff meeting at which she was to present her plan, she experienced several moments of panic. She even had to leave the room at one point because of a sudden attack of diarrhea. However, when the discussion began to favor her proposal, she was able to control herself and the panic diminished. After her plan proved successful in operation, she received much recognition and acclaim. Instead of viewing her success as a critical victory, she was able to view it only as a lucky escape from great danger.

Eventually, with continued analytic treatment, Clare was able to recognize that her self-effacement was a striving for security. She came to enjoy her successes and to take pride in her considerable abilities. A final indication of her slowly burgeoning self-confidence and realistic pride was embodied in a dream she had during the final phase of her psychoanalysis:

> . . . she drove with her friend in a strange country and it occurred to her that she, too, might apply for a driver's license. Actually she had a license and could drive as well as the friend. The dream symbolized a dawning insight that she had rights of her own and need not feel like a helpless stranger. (Horney, 1942, p. 84)

REAL SELF, ACTUAL SELF, AND IDEAL SELF: "TYRANNY OF THE SHOULDS"

Confronted by the intense conflict between their feelings of helplessness and their unexpressible hostility toward their parents, children slowly develop a characteristic *defensive* way of perceiving themselves. Their *"real selves,"* they are made to realize, are despicable, unlovable, and unworthy; their parents' inconsistent and indifferent reactions to them make that clear. The repressed hostility turns against the self to further buttress the notion that they are unlovable and unworthy. This so-called real self is not real at all. Since the picture they hold of this personage is based on *false* evaluations by others, it is "real" only to the extent that they believe it (Horney, 1945, p. 98). When their image of this "real" self is this negative, it would more appropriately be designated as the "despised self."

Children necessarily begin to develop a defensive restructuring of this image of the despised real self into an *idealized image of the self they should be* in order to survive the hostile world and gain needed love and approval.

> In contrast to authentic ideals, the idealized image has a static quality. It is not a goal toward whose attainment he strives but a fixed idea which he worships. . . . The idealized image is a decided hindrance to growth because it either denies short-

comings or merely condemns them. *Genuine ideals make for humility, the ideal-ized image for arrogance.* (Horney, 1945, p. 99; italics added)

The idealized self-image substitutes for genuine self-confidence and pride. It is based on a wishful-thinking style that is betrayed in all of its unrealistic compulsivity later in adulthood when the neurotic continually refers to his or her "shoulds":

> Forget about the disgraceful creature you actually *are* [i.e., the despised real self]; this is how you *should* be. . . . He should be the utmost of honesty, generosity, con-siderateness, justice, dignity, courage, unselfishness. He should be the perfect lover, husband, teacher. He should be able to endure anything, should like everybody, should love his parents, his wife, his country; or, he should not be attached to anything or anybody, nothing should matter to him, he should never feel hurt, and he should always be serene and unruffled. He should always enjoy life; or, he should be above pleasure and enjoyment. He should be spontaneous; he should always control his feelings. He should know, understand, and foresee everything. He should be able to solve every problem of his own, or of others, in no time. He should be able to overcome every difficulty of his as soon as he sees it. He should never be tired or fall ill. He should always be able to find a job. He should be able to do things in one hour which can only be done in two to three hours. (Horney, 1950, p. 65)

This seemingly endless list of things neurotics feel they ought to be or do was termed by Horney the "tyranny of the should" (1950, pp. 65 ff.). The contradictory and uncompromising nature of the items in the list suggests the compulsive, inexorable process of personality distortion that has resulted from the creation of the idealized self-image. With time, the idealized self-image becomes converted into an ideal self, no longer to be recognized as a fiction. It is now seen as a state of being that is nearly impossible to attain (Horney, 1950, p. 158). Nevertheless, the neurotic is compelled to strive toward this unreachable ideal in what Horney called the "search for glory" (1950, p. 23). Indeed, the ideal self slowly becomes more real to the neurotic than the "real" despised self ever was. The idealized self becomes the *comprehensive neurotic solution,* for it actualizes the fantasied image by which all problems can be solved, all difficulties surmounted. With the creation of the ideal self, the neurotic "solves" the conflict between feelings of basic anxiety and hostility; *he or she learns to deal with the world and its people through the shoulds of the ideal self.*

In writing about the tyranny of the shoulds, it is almost as though Horney were writing about her father and his rigid standards of conduct and impossible demands for moral perfection. Horney, no doubt, was expressing to some degree her experi-ence of these demands, as well as her striving to surpass her more favored brother, who served, so to speak, as another, parentally reinforced, "should" in her life.

In her later work, Horney created a further distinction among the images neu-rotics have of themselves. Originally the term *real self* was used to indicate the dam-aged self-image produced in children by their parents' reinforcement of their feelings of helplessness. Horney later changed the usage somewhat by employing "real self" to designate the true core of a person's being, his or her very center of existence. The real self harbors all the potential for growth and health: "clarity and depth of his own feelings, thoughts, wishes, interests; the ability to tap his own resources, the strength of his will power, the special capacities or gifts he may have; the faculty to express

TABLE 13.1 Horney's Conception of the Self

1. DESPISED REAL SELF
   False conceptions of one's competence, worth, and lovability based on belief in others' evaluations, especially those of the parents. Negative evaluations may reinforce one's sense of helplessness.

2. REAL SELF
   The true core of one's being, containing potential for growth, happiness, will power, special capacities and gifts, and the urge for "self-realization," that is, the need to be spontaneously what one truly is.

3. ACTUAL SELF
   Distinguished from the subjectively perceived real self as the objectively existing person, physically and mentally, independent of anyone's perceptions.

4. IDEAL SELF
   The damaged real self, hurt by negative evaluations and indifference from parents, struggles with the "tyranny of the shoulds," that is, strives to be perfect in a wishful way as a compensation for feelings of inadequacy and unlovability.

himself, and to relate to others with his spontaneous feelings" (Horney, 1950, p. 17). It is this core that is damaged by parental indifference. The goal of the real self is the striving for self-realization, that is, the accomplishment of the person's *own* values and aims in life. In this sense, Horney began to use the term "real self" to indicate a "possible self," that is, a self that the individual *can* realistically learn to express.

To a large extent, the real self is a product of the person's own perceptions, his or her own interpretations of what he or she is. To distinguish from this phenomenally real self the objective sum of what the person is at any moment in time as observed by others Horney used the term *actual self.* The actual self is thus the totality of everything, physical and mental, that the person "really" is, independent of the person's own perceptions. In summary, the real self is the core of the person's existence as he or she perceives it and perhaps despises it; the ideal self is a glorified image of what he or she should be, an image that is impossible to attain; the actual self is the sum of objectively observable characteristics of the person at one moment in time.

It should be pointed out that for Horney the goal of psychotherapy was to provide the individual with the means to free the real self, to accept its character, and to allow it full and spontaneous expression without the curtailment of learned defensiveness (Horney, 1946, pp. 202 ff.). Table 13.1 summarizes the differences among the real, actual, and ideal selves.

THE CORE NEUROTIC CONFLICT: ALIENATION FROM REAL SELF

The central neurotic conflict can now be rephrased. Recall that Horney originally described it as the contradictory trend between unexpressed hostility and anxiety over feelings of helplessness. These feelings are generalized to people at large from their original focus against the family, causing the individual to adopt one of three possible orientations to the world. On the basis of most-valued needs, the individual may adopt a strategy of compliance, aggression, or withdrawal. Now, however, the central conflict was rephrased in terms of Horney's developing ideas of the real and idealized selves.

The basic anxiety experienced in childhood and coupled with basic hostility that could not be expressed causes an alienation of the individual from his or her real self. The central neurotic conflict is furthered by the adoption of an idealized self at the expense of one's spontaneity, self-trust, and independence. In essence, neurotics attempt to mold themselves into something they are not to gain what they have lost: security. Since other people are the key agents in what has become a dangerous world, they adopt defensive strategies for dealing with them: "He feels what he *should* feel, wishes what he *should* wish, likes what he *should* like" (Horney, 1950, p. 159; italics added).

> In other words, the tyranny of the should drives him frantically to be something different from what he is or could be. And in his imagination he *is* different—so different, indeed, that the real self fades and pales still more. Neurotic claims, in terms of self, mean the abandoning of the reservoir of spontaneous energies. Instead of making his own efforts, for instance, with regard to human relations, the neurotic insists that others should adjust to him. (Horney, 1950, p. 159)

Three consequences of the individual's alienation from his or her real self can be discerned in the neurotic's feelings of being removed from him- or herself (Horney, 1950, pp. 159–161):

1. *Abandonment of self-responsibility for his behavior:* The neurotic comes to feel that "I am driven instead of being the driver" (1950, p. 159).
2. *Active moves away from the real self:* His or her own inner creative forces lie fallow as he or she succumbs to the idealized self and the search for glory embodied in "shoulds"; at all costs the ideal image must be striven for, perpetually and inexorably, since only by investing all energy in these strivings can the despised real self be left behind.
3. *Active moves against the real self:* The individual experiences bouts of self-hate, with the idea of "being oneself" becoming terrifying and appalling. The neurotic has an unconscious interest in not being him- or herself, in not having a clear self-perception. In short, the neurotic treats him- or herself *impersonally,* as an object.

INTERPERSONAL COPING STRATEGIES: MOVES TOWARD, AWAY FROM, AND AGAINST OTHERS

Unlike Freud, who saw conflict between repressed instincts and the forces of the ethical side of personality as the core of neurosis, Horney observed a different kind of conflict, interpersonal and intrapersonal conflict:

> They [i.e., the conflicts] operated between contradictory sets of neurotic trends, and though they originally concerned contradictory attitudes toward others, in time they

encompassed contradictory attitudes toward the self, contradictory qualities and contradictory sets of values. . . . (1945, p. 15)

Horney viewed the neurotic's symptoms and interpersonal strategies as attempts to "solve" basic conflicts. Compulsive and indiscriminate strivings, contradictory and conflicted needs for perfection, power, affection, and independence, are all anxiety-allaying techniques designed to maintain the alienation between the despised real self and the ideal self, and between the real self and significant others. The 10 neurotic trends or needs began to be more comprehensible to Horney as *clusters of strivings* directed toward dealing with people and their demands. Horney organized the 10 needs into three patterns of traits, illustrated by the three hypothetical personalities with which we began. It is necessary to examine those three character types from the perspective of Horney's concept of self-alienation.

Moving Toward People: The Self-Effacing Solution

Recall that the first solution to neurotic conflict that Horney described was originally termed "moving towards others" (Horney, 1945, pp. 48 ff.). This type of individual manifests the neurotic traits that are conducive to compliance, much as Clare had learned to do. These traits include intense needs for affection and approval, a need for a partner in the form of friend, husband, wife, or lover, and a necessity to be undemanding, restricting one's life within narrow borders:

In sum, this type needs to be liked, wanted, desired, loved; to feel accepted, welcomed, approved of, appreciated; to be needed, to be of importance to others, especially to one particular person; to be helped, protected, taken care of, guided. (Horney, 1945, p. 51)

The goal of the compliant type's "moving towards others" is on the surface a need to be in harmony with them, to avoid friction. But contradictory trends may also be served by this strategy. Compliance on the surface may mask a strong inner need to compete, to excel, to dominate (Horney, 1945, p. 56). Below the surface, within the real self, an unrecognized rage, anger, and residual hostile sentiment boils. The need of compliant neurotics to be liked by others thus serves to conceal their need to be aggressive. Occasionally, the repressed impulses of anger will explode into fits of irritability or into temper tantrums. Or, he or she may make demands on others only "because he is so miserable—'poor me.' " Of course, he or she never recognizes that such demands are manipulative of others, or that they are attempts to satisfy his or her aggressive strivings: "He cannot help feeling at times that he is so unfairly treated that he simply can't stand it any longer" (Horney, 1945, p. 58).

In her later statement of neurotic conflict (1950, pp. 214 ff.), Horney referred to the "moving towards others" strategy as the *self-effacing solution* to neurotic conflict. In effect, the self-effacing person has identified the ideal self with the restricted and subdued despised self:

He is *his subdued self;* he is the stowaway without any rights. In accordance with this attitude he also tends to suppress in himself anything that connotes ambition, vindictiveness, triumph, seeking his own advantage. In short he has solved his inner conflict by suppressing all expansive attitudes and drives and making self-abnegating trends predominant. (Horney, 1950, p. 216)

The self-effacing type has idealized the qualities of suffering, helplessness, and martyrdom, *for only by viewing oneself as "saintly" can one supply oneself with a good reason to endure the basic hostility one has never allowed oneself to express.* If one is a saint, then it is reasonable that one must suffer. And suffering becomes even more enjoyable if one can spread the misery to others. One thus is unable to identify with the idealized and glorified self-image. One can identify only with the victimized distortion of it. Horney felt that the self-effacing "solution" was the most damaging because intrinsic to this strategy is intense subjective unhappiness.

Moving Against People: The Expansive Solution

The aggressive, expansive solution to neurotic conflict is based on a different view of life: on a belief that the world is a hostile place and that life "is a struggle of all against all . . ." (Horney, 1945, p. 63). These individuals characteristically behave toward others in aggressive ways; they are best described as "moving against others." They have a kind of Machiavellian façade of suave politeness and good fellowship that is designed to facilitate satisfaction of their needs for control and power. Aggressive individuals need to excel by exploiting others, to attain recognition by exerting dominance and power over those they perceive to be underlings. Success and prestige are the yardsticks to their sense of self-worth.

> Any situation or relationship is looked at from the standpoint of "What can I get out of it?"—whether it has to do with money, prestige, contacts, or ideas. *The person himself is consciously or semiconsciously convinced that everyone acts this way,* and so what counts is to do it more efficiently than the rest. (Horney, 1945, p. 65; italics added)

Where the compliant types who move toward others have a need for a mate or partner stemming from their feelings of helplessness, aggressive types desire a partner who can enhance their prestige, power, or wealth.

Horney later rechristened this type who "moves against" people as the expansive solution to neurotic conflict: the appeal of mastery (1950, pp. 187 ff.). In almost every respect, the expansive solution is the direct opposite to the self-effacing solution. *The expansive type glorifies and cultivates in him- or herself everything that leads to mastery of others* (1950, p. 214).

> The appeal of life lies in its mastery. . . . He should be able to master the adversities of fate, the difficulties of a situation, the intricacies of intellectual problems, the resistances of other people, conflicts in himself. The reverse side of the necessity for mastery is his dread of anything connoting helplessness; this is the most poignant dread he has. (Horney, 1950, p. 192)

Unlike the compliant, self-effacing type who identifies with the despised real self, the aggressive person has come to believe that he or she *is* the ideal self, that he or she *is* the glorified image toward which he or she strives. All of the aggressive type's behavior can be understood as an attempt to actualize the ideal self (Horney, 1950, p. 192).

Moving Away From People: The Solution of Resignation

The third "solution" to neurotic conflict is practiced by those individuals who develop a protective "I don't care about anything" attitude. They become detached from human affairs and resigned to an emotionally flat life. For if they do not allow themselves to care about anything or anyone, they can deceive themselves that they will never be hurt. Horney characterized this individual's dominant strategy as "moving away from people" (1945, pp. 73 ff.). Resigned individuals evidence intense needs of self-sufficiency, perfection, and unassailability. They tend to restrict their lives within narrow confines much as the compliant types do, but for resigned individuals the motive is the need *never to be dependent on anyone.*

Neurotic detachment is considerably different from the normal feelings each of us experiences on those occasions when we would like to be alone with our own thoughts. The neurotic has *persistent* feelings of indifference and withdrawal based on an "intolerable strain in associating with people" (Horney, 1950, p. 73).

> What is crucial is their inner need to put emotional distance between themselves and others. More accurately, it is their conscious and unconscious determination not to get emotionally involved with others in any way, whether in love, fight, co-operation, or competition. They draw around themselves a kind of magic circle which no one may penetrate. (Horney, 1945, p. 75)

By their resigned attitudes and detachment, neurotic individuals who move away from others have removed themselves from the "inner battlefield" of their own conflicts. Their "don't care" demeanor provides them with a sense of superior distance, haughty removal from their own and others' "petty" problems. They become onlookers at themselves and their lives to the degree that even in therapy they remain detached and view the process of their own inner explorations as "fascinating entertainment" (Horney, 1950, p. 261).

A consequence of this "moving away from others" is the total lack of any striving for achievement or success in the ordinary meaning of these terms. They belittle their own assets. Unconsciously, they deny any desire to achieve success or to exert effort on their own behalf. They lack goal-centeredness. As a result, they are hypersensitive to coercion or advice, which they perceive as essentially similar, and they reject both in their attempts to remain independent.

Horney identified three modes of stilted and joyless living that characterize various subvarieties of the resigned neurotic:

1. *Persistent Resignation:* These individuals are characterized by a continual emotional inertia. They fulfill as few of the tasks of life as are necessary to guarantee their freedom. They may pass for essentially normal, though without any observable joy in living. Their persistent resignation may be only a mask covering a feeling of rebelliousness. Instead of active resistance to life, they practice passive resistance: a total uncooperation with the demands of living.

2. *Rebelliousness:* The appeal of freedom and independence from others is so strong for these individuals that they *actively* resist the "trivia" of life. They may turn the rebellion against the self and struggle against their own inner

tyrannies and shoulds. In this sense, their rebellion may actually be liberating and therapeutic.

3. *Shallow Living:* This type of individual "moves to the periphery of life"; he or she is without hope or any positive commitment. In worse condition than the persistently resigned type, the "shallow liver" finds life worthless. Eventually he or she will settle for superficial enjoyments, "high living," without meaning or direction, or will pursue opportunistic success in business. But beneath the mask of sociability he or she is merely a "well-adapted automaton" (Horney, 1950, pp. 286–287). He or she goes through the motions of life, but is without genuine concern or involvement. He or she lives with others, takes over their conventions, codes of conduct, and morals, but inwardly never accepts any of these codes as truly relevant. In short, this individual becomes other directed and completely without responsibility for his or her own life.

The common denominator that binds the three types of detached or resigned neurotic is the presence of vacillation between identification with the despised real self and identification with the glorified ideal self. Detached neurotics strive half-heartedly toward actualization of the ideal self, but fundamentally they have surrendered any hope of making the glorified image come true. In effect, they are unsatisfied with the despised self, but simultaneously afraid to strive toward the goals of the ideal self. They desire to be free *from* all demands, rather than to be free *for* the pursuit of desirable activities.

Horney's description of the three patterns of neurotic conflict-solution points up an important premise of her theory. Each of the patterns is designed to minimize anxiety in *dealing with people.* Thus Horney's conceptualizations emphasize her position that the neuroses are evidence of damaged *interpersonal processes.* Horney summarized the three attitude types in these terms:

> As we have seen, each of the basic attitudes toward others has its positive value. In moving toward people the person tries to create for himself a friendly relation to his world. In moving against people he equips himself for survival in a competitive society. In moving away from people he hopes to attain a certain integrity and serenity. As a matter of fact, all three attitudes are not only desirable but necessary to our development as human beings. *It is only when they appear and operate in a neurotic framework that they become compulsive, rigid, indiscriminate, and mutually exclusive.* (1945, p. 89; italics added)

The three attitude types are presented together with their dominant neurotic needs in Table 13.2.

AUXILIARY CONFLICT SOLUTIONS

In addition to the basic attitudes for dealing with others, Horney suggested that several secondary or auxiliary techniques might be employed by neurotic personalities in their striving for security. Each of these techniques is to be conceptualized as a "secondary defense" in the service of buttressing the primary attitudinal "solution" to neurotic conflict.

TABLE 13.2   "Solutions" to Neurotic Conflict

Self-Effacing Solution: Love "Moving Toward" (Compliance)	**Expansive Solution:** Mastery "Moving Against" (Aggression)	**Resignation Solution:** Freedom "Moving Away" (Detachment)
Need for	Need for	Need for
1. Affection and approval	4. Power and omnipotence and perfection	3. Restrictions of life to narrow borders*
2. Partner to take control	5. Exploitation of others	9. Self-sufficiency
3. Restriction of life to narrow borders	6. Social recognition and prestige	10. Perfection and unassailability
	7. Personal admiration	
	8. Personal achievement	
"If you love me, you will not hurt me."	*"If I have power, no one can hurt me."*	*"If I withdraw, nothing can hurt me."*
Identification with the despised real self	Identification with the ideal self	Vacillation between despised real self and ideal self

* Need 3 is repeated from the Self-Effacing Solution.
Based on Horney, 1945, Chapters 3, 4, 5; 1942, Chapter 2; and 1950, Chapter 3.

Externalization

Though the neurotic personality seeks to bridge the distance between the idealized self and the real self, all efforts paradoxically broaden the gap. In the most extreme case, when the gap between the idealized self and the real self becomes so great that the person can no longer tolerate the discrepancy, he or she must turn elsewhere for the solution. "The only thing left then is to run away from himself entirely and see everything as if it lay outside" (Horney, 1945, p. 116).

Externalization is the auxiliary neurotic defense technique by which individuals shift their "center of gravity" from the self to others. Although somewhat similar to the defensive technique described by Freud as projection, externalization is much more comprehensive, for it involves the shift outward to others not only of unacceptable feelings, but of *all* feelings, all emotion. Other people become the center of all the neurotic's emotional life; these external individuals become the nucleus of all important strivings that would normally be directed to and experienced by the self. Thus, one may be angry with oneself, but instead attribute the anger to another: *He* is angry with me. A profound consequence for dealings with others emerges from this tendency to externalize:

> When a person feels that his life for good or ill is determined by others, it is only logical that he should be preoccupied with changing *them,* reforming *them,* punishing *them,* protecting himself from *their* interference, or impressing *them.* . . . Another inevitable product of externalization is a gnawing sense of emptiness and shallowness. . . . Instead of feeling the emotional emptiness as such, the person experiences it as emptiness in his stomach and tries to do away with it by compulsive eating. Or he may fear that his lack of bodily weight could cause him to be tossed about like a feather—any storm, he feels, might carry him away. He may even say that

he would be nothing but an empty shell if everything were analyzed. (Horney, 1945, p. 117; italics added)

Horney's description of the emptiness of the self resembles Laing's description of what he called the experience of implosion or the vacuum of the empty self (see Chapter 10). By externalizing his or her very being, the individual can forgo any feelings of humiliation, self-hate, or self-contempt, merely assigning these damaging functions to others. He or she still feels unworthy but now has provided a rational reason for the self-hatred: Others have no use for him or her, since he or she is *nothing.*

Creation of Blind Spots

The magnitude of the difference between neurotics' ongoing behaviors and the idealized picture of themselves can sometimes be so great that outsiders marvel that they never detect the discrepancy. The fact that neurotics never consciously admit the difference is evidence for the existence of a *blind spot,* that is, the creation of a defensive "refusal to see" their own defenses.

> A patient, for example, who had all the characteristics of the compliant type and *thought of himself as Christlike,* told me quite casually that at staff meetings he would often shoot one colleague after another with a little flick of his thumb. True enough, the destructive craving that prompted these figurative killings was at that time unconscious; but the point here is that the shooting, *which he dubbed "play,"* did not in the least disturb his Christlike image. (Horney, 1945, p. 132; italics added)

Compartmentalization

Similar to blind spots, *compartmentalization* involves pigeonholing one's life into rigid and exclusive categories: Thus there is a compartment for friends, for enemies, for family, for outsiders, a compartment for professional activities separate from personal life, and so on (Horney, 1945, p. 133). The important point is that anything that occurs in one compartment cannot contradict, influence, or support what transpires in another. "Compartmentalizing is thus as much a result of being divided by one's conflicts as a defense against recognizing them" (Horney, 1945, p. 134). A widely cited example is that of the man who ruthlessly runs his business affairs during the week, taking no real interest in the hurt or humiliation he causes his competitors, and on Sunday serves as the deacon of his church. Religion and business are in separate compartments, and so too, unfortunately, is his humanity.

Rationalization

Horney treated the defense of *rationalization* pretty much as had other theorists, including Freud. "Rationalization may be defined as self-deception by reasoning" (Horney, 1945, p. 135). Thus when the person rationalizes, he or she creates a good reason for some action where the reason would be unacceptable to his or her self-esteem. For example, the compliant type offers as the reason for "giving in" to others the desire to make *them* happy, when, in fact, he or she seeks to bring them under his or her control. Where an altruistic reason is consciously offered, a desire for dominance lurks.

Excessive Self-Control

In her clinical practice, Horney found that the tendency for excessive self-control was so pervasive that she originally classed it among the 10 neurotic trends or needs: *the need to restrict one's life within narrow borders*. Individuals who are exerting excessive self-control are attempting to prevent being caught up in emotion: They "will not allow themselves to be carried away, whether by enthusiasm, sexual excitement, self-pity, or rage. . . . In short, they seek to check all spontaneity" (Horney, 1945, p. 136).

Arbitrary Rightness

Because the inner conflicts that have shaped the individual's life always produce doubt and hesitation, the individual is sometimes paralyzed, unable to take *any* course of action. All energy is spent in keeping the conflicts under control. Therefore, almost any outside influence will tip the scales, even temporarily, in one direction or another. To an outsider, it appears that the neurotic decides important events arbitrarily and then defends the decision with rationalizations.

Horney felt that the most "fertile soil" for such rigid rightness was the development of aggressive tendencies coupled with feelings of detachment from others (1945, p. 138). For example, a neurotic may end a family dispute by preemptively declaring that he will do what he has already decided to do since he is right. He then storms off, effectively ending the argument by absenting himself to pursue a course of action chosen more in spite than by reason.

Elusiveness

Sometimes the only way neurotics can avoid the inherent contradictions of their lives is to avoid making any decisions whatsoever. Completely opposite to the arbitrarily right neurotic, the *elusive* neurotic seeks never to be pinned down to anything, never to state any issue or opinion clearly. "They have a bewildering capacity to becloud issues. It is often impossible for them to give a concrete report of any incident; should they try to do so the listener is uncertain in the end just what really did happen" (Horney, 1945, p. 138).

Cynicism

To defend against the recognition of inner conflict, the neurotic may adopt a *cynical* stance toward life and its traditional moral and ethical values. By treating such issues derisively, the neurotic can forestall any conflict over deciding what his or her own position is. In effect, he or she adopts the Machiavellian attitude "Do what you please, so long as you don't get caught" (Horney, 1945, p. 140).

THE PRICE OF PROTECTION

For Horney, the development of personality is an interpersonal process involving the achievement of self-confidence and the capacity for spontaneity. The character attitudes of compliance, aggression, and withdrawal, coupled with the auxiliary defenses, constitute an entire *protective structure*. The protective structure is designed to provide neurotics with a sense of security, however falsely based, and with the means continually to fend off any potential new threats to their idealized self-images.

It must not be forgotten, however, that for these attainments of security, neurotics pay a heavy price: They must abandon the realization of their true potentialities, the fruition of their genuine skills for living, and the expression of their authentically felt needs.

MODIFICATION OF FREUDIAN PSYCHOANALYSIS

Horney's jumping-off point was, of course, traditional psychoanalytic technique and theory. She accepted, for example, Freud's orientation toward psychological determinism. For Horney, as for Freud, every mental event was caused (1939, p. 18). Furthermore, that the cause of each mental event may be found in unconscious processes and motives, another fundamental Freudian tenet, was a postulate Horney easily accepted. The basic concept of unconsciously motivated defenses against self-disturbing perceptions also was taken over from psychoanalysis by Horney, as can be seen in her list of defensive strategies for coping with others.

Where Horney radically differed from Freud was in the area of motivational *content*. She reinterpreted the Oedipus complex, for example, as a culturally determined, occasional process of jealousy and aggression within some families (1939, p. 84). For Horney, the roots of the Oedipal situation were not so much sexual as *interpersonal attitudes:*

> The typical conflict leading to anxiety in a child is that between dependency on the parents . . . and hostile impulses against the parents. Hostility may be aroused in a child in many ways: by the parents' lack of respect for him; by unreasonable demands and prohibitions; by injustice; by unreliability; by suppression of criticism; by the parents dominating him and ascribing these tendencies to love. . . . If a child, in addition to being dependent on his parents, is grossly or subtly intimidated by them and hence feels that any expression of hostile impulses against them endangers his security, then the existence of such hostile impulses is bound to create anxiety. . . . The resulting picture may look exactly like what Freud describes as the Oedipus complex; passionate clinging to one parent and jealousy toward the other or toward anyone interfering with the claim of exclusive possession. . . . *But the dynamic structure of these attachments is entirely different from what Freud conceives as the Oedipus complex. They are an early manifestation of neurotic conflicts rather than a primarily sexual phenomenon.* (1939, pp. 83–84; italics added)

Thus Horney desexualized the Oedipal conflict and transferred the dynamics of its emotional constellation into the realm of disturbed interpersonal relations.

Some years before Horney rejected the orthodox Freudian interpretation of the Oedipus complex, she applied it rather tellingly in the classic manner to the topic of marriage. Her comments contain echoes of her own marriage to Oskar Horney:

> In his paper on a case of female homosexuality, Freud says that there is nothing about which our consciousness can be so incomplete or false as about the degrees of

affection or dislike we feel for another human being. This is quite especially true of marriage, it being often the case that the degree of love felt is overestimated. . . . Once again, the relation to the Oedipus complex provides a very much deeper explanation. For we see that the commandment and the vow to love and cleave to husband or wife with which one enters into matrimony are regarded by the unconscious as a renewal of the fourth commandment ["Honor thy father and thy mother"] in relation to the parents, and in this respect also—the suppression of hate and the exaggeration of love—the earlier experiences are compulsorily repeated with exactness in every detail. (Horney, 1967, p. 88)

The reference to the "fourth commandment" is reminiscent of Horney's diary entry on the same theme with reference to her difficulties with her father and with religious doubt. In the just-quoted passage, Horney, in a paper entitled "The Problem of the Monogamous Ideal," is apparently trying to justify to herself ill-fated marriages on the basis of resurrected Oedipal themes. It is not surprising that this basic tenet of Freudian theory was reworked during her period of rebellion from psychoanalysis into the more interpersonal concept with which she had firsthand familiarity.

Along these same lines, Horney found Freud's libido theory to be a grossly inaccurate representation of feminine psychology. The concept of "penis envy" by which Freud sought to explain women's feelings of inferiority and subsequent development into the role of motherhood Horney found to be based on inadequate and biased interpretations of "evidence" from neurotic women (1939, pp. 104 ff.; see also Horney, 1967, for a selection of her early papers on feminine psychology in which she adhered more closely to the orthodox views of the psychoanalytic school).

Horney differed with Freud on other issues in personality theory, but the central distinction that divided the two theorists was Horney's resculpting of human motivation theory in cultural terms. Consequently, for Horney, personality development cannot be understood exclusively in terms of *instinctual* or biological dynamics. Personality is meaningful only when individuals' cultural settings, familial interactions, and wider interpersonal relationships are taken into account. Basic anxiety and basic hostility can be conceptualized only as interpersonal outcomes; masculinity and femininity can be understood psychologically only as cultural products.

A FINAL WORD ON KAREN HORNEY

Karen Horney, in recent years, has become the unwarranted object of neglect among students of personality theory. Her contributions have been less valued, less frequently studied, and more rarely applied by researchers than those of other neo-Freudian theorists. The reason for this narrowing of interest in Horney's writings is difficult to comprehend fully. Certainly other theorists whose contributions were of lesser magnitude have retained their popularity. In Karen Horney's case, it would be difficult to find another personality theorist with whom to compare her lucid and brilliant descriptions of neurotic misery and compulsive overstriving for imaginary and defensive self-excellence. That her lucidity and attention-compelling style derive their potency from her self-explorations should, in coming years, rearouse at least scholarly historical interest in Karen Horney's body of writings. But, as may be said of any personality theory, until the creative researcher devises an empirical way of testing or applying Horney's ideas, it is unlikely that her work will become influential outside the clinical realm of intuitive and artistic understanding of troubled people.

ERICH FROMM

FREEDOM AS FRIGHTFUL

Like Karen Horney, Erich Fromm found in psychoanalysis a rich bed of concepts by which to understand human action. He felt that classical psychoanalytic doctrine was unnecessarily constraining in its near exclusive concern with unconscious human passions. Fromm sought to broaden psychoanalytic instinct theory with a conceptualization of the human person as a social being in a culture of interacting, interdependent creatures. Where Horney had focused on the alienating and damaging effects of parental indifference and emotional coldness, Fromm stressed the deadening impact on the human spirit of the entire cultural enterprise. In Fromm's view, industrial society has the pathological potential to enforce isolating competition among human persons whose human nature desperately requires nurturing cooperation and shared caring. Fromm began his theorizing with an analysis of human freedom and its paradoxical power to numb the human will.

The rise of modern capitalism was paralleled by an expansion of people's personal freedom. Bounded by strict custom and rigidly enforced social roles, medieval people remained relatively unconcerned with problems of individual rights and freedoms. Fromm described medieval society in this way:

> What characterizes medieval in contrast to modern society is its lack of individual freedom. Everybody in the earlier period was chained to his role in the social order. A man had little chance to move socially from one class to another. With few exceptions he had to stay where he was born. He was often not even free to dress as he pleased or to eat what he liked. The artisan had to sell at a certain price and the peasant at a certain place, the market of the town. . . . Personal, economic, and social life was dominated by rules and obligations from which practically no sphere of activity was exempted. But although a person was not free in the modern sense, neither was he alone and isolated. In having a distinct, unchangeable, and unquestionable place in the social world from the moment of birth, man was rooted in a structuralized whole, and thus life had a meaning which left no place, and no need, for doubt. A person was identical with his role in society; he was a peasant, an artisan, a knight, and not *an individual* who *happened* to have this or that occupation. (1941, pp. 57–58)

Thus medieval people had no need for individual freedom because they had yet no conception of themselves as *individuals*. Each was as one with the structure of society. With Martin Luther, in the period known as the Protestant Reformation, there came a revolutionized social and psychological milieu. Emphasis was placed on *independence* from smothering institutions like the Catholic church, on *individual* decision making, and on *personal* achievement. In effect, when it came to political and social conduct, Luther and Calvin showed people that their fate was in their own hands. When it came to one's relation to God, however, Luther emphasized humans' dependence and helplessness as well as their worthlessness and need for absolute faith in God's mercy.

The notion of personal responsibility soon followed upon this conception of people's material independence. If personal effort, achievement, and independence of institutions were the basis of salvation, then personal moral responsibility was the price of this social liberation. Only upon God were humans dependent; and only in the face of the Almighty were they helpless. Consequently, as social freedom grew, there was a paradoxical growth in feelings of personal helplessness and worthlessness (Fromm, 1941, p. 124). Freedom became a burden, and the chief element of that burden was the necessity for individual competition against one's fellows. For if one were to achieve salvation by establishing a personal dependent relationship with God, one must be secure in the belief that one merited God's largesse. By demonstrating the capacity to work, to achieve, to shoulder responsibility for economic and social survival, the free, independent person asserted his or her worthiness to be God's favored—and saved—creature. But in the attempts to demonstrate his or her individual merit, the new independence of spirit fostered a sense of competition: Some are more worthy than others.

Moneyed and prestigious classes of people arose, and this aristocracy of wealth and power was the foundation of the new capitalistic spirit. Less economically favored individuals felt a sense of uncertainty, fear, and helplessness in the face of such exaggerated power and conspicuous merit. Instead of fostering cooperation, independence fostered economic competition and alienation. The middle economic classes reacted to these pressures by fighting hard against their growing sense of powerlessness at the hands of the wealthy capitalists. "The luxury of the moneyed class increased their feeling of smallness and filled them with envy and indignation. As a whole, the middle class was more endangered by the collapse of the feudal order and by rising capitalism than it was helped" (Fromm, 1941, p. 99).

The predominant feeling pervading the consciousness of the middle classes was the sense of their own insignificance. Luther's conception of religion mirrored these critical social changes. Although his doctrine freed persons from unthinking dependence on church authority, it emphasized their personal worthlessness and their dependence on God. "In psychological terms [Luther's] concept of faith means: if you completely submit, if you accept your individual insignificance, then the all powerful God may be willing to love you and save you" (Fromm, 1941, p. 100).

The Protestant Reformation thus evolved a painful dilemma for people: It permitted them to abandon reliance on institutional authority and social roles to be free and independent, but at the same time it made them more dependent on God and therefore more personally helpless. For contemporary people, the dilemma becomes more intense. The individual's insignificance in the face of powerful corporations, massive government bureaucracies, and transhuman technology has touched everyone's life.

The existence of contemporary people is marked by aloneness, fear, and bewilderment. Their freedoms are not satisfying; they are frightful. Though each is totally an individual, contemporary persons are also sometimes totally isolated. In short, contemporary people do not cherish their own individuality, their own independence. They flee from their own freedom.

THE MECHANISMS OF ESCAPE FROM FREEDOM

Clearly, Fromm's sketch of contemporary capitalistic society pictures persons as victims of their own works. The net effect of these conflicting trends toward independence and helplessness is impaired mental health. Following Freud's dictum: *"Lieben und arbeiten"* (to love and to work), Fromm characterized the normal or mentally healthy person as one who is able to work productively in the fashion demanded by his or her society, and who is able to participate in the perpetuation of that society. From the person's own perspective, however, normality is defined as "the optimum of growth and happiness of the individual" (Fromm, 1941, p. 159).

The difficulty with contemporary society is that the requirements it levels for normality often conflict with the individual's own needs for growth and happiness. Two courses of action are open to the individual as he or she tries to overcome the painful state of helplessness and aloneness. "By one course he can progress to 'positive freedom'; he can relate himself spontaneously to the world in love and work, in the genuine expression of his emotional, sensuous, and intellectual capacities; he can thus become one again with man, nature, and himself, without giving up the independence and integrity of his individual self" (Fromm, 1941, p. 161). This solution to the conflict between freedom and helplessness is essentially a healthy one.

The second course of action open to the individual involves the unhealthy strategy of relinquishing personal freedom completely. Seeking to merge with, or surrender his or her identity to the conglomerate we call society, this individual strives to "escape freedom." Fromm distinguished among three such mechanisms of escape.

Authoritarianism

To attain the desired status of strength or power, the individual may seek to fuse with another—somebody or something lying outside of self (Fromm, 1941, p. 163). In extreme form, the individual becomes submissive, passive, even masochistic. Feeling insignificant, powerless, and inferior, the individual struggling to escape freedom succeeds in the struggle when he or she is able to submit to the power of others, to provoke self-humiliation, and even to intensify his or her worthlessness with self-belittling.

A nearly opposite authoritarian mechanism is sometimes seen in those who, rather than submit to authority, attempt to become the authority. In place of masochism, a strong sadistic desire to obtain absolute and unrestricted power over others becomes the means of escape. Such an authoritarian may desire to have others dependent on him or her, or to exploit others ruthlessly, or to cause others direct physical suffering and pain.

Both the masochistic and sadistic forms of authoritarianism solve the problem of the burden of freedom by annihilating the individual self. "Psychologically . . . [sadism and masochism] are the outcomes of one basic need, springing from the inability to bear the isolation and weakness of one's own self" (Fromm, 1941, p. 180). Fromm suggested that the unconscious foundation of both these strategies be called *symbiosis*: "Symbiosis, in the psychological sense, means the union of one individual self with another self (or any power outside of the own self) in such a way as to make each lose the integrity of its own self and to make them completely dependent on each other" (Fromm, 1941, p. 180). Thus for both the masochist and for the sadist, escape from freedom involves a flight from self. For the masochist, this end is accomplished when he or she is "swallowed up" by an outside force; for the sadistic personality the same end is accomplished when he or she "swallows up" others.

Destructiveness

Like authoritarianism, destructiveness is rooted in the individual's sense of overwhelming powerlessness and aloneness. Unlike the masochistic and sadistic strategies, the destructive individual does not seek union with an external object or power over it. The destructive strategy seeks to annihilate the object.

> I can escape the feeling of my own powerlessness in comparison with the world outside of myself by destroying it. To be sure, if I succeed in removing it, I remain alone and isolated, but mine is a splendid isolation in which I cannot be crushed by the overwhelming power of the objects outside of myself. The destruction of the world is the last, almost desperate attempt to save myself from being crushed by it. (Fromm, 1941, p. 202)

When the individual is blocked by external circumstance from directing destructiveness outwardly, he or she may take the self as the target. Thus physical illness and suicide are regular outcomes of this strategy to escape from the burden of freedom.

Fromm modified Freud's notion of the death or destructive instinct by proposing a relationship between the degree to which the individual's growth strivings are thwarted and the amount of destructiveness such frustration engenders. "By this [thwarting] we do not refer to individual frustrations of this or that instinctive desire but to the thwarting of the whole of life, blockage of spontaneity of the growth and expression of man's sensuous, emotional, and intellectual capacities" (Fromm, 1941, p. 206). For this reason, Fromm proposed that the more the drive toward life is blocked, the stronger becomes the drive toward destruction: *"Destructiveness is the outcome of unlived life."*

Those institutions and social roles that, by their very nature, frustrate the individual's striving for independence and growth, are precisely those societal conditions that most engender his or her destructiveness. In this regard, Fromm's thought bears a striking similarity to the self-actualization concepts of Maslow and Rogers (cf. Chapter 15), to Carl Jung's notion of individuation (cf. Chapter 7), and to Karen Horney's concepts of the real and ideal selves.

Automaton Conformity

The two previous mechanisms of escape from freedom revolve around unconscious strategies for relinquishing the integrity of the self or around the desire to destroy the world that threatens the self. Automaton conformity, by contrast, involves a strategy of escape by default. "To put it briefly, the individual ceases to be himself; he adopts entirely the kind of personality offered to him by cultural patterns; and he therefore becomes exactly as all others are and as they expect him to be" (Fromm, 1941, pp. 208–209).

Like those animals with protective coloring, individuals who are conforming automatons take on the coloring, shading, and emotional texture of their surroundings. Because they mimic millions of other people, automatons no longer feel alone. But for this reduction in feelings of aloneness they pay the price of loss of selfhood. In their surrender of their true selves to the façade of sameness with others, individuals do not achieve the security for which they hoped. Instead, they find themselves adopting pseudo-selves to compensate for the loss of spontaneity.

Like R. D. Laing (Chapter 10), Fromm believes that the automaton conformist experiences a split between genuine feelings or spontaneous urges and the face presented to the world.

> The loss of the self and its substitution by a pseudo self leave the individual in an intense state of insecurity. He is obsessed by doubt, since, being essentially a reflex of other people's expectation of him, he has in a measure lost his identity. In order to overcome the panic resulting from such loss of identity, he is compelled to conform, to seek his identity by continuous approval and recognition by others. Since he does not know who he is, at least the other will know—if he acts according to their expectation; if they know, he will know too, if he only takes their word for it. (1941, p. 230)

Thus each of the three escape mechanisms "solves" the problem of freedom's burden only partially, only temporarily, only inadequately.

FROMM'S SOCIAL PSYCHOANALYTIC PSYCHOLOGY: SOURCES OF THE CONCEPT

Fromm (1962) has provided a uniquely revelatory account of the personal sources of his interest in the work of Sigmund Freud and of Karl Marx. It is clear from Fromm's notion of the individual's alienation from his own selfhood in the face of growing economic independence that he has attempted to blend modified Freudian concepts with Marxian economic ones. Although he credits Marx for being the more profound thinker, Fromm has found value in the complementary nature of the conceptual tools provided by Freud for understanding this alienation from self and those provided by Marx for understanding the individual's alienation from his or her fellows (Fromm, 1950, 1962, p. 12; 1959, 1970, and 1973).

An Adolescent Puzzle: Personal Interest in Psychoanalysis

Much as Erikson's (Chapter 6) concern with the crisis of identity arose from his own bewilderment and distress, Fromm's interest in psychology and social theory arose from a similar state of adolescent confusion. When Fromm was about 12 years old, an attractive young woman who was a friend of Fromm's family committed suicide:

> Maybe she was 25 years of age; she was beautiful, attractive and in addition a painter, the first painter I ever knew. I remember having heard that she had been engaged but after some time had broken the engagement; I remember that she was almost invariably in the company of her widowed father. As I remember him, he was an old, uninteresting, and rather unattractive-looking man, or so I thought (maybe my

judgment was somewhat biased by jealousy). Then one day I heard the shocking news: her father had died, and immediately afterwards she had killed herself and left a will which stipulated that she wanted to be buried together with her father. (Fromm, 1962, p. 4)

At 12, Fromm had not yet heard of the Oedipus complex or of incestuous fixations between children and parents. Yet the event deeply disturbed him. He had found the woman attractive and had developed quite a hatred for her father. "I was hit by the thought 'How is it possible?' How is it possible that a beautiful young woman should be so in love with her father, that she prefers to be buried with him to being alive to the pleasures of life and of painting?" (1962, p. 4).

In his early twenties, the haunting question "How is it possible?" finally received an answer as Fromm delved into Freud's writings. What had been a frightening and confusing adolescent experience now took on dimensions as a crucial human character problem for which psychoanalysis seemed to provide appropriate investigative tools.

An Adolescent Model: Personal Interest in Marx's Social Theory

Fromm's family was strongly religious, and he was exposed to Jewish tradition and custom at an early age. He reports that he was deeply affected by his study of the Old Testament, and in particular by the prophetic writings of Isaiah, Amos, and Hosea: "not so much by their warnings and their announcement of disaster, but by their promise of the 'end of days,' when nations 'shall beat their swords into plowshares and their spears into pruning hooks' " (1962, p. 5). Fromm suggests that the chief reason these prophets affected him so deeply was that as a Jewish boy in a Christian community he had experienced several episodes of anti-Semitism. The feelings of strangeness and of "clannishness" among Christians and Jews forced Fromm to an early dislike of isolation between people: ". . . what could be more exciting and beautiful to me than the prophetic vision of universal brotherhood and peace?"

The lessons to be learned from these experiences were intensified when Fromm was 14 years old and World War I broke out in the summer of 1914. Several of Fromm's schoolteachers expressed strongly nationalistic feelings about the war, and in one case, a Latin teacher expressed a genuine fondness for the whole concept of war. Fromm was thus provoked to ask his inevitable question: "How was it possible that a man who always seemed to have been so concerned with the preservation of peace should be so jubilant about the war?" Another puzzle had been posed.

At around the same time, a wave of hatred was sweeping through Germany with the British people as its target. Suddenly a stereotype had been created that caricatured the British as cheap mercenaries, evil and unscrupulous destroyers of German heroes (Fromm, 1962, p. 6). This stereotype and its corresponding war hysteria that was paralyzing German thinking confused and frightened the young Fromm.

An English teacher proved to be the one exceptional model of sanity and reason amid the onslaught of irrationality and hatred:

I still see him standing in front of the class, answering our protests with an ironical smile, and saying calmly: "Don't kid yourselves; so far England has never lost a war!" Here was the voice of sanity and realism in the midst of insane hatred—and it was the voice of a respected and admired teacher! This one sentence and the calm, rational way in which it was said, was an enlightenment. It broke through the crazy pattern of hate and national self-glorification and made me wonder and think, "How is it possible?" (Fromm, 1962, p. 7)

The urgency of the question "How is it possible?" grew as the war drew on, seemingly without end. The propaganda battles launched by the embattled nations depicted men of each country as mindless butchers. Fromm was overwhelmed with the senseless killing, accusations, and pointless pain of war: "How is it possible that millions of men continue to stay in the trenches, to kill innocent men of other nations, and to be killed and thus to cause the deepest pain to parents, wives, friends? . . ." (1962, p. 8).

In 1918, at the end of the war, Fromm's insistent curiosity and abhorrence had been transformed into a desire to understand the irrationality of human mass behavior.

> My main interest was clearly mapped out. I wanted to understand the laws that govern the life of the individual man, and the laws of society—that is, of men in their social existence. I tried to see the lasting truth in Freud's concepts as against those assumptions which were in need of revision. I tried to do the same with Marx's theory, and finally I tried to arrive at a synthesis which followed from the understanding and the criticism of both thinkers. (1962, p. 9)

Fromm thus adopted from Freud the conviction that *most of what is real within ourselves is not conscious, and that most of what is conscious is not real* (Fromm, 1962, p. 89). From Marx, Fromm adopted the conviction that humans are not free, and cannot be free, so long as they accept uncritically external control by social custom or institutions. Thus Freud pictured humans as determined primarily by their biological instincts and the forces of repression exerted by their own egos; Marx depicted humans as determined by the structure of their society and the forces of repression exerted by economic and political exigencies. Fromm profoundly modified both views into a social psychoanalytic theory of human character types.

CHARACTER STRUCTURE: THE NATURE OF HUMAN NATURE

Fromm's concept of individuals struggling to escape their burden of self-created freedom can now be understood in a broader context. As contemporary society grew more complex, it became less human. People sought not only to escape their growing sense of helplessness, they also struggled to regain mastery of the societal machinery that threatened to master them (Fromm, 1955a, pp. 309 ff.). In one stroke, people had created the means to subdue nature and mold it to their own needs, while at the same time they relinquished their ability to love themselves and others. In brief, contemporary capitalistic society fosters both alienation of person from person and alienation of each individual from him- or herself:

> People capable of love, under the present system, are necessarily the exceptions; love is by necessity a marginal phenomenon in present-day Western society. Not so much

because many occupations would not permit of a loving attitude, but because the spirit of a production-centered commodity-greedy society is such that only the non-conformist can defend himself successfully against it. (Fromm, 1956, p. 111)

As Fromm has pointed out, the most pressing danger is not the sudden increase of cruelty or inhumanity that a consumer society breeds. The most potent danger is that future people will become feelingless, loveless, unthinking robots (1955b, p. 105). Unable to be true to their nature, future people will be true to their "things." Acquisition, consumption, and material accumulation will claim a person's loyalties. The more pressing question, therefore, that a truly humanized psychology can ask is, *What is an individual's true nature?*

Fromm has several times attempted to answer this question in his efforts to describe how society has forced distortions of human character into existence (1947, 1964, 1968, and 1973). Rejecting Freud's view that the individual's unalterable nature is to be found within one's instinctual endowment for sexuality and aggression, Fromm has suggested that the most basic trait of human nature is a tendency toward self-actualization (1947, p. 29). Because of this tendency to become fully functioning, to exercise completely one's unique powers of reason and self-awareness, the individual's nature is not limited by one's inherited biological instincts. The single constraint governing human existence is one's need to be fully oneself.

> Man is born as a freak of nature, being within nature and yet transcending it. He has to find principles of action and decision making which replace the principles of instinct. He has to have a frame of orientation which permits him to organize a consistent picture of the world as a condition for consistent actions. He has to fight not only against the dangers of dying, starving, and being hurt, but also against another danger which is specifically human: that of becoming insane. In other words, he has to protect himself not only against the danger of losing his life but also against the danger of losing his mind. (Fromm, 1968, p. 61)

Without a frame of reference, a consistent and reliable view of oneself and one's world, the individual soon succumbs to madness, that is, to a separation from oneself. Because they have the capacity for self-awareness, humans are never free of the prospect of their own death. They are a part of nature yet set apart by their ability to reflect on it. The fundamental dichotomy of human existence is the individual's vulnerability to the laws of nature, especially to the inevitability of death, and one's painful awareness that in most other ways one has transcended one's animal heritage (Fromm, 1947, p. 49). Evolution of the human brain in directions different from those of our animal cousins has lessened human dependence on stereotyped instinctual responses. Superior cortical development has, furthermore, provided humans with the power of reason and self-reflection (Fromm, 1973, p. 223). Taken together, the lessened dependence on instinct and the superior development of the brain's cortex have freed humans from a mere survival-striving existence and have separated them from the rest of living creation. Alienated from themselves and from others by the works their intelligence has made possible, individuals strive *to be themselves,* to master their artifacts rather than be mastered by them. They struggle to allow others to be fully themselves without themselves succumbing to the extremes of apathy and nihilism.

The Uniquely Human Character Needs

To understand a person's nature it is necessary to understand his or her predicament: He or she is both animal passion and human reason. His or her most important needs, as Maslow, too, asserted, are not biological. They are, instead, distinctly human— uniquely suprabiological, and founded in human character (Fromm, 1973, pp. 230 ff.). Fromm (1955a, 1973) has defined the individual's unique nature in terms of six peculiarly human, existential needs:

1. *The Need for Relatedness and Unity:* To overcome their feelings of aloneness and isolation from nature and from themselves, humans need to love, to care for others. Love is a union with somebody or something outside of self (1955a, p. 37; 1973, p. 233).

2. *The Need for Transcendence and a Sense of Effectiveness:* Because individuals are aware of themselves and their world, they sometimes recognize how overpowering and frightening the vastness of the universe is. They may thus easily be overcome with a sense of their own helplessness and impotence (Fromm, 1973, p. 235). People need to surpass their own fear and uncertainty in the face of a hostile or indifferent universe. They may accomplish this end by actively striving to master their world and themselves. Individuals need to surpass their own potential passivity: "He is driven by the urge to transcend the role of the creature, the accidentalness and passivity of his existence, by becoming a 'creator' " (Fromm, 1955a, p. 41). In short, humans must feel that they are *effective:* "I am because I effect." The similarity to Erikson's notion of a sense of industry and a sense of initiative is obvious.

3. *The Need for Rootedness:* Throughout life humans are torn from their roots. In birth, the person is torn from the security and passivity of the womb existence. In late childhood, he or she is torn from safety of mother's care. In adulthood, each person faces the prospect of being torn from life itself as he or she faces death. Thus, throughout life, humans have needs for roots, for a sense of stability, permanency, and secure sameness similar to the security they experienced in the mother-child relationship (Fromm, 1955a, p. 43; 1973, p. 232). Erikson's notion of ego identity as a sense of continuity is similar.

4. *The Need for a Sense of Identity:* "Man may be defined as the animal that can say 'I,' that can be aware of himself as a separate entity" (Fromm, 1955a, p. 62). Humans must feel in control of their fate. Each must be able to say "I am I." In short, each person must make decisions, reflect on them, and feel that his or her life is truly his or her own.

5. *The Need for a Frame of Orientation and an Object of Devotion:* "Man needs a map of his natural and social world, without which he would be confused and unable to act purposefully and consistently" (Fromm, 1973, p. 230). Because he or she is enveloped in a universe of puzzling phenomena and frightening realities, the individual has the need to make sense of his or her life. He or she needs to be able to predict the complexities of existence. A *frame of orientation* is a set of beliefs about the ultimate course of his or her destiny. A frame of orientation is, therefore, an absolute necessity for the maintenance of sanity (Fromm, 1955a, pp. 64 ff.).

Humans need not only a frame of orientation but also an *object of devotion,* a goal or God to which they can attach meaning, to whom they can attribute the meaning of life. Where the frame of orientation provides a map of existence, the object of devotion is the goal toward which that map directs the person's search (Fromm, 1973, p. 231).

6. *The Need for Excitation and Stimulation:* Fromm (1973, p. 237) has added a sixth basic need characteristic of healthy human functioning. Surveying neurological and behavioral evidence, he concludes that the human brain is constantly active, continually functioning even in the presence of reduced external stimulation. He infers from the evidence that people need a constantly stimulating, interest-provoking environment. Fromm does not mean that humans require a chronic succession of novel stimuli. Rather, they need stimulation that induces them to *actively* construe their world, to *actively* participate in life.

Fromm thus proposed a distinction between a *simple stimulus* and an *activating stimulus:* "The simple stimulus produces a *drive*—i.e., the person is driven by it [e.g., hunger, pain]; the activating stimulus results in a striving—i.e., the person is actively striving for a goal" (Fromm, 1973, p. 240). Simple stimulation that does not engage human reason results in simple passive reactions. To avoid boredom, simple stimuli must constantly change or continually increase in intensity.

Contemporary technological society provides many simple stimuli that foster passivity and boredom. One consequence of continuous simple stimulation is that contemporary persons are driven to seek methods of boredom escape. Thus alcohol, drugs, television, and sexual promiscuity can all be means of avoiding an overwhelming sense of boredom in the face of the continual barrage of simple stimuli. The trouble with these escape mechanisms is that in themselves they are further sources of simple, boredom-producing stimulation that provide only temporary and superficial relief.

Another more pathological consequence of contemporary human boredom is *malignant aggression.* Unlike the animal who practices aggression for defense, humans are unique in their capacity to be violent, cruel, and destructive for no rational defensive purpose. To escape the ready-made patterns of behavior and the chronically unengaging entertainments offered by their technological culture, people resort to active aggression and violence. In a life without meaning, violence and destructiveness provide them with some measure of distorted mastery. Such aggression is malignant because it subverts the very essence of human character; it solves the individual's sense of despair at the meaninglessness of his or her life by allowing malignant control over the life of another. In short, boredom provokes malignant aggression.

DISTORTIONS IN HUMAN CHARACTER ENFORCED BY SOCIETY

In Fromm's view human nature is intimately bound up with self-awareness. The social form of human existence, however, is a potent shaper of that self-awareness.

Nowhere is Fromm's attempt to blend Freudian and Marxian concepts more apparent than in his treatment of this point. The content and the breadth of the individual's self-awareness are powerfully molded by the customs, taboos, and traditions of the society that engulfs him or her. To centralize this concept, Fromm proposed that each society establishes in each of its members a shared *social unconscious* (1962, pp. 88 ff.).

The social unconscious is composed of those thoughts and feelings that the society will not permit an individual to harbor in awareness. Thus Fromm combined Freud's concept of repression with Marx's concept of social illusion. Society's customs, prohibitions, and conventions enforce a kind of social repression by establishing specific cognitive categories by which every individual is expected to order his or her connection of the world. The social unconscious, therefore, is a product of a kind of *socially conditioned filtering* process that allows some thoughts to be consciously entertained and some thoughts to be forced out of awareness.

The socially conditioned filter operates through three cultural mechanisms. First, the common *language* of a culture employs a set of grammatical and syntactical rules that powerfully shape the way reality is labeled. "The whole language contains an attitude of life, is a frozen expression of experiencing life in a certain way" (Fromm, 1962, p. 118).

Second, shared *rules of logic* determine what is regarded by members of a culture as "natural" or reasonable. Thus cultures differ in the degree to which cause-and-effect, "scientific" thinking is regarded as the only appropriate way to understand the world. A good example of a vastly different view of the "proper" way to construe and relate to "reality" can be gleaned from Carlos Casteneda's fascinating accounts of the magical or mystical techniques of perception practiced by a Yaqui Indian sorcerer (e.g., Casteneda, 1968, 1971). Don Juan, the sorcerer under whom Casteneda studied, was able to manipulate situations and social cues so effectively that Casteneda was forced to concede that "reality" was not so very real. Cause and effect in the Yaqui Indian tradition do not serve as cognitive categories by which to order one's experience. Experience is structured by a more intuitive, direct contact with unseen, untouchable, unexplainable "reality." The culture shock engendered by Casteneda's apprenticeship to Don Juan nearly cost Casteneda his sanity.

The third mechanism by which the social filter shapes social character and the social unconscious is the use of taboos or *explicit prohibitions.* Certain ideas, feelings, or attitudes are treated as improper, dangerous, or forbidden to the extent that they are simply not consciously experienced.

Consequently, the social unconscious and the individual unconscious are constantly interacting, for at least part of the individual unconscious is determined or shaped by social filtering processes. Societies function in such a way that one is made to feel that one *willingly* acts the way one *ought* to act. One who successfully adapts to one's culture is convinced that *he or she wants* to behave as the culture demands because such conformity is physically and spiritually satisfying (Fromm, 1955a, p. 77). The difficulty, of course, is that the society may be pathological—that is, overtly inimical to the essence of human nature as defined by the six previously discussed needs: *relatedness, transcendence, rootedness, identity, activating stimulation,* and a *frame of orientation.* Pathological societies subvert or block the gratification of these needs. In consequence, pathological societies create pathological human character types, for only a distorted version of human nature could adapt to the distorted demands of a pathological, need-depriving culture.

Fromm has described several varieties of character type. Generally he groups them into two classes of *productive* (healthy) and *nonproductive* (unhealthy, pathological) types. In his first work on this theme he described four nonproductive character types as contrasted with a fifth, productive personality. None of these types exists in pure form because productive and nonproductive elements combine in differing proportions in particular persons. Thus the ultimate mental health or illness of a given character type depends on the ratio of positive to negative traits embodied in that individual.

The Receptive Orientation: Passivity and Dependence

It must remembered that each of the character types to be discussed represents a particular solution to the problem of adapting to social demands. Such adaptation, it will be recalled, is motivated by the human need to solve the fundamental dichotomy of existence, namely, the clash between feelings of aloneness and alienation and feelings of shared creaturehood.

The receptive personality solves this dilemma by adopting the belief that all good, all satisfactions, all worthwhile comforts and values are received from sources outside self (Fromm, 1947, p. 70). Thus receptive types feel that their central task in life is *to be loved,* not loving. They tend to be indiscriminate in their choice of love objects, desiring from nearly everyone a continual income of attention, devotion, and help. Unable to offend anyone, receptive types continuously say "yes" to everyone as if their critical faculties were paralyzed.

The receptive type may be described by the key negative trait labels of *passive, opinionless, submissive, unrealistic, cowardly, wishful, gullible,* and *sentimental* (Fromm, 1947, p. 120). On the positive side, however, the receptive type may embody enough health and productive motivation to transmute these negative traits into positive characteristics. Thus for the receptive type who harbors some productivity, passivity may become *acceptance,* opinionlessness may lead to *responsiveness,* submissiveness becomes changed into *devotion,* unrealistic perceptions may be altered to *idealistic* ones, cowardice becomes *sensitivity,* wishful thinking grows into *optimism,* and so on.

In summary, the orientation of the nonproductive receptive type is chiefly marked by passivity and by the expectancy that someone will provide.

The Hoarding Orientation: Never Let Go

The hoarding personality solves the dilemma of aloneness and the need for others in a way that is directly opposite to the receptive type. Hoarders strive to accumulate possessions, power, and love, and they struggle to avoid dispensing any of their hoard. Acting as if they had built protective fortresses around themselves, hoarding types strive to bring within their protective boundaries all that they might ever want or need. Even love is treated as a possession. To obtain love, the beloved other must be totally possessed.

Hoarding types are "tight" in nearly every physical respect: tight-lipped, tight-boweled, tight-stomached, tight-eyed—that is, they say nothing and are constipated, cramped and ulcered, and squinty. Above all else, they desire their sense of order, neatness, and cleanliness to be shared by those around them. They thus resemble closely Freud's anal retentive (erotic) character type (cf. Chapter 2).

Key traits to describe the hoarding type include *unimaginative, stingy, suspicious, cold, stubborn, obsessional, possessive* (Fromm, 1947, p. 120). In the hoarding type who possesses some degree of productivity and health, these negative traits may be changed. Thus unimaginative is changed to *practical,* stingy to *economical,* suspicious is changed to *careful,* cold to *reserved,* stubborn becomes *steadfast,* obsessional becomes *methodical,* and possessive is changed to *loyal.*

The Exploitative Orientation: Aggressive and Conceited

The exploitative personality solves the problem of aloneness by taking from others. Unlike the receptive type who *expects to receive* or the hoarder who *expects to keep,* the exploiter *expects to take, to grab, to snatch away from others* that which he or she needs or desires. He or she thus feels attracted only to people from whom he or she can steal love, or to people who themselves have to be taken from others. Intellectually, the exploiter does not create ideas; he or she steals them, plagiarizes them. In short, for the exploiters things that can be taken from someone else always seem better or more desirable than things they themselves can produce (Fromm, 1947, p. 72).

The exploiter can be described by the following key trait labels: *aggressive, egocentric, conceited, rash, arrogant, seducing.* In the exploitative character who embodies some measure of health and productivity these negative traits may be changed to more positive qualities: Aggressive thus becomes *taking the initiative,* egocentric becomes *able to make claims,* conceited is changed to *proud,* rash to *impulsive,* arrogant to *self-confident,* and seducing becomes altered to *captivating* (Fromm, 1947, p. 120).

A somewhat analogous character type has been studied by Christie and his colleagues under the descriptive label of *Machiavellian* (Christie & Geis, 1968, 1970). A Machiavellian personality is well described by most of the traits Fromm uses to define the exploitative personality. Furthermore Fromm's last nonproductive type, the marketing personality, to be described shortly, also shares some characteristics of Christie and Geis's Machiavellian personality. It is interesting that Christie and Geis's work is based on empirical measurements of personality that closely correspond to Fromm's theoretical type.

The Marketing Orientation: Selling Oneself

The marketing personality is peculiarly a product of modern industrial society. Success is measured for marketing personalities by how well they sell themselves, by how well, that is, they package their personalities in desirable qualities. Thus their family backgrounds, the clubs to which they belong, the schools they attended all have to be "right." When their personality packages fulfill the socially expected conditions of "rightness," the marketing type's skills, knowledge, or services will be in demand.

> Since modern man experiences himself both as the seller and as the commodity to be sold on the market, self-esteem depends on conditions beyond his control. If he is "successful," he is valuable; if he is not, he is worthless. (Fromm, 1947, p. 79)

The marketing personality represents the ultimate in alienation. To solve the problem of aloneness, marketing types literally become a product that will attract customers. They sell themselves without ever knowing themselves. They know only *what* will sell, not the price *they* will pay for the transaction.

Key descriptive traits for the marketing type include *opportunistic, inconsistent, childish, aimless, tactless,* and *indifferent* (Fromm, 1947, p. 121). Christie and Geis's Machiavellian type shares the traits of opportunism and indifference. When, however, the marketing type possesses some positive or productive qualities, these negative traits may undergo transformation into healthy characteristics: Opportunistic may become *purposeful,* inconsistent is modified to *able to change,* childish is changed to *youthful,* aimless is modified to become *experimenting,* tactless is changed to *curious,* and indifferent becomes *tolerant.*

The Productive Type: Personality Without a Mask

In contrast to the nonproductive orientations, productive personalities solve the problem of aloneness by becoming more fully themselves. They don no masks, erect no façades, attempt to manipulate no one. "Productiveness is man's ability to use his powers and to realize the potentialities inherent in him. . . . Productiveness means that he experiences himself as the embodiment of his powers and as the 'actor'; that he feels himself one with his powers and at the same time that they are not masked and alienated from him" (Fromm, 1947, p. 91).

Thus, Fromm, too, employed the terminology of the actor and mask to describe the ungenuineness, the hollowness, and the artificiality that the productive personality *avoids.* The productive person is independent, autonomous, integrated, spontaneous, loving, creative, and, in a word similar to Erikson's *generative* (Fromm, 1947, pp. 93 ff.). Productive people are able *to love* and *to work.* They feel at one with themselves, with their fellows, with the universe. In brief, they are *related, transcendent, rooted;* they have a strong sense of *identity* with a stable *frame of orientation* toward their lives. This description of the healthy personality is quite similar to Abraham Maslow's notion of the self-actualizing personality and to Carl Rogers's notion of the fully functioning person discussed in Chapter 15. For all three theorists, and to a lesser extent for Erikson, the healthy personality is one who finds him- or herself sufficiently acceptable and worthy as he or she really is without a protective mask.

Study of Character Types in a Mexican Village

Erich Fromm and Michael Macoby (1970) studied by means of paper-and-pencil tests, interviews, and the Rorschach projective inkblot test, a relatively large group of Mexican peasants inhabiting a single village southwest of Mexico City. Of primarily Spanish-Indian extraction, these hard-working people were mainly farmers, although some earned their living as fishermen or as expert potters. Fromm was especially interested in Mexican peasants because their modes of production are highly individualistic and barely rise above the subsistence level. By contrast, modern technologically oriented farmers run agricultural businesses whose main goal is profit, not merely survival. Moreover, the peasant is literally a "man of the land," who works closely with his family and only one or two hired hands to till soil that his government has more control over than he does. Fromm described the villagers' emotional life in this way:

> They are selfish, suspicious of each others' motives, pessimistic about the future, and fatalistic. Many appear submissive and self-deprecatory, although they have the potential for rebelliousness and revolution. They feel inferior to city people, more stupid, and less cultured. There is an overwhelming feeling of powerlessness to influence either nature or the industrial machine that bears down on them. (Fromm & Macoby, 1970, p. 37)

Poverty and frustration are the lot of peasants, and they rarely share their misery with anyone because their extreme distrust prevents the formation of close friendships.

On the positive side, peasant villagers are dignified persons with a strong sense of themselves and their heritage. They are proud, although they will, of necessity, humble themselves before powerful people. But they will also quit their jobs and risk starvation in the face of personal insult.

What impact have such ideology and existence on character formation? The most frequent character type found in the village was the *nonproductive receptive character;* the next most frequent type was the *productive hoarding character;* and the least frequent type was the *exploitative character,* consisting of both productive and nonproductive subtypes (Fromm & Macoby, 1970, p. 109). Fromm and Macoby's analysis of the social and historical origins of these three types concluded that each character had its root in a corresponding special social niche occupied by particular peasants. A given character type thus evolved as a psychological and social adaptation to the pressures of economic class. In essence, the receptive, hoarding, and exploitative characters originated as forms of coping strategies in the face of inescapable socioeconomic conditions.

The *nonproductive-receptive* character type tended to be found among landless day laborers at the bottom of the social and economic hierarchy. Such people behave submissively and passively, viewing their employers as "superiors" who have favors to bestow. These passive-receptive personalities feel and act as though they cannot control their own fate, except by winning the approval of the powerful who can.

The *productive-hoarding* type was found among 30 percent of the villagers (22 percent of the men and 39 percent of the women) (Fromm & Macoby, 1970, p. 117). The hoarding personality type was typical among villagers who were economically and socially more independent and productive. These peasants tended to be landowners, even if only of small plots that barely provided survival. Small surplus productions, when they occur, must be hoarded against the inevitable bad weather, insects, plant disease, and numerous other minor disasters that drain precious supplies "gained by slow hard work and good fortune" (1970, p. 117). Because he works his small plot alone, this productive-hoarding character must be self-reliant and independent. There is not sufficient land to hire workers, but there is enough work that only single-minded self-reliance will serve to stave off starvation. Only methodical labor, most of it by hand, will adequately redeem from the land its sparse fruits. Thus the productive-hoarding character is quite adaptive to these circumstances imposed by life (1970, p. 118).

The *exploitative character types* included 10 to 25 percent of the villagers, depending on the absolute degree of exploitativeness overtly expressed. The *unproductive-exploitative* types were found among villagers with destructive tendencies. Men of this character were likely to get into knife or pistol fights. Women who were exploitative are described by Fromm and Macoby as "the most malicious gossip mongers" (1970, p. 123). By contrast, the *productive-exploitative* villagers were a small minority of the richest and most powerful men in the village.

The productive-exploitative villagers were the modern entrepreneurs, who had been influenced by the values of contemporary capitalism through the mass media. These few individuals tended to be owners of large agricultural businesses, employing many workers and the most modern technology. These exploitative characters take advantage of the receptive, economically submissive peasants, and eventually make these powerless people even more impotent and more submissive by increasing their economic dependence. As Fromm and Macoby (1970, p. 124) point out, the productive-exploitative character is the "new man" in peasant society, viewed by his contemporaries as an important positive influence on the economy and envied because he is able to take advantage of opportunities where they lie. Thus this exploitative character is adapted to the newly emerging capitalistic society and its values of progress through schools, social mobility, and technology.

HUMAN POTENTIAL FOR DESTRUCTION: LOVE OF DEATH VERSUS LOVE OF LIFE

In his later years, Fromm sought to sharpen his hypothesis that human character types may be either productive or nonproductive. Recall that Fromm rejects the instinctivist thesis of Freud, which states that human capacities for aggression and for love are strictly biological potentials. You may remember that one of the mechanisms of an individual's escape from freedom is destructiveness. Fromm had suggested in his first major work (1947) that when the individual's self-actualizing or growth tendencies are thwarted, his or her destructive urges are intensified. The more the drive to live, to grow, to become fully what his or her nature promises is blocked, the greater the intensification of his or her destructive or aggressive tendency.

Fromm expanded and modified this fundamental tenet of the opposition of life and death strivings into a hypothesis about the essence of human evil. He proposed that certain personalities are essentially evil because they are *necrophilous,* literally, "lovers of death and decay" (1964, 1973). The opposite, healthy personality is termed *biophilous,* meaning literally "lover of life and growth." For Fromm, the necrophilous orientation is the "quintessence of evil," a truly malignant form of human existence. The malignant aggression evidenced by the necrophile is uniquely human, having no counterpart among the lower animal orders. Malignant aggression is truly destructiveness pursued for its own sake, undertaken for the enjoyment that devastation brings, practiced not for defense, but for perverse satisfaction.

The Necrophilous Character Type

The majority of people are a blend of biophilous and necrophilous traits. In extreme form, however, the necrophilous character type is defined as *"the passionate attraction to all that is dead, decayed, putrid, sickly; it is the passion to transform that which is alive into something unalive; to destroy for the sake of destruction; the exclusive interest in all that is purely mechanical. It is the passion 'to tear apart living structures' "* (Fromm, 1973, p. 332).

One easily discernible trait of necrophilous personalities is their concern with putrid or filthy aspects of their own and others' life habits. A predominant phrase in their vocabularies is "this is shitty," or "life is shitty, people are shitty," and so on (Fromm, 1973, p. 341). For the necrophile, all of life is excrement. The necrophile clearly exaggerates those traits found in the personality type that Freud called the anal sadistic.

Another observable trait of necrophilous personalities is their concern with mechanical, nonhuman gadgetry. Necrophiles who are interested in photography take pictures of people, but their interest is directed to the quality and sophistication of their *cameras;* they listen to music, but their love is for experimentation with complicated stereophonic receivers; they love time-saving appliances, but even the simplest addition is done on a calculator, even the shortest walk to a grocery store is reason to drive there by car. In effect, the necrophilous character substitutes an affinity for *technique* and for *technology* in place of the biophilous person's affinity for life, for people, for beauty (Fromm, 1973, p. 343).

Within the stream of the necrophile's life, there is a marked concern with the processes of elimination, with fecal products, and with human filth. Fromm suggests that the necrophilous person is a malignant form of the classically described Freudian anal sadistic character. Thus the distortion of development responsible for the emergence of the malignant necrophilous personality proceeds as follows: normal anal character → sadistic character → necrophilous character (Fromm, 1973, p. 349). The supreme difference between the sadistic anal type described by Freud and the necrophilous type is the latter's profound sense of alienation and detachment from everything human and alive.

Each of the previously discussed four nonproductive personality types (receptive, exploitative, hoarding, and marketing) solves the problem of his or her own sense of aloneness by establishing some kind of relationship to life. The relationship may be distorted, nonproductive, and manipulative, but at least each of these orientations remains focused on life. Each of them struggles to derive satisfaction from living people, however immoral and unethical his or her strategy may be. The necrophile, by contrast, is not interested in life, in people. His or her interest is in death, in nonliving technology, in destroying the life in others.

> [The necrophile] turns his interest away from life, persons, nature, ideas—in short from everything that is alive; he transforms all life into things, including himself and the manifestations of his human faculties of reason, seeing, hearing, tasting, loving. . . . The world becomes a sum of lifeless artifacts; from synthetic food to synthetic organs, the whole man becomes part of the total machinery that he controls and is

> simultaneously controlled by. . . . He aspires to make robots as one of the greatest achievements of his technical mind, and some specialists assure us that the robot will hardly be distinguished from living men. This achievement will not seem so astonishing when man himself is hardly distinguishable from a robot. . . . Death is no longer symbolically expressed by unpleasant-smelling feces or corpses. Its symbols are now clean, shining machines; men are not attracted to smelly toilets, but to structures of aluminum and glass. (Fromm, 1973, p. 350)

The lifeless world of 20th-century technology is a world of death, and it is a world that creates necrophilous humans just as alienated humans fabricated from their aloneness an equally dehumanizing culture.

It is important to note that Fromm's conception of the necrophilous character type is the logical extension of his early concern with the mechanism of escape from freedom. The necrophilous person is the ultimate development of schizophrenic separation of genuine feelings from public behavior. He or she behaves in a routinized, stereotyped, and unspontaneous way—a cluster of mannerisms that suggests necrophilia originates from early unbearable experiences of distrust, disinterest, and emotional coldness at the hands of the mothering one.

The Origins of Necrophilia

Fromm has hypothesized that the roots of adult necrophilia are to be found in childhood. Some children are unable to establish the normal Oedipal relationship to mother in all of its typical sexual and pleasurable manifestations. "It would seem that such infants never develop warm, erotic, and later, sexual feelings toward mother, or that they never have a desire to be near her. Nor do they later fall in love with mother substitutes. For them mother is a symbol: a phantom rather than a real person" (Fromm, 1973, p. 363).

Instead of the usual perception of mother as a symbol of earth, home, warmth, safety, life, she is to the unattached child a representation of chaos and death: "She is not the life-giving mother, but the death-giving mother; her embrace is death, her womb is a tomb" (Fromm, 1973, p. 363). What are the causes of this malignant transformation of the Oedipal situation? Fromm suggests that a definitive answer is yet unavailable, but that three factors are worth considering.

The first possibility is that some genetically determined factor that regulates the child's innate capacity to form affectional bonds is lacking or malfunctioning. Such a factor might be similar to that which operates in cases of autism. The autistic child is uncommunicative, uninterested in human contact, and fascinated with repetitive mechanical processes. Such a biologically determined factor might be physically expressed in damage to the child's central nervous system, to, for example, the ascending reticular activating system of the brain stem. Damage to this network of fibers might hinder the child's ability to form lasting memories so that its world is constantly chaotic and frightening. Emotional attachments are therefore impossible.

The second possibility is that the mother is a cold, rejecting, or inconsistent caretaker. As a potential necrophilous personality herself, the mother's interactions with a cold or detached infant would only intensify and further exaggerate its human alienation. The result would be a child unable to attach itself emotionally to mother, to father, to friends, to anyone. With time, the consequence of this early emotional abrasion or deprivation would be a defensively malignant interest in nonliving, non-reactive *things;* in short, necrophilia.

Fromm also suggests a third, and perhaps more tenuous, hypothesis. Traumatic experiences in the first years of the child's life that involve frustration of its needs for affection and safety might cause the buildup of malignant rage and hate. A child damaged in this way would have experienced outright abuse or clearly discernible rejection or hate at the hands of its caretakers. Its own resulting defensive hate and resentment eventually fester into the malignant aggression and destructive intent so characteristic of the necrophile (Fromm, 1973, p. 365).

Fromm summarized the distinction between the necrophilous personality and its opposite, the biophilous personality, in this way:

> I have tried to give a picture of the necrophilic and the biophilic orientations in their pure forms. These pure forms are, of course, rare. The pure necrophile is insane; the pure biophile is saintly. Most people are a particular blend of the necrophilous and the biophilous orientations, and what matters is which of the two trends is dominant. Those in whom the necrophilous orientation gains dominance will slowly kill the biophilic side in themselves; usually they are not aware of their death-loving orientation; they will harden their hearts; they will act in such a way that their love of death seems to be the logical and rational response to what they experience. On the other hand, those in whom love for life still dominates, will be shocked when they discover how close they are to the "valley of the shadow of death," and this shock might awaken them to life. (1964, p. 48)

EXISTENTIAL DICHOTOMY: TO HAVE OR TO BE?

Fromm's concern with the fundamentally good nature of human nature and how that nature is perverted by an insane society has also focused on the "having" and "being" orientations to life (Fromm, 1976). In technological society, according to Fromm, the emphasis is on "having," on possessing, and therefore on competitive consuming of life's resources. By contrast, it is possible to approach life with a "being" orientation, with the emphasis on participation in life, on experiencing, and on being-at-one-with life and its people. In Fromm's estimation, his previous distinction between love of life (biophilia) and love of the dead (necrophilia), combined with the having and being dichotomy, are the fundamental ways human persons experience and organize reality.

The "Having" Mode

The having orientation to life is basically consummatory. To enjoy life, we must *have* this and that; work to *possess* such and such; struggle to *obtain* success, which is only really satisfying when it is better than our neighbor Jones's success. We compare what we *have* to what he *has* or to what we will *have*.

Sometimes this orientation to life is so pervasive that we confuse nouns (an object or something to "have") with verbs (an action, process, something to experience). For example, a patient seeking a therapist's help will say: "Doctor, I *have* a problem: I *have* insomnia. Although I *have* a beautiful house, nice children, and a happy marriage, I *have* many worries" (Fromm, 1976, p. 21). Strictly speaking, this patient should say: "I *am* troubled; I *cannot* sleep; I *am* happily married." Instead, the patient begins his complaints by saying "I *have* a problem." In so doing, he avoids the realization that he *is* a problem, that he *experiences* his misery. He has transformed his experience into something he possesses, betraying an unconscious alienation from self (Fromm, 1976, p. 21):

> In the last analysis, the statement "*I* (subject) have *O* (object)" expresses a definition of *I* through my possession of *O.* The subject is not *myself* but *I am what I have.* My property constitutes myself and my identity. The underlying thought in the statement "I am I" is "*I am I* because I have X"—equaling all natural objects and persons to whom I relate myself through my power to control them, to make them permanently mine. (Fromm, 1976, p. 72)

In the having mode, both the object and the subject become things: ". . . and I have *it,* because I have the force to make it mine" (1976, pp. 72–73). The reverse relationship, of course, is implicit: "it has *me,*" because my conception of myself is predicated on possession of *it.*

Fromm, however, distinguishes between two kinds of having. There is the *characterological having* of possession, discussed thus far. There is, in contrast, *existential having,* whereby we obtain those things necessary for continued existence. By virtue of our human needs, we innately require certain commodities, such as food, shelter, and sex, for continued survival. This existential having is distinguished from characterological having because it is biological, not social; innate, not learned; and essential, not merely passion-arousing (Fromm, 1976, p. 80).

The Being Mode: Reality Beneath the Mask

Whereas having refers to objects that are fixed and hence describable, being refers to experience, to living processes within living persons not subject to description (Fromm, 1976, p. 81). If we set out to describe a person's being, we soon discover that "What is fully describable is our *persona*—the mask we each wear, the ego we present—for this persona is in itself a thing" (1976, p. 81). A human person's whole individuality, his or her uniqueness, can never be encompassed by mere description. The difference between describable having and indescribable being is the difference between possession and participation, between destruction and experience.

Fromm quotes Karl Marx's distinction between being and having: "The less you *are* and the less you express your life—the more you *have* and the greater is your alienated life. . . . Everything the economist takes away from you in the way of life and humanity, he restores to you in the form of money and wealth" (Fromm, 1976, p. 145).

The way to an understanding of being is through penetration of appearances to inner reality, the reality of human character structure. As R. D. Laing has also suggested, Fromm points to the discrepancy that may arise between people's appearance and their true motives, between their behavior and their underlying character:

> My behavior may partly reflect my being, but it is usually a mask that I have and that I wear for my own purposes. Behaviorism deals with this mask as if it were a reliable scientific datum; true insight is focused on the inner reality, which is usually neither conscious nor directly observable. This concept of being as "unmasking" . . . is the fundamental discovery of Freud. To understand the discrepancy between behavior

and character, between my mask and the reality it hides, is the main achievement of Freud's psychoanalysis. (Fromm, 1976, p. 90)

Just as Viktor Frankl (see Chapter 1) characterized Freud's work as "unmasking," Fromm, too, interprets psychoanalysis as a penetration through the mask to inner reality. But Fromm takes it a radical step further.

Not only does the unconscious beneath the mask contain repressed desires and fears, but also repressed into that domain is our knowledge of reality, our awareness of what is true (Fromm, 1976, p. 91). Our social living, the irrational passions determined by society, is not repressed. These "illusions" remain conscious and provide only a false map of reality. Our societal living assures that dangerous impulses and perceptive insights into reality will be masked in favor of "acceptable" visions of reality filtered and shaped by our culture. "The way to being is penetration through the surface and insight into reality" (Fromm, 1976, p. 92).

It is Fromm's thesis that every human person is capable of both the having and being modes, but that the society in which he or she lives determines which of the modes will prevail (1976, pp. 98 ff.). The having mode owes its existence to our biological nature and can only be diminished to its existential purity by a society that emphasizes sharing, giving, self-sacrifice, and the inherent need to be at one with others. The differences between the having and the being modes are summarized in Table 13.3.

EVALUATING KAREN HORNEY AND ERICH FROMM

Horney and Fromm shared much, both intellectually and professionally. The bitter ending to their personal relationship is one of those sad facts of history, but it does

TABLE 13.3 Having and Being Modes Contrasted

Having Mode	Being Mode
1. **Insecurity:** the anxiety of loving possessions: "I am what I have"—"I am afraid of losing everything."	1. **Security:** "I am what I am, not what I have."
2. **Antagonism:** competition with others for possessions, and fear that they will steal them.	2. **Solidarity:** sharing with others increases enjoyment of life and the experience of reality.
3. **Pleasure:** driven by passions to peaks of excitement and satisfaction by relief of tension.	3. **Joy:** becoming more fully what one is—aliveness, becoming, participating, experiencing.
4. **Sin:** fear of punishment for disobedience of authority leads to guilt; forgiveness requires repentance and submission.	4. **Sin:** alienation from self and God; loss of self-harmony or treason against self; forgiveness requires atonement, that is—"at-one-ment," or self-healing.
5. **Fear of Dying:** losing the life one possesses; fear of loss of identity—to feel lost. "I am nothing."	5. **Affirmation of Living:** focus on love for others and their love for oneself—to *be*, "I am one-ed with life."
6. **Past and Future:** time-bound focus on what I *had* and what I *can have;* submission to time.	6. **Here and Now:** timeless, eternal experiencing of what *I am*—respect for time.

Based on Fromm, 1976, pp. 100–111.

not change their accomplishments. Both theorists have expanded psychoanalysis, and had Horney lived longer, it is likely she would have shared Fromm's interest in existential thinking or perhaps Zen philosophy (Quinn, 1987).

Refutability of Horney's and Fromm's Concepts

The same evaluation, unfortunately, can be given for both theorists. Their concepts are largely, if not completely, irrefutable in the form in which they devised them. But there the similarity ends.

Horney's elegant, lucid, and nearly behavioral descriptions of neurotic misery and the conflicts underlying neurotic striving beg for translation into empirically testable concepts. At the least, personality assessment tests, based on her descriptions, could be developed by the psychometrically minded psychologist. Beyond those descriptions, her lucid synthesis of neurotic "styles" (moving toward, away from, and against) have an empirical power that is waiting to be tapped.

Fromm, much like Horney, contributed much in the way of social description, especially the elucidation of alienation. But his concepts tend toward the philosophical and existential, especially toward the end of his life. And such concepts do not have clear empirical referents. Fromm's last major theoretical effort before his death, the "having and being" modes, are existentially flavored, and probably represent ontological concepts similar to Rollo May's ideas. Although intriguing, such concepts pull Fromm's theory even further from the criterion of refutability.

Horney's and Fromm's Conception of Human Agency

Both Horney and Fromm emphasized personal freedom and autonomy. Fromm even wrote extensively about the pathological ways in which we give up our freedom. Had Horney pursued her interest in Eastern philosophy, she would, no doubt, have come to grips with the issues of human agency and determinism more clearly than she had thus far. On the whole, both of these theorists portray human agency as active, subjective, and only partly determined by drives, needs, or environmental pressures. For both thinkers, humans make free decisions, freely interpret their world, and freely make the kind of mistakes for which they suffer the burden of anxiety and alienation.

The Idiographic Emphasis of Social Psychoanalysis

Both Horney and Fromm evolved very far away from classical psychoanalysis, each for their own reasons. But despite the theoretical distance they placed between themselves and Freud, their work is as idiographic as his.

Horney clearly focused on clinical issues of psychopathology. Normal development is an afterthought in her work, and while she describes personality functioning with empathy and brilliance, her most dazzling concepts are those related to neurosis. With such a clinical perspective, it is not surprising that her theory is almost wholly focused on individual functioning and idiographic, almost phenomenological, concepts. Despite her concern with cultural differences and effects, the body of her work is idiographically focused.

Fromm, similarly, worked frequently from the clinical perspective. But his theory, you may recall, began as an attempt to blend economic theory with psychoanalysis. In a way, Fromm, more than Horney, focused on societal themes, broad-based issues of social determination, that have a nomothetic flavor. But "flavor" is not the same as substance, and in the end, the usual relationship between lack of empirical testability and strong idiographic emphasis prevails here in Fromm's theory as well.

COMPARATIVE SUMMARY

Karen Horney and Erich Fromm each took from psychoanalysis a conviction that unconscious motives shape the direction of the individual's life history. But each of these theorists modified this psychoanalytic tenet with a somewhat different concept of the social side of the human enterprise.

Karen Horney developed a psychoanalytically oriented interpersonal theory of personality and psychopathology (Or is it an object relations theory?). Fundamental to her conception of personality development and its distortion by neurotic strivings are two basic emotions: anxiety and hostility. When the parental attitude toward the child is cold, inconsistent, or abusive, the foundation is laid for the child to develop a sense of basic hostility toward the parents, and perhaps toward people at large. Because children cannot openly express their anger for fear of abandonment by these powerful "giants," they repress these dangerous feelings. Unable to recognize the hostility that boils below the surface, the child develops a façade of pleasing lovableness, a strategy Karen Horney herself had used as a child to cope with her anger and resentment toward her parents for favoring her brother. But such a strategy is usually doomed to failure, for the child's fear of abandonment and the resulting chaos of utter helplessness provoke a basic and enduring anxiety that shapes all dealings with significant people in the child's world. Compulsive, indiscriminate, and unrealistic "neurotic needs" make their appearance in the child's character as desperate means to control self and others. Horney eventually grouped these 10 needs (affection and approval; partner; restriction of life; power and omnipotence; exploitation of others; social recognition; personal admiration; personal achievement; self-sufficiency; and perfection-unassailability) into three compulsive patterns: moving compliantly *toward,* detachedly *away* from, or aggressively *against* others.

Erich Fromm likewise found human character distorted into neurotic patterns by a dehumanizing social environment that forces human beings to become alienated from self and estranged from fellow human beings. Drawing on the ideas of both Freud and Marx, Fromm sought to combine the psychoanalytic view of the person alienated from his or her own unconscious urges with the Marxian conception of people competitively isolated as they treat one another as objects of exploitation. Fromm's historical analysis attempted to show that as industrial and capitalistic growth proceeded, human character growth strangled. Increasingly freed of dependence on religious and institutional authority, human beings turned their inventiveness to the pursuit of goals beyond mere material survival. The more expansive human freedom became, the greater the burden of aloneness such independence produced. Dehumanized and alienated by their own creations, contemporary persons seek to return to more satisfying oneness with nature, with self, and with others.

To escape from such terrifying freedom, defensive maneuvers resembling Horney's neurotic needs are seized upon by people who need to avoid personhood. Such defensive character structures have a single goal embodied in their diverse adaptations to society: to default selfhood in the panic-activated striving to be secure. Thus authoritarian submission or domination, destructiveness, and automaton conformity are all attempts to numb the feelings of aloneness that inevitably accompany the responsibilities of freedom. Without a genuine self, one cannot be alienated. Without genuine selfhood, one becomes an unfeeling, and therefore unhurt, robot.

For Horney, too, the central neurotic conflict is alienation from self, a personal estrangement that has its roots in the stranglehold of the neurotic needs and coping strategies. The real self, in Horney's conception, is the source of all spontaneous personal growth toward happiness, health, and genuine love for others. Thus, for both Horney and Fromm, the individual person may be said to have a fundamentally "good," healthy, or spontaneous striving to actualize his or her unique human character. Fromm specifies that human character is a complex blend of animal passion and human reason striving for satisfaction in six unique spheres of human endeavor: relatedness and unity, transcendence and effectiveness, rootedness, identity, frame of orientation and object of devotion, and activating stimulation.

Horney conceptualizes neurotic individuals as developing idealized self-images, typically composed of a long list of things they *should* be. She wrote brilliantly of the "tyranny of the shoulds" by which the neurotic's life becomes distorted and constricted in an unending struggle to attain that which is humanly impossible. Fromm pictures neurotic distortion of human character in terms of culturally shaped types of personality that conform to the perverted standards imposed by society. Where Horney speaks of the person's alienation from real self in futile attempts to identify with an idealized and tyrannical self-image, Fromm, by contrast, describes self-alienation in terms of productive and nonproductive orientations to social living.

Consequently, the basic theme for both theorists is that feelings of aloneness and helplessness provoke caricatures of healthy human interaction that mimic adaptive interpersonal relationships. Submission or exploitation are the sad impersonations of human interaction that both Horney and Fromm picture as the unavoidable outgrowth of self-estrangement.

Fromm has taken the theme of distorted human personality a step further than Horney in his proposal of a fundamental character distinction between the lovers of life and the lovers of death. The necrophilous personality is a malignant anal-sadistic character type who prefers things to people, death to life, filth to beauty. The biophilous personality, by contrast, corresponds to what other personality theorists call the self-actualized personality. Carried even further, the existential flavor of his necrophilous-biophilous distinction has been augmented by Fromm in his analysis of the differences between the having-consumptive-destructive and the being-experiencing-participating modes of living.

Both Horney and Fromm disagreed with Freud's model of human nature on a number of points. Thus, for example, Horney "desexualized" the Oedipus complex, and Fromm "socialized" instinct theory. Horney rejected the universality of penis envy in feminine development, and she restored to personality theory an emphasis on understanding human beings as people struggling for emotional survival, identity, and security. Fromm rejected Freud's narrow focus on the war of sexual and aggressive passions, too, and he enlarged psychoanalytic theory with much needed considerations of the potent human urge for a sensible, competent existence. As Fromm has said, "If you are a thief, at least be the best possible thief that you can be" (quoted by Epstein, 1975, p. 457).

Our evaluation of Horney's and Fromm's theories reveals basic similarities. Both theories are largely nonrefutable, although some of Horney's "personality style" concepts are begging for translation into empirical referents. Both Horney and Fromm strongly emphasize active human agency, and both theories are focused mostly on idiographic issues.

FOR FURTHER READING

Karen Horney did not publish as extensively as did some of the other personality theorists. Her first book, *The Neurotic Personality of Our Time* (New York: Norton, 1937), contains lucid descriptions of neurotic coping mechanisms. She elaborated her differences from Freud and criticized fundamental psychoanalytic tenets in *New Ways in Psychoanalysis* (New York: Norton, 1939). By far the most comprehensive presentation of her thinking is to be found in her *Neurosis and Human Growth* (New York: Norton, 1950).

A collection of Horney's papers to show both her agreement and disagreement with the Freudian view of women is to be had in *Feminine Psychology* (New York: Norton, 1967). Some of Alfred Adler's ideas served as the jumping-off point for Horney's conception of basic hostility and inferiority. Adler's *The Practice and Theory of Individual Psychology* (Totowa, NJ: Littlefield, Adams, 1959) will provide some basis of comparison with Horney. Jack L. Rubins's *Karen Horney: Gentle Rebel of Psychoanalysis* (New York, Dial Press, 1978) is the first full-length biography of Karen Horney and merits attention for the light it sheds on the personal sources of Horney's emphasis on parental indifference as the root of self-alienation. Susan Quinn's *A Mind of Her Own: The Life of Karen Horney* (New York: Summit Books/Simon & Schuster, 1987) is a relatively complete and penetrating look at Horney's personal history. Horney's very personal glimpses of her own life and motives are now available in *The Adolescent Diaries of Karen Horney* (New York: Basic Books, 1980).

Two volumes edited by H. Kelman, *New Perspectives in Psychoanalysis: Contributions to Karen Horney's Holistic Approach* (New York: Norton, 1965) and *Advances in Psychoanalysis: Contributions to Karen Horney's Holistic Approach* (New York: Norton, 1964), will provide some indication of Horney's influence in psychiatry. A critical examination of her modification of psychoanalysis is provided by Benjamin Wolman in "Psychoanalysis Without Libido: An Analysis of Karen Horney's Contribution to Psychoanalytic Theory," *American Journal of Psychotherapy* (1954), **8**, 21–31. Some of Horney's ideas on social influences were shaped by Georg Simmel; his *Conflict and the Web of Group Affiliations* (New York: Free Press, 1955) will give some indication of his thought.

Erich Fromm's views are nowhere, except in textbooks, completely summarized in one volume. The place to start is with Fromm's *Escape From Freedom* (New York: Holt, 1941; also available in paperback from Fawcett, Greenwich, CT). Fromm's debts to Marx and Freud are lucidly set forth in his *Beyond the Chains of Illusion: My Encounter With Marx and Freud* (New York: Simon & Schuster, 1962). His critical attitude toward psychoanalysis may be discerned in two of his works: *The Crisis of*

Psychoanalysis (New York: Holt, 1970) and *Sigmund Freud's Mission:An Analysis of His Personality and Influence* (New York: Harper & Row, 1959).

Fromm's *The Anatomy of Human Destructiveness* (New York: Holt, 1973) contains his views on necrophilia, and an attempt to organize ethological, biological, and psychological insights on human aggression. Richard I. Evans provides another illuminating interview in his *Dialog With Erich Fromm* (New York: Harper & Row, 1966), or in condensed form in *The Making of Psychology* (New York: Knopf, 1976).

The full clinical and experimental richness of Fromm and Macoby's study of Mexican peasant villagers and their adaptive character orientations may be grasped in their *Social Character in a Mexican Village* (Englewood Cliffs, NJ: Prentice-Hall, 1970). Fromm's most recent existential-humanistic additions to his theory, the being-having modes of existence, may be read in his *To Have or to Be?* (New York: Harper & Row, 1976).

Richard Christie and Florence Geis's work on a type of personality they call the Machiavellian has some remarkable similarity to Fromm's exploitative character type. Christie and Geis's work may be found in their *Studies in Machiavellianism* (New York: Academic Press, 1970). Similarly, William H. Whyte, Jr.'s classic *The Organization Man* (New York: Simon & Schuster, 1956) deserves scrutiny for its similarity to Fromm's marketing character type. Two intellectual biographies of Fromm present various views on the significance of his work in the stream of psychology's history. Daniel Burston's *The Legacy of Erich Fromm* (Cambridge, MA: Harvard University Press, 1991) is only marginally concerned with Fromm's personal life and focuses instead on the ideological and psychological significance of Fromm's ideas. Gerhard P. Knapp's *The Art of Living: Erich Fromm's Life and Works* (New York: Peter Lang, 1993) pays slightly more attention to Fromm's personal history, but is fundamentally a history of Fromm's ideas rather than his life.

CHAPTER 14

GORDON W. ALLPORT
Humanistic Trait and Self Theory

To the S-R colleague the [eclectic] intuitionist says, "You consider the reflex (e.g., the patellar [knee-jerk]) as a basic model. Fine, but where would you locate in it the laughter of the self-transcending subject who feels silly as he watches his patella respond to the hammer?"

Gordon W. Allport, *"The Fruits of Eclecticism: Bitter or Sweet?"*

About Allport's Trait and Self Theory

Gordon Allport created American personality psychology. His emphasis on uniqueness and individuality brought him much criticism, but his central theses have enduring value. Among his core ideas are these:

1. *Personality can be understood as the mixture of major and minor "traits" by which a single life is known.*

2. *A personality "trait" is a biological, psychological, and social mixture that disposes a person toward specific kinds of action under specific circumstances.*

3. *A psychologist may say that he or she "understands" another person only when that person's entire life history is examined, only when the life course is observed, and only when the person him- or herself is permitted to contribute a thoughtful self-evaluation.*

From the tradition of the Harvard psychological clinic, in the spirit of personologists such as Henry Murray and Robert White, the contributions of Gordon Allport steered the thinking of several generations of personality theorists toward considering whole human lives rather than isolated motives, wishes, and actions.

"HOW SHALL A PSYCHOLOGICAL LIFE HISTORY BE WRITTEN?"

Within a year of his graduation from college, at the age of 22, Gordon Allport sent to Sigmund Freud a note announcing that while he, Allport, was visiting Vienna, Freud would no doubt be glad to make his acquaintance. In response to what Allport afterward labeled his "callow forwardness," Freud invited the brash young traveler to his office. The visit proved to be of lasting consequence for Allport's subsequent career as a personality theorist.

> Soon after I had entered the famous red burlap room with pictures of dreams on the wall, he summoned me to his inner office. He did not speak to me but sat in expectant silence for me to state my mission. I was not prepared for silence and had to think fast to find a suitable conversational gambit. I told him of an episode on the tram car on my way to his office. A small boy about four years of age had displayed a conspicuous dirt phobia. He kept saying to his mother, "I don't want to sit there . . . don't let that dirty man sit beside me." To him everything was *schmutzig* [filthy]. His mother was a well-starched *Hausfrau,* so dominant and purposive looking that I thought the cause and effect apparent.
>
> When I finished my story Freud fixed his kindly therapeutic eyes upon me and said, "And was that little boy you?" Flabbergasted and feeling a bit guilty, I contrived to change the subject. While Freud's misunderstanding of my motivation was amusing, it also started a deep train of thought. I realized that he was accustomed to neurotic

defenses and that my manifest motivation (a sort of rude curiosity and youthful ambition) escaped him. For therapeutic progress he would have to cut through my defenses, but it so happened that therapeutic progress was not here an issue. (1968, pp. 383–384)

Allport further commented that the experience with Freud provided a significant insight into the pitfalls of "depth" psychology: "This experience taught me that depth psychology, for all its merits, may plunge too deep, and that psychologists would do well to give full recognition to manifest motives before probing the unconscious" (1968, p. 384). It is difficult not to see in Allport's misadventure the roots of a personal distaste for psychoanalytic assessment. Indeed, Allport wryly commented in his autobiography:

> Much of my writing is critical of prevailing psychological idols. At times I have crossed swords with learning theory, dimensionalism in personality research, and with what seems to me to be an overemphasis on unconscious processes, projective tests, and simplified drive theories of motivation. I have felt that these fashionable explanatory principles are able to deal only with the peripheral or "opportunistic" layers of personality, or else that they make too much of some improbable formulations of depth psychology. (Yes, my single encounter with Freud was traumatic.) (1967, p. 22)

Often, in later years, Allport championed research and assessment strategies that emphasized exploration of the "psychic surface" of life (1960, p. 96). A direct question directly put frequently elicits as much, if not more, information about a person's motives than hours of projective testing and psychoanalytic interviewing. Commenting on the prevailing trend of motivational theory in the 1950s, Allport pointed out that psychologists often acted as if individuals' conscious verbal reports about themselves were untrustworthy. Indeed, psychologists were all too interested in indirect assessments of patients' pasts when at least some significance should have been attributed to present strivings. Allport bluntly stated his own contrary position on the matter of direct motivational assessment. It is possible to detect in his statement some residue of disappointment and anger dating from his ill-fated interview with Freud:

> When we set out to study a person's motives, we are seeking to find out what that person is trying to do in this life—including, of course, what he is trying to avoid and what he is trying to be. I see no reason why we should not start our investigation by asking him to tell us the answers as he sees them. (1960, p. 101)

It was not Allport's intention to deny the existence or significance of unconscious motives or the importance of infantile experiences. Rather, he was concerned to supplement any such one-sided emphasis on hidden, past motives with an equal emphasis on the person's conscious and contemporary self-evaluation. In the same spirit in which Harry Stack Sullivan had suggested that every scientist is a human being, Allport assumed that every person was entitled to be heard. In the same way that George Kelly had concluded that every person was a personality scientist, Allport chose to believe that every personality scientist wants to comprehend the whole person. That comprehension must, in part, rest on an understanding of what people themselves believe they are trying to do.

Allport lucidly stated the guiding questions that shaped his work in personality: "How shall a psychological life history be written? What processes and what structures must a full-bodied account of personality include? How can one detect unifying threads in a life, if they exist?" (1968, p. 377). Although these were the abiding questions that governed Allport's theorizing and research, he was forced to confess toward the end of his life:"I still do not know how a psychological life history should be written" (1968, p. 377). But Allport had learned—and taught—the important lesson that rigid reliance on abstract theories of personality should be tempered with a willingness to admit one's dogmatism, with a readiness to accept the facts however unpalatable they may prove to be, and with a firm conviction that whole persons are more complex than our explanations of them. Allport admonished psychologists to abide by two principles (1968, p. 23):

1. *"Do not forget what you have decided to neglect."* If a theory seemingly accounts for a small piece of reality, never lose sight of the fact that it does not account for all realities.
2. *"Theorize in such a way that what is true in any region of mental life can be verified to be so."* The goal of psychological science is to seek the truth, insofar as it can be known. However, the whole truth will always be the product of many workers' efforts. Therefore, no psychologist has the right to interpret his results in such a way as to block the solution of related problems.

In his own work, Allport sought to blend a scientific strategy that would yield generalizable data about human nature with a philosophic commitment to the significance of the unique individual. To achieve these complementary goals Allport postulated some very definite criteria by which to construct a theory of personality.

CRITERIA FOR A FULL-BODIED PERSONALITY THEORY: PERSONALISM

Allport found difficulty in merging science's traditional interest in universal laws with psychology's presumed focus on the uniqueness of the individual. In *Personality: A Psychological Interpretation* (1937), his first systematic treatment of the field, Allport wrote:

> The outstanding characteristic of man is his individuality. He is a unique creation of the forces of nature. Separated spatially from all other men he behaves throughout his own particular span of life in his own distinctive fashion. It is not upon the cell nor upon the single organ, nor upon the group, nor upon the species that nature has centered her most lavish concern, but rather upon the integral organization of life processes into the amazingly stable and self-contained system of the individual creature. (1937, p. 3)

Nevertheless, Allport pointed out, science seems to be embarrassed by the individual case. In its attempts to seek uniformities and regularities in nature, science has focused all of its efforts on whole classes of phenomena. From this perspective, the individual is regarded only as an instance or an example of a universal principle. For scientists, processes like intelligence, perception, and learning are regulated by general laws, and it is their job to discover how these laws apply despite particular individual differences among the subjects with whom they work.

In opposition to the classic scientific strategy, Allport identified himself with the rationale and methods of *personalistic* psychology. Personalism focuses on psychological processes as they are embodied in individuals:

> The chief tenet of [personalistic psychology] is that every mental function is embedded in personal life. In no concrete sense is there such a thing as intelligence, space perception, color discrimination or choice reaction; there are only *people* who are capable of performing such activities and of having such experiences. . . .Nor can motives ever be studied apart from their personal setting; they represent always the striving of a total organism toward its objective. (Allport, 1937, p. 18)

The distinction between the investigation of general or universal laws, and the application of such laws to the individual case occupied Allport's attention throughout his career. He adopted from the philosopher W. Windelband (in Allport, 1937, p. 22) the terms *nomothetic* and *idiographic* to describe the differences between a concern for the general principle and an interest in particular individuals.

Idiographic and Nomothetic Disciplines

As a psychologist, Allport asserted that his chief interest must by definition be the construction of methods and concepts that encompass the complexity of the individual case. As a personalistic psychologist, or personologist as Murray (1938) termed this strategy, Allport argued that idiographic (particular) and nomothetic (general) methods and concepts should be blended. "[The psychological study of individuality] will not be content with the discovery of laws pertaining to mind-in-general, but will seek also to understand the lawful tendencies of minds-in-particular. But there is no need for two disciplines. Psychology can treat both types of subjects" (Allport, 1937, p. 23).

The clear implication of Allport's argument that idiographic and nomothetic strategies can be merged is that the personologist believes "Personality . . .is a pattern that exists 'out there.' We boldly ask what a person is like in his essential nature (not merely how he affects other people, or how he behaves in different situations). Of course, his behavior is variable, but always within the limits and ranges set by the [person's] structure itself" (Allport, 1961, p. 572). Thus the personologist seeks to understand *individual consistency;* that is, personal uniformities and the regularities in behavior evidenced by the individual over time. In this sense, the personologist is concerned with "laws" of behavior. But this concern is always for the whole of personality as it exists in real people who show an endless variety of unique, novel, and matchless combinations of personality variables (Allport, 1960, pp. 146–147). Consequently, for the personologist, only laws that are applicable to the unique individual case are worth attention. If there is some measure of logical inconsistency in the concept of laws with both idiographic and nomothetic import, the personologist prefers the study of individual regularity to the investigation of a fictional "average" person.

The Meaning of Personality: Suggestions for an Adequate Theory

Allport's emphasis on the importance of the individual case, and the necessity to understand the whole person, led him to formulate five criteria by which to judge the adequacy of any personality theory (1960, pp. 20 ff.).

First, a truly satisfactory theory will *construe the human personality as integumented*—that is, as centered within the functioning organism. Personality, for Allport, is not explainable exclusively in situational terms, nor in terms of others' opinions of the person. Interpersonal theories and theories that emphasize the variability of behavior across different situations tend to confuse persons' *reputations* with the persons themselves. An adequate personality theory recognizes that *persons* are the locus of personality, that personality is *biophysical,* having both psychological and physiological components, and that persons have their own inner congruence or consistency (Allport, 1960, p. 21).

Second, the adequate personality theory will *regard the organism as replete, not empty.* Behavioristic formulations of the person tend to restrict their conceptualizations to only those aspects that are observable, measurable. Events that occur between the observable stimulus and the observable response of the organism are inadmissible to some behavioristic, positivistic theories. The result is a formulation of the human person as an "empty organism." Allport argued that the full-bodied personality theory "must assume from the onset that there is nothing scientifically shameful about postulating a well-furnished personality that is something and *does* something—a personality that has internal structures and substructures which 'cause,' or partially cause, behavior" (1960, p. 25).

Third, an adequate personality theory will *regard motivation "as normally a fact of present structure and function,* not merely as an outgrowth of earlier forces" (Allport, 1960, p. 20; italics added). Allport directed, once again, his criticism to psychoanalytic theories that tend to regard all motivation as a product of the organism's past. Such formulations pay scant attention to the uniqueness and contemporaneity of human motives. Furthermore, some formulations of personality attempt to reduce the multiplicity of human motives to a few basic drives, needs, wishes, or vectors with the implication that all personalities can be accounted for by proper application of these dimensions. Allport suggested that such formulations accomplish little that is of use in the task of understanding any single full-bodied personality: Drives, needs, wishes, and so forth merely summate to an abstraction of genuine human personality (1960, p. 27).

Fourth, the satisfactory personality theory will *employ units of analysis "capable of living synthesis"* (Allport, 1960, p. 20; italics added). Allport criticized the tendency prevalent among psychologists to reduce personality to a set of measurable variables without the foresight to plan such analytic reductions around the basic goal of resynthesizing the measurements into a whole picture: "To say that John Brown scores in the eightieth percentile of the 'masculinity-femininity' variable, in the thirtieth percentile on 'need for achievement' and at average on 'introversion-extroversion' is only moderately enlightening. Even with a more numerous set of dimensions, with an avalanche of psychometric scores, patterned personality seems to elude the psychodiagnostician" (1960, p. 30).

Fifth, the full-bodied personality theory will *"allow adequately for, but not rely exclusively upon, the phenomenon of self-consciousness"* (Allport, 1960, p. 20; italics added). Although it is true that self-awareness may be transient and ephemeral, it is equally true that "all sensing, acting and willing are, at bottom, *owned* and that self-hood is the central presupposition we must hold in examining the psychological states of human beings" (Allport, 1960, pp. 34–35). In short, as William James stated the matter, "Whatever I may be thinking of, I am always at the same time more or less aware of *myself*, of my *personal* existence" (James, 1963, p. 166). The adequate theory of personality will devote suitable attention to the person's capacity for self-attention.

The most important implication of Allport's requirements for an adequate personality theory is his insistence that no "law" of behavior is as inevitable in its application as a law of physics. The organism's active participation in life, the capacity for self-initiated organization of life, always make the inexorability of psychological "laws" suspect. Allport, therefore, advocated what he called an "open system" in personality theory (1960, Chapter 3).

An "open" personality theory, as contrasted with a "closed" one, stresses with equal emphasis past and present motives, and it includes the possibility that organisms are future-oriented. The open personality theory regards the person not only as "re-active" but as "pro-active," as well. Organisms change. The open personality theorist recognizes that his or her concepts must incorporate the fact of change as a fundamental tenet. Furthermore, whereas the closed-system formulation of personality regards the person as striving to achieve homeostasis in the face of environmental changes, the open-system approach acknowledges that organisms sometimes strive for more than mere preservation of the status quo.

As Allport succinctly stated, most closed-system personality theories are limited by their emphasis on *"being* rather than *becoming"* (1960, p. 44). Like Rogers and Maslow (see Chapter 15), Allport preferred the view that persons strive toward self-enhancement, *for* increased growth, rather than *from* a sensed deficiency, toward a state of increased appreciation of self. "If I argue for the open system," Allport stressed, "I plead more strongly for the open mind" (1960, p. 53).

Personal Sources of Allport's Emphasis on Uniqueness and Independence

Clearly, the emphasis in Allport's approach to personality is on treating persons with unquestioning respect. A human being's motives may sometimes have a convoluted personal history. Yet that human being functions adaptively in the present, giving evidence by such rational behavior that old motives frequently acquire new meanings. Present actions, although derived from dimly perceived and obsolete causes in the stream of a person's life history, may be freed from their moorings and function autonomously in new ways for new reasons in new situations. Allport appropriately called this conception of motivation "functional autonomy," a topic to be considered in detail somewhat later in this chapter. What is important in the present context of personal sources of Allport's theory is that Allport was claiming the privilege of functional autonomy for himself, as well as for personalities at large.

On Swallowing a Dictionary: Competing for Recognition

Gordon Allport was born November 11, 1897, in Montezuma, Indiana, to an enterprising physician, John Edwards Allport, and his wife, Nellie Edith Wise. Gordon was the youngest child of the family, with three brothers ranging from five to nine years older than he. Family life was marked by "plain Protestant piety and hard work" (Allport, 1967, p. 4). Allport's father stressed a humanitarian outlook on life, expressed in his fundamental rule: "If every person worked as hard as he could and took only the minimum financial return required by his family's needs, then there would be just enough wealth to go around" (1967, p. 5).

Because his brothers were so much older than he, Allport found few friends with whom to share boyhood. By his own report, it was a select few, "for I never fitted the general boy assembly. I was quick with words, poor at games." At the age of 10, a schoolmate expressed the prevailing opinion of young Gordon: "Aw, that guy swallowed a dictionary" (1967, p. 4). Allport then knew he was an "isolatc," though "I contrived to be the 'star' for a small cluster of friends."

Thus for Allport, the road to acceptance as a valued individual led through the byway of intellectual achievement. But even this avenue was fraught with unwanted competition. His older brother Floyd, destined to become an esteemed social psychologist, graduated from Harvard at about the time Gordon finished high school. Floyd suggested that Gordon attend Harvard, and though he made the decision to apply belatedly, Gordon was accepted "after squeezing through the entrance tests." After his first final examinations produced an array of D's and C's, young Gordon redoubled his efforts to earn all A's at the year-end exams.

Allport stresses in his autobiography that his career at Harvard was an intellectual revolution. There was always the silent expectation of excellence in the atmosphere: "In the course of 50 years' association with Harvard I have never ceased to admire the unspoken expectation of excellence. One should perform at the highest level of which one is capable, and one is given full freedom to do so" (Allport, 1967, p. 5). Yet, after graduation, when Allport returned from his travels and from his visit with Freud, his decision to work for the doctorate in psychology at Harvard resulted in a seemingly changed estimation: "Back at Harvard I found that the requirements for the Ph.D. degree were not stiff (not nearly stiff enough), and so with only two years' additional course work, a few examinations, and the thesis, I qualified for this degree in 1922 at the age of 24" (1967, p. 8).

Allport's ambivalent assessment of Harvard's academic excellence may have been triggered by the fact that his brother Floyd also obtained his Ph.D. there—and in psychology—and Floyd had even taught his younger brother experimental psychology during Gordon's doctoral studies. Allport's conflicting statements on Harvard's excellence, then, seem to have the flavor of minimizing the achievement that he and his brother shared, saying in effect, "It wasn't too tough; I did it too."

When brother Floyd published his classic textbook on social psychology, Gordon's comment was, "His *Social Psychology* (1924) was too behavioristic and too psychoanalytic for my taste" (1967, p. 12). Gordon and Floyd Allport rarely collaborated professionally, and they published only two papers together. With incredible under-statement, Gordon Allport commented, "Apart from these two papers we never col-laborated, even though we have occasionally helped each other with criticism" (1967, p. 12).

Atwood and Tomkins (1976) have pointed to the pattern in Allport's life of fol-lowing in his brother's footsteps:

> If we assume that this pattern of similar behavior [by Gordon imitating Floyd] was the outcome of an identification based on envy, it would mean that Allport's edu-cation and career choice were, in large measure, "functionally *dependent*," i.e., motivated by the infantile aim of participating in his brother's greatness and thereby overcoming his own feelings of inferiority. Some insight into why it should have become necessary for him to abandon this aim and make his work functionally autonomous is suggested by another concept in his theoretical writings—the *uniqueness* of the individual. To the extent that his life was directed and determined by the emulation of his brother. . . . His own identity as a separate person (his uniqueness) was likely to have been compromised. In the service of asserting his identity, then, he opposed the identification with his brother by declaring that his interests had become independent of their origins. (Atwood & Tomkins, 1976, p. 175; first italics added)

Thus Atwood and Tomkins suggest that the emphasis on personal uniqueness and the functional independence of present motives from their historical roots in All-port's theory served a defensive function in Allport's personal mental economy.

Allport's View of His Personal Uniqueness

Throughout his autobiography, Allport mentions his lack of scientific skill, his poor ability in such subjects as physics, chemistry, and experimental method. To Floyd he attributes talent in all of these subjects and more: "Floyd was a stricter logician and more systematic in his use of method than I. It should also be said that he had artis-tic, musical, and manual giftedness that I lacked" (1967, p. 12). What special talent, then, did Gordon himself possess? He hints that he and his brother differed drastically but then ambivalently withdraws the distinction: "Over the years we pursued our own ways, but because of our common and unusual surname and divergence of points of view we managed to confuse students and the public. Were there one or two Allports?" (1967, pp. 12-13).

Most emphatically, there were two. But one of them was a social psychologist, and the other was a personality psychologist, who struggled to wrest his chosen, self-created field from the domain of the social psychologists:

> In my thinking there is a sharp distinction between personality and social psychology. One must think of personality as a biophysical or biopsychical structure. It may be modified by the field, but it *is* something. Social psychology is everything else. (Allport, paraphrased by Brewster-Smith, 1971, p. 353)

Allport had singlehandedly created the field of American personality psychology with the publication of his classic book in 1937. And that personally precious field of endeavor was Allport's way of demarcating himself as a unique psychologist, as an individual, as an equal to Floyd. For him, personality *had* to be something real inside people, independently existing as a special object of study, influenced but not dependent upon the social milieu, and accessible only to the psychological specialist—the personality psychologist.

It is ironic that the psychologist whose abiding concern was "How shall a psychological life history be written?" struggled so intensely against the recognition that personal history profoundly *shapes* personality. Commenting on the individual's personal belief in religion and the sources of religious doubt, Allport dismissed the "genetic fallacy" of disproving a proposition by demonstrating its personal origins in the believer's life experiences. It is difficult to read his statement without seeing some degree of personal justification in it:

> The plain truth is that origins can tell nothing about the validity of a belief. Neither can origins characterize the mature belief as it now exists, nor explain its part in the present economy of life. One of the best musicians I know took up his profession originally, in part at least, because he was taunted in childhood for what seemed to be his tone-deafness. In psychological parlance, he "overcompensated" for the defect. But that incident has absolutely nothing to do with the present structure or dynamics of his life-absorbing interest. . . . Were we to gauge our evaluations by origins we would disparage the eloquence of Demosthenes because his oratory served as a compensation for his tendency to stammer. . . . And the fact that many psychologists take up their science because of personal maladjustments would make psychology worthless. (Allport, 1950, pp. 109–110)

The "plain truth," as Allport would say, is that he created a valuable and unique theory of personality out of his unique constellation of personal experiences and motives. The theory's validity is certainly not lessened by an examination of its personal origins. Paradoxically, such an analysis increases both the theory's uniqueness and its human generalizability. Allport's theoretical claims for uniqueness of personhood had their roots in his childhood "isolation" from peers and siblings. He followed his brother to Harvard undergraduate college, then followed him again through Harvard graduate study, even imitating his brother's field of specialization. But Gordon Allport's study of psychology was deliberately a world apart from Floyd's brand of psychology. In organizing the field of personality study, Gordon sought to rescue his special domain from the hands of his brother, the social psychologist. And he did so; in one stroke he built a theory to reflect the uniqueness and independence of the person and established his own uniqueness and independence among the Allports.

THE PERSON: TRAITS AND DISPOSITIONS

Allport's emphasis on a full-bodied and open-system personality theory was a natural outgrowth of his earliest conceptualization of personality (1937, p. 48):

> Personality is the dynamic organization within the individual of those psychological systems that determine his unique adjustments to his environment.

In devising his definition, Allport devoted a good deal of effort to synthesizing the varied usages of the term personality into a coherent and workable construct. Characteristically, Allport's definition emphasizes four of the five criteria that, as we have seen, he regarded as essential to a full-bodied view of personality. The first emphasis involves the usage of the term *dynamic organization.* Allport meant to stress that personality is always an organized whole, but a whole that is constantly changing (dynamic). Personality is thus self-regulating and continually evolving (1937, p. 48).

Second, the term *within the individual* was intended to indicate that personality is something "real"—something that resides within the skin. For Allport, as previously discussed, a personality theory or definition must imply its acceptance of the view that personality is integumented, residing as a real, though perhaps not directly observable, entity *in* people. Personality is not an abstraction, nor is it a scientifically convenient fiction. Personality *is,* and it is *in* persons.

Third, the term *psychophysical systems* was meant to convey a recognition of the fact that personality has roots in the physical, chemical processes of the body's glands and nervous system. "The term 'psychophysical' reminds us that personality is neither exclusively mental nor exclusively neural. The organization entails the operation of both body and mind, *inextricably fused into a personal unity*" (Allport, 1937, p. 48; italics added).

Fourth, and last, the phrase *unique adjustments to his environment* emphasizes both Allport's conviction that psychology must attend to the individual personality in all of its singularity and Allport's concern that psychological generalizations be understood as subject to change. Personality is a mode of survival, in Allport's view, and thus individuals adjust not merely to their geographical environment but to those aspects of their life situations that they alone construe as meaningful (1937, p. 50). To repeat Allport's apt phrase, personality is becoming, not merely being.

In his 1961 revision of his major work, Allport somewhat modified his personality definition by substituting a new phrase for the previous "unique adjustments to his environment." The modified definition now ended with the phrase, *"characteristic behavior and thought"* (1961, p. 28). It is remarkable that in the 24 years intervening between his first and second definitions of personality, Allport found so little to alter. The alteration was designed to broaden the conceptualization of personality as involving more than "adjustment" to personal and physical environments, as the first definition had implied. Thus Allport recast his definition in 1961: "We not only adjust to our environment but we reflect on it. Also, we strive to master it, and sometimes succeed. Behavior and thought, therefore, make both for survival and for growth."

Allport's definition was clearly intended to provide a definite framework for the researcher of the personality phenomena. The definition implicitly suggests that persons may be studied by investigating their unique organization of psychophysical systems, that is, by investigation of their measurable *traits.*

The Concept of Traits: Personal Consistency

Allport and Odbert (1936; cf. Allport, 1961, Chapter 14) estimated that there are nearly 18,000 words, mostly adjectives, in the English language that may be used to designate traits of personality. In fact, the language may harbor even more trait labels than this awesome number suggests, for Allport and Odbert excluded from their estimate all compound words like *nature-lover,* or *hater-of-affectation.* The problem for the psychologist lies in the embarrassment of riches that this myriad of trait names represents. Of the 18,000-plus traits indicated in the language, how many are veridical (i.e., really exist)? Allport and Odbert estimated that approximately 25 percent of the 18,000 trait names actually indicate real person characteristics if clearly evaluative items like *adorable, disgusting,* and *evil* are excluded (see 1961, p. 355).

A further limitation needs to be imposed on the wide range of possible trait names. Some of the labels embodied in the English language to indicate personality characteristics refer to transient or temporary states of mood or activity: for example, *abashed, frantic, rejoicing.* When these items are excluded, the total number of trait names indicating veridical and relatively stable personality characteristics is reduced to approximately 4,000 or 5,000 items. Of course, even this reduction does not impose limits on the number of possible combinations of trait labels that may be employed to describe various personalities. The important point, however, is that the concept of trait is clearly embedded quite firmly in our language and, therefore, in our thinking. Indeed, it is nearly impossible to think of any specific person without simultaneously calling to mind a host of characteristic traits.

For the psychologist, the concept of personality trait requires specification, and more important, the way trait is defined will determine the psychologist's mode of investigation. Allport, a strong advocate of the trait approach, defined the concept in this way:

> A trait is . . . a *neuropsychic structure having the capacity to render many stimuli functionally equivalent, and to initiate and guide equivalent (meaningfully consistent) forms of adaptive and expressive behavior.* (1961, p. 347)

Allport thus asserted that traits are indeed real, that they are rooted in nervous system functioning, and that in combination they serve as the steersmen of behavior. A trait lends consistency to personality by allowing the person to respond similarly to a wide array of situations, that is, renders diverse stimuli "functionally equivalent." For Allport, traits are rather complex enduring dispositions to respond to one's environment in particular ways. A trait is always established within the personality through a combination of innate physical attributes and acquired environmental habits (1937, p. 292). Allport illustrated his conception of trait development and function with the following example:

> A young child finding that his mother is nearly always present to satisfy his wants, develops for her an early affective attachment (conditioning). But later other social contacts likewise prove to be conducive to this child's happy and successful adjustment: playmates, for example, or family gatherings, or crowds at the circus. . . . The child gradually comes to seek people, rather than to avoid them. A trait (not an instinct) of gregariousness develops. The child grows eager for social intercourse; he enjoys being with people. When isolated from them for some time, he misses them and becomes restless. The older he grows the more ways he finds of expressing this gregarious interest. He seeks to ally himself with groups of people at the lodge, at the theater, at church; he makes friends and keeps in touch with them, often entertains them, and corresponds with them. . . . Sociability has become a deep and characteristic quality of this individual's personality. Its expression is variable; a wide range of equivalent stimuli arouse it. (1937, pp. 292–293)

Thus the child's trait of gregariousness or sociability renders many stimuli equivalent and guides many behaviors into equivalent forms of expression. In short, the trait develops motivational properties that characterize the *personal style* of the individual. The way in which Allport conceptualized a trait's mediation between diverse stimuli and the individual's characteristically uniform responses to them is illustrated in Figure 14.1.

As Figure 14.1 indicates, the child's trait of *gregariousness* allows diverse situations like theater-going, church-going, letter-writing, and family gatherings to be treated by the individual as opportunities to express his or her fundamental and pervasive enjoyment of the company of others. The behaviors that constitute personal style are all somewhat varied because they are particular responses to the specific characteristics of each social situation. But each of these behaviors shares the common denominator of gregariousness or sociability as the guiding motive. Thus the trait of gregariousness unifies an individual's "characteristic behavior and thought" in the face of diverse environmental circumstances. In commonsense terms, we often say that John or Jane did something "typical" of them. To be able to make the judgment, it was first necessary to have observed John or Jane behaving over a period of time in some *consistent* fashion despite changing situational factors. Traits are the basis of this personal consistency.

Individual and Common Traits

Allport further distinguished between *individual* and *common* traits. In theory, it is logically impossible for any two individuals to possess precisely the same trait (1937, p. 297). Because each individual is a product of a unique genetic endowment, a singular history of personally meaningful experiences, and a never-repeated

FIGURE 14.1   Trait as mediator between stimuli and responses.

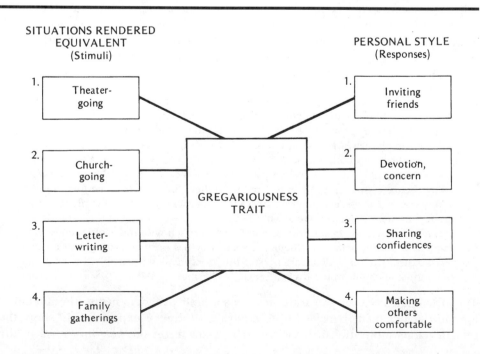

developmental progression, the totality of his or her personhood must be unique. Thus even though two individuals may be said to possess the trait of aggressiveness, the personal style with which this common trait will be translated into behavior is different in each person. In this extreme sense, then, every trait is individualistic, for total identity across individuals is nonexistent. Yet, for all practical purposes, individuals do share some similarities. It is possible to speak of *generally* aggressive personalities. That is to say, it is possible to visualize several persons who are characterized by possession of a roughly similar tendency to behave aggressively. In this more nearly commonsense meaning, traits may be described as *common*.

> The original endowment of most human beings, their stages of growth, and the demands of their particular society, are sufficiently standard and comparable to lead to some basic modes of adjustment that from individual to individual are *approximately* the same. To take an example: the nature of the struggle for survival in a competitive society tends to force every individual to seek his own most suitable level of aggression. As the saying goes, everyone *must* be either a boot or a door-mat. (Allport, 1937, p. 298)

It is clear from Allport's emphasis that only with reluctance was he willing to acknowledge the nomothetic aspects of traits. Traits may be thought of as common, but, Allport insisted, psychologists must recognize that in measuring shared traits they are assessing only some common *aspect* of the trait. A true trait is always individual in the strict sense of its role within the context of an entire personality's unique organization of many traits. Context is everything.

Cardinal, Central, and Secondary Traits

Allport allowed that, within the context of an entire network of traits that compose a personality, some traits play major directing roles and some play minor roles. In rare cases, a particular trait is so outstanding, so pervasive that nearly all of an individual's activities can be traced to its operation. A trait of this significance in the economy of a personality is apparent to even the most casual observer. Such pervasive, dominantly influential traits are termed *cardinal traits* (Allport, 1937, pp. 337 ff.). Characters drawn from the world's literature illustrate both the rarity and the uniqueness of cardinal traits. Our language has been enriched by trait names derived from outstanding fictional and historical personalities (1937, pp. 302–303):

Boswellian	Homeric	Puckish
Byronic	Lesbian	Quixotic
Christ-like	Machiavellian	Rabelaisian
Dionysian	Narcissistic	Sadistic
Falstaffian	Napoleonic	Sapphic
Faustian	Pickwickian	Shylock

A cardinal trait like *Christ-like* or *Machiavellian* is so potent and singular that all other traits embodied in the same personality seem secondary and subservient to the strength of this master steersman.

At a level of influence somewhat less than that of a cardinal trait are the *central traits.* "Central traits are those usually mentioned in careful letters of recommendation, in rating scales where the rater stars the outstanding characteristics of the individual, or in brief verbal descriptions of a person" (Allport, 1937, p. 338).

Somewhat less conspicuous, less generalized, less consistent, and frequently less influential in the overall guidance of behavior are the lowest level traits called *secondary traits.* Secondary traits are evoked by a narrower range of equivalent stimuli and direct a more restricted range of equivalent responses (1937, p. 338).

Individual Traits as Personal Dispositions (p.d.s)

In 1961 Allport introduced some terminological changes into his theory of traits. To emphasize his fundamental distinction between individual and common (aspects of) traits, Allport chose to rechristen the individual trait as a *personal disposition (p.d.)* (1961, p. 358). *Personal dispositions* followed the classification scheme of *cardinal, central,* and *secondary* traits. In fact, Allport employed a definition of p.d.s nearly identical to his definition for individual traits:

> *A personal disposition is a generalized neuropsychic structure (peculiar to the individual), with the capacity to render many stimuli functionally equivalent, and to initiate and guide consistent (equivalent) forms of adaptive and stylistic behavior.* (1961, p. 373)

Allport did not adhere to any precise distinction between his concept of individual trait and personal disposition. He did, however, suggest that the term *personal disposition* was meant to carry the supplementary meaning of "personality *form,*" and he thus offered as a synonym the term *morphogenic trait* (1961, p. 358). In all, it is clear that Allport meant to emphasize that individual traits, or p.d.s or morphogenic traits are the fundamental, objective, stable units of individual consistency.

THE STUDY OF PERSONAL DISPOSITIONS: SINGLE-CASE STRATEGY

"How shall a psychological life history be written?" This abiding question in Allport's approach to personality is clearly an idiographic query. It represents Allport's overriding concern—indeed, his own cardinal trait as a psychologist—to comprehend the complexity and novelty of the individual person fully, with satisfying attention to detail. To some of his critics, as we shall later see, the question represents at best an unanswerable paradox, and at worst, an absurdity.

Allport, perhaps sharing a professional trait with men like Jung, Maslow, and Rogers, relished paradoxes and delighted in transcending absurdities. He suggested that every psychologist is confronted with six persistent riddles. Each psychologist will linger long over different riddles, propose different solutions or means of detouring around the riddle, but more often than not will be forced to admit that he or she has come face to face with a paradox. Here are Allport's six persistent psychological riddles (1968, p. 300):

1. How is the mind you study related to its body? The *psychophysical* riddle.
2. Are the objective methods you by preference employ suited to the subjective facts that are your ultimate data? The riddle of *positivism.*
3. How do you account for such integration and unity as the human personality manifests? The riddle of the *self.*
4. Why is it that, in spite of your postulate of strict determinism, you half-believe, and nearly always act on a hypothesis of indeterminism? The riddle of *free will.*
5. Why is it that the old laws of mental connection, going back to Aristotle, seem sometimes adequate and sometimes inadequate in accounting for the organization of higher mental processes? The riddle of *association.*
6. Why is it that, after making your analyses of mental states, you are unable to find in the sum total of them any close approximation of the way mental life is uniquely and individually presented in nature? The riddle of *individuality.*

Allport proposed these riddles as part of an essay honoring the centenary of William James's birth. It was Allport's contention that James had lingered long over each of these riddles and therein lay his unique contribution to philosophy and psychology. But of course Allport wished to point up the significance of James's attitude toward these riddles for all of contemporary psychology:

> The message of James for psychology today is this: narrow consistency can neither bring salvation to your science, nor help to mankind. Let your approaches be diverse, but let them in the aggregate do full justice to the heroic qualities in man. If you find yourselves tangled in paradoxes, what of that? Who can say that the universe shall not contain paradoxes simply because he himself finds them unpalatable? (Allport, 1968, p. 323)

Allport's abiding concern: *"How shall a psychological life history be written?"* can be seen as his personal strategy for dealing with these paradoxes. Each of the six paradoxes (psychophysicalism, positivism, self, free will, association, and individuality) is reducible to that key question: *"How shall a psychological life history be written?"* For in writing the individual's life history, the psychologist attempts to answer the most fundamental riddle of them all: To what extent are any of these riddles pertinent to real persons? Or, in slightly rephrased form: Is a scientific theory of personality compatible with attempts to understand the personality of a single real person? Allport phrased it this way:

> Now the goals of science are to understand, predict, and control events. How, in dealing with a concrete person, can we expect to understand, predict, control, unless we know the individual pattern and not merely the universal tendencies of the human mind-in-general? (1965, p. 159)

Thus, Allport implied that the first five of the six riddles are answerable when the sixth, the riddle of individuality, is the psychologist's predominant concern. Indeed, for Allport, the first five are riddles only because the sixth is sometimes rejected as an unsuitable problem for science (cf. Allport, 1960, pp. 117 ff.). *"How shall a psychological life history be written?"* First and foremost it should be written from the self-revealing, though not necessarily intentionally so, evidence fabricated by the person her- or himself.

PERSONAL DOCUMENTS: A MORPHOGENIC APPROACH TO LIFE HISTORY

Individuals create self-revealing personal documents out of a variety of motives. For example, adolescents often keep detailed diaries or personal journals recounting their innermost thoughts, feelings, and aspirations. Such a document is often so revealing that the most grievous sin a parent can commit is to violate its secrecy. Personal documents may take many forms: autobiographies, diaries, letters, interviews, even literary productions (Allport, 1942, 1961). "The personal document may be defined as *any self-revealing record that intentionally or unintentionally yields information regarding the structure, dynamics, and functioning of the author's mental life*" (Allport, 1942, p. xii).

The motives that impel individuals to create self-revealing productions are varied. Allport described 13 motives that might underlie such productions (1942, pp. 69–75):

1. *Special Pleading:* to argue in a convincing way some self-serving or self-justifying premise.
2. *Exhibitionism:* a single-minded desire to display one's virtues and vices.
3. *Desire for Order:* compulsive need to record the circumstances of one's day.
4. *Literary Appeal:* desire for aesthetic and artistic satisfaction.
5. *Securing Personal Perspective:* a personal "taking stock" of one's life, achievements, failures, and so on.
6. *Catharsis:* a need to secure relief from tension and anxiety by writing when relief through direct action is unattainable.
7. *Monetary Gain:* personal revelations for prize competition, for payment in an experimental investigation, and so forth. Payment does not rule out, however, the validity of the self-revelations.
8. *Assignment:* school task imposed for some educational or therapeutic reason.
9. *Assisting in Therapy:* production of personal document for therapist to assist in one's own cure.
10. *Redemption* and *Social Reincorporation:* "confessions" of an ex-criminal, spy, alcoholic, and so on. Generally such confessions are motivated by a genuine desire for forgiveness and acceptance.
11. *Public Service:* desire to achieve public or social reform.
12. *Desire for Immortality:* "battle against oblivion," or a desire not to be forgotten after death.
13. *Scientific Interest:* though not necessarily created for this reason, personal documents sometimes are donated to psychologists with the intention of furthering science.

This diverse array of motives suggests the methodological problems that historians, sociologists, anthropologists, or psychologists face when they decide to study evidence of this sort. All of these personal documents suffer from varying degrees of lack of candor, defective recollection on the part of the writer, and from conscious or unconscious self-concealment. Nonetheless, it was Allport's conviction that personal documents were a valuable source of answers to the question: "How shall a psychological life history be written?"

To assess the value of a personal document, the psychologist must ask how useful it is in meeting the three goals of science: understanding, prediction, and control beyond the level of unaided common sense (1942, p. 148). It was Allport's judgment, after a thorough survey of the literature relating to research on personal documents, that their use was well justified.

> Personal documents are good if they serve the comparison of lives, one with another, leading to statistical generalizations and to an understanding of uniformities of behavior. But they are good also if standing one by one they provide concrete evidence of the nature of single lives from which all psychological science is derived; if they yield evidence of pluralistic causation; if they give clinicians and practitioners a sounder basis for work; and if they enhance the understanding, prediction, and control of individual lives (which is all that science ultimately demands). (Allport, 1942, p. 59)

Allport's evaluation suggests that personal documents may be treated in research with a variety of conceptualizations and methods. Analyses ranging from impressionistic characterizations, psychoanalytic hypothesizing, and direct content analysis to sophisticated statistical and factorial assessments are, in principle, possible. But two significant points about Allport's advocacy of personal document research bear mention: First, by definition, the study of personal documents is the *idiographic* strategy of assessing the unity, uniqueness, and consistency of the individual. Second, this single-case approach treats personality investigation as an attempt to comprehend the organism from the *subjective* or phenomenal perspective. In effect, the single-case approach solves the riddle of individuality by an appeal to the person's own solution.

AN ILLUSTRATIVE CASE:
JENNY GOVE MASTERSON'S LETTERS

Within four years of the publication of his monograph on the use of personal documents in psychology, Allport published a series of letters that reveal in dramatic detail the story of a mother-son relationship from the mother's point of view (Allport, 1946). The letters were presented to Allport by a young couple, identified as Glenn and Isabel, because they felt there might be some psychological value in the rather complete series of self-revelations produced by a very remarkable woman named "Jenny Gove Masterson." The correspondence between Glenn and Isabel and Jenny began in March 1926, when Jenny was 58 years old, and ran its course of 301 letters over the next eleven and a half years. In October 1937, the remarkable correspondence ended with Jenny's death at the age of 69.

In 1965 Allport made the "Jenny Masterson" letters more widely available by publishing some of them in book form along with several varieties of analyses of Jenny's personality. Allport posed the following challenges to psychologists:

To me the principal fascination of the Letters lies in their challenge to the reader (whether psychologist or layman) to "explain" Jenny—if he can. Why does an intelligent lady behave so persistently in a self-defeating manner? When and how might she have averted the tragedy of her life? Could proper guidance or therapy at an appropriate time have helped alter the rigid course of her conduct? Was the root of her trouble some wholly unconscious mechanism? (Allport, 1965, p. viii)

Some brief details about Jenny's life are in order here. Jenny Gove Masterson was born in Ireland of Protestant parentage in 1868. Migrating to Canada when Jenny was five years old, the Gove family took up residence in Montreal, but the mother worked hard to preserve the family's sense of Irish culture and tradition. Jenny was one of seven children in a family that comprised five younger sisters and one younger brother. When Jenny was 18 her father died, and to support her family, Jenny became a telegrapher. Unfortunately, Jenny and her siblings did not get along well, so by the time Jenny was 27 years old, bitter quarrels and disputes resulted in disintegration of the family. Jenny married an American railway inspector, Henry Masterson, a marriage that further outraged the family because of Masterson's previous marriage.

Jenny and Henry Masterson moved to Chicago, where Jenny found herself bored with an enforced idle existence. "She complained that she was being 'kept' by a man. She quarreled more than once with her husband over this issue, but he, like most men of his day, was firmly set against a wife seeking employment" (Allport, 1965, p. 3). The issue was not resolved at the time of Henry Masterson's death in 1897, when Jenny was 29 years old. A month after her husband's death, Jenny gave birth to her only child, a son named Ross.

Returning to work as a telegrapher to support herself and Ross, she devoted herself entirely to caring for Ross with "undivided affection." When Ross was five years old, Jenny vacationed with him in Montreal and spent some time with her sisters. Ross stayed on with Jenny's sisters for several months and "outgrew many of his 'spoiled' ways." However, when Jenny returned to Montreal, she accused her sisters of neglecting Ross; they accused her of spoiling him. The quarrel ended with another bitter separation.

Until Ross was 17 he and Jenny were closest companions, a relationship that ended when Ross left for college "back East" at Princeton. Jenny continued to work to support Ross's education and entertainment expenses. In his sophomore year, the United States entered World War I, and Ross enlisted in the ambulance corps. At his departure for France, Jenny visited Ross and met his college friends, including Glenn and Isabel, her later correspondents.

When Ross returned from France in 1919, he found himself disoriented, dissatisfied with his old ambitions and habits. For the next few years, with the exception of obtaining his college degree, Ross embarked on a series of failures in business and personal achievements. In consequence, Ross and Jenny had many grave quarrels, including one rageful encounter when Jenny learned of his secret marriage. "On his first visits to her following her discovery she drove him out of her room with violent denunciations and a threat to have him arrested if he ever tried to see her again" (Allport, 1965, p. 6).

Jenny renewed her contacts with Ross's college friends, Glenn and his wife Isabel, and requested permission to "keep in touch" with them. Her motives for this renewed acquaintance with Glenn and Isabel seem to have been a mixture of nostalgia for the days when "Ross was all hers," and a need to maintain a source of information about Ross's whereabouts.

Jenny's Personality: Samples of Her Letters

Writing to Glenn and Isabel on the occasion of Ross's visit to her room with his new wife, Jenny described the scene as follows:

> Ross brought this same woman and her brat to my house one Sunday evening and I was angry and told him that if he ever brought any more prostitutes to my house I would have them both arrested. Anyone, short of a fool, would know what she was at one glance. (Allport, 1965, p. 9).

In her letter of January 5, 1927, Jenny recalled her childhood:

> My father dropped dead one day, and had no provision made for his family—7 of them, all under 18. Not one in the house capable of earning a penny. It was my salary that kept the house going. . . . No one ever denied it, or pretended to think otherwise, and when I dared to marry the man I had been in love with for years, but dreaded to take my money out of their house . . . why, they said I was like the cow that gave the milk and then kicked the pail. (Allport, 1965, p. 27).

In June 1928, Jenny gave vent to one of her characteristic outbursts of pessimism and martyrdom:

> Anyway I am firmly convinced that I am "through" and ought to step out. I have done all, of any use, that it is possible for me to do in this world. Whether it was for good or bad it is over and done and nothing can change it now, "The moving finger writes, and having writ moves on" and my days for possible usefulness are past. I should step out, but am a coward. To suppose that Ross needs me would be indeed a joke. (Allport, 1965, p. 50)

In 1929 Ross underwent surgery for a tumor on his inner ear and for an "abscess on the outer covering of the brain." During his convalescence, he stayed with "one of his women." About two months after the operation, Jenny received word that Ross had died in a sudden relapse. She was to outlive her son by eight years. Glenn was summoned to attend the funeral and cremation of Ross's body. After the ceremony, Glenn accompanied Jenny back to her room. Ending an hour of respectful silence, Jenny spoke: "The body is consumed, now we'll have a good steak dinner" (recollection of Isabel, in Allport, 1965, p. 153). Jenny wrote to Glenn and Isabel, following Ross's death:

> After a while I shall count up all my riches—after the horror of this loss becomes blunted a bit—you know "the years roll by and on their wings bear healing"— wounds do not remain open for always—and then I shall count up my riches—such wonderful friends—*such* friends—the glory of the sun and the stars—the sigh of the sea—the laughter of little children. (Allport, 1965, p. 73)

An Analysis of Jenny's Personal Dispositions

Allport's perennial question: "How shall a psychological life history be written?" can, as always, be answered on two levels. A psychologist may decide to analyze the letters with regard to nomothetic (general-universal) results. The preferred method might be a statistical content analysis of the frequency with which Jenny used particular phrases or word combinations, or the statistical relationship between various classes of emotional response and the people mentioned in her writings. A somewhat different approach might be taken by the psychologist who wished to form an impressionistic portrait of Jenny as a unique person. This psychologist might ask a series of judges to read the Masterson letters and to record in their own words Jenny's outstanding traits. Then, eliminating items on which the judges fail to agree, a "trait portrait" might be formed.

Allport reported the results of the latter type of investigation undertaken by himself with 36 judges. These 36 people used a total of 198 trait names to characterize Jenny. Loosely clustered, the 198 items fell into nine categories:

1. *Quarrelsome-Suspicious* (e.g., distrustful, paranoid, opinionated)
2. *Self-Centered* (e.g., selfish, jealous, possessive, martyr complex)
3. *Independent-Autonomous* (e.g., hardworking, stubborn, calculating)
4. *Dramatic-Intense* (e.g., emotional, rigid, serious, violent)
5. *Aesthetic-Artistic* (e.g., intuitive, fastidious, expressive)
6. *Aggressive* (e.g., ascendant, domineering, self-assertive)
7. *Cynical-Morbid* (e.g., pessimistic, sarcastic, despondent)
8. *Sentimental* (e.g., loyal, affectionate, maternal)
9. *Unclassified* (e.g., intelligent, witty, whimsical)

(Based on: Allport, 1965, pp. 193–194)

Clearly, some of the categories are contradictory, and some overlap. Yet nearly all the judges agreed that prominent traits or p.d.s in Jenny's personality were *suspiciousness, self-centeredness, autonomy, a dramatic nature, aggressiveness, morbidity,* and *sentimentality.*

Allport reported a more elaborate study of Jenny's letters by one of his students. Jeffrey Paige (in Allport, 1965, pp. 199 ff.) used a computer lexicon of social science terms to analyze Jenny's letters. Containing nearly 3,000 items, the coding system used by Paige reduced Jenny's letters to a small number of "tag" words that summarized large classes of phrase usage in Jenny's writing. For example, Jenny employed many phrases to express her aggression, hostility, open rage, and opposition to Ross and his women. All of these phrases were coded into computer language under the tag *ATTACK.* Once programmed in this way, the computer might be asked to sort out several kinds of data from Jenny's letters.

Paige found, using the first 56 letters up to the death of Ross, eight factors that embodied Jenny's most prominent traits. Listed in order of decreasing frequency of expression, these traits were

1. aggression
2. possessiveness
3. need for affiliation
4. need for autonomy
5. need for familial acceptance
6. sexuality

7. sentience (love of art, literature, natural beauty)
8. martyrdom

(1965, pp. 200–201)

There is clearly much overlap between the judges' impressionistic analyses of Jenny's letters and the computer-derived traits.

Close analysis of other computer-derived data reveals interesting emotional reactions to the people of her life. Jenny expresses more affection for Glenn than for Isabel; she makes more requests of Glenn for advice than of Isabel. But the computer had some trouble with items tagged "Good" and "Bad." For example, the statement: "I have a truly noble son, an honor to his college, his friends, his family"—a sarcastic comment—is labeled "Good" by the computer. Apparently sarcasm is lost on computers.

It is easy to see why Allport insisted that very little is gained by sophisticated statistical and factorial analyses of individual persons. The impressionistic judgments of Jenny's personality provide as much information on most issues as the computer-derived traits. Furthermore, commonsense analysis provides some of the ineffable "flavor" of Jenny's personal dispositions, a quality not likely to be present in computer printout. Yet the more sophisticated computer analysis does accomplish tasks that are impossible for the human investigator.

Large-scale correlations of selected subclasses of statements, analysis of Jenny's attitudes toward the significant figures in her life on a comparative basis, and an assessment of Jenny's most frequently used categories of self-understanding are all possible only with the computer's help. But of course, neither common sense nor the computer can answer the ultimate question: "Are we satisfied that Jenny's life history has been adequately written?" The question can be answered only by a firsthand reading of Jenny's personal documents.

DIFFICULTIES WITH THE TRAIT STRATEGY AND SINGLE-CASE APPROACH

Allport's insistence that an adequate personality psychology must be based on attempts to understand the individual case evoked a great deal of criticism. The main issues in the controversy centered on Allport's distinctions between the idiographic and nomothetic scientific strategies. Part of the controversy, too, concerned Allport's conceptualization of traits as the fundamental units of study.

Falk (1956), anticipating later criticisms, suggested that there is no real dispute between nomothetic and idiographic goals in science. Study of *unique* events, although admissible to scientific scrutiny, is not essential to the formulation of scientific theory. Furthermore, Falk argued, the idiographic approach is a necessary *preliminary* method to the development of generalizations, for the observation of single events always precedes the construction of laws. But, Falk suggested, general laws are adequate, when properly applied, to the task of understanding the unique personality.

Robert Holt (1962) extended the objections to the idiographic-nomothetic distinction on the basis of logic. Labeling Allport's point of view a "romantic personology," Holt voiced four objections to traits and to single-case studies. First, Holt suggested that Allport had confused art and science in his attempts to achieve *comprehensive* "understanding" of single persons. The feeling of fully understanding a person is more suitable to an artist; scientists, by contrast, are satisfied when they can reliably predict and control the events they study. The intuitively satisfying "thrill of recognition" that accompanies the feeling of understanding the unique individual lies solely in art's domain. Science seeks to derive general propositions (nomothetic laws) from the study of individuals and a pure idiographic study of personality is, at best, an adjunct to this effort.

Second, Holt objected to Allport's characterization of traditional science as unconcerned with imaginative and creative accounts of phenomena. All scientists employ intuition, creativity, and imagination in choosing what to study, how to study it, and how to verify hypotheses.

Third, Holt pointed out that, strictly speaking, it is impossible to conceptualize a truly unique event. If a given personality were unique, heretofore never experienced, a totally unique trait name would have to be coined or some unique combination of existing trait names would have to be employed. In either case, personology would be a confusing Babel, although the second approach would in effect be nomothetic. Unfortunately, a combination of trait names would hardly satisfy Allport because it would fail to capture the personal element in personality.

Fourth, Holt voiced a suspicion prevalent among many scientists. The full richness of reality may be impossible to capture either artistically or scientifically. To attempt to achieve full understanding is to seek to completely identify with the observed, an act that even the most skilled phenomenologist is unable to achieve. In short, if uniqueness is to be the proper object of personology's study, then either personology will have to be a mute science without an adequate language or it will have to forgo all forms of abstraction. In all, Holt concluded that there was no logical basis for establishing a special branch of natural science for the study of the unique personality because such a study is, by definition, not scientific.

The concept of traits as the fundamental units of personality has also come in for a share of criticism. B. F. Skinner (e.g., 1953, 1974, 1975), in the tradition of radical behaviorism, objects to postulating inner mechanisms to explain observable behaviors. Traits, unconscious ids, or instincts are all equally irrelevant to explain observed responses once the environmental stimuli controlling those responses are identified.

> When we say that a man eats *because* he is hungry, smokes a great deal *because* he has the tobacco habit, fights *because* of the instinct of pugnacity, behaves brilliantly *because* of his intelligence, or plays the piano well *because* of his musical ability, we seem to be referring to causes. But on analysis these phrases proved to be merely redundant descriptions. A single set of facts is described by the two statements: "He eats" and "He is hungry." A single set of facts is described by the two statements: "He smokes a great deal" and "he has the smoking habit." (Skinner, 1953, p. 31)

Thus, from the behaviorist point of view, postulating traits of personality is merely a redundant statement of the behavior that has already been observed.

More recently, the concept of traits has come under fire for methodological reasons that involve a failure to find the reliable consistencies in personal behaviors implied by the concept. Walter Mischel surveyed the literature related to trait investigations and concluded, "With the possible exception of intelligence, highly generalized behavioral consistencies have not been demonstrated, and the concept of personality traits as broad response predispositions is thus untenable" (1968, p. 146). Mischel argued that a large proportion of studies purporting to demonstrate the existence of personality traits in the observed person actually show the contaminating effects of the observer's preconceived categories (1968, p. 70). When the reliability of a group of personality raters' judgments is high, it may spuriously suggest that the labels they have used actually indicate the existence of corresponding traits or states in the person so labeled. In short, Mischel feels that the concept of trait is not particularly useful for any scientific account of personality. His survey of the literature failed to turn up any significant evidence that adequate predictive power accrues to the psychologist who embraces trait theory. In effect, individuals show less cross-situational consistency than the concept of enduring personality traits demands.

With the exception of Mischel's commentary, Allport was aware of the criticisms directed against his theorizing. In a significant restatement and modification of his position, Allport reported that in the years intervening between his first proposal of traits as fundamental units of personality and the criticisms that followed he had come to the conclusion that ". . . my earlier views seemed to neglect the variability induced by ecological, social, and situational factors. This oversight needs to be repaired through an adequate theory that will relate the inside and outside systems more accurately" (1966, in 1968, p. 63).

"TRAITS REVISITED": A HEURISTIC REALISM

In his 1966 restatement of trait theory, Allport altered his position on the existence and research value of traits very little. Although he acknowledged the value of the criticisms that had been made, Allport reaffirmed his belief that

> Whatever tendencies exist reside in a person, for a person is the sole possessor of the energy that leads to action. Admittedly different situations elicit differing tendencies from my repertoire. I do not perspire except in the heat, nor shiver except in the cold; but the outside temperature is not the mechanism of perspiring or shivering. My capacities and my tendencies lie within. (1968, p. 47)

However, Allport conceded that trait theory would have to be made more sophisticated, more predictive, and more empirically testable if it was to survive as a useful construct in contemporary psychology. To further this aim, he proposed a safeguard for trait theory construction called *heuristic realism.*

Heuristic realism is a twofold guiding assumption. First, knowing full well that he or she may be wrong, the personologist *chooses* to believe that "the person who confronts us possesses inside his skin generalized action tendencies (or traits) and that it is our job scientifically to discover what they are" (1968, p. 49). Thus the personologist postulates that traits are *real,* but realizes the tentative nature of this assumption.

Second, heuristic realism asserts that owing to the complexity of the objects or events observed, and because present methods are not completely adequate, the goal of scientifically conceptualizing personality's realness cannot be fully successful. Yet the heuristic realist proceeds "as if" success were possible, for only by making the attempt will any progress toward knowledge of the person be attained. In short, Allport's revised position was more restrained, somewhat less enthusiastic.

Allport's emphasis on idiographic or morphogenic method thus became less unbending. He was more willing to concede that statistical and general concepts were valid ways of approaching personality. Yet, as always, Allport refused to abandon the fundamental tenet that it is the individual, the unique personality, which beckons most strongly to the personologist's curiosity.

THE SELF: PERSONALITY DEVELOPMENT

Early in his career Allport tackled at some length the third of his proposed riddles, the riddle of the self. In his 1937 statement of his position, Allport upbraided psychology's lack of interest in the mature or healthy personality.

In Allport's view, the mature personality was distinguished by three attributes that made apparent the need for some concept of personality unification. The self, as the locus of all active adaptation to life, would serve this theoretical need. First of the attributes of the healthy, mature personality is his or her capacity to defer momentary needs, pains, or desires in favor of reaching a long-term goal. Able to lose themselves in some activity regarded as important, mature personalities are not deterred by temporary setbacks or defeats. In short, the pursuit of personally meaningful goals represents an *extension of the self* (1937, p. 213). In effect, the person is going beyond self to invest energies in causes and goal-seeking that transcend his or her individual life.

The second attribute of the mature personality is what Allport called *self-objectification* (1937, p. 214). Self-objectification is "that peculiar detachment of the mature person when he surveys his own pretensions in relation to his abilities, his present objectives in relation to possible objectives for himself, his own equipment in comparison with the equipment of others, and his opinion of himself in relation to the opinion others hold of him" (1937, p. 214). The capacity of self-objectification is always tied to insight and to a sense of humor (see the quote that opens this chapter). In simplest terms, the mature person is capable of taking a hard look at self and accurately interpreting what he or she sees.

The third attribute of mature personalities is evolvement of *unifying philosophies of life.* Although their philosophies may not be expressed in words, mature persons nevertheless live their lives by some dominant guiding principles by which they place themselves in the scheme of things.

Allport's statement of these three attributes bears remarkable resemblance to Maslow's notion of self-actualizing people and to Carl Rogers's concept of the fully functioning person (cf. Chapter 15). All three of these theorists expressed an interest in understanding how the healthy personality conducts his or her life.

For Allport, the three attributes of the mature personality—self-objectification, extension of self, and a unifying philosophy of life—require that the personality theorist be able to account for their development in some personalities and for their failure to develop in the damaged personality. To achieve this aim, Allport developed an explanatory scheme to account for the emergence of the healthy self.

Emergence of the Self in Infancy

The infant, as Piaget suggested (see Chapter 9), is certainly unaware of itself as self, that is, as an active and efficacious agent. In a word, the infant lacks *self-consciousness* (Allport, 1961, p. 111). Self-consciousness is a gradual attainment during the first six years of life.

The first sense of one's self to evolve, according to Allport, is the *bodily self.* To illustrate, consider the infant of five or six months who manages to get its foot into its mouth for a two- or three-toothed bite: "If he hurts his foot he cries but has no idea at all that *he* has hurt *him*" (1961, p. 112). But with the passing of time, many such bodily sensations are experienced as recurrent and reliable aspects of *me.* Combined with these sensations are the frustrations of desires and wants that originate in external agents, like mother. "A child who cannot eat when he wants to, who bumps his head, soon learns the limitations of his too, too solid flesh" (1961, p. 112).

But bodily self is only the most basic and preliminary sense of the evolving self. By the end of the first year of life, a new aspect of selfhood begins to emerge. "Today I remember some of my thoughts of both yesterday and today; *and I am certain that they are the thoughts of the same person—* of myself" (Allport, 1961, p. 114; italics added). This emerging certainty that I am the *same me* as time passes is what Allport calls *self-identity.* Self-identity depends intimately on the child's developing capacity for language. For with the possibility of employing words to think and to communicate, the regularity, the solidity, and the sameness of existence become apparent. The most important aspect of the child's language use is the capacity to label himself with a name. "He hears constantly 'Where is Johnny's nose?' 'Where are Johnny's eyes?' 'Good Johnny,' 'John naughty' " (1961, p. 115). With the repetition of its name in various contexts, the child becomes aware of the continuity of self, and by the second year of life it understands its status as an independent agent in its family group.

The third aspect of developing selfhood to emerge is the child's feeling that it can successfully manipulate its world. It develops what Robert White (1960) calls a sense of competence and an income of *self-esteem.* Self-esteem, as an essential aspect of selfhood, begins to acquire importance near the end of the second year of life and becomes critical for healthy development in the third year. Parents often have difficulty with the two-and-a-half-year-old because it resents anyone taking over its prerogatives:

> A two-year-old went to the bathroom with his father to have his face washed. Saying, "Let me," he struggled to turn on the faucet. He persisted without success. For a time the father waited patiently, but finally "helped" the child. Bursting into screams of protest the child ran from the bathroom and refused to be washed. His father had spoiled everything. (Allport, 1961, p. 118)

Thus by the third year of life a child develops a strong need for autonomy and for a feeling of esteem when it tackles the tasks of living. At the same time the child undergoes what parents call negativism, saying "No!" to nearly every important demand that the parents make. In effect, the child regards every adult proposal or demand as a threat to its integrity. "To him it seems safer to resist any adult proposal in advance, as a protection to dawning self-esteem" (Allport, 1961, p. 119). So, by the end of the third year of life, three aspects of self have emerged: the bodily self, self-identity, and self-esteem or pride.

Emergence of Self in Later Childhood

From four to six years of age, the child consolidates and refines the three aspects of self that have already emerged. Additionally, the child's egocentric orientation to the world reaches full expression. The child believes that the world exists for its benefit. As Piaget described, the child believes that the sun follows it, "that God, or Santa Claus is a Being whose primary duty is to serve his interests" (Allport, 1961, p. 122). The child is unable to escape its own thought boundaries; only its own viewpoint exists. Slowly, however, the child experiences the fourth aspect of selfhood, the *extension of self*. It discovers that its particular likes and dislikes are an important part of what the child is. The child understands the meaning of possession: "This ball is *mine*," "He is *my* Daddy," and so on. Each of these things is seen as an extension of self.

Important during this period, too, is the developing awareness of the child that its parents want it to be a certain kind of self. The child's *self-image* begins to loom large as, at first, an uncertain, then as a more definite aspect of getting along with important others. Although conscience has not yet developed fully, the child of five or six years begins to realize the difference between being "good" and "naughty."

From ages six to twelve, the child's sense of an extended self and its self-image are enhanced by experiences with peers in the school setting. The child learns what is expected of it in regions beyond the security of the family situation. It becomes important for the child to be able to shift gears as it moves from family to outside situations so that, for example, rough-and-ready talk with peers is restrained to a more polite form of conversation at home. At this time, the child's sixth aspect of selfhood emerges, namely a conception of itself as a "rational coper" (1961, p. 124).

The *self-as-rational-coper* corresponds in Allport's view to what Freud termed the ego. The self, like the Freudian ego, attempts to mediate between the demands of one's impulses and the restraints of society (parents, teachers). In this sense, not all of the self-as-rational-coper's activities are conscious. Some of its attempts to mediate between need and reality may be unconscious and defensively oriented in its striving to maintain self-esteem. By the 12th year, furthermore, the child is capable of reflective thought and hypothetical or "as if" reasoning, and this achievement also marks the child's realization that self is a thinker and a judger—in short, a rational coper.

Emergence of Self in Adolescence: The Actor and the Masks

The period of adolescence (beginning near the age of 12 or 13) is marked by what Erikson calls an "identity crisis" (Erikson, 1950, 1959). The central question for the adolescent is: "Just who am I?" or "Am I a child or an adult?"

Parents may exacerbate the crisis by treating adolescents as dependent children, or by going to the opposite extreme of forcing overly mature responsibility onto their shoulders. Physically and sexually mature enough to play adult roles, adolescents may vacillate between adult and childhood attitudes. In attempts to discover an identity, they play various roles, trying on each for size and comfort and discarding those with which the emerging sense of self-identity clashes.

> The search for identity is revealed in the way an adolescent tries on different masks. He first develops one line of chatter, then another, one style of hairdress and then another (always within the range permitted by the peer group). He imitates one hero and then another. He is still searching for a garb that will fit. What he really wants is not yet fully present—his adult personality. (Allport, 1961, p. 125)

The problems of adolescence eventually become focused around one central issue, the last of the emerging aspects of selfhood. *Planning for the future, choosing to direct one's life into realistic and appropriate channels,* become the central concerns of the person entering adulthood. "Paring down the self-image and aspirations to life-size is a task for his adult years" (1961, p. 126). Thus the last aspect to emerge within the slowly evolving self is what Allport calls *propriate striving,* meaning literally "self-governing motivations." In its role as the hub of conscious existence, the self is the proprietor or governor that senses "ownership" and responsibility for the outcome of one's life. Propriate striving, therefore, is the culmination of a long line of development that began with the infant's realization that it *is.* The central theme of a life, the dominant and distant goals of a life history, are the essence of propriate striving. Thus propriate strivings are embodied in feelings of knowing what *I* want, who *I* want to become, and why *I* must be and have these qualities.

From the realization that one *is* to the development of a sense of self as rational coper, the maturing person who will achieve healthy selfhood accepts life's circumstances on its own terms. The unitary bond underlying the seven aspects of self is the person's continuous recognition that all of these selves are "me." *"I am the proprietor of my life."*

Personality as a Process of Becoming: The Proprium

Because each of the seven emerging aspects of self is experienced as relevant, as personal, as "owned," Allport suggested substituting the term *proprium* for the term self or ego (1955, p. 40). Thus the proprium is the embodiment of the bodily self, the self-identity, self-esteem, extended-self, self-image, self-as-rational-coper, and self-as-proprietor.

> Personality includes these habits and skills, frames of reference, matters of fact and cultural values, that seldom or never seem warm and important. But personality includes what is warm and important also—all the regions of our life that we regard as peculiarly ours, and which for the time being I suggest we call the *proprium.* The proprium includes all aspects of personality that make for inward unity. (Allport, 1955, p. 40)

The key characteristic of the proprium, according to Allport, is its warm or intimate quality, the feeling of being really a part of *me.* Recall from Chapter 10 Allport's example of the intimacy of bodily function:

> Think first of swallowing the saliva in your mouth, or do so. Then imagine expectorating it into a tumbler and drinking it! What seemed natural and "mine" suddenly becomes disgusting and alien. . . . What I perceive as belonging intimately

to my body is warm and welcome; what I perceive as separate from my body becomes, in the twinkling of an eye, cold and foreign. (1955, p. 43)

Thus another key characteristic of the proprium is that its various aspects lie within the realm of personal awareness. To the degree that we accept these aspects of self as "me" it is conscious. Yet, there is an aspect of selfhood that is far more active, far less a focal point of awareness. This aspect is the *self-as-knower.*

> This puzzling problem arises when we ask, "Who is the I who knows the bodily me, who has an image of myself and sense of identity over time, who knows that I have propriate strivings?" I know all these things and, what is more, I know that I know them. But who is it who has this perspectival grasp? (Allport, 1961, p. 128)

Recognizing the danger of creating a personality within the personality, Allport nonetheless argued that the self-as-knower is inherent to the structure of the person. The self-as-knower was not to be conceptualized as a "little man" inside the person, but rather as the *totality of the person as process,* as an entity that is *becoming* (1961, p. 130; 1955, p. 53). Yet Allport was forced to admit that this conception did not really solve the riddle of the Self:

> It seems on the whole sounder to regard the propriate functions of wanting, striving, willing as interlocked with the total personality structure. They are felt as self-relevant, but are not caused by a separate agent within the personality. As for the knower, whether it is simply an inference we make at a high level of complexity . . . or whether it is necessary to postulate a pure knower, a continuing transcendental self . . . is a riddle we have not solved. (1961, p. 138)

Consequently, Allport reserved the term *proprium* to indicate the unity of the eight aspects of self. The last of these aspects, self-as-knower, seemingly transcends and unifies the remaining seven. Table 14.1 summarizes the developmental history of the proprium.

TABLE 14.1   Aspects of the Proprium

Development Period	Proprium Characteristic	Personality Function
First year	Bodily self	Sensation-perception of physical pains, pleasures, and limitations.
Second year	Self-identity	Continuity of experience made possible through language.
Third year	Self-esteem	Pride in accomplishment; independence and negativism.
Four to six years	Self-extension	Abstract concept of possession: "mine."
Four to six years	Self-image	"Good" and "naughty" selves; sensitivity to praise and blame.
Six to twelve years	Self-as-rational-coper	Realistic solving of life's tasks; mediator between needs and reality.
Twelve years through adolescence	Propriate strivings	Ownership and acceptance of feelings, needs, thoughts; self-defined life goals.
Adulthood	Self-as-knower	The totality of all previous aspects of the proprium: awareness of self.

DEFICIT AND GROWTH MOTIVES: FUNCTIONAL AUTONOMY

Allport's belief that the concept of self or proprium is necessary in psychology combined with one of his earlier conceptions to provoke considerable controversy. The earlier conception was Allport's contention that with many repetitions, a particular motive becomes autonomous or independent of the stimulation that first aroused it. This principle, termed *functional autonomy,* underwent several modifications in Allport's thinking.

As we have already seen, Allport objected to prevailing trends in motivational theory, particularly Freudian explanations, that rely almost exclusively on the person's past unconscious needs to account for his or her present status (1960, Chapters 6, 9). Allport preferred, in keeping with his emphasis on individuality, to view adult motives in terms of the person's contemporary situation and feelings. Postulating an abstract scheme of a limited range of past motives that are responsible for all future behaviors, desires, and feelings was merely absurd to Allport:

> "Science must generalize." Perhaps it must, but what the objectors [to the study of uniqueness] forget is that *a general law may be a law that tells how uniqueness comes about.* It is a manifest error to assume that a general principle of motivation must involve the postulation of abstract or general motives. The principle of functional autonomy . . . is general enough to meet the needs of science, but particularized enough in its operation to account for the uniqueness of personal conduct. (1937, p. 194)

In Allport's original proposal of functional autonomy he pointed to a variety of everyday examples of motives that have been freed of their initial sources but continue to function as ends in themselves. "An ex-sailor has a craving for the sea, a musician longs to return to his instrument after an enforced absence, a city-dweller yearns for his native hills, and a miser continues to amass his useless hoard" (1937, p. 196). Although the sailor may have first gone to sea to earn a living, his current status as a wealthy banker precludes any need to return to the sea. Yet, he continues to desire to do so. Similarly, the miser has amassed sufficient wealth, struggling perhaps against great early deprivations, but he continues to amass money though no longer under the press of survival need.

Allport adduced a variety of experimentally studied behaviors that signified to him the perseveration of motives in the absence of their originating stimuli. To take one example, the Zeigarnik effect is a demonstration that subjects will spontaneously resume tasks that they failed to complete during an experiment (Zeigarnik, 1927). Despite the fact that the experiment is over, that the experimenter does not criticize their inability to finish the tasks, subjects desire of their own accord to return to these unfinished, and sometimes trivial, tasks to work them to completion. Working the task to its conclusion has become functionally autonomous of the original experimental requirements.

Allport's conception of functionally autonomous motives was heavily criticized by Bertocci (1950) for its all-inclusiveness. Bertocci questioned the logic of Allport's concept because it seemed to imply that *any* motive could become autonomous if repeated often enough. Furthermore, Bertocci suggested that even if motives could become functionally autonomous with repetition, there was no limiting principle to prevent the creation of a chaos of completely independent, competing motives.

In the light of these criticisms, Allport was forced to restate his concept and bring it into line with the other developments of his theory. In 1961 he defined functional autonomy more broadly:

> *Functional autonomy . . . refers to any acquired system of motivation in which the tensions involved are not of the same kind as the antecedent tensions from which the acquired system developed.* (1961, p. 229)

To modify his original conception further Allport proposed two levels of functional autonomy and a guiding or limiting principle by which to judge whether a motive was indeed autonomous.

In the most primitive form of functional autonomy, a motive becomes *perseverative* or self-repeating because of its roots in some biochemical or neurological process. For example, a rat fed reliably at one time of the day will become most active each day just before feeding time. But if the experimenter puts the rat on a starvation regimen, the fact that the rat is hungry all of the time does not prevent it from becoming most active at the time of day it was fed in the past. In effect, an autonomous rhythm has been established that persists for some time (Allport, 1961, p. 230).

Other forms of *perseverative functional autonomy* include addictions to drugs, alcohol, or tobacco, the tension induced by the Zeigarnik effect, and a child's circular activities like dropping a spoon repeatedly as long as mother returns it to his or her grasp. Each of these behaviors qualifies as functionally autonomous only in the sense specified by Allport's 1961 definition cited previously. In each of these cases, the original source of the tension under which the motive was acquired is different from the tension that maintains the motive.

Propriate functional autonomy, by contrast, does not depend directly on any feedback mechanism or biochemical processes. Propriate functional autonomy is best illustrated by somewhat more complex situations: The student who originally undertakes a field of study because it is required continues to study it beyond the externally enforced requirements; creative activities that benefit humanity earn the creative person tangible rewards, but we do not believe he or she works passionately at the tasks *for* the rewards; and the miser who hoards and amasses a huge fortune continues to do so in the absence of need. Each of these cases is governed by the propriate strivings of the self. Thus the self is the guiding principle that determines which motives will become functionally autonomous. In this sense, Allport was proposing a similar distinction to Maslow's notion of the difference between deficiency and growth motivation (cf. Chapter 15). Functionally autonomous motives are growth motives that retain their potency *because they express our most precious and most cherished self-wishes.*

Functionally autonomous motives come about, according to Allport, "because it is the essence or core of the purposive nature of man" (1961, p. 250). Three principles govern the development of such motives:

1. *Principle of Organizing the Energy Level:* There must be motives to consume one's available energies. If existing motives have been satisfied, new ones will develop. This idea is, in principle, similar to Maslow's notion that self-actualizing people are those in whom all basic biological needs are fulfilled. Self-actualizers must then turn to higher motives to achieve fulfillment. Allport cites the example of the man, well fed and rested, who looks for new worlds to conquer; or the woman whose children have all grown and who now looks "for something to do."

2. *Principle of Mastery and Competence:* Humans have motivational energies that transcend the simple need to react to their environment. They have the need to master it, to feel a sense of competence in tackling the tasks of life.

3. *Principle of Propriate Patterning:* Allport directly addressed the issue of whether functionally autonomous motives were totally independent of all personality moorings and limits in this principle. The source of the anchorage for all functionally autonomous motives is the self. "Indeed, to a large extent they constitute the self" (1961, p. 252). A young man who becomes a physician, a politician, or a hermit does not do so because he is responding to innate ambitions or to remote reinforcements of his past. These ambitions exist because "a self-image, gradually formed demands this particular motivational focus" (1961, p. 252). Thus the self or proprium is the pattern or template against which functionally autonomous motives are shaped, directed, and unified.

> We prefer to say that the essential nature of man is such that it presses toward a relative unification of life (never fully achieved). In this trend toward unification we can identify many central psychological characteristics. Among them are man's search for answers to the "tragic trio" of problems: suffering, guilt, death. We identify also his effort to relate himself to his fellow men and to the universe at large. We see that he is trying to discover his peculiar place in the world, to establish his "identity." As a consequence of this quest—which is the very essence of human nature—we note that man's conduct is to a large degree proactive, intentional, and unique to himself. (Allport, 1961, p. 252)

Like Jung, Allport believed in the self as the ultimate reconciler of opposites. Within this scheme, even the religious sentiment has its place: "A man's religion is the audacious bid he makes to bind himself to creation and to the Creator. It is his ultimate attempt to enlarge and to complete his own personality by finding the supreme context in which he rightly belongs" (Allport, 1950, p. 142).

Evaluating Gordon Allport

In a real way, Gordon Allport was the father of American personality psychology. It was his 1937 book that put "personality" on the psychology map. But Allport's conception of the discipline was controversial from the start. He emphasized the *organization* of those qualities that made up personality. He was convinced that this thing called *personality* was complex and could not be studied piecemeal. And it was he who posed the paradoxes for psychology, including the idiographic-nomothetic issue, testability of theories, and the active-passive dimension for human agency.

Refutability of Allport's Theory

In a word, yes, Allport's work lent itself to research, to experimental design, and to observational and correlational tests. How successful was the theory in withstanding the tests? Not very: The concept of traits was troublesome, especially after Walter Mischel's 1968 review of the concept showing that situational factors rather than dispositions seemed responsible for people's rather inconsistent behavior. With time, the concept of traits has evolved into a more sophisticated dimensional and interactive construct (see, for example, Eysenck in Chapter 17). Yet much of value remains in Allport's work, as even a cursory glance at the topics in the present chapter would indicate. We should not fault a theory for being testable and having had some of its main concepts refuted. The theory accomplished what a scientific theory is supposed to accomplish: It encouraged new and more precise formulations.

Human Agency

From the beginning of his encounter with Freudian psychology, Allport's conception of personality was an elegant argument for an active agency view of human motivation and human action. Not only did he rebel against what he called the "determinism" of Freudian psychology, but he was equally opposed to what he regarded as the simpleminded mechanism of behaviorism. In essence, as can be seen from his later concepts of the self, Allport's conception of personality as an "open system" stresses the human capacity for rational decision making, for substantial change despite previous history, and for creative problem solving. Like the later humanists (e.g., Maslow and Rogers), Allport stressed the human capacity for continued and active growth.

Allport's Focus on the Idiographic

Remembering that it was Allport who first brought these terms into psychology from philosophy, we need also to remember that it was he who first argued for an interactionist blend of the idiographic and nomothetic. He believed that he had accomplished that blend in his own theory. A more dispassionate view of his work, however, suggests that Allport's humanism and his interest in the individual pushed his theory largely in the direction of idiographic methods. His *Letters From Jenny* is a case in point. He encouraged the use of personal documents as research data in psychology, a method that by definition is idiographic. Although some of his students went on to conduct more generalizable laboratory studies, Allport himself did little "nomothetic" research and the theory itself has rarely been employed to generate hypotheses.

I have frequently wondered why so few contemporary psychologists pause at Allport's work and why they do not extract from it more fertile ideas to be tested. A challenge to young psychologists looking for research questions: Take a look at Allport, especially the puzzles or paradoxes he proposed. You will find much to recommend his map of the territory.

SUMMARY

Allport's early experience in an interview with Freud that he himself had engineered seemingly had lasting effects on Allport's conceptualization of the person and his or her motives. Refusing to accept the Freudian thesis that all motives can be reduced to a few basic unconscious drives, Allport proposed that motivational research should at least begin with an assessment of the individual's own estimates of his or her motives. *"How shall a psychological life history be written?"* became, for Allport, the abiding focus of his personality theory. Perhaps the single most important advice Allport had for psychologists was "Do not forget what you have decided to neglect."

Allport's emphasis on individuality led him to adopt from the philosopher Windelband the distinction between idiographic and nomothetic strategies of acquiring knowledge. Allport argued that the two strategies should be blended to achieve what he called full-bodied understanding of personality. Yet Allport's emphasis was always on the idiographic (particular) method.

Traits were conceptualized by Allport as the fundamental units of individual consistency. Distinguishing between common traits and individual traits, Allport stressed that any individual possesses a unique organization of these personal dispositions to characteristic behavior and thought. A trait functions to mediate between larger classes of stimuli and equally large classes of response. The trait of sociability, for example, serves to render many diverse situations functionally equivalent by initiating a range of meaningfully consistent behaviors. Allport was careful to stress that traits are conceptualized as neuropsychic structures, that is, as real biophysical processes existing within persons.

The concept of traits was further organized into a hierarchy of cardinal, central, and secondary traits. Cardinal traits are the master dispositions of personality, so pervasive and influential that they seem to color every activity of the person. Central traits are somewhat less pervasive and influential, but nevertheless exert strong directive influences on the person's characteristic ways of behaving. Secondary traits are the least influential forms of personal disposition.

Allport's abiding concern with the individual (idiographic) approach and with the concept of trait was heavily criticized. The main points of this criticism were that uniqueness probably lies within the range of nomothetic (general) laws and that little evidence exists for the concept of enduring dispositions to characteristic response (Holt, 1962; Mischel, 1968).

Allport's restatement of his trait concepts stressed the need for a heuristic realism in conducting research of individual personality. The heuristic realist first recognizes that though he or she may be wrong, it is better to proceed as if traits were real entities residing in real, unique personalities. Second, though it is always a matter of approximation, and success is never certain, the heuristic realist realizes that it is better to make the attempt to understand individuals than to dismiss the idea as absurd.

Allport's personality theory also stressed the importance of individual personality unity and the fact that the person is always becoming, not just being. The sense of self that characterizes the mature, healthy individual is a gradual acquisition that proceeds through eight stages:

Sense of bodily self

Sense of self-identity

Sense of self-esteem

Extension of self

Self-image

Self-as-rational-coper

Propriate striving

Self-as-knower

The proprium, for Allport, is the final sense of self that develops, in which the individual is capable of knowing and capable of knowing that he or she knows. In short, the self-as-knower poses the ultimate riddle of personality: How does the individual recognize that *he or she* is the person who is?

Closely connected with his concept of proprium was Allport's motivational theory of functional autonomy. Functional autonomy asserts that motives may continue to operate even when the original tensions on which they were based no longer operate. To modify the construct in the light of its subsequent criticism, Allport distinguished between two kinds of functional autonomy: perseverative and propriate. Perseverative functional autonomy involves biochemical or neurophysical processes that continue to operate through their own momentum or rhythm in the absence of the original deficit need that provoked them. Propriate functionally autonomous motives are those activities that serve some function of the self in its active striving for fulfillment.

Allport deserves high grades for his conception of human beings as active constructors of their lives, for his idea that idiographic and nomothetic strategies could be blended. But when the basic ideas of his theory, traits, were examined closely, they did not survive in the form that Allport proposed them (e.g., Mischel, 1968). And though he claimed a balance of idiography and nomotheticism, he in fact encouraged idiographic methods more wholeheartedly.

FOR FURTHER READING

Allport's most comprehensive work in personality theory is to be found in two successive editions of the same work: *Personality: A Psychological Interpretation* (New York: Henry Holt, 1937) was his first major contribution and continues to be valuable as an introduction to his early ideas; and *Pattern and Growth in Personality* (New York: Holt, 1961), which is a revision of the former work, reflects Allport's changing conceptions of such important concepts as functional autonomy and individual traits.

A collection of Allport's midcareer papers may be found in *The Person in Psychology* (Boston: Beacon Press, 1968). Allport's small volume, *Becoming: Basic Considerations for a Psychology of Personality* (New Haven, CT: Yale University Press, 1955), contains a historical survey of the use of the concept of self and Allport's recommendations for adopting the analogous concept of the proprium.

Allport's publication of Jenny Masterson's letters provided psychologists with raw data on a unique personality that deserves the reader's careful attention to *Letters From Jenny* (New York: Harcourt, Brace & World, 1965). In a similar vein, Allport presents the benefits and limitations of personal documents in psychological research in *The Use of Personal Documents in Psychological Science* (New York: Social Science Research Council Bulletin, No. 49, 1942).

Allport's work in the area of social psychology and the study of rumor transmission appears in his and Leo Postman's *The Psychology of Rumor* (New York: Holt, 1947). Allport's views on the crucial function of religion in the mature, healthy personality may be gleaned from his *The Individual and His Religion* (New York: Macmillan, 1962).

Criticisms of Allport's concepts abound. Walter Mischel's *Personality and Assessment* (New York: Wiley, 1968) is a thorough review of the research allegedly supporting the concept of trait. Allport's concept of uniqueness receives devastating blows at the hand of Robert Holt in "Individuality and Generalization in the Psychology of Personality," *Journal of Personality* (1962), **30**, 377–402. B. F. Skinner's *Science and Human Behavior* (New York: Free Press, 1953) may be read in part as a resounding rebuttal of Allport's trait concepts. Peter Bertocci's "Critique of Gordon W. Allport's Theory of Motivation," *Psychological Review* (1950), **47**, 501–532, cogently attacks the concept of functional autonomy.

An interview of Allport is to be found in R. I. Evans's (Ed.) *Gordon Allport: The Man and His Ideas* (New York: Dutton, 1971), or in condensed form in Evans's *The Making of Psychology* (New York: Knopf, 1976). Individual case studies in the tradition of Allport by one of his students can be had in Robert White's *Lives in Progress* (New York: Holt, 1966). William McKinley Runyan's "The Life Course as a Theoretical Orientation: Sequences of Person-Situation Interaction," *Journal of Personality*, (1978), **46**, 569–593, presents cogent arguments and evidence for understanding the study of whole lives and life histories as basic personality and clinical research strategies.

CHAPTER 15

ABRAHAM MASLOW & CARL ROGERS

Humanistic Self-Actualization Theory

and i (being at a window
in this midnight)
for no reason feel
deeply completely conscious of the rain or rather
Somebody who uses roofs and streets skillfully to make
a possible and beautiful sound . . .

e.e. cummings, "take for example this"

Even if human nature and man's behavior are absolutely determined, man's belief in his free will, ability to choose and individual responsibility would still be his "psychology" and the real object of human psychology. . . . Psychotherapy can only be based on an individualistic psychology, that is, should strive to adjust the individual to himself, which means enable him to accept himself.

Otto Rank, *Beyond Psychology*

About Rogers's and Maslow's Humanism

Maslow and Rogers each tried to shape a theory that would be an alternative to both psychoanalysis and behaviorism.

Abraham Maslow developed an early interest in personality health and exceptional human functioning. From his research with primates, college students, and eminent psychologists, Maslow developed these main themes:

1. *Personality health is more than the absence of pathology. It is a striving toward simplicity, independence, competence, and the love of beauty.*

2. *Humans develop through a hierarchy of needs, beginning with basics such as survival and safety. But once the basics are satisfied, "metaneeds" may develop that steer the person toward a search for beauty, knowledge, justice, and truth.*

3. *Self-actualization is the enhancement and full expression of what is most human, most transcendental, and most spiritual in the person. A rare few people achieve this state, but many people embark on the journey.*

Carl Rogers developed his theory essentially from his work in psychotherapy with troubled children and their parents. Like Maslow, Rogers emphasized human independence in these fundamental ideas:

1. *The core of personality is the phenomenal self, the private world of experience and personal meaning.*

2. *The self can be shaped by parental demands that level conditions under which the child feels valued or not. Trying to meet the conditions of value may alienate the developing personality from the true self, resulting in feelings of anxiety and conflict.*

3. *Psychotherapy from the Rogerian point of view is the establishment of a relationship in which the therapist has unconditional positive regard for the client, attempts to see the world as the client sees it, and is able to provide genuine empathic warmth for the client. When these conditions are met, the client's true self is freed, and the person slowly owns his or her feelings and desires.*

For both Maslow and Rogers, the dominant theme of personality is personal growth, a reaching or yearning for self-acceptance.

ABRAHAM MASLOW

THE PARADOX OF NORMALITY

The person who has achieved complete psychological health probably does not exist. Indeed, persons who merely approximate total personality integration are very rare. The vast majority of people in the world, however, must be considered to have established for themselves a balance of personality health and abnormality that leans toward health. Yet, personality theories are, for the most part, about deviant persons, about ill-conceived adaptations to life circumstances, and about major and minor personality flaws.

In consequence, the student of personality is bound to run headlong into an enduring paradox inherent in the field. Although by implication all theorists are interested in the factors that underlie the healthy functioning of the normal personality, the observational clarity—real or imagined—lent by extreme exaggeration of mental functioning in the abnormal personality presents an irresistible lure to the investigator.

The paradox is clear:

1. The majority of people are assumed to be relatively healthy.
2. Personality theorists center their studies on the abnormal personality.
3. Knowledge derived from this nonrepresentative sample of the human population serves as a pool of principles for application to the entire species.

Have we nothing to learn from direct study of the healthy personality?

Abraham Maslow, the first theorist we consider in this chapter, has in recent years focused his attention on those rare persons who are on the verge of, or who have already achieved, psychological health. Maslow prefers to think of this state of exemplary personality integration as *self-actualization.* Of course, Maslow's concern with such atypical individuals establishes an equally nonrepresentative sample of personalities as the basis of psychological generalizations, but this sample may serve as a much-needed corrective to a long history of concern with deviance. Maslow's intention was to establish the conditions under which all humans can attain their fullest degree of selfhood or health:

> Health is not simply the absence of disease or even the opposite of it. Any theory of motivation that is worthy of attention must deal with the highest capacities of the healthy and strong man as well as with the defensive maneuvers of crippled spirits. (1970, p. 33)

Like Carl Rogers, the second theorist we treat in this chapter, Maslow regards the truly healthy personality as one that possesses sufficient personal fortitude and creativity to be innocent. "Innocence," in the sense that Maslow uses the term, refers to the healthy personality's capacity to live without pretense, to be genuinely bereft of guilt in thought, in word, and in action. Creative, innocent, and healthy people are able to devote themselves completely to whatever task is at hand. They are able to free themselves from the distractions, fears, and petty influences imposed by other people, for they are in the process of becoming completely themselves, becoming more real, authentic, and less influenced by a need to placate others. Maslow used the metaphor of the actor, the mask, and the audience to portray this state of being:

> This [freedom from the influence of others] means dropping masks, dropping our efforts to influence, to impress, to please, to be lovable, to win applause. It could be said so: if we have no audience to play to, we cease to be actors. With no need to act we can devote ourselves, self-forgetfully, to the problem. (1971, p. 65)

In becoming more our real selves and less the persons we expect others want us to be, we approach closer to psychological health.

THE ORIGIN OF MASLOW'S INTEREST IN PSYCHOLOGICAL HEALTH AND STRENGTH

Maslow's original training was in experimental psychology, and he completed his doctoral thesis under Harry Harlow at the University of Wisconsin. Harlow was then (circa 1933) just beginning to set up his primate laboratory for the study of monkey behavior. Maslow's research involved a great many observational investigations of animal interaction and group affiliations. In fact, his doctoral study was concerned with the establishment of dominance hierarchies in a colony of monkeys.

Maslow noted throughout his early researches (e.g., 1936a, 1936b, 1937, in Maslow, 1973) that dominance of one animal over others was only rarely established through overt physical aggression. To Maslow it seemed rather that the dominant animal exhibited a kind of internal "confidence" or "dominance-feeling" that communicated to his less assertive cage mates that his will would prevail (1936b, p. 45).

When Maslow later applied his animal research findings and methods to the investigation of human behavior, he again employed the notion of "dominance-feeling": "If we were forced to choose a single synonym or definition for dominance-feeling, we should say that it was chiefly the evaluation of, or confidence in, the personality (self-confidence)" (1937, p. 53). Maslow extended his analysis in an Adlerian vein to suggest that a need for dominance may exist in some personalities as either a compensation for inferiority feelings, or as an inherent need in itself, or

> . . . it is possible that the most parsimonious way of treating this concept is to think of it in specific, rather than general terms. It may be possible and even desirable to speak *not* of a craving for dominance, but of craving for health *per se*. . . . Or one may crave to be free of timidity, not because of an attempt to increase self-evaluation, but simply for vocational efficiency; e.g., in order to be a better teacher or a more efficient physician. (1937, p. 64)

Dominance-Feeling in Humans

Maslow adapted his observational infrahuman primate strategies to the study of human dominance-feeling. He created a method he called "conversational probing." Conversational probing is intensive interviewing of a subject after a satisfactory rapport is established: "This meant mostly a frank, trusting, friendly relationship, resembling somewhat the transference of the psychoanalysts" (Maslow, 1939, p. 75). Maslow studied approximately 130 women and a few men in this fashion. Of these, the majority of subjects were college students between the ages of 20 and 28; 75 percent were Protestant, 20 percent were Jewish, and 5 percent were Catholic.

The interview data were organized around a basic premise: *What personality variables correlate with dominance-feeling?* Dominance-feeling was now redefined in human terms as a form of self-evaluation:

> High dominance-feeling empirically involves good self-confidence, self-assurance, high evaluation of the self, feelings of general capability or superiority, and lack of shyness, timidity, self-consciousness or embarrassment. (Maslow, 1939, p. 74)

In addition to the traits Maslow listed in defining high dominance, he also found evidence among his subjects that they were unconventional, less religious, extroverted, and, surprisingly, more hypnotizable than low-dominance subjects (1942, pp. 108 ff.). Furthermore, Maslow discovered a number of variables that were uncorrelated with high dominance. If a subject was high in dominance-feeling it was unlikely that she was "nervous," anxious, jealous, or neurotic. The high-dominance subjects began to look like the picture of psychological health.

Sexual Behavior and Attitudes of High-Dominance Women

In a later study Maslow focused attention on the sexual behavior of his subjects. He reported a wide range of impressionistic and statistical data about his high-dominance subjects' sexual preferences, but one particular phenomenon deserves a brief description.

Women of high dominance-feeling had very specific ideas about the "ideal man" and about the "ideal lovemaking situation." For the high-dominance woman, only a high-dominance man is attractive. Preferably, he should be even more dominant than she. This paragon of masculinity was described as "highly masculine, self-confident, fairly aggressive, sure of what he wants and able to get it, generally superior in most things" (Maslow, 1942, p. 126).

In contrast, women of medium to low dominance-feeling stressed qualities like kindness, amiability, and love for children, along with gentleness and faithfulness as desirable masculine traits.

Ideal lovemaking for the high-dominance woman involves a preference for

> . . . straightforward, unsentimental, rather violent, animal, pagan, passionate, even sometimes brutal lovemaking. It must come quickly, rather than after a long period of wooing. She wishes to be suddenly swept off her feet, not courted. She wishes her favors to be taken, rather than asked for. In other words she must be dominated, must be forced into subordinate status. (Maslow, 1942, p. 127)

Maslow was also interested in the preferences of the middle- and low-dominance woman. He found that women lower in dominance-feeling were repelled by the kind of "ideal man" that attracted high-dominance subjects. Middle-dominance women preferred an "adequate" rather than a superior man, "a comfortable and 'homey' man rather than a man who might inspire slight fear and feelings of inferiority" (Maslow,

1942, p. 126). In short, high-dominance women seek a good lover; middle- and low-dominance women are more interested in a good husband and father.

The Good Specimen Strategy: "Exceptional" Primates

Maslow's distinction between high dominance and low dominance may be conceptualized as the difference between relatively secure and relatively insecure personalities (1942, p. 133). He later developed from these distinctions an interest in extreme cases of the secure personality, the personality totally actualized and completely acceptant of self. People in whom dominance-feeling has come to complete fruition were later conceptualized as "most fully human," for these people share as their common trait a trust in self that is describable as general personality strength.

Maslow eventually came to describe his strategy of research with these exceptionally healthy or strong personalities as the study of the "good specimen":

> I proposed for discussion and eventually for research the use of selected good specimens (superior specimens) as biological assays for studying the best capability that the human species has. . . .What I am frankly espousing here is what I have been calling "growing-tip statistics," taking my title from the fact that it is at the growing tip of a plant that the greatest genetic action takes place. (1971, pp. 5, 6, 7)

Thus Maslow initiated the study of the "best" that human nature has to offer, the most "saintly," the wisest, most actualized human personality. He turned to a group of selected historical and contemporary figures who seemed to embody the traits he associated with this "good specimen." What is interesting, as we shall see, is that the observational data Maslow collected tended to be similar, in some cases identical to, the early data on dominance-feeling.

PERSONAL SOURCES OF THE HYPOTHESIS: IN PURSUIT OF "ANGELS"

In a rather candid statement, Maslow (1971) reported the personal sources of his interest in the self-actualizing personality (SA). Devotion to and admiration of two of his teachers, Max Wertheimer, the founder of Gestalt psychology, and Ruth Benedict, the eminent cultural anthropologist, sparked the young Maslow's interest in the exceptional person. They had impressed him with their calm acceptance of life and with their special capacity to take delight in intellectual and cultural pursuits. Yet, at the same time, Benedict and Wertheimer were something of an enigma to Maslow. In trying to ferret out the sources of Benedict and Wertheimer's approach to life and its people, Maslow embarked on a private and informal investigation of self-actualization:

> [My investigation on self-actualization] . . . started out as the effort of a young intellectual to try to understand two of his teachers whom he loved, adored, and admired and who were very, very wonderful people. It was a kind of high-IQ devotion. I could not be content simply to adore, but sought to understand why these two people were so different from the run-of-the-mill people in the world. These two

people were Ruth Benedict and Max Wertheimer. They were my teachers . . . and they were most remarkable human beings. My training in psychology equipped me not at all for understanding them. It was as if they were not quite people but something more than people. My own investigation began as a prescientific or nonscientific activity. I made descriptions and notes on Max Wertheimer, and I made notes on Ruth Benedict. When I tried to understand them, think about them, and write about them in my journal and my notes, I realized in one wonderful moment that their two patterns could be generalized. I was talking about a kind of person, not about two noncomparable individuals. . . . I tried to see whether this pattern could be found elsewhere, and I did find it elsewhere, in one person after another. (1971, pp. 41–42)

Begun as a private and informal undertaking, Maslow's interest in psychologically healthy, self-actualized people soon became a serious professional interest. It is clear that this concern with the exceptional organism, "the good specimen," was an extension of Maslow's early work with the exceptionally dominant personalities he had studied in and out of the animal laboratory. Yet, simultaneously, "good specimens" and "dominant personalities" were also reflections of Maslow's potent personal need to understand his own feelings of insecurity.

Consequently, Maslow began to develop criteria of normality or health. From his observations of personal acquaintances who might embody such qualities, Maslow was able to develop an impressionistic sketch of the exceptionally healthy person. Using biographical information on historical figures, and on some contemporary public ones, Maslow discovered nine individuals in whom he felt "fairly sure" self-actualization was well under way. Though Maslow's "fairly sure" personal acquaintances had necessarily to remain anonymous in his report of the research (except for Wertheimer and Benedict), the historical figures he chose as SA subjects were Abraham Lincoln in his last years and Thomas Jefferson. Additionally, Maslow discovered seven "highly probable" figures: Albert Einstein, Eleanor Roosevelt, Jane Addams, William James, Albert Schweitzer, Aldous Huxley, and Spinoza. Ultimately, a whole array of public and historical figures were selected as "potential cases" of SA. Among these figures were Adlai Stevenson, Ralph Waldo Emerson, George Washington, Walt Whitman, Martin Buber, and Goethe; in all a total of 37 potential cases (Maslow, 1970, p. 152).

Maslow's analysis of the personalities with whom he was directly familiar was rather different from the usual clinical-experimental investigation. Because subjects tend to freeze up when informed they are being studied as examples of exceptional psychological health, most of Maslow's observations had to be surreptitious (1970, p. 152). Therefore, the data took the form of impressionistic analyses of informal conversations and easily observable behaviors. With time, Maslow developed a definition of the self-actualizing person (SA) as one who *is* what he or she can be (1970, p. 46):

> . . . [self-actualization] may be loosely described as the full use and exploitation of talents, capacities, potentialities, etc. Such people seem to be fulfilling themselves and to be doing the best that they are capable of doing, reminding us of Nietzsche's exhortation, "Become what thou art!" (Maslow, 1970, p. 150)

In the course of his work, Maslow interviewed and studied more than 3,000 individuals, of whom only a "handful" were discovered to have potential for self-actualization. In fact, only one individual who was self-actualized in the fullest sense was found.

From Dominant Monkeys to Near-Perfect People

The question must arise: How could a psychologist trained in the best traditions of behaviorism transcend his monkey studies to explore the lives of "exceptional" people? Maslow, apparently, had a lifelong interest in famous and powerful people, persons who had reached the pinnacle of their professions. In some sense, by his deliberate seeking out of the "best" and most famous psychologists in the field to be his teachers, Maslow was vicariously identifying with their eminence. His childhood, like that of so many personality theorists, had been lonely:

> With my childhood, it's a wonder I'm not psychotic. I was the little Jewish boy in the non-Jewish neighborhood. It was a little like being the first Negro enrolled in the all-white school. I was isolated and unhappy. I grew up in libraries and among books, without friends. (Maslow, in Hall, 1968, p. 33)

As a student, Maslow not only sought out the most esteemed people in his chosen field, but he attached himself to them in the most personal ways:

> I was young Harry Harlow's first Ph.D. And they were angels, my professors. I've always had angels around. They helped me when I needed it; fed me; Bill Sheldon taught me how to buy a suit. I didn't know anything of amenities. Edward L. Thorndike was an angel to me. Clark Hull was another. (Maslow, in Hall, 1968, p. 33)

As with his relationship with Wertheimer and Benedict, Maslow chose idealizing words to describe his attachments to his professors. Graduate professors are described in many ways by their students, but until Maslow employed the term, "angel" had not seen much use. Maslow idealized his professors as angels in more than one way. Once, for example, having stood beside his philosophy professor at an adjoining urinal, Maslow's naïveté was shattered by the unwelcome revelation that academic angels need mortal bladder relief: ". . . it stunned me so that it took hours, even weeks, for me to assimilate the fact that a professor was a human being and constructed with the plumbing that everybody else had" (Wilson, 1972, p. 138). But Maslow deliberately sought out the people he thought were most eminent with such efficiency that we can only wonder at his passion for association with greatness. Indeed, Maslow described one of his own "peak experiences," a fantasy of participating in the greatest academic procession in the most astounding commencement exercise of all time:

> I was in a faculty procession here at Brandeis. I saw the line stretching off into a dim future. At its head was Socrates. And in the line were the ones I love most. Thomas Jefferson was there. And Spinoza. And Alfred North Whitehead. I was in that same line. Behind me that infinite line melted into the dimness. (Maslow, in Hall, 1968, p. 35)

Thus Maslow saw himself among the company of the best minds in civilization. Despite the seeming egocentricity of such a fantasy, Maslow tempered his wishfulness with genuine humility. He reports that a growing disaffection with behaviorism, stemming initially from his reading of philosophers and psychoanalytic psychology, reached a crisis at the birth of his son:

> . . . [W]hen my baby was born that was the thunderclap that settled things. I looked at this tiny, mysterious thing and felt so stupid. I was stunned by the mystery and by the sense of not really being in control. I felt small and weak and feeble before all

this. I'd say that anyone who had a baby couldn't be a behaviorist. (Maslow, in Hall, 1968, p. 36)

The transition of interest from dominant monkeys to nearly perfect people in Maslow's career is thus now more intelligible. Central in Maslow's life history was the clash between feelings of childhood isolation, inferiority, and powerlessness and yearnings for intellectual superiority and eminence (Maslow, 1979, pp. 101 ff.).

The first goal—intellectual superiority—could be obtained by an academic career, whose prime research interest was self-reflectively focused on dominant "best specimens." While he was among the academic behaviorists, monkeys were the best-specimen-subjects. The second goal—personal eminence—could be had only vicariously, only through association with eminent teachers, who would presumably reveal the secret of their renown. While he was among the "angels," near-perfect-people were the best-specimen-subjects (Maslow, 1979, p. 115).

Commenting on his techniques for handling critics of his life work, Maslow revealed this not-unexpected strategy:

> . . . I have worked out a lot of tricks for fending off professional attacks. . . . I have a secret. I talk over the heads of the people in front of me to my own private audience. I talk to people I love and respect. To Socrates and Aristotle and Spinoza and Thomas Jefferson and Abraham Lincoln. And when I write, I write for them. This cuts out a lot of crap. (Maslow, in Hall, 1968, p. 36)

Oedipus Against the Windmills

The theme of dominance was an enduring passion for Maslow. In a rather remarkable seminar for students at Brandeis University, in January 1963, Maslow presented his own feelings—we might say projections—about the Saul Steinberg drawing shown in Figure 15.1.

FIGURE 15.1 *"I think it expresses me very much"—Abraham Maslow.* Copyright © 1960 by Saul Steinberg.

From the book *The Labyrinth*, Harper & Row. Originally published in *The New Yorker* magazine.

Steinberg's drawing evokes a wealth of meanings and serves admirably as a kind of projective test. Maslow began the class discussion with the admission that he felt the Don Quixote–like figure represented himself: ". . . because I think it expresses me very much. Somehow I identify with it" (Maslow & Chiang, 1977, p. 241). To encourage his students to participate in this venture into self-knowledge, Maslow provided some of his own, apparently spontaneous, free associations to the drawing. These associations included the fact that when he saw the picture for the first time, he had laughed and laughed, and felt the urge to share it with his wife and friends. The geometrical objects toward which the figure on horseback seems to be proceeding reminded Maslow of something cold and bloodless, mechanistic, "just the sort of thing that I'm fighting against in the American Psychological Association" (Maslow & Chiang, 1977, p. 247). Maslow referred, of course, to his fight for recognition of humanistic psychology as an independent discipline of equal value to the mechanistic Freudian and behavioristic branches of APA. Thus Maslow saw himself as a quixotic figure tilting at the windmills of establishment.

> That is, Don Quixote, or whoever this figure with his spear is, it's all very nice. The association with me is of bravery, a kind of hopeless bravery, you might say—the ship going down with the flag flying and so on. Because this looks stronger and he can't break them—the spear isn't big enough for that—it isn't strong enough or powerful enough. So there's that kind of fundamental absurdity about the effort itself— of Don Quixote, or a Don Quixote-ish figure. I like Don Quixote, and I like that it seems like a nice thing to do. His spear will get bent, or he can't crack it or break it or anything, but the fact is that he is in a certain sense stronger, you might say, because he sees how absurd all these self-important blocks are, all puffed up with pride and solidity. (Maslow & Chiang, 1977, pp. 247–248)

Then Maslow followed his associations on tilting absurdly against the mechanists with the thought of a friend with whom he played a game involving Freud's book *Totem and Taboo.* This book contains Freud's hypothesis on the evolutionary origin of the Oedipus complex in the primal patricide of the primitive horde's father and leader by his sons in order to obtain his power and his women. In the game, apparently, his friend saw himself as one son against a horde of primal fathers, a reversal of Freud's hypothesis. Maslow went on to suggest that Freud never took his own version seriously:

> It's a myth. It's a kind of a way of saying something, just the way this cartoon is. He was trying to say that you have to *overthrow the dominant one or else you'll never be a man,* and if you're not a man you don't deserve a woman and so on. (Maslow & Chiang, 1977, p. 248; italics added)

Maslow's further associations involved his current guilt feelings at not doing rigorous experimentation in support of his work:

> I felt uneasy about all these big things without data, without support and all sorts of theories and hypotheses. A big, big balloon, and there's always the thought, Which needle is going to prick that balloon? (1977, p. 248)

Maslow was quite fearful of criticism when delivering one of his papers to an audience. In fact, his pre-presentation jitters were often so intense that immediately following his public recital he would privately take to his bed for several days to recover (Maslow, 1979, p. 99; Wilson, 1972, p. 139).

Maslow's associations to the Don Quixote–like figure with whom he identified included three elements. First, the feeling of fighting absurdly against overwhelming and cold-blooded adversaries was interpreted as nevertheless quixotically meritorious. Second, the theme of overtaking the father's power and the threat of being defeated in turn by him was interpreted as a Freudian allegory on manhood. Third, the ever-present theme of dominance emerged overtly, centering on the proposition that one has to overthrow those who are already dominant in order to be dominant.

To Be an Angel's Son

A good Freudian analyst might speculate that Maslow's extraordinary lifelong interest in dominant personalities derived from his early disappointment with his own father. It is interesting in this context that Maslow gave the following characterization of his parents in an interview:

> Both my mother and father were uneducated. My father wanted me to be a lawyer. He thumbed his way across the whole continent of Europe from Russia and got here at the age of 15. He wanted success for me.
>
> I tried law school for two weeks. Then I came home to my poor father one night after a class discussing "spite fences" and told him I couldn't be a lawyer.
>
> "Well, son", he said, "what do you want?" I told him I wanted to study—to study everything. He was uneducated and couldn't understand my passion for learning, but he was a nice man. He didn't understand that, or that I was in love, in love at the age of 16. (Maslow, in Hall, 1968, p. 33)

Maslow described his mother as "a pretty woman—but not a nice one"; and he portrayed his father as a "vigorous man, who loved whiskey and women and fighting" (Wilson, 1972, p. 131). For his mother, Maslow retained as little affection in adulthood as she had shown him in childhood, and his fondly ironic description of his father's "loves" was tempered by a strong measure of fear of the man. A maternal uncle cared for young Maslow when his mother and father were no longer interested in their children (Wilson, 1972, p. 131).

In his journal, Maslow recorded his thoughts about his mother. He had been speaking that evening with his wife about how she reacted against some aspects of her childhood with opposite behaviors now. That discussion brought these thoughts to mind:

> And suddenly it dawned on me that it had been the same thing for me & my mother (father too). What I had reacted against & totally hated & rejected was not only her physical appearance, but also her values & world view, her stinginess, her total self-ishness, her lack of love for anyone else in the world, even her own husband & children, her narcissism, her Negro prejudice, her exploitation of anyone, her assumption that anyone was wrong who disagreed with her, her lack of concern for her grandchildren, her lack of friends, her sloppiness & dirtiness, her lack of family feeling for her own parents & siblings, her primitive animal-like care for herself & her body alone, etc., etc. I've always wondered where my Utopianism, ethical stress, humanism, stress on kindness, love, friendship, & all the rest came from. I knew certainly of the direct consequences of having no mother-love. But the whole thrust

of my life-philosophy & all my research & theorizing also has its roots in a hatred for & revulsion against everything she stood for—which I hated so early that I was never tempted to seek *her* love or to want it or expect it.

All so simple, so obvious—& to discover it at the age of 61! And after all the psychoanalysis & self-analysis! (Maslow, 1979, p. 245)

It may very well have been that Maslow felt he disappointed his father as much as his uneducated father had disappointed him. Maslow wanted to be superior, and the only road he knew to that goal was the intellectual road, a journey his father could neither comprehend nor condone. To be a lawyer meant, in the elder Maslow's eyes, that education could be applied to something practical and success-making. To be an intellectual meant—what? But that was Maslow's identity; "a young intellectual," he called himself (Maslow, 1971, p. 41). His own insecurity led to his dependent attachment to and idealization of mother and father substitutes in the academic community, his "angels."

Yet the achievements he eventually won for himself did not dispel the insecurities. He was a pioneer in an area of psychology that defied rigorous experimentation. Would his critics understand his professional intentions without hard data to back them up? Would the established profession of psychology understand his efforts to be different, to be humanistic in a mechanistic discipline, to be somebody? Would they understand and esteem his passion better than his father had (Maslow, 1979, p. 101)?

Maslow's enduring concern with the theme of personal dominance and superiority, culminating with the conception of the "best human specimens" as self-actualized individuals, was probably a reflection of his own need to justify his search for heroes from whose power and eminence he could draw sustenance.

CHARACTERISTICS OF SELF-ACTUALIZERS

From his observations, interviews, and partial test results, Maslow developed a schematic picture of the self-actualizing personality. Maslow's propensity for lists of things in his writing is well known, and his description of the SA syndrome is no exception. The SA pattern consists of 15 characteristics that are positive or favorable and 5 negative (from the viewpoint of other people) traits. All 20 items have been summarized in Table 15.1 with a brief description of the meaning of each item. In addition, the 20 separate items have been grouped into seven classes where overlap and similarity permit such redistribution. To preserve the essence of continuity in Maslow's original list, the number of the item in that list is indicated in parentheses (see Maslow, 1970, Chapter 11; see also the earlier version in Moustakas, 1956, pp. 160 ff.).

From Table 15.1 it can be seen that SA people are generally characterized by independence and self-trust. They are accepting of others and self, and most important, accepting of what life holds in store for them. They are people in whom basic needs for food, shelter, and intimacy with an opposite-sexed partner have been satisfactorily met. Self-actualizers, consequently, are functioning in response to "higher" needs, needs for the classic "Goods" of the well-lived life. Beauty, Truth, Justice, and many other capitalized virtues are the very core of the self-actualizer's existence. In this sense, therefore, SA people taught Maslow an important lesson: People strive not merely for survival, not merely out of deficiencies, but *for* meaningful existence out

TABLE 15.1   Maslow's Self-Actualization Pattern

Self-Actualization Characteristic	Description
Reality (1) and Problem Centered (4)	More efficient and accurate perception of reality; unusual ability to detect the fake, phony, and dishonest; focus on problems external to self; invests energies in "causes."
Acceptance of self and others (2); Spontaneity and simplicity (3)	Accepts own nature in stoic style; accepts what cannot be changed; is spontaneous and always natural; prefers simplicity to pretense and artificiality—in self and others; conventional on surface to avoid hurting others.
Need privacy (5); Independence of culture and environment (6); Resists enculturation (15)	Relies on own judgment; trusts in self; resists pressure from others and social norms; able to "weather hard knocks" with calm; resists identification with cultural stereotypes; has autonomous values carefully considered.
Freshness of appreciation (7); Creativeness (14)	Maintains constancy for awe and wonder; ability to marvel at and enjoy the good things of life: food, sex, sports, travel; thousandth baby seen is as wonderful as first; creative in daily tasks of living; inventive and original in childlike way.
Unhostile sense of humor (13); Democratic (11); *Gemeinschaftsgefühl* (9); Intimate personal relations (10)	Does not enjoy jokes at expense of others; prefers a philosophic humor that pokes fun at the human condition; enjoys company of all people regardless of social or racial origins; Adler's *Gemeinschaftsgefühl* means "fellow-feeling" or social interest; strong interest in others' welfare; small number of intense and intimate friendships.
Peak (mystical) experiences (8); Discrimination between means and ends (12)	Has experienced mystic states characterized by feelings of limitless horizons opening, being more powerful and more helpless simultaneously, with loss of time sense; strong ethical-moral sense but not in conventional ways; discriminates between moral means and ends differently from average person; means can be ends.
IMPERFECTIONS: Unexpected ruthlessness; occasional absentmindedness; overkindliness; non-neurotic guilt and anxiety	"There are no perfect people"; SA individuals can display surgical coldness when called for in situations of betrayal; overkindliness gets them into trouble by letting others impose on them; uninterested in social "chatting" or party-going; anxiety and guilt present, but from realistic not neurotic sources; sometimes philosophical concerns cause a loss of sense of humor.

Based on Maslow, 1970, pp. 153–176.

of an innate need to be whole. The question that now occupied Maslow was, *How do such higher motivations develop to engage the self-actualizer's being?*

THE HIERARCHY OF MOTIVES: FROM DEFICIENCY TO BEING MOTIVATION

Maslow conceptualized human needs in a hierarchy of potency. Needs lowest in the scale are prepotent to needs lying above them. Prepotency means that higher needs cannot emerge until lower ones have first been satisfied. Thus lower needs exert potency in shaping an individual's behavior *before* the higher needs, and continue to be potent until satisfied.

For example, people whose every biological need is satisfied—hunger, thirst, and sex to be specific—are likely to turn to poetry, photography, art, or music to have some meaningful way of spending their energies and occupying their time.

> It is quite true that man lives by bread alone—when there is no bread. *But what happens to man's desires when there is bread and when his belly is chronically filled?* (Maslow, 1943, in 1973, p. 157; cf. 1970, p. 38; italics added)

The answer, of course, is that the "higher" needs emerge to exert potency in shaping people's strivings. The cycle continues, however, for once "higher" needs for beauty, truth, justice, and so on, are fulfilled, even "higher" needs emerge. The highest of the needs in the hierarchy are the *B-values* (Being-values), or metaneeds as Maslow termed them. We consider the metaneeds shortly, but it is important to note that the 15 metaneeds are *not* hierarchically arranged. Having reached the self-actualization step in the hierarchy, the individual experiences needs for the B-values like Beauty, Truth, and Justice more or less simultaneously, though not with equal intensity. The basic hierarchy may be schematized as in Figure 15.2 (based on Maslow, 1970, pp. 35–46).

When a lower-order need predominates—for example, hunger in the physiological step—then all behavior is directed to the fulfillment of that need. If its satisfaction is a chronic problem, then the next highest need in the hierarchy will fail to develop full potency.

FIGURE 15.2   Maslow's Hierarchy of Needs.

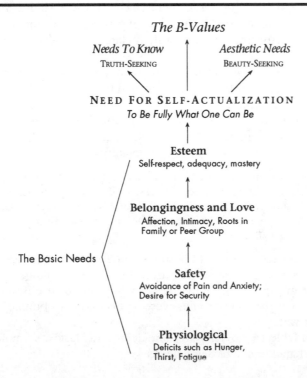

The B-Values

Needs To Know   *Aesthetic Needs*
TRUTH-SEEKING   BEAUTY-SEEKING

NEED FOR SELF-ACTUALIZATION
To Be Fully What One Can Be

Esteem
Self-respect, adequacy, mastery

Belongingness and Love
Affection, Intimacy, Roots in
Family or Peer Group

The Basic Needs

Safety
Avoidance of Pain and Anxiety;
Desire for Security

Physiological
Deficits such as Hunger,
Thirst, Fatigue

When all four levels in the hierarchy, the basic needs, are satisfied, the highest needs for self-actualization emerge. Collateral with self-actualization needs are the uniquely human desires to know, to understand the world, and to enjoy its beauty. Although Maslow was not particularly clear on the matter, he seems in the final revision of his definitive work (1970) to have intended the aesthetic and knowledge needs to be grouped with self-actualization as equal potency motives.

The term *self-actualization* was coined by Kurt Goldstein (1939) and adopted by Maslow to indicate the healthy, well-lived life previously described by the 15 characteristics attributed to self-actualizing people. In any event, it seems clear that in Maslow's scheme *satisfaction striving,* rather than deficiency motivation, is the motor of personality. Maslow construes the organism not as pushed by drives, but as pulled by the need to be fulfilled.

BEYOND SELF-ACTUALIZATION: THE B-VALUES

The rare individual who achieves the stage of self-actualization enters on a course of what Maslow called "growth motivation." In the language of needs, self-actualized people develop Being-needs or B-values. They are no longer engaged on the road to "becoming" self-actualized, for they have successfully progressed through the hierarchy of basic needs. They now embark on the growth processes of living to *enhance their being, to expand their knowledge of self and others,* and *to operationalize their personalities* in any activity that they undertake.

In this sense, Maslow proposed the further set of Being-needs that emerge at the point of self-actualization in the basic hierarchy. To these B-values Maslow often assigned the name "metamotives": "Self-actualizing people are not primarily motivated (i.e., by basic needs); they are primarily metamotivated (i.e., by metaneeds = B-values)" (1971, p. 311).

With the proposal of the B-values, Maslow recognized the possibility that some individuals may satisfy all their basic needs through to the esteem levels in the hierarchy and yet not be self-actualized. In a sense, some people suffer the neuroses of the rich, the "existential" neuroses of being affluent and directionless. To truly be self-actualizing, one must be committed to long-reaching goals: the B-values. Thus Maslow revised his definition of the self-actualizing personality:

> . . . it may turn out to be useful to add to the definition of the self-actualizing person, not only [a] that he be sufficiently free of illness, [b] that he be sufficiently gratified in his basic needs, and [c] that he be positively using his capacities, but also [d] that *he be motivated by some values which he strives for or gropes for and to which he is loyal.* (1971, p. 301; italics added)

Originally Maslow proposed a list of 14 B-values (1962, p. 78), only later to add a 15th (1971, pp. 318–319). The 15 B-values are listed in Table 15.2 along with the "deficiency diseases" or metapathologies that result when one of the B-values is unsatisfied. Thus Maslow felt that the B-values were as necessary to human existence as vitamins or food or water.

The B-values in Table 15.2 overlap to some degree. In Maslow's opinion the overlap is an essential characteristic of Being-needs:

TABLE 15.2 B-Values and Metapathologies

B-Value or Metaneed	Pathogenic Deprivation	Specific Metapathologies (Motivation Disease)
1. Truth	Dishonesty	Disbelief; mistrust; cynicism
2. Goodness	Evil	Utter selfishness; hatred, reliance only on self; disgust, nihilism
3. Beauty	Ugliness	Vulgarity; loss of taste; tension; fatigue
4. Unity-Wholeness	Chaos, atomism	Disintegration; arbitrariness
4A. Dichotomy-Transcendence	Black/White dichotomies; forced choices	Either/or thinking; seeing everything as dualistic; a simplistic view of life
5. Aliveness; process	Deadness; mechanizing of life	Robotizing; feeling totally determined; loss of zest in life
6. Uniqueness	Sameness; uniformity	Loss of feeling of individuality or being needed
7. Perfection	Imperfection; sloppiness	Discouragement (?); hopelessness
7A. Necessity	Accident; occasionalism; inconsistency	Loss of safety; unpredictability
8. Completion; finality	Incompleteness	Cessation of striving; no use trying
9. Justice	Injustice	Insecurity; anger; cynicism; mistrust
9A. Order	Lawlessness, chaos	Insecurity; wariness; loss of safety
10. Simplicity	Confusing complexity	Overcomplexity; confusion; loss of orientation
11. Richness; totality	Poverty	Depression; uneasiness; loss of interest
12. Effortlessness	Effortfulness	Fatigue; strain; clumsiness
13. Playfulness	Humorlessness	Grimness; depression; paranoid humorlessness
14. Self-sufficiency	Accident; occasionalism	Dependence upon the perceiver and others
15. Meaningfulness	Meaninglessness	Despair; senselessness of life

Condensed from Maslow, 1971, pp. 318–319.

It is my (uncertain) impression that any B-value is fully and adequately defined by the total of the other B-values. That is, truth, to be fully and completely defined, must be beautiful, good, perfect, just, simple, orderly, lawful, alive, comprehensive, unitary, dichotomy-transcending, effortless, and amusing. . . . *It is as if all the B-Values have some kind of unity, with each single value being something like a facet of this whole.* (Maslow, 1971, p. 324; italics added)

Maslow regarded the values and diseases in Table 15.2 as a kind of "psychological periodic table" that offered the possibility of discovering psychological diseases not yet observed and classified.

Maslow commented on the metapathologies to be found in everyday life: "I have used the world of television and especially of television advertising as a rich source of metapathologies of all types, i.e., of the vulgarization or destruction of all intrinsic values . . ." (1971, p. 319). A moment's thought about television commercials will confirm Maslow's opinion. Bad breath, body odor, loose dentures, psoriasis, warts, gastritis, hemorrhoids, "feminine freshness," and foot odor constitute only a partial list of television advertising's critical concerns. If this civilization is ever buried by atomic holocaust, future anthropologists who resurrect the videotapes of major network commercials are certain to conclude that as a society we were offensive to each other in a degree never before reached on earth.

PEAK EXPERIENCES AS MOMENTARILY INTENSE B-VALUE STATES

In 1902 William James published his Gifford Lectures under the title *The Varieties of Religious Experience.* In a series of 20 lectures, James surveyed from a variety of poetic, theological, and biographical writings the diversity of ways in which individuals reported experiencing God. One particular subclass of such experiences called the "mystical state" occupied James at some length. From his researches, James was able to distinguish four characteristics of the mystical experience that separated it from states of normal consciousness. Maslow accepted James's descriptive criteria as adequate characterization of *peak experiences* undergone by self-actualizing people (see Maslow, 1964; 1970, p. 164). James listed the following characteristics of the mystical experience (1902, pp. 371–373):

1. *Ineffability:* "The subject of [a mystical experience] immediately says that it defies expression, that no adequate report of its content can be given in words. It follows from this that its quality must be directly experienced; it cannot be imparted or transferred to others."
2. *Noetic quality:* The word "noetic" is based on a Greek root meaning "mind" or "intellect." James employed the term to indicate the essentially intellectual, "truth-finding" quality of a mystic experience.
3. *Transiency:* "Mystical states cannot be sustained for long. Except in rare instances, half an hour, or at most an hour or two, seems to be the limit beyond which they fade into the light of common day."
4. *Passivity:* ". . . the mystic feels as if his own will were in abeyance, and indeed sometimes as if he were grasped and held by a superior power."

Because of the generally unearthly, surreal quality of mystical experiences (peak experiences), Maslow initially felt that only self-actualizing people underwent them with any appreciable regularity (1964, p. 22). But as he became more skilled in interviewing subjects and in phrasing questions to elicit the information, Maslow discovered that most "average" people have had some peak experiences. The difficulty lay in that some persons tend to react with defensive escape strategies rather than with "openness" or acceptance. Maslow found that individuals who hold particularly materialistic, mechanistic views of life are those individuals who try to ward off and forget peak experiences. These "nonpeakers" thus deliberately cut themselves off from an important spiritual part of life.

At the other extreme, however, Maslow cautioned that contemporary cultural mores among youth tend to foster an impatience or overeager readiness to undergo the transcendent moments of a peak experience. Drugs, meditation rituals, and short-cuts of all kinds cheapen the peak experience: "The sudden insight becomes 'all' and the patient and disciplined 'working through' is postponed or devalued" (1971, p. 345). When peak experiences are sought, actively induced, or otherwise treated as a commodity to be acquired, the total value of the experience is lost. Maslow suggested that the resulting disappointment leads to an attitude of apathy or superficiality, a tendency to desanctify or *desacralize* life.

The Defense of Desacralizing

Desacralizing, a term adopted from Eliade (1961; see also 1958), was used by Maslow to indicate a defensive strategy some individuals use to cope with the demands of living. Desacralizing means to deny the awesome, marvelous, beautiful, sublime aspects of people and the universe. In effect, the desacralizer has learned to "reduce the person to the concrete object and to refuse to see what he might be or to refuse to see him in his symbolic values or to refuse to see him or her eternally" (Maslow, 1971, p. 49). Maslow has suggested that one characteristic of the self-actualizing personality that separates him from the "average" person is his ability to "resacralize" people and things. The self-actualizing person has learned to be awe-inspired by others, to marvel at and enjoy the good things of life, to accept the spiritual as well as the material.

Extending his criticism of desacralization to the domain of the sciences, Maslow found the social sciences in particular to be wanting in their treatment of persons:

> Briefly put, it appears to me that science and everything scientific can be and often is used as a tool in the service of a distorted, narrowed, humorless, de-eroticized, de-emotionalized, desacralized, and de-sanctified *Weltanschauung*. This desacralization can be used as a defense against being flooded by emotion, especially the emotions of humility, reverence, mystery, wonder, and awe. (1966, p. 139)

For some scientists, particularly those who work in the "personal" sciences of psychology, sociology, and anthropology, classical scientific method may serve the function of a defense mechanism. By abstracting, objectifying, and generally dehumanizing their human subjects, these scientific workers unconsciously seek to isolate themselves from the all-too-human failings, emotions, anxieties, and confusion they investigate in others (Maslow, 1966, p. 33).

> More than any other kind of knowledge we fear knowledge of ourselves, knowledge that might transform our self-esteem and our self-image. . . . While human beings love knowledge and seek it—they are curious—they also fear it. The closer to the personal it is, the more they fear it. So human knowledge is apt to be a kind of dialectic between this love and this fear. Thus knowledge includes the defenses against itself, the repressions, the sugar-coatings, the inattentions, the forgettings. (Maslow, 1966, p. 16)

Maslow suggested that, at least for some scientific workers, the acquisition of scientific knowledge about human persons is anxiety-instigated and therefore amounts to a "cognitive pathology." For example, when the need to know is based on a compulsive seeking after certainty rather than on enjoyment of discovery, it is pathological. Or, when individuals compulsively deny their doubts, ignorance, and mistakes, not from a position of knowledge but from a fear of confessing human fallibility, their scientific skills and knowledge are serving pathological ends. Or, when individuals feel that knowledge makes them "tough-minded," "hard-nosed," and "scientifically rigorous," they may defensively close themselves off to the tender, romantic, poetic, and spiritual aspects of the people they study.

Maslow summarized his view of the "desacralizing" tendency of some contemporary scientific efforts by indicating the directions that a new and more humanistic scientific enterprise should pursue:

> If humanistic science may be said to have any goals beyond sheer fascination with the human mystery and enjoyment of it, these would be to release the person from external controls and to make him *less* predictable to the observer (to make him freer, more creative, more inner-determined) even though perhaps more predictable to himself. (1966, p. 40)

Hence, for Maslow, the sciences, and psychology in particular, are value-laden enterprises in which the worth of the investigator becomes mingled with the virtue of the investigated.

The Effects of Peak Experiences

The B-values—Truth, Beauty, Goodness, Unity, and so on—that assume such significance for the self-actualized person are intensified in states of peak experience. The individual who has undergone such moments comes away from them feeling that the world "looks different." Maslow isolated 16 aftereffects of the peak experience. The person who has undergone a peak experience feels

1. more integrated, whole, and unified;
2. more at one with the world;
3. as if he or she were at the peak of his or her powers, more fully her or himself;
4. graceful, without strain, effortless;
5. creative, active, responsible, self-controlled;
6. free of inhibitions, blocks, doubts, self-criticisms;
7. spontaneous, expressive, innocent;
8. creative, self-confident, flexible;
9. unique, individualistic;
10. free of past and future limits;
11. free of the world, free to be;
12. undriven, unmotivated, nonwishing, beyond needs;
13. rhapsodic, poetic;
14. consumed, finished, closed, complete, subjectively final;
15. playful, good-humored, childlike;
16. lucky, fortunate, grateful.

(Based on Maslow, 1962, pp. 97–107)

In short, the peak experience is evidence that

Man has a higher and transcendent nature, and this is part of his essence, i.e., his biological nature as a member of a species which has evolved. (Maslow, 1971, p. 349)

HUMANISTIC PSYCHOLOGY: THE THIRD FORCE

Both Maslow and the second theorist we consider in this chapter, Carl Rogers, considered themselves to be *humanistic psychologists.* Humanistic psychology emphasizes human capacity for goodness, creativity, and freedom. Unlike the strictly deterministic and somewhat mechanistic views of humans to be found in Freud's psychoanalysis and in contemporary behaviorism, humanistic psychology construes the human being as a spiritual and rational, purposeful and autonomous creature. Maslow expressed this view in the preface to his definitive work:

> If I had to condense the thesis of this book into a single sentence, I would have said that *in addition* to what the psychologists of the time had to say about human nature, man also had a higher nature and that this was instinctoid, i.e., part of his essence. And if I could have had a second sentence, I would have stressed the profoundly holistic nature of human nature in contradiction to the analytic—atomistic—Newtonian approach of the behaviorisms and of Freudian psychoanalysis. (1970, p. ix)

Thus Maslow's theory represents an alternative to the two major shaping forces of contemporary psychology found in behaviorism and in Freudian psychoanalysis. For this reason, the work of Maslow and Rogers, and many others, has been christened "third force" psychology to emphasize its stature as a viable and equally comprehensive viewpoint. Toward the end of his life, Maslow emphasized that he had not intended a "sophomoric" two-valued orientation of being either pro-Freudian or anti-Freudian, or probehaviorist and antibehaviorist. He felt, rather, that he had embodied the best of both of these viewpoints and had gone beyond them to a psychology of transcendence (1971, pp. 3–4).

One evidence of his transcendent thinking was his vision of a psychological utopia in which healthy, self-actualized people would live and work in harmony. Called *Eupsychia,* this utopia would represent an attempt to blend what is godlike in our nature to what is most fully human, to actualize what Maslow saw as our inherently good being.

For Maslow, Eupsychia would attempt to provide the environment in which humans could become totally what they are (1970, p. 277).

CARL ROGERS

PSYCHOTHERAPIST AS SELF-ACTUALIZATION FACILITATOR

Unlike Maslow, Rogers began his study of human nature with troubled personalities. As a clinical psychologist, Rogers explored the human's potential for change in the therapeutic relationship. In the knotted, defensive, and anxious verbal stream of his patients, Rogers, too, found that psychological disability results when persons are prevented from being what they truly are.

Rogers's personality theory emerged slowly from his careful and exacting psychotherapeutic studies. He was among the first therapist-researchers to capture the cloistered conversation of the psychotherapeutic relationship on wire recordings in immutable and repeatedly observable form. (Recording sound on a thin thread of wire was the antecedent of the modern metallic-oxide-coated recording tape.) Along with the willingness to commit the process of therapy to scientific scrutiny, Rogers pioneered a pervasive change in the way the clinical relationship could be used to induce personality change and in the ways personality data could be derived from the relationship.

Consider the following fragments of two recorded counseling interviews with college students. They are printed side by side to facilitate direct comparisons. The left-hand transcript is of a client and a therapist who view the therapeutic situation as structured, problem-centered, and under the direct control of the therapist. The right-hand column contains the transcript of a similar client-therapist interview in a situation with a counselor who recognizes that therapeutic processes are very much person-centered.

The Key Difference: Focus on Feelings

There are significant and easily discernible differences between the two counseling interviews. The essence of the directive counselor's effort is information gathering and dispensing. The flow of communication between counselor and client tends to be one way: from counselor to client. Responsibility for the direction and outcome of the relationship implicitly lies with the authoritarian counselor. Restricted to the role of question answerer, the client is led through a series of diagnostic queries and away from any confrontation with his or her feelings, confusions, anxieties. To the degree that client feelings are mentioned at all, they are *talked about* rather than genuinely experienced or forthrightly made the focus of concern. The counselor goes so far as to summarize by assuming the "wise knower" role: "It seems to me that your problem is you want to learn more about yourself." It is a rational, perhaps even correct statement. But it is the counselor's statement; the client is reduced to a series of noncommunicative "Mm-hm's."

The second counseling transcript is immediately striking by its different emotional flavor. Most outstanding of these differences is the sheer wealth of feelings that the client is encouraged to express. In all replies, with different degrees of success, the counselor attempts to respond to the emotional content of the client's statements rather than to the cognitive or informational aspects of the situation. The nondirective counselor tried to respond to the troubled *person* by helping him or her to clarify his or her feelings: "It's a situation you've really got to face"; or, "It'll be fairly hard for you to tell them." When the counselor is successful in detecting the emotional meaning of a client remark, these rephrasings of the client's statements allow the client to examine his or her feelings "out in the open." When the counselor is unsuccessful at mirroring the emotional tone of the client's statements, the client sometimes feels that the counselor is "putting words into my mouth," or that he or she missed the boat completely. But even when mistaken, the counselor's attitude communicates to the client a genuine, if fallible, concern to understand the world as the client sees it.

The differences between these two counseling interviews are only a small sample of the insights about the counseling relationship systematized by Rogers. His development of a personality theory is so inextricably interwoven with his clinical therapeutic work that some consideration must be given to the slow development of what Rogers came eventually to call *client-centered counseling and theory* as a replacement for the original "nondirective" label.

DIRECTIVE COUNSELING
TRANSCRIPT

COUNSELOR: I noticed that you stated you enrolled in Psychology 411 [study habits course] because you didn't know how to study well enough—uh—and then I checked over the problem list, and I saw that you went rather heavy on—you worried about low grades and poor memory and so on. How well did you do in high school?

STUDENT: Well, I was just an average student.

COUNSELOR: And what major did you have there?

STUDENT: Ah, you mean—

COUNSELOR: In high school, you took college preparatory or commercial?

STUDENT: It was an academic course. I took languages and English and history.

COUNSELOR: What course did you like the best? [Student presumably answers; later in session counselor summarizes:]

COUNSELOR: It seems to me that your problem is that you want to learn more about yourself. We'll be getting all these tests back, and there are

NONDIRECTIVE COUNSELING
TRANSCRIPT

STUDENT: I haven't written to my parents about this at all. In the past they haven't been of any help to me in this respect, and if I can keep it away from them as much as possible, I'll do so. But there's a slight matter of grades to explain, and they're not good, and I don't know how I'm going to explain without telling them about this. Would you advise me to tell them about it?

COUNSELOR: Suppose you tell me a little more about what you had thought about it.

STUDENT: Well, I think I'm compelled to, because—

COUNSELOR: It's a situation you've really got to face.

STUDENT: Yes, there's no use getting around it, even if they can't take it the way they should, because I've already flunked my gym course, I just haven't come. . . .

COUNSELOR: It will be fairly hard for you to tell them.

STUDENT: Yes. Oh, I don't know if they're going to sort of condemn me. I those [study] projects, and the way we do, I see you each week at this time and you'll begin to get a little better picture—and then I'll help you check it and I'll tell you if it's right—(Laugh)

STUDENT: Mm-hm.

COUNSELOR: So we can work it out. I would suggest—I would more or less work this project out because you say you are having difficulties concentrating. . . .

(From Rogers, 1942, pp. 116–117)

think so, because that's what they've done in the past. . . .

COUNSELOR: You feel that they'll be unsympathetic and they'll condemn you for your failures.

STUDENT: Well my—I'm pretty sure my father will. My mother might not. He hasn't been—he doesn't experience these things; he just doesn't know what it's like. . . .

COUNSELOR: You feel that he could never understand you?

(From Rogers, 1942, pp. 135–136)

DEVELOPMENT OF THE NONDIRECTIVE VIEWPOINT: CLIENTS ARE PEOPLE

In 1974, as part of his address to the American Psychological Association on the occasion of receiving its Distinguished Professional Contribution Award, Rogers traced his impact on psychology. In particular, he formulated from his perspective of nearly half a century of therapeutic work the kernel of the central hypothesis that had initiated and guided his theoretical development:

> . . . the gradually formed and tested hypothesis [was] that the individual has within himself vast resources for self-understanding, for altering his self-concept, his attitudes, and his self-directed behavior—and that these resources can be tapped if only a definable climate of facilitative psychological attitudes can be provided. (1974a, p. 116)

The similarity with Maslow's conception of human nature is obvious. Both theorists regard humans as inherently good, as self-directed, and as striving toward increased autonomy. Rogers's theory, then, can be understood as the attempt to discover the conditions that foster the individual's utilization of *his or her own* powers for health and understanding.

Early Pragmatism: "If It Works, Do It"

Rogers began his career as a clinical psychologist trained in the hard-nosed empiricism of Columbia University. He was granted an internship at the newly founded Institute for Child Guidance while in doctoral training, and in the atmosphere of this clinic Rogers was exposed to a multiplicity of theoretical viewpoints. Members of the staff at the guidance clinic were largely Freudian and psychodynamic in their orientation, and the contrast to the statistical, objective atmosphere of Columbia made Rogers feel ". . . I was functioning in two completely different worlds,' 'and never the twain shall meet' " (1961, p. 9; cf. 1974c, p. 7).

The conflict of intellectual traditions was an important learning experience for Rogers, opening him to the possibility that experts differ drastically in their inter-pretations. Before completion of his doctorate, Rogers obtained a position in the Child Study Department of the Society for the Prevention of Cruelty to Children in Rochester, New York (1961, p. 9). For the next 12 years, Rogers was engaged in the application of psychological services to delinquent and underprivileged children. Many of the staff of the Rochester facility were trained in the Philadelphia School of Social Work and operated from the neopsychoanalytic viewpoint developed by Otto Rank. For some indication of Rank's theoretical orientation, the second epigraph at the beginning of this chapter is helpful, as well as this representative statement of Rank's views:

> I conceive of human help for the individual not as a planned method of psycho-therapeutic techniques with respect to a control of his stimuli and responses but as *his experiencing of the irrational forces within himself* which he has not heretofore dared to express spontaneously. (1941, p. 47; italics added)

Rogers later commented in a conversation with J. T. Hart that his own early emphasis on responding to the feelings of the client sprang from the influence of Rank and his followers at the Rochester facility (Rogers, 1966, in Hart & Tomlinson, 1970, p. 515). Most important of all, however, was the lesson to be learned from his colleagues' atti-tude toward therapeutic technique: "There was only one criterion in regard to any method of dealing with these children and their parents, and that was, 'Does it work?' " (1961, p. 10).

The lesson on pragmatism was reinforced for Rogers when his careful dynamic prodding and questioning to uncover the sexual conflicts of a young delinquent client did not prevent the boy from getting into the same difficulty with the law. On probation after therapy with Rogers, the boy again succumbed to his "propensity to set fires" (1961, p. 10). Rogers's trust in expert opinion thus received another damag-ing blow.

Insight Into the Dignity of the Individual Person: A "Failure"

Another influence that shaped Rogers's slowly developing theoretical formulations occurred during an interview with a client's mother. The boy was something of a "hel-lion," and Rogers could clearly see that the mother's early rejection of the boy was responsible. Despite repeated attempts at directing her flow of conversation toward the attainment of this insight, he could not accomplish a successful breakthrough. His report of the experience is particularly instructive:

> Finally I gave up. I told her that it seemed we had both tried, but we had failed. . . . She agreed. So we concluded the interview, shook hands, and she walked to the door of the office. Then she turned and asked, "Do you ever take adults for counseling here?" When I replied in the affirmative, she said, "Well then, I would like some help." She came to the chair she had left, and began to pour out her despair about her marriage, her troubled relationship with her husband, her sense of failure and

confusion, all very different from the sterile "case history" she had given before. Real therapy began then. . . . (Rogers, 1961, p. 11)

From this experience of "failure" Rogers learned an important lesson about the nature of the ideal psychotherapeutic experience and about the dignity of the person: ". . . it is the *client* who knows what hurts, what directions to go, what problems are crucial, what experiences have been deeply buried" (1961, pp. 11–12). Thus Rogers slowly came to the viewpoint that authoritative, directive, and diagnostically oriented psychological service was far less important than allowing the client to speak freely, feel freely, and think freely. Freud had come to much the same conclusion when Fräulein Elisabeth objected to his constant probing. But Freud developed a rather different conception of the person and his or her motives than Rogers was now developing (cf. Chapter 2).

PERSONAL SOURCES OF ROGERS'S EMPHASIS ON PERSONAL FREEDOM AND SELF-WORTH

Rogers's theory of personality, like other humanistic approaches, such as Maslow's or Allport's, stresses the dignity and worth of the individual. The accent is on the inherent capacity of the person to direct his or her own life when the interpersonal environment provides sufficient freedom from subtle and overt coercion. In Rogers's view, the primary, indeed essential, ingredient of the well-lived life is, simply, the freedom to be.

The core of Rogers's approach to personality is the belief that every individual requires freedom from coercion, from, as Karen Horney, too, had written, his or her "shoulds" and "oughts." The source of this viewpoint lay in Rogers's own coercive existence in a religiously and morally severe family.

Soda Pop as Sinful: Masters of Subtle Control

Carl Rogers was born in 1902 in a Chicago suburb as the fourth of six children of parents he described as "highly practical, 'down to earth' individuals" (Rogers, 1967b, p. 344). His father had completed an engineering degree and some advanced graduate work; and his mother had finished two years of college. Despite their relative high educational achievement, Rogers describes his parents as being "rather anti-intellectual, with some of the contempt of the practical person toward the long-haired egghead" (1967b, p. 344). Both parents were hard workers, convinced that there was no virtue higher than hard work and no problem that could not be solved by even harder work.

The family atmosphere was shaped by Rogers's mother, who was extremely religious. Among her frequently uttered biblical expressions were "Come out from among them and be ye separate"; and, "All our righteousness is as filthy rags in thy sight, oh Lord."

> The first [saying] expressed her conviction of superiority, that we were of the "elect" and should not mingle with those who were not so favored; the second her conviction of inferiority, that at our best we were unspeakably sinful. (Rogers, 1967b, p. 344)

The main result of such conflicting convictions was a pervading sense in the Rogers's family children that they were specially set apart from other families' children, and that most typical enjoyments were faintly "sinful." For example, Rogers reports that "I have a hard time convincing my [own] children that even carbonated beverages had a faintly sinful aroma, and I remember my slight feeling of wickedness when I had my first bottle of 'pop' " (1961, p. 5).

Rogers remembers both parents as extremely loving and "masters" of the art of subtle control. "I do not remember ever being given a direct command on an important subject, yet such was the unity of our family that it was understood by all that we did not dance, play cards, attend movies, smoke, drink, or show any sexual interest" (1967b, p. 344). But Rogers had some regrets. He felt for a time that his parents cared more for his next older brother than for himself, and he created the common fantasy that he therefore must be the adopted child of the family. Or, considering the range of "subtle" controls, perhaps it was wishful thinking.

The main result of this stringent upbringing was that Rogers had little social life. Yet his family independence of spirit and mixed superiority and inferiority combined somehow, in Rogers's recollection of it, to prevent the isolation from being burdensome. By high school age, however, some signs of the strain were becoming apparent. Parental demands had made it imperative to return immediately home after school to do chores:

> . . . I made no lasting associations or friendships. . . . I was a good student and never had any difficulty with the work. Neither did I have problems in getting along with the other students so far as I can recall. It is simply that I knew them only in a very surface fashion and felt decidedly different and alone, but this was compensated for by the fact that my brother and I went together much of this time and there was always the family at home. (Rogers, 1967b, p. 347)

Young Rogers's chief distraction from this sparse existence was the escape into books. He describes himself as a "dreamy," absentminded youth whose retreat into fantasy and reading troubled his parents (1967b, p. 345). The tendency to become lost in books continued through high school, and Rogers reports that he never even had a "real" date with a girl until his junior year, when he nervously asked a girl he had admired "from afar" to a school dinner-dance.

In the summer before entering college, Rogers's father secured a job for him in his own brother's lumber mill in North Dakota. With some graduation money Rogers bought a set of beautifully bound books. Throughout the summer, he worked arduously in the lumber camp without social enjoyments. But each evening he would bury himself in his newly acquired leather-bound treasures. "I realize that I lived in a world of my own, created by these books" (1967b, p. 348). With this self-created compensation, Rogers's enforced social isolation and somewhat barren childhood and youth had become tolerable to him. He learned firsthand what independence and self-responsibility could mean. Some years later, on the eve of a profound personal conflict over the issue of personal independence, Rogers evidenced the hardened, determined side of his character when he wrote in his diary of his decision to take charge of his own life, "to forge it into the kind of weapon I plan to make it" (quoted by Kirschenbaum, 1979, p. 36).

The Break With Religious and Parental Authority

During Christmas vacation of his college sophomore year, Rogers pursued his religious interests by attending a conference of student volunteers for evangelical work. "I decided at this conference that I should change my life goal and go into Christian work. . . . Having made this decision, agriculture no longer seemed to be a very suitable field. I felt that I should shift to some subject which would prepare me for the ministry. . . ." (1967b, p. 350). In his junior year of college, Rogers was selected as one of ten students to travel to Peking, China, as representatives of the World Student Christian Federation. The other members of the group were mostly young intellectuals with far more liberal backgrounds than Rogers's own. The long period of travel by ship provided Rogers with much needed social intercourse and intellectual broadening. Characteristically, he kept a journal of his personal reactions to his new acquaintances. He sent a copy to a girl he had been seeing and who was to become his fiancée upon his return. But he also, no doubt deliberately in some form of rebellion, sent a copy to his family:

> Since we did not have the benefit of airmail it took two months for a reply to arrive. Thus I kept pouring out on paper all my new feelings and ideas and thoughts with no notion of the consternation that this was causing in my family. By the time their reactions caught up with me, the rift in outlook was fully established. Thus, with a minimum of pain I broke the intellectual and religious ties with my home. (Rogers, 1967b, p. 351)

It is difficult to accept the tone of this account at face value. For one thing, considering the authoritarian nature of his childhood and the severity of his previous social isolation, it is unlikely that the break with family ties was either as nonchalant or as painless as Rogers implies.

The key element in the "rift" with his family, furthermore, centered on a rather symbolic issue of authority. One evening, aboard ship, a traveling companion, Dr. Henry Sharman, a student of the sayings of Jesus, made some provocative remarks. "It struck me in my cabin that perhaps Jesus was a man like other men—not divine! As this idea formed and took root, it became obvious to me that I could never in any emotional sense return home" (1967b, p. 351). Hence Rogers was able to transcend his family and religious ties with one stroke: by coming to the realization that Jesus was a man. In the act of demystifying divine authority, Rogers had freed himself from the bonds of parental authority.

The emotional price paid for this newly won freedom was high, despite Rogers's protestation that the rift was accomplished with minimal pain. After return from the Orient, Rogers experienced abdominal pains that led to hospitalization for duodenal ulcers:

> Something of the gently suppressive family atmosphere is perhaps indicated by the fact that three of six children [in our family] developed ulcers at some period in their lives. I had the dubious distinction of acquiring mine at the earliest age. (Rogers, 1967b, p. 352)

Rogers was apparently unable to see the internal contradictions in his account. "Gently suppressive" atmosphere does not produce ulcers. Describing the "rift" as accomplished with a "minimum of pain" falls into the same category of minimizing emotional conflict. Employing "gently suppressive" to describe what sounds like an authoritative and joyless family atmosphere gives some indication of the intensity of his conflict. Even during the period of medical treatment for his ulcers, "it was of course expected, by me as much as by my parents, that I would work" (1967b, p. 352; see, however, the somewhat less critical interpretation of this incident in Kirschenbaum, 1979, p. 31).

In 1924 Rogers married his sweetheart and set out to study for the ministry at Union Theological Seminary in New York. Union Theological Seminary had then, as it does now, a reputation for liberality, the kind of radical liberalism that Rogers's father found uncomfortable:

> Knowing my plan to go to Union, my father had made one offer which was very close to a bribe. I suspect he was not proud of himself afterward for this. Certainly I rejected it indignantly. He told me that he would pay all the expenses for both of us if I would go to Princeton Seminary, which was at that point a center of fundamentalist thinking. (Rogers, 1967b, p. 353)

Having mastered the break with his family, Rogers struck out for independence. Eventually, he transferred to Columbia University to study psychology. During this period a child was born to Rogers and his wife, and they attempted to raise him by "the book of Watsonian behaviorism, strict scheduling and the like" (1967b, p. 356). Rogers's recent experience with freedom had not yet worked its way down to the second generation.

Personal Experience of Psychotherapy

Some years after he received his doctoral degree in psychology, Rogers became the head of the counseling center at the University of Chicago. It was during this period that he experienced even more profound personal distress. A deeply disturbed schizophrenic woman threatened him with the depth of her psychotic disorganization. He recalls that he handled the case badly, vacillating between warm permissiveness and a cool, professional attitude to stave off personal threat.

> I stubbornly felt that I *should* be able to help her and permitted the contacts to continue long after they had ceased to be therapeutic, and involved only suffering for me. I recognized that many of her insights were sounder than mine, and this destroyed my confidence in myself, and I somehow gave up *my* self in the relationship. (Rogers, 1967b, p. 367)

Slowly, Rogers realized that he was approaching a complete emotional breakdown. Turning the client over to a colleague, Rogers left with his wife on a three-month "runaway" trip. But the trip did not resolve his feelings of worthlessness as a therapist. Upon return, Rogers entered therapy with a willing member of his professional group at the university counseling center. His description of that encounter lucidly reflects his personal philosophy of therapy and of personality:

> I am deeply grateful that one member of our group simply told me that it was obvious I was in deep distress, that he was not afraid of me or my problems, and he was offering me a therapeutic relationship. I accepted in desperation and gradually

worked through to a point where I could value myself, even like myself, and was much less fearful of receiving or giving love. . . .

I have often been grateful that by the time I was in dire need of personal help, I had trained therapists who were persons in their own right, not dependent upon me, yet able to offer me the kind of help I needed. I have since become rather keenly aware that the point of view I developed in therapy is the sort of help I myself would like, and this help was available when I most needed it. (Rogers, 1967b, pp. 367–368)

It is clear that the central themes of Rogers's formulation of a theory of personality stressing freedom to be self-actualized, and his theory of psychotherapy stressing the creation of an atmosphere of permissiveness and warmth, have deep roots in his personal bout with coercion and authoritarian family management. The client who faces Rogers in therapy finds himself confronted with a warm, evenhanded, nonevaluative person sincerely attempting to understand his client's meanings. Perhaps for the first time in his or her life, a Rogerian client discovers that in the presence of another human being, he or she is fully free to be. As Atwood and Tomkins (1976, p. 171–172) have pointed out:

The main dilemma faced by human beings in the theoretical world of Carl Rogers is constituted by all those interpersonal forces and pressures . . . which obstruct the emergence of what he calls the actualized and fully functioning person, and this reflects the oppressive circumstances of his own childhood.

Rogers's personal dilemma became the foundation for the nondirective undoing of many persons' dilemmas.

EARLY NONDIRECTIVE VIEW: TOO MUCH FREEDOM

In 1940 Rogers accepted a position with Ohio State University to teach graduate students about counseling. As he taught, he was forced to focus his views more sharply, in the process forming a perspective of psychotherapy that was unique. Up to this point, Rogers had felt that he was simply writing and teaching about clinical techniques that all clinicians were using (1959, p. 187). But when invited to deliver a lecture to the Psi Chi chapter at the University of Minnesota entitled "Newer Concepts in Psychotherapy," Rogers soon discovered from the furor and controversy the lecture aroused that he was indeed saying something new (1974c, p. 8).

From the Minnesota lecture, Rogers derived the second chapter of his book on counseling from the nondirective viewpoint. In *Counseling and Psychotherapy* (1942), Rogers emphasized four important principles of the "new" psychotherapy:

1. The newer therapy "relies much more heavily on the individual drive toward growth, health, and adjustment. Therapy is not a matter of doing something *to* the individual, or of inducing him to do something about himself. It is instead a matter of freeing him for normal growth and development . . ." (1942, p. 29).
2. ". . . this newer therapy places greater stress upon the emotional elements, the feeling aspects of the situation, than upon the intellectual aspects" (1942, p. 29).

3. "... this newer therapy places greater stress upon the immediate situation than upon the individual's past" (1942, p. 29).
4. The newer approach "... lays great stress upon the therapeutic relationship itself as a growth experience.... Here the individual learns to understand himself; to make significant independent choices, to relate himself successfully to another person in a more adult fashion" (1942, p. 30).

Thus the central concept in Rogers's first formulation of his views was that people have within themselves the capacity to solve their own problems, as previously pointed out. The task of the therapist is to establish the conditions that allow people to attain this insight themselves: *Attainment of insight* was, therefore, one of the key goals of nondirective therapy in the 1940s. To enable the client to achieve self-insight, the counselor's chief tool was the *clarification of feelings* through rephrasing the emotional content of the client's statements (cf. Hart, 1970, pp. 6 ff.). Rogers summarized his early view of the counselor's role in this way:

> *Effective counseling consists of a definitively structured, permissive relationship which allows the client to gain an understanding of himself to a degree which enables him to take positive steps in the light of his new orientation.* (Rogers, 1942, p. 18, emphasis in original)

Though controversial, Rogers's techniques and philosophy were widely adopted by practitioners who failed to sort out the philosophy from the techniques. The problems that followed in the application of nondirective therapy were due in part to two crucial aspects of this early formulation: (1) Little or no *explicit* theory had been developed to guide the counselor's efforts; (2) In the hands of an unskilled or inadequately trained therapist, the permissive and accepting attitude was construed by his clients as a threatening "don't care" attitude or as a directionless, disorganized relationship. Rogers felt that the difficulty lay in the tendency of some counselors to interpret his formulations too literally (1951, p. 26). In effect, some counselors supposed that their role was to be merely passive and to adopt a laissez-faire policy: "the passivity and seeming lack of interest . . . is experienced by the client as a rejection, since indifference is in no real way the same as acceptance" (Rogers, 1951, p. 27).

CLIENT-CENTERED THERAPY: EMPATHIC UNDERSTANDING

The first phase of Rogers's development of his position emphasized the warmth and acceptance of the counseling relationship. Too much acceptance, too much freedom for the client had proved to be a problem. In 1951, however, Rogers published a second major work on counseling, more carefully delineating his views. The book's title, *Client-Centered Therapy,* was meant to emphasize the new rationale of his approach: "The client, as the term has acquired its meaning, is one who comes actively and voluntarily to gain help on a problem, but *without any notion of surrendering his own responsibility for the situation*" (Rogers, 1951, p. 7n.; italics added).

Thus the publication of *Client-Centered Therapy* marked the beginning of a second phase in Rogers's thinking (cf. Hart, 1970). The focus had shifted to the counselor's efforts to be *emphatic* in understanding the client's world, and to the *communication* of that understanding to the client. The technique of reflection of feelings, though present from the first nondirective period, now assumed more importance. Reflection of feelings was not merely to be used to help the client attain insight and clarification of his or her emotions, but also to communicate the counselor's understanding of the client's inner world. In mirroring back the client's feelings, the counselor simultaneously transmits the desire to perceive the world as the client perceives it. In effect, the goal of the counselor is to achieve the *internal frame-of-reference* of the client:

> . . . it is the counselor's aim to perceive as sensitively and accurately as possible all of the perceptual field as it is being experienced by the client . . . and having thus perceived this internal frame of reference of the other as completely as possible, to indicate to the client the extent to which he is seeming through the client's eyes. (Rogers, 1951, p. 34)

Thus, by 1951, two of the three major elements that characterize Rogers's view of personality were present to his thinking. First was the necessity for the counselor to provide a warm and permissive relationship; second was the necessity for the counselor to assume the internal frame of reference of the client and to communicate emphatic understanding of the client's world.

EXPERIENTIAL THERAPY: THE CONDITIONS OF PERSONALITY CHANGE

The third element characteristic of Rogers's view of personality emerged during the third aspect of the development of client-centered theory. Hart (1970) and Gendlin (1964, 1968, 1970) have characterized this phase of Rogers's and their own work as the "experiencing" phase or as *experiential therapy.*

The focus had again shifted by 1957 to a *mutual expression of feelings* by both client and counselor. *Experiencing* became the technical term to describe the internal, directly felt emotional processes that the client and counselor struggle to put into words. Because tangled and latent feelings are the core of psychological maladjustment in Rogers's view, the tasks of learning to experience one's own distorted and trapped emotions and of learning to communicate them to oneself and to counselor became the central goals of experiential therapy.

One of the key causes of this shift in emphasis from pure verbal transactions to direct emotional experience can be found in a research effort undertaken by Rogers and his colleagues at the University of Wisconsin. Working with nonverbal, often uncooperative, schizophrenic patients in a state hospital required the radical shift in therapeutic strategy (see Rogers, 1967a; Gendlin, 1966). If psychotherapy from the client-centered framework had been a verbal interchange between a willing client and a warmly accepting therapist, it now had to be something more direct, less verbal, and increasingly experiential.

Along these lines Rogers had already provided a theoretical rationale for personality change in therapy which implied that constructive alterations in personality could occur regardless of the specific verbal techniques employed by the counselor. If six operationally defined conditions of relationship were met, then *any* person-to-person contact embodying them could promote personality growth. The six conditions postulated by Rogers (1957) were

1. *Two persons are in psychological contact* so that each of them is aware, even if in only the dimmest fashion, that the other's presence makes a difference.
2. *The first person, the client, is in a state of incongruence,* being vulnerable or anxious. Incongruence means that a discrepancy exists between the client's self-image and his or her ongoing experiences, between the actor and the mask. Any experience that threatens the self-picture will be defensively distorted.
3. *The second person, or therapist, is congruent* or integrated in the relationship. Congruence means that the therapist is genuinely him- or herself, totally free to express what he or she actually feels, positive or negative, in the situation with the client. He or she is not, however, a paragon of virtue. It is only necessary that he or she be congruent or spontaneously real in the therapeutic relationship, including the ability to express feelings that are not particularly pleasing: "I am afraid of this client"; or "I am bored with this client."
4. *The therapist experiences unconditional positive regard for the client.* Unconditional positive regard means that the counselor warmly accepts the client in all of his or her "human facets." It is unconditional: no feelings of "I like you *if* you are thus and so." Rather, the counselor "prizes" the person without evaluation, recognizing that the client is an independent human being capable of his or her own valid experiences.
5. *The therapist experiences an empathic understanding of the client's internal frame of reference and endeavors to communicate this experience to the client.* In short, the counselor tries to see the world as the client sees it and to communicate that he or she does so. The counselor does not *experience* the client's feelings: He or she *understands* them. For the counselor, it is an "as if" cognitive act, not an emotionally involving one. He or she understands the client's emotions "as if" they were his or her own without ever losing sight of the "as if" quality.
6. *The communication to the client of the therapist's empathic understanding and unconditional positive regard must be minimally achieved.* If the client does not perceive acceptance and understanding, they do not exist for him or her.

When these six conditions are fulfilled in *any* relationship, intentionally therapeutic or otherwise, personality change in a positive, healthy direction will occur. Clients who experience these conditions will be more able to accept their feelings and perceptions freely as their own; they will grow to become those idealized images that they have never before dared to strive for overtly; they will become more autonomous in their decision making. The emphasis is clearly not on the counselor's technique, nor on the specifics of verbal interchange. Crucial to personality change is the quality of the directly experienced relationship.

PERSONALITY CHANGES EVOKED BY THE THERAPEUTIC RELATIONSHIP

Rogers and his colleagues formulated a conceptualization of the specific process of personality change that occurs when these six conditions exist between two persons. From hundreds of recorded therapeutic sessions and from his own experiences, Rogers was able to discern the basic similarities of the client's progressive changes in experience within the therapeutic relationship. Rogers proposed that such personality changes may be thought of as a seven-stranded process or continuum of experience. One end of the continuum is personality or experiential *rigidity;* the opposite end is *fluidity* or psychological flow (Rogers 1958, 1961). Clients with differing degrees of personality difficulty may be conceptualized as initially occupying different positions between the two extremes. As therapy progresses, the client progresses toward the fluidity end of the spectrum.

The first three phases through which clients pass involve their initial inability to see their difficulties, a gradual dim recognition that some problem exists, and a tendency once a problem is recognized to speak of themselves as objects without a real feeling. Thus the first three stages of personality change may be identified as

1. *Rigidity of Self-Perception:* no recognition of need to change self
2. *Dim Recognition of Problem:* problem exists in others, not self
3. *Self Treated as Object:* does not own his or her feelings

In the fourth stage, there is some movement in the direction of greater flexibility. But clients continue to discuss emotions of their past lives rather than as feelings they *now* experience. Some questioning of their own interpretations also occurs and consequently anxiety and distrust of their own perceptions begin to develop. This fourth or middle phase may be identified as

4. *Partial Recognition of Feelings:* tendency to treat feelings as colorless objects

In the last three phases of the process of personality change, the client progressively approaches accurate recognition and ownership of feelings, acceptance of self, with reevaluation of personal interpretations, and finally, in the seventh phase, genuine experiencing of feelings with richness and clarity. These last three phases of the process of personality change may be identified as

5. *Improved Recognition of Feelings:* feelings of wanting to be the "real me"
6. *Acceptance of Feeling with Richness:* self is free to "own" feelings
7. *New Feelings Experienced Freely:* self is totally flexible, trustworthy, and capable of change and growth

The seven phases outlined here provide an instructive scheme by which to understand Rogers's developing conception of personality. It is easy to see that Rogers views the psychologically maladjusted personality as one who is defensively rigidified, constricted in his or her experiencing of self, and conflicted in his or her willingness to "own" his or her feelings. To describe this phenomenon, Rogers, too, employed the metaphor of the actor and the mask, for the rigid, defensive person is adopting a series of false fronts or masks to deceive others and him- or herself. In the warm and accepting empathic relationship of psychotherapy, the person

> . . . begins to drop the false fronts, or the masks, or the roles, with which he has faced life. He appears to be trying to discover something more basic, something more truly himself. (Rogers, 1961, p. 109)

The task that remains is to explore how Rogers systematized these discoveries into an explicit theory of personality.

THE FULLY FUNCTIONING PERSON: IDEAL MENTAL HEALTH

From his experience in psychotherapy, and from the consistency of the changes he observed as his clients grew toward more personal freedom, Rogers formulated a concept of the ideally free and self-accepting person. He first committed his ideas to paper during the winter of 1952–53, but they were rejected by the journal editor to whom he submitted them. The paper was finally published in original form in 1964 (see also Rogers, 1961, Chapter 9), and it presented Rogers's view of what he called "the fully functioning person."

Troubled by the question of what constitutes mental health, Rogers approached the problem by trying to decide on the traits of a person who successfully completes psychotherapy. Surely such a person may be said to be "mentally healthy," and consequently may also be said to exhibit in his or her behavior the highest goals of optimal psychotherapeutic procedure. In effect, the therapy reflects on the health of the personality; the health of the personality is taken as an indication of the value of the therapy.

Rogers distinguished three primary characteristics of the person after successful therapy, and three secondary implications. First, the fully functioning person is *more fully open to experience* (1964, p. 18). He or she has become freed of the need to distort defensively both inner and outer reality and is able to listen perceptively and unanxiously to the demands of his or her body and mind. In effect, he or she finds that his or her self is less fragile, more assertive, and more able to voice his or her true feelings.

The second characteristic of the fully functioning person is his or her *ability to live in an existential fashion* (1964, p. 20). He or she lives each moment of life more spontaneously, enjoying the exuberance and the joy of seeing life as one new moment following another. The person realizes that "What I will be in the next moment, and what I will do, grows out of that moment, and cannot be predicted in advance either by me or by others" (1964, p. 20). In essence, the person's self emerges spontaneously from his or her experiences rather than being shaped by them. He or she transcends the boundaries of life by experiencing it fully rather than anxiously anticipating its pitfalls.

The third, and last, main characteristic of fully functioning people is their *increased trust in their own organisms* (1964, p. 20). They feel free to do what "feels right" at any given moment, fully expecting that they will prove competent to meet any challenge, judge accurately any obstacle, and regulate their behavior realistically as the situation demands. They are able to engage in these complex weighing, balancing, and computational processes because their trust in their own cognitive and emotional strengths is unfaltering.

Three secondary personality characteristics flow from this conception. First, fully functioning people grow *unafraid of their own feelings;* emotions become important but not overwhelming personal experiences. Second, because they live in an existential fashion, *they are not determined;* they are free either to be themselves openly or to hide behind a façade; but they make the decision. Third, with increased trust in their own cognitive and emotional processes, these people find themselves *more creative* in devising personal and objective relationships. They are independent of conformity pressure but are able to harmonize themselves with the needs of others because they find themselves trusting human nature in general more than the uncreative person can.

Rogers's concept of the fully functioning person is clearly similar to Maslow's notion of the self-actualized personality. Maslow used a greater range of descriptive terms than Rogers does, and Maslow's SA person seems slightly more autonomous with a possibility of ruthlessness. But, nevertheless, the two concepts can be profitably compared, as illustrated in Table 15.3.

TABLE 15.3   Rogers's Fully Functioning Person and Maslow's Self-Actualized Person Compared

Rogers's Fully Functioning Person	Maslow's Self-Actualized Person
1. More fully open to experience Unafraid of own feelings	1. Reality and problem-centered Accepting of self Unexpected ruthlessness
2. More existential living Nondetermined, independent	2. Spontaneity and simplicity Freshness of appreciation Discrimination between means and ends Need for privacy
3. Increased trust in own organism More creative, nonconformist	3. Acceptance of others Resistance to enculturation Creative Unhostile sense of humor More intimate personal relations *Gemeinschaftsgefühl* (social interest)

Note: Not all of Maslow's SA traits are listed here.
Based on Rogers, 1961, Chapter 9; and 1964; also on Maslow, 1970, pp. 153–176.

Self-Actualization: Phenomenal World of the Self

It is clear from Rogers's view of the psychotherapeutic relationship that he regards the individual's subjectively felt and interpreted experience as the fundamental psychological reality. As Rogers stated this proposition, *"Every individual exists in a continually changing world of experience of which he is the center"* (1951, p. 483). The individual's experience is his or her reality (1959, p. 222). Of course it is equally true that experience is private, restricted to the person's phenomenal world. For this reason, as we shall see, Rogers and his colleagues employed a variety of indirect measures to assess the individual's private world.

The Infant's Phenomenal World: Self-Actualization

The most basic, innate tendency of the human infant is a drive toward "actualizing his organism." Instead of postulating a long list of needs or drives, Rogers chose to hypothesize that most biological functions and psychological urges could be subsumed under one major heading: a need to maintain and to enhance one's life (1951, p. 488). For Rogers, as for Maslow, self-actualization is a rather inclusive concept:

> We are talking here about the tendency of the organism to maintain itself—to assimilate food, to behave defensively in the face of threat, to achieve the goal of self-maintenance even when the usual pathway to that goal is blocked. We are speaking of the tendency of the organism to move in the direction of maturation, as maturation is defined for each species. . . . [The organism] moves in the direction of limited expansion through growth, expansion through extending itself by means of its tools, and expansion through reproduction. It moves in the direction of greater independence or self-responsibility. (1951, p. 488)

In Rogers's description of self-actualization, we recognize the same basic processes of movement toward greater autonomy and self-trust that he had described for the microcosm of psychotherapy.

Like the psychotherapy process, self-actualization is a directional concept in Rogers's scheme, for the person tends to behave in ways that enhance his or her actualization tendencies and in ways designed to avoid situations that threaten self-actualization.

As the infant develops biologically, its psychological maturation tends to keep pace through its increasing self-awareness. Gradually, a part of the infant's phenomenal world becomes differentiated and recognized as "me," "I," or "myself." From the total global mass of perceptual stimuli, the infant learns slowly and cautiously to identify itself as an independent agent. Piaget's observations and Sullivan's concept of prototaxic experience considered in Chapter 9 are similar formulations (Rogers, 1951, p. 497; 1959, p. 233; see also Mahler and White in Chapter 5).

The Development of the Self-Structure: Threat

The infant develops its picture of "me" through its interactions with significant others. Much as Sullivan had described, Rogers indicated the importance of the child's sensitivity to the praise and blame of the adults in its world. These evaluations of its behavior are assimilated to the infant's self-structure, and as socialization continues, the perceptual field continues to grow in complexity. Many behaviors consistent with its parents' conception of what it should be will be praised; a variety of behaviors that are disapproved of by its parents will be punished or responded to by them with emotionally abrasive communications.

> [The child] . . . experiences words and actions of his parents in regard to these satisfying behaviors, and the words and actions add up to the feeling "You are bad, the behavior is bad, and you are not loved or lovable when you behave in this way." This constitutes a deep threat to the nascent structure of the self. The child's dilemma might be schematized in these terms: "If I admit to awareness the satisfactions of these behaviors and values I apprehend in these experiences, then this is inconsistent with my self as being loved or lovable." (1951, p. 500)

Thus, to preserve the continuity of parental love in its world, the child must fend off threats of withdrawal of that affection. In effect, much as Sullivan had postulated the Bad-Me and the Not-Me personifications of self, Rogers hypothesized that the infant must deal with those of its behaviors that arouse parental disapproval by removing both the threat and the motive for the behavior from its awareness. For example, the infant may distort its experience of the situation: "The accurate symbolization would be 'I perceive my parents as experiencing this behavior as unsatisfying to them.' The distorted symbolization, distorted to preserve the threatened concept of self, is '*I* perceive this behavior as unsatisfying' " (Rogers, 1951, p. 500).

In short, the child learns to experience reality secondhand. It adopts not its spontaneous feelings and perceptions as guides to its behavior, but the defensively safe feelings that maintain parental love and approval. Experience is thus distorted in the service of "self" survival. The self-structure becomes "an organized configuration of perceptions of self which are admissible to awareness" (Rogers, 1951, p. 501). Threatening self-perceptions are excluded.

Healthy Self-Structure Development

How is it possible for any infant ever to develop a healthy, spontaneously natural, self-concept? Rogers suggested that three *parental* characteristics foster healthy self-structure formation: (1) ability to accept the child's feelings and strivings; (2) ability to accept own feelings that certain of the child's behaviors are undesirable; (3) and communication of acceptance of the child as a person (based on Rogers, 1951, p. 502). The child who experiences a relationship with its parents based on the three previously listed qualities experiences no threat to itself as a loved or lovable person.

THE NEED FOR POSITIVE REGARD

As the self-structure develops, a need for positive regard grows in intensity. Positive regard is, of course, the experience of feeling accepted, loved, and "prized." The source of the infant's income of positive regard is located in others' evaluations of it.

Rogers added an important corollary to this fundamental tenet: The need for positive regard is reciprocal, for "when an individual discriminates himself as satisfying another's need for *positive regard,* he necessarily experiences satisfaction of his own need for positive regard" (1959, p. 223). Satisfying another's need for love and acceptance is in itself satisfying. Rogers's concept of the reciprocity of positive regard is similar to Sullivan's notion of the empathic linkage between mother and child (cf. Chapter 9). Rogers's description of the infant's developing need for positive regard bears quoting:

> The infant learns to need love. Love is very satisfying, but to know whether he is receiving it or not he must observe his mother's face, gestures, and other ambiguous signs. He develops a total gestalt as to the way he is regarded by his mother and *each new experience of love or rejection tends to alter the whole gestalt.* Consequently, *each behavior on his mother's part such as a specific disapproval of a specific behavior tends to be experienced as disapproval in general.* So important is this to the infant that he comes to be guided in his behavior not by the degree to which an experience maintains or enhances the organism, but by the likelihood of receiving maternal love. (1959, p. 225; italics added)

As Sullivan had suggested, a kind of emotional "hot and cold" game ensues. When the infant learns to steer its behavior in relation to its tendencies to maintain others' positive regard, it is simultaneously learning another important lesson: It discovers that it must treat itself in the same ways as it is treated by others. In more technical language, it must "introject" or internalize the evaluations of significant others. In so doing, it develops a capacity for *self-regard* (1959, p. 224).

The infant gradually acquires *conditions of worth.* That is, it "understands"—however dimly at first—that only under certain conditions is it positively esteemed by others, by itself in response to others, and most important, by its parents. Conditions of worth are thus the conditions (behaviors) that provide acceptance or provoke rejection.

INCONGRUENCE BETWEEN SELF AND EXPERIENCE

As Laing had emphasized the significance of a divided self in which experience and behavior are widely separated, Rogers, too, developed a notion of *self-incongruence.*

> Because of the need for self-regard, the individual *perceives* his *experience* selectively, in terms of the *conditions of worth* which have come to exist in him.
>
> a) Experiences which are in accord with his *conditions of worth* are *perceived* and *symbolized* accurately in *awareness.*
>
> b) Experiences which run contrary to the *conditions of worth* are *perceived* selectively and distortedly as if in accord with the conditions of worth, or are in part or whole, *denied to awareness.* (1959, p. 226)

In a way similar to Sullivan's proposal of a mechanism of selective inattention, Rogers suggested that the conditions of worth by which the individual has learned to navigate his or her world serve as selective filters in screening new experiences. Those experiences that are denied access to awareness because they violate the self-structure form the foundation of potential psychological maladjustment. For once the core of experience is discrepant with the self-picture and denied to awareness, the individual is vulnerable to anxiety every time a fresh experience threatens to trigger perception of the discrepancy.

Experiences that are threatening to one's self-structure are said to be "subceived." *Subception* means that the individual perceives the threat but does not admit it to full awareness in the higher cognitive brain centers (Rogers, 1959, p. 200; see also McLeary & Lazarus, 1949). Subception of threatening discrepancies between self-structure and new experiences begins the process of defensive personality disorganization.

PERSONALITY DISORGANIZATION

When for some persons the discrepancy between self-structure and experience becomes so great that subception no longer functions with complete success, the result is personality disorganization (Rogers, 1959, pp. 228–229). Such a contingency may arise if the perception of a threatening experience arises suddenly and so force-fully that denial is impossible. Because the perception is accurately symbolized in awareness, the gestalt of the self-structure is broken by the intrusion of discrepant data (Rogers, 1959, p. 229).

Rogers offered an example of this kind of maladjustment:

> . . . take the familiar picture of a mother whom the diagnostician would term rejecting. She has as part of her concept of self a whole constellation which may be summed up by saying, "I am a good and loving mother. . . ." With this concept of self she can accept and assimilate those organic sensations of affection which she feels toward her child. But the organic experience of dislike, distaste, or hatred toward her child is something which is denied to her conscious self. The experience exists, but it is not permitted accurate symbolization. . . . Since the good mother could be aggressive toward her child only if he merited punishment, *she perceives much of his behavior as being bad, deserving punishment, and therefore the aggressive acts can be carried through, without being contrary to the values organized in her picture of self.* (1951, pp. 511–512; italics added)

At times of great provocation, such a mother might scream at her child, "I hate you." But almost in the same breath she would rush to explain that "she was not herself."

Sometimes the individual experiences psychological maladjustment when the total self-structure is founded on the evaluations of others. Since these alien values have no genuine connection with the person's own experiences, he or she may perceive him- or herself as a "nothing," as a "zero" (Rogers, 1951, p. 512). Laing's concept of *implosion* and Horney's concept of extreme *detachment* are similar (cf. Chapter 10 and Chapter 13).

OPERATIONALIZING THE CONCEPT OF SELF: Q-SORT METHODOLOGY

Rogers's reliance on the concepts of self, self-incongruence, and ideal self emerged from his experiences with patients in therapy. Often, when he had allowed clients to express their problems in their own fashion, without guidance or interpretation, they would refer to the *self* as the core of their experience: "I feel I'm not being my real self";"I never had a chance to be myself"; or,"It feels good to let myself go and just *be* myself here" (1959, p. 201).

As a consequence of their therapeutic efforts, Rogers and several of his students and colleagues mounted an early research project to investigate the individual's changing conception of self in therapy (Rogers & Dymond, 1954). The process of psychotherapeutic change seemed to be directly expressible in terms of changes in the individual's *perceived self* and movement toward the *ideal self.*

At about the time that Rogers had begun to conceptualize the self as the key element in any description of the person's experience, a colleague at the University of Chicago, William Stephenson, developed a rationale and a statistical method uniquely applicable to a study of the phenomenal world of the self. Called a *Q-sort* technique, Stephenson's procedures were applied to a variety of social and personal processes (1953). Rogers and his research team adopted Q-sort methods to operationalize the conception of self.

Essentially, the Q-sort technique involves providing a person with a large number of written statements and asking him or her to sort them into a deliberately determined number of piles. The array of categories into which the subject places his or her statements are purposefully constructed to approximate a statistically normal distribution. Printed on cards, the statements describe various aspects of a person's self. In the most widely used version, the subject is asked to sort 100 statements into nine piles ranging from "least like me" to "most like me." Other variations involve the inclusion of additional categories:"what I most would like to become," or "what I most dislike about me." A typical arrangement of a Q-sort distribution looks like this (based on Dymond, in Rogers & Dymond, 1954, p. 77):

	Least Like Me			Undecided			Most Like Me		
Pile No.	0	1	2	3	4	5	6	7	8
No. of Cards (Total: 100)	1	4	11	21	26	21	11	4	1

The criteria by which the self-statement cards may be sorted are nearly limitless. One very instructive example of a subject's card sorting responses before and after therapy is provided in Table 15.4.

In the left-hand column of Table 15.4 is a small sample of "Mrs. Oak's" statements chosen as *most characteristic* of herself before therapy. In the right-hand column are her statements describing self after therapy. The bottom half of the table contains an additional sample of Q-sort statements that were chosen before and after therapy by Mrs. Oak as *least characteristic* of herself.

The items of Table 15.4 show that before therapy, Mrs. Oak regarded herself as driven, insecure, and disorganized. After therapy, by the time of the five-month follow-up interview, she viewed herself as more in control and more secure. The items that Mrs. Oak felt were least characteristic of herself before therapy included an ability to be independent and comfortable with others. After therapy, Mrs. Oak perceived herself to be less helpless and less guilty.

The correlation between the perceived self before and after therapy was low: .30. In another Q-sort, Mrs. Oak was asked to sort the items in order of importance to

TABLE 15.4   Mrs. Oak's Changes in Perceived Self in Terms of Q-Sort Statements

Before Therapy	After Therapy
"Most Characteristic"	
I usually feel driven.	I express my emotions freely.
I am responsible for my troubles.	I feel emotionally mature.
I am really self-centered.	I am self-reliant.
I am liked by most people who know me.	I understand myself.
I am intelligent.	I feel adequate.
"Least Characteristic"	
I feel comfortable while talking with someone.	I have few standards and values of my own.
I make strong demands on myself.	I feel helpless.
I am optimistic.	I often feel guilty.

From Rogers, in Rogers & Dymond, 1954, p. 275

her for the *person she would like to be,* thus providing an estimate of her ideal self. After therapy, Mrs. Oak again sorted the items in relation to her ideal self. The before self-ideal included "I feel emotionally mature"; "I can live comfortably with people around me"; "I am a rational person." The after self-ideal included the following items: "I understand myself"; "I express my emotions freely"; and, "I am poised" (Rogers, 1954, p. 274). The degree of similarity for Mrs. Oak's self-ideal before and after therapy was great: The correlation for before and after ideal selves was .72. The key question is whether Mrs. Oak perceived her actual self to have become more like her ideal self after therapy. The correlation between her perceived self and ideal self before therapy was .21, a very low degree of relationship. Thus before therapy Mrs. Oak perceived a large discrepancy between what she was and what she would like to be. After therapy, the correlation between her ideal self and her actual self—that is, the self she felt had become—was .69 at termination, and .79 within several months after therapy (1954, p. 282). Thus the Q-sort method had shown that Mrs. Oak felt herself to be more like her ideal self after therapy than before.

Rogers and his colleagues used a variety of other assessment techniques; but in all cases the client's consistent movement in the direction of greater freedom, more independence, and more congruence between perceived self and ideal self was measurably real.

EVALUATING ABRAHAM MASLOW AND CARL ROGERS

Both Maslow and Rogers were fiercely independent men, who in their different ways tilted at windmills. Both thinkers had their share of successes and failures as they struggled against established ideas drawn from behaviorism and psychoanalysis. Rogers, for example, was instrumental in the political fight for psychologists and social workers to practice psychotherapy alongside their medical colleagues. And Maslow struggled against depersonalizing educational institutions. We could say that both men lived the ideas they espoused.

Refutability of Maslow's and Rogers's Concepts

Maslow "grew up" in psychology in a largely empirical branch of the discipline, and for a time, even practiced a kind of naturalistic behaviorism. Rogers was one of the first, if not the very first, clinicians to open the doors of the consulting room and expose psychotherapy to scientific scrutiny.

Maslow created a great wealth of ideas, most of which lack the rigor and empirical referents that would permit them to be tested. Some of his ideas, in principle, are highly testable, such as the hierarchy of motivational needs, at least up to, but not necessarily including, needs such as the need for beauty, truth, and self-actualization. But on the whole, Maslow's humanistic psychology does not attract empirically minded psychologists to create empirical translations of his ideas. Said more simply, much of Maslow is intriguing philosophy but not testable psychology.

Rogers, as mentioned, opened the process of psychotherapy to research, and under his leadership, a whole program of empirically based research on the therapeutic process, the characteristics of the helping relationship and the characteristics of the helping person was done. Studies of empathy, warmth, directiveness versus nondirectiveness, pre- and post- measures of personality, and even attempts to use client-centered therapy to aid schizophrenic people have been researched. So, in the clinical side of the enterprise, Rogers gets high grades for stimulating hypothesis testing, and for refutable therapeutic concepts.

On the down side, the theory that underlies Rogers's clinical practices is frequently vague, subjective, and not tied to empirical referents. Concepts such as the phenomenal self, conditions of worth, and "fully functioning" person are untestable in the form in which they exist in Rogers's theory. That is not to say that they are doomed to this status eternally. Rather, with considerable effort and creativity, some of these concepts could be translated into operations that lend themselves to measurement. The difficulty seems to be that few psychologists are willing to test Rogers's *theory,* although many have tested his clinical strategies.

Maslow and Rogers's Conception of Human Agency

It is fairly obvious from their humanistic stance that both theorists regard people as capable of active decision making. Rogers, early on, was even reluctant to take a clinical history with his clients or perform diagnostic testing because he felt strongly that whatever information would be needed in treatment would emerge as the client decided to communicate it. Maslow argued that human motivation is more of a "pulling" *toward* goals than it is a "pushing" by human drives. People set their own standards and discover their own paths to achieving them. When life events intervene to block pursuit of self-chosen goals, the person is frustrated but no less free to make new decisions. In short, both Maslow and Rogers picture people as active determiners of their lives rather than as passive receptacles of reality.

The Idiographic Nature of Humanistic Psychology

Rogers's theory is largely a phenomenological model of human personality, which is to say that its focus is on the subjective meanings a person lives by. Maslow, in his own way, emphasizes the same kind of subjectivity for all but the truly self-actualized personality. Almost by definition, humanistic psychology must focus on the individual and prize uniqueness above all else. Although Maslow and Rogers aspired to decipher nomothetic, even universal, "laws" of human existence, neither of their personality *theories* has sufficient empirical content to generate nomothetic principles.

COMPARATIVE SUMMARY

Carl Rogers and Abraham Maslow developed rather similar self-actualization conceptions of personality. Maslow's interests in psychological health seem to have emerged from his early work on dominance-feeling in infrahuman primates and from his interview research of dominant women. Rogers, on the other hand, developed his conceptualization of the self-actualizing nature of human motivation from his experiences in psychotherapy. For each theorist, however, an acutely felt personal inferiority and lack of self-worth were the guiding life experiences that shaped their theories of human nature.

Maslow's central concept is the growth of health-striving character of human personality. Proceeding through a hierarchy of basic needs, the individual progresses toward ultimate health and fully spontaneous expression of the self. At the lowest level of the hierarchy are the physiological needs such as hunger and thirst. These having been satisfied, the individual's behavior becomes directed by his or her needs for safety, then by needs for love and esteem. Finally, when these basic motives have been fulfilled, the need for self-actualization—to be fully what one can be—emerges.

Rogers discovered essentially the same rule of human growth from his observations of clients in therapy. In the earliest stages of his work, Rogers's central concern was to allow clients to feel warmly accepted and fully free to express themselves. Slowly, Rogers developed this nondirective orientation to include the necessity for the counselor to enter the client's phenomenal world or internal frame of reference. In order for constructive personality change to occur, the counselor must communicate an understanding of the client's internal frame of reference to the client.

Maslow's conceptualization of the self-actualizing person as independent, creative, and growth-motivated corresponds to Rogers's notion of the fully functioning person who emerges from a successful psychotherapeutic relationship. Maslow has gone further than Rogers in one respect. Specifically, Maslow has postulated that the self-actualizing person embarks on a further course of metamotives. These Being-values, as Maslow termed them, include the classic virtues like beauty, truth, justice, honesty, and freedom. When denied or frustrated, these B-values show evidence of being innate, for the frustrated individual succumbs to metapathologies.

In Maslow's theory, the motor of personality is the drive toward self-actualization, toward psychological health, toward fully accepted humanness. In Rogers's theory, the same innate striving toward enhancement and expression of one's spontaneous urges and feelings constitutes the fundamental layer of personality. In both theories, psychological maladjustments are the product of learned tendencies to subvert or block the inner self core, the spontaneous and natural expression of self.

Our evaluation of Maslow and Rogers indicates that both theorists constructed largely nonrefutable theories, although Rogers's clinical work did produce empirically testable therapeutic strategies. Human agency, from the viewpoint of both theorists, is active rather than passive, and, as we might expect from phenomenologically oriented thinkers such as these, both theories are focused on uniqueness and idiographic issues.

FOR FURTHER READING

Maslow's definitive statement of his position may be found in *Motivation and Personality* (New York: Harper & Row, 1970), 2d ed. His early papers on dominance-feeling with primates have been collected into a single volume by J. Lowry and entitled *Dominance, Self-Esteem, Self-Actualization: Germinal Papers of A. H. Maslow* (Monterey, CA: Brooks-Cole, 1973). A collection of Maslow's later papers, including a semiautobiographical account of the sources of his interest in self-actualization, is *The Farther Reaches of Human Nature* (New York: Viking, 1971). Sometimes bitter, sometimes ironic, Maslow's criticism of classical scientific method in application to persons may be found in his *The Psychology of Science: A Reconnaissance* (New York: Harper & Row, 1966). The collection of papers in Chiang and Maslow's (Eds.) *The Healthy Personality* (New York: Van Nostrand, 1977), demonstrates the application of humanistic psychology to a wide variety of fields and provides accounts of some of the personal sources of Maslow's, Rogers's, and Allport's humanistic learnings.

William James's lectures on mystical experience bear a strong similarity to Maslow's views on peak experiences. James's very readable lectures are to be found in *The Varieties of Religious Experience* (New York: Random House, 1902). For Maslow's own account of peak experiences, see *Religions, Values and Peak-Experiences* (New York: Viking, 1964). The collection of papers in R. May, E. Angel, and H. F. Ellenberger's (Eds.) *Existence: A New Dimension in Psychiatry and Psychology* (New York: Basic Books, 1958) retains its value as a thorough grounding in the history and current practice of existential psychology. A rather novel and somewhat critical view of humanistic psychology is provided by Hans Eysenck in "Reason with Compassion," *The Humanist* (March/April, 1971), 24–25.

Two of Rogers's early works adequately set forth his initial strategy and philosophy: *Counseling and Psychotherapy* (Boston: Houghton Mifflin, 1942) and *Client-Centered Therapy* (Boston: Houghton Mifflin, 1951; available in paperback). To bring Rogers's perspective on theory and therapy up to date, two recent volumes should be consulted. The first of these is a collection of research and theory papers edited by J. T. Hart and T. M. Tomlinson under the title *New Directions in Client-Centered Therapy* (Boston: Houghton Mifflin, 1970) and is, perhaps, the better of the two. The second collection of papers is to be found in David Wexler and Laura North Rice's (Eds.) *Innovations in Client-Centered Therapy* (New York: Wiley, 1974).

Rogers's definitive statement of his position is given by him in "A Theory of Therapy, Personality and Inter-Personal Relationships as Developed in the Client-Centered Framework," in S. Koch (Ed.), *Psychology: A Study of a Science,* Vol. III, *Formulations of the Person in the Social Context* (New York: McGraw-Hill, 1959). A more up-to-date survey of Rogerian method and philosophy is provided by Betty Meador (with Rogers's collaboration) in "Client-Centered Therapy," in Raymond Corsini (Ed.), *Current Psychotherapies* (Itasca, IL: Peacock, 1973), Chapter 4. A personally revealing account of Rogers's early career may be had in *On Becoming a Person* (Boston: Houghton Mifflin, 1961). *Carl Rogers on Personal Power* (New York: Delacorte Press, 1977) contains Rogers's updated views on the self-actualization motive and its political implications for personal knowledge.

Rogers's own expansion of his ideas to the field of marriage and to other two-person intimate relationships may be found in his *Becoming Partners: Marriage and Its Alternatives* (New York: Dell, 1972). The efficacy and process of encounter groups are treated to a sympathetic examination by Rogers in *Carl Rogers on Encounter Groups* (New York: Harper & Row, 1970). An interview with Rogers, along with a reprint of his ongoing debate with B. F. Skinner and one of his previously unpublished papers, are to be had in R. I. Evans's *Carl Rogers: The Man and His Ideas* (New York: Dutton, 1975). The interview in condensed version may also be found in Evans's *The Making of Psychology* (New York: Knopf, 1976). Howard Kirschenbaum has written the first full-scale biography of Carl Rogers with Rogers's and his wife's cooperation, but *On Becoming Carl Rogers* (New York: Delacorte Press, 1979) is marred by its atmosphere of uncritical hero worship. Rogers's autobiography (in E. G. Boring and Gardner Lindzey's *A History of Psychology in Autobiography,* vol. 5, New York: Appleton Century, 1967) is far more revealing. For comparison purposes, you might want to consult R. D. Laing's theory in Chapter 10. This existential thinker shares much with Maslow and Rogers's humanistic approach.

J. B. WATSON, B. F. SKINNER,
NEAL MILLER AND JOHN DOLLARD,
& ALBERT BANDURA

The Behaviorisms

In conclusion won't you then remember when you are tempted to pet your child that mother love is a dangerous instrument? An instrument which may inflict a never healing wound . . .

> J. B. Watson, *Psychological Care of Infant and Child*

I am sometimes asked, "Do you think of yourself as you think of the organisms you study?" The answer is yes. So far as I know, my behavior at any given moment has been nothing more than the product of my genetic endowment, my personal history, and the current setting. That does not mean that I can explain everything I do or have done.

> B. F. Skinner, *A Matter of Consequences*

At a recent cocktail party . . . [I] was cornered by an inquiring lady who expressed considerable puzzlement over adolescents' fascination for unusual and bizarre styles. The lady herself was draped with a sack, wearing a preposterous object on her head, and spiked high heel shoes that are more likely to land one in an orthopedic clinic, than to transport one across the room to the olives.

> Albert Bandura, "The Stormy Decade: Fact or Fiction?"

About the Behaviorisms

Radical behaviorism began with John B. Watson's declaration of independence from introspectionistic psychology. Watson wanted to make psychology a science, so he radically eliminated any attempt to study "mind" or other unobservable variables.

Following in this tradition, B. F. Skinner elevated radical behaviorism to a major orientation in psychology. Studying the behavior of single organisms in situations where their actions were instrumental in obtaining a desired effect, Skinner developed a reinforcement theory of action without resort to "inner" mental mechanisms.

Despite Watson and Skinner's insistence on the exclusion of mental variables, other behaviorists found the need to take account of what people think about their behavior. Miller and Dollard, Albert Bandura and others developed a more cognitive behaviorism where the focus is on the person's expectations and assumptions, and the capacity for people to learn by observing others.

In this chapter, the conceptual history of behaviorism's development is selectively traced by focusing on variables of interest to students of personality. Watson and Skinner would take a dim view of their work's inclusion in a book on a subject they felt they had removed from psychology.

J. B. WATSON

THE TRADITION OF RADICAL BEHAVIORISM

Freudian and humanistic solutions to the puzzles of personality demand a conscious and unconscious mind. To explain the self-division apparent in hysterical symptoms, disavowed wishes, and human anxiety, the theorists we have studied thus far picture the human mind as the inner cause of a person's actions. From Freud through Rogers, personality puzzles were solved by assuming that thought and action can oppose each other, but that *thought* causes action. John B. Watson (1878–1958), the founder of behaviorism, found such solutions puzzling.

"The time seems to have come," wrote Watson in his characteristically rebellious way, "when psychology must discard all reference to consciousness; when it need no longer delude itself into thinking that it is making mental states the object of observation" (1914/1967, p. 7). In contrast to Freud's concern with hidden wishes and thoughts, Watson chose to study only what people do:

> The behaviorist asks: Why don't we make what we can *observe* the real field of psychology? Let us limit ourselves to things that can be observed, and formulate laws concerning only those things. Now what can we observe? We can observe *behavior—* what the organism says or does. . . . (Watson, 1924/1930, p. 6)

Watson was reacting to the introspectionist tradition in psychology that preceded him, a tradition that emphasized the importance of mental states uniquely accessible in human beings by virtue of our capacity for self-report (Buss, 1978). The puzzles of conflicting personal meanings struck Watson as largely irrelevant to the aims of scientific psychology. In fact, Watson found any form of the psychological enterprise that focused on mental events to be unscientific and foolishly naive. But what aroused his scorn perhaps more than any other philosophical position was Freud's insistence on unconscious sexual and aggressive motives as the causes of human behavior.

To Watson, Pavlov's (1927, 1928) recently published work on the conditioned reflex held the scientific key to all complex human action. Mental states, especially unconscious ones, if they existed at all, were irrelevant to the scientific behaviorist. The Watsonian behaviorist could explain even emotional responses as chains of conditioned associations with demonstrable causal links between the stimuli and the responses. Table 16.1 summarizes the main Pavlovian concepts.

The way in which Watson understood Pavlovian conditioning was to think of the process—no sarcasm intended—as largely automatic and involuntary. Animals and people could acquire conditioned behaviors without their awareness or their understanding provided the right stimulus and response were carefully paired. Whether mental processes inside the organism somehow mediated this pairing of the world's stimuli with the organism's responses was a question Watson felt he could confidently ignore (Bandura, 1974; Shevrin & Dickman, 1980). Watson even made the extravagant claim:

> Give me a dozen healthy infants, well formed, and my own specified world to bring them up in and I'll guarantee to take any one at random and train him to become any type of specialist I might select—doctor, lawyer, artist, merchant-chief and yes, even beggarman and thief, regardless of his talents, penchants, tendencies, abilities, vocations and race of his ancestors. I am going beyond my facts and I admit it, but so have the advocates of the contrary and they have been doing it for many thousands of years. (Watson, 1924/1930, p. 104)

For Watson, human beings are so malleable and so trainable by proper manipulation of environmental stimuli that any behavior can be acquired or changed through conditioning. In light of this naive environmentalism, his dismissal of mental states as causal in human psychology is not surprising.

So strong was Watson's belief in the power of conditioning to shape human behavior without mediating mental events that he turned to a study of human newborns "to catalog the birth equipment of the human young" before life circumstances laid in their convoluted pattern of conditioned behaviors. He hoped to show that the infant's increasingly complex repertoire was acquired through the accumulation of layers of conditioned responses on an initial base of rudimentary reflex behavior.

PERSONAL SOURCES OF WATSON'S RADICAL BEHAVIORISM

Admitting to a strong negative reaction toward maternal expressions of affection, Watson confessed: "When I hear a mother say 'Bless its [sic] little heart' when it falls

TABLE 16.1 **Summary of Key Pavlovian Concepts**

1. UNCONDITIONED STIMULUS (UCS): *Unlearned Input* — Before conditioning, this event reliably and automatically triggers a response that does not require prior experience with the stimulus.

EXAMPLE: AIRPUFF to eyelid elicits a full eyeblink.

UCS (airpuff) $\rightarrow$ UCR (full eyeblink)

2. UNCONDITIONED RESPONSE (UCR): *Unlearned Output* — Before conditioning, this behavior, usually a reflex, is reliably and automatically elicited by the UCS.

EXAMPLE: Airpuff to eyelid elicits a full EYEBLINK.

UCS (airpuff) $\rightarrow$ UCR (full eyeblink)

3. CONDITIONED STIMULUS (CS): *Learned Input* — Before conditioning, CS is a neutral event and elicits no reliable response; but arranged so that CS precedes UCS by a fraction of a second for a number of trials, the CS will evoke a response that resembles the UCR in anticipation of the UCS, but which is reduced in magnitude and slower in response time.

EXAMPLE: Tone comes before airpuff 20 times and then elicits a REDUCED, SLOWER EYEBLINK without the airpuff on 21st trial.

For 20 times: CS (tone) + UCS (airpuff) $\rightarrow$ UCR (eyeblink)

Then on 21st trial: CS (tone) $\rightarrow$ CR (reduced eyeblink)

4. CONDITIONED RESPONSE (CR): *Learned Output* — Learned response elicited by the CS in anticipation of the UCS; but the CR only resembles the reflex UCR because its magnitude and latency (response time) are reduced.

EXAMPLE: Tone that comes before airpuff elicits a REDUCED EYEBLINK.

CS (tone) $\rightarrow$ CR (reduced eyeblink)

5. EXTINCTION: — Withholding the UCS (airpuff) while presenting the CS repeatedly (tone) until the CS no longer elicits the CR (reduced eyeblink). Organism stops blinking at the sound of the tone.

---

down, or stubs its toe, or suffers some other ill, I usually have to walk a block or two to let off steam" (Watson & Rayner, 1928, p. 82). Kissing, cuddling, and patting a child on the head constitute a "dangerous experiment" conducted by mothers who themselves are "starved for love." Such maternal "interference," Watson believed, robs the child "of its opportunity for conquering the world. . . ."

This cosmic parental malfeasance is "coddling," an emotional indulgence that deprives the child of precious time during development to learn how to conquer its world. The infant "must have time to pull his [sic] universe apart and put it together again" (Watson & Rayner, 1928, pp. 79 and 80). Instead, Watson encouraged mothers to treat their children in this more "sensible" way:

Treat them as though they were young adults. Dress them, bathe them with care and circumspection. Let your behavior always be objective and kindly firm. Never hug and kiss them, never let them sit in your lap. If you must, kiss them once on the forehead when they say good night. Shake hands with them in the morning. Give them a pat on the head if they have made an extraordinarily good job of a difficult task. (Watson & Rayner, 1928, pp. 81–82)

Emotions as the Behaviorist Fails to Feel Them

Watson's view of people—especially children—as infinitely malleable, nearly feeling-less creatures was chillingly reflected in deliberate "observations" he made with his own children. The father and mother described in the following excerpt from Watson's book *Behaviorism* are Watson and his second wife Rosalie Rayner Watson. The child "B" is Billy, the older of their two sons (Buckley, 1989). Watson was "observing" the origins of "jealousy":

The first sign of jealousy was noted in child B at about 2 years of age. It shows whenever the mother embraces the father, clings to him, kisses him. At 2 1/2 years of age this child . . . began to attack the father whenever the mother embraced the father. He [i.e., the child] (1) pulled at [the father's] coat, (2) cried out "my mama," (3) pushed his father away and crowded in between them. . . . At 3 years of age this boy was sent with his infant brother to his grandmother's. . . . He was separated from his mother for one month. During this time his strong attachment for his mother weakened. When the parents visited the child (then 37 months of age) no jealous behavior was exhibited when they made love in front of him. . . . The father then seeing the old situation failed to call it out, tried next attacking the mother, striking her on the body and head and shaking her from side to side. She on her part simulated crying, but fought back. The youngster stood this for a few minutes, then started in for his father tooth and nail and would not let up until the fight was over. (Watson, 1924/1930, pp. 189–190)

It is painful to read this passage and disquieting to comprehend the depth of Watson's insensitivity and lack of empathy. His method of provocation in studying his own child's emotions is callous and treats Billy as though he were a feelingless object. Indeed, the expression of feeling—the very notion of powerful emotions—troubled Watson from the beginning to the end of his life (cf. Buckley, 1989, pp. 120–121). His solution, reached early on, was to conceptualize feelings in himself and in others as habits that could be controlled by self-discipline or as literal behavior-objects that one could navigate around. Sometimes Watson got a hint of the distress others felt when he pushed them too far:

Next the father remained passive while the mother attacked him. She inadvertently punched below the belt, causing the father to double up in no simulated way. Nevertheless, the youngster started his attack on his father again, and continued it even after he was *hors de combat.* By this time the youngster was genuinely disturbed and the experiment had to be discontinued. (Watson, 1924/1930, p. 190)

Should we take Watson at his word? Rosalie's punch below his belt was "inadvertent"? The image bears pondering. More important, Watson is seemingly oblivious to the astonishing fact that his son continues to attack *him* even though the *attacker* is the child's mother and Watson is *"hors de combat"* (disabled). Watson terminates the "observation" because Billy has become "genuinely disturbed."

Watson's Childhood: Long-Suffering Mother, Explosive Father

Born fourth among six children in 1878, John Broadus Watson was named for John Albert Broadus, a prominent South Carolina Baptist minister-theologian. Emma Roe Watson, Watson's mother, prayed and hoped avidly that her son John would follow in his namesake's footsteps to a career in the ministry (Buckley, 1989, p. 4). Her influence shaped John's ambitions until nearly the end of his college years when he applied to Princeton Theological Seminary. Yet hers was an aspiration that John Broadus Watson found uncongenial by the end of adolescence, cleverly sabotaged by the time of his college graduation, and openly despised through adulthood (Watson, 1936).

Pickens Butler Watson, Watson's father, was somewhat of a notorious character in South Carolina. He left home at age 16 to enlist in the Confederate Army, where his reckless behavior earned him a reputation for bravado and impulsiveness. Excessively fond of whiskey and brawling, Pickens's explosive anger found targets among family, friends, and neighbors. He was an erratic, possibly abusive, spouse and an unpredictable, explosive, and frequently absent father. Pickens Watson's marriage to Emma Roe alienated him even further from his own family because the elder Watsons felt that Emma's social standing was far below their own (Buckley, 1989, p. 3). From the outset, the newly married couple was ostracized by the Watsons, and those family ties were never renewed. Isolation and poverty in a rural community were all that Emma and her children could anticipate.

By the time of John Broadus Watson's birth, Emma and Pickens Watson were virtually social outcasts. Pickens Watson was shunned by the neighbors for his aggressive, impulsive behavior. He failed at farming and at a number of other jobs, and eventually took to being a "wanderer" who would return only occasionally and only briefly (Buckley, 1989, p. 3).

> Such a father, whose absences were long and whose unpredictable presences were often volatile, had a lasting effect on Watson. As an adult, he rarely spoke of his father, and then only with resentment. Years later, when Watson had achieved a measure of success and fame, his father traveled the long distance to New York in a vain attempt to visit his son, whom he had not seen in decades. Watson responded by sending the old man a new suit of clothes—a gesture perhaps calculated to emphasize the gulf between their social circumstances—but he absolutely refused to see his father, thereby completing the circle of ostracism begun by his grandparents two generations before. (Buckley, 1989, pp. 3–4)

Emma Watson's strong religious faith served her well in the face of these difficult circumstances. She wanted more for her children than the life of poverty, loneliness, and adversity they were living. In 1890, she sold the farm and moved the family to Greenville, South Carolina, where better educational and economic opportunities might be found. Compared to the simpler rural community they had escaped, Greenville was a wonder of social and industrial activity.

Upward mobility has a cost. The young John's rural ways and naiveté made him the butt of his classmates' jokes. As a consequence, he earned a despised nickname of

"Swats" for his propensity to get in fights with his tormentors and others (Buckley, 1989, p. 7). He might have been the target of his classmates' cruelty, but Watson found scapegoats for his anger in what he called "Nigger fighting." It became one of his favorite after school activities (Buckley, 1989, p. 7). Like his father, John Broadus Watson became notorious for his unpredictable and aggressive behavior. He was arrested once for fighting with blacks, and a second time for discharging firearms within the city limits. As his biographer Kerry Buckley concludes, Watson's adolescence was a troubled time (1989, p. 7).

Watson's College Years: Arrogance Fed by Ambition

In 1894, at the age of 16, Watson entered the college prep program of Furman University. At that period, there were no public high schools in South Carolina and colleges offered "sub-freshman" programs for those students wanting to continue their education (Buckley, 1989, p. 9). Watson was an ambitious adolescent who clearly wanted to escape the contemptible poverty from which he had only partially emerged, and college was the path to that goal. Watson graduated 14th in a class of 22 from Furman in five years, earning both his undergraduate and master's degrees. He was remembered by one professor as a bright student but also as a "person who thought too highly of himself" (Buckley, 1989, p. 11).

In his autobiography, Watson (1936) tells a revealing story about his relationship with one of his professors. Gordon B. Moore, who had studied at the University of Chicago under John Dewey, was Watson's psychology professor. According to Watson, Moore told his class that any student who turned in his final examination with its pages in reverse order would fail the course. Watson, of course, did just that and promptly failed. Graduation was now delayed for at least a year. His biographer suggests that the story may be in part fictional, but it does reflect Watson's ambivalent attitude toward success. "Watson's constant striving for achievement and approval was often sabotaged by acts of sheer obstinacy and impulsiveness more characteristic of a flight from respectability" (Buckley, 1989, p. 12). Professor Moore himself was frequently engaged in disputes with the university and the church authorities who governed it. Not surprisingly, Watson seems to have genuinely admired and imitated this model of unconventional behavior. But Watson also fantasized the revenge that someday he would earn his Ph.D. in psychology and Professor Moore, who did not have a doctorate, would have to apply to him to earn it. As it happened, Watson's fantasy nearly came true years later when Moore did indeed apply to Watson at the University of Chicago but became ill and died before the fantasy was actualized.

Watson may have had other motives for arranging not to graduate from Furman University that year. He had, in accord with his mother's wishes, applied to and was accepted at Princeton Theological Seminary (Fancher, 1992, p. 288). By provoking Moore (or by colluding with him) to fail the exam, Watson postponed and eventually derailed altogether any plans for a seminary education and career in the ministry.

For a brief time after graduation, Watson worked as principal of Batesburg Institute, a private academy where Watson quickly grew tired of the tedium of enforcing trivial regulations (Buckley, 1989, p. 14). During this period, his mother became ill and after a protracted term of suffering, Emma Roe Watson died. Watson's interest in remaining in South Carolina ended with his mother's death. He burned to make something important of himself, as his mother had also wanted, but the most appealing route was preparation for a "profession" rather than a vocation in the less prestigious ministry.

Within three weeks of her passing, in July of 1900, Watson composed a letter to the president of the University of Chicago, trying to coax from him acceptance to the school as a graduate student. He described himself in the letter as poor but eager to do "advanced work in a real university" (Buckley, 1989, p. 15). Watson even convinced the president of Furman University to write a strong letter of recommendation for him, noting Watson's strength, his experience in education, and his "high character." The president of the University of Chicago granted Watson a scholarship, and the future founder of radical behaviorism found his footing on the first rung up the ladder of academic success he wanted so passionately.

Watson in Academia: Toward the Breaking Point

Initially attracted to philosophy, Watson's ambition drove him toward earning a professional degree that would confer prestige as well as a way to earn a living. He recalled angrily in his autobiography that he could not afford to enter medical school and his hopes for the prestige of the M.D. degree were blocked (Watson, 1936, pp. 273ff.). His interests turned in the direction of science, psychology, and education, areas of experience he had brought with him to Chicago.

The University of Chicago provided an intellectual milieu where the newly emerging experimental psychology could blossom in the laboratory study of the white rat. Watson took courses with Jacques Loeb, the eminent evolutionary behaviorist who insisted that scientific knowledge was the road to understanding and controlling the behavior of organisms. Unlike his earlier studies of philosophers, Watson's work with Loeb and other psychologists "took" and the seeds of radical behaviorism were being sowed "night and day" in Watson's extended series of experiments with the white rat.

In the year before he earned his doctorate, Watson's carefully managed work habits and precision self-control ground to a halt. He was working several jobs at once to support himself and simultaneously struggling to be a star student in the department. At around the same time, Watson was rejected by a young woman with whom he was in love. As a result, Watson experienced what he later called a "breakdown," or a "typical *angst*" (Watson, 1936). The symptoms he reported appear to be what now would be termed a generalized anxiety disorder and an agitated depression or dysthymic disorder (see the clinical nosology in Chapter 1). He endured weeks of not being able to sleep, followed by a need to have the lights on during those few times when he could sleep. Long walks and attempts to busy himself in academic and laboratory work, not to mention the passage of time, eventually brought an end to his anxiety attacks.

Characteristically, Watson rationalized a silver lining for this dark experience because it taught him to accept a "large part" of Freud's ideas, just as it had taught him to "watch his step" (Watson, 1936, p. 272ff.; Buckley, 1989, pp. 43 – 44). Watson's solution to his distress was to act rather than reflect. This characteristic coping style began in childhood and did not fail Watson now. He reinvested himself more fully in his work, and this pattern of action-oriented engagement with both physical and intellectual labor during times of stress marked the rest of Watson's life.

Watson's biographer (Buckley, 1989, pp. 43–44) suggests that at least part of the cause of Watson's "breakdown" was his discovery that his new professional world was fraught with competition. Driven by ambition, undermined by insecurity and fears of failure, and able to embrace success only halfheartedly, Watson found that his self-discipline and obsessive self-control were overwhelmed by his conflict, anxiety, and uncertainty. Small wonder that Freud began to make sense to the father of behaviorism. Despite his misgivings, Watson was recapturing the insight that he, too, was vulnerable.

Watson the Romantic

On the personal side, Watson's life at the university was chaotic. He presented himself as a daring, charming romantic, but privately deeply distrusted intimacy in any form (Buckley, 1989, p. 49). In somewhat cynical fashion, Watson courted young women who were impressionable and "deeply awed" by him—at least initially (Buckley, 1989, p. 49). On the rebound at the end of one such romance, Watson interested himself in 19-year-old Mary Ickes, a student at the university who may even have been a student in one of the introductory psychology classes that Watson taught. Mary's brother, Harold Ickes, an attorney, despised Watson and made no secret of his feelings. Harold profoundly distrusted Watson and thought that he was nothing more than an "unprincipled social climber" (Buckley, 1989, p. 51).

Consequently, Watson and Mary Ickes were secretly married in 1903. They did not live together for the first year of their marriage because her brother Harold intervened to separate them and sent Mary to live with an aunt. Apparently Harold Ickes was under the impression that Watson and Mary were only engaged to be married. During this time, the young woman who had previously rejected Watson returned. For a period of time, they "saw a great deal of each other," but eventually saw the futility of their relationship. Watson publicly (re)married Mary Ickes in 1904 and confessed the entire episode to his bride, admitting that his behavior had not provided "a very good foundation for marriage" (Buckley, 1989, p. 50). For once, Watson had it right—more painfully so than he could have then guessed.

Watson received his doctorate from the University of Chicago in 1903 at the age of 25 and became the University's youngest Ph.D. For the next four years Watson worked as an instructor in psychology, but other professional offers were coming in for this pioneer in animal psychology. Eventually through shrewd negotiation he received an offer from Johns Hopkins University for a full professorship at a salary of $3,500, a very large sum for the day. Watson set out for Baltimore to make psychological history and personal notoriety by founding radical behaviorism and provoking the divorce trial of the century.

Watson's marriage was not going well. Highly suspicious of Watson, Mary's brother Harold Ickes arranged to manage her financial affairs. Watson was infuriated and the result was open warfare that damaged Watson, Harold, and Mary. The Watsons had two children, a son and daughter, during the 16 years of their marriage. But Watson's romantic interests tended to wander. His "old flame" reappeared in the picture sometime during 1906–1907, and Harold Ickes hired a private detective who reported that Watson was seeing this woman regularly (Buckley, 1989, p. 55). Watson denied everything. Ickes nevertheless tried to persuade his sister to divorce Watson, and he even tried to have Watson fired from the University. Ickes failed at both enterprises thanks to the intervention of one of Watson's colleagues at the University, but Watson—with astounding arrogance and lack of gratitude—blamed his colleague for the good deed, rationalizing that it would probably have been better had the marriage ended then (Buckley, 1989, p. 55).

By 1913, Watson was ready to publish his famous paper declaring the birth of the new orientation of radical behaviorism in psychology. This paper—"Psychology as the Behaviorist Views It"—would give Watson the national prominence he had worked so hard to obtain, and its significance will be discussed later in this chapter.

Love and Hate as the Behaviorist Views Them: End of a Career

During the winter of 1919–1920, Watson and his graduate assistant Rosalie Rayner began work on conditioned emotional reactions with the infant "Little Albert B." in a series of rather primitive studies destined to add to Watson's fame. This work is described in more detail later in the chapter. For the present, it is sufficient to note that Watson regarded these experiments as definitively demonstrating that emotions were simple acquired conditioned reflexes and therefore completely controllable by the behavioristic psychologist! Publicly, at least, Watson's reputation was nearing its zenith. He was, at this time, the most influential psychologist in American psychology. But disaster was on the horizon.

Watson and Rosalie Rayner were romantically involved. As Watson's biographer aptly described it, "It was characteristic of Watson to be at once capable of sustained, concentrated, controlled behavior and impulsive, spontaneous outbursts of emotion" (Buckley, 1989, p. 123). In this instance, Watson carried poor judgment and impulsivity beyond what his personal and professional community could tolerate. The affair became public and led to a nightmare of newspaper stories and a divorce trial that fed them. Rosalie Rayner and Professor John B. Watson made the ideal couple for a scandal. Rosalie's family was prominent in the Baltimore community's political and economic life. Rosalie herself was young, a graduate student, adventurous, and determined. Watson was a prominent professor at Johns Hopkins and the founder of behaviorism. The stage was set, of course, for marital trench warfare, and Mary Watson's brother, Harold Ickes, became involved for a final assault on Watson.

Mary Watson was still embittered from her husband's earlier romantic liaisons, and she contrived to steal some of Watson's love letters to Rosalie Rayner during a visit to the Rayner home. The resulting divorce negotiations, fueled by the purloined love letters—at least one of which was published in the newspapers—and divorce trial resulted in the destruction of Watson's academic career. He was shunned by former colleagues, but Watson had seen scandal in academia before and probably thought he could ride out the storm. He was slow to realize that his chances of resuming any kind of university career were next to nil. To say that Watson was embittered and soured on academia when he finally grasped the depth of his difficulties is the grossest understatement.

Watson and Rosalie Rayner were married in 1920, after Watson's divorce became final. In the meantime, Watson had worked at pulling together the scattered debris of his life. Eventually, he secured a position with the prestigious advertising agency of J. Walter Thompson, where he brought to bear on the marketing of commercial products the same tenacity, hard-nosed empiricism, and behavioristic philosophy that had proven so successful in changing the face of psychology. Watson was a success in this business because the pragmatic style of his behaviorism was well suited to promoting product appearances while ignoring substance. But he continued to write popular and professional psychology books and articles that kept his name before the public and the academic community.

In a way, Watson was traveling two roads at once. One view is that Watson brought psychology to advertising, and he used the techniques of advertising to bring his brand of psychology to a mass audience (Buckley, 1989, p. 147). However, toward the end of his life, Watson told an interviewer over some noteworthy doses of whiskey that "psychology was irrelevant and had no effect on his [advertising] work" (Burnham, 1994, p. 68). Watson felt that advertisers were fairly rigid about their techniques, and he believed that he had little personal freedom to do other than just follow their routine ways of doing business. Coon (1994) provided some support for Watson's minimalist (perhaps depressive) view of his effect on advertising in her analysis of pre-Watson and post-Watson advertising for Pond's Facial Cream, one of Watson's accounts. It appears that, indeed, Watson made use of techniques, such as emotional appeal and "real life" testimonials to sell the product, that one could certainly rationalize as originating in or compatible with radical behaviorism. But Coon (1994) cautions that these same techniques were already in use in ad campaigns for the same product well before Watson came on the scene. Blamed for introducing unsavory "behavioristic" methods into advertising, Watson's own view of "just going along with established methods" is probably closer to the truth.

In 1935, after 15 years of marriage, Rosalie Rayner Watson died suddenly of pneumonia. Watson sent the children away to a camp and returned the following morning. The children learned of their mother's death from the cook, and Watson's youngest son recalled that it was the only time he could remember seeing his father cry (Buckley, 1989, p. 180). After his wife's death, Watson buried himself in work and drink. He withdrew more and more into social isolation. Watson left the J. Walter Thompson Company and joined the William Esty Company until his retirement in 1945. He continued to withdraw, working all hours of the day and night on his farm in western Connecticut in a splendid self-imposed isolation from all that had gone before. He had come full circle—back to the rural life of isolation and all-consuming physical labor from which he came.

His older son Billy, of the two sons he had with Rosalie, entered a difficult adolescence and frequently quarreled bitterly with his father (Buckley, 1989, p. 181). Billy decided to become a psychiatrist after graduation from college, a choice that alienated him from his father even more. Within four years of John Watson's death, this son committed suicide.

Shortly before his death in 1958 at the age of 80, John Broadus Watson burned his lifetime collection of correspondence, manuscripts, and research notes in the fireplace of his farmhouse. When his secretary protested the loss to history, he replied, "When you're dead, you're all dead" (Buckley, 1989, p. 182).

Transitional Summary: Watson Radically Shaped Behaviorism

What do the details of John Broadus Watson's life tell us about his radical behaviorism? Put directly, can Watson's life history tell us why his lifework, behaviorism, was *radical?* J. B. Watson was an angry, impulsive, and boisterous man. Sometimes arrogant, sometimes depressed, Watson spent a lifetime fighting against the appearance of inferiority and denying the existence of his own unruly feelings. He adopted a profane, salty, manly, "one of the guys" façade in his relationships with colleagues, and he seems to have earned a reputation as a "ladies man" who was something of a prodigious lover (Burnham, 1994). Undeniably, he could be charming at odd moments. But, at bottom, John Broadus Watson was an alienated human being.

Is it any wonder that the radical behaviorism he fashioned was deliberately blind to psychological causation and utterly feelingless? From the depths of his own anger, impulsivity, insecurity, and alienation, Watson fashioned a radical behaviorism that pictured people as:

- almost infinitely shapeable by environmental circumstances;
- predictable and controllable so long as one attends to what people do, not to what they think they do, and not to what they say they are doing;
- emotionless creatures who delude themselves that their desires, conflicts, and feelings guide their lives when, in fact, they are steered by only a *belief* that these mental states are real or causal.

Watson thus laid the foundations for a radically materialistic—one is tempted by the power of cliché to say "mechanistic"—philosophy of human nature that emerged from his own need to deny ordinary human vulnerability. Above all, Watson did not want to be ordinary. He struggled to make himself into something exceptional. Watson wanted to be irresistible to the women he pursued so that he could feel wanted and admired; he worked tirelessly to be an academic star in psychology, a discipline that he ardently wanted to dominate, and did; and he skillfully marketed his scientific credentials to achieve financial success in the world of big business to which he had retreated in failure and humiliation, and from which he emerged vindictive but depressed.

In the end, none of these things had provided the admiration or simple acceptance for which he longed. One by one he dissipated and then despised his own beliefs. He dismissed the religious aspirations of his childhood, corrupted the marriage he had built his life around, arrogantly misunderstood his own and everyone else's children, and clumsily discredited his cherished academic reputation in a particularly sordid fall from grace. It is doubtful that Watson ever knew how empty he had become or to whom he might turn for ordinary consolation. There had been precious little of substance to believe in from the very beginning, and with the passage of time, Watson's understanding of what he might do to diminish that lifetime of melancholy fatalism had grown increasingly clouded: "When you're dead, you're all dead."

Watson Taunts the Freudians: Little Albert B.

As part of his program to catalog the human infant's innate behavioral equipment, Watson and his wife, Rosalie Rayner Watson, applied Pavlov's conditioning methods to a nine-month-old child (Watson & Rayner, 1920). "Albert B.," as he was named for the report, was raised from birth in a children's hospital where his mother worked as a "wet nurse." Described as "stolid and unemotional," little Albert served as an experimental subject for the Watsons from his ninth month well past his first birthday. The aim of the experiments seems to have been to show that complex emotional responses, with the focus on fear, are developed in the human organism strictly through the principles of Pavlovian or classical conditioning.

Thus, at approximately nine months of age, Albert was supported on a tabletop equipped with a mattress, while John Watson successively presented the child with a white rat, rabbit, dog, monkey, costume masks with and without hair, ball of white cotton wool, and burning newspapers. In general, because Albert had no experience with such stimuli, his reaction was one of curiosity or eagerness to touch the objects. According to the Watsons, Albert showed no fear and "never cried."

When Albert was 11 months and 3 days old, the Watsons began their conditioning regimen. Previous research had shown that abrupt loud sounds such as that made by a hammer struck against a metal bar called forth a sharp fear reaction in most infants. Here was the opportunity to follow Pavlov's method: combine an *unconditioned stimulus* (loud sound) that reliably elicits an *unconditioned response* (startle, crying) with a neutral *conditioned stimulus* (white rat, for example), and wait to see whether the conditioned stimulus will eventually elicit a *conditioned response* similar to the original unconditioned response (startle, crying). The sequence can be

FIGURE 16.1   **The Pavlovian paradigm for Watson's Little Albert studies.**

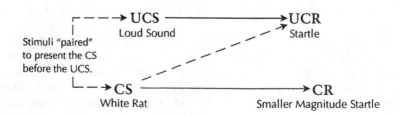

UCS = Unconditioned Stimulus
UCR = Unconditioned Response

CS = Conditioned Stimulus
CR = Conditioned Response

summarized as in Figure 16.1. Watson and Rayner described their first attempt at conditioning in this way:

> White rat suddenly taken from the basket and presented to Albert. He began to reach for rat with left hand. Just as his hand touched the animal the [metal] bar was struck [with a hammer] immediately behind his head. The infant jumped violently and fell forward, burying his face in the mattress. He did not cry, however. (Watson & Rayner, 1920, p. 8)

A second trial was conducted, and then Albert was given a week's rest. About a week later, the white rat was presented suddenly to Albert without the loud sound, and gradually brought nearer to the infant. He did not cry, but he withdrew his hand. Then Albert was exposed to a series of conditioning trials "to freshen" the conditioned responses. Rat and loud sound were paired for several trials, with the expectable result that Albert cringed, withdrew his body sharply away from the rat, and "puckered his face" while whimpering. Eventually, presentation of the white rat alone was sufficient to cause Albert to display the full range of fear responses reliably without the loud sound accompanying the rat.

Then, as the weeks wore on, Albert was presented with a variety of "new" stimuli: a white rabbit, a fur seal coat, a dog, a ball of white cotton, and even John Watson's own head of white hair lowered into the infant's face. On the whole, Albert generalized his fear responses and withdrawal efforts to all of these stimuli, presumably because of their similarity to the original conditioned stimulus of the white rat. There were differences in degree of reaction, of course, with the dog eliciting the least fear and withdrawal, but the clear conclusion was that Albert had learned these emotional responses as a generalized reaction to a known history of Pavlovian conditioning.

Watson and Rayner persisted in testing Albert's reactions, interposing longer and longer periods of rest between sessions. By the age of 1 year, 21 days, after a 31-day rest interval, Watson and Rayner exposed Albert to a Santa Claus mask, fur coat, and white rat with somewhat reduced but still detectable fear and withdrawal reactions. The Watsons also noted Albert's propensity for "compensatory blocking" behavior of thumb sucking during stressful moments of testing. So successful was Albert's self-soothing thumb sucking that the Watsons had forcibly to remove Albert's thumb from his mouth to obtain the conditioned fear responses. Despite this observation, it seems not to have occurred to Watson that there was a great deal more to Albert's "fear behavior" than simply observable withdrawal and crying. Among the conclusions that Watson drew from his work with Albert and from other observational studies of infants were these two:

1. Freud was wrong about the primacy of sexual urges as motives. Clearly, Watson felt, Albert's conditioning history demonstrated at least an equally important place for learned fears in shaping personality development.
2. Phobic disorders (irrational and inappropriately intense fears of objects, places, persons) can be explained by straightforward conditioning principles without resort to unconscious associations, wishes, or conflicts. Thus Little Albert's apparently bizarre fear of white, furry objects can be easily explained when his learning history is known.

The Watsons concluded their report with this taunt to the Freudians:

The Freudians 20 years from now, unless their hypotheses change, when they come to analyze Albert's fear of a seal skin coat—assuming that he comes to analysis at that age—will probably tease from him the recital of a dream which upon their analysis will show that Albert at three years of age attempted to play with the pubic hair of the mother and was scolded violently for it. (We are by no means denying that this might in some other case condition it.) If the analyst has sufficiently prepared Albert to accept such a dream when found as an explanation of his avoiding tendencies, and if the analyst has the authority and personality to put it over, Albert may be fully convinced that the dream was a true revealer of the factors which brought about the fear. (Watson & Rayner, 1920, p. 14)

BASIC ASSUMPTIONS OF RADICAL BEHAVIORISM

Throughout his work, Watson never faltered in the four main assumptions that guided his behaviorism:

1. *Evolutionary continuity.* Human and animal behavior are not different in kind. The Watsonian behaviorist "recognizes no dividing line between man and brute" (Watson, 1914/1967, p. 1). Human behavior differs from animal behavior only in the degree of its complexity. Natural selection shaped the human species to adapt to increasingly complex environments, but behavior is behavior, no matter the organism. Study of the "simpler" behavior of animals holds the tantalizing promise of shedding light on the more complex behavior of humans. Watson was trying to be a good Darwinian, but he carried his enthusiasm even further than Darwin would have found flattering.

2. *Reductionism.* On an evolutionary scale, behavior is behavior. But on a psychological scale, behavior is reducible to something else. All behavior is understandable ultimately as the workings of the organism's glandular and nervous systems. And the workings of the nervous and glandular systems may be traced to the biochemical processes that operate within these structures. Even the biochemistry may ultimately be understood in terms of the properties of the molecules involved. At an even lower level of reduction, molecules may be understood in terms of individual atoms, and so on. Watson believed that behavioral processes are always to be understood in terms of their constituent parts, whether the parts be at the structural level of the brain or at the molecular level of events in brain cells. A psychologist may study gross behavior, but what he or she is studying is really the behavior of electrons in atoms in molecules in cells! Viewed in this way, behavior is "nothing but" biochemistry, a view Watson found congenial because it excludes subjective experience and personal meaning from psychology (Peele, 1981).

3. *Determinism.* Every behavior is caused, and the cause can be traced to the physical links connecting the action to its biochemical bases. At the behavioral level, every response is strictly determined by the physical events (current stimuli, previous conditioned responses) that precede it. No organism behaves spontaneously or whimsically or completely freely. Behavior, strictly speaking, is never accidental (see Wolpe, 1978, p. 441 for a contemporary

statement of the same position). There is always some causal chain of physical events ultimately responsible for the observed behavior.

Most important, mental events, if they exist at all, are never causal in producing or guiding behavior. Thoughts by definition are not physical, and by themselves cannot directly trigger physical events. Instead, mental states are *epiphenomenal:* phenomena that occur as a by-product or unimportant consequence of the complexity of the organism's nervous system. Epiphenomena are wraithlike, without substance, without location, and without causal power. Ideas and subjective meanings cannot be traced link by link to their origins because they are not located in any one brain system. Thoughts are phenomena that emerge from the brain's overall complexity but are not "stored" or generated by a specifiable structure. Hofstadter (1979) provides an amusing example of how mental states can be epiphenomenal but nevertheless real:

> In the human brain, there is gullibility. How gullible are you? Is your gullibility located in some "gullibility center" in your brain? Could a neurosurgeon reach in and perform some delicate operation to lower your gullibility, otherwise leaving you alone? If you believe this, you are pretty gullible, and should perhaps consider such an operation. (1979, p. 309)

Watson was not denying the existence of mental states. He was excluding them as causal links in behavior and dismissing them as important governing influences in psychology. Like the philosopher René Descartes (1596–1650), Watson was content with a mind-body dualism that treats mental and physical as separate and different realities. Unlike Descartes, Watson further assumed that only the physical domain had explanatory power.

4. *Empiricism.* It was a logical outgrowth of Watson's stringent determinism and reductionism that he envisioned psychology as a natural science. Subjective experience and nonmaterial entities such as "consciousness" and "mind" could not be observed. And for Watson, observation was everything. His greatest impact on psychology was his insistence on experimental method. Only phenomena that could be measured and manipulated were fit subjects for a psychology aspiring to natural science status. For Watson, empiricism was equivalent to controlled observation, with one fundamental aim: ". . . to be able to predict and to control human activity" (Watson, 1930, p. 11).

At a more subtle level, as we have seen, Watson's determination to be strictly empirical led to a naive environmentalism. If subjective, "metaphysical" concepts such as mind and consciousness are unscientific, then it is equally unscientific to assume that human beings are shaped by anything but measurable, observable experiences. Human beings become solely what their history of environmental stimulation permits them to become. Personality health and pathology are similarly regulated by experience with the environment. Table 16.2 summarizes Watson's basic assumptions, but a single theme underlies all four principles. Evolutionary continuity, reductionism, determinism, and empiricism in the radical form Watson adopted exclude the study of personal meaning from psychology. For Watson, this outcome appeared to be an improvement.

TABLE 16.2   The Assumptions of Watson's Radical Behaviorism

Principle	Rationale	Influence on Psychology	Interpretation of Psychopathology
1. Evolutionary Continuity	Behavior is behavior. Humans and animals differ only in degree of complexity.	Fostered study of animal behavior as simple model of complex human responses.	Abnormal behavior is maladaptive responding in a particular situation compared to other members of species.
2. Reductionism	Behavior is analyzable into component physiologic and biochemical events in the central nervous system and peripheral musculature.	Biology and chemistry are crucial sources of knowledge about behavior; nonmaterial explanations of behavior are nonscientific.	Behavior and its supportive biology and biochemistry lie on a single dimension so that changes in one variable are reflected in changes in the other. Normal and abnormal behavior lie on a single dimension, with abnormal differing only in degree of adaptiveness.
3. Determinism	Behavior is caused by prior stimulation and is never accidental, random, or "free." Mental states are epiphenomenal, and never causal.	Goal of scientific psychology is the prediction and control of human behavior by knowledge of stimulus-response relationships.	Normal and abnormal behavior are learned, and necessary and sufficient conditions of learning are found in principles of conditioning.
4. Empiricism	Only observable, measurable events have impact on organisms; only observables can be scientifically verified.	Experimental method became the key tool of psychology. Introspective and subjective data and methods are suspect.	Symptoms are not signs of hidden unconscious conflict or disease states. Symptoms are the disorder and are changed by new conditioning.

Note: A common denominator underlying these four principles in their radical Watsonian form is the exclusion, on scientific grounds, of subjective data and methods from psychology and psychopathology.

RADICAL BEHAVIORISM AND PSYCHOPATHOLOGY

Watson extended his principles to the phenomena of abnormal behavior. He made the extension on the premise that, once "normal" emotional development was explained in behavioral terms, there was no obstacle to applying the same principles to disordered behavior. Watson gave an illuminating example of his thinking on abnormal psychology in the case of his "psychopathological dog." The case reveals not only Watson's rebellious, tongue-in-cheek view of mentalistic theories, but it also shows how strongly he believed abnormal behavior could be understood and cured through behavioral means. "Disease" and "mind" metaphors come under heavy attack in the example that follows:

> To show the needlessness of introducing the "conception of mind" in so-called mental diseases, I offer you a fanciful picture of a psychopathological dog. . . .Without taking

any one into my counsel suppose I once trained a dog so that he would walk away from nicely ground, fresh hamburg steak and would eat only decayed fish (true examples of this are now at hand). I trained him (by use of electric shock) to avoid smelling the female dog in the usual canine way—he would circle around her but would come no closer than 10 feet. . . . Again, by letting him play only with male puppies and dogs and punishing him when he tried to mount a female, I made a homosexual of him. . . . Instead of licking my hands and becoming lively and playful when I go to him in the morning, he hides or cowers, whines and shows his teeth. . . . He sleeps only two hours per day and sleeps these two hours leaning up against a wall rather than lying down with head and rump touching. He is thin and emaciated because he will eat no fats. He salivates constantly (because I have conditioned him to salivate to hundreds of objects). This interferes with his digestion. Then I take him to the dog psychopathologist. His physiological reflexes are normal. No organic lesions are to be found anywhere. The dog, so the psychopathologist claims, is mentally sick, actually insane; his mental condition has led to the various organic difficulties such as lack of digestion; it has "caused" his poor physical condition. Everything that a dog should do . . . he does not do. And everything that seems foreign for a dog to do he does. The psychopathologist says I must commit the dog to an institution for the care of insane dogs; that if he is not restrained he will jump from a 10-story building, or walk into a fire without hesitation. I tell the dog psycho-pathologist that he doesn't know anything about my dog; that, from the standpoint of the environment in which the dog has been brought up (the way I have trained him), he is the most normal dog in the world; that the reasons he calls the dog "insane" or mentally sick is because of his own absurd system of classification.

I then take the psychopathologist into my confidence. He becomes extremely angry. "Since you've brought this on, go cure him." I attempt then to correct my dog's behavior difficulties, at least up to the point where he can begin to associate with the nice dogs in the neighborhood. . . . I use behavioristic methods. I uncondition him and then condition him. Soon I get him to eating fresh meat by getting him hungry, closing up his nose and feeding him in the dark. This gives me a good start. I have something basal to use in my further work. I keep him hungry and feed him only when I open his cage in the morning; the whip is thrown away; soon he jumps for joy when he hears my step. In a few months' time I not only have cleared out the old but also have built in the new. (Watson, 1924/1930, pp. 298–300).

Watson's view of psychopathology focused on learned patterns of habit, pain-avoidance, and appetite. The dog psychopathologist was lured into the Watsonian trap of postulating a series of unobservable mental states causing the dog's "diseased" behavior. Watson's point, of course, is that the dog's conditioning history makes the psychopathologist's explanations seem ludicrous. He concluded his story with this admonition:

I am trying to show by this homely illustration *that you can by conditioning not only build up the behavior complications, patterns and conflicts in diseased personalities, but also by the same process lay the foundations for the onset of actual organic changes which result finally in infections and lesions*—all without introducing the concepts of the mind-body relation . . . or even without leaving the realm of natural science. In other words, as behaviorists, even in "mental diseases" we deal with the same material and the same laws that the neurologists and physiologists deal with. (Watson, 1924/1930, p. 300; italics in original)

Watson's psychopathological dog illustrates all of his main assumptions. First, it is clear from Watson's willingness to use an animal example of psychopathology that his belief in *evolutionary continuity* of behavior applies to abnormal behavior. In fact, Watson chose an animal example not only because such an example could sardonically illustrate his position, but also because at the time Watson created the example, only medically trained psychiatrists dealt with psychopathology. Watson therefore used a dog example both for its satiric effect and to sidestep the controversy of a psychologist proposing clinical theories. But it is also clear that Watson had no difficulty employing a dog as his subject because, in the end, behavior for Watson is behavior.

Second, one aspect of Watson's extreme *reductionism* is exemplified in his assertion that there is a direct connection between the dog's learned pathological behavior and the biologic ("organic") symptoms that it develops. Certainly, those responses that interfere with normal eating and digestion have a direct negative effect on the dog's health. For Watson, the biologic and behavioral levels of psychopathology are on a single scale or dimension so that alterations at the behavioral level are reflected in changes at the lower, biologic levels and vice versa.

Third, Watson's stringent *determinism* is shown by his insistence that the dog's behavior is completely explainable in terms of its conditioning history. Watson believed that Pavlovian conditioning is an automatic process. Manipulation of the proper sequence of stimuli and responses could always produce the desired outcome, even when pathological. Moreover, the reapplication of conditioning principles should be able to undo the original learning or replace it with new learning just as automatically. Behavior is determined. And it is lawful. The necessary and sufficient conditions of that lawful regularity can be manipulated by the conditioner.

One doubts whether a dog, or any creature, treated in the inconsistent and forceful ways that Watson imagined would ever lend itself to retraining or spontaneously "jump with joy" at his conditioner's footsteps. The dog's expectations and needs are largely ignored by Watson as if the creature were susceptible to an infinite range of Pavlovian conditioning despite its own motives and prior learning about the world. At the human level, as we shall see, this proposition has been challenged.

Fourth, Watson's *empiricism* is found in his assumption that the dog's psychopathology is not a sign of some underlying "mental disease." Symptoms are behaviors. They are not signs of unconscious conflicts. They do not reflect unobservable mental events. Symptoms do not reflect anything but the conditions under which complex behavior is learned. And, like any behavior, the maladaptive response called a symptom can be changed by altering the conditions that govern learning. The dog's observable symptoms *are* the psychopathology. In Watson's model, psychopathology is located not inside the organism but in the organism's behavior and in its environment. And, by Watson's account, the behaviorist can completely control the environment.

From Watson's point of view, the solutions created by Freud to the puzzles of psychopathology are no solutions at all. Freud merely constructed more cumbersome puzzles. And Watson's solution to Freud's puzzles aimed at ruling them out of existence. For, if pathology is to be found in the organism's behavior, problems such as self-deception, symbolic meaning, and unconscious conflict cease to be problems.

B. F. Skinner

Contemporary Radical Behaviorism

By the late 1930s, radical behaviorism was about to undergo a radical change. A young experimental psychologist at the University of Minnesota had years before found the answer to a personal crisis in the hard-nosed empiricism of John Watson. The theory and methods he would develop provided the scientific rationale for a theory of behavior that dominated psychology until the 1960s. Burrhus Frederic Skinner (1938) extended Watson's behaviorism beyond the level of Pavlovian conditioning into the more complex arena of voluntary behavior, and with that extension invited all of psychology to abandon its search for internal causes of behavior.

Like Watson, Skinner would find the term *personality* irrelevant at best, misleading at worst. Yet, like Watson, Skinner found himself resolving the puzzles that Freud had introduced. In our study of Skinner's behaviorism, of necessity, we extract only those features that have relevance to personality, a difficult task in itself. But, perhaps more important, Skinner's work has to be understood in the historical context that it helped create and which led, eventually, to cognitive behaviorism.

We begin with a behavioral illustration of voluntary behavior. In the example that follows, the main theme of Skinner's account of human behavior and the differences from John Watson's behaviorism are highlighted. The child's behavior is not reflex behavior. There is no identifiable triggering stimulus. And there are a host of possible responses that the child can make, each of them having different consequences.

When a Bookcase Is a Ladder: Behavioral Consequences

It is difficult to specify precisely what prompts a child to treat a tall set of bookshelves as if it were a ladder. But the fact that its climb to the top shelf is successful leads us to predict increased furniture climbing on this and on other heart-stopping pieces of temptation in the future. It is the *consequence* of the child's behavior—successfully reaching the top—that increases the frequency of such behavior.

Unlike Watson's little Albert, for whom a specific stimulus triggered a specific and *automatic* response, the immediate trigger for our little bookcase climber's behavior is not clear. Certainly the bookcase itself is a stimulus to action, but what action? For this child, the action is climbing. For another child, the bookcase might be a stimulus to touching, or scattering books on the floor, or running Matchbox cars on the shelves. It is the same stimulus in each case, but knowledge of the stimulus does not predict the different children's behaviors.

For our climber, the act of climbing was strictly voluntary, and it was "emitted" behavior not "elicited" by the stimulus of the bookcase. Another way to state that distinction is to say that the bookcase provided the occasion for the response, but it did not cause the response to occur. From a whole repertoire of potential responses, this child chose to treat the bookcase as a ladder. The bookcase itself, unlike little Albert's frightening loud sound, does not produce this child's climbing response.

What, then, controls climbing? For the first and successful climb, it is the consequence of reaching the top that *increases* the probability that the child will behave the same way again. A fall or an anguished parental scream are other potential consequences that will *reduce* the frequency of climbing. But for both positive and negative consequences, this voluntary, exploratory behavior can best be predicted (and controlled) by describing (and arranging) what happens to the behavior.

E. L. Thorndike and the Law of Effect

Edward L. Thorndike (1874–1949) had shown that a cat generates a great wealth of responses trying to release itself from a cagelike puzzle box to reach a dish of food just outside the door. At first, the cat roams around the box, sniffs at the corners, scratches at various points on the wall, and may even bite at the slats of the door. Eventually, all of this trial-and-error behavior accidentally results in triggering the simple latch mechanism of the door, which springs open permitting the cat to escape and to reach the food dish. On subsequent trials, the cat spends less and less time on behaviors that were more or less random attempts to escape, and more and more time scratching and pawing at the door. Those of its responses that were closest in time to actual escape (i.e., behavior directed to the door latch) had the rewarding consequence of reaching food. By the 13th or 14th trial, the cat's escape time drops from nearly three minutes on the first trial to a scant five seconds (Thorndike, 1911). At this point, the cat has "learned" to escape. In Thorndike's vocabulary, the cat has "dropped out" of its repertoire those "random" responses unrelated to escape, and has repeated only those responses instrumental in securing release. Such successful responses are "stamped in" by the pleasurable consequences of the food reward.

From studies such as these, Thorndike formulated a set of "Laws of Learning." For present purposes, Thorndike's most famous law, *The Law of Effect,* will be sufficient to show the most immediate intellectual precursor of Skinner's work. Thorndike's Law of Effect states that a response which leads to a "satisfying state of affairs" is strengthened, whereas responses that are less satisfying or "annoying" are weakened and will occur less frequently. Except for the anthropomorphic terms "satisfying" and "annoying," Thorndike was stating an observable relationship between behavior and its consequences. It is the effect a behavior produces that determines its future probability of occurrence. Like our little bookcase climber, Thorndike's cats quickly learned that nothing succeeds like success. For B. F. Skinner, nothing is more annoying than attributing "success" or "satisfaction" to a cat.

Skinner's Empirical Law of Effect

In the late 1930s, B. F. Skinner, in the tradition of John Watson and Edward Thorndike, was able to show that a broad range of behavior can be acquired, changed, and regulated by manipulating its consequences in the laboratory. But Skinner, in the tradition of Watson, preferred to avoid mentalistic terms such as pleasure and satisfaction in favor of direct description of the observable events. Where Thorndike attributed pleasurable properties to the food reward, Skinner would prefer to say simply that food "strengthens" (increases the probability of) the cat's pawing at the latch to open the puzzle box door (1938/1966). All that can be observed is that the cat behaves in a particular way, that food follows latch-pawing behavior that opens the door, and that on future trials, latch-pawing behavior increases in both speed and frequency. We cannot observe the cat's presumed "satisfaction" with escape and food nor its equally hypothetical "annoyance" should it fail to escape.

Skinner, therefore, suggested that Thorndike's Law of Effect be rechristened to the *"Empirical Law of Effect"* and be thus limited to a statement of the relationship between an observable behavior and its environmental consequences (Skinner, 1950, 1953, 1974). For the next four decades, Skinner devoted himself to a specification of these relationships, and the body of his work is often referred to as reinforcement theory. For where Thorndike spoke of rewards and punishments as key consequences shaping behavior, Skinner preferred the more descriptive and neutral terms positive and negative *reinforcers*. Very much like Watson's, Skinner's scientific style became a model of radical empiricism and determinism. But unlike Watson, Skinner avoided unnecessary reductionism, preferring to develop laws at the behavioral level that would stand independent of the organism's physiology. And, unlike Watson, Skinner was not limited to explaining complex behavior in terms of the stimulus-substitution model of Pavlovian conditioning. Voluntary behavior and the reinforcers that shape it became Skinner's focus.

Skinner (1938, 1953) pointed out that Pavlovian conditioning was very much overworked as an explanation of behavior. After all, the Pavlovian model is a reflex process in which there is a necessary and invarying connection between the stimulus and the response:

$$S \longrightarrow R$$

Both the sequence (stimulus before response) and the connection between them (autonomic nervous system pathways) are "wired" into the organism. Skinner refers to Pavlovian conditioning as *respondent* behavior to emphasize the rigidity of the stimulus-response connection. But voluntary behavior is not reflex, is not rigidly triggered by antecedent stimuli, and is instrumental in operating upon the environment to produce some effect. Furthermore, the sequence is different from Pavlovian conditioning and the variability of behavior far greater. See Figure 16.2.

Out of all the possible responses in a child's voluntary repertoire, our little athlete chose climbing the bookcase. And this response was positively reinforced ("rewarded," Thorndike would say) by safely reaching the top shelf. Note that in this sequence of what Skinner calls *operant* behavior (from "operate"), the response must occur before the reinforcing stimulus can be reinforcing. Figure 16.3 illustrates this principle. Thus Pavlovian and operant conditioning can be contrasted on their different sequences of stimulus events.

The key feature that permits a reinforcer to be effective in shaping behavior is that the reinforcing stimulus be *contingent* on the response. That is to say, every time Thorndike's cat *correctly* pawed the latch mechanism, the puzzle box door opened to permit access to food. In operant vocabulary, we say that the food was contingent (dependent upon) the latch-pawing response. Positive reinforcers (such as food, praise, money) strengthen a response by increasing its future frequency.

FIGURE 16.2   Increasing the probability of one voluntary response from a whole repertoire of potential responses.

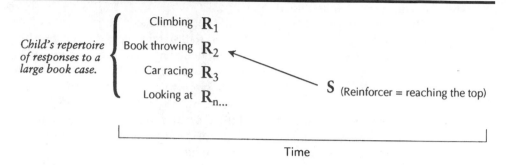

Negative reinforcers also strengthen responses by increasing their frequency, but the negatively reinforced response is one that "takes away" (terminates) the negative reinforcer. For example, if electric shock were stopped by the cat's pressing a lever in the puzzle box, the electric shock is a negative reinforcer that increases the frequency of lever pressing.

Punishing stimuli are not negative reinforcers in the technical sense because they do not strengthen the responses they are contingent upon and they may even persist throughout the contingent behavior. Punishers may be painful like negative reinforcers, but a punisher may also be the *removal* of a positive reinforcer, as when we deprive a child of a favorite television program because it climbed the bookcase. Punishers are designed, therefore, to suppress behavior. Table 16.3 contains complete definitions and examples of the main reinforcement-theory concepts.

FIGURE 16.3   Pavlovian and operant paradigms of conditioning.

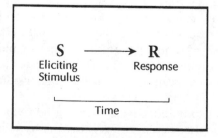

PAVLOVIAN PARADIGM
The eliciting stimulus literally triggers the involuntary response.

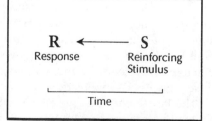

OPERANT PARADIGM
The reinforcing stimulus is a consequence of the voluntary response and occurs after it.

TABLE 16.3 Summary of Key Reinforcement Concepts

Concept	Definition	Examples
1. *POSITIVE REINFORCER* "Reward"	Any stimulus event that "strengthens" (increases the probability of) the response it follows.	Parent's praise when child shares toy with younger sibling increases sharing in future.
2. *NEGATIVE REINFORCER* "Relief"	Any stimulus event that "strengthens" (increases the probability of) the response that *removes* the negative reinforcer.	Criticism about being "chubby" is stopped or prevented by dieting.
3. *PUNISHMENT* "Pain"	Aversive or painful stimulus applied to a response to reduce its frequency to near zero. Not the same as negative reinforcer because behavior is weakened not strengthened, and punishment may continue during the behavior. Punishment may also be the *removal* of a positive reinforcer.	Slapping child's hand for reaching into cookie jar suppresses reaching-in-jar response. Revoking hospitalized patient's grounds privileges because patient assaulted a nurse.
4. *EXTINCTION*	Withholding a reinforcer while organism makes the previously reinforced response until probability of response drops to baseline levels.	Withholding praise for sharing behavior even when child calls attention to it.
5. *OPERANT*	Any voluntary behavior that can "operate" on the environment to make changes instrumental in securing reinforcements.	Walking, talking, any manipulative behavior.
6. *SHAPING*	"Molding" a final, complex response from "bits and pieces" of responses by reinforcing successively more precise approximations of the final desired response.	Driving instructor praises increasing precision of student as he or she guides car straight ahead, withholding praise for any performance that is less precise than last best approximation.
7. *PARTIAL REINFORCEMENT* "Schedules"	Delivering reinforcements on a schedule so that not every response is reinforced. Schedules may follow time patterns so that reinforcement is available only after a specific interval, or a schedule may be based on number of responses required before reinforcement is available. Time schedules are *Interval Schedules,* and response-based schedules are *Ratio Schedules.* Behavior maintained by partial reinforcement is more resistant to extinction.	*Interval Schedule:* Receiving a paycheck once a week. *Ratio Schedule:* Auto salesman who is paid by the number of cars sold.

An Illustration of Operant Conditioning

To see how behavior can be shaped and maintained by reinforcement contingencies, we can borrow and modify an example from two theorists whose work we discuss later (Dollard & Miller, 1950, pp. 26–30). Suppose we tell a six-year-old child that we want to play a special hide-and-seek game. We tell her that she can earn candy kisses, which we know are her favorite treat, by finding plastic poker chips that we will hide in a room. Of course we don't call them poker chips, but in our best scientific demeanor we refer to them as "tokens." For each token the girl finds, she will receive one candy kiss.

The child is not present when we hide the first token under the bottom edge of the center book on the lowest shelf of a small bookcase in the room. We take her to the room and tell her that the token is someplace in the bookcase to reduce the sheer wealth of possible behaviors she is likely to emit. She is excited and eager to begin.

On her first trial, she enters the room, walks immediately to the bookcase. First, she looks under several randomly chosen books on the middle shelf. Then, on tiptoes, she shuffles several books on the top shelf. No tokens. She then drops to her knees and examines books on the lowest shelf. Finding nothing, she stops for a moment and eyes the entire bookcase. The pause is not long. She is eager and hungry. With a shrug, she starts looking under books on the bottom shelf again. By our count, she has picked up 37 books at the point when she finds the token with a shriek of discovery. Total elapsed time on this first trial is 210 seconds.

With a shout of joy, the girl hands the experimenter the token and receives one candy kiss, which she devours as soon as she can remove the wrapper. To the question: "Do you want to play again?" we receive a delighted "Yes!" On the next trial, we hide the token with incredible scientific cunning under the same bottom-shelf-middle book. The little explorer examines 12 books before she tries the familiar book. Total elapsed time on the second trial is 86 seconds.

On the third trial, she goes directly to the same book, and is not disappointed. Total elapsed time is 11 seconds.

On the fourth trial, believing that we must be more sophisticated than we are, the little girl overturns 15 books before her suspicion is aroused sufficiently to look under the bottom-shelf-middle book. Total elapsed time on the fourth trial is again 86 seconds. Total candy kiss consumption: four. Girl's opinion of behavioristic psychological experimenters: simple-minded.

Secure in our scientific empiricism, we continue to hide the token under the bottom-shelf-middle book for all of the remaining trials through the 10th. Equally empirical in her strategy, bottom-shelf-middle book is now the first place she looks. Average time per trial is now reduced to a mere 3 seconds, just long enough to enter the room, kneel down, and lift the book. At this point, we might say that book-lifting behavior has been shaped from approximate responses to the one specific bottom-shelf-middle-book response by the positive reinforcer of candy kisses. What of the tokens? Tokens are technically positive *secondary* reinforcers. They cannot themselves be eaten, but they can be redeemed for the primary positive reinforcer of candy. The little girl "works" for the token because this "currency" has the value of "buying" a more direct reward. Even in behaviorism there is no free lunch.

We now turn to a discussion of the reinforcement theory concepts that are illustrated by this procedure.

Shaping

From the girl's entire repertoire of behavior, we selected the response of "examining-bottom-shelf-middle-book." All other book-examining responses went unreinforced, and although it may have seemed unchallenging to her, only one response had positively reinforcing consequences. By the fifth or sixth trial, all "random" responses were reduced in probability, and the desired response increased in probability.

Positive Reinforcement

The meaning of positive reinforcement should be fairly obvious at this point. But there is an implication in the way Skinner defines the term that needs to be spelled out. Note that his definition (see Table 16.3) does not specify *why* a positive reinforcer increases the probability of a response. In our present example the reason why candy kisses reinforce the rather aimless book-lifting behavior is that the little girl can eat them and satisfy her hunger. But positive reinforcers need not be biological drive reducers to be reinforcing. All that is necessary is empirically to observe what stimulus increases a behavior's probability to be able to describe that stimulus as a positive reinforcer. David Premack (1965) has shown, for example, that one can establish very powerful positive reinforcers solely on the basis of observing a person's differential preferences for one rather than another activity.

Premack demonstrated that a child who initially prefers watching television cartoons to playing with a pinball machine may be shaped into playing pinball if the more preferred cartoons are used as the reinforcer. To watch a cartoon, the child *must* spend a specific amount of time playing pinball.

Another child who prefers the pinball game to the cartoons can be shaped to watch the less preferred television cartoon by permitting it to play pinball *only* when he or she has spent a specific amount of time cartoon watching. Reinforcers are clearly relative, not absolute, commodities.

The *Premack Principle* states that a reinforcer can be defined in terms of the relationship between behaviors of different initial probabilities: A behavior of initially higher probability (preferred action) can be contingent on performing a behavior of initially lower probability (less preferred action). The behavior of higher probability is the reinforcer (Premack, 1965).

Skinner's point in defining reinforcers in terms of their observable effects on the frequency of behavior is that we need not make assumptions about what is "pleasurable" or "annoying" for a given creature. The Premack demonstration confirms the wisdom of Skinner's empirical strategy.

Negative Reinforcement

We could change the rules of the game so that instead of earning tokens redeemable for candy, the girl's behavior of finding the hidden token turns off a loud, blaring siren sounded into the room. In this case, although the girl would be much less motivated to play the game at all, her correct responses would be increased in frequency by the *removal* of the negative reinforcer of painfully loud sound.

Punishment

Another change in the rules of the game would make it very much less appealing. We could tell the child that for every *incorrect* response (selecting the wrong book), she will receive a mild electric shock from the electrode wired to her leg. We doubt whether this child would persist at the game at all, but for present purposes assume that she has no choice. Or, we could play the "game" with this rule: Every wrong response costs one previously earned token. Here, loss of prior positive reinforcements is punishing. In both cases, the emotional side effects are damaging to motivation, and in both cases, the behavior we aim to suppress (wrong responses) might better be eliminated by simply allowing wrong responses to be extinguished. In the original version of the game with tokens for correct responses and no consequences for wrong ones, that is precisely what happens to the wrong responses. They "drop out" of the girl's repertoire because they are not reinforced—and the game was fun.

Extinction

A simple change in procedure can extinguish the bottom-shelf-middle-book response. We change the location of the token. After several trials of no reinforcement for selecting the bottom-shelf-middle book, the girl stops "emitting" that response. Or, we could extinguish the broader behavior of "playing-the-token-finding-game" by not hiding any tokens. After several totally unsuccessful, candy-kiss-less trials, the appeal of the game will drop to zero. And so will the probability of game-playing behavior.

Partial Reinforcement: Schedules

When the game-playing routine is firmly established by having every successful response reinforced by a candy kiss, we could make the game more challenging. We tell the girl that to receive her usual candy kiss, she must now find the token three times in a row. In other words, we have scheduled reinforcements on a 3:1 ratio so that the child has to make three times as many responses to get one reinforcement as she did previously. (The possibility for using intermittent reinforcement is the reason, by the way, that we selected tokens to place under the book rather than the candy kiss itself. Even a behaviorist could not consistently yank a freshly found goody from a child's grasp fast enough to prevent immediate consumption.)

The 3:1 ratio is unchanging, although we may choose to hide the tokens under various books each time. As long, however, as the schedule demands three responses for one reinforcement it remains a *fixed ratio schedule*. The child will probably proceed at a steady pace trial after trial to earn her kisses.

But we could tell her that the game is going to get harder. Under a new rule, she must find as many tokens as possible before earning a candy, and that sometimes it will take only three tokens, sometimes five, and sometimes only two. But she will not be able to predict which contingency (three, five, or two) applies at a given moment. This schedule is still a ratio schedule (the ratios are 3:1, 5:1, and 2:1), but it is a *variable ratio schedule.* The child's best strategy, especially if she is hungry, is to work as fast as she can to build up as big a supply of tokens as she can.

We would also schedule reinforcements by establishing time limits punctuated by a buzzer and a clock we install in the room. We tell the girl that she must find the hidden token within 10 seconds or she will not receive the candy for her token. But if she finds the token before 10 seconds elapses, she must wait until the 10th second before getting the token. This schedule is called a *fixed interval* schedule because the availability of reinforcement is governed by intervals of time that remain constant from reinforcement to reinforcement. Such constant time limits encourage a steady pace of responding.

But we could speed things up by continually changing the time limits in a fashion that, from the girl's point of view, is unpredictable. We might arrange for the buzzer to sound after five seconds, then after three seconds, then after ten seconds, and then back to five seconds, and so on. This schedule is called a *variable interval* schedule because the time limits for the availability of reinforcement are continually changing. Such a schedule generates very high and very rapid rates of responding. Our little girl's best strategy under such rules would be to overturn books very rapidly and continually to beat the clock.

All of these schedules produce response rates that are more resistant to extinction than behavior maintained by continuous reinforcement (one reinforcement for every correct response). The reason is easy to understand. When she was reinforced for every correct response, an extinction contingency (no token available) is quickly detected. Within one or two trials it will be obvious to the girl that no reward is forthcoming and she will cease responding. But when the availability of tokens is less predictable, as on the variable schedules, it will take a considerably larger number of trials for the child to detect that reinforcement is not available at all. Her behavior persists, therefore, in the face of no reward for a longer time. Or, more correctly put, an intermittently reinforced response resists extinction.

Generalization

We could again add rules to our simple game by telling the child that a good clue to where a token will be found is the color of the book that was originally the bottom-shelf-middle-book-where-you-could-always-find-a-token. Assume that book was bright red. We now hide tokens only under red and near-red colored books, and never under black, yellow, or green ones. As we observe the child responding on the first trial, it is very likely that she will respond first to red books, then to light red ones, then to orange ones until she finds the token. In short, she responds similarly to stimuli that resemble a previously reinforced stimulus. This capacity for organisms to emit a learned behavior in environments that resemble the original learning environment is called *generalization.* As a rule of thumb, the more similar a stimulus is to the reinforced stimulus the more likely will it be to elicit similar behavior.

Discrimination

The girl withholds responding to stimuli that are perceptibly different from the reinforced stimulus. In terms of our game, she does not lift green, black, or yellow books to find the token because they are not sufficiently similar to the red book that always had the token. This capacity to detect the difference between stimuli associated with reinforcement and those that are not is called *discrimination*. The little girl discriminates one book from another through color cues, and she responds differently to red books than she does to yellow ones. For the behaviorist, it is the girl's differential *responding*, not her presumably perceptual distinction between red and other colors, that is the essence of discrimination. As with generalization, discrimination is more or less governed by a rule of increasing dissimilarity. The more stimuli differ on some relevant dimension, the more probable is the organism's discrimination.

The point of our lengthy example is simply to foster familiarity with the vocabulary of reinforcement theory. There are also other aspects to this illustration that we have not yet called attention to, but that serve us well toward the end of this chapter when we review the strengths and weaknesses of the behavioral paradigm.

For now, we turn to some basic applications of Skinner's work, for the puzzles of personality first described by Freud have alternative solutions.

SKINNER'S SOLUTIONS TO FREUD'S PUZZLES

For J. B. Watson, psychopathology was merely a special case of conditioned responses that proved to be maladaptive. Unfortunately, Watson's pioneering vision was limited to the principles derived from Pavlovian conditioning of reflexes. Skinner, too, conceptualizes psychopathology as maladaptive responding, but the principles by which such behavior is learned are drawn from reinforcement theory. There is considerable controversy in contemporary learning psychology over whether, in fact, Pavlovian and operant conditioning are really two very different types of learning, or if one is merely the special case of the other (Rachlin & Logue, 1983). But the distinction between operant (instrumental) and Pavlovian (classical) conditioning remains a useful demarcation. Skinner and Watson would agree, moreover, that a behavioral account of psychopathology using either set of principles rules out mental events because such unobservables are supported only by hearsay evidence.

Freud's puzzles of psychopathology and his solutions to them are unacceptable to the contemporary radical behaviorist. But unlike Watson, Skinner has never ridiculed Freud's observations (Skinner, 1953, 1974). Instead, Skinner's approach has been to accept as legitimate data the observations of psychodynamic theorists while discarding their explanations of the meaning of that data. Skinner attempts to restate the basic clinical facts of disordered human behavior in testable, empirically rigorous, and measurable terms. All references to inner agencies, conflicts, and unconscious motives as *causal* elements are excluded from a strictly behavioristic account. And, like Watson, Skinner localizes the key controls over behavior in the environment, in those consequences that the environment applies to behavior.

To grasp the nature of contemporary radical behaviorism we review the central puzzles described and explained by Freud (see Chapters 2 and 3) and resolve them in behavioristic terms. The contrast is very instructive.

Reduced to its barest skeleton, Freud's account of psychopathology revolves around three central ideas: repressed wishes, unconscious conflict among internal agencies, and the experience of anxiety as the ego's experience of its own helplessness. We now look at the contrasts between Skinner and Freud.

Repressed Wishes and Urges

Freud's Puzzle Solution
Wishes and urges seethe unrestrained in the unconscious mind, finding, from time to time, disguised expression in behavior metaphorically related to the disavowed and threatening wishes. Symptoms are, for example, compromise formations because they both symbolize *and* deny the wish—repudiate *and* gratify sexual and aggressive urges that are too painful to act on or to recognize consciously.

Skinner's Puzzle Solution
The assumption that behavior is metaphorically related to inner mental forces that have causal properties in shaping behavior is untestable, unobservable, and unnecessary. The same behavior, say a symptom, can be explained more simply and more verifiably by studying the contingencies of reinforcement under which that behavior was punished or rewarded:

> A [Freudian] wish which has been repressed as the result of aversive consequences struggles to escape. In doing so it resorts to certain devices which Freud called "dynamisms"—tricks which the repressed wish uses to evade the effects of punishment. . . . The Freudian wish is a device for representing a response with a given probability of occurrence. Any effect of "repression" must be the effect of the variables which have led either to the response itself or to the repressing behavior. . . . Where in the Freudian scheme, behavior is merely the symptom of a neurosis, in the present formulation it is the direct object of inquiry. . . . Let us say that two brothers compete for the affection of their parents and for other reinforcers which must be divided between them. As a result, one brother behaves aggressively toward the other and is punished, by his brother or by his parents. Let us suppose that this happens repeatedly. Eventually any situation in which aggressive action toward the brother is likely to take place or any early stage of such action will generate the conditioned aversive stimulation associated with anxiety or guilt. This is effective from the point of view of the other brother or the punishing parent because it leads to the self-control of aggressive behavior; the punished brother is now more likely to engage in activities which compete with and displace his aggression. In this sense he "represses" his aggression. The repression is successful if the behavior is so effectively displaced that it seldom reaches the incipient state at which it generates anxiety. It is unsuccessful if anxiety is frequently generated. (Skinner, 1953, pp. 375–376)

Repression is distraction. It is even avoidance. But in Skinner's formulation, repression is not the construction of inner mental agencies at war with one another. A punished behavior (even a verbal response) is avoided in favor of less anxiety-provoking responses. Behaviors already in the punished brother's repertoire are used as substitutes for direct aggression. By generalization, the punished brother "selects" similar but less painful responses. He can, for instance, *fantasize* killing his brother, or if that activity is still too anxiety provoking, he can fantasize killing brother substitutes, such as cousins or friends (Skinner, 1953, p. 376). Perhaps the punished brother can spend his anger in unpunished (maybe even rewarded) activities such as police work, or military service.

Repression for Skinner is not "forgetting" threatening ideas and wishes. Skinner's explanation avoids all assumptions about hidden wishes evoking anxiety. Behavior increases in frequency, ceases altogether, or remains constant because of the reinforcement contingencies to which it is exposed. When the contingencies are aversive, anxiety results. But what a person thinks about those contingencies is unimportant. What he or she *does* about them is everything. Note that Skinner is not reluctant to consider human fantasy and wishing. He is reluctant to conceptualize such unobservables as causal. Behavior, not thoughts, can be predicted and controlled.

From Freud's point of view, the difficulty with this explanation of repression is the failure to take account of the path of the displacements (substitutions). Subjective meanings govern the "choice" of substitute behaviors. Humans, in Freud's clinical experience, create substitutes not merely to avoid painful consequences, but also to symbolize their unspoken thoughts in ways far more complicated than those predicted by simple similarity generalization.

Unconscious Conflict

Freud's Puzzle Solution

Contradictory and self-deceptive behavior reflects the universal personality structure of internalized unconscious passion (id), social intelligence and reason (ego), and ethical-moral restraint through guilt (superego). It is possible for a person to be self-divided, wishing for the opposite of what he or she really wants, and to remain unaware of the self-deception because each agency has different aims and each may at various times overpower the others.

Skinner's Puzzle Solution

Again, Skinner does not dismiss Freud's clinical observations of conflicted behavior. Instead, he prefers to couch the explanation of such behavior in terms of observable variables and the principles of operant conditioning:

> In Freud's great triumvirate, the ego, superego, and id represent three sets of contingencies which are almost inevitable when a person lives in a group. The id is the Judeo-Christian "Old Adam"—man's "unregenerate nature," derived from his innate susceptibilities to reinforcement, most of them almost necessarily in conflict with the interests of others. The superego—the Judeo-Christian conscience—speaks in the "still small voice" of a (usually) punitive agent representing the interests of other people. . . . [But the superego] . . . is mainly the product of the punitive practices of a society which attempts to suppress the selfish behavior generated by biological reinforcers, and it may take the form of imitating society ("serving as the vicar of society") as the injunctions of parents, teachers, and others become part of its repertoire. The ego is the product of the practical contingencies in daily life, necessarily involving susceptibilities to reinforcement and the punitive contingencies arranged by other people, but displaying behavior shaped and maintained by a current environment. It is said to satisfy the id if it achieves a certain amount of biological reinforcement, and the superego if it does so without risking too much

punishment. We do not need to say that these archetypal personalities are the actors in an internal drama. The actor is the organism, which has become a person with different, possibly conflicting, repertoires as the result of different, possibly conflicting, contingencies. (Skinner, 1974, pp. 150–151)

Conflict, as reinterpreted by Skinner, is the result of incompatible contingencies of reinforcement. In place of Freud's internal warfare of competing mental agencies, Skinner prefers to look at the reinforcers that establish and maintain incompatible behaviors. Conflict is not *inside* the person; it is outside in the environment's (either social or natural environment's) arrangement of reinforcements and punishments. There are no metaphorical "minipersonalities" *causing* the observable conflicted behaviors. There are only learned behaviors, some of which are based in age-old traditions of social ethics and may conflict with an individual's biological needs. Nothing is gained, in Skinner's view, by replacing the external view of the organism with a hypothetical internal view of persons within a person.

For Freud, the difficulty with a behavioristic account of conflict is not the emphasis on learning. Freud himself spelled out a rather detailed formulation by which social and ethical learning takes place. Rather, the difficulty lies in localizing the causes and the controls exclusively in the environment. Freud assumed that learning has permanent or at least enduring effects on the person, and that these effects *are* enduring precisely because they are located *within* the person as persistent qualities of personality that transcend time and generalize across situations. In a real way, Freud regarded some kinds of learning history as virtually permanent, so that wishes and ideas dating from crucial experiences in childhood are "frozen" in time within the unconscious id. And such motives remain isolated from reality. Direct environmental manipulation of a person's behavior would do little if anything to modify these internalized, unchanging motives.

Skinner, on the other hand, makes no such assumptions of permanence. For the contemporary radical behaviorist, changes in the environmental contingencies, the patterns of reinforcement and punishment, have the capacity to change nearly infinitely the behavior they maintain. For Freud, a person is the sum total of his or her internalized images, experiences, and wishes; for Skinner, a person is his or her behavior.

Anxiety as a Signal of Impending Helplessness

Freud's Puzzle Solution

Anxiety is an aversive signal generated by the ego when it perceives that either external or internal threats will overpower it. The nature of anxiety experienced by the ego changes over time with development, as we discussed in Chapter 3. But by the time the child has resolved the Oedipus complex around the age of six or seven, learned standards of self-evaluation for "good" and "bad" behavior regulate the ego's vulnerability to anxiety. Freud called the sum total of those learned standards the superego. For Freud, wishes and ideas that violate the superego's standards trigger anxiety in the ego, and it is the ego's attempts to control the anxiety that result in psychopathology.

Skinner's Puzzle Solution

Anxiety is emotion, and emotions are merely special cases of involuntary behavior. Generally, Skinner argues, when a person reports that he or she is feeling anxiety, a certain class of bodily events is being described. Thus the frightened man reports feeling frightened because he detects his own sweating, rapid heart rate, and "goose pimples." But what, Skinner asks, is the causal status of such bodily states?

Skinner's answer is that anxiety (or any emotion) is not a *cause* but a reflex consequence of reinforcement contingencies. A behavior exposed to a negative reinforcer or to punishment becomes a conditioned signal that unpleasant consequences will occur again in similar situations. During our evolutionary development such automatic reactions to aversive or painful stimuli may have had adaptive effects. Certainly the organism that could learn to anticipate the negative consequences of coming close to a predator would survive longer. But the organism learns to flee to avoid being eaten, not to avoid the unpleasant bodily state of fear (Skinner, 1953, pp. 178 ff.; 1974, p. 62). In fact, the particular label a person is likely to place on the bodily arousal felt as emotion depends on the situation in which negative reinforcement or punishment has occurred:

> What a person feels when he is in a situation in which he has been punished or when he has engaged in previously punished behavior depends upon the type of punishment, and this often depends in turn upon the punishing agent or institution. If he has been punished by his peers, he is said to feel shame; if he has been punished by a religious agency, he is said to feel a sense of sin; and if he has been punished by a governmental agency, he is said to feel guilt. If he acts to avoid further punishment, he may moderate the condition felt as shame, sin, or guilt, *but he does not act because of his feelings or because his feelings are then changed; he acts because of the punishing contingencies to which he has been exposed.* (Skinner, 1974, pp. 62–63; italics added)

Like a rat in an operant chamber that learns to avoid electric shock by pressing a lever to turn off the current, people learn to avoid punishing and other aversive consequences associated with some of their behavior. Neurotic symptoms may thus be interpreted, not as compromise formations designed to appease combative internal agencies, but as learned avoidance behavior maintained by the negative reinforcement of preventing painful consequences. To control anxiety it is necessary to manipulate the environmental stimuli that are painful. It is of no help whatever to focus on the personal meanings and subjective bodily states associated with aversive stimuli.

From Freud's point of view, anxiety is developmentally progressive, changing its meanings as the infant proceeds toward maturity. And it is precisely those personal meanings that are the heart of psychopathology. Freud would not find Skinner's focus on environmental rewards and punishments at all relevant to the crux of the problem. For, in Freud's worldview, emotion is not merely correlated with behavior. Feelings are the springs of action. We act to block, change, distort, and reduce states of inner emotional tension. And of these states, anxiety is the most pathologically motivating.

PERSONAL SOURCES OF SKINNER'S RADICAL BEHAVIORISM

If we pause for a moment to consider the implications of radical behaviorism for personality theories, two interesting implications emerge. First, as we have seen in virtually all of the preceding theories in this book, the concept of *personality* has traditionally been conceptualized as something "in" a human being. For the genuinely radical behaviorist, what is inside an organism is irrelevant. Both Watson's and Skinner's views have sometimes been nicknamed "empty organism" or "black box" models of behavior for just this reason. Neither Watson nor Skinner had actually asserted that the organism was empty; but both of these radical behaviorists argued that a science of behavior could be formulated without reference to events inside the organism.

Main Themes to Be Explained

By this logic, mental events are irrelevant to understanding what organisms do. Indeed, the term *personality* is not in Skinner's technical vocabulary because it represents a metaphorical level of discourse or an inference from behavior. Consequently, if Skinner were to use the term personality, his definition would have to be something like "Personality is what an organism does, not what it thinks or feels." Pursuing this logic, the radical behaviorist looks outside people to explain why they do what they do. The causes of action are in the environment, not in the person's beliefs or feelings or needs. The environment selects behaviors by reinforcing them, and we do what we do in accord with these external selection principles (e.g., Skinner, 1987a, 1989). Motivation, from the viewpoint of the radical behaviorist, is a redundant idea, already encompassed in a person's actions and their resultant positive or negative consequences.

Ever since John B. Watson declared *prediction and control* of behavior to be the legitimate scientific goals of psychology, the second, and enduring, implication of radical behaviorism has been its insistence on an external locus of control for human agency. Concepts such as "choice," "freedom," "responsibility," "mind," and "dignity" are redefined in terms of the selection pressure a particular environment (culture) exerts on its population (Skinner, 1953, 1971, pp. 96ff., 1974). Put in crude terms, "good" (ethical) behavior and "bad" (unethical) behavior are restrained or encouraged by the person's history of reinforcement contingencies in interaction with the environment. Abstractions such as "sense of right and wrong," "conscience," or even "intention" are defined in terms of the environmental events that maintain, suppress, or enhance particular actions.

From a commonsense point of view, the puzzle of this explanation is trying to determine where responsibility lies (Skinner, 1971, pp. 70ff.). Does it lie with the person? With the environment? With the institutions that construct the environment? With the parents who initially constructed the child's first environment and first set of reinforcement contingencies? Or, perhaps, the concept of responsibility is irrelevant.

Skinner's emphasis on the external factors of human behavior, the selection pressures of the environment rather than the internal "pressures" of thought and feeling, may be a legitimate and valid scientific model of human action. But it is the *radical behaviorist's unique* view, intimately associated with Watson's and Skinner's work. We can therefore ask, what about this view of people, their motives and their obligations, is a result of Skinner's unique personal history? Can we find some explanation in Skinner's personal history for these two salient themes of radical behaviorism?

1. Human agency is localized external to the person, in the selection pressures of the environment;
2. Feelings are unimportant as causal determinants of action.

Skinner's Autobiography: Applying Behaviorism to Self

From 1976 to 1983, Skinner published three volumes of autobiography, totaling more than 1,100 pages. On the face of it, Skinner has provided historians and psychologists, more than any other theorist, with a greater quantity of personal information than anyone had a right to ask for. But the 1,100 pages consist largely of detailed, functional descriptions of his life, the same kind of descriptions of behavior that are useful in the laboratory study of reinforcement. The three volumes of autobiography contain only a few statements of personal feeling, a rare mention of intention, wish, or expectation, and, so far as I can tell, no account at all of personal meaning. At the end of the last volume of his autobiography, Skinner appended an epilogue in which he frankly explained his strategy for writing about himself. For example, on the issue of his feelings Skinner wrote,

> There are several reasons why I have not often reported my feelings. Occasionally I have said how I felt (or, more accurately, how my body felt to me) either literally ("I was angry, happy") or metaphorically ("I was stunned, shaken"), but I have not tried to "convey my feelings" in other ways—as by describing other situations which evoke the same feelings. . . . Paleontology is a science of bones, teeth, and shells because the softer parts of organisms have disappeared, and feelings are softer parts too. Only when I recorded how I felt at the time have I accepted it as part of the story.
>
> I also do not think feelings are important. Freud is probably responsible for the current extent to which they are taken seriously. . . .
>
> *Rather than tell my readers how I felt, I have left them to respond as I myself may have responded. It is the reader who must be judged warm or cold.* . . .
>
> I have also tried not to select episodes which show me as I now want my readers to see me. I have reported my failures as well as my successes. It is not easy to deal in the same way with others. I have not "honored my father and my mother"; I have described them as accurately as possible. Closer to the present, honesty about oneself is often gossip about others. (Skinner, 1983, p. 399; italics added)

Consistent with the behavioral theory that occupied his professional life for nearly a half century, Skinner dismisses the importance of feelings in his account of himself and externalizes into the environment the agency for his motives, thoughts, actions, and wishes. Readers of his autobiography, not the subject of it, "must be judged warm or cold . . . ," for Skinner believes that his feelings are irrelevant. Or to say it another way, we will feel the relevant feelings, not he.

Feelings, from the radical behaviorist's point of view, are only body states that parallel but do not cause action. Why, then, spend such great effort curtailing the report of them, concealing them from self and others? Most important, why create a *psychology* that discards feelings as important human variables and "explains" human action by not looking at the person who acts? "If I am right about human behavior, I have written the autobiography of a nonperson" (Skinner, 1983, p. 412). He also makes no claims to individuality or personal feeling: "If I am right about human behavior, an individual is only the way in which a species and a culture produces more of a species and a culture" (1983, p. 413). Above all, Skinner applies his method to himself, as indicated in the quotation that opens this chapter, but we cannot avoid speculating that he not only modeled his autobiography on his conception of scientific method, but found it congenial to do so because it is so self-protective:

> I am sometimes asked, "Do you think of yourself as you think of the organisms you study?" The answer is yes. So far as I know, my behavior at any given moment has been nothing more than the product of my genetic endowment, my personal history, and the current setting. That does not mean that I can explain everything I do or have done. (Skinner, 1983, p. 400)

In what follows, we accept Skinner's "invitation" to interpret the feelings and the meanings in his autobiography.

View of His Father: Aversion to Passivity

Born in 1904, in Susquehanna, Pennsylvania, Burrhus Frederic was the first child of William and Grace Skinner. He was called "Fred," not Burrhus, by family and friends. A second child, born two-and-one-half years later, Edward James ("Ebbie") died unexpectedly years later (probably from a cerebral hemorrhage) when Frederic was a freshman in college (more about this brother later).

Skinner's father was an attorney who worked as the counsel for the Hudson Coal Company. Skinner describes him as a man who was "unprepared" for each new step into the world (e.g., 1983, p. 20). He was a gentle man, with whom the young Frederic had a closer relationship than with his mother. Yet for all that, Skinner pictures his father as a man doomed by his own mother (Skinner's grandmother) to struggle after levels of achievement and success for which he lacked the talent and skills. He was a passive person, lacking a capacity to see how others saw him. He once successfully defended an unpopular railroad worker named Frank who had shot another worker who was picketing the railroad. The circumstances of the shooting were not clear, but the townspeople thought that Frank would at least be found guilty of manslaughter, a lesser charge than murder. Moreover, the case was invested with the additional emotional intensity of the town's divided opinion of the railroad strike. To make matters more troublesome, the Frank case involved some ethnic prejudices and resentments between Italian and Irish residents. Skinner's father's own popularity declined after his defense resulted in Frank's acquittal, and Will Skinner's political aspirations to become district attorney came to an abrupt halt. Skinner suggests that, in fact, his father's life was more or less crystallized by that time, with his remaining years spent being "worn down" by life. Depressingly, there was nothing more to aspire to:

He was then about as effective, personally and professionally, as he was ever to be. At the start of his career he began to keep a 50 cent piece in his pocket. So long as he had it, "he would never be broke," and perhaps it is a proof of his success that it was in his pocket when he died. But it was by then only a thin disk of silver, wholly unmarked, with sharp edges. For more than 50 years, it had survived the perils of loss or theft, but it had been buffeted and abraded by other coins and pocketknives and had lost its character and its value.

After the Frank trial my father suffered a similar fate. He had become a successful lawyer, but the minting was complete. The things that were to happen to him later would add no new details. Life was to abrade him, to wear him down. He struggled to satisfy that craving for a sense of worth with which his mother had damned him, but 40 years later he would throw himself on his bed, weeping, and cry, "I am no good, I am no good." (Skinner, 1976, p. 38)

For a radical behaviorist autobiographer who does not put much feeling into feelings, Skinner nevertheless manages to convey a wide range and depth of emotion in passages such as these. It is clear that he was disappointed by his father's passivity and failure to take charge of his life. Disappointment in a crucial role model frequently leads to anger. Skinner's metaphor of the coin wearing thin is about as intense an emotional expression as is possible with words while at the same time using the technique of metaphor to disclaim the feeling.

View of His Mother: Aversion to Pressure and Pretentiousness

Grace Skinner, Frederic's mother, was the dominant member of the family. Of her it had been said that she "made quite a man of Will Skinner" [Frederic's father] (Skinner, 1976, p. 45). Skinner reports that she was not unaware of her achievement. He describes his mother as a basically critical person who pressured her husband and her sons to admire her. Skinner believes that his mother was sexually inhibited, "frigid" is the word he uses, and intensely rigid about avoiding sexual topics and behavior. She was vigilant in encouraging her family to do likewise (Skinner, 1976, p. 45). Skinner believes that his father was "independent" in dealing with other women, and was probably attracted to several of his acquaintances, but Skinner also believes that his father confined such relationships to friendships.

Grace Skinner was eager for praise, just as her husband was, and she prided herself on her youthful appearance. According to Skinner, her relationships with friends and employees were close, with a good deal of loyalty demanded and received by Grace Skinner. However, he also believes that his mother received such loyalty from her friends because she liked to play the role of "bountiful Lady" who bestowed gifts and largesse on those who appreciated her.

From time to time, Skinner would be made aware that his birth had been difficult and that his mother had nearly died bringing him into the world (1976, p. 23). His mother had a way of portraying herself as a martyr. She once told Skinner the story of how she had been served ice cream by a friend at a party, but the dessert had a hair in it. "It would not have been 'right' to hurt her friend by taking the hair out of her mouth, and so she chewed and swallowed it bravely" (Skinner, 1976, p. 43). He uncharacteristically draws a further inference about his mother's intentions:

Perhaps she was thinking of my own difficult birth when she told me once that a boy who lived down the street "had no right to be alive" because his mother had died when he was born. (1976, p. 43)

Apparently, Skinner resented the pressures his mother placed on him, was critical of what he perceived to be her pretentiousness, and was alienated by her emotional restraint and inhibition.

View of His Brother: Disclaiming Feelings

Skinner reports that he felt his parents had shown more affection to his younger brother as they grew up, but claims that he was more independent and not too concerned with this disparity in parental love (1976, p. 210). What troubled him, he reports, was the painful loss of his brother and the fact that his own independence would be jeopardized as his family would draw him in closer as the "family boy," a role he had tried to escape by leaving for college.

Yet he was aware, as he wrote this explanation, that he was disclaiming his feelings. He helped the pathologist who performed the autopsy on his brother by describing "objectively" the brother's symptoms. Skinner's father was told that his elder son's "objectivity" had been helpful:

> With the same objectivity I had watched my parents as they reacted to the discovery that my brother was dead.
>
> But I was far from unmoved. I once made an arrowhead by bending the top of a tin can into a flattened cone. I fastened it to the end of an arrow, and when I shot it straight up into the air, it fell back and struck my brother in the shoulder, drawing blood. Many years later I remembered the event with a shock when I heard Laurence Olivier speaking Hamlet's lines:
>
> > . . . Let my disclaiming from a purpos'd evil
> > Free me so far in your most generous thoughts,
> > That I have shot mine arrow o'er the house,
> > And hurt my brother.
>
> (Skinner, 1976, p. 210)

It is difficult to read this description of Skinner's "external" behavior and the behavior of others without seeing some element of guilt in his quoting Hamlet's lines. Though he makes clear that Ebbie and he never competed, it is as if he were saying that he had to deny to himself that he felt jealousy or anger toward his brother—feelings that emerged only in passing and to which he gave little attention until reminded by an actor's lines.

Early Interest in Religion, Sex, and Writing: Troublesome Feelings

Summarizing his own experience of his family life, Skinner said that he was "taught to fear God, the police, and what people will think" (1983, p. 403). He was describing what he believed to be the inhibiting constraints that were imposed on him by his parents, especially by his mother. He recalls much of his later childhood and adolescence as attempts to escape these constraints, and he forthrightly admits that he could be an angry rebel at times. But most typically, his anger was suppressed in the service of creative ways to "escape" authority figures and demands, or, as Skinner prefers to put it, clever ways of circumventing aversive consequences (1983, pp. 403ff.).

In childhood, religion was a central issue for Skinner, who attended Bible classes and developed a certain degree of faith in the efficacy of religious belief. He was early made aware of the ethnic and religious differences among the Roman Catholics, Episcopalians, and Presbyterians, and like most children, wondered about the meaning of the strange customs of people who did not belong to his own faith. He received much of his formal training in religion in school in Miss Graves's Bible classes:

> We reached the story of Christ just when the sex urge had made itself felt in me. I was 12 or 13. . . . They were free, natural days. I was beginning to read and think and come in contact with earth. Religion and religious ideas bothered me and I thought a great deal about them. I had never associated freely with other boys and now my doubts about things and my sex shame drove me almost to solitude.
>
> I sensed strongly the injustice in the world. I must have been jealous and resentful. It was an uneasy age. But gradually I worked out a theory of compensation: I began to suspect that punishment or reward in afterlife brought to a balance the imbalance in this world and the theory was practical so long as I believed it. For a year at least life was perfectly happy for me. I believed that all my trouble simply made way for compensating happiness. My jealousy was not discarded (I see this now) but was rather satisfied: the happiness of my companions which I envied, simply meant, I was sure, that they would have trouble later. (Skinner, 1976, p. 110)

Skinner tested several of his religious beliefs only to have the tests result in disappointment. For example, the maxim "Faith can move mountains" didn't quite stand up to his efforts to levitate himself from a beam scale nor did any amount of faith ever achieve his fantasy of flying around a room to impress people (1976, p. 111). Later, he decided to contribute a scholarly article to a Presbyterian magazine showing that many great composers had been of that faith. When he researched the topic, he found to his dismay that there were few if any Presbyterian composers, and those he admired were Catholic. Sometime in adolescence, Skinner gave up his belief in God and organized religion, and by his account, seems never to have returned to those beliefs.

From about middle adolescence through to young adulthood, Skinner regarded himself as sexually naive and inept. He had experienced the usual "crushes" and "loves" during childhood and adolescence, and had made some rude attempts at what was then called "petting." But his first real sexual experience was not until his senior year of college. With two friends, he drove to the "red light" district, where he and his friends employed the services of a prostitute:

> This was my first unencumbered sexual intercourse, and it was over fairly quickly. The girl said that I had obviously enjoyed it more than my predecessor, but it had been surprisingly unexciting. I was no doubt a little scared, but was this indeed what I should have found if I had been successful in those attempted seductions? Was this what lay at the top of Marion Knise's leg? Would this have been the prize if I had won my wrestling match with Leslie Gilbert or had persuaded Ellen to have an affair with

me? I dressed quickly and went downstairs, pleased that my absence was attracting no more attention than if I had gone to the toilet. (Skinner, 1976, p. 244)

Although he frankly admits to being "scared," the rest of the experience was apparently devoid of feelings, a not unusual outcome given the circumstances. What is interesting in this account is Skinner's reflections on what "might have been" with other women to whom he had been attracted. One interpretation of the way he reports this episode is that it reflects his timidity and reluctance to feel. Feelings, even in retrospect, are suspect.

By the second semester of his senior year in college, Skinner had decided to attempt a career as a novelist. He asked for help from his father to support himself for one year while he made the attempt, and his father reluctantly agreed. He had gotten some encouragement from the poet Robert Frost, whom he met through an introduction by his creative writing teacher at college. Frost invited the young Skinner to send him some samples of his writing. Some months later Frost wrote to Skinner remarking on how Skinner's stories contained nice observations and that the writing was "clean." Frost gave the young would-be author warm support and the critical insight that Skinner had to learn to *care* for the things and people he wrote about (reproduced in Skinner, 1976, p. 248). Had Frost detected the same reluctance to deal with feelings?

He built a study for himself in the family house, but endured the unexpressed, sometimes overly expressed, doubts of his parents. Both parents preferred that he prepare himself for a more reliable career, and Skinner sensed their "shame" at having their college graduate son spend his time "doing nothing" but writing. He knew he had made a serious mistake. He felt trapped.

The Dark Year: Becoming a Behaviorist

By the end of that summer, it was clear to Skinner that he could not complete a novel or commercially successful stories. He decided to change his plans and "escape" writing for several years. But he had made a deal with his parents to try out this enterprise for a year, and he stuck to it. Slowly it became a "dark year" (1976, p. 265). There was little intellectual stimulation, no social support, no sign of success, and he felt pressured and criticized by his parents. He began spending long periods in the family library sitting absolutely motionless "in a kind of catatonic stupor" or making obsessive, ritualistic movements with his foot. Skinner broached the idea of seeing a psychiatrist to his father, but Will Skinner felt that it would be a waste of time and money, and the idea apparently was dropped (1976, p. 278). But the episode gives some indication of the distress in which Skinner found himself. Because he was spending more time with his father, Skinner may have realized consciously for the first time how much he did not want to become like his father, a passive, helpless, and melancholy person who had not lived up to his family's expectations.

He began clearly to see that his father was a depressed man. Will Skinner was in the second year of his private practice as a lawyer, and had several crises to face. He had been accused, erroneously, of lying about a fee he collected and a client threatened disbarment proceedings. Within recent years, his father had lost his younger son, Ebbie, lost an important job, moved his family to Scranton, and now watched his only son seemingly do nothing. Skinner's mother voiced her fear that her husband might commit suicide:

> "Others have done it for less," she said to me, and she was right. But other men had not believed so strongly in progress or had been so richly rewarded when they proved to their parents and friends that progress was possible. My father was too proud to kill himself; he could not confess failure that way. (Skinner, 1976, p. 278)

His father's luck changed for the better within the year, and he landed a job with the coal company, although it was not sufficiently important in his own eyes to constitute the sought-for success. The remainder of the "dark year" involved increasing loneliness, substituting writing personal observations for social contact. "I was confined to the autistic, not to say auto-erotic, satisfactions to be found in my notebook" (Skinner, 1976, pp. 279–280). He began to "look at myself as a person," although until then he had avoided self-observation. He realized that he was rarely satisfied when he had achieved a goal. He wrote this candid self-revelation in his notebook under the heading "What I Achieve I Despise":

> But why should I despise the things I attain [such as high grades, a reputation for cleverness]? Is it because I am secretly conscious of my inferiority and feel that if I achieve a "great" thing I must have been mistaken as to its greatness? I think not. *I think rather that I feel that greatness is merely the result of a happy combination of trivial influences, that the great man cannot help being great, the poor man cannot help being poor.* My ability to trace my own development shows this to me again and again. My only satisfaction lies in discovering that I am wrong about my "inexorable evolution"—that perhaps I have imagined it.
>   *I Ask of Life—*
>   1. Pleasurable satisfaction of desire.
>   The cardinal necessity in obtaining this is restraint. We are creatures of desire, filled with hundreds of evolved cravings, and the satisfaction of all of these is neither possible nor would it be desirable. We must make use of our knowledge and intellect to choose those desires which will give us . . . the greatest pleasure. . . . Desire may move the world but intellect may mold desire. But intellect molds desire only when desire desires to be molded. . . . (Skinner, 1976, p. 282; first italics added)

This passage was written during the dark year, when Skinner was 22. A number of features in this quotation anticipate important major themes in his later professional life and reflect his distress at that moment. First, the last lines on the nature of desire, ironically, echo Freud's views on human nature as expressed in the war between the ego and id (reason against passion), and Skinner reaches the classic Freudian conclusion that the ego (intellect) is the helpless rider of the id horse, leading the horse where it wants to go.

More important, Skinner is giving voice to a kind of nihilism in the guise of self-effacement that is uniquely characteristic of his radical behaviorism. He is depressed, but does not identify the depression as such. His struggle for success is stymied; he believes he has failed as a writer; he has watched his father fail and then react with despair to his own passivity; and he has lost his younger brother for what must have seemed like no reason at all. He concludes that personal effort and responsibility are unrelated to success or failure: Great men are great by chance, poor men are poor by chance. Happy circumstance produces happiness.

Elms (1981) has interpreted Skinner's reactions during this year as constituting an "identity crisis" as defined by Erikson (see Chapter 6). Elms believes that the issues raised during this year were resurrected later in Skinner's life, after he had become an experimental psychologist, and his identity was again threatened with frustration. At that later point, Skinner, as a form of self-therapy, wrote his best-selling utopian novel *Walden Two* to reconcile the fragments of his identity. Elms's (1981) analysis in terms of the concept of identity crisis may be at least partially correct, if we assume that part of the identity which was crumbling for the young Skinner was his identification with his father.

The crisis was resolved, if "crisis" is the correct term, in the way that Erikson indicates many identity crises are resolved, with the adoption of an ideology that gives personal and social meaning back to the person caught up in feelings of distress (Elms, 1981, p. 471). At the time, however, Skinner reached a different conclusion expressed with his usual restrained but sardonic humor and some suppressed anger: "I see now that the only thing left for me to do in life is to justify myself for doing nothing" (1976, p. 283).

Characteristically, he considered the situation from a new perspective: Had he failed as a writer, or had writing failed him as a method of studying what he was most interested in, namely, human behavior (1976, p. 291)? He concluded that writing as a method was the failure. As he began to review the reasons for the misery of the "dark year," he realized that he had been interested in psychology. The stories he had sent to Frost, for example, were largely psychological studies, and most of the reading he had done during the dark year was in the works of psychological authors such as Proust and Dostoyevsky. But, abruptly, he was sidetracked by a sudden interest in the arcane and occult. He read some books on mystical phenomena (Ouspensky, for example) and began to dabble in explanations far removed from science. Discussions with himself of the "fourth dimension," and the subjectivity of meaning made him realize "I was floundering in a stormy sea and perilously close to drowning, but help was on the way" (1976, p. 298).

The help was in the form of *The Dial* magazine, an erudite journal that published, among others, the philosopher Bertrand Russell, who at the time was writing about the work of behaviorist John B. Watson. Skinner realized that Watson's approach to meaning and knowledge, as discussed by Russell, was quite different from the occult and from the literary approach that failed him. Here, at last, was stuff you could get hold of. Inspired by Russell, Skinner bought a copy of Watson's *Behaviorism,* and within a short time, the young Skinner was identifying himself as a scientific behaviorist, even defending Watson against critics by writing to the editors of the *Saturday Review* to criticize a book critical of behaviorism. The editors did not publish his letter, but the decision was made. Skinner decided on graduate study in psychology, and his study would be focused on observables, on scientific epistemology, and on the analysis of behavior not intention.

Understanding the Personal Sources of Skinner's Radical Behaviorism

There is so much more to the story of B. F. Skinner's personal evolution as the preeminent radical behaviorist of our time that it would take an entire chapter just to outline the main features. In our review, the focus has been placed on the *personal origins* of Skinner's particular adherence to radical behaviorism. We have attempted to explain the two key themes to be found in Skinner's conception of human functioning:

1. Externalized human agency, so that the behaviorist looks outside the person for the causes of behavior.
2. Elimination or rejection of feeling as important causative variables in human psychology.

The ironies have been noted, but note one more. Skinner's interest in psychology developed out of his failed interest in becoming a creative writer. Creative writers, such as Proust whom Skinner admired, are artists who depict the range and depth of human action and thought by explicating their characters' emotions.

Aside from the ironies, what else can we conclude from this selective survey of Skinner's personal history? To answer that question we must violate Skinner's own principles and resort to educated speculation, but speculation that can serve some useful purpose in making the strengths and weaknesses of radical behaviorism clear.

First, as envisioned by Watson and Skinner, radical behaviorism makes the concept of personality obsolete and irrelevant. In a way, humans become, to use Skinner's own self-description "nonpersons." Are "nonpersons" easier to study scientifically than "persons"? Certainly, conceptualized this way, nonpeople do not have to have their nonfeelings examined.

Given the role models to whom he was exposed as a child, and the likely resentment and rebellion they triggered in him, Skinner early on adopted a kind of rationalizing style that placed blame, failure, and to be consistent, success outside personal responsibility. He was skilled at devising ways of escaping the "aversive" discipline style of his mother, but less skilled in escaping the emotional consequences of watching his mother "make quite a man of" his father. He had been taught to fear God and the police, but what he learned was to resent pressure and authority figures. Rather than confronting figures such as these directly, his adaptive strategy was to escape or to defeat them indirectly. By conceptualizing "good" and "bad" behavior, success and failure as stemming from environmental contingencies rather than from internal motives, we escape the whole issue of confrontation, responsibility—and feeling. Nonpersons do not feel. And they do not feel responsible.

Second, Skinner's insistence that feelings are only correlated bodily states, not causes, in human action reduces emotion to a mere side effect. As Watson considered thought to be an "epiphenomenon," Skinner treats feelings as trivial phenomenon. If feelings are unimportant, then we need not be concerned if our feelings momentarily hurt, or if we are momentarily threatened by emotions, or if our feelings are in painful conflict. A person can take active measures to correct or change the environment responsible for these side effects.

Skinner's book *Enjoy Old Age*, for example, is a guide for the elderly on how to cope with failing eyesight, hearing, and motor and memory skills (Skinner & Vaughn, 1983). The whole point of the book is to avoid despair and helplessness by taking an active stance to control the environment. You can't change what the ravages of old age do to your body, but you can change the environment in which you function.

Skinner, perhaps in reaction to the perceived passivity and "unpreparedness" of his father, takes nothing lying down or passively. And, whatever we think of radical behaviorism as a model of human behavior, we have to admire his courage and motives. When Skinner copes, he copes actively. When Skinner describes human coping, he *says* it is a passive response to the environment. Which one is the real Skinner?

> Can I tell you what I really think of myself? I can, at least, offer some objective evidence. In many of my notes I record my failures and mistakes, and the explanations are never excuses. . . .
>
> I do not admire myself as a person. My successes do not override my shortcomings. Last night at dinner Babs Spiegel said that I was the one person she knew who had not been changed by success. This morning I thought of a quip: "Yes, I was impossible *before* I was successful." (Skinner, 1983, p. 410)

Self-effacement or self-denial, then, is the main theme that Skinner finds in behaviorism, because we have to attribute our achievements to our genetic and environmental histories. The same themes, as Skinner points out, run through philosophy and particularly through Eastern mysticism: Self-possession out of self-abandonment, or gain freedom by abandoning the self. But, I wonder, does Skinner sometimes see, after writing three volumes of autobiography, that self-denial is also self-protection?

THE LIMITATIONS OF RADICAL BEHAVIORISM

The great scientific strength of radical behaviorism was its method. Watson's and Skinner's emphasis on observable, verifiable, and controllable variables transformed psychology into an experimental science. But the transformation that was at first so liberating eventually became limiting.

For while the practitioners of radical behaviorism scientifically demonstrated the power of Pavlovian and operant conditioning, the rest of American psychology, in its eagerness to imitate "scientific" method, lost sight of the discipline's most enduring problems: *what people think about the experiences that are thrust on them in the laboratory, and how their thinking regulates what they do.* Under the behaviorists, "thinking" became, if not a dirty word, then at least an obsolete one.

For all practical purposes, the radical behaviorists had removed the thinking organism from examining its thinking about its own psychology. Cognitive processes were treated as if they were scientifically unknowable and therefore irrelevant. As long as the observable and controllable stimuli and responses of the organism could be specified, a fully competent science of behavior would be developed. What the organism thought about its own actions had no place in this view of learning. The principles of learned behavior became almost independent of the learner. One precise statement of this viewpoint was made by Skinner, tongue-in-cheek to be sure, but in the opening to an essay entitled "Why I Am Not a Cognitive Psychologist":

> In Pavlov's experiment a hungry dog hears a bell and is then fed. If this happens many times, the dog begins to salivate when it hears the bell. The standard mentalistic explanation is that the dog "associates" the bell with food. But it was Pavlov who associated them! (Skinner, 1978, p. 97)

Pavlovian conditioning is an associative process, but the connection is not created "inside" the dog. The poor canine is merely a necessary evil in an otherwise elegant demonstration of the "laws" of learning. Skinner, and certainly Watson before him, advanced the view that it is sufficient for a science of behavior to describe the relationship between observable events. Whatever the organism's view of this relationship may be, it can safely be ignored. But can it?

Biological Limits of Conditioning

Contrary to Watson's and Skinner's enthusiastic belief in the universality and reliability of conditioning principles, it has become increasingly clear that learning is not automatic and is not organism-free. There are several limitations on the "laws" of conditioning that appear to emerge from "inside" the organism.

Pavlov's discovery that arbitrary stimuli (tones, lights, vibrations) could elicit reflex behavior when paired with the natural stimulus for such responding (for example, meat powder) led to the unsurprising but erroneous conclusion that all stimuli could serve equally well (Rachlin & Logue, 1983, p. 110). It should be pointed out, however, that neither Pavlov nor Skinner made such simplistic leaps of logic. Rather, the many researchers who followed in their footsteps tended to make these logical but wrong assumptions about the universal "lawfulness" of conditioning principles (Kling, 1971; Rescorla, 1987, 1988).

Yet not all neutral stimuli are effective conditioning stimuli. Garcia and Koelling (1966) in a landmark study exposed rats to specific light, noise, and taste stimuli as they licked water from a drinking tube. Following drinking, the rats were exposed to x-radiation of sufficient dosage to induce nausea. If Pavlovian conditioning were automatic, then each of the stimuli preceding the UCS (irradiation-nausea) would become an effective avoidance cue in the future. But, in fact, the rats learned to avoid only the sweet *taste* of the water. Sweet, but not "bright" or "noisy" water became associated with illness. A second group of rats was subjected to the same procedure, but electric shock was used in place of the radiation. This electric shock group learned to avoid the "bright" and "noisy" water, but not the sweet water. Apparently, animals are more "prepared" to associate nausea with taste cues than with auditory or visual cues. Or, more generally, rats are biologically prepared to associate specific stimuli with particular effects while selectively ignoring other stimuli (see also Garcia, McGowan, Ervin, & Koelling, 1968).

Seligman (1970, 1971, 1972) and Eysenck (1976) have argued that organisms evolved to learn some stimulus relationships more effectively than others. An animal that rapidly learns to make associations, for example, between taste and subsequent illness is likely to survive by avoiding poisonous foods after only one taste. But if all stimuli impinging on the animal at the time of the first poisoning were equally conditionable, its chances of repeatedly ingesting larger doses of the same noxious food increase.

In a similar way, human phobias reflect a limited number of feared stimuli rather than all possible objects in the neurotic person's world of dangers. Phobic people fear dangerous animals such as snakes and spiders; they fear high places, cramped places, and dark places; they only very, very infrequently have phobias of cocktail tables, stereophonic receivers, flowered wallpaper, or killer Twinkies. Our human forebears had legitimate survival needs reflected in their fears of snakes, spiders, high and dark places, so an innate *predisposition* to be fearful of and to avoid certain classes of stimuli was favored by natural selection (Rachman, 1978). Such stimuli have been called "prepared" stimuli and the fears associated with them "prepared" fears on the assumption that evolution selection pressures have somehow selected nervous systems with special sensitivities (Seligman, 1970). By the same token, such "preparation" also limits the range of effective classically conditionable stimuli.

It is well to note that alternative explanations of why some stimuli are more easily conditionable than others have been offered (Bandura, 1977b, pp. 75 ff.). There is some evidence to suggest that instead of innate "preparedness" as the facilitator in some learning, it is rather the organism's capacity to discriminate selectively among stimuli and to be sensitive to the delay between the stimulus and its noxious effects (e.g., Krane & Wagner, 1975). But the fact remains that *some* stimuli but not others are more easily learned as signals of impending events (Rescorla, 1988).

In the field of operant conditioning, similar biological and evolutionary limitations have been found. An amusing and important set of limitations on the operant shaping techniques was reported by a husband and wife team of professional animal trainers. Breland and Breland (1961) had for a number of years adopted the behavioristic spirit of the times: "If it moves, we can shape it." But they ran into trouble.

Working with a raccoon for a bank display, the Brelands tried to shape the animal to pick up coins one at a time and drop them into a container for a food reinforcement. Shaping worked well in getting the racoon to pick up two coins, but he seemed not to be able to let go of them, despite the fact that reinforcement was available only when both coins had been dropped in the "bank." As the frustrated reinforcers reported:

> He would rub [the coin] up against the inside of the container, pull it back out, clutch it firmly for several seconds. However, he would finally turn it loose and receive his food reinforcement. Then the final contingency . . . that he pick up both coins and put them in the container.
>
> Now the raccoon really had problems (and so did we). Not only could he not let go of the coins, but he spent seconds, even minutes, rubbing them together (in a most miserly fashion), and dipping them into the container. He carried on this behavior to such an extent that the practical application we had in mind—a display featuring a raccoon putting money in a piggy bank—simply was not feasible. The rubbing behavior became worse and worse as time went on, in spite of nonreinforcement. (Breland & Breland, 1961, p. 682)

The recalcitrant raccoon was merely behaving instinctually, "washing" and rubbing clean his food—or anything else that found its way into his paws.

> In a similarly frustrating fashion, attempts to train a pig to pick up a silver dollar, carry it to a "piggy bank" and deposit it were blocked by the pig's increasing slowness, his constantly dropping it to root it along the ground with his nose, toss it in the air, root it, and so on. (Breland & Breland, 1961, p. 683)

Like the raccoon's, the pig's behavior could be shaped only to the point at which its instinctual repertoire of behaviors took dominance. "Instinctual drift," as the Brelands termed it, was responsible for the human frustration in these cases of well-applied but futile operant conditioning techniques:

> The general principle seems to be that whenever an animal has strong instinctive behaviors in the area of the conditioned response, after continued running the organism will drift toward the instinctive behavior even to the delay or preclusion of the reinforcement. In a very boiled-down, simplified form, it might be stated as "Learned behavior drifts toward instinctive behavior." (Breland & Breland, 1961, p. 684)

Even the most trainable animals are not the models of environmental plasticity envisioned by the early radical behaviorists. Biological limits, species-specific behaviors, and innate predispositions all place a ceiling on the effectiveness and reliability of operant conditioning (but see Skinner, 1975). It is worth mentioning in passing that in an updated account of the "misbehavior of organisms," Marian Breland-Bailey and Robert Bailey (1993) have made clear that their experiences never caused them to dismiss reinforcement theory. Rather, in more sophisticated fashion, they had tried to understand the frustrating results they sometimes encountered as a window to understanding the limitations of operant theory.

Conditioning Is Not Automatic

For Watson and Skinner, but not for all behaviorists, there is no need to assume the existence of mental representations of the stimuli that regulate behavior. The radical behaviorist ignores the organism's cognitions on the assumption that, even if some aspect of the stimulus is encoded in the brain, it is still the behavior that must be explained (Skinner, 1950). To put the matter bluntly, the radical behaviorist proceeds with the analysis of behavior *as if* the organism were "empty" (Allport, 1960; Skinner, 1989). Only the environmental contingencies, not the organism's cognitions, expectations, knowledge, regulate behavior. At the human level, awareness does not count for much.

The first problem with this assumption developed surrounding an operant procedure in verbal shaping called the Greenspoon effect. Greenspoon (1955) reported that when subjects were asked to generate random verbal responses, a certain class of words, say, plurals ending in *s,* could be increased in frequency by the experimenter nodding approval and saying "Mmmm" whenever the subject uttered a plural word. The controversial aspect of the experiment was the initial belief that the subjects were unaware of the particular reinforcement contingency. They increased and decreased their number of plural nouns as the experimenter reinforced or extinguished the response, but they seemed not to know why they said what they said. If that claim were true, then reinforcement is clearly some mechanical, unconscious, and automatic process.

Subsequent research demonstrated that humans are not passive recipients of stimulation. Rather, they actively interpret what is happening to them, although they may not tell the experimenter about their interpretations. The original Greenspoon study had used only superficial postexperimental interview procedures to assess the subject's awareness of what the experimenter had been doing. Later studies (Dulaney, 1962; Farber, 1963; Spielberger & DeNike, 1966) with more detailed interview procedures showed that conditioning was directly related to the subject's awareness that he or she was being reinforced for a specific kind of response.

In fact, as Murray and Jacobson (1978, p. 665) point out, it is difficult to find evidence of human learning that excludes awareness altogether (but see Nisbett & Wilson, 1977; and Shevrin & Dickman, 1980, for a view of cognitive processes at the unconscious level). Perhaps the most important finding was the discovery that human awareness is directly but not simply related to the effects of reinforcement. Farber (1963) was able to show that awareness is not just a consequence of reinforcement, but a cause of what the person will do. Farber's subjects were sometimes aware of the reinforcements they received for a specific verbal response and sometimes not. Aware subjects evidenced higher rates of learning than those who were not aware, but being aware was not a foolproof predictor of a subject's conditionability. In addition to awareness, the subject, for whatever personal reasons, had also to *want* to comply with the experimenter's implicit demands that he or she utter one kind of sentence rather than another. Apparently humans can choose whether a reinforcement will be reinforcing.

It's Not What You Say or Do, but What You Think That Counts

Farber (1963) tested the radical behaviorist position that awareness is a consequence (epiphenomenon) rather than a cause of reinforcement. He had 120 subjects read through 80 index cards on which were typed four pronouns: *I, You, He, They.* Each pronoun was followed by a verb. For one-third of the subjects, the verbs were hostile (e.g., slew, hated). Another third of the subjects received pronouns with neutral verbs (e.g., touched, observed). And the final third of the subjects were given "nurturant" verbs (e.g., fondled, cherished). All subjects were instructed to make up a sentence for each card using one of the pronouns and its associated verb and to say the sentence aloud. For the first 20 cards, the experimenter remained silent. But at the end of the 20th trial, Farber scolded one half of all subjects for poor performance, lack of effort or attention, and for general incompetence. The remaining half of the subjects in all three groups were simply instructed at the end of the 20th trial with a restatement of the original directions for the task. Thus one half of all subjects in each of the three groups was given a "failure experience," and one half received "neutral" instructions.

For the remaining 60 trials, *all* subjects were positively reinforced by the experimenter saying "good" every time they chose to make a sentence beginning with the pronoun YOU, regardless of the group to which the subject belonged. The key question, of course, is whether positive reinforcement has different effects on subjects in neutral and failure conditions. And it is possible to assess whether such differences correlate with a subject's awareness or lack of awareness of the reinforcement contingency ("good" for YOU sentences). After the 80th trial, subjects were interviewed using such questions as: "Did you notice anything in particular that the experimenter did when you were making up sentences?" If the reply was affirmative, follow-up questions were asked: "How did you react to this?"

From the radical behaviorist's viewpoint, the results were startling. For the subjects in the failure (scolded) group, only 17 were aware that the experimenter had reinforced them for "YOU" sentences. But in the neutral group, 26 of the subjects were aware of the contingency. Failure experiences suppress awareness. Freud would not be surprised. More important, the aware subjects performed significantly better than the nonaware subjects. Specifically, by the 80th trial, aware subjects were getting between 43 and 50 percent of their sentence correct by using YOU to begin the sentence. The nonaware subjects, by comparison, actually demonstrated a modest *decrease* in YOU sentences over their own baseline rates by the 80th trial, and they bottomed out with a rate below 20 percent correct. The following table summarizes these results with rounded percentages supplied in a graph by Farber (1963).

	Experimental Condition	
	Neutral Instructions	*Scolding*
Aware Subjects (Percentage Correct)	50	43
Nonaware Subjects (Percentage Correct)	19	18

Note that the scolding procedure resulted in lower learning rates for *both* the aware and nonaware subjects compared to their neutral counterparts.

Further analysis of the data permitted Farber to divide the aware group into subjects who knew what they were reinforced for but who *chose* not to comply (nonconforming), and subjects who were aware and who wanted to comply (conforming). Divided in this way, the aware subjects, who had performed as a group better than the nonaware subjects as a group, now evidenced some interesting within-group differences. Conforming aware subjects showed nearly twice as many reinforced verbal responses as the equally aware but nonconforming subjects. So, not only is awareness important in verbal reinforcement, but the subject's willingness to comply with the experimenter actually determines the effectiveness of the reinforcer. Nonconforming subjects (who were aware) showed rates of correct YOU statements almost identical to subjects who had *not* been aware of what the experimenter was reinforcing. Ignorance and unwillingness are virtually equal in their power to render reinforcement ineffective!

Farber's analysis of the postexperimental interview responses for one subject at a time revealed another surprising fact about verbal shaping. Not only does the subject's awareness of the reinforcement contingency and his or her willingness to be reinforced matter, but sometimes there is a capricious rather than a simple relationship among all three variables. Thus one aware subject reported in the interview: "Everytime I said 'you' he said 'good' so naturally I said 'you' most of the time, but now and then I said something else just to break the monotony." But this subject's actual performance record showed that he "broke the monotony" only once in the last 40 trials! What a subject says, what he or she is aware of, and what he or she actually does may vary independently of each other and of the reinforcer. This sounds like Freud's view of behavior.

There were also individual aware subjects who wanted to perform well, but who began constructing *any* sentence beginning with YOU, rather than using the required verb stems on the cards. Such sentences were never reinforced. Even under this contingency of extinction, one aware subject persisted in generating incorrect YOU sentences to see if he could make the experimenter reinforce the all-important YOU pronoun! Farber summarized his findings in this way:

> Subjects may not know exactly what is going on in an experiment or, for that matter, in a therapeutic session, but very few have no ideas at all. They may be mistaken, or they may be concerned with irrelevant matters, such as whether participation is worth the time and trouble. . . .The one thing psychologists can count on is that their subjects or clients will talk, if only to themselves. And, not infrequently, whether relevant or irrelevant, the things people say to themselves determine the rest of the things they do. (Farber, 1963, p. 237)

COGNITIVE PSYCHOLOGY REINVENTS THE MIND

There are many sources of evidence from a wide variety of subfields in psychology that show what a human being thinks, expects, and plans for can directly regulate his or her behavior (e.g., Monte, 1975; Murray & Jacobson, 1978; Rachlin & Logue, 1983; but see especially Martindale's [1981] fine text for the broadest view). Gordon Allport (1961) argued almost from the beginning of his career that what a person deliberately plans has to be given as much weight as his or her actual performances. George Kelly, from the perspective of clinical psychology, said it perhaps best:

> If events, either past or expected, appear to manipulate a man it is only because, so far, he has figured out only one way to cope with them. He will continue to dance to the tune he thinks he hears them play until he contrives some other way of listening for the succession of notes.
>
> Man never waits to see what will happen; he always looks to see what will happen. (Kelly, 1967/1980, p. 27)

By the mid-1960s, it became clear to psychologists that they were faced with a choice. Either they could conceptualize thinking as an epiphenomenon in the tradition of radical behaviorism, or they could reinvent the scientific study of cognition. The main lines in the debate—to think about humans as relevantly thinking *creatures* or as irrelevantly thinking *creatures*—are illustrated in Figure 16.4. The figure is somewhat oversimplified, but the main boundaries between the various models of behaviorism are clear.

Watson and Skinner's radical behaviorism avoids any reference to cognitive (mental) representations of experience as mediators of behavior. For purebred radical behaviorists, stimuli-response sequences are sufficient, and eminently verifiable, data to explain human action. For a contemporary cognitive behaviorist, by contrast, there is a choice: Either cognition is directly *causal* in producing behavior (see Part *B* of Figure 16.4), or there is a complex correlational *and* causal relationship between cognition and behavior (see Part C of Figure 16.4). This latter and more complex reciprocal relationship between thoughts and plans and the behavior of the person has underwritten a great deal of contemporary cognitive social learning theory.

To summarize, radical behaviorism was limited in its conception of human events by some of its adherents' implicit belief that conditioning is automatic and universally

FIGURE 16.4 Behavioristic models of the status of cognition.

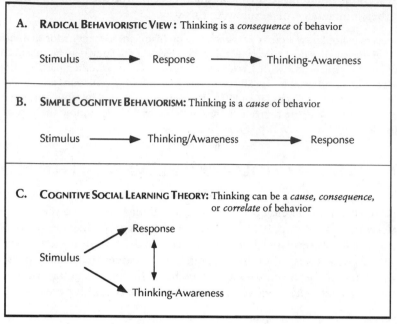

Based on Farber (1963).

applicable to living things. Cognitive events—mental states—have been shown to be clearly relevant and, as we shall see, susceptible to verifiable study.

Miller and Dollard

The Transition to Cognitive Behaviorism

Not all behaviorists were as radical as Watson and Skinner. In the 1930s through to the 1950s, a group of psychologists and social scientists studying with Clark L. Hull at Yale University began to apply the principles of conditioning to complex social behavior. Called the Yale Group, the team was composed of such eminent scientists as Neal Miller, John Dollard, O. Hobart Mowrer, and Leonard Doob. Their contributions as a group and singly have had an enduring impact on psychology, but it is to the work primarily of John Dollard and Neal Miller that we must turn briefly to understand how contemporary social learning theory emerged from behaviorism.

Miller and Dollard (1941), and to a lesser extent O. Hobart Mowrer, were interested in translating Freud's rich psychoanalytic observations into the more testable language of stimulus-response psychology. The first such effort had been a monograph entitled *The Frustration-Aggression Hypothesis* written jointly by the members of the Yale group (Dollard, Doob, Miller, Mowrer, & Sears, 1939; Miller, 1941), in which they translated Freud's concept of the aggressive instinct into a behavioral drive theory stated in formal, testable terms. The thesis of the book that aggression is always a consequence of blocking a person's efforts to reach a goal was controversial, but it triggered a wealth of research (Berkowitz, 1969; Dollard et al., 1939).

And, of course, that was the intended effect. The Yale group had demonstrated that Freud's clinical formulations could be converted into testable propositions, but they also demonstrated that a whole range of new intervening (cognitive) variables had to be invented to enrich stimulus-response behaviorism to the point at which it would be equal to the task.

Psychodynamic Social Learning Theory

Miller and Dollard persisted beyond the frustration-aggression hypothesis in modifying early behavioristic doctrine to accommodate human expectations, conflict, and defense. In 1941 Miller and Dollard published their first full account of what they termed *social learning theory.* They expanded the available principles of classical and instrumental learning with an account of learning by imitation. Social variables and the fact that much human learning occurs by watching others perform were introduced into behaviorism. But in 1950, Dollard and Miller published their masterwork *Personality and Psychotherapy,* in which they systematically set forth a behavioral translation of virtually all of Freud's main ideas about psychopathology and its treatment.

We cannot undertake here to present Dollard and Miller's psychodynamic social learning theory in its entirety. However, we need a sample of their translation strategy so that we can observe the transition from the less sophisticated behaviorism of yesterday to the cognitive social learning theory of the present.

For what Miller and Dollard's translation accomplished was nothing less than the demonstration that there were scientifically feasible ways of testing Freud's ideas, and that the clash of paradigms is not irreconcilable. The sample of their work that we examine concerns their reformulation of anxiety and repression, the key mechanisms of pathology in the Freudian scheme.

S-R TRANSLATION OF ANXIETY AND REPRESSION

Unlike the radical behaviorists, Dollard and Miller (1950) did not assume that thinking was merely an epiphenomenon. But they also did not assume, as Freud had, that such private events could be studied only by introspection and unverified self-report. Instead, they attempted to combine the strengths of behavioral methodology and psychoanalytic observations.

First Step: Anxiety as a Signal of Danger

The first step in the translation was undertaken by O. Hobart Mowrer and Neal Miller. Mowrer (1939) applauded Freud's formulation that emphasized the feeling of anxiety as a signal of danger. How to translate this conception into verifiable terms without dismissing anxiety as a *cause* of defensive behavior? Recall that Skinner attempted the same translation years later, but that he excluded anxiety and other emotions from any causal role in disordered behavior.

Mowrer's translation employed the model of Pavlovian conditioning to explain the *acquisition* of the signal of danger, and the model of reinforcement conditioning to account for the *maintenance* of the resulting avoidance (defensive) behavior. For Mowrer, physical pain is an unconditioned response (UCR) to a noxious unconditioned stimulus (UCS). Any neutral stimuli that accompany the UCS will become conditioned stimuli signaling the painful UCS:

> A so-called "traumatic" ("painful") stimulus (arising either from external injury, of whatever kind, or from severe organic need), impinges upon the organism and produces a more or less violent defense (striving) reaction. Furthermore, such a stimulus-response sequence is usually preceded or accompanied by originally "indifferent" stimuli which, however, after one or more temporally contiguous associations with the traumatic stimulus, begin to be perceived as danger signals, i.e., acquire the capacity to elicit an "anxiety" reaction. (Mowrer, 1939, p. 554)

Pavlovian conditioning—stimulus substitution by association—is used in this S-R translation to explain the "signal" function of anxiety. The heart of anxiety, for both Mowrer and Freud, is the organism's capacity to anticipate painful consequences from prior experience.

A child, for example, who has been burned by a hissing steam heater eventually fears the hissing sound and uses it as a cue to avoid the hot steam heater. But, as Mowrer cogently pointed out, Freud also suggested that once the signal of anxiety was established, certain defensive behaviors are learned to protect the organism from having ever again to experience the noxious stimulus. In short, not only must the child avoid a nearby heater that it hears hissing, it must also avoid being near the hissing sound because that signal evokes the unpleasant feeling of anxiety in the first place.

To explain the continued avoidance of the *emotion,* Mowrer proposed a second factor involved in anxiety learning, the factor of negative reinforcement. Any behavior that reduces the painful emotion of anxiety in *anticipation* of pain is functionally equivalent to the original escape from the burning heater. But note that now the escape is not from the actual burn pain; it is escape from the unpleasant emotional *signal* of potential pain. If that signal is effective in triggering defensive behavior, and the child never again is actually burned, its avoidance behavior is never reinforced. The avoidance responses should extinguish because the UCS of pain is never again experienced. Why then does the child persist in avoiding the hissing steam if it is never again burned?

The answer is that avoidance of the anxiety signal (hissing steam) *is* being reinforced by a powerful negative reinforcer. Avoidance of the hissing steam *reduces* the unpleasant feeling of anxiety. As we know from reinforcement theory, any behavior that terminates or reduces aversive stimulation *increases* in probability. Anxiety is a negative reinforcer that maintains the avoidance behavior in the absence of the original noxious UCS. To say the same thing another way, avoidance behavior is negatively reinforced by the experience of anxiety reduction.

The avoidance response may even generalize so that the child may learn not only to avoid the hissing heater, but to stay out of the room altogether. In this way, it even prevents contact with the aversive *signal* of hissing steam. Or, at a later age, the child may learn an instrumental response that also reduces anxiety. It turns the heater valve and shuts it off so that both the signal (hissing) and the noxious UCS (heat) are terminated.

> In short, *anxiety (fear) is the conditioned form of the pain reaction,* which has the highly useful function of motivating and reinforcing behavior that tends to avoid or prevent the recurrence of the pain producing [unconditioned] stimulus. (Mowrer, 1939, p. 554; italics in original)

Second Step: Fear as an Acquired Drive Called Anxiety

The second step in formulating an S-R translation of Freudian theory was to convert Mowrer's model of anxiety as a learned motive into a form testable under controlled laboratory conditions. Miller (1948) did just that by showing that rats could learn a lever-pressing response to escape from a white box where they had been shocked. After learning to make the escape response to flee the pain of electric shock, the rats were never again shocked in the white box. The mere sight of the white box was sufficiently fear arousing to provoke a rat to make the lever-pressing response that would open a door to a safer black compartment.

Then Miller changed the rules of the game. Much to the rats' dismay, he made the lever inoperative. Placed again into the white box, the rats futilely pressed the lever. The door would not drop open. After frantic scurrying, pawing, and climbing behavior, many of the rats discovered (but some did not) that turning a wheel in the wall of the white box opened the door. From that point on, within five seconds of entering the white box, rats leaped, one is tempted to say "with great relief," to the wheel, and scurried through the opened door into the safe black box. Figure 16.5 illustrates Miller's experimental arrangement.

FIGURE 16.5   Miller's acquired fear apparatus.

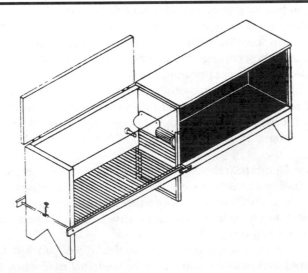

Modified from Miller (1948).

Miller had demonstrated that once fear is classically conditioned to the cue of the white box with the UCS of shock, the *learned* fear of the white color will serve as an *acquired drive* that motivates new escape learning. The acquired drive, of course, is anxiety. None of the rats ever experienced the UCS of electric shock after the initial escape response was learned. Learning the new response of wheel turning is thus motivated by the fear of the white box, and it is reinforced, not by escaping the shock, but by reduction of anxiety associated with leaving the white box.

Yet rats learning to escape white boxes, however elegant the demonstration, is still not directly comparable to the Freudian "escape" of repression. What was now needed was a demonstration that human beings learn anxiety as a signal of danger, and that conscious thinking is blocked by this avoidance learning, as Freud had described. At this level, ideas, thoughts, and words have to be considered the appropriate stimuli and responses. Thinking was about to be translated into S-R language.

Third Step: The Functional Equivalence of Words and Thoughts

The third step was to provide experimental evidence for the proposition that anxious thoughts and anxious actions are functionally equivalent. As part of his doctoral dissertation, Miller had provided just such a demonstration.

Miller's (1950) experiment showed that anxiety-motivated avoidance behavior can be attached to abstract stimuli such as words. By generalization, the anxiety attached to the words is spread to the thoughts conveyed by the words. Not-thinking the thoughts, and not-saying the words are two avoidance responses that come remarkably close to what Freud had called repression.

Miller's experimental design called for a subject to be shown the letter *T* and the number *4* in random series, with the subject required to say aloud whatever stimulus he or she was shown. Whenever the letter *T* appeared, the subject received a painful electric shock, but never received one when the number *4* was shown. The subject rapidly learned to respond with anticipatory anxiety to the letter *T*, as shown by recordings made of palmar sweating. Such a recording, one component of the multiple autonomic nervous system responses assessed by the modern "lie detector" polygraph, is called the galvanic skin response (GSR). During the learning phase, the subject's GSR recordings showed large peaks whenever *T* was followed by shock, and virtually no responses for every appearance of *4*.

In the next phase of Miller's study, the subject was shown a series of dots. He or she was required to *think,* not say aloud, *T* for the first dot, then *think 4* for the next dot, and so on, in alternating series through 25 dots. Figure 16.6 reproduces the GSR recordings in this phase of *thinking without shock* for three blocks of five-trial segments.

The tracings in Figure 16.6 show that whenever the subject *thought T,* there was a large GSR peak indicating high anxiety. Thoughts of *4,* by contrast, evoked very little GSR change. By the 25th trial in the third block, the peaks to *T* were reduced by extinction (subject had not received any more shocks), but there is a residual effect for every thought of *T* still discernible.

The anxiety had been learned in response to the UCS of shock following presentations of *T.* But it clearly became generalized to *thoughts* of *T* when the only overt

FIGURE 16.6 GSR responses to thought of letter previously shocked.

GSR RESPONSES on TRIALS 1 to 5

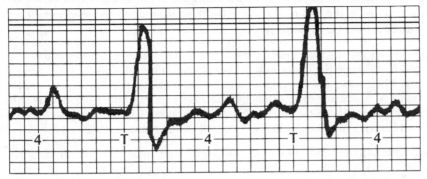

GSR RESPONSES on TRIALS 11 to 15

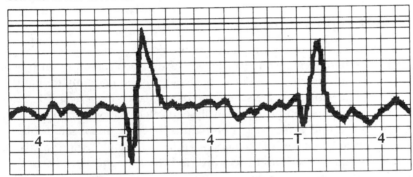

GSR RESPONSES on TRIALS 21 to 25

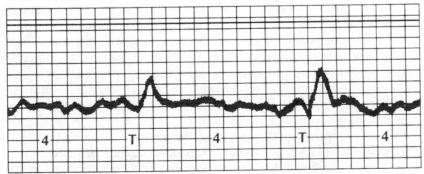

From Miller (1950), p. 464.

stimulus was a dot. Miller had shown, therefore, that there is a functional equivalence between saying a word and thinking it. Thoughts were at least as effective in mediating the GSR anxiety response as the behavior of verbalizing the shocked stimulus.

To understand the full significance of Miller's demonstration, consider the plight of a small child when she is scolded for some misdeed. When she *thinks* about similar misbehavior in the future, the same feelings of anxiety that were attached to the scolded act return. Or, even more potently,

> Sometimes parents, with their superior intelligence and experience, can tell what a child is likely to do before he says or does anything obvious. Thus they may warn the child when he has an evil thought before he had made any gross overt response. Such warnings attach fear to the thought and help to break down the discrimination between thoughts on the one hand and spoken words and acts on the other. To the small child it is as if the parents could read his mind. (Dollard & Miller, 1950, p. 207)

Thoughts could be conditioned. And, as Freud had suggested, threatening thoughts provoke defensive behavior designed to rid one of the thought. Miller had carried thinking as a cause of behavior into S-R theory. The next step was to describe the relationship between anxiety-laden thoughts and the avoidance maneuver called "repression."

Fourth Step: Repression as "Not-Thinking"

The fourth and final step in the translation of the Freudian conception of repression into stimulus-response terms required only one further small assumption. If behaviors associated with punishment or pain can be avoided, then certainly thoughts associated with "pain" are subject to the same kind of avoidance maneuver. The "not-thinking" of certain thoughts can be functionally equivalent to avoiding certain acts. In effect, thoughts that one has learned "not-to-think" become unconscious because the verbal cues are simply not part of the person's thinking. Thoughts and words, after all, are functionally equivalent. Avoid the word, and the thought ceases to exist. If the thought ceases to exist, the anxiety associated with the concept carried in the words is reduced. Here is repression in S-R language, and here are the three ways in which Dollard and Miller (1950) thought it might be mediated:

1. *Prevention of Verbal Labeling of a Drive:* A sexually aroused person does not label his erotic feelings "sexual" because he has learned to be anxious about sex from prior painful experience. Instead, he mislabels his sexual feeling "nervousness" or even "boredom." Sexual feelings arouse anxiety; "boredom" does not. Part *A* of Figure 16.7 illustrates this form of "repression."

2. *Prevention of Responses Producing a Drive:* To continue the same example, our sexually aroused but anxious person detects his own arousal by noticing that he has an erection. This bodily response means "sex" and must be avoided. Instead of increasing his sexual arousal, his own perception of his body's response increases his anxiety. He anxiously distracts his attention from his erection by declaring that he is hungry, and avidly begins preparing or eating a meal. Substitution of the eating response for the sexual one effectively blocks further *thinking* about the sexual one. Eventually, decreased anxiety results both because he no longer thinks "sex," and because, in fact, eating is an

incompatible response that has reduced his sexual arousal. Part *B* of Figure 16.7 illustrates this form of "repression."

3. *Inhibition of Responses of Mediating the Drive:* Some people learn to be afraid of their own anger through punishments for the expression of anger during childhood. When such a person perceives some cue that ought to trigger anger (a spoken insult, for example), he or she experiences both the anger appropriate to the insult *and* the learned anxiety about expressing it. He consciously suppresses the anger for the moment. But later, *thinking* about the situation renews angry feelings as well as anxiety about them. Now the person can control anxiety only by *not thinking* about the anger, for it is the *thought,* not the insult, that evokes it. He or she stops thinking about the insult. "Stopping-thinking" is functionally equivalent to the original suppression of the anger at the time of the actual insult, but it now occurs at the level of thought. Part *C* of Figure 16.7 illustrates this form of repression.

Note that all three of Dollard and Miller's explanations of repression hinge on reducing the noxious effects of anxiety that has come to be connected with particular thoughts. In each of the three instances just discussed, alternate thoughts are substituted for the threatening ones to reduce the anxiety by distraction. Anxiety, therefore, is conceptualized as a negative drive impelling escape through the expedient of "not-thinking."

These explanations of repression are far more sophisticated than any to be found in the radical behaviorism that preceded them. They give appropriate weight to the

FIGURE 16.7   The forms of repression or "not-thinking" avoidance responses in S-R terms.

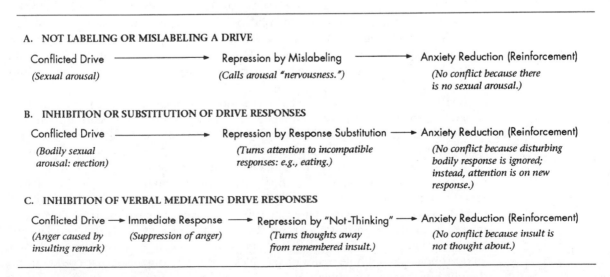

A. NOT LABELING OR MISLABELING A DRIVE

Conflicted Drive ──────────▶ Repression by Mislabeling ──────────▶ Anxiety Reduction (Reinforcement)

(Sexual arousal)   *(Calls arousal "nervousness.")*   *(No conflict because there is no sexual arousal.)*

B. INHIBITION OR SUBSTITUTION OF DRIVE RESPONSES

Conflicted Drive ──────────▶ Repression by Response Substitution ──▶ Anxiety Reduction (Reinforcement)

(Bodily sexual arousal: erection)   *(Turns attention to incompatible responses: e.g., eating.)*   *(No conflict because disturbing bodily response is ignored; instead, attention is on new response.)*

C. INHIBITION OF VERBAL MEDIATING DRIVE RESPONSES

Conflicted Drive ─▶ Immediate Response ─▶ Repression by "Not-Thinking" ─▶ Anxiety Reduction (Reinforcement)

(Anger caused by insulting remark)   *(Suppression of anger)*   *(Turns thoughts away from remembered insult.)*   *(No conflict because insult is not thought about.)*

Based on Dollard and Miller (1950).

human capacity for thinking about human experience. But there is still a drawback: Thoughts are treated statically, as if they were just one more response to stimulation. Ideas have the status in this formulation of conditioned responses analogous to the *"T"* and *"4"* responses of the subjects in Miller's (1950) GSR study.

The anticipatory function of thought by which it can be a complex *predictor* of threatening events is reduced to Pavlovian stimulus-substitution. Real human thought is complex in its network of associative relations. Real people do not think ideas in discrete, unconnected chunks, like *T*s and *4*s. Therefore, it is almost impossible, as Freud pointed out, that repression could work by eliminating discrete anxious bits of thought. All of an idea's associative and symbolic connections have somehow to be inhibited or removed from awareness as well.

Human thought also has the capacity to render some stimuli nonthreatening—not by avoiding thinking them—but by reappraisal of the threat and one's capacity to cope with or to master it. The feelings of helplessness that Freud so carefully described as the key trigger for the ego's escape through repression are given no weight at all in Dollard and Miller's S-R formulation. Anxiety is treated as the emotion that accompanies anticipations of pain. What of anticipations of feeling helpless in the face of unavoidable pain? What of anticipations of being flooded by demands with which one cannot cope? These anticipated experiences also produce anxiety, but it has a very different quality from the learned fear of electric shock at the sight of *T*. Such conditioned fears are clearly analogous to the clinical manifestations of anxiety and repression, but they are stimulus-response metaphors. The kind of distress that Freud wrote about so eloquently is not yet captured.

Dollard and Miller: The Bridge Between Radical and Cognitive Paradigms

Dollard and Miller's psychodynamic social learning theory bridged the gap between radical and cognitive behaviorism by using psychoanalytic observations and stimulus-response explanations. Dollard and Miller attempted to compromise between the richness of psychoanalytic phenomenology and the scientific need for testable hypotheses. As a historical bridge, their complex formulations had strengths and weaknesses.

On the plus side of the ledger, Dollard and Miller's greatest strength lay in their adherence to strict empirical and laboratory-based methodology. Starting with the frustration-aggression hypotheses, every one of their main formulations received extensive experimental or field testing.

On the debit side, Dollard and Miller had to invent new concepts of learning that transcended the simple stimulus-response principles at hand. In so doing, they shared Freud's greatest weakness: They raised intervening (unobservable) variables to the level of explanatory and causal mechanisms. Observable behavior became a source of inference about the unseen "inner" processes presumed at work. Like Freud, Dollard and Miller had to infer from conflicted behavior, from aggressive behavior, and from anxious behavior a whole realm of variables within the organism that could not be directly observed or manipulated.

Unlike Freud's, Dollard and Miller's formulation permitted, in fact encouraged, the direct manipulation of behavior in controlled situations to assess the effects of that manipulation on what would now be called "cognitive" events. But the leap from what could actually be manipulated to what could only be inferred troubled many psychologists.

In the end, the marriage between S-R behaviorism and psychoanalysis was less than harmonious. Psychoanalysts refused to accept the translation, and they were unmoved equally by confirmatory and disconfirmatory laboratory findings. Behaviorists were appalled by the sheer wealth of unconfirmed assumptions required to explain what transpired between the observable stimulus and the observable response. The time, apparently, had not come for adherents of the two competing paradigms to acknowledge and accept each other's contributions.

ALBERT BANDURA

COGNITIVE SOCIAL LEARNING THEORY

Albert Bandura and Richard Walters (1963) took up the task of advancing behaviorism into the realm of complex mental events without taking on what they viewed as the limitations of psychoanalytic theory. Since Richard Walters's untimely death, Bandura and his colleagues at Stanford University have worked to develop a cognitive behaviorism with the methodological rigor of radical behaviorism while nevertheless taking account of the human capacity to think about and to plan for experiences.

Many of the same clinical issues first described by Freud are dealt with in social learning theory, but there is no attempt to translate psychoanalytic concepts into another language. Rather, the attempt is to study the basic clinical phenomena with methods devised largely in the laboratory, and to explain those phenomena with concepts and language drawn from learning. The body of research literature connected with Bandura's social learning approach is now so vast that it would require a substantial handbook merely to survey it. We cannot undertake that survey here, but we can describe the main features of the paradigm.

Puzzle One: Incorporating Cognition Into the Study of Learning

One of the problems with both Watson's and Skinner's radical behaviorism (but not a problem for either Freud or Miller and Dollard) was the belief that learning occurs through direct application of reinforcement to an organism's behavior. Behavior changes because the environment, including other people, deals out consequences that say "yes" or "no" to certain behaviors. The model, of course, that served Skinner, Watson, and Pavlov so well was animal behavior. But are the principles of animal learning sufficient to account for human learning?

PUZZLE ONE: *If human learning is limited strictly to trial and error and stimulus-substitution, how do we explain the acquisition of knowledge from books, maps, teachers, and supervisors who prevent us from making*

endless random responses and who protect us from the lethal conse-
quences of error during our trials?

Consider the person learning to drive a car. A competent driving instructor does not simply turn the novice loose on the streets in some vehicle to learn by trial and error. The instructor does not simply negatively reinforce collisions and positively reinforce "near misses" until the person eventually controls the automobile.

Nor does the medical resident learn surgery by being permitted to cut into human flesh until he or she gets one operation right.

And certainly clinical psychologists do not learn to conduct psychotherapy by being allowed to talk to distressed people until they finally say the healing thing. (Although a colleague recently commented that at least for some therapists, trial and error appears to have been the method of training. But then he's a cynic.)

Complex human learning occurs with the help of reinforcement and association, but not exclusively in those ways. We also learn by imitating others who perform some response successfully. We not only attend to the details of *their* actions, but we also observe the *consequences* of their actions. And sometimes we learn through exposure to the *thinking* of other people, as, for instance, when we read a textbook that conveys the written ideas of others. In each of these instances, the learner is involved in cognitive activity. His or her behavior is not directly reinforced or paired with an unconditioned stimulus. Yet, there is learning.

The novice surgeon observes many surgical procedures before attempting to participate in small ways in a supervised operation. The beginning driver observes and listens to explanations of what to do before, under careful guidance, he or she is permitted to attempt controlling a car. And the neophyte clinical psychologist observes therapy and reads extensively about the process before conducting therapy under supervision.

In short, people learn by watching other people, and by encoding all kinds of information in symbolic form. Miller and Dollard (1941) had introduced the topic of learning by imitation into social learning theory. But Bandura took the concept one step further: Learning by watching or reading about another's performance clearly involves mental activity. The learner must

Attend to the model,

Remember what is seen and heard,

Reproduce the memory during imitation, and expect

Reinforcement for accurate performance.

Figure 16.8 summarizes these main components with their subprocesses.

Bandura's research has demonstrated a wide range of learning that is possible through observation. For example, novel responses may be acquired through observational learning so that the learner may expand his or her repertoire.

Observational learning may also serve to increase or decrease the intensity of a previously learned inhibition. When an inhibition is *increased,* the observer has learned to restrain some response more effectively by watching what happens to a model who displays self-restraint. On the other hand, when observation of a model

FIGURE 16.8   Subprocesses governing observational learning.

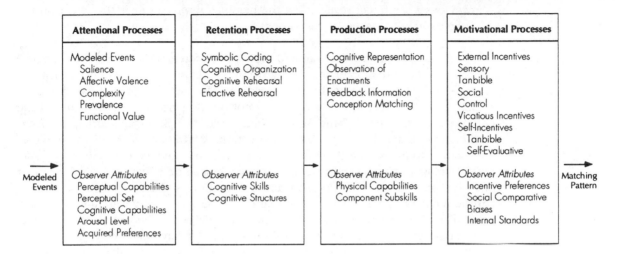

Source: Bandura (1986), p. 52.

serves to *decrease* an already established inhibition ("disinhibit" the inhibition), the observer has learned to display some behavior that he or she would ordinarily hold in check.

Finally, observational learning can include response facilitation effects whereby the presence of a model performing a particular action induces the observer to make a similar response in direct imitation. Fads in hairstyles, clothing, and diet are good examples of response facilitation effects.

Puzzle Two: The Meaning of Reinforcement

If complex behavior can be acquired by watching another's performance and its consequences, then clearly reinforcement is affecting the observer in a way that is one step removed from actual experience of the reinforcer. Yet traditional doctrine in behaviorism held that a reinforcer strengthens only the response to which it is immediately applied.

> PUZZLE TWO: *How does the observer learn when it is the model's behavior that is reinforced?*

To solve the puzzle, Bandura had to reconceptualize the nature of reinforcement in more cognitive terms. Recall that Skinner's "empirical law of effect" stated that it was necessary only to describe the observed relationship between a behavior and its consequences. The reason for the effect of a reinforcing consequence was irrelevant for a science of behavior because such reasons involved variables that could not be directly observed.

With Bandura's studies of modeling influences, the reasons why reinforcement was effective became relevant. Vicarious reinforcement raises two important questions:

1. Can a reinforcer really work backward in time to strengthen a response that has already occurred?
2. Does a reinforcer really affect the person's *responses* or is the effect on the *person* who makes the responses?

Bandura argued that the standard view of reinforcement requires the illogical assumption that a reinforcer acts backward in time to strengthen a behavior that no longer exists at the time of the reinforcement. The way out of this paradox is to assume that the effect of the reinforcer is not on the person's response but on the person's *expectations* for future responding. A reinforcer, in social learning theory, is an incentive to act, not a reward for past action. A reinforcer serves as a source of information to the person about his or her environment and its requirements for successful living, rather than as a stamping-in process. To be effective, a reinforcement must be *anticipated* by the person, and anticipation is clearly a cognitive activity. Foresight can be acquired either by direct past experience or by watching what happens to another person. Figure 16.9 illustrates the difference between Bandura's cognitive conception of reinforcement and the standard behavioristic view.

It is important to emphasize that Bandura did not dismiss the importance of direct reinforcement as a powerful determinant of learning (Bandura, 1969). Rather, his social learning formulation required the traditional view to be expanded with the

FIGURE 16.9   **Radical behavioristic and cognitive social learning views of reinforcement.**

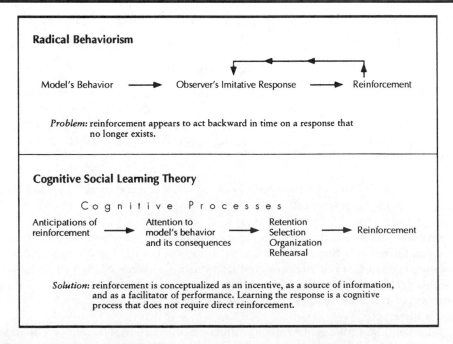

Radical Behaviorism

Model's Behavior ⟶ Observer's Imitative Response ⟶ Reinforcement

Problem: reinforcement appears to act backward in time on a response that no longer exists.

Cognitive Social Learning Theory

Cognitive Processes

Anticipations of reinforcement ⟶ Attention to model's behavior and its consequences ⟶ Retention Selection Organization Rehearsal ⟶ Reinforcement

Solution: reinforcement is conceptualized as an incentive, as a source of information, and as a facilitator of performance. Learning the response is a cognitive process that does not require direct reinforcement.

Based on Bandura (1971c), p. 9; (1977b), p. 38.

concepts of vicarious reinforcement and cognitively based learning. Once it had been demonstrated as an actual process, vicarious reinforcement made little sense without the assumption that the person thinks about and anticipates the outcomes of his or her own behavior when the time comes to imitate what was learned by observation.

Reinforcement is thus a facilitator of *performance,* not a cause of learning. Learning by watching another perform occurs cognitively without direct reinforcement. A person may choose not to display what was learned, but the absence of overt performance does not signify a corresponding absence of learning. And that learning, clearly, is cognitive.

Puzzle Three: Persons, Behavior, or Environments?

Bandura's emphasis on remembering, thinking, judging, and anticipating pulled the focus away from an exclusively environmental model of behavior that stressed reinforcement contingency more than the person experiencing the contingency. In social learning theory, people are active symbolizers of their experiences. They may choose reinforcements. And such choices are based on a person's own ethical and achievement standards. We can almost hear Watson's and Skinner's cries of outrage.

> PUZZLE THREE: *How can private events such as anticipation, memory, selective attention, and personal standards be studied scientifically?*

The cognitive social learning theorists were not abandoning the methodological rigor of the radical behaviorists. But they were not about to ignore the internal cognitive events that clearly had to be evoked to explain complex learning (Mischel, 1973b).

The social learning solution to the puzzle attempts to avoid the pitfalls of psychoanalytic internal agencies that seem to operate independently of environmental regulators. But the narrowness of radical behaviorism's "empty organism" dismisses the very clinical phenomena that require explanation. Bandura (1978a, 1986) solved the puzzles left by both psychoanalysis and radical behaviorism by proposing the existence of a cognitive-emotional set of processes *regulating and regulated by* environmental input.

The "self-system," as Bandura prefers to call these internal events, is not an autonomous, psychological agent like Freud's ego. The self-system is not autonomously isolated, is not governed exclusively by its own rules of operation, and is not a "little person" inside the person. Bandura and his colleagues have studiously avoided conceptualizing the self-system as a "thing" inside people. The self-system is a complex of processes interdependent with the person's social and physical environment (Bandura, 1977b, pp. 194ff.; 1978a, 1986, pp. 369ff.). In a rather apt phrase, Bandura calls this complex interactional viewpoint "reciprocal determinism," and it is the key to the puzzle of studying private events scientifically.

Human behavior is regulated in a reciprocally determined way as the person's behavior affects the environment, the environment in turn affects the person's behavior, and the person's awareness of these interdependencies affects behavior, environment, and changed expectations. Bandura pictures reciprocal determinism as an interactive triad of person *(P),* behavior *(B),* and environment *(E)* (Bandura, 1978a, p. 345):

FIGURE 16.10

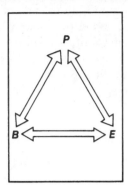

The key point in the scheme in Figure 16.10 is that:

> By their actions, individuals contribute to the nature of their situations (Bandura, 1981). People are therefore at least partial creators of their own history. Moreover, memory representation of the past involves constructive rather than reproductive processes in which events are filtered through personal meanings and biases and cognitively transformed. People thus serve as partial authors not only of their past experiences but of their memory of them as well. (Bandura, 1982, p. 167)

Bandura's principle of reciprocal determinism has received some criticism (Phillips & Oroton, 1983) on philosophical and epistemological grounds. But the essential concept is that social learning as a whole has adopted an essentially multi-causal and interactionist view of behavior regulation. There is much irony in the fact that Freud was among the first thinkers to assert that behavior was clearly multiply caused, or "overdetermined." (See Chapter 3 for a discussion of Freud's dynamic, genetic, and structural viewpoints.) The analogous principle has now been given sci-entific respectability within the intellectual tradition that first criticized him for an overly complex view of psychological events.

Within the triad of person, environment, and behavior, it is social learning the-ory's recognition of the person variables that is most unique. At the heart of the per-son is the self-system's self-regulatory processes by which people set and act upon their own standards and expectations. Figure 16.11 summarizes the main sub-processes of the self-system.

The first class of self-regulatory processes involve a person's capacity for *self-observation* of behavioral quality. Qualities such as originality, authenticity, and ethi-calness are applied as evaluative standards by the person to his or her own behavior to create incentives to act in a particular way. But note that it is the person who sets and applies such standards.

The second set of self-regulatory processes that make up the self-system are the *judgments* of excellence and goodness of one's own behavior relative to the behav-ior of others and to one's own past performances. Included among these judgments are the person's style of attributing responsibility for action to self or to external

FIGURE 16.11 **Subprocess involved in the self-regulation of behavior by internal standards and self incentives.**

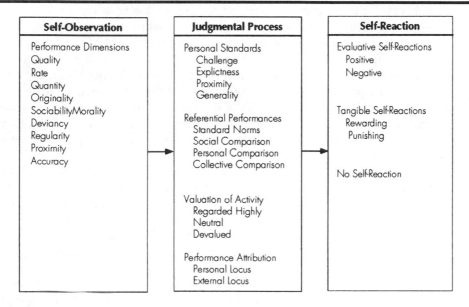

Self-Observation	Judgmental Process	Self-Reaction
Performance Dimensions	Personal Standards	Evaluative Self-Reactions
Quality	Challenge	Positive
Rate	Explictness	Negative
Quantity	Proximity	
Originality	Generality	
SociabilityMorality		Tangible Self-Reactions
Deviancy	Referential Performances	Rewarding
Regularity	Standard Norms	Punishing
Proximity	Social Comparison	
Accuracy	Personal Comparison	
	Collective Comparison	No Self-Reaction
	Valuation of Activity	
	Regarded Highly	
	Neutral	
	Devalued	
	Performance Attribution	
	Personal Locus	
	External Locus	

From Bandura (1986), p. 337.

causes. Blame for a failure attributed to self has remarkably different psychological effects from those of blame attributed to external causes.

The last set of processes in the self-system are those termed *self-reaction* processes but which would be better termed self-reward/punishment. Once the evaluations of the self-observations and judgments have been made, the person decides to reward or punish his or her own behavior with feelings of competence or with feelings of self-devaluation.

The common denominator that underlies all of these processes is the theme of competence, mastery, or self-efficacy.

Bandura (1977a, 1982) has proposed that feelings of personal competence underlie a great many behavioral phenomena, including the effectiveness of psychotherapy (e.g., Bandura, Adams, & Beyer, 1977); persistence in the face of obstacles (Bandura & Schunk, 1981); accuracy of the self-concept (e.g., Lazarus & Launier, 1978), and feelings of depression and futility (e.g., Abramson, Seligman, & Teasdale, 1978).

In Bandura's analysis, feelings of self-efficacy or personal competence have four sources:

1. *Enactive attainments,* or what Bandura used to refer to as *performance accomplishments* (Bandura, 1986, p. 399) are the most powerful regulators of self-efficacy. A person's own efforts either succeed or fail, and the outcome is instructive in planning future efforts.

2. *Vicarious experience* is derived from watching another's efforts succeed or fail. Such observations provide one with a basis of comparison by which to estimate personal competence in similar situations.

3. *Verbal persuasion* is the least powerful regulator of self-efficacy because being told that one can or cannot master a given task is far removed from the actual performance and does not engage the person's conviction as strongly.

4. *Physiological state,* or what Bandura in earlier statements referred to as emotional arousal, is the degree of apprehension and anxiety that an individual experiences in a situation that will test his or her competence (Bandura, 1986, p. 401). If a person concentrates on feelings of fear or anxiety, he or she may bring about the very failure that is dreaded. On the other hand, moderate degrees of arousal are likely to enhance performance. And Bandura (1986) points out that people read not only their anxiety levels, but their levels of physical fatigue and pain as well.

5. *Integration of Efficacy Information.* Most recently, Bandura (1997, pp. 113 ff.) has given some consideration to how the person integrates the four components of enactive attainment, vicarious experience, verbal persuasion, and physiological arousal into a personally meaningful understanding of self-efficacy. Each of the four sources may have different informational value for different people, who will weight various components differently. Indeed, some people will operate cognitively to add information from each source, whereas others may engage in a more complicated personal calculus involving multiplying some factors by others. For example, one person may more heavily weight the experience of emotional arousal from past successes and failures—how good and bad such experiences felt. Another puts primary weight on past performance accomplishments—nothing succeeds like success. And yet another person may balance feelings against performance and magnify the effects of both by factoring in others' opinions—persuade me some more.

Bandura also distinguishes between *efficacy expectations,* and *outcome expectations,* an important difference for predicting effort and persistence. An *efficacy expectation* is a personal belief that a given outcome can be personally accomplished because one possesses the requisite skills. By contrast, an *outcome expectation* is the person's estimate that a particular outcome will occur if the right combination of situational and personal processes are brought correctly to bear.

The difference between an efficacy and an outcome expectation might be stated succinctly by saying that a person may believe a certain course of action will result in a specific outcome, but that he or she is not the person to do it successfully.

It is well to repeat that social learning theory treats personal expectations and meanings as causal regulators of behavior. And the processes that regulate these expectations are susceptible to scientific study by manipulating the variables of past performance, vicarious modeling, verbal instruction, and degree of emotional arousal. These processes mediate, sometimes cause, the behavior we observe, but they are largely cognitive processes that, in the end, weight a person's thoughts equally with a person's behavior.

Self-Efficacy as Personal Control

Bandura (1997) has recently elevated the theoretical status of self-efficacy to the role of a nearly universal mediator of personality phenomena. His review of an enormous research literature aims to demonstrate how a person's belief in personal effectiveness and control shapes an extraordinary range of psychological phenomena extending from family interactions and general social transactions to the clinical phenomena of psychopathology. Three illustrative applications, drawn from Bandura's (1997) most recent statement of the theory, sample the domains of threat management, intellectual interests, and the biology of psychological stress and physical health.

Coping With Threat, Revisited

Bandura maintains his earlier conception of anxiety as "a state of anticipatory apprehension over possible deleterious happenings" (1997, p. 137). A threatening perception earns its degree of threat in a relational way: the more the person believes he or she can cope with a potentially noxious experience,

- the less threatening that experience will seem
- the less likely will the person scare self with anxiously unrealistic fantasies
- the less likely will the person dwell on unpleasant bodily arousal
- the more likely will the person transform the meaning of the threat into one that he or she believes they *can* manage.

Motivating Intellectual Interests

The process by which people develop intrinsic interests in activities at which they initially possess little or no skill is regulated by self-efficacy beliefs.

> To mountaineers, the toilsome activity of crawling over slippery rocks in foul weather is not inherently joyful. It is the self-satisfaction derived from personal triumphs over lofty peaks that provides the exhilaration. Remove the personal challenges, and crawling over rocks becomes quite boring. (Bandura, 1997, p. 219).

Personal standards and the perceived meaning of the challenge contribute to the development of interests and satisfactions in three ways:

1. Challenging personal standards *enlist sustained effort and involvement* in activities needed to build personal competencies. Only a long term investment can accomplish a worthy goal.
2. Mastering a challenge yields the *feeling of satisfaction,* a very reinforcing subjective state that enhances interest the activity leading to mastery.
3. Personal standards of high caliber are also *highly individualized markers* and like pencil marks on the closet door indicating spurts in height over time, such self-set appraisals permit monitoring of one's progress in mastery.

Most academic activities present ever-rising challenges. Whatever knowledge and cognitive skills are acquired, there is always more to learn. Past accomplishments are quickly outdistanced, and self-satisfactions are sought in higher accomplishments. Thus, in the pursuit of excellence, the higher the students' efficacy beliefs, the higher the academic challenges they set for themselves and the greater their intrinsic interest in scholastic matters. . . . (Bandura, 1997, p. 220)

Biological Effects of Self-Efficacy in Health and Psychopathology

Bandura (1997a, pp. 262 ff.) reviews an extensive and developing literature showing that a person's self-efficacy beliefs and self-appraisals exert significant changes in physiological status for physical and psychological "health." For example, strong and realistic self-efficacy beliefs appear to protect people from the deleterious bodily effects of prolonged stress. People who believe they are in control and can master even ordinarily unpredictable events maintain lower levels of blood pressure, heart rates, and stress hormone levels.

In the psychological arena, catecholamine secretions, neurotransmitters regulating important brain activities, for phobic patients fundamentally mirror the patient's self-efficacy in the face of threat. High self-efficacy—belief that the threat is easily managed—is associated with low levels of catecholamine activity and stress hormones. Low self-efficacy beliefs were associated with elevated levels of catecholamines. When threats were altogether removed, the levels of catecholamines and other stress hormones dropped in the greatly relieved phobic patients (Bandura, 1997, p. 265).

The point, of course, that Bandura and other social cognitive theorists are making is that belief in personal control shapes a person's characteristic conduct and health status across a wide variety of situations. Bandura also reviews research showing similar positive effects of high self-efficacy belief in the areas of athletic achievement, vocational goal setting, political activism and effectiveness, and several psychopathologies, including eating disorders and substance abuse. Self-efficacy, in Bandura's view, is a near-universal personality mediator of behavior.

DEVELOPMENTAL PHASES OF SELF-EFFICACY

Bandura has begun to incorporate a developmental perspective into his theory, and—big surprise—monitoring changes in self-efficacy over the life course are at the heart of the effort (1997; see the related analysis by Flammer, 1995). The course of a person's life history is portrayed in Bandura's analysis as a series of interconnected phases, each of which pulls for certain types of mastery skills at that specific moment in life. Bandura (1997, p. 163) points out that people take control of their lives only in concert with the opportunities available. Fortuitous events can materialize to form a unique constellation of circumstances and interacting people, a constellation that could not have been anticipated. Sometimes these chance encounters have little impact, but occasionally such seemingly random events profoundly alter the life course. Either way, Bandura argues, it is always the reciprocal interplay of personal qualities, such as the belief that one can control one's life, and the attributes of the social milieu that combine to launch a new life trajectory. At each stage of living from birth to old age, life itself imposes demands for specific kinds of interpersonal and personal competence.

Infancy: Linking Action With Outcome

By observing repeatedly that events happen only when some action has been performed, infants learn that actions produce effects (Bandura, 1997). But they must also learn to "self-observe" to make the crucial link: *my* actions produce effects. At first, effects produced by an infant have the character of pure trial and error. Infants flail about and generate all manner of outcomes, only some of which are intended and even fewer of which have desirable outcomes. Noncontingent—"what the hell was that?"—happenings teach infants that they cannot control their world. If enough of the infant's efforts appear to have little or no intended effect, the infant grows apathetic and loses interest in trying to exercise personal control. Under these passivizing circumstances, a darker lesson is learned: There is no benefit in anticipating consequences when most things that happen in your world are unpredictable or unreliable.

Acquiring Social Competence
Competent infants, by contrast, learn that many, but not all, of their actions have intended, anticipated, outcomes. Much of their earliest competency learning is linked to the physical environment during the early months because physical effects are unambiguous, immediate, and clear. Months later, and continuing throughout childhood, the competent infant learns to produce intended effects on the important people in its world. Learning to control the social world is more difficult because so many intended effects are delayed or hidden from the weak attentional and discriminatory abilities of the very young child. "Enabling" parents who skillfully promote mastery learning do so by intuitively reacting and sometimes overreacting to their child's efforts. In this way, even a spontaneous game of peek-a-boo can be transformed into a pivotal social transaction that teaches the child how to effect his or her social world.

Recognition and Differentiation of the Self as Active Agent
Infants acquire a sense of personal agency when they realize that they are the *doers of action.* Acquisition of this sense of a personal "me as agent" is acquired through family interactions, the use of personal names ("Oh how cute Leslie is—yes *you,* Leslie!"), and the verbal labeling of personal possessions ("It's MINE!"). By about 18 months, the typical infant has sufficient language skill to apply verbal labels to itself, indicating at least a rudimentary awareness of *being* a self (Bandura, 1997, p. 167). By 20 months, children can spontaneously describe themselves as the agents or authors of intended actions, and quickly thereafter they can describe aloud their thoughts and feelings while performing an action sequence. They are aware of personal agency at least enough to warily deny authorship of some deeds (Bart Simpson's strategic agency: "I didn't do it. No one saw me do it. You can't prove a thing"). To achieve any and all of these accomplishments, we must infer that the infant grasps the concept of self as active agent with the particular meaning of "self-as-one-who-intends-a-thing-to-happen" (see also in this context Deci & Ryan, 1995; and Epstein & Morling, 1995).

Bandura emphasizes that all competency learning is possible only through the reciprocal interaction of the child and its environment, particularly interchanges with members of the human landscape. Families that enhance a child's mastery learning are themselves changed positively by what the child learns. A family that actively promotes the competence of its younger members seems to be also a family that communicates genuine enjoyment in the personal triumphs of its members (Bandura, 1997, pp. 169 ff.). As language acquisition proceeds apace the child can use words to tell itself about the things it can and cannot do, recall encouragement and prohibition, articulate success and failure and actively, willfully engage the family's attention and admiration. In turn, the family's response can be "enabling" of the child's new-found sense of mastery, encouraging ever-wider applications, or the family can discourage, humiliate, or simply ignore such efforts.

Childhood: Comparative Self-Knowledge of Competence

The earliest efficacy learning occurs almost exclusively within the family, but as the child matures, influences beyond that immediate circle take on increasing significance.

Sibling Comparisons

First born and only children are often enriched by extra attention from parents who initially have extra time and energy to invest in mutually satisfying mastery-enabling experiences. For second and subsequent children in larger families there is often less parental time available for parental enablement, but more time and opportunity for comparisons with siblings closest in age. Initially competition and interaction with age-close siblings are the second and middle child's most important source of self-knowledge about its capabilities compared to others like itself.

Peer Comparisons and Validations

Eventually, however, peer interactions supplant the interactions of siblings as important sources of competition and comparison. The self-evaluative habits acquired in relation to brothers and sisters are extended now to comparisons with children outside the immediate family and personal efficacy is judged against their less familiar accomplishments (Bandura, 1997, p. 170). But children do not choose peers randomly. They tend to associate with children like themselves when they can. Thus friendships are more likely to be formed with children of similar ages who share a child's interests, values, gender, and experiences. Even though such choices narrow the range of comparative experiences, only direct interruption or outright blocking of peer relationships altogether is likely to obstruct the benefits of this important avenue of learning about one's own competencies relative to others.

With advancing age, beyond six years, the child's attention to comparisons becomes more focused on abstract social and psychological attributes of action and less on its immediate practical consequences. Thus, the seven- or eight-year-old child learns to compare self with similar children—sometimes preferring children who are just a *little* "better"—rather than make unmanageable and inevitably unflattering comparisons with others who are very advanced in age or skill. Similarity of self to *relevant* models grows increasingly important for the developing child in middle to late childhood and on into adolescence. Because children are curious, they are quick to try what they see others can do, quick to imitate the admired model, quick to evaluate bluntly and loudly their own and their peers' performances, and sometimes quick to mimic dangerous performances that lie outside the range of their current skills. Verbal instructions and evaluation, especially among a group of interactive peers, often serves as an important source of self-appraisal information.

Children Who Face Relentless Adversity

Even children who face childhood adversities and infirmities, such as poverty, abuse, parental alcoholism, or serious personal and familial mental disorder, can develop into efficacious and productive adults. The key appears to be the availability of caring, empathic, and attentive adult models. A close, stable bond to even one continuously trustworthy and caring adult appears to be sufficient to mobilize the child's natural resilience and promote adequate efficacy learning.

School-Age: Social Validation of Self-Efficacy

By the time the child enters school, an event that seemingly occurs earlier and earlier in our society, emphasis is placed on cognitive problem-solving skills as the chief age-appropriate competency.

Enabling Versus Discouraging Schools

The goal of attending school is to become an effective and productive member of one's culture. A child's acquired knowledge and thinking skills are put to the test— literally "tested" academically—much of the time. Institutionally sanctioned evaluations and personal comparisons with one's grade-mates are inherent to the educational enterprise. Schools and the classroom experiences they provide differ greatly in the degree to which they promote self-efficacy learning or instill self-doubt and the expectation of failure.

Student Reputation

Lockstep educational programs that ignore individual differences in ability and motivation are prone to damage a child's feelings of personal control and mastery. Programs that classify students into different ability groupings often communicate negative evaluations to those in the "lower" groupings, no matter how carefully the constituency of the group is disguised. Children assigned to the "bluebirds," the lowest reading level group, know that "robins" are "smarter" or "quicker," and children in the robins are not likely to let them forget it. Classroom teaching style is also a powerful influence over the child's acquisition of realistic self-efficacy knowledge. Group assignments that the teacher uses publicly to compare one child's performance with the others' enhance only some children's sense of mastery at the inevitable motivational expense of the less successful children with whom they are necessarily compared. Once a child's "reputation" among his peers for good, average, or poor performance is established, it is difficult for the child to alter it, even when the attributes on which the reputation supposedly rests have changed. Other children's judgments, teacher's reactions and expectations, and parental evaluations all interact to solidify an almost inescapable stereotype carved in stone.

Social Consequences of School Efficacy Learning

The lessons the child learns about intellectual performance, competition, success, and failure are not limited to the intellectual domain as the child progresses through the grades. There are repercussions for social interaction that stem from the child's belief in its power to control its own learning and master academic challenges. A sense of poor control or cognitive inadequacy that some children acquire as a result of their school experience promotes aggressive acting out (Bandura, 1997, p. 176). A child who regards him- or herself as less able than peers is less likely to engage in prosocial activities, can become alienated, and may even drift into antisocial behavior, including substance abuse. At minimum, low confidence in one's cognitive abilities inhibits the child from routine social learning about good health habits, grooming, exercise, nutritional eating, and disease prevention, an especially relevant issue as puberty approaches and prevention of sexually transmitted disease becomes crucial.

Adolescence: Risky but Proactive Transition to Adulthood

Bandura points out that many of our theories of development overpredict the incidence of psychopathology under conditions of adversity. Adolescence has become a riskier developmental period in recent years because the threats loom larger and more frequently: unprotected sex, drugs, guns, fractured families, poverty, and social displacement (Bandura, 1997, p. 177).

Competence Enablement Versus Vulnerability Protection

Self-efficacy, feelings of personal control and mastery, empowers the adolescent to navigate the transition from childhood to adulthood unscathed by exposure to risks. Bandura distinguishes the concept of "enabling competent development" from that of "protection from psychopathology." Viewed as a means to empower the developing person to construct and pursue a productive life plan, self-efficacy is the tool of an active agent rather than the "shield" of a protected victim. Enablement through self-efficacy equips adolescents:

> . . . to select and structure their environments in ways that set a successful course for
> their lives. This is the difference between proactive recruitment of sources of positive
> guidance and support and reactive adaptation to life circumstances. An agentic view
> of resilience also differs from the dualistic diathesis-stress model of psychopathology
> in which external stressors act upon personal vulnerabilities. Individuals play a
> proactive role in their adaptation rather than simply undergoing happenings in
> which environments act upon their personal endowments. The success with which
> the risks and challenges of adolescence are managed depends, in no small measure,
> on the strength of personal efficacy built up through prior mastery experiences.
> (Bandura, 1997, p. 178)

Adolescents are confronted with what seems to be an overwhelming number of changes. In rapid succession the adolescent experiences biological changes in the physical self at puberty, educational changes associated with the advancement to upper school grades, and the social stress of demands by parents and society for changes to more adult-like behavior.

Biological and Social Changes at Puberty

Learning to deal with puberty involves coping with emotionally invested partnerships associated with sexual conduct and dating rituals. Biological maturation also has an impact on physical prowess and appearance, which in turn elicit social approval or disapproval. Self-efficacy is simultaneously linked to these social evaluations and one major determinant of them. Even the timing of pubertal changes can have an impact on the adolescent's sense of self-efficacy. The advanced musculature development, height spurts, and salient sexual developments of early maturing boys earns these precocious exemplars of virility the admiration and respect of their peers of both sexes. In sharp contrast to the enhanced social status enjoyed by early maturing boys, late-maturing boys are often the subject of peers' ridicule or deliberate indifference.

But the opposite pattern is likely to prevail for girls. Precociously developed adolescent girls may have to cope with bodily changes for which they are not ready and which may attract unwanted attention. Early menstrual functioning presents its own adaptive problems. On the whole, early maturers of both genders are likely to be initiated prematurely by peer pressure into dating rituals, sexual conduct, drinking activities, and rule-breaking behaviors that have a negative impact on their educational and vocational progress.

During these transitions and exposures to risks, some adolescents experience a loss of control. Interactions with a wider, more heterogeneous peer group in high school, rotating through various class periods with different teachers, and the beginnings of familial and social pressures to start considering a vocational identity take their toll. Many adolescents deal with these transitional experiences in ways that enhance their feelings of control; others seem temporarily overwhelmed and may withdraw into self-protective social isolation. As a generalization with many exceptions, adolescent girls are more prone to feelings of depression and despondency when either academically overwhelmed or socially isolated. Boys are more prone to feelings of inefficacy over social rather than academic pressures (Bandura, 1997, p. 179). For both genders, the more adolescents yield to academic and social pressure with feelings of despondency, the more they withdraw from adaptive social interaction and the less effective they become in resisting the pressures. A vicious circle ensues. The lower the feelings of self-efficacy in the face of pressure, the more the adolescent withdraws and becomes depressed, thereby diminishing even further his or her feelings of mastery.

Managing Adolescent Sexuality and Other High Risk Behaviors

Teenagers are initiating sexual activity earlier in the life cycle than previous generations. Exposure to media models and peer pressures that portray sexual conduct in the context of uncommitted relationships without consequences accelerates sexual acting out and enforces sexual ignorance, immaturity, and interpersonal blind spots. Precocious sexual activity is more closely linked with impoverished adolescents who have poor educational attainments than with middle-class, well educated youth (Bandura, 1997, p. 179). As a society, we appear to be ambivalent in providing realistic sex education. Segments of our society lobby to maintain "a veil of silence" over sexual matters—ostensibly in the zeal to protect children. Other segments of our society aggressively advance their notion that only realistic and accurate sexual information can stem the tide of unwanted births and sexually transmitted diseases. The debate is often shrill and unproductive.

The prevailing assumption among most educators is that if teenagers are well informed, they will manage their sexuality more adaptively. However, information appears to exert little effect by itself. Bandura argues that sexual risk reduction depends on enhancing interpersonal self-efficacy to equip teenagers with the personal motivational and social skills to put protective sexual information into practice. A key component for the adolescent is to develop a heightened awareness of the significance of self-regulatory skills in managing one's own conduct. Internalized standards and values play a bigger role than mere information, especially when those standards are associated with feelings of mastery that can generalize beyond sexual to interpersonal relations.

In addition to sexuality, the adolescent has to meet the challenges of widely available, illegal substances. The temptations range from tobacco and marijuana to alcohol, cocaine, and hallucinogens. Beginning involvement in risky behaviors can often be ended by competent adult and peer guidance in concert with a network of adaptive social relationships from which the adolescent draws strength and confidence. Substance abuse, for example, weakens personal feelings of control, which in turn prompts further experimentation with substances in an effort to feel better by self-medication, and so on. To break this vicious cycle requires early intervention by parents, school personnel, and other family members. Impoverished and hazardous environments confront the adolescent with the sheer bleakness of an unrewarding life, and thereby set the stage for feelings of low self-efficacy and experimentation with risky behavior.

Adulthood: Vocation, Stable Partnerships, and Children

The demands of early adulthood bring the person face-to-face with the economic and social challenges of building a stable life. Passage into adulthood is less well marked than in the past because family patterns and structure are far less stable or predictable, and economic conditions fluctuate wildly and abruptly.

Vocation

For those young people who pursue higher education, a structured life path awaits. Such continuing students receive counseling, advice, and career information regularly, and often they have already formulated clear-cut occupational goals that require clearly prescribed tradition-bound steps. Law, medicine, the ministry, dentistry, clinical psychology, and teaching come quickly to mind in this context. Young people who do not continue their education follow a more difficult, more opaque path. The labor market is often erratic, especially for those with little skill preparation. When noncollege students leave school, they are at the mercy of the job market. They take part-time or dead-end jobs in retail or service ("To eat here or take out?") that provide no opportunity for continued training or advancement.

What is most needed, Bandura argues, is prior preparation in self-management skills that promote adaptation to the world of work. Given normal intellectual development, most job skills do not take long to master and some can be acquired during on-the-job training. Often hiring decisions are based more on the employer's perception of the candidate's reliability and maturity than on the specific skills the candidate brings. The person's beliefs about self capabilities are a powerful predictor of vocational success. A high sense of personal efficacy is linked with more successful career choices, hireability, and sustained performance that is satisfying to both worker and employer.

Partnerships, Family Roles, and Children

The "shape" of the family is undergoing enormous change. Ordinary marriage is in decline. Single-parent families, same-sex unions and parenting, and reconstituted families are commonplace. Women educate themselves more, and work full-time as a matter of personal satisfaction and identity, not just economics. All these changes are demanding, exerting pressures not only on family-building associated with young adulthood but on the individuals who constitute the potential family. Families are supported better by young adult parents who have firm self-efficacy feelings. New parents can tolerate and manage the demands of parenting more effectively when they *believe* that they will be effective. In all cases, the chain of generational parental efficacy is a good predictor of family successes. People exposed to good parenting feel efficacious in tackling parenting themselves, and in turn expose their children to a continuing tradition of successful, efficacious family building.

Middle Adulthood: Stability Versus Crisis

By midlife, a degree of stability and accomplishment is achieved. Basic economic and interpersonal issues are resolved, freeing the person to pursue new interests, retrench youthful aspirations, and sometimes reluctantly scale back, sometimes exuberantly fulfill lifelong dreams.

Declining Opportunities, New Dreams

For some, midlife may represent a period of diminishing vocational opportunities. ("When you're 40, you become undesirable; at 45, you become invisible; and at 50, you've become the walking dead in the job market.") Careers that involve physical strength or prowess are most vulnerable to decline, but certainly other occupations are sometimes in jeopardy. Popular media often portray midlife as a "crisis" period, but there is scant empirical research supporting the notion of midlife crisis. The needs to restructure the meaning of one's life and reconstrue what had been overambitious goals are not unique to the middle years. Efficacious people always see new opportunities, advance to new horizons, and envision new dreams.

Advanced Age: Reappraisals, Regrets, Reaffirmations

Old age is supposed to be a time of declining physical stamina, intelligence, and motivation. Advances in prolonging healthy life may obliterate these expectations for many people.

Cognitive Changes

Some reduction in overall intellectual functioning ordinarily does not affect daily performance observably. Indeed, the person's *expectations* may play a stronger role in diminishing performance, enthusiasm, and energy than actual biological change (Bandura, 1997, p. 199). Capacities that depend on accumulated knowledge and experience—problem solving, reasoning, forecasting—may actually improve well into advanced age. Some folks call these enhanced cognitive capacities "wisdom."

Maintaining a Sense of Control

Maintaining social connectedness is an essential aspect of adaptive advance into old age. A low sense of self-efficacy, as we have seen, is associated with increases in feelings of vulnerability and social withdrawal. Efficacious people are much more likely to socialize, to maintain a personal network of friends and contacts, and to feel better about each day's tasks. The stereotypical view of the elderly is that they invariably become increasingly dependent and dysfunctional. In reality, however, healthy but elderly people conduct quite masterful and satisfying lives, and they have every reason to expect to continue for long periods. That efficacious expectation by itself assures some degree of success, for it reflects the person's belief that he or she is still in control of life, master of personal fate.

Realistic Social Comparisons

Aging does not take place in a vacuum. The person advancing in years does so in the context of the larger society and its views of the elderly, and in the context of family expectations for its older members. Older people can sustain a high level of feeling efficacious despite real declines in physical or psychological functioning if they make realistic comparisons with those around them. Often, because of their accumulated "wisdom," mentioned previously, the comparisons with younger people are quite favorable to them. And the more those comparisons yield favorable results, the more likely the person of advanced age will be to keep up his or her skills, continuing to use them effectively and with satisfaction. Table 16.4 summarizes the life demands on self-efficacy through the developmental cycle.

Transitional Summary

Bandura's analysis of the changing demands on self-efficacy with progress through the life course brings a welcome developmental dimension to cognitive social learning theory. There are no startling or even new insights in this life course analysis that one could not encounter among the humanists, among the object relations theorists, or even among the ego psychologists. What makes Bandura's approach to the developmental process valuable is his reliance on a relentlessly active agent conception of personality functioning and his predilection for testing what are sometimes commonsense conclusions with empirical data. Generally accepted psychological truisms and common sense are thus validated and enhanced. As conceived by Bandura, self-efficacy is the backbone of personality. Indeed, coupled with the active agency on which it rests, self-efficacy eventually may very well simply assimilate the concept of personality.

SELECTIVE ACTIVATION OF SELF-CONTROLS

Bandura (1986, pp. 375ff.) has emphasized that self-controls are not automatic and unvarying. Theories such as Freud's that portray conscience, for example, as an

TABLE 16.4   Bandura's Developmental Analysis of Self-Efficacy

Life Phase	Typical Demands	Role of Self Efficacy
Infancy	LEARNING: Actions produce effects. *My* actions produce effects.	Reliable link between action and outcome builds self-efficacy. Sustained caring by parents "enable" child's self-control. Self-efficacy learning is the core of infant's self.
Early Childhood	LEARNING: Nature of family constellation Siblings' strengths and weaknesses Self-comparisons with siblings	Confidence in self permits attention to relevant models. Self-efficacious children resist risky behavior, view others' superior competence as a goal rather than as crushing competition.
School Age	Knowledge and problem-solving skills Peer pressures, peer comparisons, peer competitions	Efficacious children establish "good" reputations that generalize across situations. Self-efficacy permits child to explore new interests in physical, social, and interpersonal areas without inhibition or aggression.
Adolescence	Transitions to adult-like performances in school, dating, friendships and beginning of vocational identity explorations. Physiological changes of puberty. The temptations of risky sex, aggression, rule-breaking, and substance abuse.	Children who enter adolescence with strong self-efficacy are enabled, rather than protected, to equip themselves for a well structured path in life. Sexual, vocational, and interpersonal issues are resolved adaptively by children who feel sufficiently in control to remain engaged in prosocial behavior.
Adulthood	Vocational identity crystallizes. Stable partnerships in world of changed families. Having and raising children.	Efficacy as "enabling," i.e., equipping adults to make realistic decisions, sustain intimate relationships and good work habits, rather than as a "protector" from stress.
Advanced Age	Physical, psychological, especially intellectual decline; reduced vocational opportunities.	Efficacy aids person to see accumulated knowledge and skills as "wisdom" leading to favorable comparisons with others. Masterly older people seek new challenges, build new dreams.

Based on Bandura, 1997, Chapter 5.

"internalized" agency imply that the agency is an ever-present overseer, autonomously deciding when to act to pass judgment. The superego was sometimes described by Freud as if it were a "censor" ready to pounce at the first hint of a taboo wish or unacceptable impulse. Bandura, by contrast, pictures self-control as a process that the person is free to activate or deactivate. A given action will not be uniformly rewarded or punished because the circumstances may change sufficiently to deactivate or alter self-appraisal.

Bandura describes this flexibility as *selective activation and disengagement of internal control,* and he describes eight cognitive strategies through which a person can disengage self from condemnation during conduct he or she would ordinarily regard as worthy of self-punishment. In a way, these eight mechanisms are analogous to defense mechanisms, but with major differences. The deactivation strategies Bandura is describing are largely conscious, and they resemble the techniques of rationalization more than any other psychoanalytic defense mechanism. More important, Bandura conceptualizes these strategies as directed to the interaction of person and situation, not to the control of internal impulses, as in Freud's defense mechanisms. The eight selective activation mechanisms are

1. *Moral Justification:* By providing what appears to be a moral explanation for conduct that would be seen by a person as reprehensible, the person may "restructure" the meaning of his or her behavior sufficiently to justify the conduct. For example, persuading soldiers that "killing the enemy" serves a higher moral purpose—such as preserving freedom—can turn reluctant recruits into skilled combatants. Moral restructuring can certainly be used for self-serving purposes, as for example when terrorists justify their random killing and maiming as serving a higher moral goal. *Point of disengagement:* during or after conduct.

2. *Euphemistic Labeling:* What a thing is called substantially affects the meaning we place upon it. Convoluted verbiage is a wonderful mask for unethical conduct. For example, when the military describes an invasion of a country with its attendant killing and destruction as an "incursion" rather than as an attack, the conduct is sanitized and euphemized. Bandura (1986, p. 378) offers the example of instructors who teach business students how to lie in competitive situations by calling it "strategic misrepresentation." *Point of intervention:* during or after conduct.

3. *Advantageous Comparison:* If one chooses a sufficiently heinous standard against which to compare one's own conduct, then much of the blame can be avoided. For example, if an automobile salesperson overcharges customers, he or she can justify the deception by saying that the dealer down the street overcharges even more. Bandura provides the example of the promoters of the Vietnam war who excused the killing of thousands of people as a way of stopping their enslavement by communism. Somehow, the fact that the intended beneficiaries were being killed was obscured by the dramatic comparison with "massive communist enslavement." *Point of disengagement:* during or after conduct.

4. *Displacement of Responsibility:* If one can hide or distort the relationship between a given action and its effects, the usual self-regulatory controls can be disengaged. For example, at the Nuremberg Trials for Nazi officers accused of the concentration camp butchery, it was typical to hear "I was following orders." The officers felt little personal responsibility for their deeds because they were, in fact, following the orders of what they considered legitimate authority. And this perception was sufficient to outweigh the evidence of their own senses that they were involved in mass murder, torture, and extermination. Displacement of responsibility not only weakens personal restraints, but it also lessens concern for the well-being of others (Bandura, 1986, p. 379). *Point of disengagement:* during or after conduct, and/or at the point of observing recipients' consequences.

5. *Diffusion of Responsibility:* Similar to the displacement of responsibility, the strategy here is to confuse or "lose" a precise locus of responsibility by resorting to a kind of division of labor. Group decision making can result in inhumane treatment for others, whereas any single member of the group taken alone would not condone such conduct. A person can even go so far as to tell self that it is the other group members who are responsible. *Point of disengagement:* during or after conduct, and/or at the point of observing recipients' consequences.

6. *Disregard or Distortion of Consequences:* One can avoid facing the harm one does to others, so that the action and the outcome are disassociated. In this way, the person can disregard consequences. For example, soldiers who do battle from remote stations or who drop bombs from airplanes rarely see the effects of their conduct. They can convince themselves that they are destroying "targets," not people. The chain of command in the military or in business is another example. The person at the top of a very long hierarchy may be separated from observing the consequences of his or her decisions as people lower in the hierarchy carry them out. *Point of disengagement:* observing recipients' conscquences.

7. *Dehumanization:* One can disengage self-controls against mistreating people if one can find a way not to see them as people. Pejorative and stereotyping labels are one way to dehumanize another: "fags," or "gooks," or "grease balls." Labels such as these prevent normal empathy and permit a person to act inhumanly toward those perceived to be other than like self. The reverse, of course, is sometimes true. Some abductors find it difficult to harm their hostages once they have gotten to know them (Bandura, 1986, p. 383). *Point of disengagement:* Perception of victim or recipient.

8. *Attribution of Blame:* If a person can justify mistreatment of another by saying that the person "deserved it" or was "just asking for it," then self-controls can be disengaged. This strategy is sometimes called "blaming the victim." Sexually assaultive behavior toward women is sometimes "justified" in this way by men who subscribe to stereotyped beliefs and myths about their victims. One can also trivialize the consequences to the victim as another way of disengaging self-condemnation. Men who are prone to sexual assault may believe that women secretly enjoy being raped (Bandura, 1986, p. 385). *Point of disengagement:* Perception of victim or recipient.

Bandura points out that none of these disengagement mechanisms by itself can turn a law-abiding or ethical person abruptly into a criminal. Rather, they tend to be cumulative and interactive, so that there is a gradual disengagement of self-controls.

Puzzle Four: The Nature of Anxiety and Repression

The radical behaviorists treated anxiety as a consequence of behavior, and the psychodynamic social learning theorists attempted to treat anxiety more in the Freudian tradition as a causal variable. The problem for Bandura was to capitalize on both traditions to conceptualize anxiety as a cognitive-emotional variable that mediates avoidance and defensive behavior.

Freud's theory portrayed anxiety as the result of unconscious conflict between taboo wishes and the restraint of the ego. The ego experiences the "signal of anxiety" when a taboo impulse or thought threatens to overwhelm its coping capacities. Of course the problem in this formulation is the concept of the ego as an internal agent capable of making decisions, feeling feelings, and enacting strategies of defense as if it were a complete person within the person.

The conditioning theory of the radical behaviorists, and in part of the psychodynamic social learning theorists, portrayed anxiety in terms of the evoking stimulus. Aversive stimulation is invested with fear-provoking properties, which the person learns to avoid. In all fairness, Miller and Dollard did attempt to incorporate the concept of fearful *thoughts* as causal links in defensive behavior, but the linkage is created in their model solely by association of a thought with an unconditioned aversive stimulus. Anticipation, in this formulation, is at the level of a single thought becoming a signal for a harmful stimulus.

Left out of the S-R formulation are the components to which Freud pointed: feelings of helplessness, and complex chains of associative and symbolic links to the original noxious stimulus. Left out, too, is consideration of positive behavior that anxiety may evoke as the person not only considers defending against aversive stimulation, but also decides to muster the skills to master the threat.

Our study of the history of attempts to conceptualize anxiety and defensive behavior as key ingredients in psychopathology reveals an interesting phenomenon in the succession of paradigms. It is as if each succeeding paradigm seized upon one piece of the puzzle in its adherents' search for a workable solution. But each of these one-piece "solutions" excluded the remaining pieces as irrelevant to its formulation. Social learning theory, standing at the crossroads of behaviorism, cognition, and psychodynamic theory, is in a position to examine and synthesize all of the puzzle pieces.

> PUZZLE FOUR: *How can the signal function of anxiety, the accompanying feelings of helplessness, the causal status of anxious thoughts, and the resulting repressive-coping responses be fitted together into a verifiable explanation?*

Bandura's solution captures the clinical insight of Freud's description of the ego's helplessness and the empirical strength of behaviorism's focus on response consequences:

> From the social learning perspective, it is mainly perceived inefficacy in coping with potentially aversive events that makes them fearsome. To the extent that one can prevent, terminate, or lessen the severity of aversive events, there is little reason to fear them. (p. 136)
>
> . . . A painful event has two arousal components to it—discomfort produced by the aversive stimulation and the thought-produced arousal. It is the thought component—the arousal generated by repetitive perturbing ideation—that accounts for much of human distress.
>
> . . . people who judge themselves inefficacious dwell on their coping deficiencies and view trying situations as fraught with peril. They not only magnify the severity of possible threats but worry about perils that rarely, if ever, happen. As a result they experience a high level of cognitively generated distress. Elevated arousal, in turn,

heightens preoccupation with personal inefficacy and potential calamaties. (p. 137) (Bandura, 1982)

In Bandura's formulation, anxiety arousal and defensive behavior are *coeffects* rather than causally related. The cause of defensive behavior, including repression, is not the emotional arousal of anxiety but the cause of the anxiety in the first place: expectation of injury or pain (Bandura, 1977b, p. 61).

Bandura (1969, pp. 426ff.) has reviewed research that shows autonomic nervous system arousal and defensive behavior are frequently unsynchronized or even disassociated. For example, Miller and Dollard's explanation of anxiety as resulting through "not-thinking" the anxiety-arousing thought is based on the assumption that anxiety is an aversive stimulus with drive properties. Not-thinking the thought associated with the anxiety stimulus is negatively reinforcing because it reduces the unpleasant drive state of anxiety.

But a variety of research shows that even when autonomic nervous system arousal is blocked chemically, defensive behavior can be triggered. In the same vein, when autonomic anxiety arousal is permitted to extinguish, defensive behavior persists (e.g., Black, 1958; see the review of much of this literature by Rescorla & Solomon, 1967).

Anxiety reduction and defensive behavior may occur together, but anxiety is not the sufficient cause of defensive behavior in the social learning paradigm. Rather, in Bandura's analysis, aversive events trigger avoidance behavior because they are signals of impending pain or injury; anxiety arousal is triggered *simultaneously* with this expectation through exposure to the threatening event. But it is the person's feelings, expectations of not being able to cope with the impending dangerous event that make both the event and its associated anxiety arousal so distressing. The focus here is on the person's efficacy expectations—his or her thoughts about the meaning of anxiety stimuli and the self-evaluations of available coping skills:

> *Acquired threats activate defensive behavior because of their predictive rather than their aversive qualities.* They signal the likelihood of painful outcomes unless protective measures are taken. Defensive behavior, in turn, is maintained by its success in forestalling or reducing the occurrence of aversive events. Once established, defensive behavior is difficult to eliminate even when the hazard no longer exists. *This is because consistent avoidance prevents the organism from learning that the real circumstances have changed.* Hence, the failure of anticipated hazards to materialize reinforces the expectation that the defensive maneuvers forestalled them. This process of subjective confirmation is captured in the apocryphal case of a compulsive who, when asked by his therapist why he snapped his fingers ritualistically, replied that it kept ferocious lions away. When informed that obviously there were no lions in the vicinity to ward off, the compulsive replied, "See, it works!" (Bandura, 1977b, p. 62; italics added)

The defense of repression, in social learning theory, is therefore not an automatic response to anxiety feelings. It is an avoidance response to the aversive thoughts that accompany the anxiety. Thoughts about potential failure or pain, the inability to cope with demands, and expectations that one will not meet challenges successfully can be inhibited by focusing on an incompatible thought or behavior (Bandura, 1969, p. 592).

Thus, in the social learning paradigm, repression is conceptualized rather differently from the psychoanalytic version. For the social learning theorist, repressed ideas do not have a life of their own in the unconscious; they are not held in check by an internal agency employing psychic energy; and repressed thoughts do not have independent drive properties that regulate and necessitate substitute forms of behavior to keep them perpetually restrained and out of awareness.

Rather, repressed thoughts are treated like any other behavior that lies inert until the appropriate stimulus activates it. If the person can arrange circumstances such that incompatible responses successfully compete with the inhibited ones, then those inhibited responses will not even reach the level of thought. If an anxiety-arousing thought or behavior cannot be inhibited by substitute thoughts and acts, it may emerge sufficiently strong in the person's awareness to create anxiety and conflict (Bandura, 1969, pp. 592–593).

In essence, the social learning view draws from both the behavioristic and psychodynamic formulations those elements supported by research and susceptible to laboratory testing. Anxiety is an emotional concomitant of aversive stimulation. But the stimulation is aversive and defense-provoking because the person *thinks* about his or her capacities to master it. Low or inaccurate feelings of self-efficacy are causal in predicting a person's response to threatening ideas and stimuli.

The response to repression, as in Miller and Dollard's formulation, is actually "not-thinking" (or "not-doing") those distressing thoughts, and/or substituting incompatible thoughts (and behaviors). The difference between Bandura's and Miller and Dollard's formulation is that Bandura does not conceptualize anxiety as a negative drive that impels the person to reduce the arousal. Instead, the person is impelled to avoid the feeling of helplessness implicit in his or her low self-efficacy expectations. It is not anxiety reduction that is reinforcing; it is the reduction of feelings of helplessness. Conversely, the more one can increase a person's feelings of efficacy, the greater the reduction in his or her feelings of anxiety and fear (Bandura, 1982).

Cognitive Social Learning Theory: The Paradigm's Yield

From the way in which cognitive social learning theory deploys the workable elements from psychoanalysis and behaviorism, it is clear that its formulations of personality will be greatly different from the formulation of either of its predecessors. Table 16.5 illustrates those differences with respect to the two concepts of repression and anxiety that we have followed through each of the main paradigms.

Some Limitations of the Social Learning Paradigm

At present the social learning paradigm has the unique historical advantage of learning from the other paradigms' mistakes. Social learning, as we have seen, is empirical, laboratory oriented, nonsimplistic, and able to assimilate cognitive as well as behavioral principles.

But there is a catch-22 in these advantages. The other paradigms' "mistakes" were not made deliberately and were not made stupidly. They were made in the hard

TABLE 16.5   Comparison of Behaviorist Models on Relevant Personality Variables

	Classical Psychoanalysis	Radical Behaviorism	Psychodynamic Social Learning	Cognitive Social Learning
Theorists	FREUD	WATSON-SKINNER	DOLLARD-MILLER	BANDURA-MISCHEL
Subjective Meaning of Anxiety	Signal of different dangers at different ages; ego feels helpless to master id wishes or reality demands.	Irrelevant.	Conditioned apprehension, and anticipation of pain.	Low expectancy of self-efficacy, feelings of helplessness.
Causal Status of Anxiety	Drive status, trigger for symptoms, and defenses.	Autonomic arousal consequence of avoidance behavior; noncausal.	Drive status, trigger for symptoms, defenses, and generalization.	Unsynchronized autonomic arousal accompanies aversive stimulus, but not a cause.
Causal Mode of Anxiety	Ego acts to block, cancel, avoid anxiety ideas, wishes to reduce tension.	Consequence not cause of avoidance.	Learned avoidance response reduces anxiety, and anxiety reduction is a negative reinforcer.	Partial correlate of aversive stimulus, but not a sufficient cause.
Repression and Defensive Behavior	Ego banishes anxiety ideas, wishes from consciousness.	No such mechanism for mental content; behavior that hurts is not repeated.	Substitution of incompatible behaviors, thoughts; the anxiety-reducing response of "not-thinking" the fearful ideas.	Substitution of behavior incompatible with aversive thoughts or responses; not-thinking about feelings of helplessness triggered by aversive stimulus. Rethinking the meaning of the aversive stimulus to make it less aversive.

struggle to solve the puzzles of human behavior and psychopathology. To the degree that social learning theory assimilates workable concepts and data from these prior puzzle solutions, it is susceptible to limitation from the same obstacles. Although Bandura and Mischel have found ways to deal scientifically with unobservables—avoiding the blindness of radical behaviorism and the unverifiability of psychoanalysis—the problem of subjective experience has been attacked only piecemeal.

Social learning theory has studied expectations, self-reinforcement controls, anxiety and defense, and the variables involved in observational learning. Taken piece by piece, each of these phenomena revolutionized psychology and psychopathology. But that is the problem: "Piece by piece" is not an overall synthesis. Looking back over the classification list of psychopathology, it is obvious that each of the six categories is descriptive, not explanatory. Each category is relatively discrete, not a reflection of a coherent and interlocking set of principles.

The rich, complex, and elusive variables of personal conflict, deficits in development and interpersonal relations, and the precise contribution of biologic variables that Freud and the other psychodynamic theorists struggled with are not given any more precise or unified treatment here. The network of associations, symbolic substitutes, displacements, and condensations that make human thought so wondrous, and which at least in part regulate personality, are yet to be scientifically conceptualized.

It is not an impossible task. Some future version of social learning theory may very well set out in that direction. There is no absolute obstacle to capturing multi-causal networks in empirical terms.

In an interesting aside to the problems of synthesizing the many variables that regulate personality, Bandura (1986, p. 32) has recently devoted some attention to the effects of chance events or "fortuitous circumstances" on shaping a person's life. The idea is reminiscent of the existentialist's notion of destiny as circumstances that affect us but over which we have little control and even less foresight. Sometimes the triadic model of reciprocal influence is irrelevant because chance provides an occasion for someone to enter a "lifepath" that he or she would not even have envisioned without the "lucky accident." For example, the college student who has to meet a requirement in social science signs up for a sociology course but is placed in a psychology course when enrollments in sociology reach their ceilings. After the course, the student discovers that psychology has become a career choice.

Bandura argues that fortuitous events are not foreseeable, but, having occurred, personal factors, talents, and personal meanings then enter into the causal chain to shape behavior. Factors such as the prior skills of the person, whether the person likes or dislikes people met during a chance encounter, and personal vulnerability and emotional state all influence the degree to which a chance event *can* influence a person's life (Bandura, 1986, p. 35). But it is to the credit of social learning theory that even these unpredictable events, which can have a strong impact on personality, are recognized and studied.

EVALUATING THE BEHAVIORISMS

By the very fact of their empirical roots and the extremity with which various theorists have stated their positions, the three kinds of behaviorism we have reviewed in this chapter lend themselves to direct evaluation. Recall that we have seen the development of behavioral psychology from John B. Watson's radical behaviorism through B. F. Skinner's updated radical behaviorism to Miller and Dollard's psychodynamic behaviorism (or is it behavioral psychodynamics?) to Bandura's cognitive social learning theory. In all, there are really only three "kinds" of behaviorism represented, with minor variations along the way:

Radical behaviorism,

Psychodynamic behaviorism, and

Social cognitive behaviorism

One way to understand this list is as a developmental hierarchy, with a progression from relatively primitive views of human personality to the more sophisticated conception contained in social cognitive behaviorism.

The Refutability of the Behaviorisms

Because all three behavioral models were based, to differing degrees, on laboratory research, they each lend themselves to testing, each of them generates testable hypotheses, and each of them has had its share of confirmations and disconfirmations.

Radical Behaviorism

Watson's conception of human behavior leaned heavily on the early work in Pavlovian conditioning. And when Watson needed to make a polemical point, he was not above going beyond his data. By contrast, B. F. Skinner not only derived most of his generalizations and explanations from direct experiment, but he refused to go beyond the data to unsupportable statements. However limiting, radical behaviorism gets high grades in refutability. And to John B. Watson psychology owes at least this debt: Without his insistence on experimental method, psychology's growth as an empirical science would have been delayed.

Psychodynamic Behaviorism

Miller and Dollard based much of their theory on extensive experimentation. Most of the behaviorism that they incorporated came from the work of Clark Hull, but the tenor of the ideas is not altogether alien to Skinnerian and Watsonian behaviorism. Their work generated an astounding array of studies, but very little interest from either the behaviorist or the psychoanalytic camps. What can be said of a theory that is at once scientific, refutable, sophisticated, and synthetic but which no one wants? This much can be said: It is a highly fertile model of personality that lends itself well to testing. It is a neglected theory for reasons that are not all that clear. And, judging from the history of psychology, where the wheel is almost daily reinvented under new names, Miller and Dollard's ideas will eventually become significant again—perhaps when the current social cognitive theory turns more clearly in the direction of investigating "unconscious" processes.

Social Cognitive Behaviorism

Bandura's model is so intimately tied to laboratory and field research that we can say simply this: It is highly refutable, highly capable of generating new research ideas, and has been widely tested. Given the scope of Bandura's 1986 summary of the model, we can assume that social learning theory is capable of being fine-tuned and adjusted as new data are collected. It should also be pointed out that Bandura's cognitive conception of observational and enactive learning give due weight to the sophistication of the human organism, and the research that has been mounted in behalf of this model is equally sophisticated.

Behaviorism and Human Agency

Recall our discussion from Chapter 1 of the active-passive dichotomy in the history of personality theory. Both radical behaviorism and psychodynamic theories shared the basic assumption that reality acts upon the person. Human agency makes for strange theoretical bedfellows.

Radical Behaviorism

Watson and Skinner have pictured human agency essentially as determined by external variables. In Watson's day, the person's own view of the stimuli to which he or she was exposed was considered irrelevant. Although Skinner allows for the significance of private events, such as thinking and feeling, these variables have no causal status in Skinner's account. The radical behaviorists picture humans as passive agents, shaped by the selection pressures of the environment.

Psychodynamic Behaviorism

Oddly, despite their interest in social phenomena, Miller and Dollard share with Freud a deterministic view of human agency. The forces that act in the world of Miller and Dollard are not restricted to the external environment, certainly, but they are deterministic forces nonetheless. Human agency in psychodynamic behaviorism is passive: We are shaped by our drives and by the consequences of our attempts to satisfy them.

Social Cognitive Behaviorism

Of the three behaviorisms, only Bandura's model emphasizes, and strongly, an active conception of human agency. Bandura (1989) put it this way:

> Social cognitive theory rejects the dichotomous conception of self as agent and self as object. Acting on the environment and acting on oneself entail shifting the perspective of the same agent rather than reifying different selves regulating each other or transforming the self from agent to object. In acting as agents over their environments, people draw on their knowledge and cognitive and behavioral skills to produce desired results. In acting as agents over themselves, people monitor their actions and enlist cognitive guides and self-incentives to produce desired personal changes. They are just as much agents influencing themselves as they are influencing their environment. (Bandura, 1989, p. 1181)

It is clear that Bandura rejects any simple split between object and subject or between passive and active. The person is seen as a whole entity or agent for whom previous learning history, expectations of mastery (efficacy), and current interpretation of the world all interact to regulate behavior. Bandura's "triadic" conception of reciprocal determinism is a highly sophisticated active-reactive agency viewpoint. It gives weight to environmental, emotional, and cognitive variables in a way that no other personality theory has ever done.

Idiographic Versus Nomothetic in the Behaviorisms

Radical Behaviorism

All three behaviorisms set out to establish general "laws" or "lawlike" truisms about human psychology. And all three, as we have seen, produced nomothetic research. Of the three, Watson's radical behaviorism was perhaps least successful, largely because at Watson's time in history, the methodology of conditioning was primitive and the conceptions on which it was based were primitive. By contrast, Skinner worked for years with single organisms, a kind of idiographic approach designed to yield nomothetic data. The curves of response rates to different reinforcement schedules, based on pooled individual data, did in fact yield generalizable "laws" of conditioning schedules.

Psychodynamic Behaviorism

Miller and Dollard's psychodynamic behaviorism, on the other hand, is difficult to characterize on the idiographic-nomothetic dimension. What it shares with Freudian theory is idiographic, with a focus on the individual's drives, expectations, and avoidance maneuvers. But what it shares with behaviorism is nomothetic, including their conception of anxiety, the "rules" under which anxiety leads to "not-thinking," and Miller's elaborate conflict theory.

Social Cognitive Behaviorism

Again we find that the most sophisticated approach lies with Bandura's model. Given its empirical basis, its vast research support, and its attention to the "rules" of self-control, the theory produces nomothetic (generalizable) principles. Yet, as we have seen, Bandura's principles of self-efficacy, self-monitoring or control, and his triadic conception of determinism clearly permit empirical statements about the individual. There is a genuine balance of the nomothetic and the idiographic in Bandura's model. However, at the present stage of development, the balance leans toward the nomothetic.

Some Summary, Some Conclusions

Freud's pioneering puzzle solutions in psychopathology identified the unconscious mind as the source of the conflict, self-deception, and compromise formations he observed in his patients. Beginning with John B. Watson, psychologists have struggled to solve the same puzzles in more verifiable terms.

Watson's radical behaviorism dismissed human thought, feeling, and expectation as irrelevant to the scientific study of behavior. B. F. Skinner, in the tradition of Watson, applied the behavioristic philosophy to even more complex, voluntary behavior. And the psychodynamic S-R theorists Dollard and Miller attempted to bridge the gap between the rich clinical observations of psychoanalysis and the methodological rigor of behaviorism. In the end, adherents of each of these paradigms had solved only partially the central puzzle of personality. What is the causal status of human thought in regulating behavior? Our survey of the history of attempts within the behavioral tradition was organized around these main themes.

Watsonian behaviorism adopted the Pavlovian conditioned reflex as the fundamental "atom" of lawful behavior prediction. Watson built the behavioristic philosophy around these assumptions:

1. *Evolutionary continuity:* Animal and human behavior is not different in kind, just in degree of complexity;
2. *Reductionism:* At some ultimate level of understanding, behavior is regulated and caused by biochemical processes in the nervous, glandular, and muscle systems of the organism;
3. *Determinism:* Behavior is never random, accidental, or spontaneous. Every behavioral effect has its cause, but mental events are only epiphenomenal—wraithlike consequences or by-products of the more fundamental behavioral process.
4. *Empiricism:* If you can't measure it, see it, manipulate it, "it" doesn't exist. Watson strongly advocated experimental method for this reason, and American psychology responded with enthusiasm.

Watson conceptualized psychopathology as learned maladaptive responding. Disease metaphors, unconscious processes, and subjective experience were by definition excluded from the "scientific" conception of disordered behavior. And Watson's imaginary psychopathological dog was the case in point.

In the tradition of Watson, B. F. Skinner turned his attention to the more complex learning process introduced into psychology by Edward Lee Thorndike under the label of "trial-and-error" learning. In this paradigm, complex voluntary behavior is selectively strengthened by reinforcers. Reinforcers are stimulus events, typically rewards, that increase the probability that the response preceding them will occur again. Negative reinforcers likewise strengthen responses, but the responses are those that terminate an aversive stimulus.

Skinner argued, as had Watson, that key elements in psychopathology could be understood without reference to thought or subjective experience. Anxiety, for example, was explained as a consequence of avoidance behavior. And "repression" is the substitution of distracting and less punishing behavior for a response that has been punished. Skinner had thus succeeded in ridding psychopathology of Freud's internal mental agencies, unconscious processes, and personal meanings.

Radical behaviorism was enthusiastically adopted by psychologists who may have had more optimism than was warranted by the data. Limitations on Pavlovian and operant conditioning gradually emerged in the 1960s:

1. *Conditioning is not universally automatic:* Not all stimuli are equally associable, and not all organisms are shapeable.
2. At the human level, research was beginning to develop evidence that conditioning was heavily influenced by the person's awareness of the contingencies of reinforcement and willingness to permit the reinforcer to be effective.
3. Premack showed that reinforcers are relative not absolute commodities, so that a behavior of higher initial probability can reinforce a behavior of initially lower probability.

Dollard and Miller, and other members of the Yale Group, made the first attempt to transcend simple stimulus-response psychology. Their efforts were focused on making Freud's contributions more verifiable, and they succeeded in translating key Freudian ideas into stimulus-response-almost-cognitive psychology. Anxiety was treated as a subjective cognitive-emotional cause of defensive behavior. Repression was brilliantly translated into a functionally equivalent response that avoids painful thoughts as rats learn to avoid cues that signal electric shock. But the great achievement of Miller and Dollard was to reestablish human thought as worthy of scientific study because of its causal status in psychopathology.

Beginning in the early 1960s, Albert Bandura and Richard Walters introduced the study of observational learning into psychology. Although Miller and Dollard had considered imitation learning as early as 1941, it was Bandura and his colleagues who drew out the implications of such learning, including

1. The internal cognitive processes of *attention, retention, reproduction,* and *direct and vicarious reinforcement* that have to exist for learning from a model's behavior to occur;
2. The self-regulatory aspects of many behaviors, which demonstrate the person's capacity to reward and punish self for meeting or failing to meet self-standards.
3. The significance of a person's efficacy expectations in regulating the process of learning and the application of self-reinforcement.

Bandura has argued cogently that even the most basic conception of reinforcement must be understood in cognitive terms. A person learns to expect, to anticipate, and to predict the consequences of his or her behavior; reinforcement does not act backward in time to stamp in a response already made. Thus reinforcement is more a matter of information and performance enhancement than it is automatic response strengthening.

Bandura's social learning model is based on a multicausal perspective called reciprocal determinism, by which a person's behavior regulates and is regulated in turn by the environment, and the person's awareness of this interaction can also change the nature of the interaction. Psychopathology is thus a multicaused phenomenon, with the present focus on the principles of direct and vicarious learning responsible for the acquisition of inappropriate and maladaptive behavior.

In Bandura's scheme, the Freudian puzzles of anxiety and repression are given cognitive-behavioral explanations that appear verifiable and empirical. Anxiety is a *coeffect* of aversive stimulation that is not necessarily synchronized with autonomic nervous system arousal. Therefore, it is not anxiety itself that triggers coping and repressive behavior. It is the nature of the aversive stimulus itself: The person learns to expect pain or injury and evaluates his or her capacities to cope. If that self-evaluation reveals low-efficacy expectations, the person anticipates pain and helplessness. It is this subjective meaning that triggers the defensive behavior. As in the Miller-Dollard model, the defense of repression is a learned "not-thinking" response supplemented with distraction behavior designed to divert attention and thought from the ideas-feelings of helplessness.

Bandura has added a welcome developmental dimension to his concept of self-efficacy, tracking the unique demands on personal mastery operating at the various phases of life from infancy to old age. From infancy through adolescence, successful mastery of living demands learning not only that one can be effective, but that personal effectiveness often is linked with relationships to other people. By young adulthood, typical life demands include making vocational choices that will enhance one's sense of personal control and effectiveness and preparing for a stable intimate relationship with another to build a family. By the later years, a strong belief in personal efficacy enhances the quality of life so that the expected deterioration in cognitive and motor skills is by no means inevitable. The later years can also be a time of "wisdom," during which the older person passes along the wealth of experience and positive attitudes accumulated through a lifetime of efficacious living.

Our evaluation of the behaviorisms led to the following conclusions:

- The radical behaviorism of Skinner and Watson, the psychodynamic behaviorism of Miller and Dollard, and the social cognitive theory of Bandura are based on a great deal of empirical research. What was done with the findings, however, depended on the sophistication of the theorist. All three are refutable.

- Of the three behaviorisms, only Bandura's social cognitive theory embodies an active agent conception of the person.

- Of the three behaviorisms, only psychodynamic behaviorism is largely idiographic. Radical behaviorism and cognitive social learning theory lean in the nomothetic direction.

For Further Reading

Radical Behaviorism

A careful analysis of the meaning of empiricism and verifiability in the behavioral tradition is provided in the classic paper by Nathan Brody and P. Oppenheim: "Tensions in psychology between the methods of behaviorism and phenomenology,"

Psychological Review, 1966, **73,** 295–305. Mary Henle and G. Baltimore's criticism of "Tensions in psychology between the methods of behaviorism and phenomenology," *Psychological Review,* 1967, **74,** 325–329, provides a critique that clarifies the Brody and Oppenheim paper with humor and cogency. (See also the paper in the same issue by R. Zaner and the replies by Brody and Oppenheim.)

B. F. Skinner's *Science and Human Behavior* (New York: Macmillan, 1953) is his pioneering attempt to explain cognitive-emotional processes in behavioral terms and probably the closest he comes to a "personality theory." J. B. Watson's *Behaviorism* (New York: Norton, 1930) is the landmark statement of Watson's position. But a careful reading of Watson's "founding" paper "Psychology as the behaviorist views it," *Psychological Review,* 1913, **20,** 158–177, is, perhaps, more revealing of Watson's attitudes. Kerry Buckley's excellent biography of J. B. Watson, *Mechanical Man: John Broadus Watson and the Beginnings of Behaviorism* (New York: Guilford, 1989), is currently the most detailed account of Watson's life and personality. The definitive biography that will detail more of Watson's relationship with his mother and with his own children remains to be written. The collection of papers in James T. Todd's and Edward K. Morris's (Eds.) *Modern Perspectives on John B. Watson and Classical Behaviorism* (Westport, CT: Greenwood Press, 1994) ranges, with noticeably uneven quality, from cogent historical analyses of Watson's impact on psychology to the outcome of a rare and salty but minor interview with Watson near the end of his life.

Psychodynamic Social Learning Theory

The masterwork that spelled out the first S-R translation of Freudian ideas is to be found in John Dollard and Neal Miller's *Personality and Psychotherapy* (New York: McGraw-Hill, 1950). This book is not only interesting reading, it makes it hard to see why the Miller-Dollard theory of personality and psychopathology became more or less defunct. Paul Wachtel's *Psychoanalysis and Behavior Therapy: Toward an Integration* (New York: Basic Books, 1977) is a contemporary attempt to blend the strengths of both paradigms.

Cognitive Social Learning Theory

Albert Bandura's *Social Learning* (Englewood Cliffs, NJ: Prentice-Hall, 1977) is Bandura's most concise yet complete statement of his formulation. His more recent *Social Foundations of Thought and Action* (Englewood Cliffs, NJ: Prentice-Hall, 1986) is the definitive statement but extremely dense reading. Bandura's *Principles of Behavior Modification* (New York: Holt, Rinehart and Winston, 1969) is a survey of the empirical studies from which social learning theory was formulated. It is now a bit out of date, but retains value for what it shows of Bandura's style of theory construction from empirical studies.

Bandura's latest restatement of a major portion of his theory refocused on self-efficacy as a near-universal mediating variable is to be had in *Self-Efficacy: The Exercise of Control* (New York: Freeman, 1997). Bandura edited a companion volume of readings on self-efficacy that presents a wide range of theoretical ideas and research that tests the theory in *Self-Efficacy in Changing Societies* (New York: Cambridge University Press, 1995). Chapter 3 of this book (pp. 69–113), "Developmental analysis of control beliefs," by A. Flammer is particularly worthwhile reading for those interested in the parallels between object-relations theory and social cognition. Michael H. Kernis's (Ed.), *Efficacy, Agency, and Self-Esteem* (New York: Plenum, 1995) presents a broad spectrum of theoretical and research papers that extend the idea of personal competence into areas traditionally considered "self-esteem" variables.

Walter Mischel's "Toward a cognitive social learning reconceptualization of personality," *Psychological Review,* 1973, **80**, 252–283, is a lucid statement of the justification for cognitive constructs in the behavioral tradition. A deep understanding of contemporary empirical work in social cognition and personality can be achieved by reading nearly any chapter in Susan T. Fiske's and Shelly E. Taylor's second edition of their classic *Social Cognition* (New York: McGraw-Hill, 1991).

CHAPTER 17

HANS EYSENCK

Biological Typology

Most people of course, whatever they may say, do not in fact want a scientific account of human nature and personality at all. . . . Hence they much prefer the great story-teller, S. Freud, or the brilliant myth-creator, C. G. Jung, to those who, like Cattell or Guilford, expect them to learn matrix algebra, study physiological details of the nervous system, and actually carry out experiments rather than rely on interesting anecdotes, sex-ridden case histories, and ingenious speculation.

Hans Eysenck, *Psychology Is About People*

About Eysenck's Biological Typology

Hans Eysenck pictures personality as centered in the brain. He has constructed a multileveled model of behavior that ranges from genetics to social psychology. Eysenck's work is broad and profoundly complex, but a workable road map through this difficult terrain can be had if we emphasize these ideas:

1. *The central nervous system (CNS) is the seat of personality functioning.*

2. *Much laboratory research in learning, conditioning, perception, and drug effects shows that people can be reliably distinguished into introverts and extroverts. Introverts are "stimulus shy," because they are acutely sensitive to incoming stimulation as if their brain arousal levels were chronically high. Extroverts are "stimulus hungry" because they seek and easily process intense stimulation as if their brain arousal levels were chronically low or inhibited.*

3. *Introverts with their high chronic arousal are prone to anxiety disorders such as phobia and obsessional disorder. Extroverts with their low intellectual arousal levels are more prone to dramatic, acting-out disorders such as hysterical disorder and antisocial personality disorder.*

Unlike most of the other theories in this book, Eysenck's model lends itself, in fact demands, continuous laboratory testing.

BEHAVIORIST AS IRRITANT, AS SCIENTIST, AS PHILOSOPHER

When the young Hans Eysenck, freshly graduated from the University of London, obtained his first job as research psychologist in the wartime Mill Hill Emergency Hospital, he proceeded to alienate, shock, and generally embarrass his immediate superiors. The Mill Hill Hospital received war casualties who had succumbed to a variety of mental disturbances. Eysenck was curious to discover the reliability of the psychiatric diagnoses by which incoming airmen and soldiers were classified. If two or more physicians examined the same patient, would their diagnoses agree? Furthermore, if they did agree, would the prescribed treatments correspond? It seemed to Eysenck a simple matter to decide because all a research psychologist had to do was collect a sample of cases and perform the necessary statistical correlations. Eysenck's account of what transpired in the office of the hospital superintendent when he attempted to solicit permission to carry out this piece of research is quite revealing:

> [The Superintendent] received me in a fatherly fashion, and listened patiently to my plan. Then, to my surprise, he suggested that there were so many more interesting

things that could be done, it would be a pity to waste my time in this fashion. After all, did not everyone know that these psychiatrists had been well-trained, had medical degrees, and could therefore (almost by definition) do no wrong? When I cheerfully suggested that even such supermen might welcome definitive proof of the reliability of their judgments he became more serious. . . . And when I answered that I was not throwing doubt on anything or anybody, but just wanted to know with some precision how accurate these difficult and complex judgments could be, he told me in no uncertain terms that I was at liberty to collect these data, but I was also at liberty to look for another job. This argument seemed a winner, and I acknowledged its superior force by withdrawing from the unequal contest. I did, to be sure, collect my data but kept rather quiet about it. (1972, pp. 357–358)

Eysenck's apparently innocent desire "to know with some precision" whether traditionally accepted ideas were sound is rather characteristic of his entire approach to personality. His surreptitious research into psychiatric diagnoses, incidentally, showed such professional judgments to have very little similarity from one psychiatrist to another—even when the second psychiatrist already knew of the first psychiatrist's diagnosis. But, of course, that finding held no surprise for Eysenck.

Eysenck's philosophical position may be described as a commitment to the *hypothetico-deductive* method of classical physics (1952, p. 16; 1957a, p. 264). Beginning with basic observational data, scientists who use this method formulate a *hypothesis* or tentative explanation of the events they have observed. Controlled conditions are then established to test the validity of the hypothesis. To devise precisely the right kind of experimental situation to test the hypothesis requires that scientists *deduce* the logical, preferably quantitative, implications of their predictions.

Although a given hypothesis is derived logically from an initial set of uncontrolled observations, conclusions are never accepted solely on the basis of logic. The final criterion of acceptability for any conclusion is whether it conforms to the new observations made under the controlled conditions of the experimental test situation.

The hypothetico-deductive strategy really comes into its own when the predictions or deductions from the original observations involve the proposal of new, theretofore unexpected, propositions. To some extent these kinds of hypotheses transcend what could have been predicted on the basis of common sense. It is to this more surprising and exciting kind of prediction that Eysenck's personality formulations are directed.

As a behaviorist concerned with the measurable, quantitative aspects of personality, Eysenck has frequently criticized what he considers to be less empirical, less factual, and less scientific approaches to personality investigation. One of the chief targets of his critical attacks has been Freudian psychoanalysis, which he regards as primarily fictional and, at best, untestable (Eysenck, 1953a, 1957b, 1960, 1963b, 1965; Eysenck & Wilson, 1973; cf. Rachman, 1963, and Eysenck & Rachman, 1965). For Eysenck, the most important aspects of any psychological formulation are that it be empirical, observationally testable, and a fertile source of new hypotheses (Eysenck, 1957a, pp. 250ff.). His own efforts are exemplary in all these qualities.

PERSONAL CHILDHOOD SOURCES OF EYSENCK'S TOUGH-MINDEDNESS

In his autobiography, self-servingly but tellingly entitled *Rebel With a Cause,* Eysenck (1990) portrays himself as an angry, assertive person who collided early and frequently with established authority. His intention throughout the autobiography was to paint a portrait of himself as a tough-minded intellectual with a tender heart; but the finished portrait depicts a man who began life feeling lonely and ignored—even, perhaps, definitively unwanted by his divorced parents who went on to devote themselves exclusively to their own lives and interests in the entertainment and film industries. Eysenck recalled that he experienced their seeming indifference to him as "mean" (Eysenck, 1990, pp. 15, 228).

Childhood: Doting Grandmother, Neglectful Parents

Hans Jurgen Eysenck was born March 4, 1916, during the First World War in Berlin and grew up during Germany's period of humiliating defeat and economic crisis following its defeat. Growing up German in that era made Eysenck feel that he had to prove himself. Eysenck's mother, Ruth Werner, was born near the end of the nineteenth century in Konigshütte, a small town in what was then Silesia, now Poland. Eysenck reports that his mother's ambition was not to follow in the footsteps of her physician father but to study law. However, women were largely excluded from such careers at the turn of the century, so she followed her mother's advice and used her considerable physical assets and beauty to pursue a career in silent film acting. By age 15, Eysenck's mother was regarded as quite a beauty, and her success in an acting or modeling career seemed assured. She assumed the stage name of Helga Molander for her screen roles in the mostly silent films of the era.

Helga Molander met Anton Eduard Eysenck, also an actor, during her first professional engagement. She was a "starlet" and he was a star of stage and operettas (Eysenck, 1990, p.153). They fell in love, married, and Hans Jurgen was born shortly thereafter. They chose "Hans Jurgen" for their son's name because, in German, it "had the connotation of a simple, honest, none-too-bright youngster, reliable and trustworthy" (Eysenck, 1990, p. 10). Eysenck tells us that, with the exception of the "none-too-bright" aspect, the name viewed as destiny's cliché actually suited how he saw himself.

> . . . that was roughly how I saw myself—a large good-natured dog, always ready to be friendly, but possibly dangerous when kicked in the teeth. I was to receive many such kicks in the course of my life—but then I suppose most people do. Rebels are particularly exposed to such extremities, of course, and a rebel I was to become, more through force of circumstances than predilection. (Eysenck, 1990, p. 10)

Although neither parent was especially religious, Eysenck's father, Anton Eysenck, had been raised in a Catholic family, whereas his mother's family was Protestant. Both partners began their marriage therefore with similar career interests but had to cope with different familial histories and differing personal values. To make matters somewhat more dire, Anton was a "womanizer" (Eysenck, 1990, p. 11). The marriage was brief. By the time Hans Jurgen was age two, they were divorced (Eysenck, 1990, p. 153).

Relationship With Father

Eysenck's description of his father is unflattering. Eysenck describes Anton Eysenck as an authoritarian man with strong Germanic pride in his Aryan ancestry. During World War II, Anton Eysenck joined the Nazi party, a fact that Hans recalls with bitter distaste. A successful actor for many years, Anton eventually switched professions from stage and film actor to "conferencier," a kind of all-around stage entertainer, stand-up comic, political commentator, and master of ceremonies who traveled from one hotel, night club, or convention to another. He became very successful, and as one of the few non-Jewish conferenciers in Germany, he was accepted and admired by the Nazi regime. "My own hatred of the Nazis had led me by this time to leave Germany, and my father's hobnobbing with these people did nothing to increase my love for him" (Eysenck, 1990, p. 12).

In Eysenck's account of his childhood, he recalls both parents as essentially neglectful and unconcerned with their son, especially after their divorce. Neither parent had an interest in children and neither could communicate warmly or effectively with Hans.

> Typical perhaps of my father's method of upbringing is the occasion when he bought me a bicycle, and promised to teach me how to ride it. He took me to the top of a hill, told me that I had to sit on the saddle and pump the pedals and make the wheels go round. He then went off to release some balloons and shoot them down with the rifle he still had from the war, leaving me to learn how to ride all by myself. . . . A good training in independence, but perhaps not the behaviour of a loving father. (Eysenck, 1990, p. 12)

Relationship With Mother

Of his mother, Eysenck recalls:

> I don't think nature intended her to be a mother. I saw very little of her, except occasionally on holidays, and she never managed to treat me as a child, or show much interest in what I was doing. Conversation with her was always on strictly adult lines. (1990, p. 7)

Both parents found new spouses during Hans's childhood. His mother married an important figure in the movie industry, and his father married a considerably younger woman, also a stage entertainer, whom he met while conferenciering.

Eysenck's Maternal Grandmother

Eysenck was raised largely by his maternal grandmother, who in his account of her was warm, accepting, loving, and actively religious. Oddly, nowhere in his full autobiography (1990) or his (1980) brief autobiographical essay, not even in the photograph he includes of her in the full autobiography, does Eysenck record her name! Nevertheless, he attributes to this grandmother his salvation during childhood from what might have been a lonely and miserable existence (1990, p. 14). This grandmother later died in a Nazi concentration camp.

During childhood, neither parent provided Hans's grandmother with money to support their child, and the poverty of the maternal grandmother's home took its toll on the young Hans. But perhaps more important, Hans remembers that his parents' behavior toward his grandmother reflected a fundamental mean-spiritedness in them. "If my parents were mean toward my grandmother, I felt they were equally mean toward me. I received very little pocket-money, and they seldom agreed to pay for what I considered reasonable expenses" (1990, p. 15). He recalls how his parents' stinginess prevented him from participating in tennis and swimming at a Racquet Club where he could not pay the fees to use the facilities. In typical Eysenckian fashion, Hans found the silver lining in this cloud and thereby thumbed his nose at his neglectful parents:

> However, all this meanness had one positive side-effect; I knew that all the girls I was friendly with loved me for myself! It couldn't have been the non-existing money that might have attracted them. . . . (1990, p. 15)

School Memories: Biting the Hand or the Persistence of a Pit Bull

When Eysenck was approximately eight years old, he encountered Herr Meier, the new music teacher in school. Apparently an intense man, Herr Meier took himself and his job very seriously. At the first class meeting, he directed each student to sing aloud, whereupon the young Hans Jurgen informed his teacher that he could not sing a note, had no singing voice at all, and there was simply no point to it. Herr Meier insisted. Hans resisted. Meier shouted. Hans persisted in resistance. Meier resisted Hans's persistent refusal:

> He ordered me to go up to the dais where he was sitting, grabbed my right hand with his left, and threatened to hit me with the ruler he had in his right hand. When he brought it down I drew back my hand, and he hit the table, which seemed to infuriate him even more. He again grabbed my hand, holding it very tight, and lifted the ruler, to hit my hand really hard.
>
> Without thinking I leaned forward and sank my teeth in the fleshy part of his hand, underneath his thumb. I have always been tall and strong, and I bit him very hard indeed. He dropped the ruler, blanched (I have never seen anybody's face go so white so quickly) and tried to withdraw his hand. I hung on like a bull terrier, and the class of course started erupting in a welter of shouts, screams and jumpings up and down. (Eysenck, 1990, p. 16)

Ultimately, it took the headmaster and several teachers to separate mouth from hand, or hand from mouth, depending on your viewpoint. In any event, as Eysenck recalls with relish, Herr Meier was gone from school for the next two weeks, and when he reappeared, he did not return to Hans's music class. Eysenck aptly points out the long-term, character-reflecting significance of the event:

> In many ways what I did then was prognostic of what I was to do later on, though in rather less physical fashion. You cannot let people get away with wrongdoing just because they are strong and powerful; whatever the cost, you have to stand up for yourself. (1990, p. 17)

It is worth recalling in this context the episode with which we began this chapter: Hans J. Eysenck, the adult experimental psychologist, confronting the psychiatric establishment at the Mill Hill Hospital with his authority-defying studies of diagnosis.

Implications of Eysenck's View of Himself

Eysenck forthrightly admits that as a young man, and even later as a psychologist of some reputation, he was often confrontational, irritable and irritating, and an intolerant, impatient person (1990, p. 278). It was inevitable that he would be drawn to behaviorism with its tradition of tough-minded empiricism because he regarded himself as a tough-minded scientist and a strong-spirited rebel. But often enough throughout his career, Eysenck's intellectual battles had the character of attacking authority. Among his favorite targets: Freud, psychoanalysis, established psychiatry and clinical psychology, psychoanalysis, medical hierarchies, psychoanalysis, traditional views of intelligence, psychoanalysis, psychoanalytic treatment, traditional views of psychotherapy, and—did we mention?—psychoanalysis. Yet Eysenck admits that with age, he grew more mellow and flexible. He recalls a meeting with Gordon Allport, the dean of American personality theory, whose ideas Eysenck had criticized in his typical less than diplomatic fashion:

> [Allport] . . . had advocated a methodology which I had several times criticized as unscientific and useless. Allport was very kind and remarkably patient with my criticisms, and I still remember him telling me, at the end of our discussion: "Eysenck, one day you will write your autobiography, and you will then see how right I was!" I had not considered such a possibility then, and I was unwilling to acknowledge his wisdom, but indeed he was right—in writing one's autobiography, one inevitably has to take the idiographic path of trying to see regularities in one's own life, look for behaviour patterns that repeat themselves, and try to discover variables that are important for oneself, even though they might not be of general interest. (Eysenck, 1990, p. 3)

And so we have the familiar pattern of the personality theorist: a keen-minded person unsatisfied with his recollection of family life, feeling unwanted, angry, and impelled to disprove those early judgments by demonstrating the special worthwhileness of the self—in psychology and most especially in a scientific formulation of human personality. For Hans Jurgen Eysenck, the self-described large, good-natured and friendly dog indeed had teeth and a bite much worse than his bark. "I wish I had had brothers and sisters, and perhaps even a pair of loving parents; if I had, perhaps I would have been a nicer person!" (Eysenck, 1990, p. 278). Eysenck died on September 8, 1997, at the age of 81.

EARLY DESCRIPTIVE RESEARCHES: INTROVERSION-EXTROVERSION AND NEUROTICISM

Despite the criticism and the occasional open incredulity of the psychiatric profession, Eysenck pursued his elusive quarry of an empirical, experimentally based model of personality. One of his earliest studies involved the administration of a large number of personality, psychomotor, and performance tests to a sizable sample of neurotic and normal airmen and soldiers (Eysenck, 1947). In a kind of dragnet approach to personality assessment, Eysenck and his colleagues gathered a huge quantity of statistical data on nearly 10,000 subjects. The resulting mass of information was factor-analyzed. Factor analysis allows the researcher to correlate a group of individuals' scores on one measure with their scores on all other measures to arrive at a more limited number of factors that embody clusters of the original measurements. The clusters of associated variables that emerge from the correlation matrix are sometimes suggestive of personality trends or dimensions. Procedures for extraction of the factors are mathematically complex and need not concern us here.

What is important about Eysenck's elaborate measurement procedures in the present context is that the collection of data was undertaken to test a particular personality hypothesis.

Jung's Typology and Dimensional Hypothesis

Recall from Chapter 7 that Carl Jung, having broken with Freud, established his own analytic theory of personality. As part of his system, Jung proposed a *typological model* of personality organized around the attitude types of introversion and extroversion, and subdivided according to functional type. In addition, Jung had proposed that the two fundamental attitude types, introversion and extroversion, were associated with different forms of mental illness.

Introverts, in Jung's view, when and if they succumb to a mental illness, will likely suffer from *psychasthenia* (Jung, 1921, p. 379). Psychasthenia was the classical psychiatric label for a syndrome characterized by extreme nervousness, anxiety, and fatigue. Today psychasthenia would include more specific diagnoses of *phobia (irrational* fears of persons, places, things), or *obsessive-compulsive neurosis* (intrusion into consciousness of threatening sexual and aggressive ideas that are defended against by the performance of a compulsive series of ritual acts or magical verbalizations like repetitive hand washing or the recitation of a particular phrase in moments of anxiety), or *anxiety state* (the experience of intense physical and mental symptoms of fear without conscious knowledge of the cause of the fear).

On the other hand, Jung felt that extroverts, when and if they succumb to mental illness, are likely to suffer from *hysterical* disorders (paralyses, anesthesias or loss of feeling, blindness, tunnel vision—all without organic causes) (cf. Chapter 2, Freud's early cases; Jung, 1921, p. 336). Thus, whereas the introvert is vulnerable to intense anxiety symptoms, the extrovert develops a more "primitive" and impulsive form of neurosis based on converting the anxiety into bodily symptoms.

To understand how Jung came to these conclusions, it will be helpful to refresh our memory of Jung's descriptions of the two personality types of introversion and extroversion:

> I have . . . finally, on the basis of numerous observations and experiences, come to postulate two fundamental attitudes, namely *introversion* and *extraversion*. The first [introvert] attitude is normally characterized by a hesitant, reflective, retiring nature

that keeps to itself, shrinks from objects, is always sightly on the defensive and prefers to hide behind mistrustful scrutiny. The second [extrovert] is normally characterized by an outgoing, candid, and accommodating nature that adapts easily to a given situation, quickly forms attachments, and, setting aside any possible misgivings, will often venture forth with careless confidence into unknown situations. In the first case obviously the subject [i.e., the person himself], and in the second the object [i.e., external reality], is all-important. (1917, pp. 44–45)

It was thus Jung's opinion that extroverts are "captured" by external events and objects, and that they are ruled by the prevailing social opinion that surrounds them. Introverts, much to the contrary, give greatest weight to their own subjective reactions to external events; they devalue and deemphasize the significance of the objective world by elevating their own emotions, evaluations, and personal reactions to dominance (Jung, 1921, p. 500). Consequently, introverts are likely to succumb to the strength of their own all-important emotions with an outbreak of neurosis whose dominant characteristic is the experience of anxiety.

Extroverts, ruled by the external world, succumb to hysterical neuroses more easily because they seek to divest themselves of emotional pain; they favor the repression of unacceptable thoughts and the externalization or conversion of threatening impulses into "objectified" bodily symptoms. With the achievement of these readily observable afflictions, hysteric extroverts are in a position to profit with an income of sympathy from the social environment to which they are so sensitive. This "secondary gain," the income of sympathy and the concern of their intimates, is an important part of the hysteric's childlike impulsivity and egocentric demands for attention.

In an initial test of Jung's scheme, Eysenck and his colleagues selected a sample of 700 neurotically maladjusted patients at the Mill Hill Emergency Hospital for whom comprehensive case histories and clinical observational data were available. The psychiatrist in charge of each case prepared an "item sheet" on which the patient's familial and personal history, symptoms, diagnosis, treatment, and various social data were recorded. Eysenck selected 39 items from each of 700 such data sheets and submitted the information to a factor analysis. The resulting matrix of intercorrelations yielded two bipolar factors consisting of a number of traits.

One factor was associated with a cluster of traits that seemed to be best described as "general neuroticism." Specifically, the items that tended to be correlated on this factor were badly organized personality, dependency, abnormality before illness, narrow interests, dismissal from military service, abnormality in parents, unsatisfactory home, and poor muscular tone (Eysenck, 1947, p. 36). It must be remembered that these trait descriptions originated in the attending psychiatrist's ratings of the patient.

The second major factor that emerged from the factor analysis seemed partially to confirm Jung's hypothesis. Individuals high in the general neuroticism factor could be divided into two groups. One group was neurotically maladjusted by virtue of possessing symptoms associated with high anxiety: obsessional tendencies, headache, tremor, irritability, among others. The second group of individuals tended to have somewhat different symptoms characteristic of hysterical disorder: bodily symptoms with no organic basis, little energy, narrow interests, hypochondriasis, poor work history, sexual difficulties.

Eysenck's analysis of the item sheet data thus demonstrated that a general factor or dimension of neuroticism-normality could be used to categorize psychologically disabled patients, and that the group high in neuroticism could be further subdivided into anxiety neurotics and hysterical neurotics. The important question was whether empirical evidence could be found for a second dimension of introversion-extroversion that would cut across the two neurotic groups as Jung had suggested.

Empirical Evidence for a Dimension of Introversion-Extroversion

Starting from the premise that Jung's hypothesis was correct, Eysenck surveyed the available experimental literature on the issue of introversion-extroversion. He generally found support from a wide variety of sources that introversion was associated with anxiety, obsessive-compulsive symptoms, and reactive-depression neuroses. Similarly, the extroverted personality type seemed to be associated in a variety of investigations with the symptoms characteristic of hysterical neuroses (Eysenck, 1947, chapters 2, 7).

In his own researches with the sample of neurotic soldiers, Eysenck found direct empirical evidence on a variety of performance, metabolic, and personality measures that a dimension of extroversion-introversion could be used to distinguish between the two groups of neurotic illnesses. Coining a new term to cover the first group of neurotic symptoms (anxiety, phobia, depression, obsessive-compulsive disorders), Eysenck classified them under the heading *dysthymia* (1947, p. 37n.). Eysenck's "dysthymia" is not identical to the current use of this term in the DSM and in the clinical nosology, where it refers to reactive or "neurotic" depression (see the discussion of the clinical nosology in Chapter 1). As used by Eysenck, dysthymia is a more inclusive term incorporating *both* anxiety disorder *and* some reactive depressions. Nevertheless, Eysenck's usage is not altogether different from contemporary meanings. Recall, for example, that anxiety disorders and dysthymia, in the contemporary sense, lie at the same "neurotic" level of severity when understood in terms of changes to the person's reality testing and interpersonal relationships. Dysthymics thus corresponded to Jung's *psychasthenics* and to his introvert personality types. Eysenck retained the label *hysteric* for the second group, as Jung had proposed, and he found that hysterics tended to be extroverted in accordance with Jung's hypothesis. Eysenck's conclusions were based on a variety of experimental and questionnaire evidence that is best summarized in Eysenck's own terms:

> ... *(neurotic) introverts* show a tendency to develop anxiety and depression symptoms ... they are characterized by obsessional tendencies, irritability, apathy, and ... they suffer from a lability of the autonomic system. According to their own statement, their feelings are easily hurt, they are self-conscious, nervous, given to feelings of inferiority, moody, day-dream easily, keep in the background on social occasions, and suffer from sleeplessness. In their body-build vertical growth predominates over horizontal growth; their effort response is poor, and their choline esterase activity is high. Salivary secretion is inhibited. Their intelligence is comparatively high, their vocabulary excellent, and they tend to be persistent. They are generally accurate, but slow; they excel at finicking work (Tweezers test). Their level of aspiration is unduly high, but they tend to under-rate their own performance.

Withal, they are rather rigid, and show little interpersonal variability. Their aesthetic preferences are towards the quiet, old-fashioned type of picture. . . . They do not appreciate jokes very much, and sex jokes in particular are not much favoured. Their handwriting is distinctive. (1947, pp. 246–247)

The 30 traits that cluster together into the pattern of the neurotic introvert, as stated here by Eysenck, are characteristic of his early descriptive research. More probing investigation into the causes underlying the clustering of traits for the neurotic introvert would eventually follow. At this stage of the research, however, Eysenck was limited to specification of descriptive traits. Thus, in contrast to the neurotic introvert:

> . . . *(neurotic) extraverts* show a tendency to develop hysterical conversion symptoms, and a hysterical attitude to their symptoms. Furthermore, they show little energy, narrow interests, have a bad work-history, and are hypochondriacal. According to their own statement, they are troubled by stammer or stutter, are accident prone, frequently off work through illness, disgruntled, and troubled by aches and pains. In their body-build, horizontal growth predominates over vertical growth; their effort response is quite good, and their choline esterase activity low. Salivary secretion is not inhibited. Their intelligence is comparatively low, their vocabulary poor, and they show extreme lack of persistence. They tend to be quick but inaccurate; they are bad at finicking work (Tweezers test). Their level of aspiration is low, but they tend to over-rate their own performance. They are not very rigid, and show great interpersonal variability. Their aesthetic preferences are towards the colourful, modern type of picture. In aesthetic creation, they produce scattered designs, often having abstract subjects. They appreciate jokes, and are particularly fond of sex jokes. Their handwriting is distinctive. (Eysenck, 1947, p. 247)

Neurotic introverts and extroverts share some traits, but on the whole their patterns of responses to Eysenck's various tests and measurements are quite distinguishable. More important, the pattern of measurements for introverts and extroverts *who are neurotic* tends to resemble the two hypothetical classes of dysthymic (anxiety) neuroticism and hysterical disorder.

HISTORICAL ANTECEDENTS OF INTROVERSION-EXTROVERSION DIMENSIONS

Eysenck's early descriptive and correlational researches had established in a general way the validity of Jung's hypothesis. The direction that Eysenck's investigations were taking seemed to many psychiatrists and psychologists uninteresting, irrelevant, and, at worst, unnecessarily troublesome:

> To many, if not most, psychologists interested in personality it seemed as if I had attempted to resurrect a corpse—equivalent, perhaps, to trying to reintroduce into physics the notions of phlogiston, or aether, or a geocentric planetary system. This had many disadvantages, which will be only too obvious; no one wanted to read about extraversion, no one wanted to support research into this field, no one wanted to reconsider problems which were thought to be closed once and for all. (Eysenck, 1970, p. 3)

The concepts of introversion-extroversion were, in most psychologists' minds, associated with Carl Jung's typology. But aside from Jung's basic premise of an association between psychasthenia (dysthymia) and introversion, and between extroversion and hysteria, Eysenck accepted none of Jung's formulation. In fact, Eysenck went to great lengths to point out that the concepts of introversion-extroversion were not originated by Jung, but instead had a 2,000-year history in philosophy, medicine, and psychology (1947, 1953a, 1967, 1970).

Although it would be of some interest to trace all the roots of dimensional personality theories and speculations, our discussion is limited to the three antecedents that seem to have most influenced Eysenck. In historical order of development, we consider the influence on Eysenck's formulations exerted by Hippocrates's and Galen's classical temperament theory, by Pavlov's conception of nervous system types, and by Clark L. Hull's drive × habit theory of learning.

GALEN'S AND HIPPOCRATES'S THEORY OF TEMPERAMENTS

Two ancient Greek physicians, Hippocrates (460?–377? B.C.) and Galen (A.D. 130–200?), devised a *temperament theory* of personality and human conduct. Galen, however, is usually given credit for systematizing the previously vague notions of biological constitution and psychological character types into a coherent fourfold typology of temperaments (see Chapter 8 for a brief description of classical temperament theory in terms of Alfred Adler's typology).

In Galen's system, personality was related to four body fluids or *humors:* blood, black bile, yellow bile, and phlegm. An excess of one of the four humors was thought to determine the emotional temperament of the individual. When blood predominates, the temperament is *sanguine* (warmhearted, volatile, optimistic, easygoing); a predominance of black bile results in a *melancholic* temperament (sad, depressed, anxious); yellow bile produces the *choleric* temperament (quick to action, angry, assertive); and, finally, when phlegm predominates, the resulting temperament is, of course, *phlegmatic* (slow to action, lethargic, calm) (cf. Allport, 1937; Eysenck, 1964a, 1967, 1972; R. I. Watson, 1963, p. 80).

The German philosopher Immanuel Kant (1724–1804) amplified the classical temperament theory by proposing separate groups of verbal trait descriptions for each of the four temperaments. For example, Kant described the sanguine personality as one who is carefree and full of hope, good natured and sociable, but capricious and given to pranks (Eysenck & Eysenck, 1969, p. 12). Kant's verbal descriptions for the remaining three types of temperament may be gleaned from Figure 17.2. The important point about Kant's verbal labels was that he attempted to demonstrate how various discrete traits cluster together in a given type of temperament. The correlation among the various characteristics for a given type was thought to be high so that knowledge of any one trait would be a reliable indication of the presence of the others. Unfortunately, Kant's verbal scheme, like temperament theory itself, was of a *categorical* nature, whereby any individual was classified into one of only four possible personality types. Little or no allowance was made for overlap between types or for different *degrees* of temperamental expression in different individuals belonging to the same type. A moment's thought will indicate the obvious flaw in such a conception of personality. The four discrete, independent categories of temperament theory are clearly suitable only for classification of pure or extreme personality types—if such people exist.

Most people do not fall cleanly into only one compartment. Personalities generally possess some unique *combination* of qualities from a broader spectrum of traits than those represented by the notion of four mutually exclusive categories. To rectify the errors inherent in this system, a variety of 19th-century philosophers and psychologists sought to reconceptualize temperament theory into a more logically defensible form. They devised a series of *dimensions* or *continua* that would represent each temperament type as varying in the degree to which it possessed specific traits along some theoretical spectrum ranging from low to high.

One such dimensional modification of temperament theory was proposed by Wilhelm Wundt (1832–1920), the founding father of experimental psychology. The key to Wundt's scheme lay in his attempt to reorganize the four types according to the degree to which they each possessed two variable characteristics: degree of emotionality and degree of changeableness (Eysenck & Eysenck, 1969). Wundt suggested that the four personalities differ in the strength of their emotions and in the rate at which they change their opinions and feelings. He therefore suggested that these two continuously variable dimensions of *emotionality* and *changeability* be employed to describe subtle variations in each of the four temperaments. In Wundt's dimensional scheme, each of the two dimensions was anchored at its end points with extreme opposite types of personality. The distance between each of these bipolar extremes was conceptualized by Wundt as containing a series of continuously varying gradations. Hence the midpoint of each dimension represented the individual who possesses traits of both extremes in equal proportions.

The first of Wundt's dimensions can be termed *Non-Emotional* at one pole and *Emotional* at the opposite extreme. Similarly, the second dimension running crosswise to the first is anchored at one end with the *Unchangeable* personality type and at the other end with the *Changeable* type. (Actually, the precise terminology that Wundt used was *Weak* versus *Strong* emotional types, and *Slow* versus *Quick* reaction types. Eysenck employed the changed terminology used here in recounting Wundt's system because it makes Wundt's meaning more understandable.) The exact arrangement of Wundt's two dimensions and the position of the four classic temperaments within them can be seen in Figure 17.1. Wundt regarded the phlegmatic and sanguine personalities as having essentially weak emotions (Non-Emotional). At the opposite end of the emotionality dimension are the strongly emotional temperaments of the melancholic and choleric personalities.

The second dimension in Figure 17.1, *Unchangeable* versus *Changeable*, is orthogonal to or independent of the first dimension; that is, a person's position on the *Emotionality* dimension does not determine his or her position on the *Changeable* dimension. Consequently, according to Wundt, the melancholic and phlegmatic personalities are extreme types of the *Unchangeable* personality, whereas the choleric and sanguine personalities are extreme samples of the *Changeable* type, as illustrated in Figure 17.1. For each of the four types of temperament in this scheme, two

FIGURE 17.1   Dimensional classification of temperament.

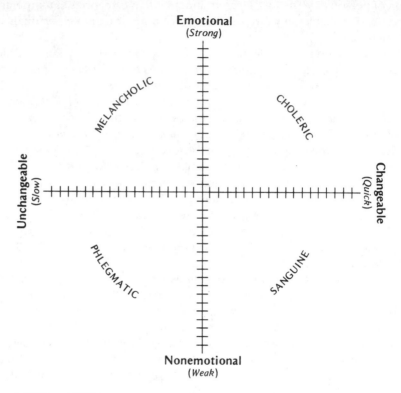

Based on Eysenck (1953a) and (1967).

continuously variable characteristics are postulated, and each of these characteristics is presumed to be independent of the other.

Eysenck realized that these early physicians, philosophers, and psychologists were essentially correct in their descriptions of personality. They attempted to order personalities on the basis of the traits they observed frequently clustering together in people who came under their scrutiny. Eysenck's own work on the introversion-extroversion and neuroticism-normality dimensions produced a comparable picture of human character types. Although the labels were changed in accordance with contemporary psychological vocabulary, Eysenck's two dimensions agreed quite closely with the dimensions introduced into classical temperament theory by Wundt. Eysenck's neuroticism-normality dimension shares a strong conceptual similarity to Wundt's emotional-nonemotional dimension; and his introversion-extroversion dimension is, in most respects, descriptively similar to Wundt's unchangeable-changeable dimension. Figure 17.2 shows these correspondences. The differences between a categorical conception of personality classification and a dimensional scheme can also be discerned in Figure 17.2.

FIGURE 17.2 **Dimensional and categorical personality classification.**

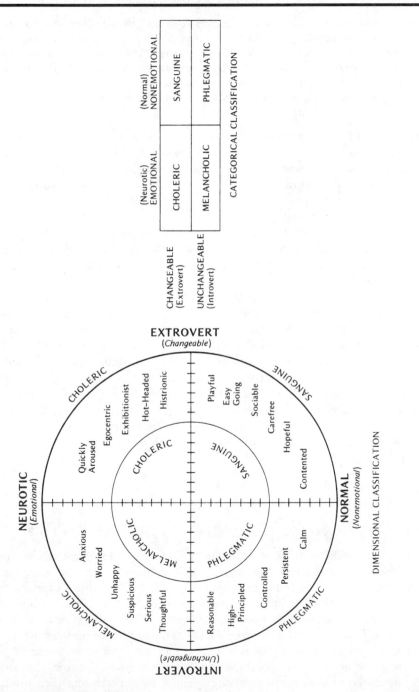

Adapted from Eysenck (1953a), p. 17; (1967), p 35.

It is important to keep in mind when comparing Eysenck's concepts with the early views of personality classification that these "classical" conceptions were subjective, speculative, and informal. Eysenck made this point well:

> . . . what these various philosophers, physicians, and psychologists were doing was to look for uniformities of conduct in the lives of the people whom they were able to observe, and reduce these uniformities to a description of a categorical or continuous type. They made no attempt to formulate specific theories about the formal structure which was so well described in their word pictures, and they made no attempt to demonstrate by experimental or statistical means the accuracy or otherwise of their hypotheses (1967, pp. 34–35)

The problem confronting Eysenck, therefore, was to discover and confirm the essence of truth contained in these early views while simultaneously expanding them to include causal explanations for the observations they embodied. Neither the categorical nor the dimensional scheme of personality classification by itself provides an explanation for the observed consistencies in behavior. To answer the question of *why* a particular personality's traits cluster together, or *why* an introvert differs from an extrovert requires that the investigator turn away from the readily observable or *phenotypical* aspects of personality. Instead, the more fundamental *genotypical* factors that produce the observed uniformities must in themselves become objects of investigation.

The problem of the actor and the mask is thus encountered, though in radically different form, once again. In the observations of the ancients and Wundt, Kant, and Jung, Eysenck found a provocative but incomplete tradition of personality investigation. Eysenck was pleased to extend this tradition into contemporary psychology by providing the experimental and statistical tests required to convert a tradition into a scientifically respectable theory. But to do so, he would have to penetrate the mask of descriptive observables through to the actor's living core of personality organization, the central nervous system. The crucial ideas that provided the key to this more fundamental genotypical aspect of personality came, surprisingly, from Ivan Pavlov's efforts with dogs to provide a physiological explanation for the classical temperaments.

Pavlov's Peculiar Dogs: Excitation-Inhibition Temperaments

At the turn of the century, the Russian physiologist Ivan Petrovitch Pavlov (1849–1936) devised an experimental situation in which to measure the secretion of digestive hormones in dogs. In the course of his work, he developed a theory of nervous system processes that greatly amplified the classical theory of temperaments.

By a careful surgical preparation, Pavlov was able to divert one of the dog's salivary ducts to an external portion of the jaw where drops of saliva could be collected and measured. Experimental dogs were also subjected to a second surgical procedure whereby the upper portion of the digestive track was severed from the stomach and then rerouted to an external fistula or opening. Food taken into the mouth, chewed and swallowed never reached the dog's stomach. It was returned instead to a collection dish near the fistula so that Pavlov could precisely measure the quantity of meat powder consumed in proportion to the saliva secreted.

Pavlov discovered that even when food did not reach the stomach, gastric secretions were still produced at a rate nearly half that of normal digestive activity. "Sham feeding" thus led Pavlov to conclude that some central brain processes were responsible for triggering of digestive activity even in the absence of real food in the stomach (Pavlov, 1927, 1928). True to his rigorous scientific and physiological training, Pavlov decided to study the problem of "psychically controlled secretions" revealed by sham feeding with the same precision of measurement and control employed in his previous investigations.

A basic experimental ground plan was followed. Dogs were isolated from distracting visual and auditory stimuli by securing them in a harness stand in a sound-deadened chamber. The experimenter, in an adjoining room, presented to the dog remotely controlled stimuli that were previously unassociated in the dog's experience with food or salivation. The sound of a ticking metronome, flashing lights of controlled intensities, and bell or buzzer sounds were used as neutral stimuli.

By presenting the neutral stimulus immediately *before* forcing meat powder into the dog's mouth, the two stimuli—buzzer and meat—became associated in the dog's central nervous system processes. The buzzer came to signal the subsequent occurrence of the event that the dog experienced as "meat-powder-in-the-mouth." After a suitable number of pairings, the unconditioned reflex of salivation-to-meat-powder was supplemented by a conditioned reflex of salivation-to-buzzer (Pavlov, 1927, Lectures II, III).

Excitation and Inhibition Processes in the Cortex

After pairing with meat powder, the buzzer had acquired the capacity to evoke salivation, although with less force than the normal stimulus. Pavlov's problem was to explain the formation of this new pathway by inferring from the dog's observable behavior the unobservable corresponding nervous processes.

Pavlov thus postulated that the cortex of the brain is composed of two types of cells or neurons. When incoming stimuli are detected by the dog's sensory receptors, the excitation is passed along to the brain, where *excitatory* cortical cells begin firing in response. When a given sequence of paired stimuli has often enough been repeated, a definite corresponding pattern of excitatory cell firing is established. The cortical process is reliably evoked each time the same stimulus pattern is repeated, allowing the dog to show the benefit of its experience by being able to anticipate one stimulus from the presence of the other. In short, excitatory cell firings are the basis of positive conditioned reflexes.

Pavlov also postulated the existence of *inhibitory* cortical cells. Inhibitory centers of the cortex function to dampen or retard the excitatory cells. In some cases, inhibitory cells even compete with excitatory processes. For example, the common-sense notion of distraction or diversion of attention corresponds to one kind of inhibition that Pavlov termed *external inhibition* (1927, p. 48). A dog thoroughly conditioned to salivate at the sound of a buzzer will cease salivation altogether if a novel stimulus like a loud bang or an unfamiliar person is suddenly introduced into the situation. The dog is said to be momentarily distracted or surprised. Its conditioned reflex is *inhibited* until the novelty of the distracting stimulus diminishes.

A second type of inhibition was postulated by Pavlov. Called *internal inhibition*, this cortical process involves a slow or gradual development of a tendency to withhold the response (Pavlov, 1927, Lecture IV). For example, the continual presentation of the conditioned stimulus without the unconditioned stimulus ever again being presented leads to a gradual termination of the conditioned response. In more concrete terms, the experimenter continues to press the buzzer without ever following it with meat powder. The dog eventually ceases to salivate at the buzzer sound. In effect, it has "unlearned" the conditioned reflex. More precisely, it has learned to inhibit its former conditioned response to the buzzer. This process is called *extinction* of a conditioned reflex, but it is more properly thought of as learning a new inhibitory response (Pavlov, 1927, p. 48).

Individual Differences in Excitation and Inhibition

Not all dogs were alike in their ability to form and maintain conditioned reflexes. Moreover, there seemed to be a correlation between a dog's innate temperament and its conditioning ability. Dogs who were most sociable, affable, and active when left to themselves proved to be the worst subjects for the establishment of positive conditioned reflexes like salivation to a buzzer. Strapped into the conditioning harness in the isolated experimental chamber, such normally active dogs soon became drowsy and fell asleep! By contrast, dogs who were quiet and "stolid" outside the experimental situation and who, therefore, Pavlov initially assumed would be poor conditioning subjects, proved to be under certain circumstances the most easily conditionable dogs (1928, p. 306).

To explain this diversity of reactions to the conditioning procedures, Pavlov initially postulated two "extreme types" of nervous system and two "balanced types." In the first extreme type of dog, excitatory cortical processes predominate, and inhibitory processes are weak or nearly absent in normal behavioral activities. Unrestrained by inhibitory cortical processes, such dogs are the affable, outgoing, always curious, sociable animals who therefore seem likely candidates for rapid conditioning. Yet, it was precisely this kind of dog that gave Pavlov the most trouble in the conditioning situation. Affable and outgoing outside the experimental chamber, the dog would paradoxically become drowsy and fall asleep during the monotony of conditioning. Pavlov initially assumed that because this dog was a "specialist in excitation," its excitatory cells were quickly exhausted. Inhibitory processes would then take over, causing the paradoxical effect of drowsiness and sleep. For such "specialists in excitation," the repetition of the same constant sequence of stimuli in conditioning rapidly depletes the easily aroused excitatory cells. Pavlov found that such dogs were good conditioning subjects if the conditioning procedure was varied so that a constant succession of novel stimuli was available (Pavlov, 1927, pp. 287ff.; Teplov, 1964, p. 14).

The second extreme type of nervous temperament is predominantly inhibitory in normal behavioral activities. Outwardly, this dog appears "cowardly," cringing in corners and slinking along the floor as if afraid of everything and everyone. However this kind of dog, contrary to expectation, conditions well in the monotonous experimental situation once it is sufficiently used to the experimenter and the equipment. But its positive conditioned reflexes are easily disrupted and extinguished. Only inhibitory reflexes (e.g., learning *not* to respond to one of a pair of stimuli that is not reinforced by meat powder) are stable and strongly established (Pavlov, 1927).

Between these two extremes of excitatory and inhibitory specialists, Pavlov found dogs that were "equilibrated" or *balanced* in their degree of inhibition and excitation (1928, pp. 374ff.). This central or balanced type of dog is found in two distinct varieties. In the first type, the balance between excitation and inhibition is well established so that the dog conditions well in both positive and inhibitory reflexes. This first balanced type tends to *behaviorally* resemble the extreme excitatory dog in its lively, outgoing manner. In the second balanced type of nervous system, excitatory and inhibitory processes reach an equilibrium but only with difficulty is this balance maintained. The balance is continually threatened with disruption at the slightest provocation or distraction (Pavlov, 1928, p. 375). Behaviorally, this second balanced type resembles the extreme inhibitory animal in its quiet, stolid, and calm temperament.

Thus Pavlov proposed four types of nervous systems to correspond with classical temperament theory's four humoral types:

Extreme Excitatory Type:	Choleric (Poor conditionability)
Extreme Inhibitory Type:	Melancholic (Good inhibitory conditionability)
Balanced (Excitatory) Type:	Sanguine (Good conditionability)
Balanced (Inhibitory) Type:	Phlegmatic (Good but easily distracted)

Experimental Neurosis: Breakdown of the Inhibition-Excitation Balance

One of the chief distinguishing features of the four nervous system types was the individual's degree of susceptibility to experimentally induced neurotic behavior. Such neurosis may be induced, for example, if a conditioning procedure is established in which *both* excitatory and inhibitory cortical processes are made to alternate rapidly so that they "collide" in the dog's nervous system. Each of the *extreme* nervous types will succumb to a different form of "nervous breakdown."

Using a mechanical vibrator applied to the dog's skin, Pavlov conditioned an *extreme excitatory* dog to salivate at 30 vibrations a minute. When the vibrator was set to oscillate at only 15 vibrations per minute, no food was presented. In this way, the dog learned to discriminate between 30 and 15 vibrations. It salivated to 30 vibrations, an excitatory response, and withheld salivation to 15 vibrations, an inhibitory response. When, however, Pavlov employed 15 and 30 vibrations in close succession, dogs of the excitatory type suffered an extreme disorganization of behavior. Their weak inhibitory processes completely failed to keep pace with the rapid alternation between 15 and 30 vibrations. Their stronger excitatory processes assumed dominance in this collision with inhibitory processes. The animal became uncontrollably excited, straining and struggling to escape the harness and bite the experimenter. In short order, the extreme excitatory type of dog showed every sign of an anxiety attack. The effect was long-lasting, often requiring months of treatment with tranquilizing drugs to effect a "cure."

Pavlov felt that this form of experimentally produced neurotic behavior in the excitatory dog was analogous to the human neurosis of psychasthenia (Pavlov, 1928, p. 375). Thus, Pavlov, too, identified excitatory processes with anxiety neurosis (dysthymia), as did Eysenck working many years later in the tradition of Jung and the classical Greek physicians. But, unlike Eysenck, Pavlov identified the extreme excitatory neurotic animal first with the sanguine temperament, then later with the choleric temperament (Teplov, 1964, p. 16). According to Eysenck's analysis of the classical temperaments, such an extreme excitatory animal would probably be classed as melancholic (see Figure 17.2).

To return to Pavlov's peculiar dogs, the inhibitory type of animal at the opposite extreme succumbed to a different type of "neurosis" when exposed to the same alternation of excitatory and inhibitory stimuli. Because the discrimination between the food-reinforced 30 vibrations and the nonreinforced 15 vibrations was made difficult as excitatory and inhibitory processes "collided," this type of animal succumbed to its stronger inhibitory tendency *not* to respond. Inhibiting all response, these dogs became rigid, drowsy, nearly hypnotized. Outside the conditioning chamber, they became withdrawn and nonreactive, easily frightened and sometimes physically ill.

Pavlov identified this pattern of "nervous breakdown" in the inhibitory dog as similar to the human hysterical disorders. He further suggested that the inhibitory neurotic animal corresponded to the melancholic temperament (1928, p. 377). In Eysenck's terms, however, such an animal would probably correspond to the choleric temperament, at the extreme extroverted end of the dimension.

Dogs of the two central or balanced types, although superficially resembling the two extreme types, do not succumb readily, if at all, to experimentally induced neuroses (Pavlov, 1928, p. 375). Pavlov later changed his system of classification and his opinion about the formation of experimental neuroses, but the details of this story go far beyond what is practical in the present context (see Teplov, 1964, for the detailed history). At this point in his work, however, Pavlov identified the two balanced types of dog as corresponding to the sanguine (stable balance) and phlegmatic (unstable balance) personalities.

Inconsistencies in Pavlov's Scheme

Eysenck (1957a, pp. 111ff.) has pointed to a variety of inconsistencies in Pavlov's descriptions of the four nervous types. Pavlov had tried to create a typology that would coordinate observable behavioral traits with underlying nervous system processes of inhibition and excitation. He then further attempted to coordinate classical temperament theory with his data on individual differences in conditioning and with susceptibility to different types of experimentally induced neuroses. It was an ambitious undertaking that was fraught with discrepancies at both the behavioral and neurological levels of explanation.

For example, Pavlov identified the extreme excitatory nervous type as a choleric personality. Presumably, in making this classification, Pavlov was focusing his attention on the dog's behavior *in the conditioning situation,* where the tedious experimental procedures made the animal drowsy and difficult to condition. But the animal's personality traits at liberty are more accurately described in temperament theory as a sanguine personality, the outgoing, friendly, emotionally demonstrative type. Yet, in Pavlov's system, this dog is classed as a choleric type. Under appropriate conditions, furthermore, the "choleric" dog succumbs to a psychasthenic (anxiety) neurosis that is more characteristic of the melancholic type. Which type is it? Is it the *sanguine* personality because it is normally outgoing and affable? Or is it *choleric* because it becomes hard to handle in the conditioning situation? Or is it *melancholic* because it succumbs to anxiety neurosis?

Because such inconsistencies exist in Pavlov's system, Eysenck was unable to adopt the classification scheme without major revision. However, Pavlov's contribution to personality was to point to the inhibition and excitation basis that underlies observable personality type and neurotic predisposition. The problem for Eysenck was to apply the conditioning data accurately and consistently to the task of personality classification. With his dimensions of introversion-extroversion and emotionality-stability, Eysenck was able to solve the problem.

Eysenck's first step in untangling the Pavlovian scheme was an assumption that Pavlov had been essentially correct in his biological strategy: Observable differences in the four personalities have their source in less observable inhibition-excitation processes of the nervous system. Eysenck adopted these concepts, but he applied them to human temperaments in a drastically different way.

For Eysenck, *the essence of the melancholic and phlegmatic temperaments is their withdrawal from social and physical stimulation,* as described by the ancients. Thus, contrary to Pavlov, Eysenck assumed that the melancholic and phlegmatic personalities are characterized by extremely sensitive excitation processes. In the melancholic, this extreme cortical arousal is coupled with high emotional reactivity so that the melancholic feels intellectually and emotionally overwhelmed by even mild social and physical stimulation. He or she succumbs to emotional despair, anxiety, and to a protective tendency to retreat from his or her surroundings. In the phlegmatic personality, however, this same high cortical excitation and sensitivity leads to withdrawal behaviors designed to escape overwhelming stimulation in the form of a protective "I don't care" apathy. Yet the phlegmatic lacks the melancholic's high emotional reactivity, and thus remains free of neurotic anxiety and despair. Eysenck therefore classified both the melancholic and the phlegmatic as introverts but *only the melancholic as neurotic.* Because both personality types have highly aroused cortical processes, the defining property of introversion in Eysenck's scheme, the melancholic and phlegmatic should, in principle, form conditioned reflexes easily and strongly.

At the other extreme, *the essence of the choleric and sanguine personalities in Eysenck's view is their responsivity and rapt attention to the social and physical environment.* The sanguine personality is fundamentally outgoing, sociable, and emotionally tranquil. He or she delights in a constant succession of novel experiences. The choleric personality is also attentive to the social environment, but finds no delight in it. He or she is more emotional, more irritable, and more prone to become irascible. The choleric may even turn mean, taking delight in manipulating or hurting others. Eysenck thus classed the choleric and sanguine personalities as extroverts but *only the choleric as neurotic.* He assumed that their cortical processes were far less sensitive, far less aroused, and considerably more inhibitory than those of introverts. In a sense, their strong inhibitory processes force the extrovert types to seek constant stimulation from the social environment to overcome their own cortical inertia. Because both personality types have strong inhibitory processes, the defining property of extroversion in Eysenck's scheme, the sanguine and choleric personalities should, in principle, form positive conditioned reflexes poorly or weakly. The similarities and differences between Pavlov's and Eysenck's explanations of temperaments are summarized in Table 17.1.

The notion that nervous systems may differ in their tolerance to stimulation has been taken up by some contemporary Russian workers whose investigations bear

TABLE 17.1   Pavlov's Types and Eysenck's Dimensions Contrasted

Classical Temperaments ←	Pavlov's Types	Behavioral Traits (Pavlov)	Eysenck's Dimensions →	Classical Temperaments
Choleric	Extreme Excitatory	1. Outgoing, affable, friendly at liberty, but becomes drowsy in monotony of experimental chamber. Conditions well only when stimuli are varied and novel. Neurosis caused by failure of inhibition and resembles human *psychasthenia*.	1. Extreme Emotional Introvert (Neurotic)	Melancholic
Melancholic	Extreme Inhibitory	2. Cowardly, cringing, nervous, this dog conditions well in the monotony of the experiment. But positive reflexes (e.g., salivation to reinforced stimulus) are poorer than negative conditioned reflexes (e.g., withholding response or discrimination). Neurosis caused by failure of excitatory cells and resembles human *hysteria*.	2. Extreme Emotional Extrovert (Neurotic)	Choleric
Sanguine	Balanced Excitatory	3. Conditions well in both positive and negative responses. Outgoing, affable, like extreme excitatory type. Resists experimental neurosis.	3. Stable Introvert	Phlegmatic
Phlegmatic	Balanced Inhibitory	4. Conditions well, but positive responses disrupted easily. Quiet, stolid, and alert, like inhibitory animal when calm. Resists experimental neurosis.	4. Stable Extrovert	Sanguine

Note reversal of classical temperaments between Eysenck's and Pavlov's schemes. Furthermore, the behavioral descriptions are Pavlov's, *not* Eysenck's, and in fact contradict Eysenck's trait descriptions of introverted and extroverted personalities.
Based on Pavlov, 1928, p. 377; Pavlov, 1927, p. 286; Eysenck, 1957a; Teplov, 1964, pp. 13, 18.

some resemblance to Eysenck's concepts. We turn next to a brief consideration of these efforts.

Weak and Strong Nervous Systems: The Work of B. M. Teplov

Pavlov developed a number of criteria by which to describe the action of the cerebral cortex in conditioning. The one criterion that has significance for an understanding of Eysenck's conception of personality dimensions is what Pavlov termed "strength of the nervous system" (Gray, 1964; Teplov, 1964).

A modern Russian worker, B. M. Teplov (1964), adopted Pavlov's concept of strength of the nervous system, restricting its meaning to the *intensity of excitatory process* in the cortex. Thus Teplov defined the *strong nervous system* as one with a large capacity to tolerate intense stimulation. A *weak nervous system,* therefore, is conceptualized as one with a small capacity to tolerate stimulation. In terms of excitation and inhibition processes, the concept of strength has particularly precise meaning. *The strong nervous system is less sensitive than the weak nervous system.* It is strong in the sense that it can operate with stimulus intensities of far larger magnitude than a weak nervous system before it must act to protectively inhibit further increases in intensity. But, for precisely this reason, the strong nervous system is insensitive to low-intensity stimulation. At low intensities, the strong nervous system's inhibitory processes overwhelm the excitation, causing such an animal to become drowsy and fall asleep.

The weak nervous system is weak only in the sense that it is operating almost continuously at its maximum excitatory strength. Therefore, any excitatory stimulus almost immediately pushes the weak nervous system beyond its excitatory capacity. To protect itself against overexcitation, it "shuts down" its excitatory centers at levels of stimulus intensity that for the strong nervous system would be only mildly arousing. Thus, as paradoxical as it may sound, the weak nervous system responds with stronger excitation to low-excitation level stimuli than the strong nervous system. Conversely, the strong nervous system, because it operates with greater levels of inhibition, is able to tolerate stronger stimuli. But these two relationships between inhibition-excitation and stimulus intensity must be kept in mind: *The strong nervous system is a specialist in inhibition;* it has a higher excitatory threshold, that is, it can endure more stimulation or more intense stimulation without protecting itself. *The weak nervous system is a specialist in excitation;* it has a low excitatory threshold, that is, it reaches and exhausts its full excitation capacity rather quickly, at relatively low levels of stimulation.

To operationalize the concept of weak and strong nervous types, Teplov and his coworkers used another one of Pavlov's concepts called *transmarginal inhibition.* Transmarginal inhibition literally means "beyond the boundary" inhibition. The basic premise underlying this concept is called the "law of strength" (Gray, 1964, p. 276). The law of strength asserts that a subject's conditioned response will increase in magnitude as the intensity of the conditioned stimulus increases. In concrete terms, a subject conditioned to blink at the sound of a tone will blink all the more sharply or more quickly if the loudness of the tone is increased. As the tone is made even louder, the conditioned response—blinking—will also increase in intensity *up to some limiting point.* At this particular point in the loudness continuum, the subject's blink response will decrease or cease altogether. The louder the tone is made beyond the point where the response has been increasing, the more response magnitude tends to decrease. This point is called the protective threshold or *threshold of transmarginal inhibition.* Pavlov thought of the transmarginal inhibition threshold as protective because the nervous system was damping itself down by inhibition before increasing-stimulus intensities overworked the cortical excitatory cells (Gray, 1964, p. 161; see Frigon, 1976 for an EEG measure of nervous system strength that supports Eysenck's theory; and Fowles, Roberts, & Nagel, 1977 for a GSR study with mixed results; and the contradictory results of White & Mangan, 1972, using drugs).

The key point about transmarginal inhibition is that *the weak nervous system reaches this threshold sooner than the strong nervous system.* In more precise terms, the weak nervous system shows signs of lessening response-intensity at lower stimulation-intensity levels than the strong nervous system. The difference between transmarginal inhibition thresholds for the weak and strong nervous systems is graphed in an idealized form in Figure 17.3.

Eysenck's introversion-extroversion dimension closely parallels Pavlov's and Teplov's weak-strong dimension. Specifically, the introvert is said to have a weak (sensitive) nervous system dominated by excitatory processes *under low levels of stimulation;* the extrovert is conceptualized by Eysenck as having a strong (stable) nervous system dominated by inhibitory processes under moderate-intensity stimulation. Under strong or intense stimulation, the introvert's nervous system responds with transmarginal or protective inhibition, whereas the extrovert's nervous system

FIGURE 17.3   Transmarginal inhibition (TMI) thresholds for "weak" and "strong" nervous systems.

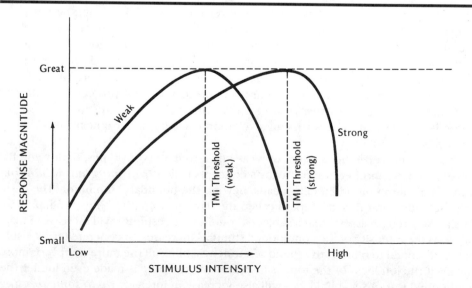

Based on Gray (1964), pp. 162, 186.

responds with increasing excitation. Thus in Eysenck's view the introvert is "stimulus-shy," and the extrovert is "stimulus-hungry." The introvert withdraws from social contacts, from prolonged interaction with the physical environment, and from all arousing stimulation because he or she is so sensitive to such excitation. The extrovert seeks social stimulation, physical arousal, and excitement to feed the never-satiated cortical lethargy.

It is possible with these conceptual tools to derive a variety of behavioral phenomena concerning the conditionability of extreme (excitatory) introverts and extreme (inhibitory) extroverts. A direct application of the notion that introverts have weaker or more sensitive nervous systems would lead to the prediction that extreme introverts condition more rapidly than extreme extroverts. Yet such a formulation would fail to take account of important conditioning variables that might be expected to change the outcome. Variables like intensity of unconditioned and conditioned stimuli and their rate of presentation should be expected to differentially affect the strong and the weak nervous system. Under certain conditions, extroverts should condition more easily or more rapidly than introverts.

In consequence, Eysenck turned to a more fully developed behavior theory that included among its concepts a more precise set of relationships between inhibition and excitation. With some modifications, Eysenck was able to adapt Clark L. Hull's *drive* × *habit* theory of learning to the task of individual personality prediction.

HULL'S DRIVE THEORY: INDIVIDUAL DIFFERENCES IN PERFORMANCE

Clark L. Hull (1884–1952) developed an influential hypothetico-deductive theory of learning and performance that incorporated basic concepts similar to excitation and inhibition. The advantage of Hull's formulation from Eysenck's point of view was its relative precision in describing the interaction of inhibition and excitation.

Hull's theory (1943, 1951, 1952) was formulated to account for a different kind of conditioning from that of Pavlov's work with dogs. Instead of involuntary reflex conditioning, Hull was more concerned with instrumental conditioning. In this variety of learning, a voluntary response of the organism like pressing a bar or making right and left turns in a maze is rewarded or reinforced to increase the likelihood that the organism will repeat the response.

The basic premise underlying Hull's formulation was that reinforcers are stimuli that reduce or satisfy an organism's biological drives. For instrumental learning to occur, an organism must first be in a state of high drive arousal (e.g., very hungry). Then, those responses that the organism uses to obtain satisfaction for the drive will become associated with the stimuli on which the drive is based. In commonsense terms, if a hungry rat discovers through trial and error that turning right into a particular alley of a maze brings it reliably into contact with food, then right turns will become habitual whenever it is hungry in that maze.

To indicate the learned connection between the stimuli of the maze's choice points and the response of turning right, Hull employed a "habit" symbol: $_SH_R$. If the rat is not in a state of drive arousal (i.e., not hungry) when placed in the maze, then its habit of turning right at a particular choice point will have a low probability of being translated into actual behavior. As the hunger drive begins to mount in intensity, it will activate the previously reinforced habit of turning right at the appropriate choice point. Hull indicated this relationship between drive and habits with a simple symbolic notation:

$$D \times {}_sH_R = {}_sE_R, \text{ where } {}_sE_R \text{ indicates observable performance}$$

In words, the formulation states that observable performance is evoked when drive (D) multiplies previously learned stimulus-response connections or habits (${}_sH_R$). Clearly this simple formulation must be modified to take account of variables that would add to or subtract from the organism's drive arousal and past habit strengths. Hull suggested two competing forms of variables: *reactive inhibition* (I_R) and *conditioned inhibition* (${}_sI_R$).

Reactive and Conditioned Inhibition

Reactive inhibition (I_R) in Hull's formulation is similar to Pavlov's concept of internal inhibition. In Hull's theory, reactive inhibition is a kind of neural fatigue that develops gradually as responses are repetitively made. Serving as a negative drive state, I_R continues to increase until the amount of nervous system fatigue is great enough to cancel the animal's positive drive to respond.

A second kind of inhibition develops as a direct consequence of I_R. As I_R increases, the animal suffers a general feeling of fatigue and discomfort associated with continued responding. When it ceases to respond as a consequence of I_R the fatigue of this "reactive inhibition" state is allowed to dissipate. Dissipation of I_R is experienced as satisfying or rewarding. But note what is being reinforced: the act of *not responding*. Thus there develops a conditioned negative habit, a tendency to not respond. This second kind of inhibition is a *learned* inhibitory response reinforced by the reduction in I_R that rest produces. Hull referred to this kind of inhibition as *conditioned inhibition* (${}_sI_R$).

Hull entered the two kinds of inhibition into his general formula for learned performance in such a way that combined I_R and ${}_sI_R$ would *subtract* from drive's activation of habit:

$$(D \times {}_sH_R) - (I_R + {}_sI_R) = {}_s\bar{E}_R$$

where ${}_s\bar{E}_R$ indicates *resultant* performance—that is, performance after total inhibition has been subtracted. It is important to emphasize that the two kinds of inhibition not only originate differently, but function differently. Whereas reactive inhibition (I_R) dissipates with time, conditioned inhibition (${}_sI_R$) is relatively enduring. Reactive inhibition is conceptualized as a negative, *innate* drive; conditioned inhibition is a *learned* negative habit.

Eysenck's Formulation of Drive, Habit, and Inhibition

The exact restructuring of Hull's formula that Eysenck adopted for his 1957 model of personality is somewhat complex and concerned with theoretical issues in learning theory that may be omitted here.[1] For present purposes it is sufficient to understand that Eysenck adopted the general Hullian notion that drive multiplies habits and that inhibition reduces the effects of positive drive. Eysenck provided a clear example of the relationship among these variables in the analogy of a person playing tennis.

> Clearly the excellence of his [tennis] performance will depend upon two things. It will depend, in the first place, on his drive; the more highly motivated he is to play well, the better his performance will be, on the whole. It also depends, of course, on his experience and on the amount of practice that he has previously put into the task, on the length of time he has been playing, and so on. In other words, it will depend on the system of bodily habits which he has built up during the past [$_sH_R$]. . . . His actual performance will be a function of both these variables; *the stronger the drive, and the more highly developed the habits which are necessary for carrying out his task, the better his performance will be.* Where does inhibition fit into this picture?
>
> The answer of course is this. If a person is carrying out a task, particularly under conditions of massed practice, then inhibition will continue to accumulate. Being a negative drive, it will subtract from the positive drive under which the organism is working. And, finally, when inhibition builds up to such an extent that it is equal to positive drive under which the person is working, he will simply cease to work altogether because now drive is equal to inhibition, and drive minus inhibition equals zero. If we put this into our general formula it will read: performance equals habit × zero. Habit × zero—or indeed, anything multiplied by zero—is, of course, zero and, therefore, performance will cease. (1964a, p. 73; italics added)

The logical deduction to be made from this conceptualization of the effects of inhibition on drive is that continued performance leads ultimately to a cessation of activity. Such a cessation may be only momentary, but if the prediction is correct, the performer will experience a fleeting block to further action. There is a good deal of experimental evidence that such blocks to performance occur. For a firsthand experience of what is sometimes termed an *involuntary rest pause (IRP),* try the following demonstration:

> Simply tap, as fast as you can, with the index fingers of your right and left hands, on the edges of the table, trying to maintain a rhythm. After a very short time, you will find that one or the other of your fingers will cease to obey your will; it will suddenly take an involuntary rest pause on its own, disrupting your performance and making

---

[1] For those of you with a strong interest in Hullian theory it may be of some benefit to record Eysenck's modified performance formula (Eysenck, 1957a, p. 58):

$$_sE_R = f(D_+ \times {}_sH_R) + f(D_+ \times {}_sI_R) + f(D_- \times {}_sH_R) + f(D_- \times {}_sI_R)$$

The important consideration about Eysenck's adaptation of Hull's formulation is that each of the components in the above notation involves a habit component ($_sH_R$ or $_sI_R$) multiplied by either a positive (D_+) or a negative drive (D_-) component. In this way, even the simplest performance is conceptualized as having complex determinants of drive, inhibition, and habit strength. The last term of the formula [$D_- \times {}_sI_R$] involves the multiplication of two negative components, that is, the multiplication of negative drive (originally called I_R) and conditioned inhibition. Such a multiplication would produce, paradoxically, a positive effect on performance. The first term of the formula [$D_+ \times {}_sH_R$] also produces a positive effect on performance. The second and third terms, however, result in a negative influence, a tendency *not* to respond.

it impossible for you to continue. This involuntary rest pause is quite brief. It is not a question of muscular fatigue, because the amount of muscular energy expended is minimal. Nevertheless, you will find that you are quite incapable, for a period of perhaps half a second to a second, of bringing the behavior of your fingers under your voluntary control. (Eysenck, 1964a, p. 74)

During the period of the IRP, inhibition will dissipate. Performance may then again continue at the rapid rate attained before inhibition reached the critical level. As we shall see, important predictions about introverts' and extroverts' performances can be made.

THE THEORETICAL YIELD: HIPPOCRATES, PAVLOV, JUNG, AND HULL

The contributions of the early Greek physicians and Pavlov, Jung, and Hull provided Eysenck with the conceptual tools to formulate a *causal* explanation of the differences between introverts and extroverts. The early temperament theory of Hippocrates and Galen suggested the basic dimensions along which individual personalities may be arranged. Pavlov's excitation-inhibition hypothesis of cortical functioning provided the first clues to the physiological basis of these personality dimensions. In addition, Pavlov's work partly confirmed Jung's clinical insight into the relationships between introversion and anxiety neuroses, and between extroversion and hysterical disorder. Hull's *drive × habit − inhibition* formulation of learning contributed the necessary theoretical relationships to bridge the gap between physiological speculation and observable performance.

With these conceptual tools at his disposal, Eysenck was able to formulate a pair of personality postulates that would combine these various antecedent theories into a coherent, yet tentative, experimental model of why introverts differ from extroverts.

INDIVIDUAL DIFFERENCES AND TYPOLOGICAL POSTULATES: AN EXPERIMENTAL THEORY

To span the distance between the theory of excitation-inhibition and personality types, Eysenck postulated that people differ in their *balance* of excitation to inhibition processes:

The Postulate of Individual Differences

Human beings differ with respect to the speed with which excitation and inhibition are produced, the strength of the excitation and inhibition produced, and the speed with which inhibition is dissipated. These differences are properties of the physical structures involved in making stimulus-response connections. (1957a, p. 114)

With the postulate of individual differences Eysenck was proposing that personality psychologists and experimental psychologists join forces in investigating a variable that had often been interpreted as having interest only for the experimentalist.

Excitation and inhibition were now to be conceptualized as fundamental to any understanding of personality differences.

To extend the logic of his position, Eysenck also proposed a relatively precise specification of these personality differences in relation to excitation and inhibition processes:

The Typological Postulate

Individuals in whom *excitatory* potential is generated *slowly* and in whom *excitatory potentials* so generated are relatively *weak,* are thereby predisposed to develop *extraverted* patterns of behavior and to develop *hysterical-psychopathic* disorders in case of neurotic breakdown; individuals in whom *excitatory* potential is generated *quickly* and in whom *excitatory* potentials so generated are *strong,* are thereby predisposed to develop *introverted* patterns of behaviour and to develop *dysthymic* disorders [anxiety, phobias, obsessive-compulsive symptoms] in case of neurotic breakdown. Similarly, individuals in whom *reactive inhibition* is developed *quickly,* in whom *strong* reactive inhibitions are generated, and in whom reactive inhibition is *dissipated slowly,* are thereby predisposed to develop *hysterical-psychopathic* disorders in case of neurotic breakdown; conversely, individuals in whom *reactive inhibition* is developed *slowly,* in whom *weak* reactive inhibitions are generated, and in whom reactive inhibition is *dissipated quickly,* are thereby predisposed to develop *introverted* patterns of behaviour and to develop dysthymic disorders in case of neurotic breakdown. (1957a, p. 114; italics added)

With the typologial postulate, Eysenck laid the groundwork for a truly hypothetico-deductive model of personality. Introverts were conceptualized as having stronger and more easily aroused excitatory processes, coupled with their rapid dissipation of inhibition. Extroverts, on the other hand, were conceptualized as having relatively weak excitatory processes and slow dissipation of inhibition. Taking only the *extreme* extrovert and the *extreme* introvert as models, the typological postulate can be summarized in the form of a table. When reading Table 17.2, it must be remembered that Eysenck's typology is dimensional, allowing for degree of expression of inhibition and excitation, whereas the summary in Table 17.2 is essentially categorical.

On the basis of the typological postulate, a number of hypotheses can be deduced about introverts' and extroverts' performance in laboratory situations. For example, if introverts do have stronger excitatory cortical processes and relatively weak inhibitory effects, they should condition more quickly than extroverts in laboratory tasks like eye-blink conditioning. Other deductions can be made along these

TABLE 17.2 Summary of Typological Postulate as Extreme Types

	Excitation	Inhibition	Neurotic Predisposition
Introverts	High (Rapid)	Low (Slow)	Dysthymia
Extroverts	Low (Slow)	High (Rapid)	Hysteria-Psychopathy

Based on Eysenck, 1957a.

same lines. For any task that requires strong excitatory processes and the rapid dissipation of inhibition, introverts should evidence superior performance. Three representative areas of study illustrate this deduction.

Eye-Blink Conditioning: Introverts Are Not Always Superior

Evidence drawn from human classical conditioning experiments contains some element of confusion. An early study of the conditioned eye-blink response by Cyril Franks (1956) was explicitly designed to test Eysenck's hypothesis of the superior conditionability of introverts. Using a precisely measured blast of air delivered through a specially prepared pair of eyeglasses, Franks conditioned 60 dysthymic, hysteric, and normal subjects to blink to the sound of a tone. Franks's procedure resembled Pavlov's work with the conditioned salivary response: the *unconditioned stimulus (UCS)* was the puff of air, the *unconditioned response (UCR)* was an electrically measured eye blink, and the *conditioned response (CR)* was, of course, the new eye-blink response to the *conditioned stimulus (CS)*, a tone presented over the subject's earphones.

Twenty subjects composed each of the three groups. Assignment to dysthymic, hysteric, or normal classification was made on the basis of psychiatric diagnoses, paper-and-pencil measures of personality, and direct observation of symptoms. Subjects in the dysthymic and hysteric groups were selected to represent extreme cases of each disorder. All subjects were presented with 30 reinforced (paired CS and UCS) trials, interspersed with 18 test trials (CS alone). The subject's participation in the experiment ended with 10 consecutive extinction trials (CS alone). Franks also measured each subject's psychogalvanic skin response (PGR), on the assumption that differences in conditionability would be reflected even in this autonomic nervous system sweat response.

The results of Franks's experiment seemed to provide evidence that dysthymics acquire a greater number of conditioned eye blinks to the tone than either normals or hysterics. Hysterics tended to resemble normals in conditioning rate. The one measure that separated dysthymics, normals, and hysterics at a statistically significant level was their measured degree of introversion-extroversion, not their type of neurosis. Dysthymics, extremely introverted, had conditioned "better" than either normals or extroverts (i.e., the hysterics). Franks's equipment thus supported Eysenck's hypothesis.

A later study by Franks (1957) confirmed his early finding that neuroticism of itself was not the basis of differing performance in the conditioning task for dysthymics and hysterics. Franks's study was considered crucial for Eysenck's theory because a variety of other workers had suggested that all neurotic subjects, having heightened emotional drive, would condition faster than normals. Franks's studies showed that introversion-extroversion, not neuroticism (or emotional drive), differentiated easily conditioned from poorly conditioned subjects.

A problem arose for Eysenck's hypothesis when Franks himself (1963) and several independent investigators were unable to replicate his original findings. Eysenck reviewed the literature reporting no differences between introverts and extroverts in conditionability and drew an important conclusion. Those investigators who had failed to establish exactly identical conditions of reinforcement rate and conditioned and unconditioned stimulus intensities were the ones who had failed to find any conditioning differences between introverts and extroverts.

Specifically, Eysenck argued that his 1957 statement of the typological postulate had specified that inhibition would rise during nonreinforced trials (CS alone). Trials in which the unconditioned stimulus is present (i.e., the air puff) provide strong excitation that prevents or disrupts the development of inhibition. Thus in Franks's procedure of interspersing test and reinforcement trials, extroverts had been provided with an opportunity to develop strong inhibitory effects. *Partial reinforcement* of this sort favors introverts because they have the capacity to dissipate quickly the small amount of inhibition they develop; extroverts, on the other hand, slowly dissipate the large amount of inhibition they have developed. Thus in Franks's (1956) investigation, extroverts conditioned more poorly than introverts because the conditioning parameters favored the introverts.

Eysenck was led to specify more carefully the theoretical assumptions from which predictions were to be made. In concrete terms, Eysenck (1966, 1967) now delineated three parameters that would favor introverts and, consequently, three opposite parameters under which extroverts would be expected to condition more rapidly. First, *partial reinforcement* procedures would favor introverts for the reasons already specified.

Second, the *strength of the unconditioned stimulus* (e.g., air puff) might be expected to act differently on introverts and extroverts. Low-strength UCS would be expected to foster the growth of inhibition, whereas relatively strong UCS should favor the development of excitation. However, as we have seen, Teplov had shown that increasing the strength of the UCS increases the intensity of the conditioned response only up to some limiting point, beyond which the response intensity decreases as transmarginal (protective) inhibition sets in. For introverts TMI is reached sooner. Thus, at levels near the transmarginal inhibition point, strong unconditioned stimuli should favor extroverts because their strong inhibitory nervous systems profit most from stimuli intensities that are disorganizing for the more sensitive introvert nervous systems.

Third, the *interval between the CS and the UCS* (i.e., between tone and puff of air) should be assumed to affect the rates of conditioning for introverts and extroverts. A short interval between CS and UCS favors introverts because their more sensitive nervous systems are able to respond to this rapid rate of presentation, whereas the extrovert's more inhibitory nervous system cannot keep pace. Furthermore, the more rapid the rate at which the UCS follows the CS, the more rapidly will reactive inhibition (fatigue) build in the extrovert's nervous system, thus causing poorer conditioning performance.

Eysenck (1966, pp. 503ff.) cited an unpublished study by A. Levey in which all three parameters were manipulated with introvert, extrovert, and ambivert (equally introverted and extroverted) subjects. Levey employed partial reinforcement (67 percent) versus continuous reinforcement (100 percent); long CS-UCS interval (800 milliseconds) versus short CS-UCS interval (400 milliseconds); and strong UCS (6 pounds of pressure per square inch) versus weak UCS (3 pounds of pressure per square inch). Levey's results were something less than completely confirmatory of Eysenck's hypotheses. Yet, on the whole, when conditions were arranged to favor the introverts, they tended to condition more rapidly than extroverts; conversely, when the three parameters were arranged to favor the extroverts, their performance was superior to introverts' performance. Figures 17.4 and 17.5 show the conditioning rates for introverts and extroverts under favorable and unfavorable conditions. Eysenck summarized the general results of Levey's study in this way:

FIGURE 17.4   Conditions favorable for introverts: Partial reinforcement, weak UCS, and short CS-UCS interval.

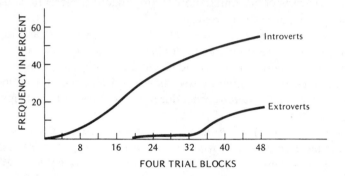

Source: A. Levey, as reported by Eysenck (1966), p. 507; curves are somewhat idealized and fitted to data points.

FIGURE 17.5   Conditions favorable for extroverts: 100 percent reinforcement, strong USC, and long CS-UCS interval.

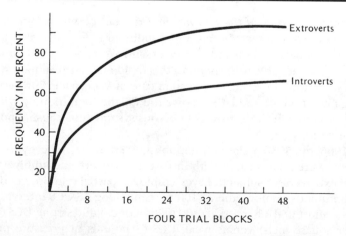

Source: A. Levey, as reported by Eysenck (1966), p. 507; curves are somewhat idealized and fitted to data points.

If the results of this experiment can be taken as representative, we might conclude that strength of the UCS was the most important parameter [separating extroverts and introverts], followed by CS-UCS interval, with reinforcement schedule last. (1966, p. 504)

Motor Movements and Involuntary Rest Pauses

Using a behavioral phenomenon with which we are already familiar, Spielmann (1963) demonstrated that extroverts develop more frequent involuntary rest pauses (IRP) than introverts on a task involving massed practice. As usual, this prediction was made on the theoretical assumption that during unrelieved responding, the extrovert's more rapid buildup of inhibitory cortical effects causes him or her to experience many of these involuntary "time-outs."

Subjects on Spielmann's investigation were required to tap repeatedly with a metal stylus on a metal plate. The time the metal stylus was in contact with the metal plate was automatically recorded, and each gap between contacts was likewise registered. From 90 working-class participants, the five most introverted and the five most extroverted were selected on the basis of personality questionnaire scores.

As expected, the average IRP scores showed that the extrovert subjects paused nearly 15 times as often as the introverts. Careful analysis of the data also demonstrated that the onset of IRPs was significantly earlier in the task for the extrovert group than for the introverts (Eysenck, 1953a, p. 432; cf. Eysenck, 1963a, 1964a, pp. 76ff., and 1964b).

Auditory Vigilance: Gaps in Attention

Another laboratory task on which extroverts and introverts may be expected to differ in performance is the vigilance or "watch-keeping" perceptual problem (Bakan, 1959; Eysenck, 1982; Mackworth, 1950, 1957). Vigilance tasks may take many forms, but they all have in common that the subject is required to detect in a long series of stimuli a particular sudden change or discrepancy in the sequence. Thus, for example, a subject may listen to a lengthy recording of someone pronouncing a seemingly endless series of digits. The task is to detect three successive odd digits—when they occur. A vigilance task may also be performed in the visual mode. A subject sits facing an electric clock device whose hands jump at one-second intervals. The goal is to detect an irregular double jump of the sweep hand—when it occurs.

On theoretical grounds it may be expected that introverts will perform better—detect more of the required stimuli—than extroverts. Because inhibition builds rapidly in extroverts and because a vigilance task is monotonous, the extrovert will experience more IRPs than the introvert. When an IRP happens to coincide with the occurrence of the stimulus that is to be detected, the extrovert will miss it. Introverts, on the other hand, who experience fewer IRPs and having greater stimulus sensitivity, should miss fewer of the designated stimuli.

Claridge (1967) used an auditory vigilance task involving the detection of three consecutive odd digits with 57 dysthymics, 48 hysterics, and 55 normal subjects. Dysthymics (introverts) were predicted to perform better than the hysterics. Besides scoring the vigilance task, Claridge also monitored subjects' physiological arousal with measurements of galvanic skin response and heart rate. Results showed that, as predicted, dysthymics were superior in total vigilance scores to hysterics and to normals. On the physiological measures, dysthymics showed a higher level of arousal (heart rate and GSR) than either normals or extroverts throughout the duration of the task.

THE BIOLOGICAL BASIS OF PERSONALITY: AROUSABILITY AND THE ARAS

The clear implication of Eysenck's proposal that individuals differ in their excitation-inhibition balance is that this difference is mediated by something in the central nervous system. Fundamentally, Eysenck's theory is biological, though of necessity most tests of the theory are behavioral. In 1967 Eysenck revised and extended his basic introversion-extroversion theory by postulating specific relationships between these personality dimensions and the *ascending reticular activating system (ARAS)* of the brain. He also now rooted the dimension of normality-neuroticism (dysthymia and hysteria) in central nervous system structures. A group of functionally related subcortical structures, including the hypothalamus, the gyrus cinguli, the hippocampus, and their interconnections, had been conceptualized by James W. Papez (1937) as mediators of bodily arousal associated with emotion. Producing their effects by activating the involuntary branch of the nervous system, these structures are responsible for changes in heart rate, respiration, blood pressure, and other signs of emotional activation. To the entire group of structures the names *visceral brain* and *limbic system* are often applied.

The relationships that Eysenck proposed can be summarized succinctly in two word equations:

Introversion-Extroversion = Difference in ARAS Arousal

Normality-Neuroticism = Differences in Visceral Brain Activation

ARAS and Cortical Arousal

The ascending reticular activating system is a network of fibers extending from the spinal cord to the thalamus of the brain at a level below the cortex. Figure 17.6 illustrates the basic location and boundaries of the ARAS. (It might be helpful for those of you unfamiliar with basic neuroanatomy to consult an introductory physiological psychology text. Thompson's [1967] is a particularly good one.)

Figure 17.6 also shows the general location of the visceral brain (VB) structures, though in reality these structures are more widely separated. The ascending arrows indicate the direction of influence of the ARAS on the cortex. Descending arrows, from the cortex toward the ARAS, indicate the reciprocal influence of the cortex on the ARAS. Generally, the ARAS serves to stimulate the cortex, to activate its cells to a state of excitability. The cortex may in turn "feed back" on the ARAS either to further increase its excitatory input or to damp it down.

Physiological interest in this arousal network or reticulum of fibers began when it was discovered in 1935 by Bremer that cutting through the brain stem at midbrain

FIGURE 17.6   Anatomical locations of ARAS and VB.

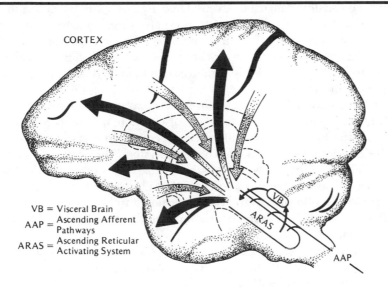

CORTEX

VB = Visceral Brain

AAP = Ascending Afferent Pathways

ARAS = Ascending Reticular Activating System

VB

ARAS

AAP

Source: Eysenck (1967), p. 231.

level caused cats to become almost permanently sleeping animals. The electrical activity of such cats' brains showed a characteristic "sleeping wave" on the electroencephalograph (EEG). In a normally sleeping cat, it is possible to induce an arousal EEG pattern by simply waking the animal or doing something to engage its attention. But in cats with transected brain stems it was possible to produce an arousal EEG pattern only for short periods lasting as long as the stimulus used to arouse the cat.

In 1949, Moruzzi and Magoun, instead of shutting down the ARAS by cutting into the brain stem, set out to stimulate it electrically. Records of EEG tracings from the cortex of stimulated cats showed that stimulation of the ARAS evokes cortical arousal.

The ARAS seems also to be involved in states of attention and concentration. Fuster (1958) was able to improve rhesus monkeys' performance on a visual discrimination task by stimulating their ARAS. This finding suggests that part of the ARAS's function may be to mediate information processing in humans (cf. French, 1957). The evidence, however, is somewhat contradictory (Eysenck, 1967; Thompson, 1967). Generally it seems safe to say that the ARAS is responsible for cortical efficiency in learning, conditioning, wakefulness, and attention. The ARAS seems to mediate states of arousal, ranging from sleep to extreme behavioral excitation.

Another portion of the ARAS, however, seems to have an inhibitory effect on the cortex. Known as the "recruiting system," this portion of the ARAS serves to damp down cortical excitation. Thus, in the ARAS, Eysenck seems to have found the physiological causes of excitation and inhibition and, therefore, the basis of introversion-extroversion. We discuss the specific relationships between ARAS arousal thresholds and introversion-extroversion shortly. It is possible, however, to recognize at this point that introverts are assumed to have higher levels of ARAS arousal (lower ARAS thresholds) than extroverts.

Visceral Brain and Emotional Activation

The second personality dimension exemplified by the extreme criterion groups of dysthymics and hysterics compared to normals is the dimension of normality-neuroticism. Eysenck assumes that this dimension consists largely of differences in emotional activation such that neurotics are more highly emotionally reactive than normals. In this sense, the structures of the visceral brain (VB) are conceptualized as the mediators of this reactivity.

Though we cannot review the relevant research relating the structures of the VB (hypothalamus and limbic system) to states of emotion, it is perhaps sufficient to point out that the hypothalamus and other visceral brain units exert their effects through the autonomic or involuntary nervous system. The range of neural effect extends from activation of glands and muscles to heart rate, respiration, and perspiration. Individuals in whom there is a low threshold of visceral brain activation (i.e., behaviorally high emotional activation) are presumed to be susceptible to neurotic disorder. Thus, in short, the visceral brain's level of activation ranges from low (normal) to chronically high (neurotic).

There is a complicating factor connected with the visceral brain and neuroticism. In states of extreme emotional activation (e.g., intense rage, or profound sadness, or extreme fear), the normal separation of functioning between the ARAS's arousal of the cortex and the VB's emotional activation of the autonomic nervous system breaks down. In effect, the dimensions of introversion-extroversion and neuroticism-normality lose their independence when the individual is emotionally active (Eysenck, 1967, p. 232). Thus, although it is possible to be intellectually aroused without emotional activation, it is impossible to be emotionally activated without simultaneous intellectual or cortical arousal.

In the first case, that of cortical arousal without VB (emotional) activation, problem-solving activity dominates the individual. For example, Eysenck cites the case of the scientist sitting quite immobile and to all appearances fast asleep. But subjectively, his mind is hard at work tackling unsolved and intricate professional problems (Eysenck, 1967, p. 232). His cortex is aroused, but his emotions are not.

In the second kind of arousal, the visceral brain and the autonomic nervous system become involved. This type of "activation" might be illustrated by the scientist sitting quietly in his bath when suddenly the long-sought solution to his "impossible" problem dawns on him. He has been *intellectually* aroused all the while that he sat in the bath. He runs screaming from the bath, shouting "Eureka!" with mad abandon, while a euphoric sense of ecstasy wells within him. Heart pounding, short of breath, profusely perspiring, this scientist now presents a clear picture of both emotional activation and intellectual arousal.

In cases where the level of emotional activation is intense, cortical arousal must also have occurred. Thus, in Eysenck's dimensional system, the separation of intellectual arousal from emotional activation holds only for normal individuals. *Neurotics evidence a capacity for emotional arousal to stimuli that would be only cortically arousing to a normal individual* (Eysenck, 1967, p. 233; 1982; Eysenck & Eysenck, 1985). In more technical terms, the neurotic individual is reaching maximum cortical and emotional arousal nearly simultaneously because the hypothalamus and other structures in the limbic system (visceral brain) are bombarding the ARAS with stimulation. At the same time, the ARAS is arousing the cortex.

TRANSLATION OF EXCITATION-INHIBITION INTO AROUSAL CONCEPTS

With the proposal that biological bases might be found for the dimensions of introversion-extroversion and for normality-neuroticism, Eysenck sharpened the causal level of his personality theory.

To make clear the transition from the 1957 theory of excitation-inhibition to the 1967 theory of biological functions, it is necessary to distinguish among four extreme types of personality. Individuals may be said to be normal or neurotic, introverted or extroverted, with of course various degrees in between these absolutes. It follows that an individual may be a normal introvert or a neurotic introvert, just as he or she may be a normal extrovert or a neurotic extrovert. The hypothetical nervous system states of ARAS arousal and VB activation that correspond to these four extreme types are indicated in Table 17.3.

It is obvious that the emphasis in this biological version of Eysenck's theory is on differences in arousal level (excitation) rather than on inhibition-level differences. In Eysenck's previous model of these personality dimensions, most of the experimental tests were directed to the hypothesized effects of inhibition (e.g., IRPs, vigilance). Experimental tests of the biological theory, however, usually spring from hypotheses about the effects of the introvert's higher cortical ARAS arousal. With this shift in theoretical emphasis came several complications. The one of immediate interest in the present context concerns a general law of motivation proposed in 1908 by Yerkes and Dodson.

The Yerkes-Dodson Law: Inverted-U Hypothesis

Yerkes and Dodson proposed a principle of motivation and performance that, with some modifications, has been widely accepted in contemporary psychology by

TABLE 17.3   Biological Basis of Personality

Dimensional Position	Level of ARAS Arousal	Level of VB Activation
Normal Introvert	High	Low
Normal Extrovert	Low	Low
Neurotic Introvert (Dysthymic)	High	High
Neurotic Extrovert (Hysteric)	Low*	High

*Note that the *neurotic* extrovert's ARAS arousal is higher than the normal extrovert's ARAS arousal because of the breakdown of separation between ARAS and VB functioning in states of high (neurotic) emotion. But the extrovert's characteristic ARAS arousal level is always lower than the introvert's level and is, therefore, simply listed as "low." Based on Eysenck, 1967.

theorists interested in states of arousal. In briefest form, Yerkes and Dodson's law states that motivation or arousal may be conceptualized as a continuum ranging from very low levels through very high levels of excitation. At the low end of the continuum, the organism is so underaroused (undermotivated) that it falls asleep. At the high end, the organism is so aroused that its behavior is disorganized, fragmented, or frenzied. Yerkes and Dodson (1908) proposed that between these two extremes lies a state of moderate arousal in which the organism is sufficiently motivated to perform well, but not so aroused as to be disorganized or distracted.

Modern theorists (e.g., Broadhurst, 1959; Hebb, 1955; Lindsley, 1951; Malmo, 1959) refer to this hypothesis at the "inverted-U hypothesis" for reasons that will be obvious after inspecting Figure 17.7.

Figure 17.7 shows in idealized form the relationship between arousal level and quality of performance. As arousal increases, performance improves until it reaches a maximum at the height of the inverted-U curve. From that point onward, increases in arousal lead to decreases in performance. This hypothesis clearly has direct relationship to Teplov's strength-of-the-nervous-system concept and the effects of transmarginal inhibition previously illustrated in Figure 17.3. A complication must be added to the inverted-U hypothesis. What happens, we might ask, when the task that the individual is performing can vary in difficulty or complexity? Will tasks of different difficulty levels require different levels of optimal arousal? The answer is a definite yes. If we confine our consideration of task difficulty to three arbitrary levels, low, medium, and high difficulty, then we can plot motivation-performance curves for each task level. Figure 17.8 illustrates the theoretical relationships among task-difficulty level, performance, and arousal level.

The three curves in Figure 17.8 are designed to indicate that the optimal level of arousal for best performance changes as task-difficulty level increases. For tasks of low difficulty, a somewhat higher level of arousal or motivation is optimal than for

FIGURE 17.7   Inverted-U law of motivation and performance.

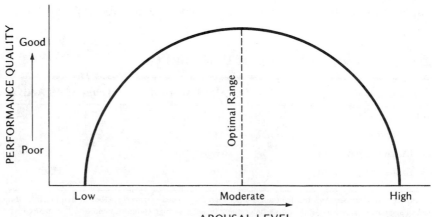

Performance is optimal at moderate levels of arousal.

FIGURE 17.8   **Yerkes-Dodson law for interaction of arousal level, performance, and task difficulty.** *As task difficulty increases, optimal level of arousal for best performance decreases.*

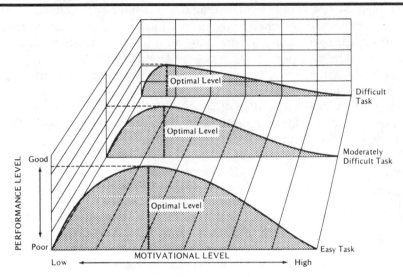

Source: Eysenck (1963a), p. 131.

tasks of moderate difficulty. Tasks of greatest difficulty require the lowest level of arousal. The general rule is: *The more difficult the task, the lower the optimum arousal.*

With the Yerkes-Dodson law in mind, predictions from Eysenck's biological model of personality not only can be more precise, but also can take account of the interaction between cortical arousal and emotional activation. Levey's results with variations of the three conditioning parameters of partial reinforcement, CS-UCS interval, and UCS intensity are more easily explained by this refined model than by the earlier excitation/inhibition account. Recall that Levey's results showed that the most important parameter manipulation separating introverts from extroverts was stimulus intensity. Extroverts conditioned better with strong UCS (air puff), and introverts were superior with the weak UCS. If UCS intensity is conceptualized as a form of arousal, the Yerkes-Dodson law predicts that introverts, having a higher level of initial arousal, will perform poorly with the additional arousal provided by a strong UCS. Extroverts, on the other hand, profit from the arousal increment because their initial cortical arousal is low.

A Test of the Yerkes-Dodson Law

An interesting question now poses itself. The four extreme types of individual (normal and neurotic introverts, and normal and neurotic extroverts) should, in principle, possess differing levels of combined cortical and emotional arousal. Presumably, neurotic introverts, in whom ARAS and VB excitation are both chronically high, should be placed at the top rank of a hierarchy of arousal. Normal extroverts, having low ARAS arousal and low VB activation, should fall at the bottom of the hierarchy of arousal. In between these extremes, normal introverts and neurotic extroverts, each having *one* form of high arousal, should evidence moderate degrees of excitation. The theory, however, does not specify whether the normal introvert is more highly aroused than the neurotic extrovert. Consequently, only an empirical investigation can provide rankings for these two personality types (cf. Eysenck, 1953b, pp. 436ff., and 1967, pp. 182ff.). It might, however, be supposed that a very neurotic extrovert would surpass a normal introvert in absolute drive level because the neurotic extrovert's emotional reactivity acts as a multiplier of habits in Hull's sense of the term.

Thus our final hypothetical hierarchy of differential combined arousal for the personality types looks like this:

Neurotic Introvert	[*highest arousal*]
Neurotic Extrovert	
Normal Introvert	↓
Normal Extrovert	[*lowest arousal*]

To illustrate this kind of experimental test of the theory, McLaughlin and Eysenck (1967) had the four different types of criterion personalities learn lists of paired nonsense syllables. One list was difficult to learn, and the other relatively easy. Results were tabulated by the number of errors a subject made in reaching a specified criterion of learning. In addition to determining the optimum level of arousal for learning, the experiment was also designed to test a hypothesis about a phenomenon called "reminiscence."

Experimental psychologists have known for a long time that memory for a learned response improves if time intervenes between the acquisition of the response and its performance. Thus, when studying for an exam in psychology, recitation of what has been learned will be better the following day when compared to immediate recitation. During the period of rest, the memory is consolidated, or made more permanent in specific neural circuits. However, while the process of consolidation is in progress, performance of the learned response is impeded. Thus memory seems to improve with rest, for rest allows consolidation to reach completion.

Eysenck hypothesized that the process of consolidation is most facilitated in individuals having high initial cortical arousal, that is, in introverts. Thus introverts should show poorest performance on memory tasks that require immediate postacquisition performance, whereas extroverts, who have low arousal and poor consolidation, will perform best immediately after acquisition (cf. McLaughlin & Eysenck, 1967, pp. 574ff.).

In the experiment conducted by McLaughlin and Eysenck (1967), tests of memory for the learned lists were conducted immediately after acquisition, and thus favored extroverts. But, as we already know, the Yerkes-Dodson law also governs performance on tasks of varying difficulty. It can be presumed that the difficult list of paired nonsense syllables would present a task requiring a moderately low level of arousal for optimal performance. Thus, taking the two effects together, the reminiscence evidence indicates that extroverts should perform better with immediate recall, whereas the Yerkes-Dodson law suggests that on the difficult list the low-arousal normal extroverts will show superior performance to neurotic extroverts, and to all highly aroused introvert personalities.

Conversely, learning the easy list should require a higher level of arousal than learning the difficult list to produce optimal performance. The prediction for the easy list thus must be that neurotic extroverts will evidence best performance because they have slightly higher arousal than normal extroverts. Neurotic introverts, having the highest level of combined ARAS and VB arousal, should, in principle, be too highly aroused to perform well on either list under conditions of immediate recall.

Figures 17.9 and 17.10 show the outcome of McLaughlin and Eysenck's investigation. The major predictions about the superiority of extroverts' performance were confirmed. Moreover, when a line is drawn through the plotted error scores for all subjects, the resulting curves resemble the inverted-U motivation-performance curve. As expected, the optimal level of arousal is shifted to the left (i.e., toward lower optimal arousal) for the difficult list.

One prediction, however, received no support. On the difficult list, neurotic introverts, although performing more poorly than normal extroverts as predicted, had fewer errors than normal introverts. The difference between neurotic and normal introverts was not significantly different. Yet is it difficult to understand why the less highly aroused normal introverts scored more poorly than neurotic introverts. A further unanswered question remains: If performance tests were administered *after* a rest period, would introverts then show superior recall? The elegance of Eysenck's

FIGURE 17.9   Easy list.

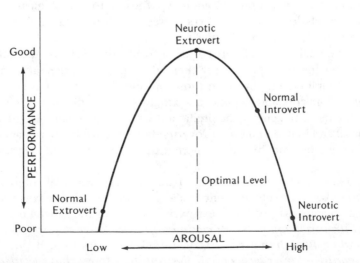

Based on McLaughlin and Eysenck (1967), p. 131.

FIGURE 17.10   Difficult list.

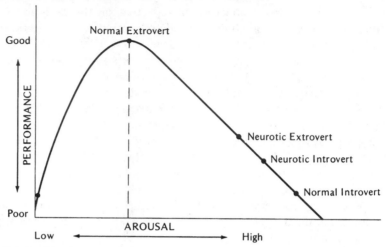

Relationship of error scores and arousal level for easy and difficult lists.

Based on McLaughlin and Eysenck (1967), p. 131.

theory is that it allows such questions to be asked (see also Alsopp & Eysenck 1974, 1975; Howarth & Eysenck, 1968; but see Schroeder & Koenig, 1978).

DIRECT TESTS OF THE AROUSAL THEORY: STIMULANT AND DEPRESSANT DRUGS

The translation of the excitation-inhibition hypothesis into its biological equivalent of ARAS arousal levels led to testable hypotheses of a somewhat different sort than those based on the usual laboratory tasks.

If ARAS bombardment of the cortex is really the basis of the introversion-extroversion dimension of personality, then stimulant and depressant drugs should produce behavioral effects similar to those produced by excitation and inhibition. Furthermore, stimulants and depressants should produce different effects in intro-verts and extroverts. "In general, the prediction would be that stimulant drugs lead to greater arousal and hence to more introverted behavior, while depressant drugs lead to greater inhibition and hence to more extroverted behavior" (Eysenck, 1967, p. 265).

The preexisting state of arousal in a particular experimental subject would, of course, have to be taken into account to allow for the fact that introverts begin any task with a higher arousal level than extroverts. Therefore, the general hypothesis can be refined: *Introverts require less of a stimulant drug to reach a specified criterion of behavioral arousal than extroverts.* In a similar vein, it can be hypothesized that *introverts require a larger dose of a depressant drug to reach a specified criterion of inhibition than extroverts* (Eysenck & Eysenck, 1985, p. 229).

A variety of research studies supports these predictions (e.g., Claridge, 1967; Laverty, 1958; Shagass & Kerenyi, 1958). Such studies generally use a measurement of "sedation threshold." A particular drug, say, a depressant, is injected intravenously at a known rate until slurred speech and specific EEG changes are noted. The amount of the drug required to reach this criterion is a measure of sedation threshold (Shagass & Kerenyi, 1958). Shagass and Kerenyi showed that subjects classified as introverts by psychiatric diagnosis and by paper-and-pencil measures had higher sedation thresholds (i.e., required a larger dosage) than extrovert subjects, thus confirming Eysenck's theory. Furthermore, subjects classified as obsessional (belonging to the dysthymic group in Eysenck's terminology) also had higher sedation thresholds than subjects classified as hysterics (see also Gupta, 1973).

ACQUISITION OF NEUROSIS: THE SOCIALIZATION OF INTROVERTS AND EXTROVERTS

Dysthymic disorders fundamentally are *learned* fears. The introvert who becomes dysthymic does so precisely because his or her high cortical and high emotional arousal facilitates rapid and strong anxiety conditioning. Dysthymic neurotic symptoms, such as phobias, obsessions and compulsions, and intense anxiety attacks are interpreted by Eysenck (1960, 1976) as *conditioned maladaptive responses* acquired by neurotic introverts in coping with the demands of life.[2]

Hysterical disorders fundamentally are *failures to learn* the anxiety-based responses that underlie "normal" socialization training. The extrovert who becomes a hysteric (or a psychopathic personality) does so precisely because his or her cortical and emotional *underarousal* impedes the learning of anxiety-based self-restraint and moral or ethical inhibitions (Eysenck & Rachman, 1965, p. 40).

Some evidence suggests that extroverts may be of two types. In the first, sociability, or outgoing, stimulus-seeking behavior predominates. In the second type of extrovert, impulsivity and an inability to keep antisocial urges and behaviors in check predominate. The first type resembles the normal personality but may succumb to hysterical disorder. Criminal or psychopathic behavior is more characteristic of the second type (Eysenck, 1964a; Eysenck & Eysenck, 1969; Eysenck & Gudjonsson, 1989, pp. 118ff.). It is this second hysterical type who seems so opposite to the dysthymic personality, for the psychopath is one who has failed to acquire by conditioning the necessary socialization restraints that in the dysthymic become exaggerated into chronic anxiety symptoms (but see Sipprelle, Ascough, Detrio, & Horst, 1977).

In effect, Eysenck is arguing that criminals are likely to score high on the extroversion dimension, but that criminals receive those high scores because of the underlying "trait" of impulsivity, which is embodied in extroversion (Eysenck & Eysenck,

---

[2] Some research suggests that neuroticism and extroversion/introversion are not independent (orthogonal) (Claridge, 1967; Eysenck & Eysenck, 1969). It would appear that introversion is more closely related to neuroticism than extroversion. Eysenck has argued that this partial breakdown in orthogonality was an artifact of the early Maudsley Personality Inventory's overinclusion of biased items. To obviate the difficulty, a new instrument called the Eysenck Personality Inventory (Eysenck & Eysenck, 1968) was devised, and results with this instrument more or less confirm the statistical independence of the two dimensions.

1985, pp. 331ff.; Eysenck & Gudjonsson, 1989). We will discuss criminality further at the end of this chapter when we discuss a third dimension of personality.

Genetic and Environmental Interactions

Eysenck's early views stressed that dysthymic neuroses could be understood in terms of Pavlovian-like conditioning processes, just as the hysterical disorders could be conceptualized as failures of Pavlovian-like conditioning. As we have seen, however, Eysenck also regards individual differences in central nervous system functioning as the foundation upon which life experiences erect a healthy or unhealthy adaptation to reality. Put into its strongest form, Eysenck's theory asserts that the dimensions of normality—neuroticism and introversion-extroversion—represent genetically transmitted features of personality.

Eysenck has several times reviewed the evidence for the genetic basis of personality dimensions (1957a; 1967; for intelligence: 1973; 1979; for psychoticism: Eysenck & Eysenck, 1976; Eaves, Eysenck, & Martin, 1989). The general argument for genetic predisposition runs along the following lines. The introvert inherits a nervous system easily able to form conditioned responses, and *if* this personality type also inherits an emotionally reactive autonomic nervous system (high neuroticism), he or she will be in an ideal position to acquire strong anxiety responses. In effect, the introvert possesses a nervous system predisposition to be acutely sensitive to all forms of stimulation and therefore to become inhibited and withdrawing in the presence of a demanding social environment.

The extrovert, by contrast, inherits the type of nervous system that is not easily conditionable, not especially sensitive to stimulation, and not prone to withdrawal from a demanding environment. In fact, the extrovert is a "stimulus-seeker" because his or her relatively high levels of inhibitory cortical processes demand constant novel and potent input of external excitation to feed the resulting "stimulus-hunger." Eysenck has summarized his position on the relative importance of biological and environmental factors in shaping personality as a "bio-social" model:

> Human behavior is rightly said to be bio-social in nature, i.e., to have both biological and social causes; it is time the pendulum started swinging back from an exclusive preoccupation with social causes to an appropriate appreciation and understanding of biological causes. . . . Biological causes act in such a way as to predispose an individual in certain ways to stimulation; this stimulation may or may not occur, depending on circumstances which are entirely under environmental control. (Eysenck, 1967, pp. 221–222)

Eysenck's theory, therefore, may be understood as an attempt to bridge two very wide gulfs: the gulf between a study of individual differences in personality and the experimental investigation of conditioning, learning, and perceptual processes, and the gulf between observable phenotype and inferred causal genotype of an organism.

Beyond the Conditioning Model: The Neurotic Paradox

Eysenck (1976) modified his views somewhat to take account of discoveries in learning theory that lie beyond the classical Pavlovian model of conditioning. In some respects, Eysenck has acknowledged that a *strict* application of *classical* Pavlovian theory to neurotic symptom learning is too simplistic to do justice to the central features of neurotic misery.

Eysenck now argues that a cardinal feature of human neurosis is the "neurotic paradox" proposed by O. H. Mowrer (1950). The neurotic person's behavior typically has consequences that are unfavorable, painful, and clearly self-defeating. Yet the neurotic persists in that same behavior for months, even years! Common sense suggests that unfavorable consequences would cause any rational person to take stock of the problem and alter his or her actions. But that illogical persistence is precisely what makes neurotic symptoms so *neurotic:* Such behavior is both self-defeating and self-perpetuating.

According to Eysenck, a strict conditioning model drawn from Pavlovian theory or even from Skinner's operant model cannot explain satisfactorily why neurotic symptoms endure unchanged in the face of punishing consequences. Moreover, some forms of neurotic behavior are founded on irrational fears, fears so removed from actuality that the dreaded outcome never materializes. Yet, despite the continual failure of the fear to be reinforced, the fear-based symptoms never extinguish as they should according to conditioning theory (Solomon, Kamin, & Wynne, 1953; Solomon & Wynne, 1954). Eysenck reviews evidence that will not be presented here that suggests that, under certain circumstances, unreinforced conditioned fears may even "incubate" with each unreinforced presentation of the conditioned stimulus.

In consequence, Eysenck believes that an adequate learning model of neurosis must include the possibility that some neurotic anxieties and fears are based on innate sensitivity to certain noxious objects or events. A similar idea first proposed by Seligman (1970, 1971, 1972; see also Rachman, 1978, 1990) suggests an evolutionary mechanism through which organisms are biologically "prepared" to respond to specific stimuli with fear. Thus, for example, there certainly would be survival value in the predisposition to be fearful of darkness, of poisonous snakes and insects, or of high places. Conditioned neurotic fears built upon any of these *prepared* survival phobias would not readily obey the ordinary "laws" of learning, including extinction. "Preparedness" might also explain why neurotic phobias tend to be restricted to a relatively small class of stimuli when, in contrast, conditioning theory predicts that *any* stimulus can be made fearsome by proper association with a noxious event. Preparedness suggests that only the "wired in" areas of life and its events can become resistant neurotic targets of anxiety.

The neurotic paradox is not so paradoxical after all. Neurotics persist in self-defeating behavior because the negative consequences of their symptoms and the failure of dreaded outcomes to materialize cannot suppress or extinguish fears that have roots in evolutionary survival mechanisms. Unfortunately for the neurotic, this "explanation" merely trades irony for paradox: Evolutionary mechanisms persist in a species because they promote environmental adaptation, but the average contemporary neurotic cannot wait eons for natural selection to catch up with our civilized existence.

Eysenck (1976, p. 264; 1982) has proposed that the failure of extinction and the possible incubation or enhancement of fear may be influenced by individual differences in personality. Thus, for example, he hypothesizes that neurotic introverts would be most susceptible to incubation and nonextinction effects, whereas the normal extrovert would be least susceptible. The important point is that Eysenck sees the need to stretch conditioning theory beyond its present constraints to account for the complexity of neurotic symptom acquisition.

PSYCHOTICISM: PSYCHIATRIC DIAGNOSIS REVISITED

Eysenck's work, you recall, began with an ill-omened investigation of psychiatric diagnostic reliability. One of the fundamental tenets of classical diagnostic systems is that neurotic and psychotic disorders are, like the schoolchild's apples and oranges, fundamentally different things. Neurotic behavior is presumed to be "discontinuous" with psychotic maladjustment; that is, psychotics possess characteristics that are possessed by *no one* who is normal and by *no one* who is neurotic (Eysenck & Eysenck, 1976, pp. 5, 157).

The dimensional model of personality, as proposed by Eysenck, suggests that "psychoticism" is not an absolute, all-or-none personality feature. There is, instead, a range of infinite gradations of psychoticism, ranging from normality at one extreme to full-blown psychotic separation from reality and thought disorder at the other extreme. Thus, in principle, it is possible for a normal person to possess some degree of those traits found in extreme form in the psychotic personality, just as it is possible for the neurotic person to possess *some* normal traits or *some* psychotic traits.

Psychoticism has entered Eysenck's theory as an additional dimension of disordered personality that, like neuroticism and introversion-extroversion, is genetically based. In Eysenck's latest addition to his theory, psychoticism as a personality dimension is mediated by a *polygenic* personality trait. "Polygenic" means that a large number of genes, each of whose individual effect is small, may be inherited by a person who will evidence a high degree of the trait they embody. Each of these "small effect" genes, in Eysenck's model of psychoticism, is additive, so that the total number inherited determines the degree of psychoticism within the personality (Eysenck & Eysenck, 1976, p. 29). Another group of genes, fewer in number than the first group and having "large effects," determine the probability that the person will not only evidence psychoticism *traits* but will also suffer a fully developed psychosis:

> A person who has a large number of genes of small value, but none of the genes of large effect, would be psychotic without demonstrating any of the classical syndromes; such persons may indeed be in the majority and create the well-known difficulties of diagnosis of sub-varieties of psychosis. When the number of genes of small value is less than that required for a proper psychosis to develop, or when external stress has not been sufficient to provide for effective interaction in producing this state, we have individuals demonstrating varying degrees of "schizoid state" or schizotype—psychopaths, sociopaths, criminals, drug addicts, etc. When genes of large effect are present (usually only one) we get the classical pictures discussed in textbooks of psychiatry. (Eysenck & Eysenck, 1976, p. 29)

Eysenck's model of psychoticism also allows that a person with a high *"P"* score who is *not* overtly psychotic may nevertheless possess traits that make him or her "unusual" but not necessarily disadvantaged socially. Some high *P* personalities may in fact evidence their "unusualness" as genius or artistic productivity, thus confirming the suspicion expressed in Dryden's couplet (Eysenck & Eysenck, 1976, p. 30):

> Great wits are sure to madness near allied
> And thin partitions do their bounds divide.

Characteristics of the High-P Scorer

Eysenck and Eysenck (1975a, 1975b, 1976) have devised a paper-and-pencil inventory called the Eysenck Personality Questionnaire (EPQ) that not only measures the neuroticism and introversion-extroversion dimensions, but also assesses the test taker's degree of psychoticism. Factor-analytic studies were the basis on which questions were selected to measure the psychoticism dimension. A "high-P" person is one who answers affirmatively a selected pattern of questions that paints the following personality portrait:

A high psychoticism scorer is a loner who cares very little for the company of other people. The high-P personality shows overt hostility to others, even to close relatives and tends to disregard dangers and social conventions. Making fools of other people is an enjoyable pastime, and this trait may be carried easily to an extreme of cruelty. The high-P scorer tends to enjoy "unusual things" and stands out as "peculiar" to his acquaintances (Eysenck & Eysenck, 1975b, p. 5).

It is important to understand that the "high-P" person on the EPQ is *not* identical with a psychotic or schizophrenic patient, although a schizophrenic person would be expected to be "high in P." The EPQ does not measure psychotic symptoms or separation from reality; it assesses psychological characteristics shown to be correlated together into a cluster in particular people who may very well also have clusters of traits unrelated to psychoticism. A high degree of psychoticism is therefore independent of the person's degree of introversion-extroversion, as measured by the same test. Some neurotics *may* have elevated "P" scores; but there is no necessary, absolute reason for neuroticism (or introversion, or extroversion) to accompany high psychoticism (Eysenck & Eysenck, 1976, pp. 38ff.).

Neurotics who also possess a high degree of psychoticism are likely to be poor candidates for psychotherapy, according to the Eysencks (1976), and the EPQ may very well become a useful screening instrument for exactly this purpose. A person's "P" score has always to be interpreted in terms of the other Eysenck dimensions. High "P" will have very different meanings when embodied in high and low introverted personalities, and even more varied meaning when associated with high, as contrasted with low, intelligence.

Thus far, the Eysencks have not proposed an underlying central nervous system mechanism for psychoticism. Some exploratory research suggests a close relationship between psychoticism and "maleness" as mediated by a person's androgen/estrogen sex hormone balance. But the evidence is merely suggestive, not definitive as discussed in the following section (Eysenck, 1982, pp. 85ff.; Eysenck & Eysenck, 1976).

PSYCHOTICISM, CRIME, AND GENETICS

Recall that Eysenck argued that the basic personality dimensions have a substantial degree of genetic loading that interacts with socialization experiences as a person develops from childhood to adulthood. When Eysenck added the psychoticism dimension to his theory, he reaffirmed this interactionist model and created several new hypotheses about the interaction of the three dimensions of extroversion, neuroticism, and psychoticism.

The person who scores high in psychoticism has inherited a *vulnerability* to psychotic disorder but may not in fact succumb to a diagnosable illness. Instead, a person who embodies a large number of the "traits" associated with psychoticism *and* who is also high in neuroticism and extroversion may develop a pattern of antisocial or criminal behavior. Eysenck argued originally that criminal or antisocial behavior was linked to extreme extroversion. The link, however, has always been modest or inconsistent in research studies (Eysenck & Gudjonsson, 1989). Eysenck, therefore, has modified his theory so that the criminal or antisocial personality is conceptualized as a person who has a high degree of the impulsivity associated with extroversion, a high degree of neuroticism, and has inherited a substantial nervous system predisposition to psychoticism.

Conceptual links between criminality (or antisocial personality disorder) and the other dimensions of personality, not to mention the interaction of socialization experiences, are complex. Eysenck's argument incorporates his arousal hypotheses, his measurements of the factors underlying the personality dimensions, and his interactionist model of socialization. The argument can be summarized in three interlocking parts.

Arousal and Hedonic Tone

Eysenck's own work and his review of the literature on criminality (Eaves, Eysenck & Martin, 1989; Eysenck & Gudjonsson, 1989) suggested to him that criminal behavior is associated with underarousal because a person with a relatively nonreactive nervous system does not condition or acquire the anxiety-based restraints of conscience as readily as do people with more highly aroused nervous systems. Therefore, during socialization, the "normal" inhibitions and restraints that are learned largely through Pavlovian conditioning and that underlie "conscience" are not acquired by the vulnerable child (Eysenck & Gudjonsson, 1989, p. 119). Figure 17.11 illustrates Eysenck's basic hypothesis. Introverts, extroverts, and ambiverts have different levels of "optimal arousal" based on the nervous system characteristics they inherited. Optimal arousal is the level of activation produced by the inherent arousal properties of the person's nervous system and the current level of stimulus input. The optimal level is the point at which a given personality type is most comfortable, most pleasantly activated, and most positively motivated. Introverts, with the highest innate arousal levels, require less stimulation to achieve the optimal level that is comfortable for them compared to extroverts. By contrast, the extrovert's chronic underarousal ensures that higher levels of stimulation will be required to reach optimal levels of arousal that are experienced as pleasant. As we discussed earlier, introverts are "stimulus shy" whereas extroverts are "stimulus hungry."

FIGURE 17.11 **Positive and negative hedonic tone for introverts and extroverts.**

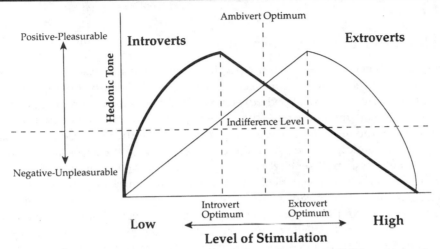

The optimal level of stimulation is higher for extroverts than for introverts both above and below the level of indifference. Eysenck predicts that levels of stimulation an introvert would find too intense would be "boring" for the extrovert. But levels of stimulation that the extrovert finds pleasurable or positively stimulating, the introvert experiences as overwhelming or painful. Most people, however, are ambiverts, and their optimal level of stimulation would fall theoretically between the optimal levels for the introvert and extrovert.

Based on Eysenck and Eysenck (1985), p. 249 and Eysenck and Gudjonsson (1989), p. 118.

The curves in Figure 17.11 indicate that the hedonic tone (pleasure or pain) of stimulation is a function of personality type. What is massive overstimulation and pain for the introvert is exciting and pleasant input for the extrovert. The "indifference level" indicated in Figure 17.11 represents a kind of "boredom" threshold, which differs for the two extreme personality types. Extroverts reach "indifferent hedonic tone" levels at much higher levels of stimulation than do introverts. Or, said another way, what an extrovert regards as boring understimulation, the introvert would find as peaceful, undemanding stimulation.

Eysenck suggests that the person destined to develop an antisocial personality is one whose arousal level is like that of the extreme extrovert in Figure 17.11. Specifically, the person would be excitement-seeking, easily distracted, and very resistant to levels of stimulation that would be regarded as painful by ambiverts or introverts. Eysenck elaborates:

> In the first place, we would expect criminals to be less reactive to pain because of their lower level of arousal. This would be directly relevant to criminal behavior, which often involves physical danger and pain, but its main effect might be on conditioning. Pavlovian conditioning, insofar as it is responsible for the creation of a "conscience," involves repeated application of painful stimuli by parents, teachers, and peers. . . . Hence, if the intensity of physical punishment is felt less strongly by extraverts, then clearly they should respond less to such types of conditioning than

would the average person, and much less so than the introvert. (Eysenck & Gudjonsson, 1989, p. 119)

The second link in Eysenck's argument involves the effects of inherited hormone levels on arousal.

Psychoticism and Male Hormones

Recall that Eysenck proposed that the psychoticism dimension was mediated by the presence of male hormones or androgens. Eysenck and Gudjonsson (1989) review literature that suggests a correlation between male androgens (testosterone) and underarousal. Androgens are produced in the adrenal glands of both sexes, in the ovaries of females and in the testes of males. Some of the evidence that Eysenck reviews indicates that high androgen levels have the effect of lowering the arousal levels in the brain's reticular system (Eysenck & Gudjonsson, 1989, pp. 130ff.). Because the pattern of androgen secretion is genetically based, a person inherits a predisposition to underarousal, to "masculinized" appearance and, perhaps, to aggressive behavior.

The evidence for these hypotheses is tentative and controversial, and for the sake of brevity, we are not detailing the intermediate links in the chain of evidence. Nonetheless, it is clear that Eysenck is proposing that criminality is mediated, in part, by the inheritance of an underaroused nervous system, which in turn is mediated by genetically regulated androgen levels. The person who fits this biological pattern would be, of course, the extreme extrovert. But how does the extreme extrovert become the "antisocial personality"? The next link in Eysenck's argument draws on the hypothesized influences of the dimension of psychoticism on the expression of extreme extroversion.

Psychoticism and Criminality

Eysenck's initial formulation of the relationship between the main personality dimensions and criminality pictured the extreme extrovert as prone to hysterical disorders and to psychopathy or criminal behavior (Eysenck, 1964a, 1976). As the evidence mounted, it became clear that hysterical disorders are more likely to occur in the neurotic ambivert than in the neurotic extrovert (Eysenck & Eysenck, 1985, p. 312). More important, the criminal, long assumed to be an extreme extrovert and also high in neuroticism, appears with more recent evidence to fall into two different categories. The *primary psychopath* is the classic antisocial personality, who evidences little conscience, anxiety or guilt, poor judgment, and intense impulsivity. By contrast, the *secondary psychopath* may engage in antisocial behavior but is highly conflicted and anxious about his or her conduct.

Eysenck's most recent formulations argue that criminals are high scorers on all three dimensions of extroversion, neuroticism, and psychoticism (Eysenck & Eysenck, 1985, pp. 330ff.). The addition of measurements for psychoticism has altered the interpretation placed on extroversion in mediating criminality. Eysenck now argues that the impulsivity component formerly associated with the extroversion dimension has to be understood as more strongly correlated to the psychoticism dimension. Thus the criminal is one who scores highly on all three dimensions because:

- as an extreme extrovert, the criminal is underaroused, sensation-seeking, poorly conditionable, and lacking in the restraints of conscience that are normally acquired through conditioning; and

- as a high scorer in neuroticism, the criminal evidences moody, irrational, and intensely emotional behavior; and

- as a high scorer in psychoticism, the criminal will lack empathy for other people, appear egocentric and impulsive, acting with poor judgment to gratify his or her needs.

The factors that determine whether the criminal will be a primary or secondary psychopath are to be found in the relationship between psychoticism and neuroticism. Generally, the theory predicts that the primary psychopath is one in whom the degree of psychoticism is higher than neuroticism; conversely, the secondary (anxious or guilty) criminal is a person who scores higher on the neuroticism dimension than on the psychoticism dimension. But in both types, the person is an extreme underaroused extrovert. Figure 17.12 summarizes the main qualities associated with Eysenck's three main personality dimensions.

FIGURE 17.12   Eysenck's three main personality dimensions in descriptive terms.

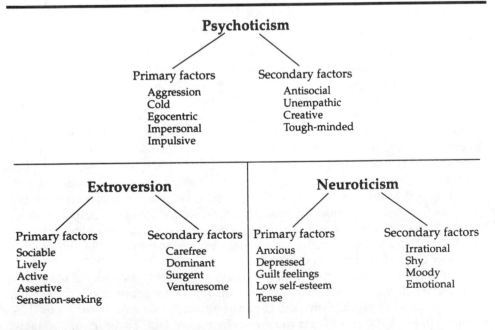

Psychoticism

Primary factors

Aggression
Cold
Egocentric
Impersonal
Impulsive

Secondary factors

Antisocial
Unempathic
Creative
Tough-minded

Extroversion

Primary factors

Sociable
Lively
Active
Assertive
Sensation-seeking

Secondary factors

Carefree
Dominant
Surgent
Venturesome

Neuroticism

Primary factors

Anxious
Depressed
Guilt feelings
Low self-esteem
Tense

Secondary factors

Irrational
Shy
Moody
Emotional

Based on Eysenck and Gudjonsson (1989), pp. 44–45.

Overview of the Psychoticism-Criminality Hypothesis

We can summarize the logic of Eysenck's hypotheses about psychoticism, arousal, and criminality in this way:

1. Inheritance of nervous system-associated hormonal regulators that establish chronic underarousal in the personality constitutes the predisposition to extreme extroversion and to antisocial behavior.
2. As the extreme underaroused extrovert matures socially, underarousal inhibits the acquisition of anxiety-based restraints, ethical behavior, and empathy, and it promotes sensation-seeking, resistance to pain, and aggressive action.
3. If the extreme extrovert also inherits a nervous system prone to neuroticism and high psychoticism, he or she is likely to develop criminal behavior. If psychoticism is higher than neuroticism, the orientation will be primary psychopathy or antisocial personality. On the other hand, if neuroticism is stronger, the orientation is likely to be more in the direction of secondary psychopathy and impulsivity.

GRAY'S REFORMULATION: IMPULSIVITY AND ANXIETY

Eysenck's formulation is based on the assumption that introversion-extroversion and stability-neuroticism are orthogonal (independent) dimensions. In principle, knowing that someone is introverted or extroverted tells us nothing about whether the person is prone to a specific psychological disorder.

Eysenckian Anomalies

To make that prediction accurately, we need information about the person's position on the second dimension of neuroticism or autonomic (anxiety) arousal. But, as we have seen, it has been shown (e.g., Gray, 1985) that the two dimensions are not independent. High levels of introversion are more closely associated with high levels of neuroticism than would be predicted from the assumption of two independent dimensions. Worse still, a subgroup of *neurotic extreme extroverts* score low on measures of neuroticism (anxiety) but high on measures of impulsivity. And this unusual combination (high extroversion and very low autonomic arousal) is associated with the acting-out disorders such as criminality, psychopathy, and conduct disorder, but not with the classic hysterias or somatoform disorders. On the whole, therefore, Eysenck's theoretical *neurotic extrovert* does not exhibit the attributes predicted by the theory. Put another way, the theory does not accurately predict the psychopathology of these exceptional extroverts.

One possibility is that the *neuroticism* (emotional arousal) dimension is not a good predictor of behavior when the levels of emotional arousal are at their lowest extreme, as they would be for psychopathic and criminal behavior. Another possibility is the lack of independence between extroversion-introversion and neuroticism-normality, mentioned previously. A third possibility is that the very concept of *neuroticism* as

Eysenck employs the term—as a virtual synonym for anxiety arousal—is not homogeneous. People who are high and low on this dimension do not differ just in amount of anxiety arousal, but also differ in some other significant ways—impulsivity, for one—that are relevant to predicting psychopathology.

Gray's Behavioral Inhibition and Approach Systems

Gray (1981, 1982, 1985) has suggested that maladaptive behavior of introverts and extroverts is better understood in terms of approach and avoidance dimensions. Some people have a highly sensitive *Behavioral Inhibition System* (*BIS*) which makes them sensitive to painful stimulation, hyper-expectant of punishment, and prone to rapid withdrawal. But others are dominated by a strong *Behavioral Approach System* (*BAS*), which makes them impulsively seek pleasure and reward while remaining relatively insensitive to potential punishment. Although the Gray model—and other biological models have been proposed—is not likely to be the final explanation of individual vulnerability to personality pathology, this formulation emphasizes an important and increasingly frequent conclusion about psychological disorder: The medium is arousal, the message is anxiety, and the name of the game is coping with helplessness (see, for example, Chapter 16 and the discussion of self-efficacy and anxiety; Amini, Thomas, Lanon, and Louie, 1996; Bandura, 1997; Cloninger, 1986).

Sensitivity to Reward and Punishment: Impulsivity and Anxiety

Gray's (1985) influential idea reconceptualizes how the limbic system and cortex of the brain function together as a kind of unified third biological system supplementing Eysenck's two systems of the "visceral brain" and ARAS-Cortex. Gray proposed that the septum and hippocampus, and more recently, the amygdala, along with parts of the frontal cortex constitute a *behavioral inhibition system* (BIS) that functions whenever the organism encounters one or more of three circumstances:

- novel stimuli violate current expectations
- a naturally threatening stimulus engages the organism's attention
- previous experience leads the organism to expect punishment

The BIS operates to arouse aversive states of fear that cause the organism to withdraw. Withdrawal, as Gray uses the term, is a kind of *inhibition* of action—slamming on the behavioral brakes—because particular responses provoke anxiety. Put another way, organisms (we can probably include people in this statement without doing violence to the formulation) differ in the sensitivity of their BIS: Some are constitutionally more prone to anxiety-inhibition and avoidance behavior than others (cf. Barlow, 1988, p. 46).

A second system proposed by Gray, the *behavioral approach system* (BAS), involves areas of the forebrain cortex, so-called "higher cognitive centers," and complements the BIS with its own sensitivity to signals of reward and safety. The two systems work interactively in this way: The BIS works with the higher centers in "checking mode" to determine what meaning a stimulus might have. If the organism's "checking" registers a threatening meaning, the BIS swings into "control" mode and prompts withdrawal; otherwise the BAS prompts approach, sometimes impulsively (Gray, 1985, p. 7). Together, the two systems regulate much of the organism's approach and avoidance behavior and can be interpreted as one way to understand the brain's construction of the experience of anxiety. Figure 17.13 shows Gray's BIS and BAS

FIGURE 17.13   Gray's behavioral inhibition (BIS) and behavioral approach systems (BAS) superimposed on Eysenck's dimensions.

The upper left quadrant represents the main agreement between Gray and Eysenck. Eysenck's highly anxious neurotic introvert and Gray's highly trait-anxious inhibition-sensitive person are virtual theoretical equivalents. But the remaining quadrants, especially the lower right quadrant, represent Gray's attempt to address the anomalous findings that don't agree with Eysenck's predictions. See text.

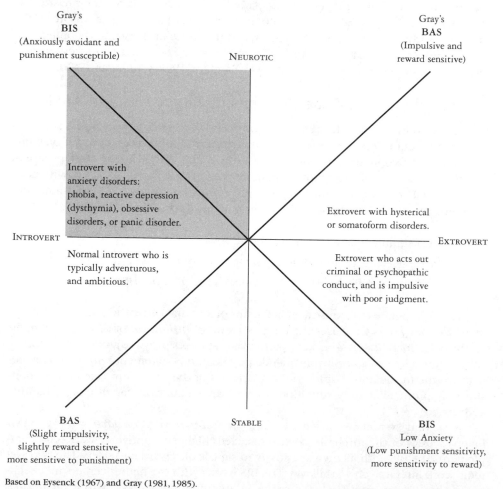

Gray's
BIS
(Anxiously avoidant and punishment susceptible)

NEUROTIC

Gray's
BAS
(Impulsive and reward sensitive)

Introvert with anxiety disorders: phobia, reactive depression (dysthymia), obsessive disorders, or panic disorder.

Extrovert with hysterical or somatoform disorders.

INTROVERT

EXTROVERT

Normal introvert who is typically adventurous, and ambitious.

Extrovert who acts out criminal or psychopathic conduct, and is impulsive with poor judgment.

BAS
(Slight impulsivity, slightly reward sensitive, more sensitive to punishment)

STABLE

BIS
Low Anxiety
(Low punishment sensitivity, more sensitivity to reward)

Based on Eysenck (1967) and Gray (1981, 1985).

dimensions superimposed on Eysenck's extroversion and neuroticism dimensions with illustrative descriptions of the associated psychopathologies.

Gray's Solution to the Eysenck Anomaly

Gray (1981) has suggested that the BIS/BAS dimension is one way out of the Eysenckian theoretical bind of *extreme neurotic extroverts* who are impulsive rather than anxious and inhibited. Gray assumes that the *behavioral inhibition system* (BIS) and the *behavioral approach system* (BAS) together constitute a third dimension that subdivides Eysenck's neuroticism dimension. A highly sensitive BIS marks the individual who is very alert to and anxious about anticipated punishment, whereas a very sensitive BAS characterizes the person who is relatively insensitive to worry about punishment and overly eager—even impulsively eager—to approach potential rewards.

Thus, an individual with *extreme BIS sensitivity* who is also *highly introverted* would be prone to psychological disorder characterized by high levels of anxiety: In essence, this person is Eysenck's *neurotic introvert.* Conversely, the individual with a *highly sensitive BAS* who is an *extreme extrovert* would be impulsive, attention seeking, pleasure seeking, and excitement prone: Eysenck's acting out *extroverted delinquent, criminal or anti-social personality.* With the BIS-BAS dimension in place, no assumptions of independence between introversion and neuroticism (anxiety) are necessary. Highly "neurotic" extroverts and introverts can be subdivided into those who exhibit anxiety symptoms (avoidance-prone) and those who display impulsivity (approach-prone). There are further implications of this theoretical reformulation, but we need not venture into that debate. Table 17.4 summarizes the links between Eysenck's and Gray's dimensions.

EVALUATING EYSENCK'S TYPOLOGY

On the face of it, Eysenck's hypothetico-deductive strategy for constructing his theory is the ideal scientific method. His conception of the three dimensions of neuroticism, introversion-extroversion, and psychoticism grew from empirical studies, was altered as more studies were done, and changed again when the research suggested new directions or disconfirmed his hypotheses. But the "theory" has some problems with its concepts that suggests a basic weakness operating in personality research. And ironically it is the same basic problem we saw when evaluating Freud at the beginning of this book. Despite the stereotypical image of "scientific" research as a kind of "truth," the fact is that research is interpretable. One person's "firm finding" is another's "dubious outcome."

Refutability of Eysenck's Model

Eysenck's model is, and was designed to be, eminently refutable. It is a research-based conception, or set of conceptions, and one of its prime goals is to provide predictions that may be tested in the laboratory. As various hypotheses were tested, Eysenck changed basic parts of the theory that were disconfirmed, strengthened those that

TABLE 17.4   Eysenck's Dimensions and Gray's Modifications

Eysenck's Dimensions	Stable Introverts	Stable Extroverts
ARAS and CNS Activation	High cortical activation	Low cortical activation
	Unstable Introverts	**Unstable Extroverts**
ANS, Limbic and Hypothalamic Arousal	High emotional arousal	High emotional arousal
Gray's Dimension	**BIS (Avoidance)**	**BAS (Approach)**
	Strong anticipation and avoidance of punishment	Strong approach to rewards. Insensitivity to punishment. Impulsivity.

Based on Eysenck (1967); Eysenck & Eysenck (1985); Gray (1964, 1981, 1985).

Features to Note
- The defining property of *introversion* for Eysenck is high cortical and ARAS arousal, so *all* introverts are listed as highly activated.
- The defining property of *neuroticism* is high ANS, limbic and hypothalamic arousal, so *all* dysfunctional personalities in Eysenck's model are listed as highly aroused. But, in fact, the unstable criminal extrovert probably has extremely low arousal and high impulsivity.
- Gray's "third dimension" of behavioral *approach and avoidance* (BAS/BIS) is intended to correct the flaws in Eysenck's model by proposing that the *unstable extrovert* type is both highly aroused and highly impulsive, thus accounting for the acting out associated with this personality style. Gray's *high BIS* type is essentially the same as Eysenck's highly neurotic introvert.

received support, and deduced new hypotheses that begin the cycle again. As he himself has pointed out:

> I have sometimes said, only half in jest, that my model of personality is the only one on the market that can claim to have been experimentally disconfirmed; this is a source of pride, not of regret. I think practically all the other models on the market are such that disconfirmation is not possible; they will remain popular for precisely this reason, but will also remain outside the pale of science. (Eysenck, 1982, p. 266)

As we saw, when the Hullian conditioning formulation could not account for the facts, Eysenck altered the model to a more physiological one that emphasizes cortical and subcortical arousal mechanisms. The problem at the present is that some basics in the current version are not as clean-cut as we would like them to be. It is not true that extroverts *always* condition more slowly than introverts, or that introverts *always* have higher sedation thresholds than extroverts, or that extreme high-P scorers are *always* psychotic. The model, in its strongest form, makes these predictions, but they do not hold under all conditions.

Eysenck has been in the position, in recent years, of "adjusting" the model, qualifying the exact conditions under which generalizations are true and when they are false (e.g., Eaves, Eysenck, & Martin, 1989; Eysenck & Gudjonsson, 1989). Eventually, if a theorist makes enough "adjustments" to bring the theory into line with all of the exceptions it must account for, it is no longer a theory. It is a collection of pieced-together, ad hoc explanations. In fairness to Eysenck, the model is complex and ranges from experimental psychology to genetics to neurophysiology to sociobiology to neurochemistry and back to social psychology. If we assume that one or two or even three uniform dimensions, and perhaps a handful of "laws" will adequately represent this vast intellectual territory, we are very much extreme extroverted, probably high-P, optimists.

Eysenck's Conception of Human Agency

Eysenck has argued, almost since the beginning of his work, for a biosocial conception of humans. He means by that label that behavior is caused by a complex interaction between inherited nervous system predispositions and social reality. But behavior is caused, not free to vary randomly. Choices a person makes are in some sense determined by the unique combination of inherited factors and personal history. A given choice may not be predictable by an outside observer, but, in principle, that choice is lawful and regulated by the sum total of biology and psychology that constitute a person.

Eysenck is not fond of vagueness, mysticism, or untestable assertions. Concepts such as active and passive agency would not spontaneously be used by him to described people. He regards himself as fundamentally a natural scientist (Eysenck & Eysenck, 1985). But if we fit Eysenck's model to our evaluation scheme, we have to place it at the passive end of the spectrum and infer from his work that people are shaped by the dual reality of inherited nervous system style and environmental experiences.

The Nomothetic Nature of Eysenck's Theory

Eysenck's theory is fundamentally a nomothetic model of personality. Study of the individual case is not part of Eysenck's interest or research methodology. It may be possible to apply some Eysenckian findings to a specific individual, but the vast bulk of the theory is derived from studying groups of people who are contrasted on the specific variables being studied.

> Modern personality theory, with its types and traits and abilities, is situated somewhere between idiographic psychology stressing *uniqueness* and experimental psychology stressing the *identity* (i.e., similarity) of human beings. What one must say, essentially, is that although human beings clearly do differ from each other, they differ along certain dimensions and their differences and similarities can therefore be quantified and measured. Measurements of traits and abilities lead us to certain *type* constructs, such as extraversion-introversion; this simply means that for certain purposes we can point to groups of people similar with respect to a given trait or ability and contrast these with groups of other people not sharing this trait or ability or showing its opposite. (Eysenck & Eysenck, 1985, p. 8)

A nomothetic theory such as this one has the advantage, as we have seen, of testability. The theory is unconcerned with subjective views of reality, and individual differences are of interest only insofar as they interact with the variables that one is trying to predict. This approach is a sound, conservative, and reasonable scientific strategy. It may, however, seem unsatisfying to clinical psychologists and others whose goal is to understand one person at a time.

SUMMARY

Eysenck's theory of personality may best be described as a hierarchical model having a minimum of three levels. At the first phenotype or observable level, personality types of introversion and extroversion are described in terms of measurable traits like sociability, shyness, impulsiveness, and activity. These traits are usually measured with paper-and-pencil instruments like the Maudsley Personality Inventory, the Eysenck Personality Inventory, or the Eysenck Personality Questionnaire.

At the second level of the hierarchy, performance on laboratory tasks such as motor movements, conditioning, and vigilance is used to define the dimensions of introversion and extroversion. Specific predictions for differential performance on a variety of these tasks are made on the basis of the hypothetical third level.

The third level is the fundamental, causal basis of the upper two divisions. Conceptualized as an excitation-inhibition balance (or ARAS arousal and inhibition of the cortex), this causal level may be classed as the genotypical basis of personality. As an inheritable dimension, excitation-inhibition (or ARAS functioning) may be thought of as the biological roots of personality. Figure 17.14 illustrates these levels of Eysenck's theory.

Eysenck's original factorial study of personality performance and physiological data derived from a large group of subjects demonstrated that two orthogonal (independent) dimensions could be used to describe their personalities. A dimension of

FIGURE 17.14   Three levels of Eysenck's theory.

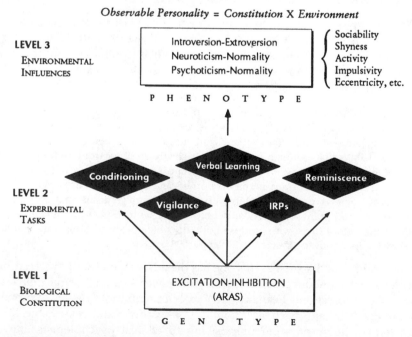

Based on Eysenck (1964a) and (1967).

introversion-extroversion and a dimension of normality-neuroticism were conceptualized as independent and continuous axes along which individuals could be arranged by degree. The typical extrovert may be described as one who likes people, is sociable, strongly attracted to novel and exciting stimuli, easygoing, and optimistic. He or she is fond of practical jokes and sometimes becomes aggressive and impulsive, unable to inhibit or control anger. The typical introvert, by contrast, may be characterized as shy, quiet, withdrawn, and somewhat detached from the social environment. He or she is a planner, always looking ahead to anticipate problems before they arise. He or she avoids overt and intense stimulation and excitement, keeping emotions under strict control. Generally pessimistic, the introvert behaves as if a well-ordered and quiet life were his or her chief desire (Eysenck & Eysenck, 1975b).

The individual who scores high in neuroticism may be characterized as emotionally reactive, anxious, moody, depressed. Sleep is disturbed, and he or she experiences chronic fatigue and assorted bodily pains. "His main characteristic is a constant preoccupation with things that might go wrong, and a strong emotional reaction of anxiety to these thoughts" (Eysenck & Eysenck, 1975b, p. 5).

Following Carl Jung's clinical insights that introverts succumb to dysthymic (psychasthenic or anxiety) disorders, and that extroverts succumb to hysterical neuroses, Eysenck was able to show that a long tradition stemming from Hippocrates and Galen through Pavlov and Hull had confirmed and refined Jung's hunches. Pavlov's conditioning investigations established the existence of excitation and inhibition as fundamental cortical processes underlying types of temperament.

Clark L. Hull's concepts of drive and habit, along with his notions of reactive and conditioned inhibition, provided Eysenck with key conceptual tools to begin devising a biological and causal account of the introversion-extroversion dimension. Introverts are individuals in whom the excitation-inhibition balance is tipped in the direction of excitation, giving them "weak" or sensitive nervous systems. Thus they condition more easily than extroverts, are more easily pained by excessive stimulation, and generally perform in a superior way on laboratory tasks requiring sustained attentiveness. Extroverts, by contrast, are individuals in whom the balance is tipped in the direction of greater inhibitory cortical functioning. For this reason, extroverts are said to have a "strong" nervous system not easily aroused by excessive stimulation, but one that is easily overcome with boredom by repetitious or monotonous tasks that rapidly build inhibition.

Eysenck has recently provided a biological translation and refinement of his excitation-inhibition theory. The ascending reticular activating system (ARAS) has been conceptualized as the basis of cortical arousal and inhibition. In this role, the ARAS is also the basis of introversion-extroversion. Introverts have more highly aroused ARAS functioning than extroverts. The dimension of neuroticism has been conceptualized as related to the functioning of the autonomic nervous system. Subcortical brain structures of the limbic system and the hypothalamus, known collectively as the "visceral brain" (VB), have been postulated by Eysenck to underlie the dimension of emotionality or neuroticism. Neurotics have a higher level of chronic VB activation than do stable or normal individuals.

In terms of socialization, Eysenck has postulated that introverts are more socialized (inhibited, ethical, anxious) than extroverts because of their greater ease of conditioning. Extroverts are less socialized and may be divided into two extreme groups. Some extroverts are characterized essentially by a trait of extreme sociability, and these individuals tend to resemble the normal personality on measures of neuroticism. On the other hand, some extroverts are characterized by a trait of extreme impulsiveness and by a lack of ethical and moral inhibitions. These individuals are generally described as criminal or psychopathic personalities.

An addition to Eysenck's personality dimensions is the continuum of "psychoticism," represented in some personalities as inheritable traits of social withdrawal, impulsivity, hostility, and a general quality of "peculiarity." The psychoticism dimension, furthermore, implies that neurotic, normal, and psychotic personalities are not categorically different entities; rather, both normals and neurotics may possess some *degree* of psychoticism without evidencing an overt psychosis, a proposition contrary to classical psychiatric diagnostic systems.

Gray has suggested that Eysenck's dimensions of extroversion and neuroticism can be fine-tuned by adding a dimension representing individual susceptibility to reward and punishment. Called the behavioral inhibition system (BIS) and behavioral approach system (BAS), these dimensions are conceptualized as brain-based systems that predict a person's impulsivity in the face of profoundly tempting rewards with little sensitivity to potential punishment or abrupt withdrawal from punishments with little regard for the possibility of enjoying reward. The behavior of the criminal or psychopathic extrovert who exhibits extreme low autonomic arousal is, perhaps, more precisely predicted by Gray's dimensions than by Eysenck's.

The advantage of Eysenck's theoretical strategy is that it allows for concrete predictions and tests of its validity. Furthermore, Eysenck's theory may eventually provide the basis for more rational and scientifically precise diagnosis and treatment of disordered behavior. The possibility of altering an individual's position on the introversion-extroversion dimension by means of depressant and stimulant drugs to alter disordered behaviors may soon be feasible.

Evaluation of Eysenck's theory shows it clearly to be a highly refutable, empirical, and scientific model of personality. Eysenck is fundamentally a biosocial theorist who believes behavior is caused by biological and psychological factors, so that human agency is essentially irrelevant. It follows from the stringently experimental approach that this theory is almost exclusively nomothetic.

For Further Reading

The development of Eysenck's continually more biological formulations may be gleaned from successive reading of three of his works: *The Scientific Study of Personality* (London: Routledge & Kegan Paul, 1952), which concerns his early descriptive measurements of introversion-extroversion; *The Dynamics of Anxiety and Hysteria* (London: Routledge & Kegan Paul, 1957), which presents his more causal inhibition theory; and *The Biological Basis of Personality* (Springfield, IL.: Charles C. Thomas, 1967), which presents the definitive statement of his cortical hypotheses of arousal. Joseph LeDoux's *The Emotional Brain* (New York: Simon and Schuster

[Touchstone], 1996) contains a very readable and comprehensive discussion of the limbic system and other brain structures involved in emotional arousal.

All four of the above-mentioned books are difficult reading. A more readable, though less comprehensive, overview of Eysenck's system is his *Crime and Personality* (London: Routledge & Kegan Paul, 1964). At a popular level of presentation, Eysenck's *Psychology Is About People* (New York: Library Press, 1972) not only provides a short account of his introversion-extroversion concepts but also surveys some of his wartime research on humor and aesthetic preferences. Another aspect of Eysenck's theory may be observed in *The Inequality of Man* (London: Temple Smith, 1973; also available from Robert Knapp, San Diego, CA), where Eysenck enters the current controversy surrounding the nature of IQ measurements. Eysenck's continued emphasis on genetic factors in personality reach their strongest expression in the sophisticated arguments of *The Structure and Measurement of Intelligence* (New York: Springer, 1979). In a similar vein, Eysenck and Eysenck's *Psychoticism as a Dimension of Personality* (New York: Crane, Russak, 1976) discusses the statistical and experimental evidence in support of a genetic model of this new personality dimension.

A three-volume collection of research papers connected to his theory was edited by Eysenck under the title *Readings in Extraversion-Intraversion* (London: Staples, 1970–1971). Eysenck's low opinion of psychoanalytic theory and method may be sampled from his *Uses and Abuses of Psychology* (Baltimore: Penguin, 1953) and from his essay "Psychoanalysis: Myth or science?" in S. Rachman (Ed.), *Critical Essays on Psychoanalysis* (New York: Pergamon, 1960).

Eysenck's position on behavior therapy for the neuroses is lucidly presented in *The Causes and Cures of Neurosis* (San Diego: Robert Knapp, 1965), which he coauthored with Stanley Rachman. Eysenck also edited a collection of research papers on the various forms of conditioning therapy, published as *Behavior Therapy and the Neuroses* (New York: Pergamon, 1960).

An interview with Eysenck, in which he discusses the implications of his work for psychotherapy and for unifying the whole of psychology, is contained in R. I. Evans's *The Making of Psychology* (New York: Knopf, 1976).

Background reading on Pavlov's changing conceptions of personality and neuroses is best begun with Pavlov's own *Conditioned Reflexes: An Investigation Into the Physiological Activity of the Cortex* (New York: Dover, 1927) and his *Lectures on Conditioned Reflexes* (New York: International Publishers, 1928). The wealth of historical information and the attempt to place Pavlov's ideas into contemporary perspective are well worth your attention to J. A. Gray's (Ed.) *Pavlov's Typology* (New York: Macmillan, 1964).

Eysenck's most recent complete statement of his theory is to be found in Hans Eysenck and son Michael Eysenck's *Personality and Individual Differences: A Natural Science Approach* (New York: Plenum Press, 1985). Eysenck's opinions about the possibility that personality style is related to physical diseases such as cancer and heart disease is well worth reading in his *Psychology Today* article "Health's character" (December, 1989, pp. 28–32, 34–35).

So, Which Theory Is Right?

To believe something is to believe that it is true; therefore a reasonable person believes each of his beliefs to be true; yet experience has taught him to expect that some of his beliefs, he knows not which, will turn out to be false. A reasonable person believes, in short, that each of his beliefs is true and that some of them are false. I, for one, had expected better of reasonable persons.

W. V. Quine, *Quiddities*

The heart has its reasons which reason does not understand.

Blaise Pascal, *Pensées*

. . . [I]ntellect molds desire only when desire desires to be molded. . . .

B. F. Skinner, from his notebooks at age 22, *Particulars of My Life*

About the Persistence of Untestable Theories

So many of the theories presented in this book, or major aspects of them, are not refutable that we are prompted to ask two questions:

1. *Is there any reasonable way to decide which theory is right?*
2. *If psychology is a science, why does it tolerate so many "unscientific" theories?*

The answer to the first question is another question: What do we want from a theory of human nature? And can we expect to get it?

The answer to the second question depends on how we define "science" and whether we are prepared to accept its findings.

All of the theories we have reviewed, from Freud to Eysenck, share some common elements. And all of the theories arrive at a small, but significant, group of human problems. Nearly all of the theorists share some common personality features and motives that guided their efforts to become eminent members of the mental health professions. Strong feelings of inferiority coupled with beliefs that they were unwanted children shaped the personal histories of the majority of theorists presented in this book.

IF THEY'RE SO UNTESTABLE, WHY DO THEY SURVIVE?

Time and again, it has been necessary to point out that a particular theory is simply untestable. With a minority of exceptions, such as the social cognitive theory of Bandura and the biological typology of Eysenck, most of the theories we have reviewed

- make no precise or testable predictions,
- generate few, if any, laboratory studies, and
- frequently lead to disputes of opinion rather than fact.

Someplace between the behaviorism of Bandura and the biology of Eysenck lies Freud's vision of humanity expressed in structural metaphors. And Freud's metaphors cloud the horizon even more. Even when a psychodynamic theory such as Freud's does generate research, there is little agreement about the adequacy or meaning of the findings. Is this any way to run a science?

Grand Theories and Classic Issues That Won't Go Away

If the purpose of a scientific theory of personality is summary and prediction, then most of the theories we have reviewed are not scientific. As history clearly demonstrates, we cannot assume from the scientific deficiencies of these theories that they will be abandoned or replaced by more scientific ones. Year after year, decade after decade, Freud's ideas continue to attract intellectuals from virtually every discipline, including psychology. I am almost persuaded that empirically minded psychologists would yell very loudly in protest at colleagues who adopt Jung's concepts for clinical practice, yet there is no shortage of Jungians. The same may be said of virtually every theory in this book: Somewhere, for some purpose, in the hands of some people, every major theorist's ideas survive and are used in some way relevant to psychology.

The issues these grand theories of human nature address are classic ones that have captured the attention of thinking people for more than 2,500 years of recorded history. Themes such as justice, truth, beauty, love, hate, and destiny have been written and thought about by philosophers, artists, and theologians well before psychology became involved with the human condition. Ideas such as these are not small. They represent core human concerns, essentials of existence, and we have a right to expect our intellectual tools, science included, to help in understanding them. These issues, concerned as they are with the *psychological meaning of human nature,* are rarely embraced by other subfields of psychology. The themes are classic and philosophical, and they generate grand theories. Personality theories are as close as psychology gets to classic questions. In a way, theories of personality are psychology's way of being psychological about psychology.

Big Potatoes, Small Potatoes

Scientific theories of human nature, rightly or wrongly, are sometimes perceived as dealing with irrelevant details rather than with the so-called big issues. When science is perceived to be irrelevant to the grand themes, thinkers turn elsewhere. Theorists such as Sigmund Freud, Abraham Maslow, Rollo May, and B. F. Skinner, to name just a few, are not satisfied with "small potatoes" on their plates. They go after the big potatoes even if they have to use imperfect implements to seize them. None of these thinkers was satisfied with piecemeal issues, such as neuronal thresholds (although Freud tried early on) or reinforcement schedules (although Skinner did invent the idea) or dominance behavior in monkeys (although Maslow began his career with this topic). All of these people turned their thoughts to the big potatoes, in one way or another: Freud tackled love and hate, life and death; May is still struggling with freedom, destiny, and beauty; and Maslow could not rest with self-actualization but had to explore truth, beauty, and the reality of peak experiences. Skinner turned his hand to the issues of societal harmony, the illusion of mind versus body, and the meaning of freedom. No small potatoes here.

None of this is surprising. Could you imagine any of the people we have studied spending their lives in pursuit of the perfect measurement of an eye-blink response? Or can you envision Skinner, Freud, Horney, Maslow, Fromm, Rogers, Allport, or White in hot pursuit of the variables that regulate color vision? Would these people really puzzle over the mysteries of rat behavior in a maze in the hope that someday the findings will have a bearing on our understanding of love, hate, destiny, or desire?

Eye-blink conditioning, color vision, and rat behavior are all important scientific topics that psychology has studied and continues to study. But they are small potatoes topics whose importance is revealed only when they are synthesized into a larger picture that reflects something about human beings *as persons.* Eysenck, for example, used eye-blink conditioning tellingly in discriminating between the introvert's and extrovert's behavior. But it is an important fact of human life that we are inherently more interested in one good life story, one good—idiographic—biography that "explains" one person's behavior than we are in a dozen nomothetic, empirical, predictive, quasi-mathematical "laws" of behavior. Nevitt Sanford had this suggestion:

> The biographical interview should be taught in high school and college, alongside of how to write a composition. If all graduate students in psychology were required to begin their work by doing such interviews and writing a case history, the whole face of psychology would be changed. (Sanford, 1985, p. 508)

In personality theory, we are dealing with thinkers who pride themselves on seeing the "big picture." They envision themselves as synthesizers, explorers, and creators of ideas. History shows that most of them were willing to forgo the benefits of scientific testing in favor of the pleasures of a good, big, compelling theory. And so, we must admit, are we.

Humans Do Not Live by Science Alone

There are some conclusions we can draw from this persistence of grand theories that cannot be tested. First, and most obvious, Popper's criterion of refutability is a stringent standard that makes powerful demands on theories, but it does not guarantee that psychologists and others will abide by it. Put a different way, perhaps it is true that we don't absolutely, positively *want* scientific theories of personality. *Scientific* theories of personality conduct business in terms of measurable, observable variables, and they generally are constructed piecemeal over long periods of research time. Such theories are not half as much fun nor half as interesting as one good Freudian metaphor. Freud's word pictures of the seething cauldron of fury known as the id and its battles against the ego are wonderfully interesting ways of talking about people as they pit reason against desire. It is more scientifically acceptable to discuss thresholds in the limbic system of the brain and its interaction with the brain's cortex and reticular system. Which of these languages, do you suppose, is likely to have the most native speakers?

WHAT WE GET FROM THEORIES OF PERSONALITY

The life histories of the theorists we have examined suggest that they share much. There is a fierce independence to be found among these thinkers, strong desires to excel and achieve greatness, and there is frequently, as Ellenberger (1970) has suggested, a personal crisis that is resolved with the creation of a "grand synthesis" that, in psychology, results in a theory of personality. If the classic theories are unscientific and if they have origins in personal issues, have they any value?

Personal Origins Speak to Personal Meanings

The answer is an unqualified yes. We continue to study these models of human nature because they contain wisdom of a special kind. They deal with the enduring themes and problems of human existence, and they provide a kind of road map for navigating these themes and problems. None of the theories has "truth" in any accepted meaning of that term; yet, all of them have sufficient truth for some purposes to satisfy important human needs. As George Kelly argued, we all need a sense that we can predict our lives and the people in them. Personality theories are ways of informally "predicting" what people will do. Put a better way, the grand theories tell us why people do what they do with sufficient everyday accuracy and sufficient attention to the big issues that we cannot imagine giving them up. These theories do not meet the standards of scientific acceptability, but then psychological science frequently does not meet our need to understand ourselves.

The personal crises faced by the theorists are not unique. As we have seen, themes of loneliness, depression, feelings of unwantedness, angry resentment toward authority figures, and strong desires to control their lives were main personality dimensions in the lives of the theorists. Accurate or inaccurate, the pictures that these thinkers painted touch on feelings, needs, and thoughts we have all experienced. It may take a hundred scientific psychologists working a hundred years to translate one page of their works into testable form so we can find out the degree of truth that lies therein. But I doubt that any of us will wait.

Common Elements in Theories of Personality

In the first chapter, we briefly saw that theories can be understood historically by momentarily backing away from the details of content and attending to how a theory portrays human agency. Buss (1978) argued that theories can be active-agent models or passive-agent models, and if you review Table 1.1, in Chapter 1, you can recapture the basic orientations of the main theories. Surprisingly, Buss's analysis indicates that psychoanalysis and behaviorism share much in common in their passive agent view, whereas social cognitive theory and humanism share some elements of an active agent view of people.

The Big Three: Psychoanalysis, Humanism, and Behaviorism

If we confine ourselves for a moment to the big three orientations in personality theory viewed historically, Buss's analysis reveals another interesting commonality among theories. The reason that Buss's analysis is so cogent in comparing the theories is that the theories lend themselves to an examination of the issue of human agency. And that in itself is an important discovery. All theories deal with the issue of human control over the world and its people. Active human agency means that the theory portrays the person as masterful, capable of having an effect on the world, and competent to detect that effect and be guided by it. Passive human agency means that the theory portrays people as shaped by effects over which they have little control. Feelings of powerlessness and incompetence are the result.

The Theme of Personal Mastery

Of the big three, classical psychoanalysis and radical behaviorism portray human control as weak in the face of reality. Freud's dictum that "reality made much of us" and his use of the metaphor of *Ananke* (destiny) reflect a fundamental theme in classical psychoanalysis: Human reason *should* take charge of inner and outer reality, but it is rarely as strong as human passion or human biology. Similarly, radical behaviorism depicts humans as almost completely determined by the sum total of their biology and environment, with very little room left for individual choice or the decisions of reason. In blunt terms, psychoanalysis and radical behaviorism picture humans as lacking control, lacking efficacy, lacking competence.

Humanism, by contrast, clearly paints the reverse picture. People are in charge of themselves and their world. Human intelligence, reason, or decision making is portrayed as an essential element of personal responsibility. It is true that this picture is based on an act of faith rather than hard evidence of any kind, but it is a picture of control that is in clear opposition to the psychoanalytic-behavioristic view.

In sum, the big three share a concern for how competent or masterful people are. They picture this issue differently, but personal competence is a common concern.

The Little Three: Ego Psychology, Existentialism, and Cognitive Behaviorism

The big three—radical behaviorism, psychoanalysis, and humanistic psychology—developed, as Buss (1978) has shown, in reaction to one another. Within the camps of each of the big three there have always been revisionist thinkers who sought to rectify mistakes or adjust concepts to be compatible with new evidence or old objections. Within psychoanalysis, Heinz Hartmann and Anna Freud led the ego psychologists to adjust the classical model to account more clearly for human intelligence, playfulness, decision, and creativity. Radical behaviorism had its synthesizers in Miller and Dollard and its innovator in Albert Bandura, who sought to reintroduce "mind" and "thinking" into scientific behaviorism. And humanism had its existential thinkers, such as Rollo May and R. D. Laing, who sought to bring some basic psychoanalytic ideas back into the model, making it clinically more relevant and philosophically less abstract. Each of the "little three" in some way "fixed" or "adjusted" one of the big three. Did the adjustments change anything?

Variations on the Theme of Personal Mastery

Ego psychology substantially changed the viewpoint of classical psychoanalysis on the issues of mastery and control. People such as Robert White and his concept of effectance motivation, Anna Freud with her notion of developmental lines of mastery, and Heinz Hartmann with his concept of ego autonomy and synthetic ego functioning placed extraordinary stress on human active mastery as a fundamental motive beyond the sexual and aggressive motives considered in classical psychoanalysis.

What Anna Freud, Heinz Hartmann, and Robert White did for classical analysis, Albert Bandura and his colleagues did for radical behaviorism. Bandura's conceptions of reciprocal determinism and active human agency place mastery motives at the core of human personality. For Bandura, people control their lives, detect external controls, react to them, and change the world they live in as they live. Mastery motivation ("efficacy" in Bandura's language) is now a central part of cognitive social learning theory. Neither Skinner nor Watson would recognize their behaviorism now. And Skinner doesn't want to.

Existentialism, as introduced into American personality psychology by Maslow, May, and Laing has always emphasized personal mastery and responsibility. These thinkers attempted to introduce into existential-humanism some of the insights of psychodynamic psychology without also incorporating its deterministic viewpoint. Rollo May (1958a,b) perhaps more than any other American theorist in this tradition, has written extensively about issues of mastery and control. His concepts of destiny, the daimonic, and will emphasize active human mastery and responsibility—all from a philosophical vantage point.

So it would seem that contemporary versions of the big three have shifted more in the direction of active human agency viewpoints. Perhaps more important, all theories of personality concentrate, with different vocabularies, on issues of personal mastery and control. If Buss (1978) is correct, we can expect at some point that there will be a "reaction" of one or more of these intellectual traditions to one or more of the others or to its own past. And, perhaps, we can anticipate a reversion, for a time, to more deterministic viewpoints.

SO, WHO BECOMES A PERSONALITY THEORIST?

To be a personality theorist is to be a keen observer of your own personality and discontent with what you find there. The prevailing pattern is found in someone who feels insecure, sometimes to the point of inferiority. Frequently, but not universally, the personality theorist-to-be felt unwanted by one or both parents.

These less than cosmic conclusions emerge when we summarize the theorists' personal sources with their resultant ideas. Table 18.1 provides this summary for 19 theorists classed in six categories:

Classical Psychoanalysis

Ego Psychology

Object Relations Theory

Neo-Freudian/Interpersonal

The Behaviorisms

Humanism/Existentialism

The parallels between theorists' personal sources and their resulting ideas in Table 18.1 are based on analyses of their work and lives in the several editions of *Beneath the Mask*. The table entries, therefore, are restricted to those 19 theorists for whom we currently have sufficiently detailed and reliable biographical information to analyze the personal origins of their intellectual creations. To understand fully the entries for a particular theorist, the personal sources section of that theorist's chapter should be consulted and reviewed.

TABLE 18.1   Nineteen Theorists' Personal Sources and Resultant Ideas

CLASSICAL PSYCHOANALYSIS

Theorists	Personal Sources	Resultant Ideas
SIGMUND FREUD	*Intense attachment to mother.* Disappointment in father. *Insecurity, inferiority.* Sensitivity to missing family members. Strivings for personal greatness.	• Oedipus complex: child-parent sexual and aggressive attachments and conflicts. • Early (1895 "Project") attempt to make psychoanalysis "scientific" with a neurological foundation. • Hunger-love, love-hate, sex-aggression, life-death drive models. • Superego as internalized parental standards, ideals, and prohibitions.

EGO PSYCHOLOGY

Theorist	Personal Sources	Resultant Ideas
ERIK ERIKSON	*Insecurity, identity confusion.* *Feelings of unwantedness* *(father abandoned family)* Inferiority feelings relative to anti-Semitism in childhood and adolescence. Feelings of "not belonging."	• Ego identity. • Psychosocial moratoria. • Ego strengths through life cycle. • Crucial importance of cultural issues in ego development: ritualizations.
ANNA FREUD	*Insecurity, inferiority, unwantedness.* Fantasies of being beaten. Feeling responsible for father. Role reversal: parenting her parent. Special attachment to and protectiveness of father. Sigmund's "Antigone."	• Developmental lines that emphasize mastery and coping in children's ego development. • Use of psychoanalytic "surrogate mothering" with war orphans. • Development of methods for child analysis. • Synthesis and explanation of ego defenses, including altruistic surrender.
M. MAHLER	*Inferiority, unwantedness, gender* *dissatisfaction (father raised her* *as a son).* Conflict with rejecting mother. Special attachment to father. Pressure from father to be totally self-sufficient.	• Importance of mother-child relationship. • Separation-individuation. • Importance of autonomy.
R. W. WHITE	*Insecurity, inferiority relative to older* *brother; acute shyness and social* *isolation.* Acute need for independence. Strong family religious values including emphasis on self-reliance and *independence.*	• Efficacy (mastery) motivation. • Needs for autonomy. • Ego pathology as failures in early parenting relationships. • Psychosexual stages reconceptualized as phases of social mastery learning.

TABLE 18.1   *(continued)*

OBJECT RELATIONS THEORY

Theorist	Personal Sources	Resultant Ideas
MELANIE KLEIN	*Unwantedness:* Told by brother and mother than she had been an "accidental" and unwanted child. *Inferiority* relative to her brother.	• Maternal centrism. • View of infants as essentially aggressive and destructive. • Feminized Freud's "male" psychoanalysis with concepts of the centrality of the breast.
D. W. WINNICOTT	*Fundamentally secure, happy childhood. Reared by multiple mothers.* Absent fathering; insensitive fathering and teasing, possibly about Winnicott's maleness. Depressed mothering.	• Emphasis on positive adaptation to facilitating environment: "No such thing as a baby." • Strong maternal identification and emphasis on role of "good enough mothering." • Little attention to role of father in development. • Concept of "False Self" as caretaker for the depressed mother who is "not good enough."

NEO-FREUDIAN/INTERPERSONAL

Theorist	Personal Sources	Resultant Ideas
ALFRED ADLER	*Insecurity, inferiority.* Childhood illness and resentment of physical vulnerability. Fear of death.	• Superiority strivings. • Organ inferiority. • *Gemeinschaftsgefühl* (fellow-feeling) • Safeguarding mechanisms.
KAREN HORNEY	*Compliant, feeling unwanted, inferior feeling, obsessive doubting of self.* Chronic depression; suicidal thoughts. Resentment of and competition with mother; competition with brother as father's favored child. Submissive to father's erratic authority.	• Basic anxiety: Lonely and helpless. • Basic hostility: Anger toward authority figures. • Tyranny of the "Shoulds." • Coping strategies: expansive, resigned, and compliant.
C. G. JUNG	*Massive feelings of insecurity, lack of personal worth.* Feelings of self-splitting: Belief in twin personalities inside self. Admitted need to avoid blame and responsibility. Feelings of derealization and depersonalization. Probable episodes of hallucinating. Compensatory grandiosity.	• Introversion-extroversion, and anima-animus as fundamental human dualisms. • Self-actualization: healing properties of the whole self. • "Synchronicity" as a noncausal explanation of reality. • Collective unconscious. • Enantiodromia: the tension of opposites.
H. S. SULLIVAN	*Insecurity, inferiority, loneliness.* Childhood alienation, feelings of unwanted-ness. Feelings of abandonment by mother. Family devaluation of father. Conflicted homosexuality.	• Interpersonal definition of personality. • Specialized treatment of schizophrenic male patients. • Interpersonal personifications.

TABLE 18.1   *(continued)*

THE BEHAVIORISMS

Theorist	Personal Sources	Resultant Ideas
J. B. WATSON	*Angry with father and mother.* *Father was unpredictable and mostly absent during childhood.* *Rebelliousness to authority.* *Strong needs to be in control of self.* *Insecure and ambivalent about success.* Strong needs to be successful, and strong fears of failure to the point of a personal "breakdown" in graduate school. Resentment of control by others, and their demands. Early rejection of mother's aspirations for him to have a career in the clergy. Belligerent and impulsive, pretentious, ambitious, and arrogant. Need to deny the importance of emotions as causal in behavior. Lifelong effort to escape poverty of his youth.	• Radical behaviorism: Mind and feelings are illusions. • Radical materialism, determinism, and reductionism. • Bitter criticism of psychoanalysis as mythology. • Goal: prediction and rational control of behavior.
B. F. SKINNER	*Rebelliousness to authority, discovery of family myth that he was a "difficult" birth who caused mother great hardship: unwantedness.* *Strong need to be in control of self.* Resentment of control, demands. Angry. Disappointment with father's perceived passivity; resentment of mother's pretentiousness and tendency to pressure her husband and sons. Insecurity during adolescence. Need to control and externalize own emotions, displacing them to the outside world.	• Semiradical behaviorism: Mind and feelings are irrelevant to understanding psychological causes. • Goal: prediction and rational control of behavior. • Semiradical determinism. • Aspiration to construct an ideal society in which control over the environment helps people want to act in their own interests. • Motivation externalized to environmental contingencies of reinforcement.
HANS J. EYSENCK	*Unwantedness:* Divorced parents had little time for or interest in their son. Described parents as "mean," ungenerous, and uncaring. *Inferiority* and self-consciousness about being German born, especially during WW II. Confrontational attitude to established authority in psychiatry/psychology. Self-described angry, dangerous "rebel."	• Intensely critical of and rebellious to authority figures in psychiatry and the status quo in psychology. • Entire theory aimed at disconfirming established conventions in diagnosis, psychotherapy and personality. • Harshly critical of psychodynamic theories. • Strong belief in material/biological basis of personality. • Reliance on stringent empiricism. • Extrovert as impulsive, sometimes acting out "rebel."

TABLE 18.1   (*continued*)

HUMANISM/EXISTENTIALISM

Theorist	Personal Sources	Resultant Ideas
GORDON ALLPORT	*Feelings of insecurity and inferiority . relative to brother, Floyd.* Struggle for recognition of his own uniqueness relative to brother. Compensatory strivings for superiority via intellectual achievement. Belief in control over one's life, ability to transcend one's history.	• Emphasis on individuality, uniqueness. • Idiographic versus nomothetic. • Proprium or self. • Functional autonomy: transcending personal history or distress.
R. D. LAING	*Feeling rejected, unwanted, and manipulated by mother.* Enforced obedience to "crazy" family rules. Resentment of parental chaos.	• Divided self: public and private. • Focus on experience, personal meaning. • Focus on interpersonal relationships and perceptions of relationships.
A. H. MASLOW	*Insecure, inferior-feeling, lacking self-confidence in the extreme.* *Rejecting mother, psychologically absent father.* Pursuit of heroes (parental substitutes?).	• Dominance-feeling in monkeys. • Studies of dominant women. • "Good-specimen" strategy. • Self-actualized people.
ROLLO MAY	*Loneliness, feelings of helplessness, isolation, massive feelings of unwantedness and rejection leading to a substantial depressive (possibly suicidal) episode.* Early exposure to discordant family life. Rebellious during adolescence. Adult confrontation with death and helplessness (tuberculosis).	• Introduction of European existential concepts to American psychology (e.g., *Dasein, Mitwelt, Eigenwelt, Umwelt*). • Psychological versions of philosophical concepts: e.g., Death, Will, Destiny, Daimonic, Freedom. • Merger of selected psychoanalytic ideas (i.e., neurotic anxiety, the unconscious) with existential concepts.
CARL ROGERS	*Insecurity, inferiority.* Resentful of parental authority. Feelings of loneliness, isolation. Rebellious to family religious and disciplinary demands as defense against feeling superior to others. Strong needs to counter dependency feelings with autonomy strivings.	• Phenomenal self; everyone has his/her own reality. • Empathic understanding of others without directive interventions. • Acceptance of children unconditionally to enable healthy development. • Fully functioning person: autonomous and spontaneous.

Creative Illness or Inferiority Loves Company?

Ellenberger's concept of "creative illness," discussed in Chapter 1, asserts that theorists resolve a personal crisis by creating a theory that universalizes their distress. No doubt Ellenberger's thesis has validity for some theorists. Carl Jung comes readily to mind in this context. Certainly Sigmund Freud, Horney, Mahler, and Sullivan universalized their personal distress in theoretical constructs that purport to describe all people. It is arguable whether these theorists were creatively *ill,* as we discussed in the first chapter. Nevertheless, it is by now abundantly clear that a theorist's personal experiences, conflicts, and idiosyncratic interpretations of social reality become that theorist's theory. Call it a "resolution of creative illness" or call it "reliance on personal sources." Either description communicates that personality theories are uniquely the harvest of the personalities that create them.

The summaries in Table 18.1 show something else. By their own account, 18 of the 19 theorists (94.7%) felt inferior during childhood (Sigmund and Anna Freud, Erikson, Mahler, White, Adler, Horney, Jung, Sullivan, Watson, Skinner, Klein, Eysenck, Allport, Laing, Maslow, May, and Rogers). It seems astounding that almost 95 percent of the personality theorists for whom we have detailed biographical information experienced significant feelings of inferiority.

Or is it so astounding? Is it not the case, as Alfred Adler proposed, that we all experience feelings of inferiority that we strive to overcome? Part of the human condition, Adler thought, was an inherent striving from minus to plus, from inferiority to superiority, from incompetence to competence. What we would most like to know is whether Adler is correct. What is the baseline rate of feeling inferior? If, as Adler claimed, most people feel inferior in *some* way, then the 95 percent of our sample of people who are personality theorists *and* who feel inferior is not so remarkable. Unfortunately, we do not have appropriate comparison groups of personality theorists or other psychologists that would help us establish a baseline.

What we need is a group of personality theorists who demonstrably *lack* these motives. Without them for comparison, we have no way of knowing what the *causal* status of inferiority feelings might be for personality theorists who feel inferior. We could make do with a group of psychologists for whom we have detailed biographical information and whose lifetime careers were spent in areas of psychology other than personality theorizing. But in the absence of even this more "neutral" baseline group, it is difficult to assess what the meaning might be of any association between professional achievement in psychology and feelings of inferiority for those in whom such an association exists. Consequently, a controlled test of any hypothesis is, for now, out of reach.

The Full Recipe for a Personality Theorist: Healing Unwantedness

But there is another way to look at it. If it were true that most of us feel inferior in some personally significant way, then why doesn't everyone create a theory of personality? Put yet another way, what is it about inferiority and the urge to understand it in self that somehow combined and motivated *this* group of people to create theories of human nature? Perhaps what is really remarkable is that they chose to strive against inferiority by becoming well-known intellectuals in the professions of *psychiatry* and *psychology.* After all, these people pursued a career and sought recognition in the mental health professions, not in art, philosophy, anthropology, or theology.

Definitive answers to these questions are not possible with the data at hand. But some educated speculation is possible. Table 18.1 contains an additional clue. Alongside nearly universal feelings of inferiority, a significant number of the theorists had the belief that they were unwanted children. A strong case for the presence of significant feelings of unwantedness can be made for:

- Erik Erikson
- Hans Eysenck
- Anna Freud
- Melanie Klein
- R. D. Laing
- Margaret Mahler
- Abraham Maslow
- Rollo May
- B. F. Skinner
- Harry Stack Sullivan

A weaker, but reasonably credible, case for the presence of feelings of unwantedness can be made for:

- Sigmund Freud
- Karen Horney
- Carl G. Jung
- John B. Watson

For four of the remaining theorists in Table 18.1—Adler, Allport, Rogers, and White—insufficient biographical information is available to decide the issue. They do not, therefore, make an adequate comparison group because we simply do not know whether they felt unwanted. The only theorist about whom we can be certain that unwantedness was not an issue during childhood is D. W. Winnicott. Yet, even with the happiest and most secure childhood of all the theorists, Winnicott was not entirely immune from what he himself called the "normal difficulties of life." Specifically, although Winnicott certainly felt wanted by his family, he felt less certain about *who* wanted him. A detached and distracted father and an apparently depressed mother led Winnicott to his classic formulations of the "good enough mother" and the caretaking role of the False Self. Thus Winnicott—and he would enjoy this immensely—is the paradoxical exception who proves the rule.

Borrowing from Karen Horney's insightful descriptions, we have a partial answer to the question of why the majority of these people chose psychiatry/psychology as a career and strove so hard for eminence and recognition in the creation of their theories. The answer is to be found in the *combination* of feelings of inferiority, unwantedness, hurt, and anger. In Horney's terms, a basic hostility emerged toward others—frequently toward the parents—for making them feel insecure, inferior, and unwanted. Specifically, these theorists achieved some degree of insight into their own feelings of distress and were angry enough to want to take control of those feelings and disprove any judgments of inferiority.

The disciplines that deal directly with "abnormal" feelings, thoughts, and behavior—psychology and psychiatry—must have had compelling attraction for such people. Personality theorists are not simply people who are dissatisfied with their own personalities for perceived inferiority. They are hurt people who have become angry and humiliated at being rejected or unwanted. They are active rather than passive people who want to heal themselves. They are proselytizers who seek to impress their colleagues in the mental health professions with their discovery that their personal pain is human pain. And they are creative intellectuals who demand answers from their science and art of the mind. The creation of a personal identity as psychologist or psychiatrist is most effective in this process of self-healing when that identity also produces publicly acclaimed achievement. And what better way to reach it than for the psychologist/psychiatrist to create and publish an influential theory of human nature? With a few strokes on well-primed canvas, personality theorists banish unwantedness to the shadow of accomplishment.

Our hypothesis comes to this: The recipe for a personality theorist is self-perceived inferiority combined with feelings of unwantedness or rejection, seasoned with dashes of anger and hurt at being made to feel "abnormal," stirred vigorously by a probing intelligence prone to self-examination, and molded by strong urges toward self-healing. All well and good for a hypothesis without firm empirical support. But would you want your daughter or son to marry one?

A FINAL EVALUATION OF THE THEORIES

The three dimensions that we have used to compare and evaluate each theory lead to some surprising conclusions when we view theories of personality from a wider perspective than the one-theory-at-a-time approach permits. Refutability, human agency, and the idiographic-nomothetic distinction are important in themselves, but they are also important for what they tell us about the persistence of these theories in human discourse.

Refutability

When Popper proposed the criterion of refutability, he had in mind the apparent universal compatibility of Adler's and Freud's theory with any human behavior he could think of. Compared to Einstein's relativity theory, it seemed to Popper that these psychological theories were too good to be true. They could explain everything—a source of pride to Adler—but a red flag to Popper.

Psychological theories can be refutable, and some are. Theories of personality, with few exceptions, are not. Some of us don't want them to be. The not so obvious secret is this: Theories of personality are theories of human nature. Understood in that way, it is easy to see that refutability is not likely to apply to any one of the "grand" theories in its entirety. One or another construct drawn from these theories may lend itself to refutation. But for every diligent empirical psychologist who makes the attempt to translate a grand idea into an empirical statement, there are a half dozen intellectuals who find something else of value in these ideas. For them a refutable theory of personality is like trying to watch a sunset with a microscope.

What can we learn from this resistance to scientific truth finding? Refutability is a good thing. It is even a necessary thing if psychology is to progress. But it is not a sufficient thing. We want more of our theories of human nature than mere refutability can provide. And, fortunately, we have no scarcity of unrefutable theories from which to choose.

Human Agency

The classic, or grand, theories, as we have seen, are a mixed lot when it comes to depicting human agency. Psychoanalysis and behaviorism fall on the side of having reality shape us. Humanism sees us as shaping reality. And social cognitive learning theory has the best of both worlds: We shape and are shaped by the changes we introduce into reality. The important point is that every theory, for better or worse, has something to say about personal mastery of the world and about our perception of that mastery. George Kelly makes personal control a central feature of his "man the scientist." And Sigmund Freud gives reality center stage instead. Alfred Adler focused on avoiding inferiority; Maslow strove for perfection. Has no one ever marvelled at the fact that there are so many theories that address mastery in its many forms because creating and using such theories is one way to master the reality of ourselves?

Idiographic Versus Nomothetic Focus

It has been pointed out that a *truly unique* "anything" would be hard to comprehend because we would have seen nothing like it before. In that sense, every person shares something with others. But the theories of personality that have survived decades of criticism and research tend to be those that apply themselves to the individual. A genuinely nomothetic theory does not exist in psychology—yet. Bandura and his colleagues are on the way toward one, but we must wait to see what can be done with cognitive social learning theory to unify psychology.

The paradox of the idiographic-nomothetic distinction is this: Every theorist aimed to create a theory that would apply to *all* humans. Who would create a theory that applies to one person, at one moment in time, in one geographic place? For example, what kind of a theorist creates a theory to explain one Bronx resident, or one highlander in Scotland, or one aborigine tribesman? The *aspiration* (literally, the hope) of every theorist is to explain all highlanders, all aborigines, and most Bronx residents.[1] But when we read a theory, our tendency is to apply it to one individual as a personal test: *Does this idea apply to me?*

---

[1] Not even the most ambitious theorist would attempt to explain *all* Bronx residents. Ever.

Even the theorists, whose aspirations are to be nomothetic, nevertheless worked from individual cases—sometimes from their own case—and then sought to generalize their findings. Although in principle the idiographic-nomothetic distinction is a sound way to characterize and compare theories, we need to be idiographic in our application of this distinction. Each theory is a case unto itself. And the grand theories, such as Freud's, Jung's, Adler's, and Skinner's, work best as art and psychology and science when we think of them idiographically: They are the creations of one person trying to find some common ground between self and others.

SUMMARY

If so many theories of personality are not refutable, why do they persist? Several answers were suggested, among them:

- Empirical research is always open to interpretation, so even when a theory is tested and refuted, some people do not accept the refutation.

- Some theorists deal with substantial issues that have enduring value in the history of humanity, and we are not very patient in waiting for "scientific" ways to understand these issues.

- Most theorists pride themselves on addressing "big potatoes" issues rather than petty but more empirically manageable concerns. And most people, including psychologists, can empathize with these concerns more readily than they can with discrete scientific variables.

Using Buss's historical analysis of passive versus active human agency, it becomes apparent that the issue of personal mastery, interpreted differently by different schools of thought, underlies all classic theories of personality. The big three—psychoanalysis, radical behaviorism, and humanism—have survived as the adjustments of the "little three" models of ego psychology, cognitive behaviorism, and existential humanism. In each case, a more active, more personally competent image of people has been introduced into the main concepts of their respective parent models.

If Buss's analysis is correct, we can expect shifts in these models as they react to each other and to their own historical developments. Each theory addresses the issue of competence or mastery in its own way, and the seeming universality of this issue raises an interesting question: Is the construction, use, and persistence of "grand" theories of personality a way we have of feeling in control of self by explaining ourselves to ourselves, not scientifically, but compellingly?

And nearly all of the theorists share some common personality features and motives that guided their efforts to become eminent members of the mental health professions. Strong feelings of inferiority coupled with beliefs that they were unwanted children shaped the personal histories of the majority of theorists presented in this book. Angry at being made to feel unwanted and "abnormal," many of the theorists constructed theories of human nature that pictured personal pain as human pain—and achieved the salvation of professional recognition in doing so.

FOR FURTHER READING

Henri Ellenberger's *The Discovery of the Unconscious* (New York: Basic Books, 1970) contains a good discussion of the personal sources of theories and expounds the author's view of "creative illness" as the source of many psychological theories. Buss's "The Structure of Psychological Revolutions" (*Journal of the History of the Behavioral Sciences*, 1978, **14,** 57–64) is worth reading for the insight it provides into the reactivity of schools of thought to each other and the importance of human agency in psychology. Along these same lines, Bandura's "Human Agency in Social Cognitive Theory" (*American Psychologist,* 1989, **44,** 9, 1175–1184) is a thoughtful analysis of human agency in psychological theory and a rationale for cognitive social learning theory. Finally, Nevitt Sanford's "What Have We Learned About Personality?" in Sigmund Koch and David Leary (Eds.), *A Century of Psychology as a Science* (New York: McGraw-Hill, 1985) is a wonderful critique of personality psychology and its various blind alleys.

Acknowledgments

Addison Wesley Longman: Excerpts from D. Winnicott, *Thinking about Children*, © 1996 by the Winnicott Trust. Reprinted by permission of Addison Wesley Longman.

Addison Wesley Longman: Excerpts from D. Winnicott, *Babies and Their Mothers*, © 1987 by the Winnicott Trust. Reprinted by permission of Addison Wesley Longman.

Addison Wesley Longman: Excerpts from D. Winnicott, *The Child, the Family, and the Outside World*, © 1964, 1957 The Estate of D.W. Winnicott. Reprinted by permission of Addison Wesley Longman.

Alfred A. Knopf: Excerpts from *Particulars of My Life* by B.F. Skinner. Copyright © 1976. Reprinted by permission of Alfred A. Knopf, Inc.

Alfred A. Knopf: Excerpts from *A Matter of Consequences* by B.F. Skinner. Copyright © 1983. Reprinted by permission of Alfred A. Knopf, Inc.

Alfred A. Knopf: Exerpts from *About Behaviorism* by B.F. Skinner. Copyright © 1974 by B.F. Skinner. Reprinted by permission of Alfred A. Knopf, Inc.

Allport: Excerpts from *Social Psychology* by Floyd H. Allport, copyright © 1924. Reprinted by permission of Floyd Allport.

Analytic Press: Extracts from *The Memoirs of Margaret S. Mahler*, compiled and edited by Paul E. Stepansky (New York: The Free Press, 1988) reprinted by permission of Paul E. Stephansky.

Archives of the History of American Psychology: Excerpts from Robert Sollod and Robert White, "Robert W. White and the Origins of the Concept of Competence: An Interview," *The Sollod Papers*, © 1980. Reprinted by permission.

Basic Books: Excerpts from *The Origins of Psychoanalysis: Letters to Wilheim Fliess, Drafts and Notes, 1897-1902*, edited by M. Bonaparte, A. Freud, E. Kris. Copyright © 1954 by Basic Books, Inc. Reprinted by permission.

Basic Books: Excerpts from *The Life and Work of Sigmund Freud, Volume 1*, by Ernest Jones, M.D. Copyright © 1953 by Ernest Jones and Basic Books, Inc. Reprinted by permission.

Basic Books: Excerpts from *Three Essays on the Theory of Sexuality* by Sigmund Freud, translated and newly edited by James Strachey. Copyright © 1962 by Sigmund Freud Copyrights Ltd. and Basic Books, Inc. Reprinted by permission.

Basic Books: Excerpts from *Studies on Hysteria* by Joseph Breuer and Sigmund Freud, translated and edited by James Strachey, published in the United States by Basic Books, Inc., by arrangement with The Hogarth Press. Reprinted by permission.

Basic Books: Excerpts from *The Interpretation of Dreams* by Sigmund Freud, translated and edited by James Strachey, published in the United States by Basic Books, Inc., by arrangement with George Allen & Unwin Ltd. and The Hogarth Press. Reprinted by permission.

Basic Books: Excerpts from "Mourning and Melancholia" (Volume IV), "On Beginning the Treatment" (Volume II), and "Further Remarks on the Defence Neuro-Psychoses" (Volume I), in *Collected Papers* by Sigmund Freud, authorized translation under the supervision of Joan Riviere, published by Basic Books, Inc., by arrangement with The Hogarth Press and The Institute of Psycho-Analysis, London. Reprinted by permission.

Basic Books: Excerpts from *The Individual Psychology of Alfred Adler: A Systematic Presentation in Selections from His Writings*, edited by H. Ansbacher and R. Ansbacher, copyright © 1956. Reprinted by permission.

Basic Books: Excerpts from *The Child's Construction of Reality* by Jean Piaget, translated by M. Cook. Copyright © 1954, 1971. Reprinted by permission.

Beacon Press: Excerpts from *The Person in Psychology: Selected Essays* by Gordon Allport, copyright © 1968. Reprinted by permission.

Brill Estate: Excerpts from *The Basic Writings of Sigmund Freud*, translated and edited by Dr. A.A. Brill. Copyright © 1938 by Random House, Inc. Copyright renewed 1965 by Gioia Bernheim and Edmund R. Brill. Reprinted by permission.

Charles C. Thomas Publisher: Excerpts and figures from *The Biological Basis of Personality* by Hans Eysenck. Copyright © 1967. Reprinted courtesy of Charles C. Thomas Publisher, Springfield, IL.

Clinical Psychology Publishing Company: Excerpts from Atwood and Tomkins, "On the Subjectivity of Personality Theory" in *Journal of the History of the Behavioral Sciences*, Vol. 12. Copyright 1976 Clinical Psychology Publishing Co., Inc., Brandon, VT. Reprinted by permission.

Doubleday: Excerpts from *Karen Horney: Gentle Rebel of Psychoanalysis* by J.L. Rubins. Copyright © 1978 by Jack L. Rubins. Used by permission of Doubleday, a division of Bantam Doubleday Dell Publishing Group, Inc.

Estate of Gordon Allport: Excerpts from *Pattern and Growth in Personality* by Gordon W. Allport. Copyright © 1961. Reprinted by permission of Robert B. Allport.

Eysenck: Excerpt from Dimensions of Personality by Hans Eysenck, copyright © 1947 Routledge Kegan Paul, London. Reprinted by permission of the author.

Free Press: Excerpts from Roger Money-Kyrle (ed.) *The Writings of Melanie Klein* by Melanie Klein, copyright © 1961, 1975.

Harcourt Brace: Excerpts from *Personality: A Psychological Interpretation* by Gordon W. Allport, copyright 1937 by Holt, Rinehart and Winston, Inc. and renewed 1965 by Grodon W. Allport, reprinted by permission of the publisher.

HarperCollins: Excerpts from *Field Theory in Social Science* by Kurt Lewin. Copyright © 1951 by Harper & Row, Publishers Inc. Reprinted by permission of the publisher.

HarperCollins: Excerpts from *The Psychological Birth of the Human Infant* by Margaret S. Mahler. Copyright © 1975 by Margaret S. Mahler. Reprinted by permission of HarperCollins Publishers, Inc.

HarperCollins: Excerpts from *To Have or To Be?* by Erich Fromm. Copyright © 1976 by Harper & Row, Publishers Inc. Reprinted by permission of the publisher.

Harvard University Press: Excerpts from Sigmund Freud, *A Phylogenetic Fantasy: An Overview of the Transference Neurosis*, 1915d from Volume 14, 1987, *The Standard Editions of the Complete Psychological Works of Sigmund Freud*. Reprinted by permission.

Harvard University Press: Excerpts from C. Winnicott, R. Shepherd, and M. Davis (eds.)*Psychoanalytic Explorations*, by D.W. Winnicott, © 1989, and excerpts from *Winnicott*, by A. Phillips, © 1988. Reprinted by permission.

Henry Holt: Excerpts from *The Anatomy of Human Destructiveness* by Erich Fromm, copyright © 1973.

Henry Holt: Excerpts from *Escape from Freedom* by Erich Fromm, copyright © 1941.

Henry Holt: Four lines from poem "Desert Places" by Robert Frost, from *The Poetry of Robert Frost*, edited by Edward Connery Lathem. Copyright 1936 by Robert Frost. Copyright © 1964 by Lesley Frost Bellantine. Copyright © 1969 by Holt, Rinehart and Winston.

Houghton Mifflin: Excerpts from *Counseling and Psychotherapy* by Carl R. Rogers, copyright © 1942; *Client-Centered Therapy* by Carl R. Rogers, copyright © 1951; and *On Becoming a Person* by Carl R. Rogers, copyright © 1961. Reprinted by permission.

Houghton Mifflin: Excerpts from *Crime and Personality* by Hans Eysenck, copyright © 1965. Reprinted by permission.

International Universities Press: Excerpts reprinted from *The Writings of Anna Freud*, Volumes 1, 2, and 4; "Ego and Reality in Psychoanalytic Theory" by Robert White, in *Psychological Issues*, Monograph #11, 1963; *On Human Symbiosis and the Vicissitudes of Individuation* by Margaret S. Mahler; *The Analysis of the Self* by Heinz Kohut; and *The Restoration of the Self* by Heinz Kohut, published with permission of International Universities Press.

International Universities Press: Excerpts reprinted from *The Maturational Processes and the Facilitating Environment, Studies in the Theory of Emotional Development* by D.W. Winnicott, published with permission of International Universities Press.

Irvington Publishers: Excerpts from "Autobiography" in *A History of Psychology in Autobiography* by Gordon Allport. Copyright © 1967.

John Wiley & Sons: Chapter "Learnable Drives and Rewards" in S.S. Stevens (ed.), *Handbook of Experimental Psychology*, copyright © 1951. Reprinted by permission.

John Wiley & Sons: Excerpts from Kurt Lewin, "Behavior and Development As a Function of the Total Situation," in Leonard Carmichael (ed.) *Manual of Child Psychology*, copyright © 1946. Reprinted by permission.

John Wiley & Sons: Excerpts from George A. Kelly, *Clinical Psychology and Personality*, edited by Brenden Maher, copyright © 1969. Reprinted by permission.

John Wiley & Sons: Excerpts and figures from Lewin and Miller, Personality and the Behavior Disorders, 2 Volume Set, edited by Hunt, copyright © 1944, 1972, 1984. Reprinted by permission of John Wiley & Sons, Inc.

McGraw-Hill: Excerpts from *Personality and Psychotherapy* by Dollard and Miller. Copyright © 1935. Used with permission of McGraw-Hill Book Company.

McGraw-Hill: Excerpts from *Psychology: A Study of a Science* by Koch and Miller, Volume II. Used with permission of McGraw-Hill Book Company.

McGraw-Hill: Excerpts from *A Dynamic Theory of Personality* by Kurt Lewin. Copyright © 1935. Used with permission of McGraw-Hill Book Company.

McGraw-Hill: Excerpts from *Principles of Topological Psychology* by Kurt Lewin. Copyright © 1936. Used with permission of McGraw-Hill Book Company.

New Yorker: Cartoon "I think it expresses me very much" — Abraham Maslow. Copyright © 1960 by Saul Steinberg. From the book *The Labyrinth*, Harper & Row Publishers, Inc. Originally published in The New Yorker Magazine. Reprinted by permission.

Open Court Publishing: Excerpts from *Psychology Is about People* by Hans Eysenck. Copyright © 1972. Reprinted by permission.

Pantheon Books: Excerpts from *Memories, Dreams, Reflections* by C.G. Jung, recorded and edited by Aniela Jaffe and translated by Richard and Clara Winston. Copyright © 1962, 1963 by Random House, Inc. Reprinted by permission of Pantheon Books, a division of Random House, Inc.

Pantheon Books: Excerpts from *Analytical Psychology: Its Theory and Practice* by C.G. Jung. Copyright © 1968 by Heirs of C.G. Jung. Reprinted by permission of Pantheon Books, a division of Random House, Inc.

Pantheon Books: Excerpts from *The Divided Self* by R.D. Laing. Copyright © 1966. Reprinted by permission.

Penguin: Excerpts from *The Facts of Life: An Essay in Feeling, Facts, and Fantasy* by R.D. Laing. Copyright © 1976 Allen Lane. Reprinted by permission.

Penguin: Excerpts from *The Politics of Experience* by R.D. Laing. Copyright © 1967. Reprinted by permission.

Penguin: Excerpts from *The Farther Reaches of Human Nature* by Abraham H. Maslow. Copyright © 1971 by

Bertha G. Maslow. Used by permission of Viking Penguin, a division of Penguin USA.

Prentice Hall: Excerpt from Social Foundations of Thought and Action by Albert Bandura. Copyright © 1986. Reprinted by permission.

Princeton University Press: Excerpts from *The Collected Works of C.G. Jung*, edited by G. Adler, M. Fordham, H. Read, and W. McGuire, translated by R.F.C. Hull. Bollingen Series XX, Vol. 8, *The Structure and Dynamics of the Psyche* (copyright © 1960 by Bollingen Foundation and © 1969 by Princeton University Press): Vol. 9i, *The Archetypes and the Collective Unconscious* (copyright © 1959 and 1969 by Bollingen Foundation), reprinted by permission of Princeton University Press.

Princeton University Press: Excerpts from *The Freud/Jung Letters: The Correspondence between Sigmund Freud and C.G. Jung*, Bollingen Series, XCIV, 1974. Reprinted by permission.

Psychoanalytic Quarterly: Excerpts and figure from *The Psychoanalytic Quarterly*, 1937, Volume 6. Reprinted by permission.

Psychology Today: Interview excerpt conducted by M.H. Hall with Abraham Maslow reprinted with permission from *Psychology Today* magazine. Copyright © 1968 Ziff Davis Publishing Co.

Random House: Excerpts from *The Voice of Experience* by R.D. Laing. Copyright © 1982 by R.D. Laing. Reprinted by permission of Pantheon Books, a division of Random House, Inc.

Random House: Excerpts from *Knots* by R.D. Laing. Copyright © 1970 by the R.D. Laing Trust. Reprinted by permission of Pantheon Books, a division of Random House, Inc.

Routledge: Excerpts from *Crime and Personality* by Hans Eysenck, copyright © 1964. Canadian rights reprinted by permission of Routledge & Kegan Paul Ltd.

Sanford Greenburger Associates: Excerpts from *What Life Should Mean to You* by Alfred Adler, copyright © 1931. Reprinted by permission.

Simon & Schuster: Excerpts from *Beyond the Chains of Illusion* by Erich Fromm. Copyright © 1962. Reprinted by permission.

Simon & Schuster: Excerpts from *Science and Human Behavior* by B.F. Skinner. Copyright © 1953. Reprinted by permission.

Taylor & Francis: Excerpts from *Through Paediatrics to Psycho-Analysis: Collected Papers* by D.W. Winnicott. Copyright © 1992 Brunner Mazel, Inc. Reprinted by permission of Taylor & Francis Publishing.

W.W. Norton: Excerpts from *Toys and Reasons* by Erik Erikson, copyright © 1977 by W.W. Norton & Company, Inc. Reprinted by permission.

W.W. Norton: Excerpts from *Conceptions of Modern Psychiatry* by Harry S. Sullivan, copyright © 1953, 1947, 1945, 1940 by The William Alanson White Psychiatric Foundation. Reprinted by permission of W.W. Norton & Company, Inc.

W.W. Norton: Excerpts from *Clinical Studies in Psychiatry* by Harry S. Sullivan, copyright © 1956 by The William Alanson White Psychiatric Foundation. Reprinted by permission of W.W. Norton & Company, Inc.

W.W. Norton: Excerpts from *Schizophrenia As a Human Process* by Harry S. Sullivan, copyright © 1962 by The William Alanson White Psychiatric Foundation. Reprinted by permission of W.W. Norton & Company, Inc.

W.W. Norton: Excerpts from *Interpersonal Theory of Personality* by Harry S. Sullivan, copyright © 1953. Reprinted by permission of W.W. Norton & Company, Inc.

W.W. Norton: Excerpts from *Personal Psychopathology* by Harry S. Sullivan, copyright © 1972. Reprinted by permission of W.W. Norton & Company, Inc.

W.W. Norton: Excerpts from *Neurosis and Human Growth* by Karen Horney, copyright © 1950. Reprinted by permission of W.W. Norton & Company, Inc.

W.W. Norton: Excerpts from *The Psychology of Personal Constructs* by George Kelly, copyright © 1955. Reprinted by permission of W.W. Norton & Company, Inc.

W.W. Norton: Excerpts from *Introductory Lectures on Psychoanalysis* by Sigmund Freud, edited by James Strachey, in *The Standard Edition of the Complete Psychological Works of Sigmund Freud*, Vol. 22, copyright © 1933. Reprinted by permission of W.W. Norton & Company, Inc.

W.W. Norton: Excerpts from *Beyond the Pleasure Principle* by Sigmund Freud, copyright © 1920, edited by James Strachey © 1961. Reprinted by permission of W.W. Norton & Company, Inc.

W.W. Norton: Excerpts from *Introductory Lectures on Psychoanalysis* by Sigmund Freud, edited by James Strachey, in *The Standard Edition of the Complete Psychological Works of Sigmund Freud*, copyright © 1916 1966. Reprinted by permission of W.W. Norton & Company, Inc.

W.W. Norton: Excerpts from *Home Is Where We Start From: Essays by a Psychoanalyst* by D.W. Winnicott. Copyright © 1986 by the Estate of D.W. Winnicott. Reprinted by permission of W.W. Norton & Company, Inc.

W.W. Norton: Excerpt from poem "Take for Example This" by e.e. cummings. Reprinted by permission of W.W. Norton & Company, Inc.

White: Excerpts from "Competence and the Psychosexual Stages of Development" by Robert White, (1960) in *Perspectives on Personality*, edited by Maddi, copyright © 1971.

Reprinted by permission of the author.

Photo Credits

Bibliography

Abramson, L. Y., Seligman, M. E. P., & Teasdale, J. (1978). Learned help-lessness in humans: Critique and reformulation. *Journal of Abnormal Psychology, 87,* 32–48.

Adler, A. (1907). The study of organ inferiority and its psychical compensation. In H. L. Ansbacher & R. R. Ansbacher (Eds.), *The individual psychology of Alfred Adler.* New York: Harper, 1956.

———. (1908). The aggression drive in life and neurosis. In H. L. Ansbacher & R. R. Ansbacher (Eds.), *The individual psychology of Alfred Adler.* New York: Harper, 1956.

———. (1910). The psychology of hermaphroditism in life and in neurosis. In H. L. Ansbacher & R. R. Ansbacher (Eds.), *The individual psychology of Alfred Adler.* New York: Harper, 1956.

———. (1912). The neurotic character. In H. L. Ansbacher & R. R. Ansbacher (Eds.), *The individual psychology of Alfred Adler.* New York: Harper, 1956.

———. (1913a). Individual-psychological treatment of neurosis. In Alfred Adler, *The practice and theory of individual psychology.* Totowa, NJ: Littlefield-Adams, 1959.

———. (1913b). Individual-psychological treatment of neurosis. In H. L. Ansbacher & R. R. Ansbacher (Eds.), *The individual psychology of Alfred Adler.* New York: Harper, 1956.

———. (1913c). The function of neurotic symptoms. In H. L. Ansbacher & R. R. Ansbacher (Eds.), *The individual psychology of Alfred Adler.* New York: Harper, 1956.

———. (1927). *Understanding human nature.* Greenwich, CT: Fawcett.

———. (1929a). *The science of living.* New York: Doubleday, 1969.

———. (1929b). *Problems of neurosis.* Philip Mairet (Ed.). New York: Harper, 1929.

———. (1930a). *The problem child.* New York: Putnam, 1963.

———. (1930b). *The science of living.* London: Allen & Unwin, 1930.

———. (1930c). *The education of children.* Chicago: Henry Regnery, 1970.

———. (1931). *What life should mean to you.* New York: Putnam.

———. (1932). The structure of neurosis. In H. L. Ansbacher & R. R. Ansbacher (Eds.), *Superiority and social interest: A collection of later writings.* New York: Viking Compass, 1973.

———. (1933). The meaning of life. In H. L. Ansbacher & R. R. Ansbacher (Eds.), *The individual psychology of Alfred Adler.* New York: Harper, 1956.

———. (1935). The fundamental views of individual psychology. In H. L. Ansbacher & R. R. Ansbacher (Eds.), *The individual psychology of Alfred Adler.* New York: Harper, 1956.

———. (1956). *The individual psychology of Alfred Adler: A systematic presentation in selections from his writings.* H. L. Ansbacher & R. R. Ansbacher (Eds.). New York: Harper.

———. (1959). *The practice and theory of individual psychology.* Totowa, N.J.: Littlefield-Adams.

———. (1964). *Social interest: A challenge to mankind.* New York: Putnam.

———. (1973). *Superiority and social interest: A collection of later writings.* H. L. Ansbacher & R. R. Ansbacher (Eds.). New York: Viking Compass.

Allport, Floyd. (1924). *Social psychology.* Boston: Houghton Mifflin.

Allport, G. (1937). *Personality: A psychological interpretation.* New York: Henry Holt.

———. (1942). *The use of personal documents in psychological science.* New York: Social Science Research Council Bulletin (No. 49).

———. (Ed.). (1946). Letters from Jenny (published anonymously in this edition). *Journal of Abnormal and Social Psychology, 41,* 315–350 and 449–480.

———. (1950). *The individual and his religion.* New York: Macmillan.

———. (1955). *Becoming: basic considerations for a psychology of personality.* New Haven: Yale University Press.

———. (1960). *Personality and social encounter: Selected essays.* Boston: Beacon Press.

———. (1961). *Pattern and growth in personality.* New York: Holt, Rinehart and Winston.

———. (1964). The fruits of eclecticism: Bitter or sweet? In G. Allport, *The person in psychology.* Boston: Beacon Press, 1968 (paper originally published in *Acta Psychological,* 1964, *23,* 27–44).

———. (Ed.). (1965). *Letters from Jenny.* New York: Harcourt, Brace & World.

———. (1966). Traits revisited. In G. Allport, *The person in psychology.* Boston: Beacon Press, 1968 (paper originally published in *American Psychologist,* 1966, *21,* 1–10).

———. (1967). Autobiography. In E. G. Boring & G. Lindzey (Eds.), *A history of psychology in autobiography,* Vol. 5. New York: Appleton.

———. (1963). *The person in psychology: Selected essays.* Boston: Beacon Press.

Allport, G., & H. S. Odbert. (1936). Trait names: A psycho-lexical study. *Psychological Monographs, 47,* (211), 1–171.

Alsopp, J. F., & Eysenck, H. J. (1975). Extraversion, neuroticism and verbal reasoning ability as determinants of paired associate recall. *British Journal of Psychology, 66,* 15–24.

———. (1974). Personality as a determinant of paired associate learning. *Perceptual and Motor Skills, 39,* 315–324.

Amacher, P. (1965). *Freud's neurological education and its influence on psychoanalytic theory. Psychological issues,* Monograph no. 16. New York: International Universities Press.

Amini, F., Thomas, L., Lannon, R., & Louie, A. (1996). Affect, attachment, memory: Contributions toward psychobiologic integration. *Psychiatry, 59,* [online] start page 213. *Available: http://www.proquest.umi.com.*

Angyal, A. (1941). *Foundations for a science of personality.* New York: Viking.

———. (1965). *Neurosis and treatment: A holistic theory.* New York: Viking.

Ansbacher, H. L., & Ansbacher, R. R. (1956). *The individual psychology of Alfred Adler: A systematic presentation in selections from his writings.* New York: Harper.

Ansbacher, H. L. & Ansbacher, R. R. (Eds.). (1973). *Superiority and social interest: A collection of Alfred Adler's later writings.* New York: Viking.

Andreasen, N. C. (1984). *The Broken brain: The biological revolution in psychiatry.* New York: Harper and Row.

Andreasen, N., & Munich, R. L. (1995). Introduction to Schizophrenia and other psychotic disorders. In G. O. Gabbard (Ed.), *Treatment of psychiatric disorders* (2nd ed., Vol. 1, pp. 943–946). Washington, DC: American Psychiatric Press.

APA. (1980). *Diagnostic and statistical manual of mental disorders [DSM-III]* (3rd ed.) Washington, D.C.: The American Psychiatric Association, 1980.

———. (1987). *Diagnostic and statistical manual of mental disorders [DSM-III-R]* (3rd ed., revised). Washington, D.C.: The American Psychiatric Association, 1987.

———. (1993). *DMS-IV draft criteria* (3/1/93). Washington, D.C., 1993.

Appignanesi, L., & Forrester, J. (1992). *Freud's women.* New York: Basic Books.

Aronson, E. (1969). The theory of cognitive dissonance: A current perspective. In L. Berkowitz (Ed.), *Advances in experimental social psychology,* Vol. 4. New York: Academic Press.

Asch, S. E. (1946). Forming impressions of personality. *Journal of Abnormal and Social Psychology, 41,* 258–290.

Atkinson, J. W. (1964). *An introduction to motivation.* New York: Van Nostrand.

Atwood, G. E., & Stolorow, R. D. (1977a). The life and work of Wilhelm Reich: A case study of the subjectivity of personality theory. *The Psychoanalytic Review, 64,* 5–20.

————. (1977b). Metapsychology, reification and the representational world of C. G. Jung. *International Review of Psychoanalysis, 4,* 197–214.

Atwood, G. E., & Tomkins, S. (1976). On the subjectivity of personality theory. *Journal of the History of the Behavioral Sciences, 12,* 166–177.

Bakan, P. (1959). Extraversion-intraversion and improvement in an auditory vigilance task. In H. J. Eysenck (Ed.), *Readings in extraversion-intraversion,* vol. 3: *Bearings on basic psychological processes.* London: Staples Press, 1971 (paper originally published in *British Journal of Psychology,* 1959, *50,* 325–332).

Balay, J. & Shevrin, H. (1988). The subliminal psychodynamic activation method. *American Psychologist, 43*(3), 161–174.

Balmary, M. (1979). *Psychoanalyzing psychoanalysis: Freud and the hidden fault of the father.* Baltimore: Johns Hopkins Press.

Bandura, A. (1961). Psychotherapy as a learning process. *Psychological Bulletin, 58,* 143–159.

Bandura, A. (1964). The stormy decade: Fact or fiction? In D. Rogers (Ed.), *Issues in adolescent psychology.* New York: Appleton, 1972 (paper originally published in *Psychology in the Schools,* 1964, *1,* 224–231).

————. (1965a). Influence of models' reinforcement contingencies on the acquisition of imitative responses. In A. Bandura (Ed.), *Psychological modeling: conflicting theories.* Chicago: Aldine-Atherton, 1971 (paper originally published in *Journal of Personality and Social Psychology,* 1965, *1,* 589–595).

————. (1965b). Behavioral modifications through modeling procedures. In L. Krasner & L. Ullman (Eds.), *Research in behavior modification.* New York: Holt, Rinehart and Winston.

————. (1967). Behavioral psychotherapy. *Scientific American,* March.

————. (1969). *Principles of behavior modification.* New York: Holt, Rinehart and Winston.

————. (1971a). Analysis of modeling processes. In A. Bandura (Ed.), *Psychological modeling: Conflicting theories.* Chicago: Aldine-Atherton.

————. (1971b). Psychotherapy based upon modeling principles. In E. Bergin & S. L. Garfield (Eds.), *Handbook of psychotherapy research* (pp. 653–708). New York: Wiley.

————. (1971c). *Social learning theory.* Morristown, NJ: General Learning Press.

————. (1973). *Aggression: A social learning analysis.* Englewood Cliffs, NJ: Prentice-Hall.

————. (1974). Behavior theory and the models of man. *American Psychologist, 29,* 859–869.

————. (1976). Conversation with Richard I. Evans. In R. I. Evans (Ed.), *The making of psychology.* New York: Knopf.

————. (1977a). Self-efficacy: Toward a unifying theory of behavioral change. *Psychological Review, 84,* 191–215.

————. (1977b). *Social learning theory.* Englewood Cliffs, NJ: Prentice-Hall.

————. (1978a). The self-system in reciprocal determinism. *American Psychologist, 33,* 344–358.

————. (1978b). "Self-reinforcement: Theoretical and methodological considerations." In Cycil M. Franks & G. Terrence Williams (Eds.), *Annual Review of Behavior Therapy,* Vol. 5.

————. (1981). In search of pure unidirectional determinants. *Behavior Therapy, 12,* 30–40.

————. (1982). Self-efficacy mechanism in human agency. *American Psychologist, 37,* 122–147.

————. (1986). *Social foundations of thought and action.* Englewood Cliffs, NJ: Prentice-Hall.

————. (1989). Human agency in social cognitive theory. *American Psychologist, 44,* 9, 1175–1184.

Bandura, A. (Ed.). (1995). *Self-efficacy in changing societies.* New York: Oxford University Press.

Bandura, A. (1997). *Self-efficacy: The exercise of control.* New York: Freeman.

Bandura, A., Adams, N. E., & Beyer, J. (1977). Cognitive processes mediating behavioral change. *Journal of Personality and Social Psychology, 35,* 125–139.

Bandura, A., Blanchard, E. B., & Ritter, B. (1969). The relative efficacy of desensitization and modeling approaches for inducing behavioral, affective, and attitudinal changes. *Journal of Personality and Social Psychology, 13,* 173–199.

Bandura, A., & Kupers, C. G. (1964). Transmission of patterns of self-reinforcement through modeling. *Journal of Abnormal and Social Psychology, 69,* 1–9.

Bandura, A., Ross, D., & Ross, S. A. (1963a). Imitation of film-mediated aggressive models. *Journal of Abnormal and Social Psychology, 66,* 3–11.

————. (1963b). A comparative test of the status-envy, social power, and secondary reinforcement theories of identificatory learning. *Journal of Abnormal and Social Psychology, 67,* 527–534.

Bandura, A., & Schunk, D. H. (1981). Cultivating competence, self-efficacy, and intrinsic interest through proximal self-motivation. *Journal of Personality and Social Psychology, 41,* 586–598.

Bandura, A., & Walters, R. H. (1959). *Adolescent aggression.* New York: Ronald Press.

————. (1963). *Social learning and personality development.* New York: Holt, Rinehart and Winston.

Bannister, D., & Fransella, F. (1971). *Inquiring man. The theory of personality constructs.* New York: Penguin Books.

Barnes, M. & Berke, J. (1971). *Two accounts of a journey through madness.* New York: Ballantine.

Barrett, W. (1958). *Irrational man: A study in existential philosophy.* New York: Doubleday Anchor.

Basch, M. F. (1975). Perception, consciousness and Freud's "project". In *The Annual of Psychoanalysis,* Vol. 3. New York: International Universities Press, 3–19.

Bateson, G. (1969). Double bind, 1969. In Gregory Bateson, *Steps to an ecology of the mind.* New York: Ballantine, 1972 (paper originally delivered at Symposium on the Double Bind, American Psychological Association, 1969).

Bateson, G., Jackson, D. D., Haley, J., & Weakland, J. (1956). Toward a theory of schizophrenia. In Gregory Batson, *Steps to an ecology of the mind.* New York: Ballantine, 1972 (Paper originally published in *Behavioral Science, 1,* 251–264).

Becker, H. K. (1963). Carl Koller and cocaine. *Psychoanalytic Quarterly, 32,* 309–373.

Bellak, Leopold, Hurvich, M., & Gediman, H. (1973). *Ego functions in schizophrenics, neurotics and normals.* New York: Wiley.

Berkowitz, L. (1969). The frustration-aggression hypothesis revisited. In L. Berkowitz (ed.), *Roots of aggression: A re-examination of the frustration-aggression hypothesis.* New York: Atherton.

Berlyne, D. E. (1968). Behavior theory as personality theory. In E. F. Borgatta & W. A. Lambert (Eds.), *Handbook of personality theory and research.* Chicago: Rand McNally.

Berman, M. (1975). Review of life history and the historical moment by Erik Erikson. In *New York Times Book Review,* March 30.

Bernstein, A. (1976). Freud and Oedipus: A new look at the Oedipus complex in the light of Freud's life. *The Psychoanalytic Review, 63,* 393–407.

Bertocci, P. A. (1950). Critique of Gordon W. Allport's theory of motivation. *Psychological Review, 47,* 501–532.

Bettelheim, B. (1967). *The empty fortress: Infantile autism and the birth of the self.* New York: Free Press.

Binswanger, L. (1958). The existential analysis school of thought. In Rollo May et al. (Eds.), *Existence: A new dimension in psychiatry and psychology.* New York: Basic Books.

Black, A. H. (1958). The extinction of avoidance responses under curare. *Journal of Comparative and Psychological Psychology, 51,* 519–524.

Blanck, G. & Blanck, R. (1974). *Ego psychology: Theory and practice.* New York: Columbia University Press.

Blos, Peter. (1962). *On adolescence: A psychoanalytic interpretation.* New York: Free Press.

————. (1970). *The young adolescent: Clinical studies.* New York: Free Press.

Bottome, Phyllis. (1957). *Alfred Adler: A portrait from life.* New York: Vanguard.

Bower, G. H., & Miller, N. (1960). Effects of amount of reward on strength of approach in an approach-avoidance conflict. *Journal of Comparative and Physiological Psychology, 53,* 59-62.

Breger, L., & McGaugh, J. L. (1965). Critique and reformulation of "Learning-Theory" approaches to psychotherapy and neurosis. *Psychological Bulletin, 63,* 338-358.

Breland, K., & M. Breland. (1961). The misbehavior of organisms. *American Psychologist, 16,* 681-684.

Breland-Bailey, M., & Bailey, R. E. (1993). "Misbehavior": A case history. *American Psychologist, 48,* 1157-1158.

Breuer, J., & Freud, S. (1893-1895). *Studies on hysteria,* Vol. II of *the standard edition of the complete psychological works of Sigmund Freud.* London: Hogarth Press, 1955.

———. (1893). On the psychical mechanism of hysterical phenomena: A preliminary communication. In J. Breuer & S. Freud, *Studies on hysteria,* Vol. II of *the standard edition of the complete psychological works of Sigmund Freud.* James Strachey (Ed.). London: Hogarth Press, 1955.

Brewster-Smith, M. (1971). Allport, Murray and Lewin on personality: Notes on a confrontation. *Journal of the History of the Behavioral Sciences, 7,* 353-362.

Broadhurst, P. L. (1959). The interaction of task difficulty and motivation: The Yerkes-Dodson law revived. *Acta Psychologica, 16,* 321-338.

Brown, Roger. (1965). *Social psychology.* New York: Free Press.

Brown, T. A., Martin, M. & Barlow, D. H. (1995). Diagnostic comorbidity in panic disorder: Effect on treatment outcome and course of comorbid diagnoses following treatment. *Journal of Consulting and Clinical Psychology, 63,* 408-418.

Bruner, J. S., Shapiro, D., & Tagiuri, R. (1958). The meaning of traits in isolation and in combination. In R. Tagiuri & L. Petrullo (Eds.), *Person perception and interpersonal behavior.* Stanford, CA: Stanford University Press.

Buckley, K. W. (1989). *Mechanical man: John Broadus Watson and the beginnings of behaviorism.* New York: Guilford.

Buckley, P. (1986). Editor's introduction. In P. Buckley (Ed.), *Essential papers on object relations.* New York: New York University Press.

Buhler, C. (1971). Basic theoretical concepts of humanistic psychology. *American Psychologist, 26,* 378-386.

Burnham, J. C. (1994). John B. Watson: Interviewee, professional figure, symbol. In J. T. Todd & Morris, E. K. (Eds.), *Modern perspectives on John B. Watson and classical behaviorism.* Westport, CT: Greenwood Press.

Buss, A. R. (1978). The structure of psychological revolutions. *Journal of the History of the Behavioral Sciences, 14,* 57-64.

Butler, R. A., & Harlow, H. F. (1957). Exploratory and related behavior: A new trend in animal research. *Journal of General Psychology, 57,* 257-264.

Campbell, D. T. (1969). Prospective: artifact and control. In R. Rosenthal & R. Rosnow (Eds.), *Artifact in behavioral research.* New York: Academic Press.

Caplan, P. J. (1979). Erikson's concept of inner-space: A data-based reevaluation. *American Journal of Orthopsychiatry, 49,* 100-108.

Carlson, R. (1971). Where is the person in personality research? *Psychological Bulletin, 75,* 203-219.

Carson, R. C. (1996). Aristotle, Galileo, and the *DSM* taxonomy: The case of schizophrenia. *Journal of Consulting and Clinical Psychology, 64,* 1133-1139.

Casteneda, C. (1968). *The teachings of Don Juan: A Yaqui way of knowledge.* New York: Ballantine.

———. (1971). *A separate reality: Further conversations with Don Juan.* New York: Simon & Schuster.

Cattell, H. E. P. (1993). Comment on Goldberg. *American Psychologist, 48,* 1302-1303.

Chapman, A. H. (1976). *Harry Stack Sullivan: The man and his work.* New York: Putnam.

Christie, R., & Geis, F. (1968). Some consequences of taking Machiavelli seriously. In E. Borgatta & W. Lambert (Eds.), *Handbook of personality theory and research.* Chicago: Rand McNally.

———. (1970). *Studies in Machiavellianism.* New York: Academic Press.

Claridge, G. S. (1967). *Personality and arousal.* New York: Pergamon.

Clarkin, J. F., Hull, J. W., Cantor, J., & Sanderson, C. (1993). Borderline personality disorder and personality traits: A comparison of SCID-II BPD and NEO-PI. *Psychological Assessment, 5,* 472-476.

Cloninger, C. R. (1986). A unified biosocial theory of personality and its role in the development of anxiety states. *Psychiatric Developments, 3,* 167-226.

Coddington, R. D. (1989). Introduction to the Adjustment Disorders. In *Treatments of the Psychiatric Disorders* (Vol. 3). Washington, DC: American Psychiatric Association.

Coon, Deborah J. (1994). "Not a creature of reason": The alleged impact of Watsonian behaviorism on advertising in the 1920s. In J. T. Todd & E. K. Morris (Eds.), *Modern perspectives on John B. Watson and classical behaviorism.* Westport, CT: Greenwood Press.

Cooper, D. (1967). *Psychiatry and anti-psychiatry.* London: Paladin and Tavistock Publications.

———. (1970). *The Death of the Family.* New York: Vintage.

Costa, P. T., & Widiger, T. A. (1994). Summary and unresolved issues. In P. T. Costa, & T. A. Widiger. (Eds.), *Personality disorders and the five-factor model of personality.* Washington, DC: American Psychological Association.

Cranefield, P. (1958). Josef Breuer's evaluation of his contribution to psychoanalysis. *International Journal of Psychoanalysis, 39,* 319-322.

Creelan, P. (1974). Watsonian behaviorism and the Calvinist conscience. *Journal of the History of the Behavioral Sciences, 10,* 95-118.

Cronbach, L. J. (1957). The two disciplines of scientific psychology. *American Psychologist, 12,* 671-684.

———. (1960). *Essentials of psychological testing* (2d ed.). New York: Harper & Row.

Deci, E. L. & Ryan, R. M. (1995). Human autonomy: The basis for true self-esteem. In M. H. Kernis (Ed.), *Efficacy, agency and self-esteem* (31-49). New York: Plenum.

Dembo, T. (1931). Der Ärger als dynamisches Problem. *Psychologische Forschung, 15,* 1-44.

Dollard, J., Doob, L., Miller, N., Mowrer, O. H. & Sears, R. (1939). *Frustration and aggression.* New Haven: Yale University Press.

Dollard, J., & Miller, N. (1950). *Personality and psychotherapy: An analysis in terms of learning, thinking and culture.* New York: McGraw-Hill.

Dreikurs, R. (1963). Individual psychology: The Adlerian point of view. In J. M. Wepman & R. W. Heine (Eds.), *Concepts of personality.* Chicago: Aldine.

Dulaney, D. E., Jr. (1962). The place of hypotheses and intentions: An analysis of verbal control in verbal conditioning. In C. W. Eriksen (Ed.), *Behavior and awareness* (pp. 102-129). Durham, NC: Duke University Press.

———. (1961). Hypothesis and habits in verbal "operant conditioning." *Journal of Abnormal and Social Psychology, 63,* 251-263.

Dyer, R. (1983). *The work of Anna Freud.* New York: Aronson.

Dymond, R. (1954). Adjustment changes over therapy from self-sorts. In C. R. Rogers & R. F. Dymond (Eds.), *Psychotherapy and personality change* (pp. 77-84). Chicago: University of Chicago Press.

Eaves, L. J., Eysenck, H. J. & Martin, N. G. (1989). *Genes, culture and personality: An empirical approach.* New York: Academic Press.

Einstein, A., & Infeld, L. (1938). *The evolution of physics: From early concepts to relativity and quanta.* New York: Simon & Schuster.

Eissler, K. R. (1978). A challenge to Professor Roazen. *Contemporary Psychoanalysis, 14,* 330-344.

Eissler, K. R. (1971). *Talent and genius: The fictitious case of tausk contra Freud.* New York: Quadrangle Books.

———. (1974). On mis-statements of would-be Freud biographers, with special reference to the tausk controversy. *International Review of Psychoanalysis, 1,* Part 4, 391-414.

Eliade, M. (1958). *Rites and symbols of initiation.* New York: Harper (originally published as *Birth and Rebirth*).

———. (1961). *The sacred and the profane.* New York: Harper & Row.

Ellenberger, H. (1970). *The discovery of the unconscious.* New York: Basic Books.

———. (1972). The story of "Anna O.": A critical review with new data. *Journal of the History of the Behavioral Sciences, 8,* 267-279.

Elms, A. C. (1981). Skinner's dark year and *Walden Two*. *American Psychologist, 36*(5), 470-479.

Epstein, L. (1975). Reminiscences of supervision with Erich Fromm. *Contemporary Psychoanalysis, 11,* 457-461.

Epstein, S. & Morling, B. (1995). Is the self motivated to do more than enhance and/or verify itself? In M. H. Kernis (Ed.), *Efficacy, agency and self-esteem* (9-30). New York: Plenum.

Eriksen, C. W., & Pierce, J. (1968). Defense mechanisms. In E. Borgatta & W. Lambert (Eds.), *Handbook of personality theory and research.* Chicago: Rand McNally.

Erikson, E. H. (1950). *Childhood and society* (2d ed.). New York: Norton, 1963.

———. (1951). Sex differences in the play configurations of preadolescents. *Journal of Orthopsychiatry, 21,* 667-692.

———. (1959). *Identity and the life cycle: Selected papers.* Psychological Issues, Monograph No. 1, Vol. 1. New York: International Universities Press.

———. (1962). *Young man Luther: A study in psychoanalysis and history.* New York: Norton.

———. (1963). Youth: Fidelity and diversity. In E. H. Erikson (Ed.), *The challenge of youth.* New York: Doubleday.

———. (1964). *Insight and responsibility.* New York: Norton.

———. (Ed.). (1968). *Identity: Youth and crisis.* New York: Norton.

———. (1969). *Gandhi's truth: On the origins of militant nonviolence.* New York: Norton.

———. (1974). *Dimensions of a new identity: Jefferson lectures, 1973.* New York: Norton.

———. (1975). *Life history and the historical moment.* New York: Norton.

———. (1977). *Toys and reasons.* New York: Norton.

———. (Ed.). (1978). *Adulthood.* New York: Norton.

———. (1982). *The life cycle completed.* New York: Norton.

Erikson, J. M. (1976). *Activity, recovery, growth: The communal role of planned activities.* New York: Norton.

Ernst, C., & Angst, J. (1983). *Birth order: Its influence on personality.* New York: Springer.

Escalona, S. (1940). The effect of success and failure upon the level of aspiration and behavior in manic-depressive psychoses. *University of Iowa Studies in Child Welfare, 16,* 199-302.

Esterson, A. (1970). *The leaves of spring.* Baltimore: Penguin (Pelican ed.).

Evans, R. I. (1975). *Carl Rogers: The man and his ideas: A dialogue.* New York: Dutton.

Evans, R. I. (1976). *Dialogue with R. D. Laing.* New York: Praeger.

Eysenck, Hans J. (1947). *Dimensions of personality.* London: Routledge & Kegan Paul.

———. (1952). *The scientific study of personality.* London: Routledge & Kegan Paul.

———. (1953a). *Uses and abuses of psychology.* Baltimore: Penguin (Pelican ed.), 1953.

———. (1953b). *The structure of human personality* (rev. ed.). London: Methuen, 1970.

———. (1957a). *The dynamics of anxiety and hysteria: An experimental application of modern learning theory to psychiatry.* London: Routledge & Kegan Paul, 1957 (American edition: Praeger).

———. (1957b). *Sense and nonsense in psychology.* Baltimore: Penguin, 1957.

———. (1959). *The Maudsley personality inventory.* San Diego, CA: Educational and Industrial Testing Service.

———. (1960). Learning theory and behavior therapy. In H. J. Eysenck (Ed.), *Behavior therapy and the neuroses.* New York: Pergamon.

———. (1963a). The measurement of motivation. *Scientific American,* May 1963, 130-140.

———. (1963b). Psychoanalysis: Myth or science? In Stanley Rachman (Ed.), *Critical essays on psychoanalysis.* New York: Macmillan, 1963.

———. (1964a). *Crime and personality.* London: Routledge & Kegan Paul, 1964 (American edition: Houghton Mifflin).

———. (1964b). Involuntary rest pauses in tapping as a function of drive and personality. In H. J. Eysenck (Ed.), *Readings in extraversion-*

intraversion, vol. 3: *Bearings on basic psychological processes.* London: Staples, 1971 (paper originally published in *Perceptual and Motor Skills,* 1964, *18,* 173-174).

———. (1965). *Fact and fiction in psychology.* Baltimore: Penguin.

———. (1966). Conditioning, introversion-extroversion and the strength of the nervous system. In H. J. Eysenck (Ed.), *Readings in extraversion-intraversion,* vol. 3: *Bearings on basic psychological processes.* London: Staples, 1971 (paper originally published in Proceedings of the 18th International Congress of Psychology, 9th Symposium, 1966).

———. (1967). *The biological basis of personality.* Springfield, IL: Charles C. Thomas.

———. (1970). Historical introduction. In H. J. Eysenck (Ed.), *Readings in extraversion-intraversion,* vol. 1: *Theoretical and methodological issues.* London: Staples.

———. (1972). *Psychology is about people.* New York: The Library Press.

———. (1973). *The inequality of man.* London: Temple Smith (American edition: Robert R. Knapp, San Diego, CA).

Eysenck, Hans. (1976). The learning theory model of neurosis—a new approach. *Behavior Research and Therapy, 14,* 251-267.

Eysenck, Hans. (1979). *The structure and measurement of intelligence.* New York: Springer.

Eysenck, Hans J. (1982). *Personality, genetics, and behavior: Selected papers.* New York: Praeger.

Eysenck, Hans J. (1993). Comment on Goldberg. *American Psychologist, 48,* 1299-1300.

Eysenck, H. J., & Eysenck, M. (1983). *Mindwatching: Why people behave the way they do.* New York: Garden Press/Doubleday.

———. (1985). *Personality and individual differences: A natural science approach.* New York: Plenum Press.

Eysenck, H. J., & Eysenck, S. B. G. (1968). *The Eysenck personality inventory.* San Diego, CA: Educational and Industrial Testing Service.

———. (1969). *Personality structure and measurement.* San Diego, CA: Robert R. Knapp.

———. (1975a). *Eysenck personality questionnaire.* San Diego, CA: Educational and Industrial Testing Service, 1975.

———. (1975b). *The manual of the Eysenck personality questionnaire.* San Diego, CA: Educational and Industrial Testing Service, 1975.

———. (1976). *Psychoticism as a dimension of personality.* New York: Crane, Russak.

Eysenck, H. J. (1980). Hans Jurgen Eysenck: Autobiographical essay. In G. Lindzey (Ed.), *A history of psychology in autobiography,* Vol. VII. New York: W. H. Freeman.

Eysenck, H. J. (1990). *Rebel with a cause: The autobiography of Hans Eysenck.* London: W. H. Allen.

Eysenck, H. J. & Gudjonsson, H. G. (1989). *The causes and cures of criminality.* New York: Plenum Press.

Eysenck, H. J. & Rachman, S. (1965). *The causes and cures of neurosis.* London: Routledge & Kegan Paul (American edition: Robert R. Knapp, San Diego, CA).

Eysenck, H. J., & Wilson, G. D. (1973). *The experimental study of Freudian theories.* London: Methuen (American edition: Harper & Row).

Falk, J. L. (1956). Issues distinguishing idiographic from nomothetic approaches to personality. *Psychological Review, 63,* 53-62.

Fancher, R. (1992). *Pioneers of Psychology* (2d ed.). New York: Norton.

Farber, I. E. (1963). The things people say to themselves. *American Psychologist, 18,* 185-197.

Feifel, H. (1961). Death—relevant variable in psychology. In R. May (Ed.), *Existential psychology.* New York: Random House.

Fenichel, O. (1945). *The psychoanalytic theory of neurosis.* New York: Norton.

Festinger, L. (1942). A theoretical interpretation of shifts in level of aspiration. *Psychological Review, 49,* 235-250.

———. (1957). *A theory of cognitive dissonance.* New York: Row, Peterson.

Fey, W. F. (1958). Doctrine and experience: Their influence upon the psychologist. *Journal of Consulting Psychology, 22,* 403-409.

Fiedler, F. (1950a). A comparison of therapeutic relationships in psychoanalytic, nondirective and Adlerian therapy. *Journal of Consulting Psychology, 14,* 436–445.

———. (1950b). The concept of an ideal therapeutic relationship. *Journal of Consulting Psychology, 14,* 239–245.

———. (1951). Factor analyses of psychoanalytic, nondirective and Adlerian therapeutic relationships. *Journal of Consulting Psychology, 15,* 32–38.

Fingarette, H. (1974). Self-deception and the "splitting of the ego". In R. Wolheim (Ed.), *Freud: A collection of critical essays.* Garden City, NY: Doubleday.

Fischer, C. T. (1977). Historical relations of psychology as an object-science and subject-science: Toward psychology as a human science. *Journal of the History of the Behavioral Sciences, 13,* 369–378.

Fowles, D. C., Roberts, R., & Nagel, K. (1977). The influence of introversion/extroversion on the skin conductance response to stress and stimulus intensity. *Journal of Research in Personality, 11,* 129–146.

Frank, J. D. (1935). Individual differences in certain aspects of the level of aspiration. *American Journal of Psychology, 47,* 119–128.

Frankl, V. (1959). The spiritual dimension in existential analysis and logotherapy. *Journal of Individual Psychology, 15,* 157–165.

———. (1963). *Man's search for meaning.* New York: Simon & Schuster (Washington Square Paperback).

——— (1978). *The unheard cry for meaning: Psychotherapy and humanism.* New York: Simon & Schuster.

Franks, C. (1956). Conditioning and personality: A study of normal and neurotic subjects. In H. J. Eysenck (Ed.), *Readings in extraversion-intraversion,* vol. 3: *Bearings on basic psychological processes.* London: Staples, 1971 (paper originally published in *Journal of Abnormal and Social Psychology,* 1956, *52,* 143–150).

———. (1957). Personality factors and the rate of conditioning. In H. J. Eysenck (Ed.), *Readings in extraversion-intraversion,* vol. 3: *Bearings on basic psychological processes.* London: Staples, 1971 (paper originally published in *British Journal of Psychology,* 1957, *48,* 119–126).

———. (1963). Personality and eyeblink conditioning seven years later. *Acta Psychologica, 21,* 295–312.

Frazer, J. George. (1963). *The golden bough.* New York: Macmillan.

Freeman, L. (1972). *The story of Anna O.* New York: Walker Press.

French, J. D. (1972). The reticular formation. *Scientific American,* May 1957 (reprinted in R. F. Thompson [Ed.], *Physiological Psychology: Readings from Scientific American.* San Francisco: Freeman, 1972).

Freud, Anna. (1922). Beating fantasies and daydreams. In Vol. 1 of *The writings of Anna Freud.* New York: International Universities Press, 1974.

———. (1927). Four lectures on Psychoanalysis. In Vol. 1 of *The Writings of Anna Freud.* New York: International Universities Press, 1974.

Freud, A. (1928). The theory of child analysis. In Vol. 1 of *The Writings of Anna Freud.* New York: International Universities Press, 1974.

———. (1929). *Anna Freud's letters to Eva Rosenfeld.* Peter Heller (Ed.). New York: International Universities Press, 1992.

———. (1936). *The ego and the mechanisms of defense* (rev. ed.). In Vol. 2 of *The writings of Anna Freud.* New York: International Universities Press, 1966.

———. (1945). Indications for child analysis. In Vol. 4 of *The writings of Anna Freud.* New York: International Universities Press, 1968.

———. (1951a). The contributions of psychoanalysis to genetic psychology. In Vol. 4 of *The writings of Anna Freud.* New York: International Universities Press, 1968.

———. (1951b). Observations on child development. In Vol. 4 of *The writings of Anna Freud.* New York: International Universities Press, 1968.

———. with Dann, Sophie. (1951c). An experiment in group upbringing. In Vol. 4 of *The writings of Anna Freud.* New York: International Universities Press, 1968.

———. (1952). The mutual influences in the development of ego and id. In Vol. 4 of *The Writings of Anna Freud.* New York: International Universities Press, 1968.

Freud, A. (1952/1992). *The Harvard lectures.* J. Sandler (Ed.). Madison, CT: International Universities Press.

———. (1953). Instinctual drives and their bearing on human behavior. In Vol. 4 of *The writings of Anna Freud.* New York: International Universities Press, 1968.

———. (1958). Child observation and prediction of development: A memorial lecture in honor of Ernst Kris. In Vol. 5 of *The writings of Anna Freud.* New York: International Universities Press, 1969.

———. (1962). Assessment of pathology in childhood. In Vol. 5 of *The writings of Anna Freud.* New York: International Universities Press, 1969.

———. (1965a). Metapsychological assessment of the adult personality: The adult profile. In Vol. 5 of *The writings of Anna Freud.* New York: International Universities Press, 1969.

———. (1965b). *Normality and pathology in childhood.* In Vol. 6 of *The writings of Anna Freud.* New York: International Universities Press, 1965.

———. (1967). Doctoral award address. In Vol. 5 of *The writings of Anna Freud.* New York: International Universities Press, 1969.

———. (1968). Indications and contraindications of child analysis. In Vol. 7 of *The writings of Anna Freud.* New York: International Universities Press, 1971.

———. (1969a). Difficulties in the path of psychoanalysis: A confrontation of past with present viewpoints. In Vol. 7 of *The writings of Anna Freud.* New York: International Universities Press, 1971.

———. (1969b). James Strachey. In Vol. 7 of *The writings of Anna Freud.* New York: International Universities Press, 1971.

———. (1970-1980). *Psychoanalytic psychology of normal development.* In Vol. 8 of *The writings of Anna Freud.* New York; International Universities Press, 1981.

———. (1970a). Problems of termination in child analysis. In Vol. 7 of *The writings of Anna Freud.* New York: International Universities Press, 1971.

———. (1970b). The symptomatology of childhood: A preliminary attempt at classification. In Vol. 7 of *The writings of Anna Freud.* New York: International Universities Press, 1971.

———. (1972). The widening scope of psychoanalytic child psychology, normal and abnormal. In Volume 8 of *The writings of Anna Freud.* New York: International Universities Press, 1981.

———. (1978). The principal task of child analysis. In Volume 8 of *The writings of Anna Freud.* New York: International Universities Press, 1881.

———. (1978). Inaugural lecture for the Sigmund Freud chair at the Hebrew University, Jerusalem. *International Journal of Psychoanalysis, 59,* 145–148.

Freud, A., & Burlingham, D. (1944). *Infants without families.* In Vol. 3 of *The writings of Anna Freud.* New York: International Universities Press, 1973.

Freud, A., Nagera, H., & Freud, W. E. (1965). Metapsychological assessment of the adult personality: The adult profile. *Psychoanalytic Study of the Child, 20,* 9–41.

Freud, S. (1894). The neuro-psychoses of defence. In Vol. III of *The standard edition of the complete psychological works of Sigmund Freud.* James Strachey (Ed.). London: Hogarth, 1962.

———. (1895). Project for a scientific psychology. In Vol. I of *The standard edition.* London: Hogarth, 1966.

———. (1896a). Heredity and the aetiology of the neuroses. In Vol. III of *The standard edition.* London: Hogarth, 1962.

———. (1896b). Further remarks on the neuro-psychoses of defence. In Vol. III of *The standard edition.* London: Hogarth, 1962.

———. (1896c). The aetiology of hysteria. In Vol. III of *The standard edition.* London: Hogarth, 1962.

———. (1897). Extracts from the Fliess papers. In Vol. I of *The standard edition.* London: Hogarth, 1966.

———. (1898). Sexuality in the aetiology of the neuroses. In Vol. III of *The standard edition.* London: Hogarth, 1962.

———. (1900). *The interpretation of dreams.* Volumes IV and V of *The standard edition.* London: Hogarth, 1953.

———. (1901). *The psychopathology of everyday life.* In Vol. VI of *The standard edition.* London: Hogarth, 1960.

———. (1905). Three essays on the theory of sexuality. In Vol. VII of *The standard edition.* London: Hogarth, 1953.

———. (1908a). On the sexual theories of children. In Vol. IX of *The standard edition.* London: Hogarth, 1959.

———. (1908b). Character and anal eroticism. In Vol. IX of *The standard edition.* London: Hogarth, 1959.

———. (1910a). *Five lectures on psychoanalysis.* In Vol. XI of *The standard edition.* London: Hogarth, 1957.

———. (1910b). The psychoanalytic view of psychogenic disturbance of vision. In Vol. XI of *The standard edition.* London: Hogarth, 1957.

———. (1911). Formulations of the two principles of mental functioning. In Vol. XII of *The standard edition.* London: Hogarth, 1958.

———. (1912). A note on the unconscious in psychoanalysis. In Vol. XII of *The standard edition.* London: Hogarth, 1958.

———. (1913a). On beginning the treatment. In Vol. XII of *The standard edition.* London: Hogarth, 1958.

———. (1913b). *Totem and taboo.* In Vol. XIII of *The standard edition.* London: Hogarth, 1958.

———. (1914a). On narcissism: an introduction. In Vol. XIV of *The standard edition.* London: Hogarth, 1957.

———. (1914b). On the history of the psychoanalytic movement. In Vol. XIV of *The standard edition.* London: Hogarth, 1957.

———. (1915a). Instincts and their vicissitudes. In Vol. XIV of *The standard edition.* London: Hogarth, 1957.

———. (1915b). Repression. In Vol. XIV of *The standard edition.* London: Hogarth, 1957.

———. (1915c). The unconscious. In Vol XIV of *The standard edition.* London: Hogarth, 1957.

———. (1915d). A phylogenetic fantasy: An overview of the transference neuroses. Cambridge, MA: Harvard University Press, 1987.

———. (1916). *Introductory lectures on psychoanalysis.* Volumes XV and XVI of *The standard edition.* London: Hogarth, 1961 and 1963.

———. (1917a). A difficulty in the path of psychoanalysis. In Vol. XVII of *The standard edition.* London: Hogarth, 1955.

———. (1917b). Mourning and melancholia. In Vol. XIV of *The standard edition.* London: Hogarth, 1957.

Freud, S. (1918). From the history of an infantile neurosis. In J. Strachey (Ed. and Trans.), *The standard edition of the complete psychological works of Sigmund Freud* (Vol. 17). London: Hogarth, 1955.

———. (1919). "A child is being beaten": A contribution to the study of the origin of sexual perversions. In Vol. XVII of *The standard edition.* London: Hogarth, 1955.

———. (1920a). *Beyond the pleasure principle.* In Vol. XVIII of *The standard edition.* London: Hogarth, 1955.

———. (1920b). A note on the prehistory of the technique of analysis. In Vol. XVIII of *The standard edition.* London: Hogarth, 1955.

Freud, S. (1921). *Group psychology and the analysis of the ego.* In J. Strachey (Ed. and Trans.), *The standard edition of the complete psychological works of Sigmund Freud.* (Vol. 18). London: Hogarth, 1955.

———. (1923a). *The ego and the id.* In Vol. XIX of *The standard edition.* London: Hogarth, 1961.

———. (1923b). The infantile genital organization: An interpolation into the theory of sexuality. In Vol. XIX of *The standard edition.* London: Hogarth, 1961.

———. (1924a). A note upon the mystic writing pad. In Vol. XIX of *The standard edition.* London: Hogarth, 1961.

———. (1924b). The dissolution of the Oedipal complex. In Vol. XIX of *The standard edition.* London: Hogarth, 1961.

———. (1924c). A short account of psychoanalysis. In Vol. XIX of *The standard edition.* London: Hogarth, 1961.

———. (1925a). *An autobiographical study.* In Vol. XX of *The standard edition.* London: Hogarth, 1959.

———. (1925b). Some psychical consequences of the anatomical distinction between the sexes. In Vol. XIX of *The standard edition.* London: Hogarth, 1961.

———. (1925c). Some additional notes on dream-interpretation as a whole. In Vol. XIX of *The standard edition.* London: Hogarth, 1961.

———. (1926a). *Inhibitions, symptoms and anxiety.* In Vol. XX of *The standard edition.* London: Hogarth, 1959.

———. (1926b). *The question of lay analysis.* In Vol. XX of *The standard edition.* London: Hogarth, 1959.

———. (1927). *The future of an illusion.* In Vol. XXII of *The standard edition.* London: Hogarth, 1961.

———. (1930). *Civilization and its discontents.* In Vol. XXI of *The standard edition.* London: Hogarth, 1961.

———. (1931). Female sexuality. In Vol. XXI of *The standard edition.* London: Hogarth, 1961.

———. (1933). *New introductory lectures.* In Vol. XXII of *The standard edition.* London: Hogarth, 1964.

———. (1936). A disturbance of memory on the Acropolis. In Vol. XXII of *The standard edition.* London: Hogarth, 1964.

———. (1940). *An outline of psychoanalysis.* In Vol. XXIII of *The standard edition.* London: Hogarth, 1964.

———. (1954). *The origin of psychoanalysis: Letters to Wilhelm Fliess, drafts and notes, 1897–1902.* Marie Bonaparte, Anna Freud, & Ernst Kris (Eds.). New York: Basic Books.

———. (1960). *The letters of Sigmund Freud.* Ernst L. Freud (Ed.). New York: Basic Books.

Freud, S. and Jones, E. (1993). *The complete correspondence of Sigmund Freud and Ernest Jones; 1908–1939.* R. A. Paskauskas (Ed.). Cambridge, MA: Belknap–Harvard University Press.

Freud, S., & Jung, C. G. (1974). *The Freud/Jung letters.* William McGuire (Ed.). Princeton, NJ: Princeton University Press.

———. (1985). *The complete letters of Sigmund Freud to Wilhelm Fliess: 1894–1904.* J. M. Masson (Ed.). Cambridge, MA: Harvard University Press, 1985.

Freud, S., & Zweig, A. (1970). *The letters of Sigmund Freud and Arnold Zweig.* Ernst L. Freud (Ed.). New York: Harcourt.

Freud, W. E. (1972). The baby profile: Part II. *The Psychoanalytic Study of the Child, 26,* 172–194.

Frigon, J-Y. (1976). Extraversion, neuroticism and strength of the nervous system. *British Journal of Psychology, 67,* 467–474.

Fromm, E. (1941). *Escape from freedom.* New York: Avon Books (also published by Holt, Rinehart and Winston).

———. (1944). Individual and social origins of neurosis. In *American Sociological Review, 9,* 380–384.

———. (1947). *Man for himself.* Greenwich, CT: Fawcett Books (originally published by Holt, Rinehart and Winston).

———. (1950). *Psychoanalysis and religion.* New Haven, CT: Yale University Press.

———. (1951). *The forgotten language: An introduction to the understanding of dreams, fairy tales and myths.* New York: Grove Press (also published by Holt, Rinehart and Winston).

———. (1955a). *The sane society.* Greenwich, CT: Fawcett Books, 1955 (also published by Holt, Rinehart and Winston).

———. (1955b). *The dogma of Christ.* Garden City, NY: Doubleday, 1955 (also published by Holt, Rinehart and Winston).

———. (1955c). The present human condition. In Erich Fromm, *The dogma of Christ.* Garden City, NY: Doubleday, 1955.

———. (1956). *The art of loving.* New York: Bantam Books (also published by Harper).

———. (1959). *Sigmund Freud's mission: An analysis of his personality and influence.* New York: Simon & Schuster, 1962.

———. (1962). *Beyond the chains of illusion: My encounter with Marx and Freud.* New York: Simon & Schuster.

———. (1964). *The heart of man: Its genius for good and evil.* New York: Harper & Row.

———. (1968). *The revolution of hope: Toward a humanized technology.* New York: Harper & Row.

———. (1970). *The crisis of psychoanalysis.* Greenwich, CT: Fawcett Books (also published by Holt, Rinehart and Winston).

———. (1973). *The anatomy of human destructiveness.* New York: Holt, Rinehart and Winston.

———. (1976). *To have or to be?* New York: Harper & Row.

Fromm, E., & Macoby, M. (1970). *Social character in a Mexican village.* Englewood Cliffs, NJ: Prentice-Hall.

Furtmüller, C. (1973). Alfred Adler: A biographical essay. In H. L. Ansbacher & R. Ansbacher (Eds.), *Superiority and social interest.* New York: Viking.

Fuster, J. M. (1958). Effects of stimulation of brain stem on tachistoscopic perception. *Science, 127,* 150.

Garcia, J., & Koelling, R. A. (1966). The relation of cue to consequence in avoidance learning. *Psychonomic Science, 4,* 123–124.

Garcia, J., McGowan, B. K., Ervin, F. R., & Koelling, R. A. (1968). Cues: Their relative effectiveness as a function of reinforcer. *Science, 160,* 794–795.

Gay, P. (1987). *A godless Jew: Freud, atheism and the making of psychoanalysis.* New Haven, CT: Yale University Press.

———. (1988). *Freud: A life for our time.* New York: Norton.

Gedo, J. E. (1976). Freud's self-analysis and his scientific ideas. In J. E. Gedo & G. H. Pollock (Eds.), *Freud: The fusion of science and humanism. Psychological Issues,* Monograph Nos. 34/35. New York: International Universities Press.

Gendlin, E. T. (1964). A theory of personality change. In P. Worschel & D. Byrne (Eds.), *Personality change.* New York: Wiley.

———. (1966). Research in psychotherapy with schizophrenic patients and the nature of that illness. In J. T. Hart & T. M. Tomlinson (Eds.), *New directions in client-centered therapy.* Boston: Houghton Mifflin, 1970 (paper originally published in *American Journal of Psychotherapy,* 1966, *20,* 4–16).

———. (1968). Focusing ability in psychotherapy, personality, and creativity. In J. M. Shlien (Ed.), *Research in psychotherapy,* vol. III. Washington, DC: American Psychological Association.

———. (1970). Existentialism and experiential psychotherapy. In J. T. Hart & T. M. Tomlinson (Eds.), *New directions in client-centered therapy.* Boston: Houghton Mifflin.

Gill, M. (1977). Psychic energy reconsidered. *Journal of the American Psychoanalytic Association, 25,* 581–597.

Goffman, E. (1959). *The presentation of self in everyday life.* New York: Doubleday.

———. (1961). *Asylums.* New York: Doubleday.

Goldberg, L. R. (1993). The structure of phenotypic personality traits. *American Psychologist, 48,* 26–34.

Goldfried, M. R. (1980). Toward the delineation of therapeutic change principles. *American Psychologist, 35,* 991–999.

Goldstein, K. (1939). *The organism.* New York: American Book Co. (Van Nostrand).

Goldman, D. (1993). *In search of the real: The origins and originality of D. W. Winnicott.* New York: Jason Aronson.

Gray, J. A. (1964). Strength of the nervous system as a dimension of personality in man. In J. A. Gray (Ed. and Trans.), *Pavlov's typology.* New York: Macmillan.

Gray, J. A. (1981). A critique of Eysenck's theory of personality. In H. J. Eysenck (Ed.), *A model for personality.* New York: Springer-Verlag.

Gray, J. A. (1985). Issues in the neuropsychology of anxiety. In A. H. Tuma & Jack D. Masser (Eds.), *Anxiety and the anxiety disorders* (5–26). Hillsdale, NJ: Lawrence Erlbaum Associates.

Greenberg, J. R., & Mitchell, S. A. (1983). *Object relations in psychoanalytic theory.* Cambridge, MA: Harvard University Press.

Greenspoon, J. (1955). The reinforcing effect of two spoken sounds on the frequency of two responses. *American Journal of Psychology, 68,* 409–416.

Grigg, K. A. (1973). "All roads lead to Rome": The role of the nursemaid in Freud's dreams. *American Journal of Psychoanalysis, 21,* 108–126.

Groddeck, Georg [1922]. *The book of the it.* New York: New American Library, 1961.

Grosskurth, P. (1986). *Melanie Klein: Her world and her work.* Cambridge, MA: Harvard University Press.

Grubrich-Simitis, Ilse. (1987). Preface to *A phylogenetic fantasy.* In S. Freud, *A phylogenetic fantasy: An overview of the transference neuroses.* Cambridge, MA: Harvard University Press.

Guastello, S. J. (1993). A two (and a half) tiered trait taxonomy. *American Psychologist, 48,* 1298.

Guntrip, H. (1973). *Psychoanalytic theory, therapy, and self.* New York: Basic Books.

Gupta, B. S. (1973). The effects of stimulant and depressant drugs on verbal conditioning. *British Journal of Psychology, 64,* 553–557.

Hall, M. H. (1968). A conversation with Abraham Maslow, In R. E. Schell (Ed.), *Readings in Developmental Psychology Today.* New York: CRM Books, 1977 (first published in *Psychology Today,* July, 1968).

Hamachek, D. E. (1988). Evaluating self-concept and ego development within Erikson's psychosocial framework: A formulation. *Journal of Counseling and Development, 66,* 354–360.

Hart, J. (1970). The development of client-centered therapy. In J. T. Hart & T. M. Tomlinson (Eds.), *New directions in client-centered therapy.* Boston: Houghton Mifflin.

Hart, J. T., & T. M. Tomlinson (Eds.). (1970). *New directions in client-centered therapy.* Boston: Houghton Mifflin.

Hartmann, H. (1939). *Ego psychology and the problem of adaptation.* New York: International Universities Press, 1958.

———. (1947). On rational and irrational action. In H. Hartmann, *Essays on ego psychology.* New York: International Universities Press, 1964.

———. (1950a). Psychoanalysis and developmental psychology. In H. Hartmann, *Essays on ego psychology.* New York: International Universities Press, 1964.

———. (1950b). Comments on the psychoanalytic theory of the ego. In H. Hartmann, *Essays on ego psychology.* New York: International Universities Press, 1964.

———. (1952). The mutual influences in the development of ego and id. In H. Hartmann, *Essays on ego psychology.* New York: International Universities Press, 1964.

———. (1955). Notes on the theory of sublimation. In H. Hartmann, *Essays on ego psychology.* New York: International Universities Press, 1964.

———. (1956). Notes on the reality principle. In H. Hartmann, *Essays on ego psychology.* New York: International Universities Press, 1964.

———. (1959). Psychoanalysis as a scientific theory. In H. Hartmann, *Essays on ego psychology.* New York: International Universities Press, 1964.

———. (1964). *Essays on ego psychology: Selected problems in psychoanalytic theory.* New York: International Universities Press.

Hartmann, H., Kris, E., & Lowenstein, R. M. (1946). Comments on the formation of psychic structure. In H. Hartmann, E. Kris, & R. M. Lowenstein, *Papers on psychoanalytic psychology. Psychological issues,* Monograph No. 14. New York: International Universities Press, 1964.

———. (1949). Notes on the theory of aggression. In H. Hartmann, E. Kris, & R. M. Lowenstein, *Papers on psychoanalytic psychology. Psychological issues,* Monograph 14, New York: International Universities Press, 1964.

———. (1953). The function of theory in psychoanalysis. In H. Hartmann, E. Kris, & R. M. Lowenstein, *Papers on psychoanalytic psychology. Psychological issues,* Monograph No. 14. New York: International Universities Press, 1964.

———. (1964). *Papers on psychoanalytic psychology. Psychological Issues,* Monograph No. 14. New York: International Universities Press.

Hebb, D. O. (1955). Drives and the C. N. S. (conceptual nervous system). *Psychological Review, 62,* 243–254.

Heinrichs, R. W. (1993). Schizophrenia and the brain: Conditions for a neuropsychology of madness. *American Psychologist, 48,* 221–233.

Henle, M. (1957). On field forces. In M. Henle (Ed.), *Documents of Gestalt psychology.* Berkeley, CA: University of California Press, 1961 (paper originally published *Journal of Psychology,* 1962, *43*).

Hoffer, A., & Hoffer, P. T. (1987). Foreword to *A phylogenetic fantasy.* In S. Freud, *A phylogenetic fantasy: An overview of the transference neuroses.* Cambridge, MA: Harvard University Press.

Hofstadter, D. R. (1979). *Gödel, Escher, Bach: An eternal golden braid.* New York: Vintage/Random House.

Holt, R. R. (1962). Individuality and generalization in the psychology of personality. *Journal of Personality, 30,* 377–402.

———. (1963). Two influences on Freud's scientific thought. In R. W. White (Ed.), *The study of lives* (pp. 365–387). New York: Atherton.

————. (1975). The past and future of ego psychology. *The Psychoanalytic Quarterly, 44,* 550-576.

Homburger, E. (Erikson, Erik). (1937). Configurations in play: Clinical notes. *The Psychoanalytic Quarterly, 6,* 139-214.

————. (1938). Dramatic productions test. In H. A. Murray, *Explorations in personality* (pp. 552-582). New York: Oxford University Press.

Hoppe, F. (1930). Untersuchungen zur Handlungs—und Affekt—Psychologie, IX. Erflog und Musserflog (Investigations in the Psychology of Action and Emotion, IX. Success and Failure). *Psychologische Forschung, 14,* 1-63.

Horney, K. (1937). *The neurotic personality of our time.* New York: Norton.

————. (1939). *New ways in psychoanalysis.* New York: Norton.

————. (1942). *Self-analysis.* New York: Norton.

————. (1945). *Our inner conflicts.* New York: Norton.

————. (1946). *Are you considering psychoanalysis?* New York: Norton.

————. (1950). *Neurosis and human growth.* New York: Norton.

————. (1967). *Feminine psychology.* New York: Norton.

————. (1980). *The adolescent diaries of Karen Horney.* New York: Basic Books.

Horowitz, M. (1989). Post-traumatic stress disorder. In *Treatments of the psychiatric disorders* (vol. 3). Washington, DC: American Psychiatric Association, 1989.

Howard, K. I., & Orlinsky, D. E. (1970). Therapist orientation and patient experience in psychotherapy. *Journal of Consulting Psychology, 17,* 263-270.

Howarth, E., & Eysenck, H. J. (1968). Extraversion, arousal and paired-associate recall. *Journal of Experimental Research in Personality, 3,* 114-116.

Hughes, J. M. (1989). *Reshaping the psychoanalytic domain: The work of Melanie Klein, W. R. D. Fairbairn, and D. W. Winnicott.* Berkeley, CA: University of California Press.

Hull, C. L. (1943). *Principles of behavior.* New York: Appleton.

————. (1951). *Essentials of behavior.* New Haven, CT: Yale University Press.

————. (1952). *A behavior system.* New Haven, CT: Yale University Press.

Jacobs, M. (1995). *D. W. Winnicott.* London, Great Britain: Sage.

Jaffé, A. (1971). *From the life and work of C. G. Jung.* New York: Harper & Row.

————. (1979). *C. G. Jung: Word and image.* Princeton, NJ: Princeton University Press.

James, W. (1902). *The varieties of religious experience.* New York: Modern Library.

————. (1963). *Principles of psychology.* Greenwich, CT: Fawcett, 1963.

Jankowicz, A. D. (1987). Whatever became of George Kelly? *American Psychologist, 42*(5), 481-487.

Jones, Ernest. (1953). *The life and work of Sigmund Freud: The formative years and the great discoveries,* vol. 1. New York: Basic Books.

————. (1955). *The life and work of Sigmund Freud: Years of maturity,* vol. 2. New York: Basic Books.

————. (1957). *The life and work of Sigmund Freud: The last phase,* vol. 3. New York: Basic Books.

Jourard, S. M. (1971a). *The transparent self* (rev. ed.). New York: Van Nostrand.

————. (1971b). *Self-disclosure: An experimental analysis of the transparent self.* New York: Wiley.

Jucknat, M. (1937). Performance, level of aspiration and self-consciousness. *Psychologische Forschung, 22,* 89-179.

Jung, C. G. (1905). The reaction time ratio in the association experiment. In Vol. 2 of *The collected works of C. G. Jung.* R. F. C. Hull (Trans.). Princeton, NJ: Princeton University Press, 1973.

————. (1907). *The psychology of dementia praecox.* In Vol. 3 of *The collected works of C. G. Jung.* Princeton, NJ: Princeton University Press, 1960.

————. (1908). The content of the psychoses. In Vol. 3 of *The collected works of C. G. Jung.* Princeton, NJ: Princeton University Press, 1960.

————. (1909a). The psychological diagnosis of evidence. In Vol. 2 of *The collected works of C. G. Jung.* Princeton, NJ: Princeton University Press, 1973.

————. (1909b). The psychological diagnosis of evidence. In Vol. 2 of *The collected works of C. G. Jung.* Princeton, NJ: Princeton University Press, 1973.

————. (1912). Symbols of transformation (2d ed.) In Vol. 5 of *The collected works of C. G. Jung.* Princeton, NJ: Princeton University Press, 1956.

————. (1913). On the doctrine of complexes. In Vol. 2 of *The collected works of C. G. Jung.* Princeton, NJ: Princeton University Press, 1973.

————. (1914). On psychological understanding. In Vol. 3 of *The collected works of C. G. Jung.* Princeton, NJ: Princeton University Press, 1960.

————. (1916). General aspects of dream psychology. In Vol. 8 of *The collected works of C. G. Jung.* Princeton, NJ: Princeton University Press, 1969.

————. (1917). Two essays on analytical psychology. In Vol. 7 of *The Collected Works of C. G. Jung.* Princeton, NJ: Princeton University Press, 1953 and 1966.

————. (1921). Psychological Types. In Vol. 6 of *The collected works of C. G. Jung.* Princeton, NJ: Princeton University Press, 1971.

————. (1931). The Structure of the psyche. In Vol. 8 of *The collected works of C. G. Jung.* Princeton, NJ: Princeton University Press, 1969.

————. (1935). The relations between the ego and the unconscious. In Vol. 7 of *The collected works of C. G. Jung.* Princeton, NJ: Princeton University Press, 1953 and 1966.

————. (1936). The archetypes and the collective unconscious. In Vol. 9i of *The collected works of C. G. Jung.* Princeton, NJ: Princeton University Press, 1959 and 1969.

————. (1938). Psychological aspects of the mother archetype. In Vol. 9i of *The collected works of C. G. Jung.* Princeton, NJ: Princeton University Press, 1959 and 1969.

————. (1939). Conscious, unconscious and individuation. In Vol. 9i of *The collected works of C. G. Jung.* Princeton, NJ: Princeton University Press, 1959 and 1969.

————. (1940). The psychology of the child archetype. In Vol. 9i of *The collected works of C. G. Jung.* Princeton, NJ: Princeton University Press, 1959 and 1969.

————. (1948). On psychic energy. In Vol. 8 of *The collected works of C. G. Jung.* Princeton, NJ: Princeton University Press, 1959.

————. (1950a). On mandalas. In Vol. 9i of *The collected works of C. G. Jung.* Princeton, NJ: Princeton University Press, 1959 and 1969.

————. (1950b). Aion: Researches into the phenomenology of the self. Volume 9ii of *The collected works of C. G. Jung.* Princeton, NJ: Princeton University Press, 1959 and 1969.

————. (1952). Synchronicity: An acausal connecting principle. In Vol. 8 of *The collected works of C. G. Jung.* Princeton, NJ: Princeton University Press, 1969.

————. (1954). On the psychology of the trickster figure. In Vol. 9i of *The collected works of C. G. Jung.* Princeton, NJ: Princeton University Press, 1959 and 1969.

————. (1957). The undiscovered self: Present and future. In Vol. 10 of *The collected works of C. G. Jung.* Princeton, NJ: Princeton University Press, 1970.

————. (1961). *Memories, dreams, reflections.* A. Jaffé (Ed.). New York: Pantheon.

————. (1968). *Analytical psychology: Its theory and practice.* (The Tavistock Lectures.) New York: Pantheon.

Kagan, J., & Berkun, M. (1954). The reward value of running activity. *Journal of Comparative and Physiological Psychology, 47,* 108.

Kahr, B. (1996). *D. W. Winnicott: A biographical portrait.* New York: International Universities Press.

Kanner, L. (1942). Autistic disturbances of affective contact. *Nervous Child, 2,* 217-250.

————. (1944). Early infantile autism. *Journal of Pediatrics, 25,* 211-217.

————. (1949). Problems of nosology and psychodynamics of early infantile autism. *American Journal of Orthopsychiatry, 19,* 416-426.

Kelly, G. A. (1955). *The psychology of personal constructs,* vols. 1 and 2. New York: Norton.

————. (1958a). Man's construction of his alternatives. In B. Maher (Ed.), *Clinical psychology and personality: Selected papers of George*

Kelly. New York: Wiley, 1969 (paper originally published: Gardner Lindzey (Ed.), *The Assessment of Human Motives.* New York: Holt, Rinehart and Winston, 1958).

———. (1958b). Personal construct theory and the psychotherapeutic interview. In B. Maher (Ed.), *Clinical Psychology and Personality: Selected Papers of George Kelly.* New York: Wiley, 1969.

———. (1963). The autobiography of a theory. In B. Maher (Ed.), *Clinical psychology and personality: Selected papers of George Kelly.* New York: Wiley, 1969.

———. (1964). The language of hypothesis: Man's psychological instrument. In B. Maher (Ed.), *Clinical psychology and personality: Selected papers of George Kelly.* New York: Wiley, 1969 (paper originally published: *Journal of Individual Psychology,* 1964, *20,* 137–152).

———. (1966). Ontological acceleration. In B. Maher (Ed.), *Clinical psychology and personality: Selected papers of George Kelly.* New York: Wiley, 1969.

———. (1967). A psychology of the optimal man. In A. W. Landfield & L. M. Leitner (Eds.), *Personal construct psychology* (pp. 18–35). New York: Wiley, 1980.

Kernberg, O. F. (1976). *Object relations theory and clinical psychoanalysis.* New York: Jason Aronson.

———. (1986). *Severe personality disorders. Psychotherapeutic strategies.* New Haven: Yale University Press.

———. (1992). *Aggression in personality disorders and perversions.* New Haven: Yale University Press.

Khan, M. (1975/1992). Introduction. In D. W. Winnicott, *Through paediatrics to psycho-analysis. Collected Papers.* New York: Bruner-Mazel (Originally published: New York: Basic Books, 1958).

Kirmayer, L. J., Robbins, J. M., & Paris, J. (1994). Somatoform disorders: Personality and the social matrix of somatic distress. *Journal of Abnormal Psychology, 103,* 125–136.

Kirschenbaum, H. (1979). *On becoming Carl Rogers.* New York: Delacorte Press.

Klein, D. F., Rabkin-Godwin, J., & Gorman, J. M. (1988). Etiological and pathophysiological inferences from the pharmacological treatment of anxiety. In A. Hussain Tuma & J. D. Masser (Eds.), *Anxiety and the anxiety disorders* (501–532). Hillsdale, NJ: Lawrence Erlbaum Associates.

Klein, M. (1921/1975a). Development of a child. In R. E. Money-Kyrle (Ed.), *The writings of Melanie Klein* (Vol I, 1–53). New York: The Free Press (Macmillan).

———. (1926/1975a). The psychological principles of early analysis. In R. E. Money-Kyrle (Ed.), *The writings of Melanie Klein* (Vol I, 128–138). New York: The Free Press (Macmillan).

———. (1927/1975a). Symposium on child-analysis. In R. E. Money-Kyrle (Ed.), *The writings of Melanie Klein* (Vol I, 139–169). New York: The Free Press (Macmillan).

———. (1928/1975a). Early stages of the Oedipus conflict. In R. E. Money-Kyrle (Ed.), *The writings of Melanie Klein* (Vol I, 210–218). New York: The Free Press (Macmillan).

———. (1929/1975a). Infantile anxiety-situations reflected in a work of art and in the creative impulse. In R. E. Money-Kyrle (Ed.), *The writings of Melanie Klein* (Vol I, 210–218). New York: The Free Press.

———. (1931/1975a). A contribution to the theory of intellectual inhibition. In R. E. Money-Kyrle (Ed.), *The writings of Melanie Klein* (Vol I, 236–247). New York: The Free Press.

———. (1932). *The psychoanalysis of children.* London: Hogarth (reissued by Delacorte Press, 1975).

———. (1932/1975b). *The psycho-analysis of children.* In H. A. Thorner (Ed.) and Alix Strachey (Trans.), *The writings of Melanie Klein* (Vol II). New York: The Free Press (Macmillan).

———. (1933/1975a). The early development of conscience in the child. In R. E. Money-Kyrle (Ed.), *The writings of Melanie Klein* (Vol I, 248–257). New York: The Free Press (Macmillan).

———. (1935/1975a) A contribution to the psychogenesis of manic-depressive states. In R. E. Money-Kyrle (Ed.), *The writings of Melanie Klein* (Vol. I, 262–289). New York: The Free Press (Macmillan).

———. (1936/1975a). Weaning. In R. E. Money-Kyrle (Ed.), *The writings of Melanie Klein* (Vol. I, 290–305). New York: The Free Press (Macmillan).

———. (1937/1975a). Love, guilt and reparation. In R. E. Money-Kyrle (Ed.), *The writings of Melanie Klein* (Vol I, 306–343). New York: The Free Press (Macmillan).

———. (1940/1975a). Mourning and its relation to manic-depressive states. In R. E. Money-Kyrle (Ed.), *The writings of Melanie Klein* (Vol. I, 344–359). New York: The Free Press (Macmillan).

———. (1945/1975a). The Oedipus complex in the light of early anxieties. In R. E. Money-Kyrle (Ed.), *The writings of Melanie Klein* (Vol. I, 370–419). New York: The Free Press (Macmillan).

———. (1946/1975c). Notes on some schizoid mechanisms. In Roger Money-Kyrle (Ed.), *The writings of Melanie Klein* (Vol III, 1–24). New York: The Free Press (Macmillan).

———. (1952/1975c). The emotional life of the infant. In Roger Money-Kyrle (Ed.), *The writings of Melanie Klein* (Vol III, 61–93). New York: The Free Press (Macmillan).

———. (1955/1975c). On identification. In Roger Money-Kyrle (Ed.), *The writings of Melanie Klein* (Vol III, 1–24). New York: The Free Press (Macmillan).

———. (1957/1975c). *Envy and gratitude.* In Roger Money-Kyrle (Ed.), *The writings of Melanie Klein* (Vol III, 176–235). New York: The Free Press (Macmillan).

———. (1958/1975c). On the development of mental functioning. In Roger Money-Kyrle (Ed.), *The writings of Melanie Klein* (Vol III, 236–246). New York: The Free Press (Macmillan).

———. (1961). *Narrative of a child analysis.* In Eliott Jacques (Ed.), *The writings of Melanie Klein* (Vol IV). New York: The Free Press (Macmillan).

Klein, M. & Riviere, J. (1964). *Love, hate and reparation.* New York: Norton.

Kline, P. (1972). *Fact and fantasy in Freudian theory.* London: Methuen, 1972 (American edition published by Harper & Row).

Kling, J. W. (1971). Learning. In J. W. Kling & L. A. Riggs (Eds.), *Woodworth and Schlosberg's experimental psychology* (pp. 551–614). (3d ed.). New York: Holt, Rinehart and Winston.

Koffka, K. (1935). *Principles of Gestalt psychology.* New York: Harcourt, Brace.

Kohut, H. (1971). *The analysis of the self.* New York: International Universities Press.

———. (1976). Creativeness, charisma and group psychology: Reflections of the self analysis of Freud. In J. E. Gedo & G. H. Pollock (Eds.), *Freud: The fusion of science and humanism. Psychological issues,* Monograph Nos. 34/35. New York: International Universities Press, 1976.

———. (1977). *The restoration of the self.* New York: International Universities Press.

———. (1984). *How does analysis cure?* Chicago: University of Chicago Press.

Kohut, H., & Wolff, E. (1978). The disorders of the self and their treatment: An outline. *The International Journal of Psychoanalysis, 59,* 413–425.

Kraeplin, E. (1905). *Lectures on clinical psychiatry* (2d, rev. ed.) London: Baillere, Tindall and Cox, 1905 (as cited by R. D. Laing, 1959).

Krane, R. V., & Wagner, A. R. (1975). Taste aversion learning with a delayed shock US: implications for the generality of the laws of learning. *Journal of Comparative and Physiological Psychology, 88,* 882–889.

Kris, E. (1954). Editor's introduction. In M. Bonaparte, E. Kris, & A. Freud (Eds.), *The origins of psychoanalysis: Letters of Sigmund Freud to Wilhelm Fliess, drafts and notes, 1897–1902.* New York, Basic Books.

Laing, R. D. (1959). *The divided self.* Baltimore: Penguin (Pelican ed.).

———. (1967). *The politics of experience.* New York: Ballantine (originally published by Pantheon, 1967).

———. (1969a). *The politics of the family.* New York: Vintage.

———. (1969b). *Self and others.* New York: Pantheon.

———. (1970). *Knots.* New York: Vintage.

———. (1976a). *The facts of life.* New York: Pantheon.

——. (1976b). Conversation with R. I. Evans. In R. I. Evans (Ed.), *R. D. Laing: The man and his ideas*. New York: Dutton.

——. (1976c). *Do You Love Me?* New York: Pantheon.

——. (1977). *Conversations with Adam and Natasha*. New York: Pantheon.

——. (1982). *The voice of experience*. New York: Pantheon.

——. (1985). *Wisdom, madness and folly: The making of a psychiatrist*. New York: McGraw-Hill.

Laing, R. D., & Cooper, D. G. (1971). *Reason and violence: A decade of Sartre's philosophy, 1950–1960*. New York: Vintage.

Laing, R. D., & Esterson, A. (1964). *Sanity, madness and the family*. Baltimore: Penguin (Pelican ed.).

Laing, R. D., Phillipson, H., & Lee, A. R. (1966). *Interpersonal perception: A theory and a method of research*. New York: Springer (This edition also includes the *IPM* test).

Langs, R. (1973). *The technique of psychoanalytic psychotherapy*, vol. 1. New York: Jason Aronson.

Laufer, M. (1965). Assessment of adolescent disturbances: The application of Anna Freud's diagnostic profile. *The Psychoanalytic Study of the Child, 20,* 99–123.

Laverty, S. G. (1958). Sodium amytal and extraversion. In H. J. Eysenck (Ed.), *Readings in extraversion-intraversion*, vol. 3: *Bearings on basic psychological processes*. London: Staples, 1971 (paper originally published in *Journal of Neurology and Neurosurgery and Psychiatry, 1958, 21,* 50–54).

Lazarus, R. S., & Launier, R. (1978). Stress-related transactions between person and environment. In L. A. Pervin & M. Lewis (Eds.), *Perspectives in Interactional Psychology*. New York: Plenum.

LeDoux, J. (1996). *The emotional brain*. New York: Touchstone (Simon and Shuster).

Leites, N. (1971). *The new age: Pitfalls in current thinking about patients in psychoanalysis*. New York: Science House.

——. (1935). *A dynamic theory of personality*. New York: McGraw-Hill.

——. (1936). *Principles of topological psychology*. New York: McGraw-Hill.

Lewis-Fernandez, R., & Kleinman, A. (1994). Culture, personality, and psychopathology. *Journal of Abnormal Psychology, 103,* 67–71.

Lindsley, D. B. (1951). Emotion. In S. S. Stevens (Ed.), *Handbook of experimental psychology* (pp. 473–516). New York: Wiley.

Little, M. I. (1990). *Psychotic anxieties and containment: A personal record of an analysis with Winnicott*. New York: Jason Aronson.

Lundin, R. W. (1963). Personality theory in behavioristic psychology. In J. M. Wepman & R. W. Heine (Eds.), *Concepts of personality*. Chicago: Aldine.

Mackinnon, D. W., & Dukes, W. F. (1962). Repression. In Leo Postman (Ed.), *Psychology in the making: Histories of selected research problems*. New York: Knopf.

Mackworth, H. N. (1950). *Researches on the measurement of human performance*. Medical Research Council Special Report, No. *268.* London: Her Majesty's Stationery Office.

Mackworth, H. N. (1957). Some factors affecting vigilance. *The Advancement of Science, 53,* 389–393.

Macleod, R. B. (1964). Phenomenology: A challenge to experimental psychology. In T. W. Wann (Ed.), *Behaviorism and phenomenology: Contrasting bases for modern psychology*. Chicago: University of Chicago Press.

Maher, B. A., & Maher, W. B. (1994). Personality and psychopathology. A historical perspective. *Journal of Abnormal Psychology, 103,* 72–77.

Mahler, M. S. (1968). *On human symbiosis and the vicissitudes of individuation: Infantile psychosis*. New York: International Universities Press.

——. (1988). *The memoirs of Margaret S. Mahler*. Paul E. Stepansky, (Ed.) New York: The Free Press.

Mahler, M. S., Pine, F., & Bergman, A. (1975). *The psychological birth of the human infant*. New York: Basic Books.

Malmo, R. B. (1959). Activation: A neurophysiological dimension. *Psychological Review, 66,* 367–386.

Marcia, J. (1966). Development and validation of ego-identity status. *Journal of Personality and Social Psychology, 3,* 551–558.

Marcia, J. (1993). The ego identity status approach to ego identity. In J. E. Marcia, A. S. Waterman, D. R. Matteson, S. L. Archer, & J. L. Orlofsky (Eds.), *Ego identity: A handbook for psychosocial research*. New York: Springer-Verlag.

Marcia, J., & Friedman, M. L. (1970). "Ego Identity Status in College Women," *Journal of Personality, 38,* 249–263.

Marrow, A. J. (1969). *The practical theorist: The life and work of Kurt Lewin*. New York: Columbia University Press.

Martindale, C. (1981). *Cognition and consciousness*. Homewood, IL: Dorsey.

Masling, J. (1983). *Empirical studies of psychoanalytical theories* (vol. 1). Hillsdale, NJ: The Analytic Press.

Maslow, A. H. (1936a). The role of dominance in the social and sexual behavior of infra-human primates: I. observations at Vilas Park Zoo. In R. J. Lowry (Ed.), *Dominance, self-esteem, self-actualization: Germinal papers of A. H. Maslow*. Monterey, CA: Brooks-Cole, 1973 (paper originally published in *Journal of Genetic Psychology, 1936, 48,* 261–277).

——. (1936b). The role of dominance in the social and sexual behavior of infra-human primates: II. An experimental determination of the behavior syndrome of dominance. In R. J. Lowry (Ed.), *Dominance, self-esteem, self-actualization: Germinal papers of A. H. Maslow*. Monterey, CA: Brooks-Cole, 1973 (paper originally published in *Journal of Genetic Psychology, 1936, 48,* 278–309).

——. (1937). Dominance-feeling, behavior and status. In R. J. Lowry (Ed.), *Dominance, self-esteem, self-actualization: Germinal papers of A. H. Maslow*. Monterey, CA: Brooks-Cole, 1973 (paper originally published in *Psychological Review, 1937, 44,* 404–429).

——. (1939). Dominance, personality and social behavior in women. In R. J. Lowry (Ed.), *Dominance, self-esteem, self-actualization: Germinal papers of A. H. Maslow*. Monterey, CA: Brooks-Cole, 1973 (paper originally published in *Journal of Social Psychology, 1939, 10,* 3–39).

——. (1942). Self-esteem (dominance-feeling) and sexuality in women. In R. J. Lowry (Ed.), *Dominance, self-esteem, self-actualization: Germinal papers of A. H. Maslow*. Monterey, CA: Brooks-Cole, 1973 (paper originally published in *Journal of Social Psychology, 1942, 16,* 259–294).

——. (1943). A theory of human motivation. In R. J. Lowry (Ed.), *Dominance, self-esteem, self-actualization Germainal papers of A. H. Maslow*. Monterey, CA: Brooks-Cole, 1973 (paper originally published in *Psychological Review, 1943, 50,* 370–396).

——. (1962). *Toward a psychology of being*. New York: Van Nostrand.

——. (1964). *Religions, values and peak-experiences*. New York: Viking.

——. (1966). *The psychology of science: A reconnaissance*. New York: Harper & Row.

——. (1970). *Motivation and personality* (2d ed.). New York: Harper & Row.

——. (1971). *The farther reaches of human nature*. New York: Viking.

——. (1979). *The journals of Abraham Maslow*. R. J. Lowry (Ed.). Lexington, MA: Lewis Publishing, 1982 (originally published as a two-volume work by Brooks-Cole Publishing, Monterey, CA, 1979.)

Maslow, A., & Chiang, Hung-Min. (1977). Laboratory in self-knowledge: A verbatim report of the workshop with Abraham Maslow. In Abraham Maslow and Hung-Min Chiang (Eds.), *The healthy personality: Readings* (pp. 240–258). (2d ed.). New York: Van Nostrand.

Masson, J. M. (1984a). Freud and the seduction theory. *The Atlantic Monthly,* February, 33–60.

——. (1984b). *The assault on truth: Freud's suppression of the seduction theory*. New York: Farrar, Straus & Giroux.

——. (Ed.). (1985). *The complete letters of Sigmund Freud to Wilhelm Fliess: 1887–1904*. Cambridge, MA: Harvard University Press.

Masterson, J. F., Tolpin, M., & Sifneos, P. E. (1991). *Comparing psychoanalytic psychotherapies*. New York: Brunner Mazel.

May, Rollo (1939/1967). *The art of counseling*. New York: Abingdon Press.

———. (1950/1970). *The meaning of anxiety.* New York: Ronald Press (paperback reissue) New York, Washington Square Press.

———. (1953). *Man's search for himself.* New York: Norton.

———. (1958a). "The origins and significance of the existential movement in psychology." In R. May, E. Angel, and H. F. Ellenberger (Eds.), *Existence: A new dimension in psychiatry and psychology.* New York: Basic Books.

———. (1958b). "Contributions of existential psychotherapy." In R. May, E. Angel, and H. F. Ellenberger (Eds.), *Existence: A new dimension in psychiatry and psychology.* New York: Basic Books.

———. (1960/1965). "Existential bases of psychotherapy." In Ohmer Milton (Ed.) *Behavior disorders: Perspectives and trends.* New York: Lippincott (originally published: *Journal of OrthoPsychiatry,* 1960, *30,* 685–695; also anthologized in R. May [Ed.], *Existential psychology.* New York: Random House, 1961; see also May, 1983, Ch. 2).

———. (1961). "The emergence of existential psychology." In R. May (Ed.), *Existential psychology.* New York: Random House.

———. (1967b/1979). *Psychology and the human dilemma.* New York: Norton.

———. (1969). *Love and will.* New York: Norton (paperback: New York, Delta Books, 1969).

———. (1972). *Power and innocence: A search for the sources of violence.* New York. Norton.

———. (1973). *Paulus: A personal portrait of Paul Tillich.* New York: Harper & Row.

———. (1975). "The courage to create." In M. Richler, A. Fortier, and R. May (Eds.), *Creativity and the university: The 1972 Gerstein Lectures at York University.* Toronto: York University.

———. (1981). *Freedom and destiny.* New York: Norton.

———. (1983). *The discovery of being: Writings in existential psychology.* New York: Norton.

———. (1985). *My quest for beauty.* Dallas, TX: Saybrook Publishing.

———. (1986a). "The destiny of america." In *Politics and innocence.* Dallas, TX: Saybrook.

———. (1986b). "The problem of evil." In *Politics and innocence.* Dallas, TX: Saybrook.

———. (1989). "Rollo May: A man of meaning and myth." Interview with F. E. Rabinowitz, Glenn Good, and Liza Cozad. *Journal of Counseling and Development, 67,* 436–441.

May, R., Angel, E., and Ellenberger, H. F. (Eds.). (1958). *Existence: A new dimension in psychiatry and psychology.* New York: Basic Books.

McCarley, R. W., & Hobson, J. A. (1977). The neurobiological origins of psychoanalytic dream theory. *American Journal of Psychiatry, 134,* 1211–1221.

McCrae, R. R. (1994). A reformulation of Axis II: Personality and personality-related problems. In P. T. Costa, & T. A. Widiger (Eds.), *Personality disorders and the five-factor model of personality.* Washington, DC: American Psychological Association.

McLaughlin, R. J., & Eysenck, H. J. (1967). Extraversion, neuroticism and paired-associate learning. In H. J. Eysenck (Ed.), *Readings in extraversion-intraversion,* vol. 3: *Bearings on basic psychological processes.* London: Staples, 1971 (paper originally published in *Journal of Experimental Research in Personality,* 1967, *2,* 128–132).

McLeary, R. A., & Lazarus, R. S. (1949). Autonomic discrimination without awareness. *Journal of Personality, 18,* 171–179.

Menninger, K., Mayman, M., & Pruyser, P. (1963). *The vital balance: The life process in mental health and illness.* New York: Viking Press.

Miller, L. (1991). *Freud's brain: Neuropsychodynamic foundations of psychoanalysis.* New York: Guilford.

Miller, N. (1941). The frustration-aggression hypothesis. *Psychological Review, 48,* 337–342.

———. (1944). Experimental studies of conflict. In J. M. Hunt (Ed.), *Personality and the behavior disorders* (pp. 431–465). Vol. 1. New York: Ronald Press.

———. (1948). Studies of fear as an acquirable drive: I. Fear as motivation and fear reduction as reinforcement in the learning of new responses. *Journal of Experimental Psychology, 38,* 89–101.

———. (1950). Learnable drives and rewards. In S. S. Stevens (Ed.), *Handbook of experimental psychology* (pp. 435–472). New York: Wiley.

Miller, N., & Dollard, J. (1941). *Social learning and imitation.* New Haven, CT: Yale University Press.

Miller, N., & Myers, A. K. (1954). Failure to find a learned drive based on hunger; Evidence for learning motivated by "Exploration." *Journal of Comparative and Physiological Psychology, 47,* 428–436.

Millon, T. (1981). *Disorders of personality: DSM III: Axis II.* New York: Wiley-Interscience.

———. (1994). Personality disorders: Conceptual distinctions and classification issues. In P. T. Costa, & T. A. Widiger, (Eds.), *Personality disorders and the five-factor model of personality.* Washington, DC: American Psychological Association.

Milne, A. A. (1926). *Winnie-the-Pooh.* New York: Dutton.

Milner, M. (1978). D. W. Winnicott and the two-way journey. In S. A. Grolnick & L. Barkin (Eds.), *Between reality and fantasy: Transitional objects and phenomena* (35–42). New York: Jason Aronson.

Mitchell, Juliet (Ed.), (1986). *The selected Melanie Klein.* New York: The Free Press (Macmillan).

Mischel, W. (1968). *Personality and assessment.* New York: Wiley.

———. (1973a). Toward a cognitive social learning theory reconceptualization of personality. *Psychological Review, 80,* 252–283.

———. (1973b). On the empirical dilemmas of psychodynamic approaches: Issues and alternatives. *Journal of Abnormal Psychology, 82,* 335–344.

———. (1985). Looking for personality. In S. Koch & D. Leary (Eds.), *A century of psychology as a science.* New York: McGraw-Hill.

Monte, C. F. (1975). *Psychology's scientific endeavor.* New York: Praeger.

———. (1993). *Still, Life: Clinical portraits in psychopathology.* Englewood Cliffs, NJ: Prentice-Hall.

Monte, C. F. (1995). *Beneath the mask: An introduction to theories of personality.* (5th ed.). New York: Harcourt, Brace Jovanovich.

Moruzzi, G., and H. W. Magoun (1949/1964). Brain stem reticular formation and activation of the EEG. In R. L. Isaacson (Ed.), *Basic Readings in neuropsychology.* New York: Harper & Row. (paper originally published: *Electroencephalography and Clinical Neurophysiology,* 1949, *1,* 455–473).

Mosak, H. H. (1958). Early recollections as a projective technique. *Journal of Projective Techniques, 22,* 302–311.

Mosak, H. H., & Kopp, R. R. (1973). The early recollections of Adler, Freud, and Jung. *Journal of Individual Psychology, 29,* 157–166.

Moustakas, C. E. (Ed.). (1956). *The self: Explorations in personal growth.* New York: Harper.

Mowrer, O. H. (1939). A stimulus-response analysis of anxiety and its role as a reinforcing agent, *Psychological Review, 46,* 553–565.

———. (1950). Identification: A link between learning theory and psychotherapy. In O. H. Mowrer, *Learning theory and personality dynamics* (pp. 69–94). New York: Ronald Press.

Murphy, G., & Kovach, J. K. (1972). *Historical introduction to modern psychology* (3d ed.). New York: Harcourt.

Murray, E. J., & Jacobson, L. I. (1978). Cognition and learning in traditional and behavioral psychotherapy. In Sol Garfield & Allen E. Bergin (Eds.), *Handbook of psychotherapy and behavior change* (pp. 661–688). (2d ed.). New York: Wiley.

Murray, H. A. (1938). *Explorations in personality.* New York: Oxford University Press.

Myers, I. B. (1972). *Myers-Brigges type indicator manual.* Palo Alto, CA: Consulting Psychologists Press.

Nisbett, R., & Wilson, T. (1977). Telling more than we can know: Verbal reports on mental processes. *Psychological Review, 84,* 231–259.

Oberndorf, C. P. (Ed.). (1953). Autobiography of Josef Breuer (1842–1925). *International Journal of Psychoanalysis, 34,* 64–67.

O'Connor, B. P. & Dyce, J. A. (1998). A test of models of personality disorder configuration. *Journal of Abnormal Psychology, 107,* 3–16.

Olds, J., & Milner, P. (1954). Positive reinforcement produced by electrical stimulation of septal area and other regions of rat brain. *Journal of Comparative and Physiological Psychology, 47,* 419–427.

Olds, J., & Olds, M. (1965). Drives, rewards and the brain. In T. M. Newcomb (Ed.), *New directions in psychology,* vol. 2. New York: Holt, Rinehart and Winston.

Orgler, H. (1963). *Alfred Adler: The man and his work.* New York: Capricorn (Putnam).

Orne, M. T. (1962). On the social psychology of the psychological experiment: With particular reference to demand characteristics and their implications. *American Psychologist, 17,* 776–783.

———. (1969). Demand characteristics and the concept of quasi-controls. In R. Rosenthal & R. Rosnow (Eds.), *Artifact in behavioral research.* New York: Academic Press.

———. (1973). Communication by the total experimental situation: Why it is important, how it is evaluated, and its significance for the ecological validity of findings. In P. Pilner, L. Kramer, and T. Alloway (Eds.), *Communication and affect* (pp. 157–191). New York: Academic Press.

Otto, R. (1923). *The idea of the holy: An inquiry into the non-rational factor in the idea of the divine and its relation to the rational.* New York: Oxford University Press.

Ovsiankina, M. (1928). Die wiederaufnahme unterbrochener Handlungen. *Psychologische Forschung, 11,* 302–379.

Papez, J. W. (1937). A proposed mechanism of emotion. *Archives of Neurology and Psychiatry, 38,* 725–744.

Parisi, T. (1987). Why freud failed. *American Psychologist, 42*(3), 235–245.

———. (1988). Freud's stance and mine. *American Psychologist, 43*(8), 663–664.

Pavlov, I. P. (1927). *Conditioned reflexes: An investigation into the physiological activity of the cortex.* G. V. Anrep (Trans.). New York: Dover.

———. (1928). *Lectures on conditioned reflexes,* vol. 1. W. Horsely Gantt (Trans.). New York: International Publishers.

Peele, S. (1981). Reductionism in the psychology of the eighties. *American Psychologist, 36,* 807–818.

Phillips, A. (1988). *Winnicott.* Cambridge, MA: Harvard University Press.

Phillips, D. C., & Oroton, R. (1983). Theoretical notes: The new causal principle of cognitive learning theory: Perspectives on Bandura's *Reciprocal Determinism. Psychological Review, 90,* 158–165.

Piaget, J. (1952). *The origins of intelligence in children.* New York: International Universities Press.

———. (1954). *The construction of reality in the child.* Margaret Cook (Trans.). New York: Basic Books.

Piaget, J., & Inhelder, B. (1969). *The psychology of the child.* New York: Basic Books.

Pollock, G. H. (1968). The possible significance of childhood object loss in the Josef Breuer–Bertha Pappenheim (Anna O.)–Sigmund Freud relationship. I. Josef Breuer. *Journal of the American Psychoanalytic Association, 16,* 711–739.

———. (1972). Bertha Pappenheim's pathological mourning: Possible effects of childhood sibling loss. *Journal of the American Psychoanalytic Association, 20,* 478–493.

———. (1973). Bertha Pappenheim: Addenda to her case history. *American Journal of Psychoanalysis, 21,* 328–332.

———. (1976). Josef Breuer. In J. E. Gedo & G. H. Pollock (Eds.), *Freud: The fusion of science and humanism. Psychological issues,* Monograph Nos. 34/35. New York: International Universities Press.

Popper, K. (1959). *The logic of scientific discovery.* New York: Basic Books.

———. (1963). *Conjectures and refutations.* New York: Basic Books.

———. (1965). *Conjectures and refutations* (rev. ed). London: Routledge and Kegan Paul.

Postman, L. (1962). *Psychology in the making.* New York: Knopf.

Premack, D. (1965). Reinforcement Theory. In M. R. Jones (Ed.), *Nebraska symposium on motivation: 1965.* Lincoln, NE: University of Nebraska Press.

Quinn, S. (1987). *A mind of her own: The life of Karen Horney.* New York: Summit Books (Simon & Schuster).

Rabinowitz, F. E., Good, G., & Cozad, L. (1989). Rollo May: A man of meaning and myth. *Journal of Counseling and Development, 1989, 67,* 436–441.

Rachlin, H., & Logue, A. W. (1983). Learning. In M. Hersen, A. Kazdin, & A. Bellack (Eds.), *The clinical psychology handbook* (pp. 107–121). New York: Pergamon.

Rachman, S. (Ed.). (1963). *Critical essays on psychoanalysis.* New York: Macmillan.

———. (1978). *Fear and courage.* San Francisco: Freeman.

———. (1990). *Fear and courage* (2d ed.) San Francisco: Freeman.

Rank. O. (1929). *The trauma of birth.* New York: Harper & Row, 1973.

———. (1932). *The myth of the birth of the hero.* New York: Vintage, 1959.

———. (1941). *Beyond psychology.* New York: Dover.

Rapaport, D. (1951). The autonomy of the ego. *Bulletin of the Menninger Clinic, 15,* 113–123.

———. (1958). The theory of ego autonomy: A generalization. *Bulletin of the Menninger Clinic, 22,* 13–35.

———. (1959). A historical survey of psychoanalytic ego psychology. *Psychological Issues, Monograph No. 1,* Vol. 1. New York: International Universities Press.

———. (1971/1972). *Emotions and memory.* New York: International Universities Press.

Redlich, F., & Kellert, S. R. (1978). Trends in American mental health. *American Journal of Psychiatry, 135,* 22–28.

Rescorla, R. A. (1987). A Pavlovian analysis of goal-directed behavior. *American Psychologist, 42*(2), 119–129.

———. (1988). Pavlovian conditioning: It's not what you think it is. *American Psychologist, 43*(3), 151–160.

Rescorla, R. A., & Solomon, R. (1967). Two-process learning theory: Relationships between Pavlovian conditioning and instrumental learning. *Psychological Review, 74,* 151–182.

Roazen, P. (1968). *Freud: Political and social thought.* New York: Knopf.

———. (1969). *Brother Animal: The story of Freud and Tausk.* New York: Knopf.

———. (1971). *Freud and his followers.* New York: Meridian Books.

———. (1977). Orthodoxy on Freud: The case of Tausk. *Contemporary Psychoanalysis, 13,* 102–115.

———. (1978). Reading, writing, and memory in Dr. K. R. Eissler's thinking. *Contemporary Psychoanalysis, 14,* 345–353.

Rogers, C. R. (1942). *Counseling and psychotherapy.* Boston: Houghton Mifflin.

———. (1951). *Client-centered therapy.* Boston: Houghton Mifflin.

———. (1954). The case of Mrs. Oak: A research analysis. In C. R. Rogers & R. F. Dymond (Eds.), *Psychotherapy and personality change* (pp. 259–348). Chicago: University of Chicago Press.

———. (1957). The necessary and sufficient conditions of therapeutic personality change. *Journal of Consulting Psychology, 21,* 95–103.

———. (1958). A tentative scale for the measurement of process in psychotherapy. In A. Rubenstein & M. B. Parloff (Eds.), *Research in psychotherapy,* vol. 1. Washington, DC: American Psychological Association, 1962.

———. (1959). A theory of therapy, personality and interpersonal relationships as developed in the client-centered framework. In S. Koch (Ed.), *Psychology: A study of a science,* Vol. III, *Formulations of the person in the social context.* New York: McGraw-Hill.

———. (1961). *On becoming a person.* Boston: Houghton Mifflin.

———. (1964). The Concept of the Fully Functioning Person. *Psychotherapy: Theory, Research and Practice, 1,* 17–26.

———. (Ed.) (1967a). *The therapeutic relationship and its impact: A study of psychotherapy with schizophrenics.* Madison: University of Wisconsin Press.

———. (1967b). Autobiography. In E. G. Boring & G. Lindzey (Eds.), *A history of psychology in autobiography,* vol. 5. New York: Appleton, 1967.

———. (1969). *Freedom to learn,* Columbus, OH: Charles E. Merrill, esp. chap. 14.

———. (1974a). In retrospect: forty-six years. *American Psychologist, 29*(2), 115–123.

———. (1974b). The emerging person: A new revolution. Mimeograph paper for private circulation. La Jolla, CA: Center for Studies of the Person (also published: Richard I. Evans, *Carl Rogers: The man and his ideas: A dialogue.* New York: Dutton, 1975).

———. (1974c). Remarks on the future of client-centered therapy. In D. A. Wexler & L. North Rice (Eds.), *Innovations in client-centered therapy.* New York: Wiley.

———. (1977). *Carl Rogers on personal power.* New York: Delacorte Press.

Rogers, C. R., & R. F. Dymond. (1954). *Psychotherapy and personality change.* Chicago: University of Chicago Press.

Rokeach, M. (1960). *The open and closed mind.* New York: Basic Books.

———.(1973). *The nature of human values.* New York: Free Press.

Rosenhan, D. L. (1973). On being sane in insane places. *Science,* January, *179,* 250–258.

Rosenthal, R., & Jacobson, L. F. (1968a). *Pygmalion in the classroom: Teacher expectations and pupils' intellectual development.* New York: Holt, Rinehart and Winston.

———. (1968b). Teacher expectations of the disadvantaged. *Scientific American,* April 1968.

Rosenthal, R., & Rosnow, R. L. (Eds.). (1969). *Artifact in behavioral research.* New York: Academic Press.

Rosenzweig, S. (1985). Freud and experimental psychology: the emergence of idiodynamics. In S. Koch & D. Leary (Eds.), *A century of psychology as science* (pp. 135–207). New York: McGraw-Hill.

Rowe, I., & Marcia, J. (1980). Ego identity status, formal operations, and moral development. *Journal of Youth and Adolescence, 9,* 87–99.

Rubins, J. L. (1978). *Karen Horney: Gentle rebel of psychoanalysis.* New York: Dial.

Rudnytsky, P. L. (1991). *The psychoanalytic vocation: Rank, Winnicott and the legacy of Freud.* New Haven: Yale University Press.

Ruesch, J. (1961). *Therapeutic communication.* New York: Norton.

Sandler, J. & Freud, A. (1985). *The analysis of defense: The ego and the mechanisms of defense revisited.* New York: International Universities Press.

Sanford, N. (1985). What have we learned about personality? In S. Koch & D. Leary (Eds.), *A century of psychology as a science.* New York: McGraw-Hill.

Sayers, J. (1991). *Mothers of psychoanalysis.* New York: Norton.

Schafer, R. (1976). *A new language for psychoanalysis.* New Haven, CT: Yale University Press.

———. (1983). *The analytic attitude.* New York: Basic Books.

Schafer, R. (1997a). *Tradition and change in psychoanalysis.* New York: International Universities Press.

Schafer, R. (Ed.). (1997b). *The contemporary Kleinians of London.* New York: International Universities Press.

Schellenberg, J. A. (1978). *Masters of social psychology: Freud, Mead, Lewin and Skinner.* New York: Oxford University Press.

Schorske, C. E. (1975). Politics and patricide. In *The annual of psychoanalysis,* vol. 2. New York: International Universities Press.

Schroeder, J. E., & Koenig, K. P. (1978). Extroversion and reminiscence following a frustrating paired-associate task. *The Journal of General Psychology, 98,* 5–14.

Schroeder, M. L., Wormworth, J. A., & Livesley, W. J. (1994). Dimensions of personality disorder and the five-factor model of personality. In P. T. Costa & T. A. Widiger (Eds), *Personality disorders and the five-factor model of personality.* Washington, DC: American Psychological Association.

Schulz, C. G. (1978). Sullivan's clinical contributions during the Sheppard Pratt era: 1923–1930. *Psychiatry, 41,* 117–128.

Schur, M. (1972). *Freud, living and dying.* New York: International Universities Press.

Sechrest, L. (1963). The psychology of personal constructs. In J. M. Wepmann & R. W. Heine (Eds.), *Concepts of personality.* Chicago: Aldine.

Segal, J. (1992). *Melanie Klein.* Great Britain, London: Sage Publications.

Seligman, M. E. (1970). On the generality of the laws of learning. *Psychological Review, 37,* 406–418.

———. (1971). Phobias and preparedness. *Behavior Therapy, 2,* 307–320.

———. (1972). *Biological boundaries of learning.* New York: Appleton-Century.

Shadel, W. G., & Cervone, D. (1993). Comment on Goldberg: The big five versus nobody? *American Psychologist, 48,* 1300–1302.

Shagass, C., & Kerenyi, A. B. (1958). Neurophysiological studies of personality. In H. J. Eysenck (Ed.), *Reading in extraversion-intraversion,* vol. 3: *Bearings on basic psychological processes.* London: Staples, 1971 (paper originally published in *Journal of Nervous and Mental Diseases,* 1958, *126,* 141–147).

Shapiro, D. (1965). *Neurotic styles.* New York: Basic Books.

Sheffield, F. (1954). A drive-induction theory of reinforcement,. In R. Haber (Ed.), *Current research in motivation.* New York: Holt, Rinehart and Winston, 1966 (paper originally read at Psychology Colloquium, Brown University, November 1954).

Shevrin, H., & Dickman, S. (1980). The psychological unconscious: A necessary assumption for all psychological theory? *American Psychologist, 35,* 421–434.

Silverman, L. H. (1976). Psychoanalytic theory: "The reports of my death are greatly exaggerated." *American Psychologist, 31,* 621–637.

———. (1983). The subliminal psychodynamic activation method: Overview and comprehensive listing of studies. In J. Masling (Ed.), *Empirical studies of psychoanalytical theories,* vol. 1. New York: The Analytic Press (Lawrence Erlbaum).

Silverman, L. H., Lachmann, F. M. & Milich, R. (1982). *The search for oneness.* New York: International Universities Press.

Silverstein, B. (1984). Psychoanalyzing psychoanalysis: Freud and the hidden fault of the father: A book review. *Review of Psychoanalytic Books, 3,* 333–343.

———. (1985). Freud's psychology and its organic foundation: Sexuality and mind-body interactionism. *The Psychoanalytic Review, 72,* 204–228.

———. (1986). "Now comes a sad story": Freud's Lost Metapsychological Papers. In P. E. Stepansky (Ed.), *Freud: Appraisals and reappraisals,* vol. 1. Hillsdale, NJ: The Analytic Press (Lawrence Erlbaum Associates).

———. (1988). Will the real Freud stand up, please? *American Psychologist, 43*(8), 662–6634.

———. (1989a). Oedipal politics and scientific creativity: Freud's 1915 phylogenetic fantasy. *The Psychoanalytic Review, 76*(3), 403–424.

———. (1989b). Contributions to the history of psychology: LVIII. Freud's dualistic mind-body interactionism: Implications for the development of his psychology. *Psychological Reports, 64,* 1091–1097.

Sipprelle, C. R., Ascough, J. C., Detrio, D. M., & Horst, P. A. (1977). "Neuroticism, extroversion, and response to stress." *Behavior Research and Therapy, 15,* 411–418.

Skinner, B. F. (1938). *The behavior of organisms.* New York: Appleton Century Crofts, 1966.

———. (1950). Are theories of learning necessary? *Psychological Review, 57,* 193–216.

———. (1953). *Science and human behavior.* New York: Free Press.

———. (1956). Critique of psychoanalytic concepts and theories. In *Minnesota studies in the philosophy of science,* vol. 1. Minneapolis: University of Minneapolis Press.

———. (1963). Behaviorism at fifty. *Science, 140,* 951–958.

———. (1968). Conversation with R. I. Evans. In R. I. Evans, *B. F. Skinner: The man and his ideas.* New York: Dutton.

———. (1971). *Beyond freedom and dignity.* New York: Knopf.

———. (1974). *About behaviorism.* New York: Knopf.

———. (1975). The steep and thorny way to a science of behavior. *American Psychologist, 30,* 42–49.

———. (1976). *Particulars of my life.* New York: Knopf.

———. (1978). *Reflections on behaviorism and society.* Englewood Cliffs, NJ: Prentice-Hall.

———. (1979). *The shaping of a behaviorist.* New York: Knopf.

———. (1983). *A matter of consequences.* New York: Knopf.

———. (1987a). What is wrong with daily life in the western world? *American Psychologist, 41*(5), 568–574.

———. (1987b). Whatever happened to psychology as the science of behavior? *American Psychologist, 42*(8), 780–786.

———. (1989). The origins of cognitive thought. *American Psychologist, 44*(1), 13–18.

Skinner, B. F., & Vaughn, M. E. (1983). *Enjoy old age: Living fully in your later years.* New York: Warner Books (W. W. Norton).

Smith-Benjamin, L. (1993). *Interpersonal diagnosis and treatment of personality disorders.* New York: Guilford Press.

Sollod, R. N., & White, R. (1980). Robert W. White and the origins of the concept of competence: An interview. Interviewed by R. N. Sollod, *The Sollod Papers.* Archives of the History of American Psychology, Box M1045, University of Akron, 1980.

Solomon, R. L., & Wynne, L. C. (1954). Traumatic avoidance learning: The principles of anxiety conservation and partial irreversibility. *Psychological Review, 61,* 353-385.

Solomon, R. L., Kamin, L. J., Wynne, L. C. (1953). Traumatic avoidance learning: The outcomes of several extinction procedures with dogs. *Journal of Abnormal and Social Psychology, 48,* 291-302.

Solomon, R. C. (1974). Freud's neurological theory of mind. In R. Wolheim (Ed.), *Freud: A collection of critical essays.* Garden City, NY: Doubleday.

Speck, R. V., & Attneave, C. (1973). *Family networks.* New York: Vintage.

Spielberger, C. D., & DeNike, L. D. (1966). Descriptive behaviorism versus cognitive theory in verbal operant conditioning. *Psychological Review, 73,* 306-326.

Spielmann, J. (1963). *The relation between personality and the frequency and duration of involuntary rest pauses during massed practice.* Unpublished doctoral dissertation, University of London; cited by H. J. Eysenck, 1953b.

Spitz, R. (1965). *The first year of life.* New York: International Universities Press.

Stagner, R. (1977). On the reality and relevance of traits. *The Journal of General Psychology, 96,* 185-207.

Stepansky, P. E. (1983). *In Freud's shadow: Adler in context.* Hillsdale, NJ: The Analytic Press (Lawrence Erlbaum Associates).

———. (Ed.). (1988). Introduction in M. S. Mahler, *The Memoirs of Margaret S. Mahler.* New York: The Free Press.

Stephenson, W. (1953). *The study of behavior: Q-technique and its methodology.* Chicago: University of Chicago Press.

Stern, D. N. (1985). *The interpersonal world of the infant: A view from psychoanalysis and developmental psychology.* New York: Basic Books.

Stern, Paul J. (1976). *C. G. Jung: The haunted prophet.* New York: Braziller.

Stolorow, R. D., & Atwood, G. E. (1976). An ego-psychological analysis of the work and life of Otto Rank in the light of modern conceptions of narcissism. *The International Review of Psychoanalysis, 3,* 441-459.

———. (1978). A defensive-restitutive function of Freud's theory of psychosexual development. *The Psychoanalytic Review, 65,* 217-238.

———. (1979). *Faces in a cloud: Subjectivity in personality theory.* New York: Aronson.

Stone, M. H. (1980). *The borderline syndromes: Constitution, personality and adaptation.* New York: McGraw-Hill.

Storr, A. (1984). Did Freud have clay feet? *New York Times Book Review,* February 1984, 3 and 35.

Strachey, J. (1966). Editor's general preface. In J. Strachey (Ed.), *The Standard Edition of the Complete Psychological Works of Sigmund Freud* (Vol. 1). London: Hogarth.

Sullivan, H. S. (1953a). *Conceptions of modern psychiatry.* New York: Norton.

———. (1953b). *The interpersonal theory of psychiatry.* New York: Norton.

———. (1954). *The psychiatric interview.* New York: Norton.

———. (1956). *Clinical studies in psychiatry.* New York: Norton.

———. (1962). *Schizophrenia as a human process.* New York: Norton.

———. (1964). *The fusion of psychiatry and social science.* New York: Norton.

———. (1972). *Personal psychopathology.* New York: Norton.

Sulloway, F. J. (1979). *Freud: Biologist of the mind.* New York: Basic Books.

Summers, F. (1994). *Object Relations Theories and Psychopathology.* Hillsdale, NJ: The Analytic Press.

Sutton, N. (1996). *Bettelheim: A life and a legacy.* New York: Basic Books.

Swick-Perry, H. (1962). Editor's introduction to H. S. Sullivan, *Schizophrenia as a Human Process.* New York: Norton.

Swick-Perry, Helen. (1982). *Psychiatrist of America: The life of Harry Stack Sullivan.* Cambridge, MA: Belknap Press of Harvard University.

Szasz, T. S. (1960). The myth of mental illness. *American Psychologist, 15,* 113-118.

———. (1961). *The myth of mental illness: Foundations of a theory of personal conduct.* New York: Harper & Row.

———. (1970). *The manufacture of madness.* New York: Dell.

Teplov, B. M. (1964). The historical development of Pavlov's theory of typological differences in the dog. In J. A. Gray (Ed. and Trans.), *Pavlov's typology.* New York: Macmillan.

Thalberg, I. (1974). Freud's anatomies of the self. In R. Wolheim (Ed.), *Freud: A collection of critical essays.* Garden City, NY: Doubleday.

Thompson, C. (1962). Harry Stack Sullivan, the man. In H. S. Sullivan, *Schizophrenia as a human process.* New York: Norton (first published in *Psychiatry,* 1949, *12,* 435-437).

Thompson, R. F. (1967). *Foundations of physiological psychology.* New York: Harper & Row.

Thorndike, E. L. (1911). *Animal intelligence.* New York: Macmillan.

Tillich, P. (1952). *The courage to be.* New Haven, CT: Yale University Press.

Todd, J. T., & Morris, E. K. (Eds.). (1994). *Modern perspectives on John B. Watson and classical behaviorism.* Westport, CT: Greenwood Press.

Torrey, F., E., Bowler, A. E., Taylor, E. H., & Gottesman, I. I. (1994). *Schizophrenia and Manic-Depressive Disorder.* New York: Basic Books.

Vaihinger, H. (1911). *The philosophy of "as if."* New York: Harcourt, Brace and World, 1925.

Vaillant, G. E. (1993). *The wisdom of the ego.* Cambridge: MA: Harvard University Press.

———. (1994). Ego mechanisms of defense and personality psychopathology. *Journal of Abnormal Psychology, 103,* 44-50.

Van der Post, L. (1975). *Jung and the story of our time.* New York: Pantheon.

Wallace, E. R. (1976). Thanatos—A reevaluation. *Psychiatry, 39,* 386-393.

———. (1977). The psychodynamic determinants of *Moses and Monotheism. Psychiatry, 40,* 79-87.

———. (1978). Freud's father conflict: The history of a dynamic. *Psychiatry, 41,* 33-56.

Walton, H. J. (1986). The relationship between personality disorder and psychiatric illness. In T. Millon & G. L. Klerman (Eds.). *Contemporary directions in psychopathology: Toward the DSM-IV.* New York: Guilford.

Watson, D., Clark, L. A., & Harkness, A. R. (1994). Structures of personality and their relevance to psychopathology. *Journal of Abnormal Psychology, 103,* 18-31.

Watson, J. B. (1913). Psychology as the behaviorist views it. *Psychological Review, 20,* 158-177.

———. (1914). *Behavior: An introduction to comparative psychology.* New York: Holt, Rinehart and Winston, 1967.

———. (1924/1930). *Behaviorism.* New York: Norton.

———. (1936). Autobiography. In C. Murchison (Ed.), *A history of psychology in autobiography,* vol. III. Worcester, MA: Clark University Press.

Watson, J. B., & Rayner, R. (1920). Conditioned emotional reactions. *Journal of Experimental Psychology, 3,* 1-14.

———. (1928). *Psychological care of infant and child.* New York: Norton.

Watson, R. I. (1963). *The great psychologists.* Philadelphia: Lippincott.

———. (1978). *The great psychologists* (4th ed.). Philadelphia: Lippincott.

Wertheimer, M. (1959). *Productive thinking* (enlarged cd.). New York: Harper & Row.

White, K. D., & Mangan, G. L. (1972). Strength of the nervous system as a function of personality type and level of arousal. *Behavior Research and Therapy, 10,* 139-146.

White, M. J. (1977). Sullivan and treatment. *Contemporary Psychoanalysis, 13,* 317-346.

White, R. W. (1959). Motivation reconsidered: The concept of competence. *Psychological Review, 66,* 297-333.

———. (1960). Competence and the psychosexual stages of development. In S. R. Maddi (Ed.), *Perspectives on personality.* Boston: Little Brown, 1971 (Originally published in M. R. Jones (Ed.), *Nebraska symposium on motivation.* Lincoln: University of Nebraska Press, 1960).

———. (1961). The dangers of social adjustment. In J. M. Lee & N. J. Pallone (Eds.), *Readings in guidance and counseling.* New York: Sheed and Ward, 1966 (Originally published: *Teacher's College Record,* 1961, January, *LXII,* 288-297.)

———. (1963a). *Ego and reality in psychoanalytic theory. Psychological Issues,* Monograph No. 11. New York: International Universities Press.

———. (1963b). Sense of interpersonal competence. In R. W. White (Ed.), *The study of lives* (pp. 73-93). New York: Atherton.

———. (1965). The experience of efficacy in schizophrenia. *Psychiatry, 28,* 199-211.

———. (1972). *The enterprise of living: Growth and organization in personality* (chaps. 3-11). New York: Holt, Rinehart and Winston.

———. (1975). *Lives in progress* (3d ed.). New York: Holt, Rinehart and Winston.

———. (1981). Exploring personality the long way: The study of lives. In A. I. Rabin, J. Aronoff, A. M. Barclay, & R. A. Zucker (Eds.). *Further exploration in personality.* New York: Wiley Interscience.

Widiger, T. A., & Costa, P. T., Jr. (1994). Personality and personality disorders. *Journal of Abnormal Psychology, 103,* 78-91.

Widiger, T. A., Trull, T. J., Clarkin, J. F., Sanderson, C., & Costa, P. T. (1994). A description of the *DSM-III-R* and *DSM-IV* personality disorders with the five factor-model of personality. In P. T. Costa & T. A. Widiger (Eds.), *Personality disorders and the five-factor model of personality.* Washington, DC: American Psychological Association.

Wilkinson, J. (1973). How good is current behavior theory? In H. Wheeler (Ed.), *Beyond the punitive society.* San Francisco: Freeman.

Wilson, C. (1972). *New pathways in psychology.* New York: Taplinger Publishing Co.

Windelband, W. (1894). *History and natural science.* Strassburg, Germany: Heitz.

Winnicott, C. (1978). D. W. W.: A reflection. In S. A. Grolnick & L. Barkin (Eds.), *Between reality and fantasy: Transitional objects and phenomena* (15-33). New York: Jason Aronson.

———. (1983/1991). Interview with M. Neve. In P. L. Rudnytsky, *The psychoanalytic vocation: Rank, Winnicott and the legacy of Freud* (181-193). New Haven: Yale University Press.

———. (1989). D. W. W.: A Reflection. In C. Winnicott, R. Shepherd, & M. Davis, *Psychoanalytic explorations.* Cambridge, MA: Harvard University Press. (For an earlier version, see C. Winnicott, 1978).

Winnicott, D. W. (1931a/1992). A note on normality and anxiety. In D. W. Winnicott, *Through paediatrics to psycho-analysis. Collected papers.* (3-21). New York: Bruner-Mazel.

———. (1931b/1992). Fidgetiness. In D. W. Winnicott, *Through paediatrics to psycho-analysis. Collected papers* (22-30). New York: Bruner-Mazel.

———. (1935/1992). The manic defence. In *Through paediatrics to psycho-analysis. Collected papers* (129-144). New York: Bruner-Mazel.

———. (1936/1992). Appetite and emotional disorder. In D. W. Winnicott, *Through paediatrics to psycho-analysis. Collected papers* (33-51). New York: Bruner-Mazel.

———. (1939/1990). Aggression and its roots. In D. W. Winnicott, *Deprivation and delinquency* (84-99). C. Winnicott, R. Shepherd, & M. Davis (Eds.). London: Routledge.

Winnicott, D. W. (1941/1992). The observation of infants in a set situation. In D. W. Winnicott, *Through paediatrics to psycho-analysis. Collected papers* (52-69. New York: Bruner-Mazel.

———. (1944/1992). Ocular psychoneuroses of childhood. In D. W. Winnicott, *Through paediatrics to psycho-analysis. Collected papers* (85-90). New York: Bruner-Mazel.

———. (1945a). Primitive emotional development. In *Through paediatrics to psycho-analysis. Collected papers* (145-156). New York: Bruner-Mazel (Collection originally published: New York: Basic Books, 1958).

———. (1945b/1996) Towards an objective study of human nature. In D. W. Winnicott, *Thinking about children* (3-12). R. Shepherd, J. Johns, & H. T. Robinson (Eds.). Reading, MA: Addison-Wesley.

———. (1948a/1996). Primary introduction to external reality: The early stages. In D. W. Winnicott, *Thinking about children* (21-28). R. Shepherd, J. Johns, & H. T. Robinson (Eds.). Reading, MA: Addison-Wesley.

———. (1948b/1996). Environmental needs; the early stages; total dependence and essential independence. In D. W. Winnicott, *Thinking about children* (29-36). R. Shepherd, J. Johns, & H. T. Robinson (Eds.). Reading, MA: Addison-Wesley.

———. (1948c/1992). Paediatrics and psychiatry. In D. W. Winnicott, *Through paediatrics to psycho-analysis. Collected papers* (157-173). New York: Bruner-Mazel.

———. (1948d/1992). Reparation in respect of mother's organized defence against depression. In D. W. Winnicott, *Through paediatrics to psycho-analysis. Collected papers.* (91-96). New York: Bruner-Mazel.

———. (1951/1992). Transitional objects and transitional phenomena. In D. W. Winnicott, *Through paediatrics to psycho-analysis. Collected papers.* (229-242). New York: Bruner-Mazel.

———. (1952). Anxiety associated with insecurity. In D. W. Winnicott, *Through paediatrics to psycho-analysis. Collected papers.* (97-100). New York: Bruner-Mazel.

———. (1954-55/1992). The depressive position in normal emotional development. In *Through paediatrics to psycho-analysis. Collected papers* (262-277). New York: Bruner-Mazel (Collection originally published: New York: Basic Books, 1958).

———. (1955/1989). Private practice. In D. W. Winnicott, R. Shepherd, and M. Davis (Eds.), *Psychoanalytic explorations* (291-298). Cambridge, Mass: Harvard University Press.

———. (1957/1965c) Advising parents. In D. W. Winnicott, *The family and individual development* (114-120). Great Britain: Tavistock.

———. (1958/1965c) Theoretical statement of the field of child psychiatry. In D. W. Winnicott, *The family and individual development* (97-105). Great Britain: Tavistock.

———. (1959/1989). The fate of the transitional object. In *Psychoanalytic explorations* (53-58). C. Winnicott, R. Shepherd, & M. Davis (Eds.). Cambridge, Mass: Harvard University Press.

———. (1960a/1965a). String: A technique of communication. In D. W. Winnicott, *The maturational processes and the facilitating environment. Studies in the theory of emotional development* (153-157). New York: International Universities Press (Originally published: *Journal of Child Psychology and Psychiatry,* 1960, *1,* 49-52).

———. (1960b/1965a). Ego integration in child development. In D. W. Winnicott, *The maturational processes and the facilitating environment. Studies in the theory of emotional development* (56-63). New York: International Universities Press.

———. (1960c/1965a). Ego distortion in terms of true and false self. In D. W. Winnicott, *The maturational processes and the facilitating environment. Studies in the theory of emotional development* (140-152). New York: International Universities Press.

———. (1961a/1989). Psycho-neurosis in childhood. In *Psychoanalytic explorations* (64-72). C. Winnicott, R. Shepherd, & M. Davis (Eds.). Cambridge, Mass: Harvard University Press.

———. (1961b/1990). Varieties of psychotherapy. In D. W. Winnicott, *Deprivation and delinquency* (232-240). C. Winnicott, R. Shepherd, & M. Davis (Eds.). Great Britain: Tavistock/Routledge.

———. (1962a/1965a). The aims of psychoanalytical treatment. In D. W. Winnicott, *The maturational processes and the facilitating environment. Studies in the theory of emotional development* (166-170). New York: International Universities Press.

———. (1962b/1965a). A personal view of the Kleinian contribution. In D. W. Winnicott, *The maturational processes and the facilitating environment. Studies in the theory of emotional development* (171-178). New York: International Universities Press.

Winnicott, D. W. (1962c/1965a). Ego integration in child development. In D. W. Winnicott, *The maturational processes and the facilitating environment. Studies in the theory of emotional development* (56-63. New York: International Universities Press.

———. (1963a/1965a). Training for child psychiatry. In D. W. Winnicott. *The maturational processes and the facilitating environment. Studies in the theory of emotional development* (193-202). New York: International Universities Press. (Originally published: *Journal of Child Psychology and Psychiatry,* 1963, *4,* 85-89).

———. (1963b/1989) D. W. W.'s dream related to reviewing Jung. In *Psychoanalytic explorations* (228-230)). C. Winnicott, R. Shepherd, & M. Davis (Eds.). Cambridge, Mass: Harvard University Press.

———. (1964a). *The child, the family, and the outside world.* Reading MA: Addison-Wesley (alternate edition: Pelican Books, 1964).

———. (1964b/1989). The squiggle game. In *Psychoanalytic explorations* (299-317). C. Winnicott, R. Shepherd, and M. Davis (Eds.). Cambridge, Mass: Harvard University Press.

———. (1964c/1987). The newborn and his mother. In D. W. Winnicott, (1987). *Babies and their mothers* (35-50). C. Winnicott, R. Shepherd, & M. Davis (Eds.). Reading, MA: Addison-Wesley.

———. (1964d/1986). The concept of the false self. In D. W. Winnicott, *Home is where we start from.* C. W. Winnicott, R. Shepherd, & M. Davis (Eds.). New York: Norton.

———. (1965a). *The maturational processes and the facilitating environment. Studies in the theory of emotional development.* New York: International Universities Press.

———. (1965b/1989). A child psychiatry case illustrating a delayed reaction to loss. In C. Winnicott, R. Shepherd, & M. Davis (Eds.), *Psychoanalytic explorations* (341-368). Cambridge, MA: Harvard University Press.

———. (1965c/1989). Notes made on the train, part 2. In C. Winnicott, R. Shepherd, & M. Davis (Eds.), *Psychoanalytic explorations* (231-233). Cambridge, MA: Harvard University Press.

———. (1966a/1987). The beginning of the individual. In Winnicott, D. W. *Babies and their mothers* (51-58). C. Winnicott, R. Shepherd, & M. Davis (Eds.). Reading, MA: Addison-Wesley.

———. (1966b/1996). Autism. In D. W. Winnicott, *Thinking about children* (197-217). R. Shepherd, J. Johns, & H. T. Robinson (Eds.). Reading, MA: Addison-Wesley.

———. (1966c/1987). The ordinary devoted mother. In D. W. Winnicott, *Babies and their mothers* (3-14). C. Winnicott, R. Shepherd, M. Davis (Eds.). Reading, MA: Addison-Wesley.

———. (1967/1996). The aetiology of infantile schizophrenia in terms of adaptive failure. In D. W. Winnicott, *Thinking about children* (218-223). R. Shepherd, J. Johns, & H. T. Robinson (Eds.). Reading, MA: Addison-Wesley.

———. (1968a/1987). Communication between infant and mother, and mother and infant, compared and contrasted. In Winnicott, D. W. (1987). *Babies and their mothers* (89-103). C. Winnicott, R. Shepherd, & M. Davis (Eds.). Reading, MA: Addison-Wesley.

———. (1968b/1989). The use of an object and relating through identifications. In *Psychoanalytic explorations* (218-227). C. Winnicott, R. Shepherd, & M. Davis (Eds.). Cambridge, Mass: Harvard University Press.

———. (1968c/1989). The use of the word "use." In C. Winnicott, R. Shepherd, & M. Davis (Eds.), *Psychoanalytic explorations* (233-235). Cambridge, MA: Harvard University Press.

———. (1968d/1989). Clinical illustration of "The use of an object." In C. Winnicott, R. Shepherd, & M. Davis (Eds.), *Psychoanalytic explorations* (235-238). Cambridge, MA: Harvard University Press.

———. (1968e/1989). Comments on my paper "The use of an object." In C. Winnicott, R. Shepherd, & M. Davis (Eds.), *Psychoanalytic explorations* (238-240). Cambridge, MA: Harvard University Press.

———. (1968f/1987). Breast-feeding as communication. In Winnicott, D. W. (1987). *Babies and their mothers* (23-33). C. Winnicott, R. Shepherd, & M. Davis (Eds.). Reading, MA: Addison-Wesley.

———. (1969a/1986). The pill and the moon. In D. W. Winnicott, *Home is where we start from* (195-209). New York: Norton.

———. (1969b/1989). The use of an object in the context of *Moses and Monotheism.* In *Psychoanalytic explorations* (240-246). C. Winnicott, R. Shepherd, & M. Davis (Eds.). Cambridge, Mass: Harvard University Press.

———. (1969c/1989). Development of the theme of the mother's unconscious as discovered in psycho-analytic practice. In C. Winnicott, R. Shepherd, & M. Davis (Eds.), *Psychoanalytic explorations* (247-250). Cambridge, MA: Harvard University Press.

———. (1969d/1989). The mother-infant experience of mutuality. In C. Winnicott, R. Shepherd, & M. Davis (Eds.), *Psychoanalytic explorations* (251-260). Cambridge, MA: Harvard University Press.

———. (1971). *Playing and reality.* Great Britain: Penguin Books.

———. (1972/1986). *Holding and interpretation: Fragment of an analysis.* New York: Grove Press.

———. (1984). *Deprivation and delinquency.* C. Winnicott, R. Shepherd, and M. Davis (Eds.). London, England: Routledge.

———. (1986). *Home is where we start from: Essays by a psychoanalyst.* C. Winnicott, R. Shephard, and M. Davis (Eds.). New York: Norton.

———. (1987). *Babies and their mothers.* C. Winnicott, R. Shepherd, & M. Davis (Eds.). Reading, MA: Addison-Wesley.

———. (1989). *Psychoanalytic explorations.* C. Winnicott, R. Shepherd, and M. Davis (Eds.). Cambridge, MA: Harvard University Press.

———. (1992). *Through paediatrics to psycho-analysis. Collected papers.* New York: Bruner-Mazel (Originally published: New York: Basic Books, 1958).

———. (1993). *Talking to parents.* Reading MA: Addison-Wesley.

———. (1996a/1996). The niffle. In D. W. Winnicott, *Thinking about children* (104-109). R. Shepherd, J. Johns, & H. T. Robinson (Eds.). Reading, MA: Addison-Wesley.

Witkin, H. A., Dyk, R. B., Faterson, H. F., Goodenough, D. R., & Karp, S. A. (1962). *Psychological differentiation.* New York: Wiley.

Wolpe, J. (1958). *Psychotherapy by reciprocal inhibition.* Stanford, CA: Stanford University Press.

———. (1973). *The practice of behavior therapy.* (2d ed.). New York: Pergamon.

———. (1978). Cognition and causation in human behavior and its theory. *American Psychologist, 33,* 437-446.

Woodworth, R. S., & Schlosberg, H. (1954). *Experimental psychology* (ref. ed.). New York: Holt, Rinehart and Winston.

Yankelovich, D., & Barrett, W. (1970). *Ego and instinct.* New York: Vintage.

Yerkes, R. M., & Dodson, J. D. (1908). The relation of strength of stimulus to rapidity of habit formation. *Journal of Comparative and Physiological Psychology, 18,* 459-482.

Yong-Bruehl, E. (1988). *Anna Freud: A biography.* New York: Summit Books (Simon and Schuster).

Zeigarnik, B. (1927). On finished and unfinished tasks. In W. D. Ellis (Ed.), *A source book of Gestalt psychology.* New York: Humanities Press, 1967 (paper originally published as "Über das Behalten von erledigten und unerledigten Handlungen." *Psychologische Forschung,* 1927, *9,* 1-85.)

Zilboorg, G. (1941). *A history of medical psychology.* New York: Norton.

Zimbardo, P. G. & Miller, N. E. (1958). Facilitation of exploration by hunger in rats. *Journal of Comparative and Physiological Psychology, 51,* 43-46.

Name Index

Subject Index